ROUTLEDGE HANDBOOK OF THE TOURIST EXPERIENCE

Routledge Handbook of the Tourist Experience offers a comprehensive synthesis of contemporary research on the tourist experience. It draws together multidisciplinary perspectives from leading tourism scholars to explore emergent tourist behaviours and motivations.

This handbook provides up-to-date, critical discussions of established and emergent themes and issues related to the tourist experience from a primarily socio-cultural perspective. It opens with a detailed introduction which lays down the framework used to examine the dynamic parameters of the tourist experience. Organised into five thematic sections, chapters seek to build and enhance knowledge and understanding of the significance and meaning of diverse elements of the tourist experience. Section 1 conceptualises and understands the tourist experience through an exploration of conventional themes such as tourism as authentic and spiritual experience, as well as emerging themes such as tourism as an embodied experience. Section 2 investigates the new, developing tourist demands and motivations, and a growing interest in the travel career. Section 3 considers the significance, motives, practices and experiences of different types of tourists and their roles such as the tourist as photographer. Section 4 discusses the relevance of 'place' to the tourist experience by exploring the relationship between tourism and place. The last section, Section 5, scrutinises the role of the tourist in creating their experiences through themes such as 'transformations in the tourist role' from passive receiver of experiences to co-creator of experiences, and 'external mediators in creating tourist experiences'.

This handbook is the first to fill a notable gap in tourism literature and collate within a single volume critical insights into the diverse elements of the tourist experience today. It will be of key interest to academics and students across the fields of tourism, hospitality management, geography, marketing and consumer behaviour.

Richard Sharpley is Professor of Tourism and Development at the University of Central Lancashire, Preston, UK. His research interests lie within two broad areas – tourism and sustainable development and the tourist experience – and he has researched and published widely in both.

ROUTLEDGE HANDBOOK OF THE TOURIST EXPERIENCE

Edited by Richard Sharpley

LONDON AND NEW YORK

First published 2022
by Routledge
2 Park Square, Milton Park, Abingdon, Oxon OX14 4RN

and by Routledge
605 Third Avenue, New York, NY 10158

Routledge is an imprint of the Taylor & Francis Group, an informa business

© 2022 selection and editorial matter, Richard Sharpley; individual chapters, the contributors

The right of Richard Sharpley to be identified as the author of the editorial material, and of the authors for their individual chapters, has been asserted in accordance with sections 77 and 78 of the Copyright, Designs and Patents Act 1988.

All rights reserved. No part of this book may be reprinted or reproduced or utilised in any form or by any electronic, mechanical, or other means, now known or hereafter invented, including photocopying and recording, or in any information storage or retrieval system, without permission in writing from the publishers.

Trademark notice: Product or corporate names may be trademarks or registered trademarks, and are used only for identification and explanation without intent to infringe.

British Library Cataloguing-in-Publication Data
A catalogue record for this book is available from the British Library

Library of Congress Cataloging-in-Publication Data
A catalog record has been requested for this book

ISBN: 978-1-032-11425-5 (hbk)
ISBN: 978-1-032-11427-9 (pbk)
ISBN: 978-1-003-21986-6 (ebk)

DOI: 10.4324/9781003219866

Typeset in Bembo
by codeMantra

To Sarah

CONTENTS

List of figures	*xii*
List of tables	*xiv*
List of contributors	*xv*
Introduction	1
Richard Sharpley	

SECTION 1
Dimensions of the contemporary tourist experience   **7**

1 Tourism, the tourist experience and postmodernity: theory, application and research   9
Craig Wight

2 Experiencing tourism: experiencing happiness?   24
Jeroen Nawijn and Wim Strijbosch

3 The emotional dimension of the tourist experience   37
Jase Wilson

4 Building the orchestra model of tourist experience, integration and examples   50
Philip L. Pearce and Zohre Mohammadi

5 The interrelationship between tourist satisfaction and experiences: how does one contribute to the other?   64
H. Kader Şanlıöz–Özgen and Metin Kozak

vii

Contents

6 Evolving authenticity into the magical realm of fantasy-based third-order simulacra 77
Jane Lovell

7 Tourist experiences: liminal, liminoid or just doing something different? 89
Richard Sharpley

8 Finding flow in the travel experience 101
Statia Elliot

9 Tourist experiences as attention products 113
Can-Seng Ooi

10 Tourist experience: a semiotic perspective 128
Richard Voase

11 Performing beyond the view: embodiment and tourist experiences 140
Jillian M. Rickly

12 Tourism: a spiritual experience? 153
Richard Sharpley

SECTION 2
Tourist demand and motivation **167**

13 The Ulysses factor revisited: consolidating the travel career pattern approach to tourist motivation 169
Philip L. Pearce

14 The experienced tourist: proposing a new tourist typology 185
Sabrina Seeler

15 Tourist motivation: a critical overview 200
Songshan (Sam) Huang

SECTION 3
Tourist roles and experiences **213**

16 Traveller, tourist and the 'lost art of travelling': the debate continues 215
Tom Sintobin

Contents

17 Mass tourism and personal experiences 235
Erik Cohen

18 Backpacker tourist experiences: temporal, spatial and cultural perspectives 249
Dallen J. Timothy and Xuan Zhu

19 Volunteer tourism: 'It's no use going back to yesterday, because I was a different person then' 262
Alexandra Coghlan

20 Feelin' Groovy: exploring slow(ness) in tourism experience 274
Julia Fallon

21 Ecotourist experience: myth or reality? 286
Stephen Schweinsberg and Louise O'Flynn

22 Is it just the music?: understanding the atmosphere in festivalgoers' experience at British rock music festivals 301
Alyssa Brown

23 The film-induced tourism experience 315
Sue Beeton

24 Remembrancing, remembrance gangs and co-opted encounters: loading and reloading dark tourism experiences 328
Tony Seaton

25 Frontier tourism: transcendence through trial 351
Jennifer H. Frost

26 Creating wellness tourism experiences 364
Melanie Kay Smith

27 Seeking the unusual but sustainable: scuba diving experience 378
Caglar Bideci and Mujde Bideci

28 Religious tourism: a spiritual or touristic experience? 391
Daniel H. Olsen

29 The contemporary cruise tourist experience 408
Jo-Anne Lester, Jennifer Holland and Catherine Palmer

Contents

30 Key components of sport tourist experiences   424
    Sean Gammon

31 Photography and the tourist experience: from cameras to smartphones   438
    Richard Sharpley

32 Accessible tourist experiences   451
    Marcus Hansen and Alan Fyall

SECTION 4
The tourist experience and place   **467**

33 Marketing a sense of place to tourists: a critical perspective   469
    Maria Lichrou and Aggelos Panayiotopoulos

34 The importance of built heritage in the English seaside experience   481
    David Jarratt

35 Island tourist experiences   498
    Godfrey Baldacchino

36 Delivering appealing and competitive rural wine tourism experiences   508
    Elisabeth Kastenholz and Bernard Lane

37 Wilderness tourism: nature-based tourist experiences in wild places   521
    Jarkko Saarinen

SECTION 5
Creating and mediating the tourist experience   **533**

38 Designing the tourist experience: a marketing perspective   535
    Dora Agapito

39 Tourist experience: a marketing perspective   549
    Serena Volo

40 Value co-creation in tourism eco-systems: operant
    and operand resources   564
    Nina K. Prebensen and Muzaffer S. Uysal

41 Place-based education, cemetery visitation and the tourist experience   577
    Siow-Kian Tan and Siow-Hooi Tan

Contents

42 Service experiences and innovation in the hospitality industry 588
Thais González-Torres, Eva Pelechano-Barahona and
Fernando E. García-Muiña

43 Tour guides as mediators of commemoration, education
and holiday making: the anthropology of the dark tourism
experience in Berlin 601
Asaf Leshem

44 Experience design in the smart tourism destination 616
Barbara Neuhofer and Dimitrios Buhalis

Index 631

FIGURES

4.1	The orchestra model of experience; a metaphor for analogic reasoning	55
5.1	Map of causes–effects and related experiential dimensions	71
5.2	Cause–effect relations and their link to experiential dimensions of memorability	71
9.1	The "I amsterdam" installation, Amsterdam	115
9.2	Paying attention: Flip-flopping between the right-facing rabbit and the left-facing duck	117
9.3	A packaged experience: Memories from a Disneyland Shanghai visitor (the author) who unexpectedly enjoyed himself *Photographs:* Can-Seng Ooi	123
13.1	An early graphical depiction of the links constituting the travel career ladder	173
13.2	The refinement to and the most used version of the travel career ladder model	174
13.3	The travel career pattern and tourists' motivation	176
14.1	Supply-side perspectives of an experienced tourist	194
16.1	Images of 'traveller'	223
16.2	The author's daughter wandering the Alps	229
22.1	The festival atmosphere	311
23.1	Media tourism as part of a circular process	321
23.2	Modelling the relationship between audience and tourist activity	321
28.1	A model of religious tourism experience	400
32.1	Destination accessibility touchpoints	455
32.2	Hierarchy of barriers to travel by people with disabilities	457
32.3	Feriecenter Slettestrand	462
34.1	Seasideness	484
34.2	Leisure health receptor model	486
34.3	Brighton's Western Bandstand – Orientalism from the Victorian period	488
34.4	Blackpool pleasure beach and casino, designed in the international modern style by Joseph Emberton and built during 1937–1940	489
34.5	The Midland Hotel, which was designed by Oliver Hill and dates to 1933, during the 2015 Vintage by the Sea Festival	492
34.6	The main stairway of the Midland Hotel with a medallion relief by Eric Gill	492

Figures

34.7	Brucciani's café window	494
35.1	Five attributes of islands	499
40.1	A destination eco-system	567
40.2	Destination resource integration framework	573
43.1	Sachsenhausen Memorial and Museum	605
43.2	Sachsenhausen Memorial and Museum	605
43.3	Memorial to the Murdered Jews of Europe	606
43.4	The social circles of the tour group	610
43.5	Tour guide position in the dark tourism experience	613

TABLES

1.1	Post-Fordism and tourism consumption	15
1.2	Types and examples of discourse analysis in tourism research	20
2.1	Journal articles within a conceptual framework of tourist experience and happiness	27
2.2	Conceptual framework for studying the tourist experience and happiness	32
5.1	Examples for the coding process	70
8.1	Experience terminology and conceptualizations relevant to tourism	105
9.1	Summary of the attraction–distraction arenas, and attention structure tactics	121
16.1	Distinctions between 'tourist' and 'traveller'	216
16.2	Mass tourism vs. new moral tourism	224
20.1	Cittaslow membership requirements	279
27.1	Studies focusing on scuba diving tourism experience	383
39.1	Synopsis of typologies of tourist experience	552
40.1	Examples of operant and operand resources in the tourism network ecosystem	570
41.1	Concepts, subthemes and themes of a cemetery tour	580
42.1	Service experience attributes in tourism research	590
42.2	Business innovation dimensions and areas	592
42.3	Innovation areas and service experience attributes	593
42.4	Summary of variables	596
42.5	Factorial exploratory analysis: results for the innovative experience	597
42.6	Business innovation dimensions and areas in hospitality firms	598
43.1	The three levels of interpretation	609

CONTRIBUTORS

Dora Agapito is an assistant professor at the University of Algarve (Faculty of Economics) and integrated researcher at the Research Centre for Tourism, Sustainability and Well-being (CinTurs), Portugal. Previously, she was a senior lecturer in Tourism and Events Management at the University of Lincoln (International Business School), UK. She holds a PhD in tourism, an MA in marketing and a BSc in communication sciences. She developed her post-doctoral studies in consumer psychology. Her research focuses on responsible tourism management, sensory-informed tourist experiences, experience design, destination marketing management, consumer behaviour and social marketing.

Godfrey Baldacchino is a professor of sociology at the University of Malta, Malta, and Malta's ambassador to small states. He served as Canada Research Chair and UNESCO co-Chair in Island Studies at the University of Prince Edward Island, Canada. He is the founding editor of *Island Studies Journal*; and president of the International Small Islands Studies Association (ISISA). His many books include *Global Tourism and Informal Labour Relations: The Small Scale Syndrome at Work* (1997) and *Archipelago Tourism: Practices and Policies* (2015).

Sue Beeton is a travel and tourism researcher and writer who became involved in tourism in the late 1980s through guiding horseback tours, and witnessed first-hand the growth of tourism and its effects on local communities. For over a quarter of a century, Professor Beeton has conducted tourism-based research into community development and public land management, but is best known for her work in film-induced tourism and pop culture. As well as producing numerous academic papers, book chapters and reports, she has published a range of research-based books, including *Ecotourism: a practical guide for rural communities, Community Development Through Tourism* and *Tourism and the Moving Image*, along with two editions of the acclaimed monograph, *Film-Induced Tourism*.

She is currently working on a new publication for Routledge on the emotions of travel. She is a visiting professor at the University of Hokkaido and in 2019 was awarded the TTRA Lifetime Achievement Award for her contribution to tourism research and scholarship.

Caglar Bideci is currently a lecturer in the marketing department at Rabat Business School at International University of Rabat and a PhD student at Swansea University, UK. His PhD project focuses on sustainability in scuba-diving tourism in terms of the tourism experience. Bideci has published tourist experience and sustainability-related papers in peer-reviewed journals and has collaborated on various projects such as a British Academy-funded project on scuba-diving experience between 2019 and 2020.

Mujde Bideci is an assistant professor in the marketing department at Rabat Business School at the International University of Rabat. Her core research interest is the consumer experience, including critical studies of sustainability applications and network analysis. Holding a PhD on the experience in sacred places, Bideci has published tourist experience-related papers in some top peer-reviewed journals.

Alyssa Brown is a senior lecturer in events and tourism and the event coordinator for the Centre for Research in Tourism Excellence (CERTE) at the University of Sunderland, United Kingdom. She holds a doctorate (PhD) in events and experience, exploring the festivalgoer's experience at UK Music Festivals. Her research areas surround managing and understanding tourist experiences considering well-being, perceptions and expectations. Other research interests include the influence of tattoos and body modifications, stakeholder experiences of niche and alternative or special interest events; business events; other types of festivals; service quality and experience management; the use of digital technology and social media in tourism, hospitality and events; and professional development.

Dimitrios Buhalis is a strategic management and marketing expert with specialization in information communication technology applications in the tourism, travel, hospitality and leisure industries. He is the director of the eTourism Lab and deputy director of the International Centre for Tourism and Hospitality Research, at Bournemouth University Business School. He is the editor in chief of the most established journal in tourism: *Tourism Review*, and the editor in chief of the *Encyclopedia of Tourism Management and Marketing*. Professor Buhalis has written and co-edited more than 20 books and 250 scientific articles. His research is referenced widely, being the second most cited for tourism and first for hospitality, twelfth on strategy and twenty-ninth in marketing on Google Scholar with more than 49000 citations and h-index 93. His research pioneers smart and ambient intelligence tourism and focuses on innovation, entrepreneurship and destination ecosystems management. For more information, books, articles and presentations, visit www.buhalis.com.

Alexandra Coghlan is an associate professor in tourism and events (Department of Tourism, Sport and Hotel Management, Griffith University, Queensland, Australia). She has a background in environmental and marine biology and has been a nature-based tour guide for most of her adult life. Her research interests are consumer psychology and its links to prosocial and environmental behaviour, particularly within an active travel, events and philanthropy. She has also written a textbook on sustainable tourism management. Her current projects include how to involve guests in resource (gas, water, electricity) savings in varied types of accommodation, as well as using mixed-reality games to build ecoliteracy in nature-based tourists, using the Great Barrier Reef as a case study. Both projects combine technology, positive psychology and consumer behaviour to foster sustainability outcomes.

Erik Cohen is the George S. Wise Professor of Sociology (Emeritus) at the Department of Sociology and Anthropology, The Hebrew University of Jerusalem. Born in 1932 in Yugoslavia, he immigrated to Israel in 1949. Cohen studied at the Hebrew University between 1954 and 1961 (BA in sociology and economics, MA in sociology and philosophy), and completed his PhD in 1968. He taught at the Hebrew University, 1959–2000, and served as dean of the Faculty of Social Science between 1988 and 1992. His principal research areas were collective settlements, tourism, folk arts and, more recently, space travel. He conducted research in Israel, Peru, the Pacific Islands and, since 1977, in Thailand. He is the author of about 250 publications. His books include *The Commercialized Crafts of Thailand* (2000), *The Chinese Vegetarian Festival in Phuket* (White Lotus 2001), *Contemporary Tourism: Diversity and Change* (Elsevier, 2004), *Explorations in Thai Tourism* (Emerald, 2008) and *Space Tourism* (edited with S. Spector, 2019). His main preoccupations were general theoretical issues in tourism theory, mobilities and mobility regimes, non-Western tourism, backpackers, animal-tourist engagement, tourism and disaster, festivals, ethnic tourism and, more recently, space tourism. Cohen is a founding member of the International Academy for the Study of Tourism. He was awarded the UNWTO Ulysses Prize for 2012. Erik Cohen presently lives in Thailand.

Statia Elliot, professor and director of the School of Hospitality, Food and Tourism Management at the University of Guelph in Ontario, teaches at the graduate level and researches tourist behaviour, destination image and e-marketing. Statia joined the School in 2007 after an extensive research career in the private and public sector, where she first worked in management consulting, then for the provincial destination management organisations of Ontario and Manitoba. She is the chair of the Ontario Tourism Education Corporation Board and a fellow of the Ontario Hostelry Institute and serves on the international Travel and Tourism Research Association's Board of Directors. Statia actively participates in academic conferences nationally and internationally, and is on the editorial boards of the *Journal of Travel Research and Tourism Management Perspectives*.

Julia Fallon is based in the Welsh Centre of Tourism Research within Cardiff School of Management at Cardiff Metropolitan University. She has a life-long interest in tourism study and transferred from working in Thomas Cook Retail to academia many years ago. Research interests include tourism and leisure experiences in watery places as well as oral history as a research technique, and these topics formed the base of her doctoral study. Nowadays, she still teaches some tourism as well as project management along with supervising projects/theses, supporting students in the UK and overseas.

Jennifer H. Frost (née Laing) is an associate professor (management/HRM) in the Department of Management, Sport and Tourism and chair of the Arts, Social Sciences and Commerce College Human Research Ethics Committee at La Trobe University, Melbourne, Australia. Her research interests include rural and regional regeneration through tourism and events, travel narratives, heritage tourism and health and wellness tourism. Jennifer's PhD, awarded in 2007, examined the motivations of frontier travellers and the implications for tourism marketing. Jennifer is a co-editor-in-chief of the *Journal of Heritage Tourism* and a co-editor of the Routledge *Advances in Events Research* book series. Her work has been published in high-quality journals in the field and she has co-written six research books, including most recently, *Royal Events: Rituals, Innovations, Meanings* (Routledge, 2018) with Warwick Frost. In 2017, Jennifer was recognized as an Emerging Scholar of Distinction by the International Academy for the Study of Tourism.

Alan Fyall is an associate dean of Academic Affairs and Visit Orlando Endowed Chair of Tourism Marketing at the Rosen College of Hospitality Management, University of Central

xvii

Contributors

Florida and is a member of UCF's National Center for Integrated Coastal Research. Alan has published widely in the areas of tourism and destination marketing and management including 22 books. His research interests revolve around destination sustainability and resilience, quality of life and well-being.

Sean Gammon is a reader in leisure and tourism management and is based in the Faculty of Business and Justice at the University of Central Lancashire. He has been writing and researching in sport tourism for over twenty-five years; and writing and managing the first undergraduate degree programme on the subject. In addition to Sean's general research interests, which mostly focus on sport tourist motives and experiences, he contributes to the literature that explores the breadth and significance of sports heritage in generating tourism. In addition to his work in sport tourism, he continues to contribute to the field of leisure studies, exploring the relationship between positive leisure experiences and subjective well-being.

Fernando E. García-Muiña is an associate professor in business administration and vice-rector for academic planning at Rey Juan Carlos University, Madrid, Spain. He is the author of several papers dealing with strategic management, in particular, the role of knowledge management in innovative activity, international business, absorptive capacity, inter-organisational networks, talent management, cultural heritage and museum management. Moreover, he is responsible for several European and Spanish competitive research projects on social sustainability and circular economy.

Thais González-Torres is a lecturer in business administration and organisation at Rey Juan Carlos University, Spain. She has recently defended her thesis, and she is the author and co-author of several papers dealing with business management, in particular innovation, intellectual capital, knowledge management and inter-firm relationships. These include various articles published in scientific journals listed in the Journal Citation Reports.

Marcus Hansen is a lecturer in hospitality, tourism and events at Wrexham Glyndwr University. Dr. Hansen is an early career researcher with research interests in the areas of adventure tourism and accessible tourism. Thus far, his research publications have focused on stakeholder collaboration and risk management in adventure tourism, as well as publications on accessible tourism in relation to travelling with a vision impairment and creating dementia-friendly destinations.

Jennifer Holland is a cruise and tourism researcher and lecturer at the University of Suffolk. She is a research fellow of the Royal Geographical Society and member of the Geographies of Leisure and Tourism Research Group and the Travel and Tourism Research Association. She is a social media editor for *Tourism and Hospitality Research*. Her research interests are consumer behaviour, marketing and risk, with a focus on the cruise sector. For her PhD, she specifically explored risk in cruising and cruise decision-making. She is an industry consultant, and her research is regularly featured in the media and industry publications, and she cruises as often as possible.

Songshan (Sam) Huang is a professor in tourism and services marketing in the School of Business and Law, Edith Cowan University (ECU). Prior to joining ECU, he worked in the School of Management at the University of South Australia from 2007 to 2016.

Dr Huang obtained his PhD from the School of Hotel and Tourism Management, The Hong Kong Polytechnic University. Before pursuing an academic career, he was a central government official in Beijing working for China National Tourism Administration (CNTA). Dr Huang's research interests include tourist behaviour, destination marketing and a wide range of China tourism issues. His publications frequently appear in top tourism, hospitality and business management journals. Dr Huang is a visiting professor to a number of universities in China, including Sun Yat-sen University and Jinan University in Guangzhou, Beijing International Studies University in Beijing and Sichuan University in Chengdu.

David Jarratt (PhD) is a senior lecturer in The Lancashire School of Business and Enterprise at the University of Central Lancashire (UCLan) in Preston, UK. He researches and writes about various aspects of the visitor economy and the consumption of leisure tourism. Much of his work to date has centred around either place/sense of place or coastal tourism. His current research interests include the links between wellness and leisure in natural environments, virtual tourism and tourism linked to popular culture. On his days off, he can be found pottering around seaside resorts.

Elisabeth Kastenholz is an associate professor at the Department of Economics, Management, Industrial Engineering and Tourism at the University of Aveiro, where she teaches tourism and marketing-related subjects. She integrates the University's Research Unit GOVCOPP (governance, competitiveness and public policies) and serves as the director at the shared international doctoral program in marketing and strategy (UA, UBI and UMinho). She holds a PhD in tourism studies, an MBA, a graduate course in tourism management and planning and a bachelor in "Public Administration – Specificity Foreign Affairs" (Germany). She has researched and published extensively and supervised several master and PhD studies, in tourist consumer behaviour and destination marketing, with particular interest in sustainable destination marketing, the tourist experience, sustainable tourism, accessible tourism, rural tourism (and related topics like wine and nature-based tourism). She is currently coordinating an FCT-funded 3-year research project TWINE (Co-creating sustainable Tourism & WINe Experiences) in rural areas (POCI-01–0145-FEDER-032259).

Metin Kozak holds a PhD degree from Sheffield Hallam University, UK. He has contributed to a wide range of articles, conference papers in more than 40 countries and over 30 books released by international publishers. As a research fellow, he was affiliated with the University of Namur, Belgium (2005–2006), Hong Kong Polytechnic University, Hong Kong SAR (2014–2015) and Bournemouth University, UK (July–August 2016). He has been invited as a guest lecturer to conduct seminars or lectures in more than 20 countries worldwide. He also has an extensive experience in taking parts in the organisation of academic organisations. He acts as the co-editor of Anatolia and the fellow of the International Academy for the Study of Tourism, Tourist Research Centre and International Academy of Culture, Hospitality and Tourism. His research interests entail destination marketing, and consumer behaviour. His current affiliation is with Dokuz Eylul University, Turkey.

Bernard Lane was the founder, and for 25 years was co-editor, of the *Journal of Sustainable Tourism,* ranked in the top 5 tourism research journals. He was on the staff of the University of Bristol for 33 years, where he directed the Rural Tourism Unit, and worked with many communities and businesses to create forums and partnerships. He is an associate of Red Kite

Environment (www.redkite-environment.co.uk), a consultancy specializing in managing, interpreting and marketing heritage sites, protected areas and rural tourism. He has also worked at Leeds Beckett and Sheffield Hallam Universities in the UK, the Western Norway Research Institute, the University of Calgary in Canada, Aveiro University in Portugal and the University of Lincoln in New Zealand. As a consultant, writer and keynote speaker, clients have included the OECD, the government of Australia, the European Union, the World Bank and businesses and communities in 28 countries worldwide.

Asaf Leshem has been guiding tours to dark tourism sites in and around Berlin since 2010. He has recently graduated with a PhD from the University of Central Lancashire, examining tour guides as interpreters of dark tourism in Berlin. Asaf's first experience in the tourism industry started in 1998 when he functioned as a tour leader of Israeli youth groups to former sites of atrocity and genocide in Poland. He then continued his work in tourism in Beijing, China, after which he started his academic studies of hotel management in New Zealand. In addition to his interest in tourism, Asaf has worked as a research fellow in Potsdam's Social Science Works, conducting deliberation workshops on a variety of social and political science issues. He has a BSc in Ecotourism from the University of Central Lancashire and an MSc of Integrated Natural Resource Management from the Humboldt University of Berlin.

Jo-Anne Lester is a principal lecturer in tourism at the University of Brighton. Within the broad context of space, place and culture, she has a particular interest in the embodied and performative dynamics of human experience and behaviour. Such focus encompasses the material, virtual and simulated spaces associated with everyday life. Her industry experience working on cruise ships underpins her continued interest in the cruise sector and cruise ships as work and leisure spaces. Her PhD investigated the architecture of cruise ship space through the medium of popular film. In so doing it acknowledged the multisensory nature of film and how the liminal realm of film space is experienced in and through the imagination, memory and emotion. She is the co-editor of several books including *Mediating Tourism: From Brochure to Virtual Encounters* (with Caroline Scarles) and *Travel, Tourism and Art* (with Tijana Rakić).

Maria Lichrou is a senior lecturer in marketing at the University of Limerick Kemmy Business School. Her research draws on critical marketing and consumer research perspectives and focuses on place, tourism and sustainability. She has explored the role of narrative in the marketing and consumption of place. Recent publications include work in *Tourism Management, European Journal of Marketing, Journal of Marketing Management* and *Journal of Place Management and Development*.

Jane Lovell worked for a decade in arts administration at the Royal Opera House in Covent Garden. She then became the tourism development officer at Canterbury City Council, where she staged international light and sculpture events. At Canterbury Christ Church University, Jane teaches Tourism and Events Management, specializing in Heritage and Creative Industry Management at undergraduate and postgraduate levels. Her research centres on authenticity, particularly in reference to literary and film geographies and their relationship to myths, storytelling and enchantment. She continues to stage light installations as part of her creative practice. She is a council member of the British Association of Canadian Studies, a visiting fellow at the British Library and an associate fellow at the UCL Institute of the Americas.

Contributors

Zohre Mohammadi is a research fellow in tourism at James Cook University, Singapore. She received her PhD in tourism management. She is a member of JCU Tropical Futures Institute and JCU's Centre for International Trade and Business in Asia (CITBA). Prior to joining JCU, she was a visiting lecturer at Allameh Tabataba'i University, Shiraz University and Yazd University. Zohre is passionate about tourism experience, marketing and new emerging markets.

Jeroen Nawijn is a senior lecturer at Breda University of Applied Sciences. His work addresses issues of well-being, sustainable tourism and cultural heritage. His main interest is to study areas or phenomena in which there is friction. This friction could relate to practical issues such as differing stakeholder objectives, tensions between visitors and residents or conceptual and methodological differences in academic interpretations and applications of theories within the field of tourism.

Barbara Neuhofer is a professor and head of experience design at the Salzburg University of Applied Sciences, Austria. Barbara's areas of expertise focus on the intersection of human experiences, experience design and transformation across the physical and digital domains. Barbara's research in the experience economy is widely published and cited in Google Scholar. She is an international keynote speaker and industry advisor on experience design and the co-founder of the award-winning Experience Design Summit Year Zero, a transformational experience event. In her recent TEDx Talk "The Global State of Awe", Barbara bridged the sciences and arts, and co-created an immersive sensory experience aimed at giving insight into the awe-inducing event and mindset transformation that astronauts have when looking at Earth from space. Barbara's work has received more than fifteen international awards, recognizing her excellence across scientific research, teaching practice and events innovation.

Louise O'Flynn has worked as a protected area practitioner in Australia and South East Asia for fourteen years, and she is an active member of the IUCN's World Commission on Protected Areas. Louise is currently part of the Industry Doctorate Program at the University of Technology Sydney, where she is exploring the sustainable financing of terrestrial protected areas with a focus on the protected area estate in New South Wales, Australia.

Daniel H. Olsen is an associate professor in the Department of Geography at Brigham Young University. His research interests revolve around religious and spiritual tourism, heritage tourism and the management of sacred sites, with secondary research interests in tourism in peripheral areas and tourism and disabilities. He is co-editor of *Religion, Tourism and Spiritual Journeys* (2006) *Religious Pilgrimage Routes and Trails* (CABI, 2018), *Dark Tourism and Pilgrimage* (CABI, 2020), *Religious Tourism and the Environment* (CABI) 2020) and the forthcoming *Routledge Handbook of Religious and Spiritual Tourism* (Routledge, 2021).

Can-Seng Ooi is a sociologist and professor of cultural and heritage tourism at the University of Tasmania. He was a professor of international business and culture industries at Copenhagen Business School. Besides tourist experiences, his other tourism research interests include tourism and the arts, destination branding, cross-cultural engagement, culture and tourism strategy, job polarization in the industry and tourism in nation-building. In his three-decade-long research career, he has published extensively and conducted research in different countries, including Australia, Singapore, Denmark, China and Malaysia. He is a firm believer of engaged scholarship; that is, scholarly knowledge should be made relevant for the community and industry. He has successfully translated his academic knowledge through his advisory board appointments and through his teaching. Subsequently, he was voted and recognised as "Best Professor" by 11 Executive MBA student cohorts at Copenhagen Business School. His website is www.cansengooi.com.

Catherine Palmer is a social anthropologist and fellow of the Royal Anthropological Institute of Great Britain and Ireland. She is an honorary research fellow in the Centre for Memory, Narrative and Histories, University of Brighton, UK, coordinating the *Heritage in the 21st Century* research theme. Her research focuses on heritage, identity and materiality, memorialization, embodiment, tourism and the coast/seaside. She is the joint book series editor for *Routledge Advances in Tourism Anthropology* (with Jo-Anne Lester), and the author of the Routledge monograph *Being and Dwelling through Tourism: An anthropological Perspective*. She is the co-editor of several books including *Tourism and Embodiment* (with Hazel Andrews), *Creating Heritage for Tourism* (with Jacqueline Tivers) and *Tourism and Visual Culture: Volume 1 Theories and Concepts* (with Peter Burns and Jo-Anne Lester).

Aggelos Panayiotopoulos is currently a senior lecturer at Liverpool Business School, Liverpool John Moores University. His research focuses on tourism development adopting a critical perspective. Drawing on political discourse theory, his work examines tourism development genealogically, unpicking the political, cultural and spatial aspects of tourism and its impact on places and people. He has also published research on (over)tourism, heritage consumption and scholar activism.

Philip L. Pearce Prior to his untimely death, Philip Pearce was the Foundation Professor of Tourism at James Cook University, Australia, and a distinguished professor of that University. He had long-standing interests in tourist behaviour and experience. His most recent book, published in 2019, was the large edited volume, *Tourist Behaviour: The Essential Companion*. Professor Pearce passed away in 2020 during the compilation of this book. Having already contributed one chapter, 'The Ulysses factor revisited: Consolidating the travel career pattern approach to tourist motivation' (Chapter 13), he then submitted a second chapter reflecting some of his latest thinking on the tourist experience. Co-authored with Zohre Mohammadi, "Building the orchestra model of tourist experience, integration and examples" (Chapter 4), this demonstrates his continuing passion for and contribution to tourism studies. He is greatly missed by friends, colleagues and the wider academic community.

Eva Pelechano-Barahona is an associate professor at the Business Administration Department in Rey Juan Carlos University, Spain. She is the author and co-author of several papers dealing with strategic management, in particular, intellectual capital, knowledge management and inter-firms networks. Numerous publications have been involved in the development of all this research activity. These include various articles published in scientific journals included in the Journal Citation Reports.

Nina K. Prebensen, PhD, is a professor in marketing at UiT The Arctic University of Norway and University of South East Norway. Prebensen has a long list of publications in highly regarded journals and books. Currently she is an associate editor in three top-tier journals. Prebensen has led the research Centre for Innovation and Management at USN, where she also had a position as professor. She has managed projects such as "Service

Contributors

Innovation and Tourist Experiences in the High North: The Co-Creation of Values for Consumers, Firms and the Tourism Industry". Prebensen has started and managed the research group "Experiential Marketing, Management and Innovation (EMMI)".

Jillian M. Rickly is a professor of tourism at the University of Nottingham and the series editor for De Gruyter Studies in Tourism. She is a tourism geographer with research interests in authenticity/alienation in tourism motivation and experience, accessibility and tourism mobilities, critical animal studies in tourism, and ethics and sustainability. Her work has been published in the *Annals of Tourism Research, Journal of Sustainable Tourism, Tourist Studies, Cultural Geographies* and *Mobilities*, among others.

Jarkko Saarinen is a professor of geography at the University of Oulu, Finland, and distinguished visiting professor (sustainability management) at the University of Johannesburg, South Africa. His research interests include sustainability, tourism and development, tourism and climate change adaptation, tourism-community relations and wilderness and nature conservation studies. Over the past 20 years, he has been working extensively in the rural and peripheral areas of southern Africa and northern (Arctic) Finland. He is editor for the tourism geographies and associate editor for the *Annals of Tourism Research* and *Journal of Ecotourism*. His recent publications include edited/co-edited books: *Resilient Destinations* (2019, Routledge), *Borderless Worlds for Whom?* (2019, Routledge) and *Political Ecology and Tourism* (2016, Routledge).

H. Kader Şanlıöz–Özgen obtained her MBA from Akdeniz University, Institute of Social Sciences, majoring in business administration in 2012, and her PhD from Dokuz Eylül University, Institute of Social Sciences, majoring in tourism management. She also gained professional experience as an employee and a manager at the front office, guest relations and marketing departments of the city and seaside hotels in Turkey between 1996 and 2011. Her research fields focus on hospitality marketing, hospitality experience, hotel information technologies, total quality management and sustainable tourism. She is currently affiliated with Özyeğin University School of Applied Sciences Hotel Management Department.

Stephen Schweinsberg is a senior lecturer in sustainable management at the UTS Business School. His current research interests include the study of tourism's place-based setting and the process of academic knowledge formation. Stephen is the co-author of two books *Ecotourism: Transitioning to the 22nd Century* and *Marketing National Parks for Sustainable Tourism*. He has authored and co-authored articles for *Annals of Tourism Research*, the *Journal of Sustainable Tourism, Tourism Management* and other leading journals.

Tony Seaton is emeritus professor of tourism behaviour at the University of Bedfordshire and visiting professor at the University of Limerick. For over 30 years, his work has combined seminal, academic papers and publications – in tourism behaviour, dark tourism/thanatourism, VFR research and travel history – with high - impact, professional research and consultancy for international organizations including the World Tourism Organization, The European Travel Commission, the European Union, USAID and NTOS in Britain and Europe. In 1990, the Queen presented his edited book on English travellers in Iceland to the President of Iceland as a gift commemorating her Royal Visit. Between 1996 and 2005, his academic work on European literary tourism led to the creation of two new cultural destinations in Britain; the book towns of Wigtown in Scotland, and Sedbergh in England.

Contributors

In the past decade, his work has included new studies of VFR, dark tourism, and currently tourism and the Industrial Revolution in the Midlands.

Sabrina Seeler is a lecturer in international tourism management at West Coast University of Applied Sciences (Heide, Germany) and a researcher and project leader at DITF – German Institute for Tourism Research. Sabrina holds a PhD from Auckland University of Technology, Faculty of Culture and Society. In her PhD, she explored factors that contribute to higher self-assessed experience levels and the identification as an experienced tourist. Before returning to her home country – German – she worked as a postdoctoral researcher at Nord University (Bodø, Norway) and was part of the team management, marketing and innovation of experiences. Sabrina is a book review editor at *Journal of Tourism Futures* and frequent reviewer for numerous tourism journals. Her research interests and expertise are consumer behaviour in tourism, experience creation and consumption, host–guest relationships, resident attitudes, sustainable destination management and resilience.

Richard Sharpley is professor of tourism and development at the University of Central Lancashire, Preston, UK. He has previously held positions at a number of other institutions, including the University of Northumbria (Reader in Tourism) and the University of Lincoln, where he was a professor of tourism and head of Department, Tourism and Recreation Management. He is co-editor of the journal *Tourism Planning & Development*, and a member of the editorial boards of a number of other tourism journals. His principal research interests are within the fields of tourism and development and the sociology of tourism, and his books include *Tourism and Development: Concepts and Issues, 2nd Edition* (2015, with David Telfer); *Tourism, Tourists and Society, 5th Edition* (2018); *The Darker Side of Travel: The Theory and Practice of Dark Tourism* (2009, with Philip Stone); *Tourism, Development and Environment: Beyond Sustainability* (2009); *Mass Tourism in a Small World* (2017, with David Harrison); and *Tourism Development in Japan: Themes, Issues and Challenges* (2020, with Kumi Kato).

Tom Sintobin is an assistant professor of cultural studies at Radboud University, Nijmegen, the Netherlands. He founded the research group Tourism, Travel and Text of the Radboud Institute for Culture and History, and coordinates the master's specialisation in tourism and culture. His research interests include Dutch and Belgian literature (1890–1970), with a special stress on travel literature and local colour fiction, tourist cultures in coastal cities in the low countries and online travel accounts. He edited volumes such as *Gender, Companionship, and Travel. Discourses in Pre-modern and Modern Travel Literature* (Routledge, 2018) and *Koninginnen aan de Noordzee: Scheveningen, Oostende en de opkomst van de badcultuur rond 1900* (Verloren 2014) and wrote a monograph on the Belgian author Stijn Streuvels (*Wie schaft er op de woorden? Vijf keer Streuvels lezen* (KANTL, 2005).

Melanie Kay Smith, PhD, is an associate professor, researcher and consultant whose work focuses on urban planning, cultural tourism, wellness tourism experiences and the relationship between tourism and well-being. She has lectured in the UK, Hungary, Germany, Austria and Switzerland. She has also been a visiting professor at the University of Tartu, Pärnu College in Estonia for more than 10 years. She has been an invited keynote speaker in many countries worldwide and was chair of ATLAS (Association for Tourism and Leisure Education) for seven years. Her most recent research focuses on the impacts of "overtourism" in cities, the changing nature of cultural tourism, spiritual tourism among younger generations, as well as digitalisation in urban environments. She has recently undertaken consultancy work for UNWTO and ETC in the field of health tourism.

Wim Strijbosch obtained both his BBA in leisure management (2014) and his MSc in leisure studies (2016) at Breda University of Applied Sciences. As part of Breda University of Applied Sciences' Experience Lab, Wim is currently working on a PhD that aims at studying the temporal dynamics of emotions in tourism and leisure experiences. In doing so, he uses measures that are relatively novel to the tourism and leisure field, such as the neuroimaging method of EEG and the electrophysiological measure of skin conductance.

Siow-Hooi Tan is an associate professor in economics at the Faculty of Management, Multimedia University. She earned her PhD from the Faculty of Economics and Management, Universiti Putra Malaysia. Her research interests focus on behavioural economics, tourism economics and corporate social responsibilities.

Siow-Kian Tan is a senior lecturer of the Faculty of Management, Multimedia University. She earned her PhD from Institute of Creative Industries Design, National Cheng Kung University, Taiwan. The focus of her research is service design, tourism management, creative and cultural tourism.

Dallen J. Timothy is professor of community resources and development at Arizona State University and senior sustainability scientist at the Julie Ann Wrigley Global Institute of Sustainability. He is also a senior research associate at the University of Johannesburg, South Africa; Furong professor at Hunan Normal University, China; visiting professor at Guangxi University and Luoyang Normal University, China; and visiting professor in the European Master in Tourism Management Program based at the University of Girona, Spain. Professor Timothy is a commissioning editor and co-editor for four book series published by Channel View Publications and Routledge, and serves on the editorial boards of 23 international social science journals. He has ongoing research projects in North America, Asia, the Middle East, Europe and Africa on many aspects of tourism, including heritage, religion, geopolitics and cross-border cooperation.

Muzaffer S. Uysal, PhD, is a professor and chair of the Department of Hospitality and Tourism Management – Isenberg School of Management at the University of Massachusetts, Amherst. He maintains an extraordinary professor title in the Research Unit: Tourism Research in Economic Environs and Society at the Potchefstroom Campus of the North-West University. He is a member of the International Academy for the Study of Tourism, the Academy of Leisure Sciences, and a founding member of the Hospitality and Tourism Management Academy. Dr. Uysal has also received over 30 awards, honors and recognitions including multiple 'best paper' and 'lifetime achievement' awards. His current research interests center on tourism development and quality of life in tourism and hospitality settings.

Richard Voase joined the University of Lincoln when its degree portfolio in tourism studies was first established. Prior to that, he enjoyed a practitioner career in destination marketing and arts management. His career has included management positions at two coastal resorts, and responsibility for arts and entertainments for one of England's major metropolitan authorities. He has also worked in France and Germany. Richard's published work centres on consumer culture, the nature of enjoyment and the role of the cultural industries

Contributors

in society. He holds a first degree in archaeology, and a postgraduate degree in the sociology of contemporary culture. Now retired from his salaried position at the University of Lincoln, he continues as an honorary visiting fellow, and is a writer and speaker.

Serena Volo is an associate professor of marketing at the Faculty of Economics and Management of the Free University of Bozen-Bolzano, Italy. She is the vice-director of the Competence Centre in Tourism Management and Tourism Economics (TOMTE) and has chaired several editions of CBTS, the Consumer Behavior in Tourism Symposium. She is editor-in-chief of the *International Journal of Culture, Tourism and Hospitality Research* published by Emerald. She is also on the editorial board of leading scientific journals in the field of tourism, hospitality and leisure. She is an elected member of the Executive Council of IATE, the International Association for Tourism Economics. Her research interests include consumer behaviour in tourism, experience and emotions in tourism, visual research methods and big data, innovation and competitiveness in tourism. She has had work, research and life experiences in Italy, Ireland, England, USA, France and Switzerland.

Craig Wight is an associate professor at Edinburgh Napier University. He has authored a number of journal articles within the field of heritage tourism, and specifically the application of a humanities lens to critique heritage as a feature of public culture and destination discourse production. His research looks variously at European Holocaust heritage, culinary tourism and immersive learning on tourism and hospitality management programmes. He has disseminated research at a number of international tourism conferences, and is currently looking at visitor narratives of Holocaust heritage across various social media channels. Craig's research is heavily influenced by post-structuralism as a research philosophy, and he has published work on the use of this kind of research philosophy in tourism in academic journals.

Jase Wilson is a doctoral researcher at Leeds Beckett University. His work focuses on high-altitude mountaineering tourism in the Himalayas on the world's highest mountains. His research investigates complex discussions of emotions and morality in typologies of tourism which involve aspects of inequality, the politicised nature of risk taking, workers' rights, indigeneity and the ethics of a researcher's ethnographic engagement with the field. Theories of emotions, he has found, provide an exceptional lens through which to view the controversies which arise as a result of dangerous, politically complex forms of consumptive leisure behaviour. Jase is a mountaineer, rock climber, ultra-marathoner, adventure traveller, passionate ethnographic photographer and writer.

Xuan Zhu is an associate professor in the Tourism College at Shanghai Normal University, China. She has been a visiting scholar at Arizona State University and at the University of Alberta, Canada. Her research interests are backpacker tourism and mobility. Her areas of expertise include social and cultural geography, tourism geography and tourism anthropology. She has directed two National Natural Science Foundation of China grants. Dr. Zhu has published many articles in peer-reviewed journals and one book on backpacker tourism. Her book received the "Outstanding Tourism Academic Research" award by China's Tourism Administration in 2011. Two of her articles have been respectively awarded Best Paper of 2019 published in *Tourism Tribune*, and the 2019 Paper of Excellence at the Annual Conference of the Tourism Geography Committee, issued by the Geographical Society of China.

xxvi

INTRODUCTION

Richard Sharpley

Introduction

It has become something of a cliché to describe tourism as one of the major phenomena of the modern era. Indeed, although the precise words used may vary, many academic publications commence with this observation, typically making reference to the exponential growth of tourism, both international and domestic, and its related contribution to the global economy. Yet, this is undeniably an accurate description. Tourism or, more precisely, travel – for it is generally acknowledged that the term 'tourism' first appeared in the English language at the end of the eighteenth century (Buzard, 1993; Feifer, 1985) – 'can trace its ancestry back to the Old Testament' (Young, 1973: 9); moreover, the roots of contemporary tourism can be found in leisure travel practices from the late seventeenth century onwards (see, for example, Towner, 1996). However, it is only over the last seven decades that tourism has evolved into what it is today: a highly significant socio-economic phenomenon.

The data that demonstrate this are well known. In 1950, just over 25 million international arrivals were recorded. With subsequent largely uninterrupted growth (as a result of the global economic crisis, 2009 was, prior to 2020, one of just three years in which global international tourist numbers witnessed a decline), by 2019 annual international arrivals reached a remarkable 1.5 billion. Equally dramatic has been the commensurate growth in the economic contribution of tourism. In 2018, international tourism receipts plus spending on passenger transport amounted to US$1.7 trillion (UNWTO, 2019) whilst, overall, the global tourism economy (direct, indirect and induced impact), including both domestic and international tourism, is estimated to contribute US$8.9 trillion, or 10.3 percent, of global GDP (WTTC, 2020a). In addition, tourism is an important source of employment; the sector typically supports around 10 percent of the global workforce, equivalent to around 330 million jobs.

At the time of writing (early 2021), however, the Covid-19 pandemic continues to wreak havoc on the tourism sector worldwide; for example, many airlines are operating limited services, hotels and other hospitality services remain closed and the future of the myriad of businesses that directly and indirectly meet the needs of tourists is in doubt. Moreover, the collapse in demand for travel and tourism during 2020 resulted in an estimated 75 percent decline in international arrivals that year (UNWTO, 2020a). As a consequence, tourism's

DOI: 10.4324/9781003219866-1

position as one of the world's most significant economic sectors has been challenged. For instance, according to the UN World Tourism Organization, the 'plunge in international tourism [in 2020] could result in an estimated economic loss of over US$2 trillion in global GDP, more than 2% of the world's GDP in 2019' (UNWTO, 2020b). Unsurprisingly, there have also been significant job losses; it has been estimated that during 2020, up to 174 million tourism-related jobs (more than 50 percent) were lost (WTTC, 2020b).

Undoubtedly it will be a number of years before the full impact of the Covid-19 pandemic on the tourism sector is known and, indeed, before business activity begins to return to pre-pandemic levels. What is also certain, however, is that although the actual demand for tourism has been temporarily suppressed by border closures, widespread restrictions on travel and the enforced closure of innumerable tourism and hospitality businesses, the latent demand for tourism remains as strong as ever. Putting it another way, as soon as people are able to participate in tourism again they will do so; their desire to be tourists, to seek or consume tourist experiences, in all likelihood remains undiminished.

The desire to travel is not, of course, new. From earliest times and as long as they have had the means to do so, people have engaged in tourism in the sense of travelling for pleasure, education, spiritual fulfilment and interest rather than for trade or warfare. As such, dromomania (initially a term referring to an uncontrollable psychological urge to roam but now used colloquially to describe wanderlust or a constant desire to travel) has arguably always been an inherent characteristic of humankind. There is, for example, evidence of early tourism in Egypt where ancient graffiti dating back to 1300 BC have been found scratched onto the great pyramids at Giza (Casson, 1974). Tourism of a sort also existed in ancient Greece, although it was normally associated with attending religious or sporting festivals or consulting oracles. Notably, following their introduction at Olympia in 776 BC, the Olympic Games attracted thousands of visitors from home and abroad who primarily sought to experience their deep religious significance. Thus, in contrast to its contemporary manifestation, tourism in ancient Greece 'was not so much a voyage of adventure as a trip in accordance with tradition and ritual. The man who travelled tightened his links rather than liberated himself from his social background' (Sigaux 1966: 10). More generally, leisure was considered by the philosophers of the time as the basis of civilized society; hence, visits to oracles or festivals were fundamental to Greek life and society whilst travel for pleasure was uncommon. In other words, this early form of tourist experience was culturally defined.

The same can be said about much contemporary tourism. Although it has evolved from an activity that for much of its history was the preserve of the privileged elite, particularly during the era of the Grand Tour (Towner, 1984, 1985), into today's mass, democratized (Urry, 1990) social phenomenon (at least in those societies that enjoy the financial, temporal and other resources that enable participation in it), tourism has always been and remains about people. As Sharpley (2018: 4) explains, tourism…

> … is about millions of individuals who comprise local, regional and national societies, travelling domestically or crossing international borders and experiencing and impacting upon different societies. It is about people who are influenced and motivated by the norms and changes in their own society, who carry with them perceptions, expectations and standards based on their own personal experience and background. Above all, tourism is about people, tourists, interacting with other places and other peoples, undergoing experiences that may influence their own or the host community's attitudes, expectations, opinions and, ultimately, lifestyles.

Introduction

In other words, why and how people engage in tourism and the experiences they enjoy (or not!) are largely socially and culturally determined. And it is for this reason that academic attention has long been paid to the social dimension or what can be broadly termed the sociology of tourism (Apostolopoulos, Leivadi & Yiannakis, 1996; Cohen, 1984, 1979a; Cohen & Cohen, 2019; Sharpley, 2018; Urry, 1989). As Dann and Parrinello (2009) reveal, the early academic study of tourism dating back to the first decades of the twentieth century – hence predating by half a century the emergence of tourism as popular and distinctive field of academic study (Dredge, Airey & Gross, 2014; Sharpley, 2011) – was firmly rooted within a sociological tradition. This laid the foundation for the subsequent development of research from the 1970s onwards into tourism as a social phenomenon, complementing and running in parallel to the study of tourism from a business/management perspective. Notably, Cohen's (1972) seminal work, based on the German sociologist Georg Simmel's (1858–1918) concept of the stranger (see Marotta, 2012), adopted a micro approach to understanding tourist choices and behavior through his widely cited (but arguably now outdated) typology of tourists. He went on to develop a phenomenology of tourism (Cohen, 1979b), arguing that not only does there exist a variety of tourist types or roles but also a variety of experiences by which tourists may be categorized. Implicit in both is the significance of tourism (and the tourist experience) in relation to the tourist's normal life, a theme taken up by others at the time in the context of, for example, motivation (Dann, 1977) and tourism as a sacred journey (Graburn, 1989). It also directly informed MacCannell's (1973, 1976) influential work on (staged) authenticity, a topic that has continued to attract much attention (for example, Olsen, 2002; Rickly, 2018; Wang, 1999).

Building on these early beginnings, the last four decades have witnessed nothing less than an explosion in the range and depth of research and literature concerned with the sociology of tourism. Traditional issue and themes, such as typologies, the motivation and demand for/consumption of tourism, authenticity, the significance of tourism in contemporary society, the social consequences or impacts of tourism and tourist–host community interaction remain popular. At the same time, the influence of wider social and cultural change on tourism has proved to be a fruitful area of research, including in particular the influence of postmodern culture on the consumption of tourism (for example, Berger, 2011; Munt, 1994; Pretes, 1995; Uriely, 1997; Urry & Larsen, 2011). Notably, however, the sociology of tourism has also come to be embraced by or, perhaps, redefined as the study of the tourist experience (Morgan, Lugosi & Ritchie, 2010; Ryan, 2002; Sharpley & Stone, 2011a, 2012), reflecting in general a wider focus on the actor – the tourist – within the phenomenon of tourism and, more specifically, a blurring of the boundaries between sociological and business/management perspectives in tourism research. As Quan and Wang (2004: 298) similarly suggest, 'there are two general approaches to the study of the tourist experience, namely, the social science approach and the marketing/management approach'. For them, the former is concerned with understanding the actual tourist experience; Ryan (2011) provides a comprehensive overview of the variety of ways in which this is conceptualized in the literature. In contrast, the latter marketing/management approach focuses upon the tourist as a consumer and the means of supporting their experience through, for example, enhancing service quality and measuring satisfaction. They go on to suggest that these approaches should be combined into a conceptual structural model of the tourist experience.

The broadening of the sociological study of tourism into the study of tourist experience or, more precisely, embracing both a sociological and business/management approach to research under the banner of the tourist experience is both beneficial and problematic. On the one hand, it highlights the inescapable relationship between tourists themselves, their needs, motives and expectations, and the providers of tourism services and products in the construction of the tourist experience. In other words, tourists depend on an enormous variety of services and goods that facilitate their consumption, from primary services such as accommodation and transport to other support services such as information centres (or more commonly nowadays, apps, destination websites and other 'smart' services), tour guides and so on that, in effect, mediate the tourist experience (O'Dell, 2007). In addition, it provides the context for research into contemporary themes such as the co-creation of experiences (Campos, Mendes, do Valle & Scott, 2018). In short, it acknowledges the fact that, when considering the tourist experience, tourists themselves cannot be conceptually divorced from the services and products that they consume.

On the other hand, it raises the inevitable questions: what is the 'tourist experience' and, for the purpose of research, what are its parameters? Simplistically, it can be suggested that, in contrast to a number of conceptual definitions summarized by Quinlan Cutler and Carmichael (2010) such as it being a function of the interaction between tourists and a place/destination, the tourist experience by definition is 'the experience of being a tourist' (Sharpley & Stone, 2011b: 3). This implies that not only are there as many tourist experiences as there are tourists – hence the predominant focus in the literature on exploring how the tourist experience might be understood rather than on specific experiences – but also that it can only be tourists themselves who can understand their experiences. And if it is 'the experience of being a tourist', what are its temporal dimensions? Is it restricted to the actual lived experience (of being on holiday), the here and now – often referred to as *Erlebnis* – or is it a post-event phenomenon (*Efahrung*), a significant or meaningful memory (Larsen, 2007)? Alternatively, the social institution of tourism is now arguably embedded in contemporary life to such an extent that being a tourist (and hence the tourist experience) is a continuous cyclical process from anticipation, through planning and actual experience to evaluation and memory, and subsequently again into the anticipatory stage.

This latter point is addressed by Quinlan Cutler and Carmichael (2010) in their discussion of the dimensions of the tourism experience. For them, understanding the experience, from anticipation through to recollection, must be framed by an exploration of the influential realm, including the social environment, the characteristics of the destination and the services provided, and the personal realm that includes both anticipation and motivational factors as well as outcomes, such as satisfaction and emotion. From this perspective, not only is the tourist experience essentially undefinable but also highly complex, multi-dimensional dynamic and individually defined. This, in turn, suggests that an understanding of the tourist experience and, hence, an understanding of the contemporary social phenomenon of tourism can be thought of as a jigsaw that will, in all likelihood, remain incomplete. Although research into various aspects of the tourist experience will produce the jigsaw pieces and, perhaps, put some of the pieces together, such is the dynamism of tourism and the socio-cultural context within which occurs the complete picture is unlikely to emerge.

The purpose of this handbook, then, is to contribute pieces of that jigsaw. Structured thematically, it comprises purposefully commissioned contributions from leading academics in the respective fields. It commences with a number of chapters that consider a variety of conceptual perspectives on the tourist experience before a shorter section addresses typologies and motivation. This is followed by chapters that, uniquely, explore the tourist experience in the context of specific tourist and roles. The relationship between experience and specific tourism places is then addressed before, finally, a number of chapters discuss the creation and

Introduction

mediation of tourist experiences. As such, this handbook is not intended to offer a complete discussion of the tourist experience; given the scope and diversity of the topic, to do so – to provide the full picture – would be an impossible task within a single volume such as this. Nevertheless, it is hoped that this collection offers an up-to-date perspective on various elements of the tourist experience, thereby enhancing our knowledge and understanding of the phenomenon that is contemporary tourism.

References

Apostolopoulos, Y., Leivadi, S. and Yiannakis, A. (Eds.) (1996) *The Sociology of Tourism: Theoretical and Empirical Investigations*. London: Routledge.

Berger, A. (2011) Tourism as a postmodern semiotic activity. *Semiotica*, 183, 105–119.

Buzard, J. (1993) *The Beaten Track*. Oxford: Oxford University Press.

Campos, A.C., Mendes, J., do Valle, P.O. and Scott, N. (2018) Co-creation of tourist experiences: A literature review. *Current Issues in Tourism*, 21(4), 369–400.

Casson, L. (1974) *Travels in the Ancient World*. London: George Allen and Unwin.

Cohen, E. (1972) Towards a sociology of international tourism. *Social Research*, 39(1), 64–82.

Cohen, E. (1979a) Rethinking the sociology of tourism. *Annals of Tourism Research*, 6(1), 18–35.

Cohen, E. (1979b) A phenomenology of tourist experiences. *Sociology*, 13, 179–201.

Cohen, E. (1984) The sociology of tourism: approaches, issues, and findings. *Annual Review of Sociology*, 10(1), 373–392.

Cohen, S.A. and Cohen, E. (2019) New directions in the sociology of tourism. *Current Issues in Tourism*, 22(2), 153–172.

Dann, G. (1977) Anomie, ego-enhancement and tourism. *Annals of Tourism Research*, 4(4), 184–194.

Dann, G. and Parrinello, G. (Eds.) (2009) *The Sociology of Tourism: European Origins and Developments*. Bingley: Emerald Group Publishing.

Dredge, D., Airey, D. and Gross, M. (Eds.) (2014) *The Routledge Handbook of Tourism and Hospitality Education*. Abingdon: Routledge.

Feifer, M. (1985) *Going Places*. London: Macmillan.

Graburn, N. (1989) Tourism: The sacred journey. In V. Smith (Ed.), *Hosts and Guests: The Anthropology of Tourism*, 2nd Edn. Philadelphia: University of Pennsylvania Press, pp. 21–36.

Larsen, S. (2007) Aspects of a psychology of the tourist experience. *Scandinavian Journal of Hospitality and Tourism*, 7(1), 7–18.

MacCannell, D. (1973) Staged authenticity: Arrangements of social space in tourist settings. *American Journal of Sociology*, 79, 589–603.

MacCannell, D. (1976) *The Tourist: A New Theory of the Leisure Class*. New York: Shocken Books.

Marotta, M. (2012) Georg Simmel, the Stranger and the sociology of knowledge. *Journal of Intercultural Studies*, 33(6), 675–689.

Morgan, M., Lugosi, P. and Ritchie, J.R.B. (2010) *The Tourism and Leisure Experience: Consumer and Managerial Experiences*. Bristol: Channel view Publications

Munt, I. (1994) The 'other' postmodern tourism: Culture, travel and the new middle classes. *Theory, Culture and Society*, 11(3), 101–123.

O'Dell, T. (2007) Tourist experiences and academic junctures. *Scandinavian Journal of Hospitality and Tourism*, 7(1), 34–45.

Olsen, K. (2002) Authenticity as a concept in tourism research: The social organization of the experience of authenticity. *Tourist Studies*, 2(2), 159–182.

Pretes, M. (1995) Postmodern tourism: The Santa Claus industry. *Annals of Tourism Research*, 22(1), 1–15.

Quan, S. and Wang, N. (2004) Towards a structural model of the tourist experience: An illustration from food experiences in tourism. *Tourism Management*, 25(3), 297–305.

Quinlan Cutler, S. and Carmichael, B. (2010) The dimensions of the tourist experience. In M. Morgan, P. Lugosi and J. Ritchie (Eds.), *The Leisure and Tourism Experience: Consumer and Managerial Perspectives*. Bristol: Channel View Publications, pp. 3–26.

Rickly, J.M. (2018) Tourism geographies and the place of authenticity. *Tourism Geographies*, 20(4), 733–736.

Ryan, C. (2002) *The Tourist Experience: A New Introduction*, 2nd Edn. London: Continuum.

Ryan, C. (2011) Ways of conceptualising the tourist experience: A review of the literature. In R. Sharpley and P. Stone (Eds.), *Tourist Experience: Contemporary Perspectives*. Abingdon: Routledge, pp. 9–20.

Sharpley, R. (2011) *The Study of Tourism: Past Trends and Future Directions*. Abingdon: Routledge.

Sharpley, R. (2018) *Tourism, Tourists and Society*, 5th Edn. Abingdon: Routledge.

Sharpley, R. and Stone, P. (Eds.) (2011a) *Tourist Experience: Contemporary Perspectives*. Abingdon: Routledge.

Sharpley, R. and Stone, P. (2011b) Introduction: Thinking about the tourist experience. In R. Sharpley and P. Stone (Eds.), *Tourist Experience: Contemporary Perspectives*. Abingdon: Routledge, pp. 1–8.

Sharpley, R. and Stone, P. (Eds.) (2012) *Contemporary Tourist Experience: Concepts and Consequences*. Abingdon: Routledge.

Sigaux, G. (1966) *History of Tourism*. London: Leisure Arts Ltd.

Towner, J. (1984) The grand tour: Sources and a methodology for an historical study of tourism. *Tourism Management*, 5(3), 215–222.

Towner, J. (1985) The grand tour: A key phase in the history of tourism. *Annals of Tourism Research*, 12(3), 297–333.

Towner, J. (1996) *An Historical Geography of Recreation and Tourism in the Western World 1540–1940*. Chichester: John Wiley & Sons.

UNWTO (2019) *International Tourism Highlights, 2019 Edition*. Madrid: UN World Tourism Organization. https://doi.org/10.18111/9789284421152.

UNWTO (2020a) Tourism Back to 1990 Levels as Arrivals Fall by More Than 70%. UN World Tourism Organization, 17 December. Available at: https://www.unwto.org/taxonomy/term/347 (Accessed 11 January 2021).

UNWTO (2020b) Impact Assessment of the Covid-19 Outbreak on International Tourism. UN World Tourism Organization, December. Available at: https://www.unwto.org/impact-assessment-of-the-covid-19-outbreak-on-international-tourism (Accessed 11 January 2021).

Uriely, N. (1997) Theories of modern and postmodern tourism. *Annals of Tourism Research*, 24(4), 982–985.

Urry, J. (1989) The sociology of tourism. In C. Cooper (Ed.), *Progress in Tourism, Recreation and Hospitality Management*, Vol. 3. London: Bellhaven Press, pp. 48–57.

Urry, J. (1990) *The Tourist Gaze*. London: Sage Publications.

Urry, J. and Larsen, J. (2011) *The Tourist Gaze 3.0*. London: Sage Publications.

Wang, N. (1999) Rethinking authenticity in tourism experience. *Annals of Tourism Research*, 26(2), 349–370.

WTTC (2020a) *Economic Impact Reports*. World Travel & Tourism Council. Available at: https://wttc.org/Research/Economic-Impact (Accessed 12 January 2020).

WTTC (2020b) 174m travel & tourism jobs could be lost due to COVID-19 and travel restrictions, says WTTC. World Travel & Tourism Council, 29 October. Available at: https://wttc.org/News-Article/174m-Travel-&-Tourism-jobs-could-be-lost-due-to-COVID-19-and-travel-restrictions (Accessed 11 January 2021).

Young, G. (1973) *Tourism: Blessing or Blight?* Harmondsworth: Penguin.

SECTION 1

Dimensions of the contemporary tourist experience

1

TOURISM, THE TOURIST EXPERIENCE AND POSTMODERNITY

Theory, application and research

Craig Wight

Introduction

The urban dictionary, a crowd-sourced online resource for slang terminologies, has this to say about postmodernity:

> My professor tried to explain postmodernism but got hung up on what words to use. He kept losing track of the meanings and saying things that nobody could understand. Finally when he was unable to speak any language at all, we all understood and went home but couldn't find it, because home is in the film The Wizard of OZ.
>
> *(Bozlog, 2008)*

This somewhat abstract initiation to the concept of postmodernity at once encapsulates both its key strength and its central weakness: that it can mean anything to anyone and that it is reassuringly, or prohibitively – depending on the reader's relationship to it – complex. The term postmodernity is used in a range of contexts with increasing frequency, and in a surprising variety of ways. Its prominent usage is perhaps a reflection of the enduring popularity of debate around the extent to which Western societies have undergone radical cultural transformation in the backdrop of the diminishing credibility of metanarratives and any shared idea of progress. As this chapter will demonstrate, postmodernity is a countermovement against the intellectual values and beliefs that dominated the modern period (seventeenth to nineteenth centuries) in the history of Western intellectual thinking. As a philosophy, its central message is the outright denial of eighteenth-century Enlightenment and the claim that logic and reason are only legitimate within the confines of the established intellectual traditions within which they are applied. It is a slippery concept, and one that consistently evades capture in terms of securing a fixed definition. Postmodernity broadly holds that the descriptive, explanatory ideas that were created and maintained around metanarratives, or 'worldviews' such as science, history and religion during the Enlightenment era, have not only failed but have floundered spectacularly to the point that postmodernists argue that there is no such thing as 'truth' at all, outside of context. And in the rarefied field of tourism in particular, postmodernity plays a disruptive, critical role as a way of understanding

DOI: 10.4324/9781003219866-3

9

tourism consumption and behaviour. It is used in this context to describe the point at which the typologically rigid classifications of tourism that emerged in the post-industrial age – such as the categorization of tourists based on simple observations about their motives and consumption – were rejected and replaced with conceptualizations that are more flexible. Postmodern thinking can also be deployed as a research philosophy that offers an alternative to the typical interdisciplinary business approaches often associated with tourism research.

The aim of this chapter, then, is to explain postmodernity, and to do so using the context of tourism so that students and academics interested in postmodern thinking for research or other purposes can take orientation from an oven-ready synthesis of the key themes and debates. As such, it seeks to offer an intellectual framework within which subsequent chapters in this volume might be located. Indeed, the chapter has a grounding in the contemporary market dynamics of tourism, so that what is happening 'now', or at least recently, and at the time of writing can be used as a reference point in discussing what postmodernity is and how it relates to tourism.

For example, the rejection of tourist typologies alluded to above, together with a repositioning of the focus in tourism research towards the idea that tourism is a multisensory and physical experience, have brought to bear the notion that the individual plays an increasingly central role in the tourist industry as an empowered consumer who interacts with digital content on a scale never witnessed before. New forms of niche and special interest tourism continue to evolve, challenging the traditional approaches to tourism supply, demand and marketing. These are emerging alongside an intellectual critique of tourism as a behaviour, a language and a pluralistic cultural industry. Postmodernity describes and accounts for these new forms of tourism and tourist experiences, and it seeks to critique tourism as a social and cultural practice using various philosophical approaches that have their roots in late-twentieth-century French philosophy. The chapter begins by introducing and exploring the concept of postmodernity before presenting a discussion of the key issues and debates that have shaped our understanding of it in tourism circles. It concludes by considering the application of postmodern thinking to contemporary tourism settings and to tourism research.

Theory: definitions and key debates in postmodernity

In attempting to answer the question 'what does postmodernism mean?' It is first necessary to bear in mind that it is only possible to describe the phenomenon, not to define it. Any attempt at coming up with a universal definition might itself be treated as a contravention of the central premise of postmodernism – that that there are no such things as absolute truths or knowledge boundaries. Postmodernity is a rejection of absolutes and is, therefore, an invitation to possibilities. Indeed, one of the central beliefs of postmodernists is relativism; the doctrine that knowledge and truth are culturally conditioned, not absolute. It is not surprising, therefore, that given its apparent vagueness of meaning and application, postmodernism is often received with some scepticism. Approached as theory, it is almost certainly more useful to think about postmodernism as a mind-set rather than a systematic movement. In this context, there is at least some agreement around the idea that postmodernism holds that truth is a relative concept. As Sire (2008: 287) puts it:

> ...no longer is there a single story, a metanarrative that holds Western culture together. The naturalists have their story, the pantheists theirs, the Christians theirs, ad infinitum. With postmodernism, no story can have any more credibility than the other. All are equally valid, being so validated by the community that lives by them.

Tourist experience and postmodernity

Postmodernists, therefore, argue that the world that is external to them is in error and that no individual or group can assert dominion over truth or over others on the basis of an authoritative truth. For some postmodernist scholars, and particularly those that apply Foucauldian thinking, truth and knowledge are contingent upon historical forces and not scientifically grounded truths. The trouble with this endless spiral towards a world in which all knowledge is relative and open to dismissal, however, is that postmodern thinkers are increasingly accused of having gone too far with their 'weapons of critique', deconstruction and relativism and... rejection of grand narratives, stable definitions and eternal truths (Salmon, 2018). Hence, it is little wonder that postmodernism has been criticized as an entirely nihilistic philosophy (Woodward, 2002) centred around the repudiation of meaning and, therefore, value. Yet to avoid reaching a hasty conclusion that dismisses postmodern thinking as singularly destructive and unproductive, it is necessary to trace its origins to understand the conditions that gave rise to its ascendency within culture and cultural studies. In other words, if we want to understand *post*modernity, it is surely useful to understand *modernity*, which it logically appears to have replaced or at least altered. However, in so doing, it is also important to heed Jennings and Graham's (1996: 269) warning that, as signifiers, modernity and postmodernity are unstable terms that have been used in 'shifting and conflicting ways', and this ambiguity has fuelled debate and created scope for dialogue.

The movement of modernity has been described as the replacement of superstitious worldviews of religion and other forms of irrationality with human reason or narratives, such as Marxism (Grassie, 1997). Kumar (1995) considers that the terms modernity and modernism are used interchangeably: the former as a comprehensive designation of change to intellectual, social and political structures and the latter as a cultural movement at the end of the nineteenth century in the west. The five hallmarks of modern thought can be summarized as:

- Humanism (humans are the source of meaning and value)
- Individualism (individuals are ethically and intellectually prior to society)
- Rationalism (there is a natural human faculty of reason)
- Secular moralism (human reason can allow moral action and moral society)
- Progressive history (human history is progressive and moderns are more humane)

Modernism was, therefore, an intellectual movement that originated in the Enlightenment at the end of the eighteenth century, a period that can be characterized by three major values. These are intellectual power of reason over ignorance, order over disorder and science over superstition. *Post*modernism is a continuation of modernism in the sense that it questions and denies prior historical beliefs. Indeed, Diepeveen and Van Laar (2001) suggest that modernists explored the implications of the decline of old systems of explaining and organizing human behaviour and turned to new forms of organization, such as Freudian psychology, anthropology and Marxism. Since the late 1970s, historiography theorists have challenged the assumption that history should be driven by the assembling of large historical truths into grand records of fact and interpretation. The progress of modernism manifested itself in material progress, the production of 'things' (i.e. industrialization) and the development of a large amount of objective and value-free scientific knowledge. Postmodern theory, conversely, is based upon a relativist theory of knowledge and the belief that there are no certain single truths about the world, only questions with infinite answers, each as valid as the next.

The term postmodernity came into popular usage after the publication of Francois Lyotard's *The Postmodern Condition* in 1979, which began challenging the salience of monolithic systems and meta-narratives that offered overarching explanations of the world. Postmodern thinking asserts, instead, that individuals create their own narrative or reality depending on different communities of knowledge. Authors including Habermas (1987) and Giddens (1990) make the argument that 'modernity' is still a work in progress, whilst Lyotard (1984) and Foucault (1980) recognize a more definitive move towards postmodernity and the role of context and community in shaping knowledge. Postmodernity, beyond the metaphysical debate, is also a discussion about society and the rapid changes that we as a society have witnessed, often at a very rapid pace, since around the 1950s. For postmodernists, societal change refers to the diminishing influence and credibility of various stable institutions and values that have historically bound 'us' together. These values and institutions include capitalism and class, urbanization, the bureaucratic nation state and authoritative scientific knowledge. These are the socio-cultural and political hallmarks of the modernity movement, and postmodernists would argue that these institutions and cultural values have been replaced to such a degree that society is now fundamentally very different to how it was before the 1950s. There are five key defining features or 'movements' that define postmodern society that are worth exploring alongside their implications for tourism. These are: globalization; media technologies; the idea of a world in fragments; consumer society; and cultural diversity.

Globalization is the evolving process of inter-connectedness between societies across the world. These points of connection include trade and cultural exchanges driven by the increased production of goods and services on a worldwide scale. Globalization is a process that has been gathering pace for hundreds of years, but it has increased exponentially over the past 50 years with the arrival of new technologies and a heightened demand for new products and services. Amongst the consequences of globalization are increased international trade, the ability of organizations to operate in several countries, a greater dependence on the global economy and the free movement of goods, services and capital. This means that the biggest companies are no longer considered national organizations, but *multinational* organizations that have subsidiaries in various other countries. Marriot, for example, is a global hotel chain that began in the 1950s in Arlington, Virginia with a service model and hospitality ethos designed around American consumer preferences. As a consequence of globalization and the ability to replicate its service culture across national borders, the chain now accounts for around 1.32 million hotel rooms worldwide. It is worth noting that whilst globalization certainly helps to generate additional wealth in developing countries, it does very little to close the gap that exists between the poorest and the richest nations in the world. In other words, it principally serves the interests of the wealthier nations who seek to dominate world trade at the expense of the developing nations that come to depend on the globalized economy that creates both the conditions for and restrictions on employment in these nations. At the time of writing, during a global pandemic caused by the Novel Coronavirus, discussions about the future of globalization have altered radically. Airlines are failing, travel plans are curtailed and car plants have halted production, all a sign of their dependence on global patterns of demand. Analysts are beginning to wonder if a consequent renewed dependence on domestic goods and services (which will almost certainly include another rise in the 'staycation') will reverse the process of globalization for good, as businesses begin to grasp the true extent of the risks involved in hedging their bets on global demand.

The post-modern age has seen a rapid expansion to the role and saturation levels of **media technologies**. Digital media and particularly the internet have driven an unprecedented increase in both the number of people who access media and the diversity of available media products. Whereas media choice was once restricted to a handful of channels, usage is now much more complex and based on picking and mixing. Consequently, there is a growing dependence on media and an apparently insatiable public appetite to find out what is going on 'now' in the world. Social networking sites have created the conditions for an ostensible breakdown in local, tangible communities that have given way to online networking that sees some people communicate regularly with strangers, but never with their next-door neighbours. The pattern resonates very clearly with the key tenets of postmodernism that include the rejection of any idea of a totalizing society and the role of individuals in constructing their own realities.

The idea of the *world in fragments* reflects the nature of a postmodern world that is dynamic and fluid and does not sit still. Sociologists have argued that modern society lacks a coherent, stable social structure as intimated in the above discussion of online interactions and disappearing communities. This is reflected in various aspects of life, such as in careers and, specifically, the notion of a 'job for life'. Those in careers are increasingly likely to initiate several career changes across their working life, whilst work more generally is also increasingly temporary with many workers on flexible or zero-hour contracts. This also accelerates the disappearance of communities, as people are more likely to move to find work and, hence, put down fewer roots. It is also reflected in fashion and music, which are perhaps the most aesthetically illuminating examples of the evolution of styles and fads, and the transience of popularity as what was popular 'last season' quickly becomes obsolete.

Postmodern society is, for all intents and purposes, a *consumer society* and the idea of consuming things is more appealing than the idea of work. The identities of individuals through the lens of postmodernity are no longer shaped purely by gender, ethnicity and class. Much more important, according to postmodernists, is what you own, who you influence and who you are influenced by. Indeed, the lifeblood of the consumer society is increasingly considered to be technology and the types of social media influences that are discussed above.

The rapid evolution of globalization over recent years has driven *cultural diversity* and the hybridization of various cultural traditions. This diversity is quite visible in a number of areas of the cultural sphere. Supermarkets offer a vivid visual depiction of globalization since they offer a diverse range of often out of season and globally diverse items that are sourced from around the world. The sheer abundance of choice and influential origins available in the fashion and music markets are a further testament to hybridization. Postmodern society is therefore an unstable and unpredictable society, and the people within it are at liberty to construct their own culture and identities in the backdrop of processes such as globalization and evolving technologies that provide instant access to information and to markets.

Based on the above discussion, the analytical lens of postmodernity can be applied to tourism as a framework for understanding transformations in (tourist) consumption behaviours or experiences. Indeed, if we want to form an understanding of developments in the tourism industry in the recent past, it is useful to consider the shifting cultural conditions that have given rise to these as part of what Coombe (1991) calls the postmodern condition. The postmodern condition describes the breaking down of barriers and boundaries, both geographic and culturally, and the subsequent expansion of a consumer society. As discussed above, this has involved the wholesale restructuring of capitalist values and processes involving new forms of media, information and communication technologies. This shift in values from productivity towards consumerism mirrors the transition from modernity to postmodernity. It reflects the end on an era of 'truth' when it comes to travel and tourism products and services, since it has replaced the methods of tourism marketing associated with the growth phase of travel and tourism (glossy brochures and consultations with travel experts in bricks and mortar high street travel agencies) with empowered consumerism and electronic consumption. Consumers are empowered because, rather than consulting the rehearsed 'propaganda' of organizationally owned commercial brochures and websites, they now consult each other through the medium of web 2.0 technologies in general and social media in particular. The consumption of travel and tourism, involving all activities from searching for a holiday to planning and booking it and, finally, reviewing it are all part of a democratic process, and the consumer wields more power than ever before over the reputation of service providers. Gone are the days of objective 'truth' and stable knowledge, particularly when it comes to the marketing of holidays. Truth, in this sense, belongs to individual consumers and to groups of consumers whose experiences of travel and tourism are relative and socially constructed. All of this, of course, resonates with the principles of postmodernity that hold that there is no such thing as a single, authoritative truth, but only truth-versions that are conditioned by cultural circumstances. The implications of this discussion for tourism consumption are considered below.

Application: postmodern tourism consumption

The emergence of tourism can be traced to the eighteenth century when travel was a novelty and something undertaken by a privileged elite (Swarbrooke & Horner, 2007). From the 1930s, however, increases in the rate of ownership of private cars along with a growth in the popularity of holiday camps further stimulated demand. The sector then settled somewhat into a predictable, homogenous pattern of supply and demand in the 1960s when air travel became more affordable and the demand for holidays, particularly in Northern Europe, grew significantly. Package holidays became the standard and the sector itself, specifically various airlines, transport providers, hotels and resorts, assumed command over their own reputations via brochures and the authoritative knowledge of intermediaries such as tour operators and travel agencies who were the primary means of interfacing with the consumer. Subsequently, with the emergence of the World Wide Web as an accessible public resource in the early 1990s, the tourism sector began to experience rapid social and technological change. These changes triggered a radical departure away from the predictability of mass tourism in terms of production and consumption. The World Wide Web and, particularly, the democratization of travel consumption through social media has since driven demand for an increasingly fragmented tourism product where outbound travel offers new possibilities for emerging destinations, each with an increasingly varied product offer.

What this brief synopsis of the evolution of tourism tells us is that the industry has experienced a number of often radical transformations since its emergence, and that these have occurred in parallel with the types of social and technological changes discussed earlier as part of a wholesale shift from modern to postmodern culture. Tourism markets continue to expand and evolve as a consequence of what Anderson (2009) refers to as a supply chain defined by endless choice and unlimited demand, and tourists themselves have become ever more demanding and lickerish in response (Dujmovic & Vitasovic, 2015). Tourism services and products have had to find new ways to compete for demand amongst an increasingly fickle and well-educated consumer base and there is a growing emphasis on emotions, aesthetics and experience as the central facets of tourism. These radical transformations and their implications for tourism consumption are introduced and discussed in more detail below.

As a consequence of globalization, modern culture characterized by mass production, mass consumption, urbanization, differentiation, rationalization, standardized production and bureaucracy has given way to a new 'post-culture' defined by flexibility, diversity, de-differentiation, internationalization and decentralization. This shift has involved a departure from traditional forms of tourism consumption, typically defined by packaging and

Tourist experience and postmodernity

standardization, to a new form of tourism consumption that is about segmentation, flexibility and customization. This dynamic reflects a shift from organized capitalism to disorganized capitalism or, to use the American automobile trope, from Fordism to post-Fordism, so that mass consumption has become gradually replaced by individualism and bespoke consumption. There is less of a preoccupation now with the descriptive aspects of tourism products (hotels, attractions, etc.) with more emphasis being placed on the quality, variety and quirkiness of tourism experiences. The search for novelty and for variety also means that tourists are presented with a number of itinerary-possibilities that means that activities that might, on the face of it, appear incompatible are bundled together to create novel and memorable experiences. Table 1.1 below summarizes what post-Fordist, disorganized capitalism

Table 1.1 Post-Fordism and tourism consumption

Characteristics of post-Fordism	*Tourism implications/examples*
Consumers are increasingly dominant, and producers must therefore be more consumer-orientated.	Mass tourism (for example, packaged holidays) no longer dominates the supply chain. The increased diversity of preferences and the search for 'new' and novel experiences drives the proliferation of a vast range of niche and special interest experiences. Often, the same services are being used (e.g. flights, accommodation), and the same resources are being consumed (e.g. transfers, food and drink). It is *how* destinations are marketed to consumers that matter, and strategies must be increasingly imaginative and tailored in this regard. Special interest tourism has emerged as one of the consequences of this characteristic.
Greater volatility of consumer preferences	Fewer repeat visits. A hunger for novel experiences, and new sights/attractions. Shorter, but more frequent holidays. A less predictable supply chain that has led to the collapse of household names and industry incumbents like Thomas Cook.
Increased market segmentation	The disappearance of the idea of the one-dimensional tourist, and the increasing recognition of visitor variety (for example: the sports tourist, the food tourist, the active tourist and the events tourist). There is also increasing recognition given to high-value tourists, so that what we spend defines us as much as what we do.
The growth of a consumer movement	Social media is often the starting point for planning a holiday, and it is also often the end point, when it comes to reviewing holidays on media such as TripAdvisor.
The evolution of new products that have shorter shelf lives	Rapid turnover of tourist sites and experiences that reflect fads and fashion changes, as well as what is happening in popular culture. Film and literary tourism, for example, create major publicity for some destinations, but their popularity can be transient.
An increasing preference for alternatives to mass tourism	Special interest tourism – the provision of customized tourism activities that appeal to specific groups is growing in popularity, as are individually tailored tourism experiences of the type seen at the top end of the luxury markets.
Consumers, as a consequence of the World Wide Web (and particularly social media) have access to peer reviews based on User Generated Content.	Producers can exert less control over their reputation as consumers increasingly take control over how we understand value and experiences of tourism. Marketing is no longer a one-way form of communication, but a conversation.

Source: Adapted from Lash and Urry (1994).

means for tourism consumption. The source from which the table is adapted is now quite dated, but the characteristics it describes are enduring. As such, the original table has been updated to reflect current market conditions and consumer behaviours.

The term that has come to be embraced to describe the type of tourism consumer portrayed above is the 'post-tourist' (Feifer, 1985; Urry, 1990). The post-tourist is both an analytical term and a vivid trope that recasts the modern-day tourist as a highly symbolic feature of postmodern consumption. Specifically, the post-tourist is the consequence of a technologically empowered world in which how we communicate and relate to other people and places is shaped by technologies that increasingly serve as a gateway to a more knowable and less enigmatic world that is accessed through media representations and simulation. As McCabe (2015) suggests, it is very hard to imagine the environment of consumption in which the tourists of the 1980s operated, when mobile phone ownership was rare and there was a very strong dependence upon the knowledge of tourism industry sales teams and representatives to provide information and shape experiences of destinations. In advance of committing to a sale, the post-tourist frantically accesses and considers a multitude of user-generated reviews of tourism experiences on social media platforms, as opposed to subscribing to the views of a handful of privileged, authoritative 'experts' such as the travel writers and television presenters that dominated the handful of available analogue media channels in the 'pre-postmodern' age. In any case, the post-tourist is not a 'tourist' at all but a 'traveller', a construct that is increasingly embraced as a much less pejorative and morally superior identifier. Even the visible appearance of the post-tourist contrasts starkly with the tourist of the 1980s. Whereas once tourists were immediately recognizable by their clothes, cameras and routines (McCabe, 2015), the post-tourist has no need for a camera as it is integrated into their phone, and their routines are far less predictable since they increasingly seek novel experiences whilst rejecting the predictability of packaged holidays and tours. The post-tourist is comfortable with technology and is particularly responsive to and dependent upon media. Indeed, it is no longer necessary for the post-tourist to leave home in order to access the objects that are typically associated with the tourist gaze (the stereotypical tourism experiences that tourists expect of destinations), since these can be summoned immediately as simulations through on-demand television, smart phones and even game consoles and virtual reality hardware.

Bigné and Decrop (2018) contemplate the consequences of the post-tourist for industry, suggesting such consumers are a puzzle for tourism producers and marketers since they are omnivorous and insatiable. The behaviour of tourists today is less rational and less predictable and it is, therefore, a challenge to locate them within various segmentation frameworks and models. What we are, therefore, dealing with in terms of contemplating the post-tourist is the fragmentation of consumption. In order to respond to such fragmented consumption, the strategies that seem to be favoured by tourism producers include customization, product flexibility and an upgrade-anything attitude. It is now possible to upgrade, personalize and customize almost any tourism product and experience and consumers in essence seek out this kind of flexibility when making purchase decisions. ICT has fuelled the growth of niche products and has allowed those in the business of tourism to profit from obscurity. The economics of today's tourism are therefore very different to the traditional format based on predictability and economies of scale to exploit mass and undifferentiated markets. The growing appetite for niche products and experiences has led to a rise in the number of low demand/low sales volume products that can often collectively exceed the value of the minority of bestsellers. This requires the aggregation of a sufficient number of products as well as the development of deep market distribution channels (Lew, 2010).

Tourist experience and postmodernity

Perhaps the two most contemporary and obvious examples of the successful aggregation and distribution of products in travel and tourism are Uber and Airbnb, both of which have grown from obscurity to command a notable proportion of the market in terms of private transport and accommodation. The thinking that has led to the introduction of disruptors such as Uber and Airbnb has its roots in Anderson's (2009) 'long tail' rhetoric; to 'make everything available'. For tourism, and speaking generally, this involves growing the diversity of the offer, including peripheral attractions and special-interest experiences whilst coming up with new and imaginative ways of reinventing destinations to appeal to as diverse a base of consumers as possible. By creating multiple versions of themselves to capture various imaginations, destinations can appeal to 'ego-tourists' who seek out travel options that reflect their pursuit of alternative, individualistic interests. As Munt (1994) notes, post-tourists are middle class consumers for whom alternative, niche travel is a kind of cultural asset. It is important to these tourists to draw a clear distinction between themselves and the 'other' mass tourists for whom authenticity is putatively frivolous. However, before getting too carried away with the idea of an elite class of post-tourists whose consumption is eccentrically more meaningful and different from the mass market, we must bear in mind that *all* tourists, regardless of their motives or interests, consume the same products and services at the level of the transaction, and also create very similar impacts. Eco-tourists, for example, do not walk to destinations; they fly. Tourists who venture 'off the beaten track' will soon beat out new and clichéd tracks in the way that Krippendorf (1987) describes in his seminal work on tourism impacts. There is also another side to the post-tourist argument. Urry (1990) suggests that tourism is a playful experience and that the post-tourist is not ultimately interested in authenticity at all. Indeed, the post-tourist is quite alert to the idea of culture as a contrived notion and has no problem embracing inauthentic and hyper-real experiences such as shopping malls, theme parks and leisure centres. However, the construct of the post-tourist is approached, what is clear is that any discussion of postmodern tourism recognizes a range of developments, including the emergence of alternatives to conventional forms of mass tourism, and a growing quest for special interest and theme-orientated tourism experiences. These radical shifts in tourism formats and consumption habits have not only changed the way that tourism markets operate; they have also created new challenges and approaches to tourism research and research methodologies, as the next and final section of this chapter explores.

Postmodernity and the study of tourism

In terms of research, the shift away from 1970s theories of 'modern' tourism towards contemporary theories of postmodern tourism is reflected in transformations in 'the style and form of theorizing within the sociology of tourism' (Uriely, 1997: 982). This shift in research values reflects the central premise of postmodern theory identified in the introduction to this chapter, that there are no such things as absolute truths or knowledge boundaries. Instead, when it comes to research, postmodern social theory challenges the modernist fixation with metanarratives/theories and, in terms of tourism, the preoccupation with categorizing and organizing (for example, creating tourist typologies and market segments). Postmodern social theory is, instead, about compromise, inconclusiveness and anti-hierarchical perceptions of the observed world. Rather than depending upon one, single approach to knowing, postmodernist researchers support a pluralistic approach to epistemology that mobilizes multiple ways of knowing.

Bauman (1987) describes postmodernist researchers as interpreters, whereas modernist theorists are legislators. Whilst the latter are concerned with categories and rules, postmodernist researchers seek to challenge the logical tidiness of order, unity and authority, and they approach the idea of objective knowledge critically. Indeed, authority and power are distrusted by postmodernists who prefer a less hierarchical approach in which authoritative sources are more diffuse. Postmodernism as a research philosophy consists of a rough alliance of intellectual perspectives that together create a disruptive critique of the core tents of modernism and, specifically, of the scientific research method preferred by positivists. Used in a research context, postmodernism encompasses a variety of research approaches, the majority of which attach value to uncertainty and disorder and regression as opposed to progress. Many of the research methods that are employed (see below) focus on spoken, written and signified texts with the aim of establishing or critiquing meaning. Central to the postmodernist research philosophy are notions of discontinuity and rupture and a rejection of the idea that science can be embraced as objective. It is no surprise, therefore, that postmodernity as a philosophical underpinning to tourism research tends to be embraced by those that value criticality as a central pursuit in knowledge creation. Indeed, postmodern research philosophies represent an alternative approach to what Tribe (2005) calls the typical interdisciplinary business approaches associated with tourism research and the fetishized analytical tools of questionnaires, SPSS and interviews that enable these.

Postmodernity, therefore, shapes tourism research as a philosophical underpinning that can inform decisions about research strategies and techniques and procedures that might later be applied in the field. The postmodern research lens represents one option amongst many competing research philosophies that can be adopted by the researcher in seeking to follow a particular set of assumptions and beliefs about how to develop knowledge (Saunders, Lewis, Thornhill & Bristow, 2015). As a research philosophy, postmodernism overlaps with the intellectual movement of poststructuralism and although there are distinctions (the former is often used to characterize features or objects whilst the latter describes a philosophical movement), the term 'postmodernism', as far as research is concerned, is increasingly accepted as a grab-bag term to describe anything that comes after modernism. Postmodernist researchers frequently attribute value to the role of language, so much so that it is not uncommon to come across social scientific research underpinned by postmodernism which is based purely on a critique of text. 'Text', in this sense refers to anything that creates meaning, not just written or spoken language, but anything symbolic that can be interpreted using Saussurean semiotic approaches to research and data. Postmodernist researchers also challenge the idea of order and the stability of knowledge, and instead argue that the world around them is fluid, and apt to change.

The theories that tend to underpin research that is framed within a postmodern philosophy include deconstruction, subjectivity, scepticism, anti-empiricism, intertextuality and relativism (Uriely, 1997). Deconstruction, for example, was applied by early poststructuralist tourism researchers such as Urry (1990) and Cohen (1972) who attacked the idea that tourism is a form of escapism from everyday life. Their deconstructive counterargument was used to make observations about the 'end of tourism' through de-differentiation; the idea that the traditional, stereotyped benefits of tourism (sightseeing and escapism, for example) are increasingly accessible in various contexts of everyday life, though, for instance, the media, simulation and, today, virtual- and augmented reality. A further, early example of deconstruction in tourism is summarized by Uriely (1997) who describes salient critiques of tourism in the 1990s and 2000s positioned around the proposition that 'tourism is everything and everything is tourism'. The proposal at this time was that the boundaries between leisure and tourism were beginning to blur as leisure and recreation began to invade workplaces in the form of gymnasia, spas and showers, and the take-off of business tourism saw workplace

Tourist experience and postmodernity

travel take place punctuated by visits to friends and relatives and to theme parks and attractions. As these examples illustrate, postmodernity can be deployed *theoretically* in research to reshape perceptions of tourism experiences and consumption. In terms of applying postmodernist thinking to primary research *in the field*, as opposed to harnessing it to create metaphysical debate as in the above examples, it is typically language and text (spoken, written or symbolic) that are the object of analyses. Given the centrality of language, it is perhaps no surprise that the methods that are typically associated with postmodern research in the field tend to involve qualitative, social constructionist investigations of texts using some form of critical discourse analysis.

Discourse analysis is an interpretive method for analyzing any communicative utterance, practice or event that may be narrative, instructive descriptive or argumentative (Titscher, Meyer, Wodak & Vetter, 2000). Discourse is an increasingly fashionable term (Jorgensen & Phillips, 2002) and one that is perhaps too often used innocently, without the essential accompaniment of an adequate definition. Discourse analysis does not describe any single analytical framework but a number of interdisciplinary approaches that can be put to use in research in a variety of social spheres (Wight, 2018). Any attempt to advocate for an objective definition is futile, and there is much to divide the philosophical underpinnings of the available approaches to take when 'doing' discourse analysis for research purposes. However, one idea that offers some unity is that discourse analysis is concerned with a certain way of talking about and indeed representing the world. In addition, discourse analysis is not simply a method but a holistic approach to research that is led by a philosophical premise, a theoretical model and a methodological strategy. Typically, the theory and methods are intertwined such that the researcher must identify with a particular theoretical perspective in order to deploy discourse analysis as a research strategy (Wight, 2018).

A cursory search of any relevant research archive reveals that neither discourse analysis, nor postmodernity are particularly common in tourism research historically, but they are beginning to emerge in more recent work. The historical dearth of discourse-focused research can perhaps be attributed to a perceived reluctance amongst researchers to abandon the convenience and safety of prescriptive research approaches, a crystallization of tourism studies (Tribe, 2005) around interdisciplinary business approaches, and an increasingly held view of the world of tourism as a technically rational, economic phenomenon. This suggests that tourism studies are at an important intersection marked by the arrival of 'new' tourism research that is defined by a humanities worldview of tourism studies that attempts to introduce critical and philosophically led approaches to knowledge creation including postmodern critique. The recent growth in the popularity of discourse analysis and its increasing recognition as a legitimate research strategy in tourism research is perhaps a response to the argument that tourism has been historically dominated by a positivist research agenda focused on business efficiency and management. A more critical tourism research agenda to address particular complexities involved in tourism, such as ethics, governance, issues of power, ulterior interests and conflict, and the evolution of tourism research and practices continues to evolve as an extension of a wider social scientific shift towards discourse analysis. The increasing use of discourse analysis in tourism research can also be attributed to the pronounced emergence and continued expansion of digital media sources in tourism over recent decades, as social media and image-sharing websites continue to dominate modes of communication, offering the social scientific researcher a fertile unit of analysis for various research purposes. Discourse analysis is not unique to postmodern research philosophies, but it is common given the fascination with critiquing texts.

Table 1.2 provides an idea of some approaches to discourse analysis that have been deployed in tourism research to date. Not all of them pertain to postmodernism. Content analysis, for example, is a quintessentially positivist endeavour, given the focus on counting instances of words. Semiotic analysis and deconstruction are very much wedded to post-structuralism, since the aim is to attack the logical tidiness and authority of texts. This is also true of some approaches to what is broadly termed textual analysis.

As Table 1.2 illustrates, almost any tourism text can be critiqued using a postmodern lens and discourse analytical methods. Narrative formats such as guided tours, destination guide resources and web content offer some examples of authoritative tourism texts that are deployed and arranged in a particular order according to the legitimated preferences of their authors. In this sense, tourism narratives can be viewed as objects of discourse that are classified according to the frameworks of knowledge that allow them to be understood. Such narratives, for the poststructuralist constitute a 'body of knowledge' that authorizes certain

Table 1.2 Types and examples of discourse analysis in tourism research

Discourse analysis approach/method	*How this method might be applied*	*Examples from the literature*
Content analysis	Counting and interpreting the content of texts to identify what is significant. For example, examining brochures over time to illuminate permanencies and variations in the representation of people and places.	Bhattacharyya's (1997) coding of photographs in the *Lonely Planet* to categorize these into broad typologies and to identify how 'people' are represented.
Textual analysis	A qualitative technique concerned with interpreting cultural meaning from texts. Less standardized than content analysis and underpinned by the idea that texts are complex sites of social construction. Themes can be created based on coding.	Halewood and Hannam's (2001) analytical framework to identify discrete references to authenticity in heritage tourism sources.
Semiotic Analysis	Concerned with the production and consumption of images, for example images within brochures or as part of web content. Examines the complex relationship between objects and representation. Can be used to analyze photographs, postcards and souvenirs. Less structured than the above and allows considerable analytical freedom and creativity in terms of how research is undertaken.	Uzzell's (1984) analysis of tourism brochures points out that photographs of wine represent the myth of a good life and symbolize a degree of freedom from everyday working life through the loss of inhibitions.
Deconstruction	A Derridean approach to texts that suggests that discourse is the outcome of a series of sometimes incoherent structures and utterances that are in conflict with one another. Enables a nuanced reading to approach texts within the wider cultural conditions in which they were produced. Useful in critiques of heritage tourism, which are often socially and culturally contested.	Edensor (1997, cited in Hannam & Knox, 2005) discusses the reception of the film *Braveheart* in Scotland in the 1990s, pointing to conflicts surrounding the authenticity of this media, but also the political uses to which a popular surge in nationalism might be put as a consequence.

Source: Wight (2019).

Tourist experience and postmodernity

discourses at the expense of others, as is the case with, for example, Uzzel's deconstruction of tourism brochures and the discursive production of wine tourism, which, through the careful arrangement of images, confers a particular, sanitized image of bucolic utopia.

In terms of the ethics of discourse analysis, the key debates reside in how knowledge is produced and in how to locate research findings between the two poles of advocacy, namely, the manufacturing of option and objective reflection. As Wrbouschek (2009: 41) puts it, if discourse analysis is understood as a kind of truth articulation then in 'pointing to these facts' the researcher effectively situates himself inside an act of truth constitution, which is itself a gesture that runs counter to the principles of postmodernism. The risk in carrying out post-structuralist discourse analysis is the possibility of constructing and advocating a particular 'truth', rather than offering an objective analysis of how knowledge is constituted in various fields, including tourism. As Jorgensen and Phillips (2002: 15) argue, 'because truth is unattainable, it is fruitless to ask whether something is true or false. Instead, the focus should be on how effects of truth are created in discourses'. If there is a practical adherence to a code of researcher ethics in terms of postmodern critique, it relates to the formation of conclusions that are acknowledged as being limited to the analytical method out of which they arise.

In sum, postmodern research has accelerated a process of the re-examination of the fixed categories and concepts of tourism that so dominated research agendas around the 1970s and 1980s. Postmodernity is a productive research philosophy that might hold appeal to anyone that seeks to critique and challenge knowledge and power and authoritative narratives (for example, guidebooks, guided tours and visitor interpretation in museums and attractions). Postmodernity is increasingly applied as a counternarrative in tourism research and an alternative to the popular interdisciplinary business approaches and fetishized analytical tools of questionnaires, SPSS and interviews that have dominated tourism research for decades. Tourism comprises a range of texts and discourses that represent a fertile ground for the application of a postmodern discursive analytic and, aside from metaphysical theorizing, discourse analysis is a common approach that is applied in the field to critique these texts through a poststructuralist lens.

Conclusion

This chapter has provided an overview of postmodernity as it applies to the theory, practice and study of tourism. Central to the concept of postmodernity is the idea of a world in flux, in which truth is fluid, contested and dependent on context. In terms of tourism, postmodernity describes a multitude of processes operating at a global scale that reaches across national boundaries, integrating cultures, capital, people, commodities, images and ideas. The traditional model of mass tourism defined by affordable package holidays that are largely standardized and which mirror the economic model of Fordist industrial production has been gradually, but not entirely, replaced with a more flexibly produced form of tourism based on consumer appetites for a wide variety of sights, attractions and increasingly novel, special interest experiences. This shift represents a paradigmatic realignment from the modern concept of mass tourism to the postmodern concept of niche, individualized tourism. It is a shift that has also been reflected in research and, as tourism consumption has grown more complex, the need for a more critical lens to examine tourism and tourism behaviours beyond the passive observations encouraged by positivism and interpretivism is now more pressing than ever before.

Tourism is more diverse that it has ever been and a host of varied interests involving visits to 'sacred, informative, broadening, beautiful, uplifting, or simply different sites' are now possible (Dujmovic and Vitasovic, 2015). The concept of the post-tourist, an idea derived from deconstructionist observations about the behaviour of tourism consumption in a globalized world, means that most people are tourists every day, given the increasing dependency and appetite for simulated experiences that now extend to virtual and augmented reality experiences that are now routine and no longer eccentric, abstract concepts in the margins of our culture. Post-tourism is a socio-cultural construct that fits the modern-day image of tourism consumption, which is built around the chaotic flux of production, consumption, reproduction, representation and commodification. Owing to the greater speed, mobility and extent of the circulation of people, cultures and objects, the process of globalization appears to be insuppressible.

However, globalization is, at the time of writing, a process that is facing an uncertain future in terms of tourism. Much that has hitherto been taken for granted, such as the freedom of movement of tourists across borders, the sheer range of options in terms of overseas travel and air travel itself, are under threat, certainly over the short-medium term as the Novel Coronavirus global pandemic continues to see almost all of the world's countries 'locked down' and unable to consume. Currently, tourism looks irrational. Business and leisure travel both seem dangerous and pointless, and many components in the supply chain are broken. In a discussion of postmodernity, one of the implications is the possibility of a partial return to modernity; to the values and practices of a form of tourism that has not been witnessed since the nineteenth century and the resurgence of the staycation at a scale far greater than that witnessed during the 2008 credit crunch. Coronavirus may do more to reshape the values of tourism consumerism over the next months and years than ecotourism ever has. The very notion of this resonates powerfully with poststructuralist theorist Jean Baudrillard's idea of the spectacle of terror (coined in response to 9/11), whereby the very system of globalization is, as a consequence of itself, under assault. Current events such as these, and the analytical horizons afforded by postmodern critique to make sense of them, add weight to the enduring centrality of this analytical lens that can be applied productively to tourism contexts to challenge perceptions and to stimulate thought.

References

Anderson, C. (2009) *The Longer Tail: How Endless Choice is Creating Unlimited Demand*. New York: Hyperion.

Bauman, Z. (1987) *Legislators and Interpreters*. Cambridge: Polity Press.

Bhattacharyya, D. (1997. Mediating India: An analysis of a guidebook. *Annals of Tourism Research*, 24(2), 371–389.

Bigné, E. and Decrop, A. (2018) Paradoxes of postmodern tourists and innovation in tourism marketing. In E. Fayos-Solà and C. Cooper (Eds.), *The Future of Tourism: Innovation and Sustainability*. Cham: Springer, pp. 131–154.

Bozlog (2008) Postmodern. Urban Dictionary, 8 May. Available at: https://www.urbandictionary.com/define.php?term=Postmodern (Accessed 2 September 2020).

Cohen, E. (1972) Toward a sociology of international tourism. *Social Research*, 39(1), 164–189.

Coombe, R. J. (1991) Encountering the postmodern: New directions in cultural anthropology. *Canadian Review of Sociology and Anthropology*, 28(2), 187–205.

Diepeveen, L. and Van Laar, T. (2000) *Art with a Difference: Looking at Difficult and Unfamiliar Art*. California City: Mayfield Publishing Company.

Dujmovic, M. and Vitasovic, A. (2015) Postmodern society and tourism. *Journal of Tourism and Hospitality Management*, 3(9–10), 192–203.

Feifer, M. (1985) *Going Places*. London. Macmillan.

Foucault, M. (1980) *Power/Knowledge*. Brighton: Harvester.

Giddens, A. (1990) *The Consequences of Modernity*. Cambridge: Polity.

Grassie, W. (1997) Postmodernism: What one needs to know. *Journal of Religion and Science*, 32(1), 83–94.

Habermas, J. (1987) *Lectures on the Philosophical Discourse of Modernity*. Cambridge: MIT Press.

Halewood, C. and Hannam, K. (2001) Viking heritage tourism: Authenticity and commodification. *Annals of Tourism Research*, 28, 565–580.

Hannam, K. and Knox, D. (2005) Discourse analysis in tourism research: A critical perspective. *Tourism Recreation Research*, 30(2), 23–30.

Jennings, L. E. and Graham, A. P. (1996) Postmodern perspectives and action research: Reflecting on the possibilities. *Educational Action Research*, 4(2), 267–278.

Jorgensen, M. W. and Phillips, L. J. (2002) *Discourse Analysis as Theory and Method*. London: Sage Publications.

Krippendorf, J. (1987) *The Holiday Makers*. Oxford: Heinemann.

Kumar, K. (1995) *From Post-industrial to Post-modern Society*. Oxford: Blackwell.

Lash, S. and Urry, J. (1994) *Economies of Signs and Space*. London. Sage Publications.

Lew, A, A. (2010) Long tail tourism: New Geographies for marketing niche tourism products. *Journal of Travel and Tourism Marketing*, 25 (3–4), 409–419.

Lyotard, J. F. (1984) *The Postmodern Condition: A Report on Knowledge*. Manchester: Manchester University Press.

McCabe, S. (2015) Are we all post-tourists now? Tourist categories, identities and post-modernity. In T. V. Singh (Ed.), *Challenges in Tourism Research*. Bristol: Channel View Publications, pp. 18–26.

Munt, I. (1994) The 'other' postmodern tourism: Culture, travel, and the new middle classes. *Theory, Culture, and* Society, 11(3), 101–123.

Salmon, P. (2018) Have postmodernist thinkers deconstructed truth? *New Humanist*, 12 March. Available at: https://newhumanist.org.uk/articles/5296/have-postmodernist-thinkers-deconstructed-truth (Accessed 2 September 2020).

Saunders, M., Lewis, P., Thornhill, A. and Bristow, A. (2015) Understanding research philosophy and approaches to theory development. In M. Saunders, P. Lewis and A. Thornhill (Eds.), *Research Methods for Business Students*. Harlow: Pearson Education, pp. 122–161.

Sire, J, W. (2008) *The Universe Next Door. A Basic Worldview Catalogue*. Illinois: Accessible Publishing Systems PTY, Ltd.

Swarbrooke, J. and Horner, S. (2007) *Consumer Behaviour in Tourism*. Oxford: Butterwoth-Heinemann.

Titscher, S., Meyer, M., Wodak, R. and Vetter, E. (2000) *Methods of Text and Discourse Analysis: In search of Meaning*. London: Sage Publications.

Tribe, J. (2005) New tourism research. *Tourism Recreation Research*, 30(2), 5–8.

Uriely, N. (1997) Theories of modern and postmodern tourism. *Annals of Tourism Research*, 24(4), 982–985.

Urry, J. (1990) *The Tourist Gaze: Leisure and Travel in Contemporary Societies*. London: Sage Publications.

Uzzell, D. (1984) An alternative structuralist approach to the psychology of tourism marketing. *Annals of Tourism Research*, 11, 79–99.

Wight, A. C. (2019) Putting Foucault to work in tourism research. *International Journal of Tourism Research*, 2(1), 122–133.

Woodward, A. (2002) Nihilism and the postmodern in Vattimo's Nietzsche. *Minerva*, 6, 51–67.

Wrbouschek, M. (2009) Discourse analysis and social critique. *Psychology and Society*, 2(1), 36–44.

2

EXPERIENCING TOURISM

Experiencing happiness?

Jeroen Nawijn and Wim Strijbosch

Introduction

Does experiencing tourism equal experiencing happiness? This is an intriguing question, and one which is of both practical and academic relevance. Its answer depends on how the concepts of happiness, experience and tourism are interpreted. And to be able to provide such an answer to this question in this chapter, it is necessary to make certain choices to limit the scope or establish the parameters of the discussion. The first choice we make is to adopt the perspective of the tourist. In doing so, we thus ignore the related work on the impacts of tourism on destinations and local communities. Then, we need to assume that academic publications on tourists are based upon roughly a similar understanding of what a tourist is; that is, we assume that these interpretations are in line with UN World Tourism Organization's (UNWTO) technical definition of who is or what constitutes a tourist (UN-WTO, 2002). We acknowledge that these assumptions are arbitrary but nevertheless legitimate given the purpose of the chapter. The first task, however, is to pay closer attention to conceptualizations of both experience and happiness, allowing us to better structure our analysis and subsequently enabling us to answer the question of whether experiencing tourism means experiencing happiness.

Conceptualizations of experience and happiness

In this section, we discuss differing interpretations of the concepts of experience and happiness. In so doing, we also acknowledge current debates and assumptions that exist in tourism studies, specifically regarding the interpretation of both concepts. Consequently, we create a framework that functions as a conceptual model that allows us to map different theoretical approaches to experience and happiness.

Experience

Experience can be regarded as one of the core constructs in the field of tourism and leisure (Mommaas, 2000; Scott, Gao & Ma, 2017). It is also one of the most complex, not least because it is prone to many different understandings from various disciplinary perspectives

24

DOI: 10.4324/9781003219866-4

Tourism: experiencing happiness?

(Carù & Cova, 2003; Jay, 2005; Snel, 2011). Yet, as Scott and Le (2017) conclude, most of the accounts of experience in the tourism literature have traditionally taken only a descriptive and rather simplistic approach towards the topic. That is, within tourism studies, experiences have mostly been described in terms of the phases or stages of a tourism product, such as the five travel phases initiated by Clawson and Knetsch (1966), categorized in terms of either managerial aspects (i.e. based on a particular descriptor of the experience environment offered by a supplier), or (inferred) aspects of the participants of an experience (i.e. based on the motivations or internal states of tourists that undergo an experience, such as hedonic experiences) (Scott & Le, 2017). Consequently, given the rather descriptive nature of these studies, the true essence of experience remains largely untreated within the field of tourism studies. Therefore, several more recent accounts in the literature have suggested that the concept of experience should be approached from a more (cognitive) psychological perspective (Bastiaansen et al., 2019; Jantzen, 2013; Scott & Le, 2017), from which various insights might shed new light on the understanding of experiences in the context of tourism and leisure.

Even from a (cognitive) psychological perspective, experience is defined and understood in a variety of different ways (Jantzen, 2013). A common factor in most studies is, however, that experience is treated as the contents of our human consciousness (Hektner, Schmidt & Csikszentmihalyi, 2007; Jantzen, 2013; Scott & Le, 2017). Hence, a principal difference between the various understandings of the phenomenon lies in its temporal dimension. On the one hand, one understanding of experience is that it refers to the moment-by-moment lived experience or, putting it another way, our consciousness of the present, our sensing and feeling in the here-and-now (Jacobs, 2006; Jantzen, 2013). One example of this is the adrenaline and thrills one may feel while riding a white-knuckle roller coaster. From this perspective, experience is denoted as a verb: you are *experiencing* something. On the other hand, an alternative understanding of experience relates to those experiences from our past that are stored in our memory and follow *after* the initial sensing and feeling; in short, remembered experience (Scott & Le, 2017). Experience here is denoted as a noun – you have had *an experience*.

However, although these two understandings of experience differ both temporally and semantically, they are not unrelated to each other. As Bastiaansen et al. (2019) explain, the constant stream of consciousness of our lived experience is constantly being divided into experiential episodes through the activation of mental models. In other words, the continuous stream of *experiencing* is constantly being divided into delimited *experiential episodes*. Yet, although we are continuously experiencing and, hence, constructing such experiential episodes, not all of these are stored in our memories as remembered experiences (Kahneman & Riis, 2005). That is, there are various factors within the process of experiencing that enhance (or diminish) the memorability of an experiential episode (see, for example, Tung, Lin, Qiu Zhang & Zhao, 2017). Of these, it is most commonly suggested that emotions are the core constituent of an experience that enhance its memorability (Bastiaansen et al., 2019; Kensinger, 2004, 2009; Kensinger & Schacter, 2008). Emotions might, thus, form the link between experience and remembered experience.

In sum, there are two understandings of experience; one that takes place in the here-and-now (experiencing) and one that is understood as memory constructs or remembered experiences from the past (an experience). In addition, a number of scholars consider anticipated experience to be a third understanding of experience (e.g. Scott & Le, 2017) – that is, how you expect you will sense and feel during a certain lived experience. However, although experiences are indeed informed and coloured by anticipated experiences (Schacter, Addis & Buckner, 2007; Wirtz, Kruger, Scollon & Diener, 2003), here we do not categorize this perspective within the concept of actual experience but, rather, under expectations or predictions that fall outside the scope of the discussion in this chapter. In a similar vein, Smith and Diekmann (2017) discuss different perspectives on well-being and order these based on the supposed duration of effects on well-being, ranging from short-term hedonic well-being to permanent utilitarian well-being. The latter interpretation does not adopt a focus on the individual, which, again, is why it is neither discussed nor applied in this chapter.

Happiness

Much like the concept of experience, 'happiness' has many different meanings and can be defined or interpreted in many different ways. However, also reflecting the discussion in the preceding section, the concept of happiness can usefully be explored within a temporal framework. In other words, there are broadly two perspectives on or understandings of happiness, namely, longer-term/cognitive happiness and shorter-term/affective happiness. These can be related to the notions of 'eudaimonia' and 'hedonia' as the constituent elements of well-being (Rahmani, Gnoth & Mather, 2018); indeed, under some circumstances, happiness can be interpreted as well-being. That is, from the longer-term, cognitive perspective, eudaimonic happiness can be equated with life satisfaction, which is commonly interpreted as an appreciation of one's life as a whole (Veenhoven, 2000). In other words, life satisfaction (or a sense of well-being) is concerned with the extent to which an individual considers he/she is leading a life that corresponds to their needs, wants and goals. This approach is also used when assessing an individual's happiness with regard to specific domains in life, such as job satisfaction (cf. Uysal, Sirgy, Woo & Kim, 2016).

In contrast, the shorter-term/affective perspective views happiness as a mood, or the difference between positive and negative emotions felt within a specific (short) time frame (e.g. Fredrickson, 2001; Sanjuán, 2011). Hence, hedonic happiness is generally considered to refer to more instant, short-term pleasure or gratification, such as experienced after a good meal. Nevertheless, a clear connection exists between cognition and affect or between eudaimonia and hedonia, primarily because affective experiences shape cognitive preferences and views over time (Baumeister, Vohs, DeWall & Zhang, 2007).

In addition to the distinction between cognition and affect, happiness can be interpreted from a number of other perspectives, most notably engagement and meaning. Engagement is currently usually considered within the context of peak experiences or flow, as first described by Csikszentmihalyi (1975). In this sense, engagement means being in a mental state of full immersion (Csikszentmihalyi, 1998). In such a state, it feels as if time is standing still; one is fully absorbed in the activity itself. Engagement is, therefore, a more affective and short-term interpretation of happiness.

Meaning is, arguably, the fuzziest conceptual interpretation of happiness and can be considered from both a short- and longer-term perspective. In other words, although there is no generally accepted way to interpret and measure meaningful experiences, one way of approaching the concept of meaning in the context of happiness is to look at meaning either in-the-moment or with respect to life as-a-whole. Regarding the latter, there is a major difference between the meaning *of* life and meaning *in* life (Baumeister, 1991). Meaning of life can be important for happiness, particularly in terms of how death is interpreted. For instance, having the belief in a pleasant afterlife will affect how someone views death and, correspondingly, their own life. In this sense, meaning is a more cognitive long-term interpretation of happiness. In contrast, meaning can also have a more short-term interpretation as in the meaning that people attach to in-the-moment experiences, such as vacations or activities during a vacation.

Tourism: experiencing happiness?

To summarize, then, an individuals' happiness can be seen as being dependent on a variety of different factors that, at risk of over-simplification, can be narrowed down to their view of life, their living conditions and their actions (Baumeister et al., 2007; Diener & Lucas, 2000; Diener, Lucas & Scollon, 2009).

Conceptual framework

Our discussion on the concepts of experience and happiness allows us to create a conceptual framework that enables us to map existing studies on the tourist experience of happiness.

Table 2.1 includes publications in *Tourism Management, Journal of Travel Research*, and *Annals of Tourism Research* for 2018. All full empirical articles published in these journals in 2018 were checked for content via their (i) abstracts and (ii) keywords. If either required further reading, the entire article was read by the authors and, if deemed appropriate, applied to the framework below.

Our review of the 2018 literature reveals that, in that year at least, there were no articles published in the three journals reviewed that considered the touristic Experiencing (in the here-and-now) of happiness within the context of domain satisfaction, engagement and peak. Furthermore, nor was Experiencing the focus of any publications on life satisfaction and meaning in life whilst An Experience (as in past, remembered experience) was not considered in any articles in the context of meaning of life and meaning.

Alternatively, in terms of Experiencing happiness, only a small number of publications explored the meaning of life (Jiang, Ryan & Zhang, 2018; Moufakkir & Selmi, 2018) and meaning (Yu & Xu, 2018). In contrast, the vast majority of publications were primarily concerned with emotions (Antón, Camarero & Garrido, 2018; Gao & Kerstetter, 2018; Li, Walters, Packer & Scott, 2018; Malone, McKechnie & Tynan, 2018; Mitas & Bastiaansen, 2018; Shoval, Schvimer & Tamir, 2018; Tassiello, Viglia & Mattila, 2018; Tucker & Shelton, 2018; Zhang, Gordon, Buhalis & Ding, 2018).

Regarding happiness in terms of An Experience, we observed that these are fewer in terms of number compared with Experiencing. Six publications deal with emotions (Antón et al., 2018; Chen & Li, 2018; Goolaup, Solér & Nunkoo, 2018; Morosan, 2018; Rahmani, Gnoth & Mather, 2018; Ribeiro, Woosnam, Pinto & SIlva, 2018) and just two deal with life satisfaction (Chen, Huang, Gao & Petrick, 2018; Hung, 2018), while one deals with meaning in life (Chen & Li, 2018; Rahmani et al., 2018).

Table 2.1 Journal articles within a conceptual framework of tourist experience and happiness

		Experiencing	*An experience*
Life as-a-whole	Life satisfaction	0	2
	Domain satisfaction	0	0
	Meaning in life	0	2
	Meaning of life	2	0
In-the-moment	Emotions	9	6
	Meaning	1	0
	Engagement	0	0
	Peak	0	0

Literature review

First, we discuss the existing work on tourists' happiness based on what is currently known. Subsequently, we go on to discuss the 2018 studies in *Tourism Management*, *Journal of Travel Research* and *Annals of Tourism Research* in more detail. Particular attention is paid to the questions of which interpretations of happiness and experience are currently applied and studied, how these are studied, and what they add to the extant knowledge prior to 2018.

State-of-the-art on tourists' experience of happiness

A recent review paper by Uysal et al. (2016) on quality of life and tourism includes a review on happiness research in tourism. Their extensive review discusses a large range of papers and identifies their samples, their methods and so on. Unfortunately, however, their paper does not distinguish between measurements taken in the moment (i.e., Experiencing) and retrospective approaches (i.e., An Experience) that ask tourists to recall an experience and assess their happiness after the recall.

Experiencing. The number of studies on happiness during a vacation is more limited because more effort is required to survey tourists while they are away on vacation. Nevertheless, the work that has been undertaken informs us that domain satisfaction (e.g., leisure) positively affects life satisfaction while on vacation (Lam & So, 2013), similar to what happens in everyday life, although tourists are not more satisfied with their lives when on vacation than when they are at home (Nawijn, 2011). This makes sense as life satisfaction in itself is a more cognitive assessment of life as a whole, which is much less affected by pleasures of the moment (Veenhoven, 1984, 2009).

Studies on tourists' reflections on the meaning of life and meaning in life are typical for studies at sites that deal with death and suffering and trips that involve extended periods of travel, such as pilgrimages. For example, Nawijn, Brüggemann and Mitas (2017) studied visitors to the former concentration camp of Sachsenhausen and found that tourists' emotional interest positively affected their meaning in life. Similarly, Thurnell-Read (2009) had found earlier that a visit to Auschwitz made tourists reflect on their life and reevaluate its meaning. Overall, such trips or activities allow tourists to reflect on their own life and the meaning of life in general (Nawijn & Biran, 2019).

In terms of emotions, studies of hedonic trips perhaps unsurprisingly tend to reveal that tourists feel better on vacation than they do in their everyday lives (Mitas, Yarnal, Adams & Ram, 2012; Nawijn, 2010, 2011; Nawijn, Mitas, Lin & Kerstetter, 2013), likely due to spending quality time with loved ones, novelty, a better match between one's needs and wants, and overall more autonomy in the choices people make about where to be, what do to and with whom to spend their time (cf. McCabe, 2002; Mitas & Bastiaansen, 2018; Nawijn et al., 2013). In contrast, non-hedonic activities or trips include a wider range of negative emotions and these carry more weight, compared with hedonic trips (Nawijn & Biran, 2019).

The concept of meaning during travel is a tricky one as it potentially relates to the interpretation of events during vacation, which could theoretically be about spirituality, social connections, learning, identity formation and so on (Iwasaki, 2008). Determining the meaning of a trip in relation to happiness is a process that seems to take place more so when reflecting on An Experience instead of reflections while Experiencing (Kirillova, Lehto & Cai, 2017).

Tourism: experiencing happiness?

Engagement during a vacation can refer to physical engagement (Mathis, Kim, Uysal, Sirgy & Prebensen, 2016) or cognitive engagement (Masberg & Silverman, 1996), next to emotional engagement as addressed earlier. Cognitive engagement is typical for learning and personal growth. Physical engagement is typical for active trips. Overall, these studies relate only in a limited way to the concept of happiness, and happiness researchers more typically resort to studying forms of extreme engagement in terms of peaks. The concept of peak experience in tourism is usually interpreted in terms of flow (Csikszentmihalyi, 1990). Flow is not typically observed in the average vacation, but it is more often found when the engagement is extreme, such as in mountaineering experiences (Tsaur, Yen & Hsiao, 2013) or when tourists are highly engaged in virtual reality tourism experiences (Huang, Backman, Backman & Moore, 2013).

An Experience. Recollections are generally pleasant when they concern memories of hedonic activities, which most vacations consist of (cf. Mitchell, Thompson, Peterson & Cronk, 1997; Wirtz, Kruger, Scollon & Diener, 2003). In line with this notion, most studies on vacations in terms of An Experience find that these contribute positively to domain satisfactions and life satisfaction (e.g., Chen, Huang & Petrick, 2016; Gilbert & Abdullah, 2004). Moreover, it appears that there are spillover effects (Sirgy, Efraty, Siegel & Lee, 2001) of these domains on life satisfaction (Sirgy, Kruger, Lee & Yu, 2011).

The body of work on the effects of vacations on meaning in life and meaning of life appears rather limited. Zahra and McIntosh (2007) address volunteer tourism and find that the experiences of the young volunteers had a sustained impact on their meaning in life. Wilson, McIntosh and Zahra (2013) studied tourism and spirituality and their work pinpoints to key moments within vacations that altered tourists' perspectives of life. In terms of meaning in life and meaning of life, it is only recently that tourism scholars have begun to uncover the essence of the relationship between vacations and existential questions of life. Kirillova et al. (2017) found that this meaning-making process includes multiple stages and, importantly, it begins after the trip. It is difficult, if not impossible, to determine the extent to which An Experience – or a series of experiences – contributes to meanings in/of life. Most likely it is about how, for whom and under which conditions this change occurs.

Recalling An Experience can lead to an emotional response related to the recollected memory of a vacation or it can reinterpret the vacation in terms of its meaning. In this regard, two studies from 2011 are insightful (Tung & Ritchie, 2011a, b). Overall, their work shows that emotional response to a recollected vacation is a main component of the memorable tourism experience (Tung & Ritchie, 2011a). Not surprisingly, the emotions that are part of this memorable tourism experience are mostly positive owing to most vacations being hedonic in nature, and most emotions are strong in terms of their felt intensity because arguably these are remembered better (Fredrickson, 2000). In terms of meanings related to An Experience, the existing work suggests that the main themes reflect the large body of work on tourism motivations (Pearce & Lee, 2005) and this thus concerns mainly social aspects, personal development, and identity formation (Tung & Ritchie, 2011b). Although there is academic work that deals with recollecting a peak experience or recollections of being very much engaged in a touristic activity, these do not have the intention to assess impacts of such recollections on happiness; rather, they attempt to explain the recollected experience itself (e.g., Filep, 2008).

2018 work on tourists' experience of happiness

Experiencing. As mentioned above, only two studies were found that fall under Experiencing and the more long-term/cognitive understanding of happiness, both pertaining to happiness as the meaning of life. These two studies were employed within the context of spiritual tourism, with Jiang et al. (2018) focusing on Zen mediation camps and Moufakkir and Selmi (2018) studying spiritual desert tourism in the Sahara. Both studies found two different nuances of the tourist experience in which meaning plays a major role. The first nuance consists of secular or nature-authentic experiences where tourists experience an enrichment of the senses, culture, human achievement and the landscape. The second nuance is that of sacred or existential-authentic experiences in which understanding the purpose of life is a main theme. It is mostly this latter nuance of the tourist experience that touches upon the understanding of happiness as meaning of life. No 2018 studies were found that employed an Experiencing approach towards the long-term/cognitive elements of life satisfaction, domain satisfaction and meaning in life.

In terms of the short-term/affective approach towards happiness, only one study explored the concept of meaning. Studying the context of literary tourism in China, Yu and Xu (2018) found that the particular tourism experience pertaining to this context may lead to tourists finding new meaning in the morality of literature, themselves, nature and the places they visit. The core focus under the 2018 works that employ a short-term/affective approach towards happiness is formed by emotions. Two studies used a traditional method of travel diaries to study emotions during a trip (Gao & Kerstetter, 2018; Mitas & Bastiaansen, 2018). Mitas and Bastiaansen (2018) found that the effect of tourism experience on positive emotions is mediated by the concept of novelty; that is, experiencing something new/not seen before. Gao and Kerstetter (2018) found that during vacations, tourists make use of several strategies to regulate their emotions and hence their level of happiness during their trip. Next to these traditional methods, several studies explored the use of novel research methods to study the concept of emotions through biometric measures such as skin conductance (Antón et al., 2018; Li et al., 2018; Shoval et al., 2018) and facial expression (Li et al., 2018). All studies found these measures to be of added value to the set of emotion measures in tourism.

As opposed to the studies mentioned above, all of which take emotions as the dependent construct, three more 2018 publications study the role of emotions in affecting other variables. Using interviews, Malone et al. (2018) found that experiencing positive emotions before, during and after the trip led to an increased customer value. In another study, using text analysis and participant observation, Tucker and Shelton (2018) concluded that different tourism narratives lead to different types of affect, which in its turn has an effect on tourists' worldview. Finally, in experimental design settings, it was found that emotions play a role in giving less negative evaluations through handwritten reviews (Tassiello et al., 2018) and that the anticipation of emotions during a vacation may mediate the effect of booking platform experience on tourists' intended level of engagement with the destination (Zhang et al., 2018).

An Experience. Whereas life satisfaction remained unstudied in 2018 from the Experiencing point of view, two studies approach the topic from the perspective of An Experience (Chen et al., 2018; Hung, 2018). Hung (2018) found that in retrospect, cruise tourists see life satisfaction and happiness with life as the ultimate experience of a cruise vacation. In a negative sense, Chen et al. (2018) found that work-related smartphone use during vacations leads to a decrease in life satisfaction. In terms of meaning in life, Chen and Li (2018) found that for inbound tourists to Switzerland, destination image was positively related to how tourists experienced the meaning of this trip in their life. Studying travel blogs, then, Rahmani et al. (2018) found that the meaning of a vacation in terms of activity and potency is strongly associated with various concepts of eudaimonia.

Besides associations between meaning of a vacation and eudaimonia, Rahmani et al. (2018) also found associations of meaning with more short-term/affective aspects of happiness, such as positive emotions of hedonia. Chen and Li (2018) found positive associations between destination image and the experience of positive emotions as well. Antón et al. (2018) found a relationship between properties of the museum visit (such as length and duration) and an overall experience of satiation. In the context of food experience, it was found that background characteristics on the side of the tourists themselves may also lead to very different emotional experiences (Goolaup, Solér & Nunkoo, 2018). Other studies, which study emotions as an independent variable affecting other constructs, have found that tourists are more likely to disclose biometric information at airports when experiencing positive emotions (Morosan, 2018), and that tourists are more likely to be loyal to a destination when experiencing positive emotions (Ribeiro et al., 2018).

Conclusion and discussion

In this final section, we apply the conceptual framework to the existing body of work on tourists' happiness, which allows us to identify potential gaps in the literature, which we discuss at the end of this section.

General conclusion

Does experiencing tourism equal experiencing happiness? In this chapter, we have sought to answer this question based on what is currently known in the academic literature. In general, we conclude that for Experiencing hedonic trips, the conclusion is that tourists feel a lot better than they do in everyday life. In terms of An Experience, recollecting vacations triggers positive feelings, adds to overall satisfaction with life and adds to finding meaning in life. Peak experiences are typical for Experiencing certain types of trips or activities, mainly when extreme physical engagement and skill are involved. Finally, tourists contemplate the meaning of life when Experiencing, but mostly when reflecting on An Experience. This phenomenon is typical for specific types of trips, such as pilgrimages or visits to sites that stimulate tourists to reflect on their own mortality.

The 2018 publications on emotions and meaning in life have added theoretically to the understanding of happiness of tourists. However, the emotion literature is, for a large part, devoted to novel methodological approaches. It remains to be seen whether these approaches will add to our theoretical understanding of tourism and happiness and/or, whether they are simply more useful for marketing practices.

Conceptual framework for future research

Earlier, we constructed a conceptual framework for analysis. We now fill the cells of this framework with our assessment of the potential of the area in question. We now discuss our reasoning in detail.

We advise not to study the effect of Experiencing on domain satisfactions and life satisfaction as these domain satisfactions and life satisfaction are more cognitive assessments of

Jeroen Nawijn and Wim Strijbosch

Table 2.2 Conceptual framework for studying the tourist experience and happiness

		Experiencing	*An experience*
Life as-a-whole	Life satisfaction	Not useful	Well studied
	Domain satisfaction	Not useful	Well studied
	Meaning in life	Gap	Gap
	Meaning of life	Gap	Gap
In-the-moment	Emotions	Well studied	Myth risk
	Meaning	Not useful	Myth risk
	Engagement	Not useful	Not useful
	Peak	Well studied	Not useful

life as a whole, which are much less affected by pleasures of the moment (Veenhoven, 1984, 2009). We therefore mark these cells as 'not useful'. Similarly, the concepts of meaning and engagement are less useful for studying happiness when Experiencing. Meaning formation seems to take place more post-trip and is this more useful to study when assessing An Experience. Engagement is more useful in its extreme form: the peak experience.

As noted earlier, studies on recalling An Experience in terms of peak experiences or recollections of being very much engaged in a touristic activity do not have the intention to assess impacts of such recollections on happiness; rather, they attempt to explain the recollected experience itself (e.g., Filep, 2008). This explains the lack of publications on An Experience in terms of peaks and engagement in 2018 and allows us to mark these cells as 'not useful' in the updated conceptual framework presented in Table 2.2. Moreover, according to psychological theory, overestimation of effects can be caused by focusing illusion (Kahneman, Krueger, Schkade, Schwarz & Stone, 2006). This phenomenon is typically present when respondents are asked to recall an event or imagine an event and consequently assess the dependent variable concerned. In this case, it means asking respondents to recall or imagine a recent/memorable vacation and then assess their happiness in order to determine the effect of vacations on happiness. Such approaches are useful to determine general patterns between concepts, such as in the study by Sirgy et al. (2011), but if done to account for the percentage of the variance in happiness explained via vacations, it is harmful in the sense that it contributes to myth-making in tourism (McKercher & Prideaux, 2014). For this reason, we have indicated these areas as 'myth-risk'.

When assessing Experiencing and An Experience in terms of happiness, it appears that there is a gap in research on meaning in life and meaning of life. The number of studies is limited, as well as the conceptual clarity regarding the constructs. Often researchers refer to meanings related to life, while it remains unclear what types of meaning are referred to (cf. Martela & Steger, 2016), or, in case of a quantitative approach, there is often no valid scale used to measure the construct.

The areas of emotions while Experiencing, domain satisfactions and life satisfaction for An Experience, and peak experiences when Experiencing are all well studied.

Specific areas for future research

Our study addressed the concept of tourists' happiness. Tourism studies have had a long-standing tradition of focusing on impacts of tourism on the destination (e.g., Ap, 1990). It is

Tourism: experiencing happiness?

therefore surprising to observe that studies on locals' happiness are still scarce. During our review of the 2018 literature, we found only one article that dealt with this issue (Lee, Ok, Lee & Lee, 2018). Future research should focus more on the perspective of the locals.

Our analysis further suggests that there is lack of clarity and consistency in the differences between meaning in life versus meaning of life and their theoretical backing. We suggest tourism researchers provide clarity and consult the publications of Martela and Steger (2016) and Martela, Ryan and Steger (2018) for theoretical work on these concepts.

References

Antón, C., Camarero, C. and Garrido, M. J. (2018) A journey through the museum: Visit factors that prevent or further visitor satiation. *Annals of Tourism Research*, 73, 48–61.

Ap, J. (1990) Residents' perceptions research on the social impacts of tourism. *Annals of Tourism Research*, 17(4), 610–616.

Bastiaansen, M., Lub, X. D., Mitas, O., Jung, T. H., Ascenção, M. P., Han, D. I., Moilanen, T., Smit, B. and Strijbosch, W. (2019) Emotions as core building blocks of an experience. *International Journal of Contemporary Hospitality Management*, 31(2), 651–668.

Baumeister, R. F. (1991) *Meanings of Life*. New York: The Guilford Press.

Baumeister, R. F., Vohs, K. D., Dewall, N. and Zhang, L. (2007) How emotion shapes behavior: Feedback, anticipation, and reflection, rather than direct causation. *Personality and Social Psychology Review*, 11(2), 167–203.

Carù, A. and Cova, B. (2003) Revisiting consumption experience. *Marketing Theory*, 3(2), 267–286.

Chen, C.-C., Huang, W.-J., Gao, J. and Petrick, J. F. (2018). Antecedents and consequences of work-related smartphone use on vacation: An exploratory study of Taiwanese tourists *Journal of Travel Research*, 52(6), 743–756.

Chen, C.-C., Huang, W.-J. and Petrick, J. F. (2016) Holiday recovery experiences, tourism satisfaction and life satisfaction – Is there a relationship? *Tourism Management*, 53, 140–147.

Chen, Y. and Li, X. R. (2018) Does a happy destination bring you happiness? Evidence from Swiss inbound tourism. *Tourism Management*, 65, 256–266.

Clawson, M. and Knetsch, J. L. (1966) *Economics of Outdoor Recreation*. Baltimore: Johns Hopkins.

Csikszentmihalyi, M. (1975). *Beyond Boredom and Anxiety: The Experience of Play in Work and Games*. San Francisco, Washington and London: Jossey-Bass Publishers.

Csikszentmihalyi, M. (1990) *Flow: The Psychology of Optimal Experience*. New York: Harper & Row.

Csikszentmihalyi, M. (1998) *Finding Flow: The Psychology of Engagement with Everyday Life*. New York: Basic Books.

Diener, E. and Lucas, R. E. (2000) Explaining differences in societal levels of happiness: Relative standards, need fulfillment, culture, and evaluation Theory. *Journal of Happiness Studies*, 1(1), 41–78.

Diener, E., Lucas, R. E. and Scollon, C. N. (2009) Beyond the hedonic treadmill: Revising the adaptation theory of well-being. In E. Diener (Ed.), *The Science of Well-Being*. Dordrecht: Springer, pp. 103–118.

Filep, S. (2008) Applying the dimensions of flow to explore visitor engagement and satisfaction. *Visitor Studies*, 11(1), 90–108.

Fredrickson, B. L. (2000) Extracting meaning from past affective experiences: The importance of peaks, ends, and specific Emotions. *Cognition & Emotion*, 14(4), 577–606.

Fredrickson, B. L. (2001) The role of positive emotions in positive psychology: The broaden-and-build theory of positive emotions. *American Psychologist*, 56(3), 218–226.

Gao, J. and Kerstetter, D. L. (2018) From sad to happy to happier: Emotion regulation strategies used during a vacation. *Annals of Tourism Research*, 69, 1–14.

Gilbert, D. and Abdullah, J. (2004) Holidaytaking and the sense of well-being. *Annals of Tourism Research*, 31(1), 103–121.

Goolaup, G., Solér, C. and Nunkoo, R. (2018) Developing a theory of surprise from travelers' extraordinary food experiences. *Journal of Travel Research*, 57(2), 218–231.

Hektner, J. M., Schmidt, J. A. and Csikszentmihalyi, M. (2007) *Experience Sampling Method: Measuring the Quality of Everyday Life*. Thousand Oaks: Sage Publications.

Huang, Y.-C., Backman, S. J., Backman, K. F. and Moore, D. (2013) Exploring user acceptance of 3D virtual worlds in travel and tourism marketing. *Tourism Management*, 36, 490–501.

Hung, K. (2018) Understanding the cruising experience of Chinese travelers through photo-interviewing technique and hierarchical experience model. *Tourism Management*, 69, 88–96.

Iwasaki, Y. (2008) Pathways to meaning-making through leisure-like pursuits in global contexts. *Journal of Leisure Research*, 40(2), 231–249.

Jacobs, M. H. (2006) *The Production of Mindscapes: A Comprehensive Theory of Landscape Experience*. PhD Thesis, Wageningen University. Available at: https://edepot.wur.nl/40182 (Accessed 11 October 2019).

Jantzen, C. (2013) Experiencing and experiences: A psychological framework. In J. Sundbo and F. Sørensen (Eds), *Handbook on the Experience Economy*. Cheltenham: Edward Elgar Publishing, pp. 146–170.

Jay, M. (2005) *Songs of Experience: Modern American and European Variations on a Universal Theme*. Berkeley: University of California Press.

Jiang, T., Ryan, C. and Zhang, C. (2018) The spiritual or secular tourist? The experience of Zen meditation in Chinese temples. *Tourism Management*, 65, 187–199.

Kahneman, D., Krueger, A. B., Schkade, D., Schwarz, N. and Stone, A. A. (2006) Would you be happier if you were richer? A focusing illusion. *Science*, 312(5782), 1908–1910.

Kahneman, D. and Riis, J. (2005) Living and thinking about it: Two perspectives. In F. A. Huppert, N. Baylis and B. Keverne (Eds.), *The Science of Well-Being*. New York: Oxford University Press, pp. 285–304.

Kensinger, E. A. (2004) Remembering emotional experiences: The contribution of valence and arousal. *Reviews in the Neurosciences*, 15(4), 241–252.

Kensinger, E. A. (2009) Remembering the details: Effects of emotion. *Emotion Review*, 1(2), 99–113.

Kensinger, E. A. and Schacter, D. L. (2008) Memory and emotion. In M. Lewis, J. M. Haviland-Jones and L. Feldman Barrett (Eds), *Handbook of Emotions*, 3rd Edn. New York: The Guilford Press, pp. 601–617.

Kirillova, K., Lehto, X. and Cai, L. (2017) Tourism and existential transformation: An empirical investigation. *Journal of Travel Research*, 56(5), 638–650.

Lam, D. and So, A. (2013) Do happy tourists spread more word of mouth? The mediating role of life satisfaction. *Annals of Tourism Research*, 43, 646–650.

Lee, J., Ok, C., Lee, S.-H. and Lee, C.-K. (2018) Relationship between emotional labor and customer orientation among airline service employees: Mediating role of depersonalization. *Journal of Travel Research*, 57(3), 324–341.

Li, S., Walters, G., Packer, J. and Scott, N. (2018) Comparative analysis of self-report and psychophysiological measures of emotion in the context of tourism advertising *Journal of Travel Research*, 57(8), 1078–1092.

Malone, S., McKechnie, S. and Tynan, C. (2018) Tourists' emotions as a resource for customer value creation, cocreation, and destruction: A customer-grounded understanding. *Journal of Travel Research*, 57(7), 843–855.

Martela, F., Ryan, R. M. and Steger, M. F. (2018) Meaningfulness as satisfaction of autonomy, competence, relatedness, and beneficence: Comparing the four satisfactions and positive affect as predictors of meaning in life. *Journal of Happiness Studies*, 19(5), 1261–1282.

Martela, F. and Steger, M. F. (2016) The three meanings of meaning in life: Distinguishing coherence, purpose, and significance. *The Journal of Positive Psychology*, 11(5), 531–545.

Masberg, B. A. and Silverman, L. H. (1996) Visitor experiences at heritage sites: A phenomenological approach. *Journal of Travel Research*, 34(4), 20–25.

Mathis, E. F., Kim, H., Uysal, M., Sirgy, J. M. and Prebensen, N. K. (2016) The effect of co-creation experience on outcome variable. *Annals of Tourism Research*, 57, 62–75.

McCabe, S. (2002) The tourist experience and everyday life. In G. Dann (Ed.), *The Tourist as a Metaphor of the Social World*. Wallingford: CABI, pp. 61–77

McKercher, B. and Prideaux, B. (2014) Academic myths of tourism. *Annals of Tourism Research*, 46, 16–28.

Mitas, O. and Bastiaansen, M. (2018) Novelty: A mechanism of tourists' enjoyment. *Annals of Tourism Research*, 72, 98–108.

Mitas, O., Yarnal, C., Adams, R. and Ram, N. (2012) Taking a 'peak' at leisure travelers' positive emotions. *Leisure Sciences*, 34(2), 115–135.

Mitchell, T. R., Thompson, L., Peterson, E. and Cronk, R. (1997) Temporal adjustments in the evaluation of events: The 'rosy view'. *Journal of Experimental Social Psychology*, 33(4), 421–448.

Tourism: experiencing happiness?

Mommaas, J. T. (2000) *De Vrijetijdsindustrie in Stad En Land. Een Studie Naar De Markt Van Belevenissen.* [The Leisure Industry in City and Country. A Study of the Market for Experiences]. The Hague: Sdu Uitgevers.

Morosan, C. (2018) Information disclosure to biometric e-gates: The roles of perceived security, benefits, and emotions. *Journal of Travel Research*, 57(5), 644–657.

Moufakkir, O. and Selmi, N. (2018) Examining the spirituality of spiritual tourists: A Sahara Desert experience. *Annals of Tourism Research*, 70, 108–119.

Nawijn, J. (2010) The holiday happiness curve: A preliminary investigation into mood during a holiday abroad. *International Journal of Tourism Research*, 12(3), 281–290.

Nawijn, J. (2011) Determinants of daily happiness on vacation. *Journal of Travel Research*, 50(5), 559–566.

Nawijn, J. and Biran, A. (2019) Negative emotions in tourism: A meaningful analysis. *Current Issues in Tourism*, 22(19), 2386–2398.

Nawijn, J., Brüggemann, M. and Mitas, O. (2017) The effect of Sachsenhausen visitors' emotions on meaning and word-of-mouth. *Tourism Analysis*, 22(3), 349–359.

Nawijn, J., Mitas, O., Lin, Y. and Kerstetter, D. (2013) How do we feel on vacation? A closer look at how emotions change over the course of a trip. *Journal of Travel Research*, 52(2), 265–274.

Pearce, P. L. and Lee, U.-I. (2005) Developing the travel career approach to tourist motivation. *Journal of Travel Research*, 43(3), 226–237.

Rahmani, K., Gnoth, J. and Mather, D. (2018) Hedonic and eudaimonic well-being: A psycholinguistic view. *Tourism Management*, 69, 155–166.

Ribeiro, M. A., Woosnam, K. M., Pinto, P. and Silva, J. A. (2018) Tourists' destination loyalty through emotional solidarity with residents: An integrative moderated mediation model. *Journal of Travel Research*, 57(3), 279–295.

Sanjuán, P. (2011) Affect balance as mediating variable between effective psychological functioning and satisfaction with life. *Journal of Happiness Studies*, 12(3), 373–384.

Schacter, D. L., Addis, D. R. and Buckner, R. L. (2007) Remembering the past to imagine the future: The prospective brain. *Nature Reviews Neuroscience*, 8(9), 657–661.

Scott, N., Gao, J. and Ma, J. (2017) *Visitor Experience Design*. Wallingford: CABI.

Scott, N. and Le, D. (2017) Tourism experience: A review. In N. Scott, J. Gao and J. Ma (Eds.), *Visitor Experience Design*. Wallingford: CABI, pp. 30–49.

Shoval, N., Schvimer, Y. and Tamir, M. (2018) Real-time measurement of tourists' objective and subjective emotions in time and space. *Journal of Travel Research*, 57(1), 3–16.

Sirgy, M. J., Efraty, D., Siegel, P. and Lee, D.-J. (2001) A new measure of quality of work life (QWL) based on need satisfaction and spillover theories. *Social Indicators Research*, 55(3), 241–302.

Sirgy, M. J., Kruger, P. S., Lee, D.-J. and Yu, G. B. (2011) How does a travel trip affect tourists' life satisfaction? *Journal of Travel Research*, 50(3), 261–275.

Smith, M. K. and Diekmann, A. (2017) Tourism and wellbeing. *Annals of Tourism Research*, 66, 1–13.

Snel, J. M. C. (2011) *For the Love of Experience: Changing the Experience Economy Discourse*. PhD Thesis, Amsterdam: Universiteit van Amsterdam. Available at: https://dare.uva.nl/search?identifier=ce-a6329e-e58f-4dff-8ab9-4a5e6b2b1c9f (Accessed 11 October 2019)

Tassiello, V., Viglia, G. and Mattila, A. S. (2018) How handwriting reduces negative online ratings. *Annals of Tourism Research*, 73, 171–179.

Thurnell-Read, T. P. (2009) Engaging Auschwitz: An analysis of young travellers' experiences of Holocaust tourism. *Journal of Tourism Consumption and Practice*, 1(1), 26–52.

Tsaur, S.-H., Yen, C.-H. and Hsiao, S.-L. (2013) Transcendent experience, flow and happiness for mountain climbers. *International Journal of Tourism Research*, 15(4), 360–374.

Tucker, H. and Shelton, E. J. (2018) Tourism, mood and affect: Narratives of loss and hope. *Annals of Tourism Research*, 70, 66–75.

Tung, V. W. S., Lin, P., Qiu Zhang, H. and Zhao, A. (2017) A framework of memory management and tourism experiences. *Journal of Travel & Tourism Marketing*, 34(7), 853–866.

Tung, V. W. S. and Ritchie, J. R. B. (2011a) Exploring the essence of memorable tourism experiences. *Annals of Tourism Research*, 38(4), 1367–1386.

Tung, V. W. S. and Ritchie, J. R. B. (2011b) Investigating the memorable experiences of the senior travel market: An examination of the reminiscence bump. *Journal of Travel & Tourism Marketing*, 28(3), 331–343.

UNWTO (2002) Definition of Tourism. UN World Tourism Organization. Available at: http://www.world-tourism.org/statistics/tsa_project/TSA_in_depth/chapters/ch3-1.htm

Uysal, M., Sirgy, M. J., Woo, E. and Kim, H. L. (2016) Quality of life (Qol) and well-being research in tourism. *Tourism Management*, 53, 244–261.

Veenhoven, R. (1984). *Conditions of Happiness*. Dordrecht: Kluwer Academic.

Veenhoven, R. (2000) The four qualities of life: Ordering concepts and measures of the good life. *Journal of Happiness Studies*, 1(1), 1–39.

Veenhoven, R. (2009) How do we assess how happy we are? Tenets, Implications and tenability of three theories. In A. K. Dutt and B. Radcliff (Eds.), *Happiness, Economics and Politics: Towards a Multidisciplinary Approach*. Cheltenham: Edward Elger Publishers. pp. 45–69.

Wilson, G. B., Mcintosh, A. J. and Zahra, A. L. (2013) Tourism and spirituality: A phenomenological analysis. *Annals of Tourism Research*, 42, 150–168.

Wirtz, D., Kruger, J., Scollon, C. N. and Diener, E. (2003) What to do on Spring break? The role of predicted, on-line, and remembered experience in future choice. *Psychological Science*, 14(5), 520–524.

Yu, X. and Xu, H. (2018) Moral gaze at literary places: Experiencing 'being the first to worry and the last to enjoy' at Yueyang Tower in China. *Tourism Management*, 65, 292–302.

Zahra, A. and Mcintosh, A. J. (2007) Volunteer tourism: Evidence of cathartic tourist experiences. *Tourism Recreation Research*, 32(1), 115–119.

Zhang, H., Gordon, S., Buhalis, D. and Ding, X. (2018) Experience value cocreation on destination online platforms. *Journal of Travel Research*, 57(8), 1093–1107.

3

THE EMOTIONAL DIMENSION OF THE TOURIST EXPERIENCE

Jase Wilson

Introduction

As Franklin and Crang (2001) note, travel has become a standard element of modern transnational living. Foreign vacations, extended sabbaticals, gap years, digital nomadism or study abroad periods have all become part and parcel of privileged citizenry in globally connected economies. As such, travel has become an explicit avenue through which it is possible to search for connections, disconnections, meaning, escape or existential realization. Furthermore, we are permitted to express our emotions *through* travel and leisure lifestyles as they have become widely acceptable modes of coping, ascertaining idealized selves or escaping when one has simply 'had enough'. For the traveller, tourism is a novel venue through which we can explore our desires, play with fantasy and, in general, seek out a set of notions that formulate our ideas of what it is to have a good life.

Emotions and affects guide individuals through the various scenes they traverse in life; they are implicated in motivation, interpretation, perception and the creation of collectives. Our emotions are felt, lived and experienced as stories. Feelings and emotions in which we are caught up are never isolated events, but part of our ongoing relations with the world. In travel, we seek to purge our deepest fears, quiet our existential anxiety or challenge the limits of our known selves. The felt, enacted, embodied stories we live (and their emotional properties) transcend dichotomies of here vs. there. The emotions we live as stories and narratives permeate through such dichotomies as we are often attempting to solve our being 'here' by travelling 'there'.

We feel, experience and interpret emotions because of our bodies. This is not only true because the body is our main instrument for sensation, but also because our gendered, ethicized bodies are the site of our relations with the world. Emotions, often viewed as categories like 'sadness' or 'melancholy', are always 'about' something; they have a story about them. The content of emotions, the 'aboutness' of emotions, is culturally, intersubjectively created between people who can understand and lay a legitimate claim to the properties of the narrative.

This chapter discusses recent works on emotions and affect from a variety of fields, and debates how these theories can contribute to both classical and current sociological debates in the field of tourism studies. It digs deeper into the propositions made above as it relates

DOI: 10.4324/9781003219866-5

to the tourist experience. Overall, this chapter provides a view of what our emotions are, discusses existing emotional research in tourism, and adds an emotional touch onto some classical discussions in the field of tourism, travel and leisure studies.

Tourism and emotions research

As the affective turn advocates (Clough, 2007), a renewed interest into the world of emotions can help us to realize how emotions shape the social world. Presently, researchers from different disciplines tackle what it is that our emotions 'do' (Ahmed, 2004). A diverse range of work, ranging from neurology (Barrett, 2017; Damasio, 2006) to cultural studies, gender studies (Ahmed, 2004; Berlant, 2011; Massumi, 1995, 2002), geography (Pile, 2010; Thrift, 2004, 2008), anthropology and sociology (Clough, 2007; Stewart, 2007) and psychology (Bondi, 2005; Wetherell, 2012), debates how our emotions and affects are formed, how emotions function and how they intervene in the present moment – often in unpredictable ways. In the wider social sciences, such writers have made efforts to show how our affects and emotions influence our daily lives, politics and reactions to current events.

Currently, writers such as Buda (2015a, b) and Tucker (2009, 2016; Tucker & Shelton, 2018) are drawing on theories of affect and emotion to bring this fruitful dimension to tourism studies. Studies that have explicitly looked at emotion or affect have done so to adopt a critical perspective on tourism in areas of social and political conflict or dark tourism (Buda, 2015b; Buda, Hauteserre & Johnston, 2014), yet also exploring specific emotions such as empathy (Tucker, 2016), fear (Fennell, 2017) or alienation and anxiety (Vidon & Rickly, 2018). Tucker (2016: 32) notes that there has been a 'dearth of attention paid to the emotional sides of tourism more generally' although more recently, and in contrast, Su, Cheng and Swanson (2020: 1) suggest that 'emotions have been widely covered in tourism literature'. However, I argue that the intervening four years have closed the gap so successfully is debatable. More specifically, although quantitative studies of emotion have become more numerous, these have primarily tied emotions to consumer behaviour modelling (Su & Hsu, 2013; Su, Huang & Pearce, 2018). While useful in some ways, such studies do not offer a more nuanced and critical exploration of the tourist's emotional experience. In other words, despite advances in emotional research in tourism, there is still a limited range and volume of such studies.

It is the argument of this chapter that much of the tourism-related research has consistently circled around debates surrounding which theories of emotions can contribute to the research; however, emotions are not always dealt with head on. For example, a great deal of tourism research has focused on ethics, ethical or moral encounters – discourses that are inevitably important to tourism (Butcher, 2003). Concepts such as morals and ethics involve instances of emotion, including feelings of shame or guilt. For example, Scarles (2013) has shown that moral judgement, reasoning and reflection are practised by would-be tourist photographers when engaging with local communities. However, not all tourists take the time to reflect upon the emotions they may spark in others as a result of their actions. For example, in 2017, one Israeli artist created a project in which he pasted images of tourists taking exaggerated selfies at Auschwitz overlaid on images taken from the same location just after the Holocaust, a project which he entitled 'Yolocaust' (Sharma, 2020). As an Israeli who had personal ties with survivors of the Holocaust, he experienced Auschwitz in a different way. As a youth, stories were transmitted to him through a process referred to as 'intergenerational hauntings' (To, 2015) that created for him a more intimately felt geography. In this way, our emotions involve an 'us' or a 'we', where the feelings evoked in a place hinge upon

Emotional dimension of tourist experience

the degree to which we (or our communities) are emotionally entangled in its historical properties. As such, tourism can be viewed as an excellent field for the study of the 'personal subjective experience' and 'collective emotional and cognitive cultures' (Picard, 2012: 12). While our emotions are our own and involve our own subjective historicity, they are also intersubjectively created based on the wider communities in which we are situated.

MacCannell's (1973) now classic work helped to cement the discussions about authenticity and staged authenticity into tourism discourse. His proposition was that an 'inauthentic modernity' (Cohen & Cohen, 2019) had alienated individuals who in turn sought authenticity through travel. The debate still holds true today and much attention has been paid to anxiety and alienation (Rickly-Boyd, 2012; Vidon & Rickly, 2018), existential authenticity (Kirillova, Lehto & Cai, 2017a), transformative experiences (Kirillova, Lehto & Cai, 2017b) and associated concepts, such as freedom (Caruana & Crane, 2011). Existential philosophy has contributed greatly to the underpinnings of tourism theory and, therefore, travel and tourism have come to be thought of as self-fashioning activities imbued with liminal, transformative properties (see also Chapter 7 in this volume). The liberation from 'structural obligations' felt at home allows tourists to play with new selves or negotiate their individual boundaries (Conti & Heldt Cassel, 2019). It is no wonder then that discussions of 'subjective wellbeing' (Holm, Lugosi, Croes & Torres, 2017) and the development of positive psychology (Filep & Laing, 2019; Vada, Prentice, Scott & Hsiao, 2020) have become recent avenues for research. The suggestion, which goes back to MacCannell's work, is that travellers are attempting to improve, solve, modify, regulate or adjust their emotional lives *through* travel experiences. However, as Crossley (2012) notes, the affective and experiential aspects of transformations in tourism, while widely written about, are often not done so employing theories of emotions or affects. Even in the more recent works by Kirillova et al. (2017a, b), the discussions often involve emotions indirectly instead focusing on 'triggering episodes' that the tourist experiences during their trip. They furthermore remark that 'transformation is not a motivation' (Kirillova et al., 2017a: 643) and attribute tourism as the main vehicle for transformative triggering events. This does not hold with the suggestion above that our emotions transcend the 'here' vs. 'there' dichotomies and fails to give weight to our emotions experienced as ongoing stories.

What are emotions?

Emotions, culturally, have been written onto female bodies (Ahmed, 2004) and are often viewed as a gendered concept (Ahmed, 2004; Bondi, 2005). Emotions are often described as tainting the rational processes of behaviour. The word 'emotion' comes from the Latin word *emover*, which means to move in or move out or be moved by (Ahmed, 2004). In this sense, emotions 'operate to "make" and "shape" bodies as forms of action which also involve orientations towards others' (Ahmed, 2004: 4) causing movement, an 'away-ness' or a 'toward-ness' creating shared, intersubjective, culturally infused attitudes to the 'historical present' (Berlant, 2011). Emotions are commonly characterized as existing beneath the faculties of thought and reason 'to be emotional is to have one's judgement affected' (Ahmed, 2004: 3). This view of emotions fails to understand how emotions, as Burkitt (2012: 461) puts it '[are] the source of all our thinking as [they are] integral to the relations we have with our world and the people within it'.

The classical view of emotions over the past half century has been greatly influenced by the work of the psychologist Sylvan Tomkins who suggested that a baseline series of prewired neurological affects exists in humans at birth; distress, enjoyment, surprise, anger, fear, shame, disgust and avoidance (Tomkins, 1962, 1963). This concept has come to be known as the 'theory of basic emotions'. However, Wetherell (2012: 43) notes that '[b]asic emotions are cut out from the flow of everyday cultural life', and that emotions appear on a broader patterning of behaviour, which is open and flowing, and evolving in a 'process of negotiation and emergence' (Wetherell, 2012: 45). The idea/concept of basic emotions, it is argued, appears to negate the process by which meaning is intersubjectively and culturally attached to feeling states (Wetherell, 2012). Barrett, Gendron and Huang (2009) further note that the theory of basic emotions cuts out the richness and complexity of everyday social life. The success of the theory of basic emotions has resulted in wider implications beyond the field of psychology and, consequentially, emotions are often viewed and treated as discreet categories in many disparate fields of research. However, as Burkitt (2018) notes, our emotions often cannot be treated as discreet categories of feeling:

> two emotions are generated together from within the same situation and there is tension between them: they may also bleed together like watercolours on a palette creating emotions like shameful love or a guilty desire.
>
> *(Burkitt, 2018: 169)*

Lisa Barrett's (2017) work on emotions, and most importantly her 'theory of constructed emotions' has challenged many of the long-held beliefs in the field of neurosciences. The theory of constructed emotions directly refutes the 'basic emotions' hypothesis. Barrett (2017) argues that our bodies' interoceptive states are translated into instances of emotions and that our act of *interpreting* our bodies' interoceptive sensations involves context and situation. A queasy stomach, for example, can mean any number of things: a nervousness to fly, love or excitement (e.g. 'butterflies'). The act of translating our bodies' feeling states and patterned embodied conduct into emotions has been widely considered by psychologists such as Bondi (2005), Wetherell (2012) and Katz (1999). As Katz (1999) notes, our emotions arrive in the present moment from distant places and are not entirely 'ours' but rather an individual take on a very public sentiment, they often have 'situation-transcending meanings of action' (Katz, 1999: 315):

> When we examine how people laugh, cry, become ashamed or get angry, we find them routinely giving a finely nuanced significance to their behaviour, even while their experience resonates with feelings of independently flowing, provocative forces.
>
> *(Katz, 1999: 309)*

The brain is *not a reactive brain*, merely reacting to the incoming phenomenon, but is active in producing and constructing an understanding of reality through the building of concepts (Barrett, 2017). What we experience of reality is actually a simulation of reality based on these concepts, or rather the 'sense' and coherence that is made from the chaos of incoming information. This simulation of reality is of huge importance to the understanding of emotions; as we experience the world, our brain increasingly adds to its 'knowingness' or its predictive capabilities of the world, we experience and interpret our interoceptive states as arising *through* our engagement with the objects we encounter. To put it another way, when we feel fear in a dark alleyway, we experience the alleyway as if it itself is imbued with the properties of fear – as Sara Ahmed so succinctly describes, we 'stick' emotions onto objects (Ahmed, 2004). This 'stickyness' of emotions onto objects, places or groups of people creates an emotional simulation of reality an 'affective realism' (Barrett, 2017).

Affective realism and the tourist imaginary

As discussed above, emotions create movement (Ahmed, 2004) and bring bodies into action. The notion of 'bodies' is not limited to a physical body, but could also be viewed as a body of thought, a narrative of place and space – take, for example, the masculine narratives of heroism tied to those who summit or climb on Mount Everest or other Himalayan peaks (Frohlick, 2006; Gugglberger, 2015) or, for that matter, the archetypal search for relaxation on a beach holiday. There is an assumption that 'nearness' to these things may help us live fuller lives even though there is no guarantee they may do so.

The emotional dimension(s) of the tourist experience is/are built up by notions of place and space, as tourists engage with their mediated forms of knowledge and become expectant of 'who' and 'what' they will encounter. Our informed, mediated knowledge of places has been otherwise described as the 'tourist imaginary' (Salazar, 2010, 2012). Salazar (2010: 864) describes that imaginaries are 'socially transmitted representational assemblages that interact with people's personal imaginings and are used as meaning-making and world-shaping devices'. More simply, White, Morgan, Pritchard and Heimtun (2019) describe the imaginary as having a loose frame for understanding something (e.g. a place) for which one has no direct contact.

The tourist imaginary is itself a form of 'affective realism', a key concept not thoroughly explored in tourism. We feel what our brain believes (Barrett, 2017) and, as such, how we experience places has a great deal to do with how we understand them, how we imagine them, or how they have been presented or told to us. The imaginary 'impacts upon our apprehension of the world and in so doing shapes the worlds we create' (White et al., 2019: 2). The concept of the tourist imaginary has been refuted by Andrews (2017), who has noted that any local imaginary often breaks down at the level of the individual tourist who ultimately makes and performs their own meanings. However, the concept of the imaginary as it relates to emotions, and especially affective realism, helps to show how the historical, imagined destination presents an emotional proposition to the traveller who ultimately embarks on a quest for feeling, or rather 'something that feels like something' (Stewart, 2007).

Tourism destinations can be viewed as 'scenes of entanglement' (Blackman, 2015: 25) in which the affective content of one's attachments to a destination's set of promises is unpacked and performed. Destinations, as 'scenes of desire' (Berlant, 2011), can be viewed as emotionscapes, or 'emoscapes' (Kenway & Fahey, 2011) as desiring bodies coalesce around and anticipate particular forms of enjoyment as practiced through leisure behaviour. Places have *feelings about them*, ways that we see and experience them. While tourists pursue their emotional needs, desires, interests en masse, destinations can become absorbed into ontological traps – seen primarily as spaces for travel consumption, laissez-faire moral engagements with local people and even the proliferation of black market emotional industries (such as the sex or narcotics trades). Emotions play a role here, much as they do with all forms of travel and leisure culture.

Language, representation and emotions

Affect 'is understood as a form of thinking, often indirect and nonreflective' (Thrift, 2004: 60). The divide in emotions and affectual research is bifurcated over the problematic nature of language. Some writers, such as Massumi (1995, 2002) and Thrift (2008) describe that affects are 'pre-signified', 'unqualified', autonomous functioning's of the body and exist *before* language. Hence, they have focused on discussing the non-representational aspects or the incapability of language to describe affects, whilst others, such as Wetherell (2012) or Barrett (2017) report that language is crucial in the translation and categorization of how we feel. Their point is that assigning language to the experience also somehow manipulates our understanding of the experience.

I will take the view of the latter and in the following comment, I will show how language filters our perception of experience. Assigning significance to a moment is a process that involves language and the stronger language used, the more we *feel it*. The comment is taken from an interview with Lianne, a woman whom I interviewed at the Mount Everest basecamp in the Spring of 2019. Lianne describes her experience of visiting the Tibetan basecamp of Mount Everest for the first time below:

> I remember it was so beautiful. You could see Everest so clearly. It was really magical, I hiked a little bit above basecamp but I could see it from far away. I remember like, full silence, as if nobody had ever been there. As if it was virgin, there was nobody, really silent, silence like, I felt disconnected from everything. It was just like… this is like… this is God. Really, like pure pure silence. Nobody. Nobody there. Completely virgin. The memory of this silence, I kept recalling, like all the time during my meditation. During the day when I was stressed and everything, all the time the silence kept coming back to re-centres me. I just felt like, this is, well, I would not say its God, but like for me like is something close from God.

This encounter, and her language used to describe it, is illustrative of how affective realism operates. Here she produces her own meaning and makes use of spiritual language to represent her feelings towards that landscape. She uses almost no emotion words in her description, yet we can certainly sense a strong feeling from her experience. It is also possible to see that her emotions can be viewed as a product of her language as a translation of her experience – her understanding of the place and the experience is formed into concepts that she knows and is familiar with using and, as such, those concepts assist her in purveying the content of the feeling. What could otherwise be described as wonder, awe, bliss, is, for her, represented by the word God rather than a feeling or emotion. Representationally, she makes use of religious connotations to describe how it is that the mountains make her feel and to explain her experience. In this instance, language is involved in the formulation and communication of abstract, ephemeral emotion concepts. She uses the lexicon available to her to explain her feelings, to communicate the feeling to others, but also to understand the feeling itself. As such, language-as-implicated in the process of formulating mental concepts, is a critical part of how we perceive places and our emotions within them.

Emotions, intersubjectivity and time

Emotions are about time, they are the very 'flesh' of time (Ahmed, 2004). 'Emotions show us how histories stay alive, even when they are not consciously remembered; how histories of colonialism, slavery, and violence shape lives and worlds in the present' (Ahmed, 2004: 202). Works on affect attempt to capture 'moments in time' as felt both individually and as publicly experienced, intersubjective atmospheres. Works such as Lauren Berlant's *Cruel Optimism* (2011), Sara Ahmed's *Cultural Politics of Emotions* (2004) or Kathleen Stewart's *Ordinary Affects* (2007) help to highlight the movement of feelings from 'I' to 'we':

> Emotions are not simply something 'I' or 'we' have [...] it is through emotions, or how we respond to objects and others, that surfaces or boundaries are made: the 'I' and the 'we' are shaped by, and even take the shape of, contact with others.
>
> *(Ahmed, 2004: 10)*

Berlant (2011: 12) asks and is also interested in how the singular 'becomes delaminated from its location in someone's story or some locale's irreducibly local history and [begins to be] circulated as evidence of something shared'. For Berlant, affect is the 'coming-into-form' of activity, or particular 'scenes of sociality', moments that portend of a shared historical consciousness that apprehends the 'historical present' (Berlant, 2011). Our emotions can be understood as moments of cultural activity as they are intersubjectively constructed interpretations of reality (Bondi, 2005).

While travellers and locals may experience interoceptive events that we would translate as instances of sadness or anger, we 'do' those emotions differently, and those emotions ultimately have a different content 'about' them. For example, in a series of interviews with women who were attempting to climb Mount Everest in the Spring of 2019, remarkably similar narratives and experiences were described to me despite them being from many different cultural, ethnic and socio-economic backgrounds. This is partly because their experience of womanhood has existed within a framework of inexplicit (or even in some cases federally administered) rules of conduct, behaviour and limitations of selfhood. There was a strong, shared sense that their experience as women involved struggle, the constant struggle for emancipation from the limiting frameworks they had found themselves in (in their own local context). Everest, symbolically, was a site of their struggling, a way of performing new selves and renegotiating the structural and philosophical boundaries that they had spent their entire lives navigating.

As per the above example, we know, or come to know, what it means to be us, as we feel and experience each day the conditions of (im)possibility that we have inherited (Berlant, 2011). As such, our emotions are tacit, inexplicit knowledge or 'feeling rules' (Hochshild, 2016) – what it means 'to be' us, to live in the gendered, ethicized, geographically and temporally located bodies in which we do. The 'aboutness' (Ahmed, 2004) of these women's emotional tensions involves these utterly pervasive narrative experiences of selfhood that are contingent upon one's psycho-social subjectivity. The performative renegotiations of selfhood that were central to many of these women's narratives is further to the point that the emotional experiences of tourists are not cut off from the flow of our everyday experience as individuals.

As another example, during one of my interviews at the Mount Everest Basecamp with Anna, the first Romanian woman to attempt to climb Everest, I asked her if being 'the first' meant something to her. The response she first gave seemed to circle around the question. However, a couple of hours after the original interview, she came back to find me again and had this to say:

> Yes... I had thought about your question, and you know its not easy to answer, when you are not prepared for a question. But, about being the first woman on Everest or the first woman to do anything, for me personally I realize that its less important to be the first, that I am the first woman from my country. But more its important that *I am part of a movement that is unstoppable.* Because the force of women, if given a chance, is incredible. Women are capable of fantastic things, but they have to be given a chance. I think this is the most important idea.

While Anna makes no reference to any emotions in this response, we can certainly sense emotions in her statement. She refers to a 'movement' of women, a gendered 'we-ness' (Ahmed, 2004) to her emotions. There is also a sense of time in this quotation, a living, gendered history that is present. The comment is imbued with a sense of hope and the suggestive promise, or attachment to the idea of a 'new world' for women. There is a futurity to Anna's activity. It says 'the world yet to come needs to be different somehow'. So we can also suggest that part of her emotions circle around optimistic attachments to the idea of new possibilities that are not entirely about her, but willfully social embodiments of 'we' (Spry, 2018). Berlant (2011) in Cruel Optimism, describes 'optimistic attachments':

> [O]ptimism is ambitious, at any moment it might feel like anything, including nothing: dread anxiety, hunger, curiosity, the whole gamut from the sly neutrality of browsing the aisles to excitement at the prospect of "the change that's gonna to come." [...] The affective structure of an optimistic attachment involves a sustaining inclination to *return to the scene of fantasy* that enables you to expect that this time, nearness to this thing will help you, or a world to become different in just the right way.
>
> *(Berlant, 2011: 2, emphasis added)*

Climbing Everest, for Anna, is about demonstrating the capability of women and about lighting the way for others – it is a return *to the scene of fantasy*. She returns to her sociality and emotional experience as a woman and plays with an optimistic fantasy of her involvement in the 'movement'. The fantasy she plays with is a form of affective realism; she sees Everest as a site of emancipation and struggle, and sees how 'nearness' not only to Everest (the object), but to the performative act, the 'doing' of herself at Everest, can shift fantasies into realities. The act can be described as a utopian performative (Spry, 2018) as it has an affective 'world shaping' performativity about it – a desire to move towards and embody the change that she feels is so desperately needed. This example shows how Anna's emotions are underpinned by her historical, shared, intersubjectively created impressions of what it is to be a woman. It shows how our emotions involve gendered, social, economic, ethnic or nationally felt stories and histories.

Many of my interview participants borrowed heavily from an existing architecture of meaning as informed by mountaineering culture that can be viewed as a set of historical embodied practices that utilize mountains as symbolic 'game spaces'. The social structure of the mountaineering produces a gestalt effect where Anna, and others, quite literally see the space (the mountain) and the game as inseparable. As such, Anna's emotions are not just tied to the space itself or her personal history, but also to the game, to the performance in the game and how she experiences setbacks, exclusions, moments of doubt or the sense of overcoming a difficult past. It is in this way that her emotional experience in this space involves what Knudsen and Stage (2015: 9) call 'object/subject/affect-assemblages'. Her emotions experienced at Everest are because of the convergence of her and its histories, the relating of her personal and intersubjectively shaped narrative(s) to Everest as a historically lived social space and the patterned embodied conduct of the game of mountaineering. So, our emotions are not only about our historical bodies, but how our bodies meet places, and social atmospheres in our current historical moment.

Surfacing emotions: boundaries and transformation

It is through experiences such as pain that the impression of a surface is created (Ahmed, 2004). The intensity of pain makes us aware of our bodily surfaces, and through the

Emotional dimension of tourist experience

experiences of intensity (such as pain) we develop a sense of ourselves as being apart from the world. However, our surfaces also connect us 'what we find the most touching is that which makes us feel (Ahmed, 2004: 28). Through pain, we experience our boundaries as surfaces, and I propose this is not just in a physical but also an emotional and psychological sense. Our emotions are often lived as a chaotic mess of interoceptive events, many of which we tend not to understand and most of which we only later attempt to tie together into coherent narratives. In this way, the 'incoherent mash' (Berlant, 2011) of emotions can arrive in the present moment as 'archaic traumas' (Buda, 2015).

For individuals who have experienced sincere pain and trauma, it is a question of how to move on when a physical knowledge of such an impressive depth of suffering is felt, lived and known each day. Many writers from the field of sports sciences lean on the theory of 'edgework' (Lyng, 1990, 2012) to discuss how people who participate in voluntary risk-taking behaviour in outdoor adventure sports seek a sense of control and mastery over their emotional anxiety. Bunn (2017) in his review of edge work discusses that it is accompanied by common sensations:

> These include a heightened sense of self and emotional states (fear and elation for instance), and a greater sense of control over particular spaces and objects through which things feel 'more real', a 'hyperreality'
>
> *(Bunn, 2017: 1311)*

Other studies have shown that those who engage in such sports do so not only for a sense of control, but also to 'access' their emotions (Woodman, Hardy, Barlow & Le Scanff, 2010). Barlow, Hardy and Woodman (2013) suggest that climbers (as an example) have difficulty regulating, and accessing their emotions, suggesting that climbers 'seek out situations of chaos, stress, and danger so as to demonstrate or reassert their agency and emotional control' (Barlow et al., 2013: 459).

Throughout these experiences, a foundational understanding of one's self-limits is developed; their physical limitations in sport, as well as their limitations to control their emotional responses to risky or dangerous situations. The limits of what one can endure emotionally and physically, creates and manifests the sense of a boundary, of a surface. The proposition of 'edgework' is around how sporting bodies test and transcend these boundaries; however, the theory of edgework can also reveal a great deal about the emotional experience of tourists and add to the already well-travelled discussions of transformative experiences. To give an example, I will draw again from my interview with Lianne to discuss how she surfaces and relives her 'archaic traumas' through mountaineering, and how she symbolically attaches her pain to a physical object (a mountain).

> Fifteen years ago, I found myself in a hospital bed, in a military hospital, when I got a brain haemorrhage. And it thought it would be the last, I thought would be the end of my life, I thought I would die. I was 25 years old. I remember they showed me the scan, the MRI, and it was like full of blood. I thought, ok, this is it. This is the end of it. I called my parents and to say 'adieu its finished, its over, I will die. And I will die here, in India. So all these experiences, like everything is connected, like ah, its a thread, yknow.
>
> So I feel like this experience brought me here. For me being here is like a spiritual experience. You go beyond your limits, you learn how to know yourself, like your limits. You are like on the limit between, if you fall, you can die. Like you touch death, but you are not dying. Its like between the two worlds. So, for me, its a spiritual thing.
>
> I'm looking like for this transformation because for me, life is about this, its about transformation of, about being aware of who we are really. I think its more about this,

who we are. I think being in the mountains in this kind of environment is about going beyond your limits. Being in this environment, I think it helps you. This is my way, its not for everybody. Its like you're purifying yourself. For me, going to Lhotse, or could be Everest, any mountain. Its a purification process. Its how I see it. So for me its like a kind of pilgrimage this climbing. Its about cleaning myself, finding myself.

Here, I will refute Kirillova et al.'s (2017a) claim that tourists are not seeking transformation as a motivation. Lianne, in her own words, is directly and intentionally seeking an act of becoming through tourism. To Lianne, a mountain is not just a mountain; it is a statement of freedom, of capability, of resolve and of a purging of pain and sadness, or a purification. Lianne's emotions become entangled with her motivations and her experience of the mountains. They become a site and space of emotional regulation, where she 'surfaces' (Ahmed, 2004) and overcomes her previously defined emotional and physical boundaries. Through tourism, Lianne partakes in an 'elective hardship' or what Ahmed would call 'border maintenance'; 'borders need to be threatened in order to be maintained, or even to appear as borders, and part of the process of "maintenance-through-transgression" is the appearance of border objects' (Ahmed, 2004: 87). Through the challenging of borders, the borders of the self, the skin, the 'edge' of one's known limits (Bunn, 2017; Lyng, 1990, 2012), we can indeed see a 'dynamic surfacing' (Ahmed, 2004) where one engages in the project of self-making, effectively reinforcing the borders of the self – the intentionality of such engagement being to continually find and renegotiate 'the edge' of one's physical and emotional self.

Conclusion

As discussed above, emotions cannot simply be viewed as categorizations of feeling states. Given that emotions hinge deeply upon perception, interpretation, motivations, the politicized body and its produced effects of affective realism, the coverage of emotions requires both a psychosocial explanation of the traveller's subjective historicity, as well as an evaluation of some level of symmetry between the visitor and visited places. It is the argument of this chapter that our emotional lives are not separated or cut off from our everyday lives and tourists often seek out novel and transformative experiences *because of* needs and desires that originate from their normal lives (and their gendered, politicized bodies). To many, travel is an instrument through which desiring bodies can attempt to manifest the ephemeral objects of our desire, though, such acts may be less-than-conscious and inexplicit. Emotions and affects operate in relation to the body, time, language, one's subjective and intersubjectively shaped historicity, the physical and historical properties of the destination (the imaginary), and the social games and events that occur in such spaces.

Interesting avenues for future research in relation to emotions can discuss 'utopian performatives' (Spry, 2018) where individuals attempt to break through barriers placed upon their politicized bodies. Research on utopian performatives would require a grounding in emotions and affect research and can use Sara Ahmed's Cultural Politics of Emotions as a guiding light as to the framing of discussions. Interest should also be turned to the collectivity of emotions; the narrativized content of emotions that is enclosed by a sense of inclusive 'we-ness', and the way in which emotions are also exclusive, dividing lines between people. Finally, discussions on edge working moments, boundary work, boundary maintenance, and the way in which travellers negotiate their physical, emotional and social selves through travel and leisure culture can add to the discussions of transformative moments in tourism.

References

Ahmed, S. (2004) *The Cultural Politics of Emotion.* Edinburgh: Edinburgh University Press.

Andrews, H. (2017) Becoming through tourism: Imagination in practice. *Suomen Antropologi,* 42(1), 31–44.

Barlow, M., Hardy, L. and Woodman, T. (2013) Great expectations: Different high-risk activities satisfy different motives. *Journal of Personality and Social Psychology,* 105(3), 458–475.

Barrett, L. (2017) *How Emotions Are Made: The Secret Life of the Brain.* New York: Houghton Mifflin Harcourt. MH Books.

Barrett, L. F., Gendron, M. and Huang, Y. M. (2009) Do discrete emotions exist? *Philosophical Psychology,* 22(4), 427–437.

Berlant, L. (2011) *Cruel Optimism.* Durham: Duke University Press.

Blackman, L. (2015) Researching affect and embodied hauntologies: Exploring an analytics of experimentation. In B. Knudsen and C. Stage (Eds.), *Affective Methodologies: Developing Cultural Research Strategies for the Study of Affect.* Basingstoke: Palgrave Macmillan, pp. 25–44.

Bondi, L. (2005) Making connections and thinking through emotions: Between geography and psychotherapy. *Transactions of the Institute of British Geographers,* 30(4), 433.

Buda, D. (2015a) The death drive in tourism studies. *Annals of Tourism Research,* 50, 39–51.

Buda, D. (2015b) *Affective Tourism: Dark Routes in Conflict.* Abingdon: Routledge.

Buda, D., Hauteserre, A. and Johnston, L. (2014) Feeling and tourism studies. *Annals of Tourism Research,* 46, 102–114.

Bunn, M. (2017) Defining the edge: Choice, mastery and necessity in edgework practice. *Sport in Society,* 20(9), 1310–1323.

Burkitt, I. (2012) Emotional reflexivity: Feeling, emotion and imagination in reflexive dialogues. *Sociology,* 46(3), 458–472.

Burkitt, I. (2018) Decentring emotion regulation: From emotion regulation to relational emotion. *Emotion Review,* 10(2), 167–173.

Butcher, J. (2003) *The Moralisation of Tourism: Sun, Sand… and Saving the World?* London: Routledge.

Caruana, R. and Crane, A. (2011) Getting away from it all: Exploring freedom in tourism. *Annals of Tourism Research,* 38(4), 1495–1515.

Clough, P. T. (Ed.) (2007) *The Affective Turn.* Durham: Duke University Press.

Cohen, S. A. and Cohen, E. (2019) New directions in the sociology of tourism. *Current Issues in Tourism,* 22(2), 153–172.

Conti, E. and Heldt Cassel, S. (2019) Liminality in nature-based tourism experiences as mediated through social media. *Tourism Geographies,* 22(2), 413–432.

Crossley, E. (2012) Affect and moral transformations in young volunteer tourists. In D. Picard and M. Robinson (Eds.), *Emotion in Motion: Tourism, Affect and Transformation.* Farnham: Ashgate, pp. 94–108.

Damasio, A. R. (2006) *Descartes' Error: Emotion, Reason and the Human Brain.* London: Vintage.

Fennell, D. A. (2017) Towards a model of travel fear. *Annals of Tourism Research,* 66, 140–150.

Filep, S. and Laing, J. (2019) Trends and directions in tourism and positive psychology. *Journal of Travel Research,* 58(3), 343–354.

Franklin, A. and Crang, M. (2001) The trouble with tourism and travel theory? *Tourist Studies,* 1(1), 5–22.

Frohlick, S. (2006) 'Wanting the children and wanting K2': The incommensurability of motherhood and mountaineering in Britain and North America in the late twentieth century. *Gender, Place and Culture,* 13(5), 477–490.

Gugglberger, M. (2015) Climbing beyond the summits: Social and global aspects of women's expeditions in the Himalayas. *International Journal of the History of Sport,* 32(4), 597–613.

Hochschild, A. (2016) *Strangers in Their Own Land. Anger and Mourning on the American Right. A Journey to the Heart of Our Political Divide.* New York: The New Press.

Holm, M. R., Lugosi, P., Croes, R. R. and Torres, E. N. (2017). Risk-tourism, risk-taking and subjective well-being: A review and synthesis. *Tourism Management,* 63, 115–122.

Katz, J. (1999) *How Emotions Work.* Chicago: University of Chicago Press.

Kenway, J. and Fahey, J. (2011) Public pedagogies and global emoscapes. *Pedagogies: An International Journal,* 6(2), 167–179.

Knudsen, B. and Stage, C. (2015) Introduction: Affective methodologies. In B. Knudsen and C. Stage (Eds.), *Affective Methodologies: Developing Cultural Research Strategies for the Study of Affect*. Basingstoke: Palgrave Macmillan, pp. 1–24.

Kirillova, K., Lehto, X. and Cai, L. C. (2017a) Tourism and existential transformation: An empirical investigation. *Journal of Travel Research*, 56(5), 638–650.

Kirillova, K., Lehto, X. and Cai, L. (2017b) What triggers transformative tourism experiences? *Tourism Recreation Research*, 42(4), 498–511.

Lyng, S. (1990) Edgework: A social psychological analysis of voluntary risk taking. *American Journal of Sociology*, 95(4), 851–886.

Lyng, S. (2012) Existential transcendence in late modernity: Edgework and hermeneutic reflexivity. *Human Studies*, 35(3), 401–414.

MacCannell, D. (1973) Staged authenticity: Arrangements of social space in tourist settings. *The American Journal of Sociology*, 79(3), 589–603.

Massumi, B. (1995) The autonomy of affect. *Cultural Critique: The Politics of Systems and Environments*, 31(Part II), 83–109.

Massumi, B. (2002) *Parables for the Virtual: Movement, Affect, Sensation*. Durham: Duke University Press.

Picard. D. (2012) Tourism: Awe and inner journeys. In D. Picard ad M. Robinson (Eds.), *Emotion in motion: Tourism, Affect and Transformation*. Farnham: Ashgate, pp: 11–30.

Pile, S. (2010) Emotions and affect in recent human geography. *Transactions of the Institute of British Geographers*, 35(1), 5–20.

Rickly-Boyd, J. M. (2012) Lifestyle climbing: Toward existential authenticity. *Journal of Sport and Tourism*, 17(2), 85–104.

Salazar, N. (2010) *Envisioning Eden: Mobilizing Imaginaries in Tourism and Beyond*. Oxford: Berghahn.

Salazar, N. (2012) Tourism imaginaries: A conceptual approach. *Annals of Tourism Research*, 39(2), 863–882.

Scarles, C. (2013) The ethics of tourist photography: Tourists' experiences of photographing locals in Peru. *Environment and Planning D: Society and Space*, 31(5), 897–917.

Sharma, N. (2020) Dark tourism and moral disengagement in liminal spaces. *Tourism Geographies*, 22(2), 273–297.

Spry, T. (2018) Autoethnography and the Other. Performative embodiment and a bid for utopia. In N. Denzin and Y. Lincoln (Eds.), *The Sage Handbook of Qualitative Research*, 5th Edn. London: Sage Publications, pp. 649–627.

Stewart, K. (2007) *Ordinary Affects*. Durham: Duke University Press.

Su, L., Cheng, J. and Swanson, S. R. (2020) The impact of tourism activity type on emotion and storytelling: The moderating roles of travel companion presence and relative ability. *Tourism Management*, 81. https://doi.org/10.1016/j.tourman.2020.104138

Su, L. and Hsu, M. K. (2013) Service fairness, consumption emotions, satisfaction, and behavioral intentions: The experience of Chinese heritage tourists. *Journal of Travel & Tourism Marketing*, 30(8), 786–805.

Su, L., Huang, S. and Pearce, J. (2018) How does destination social responsibility contribute to environmentally responsible behaviour? A destination resident perspective. *Journal of Business Research*, 86, 179–189.

Thrift, N. (2004) Intensities of feeling: Towards a spatial politics of affect. *Geografiska Annaler. Series B, Human Geography*, 86(1), 57–78.

Thrift, N. (2008) *Non-representational Theory: Space, Politics, Affect*. London: Routledge.

To, N. (2015) Diasporic montage and critical autoethnography: Mediated visions of intergenerational memory and the affective transmission of trauma. In B. Knudsen and C. Stage (Eds.), *Affective Methodologies: Developing Cultural Research Strategies for the Study of Affect*. Basingstoke: Palgrave Macmillan, pp. 69–93.

Tomkins, S. (1962) *Affect, Imagery and Consciousness* (Vol. 1). New York: Springer.

Tomkins, S. (1963) *Affect, Imagery and Consciousness* (Vol. 2). New York: Springer.

Tucker, H. (2009) Recognizing emotion and its postcolonial potentialities: Discomfort and shame in a tourism encounter in Turkey. *Tourism Geographies*, 11(4), 444.

Tucker, H. (2016) Empathy and tourism: Limits and possibilities. *Annals of Tourism Research*, 57, 31–43.

Tucker, H. and Shelton, E. J. (2018) Tourism, mood and affect: Narratives of loss and hope. *Annals of Tourism Research*, 70, 66–75.

Vada, S., Prentice, C., Scott, N. and Hsiao, A. (2020) Positive psychology and tourist well-being: A systematic literature review. *Tourism Management Perspectives*, 33. https://doi.org/10.1016/j.tmp.2019.100631

Vidon, E. and Rickly, J. (2018) Alienation and anxiety in tourism motivation. *Annals of Tourism Research*, 69, 65–75.

Wetherell, M. (2012) *Affect and Emotion: A New Social Science Understanding*. London: Sage Publications.

White, P., Morgan, N., Pritchard, A. and Heimtun, B. (2019) Framing the land of the Northern Lights. *Annals of Tourism Research*, 78. https://doi.org/10.1016/j.annals.2019.06.006

Woodman, T., Hardy, L., Barlow, M. and Le Scanff, C. (2010) Motives for participation in prolonged engagement high-risk sports: An agentic emotion regulation perspective. *Psychology of Sport and Exercise*, 11(5), 345–352.

4

BUILDING THE ORCHESTRA MODEL OF TOURIST EXPERIENCE, INTEGRATION AND EXAMPLES

Philip L. Pearce and Zohre Mohammadi

Introduction

The purpose of this chapter is to present and provide examples of the orchestra model of the tourist experience. It will be suggested that the orchestra model is both connected to philosophical traditions about understanding human existence or being (Peterson, 2019: xxi) as well as somewhat aligned with key ideas that are stressed in cognitive psychology and neuroscience (Sacks, 2017: 99). The specification of the metaphorical properties and the potential of the model will be outlined. Key (published) applications of the orchestra model will include studies of tourists experiencing Italian cathedrals in Florence and Milan, an assessment of paranormal tourist experiences in South East Asia, understanding children's travel stories in Iran, and appraising a humour-oriented tour in central Australia. Recently completed work using auto-ethnography in Europe will also be considered, together with the use of the ideas for teaching experience design. A succinct evaluation of the approach will be offered as a conclusion to the chapter.

Tourism researchers have made the study of tourists' experiences a pivotal topic area in the twenty-first century. The flourishing of this interest area is built on turn-of-the-century writing about the experience economy (Pine & Gilmore, 1999; Schmitt, 2003), which, in turn, can be linked to similar contributions in tourism (Krippendorf, 1987; Pearce, 1988; Ryan, 1997). This contemporary emphasis on experience is closely tied to the widespread adoption of the term in tourism marketing. Companies and travel bodies frequently espouse the strengths of their operations by emphasizing the way they provide access to experiences. For example, Experience Africa claims it offers 'personalised holidays which are put together with creativity and heart so that all our visitors get to truly enjoy the authentic African experience!' (Experience Africa, n.d.). Visit the USA, the official travel site for the country, uses the concept of experience days. Statements on the site advise tourists planning a trip to America to invest some time in local experiences: 'Experience days in the USA are a great way to understand the culture and history of the places you're visiting' (Local Experiences, n.d.). The term experience is employed not just at the national level but is also used to promise a rich and involving time for tourists at diverse sites. A succinct listing includes the polar bear experience in Canada (Canadian Polar Bear Experience, n.d.), the sunrise experience at Borobudur, Indonesia (Diaz, 2012), the best street food experiences in Bangkok, Thailand

50

DOI: 10.4324/9781003219866-6

(Whittington, 2017) and insights into the world of theatre through the Shakespeare experience in Stratford, England (The Shakespeare Experience, n.d.).

In considering these experience labels and in common with other frequently used tourist marketing expressions and descriptions, such as authenticity, it might be argued that the term experience no longer has a very specific meaning. It is perhaps simply a synonym for a visit, trip or tour. This apparent deterioration in the specificity of tourist language has been observed by Dann (1996, 2002), amongst others, and follows much work in the wider sphere of the changes in English language use reported in popular and contemporary culture studies (Aitchison, 2001; Bryson, 1990). The challenge for social science researchers, as Harré, Clarke and de Carlo (1985) pointed out, is to continue to use everyday terms in precise ways. Unless a strong connecting link between the public and the academic use of the terms prevails, the social science research drifts into an arcane corner where the efforts are neglected because of a lack of community understanding. Building on this argument, the development of the orchestra model of experience seeks to be precise in the way the term experience is employed; there is an explicit attempt to be accessible and understandable both to the academic community and the wider interests of tourism businesses and promoters.

Models, connections and context

There is substantial support from philosophers of science for the use of models built on metaphors and analogies (Giles, 2017). As an example, López (2006: 61) asserts: 'By linking different domains (e.g. the eye is a camera, DNA is a code), metaphorical and analogic processes are particularly useful instruments to probe the new or not yet understood'. Bridgeman (2006) specifically notes the value of models for social science research. He argues that the use of models as heuristic tools helps stimulate creative thinking and conceptual innovation. There are many precedents in tourism research for the use of metaphors in describing key processes and phenomena. Some examples include leaving home as crossing a liminal threshold (McKercher & Lui, 2014); referring to tourist attractions as magnets for visitors (Fyall, Garrod, Leask & Wanhill, 2008); and, in chaos theory, characterizing local changes due to distant actions as butterfly effects (Wattanacharaoensil & Stettler, 2020).

Metaphors can, however, both lead and mislead researchers. For example, Mulder, McElreath and Schroeder (2006) describe analogies as powerful but dangerous, whilst more specifically, Speakman (2017), commenting on the chaos theory and butterfly effects, suggests that these ideas may once have had the potential to be a key paradigm for understanding new developments and change in tourism. Nevertheless, calls for the application of this approach have been ongoing for over 20 years (Faulkner & Russell, 1997; McKercher, 1999). Arguably, the promise has not been fulfilled and the effort expended has been unproductive. As another example of the complexity of employing a metaphor as the basis for a model, Ryan (1998) criticized Pearce's travel career ladder approach to motivation (Pearce, 1988). In replying to the commentary and indeed building a more sophisticated version of the approach, Pearce and Lee (2005) and Pearce (2011a, b) noted how the analogy of a ladder had caused interpretive problems for researchers. Often the readers of the work had assumed that earlier steps in the process were left behind as tourists travelled more frequently, which was not the intended meaning. The intent was to see the lower ladder steps as still in place as the higher order motives played a bigger role, a building on the basic steps rather than abandoning them.

These concerns about the astute use of analogies in models in tourism research direct attention to four kinds of rhetorical flourishes (Lodge, 2017). Similes refer to comparisons, such that one phenomenon is seen as like or similar to another. A metaphor goes further.

It suggests that a first phenomenon is structurally matched to or is in fact equivalent to the second entity in its form. Yet again, a synecdoche considers one aspect of a phenomenon or topic and uses that to represent the whole. An example is 'the gloves were flying' to report the action of a boxing match. Additionally, metonymy uses one concept to represent another that is closely related to it. Here an example would be 'the journal accepted my paper' (Forsyth, 2013). This example also doubles as an illustration of personification. In this array of terms, the need to be precise in the formulation of the rhetorical link may not be immediately apparent. The consequences can be spelled out as follows. When a simile is employed, it is a rather weak comparison and critics may easily see that it applies in only a limited way. If synecdoche is being used, the borrowing is directed at identifying only a key part of the topic. If metonymy is preferred, then the allied topic of interest must be sufficiently well matched to add clarity to its referent. The metaphor, by way of contrast to the other rhetorical devices, implies a deeper and comprehensive comparison, one worth exploring beyond the surface level because what is being pursued here is a case of analogical reasoning (Harré, Clarke & De Carlo, 1985). As the last-mentioned authors report, 'shrewd choice of an analytical analogue is the beginning of the discovery of structure...we elicit a pattern that would have been invisible without the model' (Harré, Clarke & De Carlo, 1985: 43).

This background discussion about the choice of an analogy, with a stated preference for a metaphor, can be developed into a succinct listing of what a sound model about tourists' experience should be aiming to achieve. These requirements can be seen as a more specific version of what models, or developing theories of type 3 and 4 in tourism, should be doing (cf. Smith, Xiao, Nunkoo, & Tukamushaba, 2013). The points are offered as follows:

Epistemological integrity. A good model of tourists' experiences should access people's knowledge of their being and actions, not impose a set of views determining participants' perspectives. This requirement favours an emic, but still empirical direction. The philosophical roots are more likely to be in the realm of phenomenological inquiry rather than scientific positivism (Goolaup & Solér, 2018; McCabe, 2014).

Integrative value. The ability of a model to capture many variables and processes, that is, use a rich and appropriate metaphor rather than a synecdoche or metonym, is required to help integrate and consolidate research understanding and insights.

Directing research inquiry. A successful model of tourist experience should assist researchers to shape what is measured, desirably offer insights of general value, and potentially formulate hypotheses about the stream of human action (Smith et al. 2013).

Traverse the timeline. Tourists' experiences exist in a trajectory that covers pre-travel, on site time and post travel accounts. Ideally a model should be applicable to all phases of the timeline (Pearce, 2020).

Immediate and remembered experience. One specific conundrum lies at the heart of assessing experience, namely, the distinction between immediate experience and remembered experience – that is, the experiencing self and the remembering self. A clarity about this issue needs to be explained in presenting a tourist experience model. The difference is captured better in German than English where there are specific words for the two processes: *erlebnis* (immediate, in the moment) and *erfahrung* (remembered and processed experience) (Zare, 2019).

Appropriate for the field of study. It is quite possible to have models of experience that are conceived at the neuroscience level, attend predominantly to psychological processes or more conceptually address marketing lenses, sociological constructs and philosophical inquiry. All such approaches then have to exist within a world of analysis and criticism germane to those fields. A tourism relevant model of experiences can potentially be consistent with both these more specific and abstract approaches, but it has to serve the specific needs of researchers and practitioners who want to examine the phenomenon of tourists' reports and accounts of their holiday time (Hofstede, 1995).

The account of the orchestra model of experience, as presented in the next section, is rooted in many readings and references. In the section that follows, the portrayal of the approach is initially presented as a unified piece, not repeatedly interspersed with key references. Major influences on the ideas presented effectively follow rather than interrupt the narrative.

Specifying the orchestra model of experience for tourism study

A large, sophisticated and world class orchestra produces its work through the integrated coordination of multiple contributions from key but different components. At times, all components are in play and that combination achieves a different outcome to those times when a smaller subset of the total contributors are at work. The work of each facet of the orchestra can be understood in its own right, such as focusing on the contribution of all the string instruments, but it is the total output of all the elements that defines the full effect of the musical piece. The work of the parts is coordinated by a top-down power in the form of the efforts of the conductor. This coordinating figure is shaping the performance according to written materials and guidelines produced as a part of the cultural legacy of the world of music. No two performances are exactly the same. Local circumstances dictate mostly subtle but occasionally large and intentional differences in the work produced. The performance flows over time, although much of what is later recalled is subdivided into sections or chunks or indeed the recall may only exist at overall evaluative review.

The analogical reasoning for the orchestra model of experience can be detailed with the following points of comparison. The tourist experience is like the music produced by an orchestra with multiple contributing components. There are five contributing sections, each of which has its own elements. These sources of influence contribute different component parts at different times to achieve the full experiential (cf. musical) effect. In the tourists' experiential world, the five contributing components are (i) the sensory inputs; (ii) the affective reactions; (iii) the cognitive abilities to react to and understand the setting; (iv) the actions undertaken; and (v), the relevant relationships that define the participants' context. The component parts of these elements are sometimes more powerful than others, such as when sound rather than sight dominates the sensory sub-section of a rock concert experience. For purposes of analysis, individual components can be a focus but, for the individual, at any point in time, the integration of components is paramount. Nevertheless, the totality of the concert experience will also include affective, behavioural, cognitive and relationship contributions.

The experience can be studied as it occurs, or more usually by later recall and analysis. Immediate access tends to be largely through physiological measures or through timed prompts to ask respondents to report on their ongoing good or bad times (Kim & Fesenmaier, 2017). Just as the orchestra is shaped by the overarching influence of the conductor, the individual tourist experience is shaped by the top-down memes of the tourist's culture. Sacks (2017:99–100) conceives of this higher-order ordering of experience as an ascending process built on repeated re-categorization of inputs in line with individual values; a process defining consciousness and marrying the world of physiology and culture. In this useful account, remembering as a process exists but a fixed memory does not, as all accounts reviewing a point of time in our existence are an imaginative reconstruction for the occasion. That is, the experiential times we value are linked to the repeated mental recollection of the distinct occasions we pursue as a conductor of our own autobiography. Above all, the metaphor guiding this model likens experience itself to the hearing of the flow of the music from an orchestra; its production is seen as interlocking contributions from component parts, guided by an overarching consciousness of forms and memes, and its recall is guided by the active reconstruction involved in remembering.

These ways of thinking about experience derive from and adapt the work of multiple thinkers and researchers including Rolls (1985), Krippendorf (1987), Schmitt (2003), Baerenholdt, Haldrup, Larsen and Urry (2004), Peters (2005), Cutler and Carmichael (2010), Sacks (2017) and Peterson (2019), with lesser influences from Cohen (1979), Ryan (1997), Pine and Gilmore (1999), Gnoth and Matteucci (2014) and Ingram, Caruana and McCabe (2017).

It is often valuable to distinguish a relatively new formulation from its predecessors as well as specifying what the model does not do or aim to achieve. The orchestra model of experience is unlike the sociological models of experience originating in the work of Cohen, exemplified further in the much-cited account by Pine and Gilmore, and given fresh treatment by Gnoth and Matteucci. These approaches predominantly categorize experience in terms of labelled outcomes with such designations as educational, exploratory, aesthetic and transformative. The language differs from study to study, but the idea that there are modes of experiencing such as pure pleasure, re-discovery, existentially authentic exploration and so on run through these studies. This kind of categorization marries a holistic approach to motivation with immediate elements of the communities and materials experienced and the people encountered. The orchestra model of experience does not pre-determine any such categories. Instead it directs researchers to the contributing forces, allowing them to detect the reported strengths of various influences. Researchers can decide for themselves how to report or categorize the participants' understanding of any experience.

The orchestra model of experience is also neither an approach that tracks the sequences among the five contributing elements nor does it give priority to any one component. Focused attention to the role of emotions in tourists' experiences has been developing in the last decade (Volo, 2017). There is no argument here that emotions are not important; rather, the view is adopted that they are a part of the orchestra and whether they uniformly follow or precede other components in the tourists' experience is not directly considered in the model. To the extent that contemporary work in psychology sees the order between sensations cognition and emotions potentially varying according to context, the search for a uniform answer or the desire to plot a standard pathway in the operation of mental processes is not particularly productive (Parkinson & Manstead, 2015).

It has been noted already that like the orchestra with its divisions into cooperating units, further sub-divisions within each of the five co-acting facets can be specified. These are documented as follows with some foundation references to support their contemporary relevance in tourism.

Sensory components While the tourists' gaze and the visual components of experience have been recognized for a long time (Urry, 1990, Sontag, 2008), the additional sensory inputs related to embodied experiences has gained substantial attention in more recent writing (Baerenholdt et al., 2004; Pritchard, 2007; Selanniemi, 2003). Attention to hearing and sounds, taste and flavour, scents and smells and the value of touch and physical sensations have all been included in the sensory research lexicon. More subtly, an awareness of physical position and personal context through attention to proprioceptive sensations has been considered in the work on tourist safety and scams (Pearce, 2020).

Affective component. Expressed in broad terms, the affective components of the orchestra model embrace both emotions and the more fleeting concept of moods. The latter is of interest as an influence shaping immediate reaction to tourists' experiences, while emotions have both and at the time and post episode relevance for memory and recall (Zare, 2019). The burst of recent writing about tourists' emotions flows from both much earlier work in psychology and the adoption of those interests in marketing (Volo, 2017). Debates about how many basic emotions exist are perhaps less important in tourism study than the recognition of the rich array and shades of emotional responses depicted in work by Plutchik (2001) and others. The value of considering the rich repertoire of possible emotions in the orchestra model lies in moving beyond simple positive and negative reactions and instead being able to plot the complexity of feeling identified in such locations as visiting dark tourism sites or the realizing of life-long travel goals and achievements.

Cognitive component. All the mental operations associated with processing information can be bundled into the heading cognitive elements of the experience. Understanding places and people, learning about settings, reflecting on and savouring travel events belong in the cognitive category of the model. Trying to solve problems and coping with stress all have a cognitive as well as affective components. The literature that has most directly addressed learning and information provision in tourism includes the studies of interpretation and decision making as well as new developments in savouring and travel benefits (Falk, Ballantyne & Packer, 2012; Kahneman, 2011; Larsen, 2007; Prebensen, Woo & Uysal, 2014).

Relationships component. For a long time, tourism researchers have treated the study of tourists as if they were operating as isolated units in a dynamic world. Typically, however, the tourist experience is shared, and even when tourists travel alone, it has been suggested that they travel with their past self (de Botton, 2002). The notion that the experience is shared and influenced by an array of other persons speaks to the very social nature of contemporary tourism as the interactions with travel partners, companions, host businesses and local communities are all embedded in the experience (Pearce, 2011a).

Behavioural components. The things tourists do, the places where those activities occur and the time spent performing those actions complete the inventory of the orchestra model. The writing about flow experiences has been influential in drawing attention to the properties of activities, notably challenge and immersion, that produce distinctive experiential states (Filep, Laing & Csikszentmihalyi, 2016). Similarly, the concept of pursuing specific activities and moving from a casual to a serious interest has delineated the role of behaviours and activities in influencing experiential outcomes (Stebbins, 2014). These ideas are brought together in Figure 4.1.

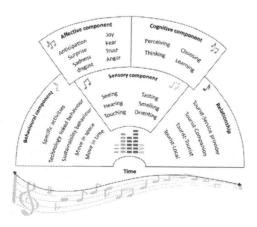

Figure 4.1 The orchestra model of experience; a metaphor for analogic reasoning

Case studies

The orchestra model of experience has been employed in a number of tourism experience studies. The cases reported in this section have attempted to develop a holistic understandings of the new, emerging markets such as Chinese travellers in European destinations (Pearce & Wu, 2016; Pearce, Wu, De Carlo & Rossi, 2013), humour-linked experiences (Pearce & Pabel, 2015), service design education (Pearce & Zare, 2017), paranormal tourism (Pharino, Pearce & Pryce, 2018), the children's market in tourism (Mohammadi, 2019; Mohammadi & Pearce, 2020), technology-linked experiences (Oktadiana & Pearce, 2020) and families with children (Mohammadi, in press).

Remembered or recalled experiences (erfahrung), some on-site and some from later periods of post- travel reporting, have been studied rather than attempting to track immediate ongoing moments (erlebnis). The orchestra model has been applied using the different ontologies and epistemologies of post-positivism, interpretivism and pragmatism. Both quantitative and qualitative approaches have been employed with the orchestra model. Specific tools to elicit the remembered experience include questionnaires, interviews, observation, autoethnography, netnography, drawing techniques, story-telling and online reviews of travellers' reports. The treatment of the data has included one-way ANOVA, Chi-square analysis, frequency analysis, content analysis and thematic analysis. Multiple tourism settings with tourists from divergent socio-cultural backgrounds have been studied: Europe, the Middle East, South East Asia and Oceania. Interestingly, the orchestra model of experience has been used to investigate both positive and negative remembered experiences.

The key case studies are presented in some more detail to document an array of insights. The first case to be considered was also underpinned by an experience economy emphasis. Pearce et al. (2013) and Pearce and Wu (2016) used the model as a holistic pragmatic approach to evaluate both Chinese independent and package tourists' experience of viewing cathedrals in Milan and Florence. The model was viewed as offering an integrated appraisal process consisting of sensory, affective, cognitive, behavioural and relationship factors. The data were collected from a survey with both closed and open-ended questions and analyzed quantitatively (one-way ANOVA, frequency analysis) and qualitatively (content analysis). The Chinese tourists mostly enjoyed the visual sensory components of the buildings, their gaze was accompanied by activities such as photography and they visited the interior and exterior parts of the site. They were not satisfied with the weather. The soundscape was reported as disruptive, even threatening. Chinese tourists described some positive emotions related to the appreciation of beauty but also expressed concerns about feeling anxious and unsafe due to the presence of African men attempting to sell souvenirs and trinkets. Relationships with companions were reported positively, although the interactions with other tourists and service providers were not so positive. Cognitively, Chinese tourists judged the sites to be as good as similar iconic European attractions. In this sample, the independent tourists explored the cathedrals more thoroughly, read the interpretation and spent longer times on-site. The group travellers evaluated the site as more satisfying with the perceived poor toilet facilities and limited interpretation affecting the lower ratings for independent tourists. Application of the orchestra model of experience in this case study relied on its strength to cover different aspects of experience and offer some insights for developing site management concerns of a site, especially for this new but large market to cities.

In a second case, the orchestra model for investigating on-site experiences was used to organize observations conducted through participation in a guided tour. A camel riding tour in central Australia, which specifically used humour to enhance the tourists' experience, was chosen for an on-site audit. Pearce and Pabel (2015) discussed the links between different facets of the model and the role of the guide's humour in shaping the camel ride experience. A detailed evaluation of the setting suggested that the humour experience was mostly derived from hearing jokes, accompanied by sights and smell in the setting. Jokes were sometimes built on the different range of emotions that visitors were experiencing, such as being scared of the camels or, conversely, being too confident. Humour was also constructed around relationships by referring to the tourists' different age levels, relationship status and traveller types. Tourists were engaged cognitively with the stories, learning something about the setting and concentrating to appreciate the light-hearted entertainment. Experiencing a humorous situation was interpreted as consisting of the sensory level (mainly visuals and smells), decoding the puns and jokes at a cognitive level and laughing with companions. The focus of the use of the model in the Pearce and Pabel study (2015) is on integration of the components, the unfolding of the experience over time and what is happening in the mind of travellers. Supportive commentary through analyzing comments on TripAdvisor from people who had been on the tour assisted with the observational insights. The orchestra model provided the researchers with a comprehensive lens to consider the features of the tour, the tourists' responses to the guide's performance and the operation of humour.

Pharino et al. (2018) used the factors from the orchestra model to explore the experience of paranormal tourism. The orchestra model was chosen for three reasons. First, the model is holistic and by including all the elements, especially the sometimes overlooked components of the sensory and relationship elements, it was anticipated that the complexity of the time spent in these special places might be adequately portrayed. Second, as all the facets are measurable, the possibility of an empirical perspective was a reason for the choice. Finally, theoretically the model is in line with the experience studies based on phenomenology, thus potentially offering comparisons with other work assessing dark tourism and unusual and challenging sites. Working in both Thailand and Indonesia, the authors surveyed tourists to ghost and spirit sites. These surveys were accompanied by the short conversations with the respondents for a better interpretation of the answers to the questionnaire. The questionnaire, which was developed after a pilot study, included Likert-scale items for emotional facets, nominal choices for the cognitive, sensory, relationship components while the behaviours were observed by the researchers. Compared with the study of Chinese tourists in Italy, this work adopted a more detailed assessment of the factors for measuring relationships by having sub-categories for companions (partner, family member, friend, colleague); it also added two senses directed at paranormal activities, such as the sense of fear and the sixth sense, and sought reactions to about 13 emotions. The cognitive aspect was limited to new information received at the site. In order of importance, the range of emotions recognized were interest, excitement, joy, surprise, eagerness, expectancy, acceptance and awe. Negative feelings and emotions, such as fear and anxiety, were also reported, although they were not common. The influence of different ghost and spirit settings on the experience was observed in the affective, sensory and behavioural components. In this foundation study about paranormal tourism, the orchestra model was used as a guide to question to understand the meaning of the visit and relate those responses to the visitors' profile and demographics.

Recently, a technology linked on-site behaviour study with a novel combination of autoethnographic and archival research strategies also used the orchestra model of experience (Oktadiana & Pearce, 2020). In contrast to the previous uses of the model, this work evaluated less positive on-site experiences. Technology-based tourism settings were reviewed by assessing the traveller's difficulties and constraints in dealing with new 'people-free' facilities. Oktadiana and Pearce (2020) tried to deepen the understanding by selecting settings in accommodation, transport and entertainment in three technologically advanced countries, Austria, the Netherlands and Spain. A 'loss of touch' was the apparent outcome in both the high-tech hotel in Vienna and the transport system in Madrid, resulting in emotional responses that included anger, frustration and uncertainty. The findings from these technologies which influenced tourist experiences conveyed the importance of being in touch with some skilled staff and locals in creating positive experiences, especially for those used to multiple service staff and only moderately comfortable with technology solutions. The autoethnographic approach, again one consistent with a phenomenological position, required the researchers to reflect on their own responses. During this reflection, a careful appraisal of the researchers' own activities, sensory awareness, understanding, emotional outbursts and their relationships were implicated. The authors used these experiential reflections to evaluate the setting and provide design implications for implementing technology interfaces for tourists.

The developing use of the orchestra model of experience has also been supported in studies of experiences recalled sometime after the events. With an emphasis on children as active agents in tourism, the orchestra model was applied to investigate remembered positive experiences about holiday places. The link between their experiences and their future travel intentions was also addressed (Mohammadi, 2019; Mohammadi & Pearce, 2020). Some recent studies in tourism have addressed the views of children on holidays, but the volume of work conducted is slight compared with other disciplines. In particular, assessing children's views of holidays directly, rather than by considering their role 'second-hand' through the opinion of adults, has been very limited. Nevertheless, some evidence exists that the holiday experiences of children can influence both their own and their families' future holiday choices and activities. Further, children's needs, well-being and happiness not only matter to tourism industry scholars, but also to a wider range of stakeholders who now understand that children are genuine social influence agents. By adopting child-centred and child-friendly techniques, specifically the drawings of a child's best holiday times and accompanying stories around such events, the researchers sought to assess the characteristics of holiday experiences that were prominent in each child's recall.

In assessing the children's views, Mohammadi (2019) proposed a 4-phased Holiday Drawing Analytical Model. The Orchestra model of tourist experience formed a deductive framework for analyzing the interpretive phase of this study. This model provided a good fit with the aims of this study. The approach captured a rich array of sensory experiences, as well as affective, cognitive, behavioural and relationship concerns. Content analysis was adopted to analyze the children's drawings and stories and this work was in greater detail compared with earlier studies. Affective and cognitive components were reported the most, followed by sensory, behavioural and relationship emphases. Positive emotions about holidays included joy, anticipation and surprise, with almost no negative emotions being depicted except for a slight fear of being lost. Cognitively, children look for information about the place, choose from the options and seek on-site learning. The dominant sense in children's experience involved vision but, in order of importance, there was regular mention of touch, taste, hearing and smell. Furthermore, the influence of sex and socio-economic background was considered on the level of experience of the children. Girls showed higher levels of affective and cognitive experience, while boys were more responsive to active behaviours. Children stemming from medium socio-economic backgrounds highlighted their cognitive elements and positive emotions more than children from a more affluent background. Adopting the orchestra model assisted the researchers to move beyond stereotypes of what adults report children think about holidays. This study offers a preface to a wider set of research efforts

The orchestra model

that will enhance the understanding of children's multi-faceted perspectives on anticipating, experiencing and reflecting on their holidays while carefully considering the ethics of research with children.

Pursuing the topic of children as a significant market, another study used the orchestra model of experience to investigate remembered experiences, but with a focus on negative memories (Mohammadi, in press). This qualitative research targeted negative travel comments from families with young children in the well-developed Asian destination of Singapore. The comments were drawn from extensive posts about Singaporean sites on TripAdvisor. It considered the experience of those families and the role of children in influencing family holiday satisfaction. Adding to the variety of settings used by Oktadiana and Pearce (2020), Mohammadi (in press) selected six less studied settings in tourism, such as urban environments, parks, museums, landmarks, food and drink outlets and shopping centres. Deductive thematic analysis was used to classify the negative experience of families with children into sensory factors, and affective, cognitive, behavioural and relationship levels. The focus in this study was on negative experiences. Comparing different tourism settings, the highest negative sensory, affective and cognitive experience was reported in outdoor/nature and parks. The most frequently reported emotions were sadness, disappointment and anger. The negative experiences were linked to cognitive appraisals. Tourists compared the experiences they received to those they had expected. They judged the site in relation to other visited places and recollected the challenges and difficulties they faced based on their children's needs and interests. All these three cognitive elements, namely, perception, choosing and thinking, led to some learning from the time spent. The main negative experiences of the family were related to a service staff, most especially if they were impolite, not being informative, unfriendly, inflexible, or there was a lack of sufficient staff on the sites. Accessibility, navigation facilities and time management are priorities for families. Unpleasant sites regarding tropical temperatures and unattractive site designs for children, as well as lack of child-friendly food places were central to the family holiday concerns. As well as reporting a sense of regret/sadness and some anger about the less than satisfactory service, families did offer some constructive thoughts about their encounters. The orchestra model of experience enabled the authors to reveal the diversity of challenges and constraints of family travellers with young children through a systematic evaluation of elements across a diversity of settings.

In a different style of work, Pearce and Zare (2017) reviewed the origins of tourism experience from the formative typology of Cohen (1979) to the underpinning works of the orchestra model of experience. The authors applied the orchestra model of experience as the basis for teaching tourism experience design. For the educational use of the orchestra model, Pearce and Zare noted the lack of a tourism service design manual for experiences. They argued that, in the next decade, competencies and skills in experience design for students in tourism, hospitality and event management are a priority. By employing the orchestra model of experience, key principles for educating students in service design were introduced. The principles articulated by Pearce and Zare were applying an emic view, keeping the business boundaries in mind, considering divergent groups of customers and respecting time/space flow. An experienced designer should be able to anticipate tourists' reactions and needs and the orchestra model can act as a systematic way of thinking of how tourists may view the setting and likely interactions. The cognitive component of experience can provide designers with some suggestions, or complaints, although sometimes they are not always malleable due to constraints such as pragmatic business concerns, sustainability issues, planning regulations and business efficiency. So, the possibility of what can be created or changed is the second principle. Third, this experience model suggests analyzing profiles of tourists and clustering markets based on common desired experiences. Finally, the behavioural facet provides insights for designing the time and space for the settings with a potential stress on involvement, capacity and skill level. Using these principles, the authors introduced a toolkit of exploratory methods to collect tourists' views. The application of the orchestra model in this work provides a framework for assessing and designing tourism and hospitality settings for educators and students that may improve the link between university learning and future–oriented employability skills.

Conclusion

The features that characterize a good model of tourists' experiences were specified in building the context for this chapter. It is useful to return to these features to appraise the existing status of the orchestra model of experience. From the perspective of epistemological consistency and integrity, the work done using the orchestra model has consistently sought the tourists' views of their holiday times. There is no single phenomenological mandate guiding the approach (cf. Goolaup & Solér, 2018), and judgements about what tourists are experiencing are not imposed during the data collection process. Further, the way tourists view the episodes and the events and sites they visit is taken as the most valid form of experiential reporting and knowledge, a view consistent with the largely constructivist and pragmatic paradigms employed. For this first criterion, it can be suggested that the orchestra model of and the way it has been used meet the criteria of epistemological integrity.

Perhaps the most dominant themes emerging from the cases reviewed and the way the model has been built do address the integrative value of the approach. Nearly all the studies stress the ability of the approach to capture a full picture of the tourists' reflections and reports. This strength provides a justification for the use of the orchestra metaphor. As an allied positive contribution to this literature on experience, the specific components articulated in the orchestra model have prompted what is measured and arguably provided insights of general value, thus leading to the conclusion that the approach has directed research about the experiential stream of human action (Smith et al. 2013).

Most of the work reported has focused on studies conducted either while the tourists were on-site or with data drawn from a later time when the participants reflected on their travels. The studies have not dealt with the pre-travel experience, but the absence of such work does not mean that engaging in pre-travel actions could not be assessed with the model nor that the anticipation of holidays is outside the range of the consideration. Indeed, opportunities rather than limitations of the work are identified in assessing this criterion of the ability of the model to traverse time. Within the studies reviewed, it is clear that the model has only been used for remembered experience. Immediate, that is, in the moment, ongoing experience (erlebnis) can be conceptualized through using the ideas of the model. This may be an advantage as an accompaniment to physiological assessment of some types but the perennial problem of converting an ongoing experience into a verbal rendition of that experience almost necessarily transforms the former into a remembered and processed experience (erfahrung). There is perhaps not a concern here as, many commentators assess remembered experience as more important in influencing satisfaction (Kahneman, 2011). There are also enduring doubts as to whether the physiological record obtained by immediate measures is insightful for the in-the-field experiences that dominate tourism and hospitality research (Pearce, 2018).

As a final evaluative remark, it can be suggested that the orchestra approach does meet the suggested goal to be accessible and understandable to the academic community and the wider interests of tourism businesses and promoters. The metaphor is not abstruse, and the components are labelled with terminology that is familiar in everyday speech (cf. Harré Clarke & de Carlo, 1985). As with all such developments, wider use in more contexts may expose frailties and issues of concern, but the promise of listening to the orchestra of experience appears to be a rewarding way to understand tourists.

References

Aitchison, J. (2001) *Language Change: Progress or Decay?* Cambridge: Cambridge University Press.

Baerenholdt, J., Haldrup, M., Larsen, J. and Urry, J. (2004). *Performing Tourist Places*. Aldershot: Ashgate.

Bridgeman, B. (2006) It is not evolutionary models, but models in general that social science needs. *Behavioral and Brain Sciences*, 29(4), 351–352.

Bryson, B. (1990) *Mother Tongue*. London: Penguin.

The Canadian Polar Bear Experience (n.d.) National Geographic Expeditions. Available at: https://www.nationalgeographic.com/expeditions/destinations/north-america/journeys/churchill-polar-bear-tour/ (Accessed 28 June 2020).

Cohen, E. (1979) A phenomenology of tourist experiences. *Sociology*, 13(2), 179–201.

Cutler, S.Q. and Carmichael, B.A. (2010) The dimensions of the tourist experience. In M. Morgan, P. Lugosi and J. R. Brent Ritchie (Eds.), *The Tourism and Leisure Experience*. Bristol: Channel View Publications, pp. 3–26.

Dann, G. (1996) *The Language of Tourism: A Sociolinguistic Perspective*. Wallingford: CABI.

Dann, G. (Ed.) (2002) *The Tourist as a Metaphor of the Social World*. Wallingford: CABI.

de Botton, A. (2002) *The Art of Travel*. London: Penguin.

Diaz, A. (2012) BOROBUDUR Sunrise Experience (The Largest Buddhist Temple in the World). *Our Awesome Planet*, 29 November. Available at: https://www.ourawesomeplanet.com/awesome/2012/11/borobudor-buddhist-temple.html (Accessed 28 June 2020).

Experience Africa. (n.d.). experience.africa. Available at: https://experience.africa/ (Accessed 28 June 2020).

Falk, J. H., Ballantyne, R. and Packer, J. (2012) Travel and learning: A neglected tourism research area. *Annals of Tourism Research*, 39(2), 908–927.

Faulkner, B. and Russell, R. (1997) Chaos and complexity in tourism: In search of a new perspective. *Pacific Tourism Review*, 1(2), 93–102.

Filep, S., Laing, J. and Csikszentmihalyi, M. (Eds.) (2016). *Positive Tourism*. Abingdon: Routledge.

Forsyth M. (2013) *The Elements of Eloquence*. London: Icon Books.

Fyall, A., Garrod, B., Leask, A. and Wanhill, S. (2008). *Managing Visitor Attractions*, 2nd Edn. Oxford: Butterworth Heinemann.

Giles, T. D. (2017) *Motives for Metaphor in Scientific and Technical Communication*. Abingdon: Routledge.

Gnoth, J. and Matteucci, X. (2014) A phenomenological view of the behavioural tourism research literature. *International Journal of Culture, Tourism and Hospitality Research*, 8(1) 3–21.

Goolaup, S. and Solér, C. (2018) Existential-phenomenology: Understanding tourists' experiences. In R. Nunkoo (Ed.), *Handbook of Research Methods for Tourism and Hospitality Management*. Cheltenham: Edward Elgar Publishing, pp. 62–71.

Harré, R., Clarke, D. and De Carlo, N. (1985) *Motives and Mechanisms: An Introduction to the Psychology of Action*. London: Methuen.

Hofstede, G. (1995) Multilevel research of human systems: Flowers, bouquets and gardens. *Human Systems Management*, 14(3), 207–217.

Ingram, C., Caruana, R. and McCabe, S. (2017) PARTicipative inquiry for tourist experience. *Annals of Tourism Research*, 65, 13–24.

Kahneman, D. (2011) *Thinking, Fast and Slow*. London: Macmillan.

Kim, J. J. and Fesenmaier, D. R. (2017) Tourism experience and tourism design. In D. Fesenmaier and X. Zhang (Eds.), *Design Science in Tourism: Foundations of Destination Management:* Cham: Springer, pp. 17–29.

Krippendorf, J. (1987) *The Holiday Makers: Understanding the Impact of Leisure and Travel*. Oxford: Heinemann.

Larsen, S. (2007) Aspects of a psychology of the tourist experience. *Scandinavian Journal of Hospitality and Tourism*, 7(1), 7–18.

Local Experiences. (n.d.). visittheusa. Available at: https://www.visittheusa.com.au/USAExperiences/local-experiences (Accessed 28 June 2020).

Lodge, D. (2017) *Writer's Luck*. London: Harvill Secker.

López, J. J. (2006) Mapping metaphors and analogies. *The American Journal of Bioethics*, 6(6), 61–63.

McCabe, S. (2014) Towards a better theory of tourism experience? A response to Gnoth and Matteucci. *International Journal of Culture, Tourism and Hospitality Research*, 8(2). Available at: https://www.emerald.com/insight/content/doi/10.1108/IJCTHR-04-2014-0026/full/html (Accessed 4 September 2020).

McKercher, B. (1999) A chaos approach to tourism. *Tourism Management*, 20(4), 425–434.

McKercher, B. and Lui, S. L. (2014) Becoming a tourist. *International Journal of Tourism Research*, 16(4), 399–406.

Mohammadi, Z. (2019) Analysing childhood travels: Perceived benefits, nostalgia, and its implications (Doctoral dissertation). Allameh Tabataba'i University, Tehran, Iran.

Mohammadi, Z (2020). Listening to children as a tourism market: The Asian context. In P. L. Pearce and A. Correia (Eds.), *Tourism's New Markets: Drivers, Details and Directions)*. Oxford: Goodfellow, pp. 176–190.

Mohammadi, Z. and Pearce, P. L. (2020) Making memories, understanding children. In H. Seraphin and V. Gowreesunkar (Eds.), *Children in Hospitality and Tourism*. Oldenbourg: DeGruyter Publishing, pp. 137–156.

Mulder, M. B., McElreath, R. and Schroeder, K. B. (2006) Analogies are powerful and dangerous things. *Behavioral and Brain Sciences*, 29(4), 350–351.

Oktadiana, H. and Pearce, P. L. (2020) Losing touch: Uncomfortable encounters with tourism technology. *Journal of Hospitality and Tourism Management*, 42, 266–276.

Parkinson, B. and Manstead, A. S. (2015) Current emotion research in social psychology: Thinking about emotions and other people. *Emotion Review*, 7(4), 371–380.

Pearce, P. L. (1988) *The Ulysses Factor: Evaluating Visitors in Tourist Settings*. New York: Springer-Verlag.

Pearce, P. L. (2011a) *Tourist Behaviour and the Contemporary World*. Bristol: Channel View Publications.

Pearce, P. L. (Ed.) (2011b). *The Study of Tourism. Foundations from Psychology*. Bingley: Emerald.

Pearce, P. L. (2018) The psychology of tourism. In C. Cooper, S. Volo, W.C. Gartner and N. Scott (Eds.), *The Sage Handbook of Tourism Management. Theories, Concepts and Disciplinary Approaches to Tourism*. London: Sage Publications, pp. 102–117.

Pearce, P. L. (2020) Smart tourists and intelligent behaviour. In Z. Xiang, M. Fuchs, U. Gretzel and W. Höpken (Eds.), *Handbook of e-Tourism*. Cham: Springer, pp. 1–17.

Pearce, P. L. and Lee, U-I. (2005) Developing the travel career approach to tourist motivation. *Journal of Travel Research*, 43, 226–237.

Pearce, P. L. and Pabel, A. (2015) *Tourism and Humour*. Bristol: Channel View Publications.

Pearce, P. L. and Wu, M. Y. (2016) Tourists' evaluation of a romantic themed attraction: Expressive and instrumental issues. *Journal of Travel Research*, 55(2), 220–232.

Pearce, P. L., Wu, M. Y., De Carlo, M. and Rossi, A. (2013) Contemporary experiences of Chinese tourists in Italy: An on-site analysis in Milan. *Tourism Management Perspectives*, 7, 34–37.

Pearce, P. L. and Zare, S. (2017) The orchestra model as the basis for teaching tourism experience design. *Journal of Hospitality and Tourism Management*, 30, 55–64.

Peters, T. (2005) *Design*. London: DK Books.

Peterson, B. (2019) *12 Rules for Life. An Antidote to Chaos*. London: Penguin.

Pharino, C., Pearce, P. and Pryce, J. (2018) Paranormal tourism: Assessing tourists' onsite experiences. *Tourism Management Perspectives*, 28, 20–28.

Pine, B. J. and Gilmore, J. H. (1999) *The Experience Economy: Work is Theatre and Every Business a Stage*. Boston: Harvard School Business Press.

Plutchik, R. (2001) The nature of emotions: Human emotions have deep evolutionary roots, a fact that may explain their complexity and provide tools for clinical practice. *American Scientist*, 89(4), 344–350.

Prebensen, N. K., Woo, E. and Uysal, M. S. (2014) Experience value: Antecedents and consequences. *Current Issues in Tourism*, 17(10), 910–928.

Pritchard, A. (Ed.) (2007) *Tourism and Gender: Embodiment, Sensuality and Experience*. Wallingford: CABI.

Rolls, E. (1985) *Celebration of the Senses*. London: King Penguin.

Ryan, C. (1997) *The Tourist Experience. A New Introduction*. New York: Cassell.

Ryan, C. (1998) The travel career ladder: An appraisal. *Annals of Tourism Research*, 25(1), 936–957.

Sacks, O. (2017) *The River of Consciousness*. London: Picador.

Schmitt, B. H. (2003) *Customer Experience Management*. Hoboken, NJ: John Wiley & Sons.

Selanniemi, T. (2003) On holiday in the liminoid playground: Place, time and self in tourism. In T. Bauer and R. McKercher (Eds.), *Sex and Tourism. Journeys of Romance, Love and Lust*. Binghampton, NY: The Haworth Hospitality Press, pp. 19–34.

The Shakespeare Experience. (n.d.). Shakespeare. Available at: https://www.shakespeare.org.uk/visit/plan-your-visit/itineraries/shakespeare-experience/ (Accessed 28 June 2020).

Smith, S. L., Xiao, H., Nunkoo, R. and Tukamushaba, E. K. (2013) Theory in hospitality, tourism, and leisure studies. *Journal of Hospitality Marketing & Management*, 22(8), 875–894.

Sontag, S. (2008) *On Photography*. London: Penguin.

Speakman, M. (2017) A paradigm for the twenty-first century or metaphorical nonsense? The Enigma of complexity theory and tourism research. *Tourism Planning & Development*, 14(2), 282–296.

Stebbins, R. (2014) *Careers in Serious Leisure: From Dabbler to Devotee in Search of Fulfilment*. London: Palgrave Macmillan.

Urry, J. (1990) The consumption of tourism. *Sociology*, 24(1), 23–35.

Volo, S. (2017) Emotions in tourism: From exploration to design. In D. Fesenmaier and Z. Xiang (Eds.), *Design Science in Tourism, Foundations of Destination Management*. Cham: Springer, pp. 31–40.

Wattanacharaoensil, W. and Stettler, J. (2020) Complexity theory in tourism: The case of Mount Rigi, Switzerland. In P. L. Pearce and H. Oktadiana (Eds.), *Delivering Tourism Intelligence: From Analysis to Action*. Bingley: Emerald, pp, 31–48.

Whittington. A. (2017) 6 Top Food Experiences in Bangkok. *Travel for Food Hub*. Available at: https://travelforfoodhub.com/6-top-food-experiences-bangkok/ (Accessed 28 June 2020).

Zare, S. (2019) Remembering. In P. L. Pearce (Ed.), *Tourist Behaviour: The Essential Companion*. Cheltenham: Edward Elgar, pp. 322–346.

5

THE INTERRELATIONSHIP BETWEEN TOURIST SATISFACTION AND EXPERIENCES

How does one contribute to the other?

H. Kader Şanlıöz–Özgen and Metin Kozak

Introduction

Satisfaction, both in general and specifically in terms of hospitality experiences, has been an increasingly popular concept that has attracted extensive attention in the literature, particularly over the last two decades. Despite this growing interest, however, the concept has not been defined clearly given its dynamic and complicated nature in relation to numerous components, antecedents and consequences (Bowen & Clarke, 2002). Studies attempt to explicate the subject of satisfaction around certain aspects of various constructs (Giese & Cote, 2000). Empirical studies in the tourism and hospitality experience have been inspired and framed by these constructs and have also primarily been based on quantitative methods as a means of revealing various attributes of satisfaction. Significantly, the majority of these studies tend to consider satisfaction as an outcome of experiences. Moreover, one major consensus is that satisfaction is a combination of cognitive and emotional evaluations. However, despite a number of studies that point to the critical role of emotions in the satisfaction and experience process (see also Chapter 3), there is still a need for further empirical research to reveal the relationship between emotions, satisfaction and experience (Ladhari, 2009).

In this respect, the purpose of this chapter is to open a discussion with regard to the interrelationship between satisfaction and experience. It is based upon a study of hospitality experiences in five-star hotels. This context for the research was selected because hotel businesses offer numerous opportunities to analyze the concepts of satisfaction and experience from a variety of perspectives that relate to complex constructs that also identify a number of hybrid sub-experiences. These experiences evoke various feelings, including satisfaction, that constitute the overall perception of experiences that enhance their memorability.

With individuals (107 participants) staying in five-star hotels and a narrative analysis of 144 statements of memorability from 78 participants, the research employed an online data collection procedure that took place in September–November 2016. The basic findings reveal various emotions, with satisfaction as the main one among various causal factors and

64   DOI: 10.4324/9781003219866-7

Satisfaction and experiences

attributes. More particularly, satisfaction appears to create mainly cognitive and emotional experiences in accordance with previous studies but also has possible relations to some other experiential dimensions.

Theoretical background

As noted in the introduction, there is no consensus on a definition of satisfaction (Bowen & Clarke, 2002) despite the significant attention that has been dedicated to it in the related literature. One reason for this is the varying perspectives adopted for the analysis of satisfaction. The disaggregative approach, for example, emphasizes the measurement of satisfaction from each component of the consumption experience whereas the gestalt approach assumes the measurement of the whole consumption experience (Czepiel & Rosenberg, 1977). Alternatively, the transaction-based approach examines satisfaction for a particular offering, which, again, contrasts with the cumulative approach implict in the overall evaluation of the consumption experience (Johnson, Anderson & Fornell, 1995). Other studies consider satisfaction as an outcome in terms of the positive disconfirmation of expectations and the actual experience or as an element of the consumption process (Yi, 1990). That is, it may differ at the attribute (process) and overall (outcome) levels according to the characteristics of consumers dependent on demographic (age, gender, income) and situational (level of the offering experienced, prior experience) differences in service-dominated offerings (Anderson, Pearo & Widener, 2008).

Despite the variety of perspectives that point to the complexity of satisfaction, it is possible to offer an explanation of what essentially constitutes it (Giese & Cote, 2000). As a psychological phenomenon falling under the research umbrella of cognitive psychology (Pizam Shapoval & Ellis, 2016), satisfaction is a cognitive or emotional response pertaining to a specific focus (the object of satisfaction, such as the consumption experience of a product or service) that occurs at a particular time (after a decision is made, after consumption, at the end of the experience). However, the role of cognitive or emotional deliberations leading to satisfaction is interchangeable because satisfaction may either occur in a summary evaluation as an emotional outcome or this outcome may be later justified by cognitive interventions (Giese & Cote, 2000). That is, satisfaction appears as the interplay recurring among cognitive and emotional components over the consumption experience (Giese & Cote, 2000; Yi, 1990).

Satisfaction as a cognitive concept

Within the academic research, earlier studies tend to consider satisfaction to be cognitive in nature (Liljander & Strandvik, 1997) and typically conceptualize satisfaction in terms of its link to the performance of mainly products. It is measured and evaluated as comparisons made with expectations through a variety of cognitive processes including objective (product-based) and subjective (expressive and implicit judgments) evaluations (Czepiel & Rosenberg, 1977; Giese & Cote, 2000; Swan & Combs, 1976; Tse & Wilton, 1988). According to these studies, satisfaction is regarded as an outcome that is the positive disconfirmation between prior expectations and actual performance. In other words, as a positive element of the post-decision process, it is a feeling that addresses the customer's evaluations based on their belief that their goals or needs have been met (Hoyer & MacInnis, 2010). In this respect, satisfaction can be a strong predictor of the quality of offerings (Kim & Severt, 2011), loyalty and profitability (Johnson et al., 1995).

Satisfaction as a blend of cognitive and emotional aspects

Despite the tendency to consider satisfaction as an outcome related to performance, other outcomes, such as the emotions evoked, a change in attitudes or particular responses/reactions (returning the products or shifting to another brand/offering) are also possible (Woodruff, Cadotte & Jenkins, 1983). In more recent years, researchers have reached an agreement that the concept of satisfaction is an emotional feeling stemming from the evaluations of expectations and performance. The reason for this shift in understanding may reflect the limitations of the cognitive approach to analyzing satisfaction with its focus on quality in order to ultimately maintain competitive advantage (Pizam et al., 2016). However, even those studies that examine the cognitive process leading to satisfaction as a resulting emotion do not focus on its conceptualization as an emotion, particularly with regard to its types and dimensions (Woodruff et al., 1983). Moreover, the consideration of satisfaction as an element of the consumption process rather than an outcome offers a deeper analysis of the entire state of an individual's consumption experience with perceptual, evaluative and psychological components of each stage (Yi, 1990).

All those studies reveal the complexity of satisfaction including the interplay between cognitive and emotional aspects. Satisfaction is, on the one hand, considered to be a cognitive process of comparative judgments about feelings, attitudes and emotions before and after the consumption or experience (Oliver, 1980). On the other hand, satisfaction is an emotional state in terms of a response triggered by cognitive evaluations or feelings about how expectations are met (Giese & Cote, 2000; Yi, 1990). In addition, it plays a transitional role around enhanced attributes from the fulfillment of needs by the expected performance based on the basic function of products to unexpected and surprising effects including delight, an extreme emotion that is highly related to higher positive disconfirmation (Rust & Oliver, 2000).

This psychological state (satisfaction) is even interpreted as a very complicated emotion that is highly correlated with, particularly, pleasantness and positivity (Mano & Oliver, 1993) as a part of a hedonic continuum that is beyond the unidimensional determination of satisfaction leading to its analysis as a multi-faceted concept (Westbrook & Oliver, 1991). Therefore, although the essence of satisfaction seems quite ambiguous, the concept has been explicated as a cognitive or emotional phenomenon in a time frame of evaluating or judging feelings or emotions with reference to expectations (Giese & Cote, 2000).

Despite extensive research into the concept of satisfaction and the additional emphasis on emotions as explained above, there exist a few studies examining the interrelations between satisfaction and experience. Given the underpinning feature of the experience, emotions are of interest as corresponding factors with satisfaction. For example, Westbrook and Oliver (1991) report an experiential base with reference to happiness/contentment, delight (pleasure/surprise) and interest in addition to the unemotional state related to the more cognitive manner of expressing satisfaction feelings. Conversely, the effect of emotions on satisfaction may not be evident in some types of offerings and, therefore, more qualitative studies are required to ascertain the role of various emotions at different stages of the experience (Liljander & Strandvik, 1997).

One noteworthy study examining the relationship between satisfaction and experience explores this link in the context of a food consumption experience in terms of utilitarian (instrumental goal of increasing gourmet self-image) and hedonic (terminal goal as the pleasure of eating) choices (Botti & McGill, 2011). Although the main focus of the study is not the experience itself, the selected examples (museum, massage, gourmet food and training

Satisfaction and experiences

camp offerings) are all experiential in essence and the findings of the study report greater anticipated satisfaction related to autonoumous and hedonic choices (Botti & McGill, 2011: 1075)

Satisfaction in the tourism and hospitality sectors

Unsurprisingly, perhaps, satisfaction is also the focus of much attention within tourism studies. To date, wide-ranging research has been undertaken that, seeking to conceptualize and enhance understanding of tourist satisfaction, employs and elaborates on a variety of approaches and measurement methods (Olivieri, Polizzi & Parocco, 2018).Various studies identify the construct of tourist satisfaction, thus measuring it as an outcome (e.g.: Alegre & Garau, 2010; Correia, Kozak & Ferradeira, 2013), whereas many others evaluate it from the perspective of both antecedents and outcomes (e.g.: del Bosque & Martìn, 2008; Ekinci, Dawes & Massey, 2008; Kim & Severt, 2011; Song, van der Veen, Li & Chen, 2012; Torres & Kline, 2006; Wang & Hsu, 2010; Yoon & Uysal, 2005). Given the multi-dimensionality and aggregation of the tourism industry or, indeed, of a single tourism offering, tourist satisfaction is also a highly dynamic and complicated subject to examine (Bowen & Clarke, 2002; Song et al., 2012), including causal relations in terms of push (internal and emotional issues such as escape, relaxation) and pull (external, situational and cognitive items such as food, cleanliness, facilities) motivations (Yoon & Uysal, 2005).

In addition to the wide range of academic works based mainly on the cognitive assessment of satisfaction by tourists, attention has also been focused beyond quality and performance issues toward emotions or affections (Bowen & Clarke, 2002; del Bosque & Martìn, 2008). More precisely, there is an interplay between emotions and cognition of satisfaction as each has an effect on the occurence of the other; that is, the cognitive evaluation of satisfaction may create some positive emotions while emotions help formulating satisfaction (del Bosque & Martìn, 2008).

A further characteristic of the extant research is the dominance of quantitative studies; the literature on tourist satisfaction arguably offers too few academic works based on qualitative methods. Yet, given the valid criticisms with regard to the limitations of quantitative methods to measure satisfaction in the most comprehensive way (i.e.: data collection with too many questions, a general tendency to ask positive and satisfaction-oriented questions), an orientation toward qualitative methods is required to explore and generate a deeper understanding of the concept, particulary in the experiential and emotional context (Bowen & Clarke, 2002).

As the core element of the tourism system, hospitality and hotel enterprises are critical places in which tourist satisfaction should be maintained and enhanced. It is not surprising, therefore, that much attention has been dedicated to tourist satisfaction within the field of hospitality (e.g:. Pizam & Ellis, 1999; Pizam et al., 2016). In this context, earlier cognitive-focused studies have evolved into more comprehensive research that includes the emotional aspects of satisfaction in hospitality businesses. More specifically, Ladhari (2009) suggests the term 'emotional satisfaction' to emphasize the emotional aspects of satistaction in terms of its positive link to service quality and behavioral intentions. Moreover, because it has been recognized that emotions evoked by hotel offerings lead to higher satisfaction, the situation tends to result in a willingness to pay higher prices and gain greater loyalty for hotel services (Barsky & Nash, 2002).

The structural analysis of satisfaction in the scope of its components and dimensions is also critical for hospitality experiences. Guests may achieve satisfaction from hotel offerings as a whole or through the consumption of specific attributes. Attribute-level satisfaction is possible either in a compensative (if the room is more critical, then food can be neglected), conjunctive (a minimum acceptance level) or disjunctive (induced number of attributes) way, whereas overall satisfaction reflects the total difference between perceived outcome and expectations regarding a group of weighted attributes (Pizam & Ellis, 1999; Pizam et al., 2016). In most cases, satisfaction with an hotel experience is the sum of satisfaction of all individual elements, thereby forming this experience as a whole (Pizam et al., 2016). Moreover, individuals may experience different levels or feelings of satisfaction from the same hospitality experience depending on their particular needs, goals and expectations (Pizam et al., 2016). Collectively, all these issues render satisfaction a more complicated and challenging concept to examine.

Given its emotional aspect, satisfaction may also play a transitional role in eliciting stronger emotions in hotels, namely delight, to raise competitiveness (Torres & Kline, 2006). The increasing focus on emotions in consumption experience studies can be seen as a response to Holbrook and Hirschman's (1982) observation almost three decades ago about the limited attention paid in the literature to the link between emotions and satisfaction. Certainly, within the wider hospitality experience, a variety of emotions that create hedonic values complement utilitarian values, thereby increasing levels of satisfaction (Yuan & Wu, 2008). Moreover, given its complicated structure, comprising holistic and hybrid experiences (Schmitt, 1999), the hospitality experience involves different emotions at various stages of the experience (Shaw, 2007).

The dominance of quantitative methods referred to above in tourist satisfaction studies in general is also prevalent in the studies of satisfaction with hospitality offerings in particular (Ekinci et al., 2008; Shanka & Taylor, 2004). Many such studies also recommend that future studies follow this orientation, viewing satisfaction as a cognitive concept within the objective offering 'an excellent and quality product' (Pizam & Ellis, 1999: 336). Therefore, there are promising opportunities to consider satisfaction in the hospitality industry through the employment of alternative methods, including qualitative approaches, in order to complement existing literature with new perspectives in both theory and practice.

In this regard, one critical research instrument to have emerged in the recent years is data mining based on the exploration of big data generated by online reviews and other relevant online content, such as online search results, GPS data and visuals. This novel type of extensive data require novel analysis methods to derive meaningful results (Li, Xu, Tang, Wang & Li, 2018; Pizam et al., 2016). These recent advanced data sources and methods offer the opportunity to analyze satisfaction in hospitality businesses, including the effects of reviews on satisfaction (Zhao, Xu & Wang, 2019), their cultural role in the satisfaction-related attributes (Liu, Teichert, Rossi, Li & Hu, 2017) and their function in contributing to satisfaction by adding some more attributes and categorizations to existing models (Zhou, Ye, Pearce & Wu, 2014). However, the methodologies employed, particularly those using textual data, may still seem limited owing to the absence of a narrative perspective to interpret and comprehend the components or aspects of people's meaning-making processes of their experiences.

The study now described in this chapter attempts to contribute to the existing literature by investigating a possible interrelationship between satisfaction and experience around the memorability aspect in tourism, particularly for accommodation experiences in five-star hotels. Experience is a phenomenon closely related to satisfaction and, for this reason, studies of hospitality experiences reveal the factors that have the highest impact on the satisfaction of hotel guests. These factors are mainly mechanic (physical/tangible/ objective/

Satisfaction and experiences

functional) – leading to utilitarian experiences – and humanic (interactional/intangible/subjective/symbolic) attributes leading to experiential consumption (Berry, Carbone & Haeckel, 2002; Carbone & Haeckel, 1994; Cetin & Dinçer, 2014; Ekinci, Dawes & Massey, 2008; Wakefield & Blodgett, 1999; Walls, Okumus, Wang & Kwun, 2011a). Moreover, those studies also reveal that hotel guests express their evaluations in both cognitive and emotional terms in accordance with the recent research on satisfaction.

Methodology

As noted in the introduction, this chapter seeks to open a discussion about the interrelationship between satisfaction and experience. Given this purpose, the focus of the study discussed below is on hospitality experiences in five-star hotels given the fact that they offer significant opportunities to analyze satisfaction and experience that comprise a plethora of factors that are part of a complex construct with a variety of hybrid sub-experiences. These experiences evoke various feelings, including satisfaction, that constitute overall perceptions of experiences that, in turn, enhance the memorability.

Memorability is one major determinant of experience and is primarily created by emotions (Pine & Gilmore, 1999). Thus, the hospitality experience is expected to create the same effect beyond satisfaction so that the hospitality businesses are able to remain profitable. For this reason, this study examines the extent to which individuals who stayed in five-star hotels (both city and resort) consider their experience to be memorable by defining the main cause–effect relations including satisfaction and their link with the experience dimensions. In order to determine such latent causes or links, a qualitative approach is adopted to identify various aspects of satisfaction (Bowen & Clarke, 2002).

The data collection process took place in September–November 2016 by approaching individuals who discussed their experience of staying in a five-star hotel located in either Antalya and İstanbul, the two capital tourism cities of Turkey and falling into the category of resort and city hotels, respectively. Those who had stayed for a minimum of three nights in these types of hotels between May 2015 and October 2016 were contacted and asked to participate in the survey that was administered via Google Documents. Accessing potential participants to elicit their evaluations of memorability following their experience is an appropriate approach as the overall emotional response to hospitality services (as an intangible offering as a whole) is best captured during the post experience period (Ekinci et al., 2008). Moreover, overall or cumulative satisfaction is the main driver of the most critical satistaction outcomes for businesses (Ekinci et al., 2008; Johnson et al., 1995). Particularly for hospitality services, which are a combination of numerous offerings, satisfaction is the sum of satisfaction with the components that comprise this experience (Pizam et al., 2016).

From the total number of individuals approched (1,252 individuals from various countries, including Turkey), 107 participated and, among those, 78 provided favorable (positive memory) answers to the open-ended question: 'Do you think this accommodation is a memorable one for you? Please explain why'. Participants providing negative responses (9 individuals) and those declaring that their experience was not memorable (20 individuals) were not included in the data analysis process, because the memorability of experiences with a positive orientation can enhance the profitablity of the business. As a result, 144 responses from 78 participants explaining why their hospitality experience was memorable were analyzed.

H. Kader Şanlıöz–Özgen and Metin Kozak

Table 5.1 Examples for the coding process

Participant expression (participant code, hotel type)	Cause	Effect	Experiential dimension expressed
"It was memorable. The reason was magnificent sea view rooms and indispensable unique view" (F111608; city hotel)	Physical/tangible attributes of the hotel – view	Emotional	Sensory (view) and emotional (magnificent-fascination)
"Yes. Clean and attentive hotel with rich variety of food where our children enjoyed their time in a comfortable way"(F091612; resort hotel)	Physical/tangible attributes of the hotel – variety of food, children facilities Interactional attributes of the hotel – employees' procedural attributes (clean, attentive)	Satisfaction and comfort	Cognitive
"Yes, it was a memorable experience with the region, sea, nature and employees" (P101601; resort hotel)	Physical/tangible attributes of the hotel – nature/beach Interactional attributes of the hotel – employees' service	Satisfaction	Cognitive, sensory (nature), relational (employees)
"Excellent people, lovely river views, great housekeeping, best bathroom, friendly atmosphere and very quiet" (F111610; city hotel)	Physical/tangible attributes of the hotel – general environment (silent), hotel and room equipment (bathroom), view Interactional attributes of the hotel – employees' service, employees' procedural attributes (housekeeping), employees' emotional attributes (friendliness)	Satisfaction Emotions	Cognitive (excellent, best), emotional (great, lovely) Sensory (view, quiet) Relational (friendly)
"Yes, the food was very good, the rooms very clean and spacious – a nice 5 star hotel" (F111667; resort hotel)	Physical/tangible attributes of the hotel – food, hotel and room equipment (spacious rooms) Interactional attributes of the hotel – employees' procedural attributes (clean rooms)	Satisfaction	Cognitive (good, clean), emotional (nice)

The analysis was conducted in two stages. Firstly, responses were carefully reviewed three times and the general structure was developed as the base of memorability (causes), what participants gained at the end (effects) and how the participants expressed this memorability (experiential dimension). Subsequently, the coding process was conducted through a narrative analysis to identify themes around participants' experiences (Riessman, 1993) with regard to the causes, effects and experiential dimensions defined by Schmitt (1999). The coding process around various themes and dimensions revealed are exemplified in Table 5.1. This coding process provided detailed tabular data, and findings were illustrated on the maps in a neural network model (Tsaur, Chiu & Huang, 2002: 401) to identify the intensity of interrelations between causes, effects and experiential dimensions (Figures 5.1 and 5.2). The analysis process and illustrations were undertaken using MS Excel.

Satisfaction and experiences

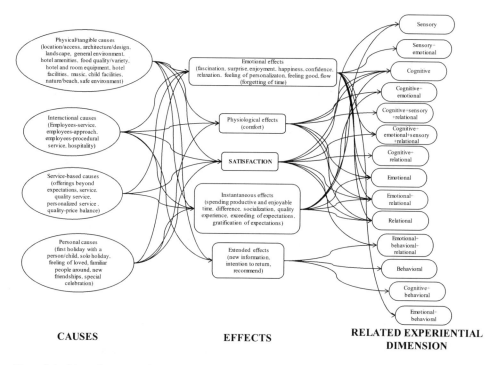

Figure 5.1 Map of causes–effects and related experiential dimensions

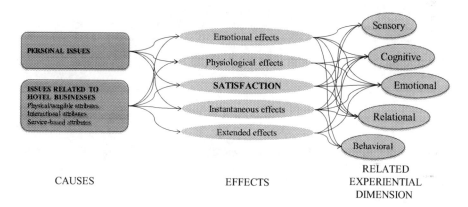

Figure 5.2 Cause–effect relations and their link to experiential dimensions of memorability

Results

The data analysis process disclosed the complicated structure of memorable hospitality experiences pertaining to various experiential dimensions that stem from a variety of issues leading to different forms of effects. Figure 5.2, summarizing the details in the tabular data generated by data analysis (see Figure 5.1 for more detail) illustrates, as a neural network map, the links among all the items of memorable hospitality experiences in hotels. The map displays the basic construct of the data analysis in terms of memorability base (causes) leading to certain gains (effects) and their overall perception as an experience around various dimensions.

As summarized in Figure 5.2, the memorability of the hospitality experience in hotels is based on two particular types of causes (personal and hotel-related), including three sub-causes in the hotel-related one (physical/tangible, interactional, service-based attributes). Effects triggered by those causes also occur in various forms, namely: emotional, physiological, instantaneous and extended. Among those effects, as satisfaction is the focus of the study, it deserves special attention given the influence of both cognitive and emotional as factors that depend on objective and subjective issues about the offering. Therefore, this effect has not been classified in any one group but explained in a separate context to highlight its significance in the hospitality experience.

Discussion

Despite its generalization of a detailed data set, Figure 5.2 reveals the major relationships with regard to the memorability of hospitality experiences in hotel businesses. The first main finding is that the majority of causes are related to conditions under the control of hotel businesses; hence, the creation of impactful experiences with memorability effects including satisfaction is in the hands of hotel professionals. Moreover, the results point toward a different interpretation of the causal relationship to that proposed by Yoon and Uysal (2005) – that is, push and pull motivations – as the personal causes revealed in this study are more situational (Anderson et al., 2008) rather than being related to other intrinsic or extrinsic factors.

One principal relationship emerging from the analysis is that the hospitality experience is considered as memorable mainly in terms of cognitive and emotional experiences. This study attempts to explicate the construct on which the hospitality experience becomes a memorable one. In this respect, the sources of these experiences are based on personal and hotel-related causes. Personal causes depend on subjective situational issues in terms of personal orientation or memories at the end of the experience. For example, it might be the first holiday with another individual (child or fiancée) or a first life experience of a child (learning to swim).

In essence, the hospitality experience is principally based on hotel-related causes in terms of the various attributes of hotel businesses:

- Physical/tangible attributes: View, nature/beach, food (variety/quality), general environment, facilities, hotel and room equipment, location and access, amenities, architecture/design/decoration, layout, children facilities, safe environment, music.
- Interactional attributes: Service of employees, their procedural service, their approach, their hospitality.
- Service-based attributes: Service/quality service, quality-price balance, personalized service, services beyond expectations, organizations for special celebrations.

This complicated structure of causes, reflecting the variety of attributes that are effective in memorability, is an unsurprising finding given the complexity of hotel offerings based around tangible and intangible elements. Therefore, this categorization of attributes as causes of memorability confirms the findings of prior studies that point to the experiential attributes around humanic and mechanic items (Berry et al., 2002; Carbone & Haeckel, 1994; Cetin & Dinçer, 2014; Ekinci et al., 2008; Walls et al., 2011a). However, this study adds another dimension, namely service-based attributes that are also offered by employees but regarded as impersonal issues by hotel guests. Another remarkable finding of the current study

Satisfaction and experiences

is that guests may find hospitality experiences memorable as a consequence of the significant performance of employees; that is, hotel guests tend to emphasize the performance of certain employees as a basis of a memorable experience. Consequently, this study contributes to the prior studies mentioned above by disclosing and specifying the perceptional differences of participants in terms of general service-based and specific employee-based causes as a part of humanic or interactional attributes.

Effects triggered by those causes also appear in various forms that can be categorized as emotional, physiological, instantaneous and extended effects. The majority of effects are emotional, involving a wide range of emotions such as fascination, happiness, pleasure, confidence/serenity, surprise, enjoyment, flow, relaxation and feeling special. In this respect, the current study reflects the experiential characteristcs of hospitality and highlights various emotions that may appear during hospitality experience (Shaw, 2007; Yuan & Wu, 2008).

Although satisfaction is the main emotional orientation of many academic studies and analyzed extensively as an outcome of offerings, its construct based on emotional and cognitive aspects to affect the overall experience is a new subject to study. The findings of the current study reveal that the perception of the hospitality experience by the participants is either an holistic (i.e.: only cognitive or emotional) or hybrid (i.e.: a mixture of cognitive and emotional) experience (Schmitt, 1999). Moreover, according to findings, the main cause of memorability is explained by the physical/tangible attributes among the hotel-related causes, which lead to principally emotions- and satisfaction-based effects that, in turn, result in the perception of the hospitality experience as being emotional and cognitive experiences. This link between physical/tangible attributes with mainly emotional but also cognitive experiences is similar to the findings of prior studies (Berry et al., 2002; Carbone & Haeckel, 1994; Wakefield & Blodgett, 1999). In addition, Figures 5.1 and 5.2 both display various links between causes, effects and experiences; this is an expected outcome regarding the variety of participants' different senses of satisfaction related to their needs, goals and expectations (Pizam et al., 2016).

Another critical aspect of the findings is the difference in the basis of memorability as expressed by various participants. That is, participants differred in the way of expressing the causes and effects of their experiences in terms of memorability. For example, some participants consider the hospitality experience as cognitive based on the quality of services offered, whereas others expressed in terms of pleasure, thus regarding it as an emotional experience. These differences can be explained by reasons such as length of stay or purpose of visit (Walls, Okumus, Wang & Kwun, 2011b).

The study also provides an insightful view of hospitality experiences in terms of the relationship among each group of attributes, effects and experiential dimensions as the findings were compiled in a neural network map. The map exhibits that hotel general environment (as an element in physical/tangible attributes) and employees' approach particularly friendliness and helpfulness (as an element in the interactional attributes) are effective in memorability. These findings suggest that memorable hotel experiences are based on emotions evoked by the hotel's general environment and employees' emotional orientation toward welcoming hotel guests.

As for the overall focus of this chapter, satisfaction, as a key output of any experience, is the only major effect item expressed by participants in relation to all experiential dimensions except for the behavioral dimension. More specifically, satisfaction is effective in creating cognitive experiences. Despite the two-folded basis of satisfaction on cognition and emotions, this study reveals the dominance of cognitive aspects followed by relational experiences but very limited effect on the emotional experience dimension. The higher emphasis on relational experience is not surprising given the nature of the hospitality experience based intensively on labor and the attitudes of the working people. Therefore, this finding partially supports prior explanations of satisfaction and the two-sided feature of the concept (Botti & McGill, 2011; Giese & Cote, 2000; Liljander & Strandvik, 1997; Rust & Oliver, 2000; Yi, 1990) but also proposes another critical dimension namely relational experience related to satisfaction. Findings also reveal that all types of the causes are evident as sources of satisfaction. Physical/tangible attributes dominantly lead to cognitive experiences, while interactional attributes naturally result in relational experiences. Following those main causes, service-related attributes generate satisfaction that is perceived mainly as cognitive experiences.

Conclusion

The aim of this chapter is to open a discussion with regard to the interrelationship between satisfaction and experience based on a study that presents an alternative way of looking at satisfaction in terms of its role on the memorability by employing narrative analysis, an effective method to examine experiences. Findings are compiled in the neural network design to exhibit the relations among causes, effects and experiential dimensions of the memorable hospitality experiences. Satisfaction, as a major outcome of all experiences, appears as an effect triggered by mainly physical/tangible and interactional causes leading to cognitive and relational experiences. Thus, this chapter introduces a new area of research to deepen the understanding of satisfaction with its focus of interrelation between satisfaction and experience through various experiential dimensions.

From a methodological point of view, this chapter also recalls the potential of qualitative studies to ascertain some latent relations of satisfaction through narrative analysis, which is an effective method to examine experiences. In this respect, another major contribution of the chapter appears as the need to analyze satisfaction deeply to identify more attributes and elements in addition to those revealed in the existing literature. Such analysis offers the possibility to comprehend satisfaction in respect for hedonic (experiential) and utilitarian (rational) aspects to design offerings for the highest degree of satisfaction in all business domains including the tourism and hospitality industry.

With this aspect, as revealed by the study in the chapter, the sensory and behavioural aspects also need consideration to incorporate into satisfaction to generate alternative perceptions of experiences. This attempt is enhanced by more qualitative or mixed methods on vast online data to derive new models and theories covering emerging trends and changing preferences of customers. Therefore, both the academia and practitioners may improve their perspective to comprehend satisfaction in the timeliest sense to develop more successful offerings that will gratify the needs of customers including hospitality guests.

Finally, this chapter opens a discussion on the interrelationship between satisfaction and experience with several limitations that may offer an opportunity for future research. First, the research area is limited to five-star hotels in the two capital cities of Turkey. Similar approach is applicable for some other destinations with different tourism resources and various types of lodging to see how satisfaction-experience interplays according to various factors. Second, although there is no limit of participants for qualitative research, longer texts with probably more questions incorporated with experience narratives may present a very insightful understanding of the satisfaction-experience interrelationship. Even instantaneous data collection through narratives during encounters, during, just after experience and sometimes after experience may present more fruitful findings.

Satisfaction and experiences

References

Alegre, J. and Garau, J. (2010) Tourist satisfaction and dissatisfaction. *Annals of Tourism Research*, 37(1), 52–73.

Anderson, S., Pearo, L. and Widener, S. (2008) Drivers of service satisfaction: Linking customer satisfaction to the service concept and customer characteristics. *Journal of Service Research*, 10(4), 365–381.

Barsky, J. and Nash, L. (2002) Evoking emotion: Affective keys to hotel loyalty. *Cornell Hotel and Restaurant Administration Quarterly*, 43(1), 39–46.

Berry, L. L., Carbone, L. P. and Haeckel, S. H. (2002) Managing the total customer experience. *MIT Sloan Management Review Spring 2002*, 43(3), 1–6.

Botti, S. and McGill, A. L. (2011) The locus of choice: Personal causality and satisfaction with hedonic and utilitarian decisions. *Journal of Consumer Research*, 37(6), 1065–1078.

Bowen, D. and Clarke, J. (2002) Reflections on tourist satisfaction research. *Journal of Vacation Marketing*, 8(4), 297–308.

Carbone, L. P. and Haeckel, S. H. (1994) Engineering customer experiences. *Marketing Management*, 3(3), 9–19.

Cetin, G. and Dinçer, F. I. (2014) Influence of customer experience on loyalty and word-of-mouth in hospitality operations. *Anatolia: An International Journal of Tourism and Hospitality*, 25(2), 181–194.

Correia, A., Kozak, M. and Ferradeira, J. (2013) From tourist motivations to tourist satisfaction. *International Journal of Culture, Tourism and Hospitality Research*, 7(4), 411–424.

Czepiel, J. and Rosenberg, L. (1977) Consumer satisfaction: Concept and measurement. *Journal of the Academy of Marketing Science*, 5(4), 403–411.

del Bosque, I. R. and Martìn, H. S. (2008) Tourist satisfaction: A cognitive–affective model. *Annals of Tourism Research*, 35(2), 551–573.

Ekinci, Y., Dawes, P. L. and Massey, G. R. (2008) An extended model of the antecedents and consequences of consumer satisfaction for hospitality services. *European Journal of Marketing*, 42(1–2), 35–68.

Giese, J. and Cote, J. (2000) Defining consumer satisfaction. *Academy of Marketing Science Review*, 1(1), 1–22.

Holbrook, M. B. and Hirschman, E. C. (1982) The experiential aspects of consumption: Consumer fantasies, feelings and fun. *Journal of Consumer Research*, 9(2), 132–140.

Hoyer, W. and MacInnis, D. (2010) *Consumer Behavior*. Boston: Cengage Learning.

Johnson, M., Anderson, E. and Fornell, C. (1995) Rational and adaptive performance expectations in a customer satisfaction framework. *Journal of Consumer Research*, 21(4), 695–707.

Kim, K. and Severt, D. (2011) Satisfaction or quality comes first: An empirical analysis. *Journal of Travel & Tourism Marketing*, 28(1), 81–96.

Ladhari, R. (2009) Service quality, emotional satisfaction, and behavioral intentions. *Managing Service Quality*, 19(3), 308–331.

Li, J., Xu, L., Tang, L., Wang, S. and Li, L. (2018) Big data in tourism research: A Literature review. *Tourism Management*, 68, 301–323.

Liljander, V. and Strandvik, T. (1997) Emotions in service satisfaction. *International Journal of Service Industry Management*, 8(2), 148–169.

Liu, Y., Teichert, T., Rossi, M., Li, H. and Hu, F. (2017) Big data for big insights: Investigating language-specific drivers of hotel satisfaction with 412,784 user-generated reviews. *Tourism Management*, 59, 554–563.

Mano, H. and Oliver, R. (1993) Assessing the dimensionality and structure of the consumption experience: Evaluation, feeling, and satisfaction. *Journal of Consumer Research*, 20(3), 451–466.

Oliver, R. L. (1980) A cognitive model of the antecedents and consequences of satisfaction decisions. *Journal of Marketing Research*, 17(4), 460–469.

Olivieri, A. M., Polizzi, G. and Parocco, A. M. (2018) Measuring tourist satisfaction through a dual approach: The 4Q methodology. *Social Indicators Research*, 146(1–2), 361–382.

Pine, B. J. and Gilmore, J. (1999) *The Experience Economy: Work Is a Theatre and Every Business a Stage.* Boston: Harvard Business School Press.

Pizam, A. and Ellis, T. (1999) Customer satisfaction and its measurement in hospitality enterprises. *International Journal of Contemporary Hospitality Management*, 11(7), 326–339.

Pizam, A., Shapoval, V. and Ellis, T. (2016) Customer satisfaction and its measurement in hospitality enterprises: A revisit and update. *International Journal of Contemporary Hospitality Management*, 28(1), 2–35.

Riessman, C. K. (1993) *Narrative Analysis*. New Bury Park: Sage Publications.

Rust, R. and Oliver, R. (2000) Should we delight the customer? *Journal of the Academy of Marketing Science*, 28(1), 86–94.

Schmitt, B. (1999) *Experiential Marketing*. New York: Free Press.

Shanka, T. and Taylor, R. (2004) An investigation into the perceived importance of service and facility attributes to hotel satisfaction. *Journal of Quality Assurance in Hospitality & Tourism*, 4(3–4), 119–134.

Shaw, C. (2007) *The DNA of Customer Experience*. New York: Palgrave Macmillan.

Song, H., van der Veen, R., Li, G. and Chen, J. L. (2012) The Hong Kong tourist satisfaction index. *Annals of Tourism Research*, 39(1), 459–479.

Swan, J. and Combs, L. (1976) Product performance and consumer satisfaction: A new concept. *Journal of Marketing*, 40(2), 25–33.

Torres, E. N. and Kline, S. (2006) From satisfaction to delight: A model for the hotel industry. *International Journal of Contemporary Hospitality Management*, 18(4), 290–301.

Tsaur, S., Chiu, Y. and Huang, C. (2002) Determinants of guest loyalty to international tourist hotels-a neural network approach. *Tourism Management*, 23(4), 397–405.

Tse, D. and Wilton, P. (1988) Models of consumer satisfaction formation: An extension. *Journal of Marketing Research*, 25(2), 204–212.

Wakefield, K. L. and Blodgett, J. G. (1999) Customer response to intangible and tangible service factors. *Psychology & Marketing*, 16(1), 51–68.

Walls, A. R., Okumus, F., Wang, Y. (R). and Kwun, D. J. (2011a) An epistemological view of consumer experiences. *International Journal of Hospitality Management*, 30(1), 10–21.

Walls, A. R., Okumus, F., Wang, Y. R. and Kwun, D. J. (2011b) Understanding the consumer experience: An exploratory study of luxury hotels. *Journal of Hospitality Marketing and Management*, 20(2), 166–197.

Wang, C. and Hsu, M. K. (2010) The relationships of destination image, satisfaction, and behavioral intentions. *Journal of Travel & Tourism Marketing*, 27(8), 829–843.

Westbrook, R. and Oliver, R. (1991) The dimensionality of consumption emotion patterns and consumer satisfaction. *Journal of Consumer Research*, 18(1), 84–91.

Woodruff, R., Cadotte, E. and Jenkins, R. (1983) Modelling consumer satisfaction processes using experience-based norms. *Journal of Marketing Research*, 20(3), 296–304.

Yi, Y. (1990) Critical review of consumer satisfaction. In V. A. Zeithaml (Ed.), *Review of Marketing 1990*. Chicago: American Marketing Association, pp. 69–123.

Yoon, Y. and Uysal, M. (2005) An examination of the effects of motivation and satisfaction on destination loyalty: A structural model. *Tourism Management*, 26(1), 45–56.

Yuan, Y. and Wu, C. (2008) Relationships among experiential marketing, experiential value, and customer satisfaction. *Journal of Hospitality and Tourism Research*, 32(3), 387–410.

Zhao, Y., Xu, X. and Wang, M. (2019) Predicting overall customer satisfaction: Big data evidence from online textual reviews. *International Journal of Hospitality Management*, 76, 111–121.

Zhou, L., Ye, S., Pearce, P. L. and Wu, M. (2014) Refreshing hotel satisfaction studies by reconfiguring customer review data. *International Journal of Hospitality Management*, 38, 1–10.

6
EVOLVING AUTHENTICITY INTO THE MAGICAL REALM OF FANTASY-BASED THIRD-ORDER SIMULACRA

Jane Lovell

Introduction

Authenticity is said to be an ever-retreating fantasy that exists in other places and times where it is sought by tourists (Bruner, 1994; Cohen, 1988; MacCannell, 1973). It is often used to describe heritage tourism, museum practices and the search for simpler lifestyles amongst other peoples and cultures (Bruner, 1994; Cohen, 1988; MacCannell, 1973; Rickly-Boyd, 2012). Authenticity is also said to be an emergent concept that reflects the requirements, tastes and values of society (Cohen, 1988). The purpose of this chapter is, therefore, to reappraise authenticity in the context of contemporary tourism studies by viewing it through the lens of the postmodern concept of simulacra (Baudrillard, 1981). More specifically, it challenges the continuing applicability of authenticity in an era that is increasingly preoccupied with permutations of real, fake and fantasy. To achieve this, the basic, foundational theories of tourism authenticity are reassessed in the context of the authentication of simulacra. In addition, the chapter expands the definition of simulacra from man-made themed spaces or objects, in so doing assessing different types of simulation, including the authentication of the world as a lived fantasy by tourists.

The foundational concepts of tourism authenticity

To understand how the concept of authenticity is applied today, it is first necessary to set the scene by revisiting some of its classic themes. First, Benjamin (1936) theorized the concept of aura in his key text *The Work of Art in the Age of Mechanical Reproduction*. Aura reflects the quality of magical fascination that is so integral to the study of simulacra. Benjamin (1936: 39) described aura as having 'cultic value' or 'a unique manifestation of a remoteness, 'no matter how near it may be'. He argued that what makes an auratic object singular is its unapproachability, and contended that people strive to bring the auratic objects of their desire closer through mass reproduction techniques, which paradoxically causes their aura of 'genuineness' to 'wobble' and fade. As we shall see later in this chapter, this is a highly relevant concept when discussing simulacra.

Discussions about authenticity in the tourism literature date from the work of Boorstin (1964), who considered that the commodification of culture involved in the production of

DOI: 10.4324/9781003219866-8

mass tourism resulted in programmed, contrived, 'pseudo-events'. In other words, he suggested that tourists prefer inauthentic performances that insulate them from the otherness of the host environment and local people. The theory of the pseudo-event is related to the standardization and commoditization of theme parks that are usually associated with simulacra (Ritzer, 1999). In contrast, MacCannell (1973) argued that tourists genuinely seek authenticity to escape their disenchantment with modernity. His work mirrors that of Benjamin's in the sense that authenticity involves the idealization (or aura) of other cultures and peoples and their 'purer and simpler lifestyles' that retreats when sought (MacCannell, (1973: 3).

MacCannell (1973) also established a key touchstone in authenticity studies. He contended that although tourists seek authenticity, they encounter 'staged authenticity' that has been contrived by the tourist industry. Following Goffman (1959), he outlined six categories of staged authenticity to indicate that tourists search for the backstage regions of destinations but are confined to the front stages of performance by the tourism industry. However, Cohen (1979: 26) critiqued MacCannell's work, arguing that tourists are not a homogenous mass and they can ignore and accept and recognize staged tourist space. His perspective was supported by Bruner (1994), who similarly stated that when tourists encounter staged authenticity, they react individually. He contended that some tourists appreciate the theatrical 'suspension of disbelief' and will accept an 'authentic reproduction' (Bruner, 1994: 240–241). The concept of tourist experiences as staged and choreographed was later elaborated upon by Edensor (2001) and is pertinent to our later discussion.

It is rare to find a publication addressing tourism authenticity that does not mention Wang's (1999) rationalization that authenticity can be divided into three separate categories: objective, constructive and existential. Looking at each of these types in turn, objective authenticity is authoritative, official and particularly pertinent to the curatorial measurement of the originality of museum artefacts (Trilling 1972, cited in Wang, 1999). In light of postmodernism (which we shall come to shortly), however, objective authenticity was argued by Reisinger and Steiner (2006) to be obsolete, although this perspective was refuted by Belhassen and Caton (2006) who outlined how object authenticity continues to be a part of tourist practitioner praxis. For example, Bruner (1994: 401) observed four distinct categories of authenticity practiced by heritage professionals in the visitor attraction of New Salem: 'verisimilitude, genuineness, originality and authority'.

Wang's second category, constructive authenticity, implies that there is no single reality but, instead, tourists assign significance to symbols, meaning that authenticity is negotiable and relative. The most influential tourist social constructivist thinkers are Cohen (1988) who alludes to authenticity as 'emergent' as values and tastes progress and Bruner (1994: 407) who also observed the continuous reinvention of cultures. The third category, 'existential authenticity', was defined by Wang (1999: 351–352) as a state of being, of 'personal or inter-subjective feelings which are activated by the liminal process of tourist activities'. Again, like MacCannell, he implied that tourists sought to escape the disenchantment of the everyday to find their 'true' selves. Perhaps the most persuasive and helpful of the responses to Wang's discussion of existential authenticity is Knudsen, Rickly and Vidon's (2016) Lacanian analysis of how existential alienation drives the touristic desire to seek authenticity. Interestingly, Cohen and Cohen (2012) have since divided Wang's three categories into the hot (emotive, elevated, spontaneous and not requiring proof) and cool (cognitive, reliant on authoritative sources) authentication of visitor attractions. They argue that constructive authenticity is not a distinct category, but informs both hot and cool typologies which exist in a world of social relations and values.

Evolving authenticity

These foundational theories (much-simplified here) tend to inform most tourism authenticity literature. Revisiting how simulacra enrich our understanding of pseudo-events, the search for authenticity, staged authenticity objective, constructive and experiential authenticity and hot and cool authentication also reveals how authenticity debates are evolving.

Simulacra

Researchers often overlook how Wang (1999) went beyond the triad of objective, constructive and existential authenticity in his seminal paper that categorizes different forms of authenticity. In fact, he also suggested that postmodernist theory deconstructs authenticity. The inference of this statement is that inauthenticity is not problematic for tourists, who are less preoccupied with seeking object-based authenticity and instead have a more playful outlook – a point alluded to earlier by Feifer (1985) in her discussion of the so-called 'post tourist'. And it is the consideration of postmodernism by Wang that speaks more to the focus of this chapter. To understand what Wang means by the postmodern deconstruction of authenticity, we need to refer to postmodern theorist Baudrillard's (1981) *Precession of the Simulacra*. Baudrillard outlines three types of simulacrum in this text: the first order (the perfect copy); the second order (the imperfect copy); and the third order, which is based on imagination and fantasy rather than an original. It *precedes* reality. Hence, there are no measurable reference points for fantasy realms. It is important to note here that, for the purposes of this chapter, fantasy is defined as stories that are derived from the magical aspects of fairytales, myths and folklore.

Now we arrive at perhaps the most important part of this section. The ultimate 'fantasy kingdom', Walt Disney World (WDW), is usually cited as the default example of a third-order simulacrum (Baudrillard, 1981; Eco, 1986; Fjellman, 1992; Lovell & Bull, 2017; Wang, 1999). Fjellman's (1992) exhaustive study of the theme park details the reason for this: the 'lines between the real and the fake are systematically blurred' (p 255). The blurring is epitomized by his description of Walt Disney World as divided into categories of 'real real, fake real, real fake, fake fake' (Fjellman, 1992: 255). In other words, simulacra dissolve the differences of equivalence between originality and replication. Neither is valued more highly.

It is important to pause here to note that Labadi (2010: 78) uses the term 'post authenticity' to describe the complex mix of restoration and recreation included in World Heritage Site nomination dossiers. Once fake and real come to possess an equivalence, researchers conclude that authenticity no longer matters. However, the lens of simulation allows us to detect how real and fake, or objective, constructive and existential authenticity, permeate one another. It is that fluidity of authenticity that is worth consideration.

At the same time, there is another dimension to our consideration of the real and fake. It is important to remind ourselves that third-order simulacra are based on fantasy narratives. Arguments have been made against the binary systems in the context of the real and imagined in the field of literary geographies (Hones, 2012; McLaughlin, 2016), cinematic geographies (Lukinbeal, 2005: 4) and combined mediatized geographies (Reijnders, 2010). Hones (2012) explains the idea further in a delineation of the concept of the 'spatial event' in literary geography, which occurs when read landscapes are co-produced between the author and the self as a 'happening.' The argument shows that texts produce spatial narratives that become experiential in the actual world.

Bearing this approach in mind, Lovell and Bull (2017: 8) have gone on to add other categories to Fjellman's heuristic types that inform our discussion. They suggest the addition of 'hyperreal' (the sensation that copies are real), 'unreal' (the impression that reality is unreal) and, lastly, 'magically real', which is the embodiment of the imagination in the actual world. Another significant category, 'irreal', has also been developed by Lovell and Griffin (2018). Irreality describes the world-building of fantasy universes, where impossible metamorphoses and transformations in the environment suspend the laws of physics. This is particularly relevant to performances and artwork that involve special effects such as light installations. These typologies highlight the interplay of the imagination in the experience of simulacra by tourists. This chapter, therefore, avoids conceptual duality. Instead, it considers third-order simulacra to encompass magical reality in the sense of '...marvellous-yet real-places' derived from the Russian 'maravilloso' (Strecher, 1999: 267), intertwining the imagined mediatized fantasy place with either its concrete adaptation in the actual world, or immaterial suggestions of fantasy.

To capture how germane postmodernism is to tourism authenticity studies, Lovell and Hitchmough (2020) conceptualize the theory of 'simulated authenticity' to capture how the increasing use of advanced technology in storytelling further obscures the differentiation between originals and copies. The television series *Westworld* is used by the authors to illustrate how simulated authenticity can produce androids that are so lifelike that they are unaware that they were manufactured. This is typified by the use of intertextuality, inter-temporality, inter-spatiality and fictional reimaginings, post-modern concepts that are relevant to our study of the construction of third-order simulacra.

Third-order simulacra continue to offer pertinent insights into the many permutations of reality that preoccupy us today. Far from the arguments of post-authenticity, the conceptual significance of authenticity to tourism studies is still being revealed.

Authenticating fantasy

The chapter now turns to the authentication of simulacra by tourists. The tourism literature frequently returns to MacCannell's idea that tourists fantasize to escape the everyday (Hemme, 2005; Knudsen, Rickly & Vidon, 2016; Lee, 2012). The search for the magical beliefs of 'purer and simpler' lifestyles that MacCannell described presupposes that there is an absence of the extraordinary in everyday life. Knudsen et al. (2016: 41–42) usefully develop MacCannell's work in their Lacanian analysis of tourist fantasies: 'In tourism, authenticity is not the "thing" that is missing, but the self-rationalization that while one's life is missing all sorts of "things", they do exist elsewhere in other places/lifestyles/cultures'. Perhaps nowhere is this impulse to capture the absent fantasy more evident than in the behaviour of so-called 'Potterheads' (Harry Potter fans). Waysdorf and Reijnders (2018) mention a common social media meme in their study of the Wizarding World of Harry Potter, where visitors to the theme park remarked that they felt as if they were still waiting for their invitation to Hogwarts wizarding school. The 'Hogwarts letter' (versions of which can be bought and personalized online) arrives for witches and wizards as a rite of passage at age 11. It signifies the awakening of an alternative, magical self and its absence plays a continued role in their lives.

MacCannell also suggested that authenticity is sought in our idealization of past cultures. Perhaps unsurprisingly, given its historical theme, Bruner (1994) found that the recreated living history town of New Salem (which, he contended, would be dismissed as a copy by postmodernists such as Baudrillard) was authenticated by tourists and heritage professionals. Research by Rickly-Boyd (2012) on tourism at Spring Hill Pioneer Village also yielded similar results. These visitor attractions are contrived by the tourist industry but, as Chhabra, Healy and Sills (2003: 715) comment, '...what is staged is not superficial since it contains

Evolving authenticity

elements of the original tradition.' This observation makes sense when applied to the living history presented in New Salem and Spring Hill. It is still more intriguing when tourists authenticate the exaggerated, hyperreal simulacra, where the 'original tradition' to which Chhabra et al. (2003) refer is situated in fantasy.

Authentication rituals resembling those practiced in living history museums can be observed in the most staged, fantastical and non-historical of visitor attractions. Embodiment has, for example, been shown to be an important factor when visiting the persuasive environment of a magical theme park (Waysdorf & Reijnders, 2018) whilst, writing of the Robin Hood festival in Nottingham, Everett and Parakoottathil (2018) indicate that cos-play can lead to a profound and transformative embodied sense of self. Buchmann, Moore and Fisher (2010) provide similar evidence of authentication practices, including re-enactments on multiple levels at the *Lord of the Rings* filming locations and sets in New Zealand. Furthermore, large-scale light installations offer overwhelming, impossible metamorphoses of space that are hotly authenticated by visitors (Lovell, 2018; Lovell & Griffin, 2019). To be clear, the *Lord of the Rings* film sets, locations and light installations are identified by their authors as simulacra. Their research conclusions surely indicate less of an attitude of postmodern touristic playfulness as suggested by Wang, which implied being 'in on the joke' of theme-park inauthenticity. Rather, they indicate a participative attitude of open-mindedness on the part of tourists that enables them to hotly authenticate fantasies and imaginatively appreciate the fluidity of reality.

A further point about the authentication of simulacra is that stories developed by tourism professionals can be powerfully evocative, tapping into hotly authentic states of being. For example, heritage interpretation has been shown to lead to a state of narrative transportation in tourists (a feeling of being present in the past) (see Chronis, 2012; Chronis, Arnould & Hampton, 2012; Green & Brock, 2000; Lovell, 2019a; Rickly-Boyd, 2012). Some narrative transportation is evoked through the use of technology that enhances visitor immersion in the story, such as through the use of virtual reality at heritage sites (Dogan & Kan, 2020). Fantasy tourists have been said to be highly emotionally invested in narratives, which suggests that they may be yet more highly charged than heritage tourists (Lee, 2012). Therefore, the potential for them to attain hotly authentic affective states is even more likely.

Yet, authentication can occur independently of the tourist industry's interpretations and stagings. A more esoteric way in which tourists authenticate simulacra is imaginatively; as a literary genre, fantasy involves world-building on the part of tourists as they exercise their imaginations. For instance, Lovell's (2019a) study on the effect of the mainstreaming of fantasy culture on visitors to historic cities reveals that tourists spontaneously compared historic streets, Gothic cathedrals, castles and statues to the fairytale tropes and schemata that they had encountered in childhood fairytales, books, films, television and gaming cities. This was reminiscent of Baudrillard's (1981) use of Borges' fable to explain simulacra, which concluded that the map (the symbol) had replaced the territory (the material world). Lovell and Thurgill's (2021) research encompasses a similar inversion; historic cities are authenticated against the archetypal collective imaginings of the inspiration for fantasy locations. Tourists behave as if the actual world is a third-order, 'magi-heritage' simulacrum. In other words, they do not differentiate between real and imagined, object and experience. This touches on constructivism because although third-order simulacra are not based on origins, the origins of fantasy reside in the collective imagination but also in the sub-conscious, manifesting in symbols and archetypes. Imaginative authentication merges the material and symbolic as lived experiences (Soja, 1996). Consequently, imaginative authentication allows for a greater degree of ambiguity, magical intervention, intersubjectivity, uncanniness and metamorphosis as a lived part of tourism.

This approach more accurately reflects how fantasy is magical and suspends the laws of physics, making the everyday world ambiguous, uncertain and unfamiliar (Feldt, 2016). For example, in Lovell's (2019a) study, quantum heritage cities unfold and appear at will and anthropomorphized buildings gaze back at tourists. By exercising their imaginations in this way, tourists 'superheat' Cohen and Cohen's (2012) theory of hot authentication to an evaporation point of enchantment, otherworldliness, transportation and poetics (Lovell & Bull, 2017: 8). Superheated authenticity does not encounter a blank canvas but a responsive, symbolic, more-than-human world. Imaginative authentication allows for the world to become a third-order simulacrum, imbricated with the unexpected possibilities of fantasy.

Yet, in complete contrast to the evaporatingly hot free-wheeling, embodied poetic authentication of the world-as-simulacrum, some authentication of the simulacrum is ice-cold. Baudrillard (1981) suggested that there are no measurable reference points for fantasy realms. However, the obsessional knowledge amongst fantasy fans about the minutiae of the texts is legendary among tour guides (Lee, 2012). Therefore, the paradox of some simulacra is that their basis in a specific fantasy universe means that they will be coolly authenticated against the sacred canon by highly informed tourists. If third-order simulacra are based on fantasy texts, then their designers often have to pay attention to detail in a granular way. It is, then, arguable whether they truly produce third-order simulacra, because the text provides a clear blueprint and origin story. However, that particular discussion must remain outside the scope of this short chapter.

To draw conclusions about how tourists authenticate simulacra, it is important to return to Cohen's (1979) impressions of staged authenticity. Tourists ignore, recognize, accept and reject staged authenticity; in other words, they co-create their experiences. This approach equally applies to even the most deeply immersive, choreographed simulacra. The other point to note is that the example of tourists apprehending historic cities as fairytale tropes indicates that simulacra may not necessarily be defined as the concretization of fantasy in the form of artworks, installations, theme parks or VR technology. Instead, tourists independently experience the 'spatial events' or 'happenings' related to their imagination. Tourists thus authenticate their fantasies by living them.

Producing authentic fantasies

The imaginative authentication emerging from the mainstreaming of fantasy culture detailed above has not only led to a more fantastic apprehension of the everyday world by tourists, but also inevitably to a proliferation of man-man third-order simulacra produced by the tourism industry. For example, the demand for child and adult re-enchantment is evident in the popularity of *Harry Potter* experiences – the theatre production of *Harry Potter and the Cursed Child* in New York was the fastest-selling play to ever open on Broadway, making over $2 million in its first full week of previews in 2018 (Cox, 2018). Hence, simulated encounters with the magical provide a (profitable) re-enchantment of the authentic self.

Third-order simulacra can be said to create magical realities by embodying the imagination in the everyday world. This is not a new phenomenon; Gaudi, for example, introduced surrealism into the architecture of Barcelona, most notably in the Dr Seuss-like Sagrada Familia Cathedral. Yet the conscious branding of magical reality is more prominent today, as used by architects such as Mona Hadid. In the same vein, large-scale hyperreal public artworks, such as Yinka Shonibare's Nelson's Ship in a Bottle (located at London's National

Evolving authenticity

Maritime Museum), introduce an increasingly common note of surreality into the environment (Lovell & Bull, 2017). These pieces are designed to act as departure points for the imagination of the viewer.

Building on this argument of an increasingly magical reality, the creation of fantasy 'place myths' (Shields, 1991) and storied landscapes have also proliferated in recent years, further encouraging imaginative authentication. Tourism producers have long created 'storyscapes' or consumption spaces focused on narratives (Chronis, et al., 2012: 266). For example, Gao Zhang and L'Espoire Decosta (2012) describe how Zhongdian County in China rebranded itself as Shangri-La County in response to the popularity of the idealized fictional place in the 1933 novel *Lost Horizon* by James Hilton. Similarly, in Canada, British Columbia draws on Haida mythology by branding itself as the *Super, Natural British Columbia* (Lovell, 2019b). In both studies, it is explicit that simulacra had been manufactured by the tourist industry to substantiate place myths.

The creation of site-specific fantasy-based landscapes has accelerated in recent years. For example, in 2017, English Heritage commissioned a series of ghost stories for some of their properties, with contributors including the authors Jeanette Winterson and Stuart Evers (English Heritage, 2017). English Heritage also actively encourages filming at their properties, such as the fairytale film *Into the Woods* (2014), which was shot at Dover Castle. Thus, intangible cultural heritage is increasingly augmented with magical references.

Conversely, the inter-referencing integral to simulated authenticity also anchors the fantasy realm in history. This is where we should pause for a moment to consider simulated authenticity as a hyperreal version of staged authenticity; it is choreographed, contrived and designed. To understand it further, let us explore the creation of the film sets that inform our magical culture. For example, the streets of Cittàgazze in the televised version of Philip Pullman's *The Subtle Knife* novel from *His Dark Materials* series were constructed in a back lot of the Bad Wolf studios in Cardiff. The design team drew their inspiration from 120 locations, purchasing windows and doors from Morocco and other places to construct a meta-Italianate Mediterranean town full of trompe d'oeil steps seeming to lead to nowhere, drawn from the paintings of M. C. Escher (Mellor, 2020). The bannisters were moulded with the emblem of the eponymous knife in *The Subtle Knife*, bricks were shaped like magpies, also reflecting the magically real architecture of Gaudi, who incorporates animals. The television series tells us that this is a simulacrum because the distance shots framing the island, Mont-Michel-like town are a portmanteau, indicating unreality. What this type of locational setting does is inform the collective imagination. Those viewers of the series may have different tourist perceptions of actual Mediterranean towns and experience an uncanny sense of Pullman's location (which is actually in a back lot in Wales) on holiday.

The translation from film set to tourist simulacrum is founded on deep research. For example, the film set furniture on display in the Warner Brothers attraction, *The Wizarding World of Harry Potter*, is designed to look antique. Display pieces such as Professor Dumbledore's chair in his study in Hogwarts have been aged to encourage the Gothic realism of the film visuals with a semblance of heritage provenance. This intricate attention to detail is reminiscent of the verisimilitude and genuineness to which heritage practitioners aspired in New Salem. However, the scale and ambition differs from staged authenticity; as part of third-order simulacra, Bruner's (1994) authentic reproductions have been transfigured into *authentic simulations*. Visitors to the attraction are aware that they are not seeing an ancient chair that has witnessed the events of history. They may not even be seeing the same chair that was used in the film. But they are not duped by it, as MacCannell suggested; rather, they are participants in a frontstage that possesses simulated, authentic references to a magical canon. Visitors can trace the fantasy lineage of the item and, thus, authenticate it.

Many third-order simulacra also authenticate the origins of fantasy. For example, Acts of Wanton Wonder was developed as one of the Hull UK City of Culture events in 2017. It was inspired by the intriguingly named Land of Green Ginger alleyway (the name was possibly derived from past imports of ginger). The event was released to the city with an announcement that a stack of crates had been discovered in a mysterious vault. An invented organization, The Green Ginger Fellowship, was asked to investigate. When they opened the vault and crates, various fantastic delights escaped. The organizer described how the event was intended to fuel 'an air of mystery which fuels the sensibilities of magic and wonder we wanted to thread throughout the story' (Fuller, 2017). The event drew on themes of English folklore enveloping distinctive elements such as the spiritually magic and the uncanny or, in other words, the unsettling, 'English eerie' (MacFarlane, 2015). Thus, the origins of fantasy can be authenticated against the event's site-specific folkloric provenance.

The proliferation of magical guided tours provides another example of simulated authenticity. While ghost tours have long been a staple product of destination tourism provision, many places now explicitly use their fantasy capital to attract tourists. Visit Oxford, for example, promotes tours of locations connected to *Harry Potter* filming locations and to the biographical sites associated with fantasy authors Tolkien, Lewis Carroll, CS Lewis and Phillip Pullman. The tours display intertextuality, a key characteristic of simulated authenticity, by mixing up the authors such as in the 'When Harry met Alice' tour (including sites associated with *Harry Potter* and *Alice in Wonderland*). The interweaving of stories constructs a simulated Oxford.

As a result of these inter-textual tours, historic landmarks such as the Bodleian Library in Oxford act as multiple portals to fantastic universes. For example, The Divinity School was filmed as Hogwarts Library in the *Harry Potter* films and Duke Humphrey's Library was a key setting in a 2018 TV dramatization of the Deborah Harness novel *A Discovery of Witches* and also in the 2019 production of *His Dark Materials* by Philip Pullman. Rowling, Pullman and Harkness rooted their works in recognizably English localities, such as Oxford colleges, London garden suburbs or King's Cross station, which is a part of their appeal as they sell a form of refracted, mythical English-magicess. Tourists often are unable to enter the library due to the teaching requirements of students, which means that tour groups sometimes simply stand outside and look through the windows, adding to its mystique. By becoming a third-order simulacrum, this one landmark can therefore simultaneously assume different fantasy magic Bodleian-nesses.

Some landmarks also become simulacra due to their inter-spatiality. Like the Bodleian Library, the Botanic Gardens in Oxford are a focal point for fantasy tours because they contain 'Lyra's Bench', featured in Philip Pullman's *His Dark Materials* series of novels. In *The Amber Spyglass*, the protagonists Will and Lyra occupy different, parallel worlds but agree to sit on the bench (which exists in both worlds) once a year on Midsummer's Day. When tour groups arrive, readings authenticate the material bench against its fictionalized description and geographical location. These parallel Oxfords also converge where fans have carved the names of Will and Lyra on the bench, which has metaphysical properties for those familiar with the stories. The opening scenes of the televisual series of *His Dark Materials* contain a sequence that reflects an important point, which is that for Pullman (and this chapter), the parallel worlds of Will's, Lyra's and our own are equivalent.

Another variation on the theme of fantasy-based third-order simulacra has emerged in the form of the exponentially growing number of exhibitions linked to magical and fantasy texts.

Evolving authenticity

These exhibitions include 'Magical Books: From the Middle Ages to Middle-earth' in the Bodleian Library in 2013 and 'Harry Potter: The Exhibition', which enabled Warner Brothers to mix the magic of film illusion with fantasy content, taking the props of The Making of Harry Potter attraction on an international tour in 2018–2019. The exhibition 'Harry Potter: A History of Magic' is particularly relevant to our discussion of simulated authenticity because of its interweaving of history with fantasy. Held at the British Library in 2017–2018, the event received a record number of 45,000 ticket pre-bookings (Harrison, 2018). The exhibition subsequently moved to the New York Historical Museum and Society in the United States.

Given its origins at the British Library, the event adopted an educational approach to the historicization of fantasy by displaying a variety of illustrated manuscripts and texts. Yet this museumesque, precise curation of originals and origins was mixed with overtly staged theming, again revealing the postmodern inter-referencing suggestive of simulated authenticity. Each of the different rooms within the exhibition focused on subjects taught at Hogwarts wizarding school in Harry Potter, including Charms, Defence Against the Dark Arts and Care of Magical Creatures. Props were used; for example, broomsticks hovered above the Charms section to reinforce the magical affordances of the space. The library itself is an otherworldly arena with its hyperreal, stories-tall, central glass archives of antique books. The effects of simulated authenticity were heightened by the deployment of genuine fakery such as a nineteenth-century mermaid and other examples of the pseudo-magi-historical. Describing his motivation for staging the event, the Lead Curator Julian Harrison (2018) explains the perennial attraction of magic:

> People have always been interested in the history of magic and in the world around them. That's what we've discovered from putting the exhibition together and the public response to it has confirmed that. There's a global fascination in things that are unexplained.

In contrast to this comment, some third-order simulacra leave nothing either unexplained, or to the imagination. The Platform Nine and Three Quarters (PNATQ) tourist attraction at London's King's Cross Station recreates the site of departure for the Hogwarts Express in the Harry Potter novels and films. A half-trolley is positioned as if moving through the wall; official photo opportunities are choreographed and comparatively expensive; there is queue management in place, and a Warner Brothers shop sells memorabilia. Cultic attractions such as Platform Nine and Three Quarters authenticate the fantasy by concretizing it. They provide approximations of the imagination, fantasy cornerstones based on nostalgia. Yet, while meaningful experiences and encounters can and do take place, there is little world-building space left to the tourist imagination. Consequently, highly overt simulacra could actually wobble and dissipate the aura that magical heritage strives so hard to cultivate.

When tourists visit a material place that has been referenced in a fantasy text, they perform a spatial act of authentication. But this type of simulacrum does not only include the overt Platform Nine and Three Quarters, but also unmarked natural sites. For example, Alan Garner's *The Weirdstone of Brisingamen* draws on the folklore of the English village of Alderley Edge but also on the topography of the mines in the Cheshire landscape. Or Susan Cooper's *The Grey King*, part of *The Dark Is Rising* series, which is inspired by Welsh mythology that blended with the mountain Calder Idris, enhancing its immanence. What makes these uninterpreted literary sites powerful simulacra for tourists is the sensation of lived fantasy when they intentionally visit and connect to the source of author inspiration.

To sum up the types of third-order simulacra in this section, they include the simplicity of the mountain with which fantasy is associated, or a bench, unadorned except for the carved names yet rife with the possibilities of the connection to parallel authentic selves and places. Third-order simulacra may also be overtly commodified, like Platform Nine and Three Quarters, or involve the complex simulated intertextual authentication of fantasy origins, as used in the *Harry Potter: A History of Magic* exhibition. In the form of fantasy tours, they enhance destinations by turning landmarks into the portals to multiple parallel fantasy simulacra, each of which is equivalent to the other. All of these permutations of place are appreciated by tourists in different ways.

Conclusion

The chapter argues that in an increasingly magical era that also dwells more on the permeability of the fake and the real, authenticity needs to evolve to embrace the imagination. The work takes the fantasies that are said to fuel tourist desires into the realm of the fantastical, by assessing simulacra that are based on narratives associated with the fantasy genre. This chapter hypothesizes that even the most fantastical of third-order simulacra induce authentication practices and rituals in tourists. Tourist sensibilities are increasingly informed by the simulated authenticity of mediatized places, such as Cittàgazze in the televised version of the novel *The Subtle Knife*. What is being authenticated is not the fake or the real, but the simulated intertextual and historical references that give fantasies provenance. The chapter raises many questions for future researchers, including whether tourist expectations of the fantastical will be raised, leading to yet more magical tourism products that are grounded in local folklore. Also, whether the magic of proliferating third-order simulacra will become normative and subsequently lose their aura, as Benjamin (1936) predicted.

Yet there is another possibility. Lovell's (2018) research illustrates how the historic environment was authenticated as an intersubjective, lived fairytale for tourists. This phenomenon occurred independently of the tourist industry. Also, the proliferation of third-order simulacra may lead to an imaginative awakening in tourists, contributing to a more magical sensibility that extends beyond their appreciation of the nuances of simulated authenticity. Tourists escape towards the fantasy of authenticity somewhere else, but there is also a magical aspect to the everyday (Bachelard, 1994). Even household spaces and domestic objects can be instilled with meaning, affection and the intersubjective poetics of 'modern magic' (Haldrup, 2017: 58). The authentic self may have been more apparent in a Covid-shaped world where domestic and local tourism, walks and nature even in the form of the urban bucolic are being rediscovered. These small touristic pleasures can reveal the previously unseen magical ordinary, the world-as-third-order-simulacrum.

References

Bachelard, (1994) *The Poetics of Space.* Cambridge: Beacon Press.
Baudrillard, J. (1981, reprinted 1994) *Selected Writings: Simulacra and Simulation.* Cambridge: Polity Press.
Belhassen, Y. and Caton, K. (2006) Authenticity matters. *Annals of Tourism Research,* 33(3), 853–856.
Benjamin, W. (1936, reprinted 2008) *The Work of Art in the Age of Mechanical Reproduction.* London: Penguin.
Boorstin, D. (1964) *The Image: A Guide to Pseudo-Events in America.* New York: Harper & Row.
Bruner, E. (1994) Abraham Lincoln as authentic reproduction: A critique of postmodernism. *American Anthropologist,* 96(2), 397–415.

Buchmann, A., Moore, K. and Fisher, D. (2010) Experiencing film tourism: Authenticity and fellowship. *Annals of Tourism Research*, 37(1), 229–248.

Chhabra, D., Healy, R. and Sills, E. (2003) Staged authenticity and heritage tourism. *Annals of Tourism Research*, 30(3), 702–719.

Chronis, A. (2012) Between place and story: Gettysburg as tourism imaginary. *Annals of Tourism Research*, 39(4), 1797–1816.

Chronis, A., Arnould, E. J. and Hampton, R. D. (2012) Gettysburg re-imagined: The role of narrative imagination in consumption experience. *Consumption Markets & Culture*, 15(3), 261–286.

Cohen, E. (1979) Rethinking the sociology of tourism. *Annals of Tourism Research*, 6(1), 18–35.

Cohen, E. (1988) Authenticity and commoditization in tourism. *Annals of Tourism Research*, 15(3), 371–386.

Cohen, E. and Cohen, S. A. (2012) Authentication: Hot and cool. *Annals of Tourism Research*, 39(3), 1295–1314.

Cox. (2018) Variety Broadway Box Office: 'Harry Potter and the Cursed Child' Hits Record Sales. Available at: https://variety.com/2018/legit/news/harry-potter-cursed-child-broadway-sales-record-1202747600/ (Accessed 30 December 2018).

Dogan, E. and Kan, M. H. (2020) Bringing heritage sites to life for visitors: Towards a conceptual framework for immersive experiences. *Advances in Hospitality and Tourism Research*, 8(1): 76–99.

Eco, U. (1986) *Faith in Fakes: Travels in Hyperreality*. London: Picador.

Edensor, T. (2001) Performing tourism, staging tourism: (Re)producing tourism space and practice. *Tourist Studies*, 1(1), 59–81.

English Heritage (2017) Top Authors Write Ghost Stories Inspired By English Heritage Sites. Available at: http://www.english-heritage.org.uk/about-us/search-news/ghost-stories-inspired-by-english-heritage-sites (Accessed 25 January 2021).

Everett, S. and Parakoottathil, J. (2018) Transformation, meaning-making and identity creation through folklore tourism: The case of the Robin Hood festival. *Journal of Heritage Tourism*, 13(1), 30–45.

Feifer, M. (1985) *Going Places*. London: Macmillan.

Feldt, L. (2016) Harry Potter and contemporary magic: Fantasy literature, popular culture, and the representation of religion. *Journal of Contemporary Religion*, 31(1), 101–114.

Fjellman, S. M. (1992) *Vinyl Leaves: Walt Disney World and America*. Boulder: Westview Press, Inc.

Fuller, K. (2017) International Arts Manager. Accessed: Available at: http://www.internationalarts-manager.com/blog/acts-of-wanton-wonder-from-the-land-of-green-ginger.html (Accessed 19 January 2021).

Gao, B. W., Zhang, H. and L'Espoire Decosta, P. (2012) Phantasmal destination: A post-modernist perspective. *Annals of Tourism Research*, 39(1), 197–220.

Goffman, E. (1959) *The Presentation of Self in Everyday Life*. New York: Doubleday.

Green, M. C. and Brock, T. C. (2000) The role of transportation in the persuasiveness of public narratives. *Journal of Personality and Social Psychology*, 79(5), 701–721.

Harrison, J. (2018) How Do You Curate an Exhibition About Magic? Available at: https://artsandculture.google.com/story/how-do-you-curate-an-exhibition-about-magic/xAJCuSa7S-VHJg (Accessed 25 January 2021).

Haldrup, M. (2017) Souvenirs: Magical objects in everyday life. *Emotion, Space and Society*, 22, 52–60.

Hemme, D. (2005) Landscape, fairies and identity: Experience on the backstage of the fairy tale route. *Journal of Tourism and Cultural Change*, 3(2), 71–87.

Hones, S. (2012) Literary geography: The novel as a spatial event. In S. Daniels, D. DeLyser, J. N. Entrikin and D. Richardson (Eds.), *Envisioning Landscapes, Making Worlds: Geography and the Humanities*. Abingdon: Routledge. pp. 279–287.

Knudsen, D. C., Rickly, J. M. and Vidon, E. S. (2016) The fantasy of authenticity: Touring with Lacan. *Annals of Tourism Research*, 58, 33–45.

Labadi, S. (2010) World heritage, authenticity and post-authenticity. In S. Labadi and C. Long (Eds.), *Heritage and Globalisation*, Abingdon: Routledge, pp.66–84.

Lee, C. (2012) 'Have magic, will travel': Tourism and Harry Potter's united (magical) Kingdom. *Tourist Studies*, 12(1), 52–69.

Lovell, J. (2018). Hyperreal light simulacra: Performing heritage buildings. In J. Rickly and E. Vidon (Eds.), *Authenticity and Tourism: Materialities, Perceptions, Experiences*. Bingley: Emerald, pp. 181–200.

Lovell, J. (2019a) Fairytale authenticity: Historic city tourism, Harry Potter, medievalism and the magical gaze. *Journal of Heritage Tourism*, 14(5–6), 448–465.

Lovell, J. (2019b) Opening the memory boxes: Magically hyperreal authenticity, tourism and the Haida People. In J. Lovell and S. Hitchmough (Eds.), *Authenticity in North America: Place, Tourism, Heritage, Culture and the Popular Imagination*. Abingdon: Routledge, pp. 96–111.

Lovell, J. and Bull, C. (2017) *Authentic and Inauthentic Places in Tourism: From Heritage Sites to Theme Parks*. Abingdon: Routledge.

Lovell, J. and Griffin, H. (2019) Fairy tale tourism: The architectural projection mapping of magically real and irreal festival lightscapes. *Journal of Policy Research in Tourism, Leisure and Events*, 11(3), 469–483.

Lovell, J. and Hitchmough, S. (2020) Simulated authenticity: Storytelling and mythic space on the hyper-frontier in Buffalo Bill's Wild West and Westworld. *Tourist Studies*, 20(4), 409–428.

Lovell, J and Thurgill, J. (2021) Extending hot authentication: Imagining fantasy space. *Annals of Tourism Research*, 87, 103–138.

Lukinbeal, C. (2005) Cinematic landscapes. *Journal of Cultural Geography*, 23(1), 3–22.

MacCannell, D. (1973, reprinted 1989) *The Tourist. A New Theory of the Leisure Class*. New York: Schocken Books.

MacFarlane, R. (2015) The Eeriness of the English Countryside. Available at: https://www.theguardian.com/books/2015/apr/10/eeriness-english-countryside-robert-macfarlane (Accessed 25 January 2021).

McLaughlin, D. (2016) The work and the world: Mobilities and literary space. *Literary Geographies*, 2(2), 122–127.

Mellor, L. (2020) His Dark Materials: Secrets of Cittàgazze and the Meaning of Pan's Different Forms. In Den of Geek. Available at: https://www.denofgeek.com/tv/his-dark-materials-behind-the-scenes-secrets/ (Accessed 21 January 2021).

Reijnders, S. (2010) Places of the imagination: An ethnography of the TV detective tour. *Cultural Geographies*, 17(1), 37–52.

Reisinger, Y. and Steiner, C. J. (2006) Reconceptualizing object authenticity. *Annals of Tourism Research*, 33(1), 65–86.

Rickly-Boyd, J. M. (2012) Through the magic of authentic reproduction: Tourists' perceptions of authenticity in a pioneer village. *Journal of Heritage Tourism*, 7(2), 127–144.

Ritzer, G. (1999) *Enchanting a Disenchanted World: Revolutionising the Means of Consumption*. Thousand Oaks: Pine Forge.

Shields, R. (1991) *Places on the Margin: Alternative Geographies of Modernity*. London: Routledge.

Soja, E. (1996) *Thirdspace: Journeys to Los Angeles and other Real-and-Imagined Places*. Oxford: Blackwell.

Strecher, M. (1999) Magical realism and the search for identity in the fiction of Murakami Haruki. *Journal of Japanese Studies*, 25(2), 263–298.

Wang, N. (1999) Rethinking authenticity in tourism experience. *Annals of Tourism Research*, 26(2), 349–370.

Waysdorf, A. and Reijnders, S. (2018) Immersion, authenticity and the theme park as social space: Experiencing the wizarding world of Harry Potter. *International Journal of Cultural Studies*, 21(2), 173–188.

7

TOURIST EXPERIENCES

Liminal, liminoid or just doing something different?

Richard Sharpley

Introduction

From an academic perspective, tourism cannot be considered a discipline. Academic disciplines, as Tribe (1997: 639) argued persuasively more than two decades ago, 'describe particular ways of analyzing the external world. However, tourism [as the object of academic study] is the material of the external world of events'. Therefore, epistemologically, tourism is a field of study. As such, 'it can…parade a number of concepts' and theories (Tribe, 1997: 643), but these are neither unique to tourism and nor do they collectively contribute to a distinctive theory of tourism. Rather, they are theories and concepts that originate elsewhere (for example, in economics, geography or sociology) but have been contextualized in or given a tourism dimension. In other words, throughout its development, tourism studies has drawn upon or appropriated existing theories residing in established disciplines as a basis of attempting to explain the practice of tourism. As Dann and Parrinello (2009) reveal, for example, the early-twentieth-century academic study of tourism was particularly informed by sociology, as indeed are many well-known more contemporary concepts such as Cohen's (1972, 1979) widely cited typologies, which are – unsurprisingly, given his own disciplinary roots – explicitly influenced by the German sociologist Georg Simmel's (1858–1918) work on strangerhood.

This borrowing of concepts and theories is not, of course, uncommon; indeed, the integrity of many areas of academic study, including tourism, is inevitably dependent upon it. However, there is a danger that, through this process, the original concepts become overused, diluted or, in a sense, evolve into a phenomenon themselves as opposed to being an explanation of a phenomenon. Putting it another way,

> the problem with concepts that become popular almost overnight is that scholars "discover" a variety of phenomena that can be labelled with a specific term…They are then incorporated as part of a terminology that usually leaves its exact significance implicit, as if a concept is self-explanatory.
>
> *(van Ginkel, 2014: 58)*

One such example is the concept of the 'tourist gaze'. Originally formulated by John Urry (1990a) in the seminal text of the same name – though, according to Jacobsen (2009: 235),

DOI: 10.4324/9781003219866-9

anticipated a decade earlier by the Danish sociologist Øllgaard – the term 'tourist gaze' is now widely applied in innumerable tourism contexts but typically with no reference to (or, arguably, awareness of) the Foucauldian origins of concept of the 'gaze' as an apparatus of power.

This, in turn, reflects a wider issue with regard to the identification and use of concepts and theories developed elsewhere. Specifically, it is often 'not questioned why a particular theory should be applied to a particular phenomenon and, more important, if it makes sense to impose a theory on that phenomenon' (Wood, Phan & Wright, 2018: 405). As a consequence, whether in an attempt to make incremental contributions to knowledge or, more simply, to demonstrate rigour in research, theories and concepts are sometimes misapplied or offer explanations of phenomena that stretch credence. Certainly, an online search of literature addressing the misuse or misapplication of theory will reveal numerous cases across a wide variety of subject areas whilst, in the specific context of tourism, the study of destination communities' perceptions of tourism is just one example of where an increasing array of concepts are drawn on to frame the research yet offer little by way of practical explanations (Sharpley, 2014).

It is not, however, the intent of this chapter to pursue this debate in more detail. Rather, it focuses on a specific concept, namely, liminality, that has not only been applied to a diversity of contexts in general, including the role of teaching assistants in primary schools (Mansaray, 2006), dance music experiences (Jaimangal-Jones, Pritchard & Morgan, 2010), health care (Jackson, 2005) and organizational behaviour (Söderlund & Borg, 2018), but in numerous tourism contexts in particular (for example, Andrews & Roberts, 2012; Foster & McCabe, 2015; Nelson, 2020; Underthun & Jordhus-Lier, 2018). Indeed, as Thomassen (2012: 22) observes, 'in taking up the concept of liminality today we have to step to step carefully... as the term is increasingly used to talk about almost *anything*' (emphasis in original). Yet, such caution has not been in much evidence in tourism. The foundations for considering tourist experiences within the conceptual framework of liminality were first established by Nelson Graburn in his contribution, *Tourism: the sacred journey*, to the first edition of the seminal *Hosts and Guests: The Anthropology of Tourism* (Smith, 1977). Republished in the second edition of that text (Graburn, 1989), it was then revised with a more explicit focus on liminality within ritual and presented as a 'general theory of tourism' (Graburn, 2001), with tourism itself being considered a contemporary social ritual. Another early work was Lett's (1983) analysis of the behaviours of charter yacht tourists in the Caribbean, one of still only few to apply the term 'liminoid' (see also Selänniemi, 2003), but it was perhaps Rob Shield's (1991) text *Places on the Margin* and, in particular, his chapter on Brighton that firmly placed liminality in the conceptual 'toolbox' of tourism researchers. Since then, it has been increasingly applied to tourism studies both explicitly (for example, Conti & Heldt Cassel, 2020; Rink, 2020) and more implicitly through general reference to the tourist experience being liminal. Typically, however, attention is paid primarily to what are claimed to be liminal tourism spaces, notably the beach and seaside resorts (Agarwal, 2014; Preston-Whyte, 2004)– although tourism destinations more generally can be thought of as liminal zones – and the liminal activities that tourists pursue whilst on holiday. Importantly, in contrast 'there is little to no research or literature on liminal experiences of tourists while in these liminal spaces' (Van Tine, 2011: 4), the assumption apparently being that if tourism spaces are liminal, then tourists' experiences of them must also be liminal.

Given this uncertainty surrounding the relevance of liminality to the tourist experience and, more generally, the widespread and arguably indiscriminate use of the concept in the tourism context, the purpose of this chapter is to consider broadly whether tourist experiences can be referred to as liminal (certainly, not all tourist experiences can be categorized as such), whether the term liminoid is more appropriate, or whether the original meaning of both has been lost in translation into tourism studies. To do so, the first task is to review briefly the origins and development of the concept of liminality, as well as the distinction between the terms liminal and liminoid. The chapter then goes on discuss the contribution of liminality to understanding the tourist experience, exploring the concept in the context of transformations in the nature, significance and practice of tourism as a form of consumption, as well as considering the extent to which tourism places and tourists' experience of them may be described or explained as liminal.

Liminality: origins and meaning

Etymologically, liminality derives from the Latin word *limen*, or threshold. To be at the threshold of something can simply mean to be at the limit or edge; a person might, for example, be at the threshold of their endurance whilst, in the UK at least, levels of income at which taxation becomes payable or increases are referred to as tax thresholds. More precisely, a stone or wooden strip at the bottom of a doorway is traditionally referred to as a threshold – hence, 'crossing the threshold'. However, crossing the threshold implies change, from one place to another, from one situation or experience to another and, therefore, to be on threshold – or in a liminal state or place – is to be between one place or condition and another.

It is in this sense of being in between that the concept (and word) liminality was proposed by the French anthropologist Arnold van Gennep more than a century ago in his book *The Rites of Passage* (van Gennep, 1960). Van Gennep was concerned with the rituals or ceremonies of societies, distinguishing in particular between those that mark the passing of time, such as new year or harvest celebrations or annual events on the religious calendar, and those marking the transition of either an individual or a society as a whole from one position or status to another or, as van Gennep (1960: 10) puts it, 'passage from one situation to another or from one cosmic or social world to another'. It is in the context of the latter that the significance of liminality lies. Singling out rites of passage as special category, van Gennep (1960: 11) subdivided these into (i) rites of separation; (ii), transition rites; and (iii) rites of incorporation, which he alternatively conceptualized as, respectively, preliminal, liminal and postliminal rites, the liminal stage representing an ambiguous state in between the ordinary and non-ordinary.

It was, however, Victor Turner who, having discovered van Gennep's work in the 1960s, explored the concept of liminality in his seminal 1967 essay *Betwixt and between: The liminal period in rites of passage* (Turner, 1987). He went on to expand his theorizing of the concept and its application to a variety of contexts, notably pilgrimage (Turner, 1973) of which, as noted later in this chapter, contemporary tourism is often considered to be a secular manifestation, as well as introducing the term 'liminoid' (Turner, 1974), which is returned to shortly. It is not surprising, therefore, that it is Turner's work that is primarily drawn upon when the concept of liminality is applied in tourism studies. His writing on the subject is extensive and is explored at length elsewhere (for example, Thomassen, 2009). For the purpose of this chapter, however, it suffices to highlight the key points emerging from Turner's work that have subsequently informed research in tourism. It must be emphasized here that liminality is a concept, not a theory; as van Ginkel (2014: 59) argues with regard to van Gennep's notion of rites of passage and Turner's subsequent work on liminality, 'they cannot and do not explain particular features of these phenomena nor what they mean for the personae conducting of undergoing rites of passage'. In other words, they do not explain the liminal experience; rather, they describe it.

Liminality: in between-ness and anti-structure

As noted above, the concept of liminality was first proposed by van Gennep (1960) who, referring to ritual-driven transitions in societies and in the social status of individuals within societies (the latter being defined as rites of passage), identified three stages in such rites, namely, separation, transition and incorporation. He termed the transition stage as the liminal stage, which, essentially, occurs when an individual crosses a temporal and/or spatial threshold and enters a state of in-betweenness – that is, in between an existing social status and a post-liminal new status. Turner (1987) went on to define this stage of liminality as an ambiguous state-of-being in which the individual is detached from the structures and rules of normal social life. In other words, liminality can be thought of as a form of 'human social existence during which the norms of everyday life are suspended and when alternatives that may be inversions are practised' (Spiegel, 2011: 13); it is a condition of anti-structure in which the norms of everyday life no longer apply. Hence, the liminal stage is one where anything is possible but where uncertainty and a loss of identity might be felt (Foster & McCabe, 2015). Paradoxically, however, although temporal or spatial liminality is characterized by the inversion of normal social structures, it is, as Spiegel (2011: 13) puts it, 'super-functional for the maintenance of...[those] ... social structure[s]'. Alternatively stated, 'Liminal phenomena tend to be collective, concerned with calendrical, biological, social-structural rhythms or with crises in social processes... They are thus enforced by social necessity' (Turner, 1974: 85) through rites of passage to maintain the structure and solidarity of society.

Transition and transformation

Key to van Gennep's (1960) original concept of liminality is its relationship with transition, arguably a fundamental facet of liminality that, as discussed below, is often lost or overlooked in its application to tourism. Rites of passage are in one way or another transformative for the individuals undergoing them; having negotiated a rite of passage, an individual may feel that, within themselves, they have benefited from some form of transformation or self-discovery, that they have been changed by the experience in the liminal stage. Equally, their status in society may also be transformed. An oft-utilized example of this is pilgrimage (Turner, 1973; Turner & Turner, 2011); not only may the physical hardship of the pilgrimage journey and its religious significance be spiritually transformative and enriching for participants but also, on their return, they may enjoy a recognized enhanced social status for having completed it.

Communitas

Communitas is a Latin word that refers both to an unstructured society or community in which people are equal and also to the spirit of community. It is, therefore, a means of understanding how members of a society relate to or perceive each other. According to Turner (1974: 79), within liminal contexts and, therefore, liberated from the structures, norms, roles and positions that may socially define (and divide) them, people may experience 'spontaneous communitas', a shared sense of community and belonging. In other words, in the unstructured condition of liminality, people become equal and share experiences and, hence, communitas describes the shared experience of liminality. This, in turn, implies that communitas is transient or short-lived; in the post-liminal stage communitas no longer occurs unless its spontaneous manifestation is replaced by normative communitas (Turner, 1974: 80), whereby it becomes transformed by a group of people into a new, permanent social structure particular to that group.

Liminal or liminoid?

Of particular relevance to this chapter is the distinction between liminal and liminoid. Liminoid is a term coined and discussed at length by Turner (1974) although, essentially, it refers to experiences that are liminal in nature (that is, occur within liminal times and spaces) but are distinctive because they occur in modern, industrialized societies in which rituals and socially determined rites of passage experiences have been replaced by contemporary departures from normal, structured life in manifestations of 'play'. More precisely, in what Turner (1974: 84) describes as small-scale 'tribal and early agrarian societies', there was little or no distinction between work and non-work or leisure; leisure, as a distinctive social institution, did not exist. Rather, interruptions to, and liminal periods within, structured agrarian life were based around annual rituals or festivals and these, as well as organized rites of passage for members of these societies, were collective, obligatory and, in a sense, socially sanctioned to maintain social structure. In contrast, in modern societies, not only has leisure (as the context for liminal periods) in all its forms become individualistic and distinctive from work, but also collective social rituals have lost their significance and role in maintaining social structure and order. Hence, liminoid experiences are distinctive in that, as Spiegel (2011: 13) suggests, they 'arise arise idiosyncratically and interstitially within society and its extant structure', they occur erratically or spontaneously rather following cyclical patterns, they are focused around the interests of the individual rather than society as a whole and they are not socially obligated but 'the product of individual or particular group efforts' (Deflem, 1991: 16). In short, liminoid experiences may occur in liminal times and places of anti-structure but are distinctive for being disconnected from traditional, society-wide ritual, significance and sanction and, perhaps, from transformative meaning for the individual.

From this perspective, it is a relatively easy task to conceptualize tourist experiences, at least in Turner's (1974) terms, as liminoid, if not liminal. The very process of travelling for a defined period of time to another (non-ordinary) place or culture means that tourists become temporarily located in what might be referred to as a liminal zone in which they are no longer bound by the norms or social structures of the home society, in which they can behave (within certain limits) as they wish. Indeed, it is this prospect of unboundedness, or freedom from social scrutiny, that underpins the long-recognized escape element of tourist motivation (Dann, 1981) manifested in compensatory or inverted behaviours while on holiday (Gottlieb, 1982; Lett, 1983; Uriely & Belhassen, 2006). However, such a generalization overlooks a number of questions that point to the need for a more nuanced understanding of the liminality–tourist experience nexus. For example, does being in a liminal place inevitably imply that experiences in or of that place are also liminal? Indeed, are tourism places truly liminal in the original meaning of the term? Airports, for instance, are descriptively liminal; they are places in between home and the destination (Huang, Xiao & Wang, 2018), but they operate according to known and expected norms and rules (or structure) to which tourists must conform. Under what conditions might participation in tourism offer transformative as opposed to restorative or recreational experiences? Or more specifically, can liminal tourist activities be logically equated with liminal experiences? And, does the contemporary significance and consumption of tourism suggest that it is no longer appropriate to refer to the tourist experience as liminal or, indeed, liminoid? It is to these questions that this chapter now turns, first by addressing the issue of the social significance of contemporary tourism.

Tourism: a contemporary ritual?

Hinting at the potentially transformative nature of the tourist experience as a sacred journey (in opposition to the profane condition of normal life), Graburn (1989: 22) observed that 'tourism…is functionally and symbolically equivalent to other institutions that humans use to embellish their lives', going on to liken it to a secular form of pilgrimage embracing three stages similar to rites of passage. In a later work, he argues more explicitly that participation in tourism is ritualistic: 'It my contention that tourism is best understood as a *kind of ritual*, one in which the special occasions of leisure and travel stand in opposition to everyday life at home and work' (Graburn, 2001: 42, emphasis in original). Fundamental to this claim is the distinction between normal, home life and being on holiday, the latter offering opportunities to experience 'ritual reversal' and 'ritual inversion' that directly reflect the anti-structure character of liminality. Nevertheless, he does not fully pursue the liminality theme, acknowledging instead that, for many tourists, their experience is neither transformative nor indeed particularly distinctive, concluding that 'tourists generally remain unchanged and demand a lifestyle not too different from that at home' (Graburn, 2001: 48). In so doing, he not only points to the arguably indisputable fact that, as discussed shortly, relatively few tourist experiences might be legitimately described as liminal, leading in turn to the question: is it possible to identify such liminal experiences? He also challenges his own assertion that viewing tourism as a secular ritual represents a general theory of tourism.

Certainly, earlier manifestations of modern-day tourism, from the evolution of seaside resorts in the UK and elsewhere perhaps through to the advent of mass international package tourism, could be considered ritualistic, not least because they occurred in places and times distinctive from normal life (for example, trips to seaside resorts during 'Wakes Weeks' in nineteenth century northern industrial towns in the UK (Barton, 2005) or the two-week 'sun-sea-sand packaged summer break in the mid- to late-twentieth century). In addition, the organization of and participation in such holidays could also considered ritualistic, following a process from anticipation / preparation / departure through to return recollection (Graburn, 2001). Interestingly, however, whether the nineteenth-century seaside resorts or their twentieth-century Mediterranean equivalents were liminal places (culturally rather than geographically) is debatable. Indeed, adopting an historical perspective, Walton (2014) argues convincingly that not only were they extensions of the industrial or metropolitan centres from which tourists originated, albeit with their own set of rules, but also that, certainly in the case of Victorian resorts, holidaying in the company – and under the scrutiny of – workmates, neighbours, friends and relatives precluded opportunities for unbounded, liminal or taboo behaviours.

The issue of tourism places being liminal is returned to shortly. The point here, however, is that, over the past four decades or so, tourism has lost its distinctiveness and, hence, the justification for being considered a ritual. That is, 'tourism is no longer a differentiated set of social practices with its distinct rules, times and places' (Urry, 1994: 234); rather, not only has it, from a postmodernist perspective (see also Chapter 1 in this handbook), merged with other social practices to the extent it is simply cultural, but also the manner and frequency with which it is consumed suggests that it can no longer be thought of as a departure from normal life. For example, with the advent of low-cost airlines, people can take international short city-breaks simply to go shopping whilst, more generally, the connectivity afforded by smartphones challenges the very notion of the tourist being separated psychologically or emotionally from their home society (Sharpley, 2018). In short, as the contemporary consumption of tourism has evolved, its significance as a distinctive, ritualistic social institution has arguably dissolved, as has, consequently, the conceptual foundation or it being considered a liminal (or liminoid) experience.

Nevertheless, it must equally be acknowledged that such a generalization is problematic. The motivation to consume tourism and the experience of it varies significantly between one person and another and transforms over time; tourism consumption is 'discretionary, future oriented, dynamic, socially influenced and evolving' (Pearce, 1992: 114). Moreover, certain touristic settings and activities evidently lend themselves to liminal / liminoid experiences more than others; a challenging Himalayan trek or engaging in so-called 'frontier tourism' (Laing & Crouch, 2011; see also Chapter 25) clearly involves participant experiences that are analytically distinctive from those on a beach holiday. Therefore, for a more nuanced perspective it is necessary to consider whether tourism places or destinations can be justifiably referred to as liminal and, subsequently, the extent to which the time tourists spend in such places and their experiences there might be referred to similarly.

Tourism places as liminal zones

Liminal spaces or places are, as discussed earlier in this chapter, both tangible (or perhaps imagined) and temporal places / spaces that lie 'in between'; people occupy them when they are in a transitional phase between one state of being another. As the central stage in a rite of passage, this lies between an existing and a new social status; for tourists, it lies between the departure from and return to normal life. Hence, the spatial and temporal elements of liminality are conceptually inseparable; for tourists, the time spent in the destination is descriptively liminal as is, arguably, the destination itself. However, as noted above, the assumption is frequently made that 'if the tourist is in a liminal space their experiences will also be liminal' (Van Tine, 2011: 4). Therefore, for the purposes of this chapter, it is essential to consider whether tangible tourism places / spaces are themselves liminal.

Immediately, the question arises: what are the parameters of what can be described as the tourism zone? More precisely, where is the *limen* or threshold that is crossed into the tourism space? Often, the coast and, more specifically, the beach / seaside resort is conceptualized as a liminal space (Gilchrist, Carter & Burdsey, 2014a; Preston-Whyte, 2004; Shields, 1991); it is seen as a place in between land and sea, a 'nebulous, ambiguous, multifaceted entity' (Gilchrist, Carter & Burdsey, 2014b: 6) between culture and nature, between the known and the unknown. In the tourism context, it is also seen as having long been, and remains, a place for liminal experiences, a place 'on the margin' (Shields, 1991) of both the land and normal structured society. However, perhaps the 'transit region' in the tourism system (Leiper, 1979) might also logically be considered to be liminal; mention has already been made of airports as arguably liminal places (Huang, Xiao & Wang, 2018). Alternatively, specific locations within a tourism destination, such as a hotel, can be described as liminal (Pritchard & Morgan, 2006).

Importantly, however, it must be remembered that a fundamental characteristic of liminality, and the potential for transformative experiences, is the anti-structure of liminal places, the inversion of normal structure and the promise of the unfamiliar, unknown and unexpected. As Beckstead (2010: 387) observes,

> The promise of travel is the possibility for personal transformation …Any journey is oriented towards the unknown future as it may become and is therefore highly ambivalent. Every step leads away from what is familiar towards unfamiliar settings and uncertain horizons which allows for novel and ambivalent experiences.

Putting it another way, liminal spaces must be unknown or unfamiliar; consequently, they should arguably be approached with a degree of expectation but uncertainty. However, for the great majority of contemporary tourism places, including geographically and culturally marginal seaside resorts or temporary, created zones such as music festival sites, this is not the case (but, see Jaimangal-Jones et al., 2010). Although the social structures and norms of the tourist's home society no longer exist, not only do such places possess their own set of structures, rules and practices (which, for economic expediency, permit or perhaps tolerate particular unbounded activities on the part of tourists), but also these are generally known and understood by the tourist, a point that Walton (2014) makes in his critique of Shield's (1991) work on Brighton. Indeed, for many tourists, the attraction or pull of a destination lies in the knowledge that they will be able to behave in particular ways free of censure from and, perhaps, shared with those around them – the concept of communitas is evidently of relevance to numerous tourism places, not least in forms of what Urry (1990b) describes as collective tourism experiences. In other words, tourists typically travel in the expectation of transitory hedonistic or, perhaps (in the broader sense of the word) deviant experiences, but not necessarily liminal, transformative experiences.

This is not to say that there do not exist tourist places / spaces that can be described or explained as liminal in the sense of being characterized by anti-structure. Tourists may, for example, find themselves in settings displaying social structures and norms that are unfamiliar or alien to them, although in a globalized and technologically connected world this is increasingly likely to be the exception rather than the rule. Equally, they may find themselves in places devoid of social structures, specifically natural areas such as wilderness or those with extreme geographical and / or meteorological conditions (for example, deserts, mountains, polar regions or, as mentioned earlier, 'frontier tourism' settings) where, in essence, the 'rules' of nature predominate. In such circumstances, tourists may encounter or be challenged by and respond to the unexpected or uncontrollable; even where there is an element of social structure (for example, organized / guided adventure trips), tourists may be in liminal places that offer the potential for liminal / liminoid experiences. Indeed, it is not surprising that much academic attention has been paid in particular to the potential for spiritual or transcendental tourist experience in wilderness and other natural areas (Ashley, 2007; Fredrickson & Anderson, 1999; Heintzman, 2003, 2010; Stringer & McAvoy, 1992). The assumption here, of course, is that spiritual experiences can be equated with those that are liminal or liminoid; this may not necessarily be the case although there are undoubtedly grounds for proposing such a relationship. That is, a liminal or transformative experience relates to an individual's pre- and post-liminality identity and social status and, similarly, 'living with an awareness of one's relationality is the essence of human spirituality' (de Souza, 2012: 292). A more detailed consideration of this is beyond the scope of this chapter but it nevertheless points to the final issue to be addressed here, namely, the extent to which tourist experiences might justifiably be explained as liminal or liminoid.

The liminality of tourist experiences

There are two ways of exploring the liminality of the tourist experience: first, from the perspective of tourists themselves and the experiences they seek and, second, in the context of the destination (as a potentially liminal tourist zone) and the activities tourists participate in whilst there. The focus in this section is primarily on the latter, not least because only broad generalizations are likely to emerge from a discussion of the former. Nevertheless, it is worth noting that, as Cohen (1979) conceptualized in his seminal paper more than four decades ago, the type of tourism that people consume or, more precisely, the experiences they seek is determined by the location of their 'spiritual centre'. At one extreme, those who are satisfied or identify with their normal home environment and life (and hence, feel no need to 'find themselves' or undergo transformative experiences) seek recreational experiences; they consume forms of tourism, as Graburn (2001) acknowledges, that differ little from their normal lifestyle. At the other extreme, however 'existential' (Cohen, 1979) tourists, experiencing a sense of alienation in the normal lives, seek meaning, identity and fulfilment through immersing themselves in other places and cultures in which they believe their spiritual centre might be located. In principle, therefore, only existential tourists might seek or go through liminal, transformative experiences; in reality, however, the majority of tourists are likely to be found somewhere between these two extremes. Where and when, then, might tourist experiences be liminal?

It has already been argued that the tourism zone – that is, the places that tourists find themselves between departure from and return to their normal home and life – are descriptively but not typically analytically liminal. This particularly applies to places that are socially structured and organized (resorts, tourist cities and so on). In contrast, as suggested above, unstructured places may both be liminal in character and offer opportunities for liminal experiences, though much depends on the expectations, motives and behaviours/ activities of tourists. Yet, relating the potential for liminal tourist experiences to a simple distinction between socially structured and unstructured places does not stand up to scrutiny; wilderness tourism experiences might be exciting, challenging (or even unpleasant) but not necessarily liminal in the transformative sense; equally some activities in organized tourism zones have the potential to be transformative for participants. For example, Thomassen and Balle (2012), likening the popular activity of bungee jumping to traditional jumping rituals in non-modern societies, propose that not only can it be seen as a modern touristic ritual associated with a number of well-known destinations, such as Queenstown in New Zealand, but also it can be transformative – a leap into the void comes with social status: 'Being seen and being recognized and becoming accepted into a group is an important part of the jumping' (Thomassen & Balle, 2012: 86). Indeed, in identifying the correlation between modern bungee jumping and traditional jumping rites, they acknowledge that the bungee experience can be described as liminoid but go on to coin the term 'limivoid' to emphasize crossing the threshold into, literally, the void.

Other organized tours activities, such as white-water river rafting (Arnould & Price, 1993; Beckman, Whaley & Kim, 2017), might equally be legitimately conceptualized as liminal or, more precisely, limioid experiences; tourists enter a liminal space beyond their normal frame of reference and not only achieve self-identity from participation but also enjoy the 'communitas' of the shared 'white knuckle' experience. Less certain, however, is the extent to which other tourist activities, claimed by some to be liminal, can be considered as such.

Richard Sharpley

Conclusion

Since Graburn (1989) conceptualized it as a secular journey similar in form and function to traditional rituals, contemporary tourism has increasingly been considered a liminal experience. And at first sight, it is easy to understand why this is so. Not only does tourism occupy an in-between, liminal temporal space in people's lives, a space in which the structures and norms of their day-to-day lives are temporarily suspended or inverted, but the tourism place can also be considered liminal, between the place departed from and returned to. Moreover, the overall tourism process, embracing preparation/departure, the time in the destination and the return, shares similarities with the three stages of ritual journeys or rites of passage, whilst tourist engage in activities that, unbounded by social scrutiny, might equally be thought of as liminal. Hence, it is logical to suggest that, overall, the tourist is liminal or, according to Turner's (1974) reasoning, liminoid.

However, as this chapter has demonstrated, this is rarely likely to be the case. In other words, although participation in tourism is descriptively liminal, the tourist experience cannot analytically be considered as such; occupying a liminal tourism zone and engaging in liminal activities does not immediately imply that the tourist experience will also be liminal or liminoid (in the original, anthropological sense of the word). Indeed, it would appear from the discussion in this chapter that only certain, physically challenging activities might elicit a sense of identity, communitas and potential transformation, all fundamental elements of liminality as originally conceptualized. This leads to two inevitable conclusions. First, the essence of the concept of liminality has been lost in its application to tourism, the emphasis primarily being on the alternative social structures and norms of 'in between' times and places. And second, contemporary tourists typically participate in tourism in the expectation and knowledge of doing something different from normal, of having experiences that are recreational, physically and emotionally restorative, compensatory, hedonistic and perhaps even transgressive but, for the most part, neither liminal nor liminoid.

References

Agarwal, S. (2014) Managing liminality in coastal tourism resorts. In P. Gilchrist, T. Carter and D. Burdsey (Eds.), *Coastal Cultures, Liminality & Leisure*. LSA Publication No.126. Eastbourne: Leisure Studies Association, University of Brighton, pp. 65–85.

Andrews, H. and Roberts, L. (2012) *Liminal Landscapes: Travel, Experience and Spaces In-between*. Abingdon: Routledge.

Arnould, E. and Price, L. (1993) River magic: Extraordinary experience and the extended service encounter. *Journal of Consumer Research*, 20(1), 24–45.

Ashley, P. (2007) Toward an understanding and definition of wilderness spirituality. *Australian Geographer*, 38(1), 53–69.

Barton, S. (2005) *Working-Class Organisations and Popular Tourism, 1840–1970*. Manchester: Manchester University Press.

Beckman, E., Whaley, J. and Kim, Y. (2017) Motivations and experiences of whitewater rafting tourists on the Ocoee River, USA. *International Journal of Tourism Research*, 19(2), 257–267.

Beckstead, Z. (2010) Liminality in acculturation and pilgrimage: When movement becomes meaningful. *Culture & Psychology*, 16(3), 383–393.

Cohen, E. (1972) Towards a sociology of international tourism. *Social Research*, 39(1), 64–82.

Cohen, E. (1979) A phenomenology of tourist experiences. *Sociology*, 13, 179–201.

Conti, E. and Heldt Cassel, S. (2020) Liminality in nature-based tourism experiences as mediated through social media. *Tourism Geographies*, 22(2), 413–432.

Dann, G. (1981) Tourist motivation: An appraisal. *Annals of Tourism Research*, 8(2), 187–219.

Dann, G. and Parrinello, G. (2009) Setting the scene. In G. Dann and G. Parrinello (Eds.), *The Sociology of Tourism: European Origins and Developments*. Bingley: Emerald Group Publishing, pp. 1–64.

Tourist experiences: liminal or liminoid?

de Souza, M. (2012) Connectedness and connectedness: The dark side of spirituality–implications for education. *International Journal of Children's Spirituality*, 17(4), 291–303.

Deflem, M. (1991) Ritual, anti-structure and religion: A discussion of Victor Turner's processual symbolic analysis. *Journal for the Scientific Study of Religion*, 30(1), 1–35.

Foster, C. and McCabe, S. (2015) The role of liminality in residential activity camps. *Tourist Studies*, 15(1), 46–64.

Fredrickson, L. and Anderson, D. (1999) A qualitative exploration of the wilderness experience as a source of spiritual inspiration. *Journal of Environmental Psychology*, 19(1), 21–39.

Gilchrist, P. T., Carter, T. and Burdsey, D. (Eds.) (2014a) *Coastal Cultures, Liminality & Leisure*. LSA Publication No.126. Eastbourne: Leisure Studies Association, University of Brighton.

Gilchrist, P. T., Carter, T. and Burdsey, D. (2014b) Costal cultures: Leisure and liminality – Introduction. In P. Gilchrist, T. Carter and D. Burdsey (Eds.), *Coastal Cultures, Liminality & Leisure*. LSA Publication No.126. Eastbourne: Leisure Studies Association, pp. 1–12, University of Brighton, pp. 65–85.

Gottlieb, A. (1982) Americans' vacations. *Annals of Tourism Research*, 9(2), 165–187.

Graburn, N. (1989) Tourism: The sacred journey. In V. Smith (Ed.), *Hosts and Guests: The Anthropology of Tourism*, 2nd Edn. Philadelphia: University of Pennsylvania Press, pp. 21–36.

Graburn, N. (2001) Secular ritual: A general theory of tourism. In V. Smith and M. Brent (Eds.), *Hosts and Guests Revisited: Tourism Issues of the 21st Century*. New York: Cognizant Communications, pp. 42–50.

Heintzman, P. (2003) The wilderness experience and spirituality what recent research tells us. *Journal of Physical Education, Recreation & Dance*, 74(6), 27–32.

Heintzman, P. (2010) Nature-based recreation and spirituality: A complex relationship. *Leisure Sciences*, 32(1), 72–89.

Huang, W. J., Xiao, H. and Wang, S. (2018) Airports as liminal space. *Annals of Tourism Research*, 70, 1–13.

Jackson, J. E. (2005) Stigma, liminality, and chronic pain: Mind–body borderlands. *American Ethnologist*, 32(3), 332–353.

Jacobsen, J. (2009) Early tourism research in Scandinavia. In G. Dann and G. Parrinello (Eds.), *The Sociology of Tourism: European Origins and Developments*. Bingley: Emerald Group Publishing, pp. 221–242.

Jaimangal-Jones, D., Pritchard, A. and Morgan, N. (2010) Going the distance: locating journey, liminality and rites of passage in dance music experiences. *Leisure Studies*, 29(3), 253–268.

Laing, J. and Crouch, G. (2011) Frontier tourism: Retracing mythic journeys. *Annals of Tourism Research*, 38(4), 1516–1534.

Leiper, N. (1979) The framework of tourism: Towards a definition of tourism, tourist, and the tourist industry. *Annals of Tourism Research*, 6(4), pp. 390–407.

Lett, J. (1983) Ludic and liminoid aspects of charter yacht tourism in the Caribbean. *Annals of Tourism Research*, 10(1), 35–56.

Mansaray, A. (2006) Liminality and in/exclusion: Exploring the work of teaching assistants. *Pedagogy, Culture & Society*, 14(2), 171–187.

Nelson, V. (2020) Liminality and difficult heritage in tourism. *Tourism Geographies*, 22(2), 298–318.

Pearce, P. (1992) Fundamentals of tourist motivation. In D. Pearce an R. Butler (Eds.), *Tourism Research: Critiques and Challenges*. London: Routledge, pp. 113–134.

Preston-Whyte, R., (2004) The beach as a liminal space. In A. Lew, C. M. Hall and A. Williams (Eds.), *A Companion to Tourism*. Oxford: Blackwell Publishing, pp. 349–359.

Pritchard, A. and Morgan, N. (2006) Hotel Babylon? Exploring hotels as liminal sites of transition and transgression. *Tourism Management*, 27(5), 762–772.

Rink, B. (2020) Liminality at-sea: Cruises to nowhere and their metaworlds. *Tourism Geographies*, 22(2), 392–412.

Selänniemi, T. (2003) On holiday in the liminoid playground: Place, time, and self in tourism. In T. Bauer and B. McKercher (Eds.), *Sex and Tourism: Journeys of Romance, Love, and Lust*, Binghampton: The Howarth Hospitality Press, pp. 19–31.

Sharpley, R. (2014) Host perceptions of tourism: A review of the research. *Tourism Management*, 42(1), 37–49.

Sharpley, R. (2018) *Tourism, Tourists and Society*, 5th Edn. Abingdon: Routledge.

Shields, R. (1991) *Places on the Margin: Alternative Geographies of Modernity*. London: Routledge.

Smith, V. (Ed.) (1977) *Hosts and Guests: The Anthropology of Tourism*, 1st Edn. Philadelphia: University of Pennsylvania Press.

Söderlund, J. and Borg, E. (2018) Liminality in management and organization studies: Process, position and place. *International Journal of Management Reviews*, 20(4), 880–902.

Spiegel, A. D. (2011) Categorical difference versus continuum: Rethinking Turner's liminal-liminoid distinction. *Anthropology Southern Africa*, 34(1–2), 11–20.

Stringer, L. and McAvoy, L. (1992) The need for something different: Spirituality and wilderness adventure. *Journal of Experiential Education*, 15(1), 13–20.

Thomassen, B. (2009) The uses and meaning of liminality. *International Political Anthropology*, 2(1), 5–28.

Thomassen, B. (2012) Revisiting liminality: The danger of empty spaces. In H. Andrews and L. Roberts (Eds.), *Liminal Landscapes: Travel, Experience and Spaces In-between*. Abingdon: Routledge, pp. 21–35.

Thomassen, B. and Balle, M. (2012) From liminoid to limivoid: Understanding contemporary bungee jumping from a cross-cultural perspective. *Journal of Tourism Consumption and Practice*, 4(1), 59–93.

Tribe, J. (1997) The indiscipline of tourism. *Annals of Tourism Research*, 24(3), 638–657.

Turner, V. (1973) The centre out there: The pilgrim's goal. *History of Religions*, 10, 191–230.

Turner, V. (1974) Liminal to liminoid, in play, flow, and ritual: An essay in comparative symbology. *Rice Institute Pamphlet: Rice University Studies*, 60(3), 53–92. Available at: https://scholarship.rice.edu/bitstream/handle/1911/63159/article_RIP603_part4.pdf (Accessed 16 April 2020).

Turner, V. (1987) Betwixt and between: The liminal period in rites of passage. In L. Mahdi, S. Foster and M. Little (Eds.), *Betwixt and Between: Patterns of Masculine and Feminine Initiation*, Peru: Open Court Publishing, pp. 3–19.

Turner, V. and Turner, E. (2011) *Image and Pilgrimage in Christian Culture*. New York: Columbia University Press.

Underthun, A. and Jordhus-Lier, D. C. (2018) Liminality at work in Norwegian hotels. *Tourism Geographies*, 20(1), 11–28.

Uriely, N. and Belhassen, Y. (2006) Drugs and risk-taking in tourism. *Annals of Tourism Research*, 33(2), 339–359.

Urry, J. (1990a) *The Tourist Gaze*. London: Sage Publications.

Urry, J. (1990b) The consumption of tourism. *Sociology*, 24(1), 23–35.

Urry, J. (1994) Cultural change and contemporary tourism. *Leisure Studies*, 13(4), 233–238.

van Gennep, A. (1960) *Rites of Passage* (Trans. M. Vizedom and G. Caffee). London: Routledge & Kegan Paul Ltd.

van Ginkel, R. (2014) The cultural seascape, cosmology and the magic of liminality. In P. Gilchrist, T. Carter and D. Burdsey (Eds.), *Coastal Cultures, Liminality & Leisure*. LSA Publication No.126. Eastbourne: Leisure Studies Association, University of Brighton, pp. 45–64.

Van Tine, R. (2011) Liminality and the short term study abroad experience. MSc Thesis, University of Illinois at Urbana-Champaign. Available at: https://www.ideals.illinois.edu/bitstream/handle/2142/26278/VanTine_Rebecca.pdf?sequence=1 (Accessed 1 June 2020).

Walton, J. (2014) Histories of liminality on the coast. In P. Gilchrist, T. Carter and D. Burdsey (Eds), *Coastal Cultures, Liminality & Leisure*. LSA Publication No.126. Eastbourne: Leisure Studies Association, University of Brighton, pp. 13–30.

Wood, G., Phan, P. H. and Wright, M., 2018. The problems with theory and new challenges in theorizing. *Academy of Management Perspectives*, 32(4), pp. 405–411.

8

FINDING FLOW IN THE TRAVEL EXPERIENCE

Statia Elliot

The best moments in our lives are not the passive, receptive, relaxing times – although such experiences can also be enjoyable, if we have worked hard to attain them. The best moments usually occur if a person's body or mind is stretched to its limits in a voluntary effort to accomplish something difficult and worthwhile. Optimal experience is thus something that we make happen...For each person there are thousands of opportunities, challenges to expand ourselves. (Csíkszentmihályi, 1990: 3)

Introduction

Some 3,000 years ago Plato philosophized what might be considered the best tourism brand slogan ever: *live life as play*. Fast forward to Csíkszentmihályi's 1970s observations of artists painting, children playing, chess players competing, even doctors performing surgeries, and his concept of flow as episodes of intrinsic joy that stand out as the best moments of life, and you have a modern day, positive psychologist's interpretation of Plato's perspective.

Csíkszentmihályi (1997) believes that flow can be achieved not only during play or leisure times, but also in the context of work and even during everyday moments. It is not just the behaviour or activity that produces flow, it is the psyche; a state of consciousness 'where we feel a sense of exhilaration, a deep sense of enjoyment that is long cherished, does not come through passive, receptive, relaxing times' (Csíkszentmihályi 1990: 2). Over the past five decades, he and his co-authors have applied the concept of flow to studies of work (Seligman & Csíkszentmihályi, 2000), sport (Jackson & Marsh, 1996), leisure and adventure (Csíkszentmihályi & Selega, 1990), family, school and society (Csíkszentmihályi & Csíkszentmihályi, 1988). Flow has been developed and used in numerous studies of consumption and is of particular relevance to travel, recreation and leisure consumption (Arnould & Price, 1993; Celsi, Rose & Leigh, 1993; Tinsley & Tinsley, 1986), where flow is claimed to be the leading explanation for positive subjective experiences (Elkington, 2010). And in studies of experiential marketing, flow is held up as the ideal consumer experience (Hoffman & Novak, 2009).

Comparatively, flow has received limited mention in the tourism literature, despite its applicability to understanding tourist behaviour, satisfaction and dissatisfaction (Ryan, 1995). Ryan (2011: 15) brings flow into focus in his literature-based review of the tourist

DOI: 10.4324/9781003219866-10

experience, highlighting that flow (and arousal theory) 'may deserve more attention than they currently appear to attract within the academic tourism literature'. When flow emerges periodically in the tourism literature, as happens (Ayazlar & Yuksel 2018; Tsaur, Yen & Hsiao, 2013), the passage of five decades of research advancement in other fields is missing, as if a concept termed flow were, ironically, static. As our understanding of tourism expands from travel as guilty pleasure to a more meaningful experience, so too must our theoretical reflections. The theory of flow is one with strong relevance to the tourism experience. Well beyond the impact of customer satisfaction – perhaps the most commonly studied outcome of travel experiences – flow not only results in optimal performance but has been found to produce longer-term psychological and physical benefits (Demerouti, Bakker, Sonnentag & Fullagar, 2012; Farber & Hall, 2007). To consider the value of this concept to tourism research, this chapter summarizes its theoretical origins and multidisciplinary applications in a focused review of flow in relation to the travel experience.

Csíkszentmihályi's flow

Csíkszentmihályi (1975) first identified the concept of flow as a condition among artists during their creative process characterized by a total absorption in the moment at the expense of any other activity (e.g., physiological needs, sense of time). In *Beyond Boredom and Anxiety* (1975), he builds a theoretical model of enjoyment by first exploring intrinsic motivation and the rewards of autotelic activities as key elements of individual happiness. Through interviews with composers, chess champions and surgeons, a particular state of experience emerged as the concept he termed flow, defined by several dimensions: (i) merging of action and awareness; (ii) centering of attention on limited stimulus field; (iii) transcendence of ego boundaries; (iv) feelings of competence and control; (v) unambiguous and immediate feedback; and (vi) an autotelic nature.

Firstly, flow merges action and awareness so that one's attention is undivided and centred on a limited stimulus field. For this to occur requires clearly established rules or structure, a second characteristic of flow where the level of ability to perform the activity allows for complete involvement. Whether in work or play, a foundational characteristic of flow is that there must be a balance between challenge and skill, otherwise the result may instead be boredom or anxiety. A third characteristic is the loss of self-consciousness or ego, whereby flow occurs. Fourthly, flow requires being in control of one's actions and of the environment, without worry. A fifth characteristic is that flow experiences provide unambiguous feedback as evaluation of performance. Lastly, flow experiences are autotelic in nature rather than dependent on external reward. These interconnected characteristics led to the modelling of flow (Csíkszentmihályi 1975: 49) whereby flow is achieved when challenge and skill are balanced: too demanding a challenge results in worry; a challenge below one's skill results in boredom.

Across disciplines, flow is widely accepted as positive, defined as a 'state in which people are so involved in an activity that nothing else seems to matter: the experience itself is so enjoyable that people will do it at great cost, for the sheer sake of doing it' (Csíkszentmihályi, 1990: 4). In flow, an activity is perceived as rewarding and productivity is described as maximum. Individuals experiencing flow develop a sense of hyper-concentration that makes them feel good. Stimulating spontaneous energy, the activity can be sustained for a longer period without effort. The cares of daily life are temporarily erased, which induces post-positive emotions. There is a loss of self-awareness; individuals act but without being self-conscious of their actions. The individual is totally immersed in the present moment with a distorted perception of time (Csíkszentmihályi, 1975).

Finding flow in the travel experience

Flow and play

While achievable in many contexts, such as travel, flow is beyond normal or everyday life. Travel is planned and executed, akin to structured play. It is not driven by extrinsic reward, requiring resources to partake, but is driven by the rewards from travel itself. These dimensions of challenge and reward, absorption and immersion and energy and emotion are all significant to the experience of travel, calling for a closer examination of the flow–tourism relationship.

In a tourism context, the concept of flow is found predominantly in two streams of research and, most notably, in studies of adventure travel, a logical extension of Csíkszentmihályi's (1975) early reports of mountain climbers finding happiness and understanding in flow. Travel typically affords more time for leisure pursuits not enjoyed during daily life, and often physical adventures are the primary trip purpose as an opportunity to experience something special, even meaningful.

> Extended service encounters such as those found in activities like golf, tennis or perhaps sailing are capable of producing a flow experience because they provide a clear-cut challenging goal, especially for those who know the rules and the intricacies of the activity.
> *(McGinnis, Gentry & Gao, 2008: 76)*

The second stream of tourism-flow research, to a much lesser extent, is found in studies of the online environment (Hoffman & Novak 2009), reflecting the increasing market share of e-transactions in travel purchases from lodging to transportation and the importance of positive online experiences to commerce.

To begin in the realm of adventure, Csíkszentmihályi (1975) studied extreme mountain climbing as an ideal example of flow: it is autotelic, offering no material reward; it requires high awareness and attention, competence and control and transcendence of ego for clear and immediate feedback of one's climbing performance. In flow, Csíkszentmihályi's climbers reported feelings of happiness, true understanding, oneness with nature and a sense of one's place in the universe. These psychological 'highs' can be habit forming and even seductive, making flow potentially addictive (Csíkszentmihályi, 1975: 139) and more powerful than extrinsic return. Like climbing enthusiasts, the so called 'travel junkie' is hooked on the experience drug, with effects that are by no means limited to the mountains.

Flow has become the leading explanation for positive subjective experience in the study of leisure, specifically that of serious leisure (Elkington, 2010) defined as 'the systematic pursuit of an amateur, hobbyist, or volunteer activity sufficiently substantial and interesting for the participant to find a career there in the acquisition and expression of a combination of its special skills, knowledge, and experience' (Stebbins 1992: 3). The concept of flow has been used by leisure theorists as the object of interest in studies pertaining to white water rafting (Arnould & Price, 1993), sky diving (Celsi et al., 1993), paragliding (Ayazlar & Yuksel, 2018) and adventure tourism (Beedie & Hudson, 2003; Jones, Hollenhorst & Perna, 2003). Overall, the study of flow has been largely associated with physical activities and the wilderness/adventure setting (McGinnis et al., 2008; Tinsley & Tinsley, 1986; Tsaur et al, 2013). Analogous to flow occurrence in serious leisure is flow in 'serious tourism'. Ryan (2011: 15) describes the 'tourist as an actor in the process of holiday making rather than simply holiday taking', or co-created experiences. Stebbins (2007) attributed the experience of flow during serious leisure to its requirements of a proactive attitude and a significant effort from participants, or as Csíkszentmihályi (1997) describes, an activation energy is required for flow. Simply put, flow takes effort to reach the experience of ease.

Kreziak and Frochot (2011) identified that the delicate balance between boredom and anxiety necessary to experience a state of flow is also at work in the challenge of skiing with skiers of a different level. In a group, the likelihood of achieving flow is greater if people of the same level ski together. Time can also influence the flow experience. First, flow happens when a person's skills are fully involved in overcoming a challenge that is just about manageable, so it acts as a magnet for learning new skills and increasing challenges. If challenges are too low, one gets back to flow by increasing them. If challenges are too great, one can return to the flow state by learning new skills.

The concept of matching skill and challenge can help explain vast differences in travel preferences, whereby some tourists may enter flow while strolling the shore while others would be bored unless surfing the waves. Csíkszentmihályi (1975) incorporates this variance by constructing flow as a continuum, ranging from low to high complexity or from repetitive automatic acts to those requiring a person's full physical and intellectual potential. He describes these patterns as micro flow and macro flow. Both are above the normal, everyday level of activity but differ greatly in terms of their relative degree of complexity and structure of experience, and of pleasure and enjoyment produced. Both may be indispensable to positive well-being and, perhaps, to travel satisfaction. Interestingly, however, in the relatively few tourism studies that have incorporated flow in analyses of travel experiences, the focus has been at the macro end and almost exclusively in the context of mountaineering (Beedie & Hudson, 2003; Faullant, Matzler & Mooradian, 2011; Noy, 2004; Pomfret, 2006, 2011; Tsaur et al., 2013), perhaps because even the existence of mountain scenery can foster emotional outcomes (Farber & Hall, 2007).

Flow and experiences

In consumer behaviour, another field that has grasped the concept of flow, the potential of experiences to influence customer attitudes and behaviours has long been explored (Holbrook & Hirschman, 1982), particularly in the online environment where engagement can be complete (Hoffman & Novak, 2009). Flow produces 'a state of transcendence, a suspension of temporal reality, a sense of separation from the mundane, and a sense of unity with some higher plane of experience' (Schouten, McAlexander & Koenig, 2007: 357). Marketers desire this consumer state to strengthen brand community and loyalty, and to bring the consumer back over and over again (Schouten et al, 2007). Thus, marketing studies have focused on the triggers that might stimulate flow experiences, such as sights, sounds and smells, unexpected gratifying interpersonal encounters with staff and with other customers, and personal achievements that exceed expectations (Schouten et al., 2007).

Rituals can also be affective triggers of emotional, social and psychic connections (Schouten et al., 2007), stronger than more traditional loyalties developed by frequent product usage. The potential dark side of such strong connections is addiction, as in the case of gamblers or shopaholics, where repetitive consumer behaviour becomes out of control and harmful. For most, however, flow experiences simply transcend the mundane and strengthen ties. Consider, for example, an annual ski trip (ritual), where a guide finally helps you conquer the black diamond mogul run (psychic), followed by an après-ski celebration with family and friends (social). The emotional atmosphere triggers flow and, very likely, will bring you back. The appeal is best described by Csíkszentmihályi (1997):

> Imagine that you are skiing down a slope and your full attention is focused on the movements of your body, the position of the skis, the air whistling past your face and the snow-shrouded trees running by. There is no room in your awareness for conflicts

Finding flow in the travel experience

or contradictions; you know that a distracting thought or emotion might get you buried face down in the snow. The run is so perfect that you want it to last forever.

The strong focus on experiences in tourism research and practice is evidenced by the range of terminology used to describe exceptional experiences. While not inclusive, Table 8.1 summarizes a number of concepts, each uniquely defined, though their boundaries are far from definitive and at least a few attributes are shared across their fuzzy borders. The majority involve some positive state (e.g. cathartic provides relief; peak stimulates happiness; extraordinary provokes pleasure; mystical excites the divine), and almost all involve a degree of absorption beyond normal (e.g. re-enchantment takes the consumer away; emotion-high requires focused attention; transcendence expands awareness). And while macro flow may have similar characteristics to many other experience phenomenon, such as cathartic (Ryan & Deci, 2001), emotion-high (Farber & Hall, 2007), extraordinary (Arnould & Price 1993), hedonistic (Kraut, 1979), luminal (Pritchard & Morgan, 2006), mystical (James, 1917), optimal (Csíkszentmihályi & Csíkszentmihályi, 1988), peak (Privette, 1983), spiritual (Fredrickson & Anderson, 1999) and transcendent (Levin & Steele, 2005), an important differentiating characteristic of flow is its pattern at the micro end of a continuum.

Table 8.1 Experience terminology and conceptualizations relevant to tourism

Concept	Definition	Dimensions	Relationships
Cathartic	Providing psychological relief through open expression of strong emotions; life-changing; not the norm (Ryan, 1997)	1. life affirming 2. emotional release 3. well-being 4. self-efficacy 5. meaningful (Zahra & McIntosh, 2007)	Volunteer tourism → cathartic experience (Zahra & McIntosh, 2007)
Emotion – High	Complex episodes involving objects of attention, appraisal and phenomenological experiences (in Farber & Hall, 2007)	1. Scenery 2. Recreational activity 3. Wildlife 4. Social interaction 5. Novelty (Farber & Hall, 2007)	Special experiences → positive affect (Farber & Hall, 2007)
Extraordinary	Strong positive emotions (high pleasure & arousal), transitory or rare; spontaneous (Arnould & Price, 1993)	1. Communion with nature 2. Group connectivity 3. Personal growth (Arnould & Price, 1993)	Extraordinary experience → trip satisfaction (Arnould & Price, 1993)
Flow	The holistic sensation people feel when they act with total involvement, characterized by a sense of self-control and pleasure (Csíkszentmihályi, 1975)	1. Challenge-skill balance 2. Clear goals 3. Unambiguous feedback 4. Concentration on task 5. Sense of control 6. Loss of self-consciousness 7. Autotelic experience 8. Action awareness merging 9. Transformation of time (Jackson & Marsh, 1996)	Flow → Quality of experience (LeFevre, 1988) Flow → Happiness → Well-being & Energy (Demerouti et al., 2012) Flow → Peak physical performance (Jackson & Marsh, 1996)

(Continued)

Statia Elliot

Concept	Definition	Dimensions	Relationships
Hedonistic	Positive effects that accompany getting or having the material objects and action opportunities the individual wishes to possess or experience (Kraut, 1979)	1. Pleasure 2. Enjoyment 3. Satisfaction 4. Feeling good 5. Feeling of warmth 6. Feeling happy (Tsaur et al., 2013)	Transcendence → Flow → Happiness (Tsaur et al., 2013)
Immersion	Feeling of well-being, development & satisfaction (Carù & Cova, 2006). Appropriation of the service environment (Aubert-Gamet, 1997)	1. Nesting 2. Exploring 3. Tagging (Carù & Cova, 2006)	Immersion → Satisfaction (Carù & Cova, 2006) Immersion → Optimal experience (Frochot, Elliot & Kreziak. 2017)
Mystical	Experiencing a connection with the divine; a state of consciousness that transcends normal reality (James, 1917)	1. Ineffability 2. A noetic quality 3. Transience 4. Passivity (James, 1917)	Mystical experiences → Psychological well-being (Levin & Steele, 2005)
Optimal	The highest level of subjective experience relative to other psychological states (Csíkszentmihályi, 1990)	1. Positive affect (joy) 2. Activation (aroused) 3. Cognitive efficiency 4. Motivation (Csíkszentmihályi & Larson, 1987)	Cognitive involvement → Flow (Lambert, Chapman & Lurie, 2013)
Peak	Moments of highest happiness and fulfillment, surpassing usual psychological levels in intensity, meaning and richness (Maslow, 1962)	1. Intense 2. Highly valued moment (Privette, 1983)	Peak experience → Transcendence (Schouten et al., 2007) Peak experience → Ties to consumption activity (Ryan et al., 2003)
Transcendent	A state of consciousness characterized by altered or expanded awareness (Levin & Steele, 2005)	1. Emotional intensity 2. Epiphany 3. Singularity of experience 4. Extreme enjoyment 5. Oneness 6. Ineffability 7. Extreme focus 8. Test of personal limits (Schouten et al., 2007)	Flow → Transcendence → brand community (Schouten et al., 2007) Transcendence → Flow → Happiness (Tsaur et al., 2013) Transcendence → relationship with nature & service providers (Arnould & Price, 1993) Natural environment → Transcendence (Farber & Hall, 2007) Transcendence → Flow (Williams & Harvey, 2001)

Finding flow in the travel experience

Privette (1983) detailed the commonalities between peak experience, peak performance and flow as absorption, valuing, joy, spontaneity, power, personal identity and involvement. She also noted their distinguishing characteristics, finding peak experience to be mystic and transpersonal; peak performance to be transactive and self-focused; and flow to be fun (Privette, 1983). Looking at the dimensions listed in Table 8.1 for each experience, it is more than fun that differentiates flow. With clear goals, a sense of control and unambiguous feedback, flow is more planned and structured than other experiences. And while flow is pleasurable, unlike the extreme highs of peak, mystical, optimal and others, it can happen at a micro level as long as challenge and skill are balanced and the other dimensions met. Transcendence is another experience with subtypes, namely, green and mature transcendence (Levin & Steele, 2005). Green transcendence can be described as ecstatic and profound as well as transitory, much like peak and mystical experiences. In contrast, mature transcendence, while profound and mystical, is long lasting, transporting one to a new state of awareness (Levin & Steele 2005). None of these experiences, however, mirrors flow at the micro level.

At the more micro level, Csíkszentmihályi (1975) argues that flow can be present even in everyday life, through a range of activities from daydreaming to smoking. Rather than trivial, he believes these behaviours facilitate a type of flow, turning the ordinary into something more rewarding. In a study of 20 students, Csíkszentmihályi (1975: 147) identified six categories of micro flow activities: imagining (e.g. humming); attending (e.g. listening to music); oral (e.g. snacking); creative (e.g. writing); kinesthetic (e.g. walking); and, social (e.g. talking), with the last two most common. So satisfying are these micro flow activities that deprivation causes negative feelings (Csíkszentmihályi 1975: 176), supporting the importance of micro flow activities, from daydreams to more structured leisure, for happiness.

For a travel experience occurring over an extended period of time, sustaining macro flow is not possible. However, micro flow behaviour can feasibly occur throughout a trip, given the additional 'free' time and sense of freedom one feels when away from the home environment. Many travel activities are structured and patterned and even a morning breakfast, for example, may have added challenges (e.g. finding a restaurant) and goals (e.g. trying a new food) that stimulate a degree of flow beyond ordinary life. While macro flow may be experienced at extreme travel moments, micro flow may occur throughout the travel journey.

Closely related to flow is the concept of immersion. Indeed, what is particularly interesting in the study of flow is its ability to act as an accelerator to the immersion experience (Frochot, Elliot & Kreziak, 2017). Flow, then, presents opportunity to accelerate and ensure immersion, improving tourist welfare and enhancing the stay experience. In this perspective, certain travel experiences may act as accelerators to this process, of interest to help clarify theoretical definitions. Another dimension of the flow experience, refuting the long-held belief that most memorable travel moments are the result of spontaneous events or serendipitous moments (Hom Cary, 2004), is the structured and planned nature of flow. Like 'the trip of a lifetime', expending energies to prepare for an activity often results in the highest of highs, or deep flow. In this regard, flow brings cognitive elements to the forefront of the experience, calling for clear goals, unambiguous feedback, control and concentration; it is much like appraisal theory (Scherer, Schoor & Johnstone, 2001), whereby emotional responses are shaped by cognitive responses to stimuli. In summary, the concept of flow supports our understanding of the travel experience.

Flow and work

As work is a reality for most who desire travel, it is important to consider the experience of flow in this life realm. Logically, the field of psychology has grasped the flow concept, particularly as the positive branch of psychology has grown, along with valuing subjective experiences such as past well-being, future hope and present happiness (Seligman & Csíkszentmihályi, 2000). Studies of quality of life and the relationship between work and satisfaction incorporate the flow concept to understand how 'anti-flow' – feelings of boredom and frustration – might be avoided in the workplace. Work by definition is paid activity, an extrinsic motivator. Yet, if employees find intrinsic motivation in work activities, particularly in what Stebbins (2007) termed 'devotee' occupations, intense flow experiences are possible (Allison & Duncan, 1988).

LeFevre (1988) also found a correlation between flow and work that ultimately can enhance productivity, but she questions the direction of causation. Does increased time in flow make people happy, or are happy people able to find more time for flow? Further confounding the issue, her results indicate that more flow is experienced during work than during leisure time, meaning that the conditions for flow are more important than the context. The choice of relatively low-challenge, low-skill activities during one's free time (e.g. watching TV), supports the notion that deep flow may not be sustainable for extended periods. Additionally, time spent in flow seems to carry over, positively affecting rest-of-life experiences (LeFevre, 1988).

Whatever the causation, with flow comes not only positive psychological feelings of happiness, satisfaction, motivation and creativity but also increased physical resources and resiliency (Demerouti et al., 2012). It is puzzling, then, that some individuals choose to spend free time in states closer to apathy than flow (Csíkszentmihályi, 1988), pointing to the influence of personality or the autotelic characteristic of flow, similar to tourist motivation studies that align personality with trip preferences, notably Plog's (1974) allocentric-psychocentric continuum among others. Those individuals autotelic in nature may be more inclined to travel during leisure to experience deeper flow.

Measuring flow

Csíkszentmihályi's (1975) early observations of flow were captured by means of in-depth interviews with hundreds of individuals identified as intrinsically motivated, from amateur athletes to music composers. While interviews are effective to research the subjective dimensions of experience, they are limited by respondents' memory and reconstruction. Diary methods were an attempt to capture thoughts and feelings, but still lacked spontaneity. The Experience Sampling Method (ESM) developed by Csíkszentmihályi and Larson (1987) signals respondents, typically via a pager or transmitter, to record their activities and corresponding states at random times throughout a typical day over a period of days. This in situ self-reporting technique calls for respondents to answer open-ended or numerical scale items to assess flow 'on the spot'.

Another early advancement in flow methodology came when Massimini and Carli (1988) developed the Four Channel Model to denote the states of anxiety, apathy, boredom and flow, whereby flow is only achieved at the high-challenge, high-skill level. The authors, however, recognized that moment-to-moment daily life experiences may not be captured so simplistically. Employing ESM, they set out to capture a fuller range of personal experiences. Massimini and Carli's (1988) findings, still based on the ratio of challenge to skill, led to the development of the Experience Fluctuation Model with eight channels: arousal, flow, control, boredom, relaxation, apathy, worry and anxiety. While the optimal experience is still considered to be flow, this model recognizes the existence of other positive states, such as

Finding flow in the travel experience

relaxation and arousal. Subsequent studies of flow and methods of measurement advanced in a range of research domains, notably sport, where psychologists strive to understand the contributing factors to peak performance. Translating the dimensions of flow into numerically measurable items, Jackson and Marsh (1996) developed the Flow State Scale (FSS). After testing the psychometric properties of second-order factor models, a nine-factor first-order solution demonstrated the best fit, confirmed by later tests (Stavrou & Zervas, 2004). The FSS consists of 36 items measuring nine dimensions of flow:

i   Challenge–skill balance;
ii   Action–awareness merging;
iii Clear goals;
iv Unambiguous feedback;
v   Concentration on task at hand;
vi Sense of control;
vii Loss of self-consciousness;
viii Transformation of time; and
ix Autotelic experience.

While Csíkszentmihályi's concept of flow is largely accepted, its operationalization and measurement vary. From narrative analysis (Laing & Crouch, 2009) to quantitative scales (Tsaur *et al.* 2013), what has emerged in flow research is a mix of methodological approaches. A notable example is Arnould and Price's (1993) study of extraordinary experiences while white water rafting that uses a range of tools, including interviews, survey, observation and focus groups over a two-year period to illustrate the complex nature of extended service encounters. Others use scales to quantify relationships between flow, experience and resulting outcomes such as happiness (Tsaur *et al.* 2013). Hoffman and Novak (2009) summarize 22 conceptual and structural models of flow and detail the range of uni-dimensional approaches to its measurement, from direct self-report to derived scales, and multidimensional approaches with sets of constructs. Interestingly, ESM, while being the popular method to measure flow in the psychology field and often applied in leisure behaviour studies (Lee, Dattilo & Howard, 1994; Jones et al., 2003), is not common in tourism research where more traditional survey methods dominate.

Jackson, Martin and Eklund (2008) revisited the FSS and developed a short scale of nine items, one item to measure each dimension, to contribute a scale that is theory-based yet pragmatic. In tourism research, flow is most typically measured by some limited number of measures such as (i) pleasure; (ii) focus and (iii) control (Gao, Bai & Park, 2017), or by (i) time, (ii) purpose and (iii) reward (Ayazlar & Yuksel, 2018) for example. A useful table of flow measures, antecedents and outcomes in Bilgihan, Okumus, Nusair and Bujisic's (2014) study highlights the inconsistencies across 44 studies examined. Despite its appeal across a diversity of fields, most notably serious leisure, information technology and, increasingly, tourism, a standard conceptualization is lacking.

Conclusion

The concept of flow, perhaps more so than many other experience concepts, develops our understanding of a range of travel experiences and, most notably, the everyday of travel that is beyond the everyday of daily life. Following this review of flow research through the years

Statia Elliot

and across disciplines, the relevancy of incorporating flow in travel experience research is summarized as follows:

i   The flow–travel relationship connects on several dimensions; extrinsic rewards, absorption, autotelic and matching challenge and skill;

ii The benefits of flow-travel extend from an immediate reward of optimal performance to post-trip psychological and physical well-being;

iii More than other experience concepts, micro flow helps to explain how seemingly ordinary activities such as walking and listening to music can be highly rewarding during free time spent away from the home environment;

iv Flow combines cognitive and affective dimensions to help explain the rewards of planned and structured travel experiences that although not spontaneous, exceed expectations;

v   Marketing research has identified triggers to flow, including sights, sounds, smells, encounters and rituals, from which tourism service providers can benefit;

vi Research of flow in several domains has led to a rich toolbox of measures, including ESM and the FSS, from which tourism experience research can benefit.

Apropos of our times, Csíkszentmihályi (1975) concluded his original text on flow with a warning that 'if we continue to ignore what makes us happy, what makes our life enjoyable, we shall actively help perpetrate the dehumanizing forces which are gaining momentum day by day' (p. 197). He saw crime, mental disease, drug abuse and general discontent worsening, and idealistically hoped to 'maximize flow involvement in as many people as possible' (p. 203), harkening the utopian planners – Plato, Comte, Huxley – before him. 'It is through the flow experience that evolution tricks us to evolve further' (Csíkszentmihályi 1988: 367). Incorporating flow to elevate the tourist experience of discovery and exploration to its fullest potential seems a good place to start

References

Allison, M. T. and Duncan, M. C. (1988) Women, work, and flow. In M. Csíkszentmihályi and I. S. Csíkszentmihályi (Eds.), *Optimal Experience: Psychological Studies of Flow in Consciousness*. New York: Cambridge University Press, pp. 118–137.

Arnould, E. J. and Price, L. L. (1993) River magic: Extraordinary experience and the extended service encounter. *Journal of Consumer Research*, 20(1), 24–45.

Aubert-Gamet, V. (1997) Twisting servicescapes: Diversion of the physical environment in a re-appropriation process. *International Journal of Service Industry Management*, 8(1), 26–41.

Ayazlar, R. A. and Yuksel, A. (2018) Flow experience in paragliding: Effects on experience and life satisfaction. *Tourism Analysis*, 23(4), 461–443.

Beedie, P. and Hudson, S. (2003) Emergence of mountain-based adventure tourism. *Annals of Tourism Research*, 30(3), 625–643.

Bilgihan, A., Okumus, F., Nusair, K. and Bujisic, M. (2014) Online experiences: Flow theory, measuring online customer experience in e-commerce and managerial implications for the lodging industry. *Information, Technology and Tourism*, 14(1), 49–71.

Carù, A. and Cova, B. (2006) *Consuming Experiences*. London: Routledge.

Celsi, R. L., Rose, R. L. and Leigh, T. W. (1993) An exploration of high-risk leisure consumption through skydiving. *Journal of Consumer Research*, 20(1), 1–23.

Csíkszentmihályi, M. (1975) *Beyond Boredom and Anxiety*. San Francisco: Jossey-Bass.

Csíkszentmihályi, M. (1990) *Flow: The Psychology of Optimal Experience*. New York: Harper and Row.

Csíkszentmihályi, M. (1997) *Finding Flow*. New York: Perseus Books.

Csíkszentmihályi, M. and Csíkszentmihályi, I. S. (1988) *Optimal Experience: Psychological Studies of Flow in Consciousness*. New York: Cambridge University Press.

Csíkszentmihályi, M. and Larson, R. (1987) Validity and reliability of the experience-sampling method. *Journal of Nervous and Mental Disease*, 175(9), 526–536.

Csíkszentmihályi, M. and Selega, I. (1990) Adventure and the flow experience. In J. Miles and S. Priest (Eds.), *Adventure Education*. State College: Venture Publishing, pp. 149–155.

Demerouti, E., Bakker, A. B., Sonnentag, S. and Fullagar, C. J. (2012) Work-related flow and energy at work and at home: A study on the role of daily recovery. *Journal of Organizational Behavior*, 33(2), 276–295.

Elkington, S. (2010) Articulating a systematic phenomenology of flow: An experience-process perspective. *Leisure*, 34(3), 327–360.

Farber, M. E. and Hall, T. E. (2007) Emotion and environment: Visitors' extraordinary experience along the Dalton Highway in Alaska. *Journal of Leisure Research*, 39(2), 248–270.

Faullant, R., Matzler, K. and Mooradian, T. A. (2011) Personality, basic emotions, and satisfaction: Primary emotions in the mountaineering experience. *Tourism Management*, 32(6), 1423–1430.

Fredrickson, L. M. and Anderson, D. H. (1999) A qualitative exploration of the wildness experience as a source of spiritual inspiration. *Journal of Environmental Psychology*, 19(1), 21–39.

Frochot, I., Elliot, S. and Kreziak, D. (2017) Digging deep into the experience – flow and immersion patterns in a mountain holiday. *International Journal of Culture, Tourism and Hospitality Research*, 11(1), 81–91.

Gao, L., Bai, X. and Park, A. (2017) Understanding sustained participation in virtual travel communities from the perspectives of IS success model and flow theory. *Journal of Hospitality & Tourism Research*, 41(4), 475–509.

Hoffman, D. L. and Novak, T. P. (2009) Flow online: Lessons learned and future prospects. *Journal of Interactive Marketing*, 23(1), 23–34.

Holbrook, M. B. and Hirschman, E. C. (1982) The experiential aspects of consumption: Consumer fantasies, feelings, and fun. *Journal of Consumer Research*, 9(2), 132–140.

Hom Cary, S. (2004) The tourist moment. *Annals of Tourism Research*, 31(1), 61–77.

Jackson, S. A. and Marsh, H. W. (1996) Development and validation of a scale to measure optimal experience: The flow state scale. *Journal of Sport & Exercise Psychology*, 18(1), 17–35.

Jackson, S. A., Martin, A. J. and Eklund, R. C. (2008) Long and short measures of flow: The construct validity of the FSS-2, DFS-2, and new brief counterparts. *Journal of Sport and Exercise Psychology*, 30(5), 561–587.

James, W. (1917) *The Varieties of Religious Experience: A Study in Human Nature*. New York: Longmans, Green and Co.

Jones, C. D., Hollenhorst, S. J. and Perna, F. (2003) An empirical comparison of the four-channel flow model and adventure experience paradigm. *Leisure Sciences*, 25(1), 17–31.

Kraut, R. (1979) Two conceptions of happiness. *The Philosophical Review*, 88(2), 167–197.

Kreziak, D. and Frochot, I. (2011) Co-construction de l'expérience touristique: Les stratégies des touristes en stations de sport d'hiver. *Décisions Marketing*, 64, 23–33.

Laing, J. H. and Crouch, G. I. (2009) Myth, adventure and fantasy at the frontier: Metaphors and imagery behind an extraordinary travel experience. *International Journal of Tourism Research*, 11(2), 127–141.

Lambert, J., Chapman, J. and Lurie, D. (2013) Challenges to the four-channel model of flow: Primary assumption of flow support the moderate challenging control channel. *Journal of Positive Psychology*, 8(5), 395–403.

Lee, Y., Dattilo, J. and Howard, D. (1994) The complex and dynamic nature of leisure experience. *Journal of Leisure Research*, 26(3), 195–211.

LeFevre, J. (1988) Flow and the quality of experience during work and leisure. In M. Csíkszentmihályi and I. S. Csíkszentmihályi (Eds.), *Optimal Experience: Psychological Studies of Flow in Consciousness*. New York: Cambridge University Press, pp. 307–318.

Levin, J. and Steele, L. (2005) The transcendent experience: Conceptual, theoretical, and epidemiologic perspectives. *Explore*, 1(2), 89–101.

Maslow, A. H. (1962) *Towards a Psychology of Being*. Princeton: Van Nostrand.

Massimini, F. and Carli, M. (1988) The systematic assessment of flow in daily experience. In M. Csíkszentmihályi and Csíkszentmihályi, I. S. (Eds.), *Optimal Experience: Psychological Studies of Flow in Consciousness*. New York: Cambridge University Press, pp. 266–278.

McGinnis, L., Gentry, J. W. and Gao, T. (2008) The impact of flow and communitas on enduring involvement in extended service encounters. *Journal of Service Research*, 11(1), 74–90.

Noy, C. (2004) This trip really changed me: Backpackers' narratives of self-change. *Annals of Tourism Research*, 31(1), 78–102.

Plog, S. C. (1974) Why destination areas rise and fall in popularity. *Cornell Hotel and Restaurant Administration Quarterly*, 14(4), 55–58.

Pomfret, G. (2006) Mountaineering adventure tourists: A conceptual framework for research. *Tourism Management*, 27(1), 113–123.

Pomfret, G. (2011) Package mountaineer tourists holidaying in the French Alps: An evaluation of key influences encouraging their participation. *Tourism Management*, 32(3), 501–510.

Pritchard, A. and Morgan, N. (2006) Hotel Babylon? Exploring hotels as liminal sites of transition and transgression. *Tourism Management*, 27(5), 762–772.

Privette, G. (1983) Peak experience, peak performance and flow: A comparative analysis of positive human experience. *Journal of Personality and Social Psychology*, 45(6), 1361–1368.

Ryan, C. (1995) *Researching Tourist Satisfaction: Issues, Concepts, Problems*. New York: Routledge.

Ryan, C. (1997) The chase of a dream, the end of play. In C. Ryan (Ed.), *The Tourism Experience: A New Introduction*. London: Cassell, pp. 1–24.

Ryan, C. (2011) Ways of conceptualizing the tourist experience: A review of literature. In R. Sharpley and P. R. Stone (Eds.) *Tourist Experience: Contemporary Perspectives*. New York: Routledge, pp. 9–20.

Ryan, R. M. and Deci, E. L. (2001) On happiness and human potentials: A review of research on hedonic and eudaimonic well-being. *Annual Review of Psychology*, 52(1), 141–166.

Ryan, R. M., Trauer, B., Kave, J., Sharma, A. and Sharma, S. (2003) Backpackers – What is the peak experience? *Tourism Recreation Research*, 28(3), 93–98.

Scherer, K. R., Schoor, A. and Johnstone, T. (2001) *Appraisal Processes in Emotion*. New York: Oxford University Press.

Schouten, J. W., McAlexander, J. H. and Koenig, H. F. (2007) Transcendent customer experience and brand community. *Journal of the Academy of Marketing Science*, 35(3), 357–368.

Seligman, M. E. P. and Csíkszentmihályi, M. (2000) Positive psychology: An introduction. *American Psychologist*, 55(1), 5–14.

Stavrou, N. A. and Zervas, Y. (2004) Confirmatory factor analysis of the flow state scale in sports. *Journal of Sport and Exercise Psychology*, 2(2), 161–181.

Stebbins, R. (1992) *Amateurs, Professionals, and Serious Leisure*. Canada: McGill-Queen's University Press.

Stebbins, R. (2007) *Serious Leisure: A Perspective for Our Time*. New Brunswick: Transaction.

Tinsley, H. E. A. and Tinsley, D. J. (1986) A theory of the attributes, benefits and causes of leisure experience. *Leisure Sciences*, 8(1), 1–45.

Tsaur, S., Yen, C. and Hsiao, S. (2013) Transcendent experience, flow and happiness for mountain climbers. *International Journal of Tourism Research*, 15(4), 360–374.

Williams, K. and Harvey, D. (2001) Transcendent experience in forest environments. *Journal of Environmental Psychology*, 21(3), 249–260.

Zahra, A. and McIntosh, A. J. (2007) Volunteer tourism: Evidence of cathartic tourist experiences. *Tourism Recreation Research*, 32(1), 115–119.

9

TOURIST EXPERIENCES AS ATTENTION PRODUCTS

Can-Seng Ooi

Introduction

Individuals have different tourist experiences even if they are doing similar things at the same place. And even if they say that they are enjoying themselves, it does not necessarily mean that they are all having the same positive experiences (Lengkeek, 2001). Social and cultural backgrounds also affect the tourist experience. How, then, is it possible to produce an experience product that will be of wide appeal, interesting and exciting to a myriad of distinct individuals?

A tourist experience is a process that has to be managed. Tourism mediators play an important role in the process of shaping the tourist experience. This chapter presents the attention structure approach to understanding tourist experiences and explains why the control and structuring of visitor attention is at the centre of the tourist experience. As such, it complements the many concepts and theories related to the tourist experience. The attention structure framework also situates the production and consumption of tourist experiences in the 'attention economy' (Davenport & Beck, 2001), and frames tourist experiences as attention products in the context of the experience economy (Hansen & Mossberg, 2017; Mossberg, 2008; Ooi, 2005; Pine & Gilmore, 1999).

The attention structure framework in context

There are at least six overlapping streams of tourist experience research. Each contributes to an understanding of how desired tourist experiential responses are framed, invoked, generated and managed.

The first stream focuses on the importance of cognition. Cognition – that is, knowledge, preconceptions and information – shapes tourist experiences (Jolliffe & Piboonrungroj, 2020; Lee & Shafer, 2002; Ma, Ooi & Hardy, 2018; Wong & Ng, 2020). Stories and themes help visitors make sense of and organize their experiences (Dahles, 2002; Jolliffe & Piboonrungroj, 2020; Ooi, 2002). Destination branding and marketing campaigns, for example, are geared towards shaping visitor pre-conceptions as well as offering them gaze lenses in order to experience a place in a desired manner (Lai & Ooi, 2015). Mass and social media have also become important sources of information that will affect how a tourist

DOI: 10.4324/9781003219866-11

113

interprets and experiences a site (Munar & Ooi, 2012; Ooi & Munar, 2013). Incorrect preconceived knowledge can similarly shape the experience. For instance, in Japan, the swastika is a Buddhist symbol and was until recently used to mark out Buddhist temples on tourist maps. Reactions from visitors were, however, varied, with many remaining uncomfortable even after they had been told that the sign is an old Buddhist symbol. Nevertheless, amid criticisms of pandering to tourist ignorance, the symbol was replaced with a pagoda in tourist maps in time for the 2019 Rugby World Cup and 2020 (rescheduled in 2021) Tokyo Olympics (McCurry, 2016). Our knowledge and preconceptions often define our experience.

The second stream of tourist experience research focuses on personal benefits and identification. Some tourist activities enable tourists to gain experiences that fulfill their personal goals, serve a purpose in their lives and assert their sense of self. Bucket list tourism in particular reflects this personal drive and motivation to experience something at least once, as part of one's identity or being (Thurnell-Read, 2017). Another example is the gay man tourist experience, which does not just involve sexual activities during travels but also includes performing and claiming the gay identity (Vorobjovas-Pinta, 2021; Waitt & Markwell, 2006). Some tourist activities improve the individual's psychological mood and well-being, and/or are highly educational and yet fun (Boksberger, Dolnicar, Laesser & Randle, 2011; Lee & Shafer, 2002; Prentice, Witt & Hamer, 1998). Besides looking at the cognitive dimension in shaping tourist experiences, these personal and felt experiences are sometimes studied through the phenomenological approach that attempts to capture a range of personal experiences that reflect on the individual's sense of who they are, who they want to be and what they want to realize (Cohen, 1979; Goolaup & Solér, 2018; Lengkeek, 2001; Pernecky & Jamal, 2010; Thurnell-Read, 2017). Such an approach highlights the immediacy of personal experiences and how some experiences constitute an individual's being, identity and self.

The third stream focuses on the depth of experiences and the different states of consciousness (Ellis, Morris & Voelkl, 1994; Hansen & Mossberg, 2017; Kuo, Chang, Cheng & Lin, 2016; Wöran & Arnberger, 2012). The most engaging is the 'flow' or 'optimal experience'. It is the mental state that people often describe as immersive, special, meaningful or out-of-the-ordinary (Walker, Hull & Roggenbuck, 1998). These experiences are not only engaging but are also emotionally intense. People may feel a sense of transcendence, spiritualism or even an expansion of their boundaries of self (Csikszentmihalyi, 1993; Sharpley & Jepson, 2011). For example, with the help of mediators, tourists may feel that they are intellectually challenged while they become deeply attentive or lose their sense of time when engaging in an activity (Gyimóthy & Mykletun, 2004; Hansen & Mossberg, 2017; Kuo, Chang, Cheng & Lin, 2016; Wöran & Arnberger, 2012). Optimal experiences highlight the varied depths of tourist experiences. Flow experiences, however, are not necessarily the 'best'; rather, experiences must be understood in context and that different levels of engagement are appropriate for different types of tourist activities.

The fourth stream focuses on the gaps between locals and tourists and how that gap defines the tourist experiential encounter. Through the tourist gaze, Urry (1990) highlighted that visitors notice things that are different from their daily life. Tourists also lack the local knowledge to experience the destination in the same way as residents, which means that tourist experiences are largely reflections of their own backgrounds. Interaction with residents, for instance, is then taken as an important indication of a more authentic experience (Johnson & Neuhofer, 2017; Makkar & Yap, 2020; Wiegerink & Huizing, 2020). At the same time, guest–host interactions also provide new experiences for members of the host community. Some school programs in Kenya, for example, create opportunities for young people to engage with tourists and, in that process, help in skill building, value cultivation

Tourist experiences as attention products

and personal reflection (Jernsand & Goolaup, 2020). Similarly, in the Children's University Tasmania programs, tourist attractions become learning destinations for young people in the community, where they learn about their own (but still 'foreign') heritage, culture, art and history, transforming their local tourist experiences into educational opportunities (Ooi & Shelley, 2019).

The fifth stream concentrates on props and the staging of experiences (Pine & Gilmore, 1999). Unlike other approaches that emphasize personal interpretations and the personal relationship with the product, the staging approach employs the performative and dramaturgical metaphor to argue that engaging experiences depend on the degree to which people actively interact with the product. The atmospherics, physical design and environment and social interaction with other people affect the depth of engagement and the experience (Baker & Kim, 2020). With guidance, props offer the space for performance and the embodied tourism experience, such as dog-sledding in a cold and white Arctic day or interacting playfully with a public art installation (Haanpää & García-Rosell, 2020). The gigantic 'I amsterdam' installation outside the Rijksmuseum in the Dutch capital invited people to play with it (Figure 9.1). It was however, removed, in 2018 because it was too popular and became a symbol of mass tourism (Hitti, 2018).

The sixth stream focuses on the invocation of bodily reactions. Intended experiences are designed through a methodological approach (Smit & Melissen, 2020). It starts from defining the overall problem to testing, improving and creating the solution. For instance, with the help of Electro Dermal Activity sensors and GPS location services, a tour experience can be designed and optimized through a series of touch points, attractions and activities targeted at certain groups of visitors. This approach identifies the latent experiential responses of visitors, tests their responses and then provokes these responses to create the desired experience. Such an approach highlights how experiences can be stimulated, invoked and provoked and

Figure 9.1 The "I amsterdam" installation, Amsterdam
Source: Andrew Watts (Flickr, image originally in colour, https://www.flickr.com/photos/dandrewwatts/3568527081/).

uses similar brain science technology in neuromarketing (Harrell, 2019). There are, however, ethical issues related to the intrusive nature of such research.

These different approaches to understanding tourist experiences complement each other. They are used variedly to design tourist experiences. Attractions like Disneyland and the Louvre, as well as ghost tours and wine tours, are designed to please visitors (Jensen & Sundbo, 2020; Seraphim & Haq, 2020; Smit & Melissen, 2020; Strickland, Jennifer, Frost & Williams, 2020). They tap into cultural backgrounds, personal identities and bodily reactions in producing the sought-after experience. For instance, in the design of wine tours for millennials in Victoria, Australia, these tourists engage in hedonistic activities that appeal to them at different levels. First it is getting to know and appreciate specific wines and coaxing these younger visitors to find related information on the Internet whilst providing other pleasurable activities, such as concerts, art displays and tractor rides (Strickland et al., 2020). Engaging them via social media and providing Internet facilities during the tour is important because that is the dominant channel of access and communication for them. Such a design approach focuses on what the targeted audiences are familiar with, what they want and how to stimulate their senses.

Tourists choose experiences (Jensen & Sundbo, 2020). Commonly, destinations offer a smorgasbord of pleasing activities and facilities to allow tourists to engage and enjoy themselves. However, tourists may also make unexpected decisions. In a study of a four-star hotel in Slovenia, the pro-environmental appeal of the hotel failed to reduce towel reuse and room electricity consumption among guests; the championed green experience in this tourist accommodation may require more tangible benefits for the guests (Dolnicar, Knezevic Cvelbar and Grün, 2017). Providing a range of potential experiences to let tourists choose has its limits. Tourism businesses and tourists choose and evaluate experience elements from different perspectives (Jensen & Sundbo, 2020).

The attention structure framework attempts to bring these different ways of understanding experiences together. The mediation of tourist experiences is important, and the ability to direct tourist attention to relevant and desired details will invoke the desired experience. But there are also distractions that compete for attention. Tourism mediators must manage what to focus on, what to ignore and how to mitigate distractions in a dynamic fashion. It is with this that the following section is concerned.

Experiences as attention products: Three basic elements

Davenport and Beck (2001: 20) define attention as 'focused mental engagement on a particular item of information. Items come into our awareness, we attend to a particular item, and then we decide whether to act.' Our immediate experience depends on what we pay attention to at any given moment, because it is then that we become explicitly aware of the situation. As observed in marketing and advertising, and also during public debates and negotiation, the ability to structure and control people's attention is important. In going beyond awareness, the ability to make people focus on desired details and messages will shape their decisions and actions. Road safety campaigns highlighting the dangers of motorists using their mobile phones are an example of the importance of getting drivers to focus on what they do. The attention economy is particularly fierce on the Internet (Williams, 2018; Wu, 2017). Social media compete to make users stay on their platforms. And for educators who teach online, their recorded lectures may have to compete with funny cat videos on YouTube! Tourism mediators are in the same business of crafting tourist attention and are, thus, attention merchants (Wu, 2017). There are three interrelated elements in capturing and structuring people's attention.

Tourist experiences as attention products

Figure 9.2 Paying attention: Flip-flopping between the right-facing rabbit and the left-facing duck

First, as human beings, we do not and cannot notice everything around us at the same time. Our neuro-physiological make-up entails that we can only focus on one thing at any given moment (Nijboer, Borst, van Rijn & Taatgen, 2014; Polanyi, 1958; Rothbart & Posner, 2015). To illustrate this, Figure 9.2 is a classic picture of two different images. Depending on how we each frame the picture, we can either see a duck facing left or a rabbit facing right. While we may flip our visual attention between the duck and the rabbit, we can still only see one of them at any one fleeting moment in time. This does not deny that we multi-task in our everyday lives; however, it is the result of task-specific interactions and there is no region in the brain that is known for multitasking (Nijboer et al., 2014). Physiologically, we are constrained by what we can focus at any one moment, and that makes attention 'scarce'.

Second, our felt experience is dependent on what we pay attention to and, when our attention shifts, how we feel and sense changes accordingly (Alberts, Martijn, Nievelstein, Jansen & de Vries, 2008). For instance, as a treatment for chronic pain, patients are taught how to switch attention to manage their pain (Eccleston, 1995). While what we pay attention to shapes our experience, this also means that there are things that we have ignored that would change the experience. The many accidents visitors have while taking selfies are examples of people not paying attention to the dangers; their intense excitement in wanting to capture the moment would change drastically if they were to pay attention to the danger they have put themselves in. Tourism mediators who are able to control, shift and structure the attention of visitors will be better placed to craft the tourist experience in the desired direction (Hansen & Mossberg, 2017; Ooi, 2002); they focus the minds of tourists on desired elements, while ignoring less desirable ones.

Third, there are internal-push and external-pull factors in the competition for attention; these factors are interrelated and complementary. Internal-push factors refer to a person's motivation for paying particular attention to certain details to achieve a goal or to enhance and receive pleasure. They may pick up details with which they are already familiar as they make sense of the new situation. As already pointed out, different visitors have their own preconceptions that influence what they pay attention to. For instance, many Chinese visitors to Port Arthur Historic Site in Tasmania, Australia, focus on the beautiful scenery and largely ignore the rich convict built heritage there (Ma, Ooi & Hardy, 2018). The natural beauty resonates more to them than the site's esoteric and seemingly alien convict past. Niche tourism activities, such as in dark tourism, gay tourism and adventure tourism, cater to people who are already drawn to certain things. Besides beautiful sights and pleasant weather, external-pull factors can be negative, such as a screeching noise, pungent smells and dirty streets. Distress distracts from and affects the desired visitor experience. A sense of tourist adventure is often balanced between the fearful unknown and the safe and secure. For example, eating street food in Asia can be a gamble, but authorities in Singapore have sanitized the island's street food culture and have effectively removed the anxiety in tourists as they can experience a form of Oriental exoticism in a hygienic eating environment (Ooi & Tarulevicz, 2019; Tarulevicz & Ooi, 2019).

To summarize, the three interrelated elements in structuring the attention of a human are: one, we can only pay attention to one thing at any one moment in time and that is why attention is scarce; two, what we pay attention to and how our attention shifts affect our immediate felt experience; and three, our attention is drawn by different factors – some stimulate us positively and others negatively. As attention merchants, tourism mediators draw and direct the attention of their customers. These mediators strive to make tourists pay attention to some things and not to some others.

Managing the attention product: attractions and distractions

If tourist experiences are attention products, then how are these products managed? Besides drawing attention to desired elements, the attention product has to be managed as a process. As pointed out in the third characteristic of the human attention structure, tourists pay attention to attractions and distractions. And there are at least four attraction-distraction arenas that tourism mediators have to manage: (i) between different products; (ii) the social cultural contexts in which the product is embedded; (iii) the physical environment in which the product is situated; and (iv), tourist preconceptions of the product. The competition for attention can result in the derailment of desired tourist experiences but also creates opportunities for new and interesting ones.

Attractions and distractions 1: competing and complementing tourist products

Different tourist products compete for attention, and at different levels: destinations compete to draw tourists, attractions in the same city compete for visitors, shops in malls compete for shoppers and different rides in theme parks compete for customers. Even within a museum, exhibits may compete with each other. For example, many visitors to the Vatican Museum are overwhelmed by the variety and number of collections, and many seek out only those they already know, such as Leonardo da Vinci's paintings in the Sistine Chapel.

Some tourist products may not only compete but also send out contradicting or conflicting messages. For instance, many tourist brochures for diverse attractions, ranging from theme parks to nature walks, family restaurants to adult entertainment, are found side-by-side on the brochure rack at visitor centres. The array of and competition between products and attractions can nonetheless generate a sense of excitement and possibilities for visitors. Many cities, such as Copenhagen, Sydney and San Francisco, overwhelm tourists with choices. Such destinations are attractive precisely because of its hustle and bustle. Tourists are bombarded with options, and are able to pick and mix from the diverse range of attractions, and construct their own itinerary and destination experience.

The smorgasbord of tourism offerings in a destination can also lead to confusion. Destination brands are often used to help visitors make sense of a place by providing a brand narrative to bring things together. It provides a set of gaze lenses to structure the visitor experience. For instance, in Malaysia, the diverse offerings reflecting multicultural fabric, its modern cities and tropical rainforests, and the old and the contemporary are framed as 'Truly Asia' (Lai & Ooi, 2015). The destination brand draws attention to a narrative that brings disparate manifestations together to help visitors make sense and have a more engaging and curated experience of an emerging modern Malaysia with strong ties to its rich Asia-wide migrant pasts.

Attractions and distractions 2: noticing contrasting contexts in tourism

Secondly, a tourist product is embedded in social contexts, and these contexts may clash. Commonly, for example, tourists and researchers are concerned with host–guest relations, staged authenticity and the touristification of society; these highlight the discords arising from diverse economic, political and social cultural interests embedded in cultural tourism products (Chhabra, Healy & Sills, 2003; MacCannell, 1992; Ooi, 2013). The increased interest in responsible and ethical tourism challenges tourists and the industry (Jamal, 2019). Those tourists who want to be more responsible may suffer from 'experiential dissonance' (Sundbo, 2020) that occurs when a visitor desires and pursues one tourist experience but another contrasting experience is crucial to the total desired experience. For example, the flight shame movement creates ambivalence and experiential tensions for many environmentally conscious holiday makers (Gössling, Humpe and Bausch, 2020). Likewise, conscience-driven tourists appreciate the affordable warm hospitality they receive, but when they focus on the precarious work situation and the heavy emotional labour in the industry, they feel uncomfortable (Ek, Hardy, Larson & Ooi, 2020; Ooi & Ek, 2010).

Conversely, contrasting social, cultural and economic contexts are sometimes intentionally brought together and accentuated so as to generate interesting experiences. For example, Berlin's Kaiser Wilhelm Memorial Church is resurrected with multiple layers of history coming together in a spectacular manner (depending on one's perspective). It was a neo-Gothic city icon that was bombed during the Second World War and rebuilt in a seemingly incongruent architectural mix of the past and the contemporary. Inevitably the new structure draws controversy and also demonstrates Germany's rebirth and confidence (Zill, 2011). The rebuilt memorial is contentious and confusing for many because of the clash of styles: a sacred place that has become a popular tourist site and a historical site that represents history through disrespectful contemporary interventions. Whether one likes it or not, the historical, social, economic and political layers of interpretations allow visitors to reflect, interpret and appreciate the church, Berlin and Germany in multiple and divergent ways.

Attractions and distractions 3: embodied tourists and the physical environment

Our bodily senses can be distracting, whether that is the need to use the toilet, being ill-prepared for blustery weather or recovering from a hangover. The surrounding environment can also generate bodily reactions that distract. For example, visitors driving around Tasmania are often shocked when they see dead wild animals by the road; this detracts and diminishes their scenic drive experience (Leurs, 2020). The physical environment and conditions often draw attention away from the promoted product if they trigger or aggravate undesirable embodied responses. People pay attention not only to attractive stimuli, but also to stimuli that bring about physical discomfort and psychological stress. Alternatively, visitors to Ribe Viking Museum in Denmark will encounter the pungent smell of dried fish as soon as they enter a re-constructed Viking fishing village in a gallery; this is however considered appropriate and is intentional.

Feeling unsafe and anxious detracts from the intended experience. Allaying anxiety is important in crafting the tourist experience (Ma et al., 2018; Tjiptono & Yang, 2018; Yang, Khoo-Lattimore & Arcodia, 2017). Different people have different levels of travel anxiety, and markets have been segmented accordingly (Dolnicar, 2005; Seabra, Dolnicar, Abrantes & Kastenholz, 2013). So unless it is part of the intended experience, such as going on a ghost tour or taking a thrill ride, feeling comfortable and not being anxious in the environment are conditions that are needed to craft the desired experience.

Attractions and distractions 4: reference points and searching for the expected

Fourthly, what a product tries to offer may be ignored because tourists have their own expectations and preconceptions. Tourists judge tourism products through their own observations and imaginations. McIntosh and Prentice's (1999) study of visitors to three English heritage sites shows that tourists judge the authenticity of their experience by affirming their preconceptions. Tourists notice what they expect and what they already know. These are their reference points, which are cognitive and emotional details that resonate and provoke spontaneous interpretative and evaluative responses from individuals (Rosch, 1975; Walmsley & Jenkins, 1992). Narrating a web of familiar reference points enables tourism mediators to weave a narrative that is more entwined in the visitor's worldviews. Some preconceptions can be wrong; for example, the popular depiction of Vikings wearing horned helmets has created souvenirs that are popular, and Viking museums in Denmark, Norway and Iceland find it an uphill task to correct this misconception. Similarly, tourists' propensity to seek out what they are already familiar explains why many destinations are offering similar experiences and products (Ooi, 2011, 2014). For example, cities compete to host the Olympics, create similar art biennales and build globally recognized theme parks such as Universal Studios. Visitors are familiar with these references, and have preconceptions and expectations of these events and products.

Crafting attention products

These four attraction–distraction arenas are resources for the crafting of the attention product. Besides drawing attention to desired elements, potential distractions and distractions have to be managed. The crafting process invokes latent elements (e.g. cultural reference points, potential controversies) and overt ones (e.g. confront the senses, pointing out potential dangers).

There are distractions that cannot be hidden or crafted away. The Singapore Tourism Board (STB), for instance, has always been quite transparent with environmental and health crises in the city-state. The almost annual smog that engulfs large swathe of Southeast Asia is unhealthy and detracts tourists from enjoying themselves. The Singaporean authorities have since set up a dedicated website to inform residents and visitors about the island's air quality (www.haze.gov.sg). If necessary, STB provides health advice to visitors, even though such information highlights the severity of the pollution and discourages visitation. For the Formula One races in 2019, the authorities were ready to provide respiratory masks because the air quality was seriously then threatened by land-clearing fires in Sumatra. The dire situation was made public globally and spectators were informed through the smog-tracking website (Illmer, 2019). Visitors have to decide if they want to visit or not.

Marketing materials feature only beautiful shots, and they are often misleading. People know that. Regardless, less desirable elements of the experience that cannot be mitigated, such as the smog in Singapore, can be reframed as a lesson on transnational environmental challenges. Narratives are used by mediators to craft the tourist experience to weave the diverse elements that attract and distract the attention of visitors. The crafting process will always have room for co-creation and alternative interpretations by tourists because a

Tourist experiences as attention products

tourist's own interests and background are part of the experience. Nevertheless, the attention structure approach dissects the tourist experience, and frames the dynamic emergence of the experience. Table 9.1 summarizes the arguments, and also presents certain attention structure tactics to craft desired experiences.

Table 9.1 Summary of the attraction–distraction arenas, and attention structure tactics

	Potential distractions	Attention product tactics	
		Attracting and keeping tourists' attention	Appropriating (potential or otherwise) distractions
Competition between tourist products	• Tourists lack awareness of the products • Unaware of significance and details of the products • Distraction from other products	• Advertising and marketing to raise awareness • Offer information and narratives to interest tourists • Accentuate selected elements of the products	• Generate excitement through the variety of products • Combine different products into a broader "supermarket" mix of exciting tourism experiences
The environment and amenities: Minimize psychological and physical distractions	• Personal responses: costs, hunger, discomfort, fear, insecurity • Environmental distractions, e.g. weather, traffic, physical conditions	• Transparency about costs, and offering facilities and amenities. • Enhance sense of security, e.g. provide information for emergency help • Comfortable environment to eliminate or mitigate physical discomforts, e.g. air conditioning, amenities and facilities (toilets, etc.)	• Mitigate discomfort or at least address environmental distractions by setting expectations or storying it into the narrative • Appropriate environmental distractions into the experience product, e.g. providing rain gear at a usually wet place
Competing and contrasting contexts: scepticism arising from tourism motive in activities	• Commercial interests inevitably embedded in tourist cultural and environmental activities • Modern presentation of heritage products	• Offer detailed information to incorporate different social contexts into understanding the product • Help tourists go native	• Create a dynamic product by bringing contrasting elements and contexts together • Engage tourists by layering the stories, and making them think about their role in the host society
Preconceptions and reference points: Expectations and cognitive dissonance	• Tourists have correct and/ or wrong pre-conceptions • Tourists have unrealistic expectations	• Control attention and make them notice things that will correct their misconceptions • Accentuate selected sensory perceptions to mark desired experience, e.g. stop to smell the forest	• Set and reframe expectations by addressing preconceptions • Highlight misconceptions and story into the experience.

Lessons

The various approaches to studying tourist experiences as presented in the brief literature review highlight the importance of understanding tourist experiences in different ways. These approaches are important because tourists' expectations, preconceptions and preferences affect what tourists notice and how they interpret and experience the product. The attention structure framework acknowledges the importance of tourists' cognition and psychological make-up. It also acknowledges the existential nature of experiences and shows how experiences may diverge from what is planned because of different types of distractions. These distractions are not necessarily disruptive, but can be mitigated, appropriated into the experience product or made into attractions themselves. The framework also alerts us to the social context of tourism consumption, tourist responses to the physical environment and the competition for attention between products. In other words, what is considered an attraction or a distraction is negotiated, depending on how the element is framed and interpreted by tourists and tourism mediators.

In the first paragraph of this chapter, a question was posed: how is it possible to produce an experience product that is widely appealing, interesting and exciting to a range of different individuals with different backgrounds? The attention structure framework points to a fluid, dynamic and holistic way of understanding the emergence of experiences. In the competition for attention, the negotiation between tourist products and other competing elements can generate interesting tourist experiences. No two persons will have the same experience but, by directing their attention to selected elements and responding to their backgrounds and reactions, tourism mediators are at least able to craft experiences in the desired direction. And some lessons can be learned from the attention structure framework.

One, tourism mediators are attention merchants. They play a vital role in the crafting of experiences. They play the role of selecting and accentuating items for tourist consumption. Tourists visit a place for only a short period of time, lack local knowledge and are unlikely to invest much time and effort in getting to know a destination in any depth. Tourism mediators offer a shortcut by drawing attention to sights and sites that are interesting and significant. These mediators also educate tourists with information and details, which enriches the experience. This also means that products that are not mediated can lead to unintended tourist experiences because the visitors will notice and interpret the attraction in their own ways.

Two, distinctive local products may not attract or engage visitors in meaningful ways. Tourists do not normally have the luxury or the desire to do the necessary research and to acquire the deep knowledge to engage with the host community. Tourists will inevitably appreciate attractions with their own backgrounds, which may make the attraction less distinctive in their own judgment. But ironically that experience may be more engaging because it is endeared to the tourist's own worldview.

Three, there are different ways to draw attention. For instance, during a ghost tour, the guide may whisper and then raised her voice when telling an eerie story to create the shock effect. Similarly, a big structure that stands out from the surrounding has a special quality in itself, like the Eiffel Tower and the Pyramids. People notice. The competition to being the loudest, biggest and best may just create a carnivalesque mess at a destination unless an attention-drawing narrative, such as a brand story, is at hand to pull all together.

Four, many tourist experience accounts can be reconfigured. An experience is constituted by a series of moments. Each series of moments is shaped by what the tourist pays attention to. Williams presented the two broad meanings of experience: '(i) knowledge gathered from past events, whether by conscious observation or by consideration and reflection; and (ii) a

Tourist experiences as attention products

Figure 9.3 A packaged experience: Memories from a Disneyland Shanghai visitor (the author) who unexpectedly enjoyed himself *Photographs:* Can-Seng Ooi

particular kind of consciousness, which can in some contexts be distinguished from "reason" or knowledge' (Williams, 1976: 126). The two different framings highlight the temporal dimension of experiencing. The first refers to the building up and the subsequent reflection and evaluation of a series of encounters, such as someone talking about her two-week experience in Spain. The second framing is about the immediate and felt consciousness that is subjective and emotional. The second is not rational but personally felt at the moment in time. Both types of experiences are interrelated. A series of immediately felt experiences during a visit to Disneyland, for instance, can be packaged into an enjoyable day-trip experience. I was a (reluctant) visitor to Disneyland Shanghai and enjoyed myself thoroughly (Figure 9.3). The diverse experiences from the Caribbean of the Pirates thrill-ride, encounter with Darth Vader, seeing Mickey Mouse and friends performing made for an enjoyable day. In other words, experiences can be packaged and repackaged.

Five, ignoring salient issues does not mean that tourists will not be distracted. Marketing materials do not usually highlight bad weather conditions and that may set unrealistic expectations. Distractions have to be mitigated, addressed and even appropriated. Offering shelter and equipment for people to move around a natural park in bad weather would enhance the experience. Talking to misconceptions directly will provide for educational and interesting experiences. And distractions can even be turned into attractions, such as doing the challenge of crossing the busy and haphazard roads of Ho Chi Minh City in Vietnam in a safe way.

These five lessons demonstrate how the attention structure framework complements and builds on the different streams of tourist experience research. The tourist experience is one that can be crafted even though it would not be possible to ensure that two visitors will have the same positive experience.

References

Alberts, H. J. E. M., Martijn, C., Nievelstein, F., Jansen, A. and de Vries, N. K. (2008) Distracting the Self: Shifting Attention Prevents Ego Depletion. *Self and Identity*, 7(3), 322–334.

Baker, M. A. and Kim, K. (2020) The service experiencescape. In S. K. Dixit (Ed.), *The Routledge Handbook of Tourism Experience Management and Marketing*. Abingdon: Routledge, pp. 150–158.

Boksberger, P., Dolnicar, S., Laesser, C. and Randle, M. (2011) Self-congruity theory: To what extent does it hold in tourism? *Journal of Travel Research*, 50(4), 454–464.

Chhabra, D., Healy, R. and Sills, E. (2003) Staged authenticity and heritage tourism. *Annals of Tourism Research*, 30(3), 702–719.

Cohen, E. (1979) A phenomenology of tourist experiences. *Sociology*, 13, 179–201.

Csikszentmihalyi, M. (1993) *The Evolving Self: A Psychology for the Third Millenium*. New York: Harper Collins.

Dahles, H. (2002) The politics of tour guiding. *Annals of Tourism Research*, 29(3), 783–800.

Davenport, T. H. and Beck, J. C. (2001) *The Attention Economy: Understanding te New Currency of Busines*. Boston: Harvard Business School Press.

Dolnicar, S. (2005) Understanding barriers to leisure travel: Tourist fears as a marketing basis. *Journal of Vacation Marketing*, 11(3), 197–208.

Dolnicar, S., Knezevic Cvelbar, L. and Grün, B. (2017) Do pro-environmental appeals trigger pro-environmental behavior in hotel guests? *Journal of Travel Research*, 56(8), 988–997.

Eccleston, C. (1995) Chronic pain and distraction: An experimental investigation into the role of sustained and shifting attention in the processing of chronic persistent pain. *Behaviour Research and Therapy*, 33(4), 391–405.

Ek, R., Hardy, A., Larson, M. and Ooi, C. (2020) The emotional labor of the co-created tourism experience. In S. K. Dixit (Ed.), *The Routledge Handbook of Tourism Experience Management and Marketing*. Abingdon: Routledge, pp. 550–559.

Ellis, G. D., Morris, C. and Voelkl, J. E. (1994) Measurement and analysis issues with explanation of variance in daily experience using the Flow Model. *Journal of Leisure Research*, 26(4), 337–356.

Goolaup, S. and Solér, C. (2018) Existential-phenomenology: Understanding tourists' experiences. In R. Nunkoo (Ed.), *Handbook of Research Methods for Tourism and Hospitality Management*. Cheltenham: Edward Elgar Publishing., pp. 62–71.

Gössling, S., Humpe, A. and Bausch, T. (2020) Does 'flight shame' affect social norms? Changing perspectives on the desirability of air travel in Germany. *Journal of Cleaner Production*, 266. https://doi.org/10.1016/j.jclepro.2020.122015

Gyimóthy, S. and Mykletun, R. J. (2004) Play in adventure tourism. *Annals of Tourism Research*, 31(4), 855–878.

Haanpää, M. and García-Rosell, J.-C. (2020) Understanding performativity and embodied tourism expeirences in animal-based tourism in the Arctic. In S. K. Dixit (Ed.), *The Routledge Handbook of Tourism Experience Management and Marketing*. Abingdon: Routledge, pp. 229–237.

Hansen, A. H. and Mossberg, L. (2017) Tour guides' performance and tourists' immersion: Facilitating consumer immersion by performing a guide plus role. *Scandinavian Journal of Hospitality and Tourism*, 17(3), 259–278.

Harrell, E. (2019)Neuromarketing: What you need to know. *Harvard Business Review*. Available tat https://hbr.org/2019/01/neuromarketing-what-you-need-to-know

Hitti, N. (2018, December). Amsterdam council removes "I amsterdam" sign after it becomes selfie spot. *De Zeen*, 5 December. Available at: https://www.dezeen.com/2018/12/05/i-amsterdam-sign-removed-council-mass-tourism/ (Accessed 21 November 2020).

Illmer, A. (2019). Singapore Grand Prix: How will haze affect the drivers and fans? *BBC News*, 20 Septemebr. Available at: https://www.bbc.com/news/world-asia-49737216 (Accessed 21 November 2020).

Jamal, T. (2019) *Justice and Ethics in Tourism*. Abingdon: Routledge.

Jensen, J. F. and Sundbo, J. (2020) Experiential choice in tourism. In S. K. Dixit (Ed.), *Routledge Handbook of Tourism Experience Management and Marketing.* London: Routledge, pp. 140–149.

Jernsand, E. M. and Goolaup, S. (2020) Learning through extraordinary tourism experiences. In S. K. Dixit (Ed.), *The Routledge Handbook of Tourism Experience Management and Marketing.* Abingdon: Routledge, pp. 173–182.

Johnson, A.-G. and Neuhofer, B. (2017) Airbnb: An exploration of value co-creation experiences in Jamaica. *International Journal of Contemporary Hospitality Management,* 29(9), 2361–2376.

Jolliffe, L. and Piboonrungroj, P. (2020) The role of themes and stories in tourism experiences. In S. K. Dixit (Ed.), *The Routledge Handbook of Tourism Experience Management and Marketing.* Abingdon: Routledge, pp. 218–228.

Kuo, N.-T., Chang, K.-C., Cheng, Y.-S. and Lin, J.-C. (2016) *Journal of Travel & Tourism Marketing,* 33(supp.1), 103–122.

Lai, S. and Ooi, C.-S. (2015) Branded as a World Heritage city: The politics afterwards. *Place Branding and Public Diplomacy,* 11(4), 276–292.

Lee, B. and Shafer, C. S. (2002) The dynamic nature of leisure Eeperience: An application of affect control theory. *Journal of Leisure Research,* 34(3), 290–310.

Lengkeek, J. (2001) Leisure experience and imagination: Rethinking Cohen's modes of tourist experience. *International Sociology,* 16(2), 173–184.

Leurs, E. (2020) Bloody tourism: Roadkill and tourists on Tasmanian roads. In C. Ooi and A. Hardy (Eds.), *Tourism in Tasmania.* Hobart: Forty South, pp. 52–60.

Ma, Y., Ooi, C.-S. and Hardy, A. (2018) Chinese travelling overseas and their anxieties. In E. Yang and C. Khoo-Lattimore (Eds.), *Asian Cultures and Contemporary Tourism. Perspectives on Asian Tourism.* Singapore: Springer, pp. 201–220.

MacCannell, D. (1992) *Empty Meeting Grounds: The Tourist Papers.* London and New York: Routledge.

Makkar, M. and Yap, S.-F. (2020) Managing hearts and minds: Romanticizing Airbnb experiences. *Current Issues in Tourism,* 1–20. Online: https://doi.org/10.1080/13683500.2020.1792855

McCurry, J. (2016) Japan to drop the swastika from its tourist maps, *The Guardian.* 21 January. Available at: https://www.theguardian.com/world/2016/jan/20/japan-to-drop-the-swastika-from-its-tourist-maps

McIntosh, A. J. and Prentice, R. C. (1999) Affirming authenticity: Consuming cultural heritage. *Annals of Tourism Research,* 26(3), 589–612.

Mossberg, L. (2008) Extraordinary experiences through storytelling. *Scandinavian Journal of Hospitality and Tourism,* 8(3), 195–210.

Munar, A. M. and Ooi, C.-S. (2012) The truth of the crowds: Social media and the heritage experience. In L. Smith, E. Waterton and S. Watson (Eds.), *The Cultural Moment in Tourism.* Abingdon: Routledge, pp. 255–273.

Nijboer, M., Borst, J., van Rijn, H. and Taatgen, N. (2014) Single-task fMRI overlap predicts concurrent multitasking interference. *NeuroImage,* 100, 60–74.

Ooi, C.-S. (2002) *Cultural Tourism and Tourism Cultures: The Business of Mediating Experiences in Copenhagen and Singapore.* Copenhagen: Copenhagen Business School Press.

Ooi, C.-S. (2005) A theory of tourism experiences. In T. O'Dell and P. Billing (Eds.), *Experiencescape: Culture, Tourism and Economy.* Copenhagen: Copenhagen Business School Press, pp. 51–68.

Ooi, C.-S. (2011) Branding and the accreditation approach: Singapore. In N. J. Morgan, A. Pritchard and R. Pride (Eds.), *Destination Brands: Managing Place Reputation.* Oxford: Elsevier, pp. 185–196.

Ooi, C.-S. (2013) Tourism policy challenges: Balancing acts, co-operative stakeholders and maintaining authenticity. In M. Smith and G. Richards (Eds.), *Routledge Handbook of Cultural Tourism.* Abingdon: Routledge, pp. 67–74.

Ooi, C.-S. (2014) The making of the copy-cat city: Accreditation tactics in place branding. In P. O. Berg and E. Bjoerner (Eds.), *Branding Chinese Mega-Cities.* Cheltenham: Edward Elgar Publishing, pp. 232–248.

Ooi, C.-S. and Ek, R. (2010) Culture, work and emotion. *Culture Unbound: Journal of Current Cultural Research,* 2(3), 303–310.

Ooi, C.-S. and Munar, A. M. (2013) The digital social construction of Ground Zero. In A. Maria Munar, S. Gyimothy and L. A. Cai (Eds.), *Tourism Social Media: Transformations in Identity, Community and Culture.* Bingley: Emerald, pp. 159–175.

Ooi, C.-S. and Shelley, B. (2019) The Children's University Tasmania: The Transformative Power of Tourism. In T. Jamal (Ed.), *Justice and Ethics in Tourism.* Abingdon: Routledge, pp. 222–228.

Ooi, C. and Tarulevicz, N. (2019) From Third World to First World: Tourism, food safety and the making of modern Singapore. In E. Park, S. Kim and I. Yeoman (Eds.), *Food Tourism in Asia*. Singapore: Springer, pp. 73–88.

Pernecky, T. and Jamal, T. (2010) (Hermeneutic) phenomenology in tourism studies. *Annals of Tourism Research*, 37(4), 1055–1075.

Pine, B. J. and Gilmore, J. H. (1999) *The Experience Economy: Work is Theatre and Every Business a Stage*. Boston: Harvard Business School Press.

Polanyi, M. (1958) *Personal Knowledge: Towards a Post Critical Philosophy*. Chicago: University of Chicago Press.

Prentice, R. C., Witt, S. F. and Hamer, C. (1998) Tourism as experience : The case of heritage parks. *Annals of Tourism Research*, 25(1), 1–24.

Rosch, E. (1975) Cognitive reference points. *Cognitive Psychology*, 7(4), 532–547.

Rothbart, M. K. and Posner, M. I. (2015) The developing brain in a multitasking world. *Developmental Review*, 35(March), 42–63.

Seabra, C., Dolnicar, S., Abrantes, J. L. and Kastenholz, E. (2013) Heterogeneity in risk and safety perceptions of international tourists. *Tourism Management*, 36, 502–510.

Seraphim, J. and Haq, F. (2020) Experiential heritage tourism designing in the United Arab Emirates. In S. K. Dixit (Ed.), *The Routledge Handbook of Tourism Experience Management and Marketing*. Abingdon: Routledge, pp. 195–206.

Sharpley, R. and Jepson, D. (2011) Rural tourism: A spiritual experience? *Annals of Tourism Research*, 38(1), 52–71.

Smit, B. and Melissen, F. (2020) Understanding the experience design process. In S. K. Dixit (Ed.), *The Routledge Handbook of Tourism Experience Management and Marketing*. London: Routledge, pp. 131–139.

Strickland, P., Jennifer, L., Frost, W. and Williams, K. M. (2020) Trends in experience design: Strategies for attracting millennials to wineries in Victoria, Australia. In S. K. Dixit (Ed.), *The Routledge Handbook of Tourism Experience Management and Marketing*. Abingdon: Routledge, pp. 207–217.

Sundbo, J. (2020) Experiential dissonance. In S. K. Dixit (Ed.), *The Routledge Handbook of Tourism Experience Management and Marketing*. Abingdon: Routledge, pp. 238–245.

Tarulevicz, N. and Ooi, C.-S. (2019) Food safety and tourism in Singapore: Between microbial Russian roulette and Michelin stars. *Tourism Geographies*, 1–23. https://doi.org/10.1080/1461668 8.2019.1654540.

Thurnell-Read, T. (2017) 'What's on your Bucket List?': Tourism, identity and imperative experiential discourse. *Annals of Tourism Research*, 67, 58–66.

Tjiptono, F. and Yang, L. (2018) To go or not to go: A typology of Asian tourist destination avoidance. In E. Yang and C. Khoo-Lattimore (Eds.), *Asian Cultures and Contemporary Tourism. Perspectives on Asian Tourism*. Singapore: Springer, pp. 183–200.

Urry, J. (1990) *The Tourist Gaze: Leisure and Travel in Contemporary Societies*. London: Sage Publications.

Vorobjovas-Pinta, O. (Ed.) (2021) *Gay Tourism: New Perspectives*. Bristol: Channel View Publications.

Waitt, G. and Markwell, K. (2006) *Gay Tourism: Culture and Context*. London: Routledge.

Walker, G. J., Hull IV, R. B. and Roggenbuck, J. W. (1998) On-site optimal experiences and their relationship to off-site benefits. *Journal of Leisure Research*, 30(4), 453–471.

Walmsley, D. J. and Jenkins, J. M. (1992) Tourism cognitive mapping of unfamiliar environments. *Annals of Tourism Research*, 19(2), 268–286.

Wiegerink, K. and Huizing, J. (2020) Resident-driven city hospitality design and delivery. In S. K. Dixit (Ed.), *The Routledge Handbook of Tourism Experience Management and Marketing*. Abingdon: Routledge, pp. 183–194.

Williams, J. (2018) *Stand Out of Our Light: Freedom and Resistance in the Attention Economy*. Cambridge: Cambridge University Press.

Williams, R. (1976). Culture. In *Keywords* (pp. 87–93). London: Fontana Press.

Wong, B. K. M. and Ng, C. Y. N. (2020) Exploring image, perception and motivation in tourism experience. In S. K. Dixit (Ed.), *The Routledge Handbook of Tourism Experience Management and Marketing*. Abingdon: Routledge, pp. 159–172.

Wöran, B. and Arnberger, A. (2012) Exploring relationships between recreation specialization, restorative environments and mountain hikers' flow experience. *Leisure Sciences*, 34(2), 95–114.

Wu, T. (2017) *The Attention Merchants*. London: Atlantic Books.

Yang, E. C. L., Khoo-Lattimore, C. and Arcodia, C. (2017) A systematic literature review of risk and gender research in tourism. *Tourism Management*, 58, 89–100. https://doi.org/10.1016/j.tourman.2016.10.011

Zill, R. (2011) 'A true witness of transience': Berlin's Kaiser-Wilhelm-Gedächtniskirche and the symbolic use of architectural fragments in modernity. *European Review of History: Revue Europeenne d'histoire*, 18(5–6), 811–827.

10

TOURIST EXPERIENCE

A semiotic perspective

Richard Voase

Semiosis and the human habitat

…Humans…live in a forest of symbols…and to understand what makes humans tick, it is necessary to understand how those symbols work.

(Renfrew, 2007: 107)

The capacity to think in symbolic terms is definitive of *homo sapiens*. Thus, any attempt to understand the tourist experience requires an understanding of how this peculiarly human facility works. Urry (1990: 139) suggested the tourist could be considered an 'amateur semiotician' who travels the world, creates a photographic record, selects and makes purchases representative of the trip and collects mementos. The intention in this chapter is to equip the reader with an understanding of what will be termed the 'semiotic toolbox': that is to say, the body of concepts and terminology by which semiotic analysis can be undertaken. Thereafter, a selection of semiotic practices will be surveyed. These practices include the deployment of semiotics in advertising, the tourist's own semiotic practices as represented in the acquisition of souvenirs, mementos and photographs, and the acquisition and use of holiday clothing. A recurring theme will be the array of semiotic connotations known as 'lifestyle'. Finally, attempts to engineer symbolic image for tourist destinations – the poorly understood matter of 'branding' – will be subjected to critical review.

Prior to embarking on this journey, however, an understanding of terminology needs to be established. In other words, two terms, namely 'semiotics' and 'semiology', are in currency. While they are for the most part synonymous, this author will speak of 'semiotics' as the usage and analysis of symbols, and 'semiology' as the study of the nature and appearance of symbols. A 'symbol' itself, as explained further below, is a sign for which a secondary meaning has been pre-learned. Symbols 'work' when human subjects share an understanding. The exposition in the chapter draws on a selection of established sources that outline the concepts and contexts of semiology, whilst recent sources offering similar treatments include Echtner (1999), Metro-Roland (2009), Tresidder (2011) and Knudsen, Rickly and Metro-Roland (2016).

128

DOI: 10.4324/9781003219866-12

Introducing the semiotic toolbox

Grounded in work undertaken in the twentieth century by Ferdinand de Saussure and Charles Sanders Peirce, semiology posits a relationship between a *signifier* as a vehicle of meaning, and a *signified*, which is the concept conveyed by the vehicle (Dyer, 1982: 118; Lash, 1990: 5; Myers, 1994: 137). The signifier and signified, together, constitute a *sign*. For example, he who writes these words has a name: Richard Voase. The words 'Richard Voase' are not the same as the sentient being who is typing these words into a keyboard. 'Richard Voase' is a combination of words that serves as a signifier of that being. The connection with the author is *signified* wherever it appears, for example, at the head of this chapter as the named author. A more prosaic example may be the presence of the words 'Richard Voase' on an office door at the University of Lincoln. What is signified, by the presence of the signifier on the door, is that the author occupies that room. Put simply, I have a sign on my door.

Of particular interest are the relationships *between* signs. A *paradigmatic* relationship can be understood as the relationship between a particular sign and other possible substitutes. For example, when a human subject gets dressed in the morning, paradigmatic decisions are taken in terms of choice of clothing. Weather conditions will influence the choice, but most human subjects will have a range of options available and will make the decision according to mood, and the anticipated requirements of the day. Should one wear the Harris Tweed jacket or the corduroy jacket? Accompanying such a paradigmatic decision may be some consideration as to what to wear *with* the jacket. That decision is *syntagmatic* in character. Syntagmatic relationships are the way in which a particular sign joins with other related signs to generate meaning (Mick, 1986: 197). Weather conditions may continue to influence the choice, but 'what it looks like with the jacket' will play some role. Therefore, despite having only just got out of bed, the author has become an amateur semiotician. 'Style' is about the construction of sign-systems: the practice of making effective paradigmatic and syntagmatic choices when selecting clothing. This topic will be revisited later in the chapter, when the matter of the purchase and selection of holiday clothing is addressed.

From the work of Peirce come other useful terms: the *iconic, indexical* and *symbolic* sign (Dyer, 1982: 139; Mick, 1986: 199). The term 'iconic' has become over-used in recent years to indicate something that is distinctive and well-recognized. For example, one may speak of an 'iconic building'. However, in the technical sense used by Peirce, an *iconic* sign enjoys a direct link with its subject matter; it is pure or direct representation. For example, an application for a passport must be accompanied by a photograph that directly represents the intended passport-holder. An *indexical* sign, by contrast, is one step removed from the object of representation. It represents the object through some associated link. For example, show a photograph of the Eiffel Tower to an audience and ask them what comes into their heads, and they will say, 'Paris'. The Eiffel Tower serves as an indexical sign of Paris. Like the index finger, it points to something else.

A symbolic sign, by contrast, may have no iconic or indexical connection with the meaning that readers generate from it. The illustration offered by French literary theorist and semiotician Roland Barthes is that of the red rose (Barthes, 1972: 113). A single red rose, seen as one illustration alongside many others in an encyclopaedia of flora, would have no special significance. But purchased as a gift on St Valentine's Day, and handed from one person to another, a red rose generates a special meaning. Putting it another way, at one level a red rose is a mere plant. At a second level that we will explore shortly, namely the level of *signification*, the rose enjoys a second status, as a signifier of love. Handed from the one to the other, that which is signified is a state of love, or proclaimed love. The presentation of the rose is thus a *sign* of love. The crucial element is that the intended meaning of the rose-as-signifier-of-love is shared by giver and recipient. This is why the giving of the rose is a *symbolic* act. If the significance of the rose has not pre-learned and understood by both parties, the gesture means no more than one person handing a plant to another.

Semiosis in advertising

Barthes (1972: 112) accepted de Saussure's premise that semiology suggests a relationship between a signifier and signified. However, he explored the idea that, as in the case of the red rose, signs can work at two levels: the *denotative* level and the *connotative* or *mythical* level (1972: 114, 1977: 37; Woollacott, 1982: 99). Barthes (1972: 117) uses the term *signification* to refer to this connotative, second-level sign. Applying the ideas of De Saussure, Peirce and others to the interpretation of advertisements, he introduced two terms by which the relationship between text and image can be understood. *Anchorage* refers to the way in which text and image are juxtaposed to 'anchor' the meaning of the advertisement, whilst *relay* refers to the way in which, in some advertisements, the reader is led back and forth from text to image in the attempt to convey the intended meaning, as in the case of cartoon strips (Barthes, 1977: 38–41; Myers, 1994: 142). Where text and image are in turn anchored by a third discursive form, such as music as in televisual and cinematic advertisements, the effect can be referred to as 'intertextuality'.

These concepts are deployed to considerable effect in an engagingly simple advertisement for P&O cruises reproduced by Finn, Elliott-White and Walton (2000: 153). An image of a cruise ship is shown at night, on a calm sea, with a large moon behind. The legend at the top reads, 'Cannes, Rome, Casablanca, via the Sea of Tranquillity'. The selling proposition at the foot is aimed primarily at those who have not yet taken a cruise holiday. It concludes by advising that, 'Before making such a giant leap, however, you must take that one small step'. The calm sea is anchored by the mention of the 'Sea of Tranquillity'. The moon is anchored both by the reference to the 'Sea of Tranquillity' and the allusion to astronaut Neil Armstrong's words when stepping onto the moon for the first time: 'One small step for man, one giant leap for mankind'. However, the symbolic significance only works if it is pre-learned. The advertisement, to work to full effect, relies on the reader (a) knowing there is a feature on the moon known as the Sea of Tranquillity and (b) familiarity with Neil Armstrong's words (Finn, Elliott-White and Walton, 2000: 152–3).

That leads to the need to comprehend the means by which the reader understands the symbolic message. Reference has been made to an understanding that is shared and pre-learned. This is where a third element, termed the *referent* or *interpretant*, becomes a crucial factor. The referent is pre-loaded, so to speak, in the mind as a result of previous exposure. Frequently, referents will be mythological in character and representative of, and embedded in, the cultures of the societies that produce them (Barthes, 1977: 49; Hall, 1980: 133; Williamson, 1978: 19–20). For example, the status of the red rose as a signifier of love has antecedence in as much as the Scottish poet Robert Burns wrote, in 1794, that *My Love is Like a Red Red Rose*. Barthes' term for the operation of signification at the mythical level is the *rhetorical system* (Barthes, 1977: 49; Culler, 1983: 75). The giving of the red rose is a *symbolic sign* that requires both parties to be aware of the 'myth' that surrounds the red rose. Meaning is not 'out there'; it is generated in the mind. The post-structuralist thinker Jacques Derrida memorably pointed out that *il n'a pas de hors-texte* (Derrida, 1997: 158). This does

Tourist experience: a semiotic perspective

not translate readily into English, but Derrida's point is that a visual image is nothing more than representation and text is nothing more than words on a page. Meaning is generated only when the image is viewed, or the words are read, or heard. This insight was not lost on William Shakespeare, who concludes one of his more famous sonnets, written to an imagined lady-friend, *Shall I Compare Thee to a Summer's Day?* (sonnet XVIII) with these lines:

> Nor shall Death brag though wander'st in his shade
> When in eternal lines to time thou growest;
> So long as men can breathe, or eyes can see
> So long lives this, and this gives life to thee.

Shakespeare (1958: 1045)

There are two other points to note. First, Derrida points out that meaning is seldom structurally stable (see Brown, 1995: 82–3). For example, the words of the German phrase 'Vorsprung durch Technik', used as an UK advertising strapline for *Audi* cars from the 1980s until the present, denotes little because it will not be generally understood by an Anglophone audience (Rice-Oxley, 2012). But at the level of signification, the signifier is the use of German language, that which is signified is a German origin for the car, and the referent is 'Germanicity' (or in the comparable case of Barthes' tortuously analyzed pasta advertisement, *Italianicity*; see Barthes, 1977: 33–37). However, 'Germanicity' is both the referent *and* another signifier. Various connotations of sound engineering, reliable components and good-quality after-sales service combine to enable an Anglophone audience to author a positive meaning from the strapline. At the level of signification, meaning is located along 'chains of signifiers' (Barthes, 1977: 39; Dyer, 1982: 123).

Second, contemporary advertisements are painstaking constructs in which the agencies responsible for their production seek not only to reflect, but to exceed, the expectations of their intended audiences (Lury, 1994: 93). In this sense, the content of advertising is generically aspirational. Its purpose is to convince the reader that he/she is in need. It needs to be said that not all advertisements use a semiotic approach to get their message across. For example, an advertisement portraying a photograph of a product, such as a vacuum cleaner, accompanied by claims as to its technical prowess and favourable price, may rely entirely on substance over style. That said, if a decision is taken to portray the vacuum cleaner in use by a human subject, then paradigmatic decisions present themselves – should the human subject be male or female, how should he or she be dressed, in what kind of domestic context should the subject and the machine be situated and so on. The signifying content of advertisements is orchestrated to create, to adapt a term used by Lash (1990: 11; 1988), a microcosm of a 'regime of signification'.

The value of semiotic analysis lies in its facility to uncover and reveal the character of the 'regime' in any one particular case. However, a pure analysis of sign-value is of itself inadequate in explaining the meaning of the specific 'regime'. There are two reasons for this. First, contemporary marketing practice sets much store by the sending of specific promotional messages to particular target markets in the process known as segmentation. For example, the P&O advertisement, mentioned earlier, offers a primary message to readers who have yet to purchase a cruise. It is an *exposure* advertisement, in that its purpose is, literally, to expose the product in a romantic and inviting guise. It seeks to win hearts, and then minds. Second, a prime vehicle for targeting specific markets is through a discursive adaptation known as *lifestyle advertising* in which it is the significatory array that the advertiser creates around the product, rather than the product itself, that 'sells' the product or service. It is for this reason that a pure analysis of sign-value cannot be expected to yield a full range of insights into advertising content, unless accompanied by an analysis of the *referent systems*, that is to say, the constituted social context, of the intended target market.

Tourism as a lifestyle array

Tourism can be thought of as an exemplary lifestyle product inasmuch as it is the opportunity for human subjects to be who they are, or aspire to be, free from the constraints of paid employment and the demands of domesticity. Unsurprisingly therefore, tourism motifs and settings appear in a range of product advertising contexts, from cocktails to cars. Having already mentioned Audi vehicles, it may be useful to stay with that product and refer to a very unusual televisual lifestyle advertisement that was produced for one of their passenger vehicles in the mid-1990s. It is of interest because it made use of a 'regime of signification' that was derived from the aspirational tourism motifs of the day. The 30-second advertisement, named 'Dress' (Bartle, Bogle & Hegarty, 1995a), produced for the UK market and filmed in monochrome, portrays the vehicle parked outside an old farmhouse of multi-period origin. The house is surrounded by cattle in a field. A farm dog races to the house to alert the farm owner, a young woman in her 30s, of the approach of dinner time. She completes her payment of bills in her somewhat shabby office and walks to a room full of clothes, choosing, for the evening out, the Little Black Dress. Her voice-over tells us that the concept of the black dress originated with Coco Chanel in the 1920s. Her voice is accent-neutral, but with a very vague hint of north-eastern England. She walks past the sepia photograph of a male ancestor, leaves the house and gets into the vehicle: an Audi passenger car. The advertisement's strapline, spoken at the end of her voice-over, is that 'Fashion fades, only style remains'. The analysis follows.

The 1980s and 1990s were decades when, in the broadest terms, a so-called 'new tourism' was emerging (Poon, 1989). This was identified by the sociologists of the day as a diversification away from beach holidays toward heritage, rural environments and cultural experience. Central to this cultural shift was the aspirational taste regime of what became termed the 'service class', an expanding group of educated, credentialed employees whose jobs involved mediating information – through education, advertising, the media, the arts – throughout the population (Munt, 1994; Urry, 1990). Bourdieu's term, the 'new cultural intermediaries', perhaps reflects more accurately who they were (1984: 325, 345; Voase, 2007: 541–543). This class was linked, in terms of aspiration and consumption, with what Thrift (1989) termed the 'countryside and heritage traditions'. The car appears in the advertisement for only nine seconds. The objects of exposure – the 'lifestyle array', as termed earlier – are the countryside, the ancient house and above all, the unflashy but educated tastes of the young woman who had, we assume, inherited the farm from her male ancestor. Audi were seeking, at that time, to differentiate their product from flashier competitors by establishing a case that the car was stylish through an enduring simplicity of substance. The 'Little Black Dress' is the symbolic representation of the car. The appeal is not to the ephemerality of fashion but to the enduring qualities of 'style'. At the denotative level, the advertisement shows a spinster operating a run-down farm in the north-east of England who, perplexingly, drives an Audi car rather than a Land Rover. But that is not the point. At the connotative level, it is a regime of signification intended to engage the attention and approval of a growing group within the middle class who, impelled by the creative nature of their professional roles, share and make themselves distinctive with cultivated tastes.

Tourist experience: a semiotic perspective

The multiple paradigmatic choices that had been made in the production of the advertisement – to film in monochrome, to select an old house, to set it in the countryside, to identify a male ancestor photographically, to position the Little Black Dress as a choice of enduring style over the ephemerality of fashion – all work in syntagmatic relationship to anchor the Dress/Audi in the tasteful past. Intriguingly, a viewer in 1995 could have seen, during the same evening's viewing, a parallel advertisement featuring a character with contrasting values. An executant young man, named 'Number One' by the advertising agents who produced the piece, is portrayed working, we assume, in the financial sector in the City of London. He takes a test drive in the Audi, during which he outlines his personal philosophy in a soliloquy to camera – 'Every man for himself, right?' – and rejects the vehicle after a test drive: 'Not really my style. Know what I mean?' (Bartle Bogle Hegarty, 1995b). The advertiser's message in the *Dress* was to link the vehicle with a particular set of values. In the second advertisement, *Number One*, the advertiser seeks to actively de-couple the vehicle from values at variance. This is arguably an example of an act of symbolic violence in what Bourdieu (1984: 330) termed the 'symbolic struggle'.

We now move to consider the ways in which the tourist, as amateur semiotician, documents his/her trip through the creation of his/her own significatory array of souvenirs, mementos and photographs.

Souvenirs, mementos and photographs

The tourist undergoes an experience-apart in a place-apart. Urry (1990: 11) suggests that tourism can be understood as a step from the ordinary into the extraordinary, whilst MacCannell (2001) presents a complementary view, arguing that it is the unexpected, rather than the extraordinary, that provides the stuff of stories. It is not the purpose here to excavate the niceties of this debate, except to make the point that the tourist undergoes an experience that he/she wishes to conserve and revisit after the experience itself is complete. The human episodic memory is the repository of experiences, but is notoriously fickle. Minor incidents may be sealed in the memory for a lifetime for no apparent reason; conversely, important events in the life of the human subject may become a blur very quickly. For this reason, the human subject takes no chances. Important life events such as weddings, significant birthdays and holidays are documented through photography and through the acquisition of memorial objects. We now examine the semiotic dimensions to these behaviours.

First, we deal with material acquisition in the form of souvenirs and mementos. It is important to understand that these are not the same (Gordon, 1986). A souvenir is best understood as a purchasable item that proclaims its origins; thus, for example, a model of the Eiffel Tower may well bear the legend 'Eiffel Tower' or 'Paris'. Therefore, a souvenir is in a sense outside of the semiotic system because it operates at the denotative level; it is an iconic representation. A memento, by contrast, is best understood as an object collected by the tourist to which is ascribed a symbolic meaning that is strictly personal and may be unknown and unapparent to others. So, for example, the tourist may pick up a shell from a beach, take it home and display it, but its provenance will be apparent only to its collector, and those to whom the collector reveals its provenance. As such, to the casual viewer, the shell is simply a shell, just as the red rose is simply a plant. To the collector, it is the vehicle of connotations of pleasures and feelings encountered at the time of collection. Its function is indexical; it points backwards, facilitating recollection.

The taking of photographs is at first sight a more explicit method of documenting a visit. However, again, the tourist finds him/herself in the role of amateur semiotician. The archive is likely to be shared with others. For that reason, the tourist has a two-fold purpose – first, to prove that s/he has 'been there' by including photographs of the extraordinary in the sense of the well-known and expected and second, to complement these with pictures of the unexpected, whether the making of new friends, the witnessing of an unusual incident, whatever. The 'official' normative shots of extraordinary sites, known as 'stock' photographs (Feighery, 2009), that are commonly reproduced on websites, in brochures and on postcards, will normally provide inspiration, but the tourist will usually make such iconic scenes indexical in character by featuring him/herself and his/her companions in the photograph. One of the most resonant and highly publicized examples was the photograph of the late Princess Diana of Wales seated, alone, in front of the Taj Mahal (Edensor 1998: 1 & 131). In recent years, the replacement of analogue photography with digital photography, coupled with the arrival of Web 2.0 and portable communications devices, have created the facility for unconstrained photographic acquisition and immediate sharing (Larsen & Sandbye, 2014). This has not, *per se*, created a significant difference in the semiotic practices involved in tourist photography, but it has brought about an intensification of the need to document the trip in favourable semiotic terms. The extent of this can be troublingly perverse. For example, a recent media report indicates the amount of time that tourists are prepared to invest to acquire photographs of themselves in an idealized location for the purpose of exposure on *Instagram* (Roy, 2018).

A fourth form of semiotically influenced tourist material culture is the acquisition of clothing prior to the holiday and its use during the holiday. It is to this that we now turn.

'Dressing for Planet Holiday'

'Style', as suggested earlier, can be understood as the combination of individual signifiers, in syntagmatic relationship, in order to create an appearance that will be 'read' as meaningful and satisfying by persons possessed of the required aesthetic judgment. Renfrew (2007), cited at the head of this chapter, was not exaggerating when he suggested that humans live in a 'forest of symbols', whilst the anthropologist Leslie White suggested that culture, which we can think of as human subjects' non-functional mode of expression, can be understood, in the broadest terms, as 'man's extra-somatic [read: 'outside of the body'] means of adaptation' (White, 1959: 8). Thus, the naked human, as soon as he or she decides to have body art applied to his or her person, is making a paradigmatic decision as to what kind of art, where to have the art applied, and so on. Such expressions are 'read' by other humans, who negotiate the cultural position of the bearer in relation to themselves. The paradigmatic and syntagmatic choices that are made in the decoration of a room, or the selection of an ensemble of clothing, or indeed in the application of facial make-up to the female person (Ogilvie & Mizerski, 2011), are undertaken to establish an aesthetic array that will satisfy the originator, and also establish a position relative to others. Cultural expressions are thus a means of navigation, whereby humans negotiate their way through the symbolic forest. Stuart Hall (1980: 134) usefully termed cultural expressions 'maps of meaning'; they show the way, they please, they repel and, sometimes, they warn. Special, therefore, to the tourist experience is the preparation of the person through the purchase and selection of clothing.

'Dressing for Planet Holiday' was the descriptor of choice of one female research subject, when invited to speak about the 'embodied transition to the extraordinary holiday realm' (Banim, Guy & Gillen, 2005). Reporting the results of research into the nature of women's clothing acquisition and bodily preparation prior to vacation, the researchers show how such preparations enhanced the pleasures of anticipation prior to the actual holiday. New clothing acquisitions were carefully chosen for their facility to combine with already-owned items; the holiday was the opportunity to present themselves as the woman they aspired to be, shorn of the demands of employment and domesticity; and evening wear in particular was chosen in the knowledge that their style would be the object of critical appraisal by others, including their own companions. Bodily preparations included attention to hairstyle and, in some cases, the acquisition of a pre-tan (Banim et al., 2005). The article makes no mention of semiosis, but there is no doubt that the women are exercising agency as amateur semioticians. Paradigmatic and syntagmatic decisions are made in preparation for their adventure into an unfamiliar part of the symbolic forest. The techniques of iconicity, indexicality and anchorage are all deployed to create, to revisit Hall's term from earlier, 'maps of meaning' by which they will position themselves relative to others. What is more, an earlier study on the same topic by the authors revealed that, *contra* expectation, the overall aim was not the achievement of an 'effortless' style. The female research subjects positively wanted their efforts to be analyzed, recognized and valued (Guy & Banim, 2000).

Banim et al.'s (2005) study, while it reported that bodily preparations accompanied the assembling of clothing for the holiday, was essentially a study of clothing choice. By contrast, Small's (2016) study, while reporting on clothing choice, focused on bodily preparation. While, again, no reference is made to semiosis, it is clear that the female research subjects compared the success of their efforts with those of other women by means of detailed surveillance and self-surveillance. This surveillance involved not just an overall view of bodily appearance, but a detailed analysis of how various components came together to create that appearance. Matters such as the size of body parts, skin tone, tanned skin and the like were reported in considerable detail. The critique and self-critique was a study of paradigmatic elements, and the extent to which those elements created an overall appearance in syntagmatic relationship (Small, 2016). Indeed, the matter of clothing choice and bodily appearance can be studied via the theoretical concept termed symbolic interactionism, whereby socially understood collective meanings are held to emerge through the trading of symbolic messages (Kaiser, 2001), and also via 'the gaze' as theorized by Foucault (1980) and discussed in relation to female clothing practices by Tseëlon (1995). Exploration of these topics in detail lies beyond the scope of this chapter, but it is perhaps useful to mention how the *absence* of the exercise of choice can also be a *de facto* vehicle for symbolic meaning.

The relationship with personal clothing is considered to be an area of human experience that varies between the sexes. This is revealed, for example, in the different approaches of men and women to the practice of shopping, as revealed by Campbell's research (1997). A study of work clothing choices by Dutch males, undertaken by van der Laan and Velthuis (2016), suggested, first, that in getting dressed for the working day, the initial choice of garment is governed by weather conditions. Thereafter, the choice of workplace clothing is governed by the desire to project a deliberate style of routine and conformity; the males did not wish to be thought of as using the workplace as a setting for sartorial expression. In public life, this approach is probably best exemplified by the founder of Facebook, Mark Zuckerberg, who routinely wears the same T-shirt as daywear for the workplace. His rationale, when asked, is that he wishes to concentrate his mental efforts on his work. To remove the matter of clothing choice from his personal daily agenda was one contributing factor to this effort (Saul, 2016). Nevertheless, his sartorial choice was noticed and became a matter of media enquiry. This shows how, in the forest of symbols, one cannot escape.

Richard Voase

The 'brand' illusion

Finally, a topic is addressed that some may think, at first sight, belongs more properly in an appraisal of tourism marketing techniques. However, the essence of a brand is *symbolic value*. Symbolic value, as we have seen, is a construct of the mind. For that reason, brands, and rumours of brands, are necessarily a component of a semiotic perspective. This author argues that 'brand' is an over-used term that has become emptied of its meaning through frequency of exposure. An informed understanding is required and, thus, the topic fits within the parameters of this chapter.

The American Marketing Association's (AMA) definition of a brand is that it serves to differentiate the products and services of one seller from those of another (AMA, 2019). However, this definition does not explain, for example, a £50 price difference between near-identical pairs of men's blue jeans from trusted UK retailer Marks and Spencer and Levi-Strauss. Both companies were founded in the late nineteenth century, and both enjoy an enduring reputation for quality. The products, when shorn of their identifying labels, are almost indistinguishable. The author's students might say that the purchaser of the Levis is 'paying for the label', but that is only part of the story. The label is a visual representation of the symbolic value that has been added to the product, and for which the buyer is paying the additional £50. Some years ago, when the nature of the brand was perhaps better understood than at present, Gardner and Levy (1955: 35) argued the following:

> …a brand name is more than the label employed to differentiate among the manufacturers of a product. It is a complex symbol that represents a variety of ideas and attributes… via the body of associations it has built up and acquired as a public object over a period of time.

Meaning, as established earlier, is generated in the mind. This is the central insight of post-structuralism. There is no *hors-texte*. Thus, a man gazing upon a pair of men's Levi jeans is not looking at a brand. He is looking at a pair of trousers. The brand, defined as symbolic value, is generated in his brain, like the meaning of the red rose as a signifier of love, from pre-learned exposure (see Moisander, 2009, 338–339). Branding is a useful device for creating a differential *persona* around simple products, such as cola drinks, chocolate and washing powder. Such products are little more than commodities, and virtually indistinguishable, the one from the other (Hatch & Rubin, 2005: 52; Kniazeva & Belk, 2007: 63). The purchasing decision is rapid. Who agonizes for long over what bar of chocolate to purchase? That is why the brand is so suited to the bland. The human response to a symbol is *instinctive and immediate*. Who, for example, when driving a vehicle and encountering a red light, reflectively considers what the red light might mean? Red means stop. Green means go. *Nike's* guileless dictum is, 'Just Do It'. Whatever you do, don't think about it. The brand, as a device, is reductionist in nature.

The problem with the application of 'branding' to tourist destinations is that the purchasing decision for a holiday is not immediate and instinctive. The process is reflective, exploratory and is often the object of detailed research. A bar of chocolate can be consumed in two minutes, but a holiday can take two weeks. The nature of the act of consumption is dramatically different. That is why any successful attempt to 'brand' a tourist destination can be expected to cause harm. The brand is designed, not to encourage reflective thought, but to discourage it.

Tourist experience: a semiotic perspective

In the case of Scotland, a destination for which distinctive imagery is very well known and recognized, the national tourist board found it necessary to limit, and in some cases to not deploy, this familiar imagery in its promotional activities (Voase, 2012: 80–82). We all know about Scotland, don't we? Think Scotland: think tartans, kilts, cabers, bagpipes, whisky. End of. Could there just, perhaps, be more to Scotland than these over-familiar images? I shall not even start on referring to the endless literature on the tourist quest for 'the authentic', save to make the point that potential visitors can be expected to fill up a two-week vacation with something more than the already-known and over-familiar. Elsewhere, this author offers a detailed exposition of the Scotland example, together with a comprehensive appraisal of what brands can and cannot do (Voase, 2012; see also Mundt, 2002). However, by means of addendum, a recent offering from Medway and Warner (2014) offers a critique of place-branding from a very different angle. They show how naturally evolved place-names are the consequence of associations that have accumulated over long periods. An attempt to superimpose an artificial set of symbolic attributes not only risks the consequences above, but destroys the symbolic value of that which has been accumulated over time.

Conclusion

Human subjects have been described by the American anthropologist Leslie White as 'symboling animals' (cited in Renfrew, 2007:107). Clumsy though this descriptor may be, it captures the essence of a creature that, as soon as he or she gets out of bed in the morning, makes paradigmatic decisions as to what to wear or not wear, and those decisions are influenced by form as well as function. Similarly, we have seen how the female human subject, once she has decided on the destination for an annual holiday, reveals herself to be an amateur semiotician in making clothing acquisitions for the purpose. Advertisers, as we have seen, use semiotic techniques to create an aesthetic array to engage potential tourists. Tourists themselves create their own arrays through the acquisition of souvenirs and mementos, and photography. The deployment of the contents of the semiotic toolbox enable one, if one may extend the 'forest of symbols' metaphor, to stand back from the wood and look at the trees, one by one: what species they may be, why they are there and how they relate to their companion trees; and how the shrubs that inevitably accompany the trees anchor, or otherwise, the arboreal landscape. The utility of semiotic analysis subsists in its facility to answer the question, not just 'what', but 'why'. For those occasions when 'That looks good' and 'This reminds me of last year's holiday' does not suffice, semiotic analysis offers a method to uncover, in analytical detail, the reality behind the rhetoric.

References

AMA (2019) *Resource Library: Dictionary,* American Marketing Association. Available at http://www.marketingpower.com/_layouts/dictionary.aspx?dletter=b. (Accessed 6 February 2019)

Banim, M., Guy, A. and Gillen, K. (2005) "It's Like Planet Holiday": Women's dressed self-presentation on holiday. *Fashion Theory,* 9(4), 425–444.

Barthes, R. (1972) *Mythologies.* London: Vintage Books (edition 1993).

Barthes, R. (1977) *Image, Music, Text.* London: Fontana.

Bartle Bogle Hegarty (1995a) *Dress.* Televisual advertisement for Audi car. Not publicly available at the time of writing.

Bartle Bogle Hegarty (1995b) *Number One,* televisual advertisement for Audi car. Available from: https://www.youtube.com/watch?v=pIQ-283wKgg (Accessed 3 June 2019).

Bourdieu, P. (1984) *Distinction: A Social Critique of the Judgement of Taste.* London: Routledge.

Brown, S. (1995) *Postmodern Marketing.* London: Routledge.

Campbell, C. (1997) Shopping, pleasure and the sex war. In P. Falk and C. Campbell (Eds.), *The Shopping Experience.* London: Sage, pp. 166–176.

Culler, J. (1983) *Barthes.* London: Fontana.

Derrida, J. (1997) *Of Grammatology*, Corrected Edn. London: John Hopkins University Press.

Dyer, G. (1982) *Advertising as Communication.* London: Routledge.

Echtner, C. (1999) The semiotic paradigm: Implications for tourism research. *Tourism Management*, 20(1), 47–57.

Edensor, T. (1998) *Tourists at the Taj: Performance and Meaning at a Symbolic Site.* London: Routledge.

Feighery, W. (2009) Tourism, stock photography and surveillance: A Foucauldian approach. *Journal of Tourism and Cultural Change*, 7(3), 161–178.

Finn, M., Elliott-White, M. and Walton, M. (2000) *Tourism and Leisure Research Methods: Data Collection, Analysis and Interpretation.* Harlow: Longman.

Foucault, M. (1980) The eye of power. In C. Gordon (Ed.), *Michel Foucault: Power/Knowledge,* Hemel Hempstead: Harvester Wheatsheaf, pp. 146–165.

Gardner, B. and Levy, S. (1955) The product and the brand. *Harvard Business Review*, 33(2), 33–39.

Gordon, B. (1986) The souvenir: Messenger of the extraordinary. *Journal of Popular Culture*, 20(3), 135–146.

Guy, A. and Banim, M. (2000) Personal collections: Women's clothing use and identity. *Journal of Gender Studies*, 9(3), 313–327.

Hall, S. (1980) Encoding/decoding. In S. Hall, D. Hobson, A. Lowe and P. Willis (Eds.), *Culture, Media, Language.* London: Routledge, pp. 128–138.

Hatch, M. and Rubin, J. (2005) The hermeneutics of branding. *Brand Management*, 14(1–2), 40–59.

Kaiser, S. (2001) Minding appearances: Style, truth, and subjectivity. In J. Entwistle and E. Wilson (Eds.), *Body Dressing.* Oxford: Berg, pp. 79–102.

Kniazeva, M. and Belk, R. (2007) Packaging as vehicle for mythologizing the brand. *Consumption, Markets and Culture*, 10(1), 51–69.

Knudsen, D., Rickly, J. and Metro-Roland, M. (2016) Touring as a Peircean Habit. *Annals of Tourism Research*, 57, 246–248.

Larsen, J. and Sandbye, M. (2014) Introduction: The new face of snapshot photography. In J. Larsen and M. Sandbye (Eds.), *Digital Snaps: The New Face of Photography.* London: Tauris, pp. xv–xxxii.

Lash, S. (1988) Discourse or figure? Postmodernism as a 'regime of signification'. *Theory, Culture & Society*, 5(2–3), 311–336.

Lash, S. (1990) *Sociology of Postmodernism.* London: Routledge.

Lury, A. (1994) Advertising: Moving beyond the stereotypes. In R. Keat, N. Whiteley and N. Abercrombie (Eds.), *The Authority of the Consumer.* London: Routledge, pp. 91–101.

MacCannell, D. (2001) Tourist agency. *Tourist Studies*, 1(1), 23–37.

Medway, D. and Warner, G. (2014) What's in a name? Place branding and toponymic commodification. *Environment and Planning A*, 46(1), 153–167.

Metro-Roland, M. (2009) Interpreting meaning: An application of Peircean semiotics to tourism. *Tourism Geographies*, 11(2), 270–279.

Mick, D. (1986) Consumer research and semiotics: Exploring the morphology of signs, symbols and significance. *Journal of Consumer Research*, 13(2), 196–213.

Moisander, J. (2009) Personal interviews in cultural consumer research – post-structuralist challenges. *Consumption, Markets & Culture*, 12(4), 329–348.

Mundt, J. (2002) The branding of myths and the myths of branding. *Tourism-Zagreb*, 50(4), 339–348.

Munt, I. (1994) The 'Other' postmodern tourism: Culture, travel and the new middle classes. *Theory, Culture & Society*, 11(3), 101–123.

Myers, G. (1994) *Words in Ads.* London: Arnold.

Ogilvie, M. and Mizerski, K. (2011) Using semiotics in consumer research to understand everyday phenomena. *International Journal of Marketing Research*, 53(5) 651–668.

Poon, A. (1989) Competitive strategies for a 'new tourism'. In C. Cooper (Ed.), *Progress in Tourism, Recreation and Hospitality Management* (Vol. 1). London: Belhaven Press, pp. 91–102.

Renfrew, C. (2007) *Prehistory: The Making of the Human Mind.* London: Weidenfeld & Nicolson.

Rice-Oxley, M. (2012) Vorsprung durch Technik – ad slogan that changed how we saw Germany. *The Guardian*, 18 September. Available at: https://www.theguardian.com/world/2012/sep/18/vorsprung-durch-technik-advertising-germany (Accessed 14 May 2019).

Roy, E. (2018) Instacrammed: The big fib at the heart of New Zealand picture-perfect peaks. *The Guardian*, 06 December. Available at: https://www.theguardian.com/world/2018/dec/07/instacrammed-the-big-fib-at-the-heart-of-new-zealand-picture-perfect-peaks (Accessed 9 June 2019).

Saul, H. (2016) Why Mark Zuckerberg wears the same clothes to work every day. *The Independent*, 26 January. Available from: https://www.independent.co.uk/news/people/why-mark-zuckerberg-wears-the-same-clothes-to-work-everyday-a6834161.html (Accessed 1 July 2019).

Shakespeare, W. (1958) *The Complete Works of William Shakespeare*. London: Hamlyn.

Small, J. (2016) Holiday bodies: Young women and their appearance. *Annals of Tourism Research*, 58, 18–32.

Thrift, N. (1989) Images of social change. In C. Hamnett, L. McDowell and D. Sarre (Eds.), *The Changing Social Structure*. London: Sage, pp. 12–42.

Tresidder, F. (2011) The semiotics of tourism. In P. Robinson, S. Heitmann and P. Dieke (Eds.), *Research Themes for Tourism*. Wallingford: CABI, pp. 59–68.

Tseëlon, E. (1995) *The Masque of Femininity*. London: Sage.

Urry, J. (1990) *The Tourist Gaze: Leisure and Travel in Contemporary Societies*. London: Sage.

van der Laan, E. and Velthuis, O. (2016) Inconspicuous dressing: A critique of the construction-through-consumption paradigm in the sociology of clothing. *Journal of Consumer Culture*, 16(1), 22–42.

Voase, R. (2007) Individualism and the 'new tourism': A perspective on emulation, personal control and choice. *International Journal of Consumer Studies*, 31(5), 541–547.

Voase, R. (2012) Recognition, reputation and response: Some critical thoughts on destinations and brands. *Journal of Destination Marketing and Management*, 1(1–2), 78–83.

White, L. (1959) *The Evolution of Culture*. New York: McGraw-Hill.

Williamson, J. (1978) *Decoding Advertisements*. London: Marion Boyars.

Woollacott, J. (1982) Messages and meanings. In M. Gurevitch, T. Bennett, J. Curran and J. Woollacott (Eds.), *Culture, Society and the Media*. London: Methuen, pp. 91–111.

11

PERFORMING BEYOND THE VIEW

Embodiment and tourist experiences

Jillian M. Rickly

Introduction

Anyone new to tourism studies and eager to learn the foundational theories of tourist experience will read Urry's (1990, 2002; Urry & Larsen, 2011) *The Tourist Gaze*. This foundational text solidified the concept of the tourist gaze as a form of visual consumption and power dynamics of sightseeing. Importantly, Urry's focus on the visual also had the effect of inspiring researchers to reconsider the role of the other senses, and the body holistically, in the touristic experience. This chapter works from the tourist gaze as a springhead moment in tourism studies. Rather than challenge Urry's concept, I wish to embrace it for its importance to the field as a key concept but also as a contentious point that, along with major theoretical developments in the 'performative turn', inspired scholars to challenge the basic assumptions of the tourist gaze, thereby yielding tremendous insights into the *embodied* experience of tourism.

In their recent edited text, *Tourism and Embodiment*, Palmer and Andrews (2019) posit that the body and processes of embodiment are experiencing a resurgence in scholarly attention in tourism studies. While Veijola and Jokinen (1994) may have been among the first to note the absence of the body in tourism theories, it has been some of the latest theoretical advances in performance theories, non-representational theory, actor network theory and post-phenomenological perspectives that have renewed our interest and offered novel insights. As Palmer and Andrews aptly summarize,

> ...the body of the tourist is a social body, it engages with other bodies, things and activities, with other places and ways of living. The body is also affected by the experience of and engagement with nature and the natural world. It shapes and is shaped by technology and may be subject to out of body experiences. In addition, there is not one tourist body but a range of bodies, male, female, transgender, transsexual and [...] bodies that are physically and/or sensory impaired.
>
> *(Palmer & Andrews 2019: 1)*

In what follows is a brief summary of the trajectory of tourism theory from a focus on the visual to the reactions of tourism scholars that led to a re-consideration of the body. Next,

140

DOI: 10.4324/9781003219866-13

Performing beyond the view

the discussion moves more deeply into the ways embodiment is studied within the field, importantly taking note of how the body is experienced through tourism, but also how the body is involved in the performance of place. Then, there is a quick rumination about potential future research directions before the chapter concludes with some thoughts about how far the field has come in the past several decades.

From sightseeing to embodied encounters

The tourist experience has always been an embodied experience. Owing to the theoretical significance of Urry's *The Tourist Gaze*, much of the earlier research on touristic experience leaned heavily upon the visual dimensions. Although it is indeed true that sightseeing plays an important role in modern (and postmodern) tourism, many forget that there was a time when visual consumption was not the primary means of experiencing and recounting travel. As Adler (1989: 8–9) explains, 'travel was first widely proclaimed as an art', as sixteenth century travellers were taught to experience the world through the ear and the tongue. Rather than collecting sights, travellers sustained themselves on local culinary traditions and filled their 'album amicorum' with words inscribed by wise men of reputation. In fact, the preparation for travel abroad, Adler argues, involved 'learning foreign languages, compiling systematic lists of questions, obtaining the letters of introduction necessary for access to high status settings of conversation, and, above all, reading (Adler, 1989: 10).

Over time, however, viewing offered a more distant and detached means of experience that also corresponded to changing attitudes about the value of 'eye witness' accounts and verification of the seventeenth century turn to empiricism (Adler, 1989). This had a tremendous effect on the Grand Tour and the cultural artefacts that it produced. Before departing, Grand Tourists learned about landscape aesthetics, in addition to languages and politics. They hired artists to capture the views and their diaries formed some of the earliest iterations of travel guidebooks, noting unique aspects of places worth seeing (Rickly-Boyd, Knudsen, Braverman & Metro-Roland, 2014; Towner, 1985). This, no doubt, greatly influenced the visual consumption practices of subsequent tourists. Not only was sightseeing increasingly prioritized, but tours were devoted to particular views, while new inventions informed how these views were to be seen, including the development of the Claude glass in the eighteenth century and, of course, the camera in the nineteenth century led to the 'search for the photogenic' (Urry & Larsen, 2011: 178).

However, this emphasis on the visual does not happen at the exclusion of the body. As Urry and Larsen (2011) explain, photography is an embodied practice performed by those on both sides of the lens. The photographer does not simply point and click but bends, squats and leans to produce the preferred angle and, similarly, those being photographed pose and posture (Haldrup & Larsen, 2003; Pearce & Wang, 2019). While photographs might capture the visual elements of the tourist gaze, researchers are now fully aware that experientially tourism involves all of the body. 'Landscapes are not merely visionscapes', argue Morgan and Pritchard (2005: 41), but they are also 'touchscapes, soundscapes, and smellscapes' (see also Dann & Jacobsen, 2002, 2003). In fact, Dann and Jacobsen (2003: 5) observe that contemporary travel writers follow the 'literary aromatic tradition' by characterizing destinations according to their most prevalent odours – 'nice places smell good, nasty places smell bad'. Relatedly, while the rise of social media might lend support to the importance of the visual, a closer look at the travel images tourists produce reveals photographs of food and drink, active bodies and bodies engaged with the tactile – splashing in waves, toes in sand. In these ways, 'photographic performances are always *more*-than-just representational' (Urry &

Larsen, 2011: 209). The visual is integral to many tourists' pursuits, but it is also accompanied by and 'subjugated by sonic, tactile, and olfactory sensations' (Edensor, 2018: 1).

Embodiment and experience

Attempting to overcome the mind–body dichotomy of Cartesian thought, Merleau-Ponty's phenomenology emphasizes embodied lived experience by arguing that experiences exist *between* the mind and the body. He articulated, 'the body is the vehicle of being in the world [...] I am conscious of the world through the medium of my body' (Merleau-Ponty 1962 [2004]: 93). Therefore, the body should not be viewed as an object but, rather, as the condition and context of experience (see also Grosz, 1994; Leavy, 2008). Csordas (1993: 135) further developed the concept of embodiment as one that takes 'embodied experience is the starting point for analyzing human participation in a cultural world'; as such, embodiment does not supplant textual and representational approaches, but aims to complement them by attending to the experience of being-in-the-world (Csordas, 1994).

The 'performative turn' in geography, and the rise of non-representational theory (NRT) in particular, has incorporated these aspects of phenomenology towards understanding embodiment and experience (see Anderson & Harrison, 2010; Obrador-Pons, 2003, 2007; Thrift, 1996, 1999, 2000, 2008; Wylie, 2007). Specifically, Laurier and Philo (2006: 353) note that NRT is interested in 'matters that mark the end of representation: things, events, encounters, emotions and more that are unspeakable, unwriteable, and of course, unrepresentable'. Indeed, Game (1991: 177) explains, 'the desire to put one's feet or body in the sand, to be in the water, can be understood as meaning embodied – feel, touch, fluid – and possibly not speakable'. As such, NRT is actually considered post-phenomenological because it extends beyond the body to how and why our bodies are put into motion or emotion. Thus, the context of embodiment is important. Bodies are performances that occur in conjunction with landscapes, objects and contexts, informed by habits, sensations and materiality (Macpherson, 2010). The body is 'always both subject and object [...] observer and observed, seer and seen' (Wylie, 2007 151).

As a result, NRT has found considerable value in elucidating tourist experiences (Obrador-Pons, 2003, 2007; Palmer & Andrews, 2019). Indeed, Obrador-Pons (2003: 55) summarizes the complexity of the tourist body:

> The tourist body is neither only a thing through which we tour the world, nor only an object of representation, cultivation or exhibition. The body is also active, expressive and sensual, that is, it is always at the same time social and natural, object and subject, active and passive.

In what follows, the role of embodiment in tourist experience is approached from two distinct, but related perspectives. Beginning with the ways one's body is brought to the forefront of touristic experience, the discussion then progresses to the role bodies play in performing places.

The tourist body

According to Csordas (2011), embodiment is the fundamental existential condition. In other words, 'the body is the means through which we are practically involved in the world' (Obrador-Pons, 2003: 53). The concept of embodiment is of particular significance in research that aims to understand the ways the body is experienced through tourism. In many ways, this research is a direct reaction to the emphasis on the visual aspects of tourism – that tourism is an act of sightseeing – and as a result emphasizes tourism as a means to come to know one's body: its sensations and strength, privilege and power.

Indeed, such realizations of one's own body can come as a surprise to some tourists, who set out to 'see the sights' of exotic destinations. Huberman (2019) aptly captures the surprise moments of tourists' own bodily awareness as they travel to Banaras, India, and interact with the children who work as unlicensed peddlers and guides:

> It was not just the case that their visits to India were profoundly mediated *through* the body and experiences of 'sensory overload', it was also the case that being in India frequently made tourists *aware* of their body and senses in new ways. Bodily attributes often taken for granted at home, such as size, skin, hair or eye colour, came to be fore-grounded and in some cases, *experienced* as new sources of power, privilege and pleasure.
>
> *(Huberman, 2019: 12)*

Similarly, others have found tourists expressing new perceptions and experiences of their own bodies. While Merchant (2011) explores the ways scuba divers learn and adjust their sensory skills for underwater environments, Speier (2019) reports on yoga tourists who were motivated by the landscape imagery of a yoga retreat, finding, in the end, that they were mentally and bodily challenged in positive ways, pushing their own bodies' limits and feeling surprised at what their bodies were capable of. At the heart of these disparities of expectation and experience are the roles of intentionality, action and cognition. Haldrup (2019: 144) reminds us that cognition and action are intentional, that 'action and cognition are embodied, habitual and contextual. We act as we do because our bodies "know" what to do in a particular context' (see also Somdahl-Sands, 2013). When that context changes, our bodies are sometimes able to push beyond the habitual to reveal previously unrealized abilities. This can be an empowering and/or a troubling experience.

Applying Assemblage Theory to wilderness hiking, Barry (2019) witnesses hikers gaining body awareness in relation to the material assemblage of their backpack. In preparing for multi-day, off-grid hiking and camping, they carried all the necessities on their backs – equipment, clothing, food and other supplies. Not only was it the weight of the pack that brought awareness to one's body, but the more subtle strategies of how it was packed for balance on one's back, the adjustment of harnesses and placement of straps (for example, wider hip straps for women) so that it fits the hiker's body and moves with them, minimizing chaffing. Barry (2019) observes the hikers re-familiarizing themselves with their pack-body assemblage:

> With each step, the tourist body recalibrates and adjusts as the assemblage of objects – hiking boots, backpack, food, first aid kits, water and so on – is bounced around, shifting the distribution of weight, and therefore forcing the walking tourist body to re-act and redistribute their actions in accordance with these co-produced movements.
>
> *(Barry, 2019: 80)*

However, in the case of medical tourism, awareness of the body is foregrounded and, in fact, is central to touristic motivation. The motivation of medical tourists is 'not the onslaught of modern life that these tourists wish to escape, but the current reality of their body or how they experience this body' (Cook, 2010: 147). Although related to health tourism, which

Jillian M. Rickly

is often associated more broadly with leisure, recreation, pleasure and well-being, medical tourism, on the other hand, situates medical intervention at the centre of tourism motivation. Thus, in this case, the tourist body is also the 'medicalized body', as Cook (2010) summarizes:

> Medical tourism is based on the tourist's embodiment *as it exists* and as they *want it to be*. They travel for a service and a product that is focused on and marketed toward their current embodied state and what they desire it to be. The outcome of their tourist experience is located within their body.
>
> *(Cook, 2010: 149, emphasis in original)*

While tourism can be a means to reconnect with one's body, to be surprised by one's bodily abilities or to change one's body, understanding embodiment in the context of tourism also requires an understanding that 'the body is not only written, but it also writes (Obrador-Pons, 2003: 55). It is active in exploring, knowing and producing the spaces of tourism. As Crouch (2002: 214) argues, 'we "know" places bodily and through an active intersubjectivity'. Human bodies are spatialities of position and situation – our bodies are not in space/time but inhabit it (Simonsen, 2005, 2008, 2010). 'Body and space are mutually defining' (Obrador-Pons, 2003:55, see also Grosz, 1994; Rickly, 2017; Simonsen, 2005, 2008, 2010). Thus, the concept of dwelling derives from a recognition that 'being is always being-in-the-world'; as such, Obrador-Pons (2003: 49) understands tourism as 'live, sensible, situated, embodied and relational' developing out of our inherent mobile nature and simultaneous desire to be in place.

Conceptually, dwelling developed alongside broader developments in non-representational theory that aim to re-evaluate the emphasis on representation by focusing, instead, on the relational qualities of place through materialities, movements, gestures *and* representations as 'enactments, neither subjects nor objects, signs or referents, but processual registers of experience [...] as performative in themselves; as doings' (Dewsbury, Harrison, Rose & Wylie 2002, 437–8). Because NRT is intended to push beyond examinations of representations, to be 'more-than-representational' (Dewsbury et al., 2002; Lorimer, 2005), Thrift (1999) terms NRT, a theory of practices, as non-representational approaches, such as the concept of dwelling, that recognize the agency of landscape. According to Rose (2002: 457), NRT foregrounds the notion of 'how the landscape "comes to matter"—how it comes to be relevant through practice'. It is thoroughly materialist; everything acts (Anderson & Harrison, 2010). Thus, Spinney (2006: 713) suggests that by focusing on 'doing and acting', that is, 'the practice of movement and the movement of practice', a space by which to examine the ongoing dialectic between body and landscape, the construction of meanings and the constitution of place is opened up.

The embodied practice of dwelling and the agency of landscape are illustrated in Wylie's (2005) account of walking the South West Coast Path. The journey begins 'in the woods' with experiences of anxiety upon entering the tangles of the woods' branches, leaves and undergrowth. Pausing for a moment amongst the woods, however, reveals the intimacy of 'this tree, these branches' and a sense of solitude and enmeshment with the wooded landscape. Following a small, mud path through wet, thick blankets of ferns finds his '[l]imbs and lungs working hard in a haptic, step-by-step engagement with nature-matter' (Wylie, 2005: 239). Despite what may seem like a description of 'being-in-the-world', Wylie argues in this moment he feels as much 'in' the landscape as up against it. The long distance journey produces pains that are relational and therefore difficult to locate. 'Pain occurs neither "in me" nor "in

Performing beyond the view

that"—the externalized body—but "between me and it", in this step, this next step. And so the landscape emerges as malignant' (Wylie, 2005: 244).

Such a post-phenomenological approach sheds light on the relationality of the body and landscape in practice, body–landscape becoming together. Importantly, though, for the tourist body, 'moving does not simply mean leaving one place behind and encountering another' (Howard & Kupers, 2019: 207). Rather, 'places accompany travellers in embodied forms', from the objects carried or worn to the diseases encountered and the bones broken (Howard & Kupers, 2019: 207; see also Germann Molz, 2006; Rickly, 2017). Rickly's (2017) account of the climbing body illustrates this relationality of bodies shaped by the practice of climbing and the rock faces transformed into climbing routes through the trained eyes of climbers. Thus, Howard and Kupers (2019: 207) suggest the concept of inter-place to account for places as mobile, in which lives often transcend boundaries but also carry them as 'embodied, materialised and socially constituted'.

Performing places

In addition to advancing our understanding of body–landscape relationality, the performative turn also significantly affected the way scholars think about place. Rather than static containers of meaning to be read through textual approaches, place came to be understood as enactments of the dynamic social, cultural, political, economic *and* ecological connections that feed into and through particular spaces. This is why NRT is, in fact, better characterized as a 'more-than-representational' theory, as it maintains 'a firm belief in the actuality of representation [...] not as a code to be broken or as an illusion to be dispelled rather representations are apprehended as performative in themselves; as doings' (Dewsbury, et al., 2002: 438). The act of representing, whether by speaking, writing or creating, argues Wylie (2007: 164), is understood to be 'in and of the world of embodied practice and performance, rather than taking place outside of that world, or being anterior to, and determinative of, that world.'

The concept of emplacement, developed by Casey (1993, 1996, 2001), stresses the interplay of place with the body. There can be 'no places without bodies [...] bodies build places' (Casey, 1993: 103). Indeed, place is not construed out of 'nowhere' (Bærenholdt & Granas, 2008). Rather, places are enacted points of encounter, mooring and connection. Simonsen (2008: 16) explains, 'place is a specific conjunction of social practices and social relations, it will consist of particular interweavings or networks which have over time been constructed, consolidated, decayed, and renewed'. As points of encounter, connections are vital to the enactment and existence of place; '[w]ithout enacted connections, the place would simply not "happen"' (Johannesson & Bærenholdt, 2008: 155). Embodied performances of these connections form the foundations of touristic experience, evidencing the argument that tourism is about much more than sightseeing. As Casey (1996) asserts, the body subject is the fabricating agent in enacting place, as emplaced being entails moving, feeling, sensing, thinking and (re)acting.

In early efforts to move beyond the tourist gaze (Urry, 1990) and staged authenticity (MacCannell, 1973) to investigate the ways tourists perform places, Edensor (2000, 2001) developed dramaturgical and theatrical metaphors. Indeed, tourists' interactions with staging, directors, scripts, choreographers and scenography can all be observed. In this approach, 'tourist places are conceived as made through the interrelated actions of tourists, tourist workers and local people, acting within bounded settings controlled by regulations and social codes of conduct' (Prince, 2019: 173; see also Bærenholdt et al., 2004;

145

Edensor 2000, 2001; Larsen 2010, 2012; Rickly-Boyd et al., 2014). Indeed, Edensor (2001: 64) asserts that most tourism destinations are heterogeneous spaces in which tourist activities 'may be performed alongside the everyday enactions of residents, passersby and workers'. As a result, tourists often must improvise in navigating destinations. In so doing, place is made through embodied performances accompanied by discourses and texts, bodies and objects, affects and percepts, and technologies and mediums (see Bærenholdt et al., 2004; Coleman & Crang, 2002; Rickly-Boyd et al., 2014). Rink (2019), for example, demonstrates the intersections of place and the body used to both produce tourist maps and perform destinations. By examining the *Pink Map* of Cape Town, a tourist map highlighting the queer spaces of the city, the author notes the role of embodiment in the socio-cultural construction of city as tourism place:

> More than simply serving as the container of the tourist subject, the body is represented in the *Pink Map*, on the one hand, as the site of tourism that attracts tourists for pleasure and leisure activities, and, on the other hand, the body serves as a representation of destination space.
>
> *(Rink, 2019: 41)*

Yet, in following the *Pink Map*, tourists in Cape Town enact an 'uneven terrain of representation', as this map foregrounds gay spaces, while many other queer bodies, particularly lesbian, bisexual and transgender, remain invisible (Rink, 2019). As such, these tourists are engaging with a particular representation of the city; they can choose to follow or improvise on whim, allowing them to explore and perform their own versions of Cape Town as tourism place.

However, some tourism spaces are more homogenous, with specific choreography, staging, direction, scripts and actors that limit tourists' potential enactments of the space (Edensor, 2001). Despite efforts to choreograph and direct tourists, these dramaturgical landscapes cannot *determine* performance and experience (Edensor, 2000, 2001). Indeed, more recent work by Haldrup (2019) and Chronis (2015) re-infuses the body into enclavic tourism spaces, such as museums and heritage sites, demonstrating that even when improvisation is limited, the body acts, it has agency – it is doing, touching, seeing, sensing, being in place. So, while Haldrup (2019) observes that museums are full of signs and markers instructing our bodies to 'stop, look and listen', he also notes that visitor bodies are rather absent from museum studies. Thus, Haldrup's work in the Viking Ship Museum, Denmark, foregrounds the body and the embodied experience of the museum's hands-on, sailing experience in a replica of a 1,000-year old Viking ship. In so doing, he captures the embodied experience of 'becoming-Vikings' through the practice of sailing – or learning to sail. In the 'nauseating' space produced 'in the encounter between, or assemblage of, water, boats and bodies', Haldrup observes, the assemblage also yields a sense of collectivity among the participants, who are, in fact, rowing the boat and attempting to find a collective rhythm, and sometimes failing to do so.

Relatedly, Chronis (2015) approaches the guided tours of Gettysburg National Park, USA, from the perspective of the body and emplacement. He suggests that the 'strategic use of the body is intertwined with discursive techniques in the purposeful construction of a tourist place', so that 'walking is an act of "enunciation"' that emplaces the narratives told by the guides (Chronis, 2015: 125). However, this research does much more than illustrate embodiment processes in guided tours; it contributes to our understanding of tourism performances more broadly. While much of the literature on tourism and performance has

Performing beyond the view

made good use of dramaturgical metaphors, the body has not been given thorough consideration. Of course, it is included as one of the actors in the tourism scene, but the agency of the body has not been fully realized. Chronis (2015) notes three important strategies of body–space tourism staging – spatialization, emplacement and regulation. *Spatialization* occurs in the kinaesthetic mapping of the tourism space brought about by the tourist's movement in relation to the affordances of the landscape. The landscape affordances, however, may require a mediator, such as a guide, to bring landscape elements together into a story that suggests how the landscape was or is to be interacted with. *Emplacement*, then, embeds the tourist within the dramatic stage, while their embodied agency in the landscape facilitates the transformation of an 'un-prepossessed geographical locale' to an emplaced historical drama (Chronis, 2015: 137). Thus, Chronis (2015) is relying on Casey's (1993, 1996, 2001) concept of emplacement to relate this body–space strategy to tourism performance, as Casey maintains that through movement we are able to link places in proximity into a coherent path. The third strategy, Chronis (2015) notes, is *regulation*. This importantly denotes the limitations on the body–space performance, as particular spaces are off-limits and behaviours not allowed. Hence, regulation demonstrates that the body is never completely free in tourism spaces.

Thus, Chronis (2015) observes these three body–space strategies coming together during the battlefield memorial tours, such that visitors came away with an embodied sense of the landscape that contextualizes the historical narrative:

> Walking the mile-long Pickett's Charge with its undulated terrain or ascending Little Round Top under the sweltering sun produces sensory knowledge that cannot be gained through signs or texts. It is not rare, for example, to hear tourists experiencing the 'heat', 'odors' and 'noise' of the battle.
>
> *(Chronis, 2015: 138)*

Indeed, it is through moments such as these that tourists most often describe authentic experiences, as well as anxious experiences and embodied alienation (Sharma & Rickly, 2019; Vidon & Rickly, 2018).

Despite the debated meanings and uses of authenticity in tourism studies, it is argued that authenticity is a relational concept that draws upon objective, constructive and existential dimensions of tourist experiences (Rickly-Boyd, 2012a, b). So while tourism often engages aspects of fiction, fantasy and imagination, it is through the body that tourists are able to add a sense of objectivity. They experience tourism places through the body; through its senses the body offers feedback as to where one is located and what one is doing (Rickly-Boyd, 2013). As a result, even in the most fantastical of tourism scenarios, tourists report authentic experiences, including in Buchmann, Moore and Fisher's (2010) study of *Lord of the Rings* tourists in New Zealand. These tourists are motivated by the film series that was developed from Tolkien's works, who partake in tours of the associated mediated hyperreal simulacra – the landscapes of filming that were then enhanced through CGI technologies. Nevertheless, the tourists report that they are able to connect to the themes of Tolkien's stories – fellowship, adventure and sacrifice – through the tour. They experience the adventure of travelling far distances to places only imagined, while a sense of fellowship comes from forming a touring community with others of common motivation. In fact, being in the landscape that was used as background to portray the Tolkien stories on film, tourists describe being able to experience a material place, its terrain and climate, but also use their imaginations. This embodied experience is essential to their authentic experiences of place, as embodiment 'helps counteract feelings of surreality that many tourists reported when arriving' (Buchmann et al., 2010: 241).

Embodiment is about 'culture and experience insofar as these can be understood from the standpoint of bodily being-in-the-world' (Csordas, 1999: 143). Thus, an embodied approach to tourism, assert Palmer and Andrews (2019: 3), means that 'the body is not something to be studied in relation to culture as if it were an object, it is the very subject of culture'. In the performance of tourism places, representations matter, but the matter as doings in which the tourist body enacts the connections that weave through places. Tourists are 'situated and embodied subjects whose lives unfold in reciprocal interactions with their environment' (Obrador-Pons, 2003: 47).

Future directions

In Veijola and Jokinen's (1994: 129) call for greater attention to the body in tourism, the authors encouraged us to engage with 'embodiment, radical otherness, multiplicity of differences, sex and sexuality in tourism'. In the intervening years, tourism studies has made considerable strides towards this, along with developing much more theoretical richness for addressing these issues. Yet, particular aspects of tourism and embodiment remain under-examined, of which two – critical disability studies and critical animal studies – come to mind.

Critical disability studies is a welcome addition to the tourism studies cannon. Researchers in this area are continually pushing forward our understanding of enabling environments, accessibility, inclusivity and diversity (Buhalis & Darcy 2011; Buhalis, Darcy & Ambrose, 2012). While this research contributes greatly to practical aspects of destination management, as well as travel and transport mobilities, much has yet to be examined in terms of disability, embodiment and tourist experience. There are notable exceptions, however, including Macpherson's (2009) work with vision-impaired hiking tourists who describe the tactile significance of feeling the countryside, as well as Portales and Nogues-Pedregal (2019) who investigate the embodied experience of travelling for mobility-impaired tourists, noting the ways they are ignored and overlooked, as well as objectified as 'problems' for staff to solve. Indeed, as the authors remind us going forward:

> We must not ignore the fact that the embodiment of tourists with disabilities is not a homogenous construct since it manifests itself in a variety of ways, namely, mobility, hearing, vision, learning, sensitivities, and mental health (Buhalis and Darcy 2011). Each one of these embodied expressions is affected by the level of support and the assistive technology required. Both of which help to construct an embodied identity for the individual disabled traveller.
>
> *(Portales & Nogues-Pedregal, 2019: 60)*

An additional area worth further consideration from the perspective of embodiment is critical animal studies and the human–animal relations facilitated by tourism. Critical animal studies is increasingly incorporated into tourism research, exploring the ways tourists interact with animals, including as performers for tourists (Markwell, 2015; Rickly & Kline, 2021), as food through tourists' consumption (Kline, 2018a, 2018b) and through outdoor leisure and recreation (Carr & Young, 2018). So while the above discussion of embodiment and experience has summarized how tourism researchers address the experiences of the body through tourism, body–landscape interactions and embodied performances of place,

Performing beyond the view

there remains a dearth of research on the ways in which human–nonhuman bodies come into contact through tourism encounters. We only need to think about the popularity of elephant rides and swimming with dolphins, as well as donkeys as pack animals or guide dogs for vision-impaired tourists to begin to imagine the significance of this embodied intersubjectivity for the tourists' experiences (Rickly & Kline, 2021). Further, considering animals as food and animal consumption through tourism clearly has significant implications for tourist bodies in terms of health and nutrition, but also potential disease. Additionally, such examples raise ethical questions of the tourism industry and tourists themselves, offering opportunities to bring ethical debates and embodiment into conversation.

Conclusions

While Urry and Larsen (2011) have updated and revised *Tourist Gaze 3.0*, they maintain an emphasis on the visual, albeit in relation to other senses and sensations. Such a revision supports the extensive research on the body in tourism as important and significant to understanding the tourist experience. From Veijola and Jokinen's (1994) call for greater attention to the body in tourism studies to Palmer and Andrews (2019) latest edited volume on *Embodiment and Tourism*, this area of tourism research has developed at a fever pitch. Accompanied by major theoretical strides in performance studies, non-representational theory and (post)-phenomenology, we now have much richer understandings of the body *doing* tourism. Yet, we are also more aware than ever that the tourist experience has always been a practice of embodiment, from pre-modern travellers' emphasis on the ear and the mouth to our postmodern social media practices in which we use visual media as the means to communicate bodily enactments. As such, our steady technological advances, greater global connectivity and mobilities, along with increased demands for fairness, diversity and ethics in tourism, point the fact that there remains much work ahead for scholars of tourism and embodiment.

References

Adler, J. (1989) Origins of sightseeing. *Annals of Tourism Research*, 16(1), 7–29.

Anderson, B. and Harrison, P. (Eds.) (2010) *Taking-Place: Non-Representational Theories and Geography*. Aldershot: Ashgate.

Bærenholdt, J. O. and Granas, B. (Eds.) (2008) *Mobility and Place: Enacting Northern European Peripheries*. Burlington: Ashgate.

Bærenholdt, J. O., Haldrup, M., Larsen, J. and Urry, J. (2004) *Performing Tourist Places*. Burlington: Ashgate.

Barry, K. (2019) Material-bodily assemblages on a multi-day wilderness walk, In C. Palmer and H. Andrews (Eds.), *Tourism and Embodiment*. Abingdon: Routledge, pp. 172–186.

Buchmann, A., Moore, K. and Fisher, D. (2010) Experiencing film tourism: Authenticity and fellowship. *Annals of Tourism Research*, 37(1), 229–248.

Buhalis, D. and Darcy, S. (Eds.) (2011) *Accessible Tourism: Concepts and Issues*. Bristol: Channel View Publications.

Buhalis, D., Darcy, S. and Ambrose, I. (2012) *Best Practices in Accessible Tourism. Inclusion, Disability, Ageing Population and Tourism*. Bristol: Channel View Publications.

Carr, N. and Young, J. (Eds.) (2018) *Wild Animals and Leisure: Rights and Wellbeing*. Abingdon: Routledge.

Casey, E. S. (1993) *Getting Back into Place: Towards a Renewed Understanding of the Place-world*. Bloomington: Indiana University Press.

Casey, E. S. (1996) How to get from space to place in a fairly short stretch of time: Phenomenological prolegomena. In S. Feld and K. H. Basso (Eds.), *Senses of Place*. Seattle: University of Washington Press, pp. 13–52.

Casey, E. S. (2001) Body, self and landscape: A geophilosophical inquiry into the place-world. In P. C. Adams, S. D. Hoelscher and K. E. Till (Eds.), *Textures of Place: Exploring Humanist Geographies.* Minneapolis: University of Minnesota Press, pp. 403–425.

Chronis, A. (2015) Moving bodies and the staging of the tourist experience. *Annals of Tourism Research,* 55, 124–140.

Coleman, S. and Crang, M. (Eds) (2002) *Tourism: Between Place and Performance.* New York: Beghahn Books.

Cook, P. S. (2010) Constructions and experiences of authenticity in medical tourism: The Performances of places, spaces, practices, objects and bodies. *Tourist Studies,* 10(2), 135–153.

Crouch, D. (2002) Surrounded by place: Embodied encounters. In S. Coleman and M. Crang (Eds.), *Tourism: Between Place and Performance.* New York: Berghahn Books, pp. 207–218.

Csordas, T. J. (1993) Somatic modes of attention. *Cultural Anthropology,* 8(2), 135–156.

Csordas, T. J. (1994) *Embodiment and Experience: The Existential Ground of Culture and Self.* Cambridge: Cambridge University Press.

Csordas, T. (1999) Embodiment and cultural phenomenology. In G. Weiss and H. F. Haber (Eds.), *Perspectives on Embodiment: The Intersections of Nature and Culture.* New York: Routledge, pp. 143–162.

Csordas, T. J. (2011) Cultural phenomenology: Embodiment: Agency, sexual difference, and illness. In F. Mascia-Lees (Ed.), *A Companion to the Anthropology of the Body and Embodiment.* Chichester: Wiley-Blackwell, pp. 137–156.

Dann, G. and Jacobsen, J. K. S. (2002) Leading the tourist by the nose. In G. Dann (Ed.), *The Tourist as a Metaphor of the Social World.* Wallingford: CABI, pp. 209–235.

Dann, G. and Jacobsen, J. K. S. (2003) Tourism smellscapes. *Tourism Geographies,* 5(1), 3–25.

Dewsbury, J. D., Harrison, P., Rose, M. and Wylie, J. (2002) Enacting geographies. *Geoforum,* 33(4), 437–440.

Edensor, T. (2000). Staging Tourism. *Annals of Tourism Research,* 27(2), 322–344.

Edensor, T. (2001) Performing tourism, staging tourism: (Re)producing tourist space and practice. *Tourist Studies,* 1(1), 59–81.

Edensor, T. (2018) The more-than-visual experiences of tourism. *Tourism Geographies,* 20(5), 913–915.

Game, A. (1991) *Undoing the Social: Towards a Deconstructive Sociology.* Buckingham: Open University Press.

Germann Molz, J. (2006) Cosmopolitan bodies: Fit to travel and travelling to fit. *Body and Society,* 12: 1–21.

Grosz, E. (1994) *Volatile Bodies. Toward a Corporeal Feminism.* Bloomington: Indiana University Press.

Haldrup, M. (2019) Bodies at sea: 'Water' as interface in Viking heritage communication. In C. Palmer and H. Andrews (Eds.), *Tourism and Embodiment.* Abingdon: Routledge, pp. 121–139.

Haldrup, M. and Larsen, J. (2003) The family gaze. *Tourist Studies,* 3(1), 23–45.

Howard, C. A. and Kupers, W. (2019) Phenomenological anthropology of interactive travel: Mediated responsivity and inter-placed mobilities. In C. Palmer and H. Andrews (Eds.), *Tourism and Embodiment.* Abingdon: Routledge, pp. 187–202.

Huberman, J. (2019) Re-encountering bodies: Tourists and children on the riverfront of Banaras. In C. Palmer and H. Andrews (Eds.), *Tourism and Embodiment.* Abingdon: Routledge, pp. 9–22)

Johannesson, G. T. and Baerenholdt, J. O. (2008) Enacting places through the connections of Tourism. In J. O. Baerenholdt and B. Granas (Eds.), *Mobility and Place: Enacting Northern European Peripheries.* Burlington: Ashgate, pp. 155–166.

Kline, C. (Ed.) (2018a) *Animals, Food & Tourism.* Abingdon: Routledge.

Kline, C. (Ed.) (2018b) *Tourism Experiences and Animal Consumption: Contested Values, Morality and Ethics.* Abingdon: Routledge.

Larsen, J. (2010) Goffman and the tourist gaze: A performative perspective on tourism mobilities. In M. H. Jacobsen (Ed.), *The Contemporary Goffman.* New York: Routledge, pp. 313–332.

Larsen, J. (2012) Performance, space and tourism. In J. Wilson (Ed.), *The Routledge Handbook of Tourism Geographies.* Abingdon: Routledge, pp. 67–73.

Laurier, E. and Philo, C. (2006) Possible geographies: a passing encounter in a cafe. *Area,* 38(4), 353–363.

Leavy, P. (2008) Performance-based emergent methods. In S. N. Hesse-Biber and P. Leavy (Eds.), *Handbook of Emergent Methods.* New York: The Guilford Press, pp. 343–359.

Lorimer, H. (2005) Cultural geography: The busyness of being 'more-than-representational'. *Progress in Human Geography,* 29(1), 83–94.

MacCannell, D. (1973) Staged authenticity: Arrangements of social space in tourist settings. *American Journal of Sociology*, 79(3), 589–603.

Macpherson, H. M. (2009) Touch in the countryside: Memory and visualization through the feet. *Senses and Society*, 4(2), 179–195.

Macpherson, H. M. (2010) Non-representational approaches to body-landscape relations. *Geography Compass*, 4(1), 1–13.

Markwell, K. (Ed.) (2015) *Animals and Tourism: Understanding Diverse Relationships*. Bristol: Channel View Publications.

Merchant, S. (2011) Negotiating underwater space: The sensorium, the body and the practice of scuba-diving. *Tourist Studies*, 11, 215–234.

Merleau-Ponty, M. (1962[2004]) *Phenomenology of Perception* (C. Smith, Trans.) New York: Humanities Press.

Morgan, N. and Pritchard, A. (2005) On souvenirs and metonymy: Narratives of memory, metaphor and materiality. *Tourist Studies*, 5(1), 29–53.

Palmer, C. and Andrews, H. (Eds.) (2019) *Tourism and Embodiment*. Abingdon: Routledge.

Pearce, P. L. and Wang, Z. (2019) Human ethology and tourists' photographic poses. *Annals of Tourism Research*, 74, 108–120.

Obrador-Pons, P. (2003) Being-on-holiday: Tourist dwelling, bodies and place. *Tourist Studies*, 3(1), 47–66.

Obrador-Pons, P. (2007) A haptic geography of the beach: Naked bodies, vision and touch. *Social & Cultural Geography*, 8(1), 123–141.

Portales, R. C. and Nogues-Pedregal, A.M. (2019) Rethinking the body in the touristic scenario: The elusiveness of embodying disability into tourism. In C. Palmer and H. Andrews (Eds.), *Tourism and Embodiment*. Abingdon: Routledge, pp. 41–54.

Prince, S. (2019) Clay, glass and everyday life: Craft-artists' embodiment in the tourist landscape. In C. Palmer and H. Andrews (Eds.), *Tourism and Embodiment*. Abingdon: Routledge, pp. 158–171.

Rickly, J. M. (2017) (Re)production of climbing space: bodies, gestures, texts. *Cultural Geographies*, 24(1), 69–88.

Rickly, J. M. and Kline, C. (Eds.). (2021) *Exploring Non-human Work in Tourism: From Beasts of Burden to Animal Ambassadors*. Berlin: Walter de Gruyter GmbH & Co KG.

Rickly-Boyd, J. M. (2012a) Authenticity & aura: A Benjaminian approach to tourism. *Annals of Tourism Research*, 39(1), 269–289.

Rickly-Boyd, J. M. (2012b). Lifestyle climbers: Towards existential authenticity. *Journal of Sport & Tourism*, 17(2), 85–104.

Rickly-Boyd, J. M. (2013) Existential authenticity: Place matters. *Tourism Geographies*, 15(4), 680–686.

Rickly-Boyd, J. M., Knudsen, D. C., Braverman, L. C. and Metro-Roland, M. M. (2014) *Tourism, Performance, and Place: A Geographic Perspective*. Aldershot: Ashgate.

Rink, B. (2019) Queer bodies and the construction of tourism destination space, In C. Palmer and H. Andrews (Eds.), *Tourism and Embodiment*. Abingdon: Routledge, pp. 23–40.

Rose, M. (2002) Landscape and labyrinths. *Geoforum*, 33(4), 455–467.

Sharma, N., & Rickly, J. M. (2019). 'The smell of death and the smell of life': Authenticity, anxiety and perceptions of death at Varanasi's cremation grounds. *Journal of Heritage Tourism*, 14(5–6), 466–477.

Simonsen, K. (2005) Bodies, sensations, space and time: The contribution from Henri Lefebvre. *Geografiska Annaler: Series B, Human Geography*, 87(1), 1–14.

Simonsen, K. (2008) Place as encounters: Practice, conjunction, and co-existence. In J. O. Baerenholdt and B. Granas (Eds.), *Mobility and Place: Enacting Northern European Peripheries*. Aldershot: Ashgate, pp. 13–26.

Simonsen, K. (2010) Encountering O/other bodies: Practice, emotion and ethics. In B. Anderson and P. Harrison (Eds.), *Taking-Place: Non-representational Theories and Geography*. Burlington: Ashgate, pp. 221–240.

Speier, A. (2019) Yoga as an embodied journey towards flexibility, openness and balance. In C. Palmer and H. Andrews (Eds.), *Tourism and Embodiment*. Abingdon: Routledge, pp. 54–70.

Somdahl-Sands, K. (2013) Non-representational theory for the uninitiated: Come JUMP with me! *Geography Compass*, 7(1), 1–6.

Spinney, J. (2006) A place of sense: a kinaesthetic ethnography of cyclists on Mont Ventoux. *Environment and Planning D: Society and Space*, 24(3), 709–732.

Thrift, N. (1996) *Spatial Formations*. London: Sage Publications.

Thrift, N. (1999) Steps to an ecology of place. In D. Massey, J. Allen and P. Sarre (Eds.), *Human Geography Today*. Cambridge: Blackwell, pp. 295–321.

Thrift, N. (2000) Afterwords. *Environment and Planning D: Society and Space*, 18(2), 213–255.

Thrift, N. (2008) I just don't know what got into me: Where is the subject? *Subjectivity*, 22(1), 82–89.

Towner, J. (1985) The Grand Tour: A key phase in the history of tourism. *Annals of Tourism Research*, 12(2), 297–333.

Urry, J. (1990) *The Tourist Gaze*. London: Sage Publications.

Urry, J. (2002) *The Tourist Gaze*, 2nd Edn. London: Sage Publications.

Urry, J. and Larsen, J. (2011) *The Tourist Gaze 3.0*. London: Sage Publications.

Veijola, S. and Jokinen, E. (1994) The body in tourism. *Theory, Culture & Society*, 11(1), 125–151.

Vidon, E. S. and Rickly, J. M. (2018) Alienation and anxiety in tourism motivation. *Annals of Tourism Research*, 69(1), 65–75.

Wylie, J. (2005) A single day's walking: Narrating self and landscape on the South West Coast Path. *Transactions of the Institute of British Geographers*, 30, 234–247.

Wylie, J. (2007) *Landscape*. London: Routledge.

12

TOURISM

A spiritual experience?

Richard Sharpley

Introduction

In the introduction to a recent special issue on spiritual tourism, Cheer, Belhassen and Kujawa (2017: 252) propose that:

> If spirituality is the goal, traveling seems like an ideal setting within which it can be sought and, sometimes, even found. If spirituality is a practice or an attitude of connectivity then, again, travel offers many opportunities to experience our renewed connection with others, with life in general and, most importantly, with ourselves.

In so doing, they allude to an argument long put forward in tourism studies, that the contemporary tourist experience is akin to a sacred journey (Graburn, 1989). More specifically, following Durkheim's observation over a century ago, that when traditional religious institutions and rituals succumb to science and rationality (Durkheim, 2008), people turn to other social practices in their quest for meaning, it has been suggested that tourism represents one such 'secular substitute' for religion (Allcock, 1988: 35). Hence, reflecting Brown's (1998: 1) assertion that 'the spiritual search has become a dominant feature of late twentieth-century life; a symptom of collective uncertainty', MacCannell (1976) famously argued that the modern alienated tourist is a secular pilgrim seeking meaning (or authenticity) in other places and other times whilst similarly, though adopting a more nuanced perspective, Cohen (1979) proposed a typology of tourists based on the location of their spiritual centre. For those (existentialist) tourists who feel alienated within their home society and culture, tourism becomes a quest for an 'elective' spiritual centre elsewhere, for a meaningful life not experienced in the 'exile' of the home environment (Cohen, 1979: 190). At the same time, Graburn (1989: 22) has suggested more generally that tourism is 'functionally and symbolically equivalent to other institutions that humans use to embellish and add meaning to their lives' and thus, in short and paraphrasing Cheer et al. (2017) above, contemporary tourism may, on the one hand, be motivated by a search for spiritual experiences and, on the other hand, offer the opportunity for such experiences to those open to the notion of spirituality.

Immediately, however, a number of points emerge. First, by aligning the spiritual quest in tourism with the widely acknowledged decline in adherence to institutionalized religious

DOI: 10.4324/9781003219866-14

153

practices (Heelas & Woodhead, 2005; Houtman & Aupers, 2007; Stark, Hamberg & Miller, 2005), a distinction is explicitly made between 'spirituality' and 'religion' and, by association, between spiritual and religious tourism experiences. Such a distinction, however, may not be clear cut and, therefore, a precise definition of spirituality and religion is required both generally and in the context of tourism in particular to establish the parameters of the concept of spiritual tourism. Second, the spiritual dimension of tourism is considered in the literature from two opposing perspectives. For MacCannell (1976) and others, it is seen as the purposeful quest for spiritual experiences or, as Norman (2012: 20) puts it, 'tourism characterised by a self-conscious project of spiritual betterment'. In other words, it is assumed that there exists an identifiable form of tourism – spiritual tourism – and, hence, there also exist spiritual tourists who are motivated by the need or desire for spiritual experiences. However, such experiences are not, in a sense, guaranteed and, as a consequence, the 'spiritual tourist' categorization can be challenged – not least because a spiritual experience may be the outcome of more tangible forms of tourism such as adventure or rural tourism (Sharpley & Jepson, 2011). Conversely, the claim that contemporary tourism is in both form and function similar to a religious journey, in essence a secular pilgrimage (Digance, 2006), suggests that not only is a spiritual experience a serendipitous outcome of travel, but also participation in any form of tourism may, in principle, offer opportunities for spiritual experiences.

Lastly, it is important to acknowledge that the socio-cultural environment within which tourism occurs is in a constant state of flux, as is the significance of tourism within that dynamic environment and the manner in which it is consumed or performed. Hence, any consideration of the spiritual dimension of tourism must be informed by its wider socio-cultural context. Putting it another way, the early debates surrounding tourism as a spiritual experience/quest were framed by a particular socio-cultural condition that perhaps no longer exists (or has considerably transformed) whilst relatedly, the significance of tourism has arguably evolved to the extent that it is, as John Urry (1994: 234) put it more than two decades ago, 'no longer a differentiated set of social practices with its own and distinct rules, times and spaces'. People are, or can be, tourists most of the time. Moreover, the performance of contemporary tourism is shaped by other 'external' factors, not least the pervasive influence of digital technology and social media. This implies that the potential of tourism as a generator of spiritual experiences may be questioned whilst, collectively, the above points suggest that the relationship between tourism and spirituality demands more critical interrogation than has been in evidence to date.

This chapter seeks to address this need. Following a brief review of the distinction between religion and spirituality and models that conceptualize this distinction in the tourism context, it explores contemporary perspectives on the spiritual dimension of tourism. Subsequently, it draws a number of conclusions with regard to the extent to which tourists and/ or their experiences may legitimately be referred to as spiritual.

Religion, spirituality and tourism

As noted above, the notion that, irrespective of whether it is purposefully sought or not, participation in tourism may offer a spiritual experience is founded on the argument that, in modern societies at least, increasing secularization manifested in the decline in the perceived relevance of traditional religious institutions and practices (Sharpley, 2009: 240) has resulted in a quest for spiritual fulfilment through other means and practices. This, in turn, suggests that a distinction exists between the concepts of religion (or religiosity) and spirituality, that the former is increasingly being rejected in favour of the latter.

Tourism: a spiritual experience?

Whether this is indeed the case depends to a great extent on definition whilst, in contrast, some have pointed to a religious revival around the world (Tilson, 2001). Nevertheless, the evidence suggests that, certainly in Western societies, traditional religion and religious practices continue to decline in popularity. For example, a recent study in the UK reveals that membership of the Church of England has fallen to an all-time low; not only does a majority of the population (56 percent) claim to have no religion, but also just two percent of adults in the 18–24 age bracket in particular admitted to affiliation to the Church (Baynes, 2018). Although the figures are less stark, a similar picture is also in evidence in the US, where 26 percent of the population claims to be religiously unaffiliated (Pew Research, 2019).

However, this increasing secularization of modern societies does not necessarily imply the emergence of a religious vacuum; rather, many suggest that societies remain religious, but religion is taking on a different form (Tomasi, 2002). In other words, there has been what Heelas and Woodhead (2005: 2) refer to as a spiritual revolution, a 'shift in the spiritual landscape' in which there is increasing evidence of a need and desire amongst people to maintain and nurture their spiritual health or, as Wuthnow (1998: 138) alternatively observes, there has been a major shift in religious practices manifested in 'the traditional spirituality of inhabiting sacred spaces giving way to a new spirituality of seeking'. Is it possible then, to distinguish between religion/religiosity and spirituality? If to be religious is by definition to be spiritual, is it possible to be spiritual without being religious? And in the context of this chapter, can religious tourism be categorized as a form of spiritual tourism and *vice versa*, particularly as in contrast to the acknowledged decline in religion referred to above, religious tourism is widely considered to be a growth market (Griffin & Raj, 2017). As now discussed, the answers to these questions lie in definitional (and perceptual) distinctions.

Religion/religiosity

According to Vukonić (2000: 497), religion cannot 'be described in a simple definition'; not only are there competing sociological and theological perspectives on religion, but there also exist numerous manifestations of the phenomenon. Nevertheless, as Durkheim (2008) established in his seminal work *The Elementary Forms of Religious Life*, originally published (in French) in 1912, religion is the product of society, a social construct manifested in an institutionalized system of beliefs and practices observed by some or all members of society. Moreover, Durkheim also identified beliefs, practices, rituals and objects within the religious realm as being sacred; in contrast, he described all other things within society not having a religious function or significance as profane. A belief in the supernatural is not an inevitable ingredient of the sacred realm although, as Vukonić (2000: 497) notes, 'almost all people who follow some form of religion believe that a divine power created the world and influences their lives'.

Thus, in many societies religion is an integral element of the social structure (Vukonić, 1996) and plays a fundamental role in what Durkheim termed the solidarity of societies. That is, religion reinforces the values, morals and behaviours that bind societies together, maintaining their structure and cohesion and, hence, is reflected in the culture of those societies (Lupfer, Brock & DePaola, 1992). Specifically, adherence to religious codes not only requires participation in particular rituals and practices but may also impose obligations or restrictions upon the more general behaviour of believers, such as with regard to dress or to the consumption of food and drink. And it is in this context that a distinctive understanding of religion/religiosity emerges. That is, for some, religion has come to be seen narrowly as 'religious institutions and prescribed theology and rituals' (Zinnbauer et al., 1997: 551), a set of practices that believers must adhere to. In other words, religiosity requires unquestioned submission to such practices, reflecting the argument that, throughout history, 'the power and force of religion... have been beyond question, analysis or inspection' (Wellman & Tokuno, 2004: 294) but also competing with the postmodern search for individual freedom and expression (Tomasi, 2002). Hence, religion is increasingly perceived negatively as a barrier to a more personal, individualistic search for and experience of the sacred or spiritual and, as a consequence, it is being rejected by increasing numbers of people who prefer to define themselves as spiritual (Lambert, 2004). In short, religion or religiosity can be thought of as passive collective adherence to the organized rigidity of traditional practices, and it is this required adherence to such practices, rather than religious/spiritual beliefs, that societies are increasingly turning away from. In its place, a 'new' religion is allegedly emerging, manifested in the proactive, individualistic search for meaning or spirituality. Yet, is it possible to define spirituality?

Spirituality

According to research in the UK,

> 'it is clear that spiritual beliefs are not the preserve of the religious... a majority of non-religious people hold spiritual beliefs. This is particularly evident when it comes to non-traditional forms of religious beliefs, where it seems to make very little difference whether someone considers themselves religious or not'.
>
> *(Theos, 2013: 25)*

In other words, not only does the concept of spirituality extend beyond the restrictive definitional parameters of religion/religiosity but also, as Vukonić (1996) observes, it is implicitly a fundamental element of human existence. Indeed, some support the argument, often attributed to the French philosopher Pierre Teilhard de Chardin (but see QI, 2019), that 'We are not human beings having a spiritual experience. We are spiritual beings having a human experience'. More simply perhaps, to be human is to be spiritual or, as Hay and Socha (2005: 607) suggest, 'spiritual awareness [is] natural and universal within the human species'.

Irrespective of such philosophical debates, however, it is acknowledged that, on the one hand, there remains a degree of congruence between religiosity and spirituality (Zinnbauer et al., 1997) – those who consider themselves to be religious also consider themselves to be spiritual whilst spirituality is often defined in religious terms, such as a belief in God or ritual performance – whilst, on the other hand, the quest for the spiritual is, in practice and belief, distinctive from a religious quest. That is, it is arguably concerned broadly 'with things of the spirit as opposed to the material' (Stark et al., 2005: 7) although, as proposed shortly, it may also be found in the material, and is manifested in a wide variety of contemporary practices – including, of course, tourism – beyond the constraints of traditional religious ritual. It is also generally accepted that the need for spiritual nourishment is prevalent within contemporary society yet, significantly, achieving definitional consensus on spirituality remains problematic. In a workplace-based study, for example (Kinjerski & Skrypnek, 2004: 31), respondents not only found difficulty in defining it, but some also suggested that 'defining spirituality concretizes it and treats it like a scientific thing', which they did not perceive it to be. Similarly, respondents in Sharpley and Jepson's (2011) research amongst rural tourists initially struggled to articulate their understanding of spirituality although, in subsequent group

Tourism: a spiritual experience?

discussions, they related it to 'concepts of connectedness, one-ness, insightfulness and inner well-being' (Sharpley & Jepson, 2011: 61).

Connectedness, in particular, is central to many definitions of spirituality; it is considered to be a 'feeling of being connected with one's complete self, others, and the entire universe' (Mitroff & Denton, 1999: 83). Conversely, as Moufakkir and Selmi (2018) observe, spirituality also embraces a more specific inward focus on the self, achieving one's potential or, in Maslow's (1943) terms, self-actualization. To an extent, this coincides with Heelas and Woodhead's (2005) conceptualization of spirituality as what they refer to as a 'subjective life', a 'life lived in accordance with an individual's inner needs, desires and capabilities' (Sharpley & Jepson, 2011: 55); hence the spiritual quest is 'not to become what others want one to be, but "to become who I truly am"' (Heelas & Woodhead, 2005: 3). Significantly, Heelas and Woodhead (2005) also suggest that such subjective-life spirituality can be found in the material world, not necessarily in a transcendental 'other', in so doing further emphasizing a distinction between humanistic spirituality and traditional religiosity.

Also adopting a more humanistic perspective, Fisher, Francis and Johnson (2000: 135) propose four domains within which connectedness or harmonious relationships are fundamental to spiritual well-being:

i   Personal domain (connectedness with the self); seeking self-awareness, identity, esteem.
ii Communal domain (connectedness with others); seeking meaning through interpersonal relationships.
iii Environmental domain (connectedness to the natural world); developing a sense of awe and wonder.
iv Transcendental domain (connectedness with a spiritual 'other'); relating to 'some-thing or some-One beyond then human level' (Fisher et al., 2000: 135.)

Typically, people give precedence to one domain over the other, reflecting individual values, needs and experiences and, certainly within the first three listed above, it is evident that the distinction between spiritual and emotional well-being, the latter perhaps synonymous with the concept of eudaimonia (Knobloch, Robertson & Aitken, 2017) or contentedness, is rather fuzzy. In other words, the experience of particular forms of connectedness may be interpreted differently by different people, not least reflecting an individual's openness to notions of spirituality. For example, Jepson and Sharpley (2015) found that rural tourists typically considered their environmental connection with place to be emotional as opposed to spiritual.

This implies that, unlike the social construct of religion (as defined above) with its established role, rituals and practices, spirituality is a more nebulous, affective concept that is uniquely sought, understood, experienced or even denied by the individual. In other words, although generally considered to be some form of connectedness with the material and/or non-material world, that connectedness is experienced, felt or interpreted privately by the individual. It may also, particularly in the tourism context, be a fleeting, temporary experience whilst, for religious adherents, a sense of connectivity to a higher power may be more permanent. Hence, spirituality defies precise definition yet, for the purposes of this chapter, can be thought of literally as being concerned with the human spirit. This then suggests that, as the following section discusses, although religious tourism is distinctive, identifiable form of tourism, the same cannot be said for what some refer to as spiritual tourism.

Richard Sharpley

From religious to spiritual tourism

As many claim (Digance, 2006; York, 2001), the phenomena of religion and tourism have long been closely aligned; not only is travel for religious purposes widely considered to be one of the earliest forms of tourism (Kaelber, 2006) but, throughout history, the growth in tourism in general has, to some extent, reflected the expansion of religion in particular (Vukonić, 1996: 17–19). Alternatively, as Collins-Kreiner and Gatrell (2006: 33) note, 'it is impossible to understand the development... of tourism without studying religion and [specifically] the pilgrimage phenomenon', pilgrimage being both an early and major contemporary manifestation of religiously motivated travel.

A detailed discussion of religious tourism and the religious tourist experience is beyond the scope of this chapter (but, see Chapter 28). Suffice to say, religious tourism takes numerous forms – in addition to pilgrimage and visits to sites of religious significance, it also embraces activities such as missionary travel, attendance at religious events/gatherings and fellowship travel (Nolan & Nolan, 1989; Wright, 2008) – and nowadays constitutes a major (and economically important) sector of the global tourism market. It is also distinctive for being a form of tourism 'whose participants are motivated in part or exclusively for religious reasons' (Rinschede, 1992: 52); that is, whether a trip is wholly (for example, a pilgrimage) or partly (for example, visiting a sacred site whilst on holiday) religious, it is undertaken for religious purposes.

Recognizing the variations in the intensity of motivations, purpose or beliefs amongst religious tourists, Smith (1992) was the first to conceptualize what she refers to as the 'quest in guest', or the search for religious /spiritual fulfilment through tourism. At one end of her widely cited continuum lies the 'true' pilgrim undertaking a journey motivated by faith, adherence to ritual and the potential for a transformative spiritual experience; at the other lies the secular tourist seeking personal/spiritual fulfilment through tourism. Between these extremes can be found various forms of religious tourism defined by the individual tourist's religious or other needs, though common to all points on the continuum is an assumed search for spiritual fulfilment or meaning on the part of the tourist. Such a search is also implicit in a more recent conceptual framework for spiritual tourism offered by Cheer et al. (2017: 255) although, mirroring the definitions of religiosity and spirituality proposed above, a distinction is made between religious tourism with a focus on the social institution of religion and spiritual tourism with a focus on the self. In other words, it is assumed that, for religious tourists, spiritual fulfilment or connectivity with a higher power is achieved through participation in ritualized religious practices whilst, for spiritual tourists, the 'focus tends to be on the attainment of some kind of spiritual benefit, such as getting in touch with one's inner self' (Cheer et al., 2017: 254) through participation in specific types of secular tourist activity. Interestingly, Cheer et al. (2017: 254) also distinguish spiritual tourism as being 'consumptive by nature', or based on commodified tourist experiences.

This latter claim can be easily challenged. That is, religious tourism experiences (as defined in this chapter) are no less commodified than their spiritual counterpart, reflecting what some consider to be the increasing commodification of religion (Einstein, 2008) or what Carrette and King (2005) describe as the rebranding and marketing of religion for profit. The point here, however, is that spiritual tourism is typically considered distinctive from religious tourism, thereby answering a question posed earlier: religious tourism is clearly a form of spiritual tourism (or is spiritual in nature), but spiritual tourism cannot be categorized as a form of religious tourism. Rather, the (spiritual) tourist experience is based upon the individual, non-institutionalized quest (assumedly amongst tourists with no traditional religious beliefs or conviction) for meaning through purposeful participation in specific forms of touristic activity. However, as suggested in the introduction to this chapter, not only might such a quest be unsuccessful but also meaningful or spiritual experiences may be an unanticipated outcome of participation in any form of tourism. This suggests that identifying or defining a particular form of tourism as 'spiritual' may be inappropriate. Hence, by way of commencing a critique of the concept, the following section considers a number of contemporary perspectives on the spiritual tourist experience.

The spiritual tourist: contemporary perspectives

As observed earlier, the notion that participation in tourism offers, in principle, opportunities for spiritual fulfilment was first proposed around four decades ago. Nevertheless, in contrast to the substantial literature on religious tourism that has since emerged, few attempts have been made to address empirically the validity of this claim (Moufakkir & Selmi, 2018; Sharpley, 2009; Sharpley & Jepson, 2011; Sharpley & Sundaram, 2005). Arguably, this paucity of research reflects the ambiguity of the concept of spiritual tourism and the potential difficulty in exploring an experience that tourists themselves may neither be consciously seeking nor easily recognize. Moreover, as Willson, McIntosh and Zahra (2013: 164) imply, some of the factors that influence the degree of meaning attached to a tourist experience are 'private' and, hence, avoided by researchers.

Usefully, however, Norman (2012) provides a conceptual overview of the spiritual tourist experience in which he proposes five inter-related varieties of experience that represent a framework for identifying and understanding the form and function of specific types of tourism that offer a spiritual dimension. Interestingly, he also suggests that, typically, a spiritual tourist will exhibit two or more of these characteristics, under which headings relevant perspectives are now discussed.

Healing

According to Norman (2012: 28), the spiritual tourist experience is associated with spiritual healing, or 'practices that seek to correct or ameliorate elements of everyday life perceived as problematic'. This is immediately open to debate, for many forms of tourism might fall under this heading, particularly as a long-recognized motivation to participate in tourism is the need to not only escape (Iso-Ahola, 1982) but to regenerate, or 'heal'. Putting it another way, 'tourism is social therapy, a safety valve keeping the everyday world in good working order' (Krippendorf, 1986: 525); it plays a healing, or re-creational, role in societies. Beyond this broad observation, however, a variety of types of tourism and significantly, places where tourism occurs can be directly related to a potential healing process.

Addressing the latter first, tourism is all about place; it involves the temporary movement from one place or centre of meaning – typically ordinary home life – to another place, a centre 'out there' (Cohen, 1979: 180) that offers the potential for new, meaningful experiences. Hence, tourists arguably choose to travel to particular places in the hope or expectation of such meaningful experiences, including psychological (or spiritual) healing. Throughout history, it has been acknowledged that the experience of natural places in particular may elicit a positive spiritual response (Szerszynski, 2005) whilst in recent years, a growing body of research has demonstrated the restorative effects on mental health of both viewing and engaging physically with green spaces in general. For example, MacKerron and

Mourato (2013) have found that being in green space of all kinds induces greater levels of happiness than in built environments.

In the particular context of tourism, the designation of national parks and other public green spaces from the nineteenth century onwards reflected understanding that nature and access to green spaces is conducive to both physical and psychological health and well-being (Conway, 1991). More specifically, a number of studies have focused on the extent to which spiritual or emotional outcomes may result from participating in tourism and leisure in a variety of natural environments, most notably exploring the connection between spirituality and wilderness experiences (Ashley, 2007; Fredrickson & Anderson, 1999; Heintzman, 2003; Stringer & McAvoy, 1992). In addition, others have considered the potential for spiritual experiences in forest (Williams & Harvey, 2001) and mountain environments (Pomfret, 2006) as well as in outdoors more generally (Allcock, 2003). Whilst tourists' responses have, inevitably, been found to vary according to individual expectations, motivations and experiences (Heinzman, 2010), most studies reveal that being in and interacting with the natural environment is a significant factor in stimulating spiritual responses; being in green space offers opportunities to develop not only a 'spiritual connectedness to the landscape' (Gelter, 2000: 78) but also 'intimate contact with this environment leads to thoughts about spiritual meanings and eternal processes' (Kaplan & Talbot, 1983: 178). Although a specific healing process might not be explicit, such responses undoubtedly bring restorative benefits.

And it is not only green spaces that have attracted academic attention; a study by Jarratt and Sharpley (2017) explores tourists' spiritual responses to the seaside, reflecting work that has considered the restorative benefits of blue spaces more generally (Purcell, Peron & Berto, 2001). Together with the green space research, this suggests that participation in many types of tourism activity in natural places, such as ecotourism, rural tourism, adventure tourism or marine-based to name but a few, may provide psychological/spiritual healing benefits. In addition, other non-environment specific forms of tourism, such as those falling under the umbrella of holistic or wellness tourism (Smith & Puczkó, 2009) are undertaken with, assumedly, the explicit desire to improve both physical and spiritual health and well-being.

Collectively, these points imply that many forms of tourist experiences may have restorative or healing effects, the list being longer if intent is taken out of the equation (see 'quest' below). In turn, this suggests that tourism generally, rather than activities that are implicitly spiritual in form, may possess healing qualities, even if these are not expressly sought or even recognized by tourists.

Experiment

The second variety or characteristic of spiritual tourist experience is experiment or, more precisely, 'tourists trying out alternatives when normal lifeways appear problematic' (Norman, 2012: 29). Broadly, this may be understood as experimenting with different lifestyles through tourism, such as in the case of Western tourists staying in an ashram and experimenting with different activities, such as yoga or meditation, whether intentionally or simply because the opportunity exists (Sharpley & Sundaram, 2005). Indeed, Norman (2012) observes that documented examples of such experimentation focus primarily on Western tourists in the East, implicitly engaging in alternative religions/spiritualities (see Brown, 1998). For the purposes of this chapter, however, such experimentation may be interpreted more broadly as engaging in activities not normally undertaken at home or experimenting with one's own abilities or limitations. For example, in the research amongst rural tourists participating in active rural pursuits, such as hill walking, Jepson and Sharpley

(2014) found that, for some, emotional or spiritual fulfilment was achieved through not only by being on the mountain tops but also through overcoming the physical challenge of the climb. In a similar vein, what Laing and Crouch (2006) refer to as frontier tourism is revealed to be often a spiritual or transformative experience. Moreover, if the notion of frontier is adapted to refer to the extent of an individual's experience as opposed to frontier places, then any new or challenging experience through tourism may equally be considered meaningful of transformative.

Quest

Perhaps extending MacCannell's (1976) argument that the contemporary tourist is a secular pilgrim seeking meaning, Norman (2012: 30) proposes that the quest in tourism, 'the act of finding [the self] in and for itself as a spiritual experience, is an ideal form of spiritual tourist experience'. This spiritual quest through tourism may be described as a transformative 'voyage of discovery' (Robledo, 2015), implicit to which is intent or purpose. In other words, if tourism is to be referred to as a quest, such as quest should be intentional. However, it is uncertain how many tourists consciously embark on a journey with this specific objective in mind – none of the respondents in Sharpley and Jepson's (2011) study, for example, had done so – whilst if that quest is ultimately unsuccessful, can the traveller then be legitimately referred to as a 'spiritual tourist'?

Retreat

Described as an 'experience characterized as one of escape from the everyday' (Norman, 2012: 32), tourism as retreat can, from this perspective, be related to most forms of tourism. However, Norman goes on to identify specific forms of tourism, such as so-called slow tourism, which, although a contentious concept (for example, Fullagar, Markwell & Wilson, 2012; McGrath & Sharpley, 2018), offer retreat from the fast pace of modern urban life. At the same time, so-called retreat tourism is a recognized touristic activity engaged in 'by people in search of peace, quiet and spiritual input' (Shackley, 2004: 227). Often utilizing secular locations, such as historic cultural properties or purpose-built facilities, but more typically in places associated with a particular religious tradition, tourists are provided with accommodation, food, spaces for quiet contemplation and opportunities to participate in organized religious or spiritual activities. In this case, the distinction between religious and spiritual tourism becomes blurred.

Collective

Noran's final variety of spiritual tourist experience is being part of a collective, or sharing the experience 'with others of like persuasion' (Norman, 2012: 32). A common example is that of participation in walks on traditional pilgrimage routes, such as the Camino de Santiago in Spain (Lois-González & Santos, 2015) or the Kumano Kodo in Japan (Kato & Progano, 2017), where walking in the footsteps of innumerable pilgrims may in itself evoke a sense of connection or spirituality, but one that is enhanced by sharing it with others undertaking the route – perhaps a manifestation of the 'communal domain' referred to earlier. There are evident links here with the concept of communitas, or equality and sharing of experiences amongst an unstructured community, as experienced by hill-walking tourists in Sharpley and Jepson's (2011) study. For them, the physical experience and connectivity with place was significantly enhanced by the connectivity with other hikers. And again, collective meaningful experiences arguably occur in many forms of tourism, from the shared excitement of, for example, 'white-knuckle rides' at theme parks to the more general sharing of tourist spaces, referred to by Urry (1990) as collective tourism, where the tourist experience is enhanced by the presence of others. In this case, and as discussed in more detail in the following conclusion, this is yet another instance where identifying a 'spiritual tourist experience' as distinctive from tourist experiences more generally again becomes problematic.

Conclusion: is there a spiritual tourist experience?

The purpose of this chapter has been to undertake a critical review of the concept of the spiritual tourist experience. In other words, it has long been suggested that not only may tourism offer the opportunity for meaningful, spiritual or even transcendental experiences but also that, for many, tourism has become the focus of a quest for such experiences, that there is a 'spiritual tourist' seeking spiritual fulfilment through tourism. However, only few attempts have been made to verify empirically this claim, the outcomes of which tend to be ambiguous. Hence, this chapter has sought to offer a more nuanced consideration of the spiritual tourist, questioning in particular whether there is indeed a distinctive tourist experience that can be labelled or understood as spiritual.

What is beyond doubt is that, through participation in tourism, people benefit from experiences related to the human spirit, such as happiness (hedonic and/or eudaimonic), awe, wonder, a state of mindfulness or peacefulness, a sense of connectedness to others or to nature, or even a feeling of self-discovery. Indeed, the regularity with which many people consume tourism would imply the existence of such experiences. However, less certain is the extent to which they can be referred to collectively as 'spiritual', particularly within the context of spirituality being understood as the contemporary substitute for traditional institutionalized religion. As previously noted, spirituality for many remains an undefinable concept often related to a belief in a higher power and, consequently, responses to particular places, events or experiences are typically considered to be emotional rather than spiritual (Jepson & Sharpley, 2014).

At the same time, the tourism contexts within which such experiences might occur are numerous – they are not necessarily restricted to specific touristic places and activities that are potentially 'spiritual' in nature' – and nor are they necessarily the preserve of the 'spiritual tourist' purposefully seeking meaning, authenticity or spiritual refreshment. Putting it another way, all tourists might, at some time or another and in all likelihood serendipitously, experience feelings and emotions that some might describe as spiritual. Moreover, also less certain is the extent to which they are unique to tourism. That is, whilst the explicit act of being a tourist, of temporarily substituting the normal, home environment for another, may enhance the potential for such experiences, they might equally occur in the course of day-to-day life.

This is not to say, of course, that participation in particular forms of tourism, such as retreat tourism, temple-stay tourism, wellness tourism, secular pilgrimage tourism or even adventure tourism, is not motivated by the expectation of or hope for meaningful or even transcendental experiences. Indeed, the tourists in Moufakkir and Selmi's (2018) research are described as purposefully seeking spirituality although interestingly, many of their responses correspond to the categories of humanistic connectedness referred to earlier in this chapter whilst, more generally, there is no guarantee of such experiences as an outcome. Hence

Tourism: a spiritual experience?

much again depends on individual understandings or interpretations of the concept of spirituality, as well as the wider life-world context of individual tourists (Willson et al., 2013).

Collectively, these points lead to the inevitable conclusion that care must be taken in categorizing certain tourists and their experiences as spiritual as defined in this chapter. In other words, it is perhaps erroneous to suggest there is a distinctive type of 'spiritual' tourist seeking or enjoying a distinctive 'spiritual' experience. Undoubtedly, the potential exists for all tourists at some time to enjoy meaningful experiences; such experiences are, however, neither necessarily sought nor the inevitable outcome of being a tourist; moreover, they are unique to the individual in terms of their significance and the manner in which they are understood and, indeed, may also occur in non-touristic contexts. Hence, ultimately, it is only the religious tourist who can also be legitimately referred to as a spiritual tourist.

References

Allcock, D. (2003) From the plains to the peaks: The outdoors as a repository of spirituality. *Horizons*, 21, 10–12.

Allcock, J. (1988) Tourism as a sacred journey. *Loisir et Société*, 11, 33–48.

Ashley, P. (2007) Toward an understanding and definition of wilderness spirituality. *Australian Geographer*, 38(1), 53–69.

Baynes, C. (2018) Church of England staring at oblivion as just 2% of young Britons say they identify with it. *The Independent*, 7 September. Available at: https://www.independent.co.uk/news/uk/home-news/church-england-uk-young-adults-identify-british-social-attitudes-a8527136.html (Accessed 24 October 2018).

Brown, M. (1998) *The Spiritual Tourist*. London: Bloomsbury.

Carrette, J. and King, R. (2005) *Selling Spirituality: The Silent Take-over of Religion*. Abingdon: Routledge.

Cheer, J., Belhassen, Y. and Kujawa, J. (2017) The search for spirituality in tourism: Toward a conceptual framework for spiritual tourism. *Tourism Management Perspectives*, 24, 252–256.

Cohen, E. (1979) A phenomenology of tourist experiences. *Sociology*, 13(2), 179–201.

Collins-Kreiner, N. and Gatrell, J. (2006) Tourism, heritage and pilgrimage: The case of Haifa's Bahá'í Gardens. *Journal of Heritage Tourism*, 1(1), 32–50.

Conway, H. (1991) *People's Parks: The Design and Development of Victorian Parks in Britain*. Cambridge: Cambridge University Press.

Digance, J. (2006) Religious and secular pilgrimage: Journeys redolent with meaning. In D. Timothy and D. Olsen (Eds.), *Tourism, Religion and Spiritual Journeys*. Abingdon: Routledge, pp. 52–64.

Durkheim, E. (2008) *The Elementary Forms of Religious Life* (Trans. C. Cosman). Oxford: Oxford University Press.

Einstein, M. (2008) *Brands of Faith. Marketing Religion in a Commercial Age*. Abingdon: Routledge.

Fisher, J., Francis, L. and Johnson, P. (2000) Assessing spiritual health via four domains of spiritual wellbeing: The SH4DI. *Pastoral Psychology*, 49(2), 133–145.

Fredrickson, L. and Anderson, D. (1999) A qualitative exploration of the wilderness experience as a source of spiritual inspiration. *Journal of Environmental Psychology*, 19(1), 21–39.

Fullagar, S., Markwell, K. and Wilson, E. (Eds.) (2012) *Slow Tourism: Experiences and Mobilities*. Bristol: Channel View Publications.

Gelter, H. (2000) Friluftsliv: The Scandinavian philosophy of outdoor life. *Canadian Journal of Environmental Education*, 5(1), 77–92.

Graburn, N. (1989) Tourism: The sacred journey. In V. Smith (Ed.), *Hosts and Guests: The Anthropology of Tourism*, 2nd Edn. Philadelphia: University of Pennsylvania Press, pp. 21–36.

Griffin, K. A. and Raj, R. (2017) The importance of religious tourism and pilgrimage: Reflecting on definitions, motives and data. *International Journal of Religious Tourism and Pilgrimage*, 5(3) Article 2. Available at: https://arrow.dit.ie/ijrtp/vol5/iss3/2 (Accessed 24 October 2019).

Hay, D. and Socha, P. (2005) Spirituality as a natural phenomenon: Bringing biological and psychological perspectives together. *Zygon*, 40(3), 589–612.

Heelas, P. and Woodhead, L. (2005) *The Spiritual Revolution: Why Religion Is Giving Way to Spirituality.* Oxford: Blackwell Publishing.

Heintzman, P. (2003) The wilderness experience and spirituality what recent research tells us. *Journal of Physical Education, Recreation & Dance*, 74(6), 27–32.

Heinzman, P. (2010) Nature-based recreation and spirituality: A complex relationship. *Leisure Sciences*, 32(1), 72–89.

Houtman, D. and Aupers, S. (2007) The spiritual turn and the decline in tradition. The spread of post-Christian spirituality in 14 Western countries, 1981–2000. *Journal for the Scientific Study of Religion*, 46(3), 305–320.

Iso-Ahola, S. (1982) Toward a social psychological theory of tourism motivation: A rejoinder. *Annals of Tourism Research*, 9(2): 256–262.

Jarratt, D. and Sharpley, R. (2017) Tourists at the seaside: Exploring the spiritual dimension. *Tourist Studies*, 17(4), 349–368.

Jepson, D. and Sharpley, R. (2015) More than sense of place? Exploring the emotional dimension of rural tourism experiences. *Journal of Sustainable*, 23(8–9), 1157–1178.

Kaelber, L. (2006) Paradigms of travel: From medieval pilgrimage to the virtual tour. In D. Timothy and D. Olsen (Eds), *Tourism, Religion and Spiritual Journeys*. Abingdon: Routledge, pp. 65–79.

Kaplan, R. and Talbot, J. (1983) Psychological benefits of a wilderness experience. In I. Altman and J. Wohlwill (Eds), *Behavior and the Natural Environment*. Boston: Springer, pp. 163–203.

Kato, K. and Progano, R. (2017) Spiritual (walking) tourism as a foundation for sustainable destination development: Kumano-kodo pilgrimage, Wakayama, Japan. *Tourism Management Perspectives*, 24, 243–251.

Kinjerski, V. and Skrypnek, B. (2004) Defining spirit at work: Finding common ground. *Journal of Organizational Change Management*, 17(1), 26–42.

Knobloch, U., Robertson, K. and Aitken, R. (2017) Experience, emotion, and eudaimonia: A consideration of tourist experiences and well-being. *Journal of Travel Research*, 56(5), 651–662.

Krippendorf, J. (1986) Tourism in the system of industrial society. *Annals of Tourism Research*, 13(4), 517–532.

Laing, J. and Crouch, G. (2006) From the frontier: Sacred journeys in faraway places. *Tourism: The Spiritual Dimension Conference*, 5–8 April, University of Lincoln, Lincoln.

Lambert, Y. (2004) A turning point in religious evolution in Europe. *Journal of Contemporary Religion*, 19(1), 29–45.

Lois-González, R. and Santos, X. (2015) Tourists and pilgrims on their way to Santiago. Motives, Caminos and final destinations. *Journal of Tourism and Cultural Change*, 13(2), 149–164.

Lupfer, M., Brock, K. and DePaola, S. (1992) The use of secular and religious attributions to explain everyday behavior. *Journal for the Scientific Study of Religion*, 31(4), 486–503.

Maslow, A. (1943) A theory of human motivation. *Psychological Review*, 50, 370–396.

MacCannell, D. (1976) *The Tourist: A New Theory of the Leisure Class*. New York: Schocken Books.

MacKerron, G. and Mourato, S. (2013) Happiness is greater in natural environments. *Global Environmental Change*, 23(5), 992–1000.

McGrath, P. and Sharpley, R. (2018) Slow travel and tourism: New concept or new label? In M. Clancy (Ed.), *Slow Tourism, Food and Cities: Pace and the Search for the 'Good Life'*. Abingdon: Routledge, pp. 49–62.

Mitroff, I. and Denton, E. (1999) A study of spirituality in the workplace. *Sloan Management Review*, 40(4), 83–92.

Moufakkir, O. and Selmi, N. (2018) Examining the spirituality of spiritual tourists: A Sahara Desert experience. *Annals of Tourism Research*, 70, 108–119.

Nolan, M. and Nolan, S. (1989) *Christian Pilgrimage in Modern Western Europe*. London: University of North Carolina Press.

Norman, A. (2012) The varieties of the spiritual tourist experience. *Literature & Aesthetics*, 22(1), 20–37.

Pew Research (2019) In U.S., decline of Christianity continues at rapid pace. *Pew Research Centre: Religion & Public Life*. Available at: https://www.pewforum.org/2019/10/17/in-u-s-decline-of-christianity-continues-at-rapid-pace/ (Accessed 24 October 2019).

Pomfret, G. (2006) Mountaineering adventure tourists: A conceptual framework for research. *Tourism Management*, 27(1), 113–123.

Purcell, T., Peron, E. and Berto, R. (2001) Why do preferences differ between scene types? *Environment and Behavior*, 33(1), 93–106.

Tourism: a spiritual experience?

QI (2019) You are not a human being having a spiritual experience. You are a spiritual being having a human experience. *Quote Investigator.* Available at: https://quoteinvestigator.com/2019/06/20/spiritual/ (Accessed 28 October 2019).

Rinschede, G. (1992) Forms of religious tourism. *Annals of Tourism Research*, 19(1), 51–67.

Robledo, M. A. (2015) Tourism of spiritual growth as a voyage of discovery. In D. Chambers and T. Rakić (Eds.), *Tourism Research Frontiers: Beyond the Boundaries of Knowledge*. Bingley: Emerald Publishing, pp. 71–86.

Shackley, M. (2004) Accommodating the spiritual tourist: The case of religious retreat houses. In R. Thomas (Ed.), *Small Firms in Tourism: International Perspectives*. Oxford: Elsevier, pp. 225–237.

Sharpley, R. (2009) Tourism, religion and spirituality. In T. Jamal and M. Robinson (Eds.), *Sage Handbook of Tourism Studies*. London: Sage Publications, pp. 237–253.

Sharpley, R. and Jepson, D. (2011) Rural tourism: A spiritual experience? *Annals of Tourism Research*, 38(1), 52–71.

Sharpley, R. and Sundaram, P. (2005) Tourism: A sacred journey? The case of ashram tourism, India, *International Journal of Tourism Research*, 7(3), 161–171.

Smith, V. (1992) Introduction: The quest in guest. *Annals of Tourism Research*, 19(1), 1–17.

Smith, M. and Puczkó, L. (2009) *Health and Wellness Tourism*. Oxford: Butterworth-Heinemann.

Stark, R., Hamberg, E. and Miller, A. S. (2005) Exploring spirituality and unchurched religions in America, Sweden, and Japan. *Journal of Contemporary Religion*, 20(1), 3–23.

Stringer, L. and McAvoy, L. (1992) The need for something different: Spirituality and wilderness adventure. *Journal of Experiential Education*, 15(1), 13–20.

Szerszynski, B. (2005) *Nature, Technology and the Sacred*. Oxford: Blackwell Publishing.

Theos (2013) *The Spirit of Things Unseen: Belief in Post-Religious Britain*. London: Theos.

Tilson, D. (2001) Religious tourism, public relations and church-state partnerships. *Public Relations Quarterly*, 46(3), 35–40.

Tomasi, L. (2002) Homo viator: From pilgrimage to religious tourism via the journey. In W. Swatos and L. Tomasi (Eds.), *From Medieval Pilgrimage to Religious Tourism: The Social and Cultural Economics of Piety*. London: Praeger, pp. 1–25.

Urry, J. (1990) The consumption of tourism. *Sociology*, 24(1), 23–35.

Urry, J. (1994) Cultural change and contemporary tourism. *Leisure Studies*, 13(4), 233–238.

Vukonić, B. (1996) *Tourism and Religion*. Oxford: Pergamon.

Vukonić, B. (2000) Religion. In J. Jafari (Ed.), *Encyclopedia of Tourism*. London: Routledge, pp. 497–500.

Wellman J. and Tokuno, K. (2004) Is religious violence inevitable? *Journal for the Scientific Study of Religion*, 43(3), 291–296.

Williams, K. and Harvey, D. (2001) Transcendent experience in forest environments. *Journal of Environmental Psychology*, 21(3), 249–260.

Willson, G., McIntosh, A. and Zahra, A. (2013) Tourism and spirituality: A phenomenological analysis. *Annals of Tourism Research*, 42, 150–168.

Wright, K. (2008) *The Christian Travel Planner*. Nashville: Thomas Nelson.

Wuthnow, R. (1998) *After Heaven: Spirituality in America since the 1950s*. Berkeley: University of California Press.

York, M. (2001) New age commodification and the appropriation of spirituality. *Journal of Contemporary Religion*, 16(3), 361–372.

Zinnbauer, B., Pargament, K., Cole, B., Rye, M., Butfer, E., Belavich, T., Hipp, K., Scott, A. and Kadar, J. (1997) Religion and spirituality: Unfuzzying the fuzzy. *Journal for the Scientific Study of Religion*, 36(4), 549–564.

SECTION 2

Tourist demand and motivation

13

THE ULYSSES FACTOR REVISITED

Consolidating the travel career pattern approach to tourist motivation

Philip L. Pearce

Introduction

Many individuals – academics, tourism professionals and tourists themselves – have clear views about what motivates tourists. In this chapter, credibility is given to a range of views about tourists' desire to travel, but one long-standing approach occupies centre stage. Most attention will be given to the travel career pattern approach to tourist motivation. This model, which has been crafted and developed through collecting data from multiple markets, originated with work in the 1980s and continues to be trialled and tested in a number of contemporary studies. The first aim of the chapter is to provide readers with a concise academic history of the development of this moderately influential set of tourist motivation ideas. The material discussed covers the criticisms and the modifications to the early phases of the approach and, as a by-product of that discussion, reveals some of the forces that shape academic inquiry. The central section of the chapter turns from the academic history to the more immediate attributes of the travel career pattern for assessing and categorizing contemporary tourist demand at several different scales of analysis. The penultimate section offers examples of using the approach. The final component of the work reflects on the development of the ideas and offers subtle directions for its further refinement.

It is valuable at the start of the chapter to explain the use of the expression 'The Ulysses factor'. The expression was first used in tourism studies as the title of a book written by the author (Pearce, 1988). In summarizing the work, the following sentence appeared in the last pages of that volume:

> The Ulysses factor, in brief, is the multi-faceted motivational dynamic of those who leave their homes to venture into new worlds.
>
> *(Pearce, 1988: 227)*

As the international diversity of tourism scholars has evolved over the past 30 years, the reference to the mythical hero Ulysses from classical literature might be somewhat obscure to those with non-western educational backgrounds. Ulysses is the Roman adaptation of the Greek name Odysseus. Both names are still used to refer to the hero of a fantastic set of mythical travel adventures around the Mediterranean that takes Ulysses 19 years to

DOI: 10.4324/9781003219866-16

complete. The voyages were described by Homer in his epic poem *The Odyssey*, and then revisited by other authors including the English poet Alfred Lord Tennyson whose work was simply entitled Ulysses.

The tale of Ulysses appeals as an archetypal image of the desire for and complexity of travel motivation. During the voyages, multiple motives are displayed; there is the enjoyment of sensual pleasures, the documentation of achievement, the social pleasure associated with travelling with others and the realization and development of personal strength through self-discovery. Ulysses travels in a very unsafe world; he has to battle the Cyclops, a fearsome one-eyed monster, deal with the lustful intentions of the Sirens and reconcile his love of home and wife with his attraction to both the nymph Calypso and the beguiling Circe. Bad weather and fearsome storms disrupt his journeys and he alone survives the whole 19 years as his companions perish in a set of gruesome ways.

As a character, Ulysses is flawed and very human; he is arrogant yet determined, self-interested but close to his companion travellers, and independent-minded, although he is sometimes seduced by those seeking to exploit his desires. He craves the freedom of travel and searches for meaning. Tennyson, interpreting the Ulysses story, writes that on his return home, Ulysses pines for more adventures and his many experiences drive him to seek fresh worlds: The lines are:

> I am a part of all that I have met;
> Yet all experience is an arch wherethro'
> Gleams that untravelled world, whose margin fades
> For ever and ever when I move.

The relevance of referring to the Ulysses voyages in tourism research, and specifically in this chapter, is as a short-hand way of introducing the travel career pattern approach. The ideas about Ulysses are from classical and nineteenth-century literature but the focus on experience is very much a part of twenty-first century thinking. The central point is to appreciate the changing motives of Ulysses across the timeline of his travels and understand how previous experiences change the pattern of travel motives.

The early context

In the early years of what we now know as tourism research, there were few scholars interested in motivation and the drivers of tourist experience. Economists and industry analysts viewed demand, as measured by visitor arrivals and statistics, as an adequate way to capture tourists' interests in destinations (Young, 1973). The social forces and psychological needs that built these numbers were of little concern and were neglected. It was the sociologists interested in tourism who stepped in to fill the void. Dean MacCannell (1973, 1976) proposed that tourists seek authenticity; in this view tourists were on a quest for the real, backstage and genuine features of the setting they visit. This quest was seen as driven by the tourists' alienation from their everyday modern world. Graham Dann (1977, 1981) also identified generic themes. He argued that tourists are driven by both anomie, the alienation from their own society and self enhancement, which was conceived as a need to develop their status. Erik Cohen (1979) argued for a more differentiated view of tourists' desired experiences. He recognized that some tourists may not seek authenticity and formulated five kinds of tourists' experience: recreational, diversionary, experiential, experimental and existential. His classification was driven by an explicit reference to literature about the meaning of pilgrimage

(Eliade, 1969). Cohen's categories are arranged as sequence from less concerned with seeking the meaning of existence and identity to more fully engaged in such a quest. Many of these foundation ideas from the sociology of tourism have been used widely by later scholars (Cohen & Cohen, 2012).

The prevailing ways in which tourist motivation was being conceived in tourism studies at the start of the 1980s did not sit comfortably with my own views and experience as an emerging tourism researcher. I had completed a doctorate at the University of Oxford in psychology in 1977 and was engaged in writing my first book on tourism, *The Social Psychology of Tourist Behaviour*, which was then published in 1982 (Pearce, 1982). My concerns were first, that the approaches were generic – typically all tourists were treated the same way. Second, the work ignored the long and detailed treatment of motivation in psychology, which had a rich history of developing an understanding of motivation with a variety of theories. As a third concern, the notions were put forward with little empirical evidence, an anathema to the way psychologists approached topics in human behaviour. And as a fourth and final concern, the theories were mostly static with no prospect of change or the evolution of tourists' motivation over time. Some of these views were articulated in the 1982 book and other psychologists noted similar concerns (Iso-Ahola, 1982).

The uneasiness with the existing studies was not universal. Some of the leisure and recreation researchers in the United States were undertaking work partly linked to tourism and they used more empirical approaches. The often quoted phrase from John Crompton, that tourist motivation is hard to measure, was a part of his 1979 paper that did formulate a listing of suggested motivational factors from a survey (Crompton, 1979). The contribution of Crompton, together with that of Graham Dann, did result in the identification and early use of a distinction between push (internally driven) and pull (external features of the destination or experience) motives. That distinction has endured and continues to be useful in specifying what is being measured (Crompton, 1979; Dann, 1977, 1981). A little later, Beard and Ragheb (1983) developed a leisure motivation scale that was used with some enthusiasm by those seeking a quick account of tourists' motives. Again though, the work provided only a static snapshot and incorporated little of the accumulated knowledge about human motivation from the decades of psychological inquiry.

The absence of specific tourist motivation systems in the literature had one unusual consequence. One system, which emphasized the level of anxiety felt by tourists in their destination choice, was offered by Stanley Plog, a United States based marketing and business consultant who had a broad social science background (Plog, 1974, 2011). The poles of this one-dimensional continuum were given the labels psychocentric (home seeking and travel averse) and allocentric (outward looking and adventurous). The curve that depicted a normal distribution of individuals along this dimension became standard fare in tourism teaching, especially because it was used in one of the first and very widely used textbooks entitled *Tourism: Principles, Practices, Philosophies* (McIntosh, 1977). The work by Plog had originated in consulting studies done for the airlines in the United States and its details and methodology were therefore confidential and unavailable for academic scrutiny. There were some forceful and far-reaching criticisms of the one-dimensional, sector-specific and regionally localized views (Smith, 1990a, 1990b). Plog's analysis had a commercial imperative and was built to describe one culture with attendant limitations, even though it was applied for universal use. Nevertheless, his ideas persisted for many years in tourism textbooks and became an established core of tourism study. In the mid-1990s, Robert McIntosh explained to the author that the ideas were used because there was nothing else to fill the motivation chapter. This conversation resulted in the present author taking on that responsibility from the 7th edition onwards (Pearce, 1995).

These early efforts to account for tourist motivation can be encapsulated by Hofstede's formulation of a levels of analysis problem (Hofstede, 1995). The leisure researchers were interested in a slightly different phenomenon to that of tourism, with the consequence that their vision of the possibilities of why people travel was limited. The sociologists, notably MacCannell, Cohen and Dann, were mostly interested in developing broad commentaries about tourists by integrating motivation, activities and experiences in relation to large social forces and the characteristics of (western) society. The limitations of their approaches were exposed when a more fine-grained approach directed at the internal push factors was required for specific tourist groups. If they were aware of the efforts of psychologists, including Allport (social learning theory), McClelland and Atkinson (achievement motivation), Murray (multiple human needs), Maslow (hierarchy of needs), Rogers (self-development), Csikszentmihalyi (peak experiences), as well as social status concepts from writers with a philosophical leaning such as Harré, or a clinical and psychoanalytic orientation such as Freud, Jung and Adler, they did not attempt to include such ideas in their broader motivational systems and portrayals of experience (Pearce, Morrison & Rutledge, 1998: 37).

A first iteration

The foundation components for the travel career concept were first articulated in a chapter on motivation in 1982 and a co-authored article in 1993 (Pearce, 1982; Pearce & Caltabiano, 1983). The material used to understand motivation included 400 descriptive accounts provided by experienced tourists drawn primarily from members of the North American Travel and Tourism Association (TTRA) supplemented by less experienced tourists represented by students from Australian University classes. In the 1982 chapter, a rich descriptive account was provided about the range of experiences and the implicit motivations driving these pursuits. In the 1983 article, the experiences were coded by referring to their links to the five levels of Maslow's hierarchy of needs. Further, and importantly, the notion that tourists changed their motives with experience and held multiple motives at once was expressed in the paper. The precise words used were:

> The argument that tourists may be thought of as having a motivational career in travel was also sustained by the data. In particular, the two experienced travel groups (those who had visited either more than three, or more than 10 countries) were shown to be more concerned with higher order needs (notably love and belongingness and self-actualisation) than were less experienced travelers. The view that these differences reflect age or sex differences was ruled out by separate analyses of these variables which did not generate the above motivational differences.
>
> *(Pearce & Caltabiano, 1983: 19)*

Further work linking the patterns of motives to the need for authenticity and the role of motives in visiting theme parks found some continuing support for these ideas (Pearce & Moscardo, 1985). They were brought together in the clearest and simplest way in the 1988 book *The Ulysses Factor* using the label the travel career ladder (TCL) approach to tourist motivation (Figure 13.1).

A second and more often cited version of the travel career ladder was also drawn. In this second version, the work of Mills (1985) and Groves, Kahalas and Erickson (1975) were both influential. In the study by Mills, changing a pattern of motivation amongst skiers with

The Ulysses factor revisited

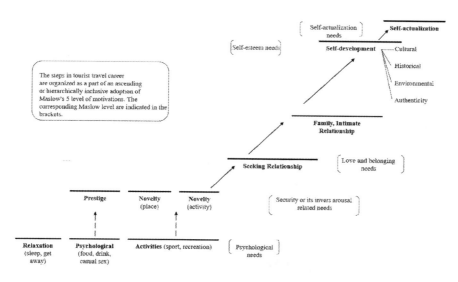

Figure 13.1 An early graphical depiction of the links constituting the travel career ladder

different levels of travel experience was shown to be in accord with the TCL ideas, while the work of Groves, Kahalas and Erikson suggested differentiating each Maslow level by building in an intrinsic (self-driven) and an extrinsic (socially influenced) level for each of the first four Maslow-linked stages. Only the self-actualization stage was seen as fully internally determined. The second variant of the TCL offering a minor refinement to the first illustration is depicted in Figure 13.2.

During the following 10 years, the approach was used intermittently by a variety of scholars and practitioners. The TCL appeared in conference presentations, consultancy projects, students used the travel career ladder and reviews cited it (Kim, 1997; Kim, Pearce, Morrison & O'Leary, 1996; Loker-Murphy, 1997; Oppermann, 1998). Perhaps in common with the earlier influence of Plog's work, there were few major competitors to the notions proposed. Yet all was not well. As Ryan (1998) pointed out in a solid appraisal of the approach, more evidence was needed and refinement of the categories required. This was an important and powerful criticism and prompted a period of reflection and reconsideration of how to produce a more adequate conceptualization while retaining some of the existing positive features. For example, most of the commentary did seem to ignore the influence on the travel career ladder of the notion of a career, a changing array of desired experiences across a timeline (cf. Harré, 1980; Hughes, 1937; Marsh, Rosser & Harré, 1978). Further, desirable features of a good tourist motivation theory had already been outlined in a paper on the fundamentals of tourist motivation and these principles acted as reference points for improvement (Pearce, 1992).

That framework and Ryan's helpful and instructive critique suggested the keys to building a sound theory of tourist motivation were: to make sure that it could act as a theory with integrative and some predictive power, not merely serve as a 'state of play' description; that the theory would be both appealing to users and relatively easy to communicate so it could be adopted; that it was able to be measured; and that a multi-motive approach was used. Further, the approach should be dynamic, that is, being able to monitor change in individuals and social forces over time, and that extrinsic and intrinsic factors should be incorporated.

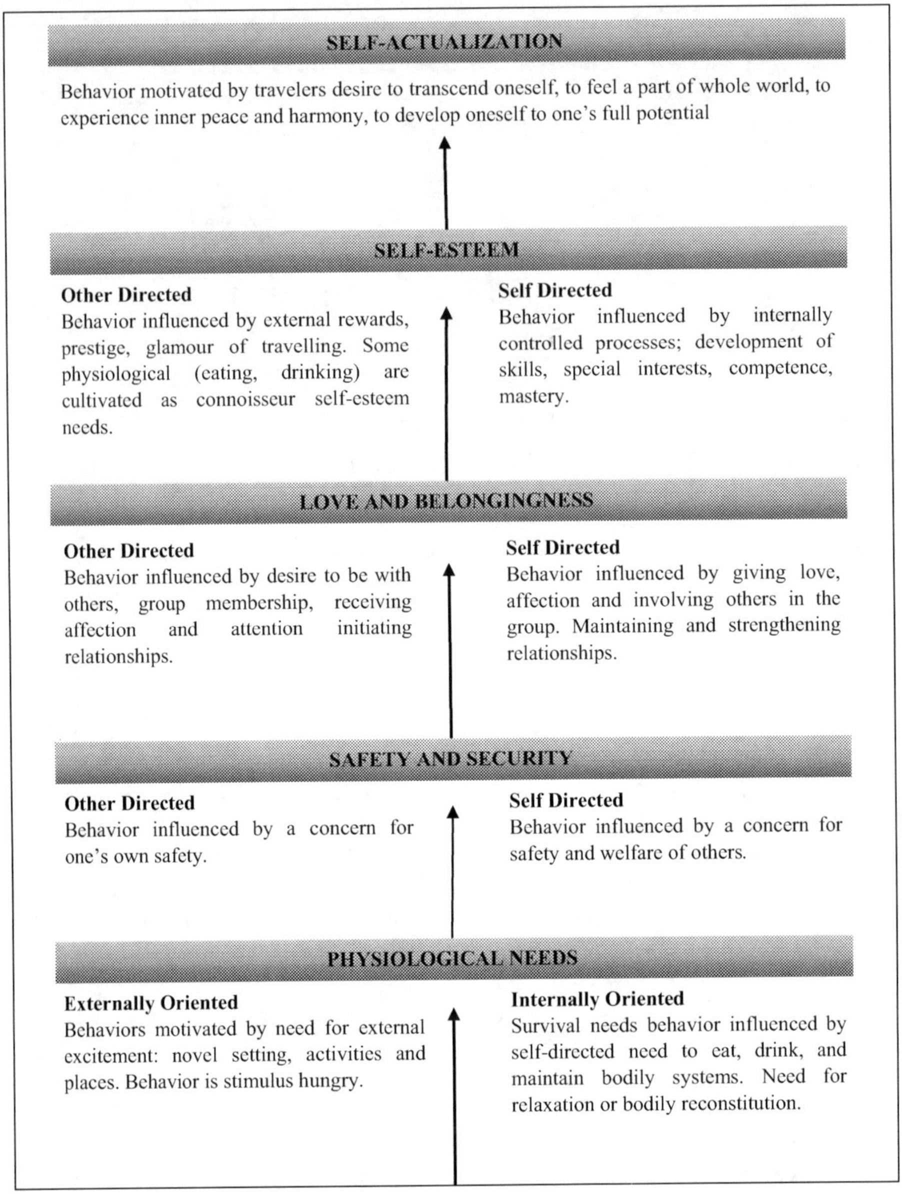

Philip L. Pearce

SELF-ACTUALIZATION

Behavior motivated by travelers desire to transcend oneself, to feel a part of whole world, to experience inner peace and harmony, to develop oneself to one's full potential

SELF-ESTEEM

Other Directed
Behavior influenced by external rewards, prestige, glamour of travelling. Some physiological (eating, drinking) are cultivated as connoisseur self-esteem needs.

Self Directed
Behavior influenced by internally controlled processes; development of skills, special interests, competence, mastery.

LOVE AND BELONGINGNESS

Other Directed
Behavior influenced by desire to be with others, group membership, receiving affection and attention initiating relationships.

Self Directed
Behavior influenced by giving love, affection and involving others in the group. Maintaining and strengthening relationships.

SAFETY AND SECURITY

Other Directed
Behavior influenced by a concern for one's own safety.

Self Directed
Behavior influenced by a concern for safety and welfare of others.

PHYSIOLOGICAL NEEDS

Externally Oriented
Behaviors motivated by need for external excitement: novel setting, activities and places. Behavior is stimulus hungry.

Internally Oriented
Survival needs behavior influenced by self-directed need to eat, drink, and maintain bodily systems. Need for relaxation or bodily reconstitution.

Figure 13.2 The refinement to and the most used version of the travel career ladder model
Source: Redrawn from the version in Pearce (1988: 31).

A second system: the travel career pattern approach

By the year 2000 much had been learnt about building a viable travel motivation theory. Not only were there requirements to build a genuine theoretical approach and collect more data, but also the original metaphor of a ladder had misled some commentators into thinking that motives were dominated by one level in the system. In such an interpretation, the 'lower

The Ulysses factor revisited

levels' of the ladder, once used, were no longer important. That was not intended. And it was not really intended by Maslow either, who had always adopted a hierarchically inclusive approach in his own formulations. It can be pointed out for the sake of academic clarity that it was the textbook personnel who used his ideas and drew a ladder like diagram of the hierarchy – that figure does not appear in Maslow's own works (Maslow, 1943, 1954).

It was decided to rebuild the travel career approach. As Head of a School of Business by that time, and working closely with PhD students in the development of ideas, the author was able to build a partnership with Uk-il (Lui), Lee a Korean PhD student. His role in the travel career pattern story is both important and sad. He contributed a number of good ideas and collected much data. He was able to provide a first conference presentation in 2003 of our reformulation of the approach into the travel career pattern (Lee & Pearce, 2003). This work was then published and reached a wider audience in a key article in 2005 supported by a book chapter covering the same material in a more expansive format (Pearce, 2005; Pearce & Lee, 2005). Most regrettably, the entertaining and smart Lui, as he was widely known, suffered from a fatal form of cancer towards the end of this period and the work with his name on it was published posthumously.

The reformulation offered a number of new perspectives. The core idea that experience changed the tourists' motivations was preserved but the notion that it was vertical ladder was disbanded. Instead, the data collected for both western and Asian samples suggested changing emphasis on motives in an array of patterns. Fourteen motive factors were identified from two large-scale surveys. Starting with a 140-item array of motives that was whittled down to 74 after virtual synonyms were eliminated, the research team sought responses from a sample of over 1,000 western tourists and more than 800 Asian tourists. Factor analysis of the responses to the items produced 14 highly consistent factors that differed in the ratings of importance. These differences in importance were used to build an image of a core of motives surrounded by layers of decreasing importance. An image constructed from these results is displayed in Figure 13.3.

The travel career pattern approach conceptualizes motivation as involving a core of common, almost invariant, motives – to escape, relax and build close relationships – surrounded by two further layers. In the outer layer, several peripheral and less important motives such as the desire for autonomy, nostalgia and romance exist while the inner middle layer is more concerned with fulfilment, a desire to learn and to build knowledge of local people and settings. Within this middle layer, a differentiation of more intrinsic motives and more externally influenced motives is depicted. The empirical work demonstrated that while the core layer was common and stable, inexperienced tourists rated all layers as quite to very important, and tourists with greater travel experience placed extra emphasis on the middle layer.

The approach began to be used. O'Reilly (2006) used travel career patterns to understand gap year travel; Morgan and Xu (2009) and Xu, Morgan and Song (2009) employed the concepts to assess student travel; Paris and Teye (2010) used the ideas to study backpackers; Smed (2009) explored identity changes emerging through the motive patterns; and Getz and Anderson (2010) applied the system to festivals and event participation. There were multiple other uses, including in student theses and conference presentations. Filep and Greenacre (2007) offered some small modifications to the work, as did Williams and McNeil (2011). Hsu and Huang (2008) and Huang and Hsu (2009) accorded the travel career pattern approach a prominent place in their comprehensive reviews of travel motivation theories.

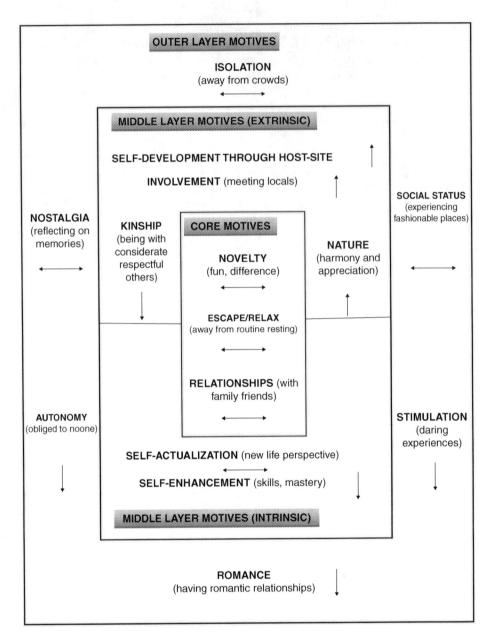

Figure 13.3 The travel career pattern and tourists' motivation
Source: Redrawn from the version in Pearce (2011: 62).

Linking concepts

By 2011, the need to address two further themes emerged. As the study of tourism became more sophisticated, an increasing number of researchers recognized the diversity of approaches to human behaviour and experience. As Hofstede (1995) had suggested, different levels of contribution to studying a topic are possible. Attention was beginning to be directed towards the value of positive psychology, as well as the work of neuroscientists and brain-based researchers. Both approaches offered something of interest to tourist motivation research.

Positive psychology is often depicted as starting in the year 2000 with the keynote address to the American Psychological Association by its then President Martin Seligman (Csikszentmihalyi & Seligman, 2000). The vision in that address was to orient some of the research world in psychology towards enhancing human well-being, rather than only correcting psychological deficits and problems that had begun to be the major pre-occupation of the discipline. Several lines of inquiry developed. Key directions captured by the rubric of positive psychology included an emphasis on flow experiences (Snyder & Lopez, 2009), an understanding of human virtues and character strengths (Peterson & Seligman, 2004) and the development of the PERMA model for building and assessing the quality of life (Park, Peterson, & Seligman, 2004; Seligman 2012). PERMA emphasizes being *positive*, *engaged* with the world, having quality *relationships*, developing *meaning* for activities and acknowledging *achievements*. A primary orientation in the literature concerned with positive psychology is teleological: a view that human well-being or flourishing is driven by a forward looking approach to life's possibilities (Harré, 1980). This perspective was noted in work by the author and colleagues as they sought to introduce positive psychology ideas to tourism (Filep & Pearce, 2014; Pearce, 2009; Pearce, Filep & Ross, 2011). All importantly, the motives used in building the travel career pattern model already contained a blend of forward looking perspectives and deficit correcting needs. The fit between the travel career pattern work and positive psychology is more than an academic coincidence. Maslow and Harré amongst others, whose ideas were pivotal in developing the travel career pattern view of motives and human aspirations, were key figures in the twentieth-century psychology who provided a groundwork of ideas on which positive psychology could be constructed. This connection has meant that researchers seeking to develop an understanding of how travel motives reflect human aspirations and underlie choices have a dynamic and contemporary but above all hopeful orientation to their work (cf. Pritchard, Morgan & Ateljevic, 2011). This is not to deny that anxieties and alienation, and at times a desire to escape, are necessarily unimportant, and they too appear in the model and in Figure 13.3, but such corrective imperatives are not the only ones that drive tourists. The increasing interest in well-being, happiness and transformative times in tourism studies can be very closely aligned with the travel career pattern work and the multifaceted view of what drives holiday behaviour (Garcês, Pocinho, Jesus & Rieber, 2018).

In the past 20 years, neuroscience has emerged as a major research enterprise. Researchers in this field seek to understand biophysical determinants of behaviour and develop models of brain function. This neuroscience work provides a contemporary link to the biological needs that shape some tourist motives and is congruent with the definition of travel motivation offered by the author and colleagues some time ago (Pearce, Morrison & Rutledge, 1998). In that book, tourist motivation was defined as the 'the total network of biological and cultural forces which give value and direction to travel choice, behaviour and experience' (Pearce, Morrison & Rutledge, 1998: 33). By working with the close analysis of cases with specific problems, and by using cortical stimulation of parts of the brain, as well as examining the effects of drugs on behavioural responses, neuroscientists have provided some clarity about the motivational systems in both animal and human brains that shape behaviour (Panksepp, 1992, 1998, 2005; Panksepp & Biven, 2010; Sacks, 1991, 2016; Sacks & Sacks, 1998; Volkow, Fowler & Wang, 2002). For the present purposes, some key findings have emerged. In particular, there appear to be specific locations in the cortex and lower brain for fear, anger, curiosity and the need to have social contact. In the original versions of the work, the emotional circuits are capitalized to distinguish them from everyday uses of the terms (Panksepp, 2005). The expressions used for these circuits include seek, relate, care, lust, play, fear and rage. The knowledge about these systems comes from closely monitoring the rates of neural firing when these circuits are activated. Of particular interest to this chapter is the apparently rewarding and satisfying nature for species when the curiosity and social stimulation circuits are being stimulated (Panksepp & Biven, 2010). It is not the point of this review to initiate or follow a reductionist approach when considering tourist motivation. It is, however, appropriate to note that in the neuroscience realm there is evidence that the biological roots of some behaviour are in accord with the core motives of the travel career pattern; specifically the desire for novelty and the pleasure and excitement it brings (seeking), and the centrality of the need for social contact (relate and care). By tracing links to contemporary, world-leading neuroscience work that appear to be consistent with the tourism and psychological level of analysis, the overall credibility of the travel career pattern approach is consolidated.

In an associated development about human biology and physiology, advancements in the understanding of stress have also been achieved in the past 20 years. In early work, stress was largely conceived as a matter of the overuse of tissues, muscles and the nervous system. This approach is referred to as systemic stress (Selye, 1956; Viner, 1999). Later research highlighted the power of perceived or psychological stress to affect human functioning, with some researchers pointing out that not all stress is negative (Cohen, Gianaros & Manuck 2016; Kupriyanov & Sholokhov, 2014). Perceived stress, in both a positive (eustress) and negative sense, can be conceived as arising from our cognitive interpretation of life's experiences. Approaches adopting this perspective are usually linked together under the heading of cognitive appraisal theory (Moors, Ellsworth, Scherer & Frijda, 2013). As Sacks (2016) has argued in his rich and accessible work about human consciousness, individual awareness of these psychological processes and the role of everyday life stress can vary. At times, individuals may feel very aware of the stressors and the consequential emotional states that are induced by the situations they find challenging. Yet again, stress can be built up with individuals feeling unaware of the daily impacts on their moods and emotional reactions. Perceived stress is now acknowledged as a genuine source of physical malaise (Cohen, Murphy & Prather, 2019; Rohleder, 2014). One way to relieve the impact of stress on our systems and lives is to escape, to relax in different settings, and more specifically, to take holidays. In the travel career pattern work, the need to escape and relax are cast as core motives. Again, a congruence with biological imperatives and recent research work in an allied field strengthens the patterning of motives found through the previous tourism-based survey and factor analytic studies of motives.

Recent studies and uses

Following the development of the travel career pattern model in 2005, and the discussion about its links to other types of emerging research (Pearce, 2011, Pearce & Packer, 2013), a number of researchers employed the system. By the end of 2019 approximately 1000 Google scholar citations exist for the TCP work. Two dominant ways of using the full 74 motives and the 14 factors emerged. The examples of the first use are spread across several research teams but the two examples cited here directly involve the author. In one illustration of the use of the TCP, Pearce and Panchal (2011) were able to show that further specific questions about travelling for health reasons could be added into the TCP work as additional codes. Respondents from a number of Asian countries ranked a small set of health needs as well

The Ulysses factor revisited

as the existing TCP items. It was found that the health needs were given about the same level of importance as the middle level self-development motives. In a similar illustration of the use of the TCP as a deductive or top-down coding scheme, Mohammadi and Pearce (2020) examined drawings by children, responses to a cartoon based set of pictorial images representing potential motives, and text from interviews. These sources were employed to ascertain the children's implicit motives for taking holidays. The combination of the visual and verbal techniques reduced the weakness of each individual approach and added credibility to the outcomes. The visual images in the drawings and the oral methods of narration and cartoon selection were closely aligned in revealing the children's perceived travel needs and benefits. The core motives that were most important for children were novelty, nature, social relationships, personality excellence and excitement. The second layer of less important motivations includes comfort and escape, independence, recognition, loneliness and self-esteem, and the third layer with substantially reduced importance consisted of only two motives —romance and nostalgia. The continuing and further use of the TCP as a pre-existing coding scheme for researchers conducting tourist motivation studies appears to be warranted because it offers a wide array of themes and allows benchmarking of the results with previous work.

A second way of using the travel career pattern work has also been developed. In this approach, a specific tourist market segment and its within group variability is examined. The patterns of tourists' motives permit an appraisal of the differences within the overall market and may offer a vision of the needs of the group in the future. Li, Pearce and Zhou (2015) studied over 600 respondents from the large Chinese-outbound market and assessed group differences for younger and older, and more versus less experienced, travellers. Using a four cell model (older and experienced, older and less experienced, younger and experienced, and younger and less-experienced travellers), they uncovered some clear differences in the intergroup motive patterns. The core motives remained highly similar for all four groups. The identification of the 14 motivation factors for the Chinese tourists were very much like the 14 factors uncovered among the western and Korean samples studied previously. Younger and older inexperienced travellers differed from each other, and well-travelled younger and older tourists both differed from their more inexperienced counterparts. Personal development and host site involvement are the two factors that consistently differentiated the four groups and they increase in importance for each age group as travel experience develops. Strengthening relationships appears to matter less to the Chinese as a holiday motive, possibly because it is already seen as an aspect of life highly developed in the tourists' socially tight worlds. Nature is given a particular prominence as a factor in the inner core of the Chinese motives.

Overall, these differences in the travel motivation patterns are subtle but arguably reflect two important points. Chinese life has an array of different values and emphases, including different approaches to personal development, relationships and nature that might partly generate the higher level of importance noted in ordering the importance of the factors. Additionally, a major consideration is that the terms reported here are all in English. The substantial difficulty in exactly translating and understanding some of these concepts in Mandarin represents a degree of complexity in cross-cultural work that must be directly acknowledged.

The further use of the TCP in examining a specific market lies in the work of Oktadiana, Pearce, Pusiran and Agarwal (2017) and Oktadiana and Pearce (2018). Muslim tourists from Malaysia and Indonesia were the target groups for this study. An innovative feature of this study was the reduction of the TCP to a reduced number of 26 items. This was achieved by considering only the two highest loading items from the 13 factors deemed to be relevant and culturally appropriate for examining this market. The Romance factor, which contains an item about sexual relationships, was deemed to be potentially offensive to Muslim respondents and was not collected in these studies. The results from the Malaysian and Indonesian Muslims were aligned in terms of the contributions of the items to the factors. It appeared that self-development (host-site involvement), personal development and self-actualization were closely integrated for both the Malaysian and Indonesian samples, thus building the case that there are generic trends for Muslim tourists from the region. All importantly, there was a close correspondence in the ordering of the importance of the motives. The factors of strengthening relationships, appreciating nature and novelty headed the importance list for both samples. Nostalgia and recognition were also the least important motives for both groups.

As was illustrated in the Chinese study, the TCP appears to be sensitive enough to reveal intragroup differences. There were some minor differences in the structure of the factors for the Malaysian and Indonesian samples. For the Malaysians, appreciation of nature was enriched with self-development (experiencing a different culture). For the Indonesian sample, being safe when travelling by being with other well-known people was more prominent. Potentially such concerns reflect some overarching themes in the lives of Muslim adherents in the two countries where the boundaries among culture, nature and human existence are less rigid than in western societies, but within Indonesia, safety and security issues have a more visible face (Pisani, 2014).

One key study that offers a link to another long-standing idea in leisure and tourism research is offered in the work of Wen (2017). He connected the travel career pattern work with the concepts of casual, project and serious leisure (Stebbins, 2015). The connections proved to be solid. More specifically, Wen found a strong link between the TCP model and Stebbins' (1982, 2015) leisure involvement theory. The context for the work was astronomy tourism, a topic built on travel to a particular destination where 'the environment is suitable for observing and/or photographing celestial bodies or periodic astronomic phenomena/events' (Wen, 2017:16). The work was built on a quantitative analysis of 866 respondents from a world-wide sample. An array of findings were reported by assessing tourists' general travel experience, determinants in decision making, tourist motivation, leisure involvement, on-site activity participation, tourist satisfaction, recollection behaviour and learning outcomes. A key conclusion was drawn that the travel career patterns in the astronomy tourism context corresponded closely to rising levels of serious leisure involvement. A growth in leisure involvement was significantly reflected in higher-level motivations pertaining to self-actualization or self-development needs.

Reflection and conclusion

This chapter has traced the academic history of a conceptual scheme in tourism study. As noted, the ideas and approach continue to evolve with an active set of researchers finding uses for the full approach, modified shorter-scale versions and value in employing the work as a guiding a priori coding framework. A contribution of the chapter lies in bringing together much work that has perhaps been scattered for some readers. For example, the travel career pattern approach, despite the number of citations recorded, was not included among the 17 measures for motivation in the *Handbook of Scales in Tourism and Hospitality Research* (Gursoy, Uysal, Sirakaya-Turk, Ekinci & Baloglu, 2014). This kind of omission is puzzling, and while seeking to avoid overly harsh speculation about why such gaps occur, the failure to include the TCP may be indicative of a view about motivation oriented not towards generic theoretical perspectives but working only for specific contexts. It is hoped that the present chapter offers a review that will at least capture the fullness and potential of the TCP for readers.

The development of the ideas has been traced in part through the views and experiences of the author, so the review is partly autobiographical. As such, while they are not abundant, strong doubts about the TCP have not been exhaustively pursued. It is clear that there are some researchers who feel responses to scales do not capture the subtle motives of participants. Such perspectives underpin some recent discussions by Dolnicar who seeks to boost multiple research methods and Moscardo who has argued for a greater narrative approach (Dolnicar, 2013, 2018; Moscardo, 2011). Both researchers advocate closer connections between well-being and tourist motivation (Pearce, 2016). This push is a positive direction for further alignment of the motives expressed in the TCP and teleological and value-oriented approaches. Studies linking the TCP to research concerned with wellness and flourishing are recommended. In many ways these commentaries reiterate opinions expressed to the author by MacCannell in conversation in the early 1990s when he wondered if tourists could ever articulate what motivated them. These views are not particularly troubling to the author. The origins of the TCP and some of the current uses are employing creative and non-traditional techniques (cf. Mohammadi & Pearce, 2020). Mixed methods approaches are certainly a desirable part of using and developing the TCP further. Additionally, the limitations of empirical work built on scales can still be acknowledged without casting destructive doubt on what can be achieved using solid samples and then cross-checking the results across populations. Tourist motivation studies have come quite a long way from the early unsupported speculation about what drives people to take holidays. The travel career pattern story is a continuing part of that evolving narrative.

Acknowledgement: The author thanks Dr Zohre Mohammadi for her assistance in redrawing the TCP models used in the text.

References

Beard, J. G. and Ragheb, M. G. (1983) Measuring leisure motivation. *Journal of Leisure Research*, 15(3), 219–228.

Cohen, E. (1979) A phenomenology of tourist experiences. *Sociology*, 13(2), 179–201.

Cohen, E. and Cohen, S. A. (2012) Current sociological theories and issues in tourism. *Annals of Tourism Research*, 39(4), 2177–2202.

Cohen, S., Gianaros, P. J. and Manuck, S. B. (2016) A stage model of stress and disease. *Perspectives on Psychological Science*, 11(4), 456–463.

Cohen, S., Murphy, M. L. and Prather, A. A. (2019) Ten surprising facts about stressful life events and disease risk. *Annual Review of Psychology*, 70, 577–597.

Crompton, J. (1979) Motivations for pleasure vacation. *Annals of Tourism Research*, 6(1), 408–424.

Csikszentmihalyi, M. and Seligman, M. E. (2000) Positive psychology: An introduction. *American Psychologist*, 55(1), 5–14.

Dann, G. M. S. (1977) Anomie, ego-enhancement and tourism. *Annals of Tourism Research*, 4(4), 184–194.

Dann, G. M. S. (1981). Tourist motivation: An appraisal. *Annals of Tourism Research*, 8(2), 187–219.

Dolnicar, S. (2013) Asking good survey questions. *Journal of Travel Research*, 52(5), 551–574.

Dolnicar, S. (2018) A reflection on survey research in hospitality. *International Journal of Contemporary Hospitality Management*, 30(11), 3412–3422.

Eliade, M. (1969) *The Quest. History and Meaning in Religion.* Chicago and London: University of Chicago Press.

Filep, S. and Pearce, P. L. (Eds.) (2014) *Tourist Experience and Fulfilment: Insights from Positive Psychology*. New York: Routledge.

Filep, S. and Greenacre, L. (2007) Evaluating and extending the travel career patterns model. *Turizam: međunarodni znanstveno-stručni časopis*, 55(1), 23–38.

Garcês, S., Pocinho, M., Jesus, S. N. and Rieber, M. S. (2018) Positive psychology & tourism: A systematic literature review. *Tourism & Management Studies*, 14(3), 41–51.

Getz, D. and Anderson, T. D. (2010) The event-tourist career trajectory: A study of high-involvement amateur distance runners. *Scandinavian Journal of Hospitality and Tourism*, 10(4), 468–491.

Groves, D. L., Kahalas, H. and Erickson, D. L. (1975) A suggested modification to Maslow's need hierarchy. *Social Behavior and Personality: An International Journal*, 3(1), 65–69.

Gursoy, D., Uysal, M., Sirakaya-Turk, E., Ekinci, Y. and Baloglu, S. (2014) *Handbook of Scales in Tourism and Hospitality Research*. Wallingford: CABI.

Harré, R. (1980) *Social Being: A Theory for Social Psychology*. London: Rowman and Littlefield.

Hofstede, G. (1995) Multilevel research of human systems: Flowers, bouquets and gardens. *Human Systems Management*, 14(3), 207–217.

Hsu, C. H. C. and Huang, S. (2008) Travel motivation: A critical review of the concept's development. In A. Woodside and D. Martin (Eds.), *Tourism Management Analysis, Behaviour and Strategy*. Wallingford: CABI, pp. 14–27.

Huang, S. and Hsu, C. H. (2009) Travel motivation: Linking theory to practice. *International Journal of Culture, Tourism and Hospitality Research*, 3(4), 287–295.

Hughes, E. C. (1937) Institutional office and the person. *American Journal of Sociology*, 43, 404–413.

Iso-Ahola, S. (1982) Towards a social psychological theory of tourist motivation: A rejoinder. *Annals of Tourism Research*, 9(2), 256–262.

Kim, E. Y. (1997) Korean outbound tourism: Pre-visit expectations of Australia. *Journal of Travel & Tourism Marketing*, 6(1), 11–19.

Kim, Y. E., Pearce, P. L., Morrison, A. M. and O'Leary, J. T. (1996) Mature vs. youth travelers: The Korean market. *Asia Pacific Journal of Tourism Research*, 1(1), 102–112.

Kupriyanov, R. V. and Sholokhov, M. A. (2014) The eustress concept: Problems and outlooks. *World Journal of Medical Sciences*, 11(2), 179–185.

Lee, U. and Pearce, P. L. (2003) Travel career patterns: Further conceptual adjustment of travel career ladder. In *Second Asia Pacific Forum for Graduate Student' Research in Tourism*. Busan: The Korea Academic Society of Tourism and Leisure, pp. 2–4.

Li, H., Pearce, P. L. and Zhou. L. (2015) Documenting Chinese tourists' motivation patterns [online]. In: E. Wilson and M. Witsel (Eds.), *CAUTHE 2015: Rising Tides and Sea Changes: Adaptation and Innovation in Tourism and Hospitality*. Gold Coast: School of Business and Tourism, Southern Cross University, pp. 235–246.

Loker-Murphy, L. (1997) Backpackers in Australia: A motivation-based segmentation study. *Journal of Travel & Tourism Marketing*, 5(4), 23–45.

MacCannell, D. (1973) Staged authenticity: Arrangements of social space in tourist settings. *American Journal of Sociology*, 79(3), 589–603.

MacCannell, D. (1976) *The Tourist: A New Theory of the Leisure Class*. New York: Schocken Books.

Marsh, P., Rosser, E. and Harré, R. (1978) *The Rules of Disorder*. London: Routledge.

Maslow, A. (1943) A theory of human motivation. *Psychological Review*, 50(4), 370.

Maslow, A. (1954) *Motivation and Personality*. New York: Harper and Brothers Publishers.

McIntosh, R. W. (1977) *Tourism: Principles, Practices, Philosophies*. Columb: Grid Publishing, Inc.

Mills, A. S. (1985) Participation motivations for outdoor recreation: A test of Maslow's theory. *Journal of Leisure Research*, 17(3), 184–199.

Mohammadi, Z. and Pearce, P. L., (2020) Making memories: An empirical study of children's enduring loyalty to holiday places. In H. Seraphin and G. Gowreesunkar (Eds.), *Children in Hospitality and Tourism*. De Gruyter Studies in Tourism, 4. Berlin: de Gruyter, Berlin, pp. 137–156.

Moors, A., Ellsworth, P. C., Scherer, K. R. and Frijda, N. H. (2013) Appraisal theories of emotion: State of the art and future development. *Emotion Review*, 5(2), 119–124.

Morgan, M. and Xu, F. (2009) Student travel experiences: Memories and dreams. *Journal of Hospitality Marketing & Management*, 18(2–3), 216–236.

Moscardo, G. (2011) Searching for well-being: Exploring change in tourist motivation. *Tourism Recreation Research*, 36(1), 15–26.

The Ulysses factor revisited

O'Reilly, C. C. (2006) From drifter to gap year tourist: Mainstreaming backpacker travel. *Annals of Tourism Research*, 33(4), 998–1017.

Oktadiana, H. and Pearce, P. L. (2018) Motivated muslims: Exploring travel career patterns among Indonesian tourists. In E. Yang, J. Lee, and C. Khoo-Lattimore (Eds.) *Asian Cultures and Contemporary Tourism*. Springer, Singapore, pp. 101–119.

Oktadiana, H., Pearce, P. L., Pusiran, A. K., and Agarwal, M. (2017) Travel career patterns: The motivations of Indonesian and Malaysian Muslim tourists. *Tourism Culture & Communication*, 17(4), 231–248.

Oppermann, M. (1998) Travel horizon: A valuable analysis tool? *Tourism Management*, 19(4), 321–329.

Panksepp, J. (1992) A critical role for affective neuroscience resolving what is basic about basic emotions. *Psychological Review*, 99(3), 554–560.

Panksepp, J. (1998) *Affective Neuroscience: The Foundations of Human and Animal Emotions*. London: Oxford University Press.

Panksepp, J. (2005) Affective consciousness: Core emotional feelings in animals and humans. *Consciousness and Cognition*, 14(1), 30–80.

Panksepp, J. and Biven, L. (2010) *The Archaeology of the Mind*. New York: W.W Norton.

Paris, C. M. and Teye, V. (2010) Backpacker motivations: A travel career approach. *Journal of Hospitality Marketing & Management*, 19(3), 244–259.

Park, N., Peterson, C. and Seligman, M. E. (2004) Strengths of character and well-being. *Journal of social and Clinical Psychology*, 23(5), 603–619.

Pearce, P. L. (1982) *The Social Psychology of Tourist Behaviour*. Oxford: Pergamon.

Pearce, P. L. (1988) *The Ulysses Factor: Evaluating Visitors in Tourist Settings*. New York: Springer-Verlag.

Pearce, P. L. (1992) Fundamentals of tourist motivation. In D. Pearce and R. Butler (Eds.), *Tourism Research: Critiques and Challenges*. London: Routledge, pp. 113–134.

Pearce, P. L. (1995) Chapter 9: Pleasure travel motivation. In R. W. McIntosh, C. R. Goeldner and J. R. Brent Ritchie (Eds.), *Tourism: Principles, Practices, Philosophies*, 7th Edn. New York: John Wiley, pp. 167–190.

Pearce, P. L. (2005) *Tourist Behaviour: Themes and Conceptual Schemes*. Clevedon: Channel View Publications.

Pearce, P. L. (2009) The relationship between positive psychology and tourist behavior studies. *Tourism Analysis*, 14, 37–48.

Pearce, P. L. (2011) *Tourist Behaviour and the Contemporary World*. Bristol: Channel View Publications.

Pearce, P. L. (2016) Australian contributions to tourist behaviour research. *Journal of Hospitality and Tourism Management*, 26, 84–90.

Pearce, P. L. and Caltabiano, M. L. (1983) Inferring travel motivation from travellers' experiences. *Journal of Travel Research*, 22(2), 16–20.

Pearce, P. L., Filep, S. and Ross, G. (2011) *Tourists, Tourism and Well Being*. New York: Routledge.

Pearce, P. L. and Lee, U. I. (2005) Developing the travel career approach to tourist motivation. *Journal of Travel Research*, 43(3), 226–237.

Pearce, P. L., Morrison, A. M. and Rutledge, J. L. (1998) *Tourism: Bridges across Continents*. Sydney: McGraw-Hill.

Pearce, P. L. and Moscardo, G. M. (1985) The relationship between travellers' career levels and the concept of authenticity. *Australian Journal of Psychology*, 37, 157–174.

Pearce, P. L. and Packer, J. (2013) Minds on the move: New links from psychology to tourism. *Annals of Tourism Research*, 40, 386–411.

Pearce, P. L. and Panchal, J. (2011) Health motives and the travel career pattern (TCP) model. *Asian Journal of Tourism and Hospitality Research*, 5(1), 32–44.

Peterson, C. and Seligman, M. E. (2004) *Character Strengths and Virtues: A Handbook and Classification* (Vol. 1). Oxford: Oxford University Press.

Pisani, E. (2014) *Indonesia, Etc.: Exploring the Improbable Nation*. WW Norton & Company.

Plog, S. C. (1974) Why destination areas rise and fall in popularity. *Cornell Hotel and Restaurant Administration Quarterly*, 14(4), 55–58.

Plog, S. C. (2011) Tourism research: A pragmatist's perspective. In P. L. Pearce (Ed.), *The Study of Tourism: Foundations from Psychology*. Bingley: Emerald, pp. 45–62.

Pritchard, A., Morgan, N. and Ateljevic, I. (2011) Hopeful tourism: A new transformative perspective. *Annals of Tourism Research*, 38(3), 941–963.

Rohleder, N. (2014) Stimulation of systemic low-grade inflammation by psychosocial stress. *Psychosomatic Medicine*, 76(3), 181–189.

Ryan, C. (1998) The travel career ladder: An appraisal. *Annals of Tourism Research*, 25(1), 936–57.

Sacks, O. (1991) *Awakenings*. London: Pan Macmillan.

Sacks, O. (2016) *On the Move: A Life*. London: Pan Macmillan.

Sacks, O. and Sacks, O. W. (1998) *A Leg to Stand On*. London: Simon and Schuster.

Seligman, M. E. (2012) *Flourish: A Visionary New Understanding of Happiness and Well-being*. New York: Simon and Schuster.

Selye, A. (1956) *The Stress of Life*. New York: McGraw-Hill.

Smed, K. M. (2009) Tourism and identity–accumulated tourist experience and travel career narratives in tourists' identity construction. *Institut for Historie, Internationale Studier og Samfundsforhold, Aalborg Universitet*.

Smith, S. L. (1990a) A test of Plog's allocentric/psychocentric model: Evidence from seven nations. *Journal of Travel Research*, 28(4), 40–43.

Smith, S. L. (1990b) Another look at the carpenter's tools: A reply to Plog. *Journal of Travel Research*, 29(2), 50–51.

Snyder, C. R. and Lopez, S. J. (Eds.) (2009). *Oxford Handbook of Positive Psychology*. Oxford: Oxford Library of Psychology.

Stebbins, R.A. (1982) Serious leisure: A conceptual statement. *Pacific Sociological Review*, 25(2), 251–272.

Stebbins, R. A. (2015) *Serious Leisure: A Perspective for Our Time*. New Brunswick: Transaction Publishers

Viner, R. (1999) Putting stress in life: Hans Selye and the making of stress theory. *Social Studies of Science*, 29(3), 391–410.

Volkow, N. D., Fowler, J. S. and Wang, G. J. (2002) Role of dopamine in drug reinforcement and addiction in humans, results from imaging studies. *Behavioural Pharmacology* 13(5&6), 355–366.

Wen, J. (2017) *Astronomy Tourism: Exploring an Emerging Market. Group Culture, Individual Experience and Industry Future*. Unpublished PhD thesis, James Cook University Townsville, Australia.

Williams, J. A. and McNeil, K. R. (2011) A modified travel career ladder model for understanding academic travel behaviors. *Journal of Behavioral Studies in Business*, 4, 1.

Xu, F., Morgan, M. and Song, P. (2009) Students' travel behaviour: A cross-cultural comparison of UK and China. *International Journal of Tourism Research*, 11(3), 255–268.

Young, G. (1973) *Tourism: Blessing or Blight?* Harmondsworth: Penguin.

14

THE EXPERIENCED TOURIST

Proposing a new tourist typology

Sabrina Seeler

Introduction

The tourist takes centre stage in the creation and realization of the tourism product and is of critical importance for the tourism industry's overall success. As a result, understanding the tourist has attracted much research interest from scholars from different disciplinary backgrounds, translating into a plethora of models and theories. Jafari (1987: 151) noted more than 30 years ago that 'tourists are among the least understood collectivities, despite their ubiquitiousness and still growing number worldwide'. Jafari's proposition still remains valid today. Similarly, Pearce (2005: 4) argues that 'the very word "tourist" is its own definitional problem child' and Cary (2004: 62) postulates that 'the figure of the tourist will never be easily grasped'. While the number of tourists continues to grow (in 2019, some 1.5 billion international arrivals were recorded), there is the realization that tourists are heterogenous regarding their socio-demographics, psychographics, travel behaviour, motivation and roles when travelling (Eisenstein, 2017). This impedes a satisfactory conceptualization of the tourist and results in the need for a segmented approach.

Historically, with the growth in package holidays and mass tourism, discussions around the often synonymously used terms *tourist* and *traveller* evolved and subsequently scholars developed tourist typologies to distinguish between different segments of the market. Despite flaws and weaknesses associated with established models, tourist typologies, such as Cohen's (1972) model based on a familiarity–strangerhood continuum, are still commonly applied and referred to. At the same time, however, there is the realization that tourists can no longer be segmented in internally homogenous and externally heterogenous groups as they are increasingly hybrid, meaning that their motivation and behaviour changes between and during trips (Boztug, Babakhani, Dolnicar & Laesser, 2015; Csikszentmihalyi & Coffey, 2017). In this vein, scholars also discuss the influential role of past experience on motivation, decision-making and behaviour (Pearce & Lee, 2005), and the concept of an experienced tourist has received research attention as this segment of the market is believed to behave more ethically and socially responsibly when travelling (Lee, Bonn, Reid & Kim., 2017; Seeler, Lück & Schänzel, 2021). As individuals constantly accumulate experience, both in their living environment and while travelling, experience levels continuously evolve yet,

DOI: 10.4324/9781003219866-17

owing to the subjectivity and dynamic nature of experiencing, an operationalization of experience accumulation is challenged (Filep & Greenacre, 2007). Most studies define the level of experience based on a few predefined variables without exploring the factors that eventually contribute to an individual's self-perceived experience level and identification as an experienced tourist. This knowledge gap is addressed in this chapter, and empirically grounded ideas of an experienced tourist as a potential new and promising tourist typology are introduced. First, however, the chapter discusses the traveller–tourist dichotomy and briefly introduces some of the most established and prominent tourist typologies. It then turns its lens towards the term *experience* and the role of experience in tourism research, before briefly describing the research project to explore the dimensions of an experienced tourist. Lastly, the findings are synthesized, and the proposed experienced tourist is compared with other tourist typologies.

The traveller–tourist dichotomy

The concept of the tourist remains one of the most discussed, discordant and misconceived in tourism literature (Bowen & Clarke, 2009). Early attempts to define a tourist were mostly driven by organizational interests and, thus, an economic perspective, while socio-psychological determinants were largely overlooked. Alongside the challenge to clearly define a tourist, discussions emerged around the oftentimes interchangeably used terms *tourist* and *traveller* (Sharpley, 2018). With the democratization of travel, the growth in mass tourism and the emerging discrepancies between tourist and traveller, scholars called for the two terms to be more clearly differentiated and unambiguously defined (Buzard, 1993; Urry, 1995).

In one of the earliest studies on the topic, Cohen (1974) describes a tourist as part of the general traveller's realm. He proposes a conceptual tree consisting of six distinctive factors to differentiate between roles of traveller and tourist. He further suggests that a tourist is 'a voluntary, temporary traveller, travelling in the expectation of pleasure from the novelty and change experienced on a relatively long and non-recurrent round-trip' (Cohen, 1974: 533). This influential scholar also identifies vacationers and sightseers as tourist typologies and notes that these roles tend to approximate as boundaries blur. In later studies, scholars demarcate a tourist from a traveller and negate the blurring of boundaries as specific impressions are evoked, and different behaviours and travel forms are identified. For example, Buzard (1993: 2) maintains that 'the traveller exhibits boldness and gritty endurance under all conditions [...]; the tourist is the cautious, pampered unit of the leisure industry'. In a similar vein, Rojek (1993) defines a traveller as a novelty-seeker and endeavourer of self-realization and a tourist as a consumer of the predefined reality. The distinguishing factor here is the mentality and the realization that a traveller is seeking transformative moments, while a tourist's motivation is more aligned with the fulfilment of hedonic needs. Although links to tourist typologies and roles are missing, the concepts of eudaemonia and hedonia have more recently gained increased attention in tourism research (Csikszentmihalyi & Coffey, 2017; Knobloch, Robertson & Aitken, 2017). Wang (2000) claims that a tourist consumes experiences that are specifically prepared for them, while a traveller individually and autonomously designs them. This view resembles Boorstin's (1992) assumption of a fabrication of reality through pseudo-events mirrored in mass tourism, in isolation from the actual landscape. Thus, a tourist more passively consumes mass-produced, pre-paid and packaged tourism products and services (McCabe, 2005). In this vein, Reif, Harms and Eisenstein (2020) illuminate negative connotations, adjectives, visual appearance and stereotypical assumptions associated with the tourist and unveil common comparisons with animals such as ants or bacteria. However, negative connotations with the term tourist cannot be confirmed in their empirical research based on a representative German sample (Reif, Harms & Eisenstein, 2020).

Buzard (1993) sees a traveller as someone who fully immerses themselves in a situation, aims to explore off the beaten track, seeks freedom and adventure to express individuality. This is in line with MacCannell's (1976) ideas of tourist and traveller that he distinguishes based on the degree of authenticity sought by an individual. In this vein, MacCannell (1976) describes frontstage and backstage experiences, the former catering mostly for tourists and the latter being the playground for travellers. Sharpley (2018) explains that a traveller seeks adventure, authentic experiences, freedom, self-realization and individuality through long-term travel. However, with the growth of mass tourism throughout the twentieth century, the traveller's desire for self-realization through full immersion was impeded and the (perceived) gap between tourist and traveller deepened. Those who identified themselves as a traveller rejected being labelled as tourists. Sharpley (2018: 95 & 87) describes this conflict as a 'kind of social arrogance' and notes that 'most people have tried to distance or disassociate themselves from other tourists, convincing themselves that they are somehow better or enjoying a more meaningful experience'. While the excitement of travel is often glorified in travel writing, tourism is portrayed as the mundane and unexciting practice of touring. This glorification of travel as a form of (self-)exploration and adventure also attracts others to follow the newly beaten track, which in turn contributes to the massification of experiences (Seeler, Lück & Schänzel, 2021).

Galani-Moutafi (2000) notes a processual nature and suggests that traveller and tourist should not be understood as opposites, but as a process in which one role acts as predecessor for the other. The advances in online technologies and social media accelerate the pace of information exchange, which has also contributed to the emergence of over-tourism situations and tensions between hosts and guests, but also different types of guests. As destinations become more accessible and touristificated, Sharpley (2018: 93) notes that 'for travellers it is not where but how that has become important'.

In an earlier study, Jacobsen (2000) observes that anti-tourist attitudes developed with the tourist who worries about negative perceptions, while the traveller is generally less concerned about the perceptions of others. Dann (1999) discusses this distancing beyond the traveller–tourist dichotomy. He argues that tourist disidentification is on the one hand between the tourist and others, while on the other hand also a criticism of the tourist's own being through self-reflection. McCabe (2005: 95) shares this view, claiming that the term tourist is exploited as 'a rhetorical apparatus' and suggests that self-assessment and self-reporting based on behaviour and experience enable a more emic perspective of the concept of tourists and their roles. Considering the multifaceted nature of people involved in travelling and the different types of travel, Sharpley (2018) raises the question of whether an unambiguous definition of the term tourist is feasible, particularly as distinctions between traveller and tourist are mostly self-imposed. Instead of defining and generalizing the term, Sharpley (2018: 88) contends that an advanced understanding is needed that goes 'beneath the all-encompassing label of "tourist"' and explores the different types of tourist, as this can assist in more nuanced market segmentation, product development and thus competitiveness.

Tourist typologies

The existence of a unitary type of tourist limited to a tourist bubble is negated. Instead, scholars attempt to develop tourist typologies that assist in distinguishing different types of tourist that then help to understand the intricacies of travel motivation and behaviour (Gibson & Yiannakis, 2002). Typologies segment tourists into internally homogenous and externally heterogenous groups. These classifications and segmentations are regarded as prerequisites for understanding, explaining and predicting motivation, decision-making and behaviour. Segmentation approaches were traditionally based on socio-demographic variables as these are accessible, intelligible and measurable. However, criticism emerged as socio-demographic factors are unable to depict the dynamics of modern societies and fail to provide insights into consumer preferences. Socio-psychological and behavioural approaches more recently gained in importance, and tourist typologies were implemented that support market segmentations based on psychographic (e.g. travel motivation, personality) or behavioural factors (e.g. type of travel) (Kotler, Bowen, Makens & Bagloglu, 2017).

Making a distinction between *sunlust* and *wanderlust* tourism, Gray (1970) was one of the first scholars to distinguish between tourists based on their motivation, behaviour and purpose of trip. A sunlust tourist desires to relax and rest with sun, sea and sand (three Ss), while a wanderlust tourist aims to explore new cultures and people. In his conceptualization, Gray (1970) discusses a tourist in isolation from their environment and disregards potential relationships with the host community, destination or tourism business. Based on a sociological approach, Cohen (1972) classifies the tourist with reference to the degree of institutionalization and identifies four types of tourist based on a familiarity–strangerhood continuum: (i) organized mass tourist, (ii) individual mass tourist, (iii) explorer and (iv) drifter. The first two types are aligned with more institutionalized forms of travelling and approximate to the stereotypical image of the mass tourist. Explorers and drifters, in contrast, are independent and non-institutionalized tourists seeking novelty and authenticity. With this classification, Cohen challenges Boorstin's (1992) unilateral view of tourists being an entirely homogenous group of mass tourists. Cohen (1972) argues that a tourist is never fully detached from their home environment and culture and that they travel in an environmental bubble. However, their degree of attachment to their home bubble varies, which can be expressed by their desire to either remain close to their familiar environment or to aim to break free and escape from the bubble by seeking novelty in strangerhood.

Cohen (1972) further assumes that a tourist can adapt and progress from the familiarity end to the strangerhood/novelty end of the continuum, and proposes that the explorer and drifter is often the pathfinder and spearhead for the organized or individual mass tourist, therewith paving the way for mass tourism. In a similar vein, Sharpley (2018: 99) remarks that 'independent travel has [...] become as institutionalized as mass tourism' and critically questions whether Cohen's typology based on a simplified continuum and dichotomy still fits in the context of the contemporary independent tourist. While Cohen focused on the observable tourist behaviour, Smith (1989) bore the tourist's impact on the host destination in mind when introducing seven different types of tourist: (i) explorer, (ii) elite tourist, (iii) off-the-beaten-track tourist, (iv) unusual tourist, (v) incipient mass tourist, (vi) mass tourist and (vii) charter tourist. Although widely adopted and cited in the literature, both taxonomies attracted criticism for their static nature, their limitations to a researcher-dependent set of behavioural factors and lack of explanation of the actual influence of the social environment on the tourist's behaviour (Sharpley, 2018).

By 'rethinking' the sociology of tourism and reassessing the taxonomic model, Cohen (1979) introduces a new typology in which he acknowledges the tourist's past experience as an important influencing factor. His re-evaluation and development of a new typology was driven by the growing critique that his familiarity–strangerhood continuum was too simplistic. In his revised model, Cohen (1979) understands 'other' and 'centre' as the two extremes on the continuum and thereby refers to the individual's spiritual centre in the context of the home environment and thus tourism-generating society. Hereby, the 'centre' is within the home society, meaning that this individual is satisfied and fulfilled without immersing themselves into foreign cultures and interacting with other people. The 'other', in contrast, means that the individual seeks happiness, fulfilment and satisfaction through travelling and learning about other cultures and people. Thus, this individual locates their inner centre elsewhere and detached from the home society. Cohen (1979) goes beyond the previously criticized observable behaviour and bases his typology on cognitive–normative dimensions related to the tourist's desired experience. Hereby, he distinguishes five categories of tourist: (i) recreational, (ii) diversionary, (iii) experiential, (iv) experimental and (v) existential (Cohen, 1979). As the recreational tourist's centre is situated in the home society, they are less interested in the society and culture of the destination visited, making them comparable to Boorstin's inauthentic (mass) tourist. In contrast, an existential tourist is searching for their centre somewhere else and immerses themselves in the local population and foreign culture, which brings them closer to MacCannell's (1976) understanding of the authenticity-seeking tourist. Despite its advancements, the typology attracted critique owing to its theoretical nature and lack of empirical evidence, as well as its failure to acknowledge the tourist's broader social environment (Sharpley, 2018).

Alongside Cohen's theoretical contributions to advance the understanding of tourist roles and typologies, Plog (1974) bases his tourist typology on empirical information derived from interviews with non-flyers in the U.S. By linking personality traits to tourist types and roles, he classifies tourists along a continuum ranging from allocentric to psychocentric. Between these taxonomic poles, he introduces three other types: 'near-allocentric', 'mid-centric' and 'near-psychocentric' (Plog, 1974). The allocentric is defined as novelty-seeker and risk-taker, searching for new, exotic destinations to explore and immerse themselves in. Psychocentrics prefer the familiar and are considered the less adventurous, passive traveller, frequently visiting mass tourist resorts. Lowyck, Langenhove and Bollaert (1992: 19) imply that psychocentrics feel almost pressured to travel, as they see travelling as compulsory and a 'cultural norm, imposed by the legal system of paid holidays'. Differentiating tourists according to their desire for novelty-seeking or familiarity-preferring, Plog's model is analogous to Cohen's and Smith's continua. However, Plog's allocentric–psychocentric taxonomy, which he later reformulated into a dependable–venturer continuum (Plog, 2001), differs from previous typologies as it constitutes the relationship between the tourist's motivation to travel, their actual travel behaviour and destination choice. Allocentrics/venturers, for instance, are the first to visit a destination regardless of whether any form of tourist infrastructure or only primitive circumstances exist. Similar to other typologies, Plog's (1974, 2001) allocentric/venturer–psychocentric/dependable typology was critiqued for its static nature and negligence of the fact that tourists themselves mature, and tourist destinations and other external factors change as well, which influences destination choice and behaviour. This further raises the question of how a non-institutionalized tourist, regardless of whether they are called allocentric, venturer, explorer, drifter or novelty-seeker, will be able to satisfy their desires and needs in the future.

Despite the prominence of these typologies, criticism emerged as typologies are based on circular arguments, etic and heuristic devices and theoretical knowledge, while often missing empirical data (Dann, 2014). Although labelled differently, these widely adopted typologies generally refer to similar criteria, such as novelty and familiarity, and propose similar types of tourist, such as mass tourist versus free independent tourist (FIT). Sharpley (2018: 114) summarizes these stereotypical grouping and generalization as follows:

> The explorer-wanderlust-allocentric tourist is typecast as being bold, adventurous, independent and empathetic to new cultures and societies, whereas the mass, institutionalised tourist is unadventurous, indecisive, easily pleased by staged, inauthentic events and has little or no interest in expanding his or her cultural horizons beyond the limits of the environmental bubble.

Alongside tourist typologies that aim to distinguish tourists along a continuum in general, several approaches have evolved that explore specific types of tourists with reference to a (current) touristic topic. For instance, scholars have attempted to define an ecotourist (Tao, Eagles & Smith, 2004) as well as an ethical, sustainable and responsible tourist (Dolnicar & Leisch, 2008; Weeden, 2011). Although this sustainable and responsible tourist is often deemed to be a 'good tourist' and desirable market segment favoured over the mass tourists who are a threat to the destination, the partly oxymoronic nature of sustainable and responsible travel behaviour, the prevailing attitude–behaviour gap, as well as paradoxes related to altruistic motives, moral hypocrisy and an overemphasis on environmental sustainability remain (Juvan & Dolnicar, 2016; Mkono, 2020) and a unifying definition is lacking to date. Mkono (2020) describes an ecotourist as a controversial figure and offers different scholarly viewpoints on the ecotourist, such as ego-tourist or feel-good tourist. She further addresses the constant tensions between being a good citizen and the desire to fulfil personal aspirations, and eventually concludes that a tourist can only be fully eco-conscious if they refrain from travelling altogether (Mkono, 2020).

In response to the evolving criticism around the eco-conscious and responsible tourist, scholars draw attention to the need for more mindful consumption and explore the mindful tourist. According to Fischer, Stanzus, Geiger, Grossmann and Schrader (2017: 547), mindful consumption is a form of attentiveness that 'refers to the act of cultivating unbiased awareness of all moment-to-moment perceptible experience'. Although the topic has become of increasing importance in the tourism context, empirical data is scarce and a unifying definition of a mindful tourist is also absent. Mindfulness and mindful consumption have also been discussed regarding advances in information and mobile technologies with the dual emergence of the digital-free tourist and digital-immersed tourist (Stankov, Filimonau & Vujičić, 2020). With reference to the degree of immersion in or detachment from the digital world, Fan, Buhalis and Lin (2019) propose six types of digital travellers: social media addict, daily life controller, dual zone traveller, diversionary traveller, digital detox traveller and disconnected immersive traveller. Other scholars identity, for instance, the cultural tourist (McKercher & du Cros, 2003), golf tourist (Kim & Ritchie, 2012) or crisis-resistant tourist (Hajibaba, Gretzel, Leisch & Dolnicar, 2015), and therewith concentrate on very narrow segments of the market based on motivation and behaviour.

Most of these topic-related typologies adopt motivation-based segmentation approaches as these facilitate effective and targeted marketing. However, they often fail to incorporate the *why* behind motivation and simplify the complex topic as they fail to take the broader social context into account. The unique nature of the tourism product and multifacetedness of tourists reveals a paradox associated with tourist typologies: they are established to understand complexities but are criticized for being too static in breadth and time (Decrop, 2006). Given the multidimensionality and increasing hybridity of tourists, as well as the awareness that tourists themselves are constantly evolving without following a predefined path, leading to blurring boundaries between typologies, scholars critically question whether segmentation into homogenous groups based on certain characteristics is feasible (Boztug et al., 2015; Csikszentmihalyi & Coffey, 2017). Furthermore, the longevity of tourist typologies is challenged, as existing typologies prove beneficial for tactical decisions but are deemed less appropriate for strategy formation (Decrop, 2006). At the same time, scholars acknowledge the centrality of tourist typologies in product development, marketing and distribution (Sharpley, 2018). Thus, there is a call for more innovative approaches that concede the complexity and multidimensionality of the constantly changing and evolving tourist. These new approaches also need to take broader environmental developments and the need for more sustainable tourism futures into account. In this vein, scholars propose that the experienced tourist is a promising market segment as they are believed to travel more sustainably, and are ethically responsible and respectful of foreign cultures (Lee et al., 2017; Seeler, Lück & Schänzel, 2021).

Advancing tourist typologies – the experienced tourist

The growing middle class, improved global mobility and continued importance of travelling for a fulfilling life have not only contributed to a sustained growth in international tourist arrivals, but have also resulted in the emergence of the increasingly experienced tourist. The term *experienced tourist* is commonly applied in academic literature to distinguish between the behaviour of tourists with higher and lower levels of experience (Pearce & Caltabiano, 1983; Pearce & Lee, 2005). For instance, the experienced tourist is identified as being more risk averse (Lepp & Gibson, 2003; Smed, 2012) compared with their less experienced counterparts. Despite the awareness that past experiences are influential in predicting motivation, behaviour and decision-making, and the general assumption that today's tourist is more experienced compared with the past, a unifying understanding of the term experienced tourist remains missing. Instead, measurements of experience levels are ambiguous, and scholars base their discrimination between experienced and inexperienced tourists on different input variables. Challenges related to a unifying definition are also discussed with reference to the general ambiguities related to the term experience.

The role of experience in tourism research

The creation of memorable experiences has become of increasing importance in the increasingly competitive environment of tourism and is understood as a key driver in today's complex tourism system (Jensen, Lindberg & Østergaard, 2015; Kim & Chen, 2018). Thus, following Pine and Gilmore's (1999) principles of the experience economy, experience creation is focused. A management/marketing approach to the topic is largely adopted and experiences are understood as objects of consumption and commercial exchange. Thus, experiences are understood as immediate lived and partaking experiences that equal countable events. However, with the progression of economic value towards transformation (Pine & Gilmore, 2013) and the growing importance of the subjective dimensions of experience (Knobloch, Robertson & Aitken, 2017), research has shifted towards more social scientific approaches. From this perspective, experiences are seen as a form of knowledge accumulation based on continuous subjective reflections and evaluations of the lived experiences and, thus, take on a reminiscing function over the lifetime (Jantzen, 2013).

Owing to difficulties in unambiguously demarcating the two meanings of the term inherited in the semantic differences and linguistic subtleties, scholars frequently use the German terms *Erlebnis* (partaking) and *Erfahrung* (reminiscing). Scholars also address the mutual dependence of the two meanings of the term (Seeler, Lück & Schänzel, 2018; Smed, 2012), which Jantzen (2013: 151) summarizes as follows: '[...] the impurity of immediate experiences implies that *Erfahrungen* have already informed an Erlebnis. *Erfahrungen* are not only outcomes of *Erlebnisse*, they are also sources of *Erlebnisse*.' Hence, an *Erlebnis* is understood in the present tense and *Erfahrung* in the past tense (Seeler, Lück & Schänzel, 2019). Several attempts have been undertaken to provide an intelligible and unambiguous definition of the term experience in the tourism context, yet no generally accepted definition exists (Seeler, Lück & Schänzel, 2018). Scholars accept the fact that experiences are multi-layered, comprise intangible and tangible assets, and are subjectively perceived. Thus, they are highly personal phenomena. As they are accumulated over time and are constantly changing, the experience levels of individuals develop. These accumulated experiences are assumed to have an impact on tourist expectations and satisfaction, information search, decision-making and behaviour (Crouch, Huybers & Oppewal, 2016; Han & Hwang, 2018; Smed, 2012).

The Travel Career Ladder (TCL), later refined as the Travel Career Pattern (TCP) framework (Pearce & Caltabiano, 1983; Pearce & Lee, 2005), is one of the most prominent models applying the level of an individual's experiences as the antecedent to predict motivation. Inspired by Maslow's (1954) hierarchy of needs, Pearce and Lee (2005) ground their analysis on the demographic factor of age and the number of past trips (domestic and international). They propose that higher age and more domestic and international past travel experience translate into higher experience levels, which are then reflected in travel motivation and behaviour. While the TCL was critiqued for its static nature and assumption of linearity (Ryan, 1998), the previously contested use of the variable of age, which was added in the revised TCP, received criticism. Filep and Greenacre (2007) critically question whether higher age translates into higher experience levels, as older segments of the market might have had more opportunities to travel but might not have made use of it. Statistics also reveal that the travel propensity of younger age cohorts has increased within the past decades (Kožić, Mikulić & Krešić, 2016) and the centrality of age to predict quantitative travel experiences can be challenged. Scholars use various variables to measure the experience level, such as the number of past visits to specific destinations (Jørgensen, Law & King, 2018; Lee & Tussyadiah, 2012) or follow a specialization approach (Han & Hwang, 2018; Pröbstl-Haider & Haider, 2014). This demonstrates the vagueness of the concept of tourist experience levels and being an experienced tourist. Studies share treating the level of experience as an antecedent to predict and explain motivation, decision-making and behaviour, and measuring the level of experience based on a few predefined and objectified variables. However, scholars fail to explore the factors that eventually contribute to higher experience levels. Instead, they rely on one-dimensional measures and assume a linear progression, despite the awareness that experiences are multidimensional and that several factors need to be incorporated when developing tourist typologies (Sharifpour & Walters, 2014; Sharpley, 2018).

Past studies also fail to acknowledge that identification as an experienced tourist is a self-perceived mental process owing to the subjective nature of experience (Knobloch, Robertson & Aitken, 2017; Smed, 2012). Most studies are narrow in their approach with regard to their target sample and concentrate on tourist perspectives. Given the mutual dependence of experience creation and consumption (Jensen, Lindberg & Østergaard, 2015; Seeler, Lück & Schänzel, 2018) and therewith the strong relationship between the demand-side and supply-side of tourism, industry voices are needed alongside those of the tourist. These can contribute to closing perception–reality gaps and thereby provide important insights for effective product development and marketing. In this chapter, an advanced theory of the experienced tourist is proposed and a valuable contribution to tourist typologies is made, based on empirical data.

Methods

Given that little is known about the factors contributing to a tourist's self-perceived experience level, an exploratory and inductive research design was adopted and a sequential mixed-methods approach followed. Both research phases were implemented in Germany and New Zealand. To gain insights from the supply-side, 15 semi-structured interviews with 18 representatives from destination marketing/management organizations (DMOs) were conducted between May and August 2016. Participants were selected based on a purposive sampling strategy and were invited through direct emails. They were asked to define an experienced tourist and elaborate on the factors contributing to higher levels of experience. Interviews were audio-recorded and transcribed, and thematic analysis was applied to identify core themes. These built the basis for the development of the online survey implemented in the second stage of data collection. A non-probability sampling strategy was adopted and a total of 1,000 German and New Zealand tourists were surveyed though a web-access panel in January 2017. Central to the survey was the question of how tourists self-assess their experience level as a tourist on a scale from 1 = not experienced at all to 10 = extremely experienced. This variable became the dependent variable in the stepwise multiple regression analysis to explore the independent variables that significantly contribute to an individual's self-assessed experience level. Given the developmental nature of this research and the realization that participants in the first research phase shared the fact that the experienced tourist travels independently, a reduced dataset was used for the multivariate analyses and only respondents that fit the requirement of a FIT were considered.

The experienced tourist: a supply–demand perspective

Representatives from DMOs shared similar ideas about the experienced tourist and identified numerous possible influencing factors. Thereby they negated the previous dominance of the number of trips as a core predictor of higher experience levels. Instead, there was the realization that breadth of experience is decisive and that today's younger generation accumulates experiences earlier in their lives. Participants were inconclusive regarding the influence of age. While some argued that there is a higher likelihood that the experienced tourist is older, others emphasized the breadth and depth of experiences of the younger segments of today's market:

> Participant 2_GER: [...] the accumulation process of the generation of your parents differs from people who are 20 years old [...] the horizon of experience does not grow with the number of trips when the travel pattern remains unchanged.

Alongside socio-demographic factors, participants also discussed the role of social identity and personality. The experienced tourist is assumed to be more risk averse, open-minded and curious, which is mirrored in their travel motivation and behaviour:

> Participant 3_NZ: They want to understand, they want to learn, they want to be educated, and feel enriched on a mental level not only a superficial level of telling their friends they have been here.

Although the personal travel biography and past experiences were believed to be influential, participants highlighted the role of the home environment and discussed the influence of changes in the living environment or with regard to living standards as well. Generally, participants distinguished between internal and external factors and emphasized the influential role of the wider environment. They discussed the role of technological advances and online media, personal reference groups, broader societal and political factors, and the improved professionalism of the tourism industry itself. Alongside active past experiences, there is also the assumed influence of secondary experience passively consumed through other people's eyes, that contributes to an individual's self-assessed experience level (see also Seeler et al., 2019):

> Participant 7_NZ: *So that whole social media world means that they probably have secondary experiences through other peoples' interactions.*

Thus, from a supply-side perspective, an experienced tourist can be defined by eight overarching topics that can be summarized as personal identifiers and external facilitators see Figure 14.1).

Tourists surveyed in the second phase of the research were asked to self-rate their experience level on a scale from 1 (not experienced at all) to 10 (extremely experienced). Results reveal that the majority of German tourists (M = 6.18; SD = 2.103) and New Zealand tourists (M = 5.77; SD = 2.438) considered themselves as experienced tourists. Results from stepwise multiple regression analyses reveal differences and similarities between the two samples, yet overall resulted in multi-dimensional accumulation sets of experienced tourists. The German experienced tourist is predicted by 18 variables from which 17 are statistically significant, explaining 47.7% of the variance ($F(18, 300) = 15.199$, $p = 0.000$, R^2_{adj}: 0.445). In the case of New Zealand, 19 independent variables were identified as predictor variables from which 14 were statistically significant, explaining 45.8% of the variance (($F(19, 308) = 13.721$, $p = 0.000$, R^2_{adj}: 0.425). Results from the regression analyses also allowed a

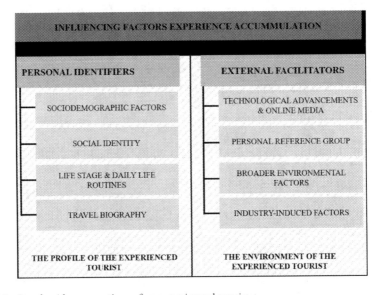

Figure 14.1 Supply-side perspectives of an experienced tourist

distinguishing between variables with a positive and a negative influence on the experience level. This possible negative influence has been neglected in previous research, yet contributes to a more nuanced understanding of an experienced tourist.

The variable 'higher age', for instance, did not remain in any of the two regression equations, yet a negative contribution was found for the counter group 'young adults' in the German regression analysis. Statistical results reveal the importance of retrospective and prospective predictors that can be summarized in three overall categories: (1) general profiling factors (socio-demographic factors, aspects of the social identity) (2) travel profiling factors (past travel, role of travel) and (3) factors related to the travel journey (inspiration and decision-making, holiday trip behaviour, future holiday intentions). The variable with the highest statistical power in both regression equations relates to the subjective importance of travelling in an individual's life. Findings from the sequential developmental mixed-method research led to the proposition of an advanced theory of an experienced tourist and expansion of existing tourist typologies.

Synthesizing an experienced tourist and advancing tourist typologies

With the aim of delivering more effective and targeted marketing as well as product development, tourism scholars attempt to distinguish between tourists based on, for instance, observable and actual behaviour and socio-demographic or psychographics factors (Eisenstein, 2017). However, with the increasing hybridity of tourists between and during holiday trips (Boztug et al., 2015; Csikszentmihalyi & Coffey, 2017), the existence of internally homogenous and externally heterogenous market segments is challenged. While the need for more fluid and dynamic frameworks grows, there exists the realization that today's tourist is increasingly experienced compared with those in the past, and the question emerges: Who is an experienced tourist? As the process of experience accumulation is infinite and comprises experiences made in the home environment and destination, a more all-encompassing approach is needed. Furthermore, the level of experience remains an individual's self-perception and, thus, a realistic understanding of being experienced requires the acknowledgement of tourist self-evaluation. In this chapter, an advanced understanding of an experienced tourist as a new tourist typology is introduced that addresses the existing research gaps: (i) it treats the level of experience as an outcome instead of an antecedent; (ii) it adopts a supply–demand perspective; and (3) it is based on a tourist's self-evaluation of being experienced.

The identification of an experienced tourist as a promising tourist typology in support of more sustainable tourism futures remains context-dependent, as the derived accumulation sets of German and New Zealand experienced tourists differed. Cohen's (1972) influential model of tourist typologies acknowledged the home environment through the familiarity–strangerhood continuum. The emphasis here was on the influence of the home environment on the individual, yet it was not the aim to uncover differences between nations or cultures. However, the experienced tourist from Germany and New Zealand introduced in this chapter shares commonalities with Cohen's (1972) drifter and also explorer Plog's (1974, 2001) allocentric/venturer typologies. The experienced tourist travels independently, is curious and open-minded, wants to explore new regions and immerse themselves in new cultures, while travelling off the beaten track with self-confidence and therewith becoming a role model and pioneer (Seeler, Lück & Schänzel, 2021). Plog (2001) also found that venturesomeness predicts travel propensity. The number of trips was also frequently defined as a central element to measure an individual's level of experience (Pearce & Lee, 2005). Based on findings from the mixed-methods research, this chapter proposes that the number of trips is unsatisfactory in distinguishing an experienced from an inexperienced tourist. While the number of past trips had a positive influence on the experience level of Germans, it did not contribute to the prediction of the New Zealand experienced tourist. This underlines that being identified as an experienced tourist is context dependent. Similarly, the assumed relationship between higher income, travel propensity, higher experience levels and venturesomeness (Plog, 2001; Kožić, Mikulić & Krešić, 2016) could not be directly confirmed in this empirical research.

Cohen's (1972) drifter and explorer can also be considered in light of Fan, Buhalis and Lin's (2019) digital detox traveller and disconnected immersive traveller. Fan, Buhalis and Lin (2019: 13) describe these tourists also as 'experienced, international travellers' that are 'motivated by self-fulfilment and self-development needs'. In this context, the term experienced is used without describing what it means to be an experienced international traveller. However, this empirical research reveals that an experienced tourist resembles Fan, Buhalis and Lin's (2019) dual zone traveller and not the digital detox or disconnected immersive traveller. The experienced tourist aims to be both connected and disconnected throughout the travel journey, which means they behave like the dual zone traveller. It also provides further evidence for the hybridity and fluidity of today's increasingly experienced tourist and the need for more dynamic tourist typologies. Most past tourist typologies lacked empirical evidence and were one-dimensional. The same applies for models aiming to predict motivation or behaviour based on level of experience and following Pearce and colleagues' TCL/TCP frameworks (Pearce & Caltabiano, 1983; Pearce & Lee, 2005). Here, experience levels were also simplified by the number of past trips and age. The empirical exploration of an experienced tourist reveals that the self-perception of being experienced is based on a multidimensional accumulation set that negates previous narrow approaches. It also highlights the role of subjectivity and centrality of self-perception that has largely been neglected in previous research. With the limitation of this one-off cross-sectional research in mind, this chapter on the one hand demonstrates the commonalities with past typologies, yet on the other hand underlines the necessity of more comprehensive approaches that go beyond simplified approaches. Future research is needed to test and potentially extend the multidimensional accumulation set introduced in this chapter. Further future avenues can be identified as the power of transformative moments for an individual's self-development as a tourist need further exploration.

References

Boorstin, D. J. (1992) *The Image: A Guide to Pseudo-Events in America*. New York: Vintage.

Bowen, D. and Clarke, J. (2009) *Contemporary Tourist Behaviour: Yourself and Others and Tourists*. Wallingford: CABI.

Boztug, Y., Babakhani, N., Dolnicar, S. and Laesser, C. (2015) The hybrid tourist. *Annals of Tourism Research*, 54, 190–203.

Buzard, J. (1993) *The Beaten Track: European Tourism, Literature, and the Ways to 'Culture', 1800–1918*. Oxford: Oxford University Press.

Cary, S. H. (2004) The tourist moment. *Annals of Tourism Research*, 31(1), 61–7.

Cohen, E. (1972) Toward a sociology of international tourism. *Social Research*, 39(1), 164–182.

Cohen, E. (1974) Who is a tourist? A conceptual clarification. *The Sociological Review*, 22(4), 527–555.

Cohen, E. (1979) Rethinking the sociology of tourism. *Annals of Tourism Research*, 6(1), 18–35.

Crouch, G., Huybers, T. and Oppewal, H. (2016) Inferring future vacation experience preference from past vacation choice: A latent class analysis. *Journal of Travel Research*, 55(5), 574–587.

Csikszentmihalyi, M. and Coffey, J. (2017) Why do we travel? A positive psychological model for travel motivation. In S. Filep, J. Laing and M. Csikszentmihalyi (Eds.), *Positive Tourism*. New York: Routledge, pp. 122–132.

Dann, G. (1999) Writing out the tourist in space and time. *Annals of Tourism Research*, 26(1), 159–187.

Dann, G. (2014) Why, oh why, oh why, do people travel abroad? In N. K. Prebensen, P.-T. Chen and M. Uysal (Eds.), *Creating Experience Value in* Tourism. Wallingford: CABI, pp. 48–62.

Decrop, A. (2006) *Vacation Decision Making*. Wallingford: CABI.

Dolnicar, S. and Leisch, F. (2008) Selective marketing for environmentally sustainable tourism. *Tourism Management*, 29(4), 672–680.

Eisenstein, B. (2017) Destinationsmarktforschung – Relevanz und Grundlagen. In B. Eisenstein (Ed.), *Marktforschung für Destinationen: Grundlagen - Instrumente – Praxisbeispiele*. Berlin: Erich Schmidt Verlag, pp. 11–70.

Fan, D. X. F., Buhalis, D. and Lin, B. (2019) A tourist typology of online and face-to-face social contact: Destination immersion and tourism encapsulation/decapsulation. *Annals of Tourism Research*, 78 doi.org/10.1016/j.annals.2019.102757

Filep, S. and Greenacre, L. (2007) Evaluating and extending the Travel Career Patterns model. *Tourism: An International Interdisciplinary Journal*, 55(1), 23–38.

Fischer, D., Stanzus, L., Geiger, S., Grossmann, N. P. and Schrader, U. (2017) Mindfulness and sustainable consumption: A systematic literature review of research approaches and findings. *Journal of Cleaner Production*, 162, 544–558.

Galani-Moutafi, V. (2000) The self and the other: Traveler, ethnographer, tourist. *Annals of Tourism Research*, 27(1), 203–224.

Gibson, H. and Yiannakis, A. (2002) Tourist roles: Needs and the Lifecourse. *Annals of Tourism Research*, 29(2), 358–383.

Gray, H. P. (1970) *International Tourism – International Trade*. Lexington: DC Heath Books.

Hajibaba, H., Gretzel, U., Leisch, F. and Dolnicar, S. (2015) Crisis-resistant tourists. *Annals of Tourism Research*, 53, 46–60.

Han, H. and Hwang, J. (2018) Growing competition in the healthcare tourism market and customer retention in medical clinics: New and experienced travellers', *Current Issues in Tourism*, 21(6), 680–702.

Jacobsen, J. K. S. (2000) Anti-tourist attitudes: Mediterranean charter tourism. *Annals of Tourism Research*, 27(2), 284–300.

Jafari, J. (1987) Tourism models: The sociocultural aspects. *Tourism Management*, 8(2), 151–159.

Jantzen, C. (2013) Experiencing and experiences: A psychological framework. In J. Sundbo, and F. Sørensen (Eds.), *Handbook on the Experience Economy*. Cheltenham: Edward Elgar Publishing, pp. 146–177.

Jensen, Ø., Lindberg, F. and Østergaard, P. (2015) How can consumer research contribute to increased understanding of tourist experiences? A conceptual review. *Scandinavian Journal of Hospitality and Tourism*, 15 (Supp 1), 9–27.

Jørgensen, M. T., Law, R. and King, B. (2018) Beyond the stereotypes: Opportunities in China inbound tourism for second-tier European destinations. *International Journal of Tourism Research*, 20(4), 488–497.

Juvan, E. and Dolnicar, S. (2016) Measuring environmentally sustainable tourist behaviour. *Annals of Tourism Research*, 59, 30–44.

Kim, H. and Chen, J. S. (2018) The memorable travel experience and its reminiscence functions. *Journal of Travel Research*, 58(4), 637–649.

Kim, J. H. and Ritchie, B, W. (2012) Motivation-based typology: An empirical study of golf tourists. *Journal of Hospitality & Tourism Research*, 36(2), 251–280.

Knobloch, U. Robertson, K. and Aitken, R. (2017) Experience, emotion, and eudaimonia: A consideration of tourist experiences and well-being. *Journal of Travel Research*, 56(5), 651–662.

Kotler, P., Bowen, J. T., Makens, J. C. and Bagloglu, S. (2017) *Marketing for Hospitality and Tourism*. Boston: Pearson.

Kožić, I., Mikulić, J. and Krešić, D. (2016) Propensity to travel: What is the macro-data telling us? In Á. Matias, P. Nijkamp and J. Romão (Eds.), *Impact Assessment in Tourism Economics*. Cham: Springer International Publishing, pp. 9–22.

Lee, G. and Tussyadiah, I. (2012) Exploring familiarity and destination choice in international tourism. *Asia Pacific Journal of Tourism Research*, 17(2), 133–145.

Lee, H. Y., Bonn, M. A., Reid, E. L. and Kim, W. G. (2017) Differences in tourist ethical judgment and responsible tourism intention: An ethical scenario approach', *Tourism Management*, 60, 298–307.

Lepp, A. and Gibson, H. (2003) Tourist roles, perceived risk and international tourism. *Annals of Tourism Research*, 30(3), 606–624.

Lowyck, E., Langenhove, L. and Bollaert, L. (1992) Typologies of tourist roles. In P. S. Johnson and R. B. Thomas (Eds.), *Choice and Demand in Tourism*. London: Mansell, pp. 13–32.

MacCannell, D. (1976) *The Tourist: A New Theory of the Leisure Class*. New York: Schocken Books.

Maslow, A. H. (1954) *Motivation and Psychology*. New York: Harper and Row.

McCabe, S. (2005) Who is a tourist? A critical review. *Tourist Studies*, 5(1), 85–106.

McKercher, B. and du Cros, H. (2003) Testing a cultural tourism typology. *International Journal of Tourism Research*, 5(1), 45–58.

Mkono, M. (2020) Eco-hypocrisy and inauthenticity: Criticisms and confessions of the eco-conscious tourist/traveller. *Annals of Tourism Research*, 84. doi.org/10.1016/j.annals.2020.102967

Pearce, P. L. (2005) *Tourist Behaviour: Themes and Conceptual Schemes*. Clevedon: Channel View Publications.

Pearce, P. L. and Caltabiano, M. L. (1983) Inferring travel motivation from travelers' experiences. *Journal of Travel Research*, 22(2), 16–20.

Pearce, P. L. and Lee, U.-I. (2005) Developing the travel career approach to tourist motivation. *Journal of Travel Research*, 43(3), 226–237.

Pine, B. and Gilmore, J. (1999) *The Experience Economy: Work is Theatre & Every Business a Stage*. Boston: Harvard Business School Press.

Pine, B. and Gilmore, J. (2013) The experience economy: Past, present, and future. In J. Sundbo and F. Sørensen (Eds.), *Handbook on the Experience Economy*. Cheltenham: Edward Elgar Publishing, pp. 21–44.

Plog, S. C. (1974) Why destination areas rise and fall in popularity. *Cornell Hotel and Restaurant Administration Quarterly*, 14(4), 55–58.

Plog, S. C. (2001) Why destination areas rise and fall in popularity: An update of a *Cornell Quarterly* classic. *Cornell Hotel and Restaurant Administration Quarterly*, 42(3), 13–24.

Pröbstl-Haider, U. and Haider, W. (2014) The role of protected areas in destination choice in the European Alps. *Zeitschrift für Wirtschaftsgeographie*, 58(2–3), 144–163.

Reif, J., Harms, T. and Eisenstein, B. (2020) Tourist-Sein oder nicht Tourist-Sein? *Zur Reputation Zeitschrift für Tourismuswissenschaft*, 11(3), 381–402.

Rojek, C. (1993) *Ways of Escape: Modern Transformations in Leisure and Travel*. Lanham: Rowman & Littlefield.

Ryan, C. (1998) The travel career ladder: An appraisal. *Annals of Tourism Research*, 25(4), 936–957.

Seeler, S., Lück, M. and Schänzel, H. A. (2018) The concept of experience in tourism research: A review of the literature. In. A. Ali and J. Hull (Eds.), *Multi-stakeholder Perspectives of the Tourism Experience: Responses from the International Competence Network of Tourism Research and Education (ICNT)*. Frankfurt am Main: Peter Lang, pp. 203–226.

Seeler, S., Lück, M. and Schänzel, H. A. (2019) Exploring the drivers behind experience accumulation – The role of secondary experiences consumed through the eyes of social media influencers. *Journal of Hospitality and Tourism Management*, 41, 80–89.

Seeler, S., Lück, M. and Schänzel H. (2021) Paradoxes and actualities of off-the-beaten-track tourists, *Journal of Hospitality and Tourism Management*, https://doi.org/10.1016/j.jhtm.2021.06.004

Sharifpour, M. and Walters, G. (2014) The interplay between prior knowledge perceived risk and the tourism consumer decision process: A conceptual framework. *The Marketing Review*, 14(3), 279–296.

Sharpley, R. (2018) *Tourism, Tourists and Society*, 5th Edn.. Abingdon: Routledge.

Smed, K. M. (2012) Identity in tourist motivation and the dynamics of meaning. In R. Sharpley and P. Stone (Eds.), *Contemporary Tourist Experiences: Concepts and Consequences*. New York: Routledge, pp. 130–146.

Smith, V. L. (1989) *Hosts and Guests: The Anthropology of Tourism*. Philadelphia: University of Pennsylvania Press.

Stankov, U., Filimonau, V. and Vujičić, M. D. (2020) A mindful shift: An opportunity for mindfulness-driven tourism in a post-pandemic world. *Tourism Geographies*, 22(3). doi.org/10.1080/14616 688.2020.1768432

The experienced tourist

Tao, C-H, Eagles, P. and Smith, S. (2004) Profiling Taiwanese ecotourists using a self-definition approach. *Journal of Sustainable Tourism*, 12(2), 149–168.

Urry, J. (1995) *Consuming Places*. New York: Routledge.

Wang, N. (2000) *Tourism and Modernity: Sociological Analysis*. Amsterdam: Pergamon.

Weeden, C. (2011) Responsible tourist motivation: How valuable is the Schwartz value survey? *Journal of Ecotourism: Ecotourism and Ethics*, 10(3), 214–234.

15

TOURIST MOTIVATION
A critical overview

Songshan (Sam) Huang

Introduction

This chapter provides a critical overview of tourist motivation as one of the key concepts in the tourism literature. As the ultimate driving force for tourist behaviour, tourist motivation has been studied as a core concept in understanding different types of tourist behaviour (Pearce, 2005). While it is more evident to study and describe the who, when, where and how of tourism phenomena, the issue of why people travel to a certain destination and consume certain tourism forms and products seems to be more complicated and challenging to researchers (Crompton, 1979). As a matter of fact, early studies in the field of tourism seem to have taken tourist motivation as a focus (cf. Crompton, 1979; Dann, 1977; Pearce, 1982) and, until the present time, tourist motivation has not only remained a critical construct in tourist behaviour studies but also become a familiar term to most tourism researchers (e.g., Lu, Hung, Wang, Schuett & Hu, 2016; Rita, Brochado & Dimova, 2019; Wong, Law & Zhao, 2018). From a critical perspective, however, the literature on tourism motivation appears to be mostly atheoretical. This chapter thus adopts a theoretical lens to assess the developments of conceptual or theoretical frameworks and schemes around tourist motivation. It then goes further to review the methodological issues in measuring tourist motivations and elaborate on the three streams of tourist motivation research in the recent literature.

Theoretical frameworks of tourist motivation

There is no single dominant theory or theoretical framework of tourist motivation in the literature. Rather, several conceptual frameworks exist, and these are generally well received by tourism researchers (Hsu & Huang, 2008). These include the Push-Pull model, the Escaping-Seeking conceptual framework, and the Travel Career Ladder (TCL) and Travel Career Patterns (TCP) models. Some scholars, such as Hsu and Huang (2008), have also classified Plog's Allocentrism/Psychocentrism model (Plog, 1974, 2001) as a tourism motivation framework. However, upon close examination, Plog's model was found to be more about the general propensity to travel in the context of different personality types. Therefore, from a stricter viewpoint, although helpful in understanding tourist motivation, Plog's model is not directed at tourist motivation and is thus not included in this review.

DOI: 10.4324/9781003219866-18

The Push-Pull Model

The Push-Pull Model appeared early in the tourism literature (Crompton, 1979; Dann, 1977) and has been adopted by many tourism scholars in studying tourist motivations (e.g., Jang & Cai, 2002; Hsu & Lam, 2003; Sangpikul, 2008; Whyte, 2017; Zhang & Lam, 1999). Yet, the model seems to be derived from common sense reasoning rather than systemic theorizing. The push-push dynamism can be found in multiple disciplines including marketing, management and education (e.g., Horbach, Rammer & Rennings, 2012; Mazzarol & Soutar, 2002; Olver & Farris, 1989). In the tourism literature, push motivational factors refer to those internal psychological forces that drive a person to move away from his/her home and travel to a destination, while pull factors are those destination-associated features and characteristics that are attractive to potential tourists (Gnoth, 1997; Uysal & Jurowski, 1994).

Early tourist motivation studies tend to embrace the Push-Pull framework. In his seminal work based on unstructured interviews, Crompton (1979) identified two categories of tourist motivations: socio-psychological motivations and cultural motivations. There are seven socio-psychological motivations, including: escape from a perceived mundane environment; exploration and evaluation of self; relaxation; prestige; regression; enhancement of kinship relationships; and, facilitation of social interaction. The two cultural motivations are novelty and education. In an implicit way, Crompton (1979) would like to link the socio-psychological motivations to push factors while claiming that the cultural motivations can be 'at least partially aroused by the particular qualities that a destination offered' (Crompton, 1979: 408) and thus linked to pull factors. However, Hsu and Huang (2008) argued that novelty can be driven by the innate desire of curiosity, as mentioned by Maslow (1970) as a basic human need, and thus should be more like a push factor.

From a sociological perspective, Dann (1977) elaborated on two socio-psychological constructs which serve well as two pertinent travel motivations across different cultural denominations. These two motivational factors are anomie and ego-enhancement. On the one hand, anomie, not a familiar term to lay people, represents an individual's psychological state of being which is believed to be generated from everyday life and, more precisely, the social isolation from everyday life. In most post-modern societies, anomie would be a socio-psychological mechanism that pushes people to 'get away from it all' and therefore become a tourist (Dann, 1977: 187). Dann (1977) also argued that in order to counteract the influence of anomie, an individual would seek 'love and affection and the desire to communicate to his fellow man [sic]' (Dann, 1977: 187), indicating that relationships and socialization could be the needs underlying such a state. Dann's use of the term anomie has far-reaching theoretical and practical relevance and should not be easily neglected by scholars. For example, in countries such as China which has been a latecomer to the process of industrialization, urbanization has witnessed over half of its population now living in cities. It is apparent that the subsequent urban lifestyle and living conditions might lead to the emergence of anomie as a modern life 'symptom' and, consequently, tourism seems to offer a means of releasing the societal tension.

On the other hand, ego-enhancement is derived from the need to have social interaction and recognition and, perhaps, to boost one's ego to achieve a perceived status that might be considered superior to that of fellow human beings. As such, ego-enhancement is closely related to the needs of achievement, self-actualization and self-fulfilment, and can be congruent with the need of self-esteem (Chen, Huang & Hu, 2019; Hsu & Huang, 2008). As a basic motive that pushes people to travel, ego-enhancement can be reflected in multiple motivational factors such as, for example, status seeking and prestige (Zhang & Lam, 1999).

Dann (1977) deemed both anomie and ego-enhancement to be push factors and, through empirical tests, attempted to align anomie and ego-enhancement as the two polar coordinates in a continuum. Similarly, Crompton (1979) also tried to conceptualize his identified nine travel motivations as being located along a continuum ranging from cultural to socio-psychological.

In essence, the Push-Pull Model represents a dichotomous typology of travel motivations. As noted above, the model has been widely adopted and discussed in the tourism literature (e.g., Hsu & Lam, 2003; Sangpikul, 2008; Turnbull & Uysal, 1995; Whyte, 2017; Zhang & Lam, 1999). However, while conceptually researchers can label a motivational factor as either a push or a pull factor based on their judgement of whether it represents an internal personal need or is an external feature in the destination, such a simple dichotomous approach may arguably overlook the essential meaning of tourist motivation. Hence, some researchers, such as Pizam, Neumann and Reichel (1979), recognize that only push factors can be considered to underpin tourist motivations while 'pull factors, in many cases, do not play any role in motivations of a certain touristic activity' (Pizam, Neumann & Reichel, 1979: 195). Certainly, empirical tests often reveal that one push factor may be correlated to multiple pull factors whilst one pull factor can correlate to multiple push factors (Baloglu & Uysal, 1996; Klenosky, 2002; Pyo, Mihalik & Uysal, 1989). Such relationships between push and pull factors question the validity of the dichotomy model and, furthermore, raise doubts about whether pull factors (as, essentially, characteristics of a destination that might satisfy a motivational need) can be conceptually argued to be motivations. Reflecting the arguably more general uncritical tendency to adopt concepts and theories in tourism studies (see also Chapter 7 in this volume) unfortunately very few researchers have questioned conceptually the push-pull dichotomy of tourist motivations.

The Escaping-Seeking framework

The Escaping-Seeking framework is another conceptual framework in the literature that can be used to offer explanations on tourist motivations. This framework is developed from the understanding of leisure motivation in leisure studies (Hsu & Huang, 2008; Mannell & Iso-Ahola, 1987). Mannell and Iso-Ahola (1987) present this two-dimensional motivation model to explain an individual's tourism and leisure experiences. According to them, individuals are constantly subjected to two motivational forces that simultaneously influence their tourism and leisure behaviours; more specifically, they are either escaping from daily routines and a stressful life or are seeking recreational experiences that are rewarding to them. Along with these seeking and escaping forces, there may also exist related personal and interpersonal issues. So, for example, an individual's motivation in leisure and tourism can vary from escaping personal environments to seeking personal rewards on one axis and, on another intersecting axis, range from escaping interpersonal environments to seeking interpersonal rewards.

Upon close examination, one may find that the Escaping-Seeking framework is in essence little different from the Approach-Avoidance motivation model (Elliot, 2006; Elliot & Thrash, 2002) in which an individual's behaviour is seen to be influenced by, respectively the potential for positive, desirable experiences and for negative, undesirable experiences. What determines whether an individual tends to seek or escape through participating in tourism seems to be the stimulating or arousal state of the individual's daily life. Therefore, the construct of optimal arousal seems to be important in understanding tourist motivation (Mannell & Iso-Ahola, 1987); for example, if an individual is facing overstimulating life

Tourist motivation: a critical overview

situations, it is likely he or she will escape this type of daily life by taking vacations. It is also possible for an individual to escape an under-stimulating environment by seeking excitement in vacations. In general, people take vacations to either seek more stimulation if their daily life does not provide them with an optimal level of simulation, or reduce overstimulation to achieve optimal arousal level (Mannell & Iso-Ahola, 1987).

With its resemblance to the Approach-Avoidance motivation model referred to above, the Escaping-Seeking model is related to people's more fundamental socio-psychological motives. In particular, its conceptual connection to various experience constructs such as flow or peak experience, optimal arousal and personality would appear to offer some potentially fruitful streams of research in the study of tourist motivation and experience. However, the further development of the Escaping-Seeking framework and its application in conjunction with tourist experience research has, to date, been limited and largely disappointing.

Nonetheless, some researchers have tried to verify empirically the Escaping-Seeking framework. For instance, Wolfe and Hsu (2004) applied the Escaping-Seeking framework to tourist motivation and found that motivational factors can be generally aligned with the personal/interpersonal seeking/escaping paradigm. In another attempt, Kay (2009) applied the framework in an examination of both Western and Asian tourists' cultural experiences and tourist motivations. Unfortunately, however, in most cases, the framework has been used in a rather uncritical manner and, as a consequence, potential theoretical insights emerging from its application have not been forthcoming. Indeed, some researchers simply see the framework as a seeking/avoiding dichotomy theory or a typology of tourist motivations (Kay, 2009), thereby largely overlooking its theoretical underpinning. The seeking and escaping dimensions of tourist motivation may in fact be informed by the social and cultural realities of a home society and, hence, the variations in the magnitude and number of seeking/escaping dimensions may offer a truthful reflection of the home society. Therefore, more theoretical explorations and verifications are required with regards to the further development and application of the Escaping-Seeking framework in tourism.

The Travel Career Ladder (TCL) and Travel Career Pattern (TCP) models

Pearce and his colleagues advanced another line of theoretical explorations of tourism motivations (e.g., Moscardo & Pearce, 1986; Pearce, 1982, 1988; Pearce & Caltabiano, 1983; Pearce & Lee, 2005) – see also Chapters 4 and 13 in this volume. Holding an academic background of psychology (social psychology), Pearce (1982) commenced his inquiries of tourist motivation following Maslow's (1970) hierarchy of needs motivation theory. Based on travel narratives of both positive and negative experiences of some 200 tourists from multiple countries, Pearce (1982) found the occurrence rates varied along the different basic human needs in Maslow's model across the positive and negative experiences. A general pattern to emerge was that higher-end needs like self-actualization appeared more often (35%) in the positive experience narratives than in the negative experience narratives (1%). Probably based on this observation, Pearce (1982) developed the Travel Career Ladder (TCL) model, the overall proposition of which is that people who have more travel experiences tend to demonstrate more motivations relating to the higher end of Maslow (1970)'s model, such as love and belongingness and self-actualization, than those with less travel experiences.

Despite being a worthwhile attempt to theorize travel motivations, the TLC model is, according to Ryan (1998), difficult to validate empirically. Hence, Pearce and his colleagues went further and developed the Travel Career Pattern (TCP) model based on further empirical works on tourist motivation (Pearce & Lee, 2005). Unlike TCL, TCP does not follow the needs hierarchy structure; like TCL, however, TCP continues to relate tourist motivations to travel experience (that is, a travel career). Empirical results leading to TCP reveal that some motivational factors, such as host-site involvement, and nature-related factors are more important to the more experienced travellers, while other motivation factors such as stimulation, personal development, relationship, self-actualization, nostalgia, romance and recognition appear to be more important to less experienced travellers. In addition, there exists a core set of motivations including escape, relaxation, relationship enhancement and self-development that seem to be equally important to both experienced and inexperienced travellers (Pearce & Lee, 2005).

Pearce should be praised for his continuing, relentless effort in advancing the theoretical explorations of tourist motivations (again, see Chapters 4 and 13 in this volume). However, while levels of travel experience do seem to be a relevant covariate to tourist motivations, there remains to a larger gap in theorizing tourist motivation. As mentioned above in the discussions of the Escaping-Seeking framework, relevant constructs such as optimal arousal, flow state and mindfulness may be adopted as an external calibrating concept to better understand tourism motivation.

Arguably, the field of tourism studies can be seen as lacking good theorizing scholars. (Pearce may be a notable exception). However, even TCP lacks theoretical clarity and can be regarded at most as a theoretical framework rather than a theory. Few applications of the TCP model can be traced in the literature, although as one example, Paris and Teye (2010) applied the TCP model to study the relationship between backpacker motivations and previous travel experience. Two dimensions of motivation, cultural knowledge and relaxation, were identified as core motivations that do not vary across travel experience level, while four motivations, namely, personal/social growth, experience seeking, budget travel and independence, were found to vary with different levels of travel experience. In another study, Song and Bae (2018) applied the TCP in examining the travel motivation patterns of international students in Korea. Latent profile analysis (LPA) identified four profiles, labelled as 'core', 'longing', 'middle' and 'veteran' respectively whilst, more generally, Wu, Law, Fong and Liu (2019) compared the concept of travel life cycle with TCP and found that the travel life cycle cannot be equated to family life cycle and, consistent with the proposition of TCP, there are core travel motives that do not vary over different stages of travel life cycle.

Methodological issues in researching tourist motivation

Tourist motivation is generally perceived to be a multi-dimensional psychological construct, subject to the influences of one's social environment (Chen, Bao & Huang, 2014; Hsu & Huang, 2008; Hsu & Lam, 2003; Huang & Hsu, 2005; Sangpikul, 2008; Turnbull & Uysal, 1995; Whyte, 2017; Zhang & Lam, 1999). Measuring tourist motivation as a latent social psychological construct is always challenging (Dann, 1981). In the literature, numerous studies adopt a post-positivistic approach to measuring tourist motivations. In contrast, a pure quantitative method would involve generating relevant tourism motivation measurement items from previous studies in the literature and presenting these items to the study respondents to ask to what extent (normally on a 1–5 or 1–7 scale) they agree with the statements (the agreement approach) or they think the statement is important (the importance approach) (see Huang, 2010). Either way, the measurement would be subject to researcher selection bias (Lowyck, Langenhove & Bollaert, 1992) whilst, as Huang (2010) elaborates, both approaches may have the common method bias.

The literature also indicates that tourist motivations may be highly situational and context specific (cf. Hung & Petrick, 2011; Kluin & Lehto, 2012; Mak, Wong & Chang, 2009). In measuring tourist motivations in different travel and tourism contexts, different studies confirm this with numerous combinations of factor numbers and measurement item numbers. In other words, there does not seem to be a universal tourist motivation scale that can be applied across different contexts. As a matter of fact, new tourist motivation scales in novel tourism or travel contexts keep emerging, reinforcing the impression that the field has not been attended to well from a theoretical perspective. While a universal tourist motivation scale may be possible epistemologically and ontologically, this has been largely unavailable. This may be partly attributed to the atheoretical development of the area. As shown above, some of the widely adopted models, such as the Push-Pull Model, appear to lack a strong theoretical foundation. Indeed, as the Push-Push Model allows destination features to be classified as tourist motivations, this apparently over-lenient conceptualization allows internal psychological forces to become entangled with external situational and contextual factors, making it difficult for a universal tourist motivation scale to be developed.

Dann (1981) considers the reasons why it is difficult to measure tourist motivation. In particular, he suggests that tourist motivation, as a deep-mind driving factor behind an individual's deciding to participate in tourism, may be rooted in the subconscious and thus be unspeakable. Consequently, he notes that one major issue in measuring tourist motivation is that some respondents may not be aware of their real motives of travel. Tourists may not wish or be able to reflect on their real travel motives; more precisely, tourists may not wish or be able to express their real travel motives (Dann, 1981).

More generally, as a deep-mind psychological construct, tourist motivation may not lend itself to effective measurement through the commonly used survey techniques in tourism research. Apart from the researcher selection bias in the adoption of measurement items, measuring tourist motivations in a new context would always bear the risk that some unique motivational factors relevant to that context could be missed in the measurement items pool. Therefore, it is always prudent to have some explorative investigation, most effectively in a qualitative emic approach, to identify these unique context-specific motivational factors. In-depth personal interviews are recommended as a preparatory step prior to administering a questionnaire survey. Even with interviews, however, some special techniques may be required to explore motivations. For example, following the means–end approach, Jewell and Crotts (2002, 2009) used the Hierarchical Value Map (HVM) technique to explore the underlying motives of heritage tourists. A specific interview technique called 'laddering' was applied to continue asking the respondent to justify their answer to the previous question until they can no longer justify the answer. The means–end approach and its associated HVM technique have also been adopted by other researchers in studying tourist motivation (e.g., Jiang, Scott & Ding, 2015; Wen & Huang, 2020). It should be noted that as the analysis of any interview transcripts would involve the researcher's own understanding of the background and the central issue under examination, there is always a degree of researcher bias in such research work.

Recent developments in tourist motivation research

Tourist motivation remains a core concept in tourism research, and the recent tourism literature offers different types of tourist motivation studies. Generally, these studies can be classified into three categories: (i) studies exploring tourist motivations in different tourism forms and contexts; (ii) studies applying tourist motivation in integrated tourist behaviour models; and (iii), studies endeavouring to examine the relationship between motivation and some even deeper-mind constructs such as cultural values.

There are a number of studies examining the motivations of different types of tourists or of tourists in different forms/context of tourism. Mak et al. (2009), for example, examined the motivations of spa-goers in Hong Kong and found that relaxation and relief, escape, self-reward and indulgence, and health and beauty are important motivational factors for people to visit spas. Applying a mixed method design including both questionnaire survey and follow-up interviews, Rittichainuwat and Rattanaphinanchai (2015) examined the travel motivations of film tourists visiting a film-shooting destination. Ritchie, Tkaczynski and Faulks (2010) investigated cycle tourists' motivations and travel behaviour using their involvement profiles whilst Hung and Petrick (2011) followed Churchill's (1979) scale development procedure and developed a scale to measure cruise tourist motivations; Ye, Qiu and Yuen (2011) examined the motivations of mainland Chinese medical tourists in Hong Kong. While such studies produce context-specific knowledge about particular forms of tourism (e.g., medical tourism, cruising tourism), the motivational factors identified tend to be the same factors discussed more generally in the literature. That is, it is common to see some core travel motivations, such as relaxation, novelty seeking, relationships and prestige, being identified as factors across multiple studies. Nevertheless, it can be argued that studying the motivations of tourists engaged in a specific form of tourism may at least enhance knowledge and understanding of that tourism form or phenomenon. However, in terms of deepening the theoretical understanding of tourist motivation per se, the contribution of these studies is typically more limited.

The second stream of tourist motivation research views motivation as one of the key tourist behaviour constructs within integrated tourist behaviour models. In this regard, this type of research tends to be more theoretical, typically following a theory testing approach (Colquitt & Zapata-Phelan, 2007). In such studies focusing on theory construction and testing, researchers tend to seek theoretical clarifications and correlations between tourist motivation and other tourist behaviour constructs, such as attitude, destination image, perceived value, constraints, expectation, satisfaction, behavioural intention and tourist loyalty (e.g., Hsu, Cai & Li, 2010; Huang & Hsu, 2009; Lee, 2009; Yoon & Uysal, 2005). For instance, employing the theory of planned behaviour (Ajzen, 1991) as a theoretical foundation, Huang and Hsu (2009) developed and tested a model examining the effects of travel motivation, perceived constraints, past experience and attitudes on tourists' intention to revisit a destination. Travel motivation was conceptualized and operationalized as a multi-dimensional construct, and it was found that motivational factors exerted different influences on attitudes, which, in turn, further affected revisit intention. While novelty and relaxation had significant positive effects on tourists' attitudes towards revisiting the destination, shopping and knowledge as travel motivations had no direct effect on attitude. However, shopping, as a destination-specific (Hong Kong) motivation, had a significant positive effect on revisit intention. In another study of similar type, Hsu et al. (2010) interrogated the relationships between expectation, motivation and attitude. It was found that motivation played a partial mediating effect on the relationship between expectation and attitude.

As tourist motivation is conceptually multi-dimensional, the internal structure and relationships amongst the different dimensions of tourist motivation can be theoretically critical. Although Pearce and his colleagues have attempted to explore these internal relationships among tourist motivation constructs in their TCL and TCP theorizing works, discussed above (Pearce, 1982, 1988; Pearce & Caltabiano, 1983; Pearce & Lee, 2005; Ryan, 1998), the relationships between different tourist motivational factors are still not crystal clear.

Tourist motivation: a critical overview

For example, through common-sense reasoning, relaxation can be considered very different from novelty seeking as a specific tourist motivational factor. Each factor (e.g., novelty seeking) can be a standalone tourist psychological construct; indeed, novelty seeking has been studied as an independent tourist motivational factor in tourism studies (cf. Assaker, Vinzi & O'Connor, 2011; Chang, Wall & Chu, 2006; Jang & Feng, 2007; Lee & Crompton, 1992). Therefore, in the second stream of tourist motivation studies elaborated on here, there is a theoretical caveat that the internal structure of overall tourism motivation and the relationships among the composing motivation dimensions may be overlooked.

The third stream of tourist motivation studies explores the relationship between motivation and cultural values (Hsu & Huang, 2016; Li & Cai, 2012; Wong & Lau, 2001). Comparing with the first two streams of tourist motivation research, the number of studies in this stream is more limited and, indeed, some do not explicitly touch on the issue of travel motivation when examining the influence of cultural values on travel behaviour (e.g., Wong & Lau, 2001). More specifically, researchers may not easily discern the difference between the second stream and the third stream studies. While those in second stream studies usually take tourist motivation, together with other behavioural constructs, as a determinant to predict some outcome behavioural constructs such as attitude, satisfaction, behavioural intention and loyalty, the third stream studies explore the possible effect of values as a determinant of tourist motivation. Broadly, it is suggested in the literature that tourist motivation could be determined by national cultural values (Kim & Lee, 2000; Kozak, 2002). In one study, Kim and Lee (2000) compared the travel motivations of Anglo-American and Japanese tourists, finding that while Japanese tourists exhibit stronger motivations related to prestige/status and family togetherness than their Anglo-American counterparts, they rate novelty as a travel motivation significantly lower than Anglo-American tourists. Similarly, by comparing the travel motivations of British and German tourists visiting two distinctive destinations (Turkey vs. Mallorca), Kozak (2002) found that motivations of the two nationalities of tourists varied in their strengths in most of the motivational factors, and also across the destinations.

A more recent study provides stronger evidence that national cultural values exert a significant influence on tourist behaviour. Huang and Crotts (2019) identified consistent relationships between Hofstede's six cultural dimensions (power distance; individualism/collectivism; masculinity/femininity; uncertainty avoidance; long-term orientation/short-term orientation; and indulgence/restraint) and tourist satisfaction across different country samples. Although tourist motivation is not directly tested with the cultural dimensions in their study, as it has been shown elsewhere in the literature that travel motivation (push motivation) positively affects tourist satisfaction (Battour, Ismail, Battor & Awais, 2017; Yoon & Uysal, 2005), the relationships between these cultural dimensions and tourist motivation can be reasonably speculated.

Examining the relationship between cultural values and tourist motivation would be valuable to advance our understanding of tourist motivation per se. However, as both cultural values and tourism motivation are deep-mind level constructs, the inherent difficulty in undertaking such research is immediately apparent. Perhaps unsurprisingly therefore, to date very few attempts have been made to explicitly examine the relationship between cultural values and tourist motivation. Notably, Hsu and Huang (2016), using focus group interviews, identified 40 Chinese cultural values items within the contemporary society in China and explored the links between these cultural values and travel behaviours/preferences of Chinese tourists. Similarly focusing on Chinese tourists, Li and Cai (2012) examined the effects of personal values (internal vs. external) on travel motivation and behavioural intention. They found that internal values had significant relationships with the motivations of novelty and knowledge, and self-development, but not with prestigious and luxury experience, exciting experience and escape and relationship. External values related to all other motivation factors except novelty and knowledge. Such a result suggests that the internal structure of tourist motivations should be clarified before a better understanding of the relationship between values and tourist motivations can be rendered.

As both cultural values and tourism motivation are multi-dimensional, the relationships between the two might logically be considered to be multifaceted. Employing the means–end approach and laddering interview technique with 60 Chinese respondents, Jiang, Scott, Tao and Ding (2019) identified 15 travel motivations at the value level and classified these motivations into three themes: self-enhancement, nurturing the soul and harmonious relationships. However, Jiang et al.'s (2019) findings are conceptually confusing as they did not clearly differentiate motivations from values. Wen, Huang and Ying (2019) went further to apply quantitative tests on the relationship between values and motivations. Using canonical correlation analysis, they found that Chinese tourists' specific motivations for visiting Israel for business development and self-fulfilment are correlated to modern personal values, while sightseeing as a tourist motivation is associated with the value of life enrichment and quality.

Despite the above-mentioned studies, the relationship between cultural values and tourist motivation is not yet clear. Hence, this will remain on the future agenda for tourist motivation studies. In addition, the few investigations to date appear to be *a posteriori*. There have been no theoretical speculations or assumptions made on the structural relationships between cultural values and tourism motivation dimensions. Overall, then, there needs to be more dedicated studies exploring the relationship between cultural values and tourist motivation. It is believed this stream of research may better advance the theoretical development of tourist motivation studies although researchers are, however, advised to refer to the above-mentioned theoretical frameworks of tourist motivation in furthering their studies.

Conclusions

This chapter has reviewed the development of tourist motivation research. It has focused on three areas of development: (i) the development of theoretical frameworks of tourist motivation; (ii) methodological development issues; and (iii) recent developments in tourist motivation studies. It has revealed that the Push-Pull model, the Escaping-Seeking framework and the TCL and TCP models are arguably the dominant theoretical frameworks employed in the literature and, although commonly adopted in tourist motivation studies, the post-positivistic survey approach seems to be limited as a method to measure tourist motivations. Hence, mixed-method approaches incorporating both quantitative survey and qualitative interviews are recommended as a means of more thoroughly studying tourist motivations in new tourism contexts.

The chapter has also identified three distinctive streams of tourist motivation research. The first stream of research focuses on identifying tourist motivations in specific new contexts. In these studies, some core motivational factors evident in most if not all tourism contexts are usually confirmed while some context-specific motivations may be an outcome. The second stream positions tourist motivation as one of the many tourist behaviour predictors alongside other behaviour constructs in structural models to understand tourist behaviour. The third stream focuses on examining the relationship between cultural values and motivation.

Although tourist motivation has been a core concept in tourism research, studies on tourist motivation have been mostly atheoretical. More theorizing efforts are thus welcomed in this important sub-field of tourism research. Future efforts on the development of tourist motivation theoretical frameworks could further look upon the internal structure and relationships among the composing dimensions or constructs of tourism motivations. A better understanding and knowledge of tourist motivation may also be developed by clarifying the relationship between cultural values and tourist motivation. Indeed, cultural values could be used as a useful external nomological concept to further develop the knowledge of tourist motivation.

References

Ajzen, I. (1991) The theory of planned behaviour. *Organizational Behavior and Human Decision Processes*, 50, 179–211.

Assaker, G., Vinzi, V. E. and O'Connor, P. (2011) Examining the effect of novelty seeking, satisfaction, and destination image on tourists' return pattern: A two factor, non-linear latent growth model. *Tourism Management*, 32(4), 890–901.

Baloglu, S. and Uysal, M. (1996) Market segments of push and pull motivations: A canonical correlation approach. *International Journal of Contemporary Hospitality Management*, 8(3), 32–38.

Battour, M., Ismail, M. N., Battor, M. and Awais, M. (2017) Islamic tourism: An empirical examination of travel motivation and satisfaction in Malaysia. *Current Issues in Tourism*, 20(1), 50–67.

Chang, J., Wall, G. and Chu, S.-T. (2006) Novelty seeking at aboriginal attractions. *Annals of Tourism Research*, 33(3), 729–747.

Chen, G., Bao, J. and Huang, S. (2014) Segmenting Chinese backpackers by travel motivations. *International Journal of Tourism Research*, 16(4), 355–267.

Chen, G., Huang, S. and Hu, X. (2019) Backpacker personal development, generalized self-efficacy, and self-esteem: Testing a structural model. *Journal of Travel Research*, 58(4), 680–694.

Churchill, G. A. (1979) A paradigm for developing better measures of marketing constructs. *Journal of Marketing Research*, 16(1), 64–73.

Colquitt, J. A. and Zapata-Phelan, C. P. (2007) Trends in theory building and theory testing: A five-decade study of the Academy of Management Journal. *Academy of Management Journal*, 50(6), 1281–1303.

Crompton, J. (1979) Motivations for pleasure vacation. *Annals of Tourism Research*, 6(4), 208–424.

Dann, G. (1977) Anomie, ego-enhancement and tourism. *Annals of Tourism Research*, 4(4), 184–194.

Dann, G. (1981) Tourist motivation: An appraisal. *Annals of Tourism Research*, 8(2), 187–219.

Elliot, A. J. (2006) The hierarchical model of approach-avoidance motivation. *Motivation and Emotion*, 30, 111–116.

Elliot, A. J. and Thrash, T. M. (2002). Approach-Avoidance motivation in personality: Approach and avoidance temperaments and goals. *Journal of Personality and Psychology*, 82(5), 804–818.

Gnoth, J. (1997) Tourism motivation and expectation formation. *Annals of Tourism Research*, 24(2), 283–304.

Horbach, J., Rammer, C. and Rennings, K. (2012) Determinants of eco-innovations by type of environmental impact – The role of regulatory push/pull, technology push and market pull. *Ecological Economics*, 78, 112–122.

Hsu, C. H. C., Cai, L. A. and Li, M. (2010) Expectation, motivation, and attitude: A tourist behavioural model. *Journal of Travel Research*, 49(3), 282–296.

Hsu, C. H. C. and Huang, S. (2008) Travel motivation: A critical review of the concept's development. In A.G Woodside and D. Martin (Eds.), *Tourism Management: Analysis, Behaviour and Strategy*. Cambridge MA: CABI Publishing, pp. 14–27.

Hsu, C. H. C. and Huang, S. (2016) Reconfiguring Chinese cultural values and their tourism implications. *Tourism Management*, 54, 230–242.

Hsu, C. H. C. and Lam, T. (2003) Mainland Chinese travelers' motivations and barriers of visiting Hong Kong. *Journal of Academy of Business and Economics*, 2(1), 60–67.

Huang, S. (2010) Measuring tourism motivation: Do scales matter? *Tourismos*, 5(1), 153–162.

Huang, S. and Crotts, J. (2019) Relationships between Hosftede's cultural dimensions and tourist satisfaction: A cross-country cross-sample examination. *Tourism Management*, 72, 232–241.

Huang, S. and Hsu, C. H. C. (2005) Mainland Chinese residents' perceptions and motivations of visiting Hong Kong: Evidence from focus group interviews. *Asia Pacific Journal of Tourism Research*, 10(2), 191–205.

Huang, S. and Hsu, C. H. C. (2009) Effects of travel motivation, past experience, perceived constraints, and attitude on revisit intention. *Journal of Travel Research*, 48(1), 29–44.

Hung, K. and Petrick, J. F. (2011) Why do you cruise? Exploring the motivations for taking cruise holidays, and the construction of a cruising motivation scale. *Tourism Management*, 32, 386–393.

Jang, S. C. and Cai, L. A. (2002) Travel motivations and destination choice: A study of British outbound market. *Journal of Travel and Tourism marketing*, 13(3), 111–133.

Jang, S. C. and Feng, R. (2007) Temporal destination revisit intention: The effects of novelty seeking and satisfaction. *Tourism Management*, 28(2), 580–590.

Jewell, B. and Crotts, J. (2002) Adding psychological value to heritage tourism experiences. *Journal of Travel and Tourism Marketing*, 11(4), 13–28.

Jewell, B. and Crotts, J. (2009) Adding psychological value to heritage tourism experiences revisited. *Journal of Travel and Tourism Marketing*, 26(3), 244–263.

Jiang, S., Scott, N., Tao, L. and Ding, P. (2019) Chinese tourists' motivation and their relationship to cultural values. *Anatolia*, 30(1), 90–102.

Jiang, S., Scott, N. and Ding, P. (2015) Using means-end chain theory to explore travel motivation. *Journal of Vacation Marketing*, 21(1), 87–100.

Kay, P. L. (2009) Cultural experience tourist motives dimensionality: A cross-cultural study. *Journal of Hospitality Marketing and Management*, 18(4), 329–371.

Kim, C. and Lee, S. (2000) Understanding the cultural differences in tourist motivation between Anglo-American and Japanese tourists. *Journal of Travel and Tourism Marketing*, 9(2), 153–170.

Klenosky, D. B. (2002) The 'pull' of tourism destinations: A means-end investigation. *Journal of Travel Research*, 40(4), 385–395.

Kluin, J. Y. and Lehto, X. Y. (2012) Measuring family reunion travel motivations. *Annals of Tourism Research*, 39(2), 820–841.

Kozak, M. (2002) Comparative analysis of tourist motivations by nationality and destinations. *Tourism Management*, 23, 221–232.

Lee, T. H. (2009) A structural model to examine how destination image, attitude, and motivation affect the future behaviour of tourists. *Leisure Sciences*, 31(3), 215–236.

Lee, T. H. and Crompton, J. (1992) Measuring novelty seeking in tourism. *Annals of Tourism Research*, 19(4), 732–751.

Li, M. and Cai, L. A. (2012) The effects of personal values on travel motivation and behavioural intention. *Journal of Travel Research*, 51(4), 473–487.

Lowyck, E., Langenhove, L. V. and Bollaert, L. (1992) Typologies of tourism roles. In P. Johnson and B. Thomas (Eds.), *Choice and Demand in Tourism*. London: Mansell, pp. 13–32.

Lu, J., Hung, K., Wang, L., Schuett, M. A. and Hu, L. (2016) Do perceptions of time affect outbound-travel motivations and intention? An investigation among Chinese seniors. *Tourism Management*, 53, 1–12.

Mak, A. H. N., Wong, K. K. F. and Chang, R. C. Y. (2009) Health or self-indulgence? The motivations and characteristics of spa-goers. *International Journal of Tourism Research*, 11(2), 185–199.

Mannell, R. C. and Iso-Ahola, S. E. (1987) Psychological nature of leisure and tourism experience. *Annals of Tourism Research*, 14(3), 314–331.

Maslow, A. (1970). *Motivation and Personality*, 2nd Edn. New York: Harper and Row.

Mazzarol, T. and Soutar, G. N. (2002) 'Push-pull' factors influencing international student destination choice. *International Journal of Educational Management*, 16(2), 82–90.

Moscardo, G. M. and Pearce, P. L. (1986) Historical theme parks: An Australian experience in authenticity. *Annals of Tourism Research*, 13(3), 467–479.

Olver, J. M. and Farris, P. W. (1989) Push and pull: A one-two punch for packaged products. *Sloan Management Review*, 31(1), 53–61.

Paris, C. M. and Teye, V. (2010) Backpacker motivations: A travel career approach. *Journal of Hospitality Marketing and Management*, 19(3), 244–259.

Pearce, P. L. (1982) *The Social Psychology of Tourist Behaviour*. Oxford: Pergamon.

Pearce, P. L. (1988) *The Ulysses Factor: Evaluating Visitors in Tourism Settings*. New York: Springer-Verlag.

Pearce, P. L. (2005) *Tourist Behaviour: Themes and Conceptual Schemes*. Clevedon: Channel View Publications.

Pearce, P. L. and Caltabiano, M. L. (1983) Inferring travel motivating from travelers' experiences. *Journal of Travel Research*, 22(2), 16–20.

Pearce, P. L. and Lee, U. (2005) Developing the travel career approach to tourist motivation. *Journal of Travel Research*, 43(3), 226–237.

Pizam, A., Neumann, Y. and Reichel, A. (1979) Tourist satisfaction: uses and misuses. *Annals of Tourism Research*, 6(2), 195–197.

Plog, S. C. (1974) Why destination areas rise and fall in popularity. *Cornell Hotel and Restaurant Administration Quarterly*, 14(4), 55–58.

Plog, S. C. (2001) Why destination areas rise and fall in popularity: An update of a Cornell quarterly classic. *Cornell Hotel and Restaurant Administration Quarterly*, 42(3), 13–24.

Pyo, S., Mihalik, B. J. and Uysal, M. (1989) Attraction attributes and motivations: A canonical correlation analysis. *Annals of Tourism Research*, 16(2), 277–282.

Rita, P., Brochado, A. and Dimova, L. (2019) Millennials' travel motivations and desired activities within destinations: A comparative study of the US and the UK. *Current Issues in Tourism*, 22(16), 2034–2050.

Ritchie, B. W., Tkaczynski, A. and Faulks, P. (2010) Understanding the motivation and travel behaviour of cycle tourists using involvement profiles. *Journal of Travel & Tourism Marketing*, 27, 409–425.

Rittichainuwat, B. and Rattanaphinanchai, S. (2015) Applying a mixed method of quantitative and qualitative design in explaining the travel motivation of film tourists in visiting a film-shooting destination. *Tourism Management*, 46, 136–147.

Ryan, C. (1998) The travel career ladder: An appraisal. *Annals of Tourism Research*, 25(4), 936–957.

Sangpikul, A. (2008) Travel motivations of Japanese senior travellers to Thailand. *International Journal of Tourism Research*, 10(1), 81–94.

Song, H. and Bae, S. Y. (2018) Understanding the travel motivation and patterns of international students in Korea: Using the theory of travel career pattern. *Asia Pacific Journal of Tourism Research*, 23(2), 133–145.

Turnbull, D. R. and Uysal, M. (1995) An exploratory study of German visitors to the Caribbean: Push and pull motivations. *Journal of Travel and Tourism Marketing*, 4(2), 85–91.

Uysal, M. and Jurowski, C. (1994) Testing the push and pull factors. *Annals of Tourism Research*, 21(4), 844–846.

Wen, J. and Huang, S. (2020) Chinese tourists' motivations of visiting a highly volatile destination: a means-end approach. *Tourism Recreation Research*, 45(1), 80–93.

Wen, J., Huang, S. and Ying, T. (2019) Relationships between Chinese cultural values and tourist motivations: A study of Chinese tourists visiting Israel. *Journal of Destination Marketing and Management*, 14. DOI: /10.1016/j.jdmm.2019.100367

Whyte, L. J. (2017) Understanding the relationship between push and pull motivational factors in cruise tourism: A canonical correlation analysis. *International Journal of Tourism Research*, 19(5), 557–568.

Wolfe, K. and Hsu, C. H. C. (2004) An application of the social psychological model of tourism motivation. *International Journal of Hospitality & Tourism Administration*, 5(1), 29–47.

Wong, I. K. A., Law, R. and Zhao, X. (2018) Time-variant pleasure travel motivations and behaviours. *Journal of Travel Research*, 57(4), 437–452.

Wong, S. and Lau, E. (2001) Understanding the behavior of Hong Kong Chinese tourists on group tour packages. *Journal of Travel Research*, 40(1), 57–67.

Wu, J., Law, R., Fong, D. K. C. and Liu, J. (2019) Rethinking travel life cycle with travel career patterns. *Tourism Recreation Research*, 44(2), 272–277.

Ye, B. H., Qiu, H. Z. and Yuen, P. P. (2011) Motivations and experiences of Mainland Chinese medical tourists in Hong Kong. *Tourism Management*, 32(5), 1125–1127.

Yoon, Y. and Uysal, M. (2005) An examination of the effects of motivation and satisfaction on destination loyalty: A structural model. *Tourism Management*, 26(1), 45–56.

Zhang, H. and Lam, T. (1999) An analysis of mainland Chinese visitors' motivations to visit Hong Kong. *Tourism Management*, 20(5), 587–594.

SECTION 3

Tourist roles and experiences

16

TRAVELLER, TOURIST AND THE 'LOST ART OF TRAVELLING'

The debate continues

Tom Sintobin

An agelong opposition

The opposition between a tourist and a traveller is generally assumed to be one of the most powerful dichotomies to structure tourism discourse. Already in the early stages of modern tourism, 'people on the move' (for lack of a better word) were often divided into categories. Even when other terms were used, a distinction was often made between two kinds of 'travelling'. A good example is a review for the Dutch magazine *Vaderlandsche Letteroefeningen* from 1861, in which the reviewer explicitly mentions that he does not understand why the author of the book under review uses the word 'tourist' instead of 'traveller', seemingly for linguistic and nationalist reasons; there is a proper Dutch word, so why not use it? However, even this reviewer installs a dichotomy between an 'ordinary fun-traveller', who is looking for entertainment and pleasure only, like for instance 'the English spleen-sufferers' and others, whose travelling implies hard work, such as 'to collect material for a book' (R. V. 1861: 455).

Numerous scholars have attempted to chart this opposition (e.g.: Boorstin, 1961: 77–117; Butcher, 2003: 34–49; Buzard, 1993: 18–79; Fussell, 1980: 37–50). The American historian Daniel Boorstin argues in the chapter 'The lost art of travel' from his tremendously influential book *The Image. A Guide to Pseudo-events in America* (Boorstin, 1961) that travel used to be a demanding[1] but worthwhile educational practice that functioned as a 'universal catalyst'. In Boorstin's view, the 'conquest' of the Americas helped to create the Renaissance whereas the travels of the seventeenth century led to the Enlightenment. However, despite the fact that 'there is about five times as much foreign travel by Americans nowadays as there was a hundred years ago', he states, 'all this travel has made so little difference in our thinking and feeling' (Boorstin, 1961: 79). He concludes that the travelling experience itself must have been transformed – and he marks this belief by putting the word 'travel' to indicate the contemporary phenomenon between quotation marks and switching to the word 'tourist':

> Formerly travel required long planning, large expense, and great investments of time. It involved risks to health or even to life. The traveler was active. Now he became passive. [...] The traveler, then, was working at something; the tourist was a pleasure seeker. The traveler was active; he went strenuously in search of people, of adventure,

DOI: 10.4324/9781003219866-20

of experience. The tourist is passive; he expects interesting things to happen to him. He goes 'sight-seeing' [...]. He expects everything to be done to him. Thus foreign travel ceased to be an activity – an experience, an undertaking – and instead became a commodity.

(Boorstin, 1961: 84–85)

This new situation, characterized by superficiality, comfort, pleasure-seeking, laziness, in-authenticity and consumerism, was enabled by important changes in society in the second-half of the nineteenth century: the rapidly improving and democratizing means of long-distance transportation, the commodification of conducted tours that become collective events, the invention of traveller's cheques, insurances, installment plans to finance the trip and the lowering cost of the enterprise. This new way of touring the world is fake, according to Boorstin. It is a pseudo-event that keeps the tourist away from 'the real thing': the 'natives', 'the landscape he traverses' (Boorstin, 1961: 94), the discomforts of true travel that insulate him in pseudo-places like hotels and cruise ships simulating 'local atmosphere', museums that radically decontextualize cultural artefacts, and staged tourist attractions ('pseudo-events'). Tourists could not care less; they prefer their 'own provincial expectations' informed by popular culture and tourism advertising over the real (Boorstin, 1961: 106). They lack freedom and individuality as well, since they obey codes prescribed in guidebooks: how to behave, how to dress, what to like (Boorstin, 1961: 105–106). Space and culture have become homogenized all over the globe so there is nothing left to discover, but for a few 'adventuring travelers who still exist' (Boorstin, 1961: 117) by fabricating 'risks and dangers', reliving 'ancient adventures' – who then proceed to publishing them and have their 'mystery abolished' (Boorstin, 1961: 117).[2]

The American journalist, author and historian Paul Fussell laments the same loss along rather similar lines in his book *Abroad. British Literary Traveling Between the Wars.* Tourists are passive and without initiative (Fussell, 1980: 39), they lack individuality, autonomy and even humanity (Fussell, 1980: 40–41). They are characterized by inauthenticity and consumerism:

What distinguishes the tourist is the motives, few of which are ever openly revealed: to raise social status at home and to allay social anxiety; to realize fantasies of erotic freedom; and most important, to derive secret pleasure from posing momentarily as a member of a class superior to one's own, to play the role of a "shopper" and spender whose life becomes significant and exciting only when one is exercising power by choosing what to buy.

(Fussell, 1980: 42)

Table 16.1 Distinctions between 'tourist' and 'traveller'

Tourist	Traveller
Inauthentic, fake	Authentic, original
Passive	Active
Lacking autonomy	Independent
Sightseeing	Experiencing
Superficial	Fundamental
Collective	Individual
Leisure, uninformed	Work, educated
Confirms worldviews, risk-avoiding	Challenges worldviews
Consumer	Worker

Traveller or tourist

Their habitat consists of pseudo-places, that 'entice by their familiarity and call for instant recognition' (Fussell, 1980: 43) and do not call for the work of the imagination (Fussell, 1980: 45). The above can be schematized as in Table 16.1 above.

Problematizing the dichotomy

Not an opposition

In his often quoted essay 'The Semiotics of Tourism', the literary critic Jonathan Culler is wondering why Boorstin and Fussell have identified the exact moment when the 'age of travel' ended differently. Whereas Fussell situates it around 1939, Boorstin sees 'the decline of the traveler and the rise of the tourist' already in the middle of the nineteenth century (Culler, 1988: 156). Culler adds an example from his own reading of Stendhal, who complained about mass tourism in Florence as early as 1826. This leads Culler to the conclusion that:

The true age of travel has, it seems, always already slipped by; other travellers are

always tourists. This repetition and displacement of the opposition between tourist and traveler suggests that these are not so much two historical categories as terms of an opposition integral to tourism. The historical explanations are excuses for what travelers always do: feel superior to other travellers.

(Culler, 1988: 157)

Travelling as dreamt of by both scholars, characterized by direct contact with authentic reality, has, however, always been impossible, for 'authenticity is a sign relation'. It depends on markers and mediation to exist: '"the real thing" must be marked as real, as sight-worthy; if it is not marked or differentiated, it is not a notable sight' (Culler, 1988: 161). He recollects a story from Walker Percy's *The Message in a Bottle* of a couple that accidently ends up in a Mexican village where a native ritual is in progress. Although they are supposedly as close to authentic reality as one can imagine, they only manage to fully enjoy it after returning with an ethnologist friend who assures them that their experience was indeed genuine and, in doing so, provides them with markers of authenticity. Culler calls this the paradox of authenticity:

to be experienced as authentic it must be marked as authentic, but when it is marked as authentic it is mediated, a sign of itself, and hence lacks the authenticity of what is truly unspoiled, untouched by mediating cultural codes.

(Culler, 1988: 164)

No one ever really leaves the script, or rather, the beaten track, for leaving them is already a function of the system (Culler 1988: 165). The main goal of the traveller – to encounter authenticity in the sense of unmediated phenomena – is an impossible one, which puts every traveller automatically on a par with a tourist. What the tourist industry is selling to aspiring travellers (Culler, 1988: 165) is the carefully crafted illusion of an unmediated experience – and the right to call themselves travellers. So-called authenticity is a commodity that hides its own transactional and mediated nature.

If there is one pair of terms that echoes the traveller/tourist dichotomy in present-day discourse, it must be the one between backpackers (or budget travellers) and mainstream tourists.

Several of the characteristics that are generally ascribed to backpackers – mostly middle class, white and originating from what is conventionally considered to be the West – can easily be linked to Boorstin's and Fussell's 'traveller', such as their concern with authenticity (Noy, 2004), learning opportunities (O'Reilly, 2006: 999; Pearce & Foster, 2007), meeting other people, independently organizing their own travel itineraries (Larsen, Torvald & Brun, 2011: 697) and openness to change of plan (O'Reilly, 2006: 999), and less with risks and worries. They also tend to 'dislike being called "tourists", usually reserving this epithet for package tourists only' and call themselves 'travelers, or simply backpackers' (O'Reilly, 2006: 999–1000). Research on 2000 tourists to Norway from 48 countries, however, suggests that these groups are much more similar than one would assume. Both seemed to be equally motivated 'by social motives and by knowledge/cultural motives' and were 'equally worried about travel related issues' (Larsen et al., 2011: 701). The study concludes that although backpackers indeed travel on lower budgets,[3] they 'are similar to mainstream tourists in most *motivational* issues investigated in this study' – with some differences as far as the needs for luxury and relaxation are concerned (Larsen et al., 2011: 702). There was, however, a difference between budget travellers' subjective perceptions concerning the tourist role, viz. 'a tendency in these travellers to view themselves as less institutionalized tourists' and what they actually did: 'It may be that this finding simply reflects a self-perception as "more individualized" and "more independent", and that this [...] may be something of a social construction in backpackers mythologies about themselves' (Larsen et al., 2011: 703). In other words, this kind of research also leads to the insight that the difference between both categories is (or has become (O'Reilly 2006: 1006–1009)) a rhetorical construction, a stereotype not based in reality.

The need for empirical research

Another line of critique is to be found in James Buzard's book *The Beaten Track: European Tourism, Literature, and the Ways to Culture, 1800–1918*, in which he rightly remarks that the 'rough consensus' (Buzard, 1993: 1) on the meaning of both terms is highly problematic because it is often taken for granted and a-historical. Neither Fussell nor Boorstin base their theory on the motivations and feelings of real people, but in fact reproduce 'nearly two hundred years of concerted cultural stereotyping' (Buzard, 1993: 3). Yet Fussell and Boorstin, but also Culler and Buzard himself, all rely on written texts. On the one hand, this means that their conclusions are based on testimonies from people that were literate and had access to the public forum. The majority of these were male and white. Fussell's (1980: 39–40) chapter 'Exploration to travel to tourism' quotes from Anthony Burgess, Paul Theroux, Lawrence Durrell, Charles Lever, Francis Kilvert, Osbert Sitwell and Frederic Harrison. Only two of his quotes are from female voices: one from Hugh *and* Pauline Massingham and one from Sitwell's 'sister Edith'– but the source is, tellingly, not in the bibliography. None of the quotes stems from people of colour. The same observation can be made for Boorstin (quoting from John Ruskin and 'a British consul in Italy' (viz. Charles Lever) (Boorstin, 1961: 87)), Butcher (Kilvert), Buzard (William Wordsworth, Adam Walker, Evelyn Waugh, Kilvert), and Culler (Ruskin, Lever, and Stendhal).

On the other hand, these texts often belong to genres often prioritizing identity politics: travelogues and diaries. This double observation could well cloud the entire argument that the traveller/tourist dichotomy is ubiquitous in tourism discourse: these scholars are relying on a limited number of very specific sources and genres, so their observations are only valid within those limits. It is intriguing to see that the words tourist and traveller seem to function as synonyms in other types of text, such as grammars or dictionaries. One of the earliest entries for

Traveller or tourist

the word 'tourist' in the *Oxford English Dictionary* is from Samuel Pegge's *Anecdotes of the English language* and goes as follows: 'A Traveller is now-a-days called a Tour-ist' (1814²). The phrase is unaccompanied by any value judgment, which seems to suggest that the terms essentially designate the same thing (Buzard, 1993: 1). And in an old Dutch dictionary, *Beknopt kunstwoordenboek*, originally published in 1865, a tourist is defined a subcategory of the traveller: 'tourist, m. (tourists), traveller who visits many countries for his pleasure' (Calisch & Calisch, 1882: 276).

What happens if one decides to shift the focus from texts to real people, located in time and space? Several scholars have attempted to make convincing typologies of tourists making use of different sources and criteria, and avoiding normative standpoints. An early example is the model that social psychiatrist Stanley Plog published in his article 'Why Destination Areas Rise and Fall in Popularity'. Plog and his team wanted to understand 'the psychology of travel' (Plog, 1974: 55); more specifically, they wanted to know why some people were not making use of airplanes. They relied on the review of existing research, psychological in-depth interviews and the monitoring of telephone calls to airlines. The sample consisted of 1600 respondents from the United States with minimum incomes of US$9000. Based on their research, they came up with the opposition between two 'psychograph types'. On the one hand, there is the 'psychocentric', 'a self-inhibited, nervous, and non-adventuresome type of person' (Plog, 1974: 55), and on the other the 'allocentric',

> characterized by a considerable degree of adventuresomeness, self-confidence, a lack of the general anxieties common among Psychocentrics, and a willingness to reach out and experiment with life. Travel is a way of expressing his inquisitiveness and curiosity. He wants to see and do new things, to explore the world around him.
>
> *(Plog, 1974: 56)*

The psychocentric and the allocentric are at opposite ends of a continuum. In between, Plog locates the 'near psychocentric', the 'mid-centric' and the 'near allocentric'. They differ in many respects: preferred media and genres, income, purchase habits, and travel characteristics. Whereas psychocentrics highly esteem familiarity, relaxation, low activity levels, travelling by car, well-developed tourist infrastructure and a high degree of tour packaging and scheduling, allocentrics prefer interacting with 'people from a strange or foreign culture', non-touristy areas, a sense of discovery, novelty, high activity levels, traveling by plane, few tourist attractions and accommodation, and 'considerable freedom and flexibility' (Plog, 1974: 57). It is not difficult to recognize the classical traveller–tourist opposition, although different terms are used[4] and value judgment is lacking. This means that if Plog's research is valid, there indeed exist travellers and tourists (at least within his sample) – not just as discursive positions but as real-life behaviours and psychological characteristics.

Plog's model was, however, severely criticized (Smith, 1990). One of the main points of critique was that it does not accurately predict travel behaviour for numerous reasons; the model was based on US-based travellers; people are more complex than this model suggests, and practical circumstances (for instance, financial) may force people to behave differently than one would expect based on their psychological profile (Litvin, 2006). The model nevertheless proved to be very influential. For instance, it provided Richard Butler with a blueprint of his well-known Tourist Area Life Cycle-theory (Butler, 1980) who claims that 'pioneers' visit the tourist area in the first phase of its development ('exploration'), only to be replaced by less adventurous visitors in the later phases. Despite all this, Plog was one of the first to try and base the categorization of tourists on real people's behaviours and attitudes.

Tom Sintobin

Other typologies

In his paper 'A Phenomenology of Tourist Experiences', social anthropologist Erik Cohen (1979: 179) highlights the difference between Boorstin (1961) and MacCannell (1976). Whereas the former claims that tourists are engaged in 'a trivial, superficial, frivolous pursuit of vicarious, contrived experiences, a "pseudo-event"', the latter says that they are on 'an earnest quest for the authentic'. According to Cohen (1979: 180), they are both wrong and right at the same time; they assume that '"*the* tourist" as a general type' exists and neglect that there are several different types of tourist. Cohen proceeds in developing a phenomenological typology of tourist experiences based on five modes in which a person can travel, depending on their relationship to a 'centre' – defined as a 'spiritual', but not necessarily a religious nexus of moral values. This results in a continuum with five positions. At the one end there is the pilgrim, travelling in the existential mode and 'fully committed to an 'elective' spiritual centre' (Cohen, 1979: 190). They are, thus, looking for a place that will restore meaning and authenticity – and that place can be one 'external to the mainstream of his native society and culture', a 'traditionally given centre' or somewhere in between (Cohen, 1979: 191). At the other end stands the tourist travelling in the recreational mode, for whom authenticity is irrelevant because all they want is to have 'physical and mental powers' restored by means of 'recreation' (Cohen, 1979: 183). This tourist is not challenging the existing centre of their world, because this kind of travel in fact 'restitutes the individual to his society and its values' by serving as a kind of 'pressure valve' to let off steam within the constraints of a holiday-away-from-the centre (Cohen, 1979: 185). In between these two poles, Cohen (1979: 186–189) situates the divisionary mode (the trip 'a centre-less person' undertakes purely for pleasure), the experiential mode (the alienated individual who travels 'to look for meaning in the life of others' who are presumed to have preserved authenticity, however without converting to that other lifestyle), and the experimental mode (travellers 'pre-disposed to try out alternative life-ways in their quest for meaning'). All modes have different subcategories, and there are some reminiscences of the old dichotomy in the sense that the recreational mode could be linked to 'the tourist' and the other three modes to 'the traveller'.

In his earlier work 'Toward a Sociology of International Tourism', Cohen (1972) proposed four categories: the organized mass tourist, the individual mass tourist, the explorer and the drifter. They differ in their use or refusal of the facilities of the tourist industry and in their appraisal of either novelty ('strangeness' (Cohen, 1972: 177)) or familiarity while travelling. Attempts to empirically verify this typology rendered interesting results. Eugenia Wickens, for instance, interviewed and observed British holidaymakers in the Greek region of Chalkidiki and came to the conclusion that these people were characterized 'by a highly diversified pattern of interests and activities' (Wickens, 2002: 849), despite the fact that they all qualified as 'individual mass tourists in Cohen's sense' (Wickens, 2002: 836). According to her, there are five subtypes of which several do interact with the locals, contrary to the assumption that individual mass tourists 'are both physically and socially segregated from the host community' (Wickens, 2002: 846).

Cohen's types can easily be linked to the dichotomy between the tourist and the traveller, as both ends of a continuum. That is no longer the case with the typology suggested by Philip Pearce (1982) in his book *The Social Psychology of Tourist Behaviour* that consists of 15 'travel-related roles' and is based on real tourists' behaviour. Pearce ordered these roles in five clusters, plus two (the migrant worker and the international athlete): ''Environmental Travel' (anthropologist, conservationist, and explorer), 'High Contact Travel' (traveller, overseas student, overseas journalist), 'Spiritual Travel' (hippie, religious pilgrim, missionary), 'Pleasure First Travel (jetsetter, tourist, holidaymaker) and 'Exploitative Travel' (businessman, jetsetter)' (Yiannakis & Gibson, 1992: 289). The tourist and the traveller are just two of the 15 roles people can fulfill. Interestingly, Yiannakis and Gibson suggest that the jetsetter, the hippie and the holidaymaker 'are simply subcategories of the broader tourist construct' whereas some other roles are 'clearly not touristic in nature'. They distinguish between 'leisure-based and work-based travel roles' (Yiannakis & Gibson, 1992: 290) and, based on interactions with several carefully composed sets of respondents, eventually compile a typology containing 14 'leisure-based tourist roles', also including types from both Cohen and Pearce. They conclude that there exist 'three bipolar dimensions which [...] point to an underlying structure characterized by Stimulation-Tranquility [...]. Strangeness-Familiarity [...], and Structure-Independence' (Yiannakis & Gibson, 1992: 299) and which enable categorizing tourists. Their list contains types reminding us of the old 'traveller', such as 'the Explorer' who '[p]refers adventure travel, exploring out of the way places and enjoys challenges involved in getting there', the 'Seeker of spiritual and/or personal knowledge to better understand self and meaning of life' and the 'Anthropologist', '[m]ostly interested in meeting local people, trying the food and speaking the language'.

In later publications, Pearce tries to take the full Maslow's (1943) hierarchy of needs into account by formulating his well-known Travel Career Ladder (Pearce 1988, 1991, 1993, 2005) – see also Chapter 13 in this volume. At the top there are 'fulfillment needs', and descending we find 'self-esteem/development needs', 'relationship needs' and 'safety/security' needs to reach the lowest stair with the 'physiological needs'. The more travel experience a person has, the higher up the ladder their motives tend to be situated, but it is also possible to descend. This also implies that the motives of experienced travellers assumedly are more diverse than those of less experienced travellers because, according to Pearce (1991), the higher-level motives include lower-level motives, although 'one motive at a time tends to be dominant'. It is interesting to see that the classical hierarchical opposition between the traveller and the tourist is to a certain extent reflected in this model, for the higher up the ladder we get, the more the specific needs resemble the characteristics Fussell and Boorstin ascribed to their 'superior' traveller. Take, for instance, the needs for self-actualization and development and the need for curiosity/mental stimulation, as opposed to the need for relaxation and the need to predict and explain the world. However, some of the needs higher up on the ladder, such as the need for status, remind us of Fussell's claim that tourists are yearning for a higher social status. The ladder also mentions needs that do not seem to play any role whatsoever in the classical opposition, such as the need to give love and affection. An important observation to come out of this kind of research is that 'types' are just that. Scholars have increasingly become aware that tourists are complex beings, not just driven by a single motive to travel but by a wide range of needs on very different levels that may be co-present in one tourist or trip or show variation throughout the years.

Powerscapes

Why are scholars like Boorstin and Fussell blindly relying on these stereotypes without questioning them? Fussell, Culler (1988: 156) claims, is so vehement in his description of tourists because he was afraid to be taken for a tourist himself when visiting England as an American. Perhaps the same goes for Boorstin, who stemmed from a well-off family of lawyers and was a full professor at the University of Chicago at the time he wrote his book. The privileged world of highly educated, wealthy global citizens that these people thought was getting lost was the world they called their own. In embracing the stereotypical rejection of tourists, these scholars in fact participate in and (re)produce the discourse they are claiming to analyze, which tells more about their own identity politics than about reality.

Clearly the categories of the traveller and the tourist imply a hierarchy: the traveller enjoys a higher status than the tourist. This comes at a cost; to be able to successfully claim this identity, a person needs to have the means to do that. That meant time (travelling means not working so not earning money), mobility (it took Thomas Cook and his chartering of a train to enable ordinary people to make use of the railways), skills (language), money and above all access to media to promote this self-image. It is therefore not surprising that the 'identity' of the traveller has not been available to each and every one.

A non-inclusive cliché

For a long time, 'the status of the traveler has been assigned predominantly to the economically well-off, white, European male who has embarked on voyages motivated by heroic, educational, scientific, and recreational purposes' (Galani-Moutafi, 2000: 204). Although people of lower classes and/or of colour undertook very similar projects, it proved hard to be recognized by the dominant discourse as successful travellers: 'A host of servants, helpers, companions, guides, and bearers have been excluded from the role of proper travellers because of their race and class, and because theirs seemed to be a dependent status in relation to the supposed independence of the individualist, bourgeois voyager' (Clifford, 1986: 33). Clifford gives the example of Matthew Henson, in 1909, the first to reach the North Pole together with Robert Peary. The black explorer had to wait until the publication of S. Allen Counter's *North Pole Legacy. Black, White, and Eskimo* (1991) to be recognized as such, since a long list of accounts by 'Peary, a host of historians, newspaper writers, statesmen, bureaucrats, and interested institutions such as *National Geographic* magazine' preferred to focus on his white companion (Clifford, 1986: 33).

Women often suffered a similar fate. Although many travellers throughout the ages were female, existing travel accounts and media often tended to marginalize them, for instance by depicting them in the company of male protectors, or by leaving them out altogether (Meens & Sintobin, 2019: 6). Ann Lister, the first person to make it to the summit of the Vignemale in 1838, even needed a lawyer to be able to claim her achievement from a prince who made the ascent a few days later (Lyons, 2019: 166). The higher altitudes of the mountains were considered to be male territory for a long time; women were supposed to prefer 'less strenuous excursions in the foothills' while men 'as individuals sought the distinction of making the first ascent or "conquest" of those surrounding peaks which still enjoyed "virgin" status' (Lyons, 2019: 165).

One of the most iconic symbols of the heavily scripted figure of the traveller must be the *Rückenfigur* on the painting Der Wanderer über dem Nebelmeer, which Caspar David Friedrich pained in around 1817. It shows a solitary male figure, looking out over a vast moutainscape from a panoramic position. It suggests individuality, autonomy, control and adventurousness. The work has triggered many different interpretations (Keck, 2007: 35–37). Some interpret it as a patriotic statement, since the man seems to be wearing a uniform from the time of the Napoleonic wars. Others have claimed that the figure is the painter himself taking refuge in nature to escape industrialization. Yet others see it as a depiction of mankind in the peak of its life and akin to God, or as a visualization of an aesthetic program centralizing the sublime.

Figure 16.1 Images of 'traveller'
Source: Snapshot from Google Images – 7 October 2020 (Nijmegen).

Interestingly, the painting refers to the genre of the veduta (a large, highly detailed painting, often a cityscape) that played an important role in the Grand Tour since painters provided the visitors with depictions of the cities and landscapes they consumed. Friedrich's biographer Jens Christian Jensen (1999) claimed that this painting depicted real trips the painter undertook – which in a sense implies that he was painting his own vedute. Friedrich nevertheless could not have foreseen that this particular work would haunt the imagination and social media of so many twenty-first century travellers. It suffices to enter the term 'traveller' as a search term in Google Images to generate a 'random' sample and see how often this painting functions online as an intertext (see Figure 16.1).

Whether it is bloggers such as Nomadic Matt, Brook Verlini and Nikolaj Salinger of mytravelbackpack.com or Rob from atraveler.world,[5] podcasters such as Nativetraveler.com,[6] traditional media such as Turkey Daily Sabah,[7] promotional and commercial websites such as Worldlyadventurer.com, Dreams Voyager, bustickets.com, reviewpro.com, McKinsey and Keys Hotels,[8] or www.pandotrip.com,[9] or lifestyle magazines such as The Ascent, Fortune and Jetsetter,[10] in their visual language they all consciously or unconsciously refer to Friedrich's Wanderer. Smith (2019) has identified the 'promontory witness' as one of the visual tropes on Instagram, echoing both colonial and Romantic iconography.

Evidently, there are differences from the original painting. The landscape does not necessarily consist of mountains; there are also skylines of cities, ocean fronts, forests, and lakes, for the modern sublime clearly has many faces. Quite often, the male traveller is replaced by a woman and occasionally even by a couple[11] facing the camera.[12] To claim that this goes to show that the role of the traveller is now open to everyone seems, notwithstanding, to be still largely an illusion, since there are no people of colour featuring in my random sample – not even in the Turkish newspaper that depicts a white man and a white dog. Studying lists of successful travel influencers online[13] leads to a similar conclusion. Successful travel influencers on these lists usually originate from wealthy, Western countries or from one of the new economic powers globally, such as Brazil or India. The

Forbes-list from 2017, for instance, mentions one woman of colour (as part of a travelling duo that is half American and half Brazilian).[14]

Although it has been claimed that modern tourism implied a democratization of the practice, 'a broadly accessible form of leisure travel no longer based in the overt class and gender prerogatives of the Grand Tour' (Buzard, 1993: 18), it may be clear that even nowadays 'the right to travel' is still the privilege of the wealthy 'while the poor and the marginalized serve and host them on their holidays, in order to eke out a living, try to pay off the debts fostered by capitalist globalization and hopefully eventually to enjoy their moment as consumers' (Higgins-Desbiolles, 2010: 124). The United Nations telecommunications agency ITU estimated that in 2018, 51.2 percent (3.9 billion people) of the global population had access to the Internet.[15] According to recent statistics, 2.65 billion of those people were using social networks in that same year. This means that about half the planet's population is theoretically able to produce and/or consume travel images and stories online, whereas the other half are unable to participate. The sociologist and philosopher Zygmunt Bauman has even argued that there are only two categories of people in our modern societies: tourists and vagabonds. 'The tourists', claims Bauman, 'travel because *they want to*; the vagabonds because *they have no other bearable choice*' because '"staying at home" in a world made to the measure of the tourist feels like humiliation and drudgery' (Bauman, 1998: 93). Tourists are welcomed everywhere, they have the papers and the funds to move at will – whereas the vagabonds 'are the waste of the world which has dedicated itself to tourist services' (Bauman, 1998: 92). A vagabond is anyone unable to meet the demands of consumerism: tramps, emigrant, refugees – but also former tourists who descended into poverty (Bauman, 1998: 97). Bauman later restored part of the dichotomy in an interview, when contrasting '"standardized" tourism', which aims for 'the right proportion of genuine or pretended "otherness" […] and reassuring familiarity', and he who travels 'to learn, […] to understand, […] to get in touch with alien people and to embrace and imbibe and assimilate untold riches stored in their heads, in their timeless cultural lore' (Franklin, 2003: 213).

New moral tourists

In his book *Sun, Sand… and Saving the World. The Moralization of Tourism*, Jim Butcher (2003) studies new types of tourism that are contrasted to mass or package tourism: 'new tourism', ethical tourism, responsible tourism, sustainable tourism and ecotourism. He brings those new forms together under the umbrella term 'New Moral Tourism', summarized in Table 16.2.

Table 16.2 Mass tourism vs. new moral tourism

Mass tourism	New moral tourism
Sameness (not interested in cultural differences)	Difference (interested in cultural and environmental differences)
Crude (lacks self-restraint; pleasure-seeking only)	Sensitive (tries to learn the host's culture and language)
Destructive (disregards the host's environment and culture)	Constructive (tries to support and preserve local cultures)
Modern	Critical of modern 'progress'

Source: Adapted from Butcher (2003, 21–22).

Traveller or tourist

Butcher suggests that in a sense the New Moral Tourist has always been around, 'in the guise of the traveller' from the nineteenth century: he claims to be

> a "thinking tourist" – someone prepared to strike out, experiment with different ways of life, and not be part of a packaged product put together by global companies. He is someone who takes interest in the culture and the environment of the host.
>
> *(Butcher, 2003: 41)*

as opposed to the mainstream tourist. Butcher does not just argue that this self-perception is false (in reality both categories are very similar in their actual behaviour and the resulting effects (Butcher, 2003: 41–49)), but also deconstructs the very claim that New Moral Tourism could be wholesome. Wealthy Westerners, discontented with their own lives, indulge in fantasies about unspoiled but fragile authentic places and cultures and project them on the Other, who is assigned the role of 'guardian of nature'. This not only departs from the false premise that carrying capacities of sites cannot be extended if managed well, claims Butcher, it also denies the Other access to global culture and progress. Butcher gives the example of a project in India where the so-called 'reverence and "respect" for tradition provide an obstacle to a critical examination of the grinding poverty of the people of Ladakh' (Butcher, 2003: 30). Another tendency of New Moral Tourism is that its practitioners believe that there are 'individual solutions to social inequalities':

> They effectively take people's aspirations to do good and convert them into personal guilt at the poverty evident in Third World destinations. Yet to travel or not to travel, to stay in a hotel or in a village, to enjoy the culture or just the climate, will make no difference to the broader inequality that exists between nations and peoples. More importantly, it is an agenda that discourages a critical examination of the causes of poverty by presenting individual behaviour as a strategy to bring positive change to the Third World. This makes for degraded politics, and a diminished travel experience too.
>
> *(Butcher, 2003: 109–110)*

In other words, the identity politics of New Moral Tourists/travellers, embracing stereotypical beliefs about hosts and other tourists, have far-reaching real life consequences. They not only spoil the fun travelling is supposed to be, but also deny the 'Other' access to the modern world.

It is not difficult to find more examples of this mechanism. All over the internet, travellers are vlogging and blogging with the best intentions, largely unchecked. Reproducing old colonial tropes, they frame their trips as unique encounters with authentic Others who are savage and even dangerous but noble, or as explorations into the last wildernesses of this planet. They largely remain silent about the financial transactions that enabled these visits because they claim to be on friendly terms with locals and to not make use of existing tourism infrastructure. In doing this, they construct identities for themselves as worthy travellers and gain money with it, but forget about the real world effects their representations have on the people and places they visited (Sintobin & Tonnaer, 2020).

Twenty-first century trends

In contemporary travel discourse online, the opposition between traveller and tourist is definitely very present. The internet is full of manifestos,[16] quizzes,[17] blogs,[18] lists of characteristics,[19] opinion articles and so on that are explicitly using it. It is not difficult to recognize many of the conventional characteristics in them, for instance by reading the 'about me' sections of influential bloggers. They describe themselves as active, adventurous, independent, hardworking travellers (never tourists), who have a lot of individual agency, are very reflexive about what they are doing and travel to learn new things. In this section, I will give a brief overview of what could be seen as problems typical for twenty-first century tourists.

Overtourism

In the years before the pandemic, overtourism had clearly become one of the central tourism-related problems. The internet was flooded with pictures of huge crowds in tourist attractions such as beaches, nature reserves, heritage sites and evidently cities (Amsterdam, Barcelona, and Venice became exemplary cases) and many a newspaper published series of before/after- or advertising/reality pictures. This was generally considered to be destructive to cultural and natural ecosystems,[20] and triggered well-mediated protests (Hughes 2018; Milano, Cheer & Novelli, 2019; Zemla 2020). The discourse was strikingly similar to its nineteenth-century counterpart, with metaphors of flooding, invasion and dehumanization. Evidently, overtourism also radically ended the Wanderer's fantasies of discovery and solitude.

Strategies proposed to try and deal with overtourism included the limiting of platforms such as Airbnb, the regulation of low-cost airlines and cruise ship tourism, enhancing the carrying capacity of sites and, relevant to this chapter, trying to redistribute visitors by opening up more spaces than just the conventional hotspots. *Iamsterdam*, for instance, encourages visitors on its website 'to get off the beaten track and discover some of Amsterdam's lesser known attractions'.[21] Other cities brand themselves as places that are off the beaten track in their entirety.[22] Unofficial tourism discourse contributed greatly to this effort; travel magazines, tour operators, influencers, travel authors, TV shows, travelogues, and so on are all promoting alternative sites to avoid crowds.

This is evidently not a new phenomenon, as we have seen above; drifters, travellers, allocentrics, backpackers or whatever one wishes to call them were all characterized by the wish to leave the beaten track. However, with the arrival of Web 2.0 and the resulting proliferation of travel writing and filming, this state of mind does seem to have become even more prominent and mainstream than ever before (Matoga & Pawlowska, 2018). TV shows dedicated to non-mainstream travelling abound, such as Anthony Bourdain's *No Reservations* and Michael Palin's work, and so do Netflix-series and documentaries. All over the internet, people are writing about their passion for 'off the beaten path places'[23] and 'discovering hidden gems',[24] compiling endless lists of alternative must-sees for their readers or even developing cunning apps to identify 'where the locals go'.[25] News media do exactly the same in similar terms,[26] specialized travel agencies offer 'Off-the-beaten-track holidays'.[27] Even companies exploiting the most conventionalized sites find ways to commodify the illusion of adventure and discovery on site. The cruise ship company Royal Caribbean offers their customers at the totally artificial peninsula of Labadee the opportunity to book 'a private beach' in 'a remote cove' – and even experienced travel bloggers are writing about that highly staged experience as if they have discovered something new (Labrousse, 2015: 28).

Some of these popular media productions are in fact very similar to earlier bestselling projects, such as Richard Halliburton's reliving of ancient travels (Boorstin, 1961: 116–117). Extreme travel TV, as it has been called, represents these trips as adventurous, authentic and potentially even lethal. *Don't crack under pressure*, so we are told, is about travellers who 'risk their lives for it by dodging avalanches, free-diving with sharks, and surfing inches above a razor sharp coral reef'.[28] Whether all of this is true or not remains to be seen. The Belgian traveller Tom Waes, of the Reizen Waes show on national television, claimed in 2013 that he was the first to visit the Caño Canoas waterfall in the Colombian rain forest, previously controlled by the rebel group FARC. He lost quite some credibility after it became clear that thousands of tourists had been visiting that site for years. Waes tried to explain away the problem afterward by saying that he had been misled himself: 'our local guide claimed that we were the first. He even had special negotiations with the military to be allowed to bring us to the waterfalls'.[29] Waes later apologized for his naivité, but the example shows the radical commodification of exclusivity and remoteness, no matter how far one ventures. One pays for the right to call oneself a traveller or even an explorer.

Several forms of niche tourism that are becoming more popular in recent years also can be related to the urge to leave the beaten path. Urban explorers, for instance, focus on sites and sights '*beyond* the radar of commercial tourism', such as 'abandoned places (e.g., industries, hospitals, residential buildings and sites of leisure and tourism)' and 'places that are hidden or difficult to access (e.g., urban rooftops, subterranean spaces and military complexes)' (Jansson, 2018: 105). As Jansson (2018) shows, some of them are well aware of the double bind they find themselves in: the quest for the extraordinary, pristine and genuine leads ironically enough to the erosion of what is unique (places, experiences and identities). This is all the more so since many urban explorers are sharing their pictures on social media or even in one of the numerous books on 'Abandoned places'.[30] Another example is dark tourism, also called thanatourism, grief tourism and so on that allows increasing numbers of people to claim adventurous identities. The number of visitors to Chernobyl, for instance, has been rising for years (Bordun & Komar, 2018). A big surge came after the TV-series *Chernobyl* was aired in 2018, but the site had been successfully exploited as a tourist attraction before that. The same can be said of many of the trips undertaken for the Netflix-series *Dark Tourist*. The episode shot on the Mexico–US border is exemplary; although it is represented as a dangerous adventure, in reality, it is a simulation taking place over 500 miles away from the border that had been open since 2004.[31] Research on motivations for visiting such sites has identified some factors that can be connected with the stereotypical traveller, such as the quest for 'authenticity', 'self-discovery and the intrinsic desire to learn' (Robinson 2015: 28–29), although curiously the dream of leaving the beaten path is not present. Sharpley and Stone (2009: 18–19) do mention the possibility that tourists are visiting such places to enhance their status by having undertaken 'forms of travel [...] that are dangerous for the tourist', and specialized travel agencies use it for their branding.[32] Interestingly, there is already a new distinction within this discourse, the one between real and fake dark tourists. The former is defined as: 'sober, unsensationalist engaging with the real, and often difficult, contemporary world, without any recourse to cheap thrills of horror and disgust, or anything actually dangerous, or anything "paranormal"'.[33]

Redefining the traveller

In May 2019, pictures taken by the mountaineer Nirmal Purja of a people queuing up to reach the summit of Mount Everest hit global news. These pictures made clear that there no longer was an off the beaten track where solitary wanderers would be able to find refuge. Even the most remote or desolate places on this planet are part of the tourist circuit – exploited as a tourist site and mediatized as such. There are *Lonely Planet*s for every spot, even for 'dark lands' ruled by dangerous regimes[34] and, apocryphal of course, for the caliphate.[35] Several styles of tourism seem to be well aware of the fact that there is nowhere left to travel and that an anti-tourist attitude does not make sense in a world where we are all tourists (MacCannell 1999: 9). To conclude this chapter, I will discuss some tendencies.

New eyes

In the spring of 2020, Covid-19 abruptly halted an industry that had been projected to keep growing exponentially. International mobility was greatly reduced, which led to more interest in domestic tourism and a reflection on the future of tourism with many considering the pandemic a 'transformative opportunity', a chance to reform the industry and people's mentality. Early on in the crisis Freya Higgins-Desbiolles wrote:

> Staying closer to home could be a catalyst awakening us to the value of eating locally, travelling less and just slowing down and connecting to our community. After this crisis passes, we might find the old business as usual less compelling. We might learn that not travelling long distances didn't stop us travelling; it just enlivened us to the richness of local travel.
>
> *(Higgins-Desbiolles, 2020a)*

Although the industry itself seems to prefer the idea of a return to business as usual and Higgins-Desbiolles was attacked online by Jim Butcher (2020) for her ideas,[36] her words reflect a sentiment that is shared more broadly. We find it on social media, where travel influencers, unable to leave their countries, are actively promoting domestic travel by making lists of reasons to travel in one's own country during Covid-19.[37] *Girlswanderlust* claims that 'traveling and exploring your own country is beautiful and worthy', because 'it will make you realize that there is so much more to see than you once thought.'[38] A quote by Marcel Proust is trending: 'The real voyage of discovery consists not in seeking new landscapes, but in having new eyes.' Real travellers are not those desperately trying to get off the beaten track, but those who manage to discover something new on conventional sites.

This movement was, in fact, already present before Coronavirus struck the planet, under the name of slow travel. Mainstream tourism, it was argued, is 'based on the principles of the supply chain' (Dickinson & Lumsdon, 2010: 6), relying on speed, efficiency and disregard for the environment. The unsustainability of this enterprise, it was predicted, would eventually lead to new forms of tourism in which people would be prepared 'for more locally-based recreation near to our homes' and 'where the supply sector becomes more educational and inspirational than simply selling tourist products' (Dickinson & Lumsdon, 2010: 12). This opposition between commercial/superficial and educational/inspirational echoes the traveller/tourist dichotomy.

Authenticities

In 1985, Maxine Feifer proposed a new category in her book *Going Places*: the post-tourist (Feifer, 1985). Although scholars have attempted to broaden the scope of the definition to include other new phenomena (Jansson, 2018; Munt, 1994), one of the key elements characterizing such tourists remains a postmodern sense of irony. They are aware of the radically commodified, staged and mediatized nature of any tourist activity, but they eclectically play along anyway, tongue in cheek. 'The post-tourist or post-modern tourist is a consumer who

Traveller or tourist

Figure 16.2 The author's daughter wandering the Alps
Source: T. Sintobin.

embraces openly, but with some irony, the increasingly inauthentic, commercialized and simulated experiences offered by the tourism industry' (Smith, Macleod & Hart Robertson, 2010: 129). Post-tourists' irony tends to be explicitly marked as such; a good example are the many pictures of people performing in humorous ways in front of well-known flagship attractions (Edensor, 2009: 548). The fact that at some sites, such as the Leaning Tower of Pisa, such pictures outnumber more conventional ones, shows that this behaviour has become mainstream and heavily scripted as well.

There also exists a style of conscious tourism that is not ironical. The ethnographer Eduard Bruner relates an experiment he did when working as a tour guide-lecturer in Indonesia. He tried to educate his group of tourists – much to the dislike of the owner of the company that hired him – on the way tourism worked by taking photographs of them and by contextualizing and deconstructing the so-called traditional performances they had attended. This could be called metatourism: tourists travelling to see how the tourist industry works. Bruner (2005) claims that even the most staged tourist ritual is authentic (because it is a new form of cultural ritual that merits study), which means that the metatourist is, in a sense, always dealing with authentic reality. This attitude also reinstalls the association of travelling with learning and (anthropological) work. Perhaps the aestheticizing of tourist crowds – analogous with festival crowds[39] – will be the next step, although for now tourists seem quite keen on maintaining the illusion of solitude.[40]

Bruner is not the only one to question existing definitions of authenticity. Ning Wang described the concept of 'existential authenticity', 'a special state of Being in which one is true to oneself' (Wang, 1999: 358). This kind of authenticity often has nothing to do with 'realness' of toured objects, but rather with '*the existential state of Being* activated by certain tourist activities' – 'derived from tourists' participation in the event rather than from merely being spectators of it' (Wang, 1999: 59). In other words, true travellers are those who experience this state of being, which can, in principle, be evoked by tourist hotspots and places off the beaten path alike. This is, again, an idea that online influencers frequently evoke when they state that they are 'a passionate traveler' for whom 'it's not about ticking destinations off the bucket list but experiencing each one of them to the fullest',[41] or wonder rhetorically: 'But is it not the ultimate goal of the traveler to experience a place in a manner that is his, no matter how many others have treaded there?'[42]

Go offline

Evidently, the arrival of social media brought enormous changes to the world of the traveller. The permanent and ubiquitous connectivity to the internet radically altered his or her state of being; people are now 'actually-locally absent' to be 'virtually-globally present' (Oosterling, 2000). 'The new temporal order of tourist photography', Larsen (2006: 255) writes, 'seems to be "I am here" rather than "I was here"'. On the one hand, this could be seen as an opportunity. People no longer need to leave their house to visit the entire world – as the virtual and imaginative travellers Urry and Larsen noted but did not yet see 'replacing corporeal travel' (Urry & Larsen, 2011: 23). Many museums did promote virtual tours in 2020, to receive visitors despite the strict lockdown restrictions – so perhaps that time has come at last.[43] For those who keep travelling physically, the internet offers equal opportunities to everyone who has access to it, which means that the media in which to proclaim oneself a traveller are more broadly available than ever. It is up to the individual to use his or her creativity to come up with a convincing identity. Successful travel influencers now have the chance to actually make a living out of their travelling. On the other hand, however, this situation also radically destroys any fantasies a traveller may have about being a solitary individual who goes where no one has gone before. Actual solitude is forever gone; tourists are constantly live-performing in front of potentially vast audiences online. It also means that wherever one goes, one is simultaneously consuming and producing mediated places.

Tourists are struggling to deal with this. 'I will remember to get off Facebook, put my camera down, and enjoy the moment', is one of the '26 ways to be a traveler, not a tourist', but this 'manifesto' is, paradoxically, online.[44] Travellers who participated in research on digital-free travel responded in emotionally very different ways. Some of the reported feelings were negative, such as frustration regarding navigation and information acquisition, a sense of isolation from significant others and boredom in empty moments. There were many positive feelings as well, however; people felt liberated, 'started to perceive and actualize other environmental affordances and engaged in more social interactions at the destination that they previously ignored' and got the feeling that they 'learned more about sights, places, and beaches that were not on any tourism websites or guidebooks, but were beautiful and a highlight of their trips' (Cai, McKenna & Waizenegger, 2020: 920). All these aspects can be linked to the identity of the traveller dreamt of by Boorstin and Fussell.

Notes

1 'The Old English noun 'travel' (in the sense of a journey) was originally the same word as 'travail' (meaning 'trouble', 'work' or 'torment')'(Boorstin 1961: 85).
2 Interestingly, Boorstin's contemporary, Max Kaplan, a sociologist, identifies the opposite evolution in his *Leisure in America: a Social Inquiry*. The 'American tourist abroad', he writes, used to trigger some very bad publicity, with his inclination to exhibit a sense of superiority 'over people with less material advantages', but this is improving as the category of the 'comparative strangers', who 'never, or seldom, leave their own familiar ideas and judgments' while travelling and who 'view, but do not understand' is being replaced by the category of 'the empathic natives', who 'become native as much as their backgrounds, study and empathy permit' and in doing so gain real knowledge – 'not particulars but universals' (Kaplan 1960: 216).

Traveller or tourist

3 The relationship of the tourism-traveler dichotomy to funding is rather complex. Boorstin claimed that travelling was expensive, as opposed to tourism. Travel agencies such as Thomas Cook and Henry Gaze & Son and books advising people how to travel low budget, like Henry Gaze's *Switzerland: how to see it for ten guineas* (1861) or its twentieth century counterpart *Europe on 5 dollars a day* (Arthur Frommer 1957), brought more and more people on the road and destroyed the exclusivity of travelling. Another line of thinking, however, claims that the lower the budget the more authentic a travel experience is. A good example is the hitchhiking movement, that started in the early twentieth century with Tickner consciously avoiding 'any of the wonted means of conveyance beloved of tourists' (Tickner, 1910:vi) and became synonymous with adventurous in the course of the century.

4 In an update of his article he uses the terms dependables and venturers (Plog, 2001).

5 https://www.nomadicmatt.com/travel-blogs/new-traveler-advice/, https://www.mytravelbackpack.com/category/guides-resources/, https://www.atraveler.world/a-traveler/a-little-bit-about-me/

6 https://www.nativetraveler.com/blog-main/2017/9/20

7 https://www.dailysabah.com/travel/2019/09/28/a-journey-into-becoming-a-mindful-traveler

8 https://www.worldlyadventurer.com/about-me/, https://www.dreamsvoyager.com/what-kind-of-traveler-are-you/, https://bustickets.com/bus-travel/10-items-every-solo-traveler-needs/, https://www.reviewpro.com/blog/high-season-traveler-types/, https://www.mckinsey.com/industries/travel-logistics-and-transport-infrastructure/our-insights/how-to-serve-todays-digital-traveler#, https://www.keyshotels.com/blog/travel/solo-woman-traveler-destinations

9 https://www.pandotrip.com/awesome-destinations-for-solo-female-travelers-and-their-lesser-known-alternatives-30666/

10 https://medium.com/the-ascent/what-type-of-traveler-are-you-d7f09e00af11, https://fortune.com/2019/09/01/travelers-foodies-perks-rewards/, https://www.jetsetter.com/magazine/products-for-solo-travelers/

11 https://blog.virtuoso.com/uncategorized/5-trends-know-today-millennial-traveler/; https://traveler.marriott.com/tips-and-trends/holiday-travel-gift-ideas/

12 https://travelfave.com/mystery-traveler-guizhou/

13 https://www.amraandelma.com/100-top-travel-influencers/; https://www.under30experiences.com/blog/top-10-travel-bloggers-you-should-already-be-following; https://www.wanderlust.co.uk/content/the-top-travel-blogs-you-must-read/; https://medium.com/wearewoop/10-travel-influencers-that-you-may-not-know-to-include-on-your-digital-strategy-aa2e205b1160

14 https://www.forbes.com/top-influencers/2017/travel/#14dddf1d6d04

15 https://www.itu.int/en/mediacentre/Pages/2018-PR40.aspx

16 http://www.pandatraveller.com/a-travelers-manifesto-30-travel-rules-to-live-by/; https://thoughtcatalog.com/matthew-kepnes/2015/08/the-travelers-manifesto/

17 https://blog.flyporter.com/quiz-are-you-a-tourist-or-a-traveller/

18 https://777cebuadventures.blogspot.com/2013/08/traveler-or-tourist.html; https://hoponboard-blog.wordpress.com/2017/06/12/tourist-or-traveller/

19 https://www.boredpanda.com/traveller-vs-tourist-differences-holidify/?utm_source=bing&utm_medium=organic&utm_campaign=organic

20 E.g. *Bye Bye Barcelona* (Eduardo Chibas, 2014).

21 https://www.iamsterdam.com/en/see-and-do/things-to-do/itineraries/off-the-beaten-track

22 https://www.thisiseindhoven.com/en/visit/eindhoven-wanted/top-picks/de-ultimate-eindhoven-bucketlist

23 https://www.anitahendrieka.com/off-the-beaten-path-places/

24 https://mypathintheworld.com/unusual-things-to-do-in-barcelona/

25 https://www.theguardian.com/cities/2017/sep/15/authentic-tourist-app-instagram-holiday?CMP=twt_gu

26 'They're off-the-beaten-track, under-appreciated... and utterly fantastic. Welcome to the hidden gems you never thought to visit, but really should if you're planning a trip.' - https://www.thetimes.co.uk/expert-traveller/experiences/adventure/adventurous-destinations-you-shouldnt-overlook

27 https://www.audleytravel.com/inspiration/off-the-beaten-track

28 https://www.themanual.com/travel/best-travel-documentaries-on-netflix/

29 https://www.standaard.be/cnt/dmf20130919_007

30 E.g. Kieron Connolly, *Abandoned places: A photographic exploration of more than 100 words we have left behind* (2017); Mathew Growcoot, *Abandoned: The most beautiful forgotten places from around the world* (2018); Henk van Rensbergen, *Abandoned places* (2007, 2010, 2012, 2014, 2016, 2019).

31 https://www.nytimes.com/2007/02/04/travel/04HeadsUp
32 https://www.youngpioneertours.com/dark-tourism/
33 https://www.experiencetravelgroup.com/blog/2018/09/dark-tourism-explained-by-a-real-dark-tourist/
34 Tony Wheeler, *Badlands. A tourist on the axis of evil Lonely Planet* (2010).
35 https://www.nytimes.com/2015/03/22/world/middleeast/from-minneapolis-to-isis-an-americans-path-to-jihad.html
36 See Higgins-Desbiolles (2020b) for an overview of the debate.
37 https://www.bucketlistly.blog/posts/travel-in-our-own-country#why-you-should-travel-in-your-own-country
38 https://girlswanderlust.com/why-travel-in-your-own-country/?utm_source=rss&utm_medium=rss&utm_campaign=why-travel-in-your-own-country
39 E.g. Rutger Geerling, *This is my church* (2020).
40 https://digital-photography-school.com/taking-photos-in-busy-tourist-destinations-with-no-people-in-the-shot/; https://krijnvandergiessen.com/2018/01/travel-photography-without-tourists/; https://www.digital-photo-secrets.com/tip/2530/amazing-photography-tricks-how-to-get-a-people-free-picture-at-a-tourist-trap/
41 https://mypathintheworld.com/unusual-things-to-do-in-barcelona/
42 https://777cebuadventures.blogspot.com/2013/08/traveler-or-tourist.html
43 https://www.travelandleisure.com/attractions/museums-galleries/museums-with-virtual-tours
44 https://thoughtcatalog.com/matthew-kepnes/2015/08/the-travelers-manifesto/

References

Bauman, Z. (1998) Tourists and vagabonds. In *Globalization: The Human Consequences*. New York: Columbia University Press, pp. 77–102.

Bordun, O. and Komar, R. (2018) Current state and prospects of dark tourism flows organization in Ukraine. *Current Issues of Tourism Research* 4(2), 4–13.

Boorstin, D. (1987) [1961] *The Image. A Guide to Pseudo-events in America*. New York: Random House.

Bruner, E. (2005) *Culture on Tour. Ethnographies of Travel*. Chicago & London: Chicago University Press.

Butcher, J. (2003) *The Moralization of Tourism. Sun, Sand… and Saving the World*. Oxford/New York: Routledge.

Butcher, J. (2020) The war on tourism. Available at: https://www.spiked-online.com/2020/05/04/the-war-on-tourism/ (Accessed 24 January 2021)

Butler, R. (1980) The concept of a tourism area cycle of evolution. *Canadian Geographer*, 24, 5–12.

Buzard, J. (1993 [2001]) *The Beaten Track. European Tourism, Literature, and the Ways to Culture, 1800–1918*. Oxford: Clarendon Press.

Cai, W., McKenna, B. and Waizenegger, L. (2020) Turning it off: Emotions in digital-free travel. *Journal of Travel Research* 59(5), 909–927.

Calisch, I. and Calisch, N. (1882) *Beknopt kunstwoordenboek*. Tiel: Campagne.

Chibás, E. (2014) *Bye bye Barcelona*. Available at: https://www.youtube.com/watch?v=kdXcFChRpmI November 2014 (Accessed 24 January 2021)

Clifford, J. (1986) On ethnographic allegory. In J. Clifford and G. Marcus (Eds.), *Writing Culture: The Poetics and Politics of Ethnography*. Berkley and Los Angeles: University of California Press, pp. 98–121.

Cohen, E. (1972) Towards a sociology of international tourism. *Social Research*, 39(1), 164–182.

Cohen, E. (1979) A phenomenology of tourist experiences. *Sociology*, 13(2), 179–201.

Culler, J. (1988) The semiotics of tourism. In *Framing the Sign: Criticism and Its Institutions*. Oxford: Basil Blackwell, pp. 153–167.

Dickinson, J. and Lumsdon, L. (2010) *Slow Travel and Tourism*. London: Earthscan.

Edensor, T. (2009) Tourism and performance. In T. Jamal, T. and M. Robinson (Eds.), *The Sage Handbook of Tourism Studies*. London: Sage Publications, pp. 543–557.

Feifer, M. (1985) *Going Places. The Ways of the Tourist from Imperial Rome to the Present Day*. London: MacMillan.

Franklin, A. (2003) The tourist syndrome. An interview with Zygmunt Bauman. *Tourist Studies*, 3(2), 205–217.

Frommer, A. (1957) *Europe on 5 Dollars a Day*. Greenberg: Trade Distributors.

Fussell, P. (1980) *Abroad: British Literary Traveling Between the Wars*. New York/Oxford: Oxford University Press.

Galani-Moutafi, V. (2000) The self and the other. Traveler, ethnographer, tourist. *Annals of Tourism Research*, 27(1), 203–224.

Higgins-Desbiolles, F. (2010) The elusiveness of sustainability in tourism: the culture-ideology of consumerism and its implications. *Tourism and Hospitality Research*, 10(2), 116–129.

Higgins-Desbiolles, F. (2020a) The end of global travel as we know it: an opportunity for sustainable tourism. Available at: https://theconversation.com/the-end-of-global-travel-as-we-know-it-an-opportunity-for-sustainable-tourism-133783 March 17 (Accessed 24 January 2021)

Higgins-Desbiolles, F. (2020b) The 'war over tourism: Challenges to sustainable tourism in the tourism academy after COVID-19. *Journal of Sustainable Tourism*, 29(4), 551–569.

Hughes, N. (2018) 'Tourists go home': Anti-tourism industry protest in Barcelona. *Social Movement Studies*, 17(4), 471–477.

Jansson, A. (2018) Rethinking post-tourism in the age of social media. *Annals of Tourism Research* 69, 101–110.

Jensen, J. (1999) *Caspar David Friedrich. Leben und Werk*. Köln: DuMont.

Kaplan, M. (1960) *Leisure in America: a Social Inquiry*. New York: Wiley.

Keck, M. (2007) 'Kindred Spirits' in romantic vein: Durand's Kindred Spirits compared to Friedrich's Wanderer über dem Nebelmeer. *Amerikastudien/American Studies* 52(1), 35–46.

Labrousse, S. (2015) *Cruise Ship Tourism in Labadee, Haiti*. Nijmegen: Radboud University.

Larsen, J. (2006) Geographies of tourist photography. Choreographies and performances. In J. Falkheimer and A. Janssen, A. (Eds.), *Geographies of Communication: The Spatial Turn in Media Studies*. Göteborg: Nordicom, pp. 241–257.

Larsen, S., Torvald, O. and Brun, W. (2011) Backpackers and mainstreamers. Realities and myths. *Annals of Tourism Research*, 38(2), 690–707.

Litvin, S. W. (2006) Revisiting Plog's Model of allocentricity and psychocentricity...One more time. *Cornell Hospitality Quarterly*, 47(3), 245–253.

Lyons, M. (2019) Companions and competitors: Men and women travelers and travel writing in the mid-nineteenth-century French Pyrenees. In F. Meens and T. Sintobin, T. (Eds.), *Gender, Companionship, and Travel. Discourses in Pre-modern and Modern Travel Literature*. Abingdon and New York: Routledge, pp. 154–170.

MacCannell, D. (1976) *The Tourist: A New Theory of the Leisure Class*. New York: Shocken Books.

MacCannell, D. (1999) *The Tourist: A New Theory of the Leisure Class*. Berkeley: University of California Press.

Maslow, A. (1943) A theory of human motivation. *Psychological Review*, 40(4), 370–396.

Matoga, L. and Pawłowska, A. (2018) Off-the-beaten-track tourism: A new trend in the tourism development in historical European cities. A case study of the city of Krakow, Poland, *Current Issues in Tourism*, 21(14), 1644–1669.

Meens, F. and Sintobin, T. (2019) Who is carrying the luggage? Gendered discourses on companionship in travel writing: an introduction. In F. Meens and T. Sintobin (Eds.), *Gender, Companionship, and Travel. Discourses in Pre-modern and Modern Travel Literature*. Abingdon and New York, Routledge, pp. 1–16.

Milano, C., Cheer, J. and Novelli, M. (Eds.) (2019) *Overtourism: Excesses, Discontents and Measures in Travel and Tourism*. Wallingford: CABI.

Munt, I. (1994) The 'other' postmodern tourism: Culture, travel and the new middle classes. *Theory, Culture and Society*, 11(3), 101–123.

Noy, C. (2004) 'This trip really changed me'. Backpackers narratives of self-change. *Annals of Tourism Research*, 31(1), 78–102.

O'Reilly, C. (2006) From drifter to gap year tourist: Mainstreaming backpacker travel. *Annals of Tourism Research*, 33(4), 998–1017.

Oosterling, H. (2000) *Radicale middelmatigheid*. Amsterdam: Boom.

Pearce, P. L. (1982) *The Social Psychology of Tourist Behaviour*. New York: Pergamon Press.

Pearce, P. L. (1988) *The Ulysses Factor: Evaluating Visitors in Tourist Settings*. New York: Springer.

Pearce, P. L. (1991) Analyzing tourist attractions. *Journal of Tourism Studies*, 2(1), 46–52.

Pearce, P. L. (1993) Fundamentals of tourist motivation. In D. Pearce and R. Butler (Eds.), *Tourism Research: Critiques and challenges*. London: Routledge, 113–134.

Pearce, P. L. (2005) *Tourist Behaviour. Themes and Conceptual Schemes*. Clevedon: Channel View Publications.

Pearce, P. L. and Foster, F. (2007) A 'university of travel': Backpacker learning. *Tourism Management* 28(5), 1285–1298.

Plog, S. C. (1974) Why destination areas rise and fall in popularity. *Cornell Hotel and Restaurant Administration Quarterly*, 14(4), 13–16.

Plog, S. C. (2001) Why destination areas rise and fall in popularity: An update of a Cornell quarterly classic. *Cornell Hotel and Restaurant Administration Quarterly*, 42 (3), 13–24.

R. V. (1861) Een zomer in het Noorden door Gerard Keller. *Vaderlandsche letteroefeningen*, 454–457.

Robinson, N. (2015) *Dark Tourism Motivations. An investigation into the Motivation of Visitors to Sites Associated with Dark Tourism*. PhD Thesis, University of Salford. Available at: http://usir.salford.ac.uk/id/eprint/36776/5/dark%20tourism.pdf (Accessed 27 January 2021)

Sharpley, R. and Stone, P. (2009) *The Darker Side of Travel: The Theory and Practice of Dark Tourism*. Bristol: Channel View Publications.

Sintobin, T. and Tonnaer, A. (2020) Tourists' filmic representations on YouTube: A case study analysis of two mediatized visits to the Mursi in Ethiopia. In M. Mansson, A. Buchmann and C. Cassinger, C. (Eds.) *The Routledge Companion to Media and Tourism*. Abingdon: Routledge, pp. 245–254

Smith, M., Macleod, N. and Hart Robertson, M. (2010) *Key Concepts in Tourist Studies*. London: Sage Publications.

Smith, S. (1990) A test of Plog's allocentric/Ppychocentric model: Evidence from seven nations. *Journal of Travel Research*, 28(4), 40–43.

Smith, S. (2019) Landscapes for 'likes': Capitalizing on travel with Instagram. *Social Semiotics*. Available at: https://doi.org/10.1080/10350330.2019.1664579

Tickner, E. (1910) *Lift-luck on Southern Roads*. New York: The Macmillan Company.

Urry, J. and Larsen, J. (2011) *The Tourist Gaze 3.0*. London: Sage Publications.

Wang, N. (1999) Rethinking authenticity in tourism experience. *Annals of Tourism Research*, 26(2), 349–370.

Wickens, E. (2002) The sacred and the profane: A tourist typology. *Annals of Tourism Research*, 29(3), 834–851.

Yiannakis, A. and Gibson, H. (1992) Roles tourists play. *Annals of Tourism Research*, 19(2), 287–303.

Zemla, M. (2020) Reasons and consequences of overtourism in contemporary cities: Knowledge gaps and future research. *Sustainability*, 12(5), 1729.

17
MASS TOURISM AND PERSONAL EXPERIENCES

Erik Cohen

Introduction

Frequently, 'mass tourism' is referred to uncritically as a 'self-explanatory concept' (Vainikka, 2013b: 318). However, the term is conceptually ambiguous (Vainikka, 2013a) and few efforts have been made to clarify it. Indeed, although it is widely considered to be the principal type of contemporary tourism, mass tourism has been subjected to relatively limited empirical study. Moreover, a perusal of the literature reveals that, surprisingly, the experiences of so-called 'mass tourists' are more often stereotypically assumed rather than systematically examined. The purpose of this chapter, therefore, is to address the lack of critical attention, particularly from an experiential perspective, paid to one of the most widely used but arguably misunderstood terms in tourism. First, it briefly considers the nature of the tourist experience before examining the concept of mass tourism in light of contemporary attempts at its reconceptualization. It then turns to its principal topic, the mass tourist experience, which it discusses in light of three basic questions:

i   Are there differences between the prevalent personal experiences of different types of tourists, particularly between mass tourists and those travelling independently, such as backpackers?
ii Are mass tourists, despite the co-presence of many other participants in a particular situation, able to attain the intensive, unique high or deep 'peak' (Maslow, 1964) experiences that are often assumed to be the privilege of solo travellers?
iii How does the ongoing commodification and medialization of tourism impact upon mass tourist experiences?

Tourist experiences

The term 'experience' is used in tourism studies in two distinct senses, namely, intrinsic and extrinsic. The former marks the more theoretical, phenomenological approaches to the topic, the latter the more empirical ones. It is important to note that there is a significant gap between the theoretical discourse in the study of tourist experiences and the empirical research into the topic. More specifically, the theoretical discourse on intrinsic tourist

DOI: 10.4324/9781003219866-21

experiences focuses primarily on intensive 'peak' experiences (Maslow, 1964) rather than on the more mundane experiences, such as satisfaction with services, accommodations or leisure activities (Quan & Wang, 2004), that empirical studies tend to explore.

This discourse unfolded from MacCannell's (1973, 1976) well-known argument that moderns are alienated and, hence, are on a quest for authenticity in other places or other times. Yet, that quest is frustrated by the staged authenticity of the attractions they encounter on their trip. Building on MacCannell's work, Cohen (1979) proposed a phenomenological typology of tourist experiences, ranging from diversionary and recreational to existential. This implied a hierarchy of experiences of authenticity in terms of their intensity, the 'existential' being assumedly the most intensive one. That approach was further developed by Ning Wang (1999), who distinguished between object authenticity (i.e. the authenticity of attractions or of the life of others observed by the tourist) and existential authenticity, a feeling of 'really living' experienced in the course of a trip. The latter resembles Maslow's (1964) notion of 'peak experiences' or Csikszentmihalyi's notion of 'flow' (Csikszentmihalyi & Csikszentmihalyi 1988). This line of conceptual work was taken further by Reisinger's application of Heidegger's existentialist philosophy to tourism, ascribing to it a transformational potential that enables the individual to achieve 'self-actualization' (Reisinger, 2013, 2015; see also Cohen, 2018b). 'Peak' experiences of self-realization or transformation in tourism are believed to be serendipitous events, occurring spontaneously and surprisingly in unexpected 'moments' (Cary, 2004) and, hence cannot be planned as part of a tour. This view fits, and is possibly supported by, reports from tourists that their most memorable experiences occurred in unplanned moments of their trip (Birenboim, 2016, Filep, 2014: 269, Ritchie & Hudson, 2009: 112).

It is important to note that the study of experience in the intrinsic sense is a difficult enterprise, not least because personal experiences are unfathomable; they are not given to direct access by others, but can only be gauged indirectly from subjects' reports. In fact, little empirical research has been undertaken into 'peak' experiences in tourism, whilst critics have claimed that the meaning of terms, such as 'peak' (or 'memorable,' a term current in tourism managerial and marketing research), are problematic and that 'the nature of the experience to which they refer varies widely' in the literature (Knobloch, Roberson & Aitken, 2014: 599). Hence, as Tung and Ritchie (2011: 1367) point out 'more research must be done to uncover the essence of what exactly makes certain experiences special, spectacular and... memorable.'

In contrast, the term 'experience' in the extrinsic sense is used in many of the empirical marketing or management studies as a synonym for attractions (sites, sights or other stimuli) to which tourists are exposed on a planned trip. The introduction of the concept of the 'experience economy' (Pine & Gilmore, 1999) into tourism studies deflected the attention of researchers in marketing and management from the 'objective' qualities of such attractions to the manner in which they are subjectively experienced by customers. Their research is mainly intended to find out which stimuli have provoked positive responses on part of tourists, often framed in terms of 'satisfaction' (e.g. Hosany & Prayag, 2013) or memorability (Tung & Ritchie 2011; Zhong, Busser & Baloglu 2017). It does not, however, dwell on the personal significance, intensity or depth of those experiences.

Mass tourism

'Mass tourism' is a widely used term but, despite its centrality in the tourism discourse, its theoretical and ideological roots have by and large gone unnoticed, even in the most recent

Mass tourism and personal experiences

literature on the topic (e.g. Harrison & Sharpley, 2017a; Vainikka, 2013a); one exception is Sharpley's (2018: 106–109) discussion of the phenomenon. In particular, it has not been noted that the concept of mass tourism is rooted in the broader concept of 'mass society', which was central to the sociological discourse of modernity up to about the middle of the twentieth century (e.g. Bell, 1956; Shils, 1962; Thompson, 2005). This is significant not merely for the history of the idea of mass tourism but for its routinely assumed connotation.

Drawing on classical sources, mid-twentieth century commentators characterized 'mass society' as an 'inert and formless mass' (Shils, 1962: 45) in which 'individuals have grown estranged from one another' (Bell, 1956: 75). This image of 'mass society' as a dehumanized assemblage of disconnected and lonely individuals has been implicitly injected into the concept of 'mass tourism' as used by Cohen (1972) and more recent writers, such as Harrison and Sharpley (2017a, b). This had an important practical consequence; the actual social relations between 'mass tourists' remain under-researched to this day.

Reconceptualizing mass tourism

Mass tourism, as a dominant form of tourism, is said to have emerged in the 1950s and 1960s in Europe (e.g. Vainikka, 2013a: 272). At the time, it was principally manifested in 'package tours' (Sezgin & Yolal, 2012: 73), bringing the inhabitants of cool northern European countries to the warm Mediterranean beaches in quest of sun, sea and sand (Turner & Ash, 1975). Such 'package tours' remained the dominant form of mass tourism for decades (Chen, Schuckert, Song & Chon, 2016) and, even as Western tourism underwent increased individualization, they came to dominate the emergent Asian tourism markets (Chen et al., 2016; Lee & Wilkins, 2017). Moreover, the Asian version of the 'package tour' was more comprehensive than that in the West; while 'in Western countries, package tours provided [merely] basic elements for the trip, Asian package tours normally include almost all elements, including organized schedules, meals, a tour guide as well as…accommodations and bus tours' (Lee & Wilkins, 2017: 5).

The traditional self-contained 'package tour' fostered the prevailing negative stereotype of mass tourism (Vainikka, 2015; Wang, Weaver & Kwek, 2016), and was even unreflectively adopted by tourism researchers. As Vainikka (2013b: 318) notes, 'the widely used term "mass tourism" is often considered as a self-explanatory concept that refers to an unpleasant and an overcrowded form of tourism'. Moreover, although this stereotype was criticized as judgmental and deterministic, thus preventing a more nuanced and flexible view of mass touristic phenomena (Vainikka 2013a), it continued to influence the prevalent image of mass tourism both in popular writings and even in scientific studies. The stereotype has also kept researchers from paying due attention to the transformations that mass tourism has undergone, particularly in the West, over the course of the past few decades (Vainikka, 2013a, Wang, Weaver & Kwek, 2016) and has impeded a more nuanced, less judgmental analysis of mass tourist phenomena. More specifically, deterministic modernist discourses (Vainikka, 2013a: 271–275) have perceived 'mass tourism' in terms of a bundle of common, interrelated traits (e.g. Harrison & Sharpley, 2017a). In contrast, flexible post-modernist discourses (Vainikka, 2013a: 275–279) deconstruct that bundle, allowing for a plurality of diverse configurations of traits in mass touristic phenomena.

Adopting a broad mobilities perspective, I conceive of 'mass tourism' as a movement of great numbers of tourists along well-trodden routes through big, versatile moorings, to popular destinations and attractions. This definition covers the growing variability of mass tourist phenomena; since its initiation in 'package tours,' mass tourism became socially fractured, ranging from organized groups to individual mass travelers, mass back-packers and mass eco-tourists (Weaver, 2005). The concept can also be extended to some massive counter-cultural phenomena, such as the Burning Man festival (Kozinets, 2002; Sherry & Kozinets, 2007; St John, 2018), and even to its various smaller-scale, 'no spectators' permutations (Robinson, 2015). It is important to note that the modes of movement of mass tourists also became diversified, ranging from airlines (often in charter flights), buses and trains, to cruise ships and charter yachts (Lett, 1983). Their destinations became similarly varied, ranging from heterogeneous concentrations of hotels and guest houses in sea-side resort cities, to capacious, heterotopic, self-contained tourist enclaves (Edensor, 1998), which typically provide inclusive services to mass-vacationers, consisting of a combination of accommodation, facilities (such as restaurants, bars, shops and beauty parlours) and amenities (such as beaches, pools, saunas or golf course). While these often constitute the principal attractions for vacationing tourists, such destinations also serve as a basis for sightseeing excursions to natural or cultural attractions.

Over recent decades, mass tourist activities have also become more heterogeneous, ranging from long-established sun, sea and sand vacationing tourism (Obrador Pons, Crang & Travlou, 2009), cultural mass tourism (Jovicic, 2016), such as mass-excursions to famous old European cities such as Venice, Amsterdam and Barcelona and mass eco-trips, to mass attendance in popular cultural or even counter-cultural, events. In other words, mass tourism can perhaps be thought of, in an era of mass mobility, as 'tourism enjoyed by the masses' (Sharpley, 2018: 108).

Mass tourist experiences

Vainikka's reconceptualization of 'mass tourism' has not yet significantly influenced current writings on the topic; the business and marketing literature in particular still conceives 'mass tourism' as a distinct, bounded category of organized groups travelling within an 'environmental bubble' (Cohen, 1972) of their familiar environment (for example, Cortini & Converso, 2018; Lee & Wilkins, 2017: 3–4). Mass tourists are described as seeking protection and familiar foods in the bubble, while avoiding interaction with the hosts (Lee & Wilkins 2017: 14). Cortini and Converso (2018: 54) even argue that residents form 'counter-environmental bubbles' to 'defend their own culture and identity from the attacks of mass tourism'. Mass tourists are consequently believed to have merely 'an inferior experience' on their trip (Lee & Wilkins, 2017: 6).

The standardized 'experiences' (stimuli) offered to mass tourists by tourism establishments assumedly prevent them from achieving the personal, spontaneous and unfathomable experiences as conceived in extant theoretical discussions of 'peak'(Maslow), 'existential' (Wang) or 'transformative' (Reisinger) tourist experiences. These authors do not generally specify the type of tourists having the opportunity for such heightened experiences, but they implicitly relate to solo travelers rather than to mass tourists. Shepherd (2015: 61) points out that, in the early literature, there were 'various attempts to chart and classify the experiences and practices of travelers in contrast to tourists, with the former typically framed as active seekers of meaning, the latter as passive observers of staged performances'. That assumption is also implicit in Cohen's (1972) typology of non-institutionalized and institutionalized tourist roles. Surprisingly, however, a search of the relevant literature reveals that the relationship between type of tourists and their experiences has been rarely empirically documented (but see Uriely, Yonay & Simchai, 2002). Moreover, McCabe (2005: 87) has argued that 'There appears to be little correlation between typologies of "tourist" and the

Mass tourism and personal experiences

actual category constructions of tourist experiences used by tourists'. This suggests that mass tourist experiences might not differ categorically from those of other kinds of tourists. But as already noted, mass tourist experiences have not been much studied empirically, and do not figure significantly even in recent treatments of the topic, such as Harrison and Sharpley's (2017b) edited volume. The question is, therefore, whether mass tourists might have intensive 'peak' experiences, and if so, under what circumstances?

In the absence of studies of *experiences*, this question could be approached indirectly by way of the psychological research on tourist *motivations*: We could ask what mass tourists want to experience on their trip, and if and how mass tourists differ from more individual travellers in their motivations? As an initial response to such a question, the empirical study of tourist motivations (and hence, implicitly, preferred experiences) indicates that their principal common trait is a quest for distinction: that their experience be distinct and unique, different from the common experience of other tourists. For example, Doran, Larsen and Wolff (2015: 561), in their study of people's self-perception while on vacation, claim that tourists perceive themselves 'to be authentic (or individualistic) travellers with characteristics different from those represented in the mainstream tourist population.' They therefore conclude that, 'when considering psychological variables, such as travel motivation, categorizations between non-institutionalized and institutionalized forms of tourism seem not necessarily to be in accordance with people's self-perception.' They explain that

> differences in the perception of the self and typical tourists may allow people to maintain a positive sense of personal identity (i.e. to be an authentic traveler rather than a stereotypical tourist) despite the fact that they are involved in tourism activities that are simultaneously shared by many others.
>
> *(Doran et al., 2015: 561; parenthesis in original)*

Some other studies, referred to by these authors, seem to support these claims. Thus, Prebensen, Larsen and Abelsen (2003) found, in a study of German tourists visiting Norway, 'that almost 90% ...considered themselves to be non-typical German tourists' (cited in Doran et al., 2015: 557). It is important to note, however, that the term 'authentic' has been introduced by Doran et al. (2015) in their discussion of the findings but was not deployed by the subjects of their study. They (the tourists) simply sought to distinguish themselves from the stereotype of 'the tourist' and, thus, reflect a general Western urge to affirm one's distinct, unique, individual personhood.

McCabe (2005: 92), following Jacobsen (2000), lends further support and amplifies Doran et al.'s argument by pointing out that the tendency of tourists to distance themselves from the tourist role and adopt an anti-tourist attitude, 'becomes a means of maintaining a feeling that individuals' experiences are distinct from all the other occupants and players of a [tourist] role.'

Doran et al. (2015) and McCabe's (2005) claims indicate that all kinds of (Western) tourists seek distinct, personal experiences on their trip, though they might feel disturbed by other tourists. This, in turns, suggests that mass tourists might desire 'peak' or existential experiences, just like solo travellers. Strangely, however, there exist no detailed phenomenological studies of mass tourist experiences that could be of assistance to deal with this question.

Quan and Wang (2004) help us to understand the reason for this absence by their introduction of an important distinction into the study of tourist experiences. Arguing that the tourist experience is multi-dimensional, they point out the contrasting disciplinary approaches to it:

> In social science literature…most researchers focus on the [tourist] experience *in sharp contrast* to the daily experience. The tourist experience is thus understood as the "pure", "net" or "peak" experience, usually derived from the attractions, rather than "mixed", "gross" or "supporting" experience such as eating, sleeping and so on.
>
> (Quan & Wang, 2004: 297)

In contrast, 'such "secondary", "derisive" and "supporting" experiences have caught the full attention…in the literature on hospitality' (ibid, p. 297). Hence, 'there is a discrepancy between the social science approach and the marketing/management approach [to the tourist experience]. The latter treats the tourist experience as *consumer experience*, whereas the former regards the tourist experience as *'peak experience'* (ibid, p. 298). It stands to reason to argue that the social science approach was primarily interested in the intensive, 'peak' experiences of individual tourists, whereas the marketing/management approach was concerned primarily with the degree of satisfaction of mass tourists with the auxiliary services provided (Hosany & Prayag, 2013; Quan & Wang, 2004). This leaves a lacuna in the literature: The question of whether mass tourists could have intensive 'peak' experiences has not been systematically studied.

To approach this question, several preliminary points have to be taken into account. First, in contrast to the conventional view of 'mass tourism', its heterogeneity, stressed by Vainikka (2013a, 2015), indicates that not all of its manifestations are equally ensconced in an environmental bubble. For example, mass ecotourists (Weaver, 2005) are certainly more exposed to the host environment than package tour vacationers. Second, even within mass tourism, including participants in 'package tours', there may be a considerable diversity of interests and activities (Wickens, 2002; see also McCabe, 2005: 93; Uriely, 2005: 205). Third, exposure to the same 'experiences' (stimuli, attractions) may provoke very different personal experiences in participants, according to how they resonate with their biographies and memories. And finally, the exposure of mass tourists to 'experiences' occurs in various contexts, what Mossberg (2007) called 'experiencescapes'; a physical environment, tourism personnel and other tourists. These contextual factors and, especially, the last one, might significantly influence the quality and intensity of personal experiences.

The conventional concept of mass tourism implies the co-presence of many individuals facing the same attractions or doing the same thing, but without being socially mutually engaged. Hence, the co-presence of other tourists is assumed to be a disturbing factor, impeding the individual tourist's ability to have a unique, intensive, peak experience. This is not a self-evident assumption; a counter-example could be given from the field of music, whereby a person at a concert is generally not disturbed by the presence of other listeners from having a deep, even existential, experience. However, while researchers have engaged in the study of relations between mass tourists and their hosts (for example, Lee & Wilkins, 2017; Peters, 2017; Wai & Hitchcock, 2017), the interaction between mass tourists themselves has gained little attention. In particular, sociality or the tendency of being social on holidays, remains an under-researched dimension of mass tourism (Blitchfeldt & Mikkelsen, 2013: 235). Although the marketing literature (for example, Jennings, 2006; Nickerson, 2006) lists a range of factors influencing the (mass) tourist experience, sociality is not among them.

I suggest that mass tourists tend to have an ambiguous attitude to their co-travellers. On the one hand, they disturb their privacy and compete for getting the best view of attractions;

Mass tourism and personal experiences

hence, mass tourists seek to distance themselves physically and socially from co-travellers, to be able to experience the attractions and use the conveniences of the trip in privacy. On the other hand, mass tourists are interested in sociality (Jacobsen, Skogheim & Dann, 2015) and share experiences with their co-travellers, not least to get confirmation of their 'uniqueness'. I further suggest that the patterns of sociality will vary considerably between the diverse manifestations of mass tourism, stressed by Vainikka (2013a). Particularly, the patterns of sociality in organized mass tourism ('package tours') might differ from those among individually travelling mass tourists, who have a greater freedom than the former to choose with whom to associate, and to disengage themselves from the company of other tourists. The question then emerges, how are the patterns of sociality related to mass tourists' ability to achieve intense 'peak' experiences? Unfortunately, even those few authors concerned with the influence of the co-presence of other tourists on a given individual's experience (Mossberg, 2007; Yin & Poon, 2016) did not discuss the intensity of that experience.

It can be argued that the chances for such experiences are related to the degree of sociality among mass tourists; specifically, that the extremes of a high degree of sociality on the one hand and a low degree of sociality on the other, enhance the mass tourists' chances for 'peak' experiences, albeit of very different kinds: *collective* peak experiences in the former case, and *individual* peak experiences in the latter.

Collective 'peak' experiences

Building on anthropological theories of the emergence of collective effervescence and of a sense of 'communitas' in the liminal phase of ritual processes (Olaveson, 2001; V. Turner 1969; E. Turner, 2012), I suggest that tourists, even mass tourists, could in some instances be carried away, and become participants (rather than mere observers) in communal celebrations and festivals, momentarily reaching a 'peak' experience of communitas among themselves or with the locals. The evidence for such situations is admittedly rare, but a phenomenological study of apparent mass tourists to the Limassol carnival in Cyprus by Zakas and Boukas (2013) indicated that the tourists' experiences were shaped 'by the generalized sociality and perceived community metamorphosis' of the festival, though they were constrained by interfering organizational factors.

A very different variant of collective effervescence leading to 'peak' experiences has been shown to emerge at mass tourists' beach-side drinking bouts. Munar (2013) claims that German beach vacationers' nocturnal group beer drinking on Mallorca's *Beerstrasse* engender joint affirmation, social enjoyment and mutual trust, and that beer tourism provides a stage where people connect with each other (resembling communitas) and attain authentic existential experiences in Wang's (1999) sense of the term.

However, the scarcity of good examples of collective 'peak' mass tourist experiences in the literature possibly reflects a general scarcity of opportunities in contemporary tourism for group effervescence and blending of individuals into communitas. Hence, mass festivals, such as the Burning Man (*Black Rock City*) (Kozinets, 2002; Sherry & Kozinets, 2007; St John, 2018), while spurning 'tourists,' could be seen as offering compensatory opportunities to experience sociality among strangers, effervescence and communitas in a large-scale counter-cultural framework. The *Burning Man*, an anti-consumerist (but expensive) annual festival that presently draws about 70,000 participants (St John, 2018: 4), is intended to reverse 'the commercial world of formal institutions', by initiating the participants, called 'pilgrims' (in contrast to the merely observing 'tourist[s]' [St John, 2018: 15]) into an 'antistructural world' (Sherry & Kozinets, 2007: 123). Unlike in conventional mass tourist events, in the

Burning Man sociality is encouraged, and 'participants are even entreated to "welcome the stranger [i.e. tourist]", though he/she is a derided figure (St John, 2018: 4). The event, which focuses on artistic creativity, is rich in interaction between participants, and culminates in a bacchanalian concluding ritual of burning the Man; the fire is reportedly accompanied by a symbolic 'stripping of the self' (St John, 2018: 128–9) in a communal purification ritual, remindful of the rites-of-passage in tribal societies (Turner, 1969). Somewhat paradoxically, however, the very success of the Burning Man festival transformed it into a tourist attraction, with expensive 'turnkey' camps offering luxury habitations for the super-rich who come to the festival to increase their popularity, but not to participate in the events (Pierpoint 2019).

The multiplication of Burning Man-like festivals around the world (Jahn, Cornwell, Drengner & Gaus, 2018), in which the formation of communitas is a major attraction, testifies to a thirst among contemporary Westerners for 'peak' collective experiences that are not readily available in conventional mass tourism. Alternative mass tourism is spreading, but has not yet been recognized as such in the tourism literature.

Individual peak experiences

While the preceding examples indicate that mass tourists could achieve 'peak' experiences as a result of intensified sociality, I suggest that mass tourists could attain individual peak experiences by way of disengagement from sociality and distancing themselves from the co-presence of other tourists. Stretching out leisurely in the sun on the sand on a sea-beach is often denigrated as a banal and dull mass tourist activity with potentially harmful environmental consequences (Aguiló, Alegre & Sard, 2005). But an alternative view is emerging. Jarratt and Sharpley (2017: 350), for example, have recently pointed out that the sea-side is a 'liminal space' and that visits to the sea-side might have a spiritual significance (though people in their study of a northerly English seaside resort only visit the beach, but are not sun-bathing).

A similar argument could be made for sun-sea-and-sand tourism on the warm southern beaches. Baldacchino (2010: 763) claims that [beach] sand 'offers a complex, multi-layered experience, where the real and the fictive are mutually constituted', a powerful description of the between-and-betwixt character of liminal situations (Turner, 1967). Lying motionlessly in the sun on the sand, even the mass tourist might spontaneously fall into a half-conscious state of mind in which he/she experiences a moment of deep, mystical unity with their surroundings, Earth or the world. Unfortunately, however, the stereotypical perception of sea-side leisure as a superficial hedonistic activity has as yet prevented the investigation of its deeper experiential potentialities.

The commodification of mass tourist experiences

The commodification of tourist experiences was intensified by the growing attention in tourism management and marketing to the experiential nature of consumption, expressed in the notion of the 'experience economy' (Pine & Gilmore, 1999). Tourism practitioners consequently set upon the commodification of experiences for mass tourist consumers, and destinations or attractions came to be marketed as detailed packages of promised 'experiences'. Ritchie and Hudson (2009: 111), for example, argued that 'the central challenge facing tourism planners [is] the design [of] effective touristic experiences'. While this development probably serves to ensure that prospective tourists will get value for their money, it further 'disenchanted' the tourist products themselves. They came increasingly to resemble the products people consume in their daily life.

In a similar vein, Park and Santos (2017: 17) emphasize that 'positive emotions and feelings associated with experiences, such as excitement, are a critical component of memorable tourist experiences.' However, exciting or intensive 'peak' tourist experiences are often serendipitous, surprising events, occurring outside the planned program of a trip; in an early paper, Cary (2003) pointed to the spontaneous nature of the 'tourist moment.' Park and Santos (2017) cite the *Lonely Planet*'s (2000: 18) statement that '…we believe the most memorable tourist experiences are often those that are unexpected, and the finest discoveries are those you make yourself'. And Ritchie and Hudson (2009: 112) state that 'we seem to appreciate most those moments we can say afterward were big – but which stole upon us and took us unawares'.

Tourism professionals thus realized the significance of surprising or unexpected tourist experiences. The extraordinary character of such experiences inspired some professionals to suggest a planned inclusion of surprise into the tourism product. Thus, Park and Santos (2017: 25) advise that: 'Promotional strategies should consider the incorporation of serendipity and fortuity narratives [into tourism products]'. Paradoxically, surprise would thus become a hidden ingredient of the commodified mass tourist product!

Medialization

The rapid development of Information and Communications Technologies (ICT) is having a growing impact on tourism, and might transform the nature of mass tourist experiences in the near future. Neuhofer, Buhalis and Ladkin (2012) have already noted the potential of such new technologies to co-create enhanced, personalized tourist experiences. Since then, the concept of (technological) 'smartness', which emerged in the development of Smart Cities (Buhalis & Amaranggana, 2014: 553–554), was introduced into the tourism discourse. According to Boes, Buhalis and Inversini (2015: 391), 'the term "smart" represents a marketing word for all things that are embedded or advanced by technology,' such as the Internet, Augmented Reality, Cloud Computing and the Internet of Things (IoT)'. In the tourism discourse, the concept was specifically deployed in the notions of 'Smart Tourism Destinations' (STD) (Boes, et al., 2015; Buhalis & Amaranggana, 2014), Smart Tourists and Smart Tourist Experiences (Femenia-Serra, Neuhofer & Ivars-Baidal, 2018). Buhalis and Amaranggana (2014: 557) maintain that the establishment of Smart Tourist Destinations requires 'dynamically connecting stakeholders through a technological platform on which information relating to tourism activities could be exchanged instantly'. This platform will be used as a neural system 'to enhance [the] tourism experience and improve the effectiveness of resource management towards maximizing both destination competitiveness and consumer satisfaction'.

Arguing along similar lines, Femenia-Serra, Neuhofer and Ivars-Baidal (2019) recently proposed the notion of the 'smart tourist', a new type of tourist, emerging under the impact of the penetration of the latest ICTs into tourism. They claim that the multiple forms of ICT will enable tourists to achieve 'tailored and richer experiences' (n.p.) The authors' primary concern is 'to provide tourists with higher satisfaction, improved experiences and a better achievement of their individual preferences, through varied "smart solutions"' (Femenia-Serra, et al., 2019: n.p.). Since in smart destinations 'technology is centrally embedded in all elements, thanks to new [technological] developments,' technology 'becomes *the space* where all the interactions between the stakeholders happen' (ibid: n.p.). The new smart technologies are believed to be 'a crucial element for the creation of better experiences in SDs', since they will 'open possibilities of greater personalization and dynamic real-time co-creation' of *smart experiences*. For that, however, it will be necessary to 'establish underlying attitudes and behaviours of tourists who fit into the smart destination scenario' (ibid: n.p).

Some authors are aware of the limitations to spontaneity that the medialization of tourism in Smart Destinations imposes upon the tourist. For example, Buhalis and Amaranggana (2014: 561) concede that

> Although tourism often incorporates elements of spontaneity and exploration, [it] seems that tourism industries in general are assuming that uncertainty reduction is preferable. In fact, tourists may actually seek out risk and opportunity to get lost and explore. To this end some intelligent systems are now being developed…to stress the importance to inspire rather than precisely matching tourists,

thus introducing a degree of openness into the 'neural system' enfolding the smart tourist, and creating a 'programmed spontaneity', which, to my mind, will constitute the postmodern counterpart of the 'staged authenticity' (MacCannell 1973) in modern tourism.

This raises the question: how will the comprehensive and sophisticated medialization of tourism by the revolutionary ICT developments impact upon mass tourism and mass tourists' experiences? I suggest that the processes discussed above will lead to three inter-related future developments:

i   As growing numbers of 'smart mass tourists' learn how to tour independently by using ICT, they would become less dependent on others on their trip. This would in the first place affect guided tours, and dispense more generally with guiding services. The proliferation and wide adoption of ICT might also lead to a gradual disuse of comprehensive 'package tours' and a concomitant increase of individual mass tourists.

ii The increased use and dependence on ICT will affect the social interaction between mass tourists, and their accompanying sociality, just as medialization affected sociality in backpacker enclaves (Cohen, 2018a). Mass tourists will become more preoccupied with mediating devices and be less aware of, concerned with (or disturbed by), co-present tourists; they might also become less willing to participate in joint activities.

iii Mass tourists will get better value for their money and derive greater satisfaction from their trip, but their experiences will increasingly resemble the satisfaction derived from ordinary consumer products. Opportunities for un-preplanned serendipitous, surprising and spontaneous 'peak' experiences will decline, since the medialization of mass tourism offers tourists the opportunity to co-create ever more predictable experiences. An awareness of the programmed nature of apparently serendipitous, surprising and spontaneous experiences might fundamentally devalue them as 'peak' or even 'memorable', experiences. Ensconced from all sides by the comprehensive ICTs, the mass tourist will find no exit to escape their hold.

Conclusion

In this chapter I have adopted Vainikka's (2013a) broad definition of mass tourism that encompasses many variants beyond the stereotype of 'package tours', including some counter-cultural mass tourist phenomena. Considering that variety, it is hard to offer unambiguous

Mass tourism and personal experiences

answers to the questions regarding mass tourists' personal experiences posed in the intro-duction to this chapter. Nevertheless, I shall try to extricate briefly some principal points emerging from the preceding discussion.

The first question relates to the widely held assumption that there are significant differences in travel experiences between different types of tourists. Thus, Park and Santos (2017: 25) stated that 'the tourist experiences of backpackers might be significantly different from those of mass tourists'. The prevailing assumption is that the intensity, 'depth' or 'height' of tourist experiences is inversely related to the degree of the institutionalization of tourist roles, and predicts that the more freedom the tourist enjoys, the better his/her chances for 'peak' experiences. Such experiences will be the prize for the efforts and discomforts suffered by the lonely traveller (drifter or backpacker), and denied to the mass tourist travelling in his/her comfortable 'environmental bubble'.

However, this assumption has not been systematically investigated in comparative studies of different types of tourists, while the scarce research on this issue does not provide it with empirical support. Existing psychological research indicates that the *motivation* for distinct and unique (or authentic) experiences is independent from the type of tourists, but no find-ings exist about the relative chances of *realization* of such motivations by different types of tourists.

Moreover, the work of Vainikka (2013a) and others, which deconstructs the category of the 'mass tourist' and points out that it is loosely bounded and internally heterogeneous, in-dicates that wide differences in the intensity, 'depth' or 'height' of experiences might prevail between various concrete kinds of mass tourisms.

The second question relates to the ability of mass tourists to attain intensive 'peak' (Maslow, 1964) experiences, despite the co-presence of many other participants in a situ-ation. To the best of my knowledge, this question has not been studied empirically. I have therefore suggested in this chapter that the chances for such experiences are related to the state of sociality among mass tourists; that is, situations of intensive group sociality fostering exuberance among participants (for example, at celebrations or festivals), will lead to the emergence of collective 'peak' experiences, resembling the sense of communitas in rites-of-passage. Equally, situations of low sociality, such as sun-bathing on beaches, will enable the individual mass tourist to disengage temporarily from his/her companions, and facilitate the achievement of individual 'peak' experiences. However, conventional mass tourists seem to encounter few occasions for collective 'peak' experiences, but such experiences are provided by increasingly proliferating counter-cultural mass events, based on the model of the Burn-ing Man.

The third question relates to the impact of the ongoing commodification and medializa-tion of tourism on mass tourist experiences, particularly on the chances of mass tourists for intense 'peak' experiences. I have argued that the ongoing processes of commodification of tourist experiences and the medialization of tourism by ICT technologies, while helping to enhance the mass tourists' *satisfaction*, will reduce their chances for intensive 'peak' experi-ences, since such experiences tend to be serendipitous, emerging spontaneously and unex-pectedly in the course of a trip. Hence, the greater the ability of the 'smart' tourist to plan his or her trip in 'smart' destinations, the lesser the chances for such spontaneous moments. Realizing the importance of serendipity in the tourist experience, some experts suggest integrating it into mass tourism programs. However, I have argued that such attempts will lead to 'planned spontaneity', which could be seen as a post-modern equivalent of modern 'staged authenticity'.

Erik Cohen

References

Aguiló, E., Alegre J. and M. Sard (2005) The persistence of the *sun and sand* tourism model. *Tourism Management*, 26(2), 219–231.

Baldacchino, G. (2010) Re-placing materiality: A Western anthropology of sand. *Annals of Tourism Research*, 37(3), 763–778.

Bell, D. (1956) The theory of mass society. *Commentary*, 22(1), 75–83.

Birenboim, A. (2016) New approaches to the study of tourist experiences in time and space. *Tourism Geographies*, 18(1), 9–17.

Blitchfeldt, B. S. and Mikkelsen, M. V. (2013) Vacability and sociability as touristic attractions. *Tourism Studies*, 13(3), 235–250.

Boes, K., Buhalis, D. and Inversini, A. (2015) Conceptualizing smart tourism destinations. In I. Tussyadiah and A. Inversini (Eds.), *Information and Communication Technologies in Tourism 2015*. Cham: Springer International Publishing, pp. 391–403.

Buhalis, D. and Amaranggana, A. (2014) Smart tourism destinations. In Z. Xiang and I. Tussyadiah (Eds.), *Information and Communication Technologies in Tourism 2014*. Cham: Springer International Publishing, pp. 553–564.

Cary, S. H. (2004) The tourist moment. *Annals of Tourism Research*, 31(1), 6–77.

Chen, Y., Schuckert, M, Song, H. and Chon, K. (2016) Why can package tours hurt tourists? Evidence from China's tourism demand in Hong Kong. *Journal of Travel Research*, 55(4), 427–439.

Cohen, E. (1972) Towards a sociology of international tourism. *Social Research*, 39, 164–182.

Cohen, E. (1979) A phenomenology of tourist experiences. *Sociology*, 13, 179–182.

Cohen, E. (2018a) Backpacker enclaves research: Achievements, critique and alternative approaches. *Tourism Recreation Research*, 43(1), 105–116.

Cohen, E. (2018b) The philosophical, ethical and theological groundings of tourism: An exploratory inquiry. *Journal of Ecotourism*, 17(4), 359–382.

Cortini, M. and Converso, D. (2018) Defending oneself from tourists. *Frontiers in Psychology*, 9: Article 354. https://doi.org/10.3389/fpsyg.2018.00354

Csikszentmihalyi, M. and Csikszentmihalyi, I. S. (1988) *Optimal Experience: Psychological Studies of Flow in Consciousness*. Cambridge: Cambridge University Press.

Doran, R., Larsen, S. and Wolff, K. (2015) Different but similar: Social comparison of travel motives among tourists. *International Journal of Tourism Research*, 17(6), 555–563.

Edensor, T. (1998) *Tourists at the Taj*. London: Routledge.

Femenia-Serra, F and Neuhofer, B. (2018) Smart tourism experiences: Conceptualization, key dimensions and research agenda. *Investigaciones Regionales – Journal of Regional Research*, 42, 129–150.

Femenia-Serra, F., Neuhofer, B. and Ivars-Baidal, J. A. (2019) Towards a conceptualization of smart tourists and their role within the smart destination scenario. *The Service Industries Journal*, 39(2). https://doi.org/10.1080/02642069.2018.1508458

Filep, S. (2014) Moving beyond subjective well-being: A tourism critique. *Journal of Heritage and Tourism Research*, 6(1), 266–274.

Harrison, D. and Sharpley, R. (2017a) Introduction: Mass tourism in a small world. In D. Harrison and R. Sharpley (Eds.), *Mass Tourism in a Small World*. Wallingford: CABI, pp. 1–14.

Harrison, D. and Sharpley, R. (Eds.) (2017b) *Mass Tourism in a Small World*. Wallingford: CABI.

Hosany, S. and Prayag, G. (2013) Patterns of tourists' emotional responses, satisfaction and intention to recommend. *Journal of Business Research*, 66(6), 730–737.

Jacobsen, J. (2000) Anti-tourist attitudes: Mediterranean charter tourism. *Annals of Tourism Research*, 27(2), 284–300.

Jacobsen, J., Skogheim, R. and Dann, G. (2015) Sun, sea, sociability, and sightseeing: Mediterranean summer holidaymaking revisited. *Anatolia*, 26(2), 186–199.

Jahn, S., Cornwell, T. B., Drengner, I. and Gaus, H. (2018) Temporary communitas and willingness to return to events. *Journal of Business Research*, 92, 329–338.

Jarratt, D. and Sharpley, R. (2017) Tourists at the seaside: Exploring the spiritual dimension. *Tourist Studies*, 17(4), 349–368.

Jennings, G. (2006) Perspectives on quality tourism experiences: An introduction. In G. Jennings and N. P. Nickerson (Eds.), *Quality Tourism Experiences*. Burlington: Elsevier Butterworth-Heinemann, pp. 1–21.

Jovicic, D. (2016) Cultural tourism in the context of relations between mass and alternative tourism. *Current Issues in Tourism*, 19(6), 605–612.

Mass tourism and personal experiences

Knobloch, U., Roberson, K. and Aitken, R. (2014) (Mis)understanding the nature of tourist experiences. *Tourism Analysis*, 19(5), 599–608.

Kozinets, R. V. (2002) Can consumers escape the market? Emancipatory illuminations from Burning Man. *Journal of Consumer Research*, 29(1), 20–38.

Lee, H. J. and Wilkins, H. (2017) Mass tourism and destination interaction avoidance. *Journal of Vacation Marketing*, 23(1), 3–19.

Lett, J. W. (1983) Ludic and liminoid aspects of charter yacht tourism in the Caribbean. *Annals of Tourism Research*, 10(1), 35–56.

Lonely Planet (2000) *Australia* (O'Byrne, D. et al.). Melbourne: Lonely Planet Publications.

MacCannell, D. (1973) Staged authenticity: Arrangements of social space in tourist settings. *American Journal of Sociology*, 79(3), 589–603.

MacCannell, D. (1976) *The Tourist: A New Theory of the Leisure Class*. New York: Schocken Books.

Maslow, A. H. (1964) *Religious Values and Peak Experiences*. Columbus: Ohio Stet University Press.

McCabe, S. (2005) 'Who is a tourist?' A critical review. *Tourist Studies*, 5(1), 85–106.

Mossberg, L. (2007) A marketing approach to the tourist experience. *Scandinavian Journal of Hospitality and Tourism*, 7(1), 59–74.

Munar, A. M. (2013) Sun, alcohol and sex: Enacting beer tourism. In J. Gummelgaard and C. Dörrenbächer (Eds.). *The Global Brewery Industry: Markets, Strategies and Rivalries*. Cheltenham: Edward Elgar, pp. 310–334.

Neuhofer, B., Buhalis, D. and Ladkin, A. (2012) Conceptualizing technology enhanced destination experiences. *Journal of Destination Marketing & Management*, 1(1–2), 36–46.

Nickerson, N. P. (2006) Some reflections on quality tourism experiences. In G. Jennings and N. P. Nickerson (Eds.), *Quality Tourism Experiences*. Burlington: Elsevier Butterworth-Heinemann, pp. 227–236.

Obrador Pons, P., Crang, M. and Travlou, P. (2009) *Cultures of Mass Tourism: Doing the Mediterranean in the Age of Banal Mobilities*. Farnham: Ashgate.

Olaveson, V. (2001) Collective effervescence and communitas: Processual models of ritual and society in Emile Durkheim and Victor Turner. *Dialectical Anthropology*, 26, 89–124.

Park, S. and Santos, C. (2017) Exploring the tourist experience: A sequential approach. *Journal of Travel Research*, 56(1), 16–27.

Peters, R. F. (2017) The role of tour operators and suppliers in the resident-visitor relationship. *Tourism, Culture and Communication*, 17(4), 289–297.

Pierpoint. G. (2019) Are the super-rich ruining Burning Man? *BBC News* 18 February. Available at: https://www.bbc.com/news/world-us-canada-47203978

Pine, B. J. and Gilmore, J. H. (1999) *The Experience Economy: Work Is Theater and Every Business a Stage*. Boston: Harvard Business School Press.

Prebensen, N. K., Larsen, S. and Abelsen, B. (2003) I'm not a typical tourist; German tourists' self-perception. *Journal of Travel Research*, 4(4), 226–246.

Quan, S. and Wang, N. (2004) Towards a structural model of the tourist experience: An illustration from food experiences in tourism. *Tourism Management*, 25(3), 297–305.

Reisinger, Y. (Ed.) (2013) *Transformational Tourism: Tourist Perspectives*. Wallingford: CABI.

Reisinger, Y. (2015) Personal transformations and travel and tourism. In Y. Reisinger (Ed.), *Transformational Tourism: Host Perspectives*. Wallingford: CABI, pp. 6–13.

Ritchie, J. R. B. and Hudson, S. (2009) Understanding and meeting the challenges of consumer/tourist experience research. *International Journal of Tourism Research*, 11(2), 111–126.

Robinson, R. (2015) *Music Festivals and the Politics of Participation*. Farnham: Ashgate.

Sezgin, E. and Yolal, M. (2012) Golden age of mass tourism: Its history and development. In M. Kasimoglu (Ed.), *Visions for Global Tourism Industry: Creating and Maintaining Competitive Strategies*. London: Intech Open, pp. 73–90.

Sharpley, R. (2018) *Tourism, Tourists and Society*, 5th Edn. Abingdon: Routledge.

Shepherd, R. J. (2015) Why Heidegger did not travel? Existential angst, authenticity, and tourist experience. *Annals of Tourism Research*, 52, 60–71.

Sherry, J. and Kozinets, R. (2007) Comedy of the commons: Nomadic spirituality and the Burning Man festival. *Research in Consumer Behavior*, 11, 119–147.

Shils, E. (1962) The theory of mass society: Prefatory notes. *Diogenes*, 10(39), 45–66.

St. John, G. (2018) Civilised tribalism: Burning Man, event-tribes and maker culture. *Cultural Sociology*, 12(2), 3–21.

Thompson, I. (2005) The theory that won't die: From mass society to the decline of social capital. *Sociological Forum*, 20(3), 21–448.

Tung, V. W. S. and Ritchie, B. (2011) Exploring the essence of memorable tourist experiences. *Annals of Tourism Research*, 38(4), 1367–1386.

Turner, E. (2012) *Communitas: The Anthropology of Collective Joy*. New York: Palgrave Macmillan.

Turner, L. and Ash, J. (1975) *The Golden Hordes*. London: Constable.

Turner, V. (1967) Betwixt and between: The liminal period in rites of passage. In V. Turner (Ed.), *The Forest of Symbols*. Ithaca: Cornell University Press.

Turner, V. (1969) *The Ritual Process: Structure and Anti-structure*. New York: Aldine.

Uriely, N. (2005) The tourist experience: Conceptual developments. *Annals of Tourism Research*, 32(1), 199–216.

Uriely, N., Yonay, Y. and Simchai, D. (2002) Backpacking experiences: A type and form analysis. *Annals of Tourism Research*, 29(2), 519–537.

Vainikka, V. (2013a) Rethinking mass tourism. *Tourist Studies*, 13(3), 268–286.

Vainikka, V. (2013b) Travel agent discourses of mass tourism: Beyond stereotypes? *Tourism Geographies*, 16(2), 18–332.

Vainikka, V. (2015) Stereotypes and professional reflections on mass tourism: Focusing on tour operators, mass tourism destinations and mass tourists. *Études caribéennes* No. 31–32. Available at: https://journals.openedition.org/etudescaribeennes/7609

Wai, L. T. K. and Hitchcock, M. (2017) Local reactions to mass tourism and community tourism development in Macau. *Journal of Sustainable Tourism*, 25(4), 451–470.

Wang, N. (1999) Rethinking authenticity in tourist experience. *Annals of Tourism Research*, 26(2), 349–370.

Wang, Y., Weaver, D. B. and Kwek, A. (2016) Beyond the mass tourism stereotype: Power and empowerment in Chinese tour packages. *Journal of Travel Research*, 55(6), 724–736.

Weaver, D. B. (2005) Mass and urban ecotourism: New manifestations of an old concept. *Tourism Recreation Research*, 30(1), 19–26.

Wickens, E. (2002) The sacred and the profane: A tourist typology. *Annals of Tourism Research*, 29(3), 835–851.

Yin, C. Y. and Poon, P. (2016) The impact of other group members on tourists' travel experiences: A study of domestic package tours in China. *International Journal of Contemporary Hospitality Management*, 28(3), 640–658.

Zakas, V. and Boukas, N. (2013) Extracting meanings of event tourist experiences. A phenomenological exploration of Limassol carnival. *Journal of Destination Marketing & Management*, 2(2), 94–107.

Zhong, Y. Y. S., Busser, J. and Baloglu, S. (2017) A model of memorable tourist experiences: The effects of satisfaction, affective commitment, and story telling, *Tourism Analysis*, 22(2), 201–217.

18
BACKPACKER TOURIST EXPERIENCES
Temporal, spatial and cultural perspectives

Dallen J. Timothy and Xuan Zhu

Introduction

Backpacker travel has a long history, dating back perhaps thousands of years as early people wandered, foraging for food and engaging in trade with their 'backpacks' in tow. Some have noted how the medieval Grand Tour in many ways resembles the modern-day notion of the 'gap year' and its associated backpacking experiences (Bagnoli, 2009). The modern precursor of backpacking tourism developed in the United States after the widespread adoption of the automobile in the 1920s: the phenomenon of hitchhiking. Hitchhiking soon spread to Europe and other parts of the world as automobiles became more common and as roads and highways developed. By the 1950s, backpacking-oriented hitchhiking was rather routine for people who were unable or unwilling to pay for transportation, had no other means of getting around or were seeking adventure, or a combination of these. By the 1940s, hitchhiking 'remained one of America's favourite forms of adventure' (Schlebecker, 1958: 318).

Following the Second World War, the backpacker phenomenon continued to evolve in the 1950s and 1960s with the development of the hippie subculture and its reputation for carefree and freestyle living. This subcultural movement contributed a great deal to the idea of spontaneous travel and globetrotting on only pennies a day. People began travelling on tight budgets with a few belongings in tow to already popular destinations in Europe and North America, but their interests soon extended into far less explored areas of Asia, Latin America and Africa. Eventually, certain global localities became famous destinations for hippies and other budget travellers (e.g. Kathmandu, Nepal), and prescribed routes were set that backpacker tourists were expected to follow, including the Hippie Trail, which extended from the UK, through Asia Minor, South Asia and into Southeast Asia (Gemie & Ireland, 2017; Liechty, 2005). The 'trail' ended in the 1970s as several governments and warring tribes became hostile to Westerners and the idea of tourism. Nevertheless, the legacy of the Hippie Trail and the vagabondage that it inspired continue to live on today in the form of backpacker tourism.

What the hitchhikers in early twentieth-century America and later in other areas of the world sought was an inexpensive adventure, opportunities for cultural immersion and the chance to see far-flung places they had only read about in magazines or seen in movies. Today, the backpacker tourism phenomenon involves many motivations, experiences and

DOI: 10.4324/9781003219866-22

249

place identities. This chapter sheds some light on the phenomenon of backpacker tourism and the experience it provides to those who participate. It aims to highlight some of the time frames, geographical contexts and cultural norms that affect backpackers' travel experiences. It first examines the broad concept of backpacker tourism, followed by an in-depth description of backpacker experiences in certain temporalities, spatialities and culturalities as manifested in gap year travel; the Chinese notion of *qiongyou*; rail travel, especially the idea of European Interrailing; backpacker service clusters, or enclaves; and trail/route-based backpacking experiences.

Backpacking tourism

Backpacking as a form of tourism has grown enormously since the 'hippie days' of the 1960s and 1970s. Today, it is a prominent form of tourism in many parts of the world, and certain regions have become extremely popular backpacker destinations (e.g. Western and Eastern Europe, Australia, South Asia and Southeast Asia). Backpacking generally has several unique features that differentiate it from other manifestations of tourism. Although various authors have used different criteria to define backpacker tourists (Dayour, Kimbu & Park, 2017), the phenomenon is generally characterized by independent, low-budget forms of travel in which people overnight in low-cost accommodations, such as campgrounds, hostels, homestays and, more recently, CouchSurfing and shared Airbnb rentals. They eat inexpensive food, preparing their own meals as much as possible, or buying from street vendors and local markets. They typically use local public transportation, walk, cycle or hitchhike. They normally stay away from home longer than other holidaymakers do, and they carry all of their belongings in a backpack (Loker-Murphy & Pearce, 1995).

Long-term backpackers, or lifestyle travellers, 'style their lives around the enduring practice of backpacking' (Cohen, 2011: 1550), thereby blurring the distinction between holiday and daily life. Maoz (2004) details one cohort of Israeli backpackers, which she calls 'settlers'. These lifestyle travellers stay in a place longer, sometimes months or years, and become immersed in the local community. The extreme mobilities of 'global nomads' challenge the concept of travel itself and the related ideas of citizenship and nationality, home and homelessness by choosing to be location-independent wanderers (Kannisto, 2016).

Since the 1960s, backpacker tourism has been largely associated with young people under age 30 seeking adventure during their gap years, summer holidays or as an appendage to overseas volunteer service (Loker-Murphy & Pearce, 1995; O'Reilly, 2006; Wearing & McGehee, 2013). Today, however, older people, including retirees, are participating in far greater numbers. This is especially true with the baby-boomer generation, many of whom retire earlier, are better educated and more affluent than their predecessors were. Older backpackers are also motivated by the desire to see the world and relive their youth by travelling how they might have done many years earlier (Oliveira-Brochado & Gameiro, 2013). Upmarket and more mature backpacker travel is sometimes referred to as poshpacking or flashpacking. One of the characteristics that defined them a decade ago was their tech savviness and their constant contact with home through the mobile devices they brought with them (Germann Molz & Paris, 2015; Hannam & Diekmann, 2010; Paris, 2012). Flashpackers choose to backpack for the immersive experience rather than because of budget constraints, although they also continue to seek bargain travel. Flashpackers epitomize the new 'mobile elites' who are in continuous contact with home through their mobile devices (Hannam & Diekmann, 2010), but this is less of a distinguishing characteristic today since most backpackers now travel with smartphones and laptops (Dayour, 2019).

Backpacker tourist experiences

Despite the emphasis on low-budget travel, most backpackers traditionally have come from the affluent countries of Western Europe and North America, as well as Australia and New Zealand. In these prosperous countries, people had the freedom, time, financial means and interest to take a break from work and school and embark on extended journeys away from home. Their citizenships enable lifelong travel by allowing them to cross most national borders easily. This also partly explains why some countries that have easier visa policies are more popular destinations than others. Since the collapse of communism in Eastern Europe, the 'open door policy' of China and its resultant freedoms and growing economic affluence there, as well as the increasing affluence and growing sense of individualism among younger generations in other East Asian countries, other nationalities have joined the backpacker ranks and are some of the most passionate backpackers today (Bui, Wilkins & Lee, 2014; Maoz, 2007; Zhang, Tucker, Morrison & Wu, 2017; Zhu, 2018).

There are as many motivations for undertaking a backpacking journey as there are backpackers. First, many studies have shown that sightseeing and leisure are the most prominent motivations (Bui et al., 2014; Ooi & Laing, 2010; Paris & Teye, 2010). Many backpackers see their trips as holidaymaking, and their experiences serve the same purposes as any other type of vacation: sightseeing, relaxation, stress relief, escape from mundane home life and meddling parents, seeking adventure and having fun.

Second, many backpackers desire to learn and become educated about the world. Backpackers often stress their desire to visit cultural attractions as a means of learning about people, places and history (Maoz, 2004; Richards, 2015). Part of this experience is a strong desire to become immersed in authentic foreign cultures (Cederholm, 2004; Huxley, 2004; Paris & Teye, 2010; Richards & Wilson, 2004). According to many backpackers, their propensity to travel off the beaten tourist path and seek authentic places and experiences is what differentiates them from traditional 'tourists'. In the views of many backpackers, their search for knowledge and authentic experiences 'distances them from the more superficial and "en masse" tourists' (Bagnoli, 2009: 331).

The third overarching motive is a longing for personal growth, self-awareness and self-actualization. This is something that almost all backpackers have in common (Canavan, 2018; Noy, 2004; Shulman, Blatt & Walsh, 2006). Many set out on a journey to 'discover' themselves and become more deeply rooted in their existential lives or to abandon their normative lived experiences entirely (Bagnoli, 2009; Binder, 2004). This often manifests in expressions of liberation or freedom – freedom to make their own choices away from the bonds of home (Ooi & Laing, 2010). This is also reflected in the empowerment they achieve by facing stressful situations on their own and having to solve their own problems, which may strengthen their self-confidence and enhance their personal growth. The experiences they gain, the personal transformations they undergo and the confidence they develop endures for many years and informs their life choices far beyond the end of the physical journey (Collins-Kreiner, Yonay & Even, 2018; Leinonen, 2012; Noy, 2004).

Fourth, many backpackers aim to extend their realm of friendships and global contacts by meeting other backpackers with similar interests along the way (Bagnoli, 2009; Binder, 2004). Becoming part of a community of like-minded adventurers is, for many, an important part of developing self-esteem and a means of achieving personal growth and 'global citizenship' (Dayour, 2019). Other motives include, but are not limited to, volunteering, learning practical life skills and practicing a foreign language.

Studies have shown that motivations and experiential expectations of backpackers may be mitigated by their cultural backgrounds and nationalities (Enoch & Grossman, 2010; Maoz, 2007; Zhu, 2018; Zhu & Xie, 2016). Social mores or structures (individualism, collectivism or xenophobia), belief systems (aversions to certain places or activities), familial traditions (filial piety or parental control), nationalism (patriotism or superiority complex) and similar constructs may determine backpackers' experiences in the destination, their interactions with other travellers, their perceptions of authenticity and service quality and their dealings with destination inhabitants.

Backpacker temporalities, spatialities and culturalities

Backpacker tourism (and other mobilities) has thrived in many social and geographical contexts. For example, gap year has a long history in Europe associated with the Grand Tour and tramping, while *qiongyou* has emerged in China since the early 21st century. Working holidays are an important forum for international backpacker experiences in Australia and New Zealand, while volunteer tourism is an alternative way for backpackers to visit less developed areas. Backpacking experiences are strongly influenced by time, space and culture and, therefore, they demonstrate characteristics of temporality, spatiality and culturality. In the sections that follow, five backpacking forms, settings and venues are described, including elements of these three dimensions. The timing and temporal opportunities are key for most young backpackers and their experiences are mitigated largely through their own cultural baggage and the cultural encounters on the way. Spatially, backpackers move from moorings to mobility through various transportation modes, accommodations and service clusters and destination activities. Thus, their experiences during gap year, with the new phenomenon of *quiongyou*, during railway journeys, in backpacker enclaves and on hiking trails are described below as manifestations of spatialities, temporalities and culturalities.

Gap year backpacking

'Gap year' (also overseas experience (OE) in New Zealand), or an extended period of time taken off between high school and university, or between university and full-time employment (Bagnoli, 2009; Huxley, 2004) is a typical backpacking phenomenon for Europeans, Australians and New Zealanders. This extended time away from formal education and work is typically spent seeing the world and seeking adventures before 'real life' sets in. It usually lasts a year and is a chance for youth to become emancipated and get it (whatever 'it' is) 'out of their systems'. Some youth spend their gap years volunteering for social or environmental causes. Others work as domestic helpers or farmhands; many enroll in foreign language courses. Regardless of how a gap year is spent, however, it usually involves independent travel. Sometimes these purposeful experiences are supplemented by backpack travel and sometimes the volunteer work is done as a means to enable backpacking. These gap year experiences often involve low-budget travel in a state of boundlessness and self-actualization without interference from parents or other authority figures. Some people spend their time traipsing through various parts of the world, aimlessly or purposively trying to collect as many localities as possible.

Many backpackers work their way through a country or region doing odd jobs to pay for the continuation of their journey or volunteering on farms in exchange for room and board, known as WWOOFing (World Wide Opportunities on Organic Farms) (Deville, Wearing & McDonald, 2016; Mosedale, 2009). Bernstein (2019) reports how the popular media in certain developing countries has coined the term 'begpacking' to denote the increasingly common practice of backpackers panhandling for change on street corners,

Backpacker tourist experiences

selling postcards or other small trinkets, or street performing – all ways of begging for money to support their ongoing travel.

In some parts of the world, the gap year has become a social institution, doubling as a rite of passage from childhood into adulthood (Noy & Cohen, 2005; Shulman et al., 2006). Some countries have formalized it as allowable vacation time, granting individuals a year's leave from their employment to avoid workplace burnout (Van Mol & Timmerman, 2014). Young Israelis are avid backpacker tourists. Taking an extended time between mandatory military service and beginning university studies or employment is customary and expected (Noy & Cohen, 2005; Shulman et al., 2006). However, gap year travelling is not a recognized phenomenon in equally affluent but more work ethic-oriented countries such as Canada and the United States. Although Canadians and Americans have become one of the largest and most active backpacker segments, this activity is far less institutionalized in these countries than in places such as Europe, Australia and Israel, where backpacking trips have become an identifiable (and somewhat requisite) part of the Western youth experience (Huxley, 2004). In the United States and Canada, there is no regimented 'gap year' or even expectations that youth will pursue backpacking experiences overseas. However, the related notions of volunteer travel and study abroad are increasingly valued. In conjunction with this, backpacking has become more mainstream among North Americans in the past quarter century, but youth undertaking these journeys as thresholds into adulthood are still the exception rather than the rule. It is believed that a strong commitment to home through a sense of filial piety in some East Asian countries is a barrier for many youths from that region who desire to participate in gap year travel (Bui et. al., 2014). Their economic dependence on, and tight bond with, their parents is a constraint, especially in China among the one-child-only generation (Zhu, 2009) where parental permission is socially required, and high achievement in work and education at an early age are valued more than taking time off to travel.

Qiongyou

'Qiongyou' is a two-character phrase in Chinese that is both a verb and a noun. 'Qiong' means poor and 'you' means travelling. Together, they form the word 'backpacking' as a means of travelling on a shoestring. Qiongyou has become a widely recognized phrase in China since Xiao Yi, the founder of the Qiongyou website, established the Qiongyou European Forum in 2004. Back then, Xiao was an overseas student in Germany, and the forum was created as a communication platform for Chinese overseas students who wanted to travel independently throughout Europe on a tight budget. The forum gained over 10,000 registered users in its first month and its name was shortened simply to 'Qiongyou' in 2006, merging independent travelling themes from other continents. Xiao returned to China in 2008 to start the business operations of the qiongyou website, which aimed to provide 'quality travel services and better life experiences for outbound Chinese travellers'. Though the term 'qiongyou' was originally created to denote Chinese budget travel abroad, it is now commonly used to refer to independent low-budget travel in China.

An interesting comparison is that in Chinese, there is another equivalent phrase, *bei bao lv xing*, which means 'backpacking travelling', with *bei bao* referring to a backpack and *lv xing* referring to travel. This idea originated from backpacking, hiking and camping as an outdoor recreational practice in the 1990s (Zhu, 2009). Both backpacking travel and qiongyou are booming in China, and those who engage in these activities are all called *lv you* (donkey friends), because of the homophonic pronunciation of 'travelling' (*lv*) and 'donkey' (*lv*) in

Chinese and the symbolic meaning of a donkey's endurance, perseverance and resilience similar to the travellers.

A few scholars have described donkey friends in China but not distinguished Chinese backpackers from qiongyou participants (Chen & Weiler, 2014; Luo, Huang & Brown, 2015). According to Xie and Zhu (2019), previous studies on qiongyouers tend to equate this group with normative backpackers or low-budget travellers, overlooking the unique identity of qiongyouers. Although the idea of qiongyou surfaced first to denote Chinese outbound budget travel, as noted earlier, at present, it also entails domestic budget travel.

Qiongyouers are mainly students or other youth, low-skilled, low-paid itinerant workers who admire the life of hippies. Most qiongyouers have middle to low incomes. In contrast, most Chinese backpackers are young professionals who have middle or high incomes and come from more affluent families. Most backpackers, thus, refuse to be identified as 'qiongyouers' because this is a socio-economic and class distinction in the Chinese budget travel marketplace. Backpackers do not consider themselves poor, although both groups undertake independent travel on a tight budget. In addition, qiongyouers prefer long-term, long-haul travel without a clear return plan, which sharpens the contradiction between their low incomes and their travel costs. As a result, saving every yuan becomes the only strategy for qiongyouers, who are significantly less concerned about the recreational aspects of travel. Instead, they understand the journey as a way to reflect on themselves. Many qiongyouers begin travel during or immediately after a life crisis, such as divorce or losing a job or, in common with other nationalities, during their transition to adulthood and independence. This journey is their opportunity to escape from their routine lives and pursue a new lifestyle. This new lifestyle is different from mainstream adulthood, which encourages them to find a stable job and settle down.

Some qiongyouers no longer believe that the normative and most socially accepted lifestyle of today is the only desirable way of life. Qiongyouers reflect on existential questions such as 'who am I?' and 'what life do I want to live during the journey?' In this sense, their existential self-identity becomes a reflexively organized endeavour or 'life politics' as suggested by Giddens (1991). On one hand, this nomadic living becomes qiongyouers' means of fighting against the drudgery of their old life. On the other hand, long-term immersion in qiongyou increases self-reflection among the younger generations and empowers them to seek alternative lifestyles. More importantly, qiongyou is advocated and practised by lower social classes as a means of voicing and justifying their life decisions. Their right of mobility is determined by their social identity; hence, further issues, such as the relationship between life politics and emancipatory politics, the real meaning of travelling, need to be understood better in the context of qiongyou. Qiongyouers, restrained by their education levels, low budgets and foreign visa requirements, typically remain in mainland China and Southeast Asia, while regular backpackers frequently go as far as Europe and North America. Qiongyouers laugh at themselves and claim not be *diao si*, a term coined first by single young men who feel they have dead-end lives; it was later applied to those who are not good-looking, wealthy or part of the 'right' social group.

Although qiongyou is a relatively new phenomenon in China, it somewhat resembles the Western hippies of the 1970s. However, hippies normally came from white, middle-class families in developed societies, whereas qiongyouers come from the lower rungs of society, usually peasant families. The manifestation of qiongyouers in China raises questions about the classical (and now-debunked) notion that money and leisure time are the preconditions of tourism. It reflects changes in travel culture and mirrors some of the dramatic social and cultural changes occurring in China. Its mantra, 'one can travel even though he has no

Backpacker tourist experiences

money', not only challenges the traditional Chinese travel culture of *qiong jia fu lu*, which indicates that one must be financially equipped during a trip in spite of being thrifty in everyday life. It also reveals that backpacking itself might be an approach to realizing upward social mobility.

Interrailing

One of the most prevalent, easiest and least expensive modes of long-distance backpacker mobility is rail travel, which is especially popular in Asia and Europe (Bae & Chick, 2016; Johnson, 2010). Europe has been a significant backpacker destination with London and Amsterdam as original drifter centres (Cohen, 1973; Johnson, 2010). Backpacking around Europe is facilitated and strongly associated with the region's widespread railway network. In Western Europe, since the 1970s, there has been a long-held practice of 'Interrailing'. Interrail passes are inexpensive train tickets that are only available to citizens or residents of Europe. They allow virtually unlimited, inexpensive train travel throughout most of the continent (today Interrail includes travel in 33 countries). From 1972 to 1998, only Europeans under the age of 21 were eligible to purchase Interrail passes. In 1998, however, the passes became available to Europeans of all ages. Interrailing is one of the most common ways in which Europeans backpack around the continent for a period of time, from a couple of weeks to a few months, usually over the summer holidays after high school graduation. The Interrail program was established in the 1970s to provide European youth an inexpensive means of seeing Europe and stimulating intra-European tourism. Recent support of the program by the European Commission focuses on how Interrailing can help foster common European identities and values.

Among many Europeans, Interrailing is an expected life event and an important rite of passage, which helps identify who they are as Europeans (Bagnoli, 2009; Leinonen, 2012). Interrailing is often Europeans' first experience with extended and independent international travel and marks their foray into the global travel sphere. Interrailing is encouraged by national governments, the European Commission, educational organizations and the Interrail Eurail organization as a means of stimulating tourism, building awareness of European issues, and helping develop a European identity. Eurail passes are available for travellers from outside Europe and offer some of the same benefits as the Interrail pass, although they are more expensive.

Most tourism research focuses on happenings in the destination, but there is an increasing interest in understanding the experience in transit times and spaces, including train journeys. Several scholars have debunked the notion that transit is an empty or wasted space and time, ensconced by boredom and wielding little of interest to transit passengers (Megerle, Hildinger & Ernst, 2015). Indeed, rail-based mobility is now frequently regarded as an important part of the experience with many sensualities associated with the sights, sounds and smells of trains being a salient part of the entire experience (Jensen, Scarles & Cohen, 2015). It may be argued that the discomfort and challenges brought up by the rhythemscapes, soundscapes, thermalscapes and smellscapes (Jensen et al, 2015; Mertena, 2015) during frequent train travel and nocturnal Interrailing strengthen travellers' feeling of being 'on the road', thus fulfilling their identity as experienced travellers in Europe. Likewise, the fleeting times and mobile spaces of Interrailing capture the mundane and ordinary wherein Interrailers and locals share the same mobile spaces (Franklin & Crang, 2001), lending yet additional doses of authenticity behind the stages built for the tourist gaze.

Multisensory research techniques have been employed to explore how train spaces are embodied as tourists inhabit, (co)produce and practice time–space while being 'on the move'

(Jensen et al, 2015; Mertena, 2015). The idea that as transport technologies advance, transportation becomes less of a sensual experience is not entirely true (Johnson, 2010; Megerle, Hildinger & Ernst, 2015). Though modern railways attempt to provide passengers with comfort, the embodied act of Interrailing accompanied by long and exhausting trips, the depth of socialization involved, and backpackers' personal challenges become part of their identity and self-actualization through their hardship narratives and story-telling (Leinonen, 2012).

Backpacker enclaves

Compared with the perspectives of mobilities and transit times and spaces, backpacker enclaves have received considerable research attention (e.g. Cohen, 2003, 2018; Johnson, 2010; Maoz, 2004, 2005; Richards, 2015). Spatially and temporally, backpacker enclaves are important moorings that facilitate mobility and stability during backpacker journeys. In the most popular backpacker destinations, special backpacker zones have developed both organically and purposefully. These backpacker enclaves have been well researched for their unique characteristics and the important role they play in the backpacker experience. These zones have specific physical characteristics: intensive tourism services, foreign language norms, cheap eateries and plethoric tour agencies, souvenir shops, youth hostels and internet cafes (Ateljevic & Doorne, 2005).

These spaces deliver respite from the challenges (e.g. poverty, crowdedness and hyperforeignness) of the destination and are, in the words of Richards and Wilson (2004: 261), 'quintessential "refueling station[s]" where road-weary travellers can take a hot shower, buy an imported beer, use the Internet and watch the latest movies'. These tourist zones are frequently the most sought-after attractions in the destination – sometimes wielding more attractiveness than local culture, natural landscapes and historic monuments (Cohen, 2003, 2018). They are also the best venues for meeting other backpackers and maintaining the subculture and backpacker identity (Cohen, 2018; O'Regan, 2010; Richards & Wilson, 2004). In essence, they become spaces suspended 'between local and global culture, between a totally tourist culture and a totally local culture, in a space that is neither homogeneous nor totally heterogeneous' (Wilson & Richards, 2008: 192). In countries of the Global South, these enclaves and their ubiquitous hostels provide a taste of home, where Western food can be bought and wireless internet is plentiful and strong. They are refuges against culture shock and homesickness, where the comforts of home are extended to those who need them. By the same token, these enclavic territories are also quasi-foreign spaces where locals can experience the exotic otherness of the foreign cultures carried in by the backpackers (Wilson & Richards, 2008: 187).

For the most part, these urban backpacker districts provide a great deal of social support and cultural exchange as they become temporary homes to multitudes of nationalities and where friends are made and travel stories shared with co-travellers from every corner of the globe (Cohen, 2018; O'Regan, 2010). Although backpacker enclaves are relatively heterogeneous from cultural and nationality perspectives, some have developed into hubs for certain nationalities, such as the Israeli enclaves in Goa and other Indian destinations along the nicknamed 'Hummus Trail'. This popular Israeli circuit throughout India links together popular Israeli backpacker zones where local merchants, vendors, tour guides and food service providers speak Hebrew, serve Israeli food and cater in other ways to the tastes of mainstream Israelis (Maoz, 2004).

On the downside, some backpacker enclaves in popular destinations have come to be known as centres of hedonism, where drunkenness and a party atmosphere contrast with the

Backpacker tourist experiences

normative environment of the destination, leading many residents to conclude that backpackers are self-centred, arrogant and irresponsible (Scheyvens, 2002). Furthermore, the backpacker 'enclaves...and environmental bubbles are very solid and closed, and no one, especially no local, can invade. The locals are there for décor and service only and they are mostly used as porters and errand servants' (Maoz, 2004: 112). In true colonialist fashion, many Western backpackers spend most of their time in these enclaves, showing little empathy for local living conditions (Canavan, 2018: 561) and largely avoiding truly immersive cultural experiences (Enoch & Grossman, 2010).

Trail-based backpacking

Hiking on trails has long been an important undertaking for backpackers. Cultural routes and nature trails have been a fundamental backpacker tourism space since the Middle Ages. Thousands of heritage trails all over the world have become an important part of the long tradition of backpacker tourism. Increasing numbers of purposive trails are being designed and demarcated on the ground, providing additional linear resources for this type of independent travel with the intent of developing local economies. The Council of Europe has been heavily involved in establishing long-distance purposive trails that connect thematic sites in clusters of countries in Europe (Timothy & Saarinen, 2013). Most of the Council's trails cover hundreds or thousands of kilometres with important nodes, or representative localities, along the way. Trails including the Routes of the Olive Tree, the Viking Routes, the European Route of Jewish Heritage, Destination Napoleon and the Iron Curtain Trail have recently become a focus for backpacker tourists owing to their thematic itineraries, which can be followed for the most part by public transportation in combination with cycling and trail walking (Timothy & Boyd, 2015).

In addition to purposive routes, many organic trails have also become important travel venues for backpacker tourists. These linear corridors were not designed to be tourist trails. Instead, their original purposes were utilitarian and because of their linear characteristics, they developed into hiking or cycling trails. Pilgrimage paths, railways and international borders are among the most pervasive examples of organic tourism trails today, with rail-trails and border trails becoming increasingly popular backpacker tourism assets (Scherrer, Dimmock, Lamont & Ripoll González, 2021; Stoffelen, 2018; Taylor, Frost & Laing, 2019). Likewise, many ancient pilgrimage trails have now become culture and nature trails for non-pilgrim tourists. In Europe, two of the most prevalent examples are the Via Francigena and the Camino de Santiago (Way of St James), both of which were originally early medieval Christian routes that led from many areas of Europe to the sacred destinations of Rome and Santiago de Compostela (Ron & Timothy, 2019; Timothy & Boyd, 2015).

Along with the development of trekking and hiking trails, backpackers' trail-based experiences have been studied by many tourism scholars. Affinity with nature and the outdoors, the mental and physical benefits of walking and hiking, interactions with others and the development of self-knowledge are four of the main walking experiences associated with nature trails (Roberson & Babic, 2009). In addition to these same outcomes, appreciating culture and nature, achieving a sense of oneness with the world, growing spiritually and learning about the cultural geography of places are part of backpackers' experiences on cultural/heritage trails (Timothy & Boyd, 2015).

Cutler, Carmichael and Doherty (2014) found that hiking on the Inca Trail holds deep meaning for those who undertake it, as they encounter the frailties and strengths of their corporeal selves and achieve a certain degree of self-actualization. Through the pain and physical struggle of the trail, memorable emotional, educational and physical elements of the mobile experience eclipse the actual site of Machu Picchu for many backpackers. The treacherous journey itself is an important marker of identity and personal growth derived from the experience of hardship and difficulty hikers face along the trail. Collins-Kreiner and Kliot (2017) conclude that Israeli backpackers establish a stronger place attachment to their home country and greater sense of patriotism by hiking the Israel National Trail. As well, natural landscapes and human interaction on trails can trigger backpackers' moral self-reflection (Zhu & Jiang, 2019).

Xie and Fan (2017) analysed trekking experiences based on Chinese travel blogs to build a trekking experience model, comprising four sequences: (1) corporeal arousal, (2) body–mind unity, (3) co-presence with other wanderers and nature and (4) a sense of individual 'becoming' – a process of self-renewal, self-development and self-creation by sharpening the mind and body, gaining knowledge and purifying the soul. While Israeli backpackers' experiences appear to reinforce their support for their homeland (Collins-Kreiner & Kliot, 2017), the experience model of Xie and Fan (2017) has a universal application to explain how a trekker's experience is formed through the embodied practice of trail-based backpacking.

Conclusion

Although backpacking is no longer the sole province of youth, this chapter has focused primarily on the youth experience. Backpacker experiences are as diverse as the backpackers themselves, yet they share many common goals, expectations and outcomes, which are embodied and performed within temporal, spatial and cultural spheres. Temporalities are uniquely manifested in the prescribed threshold leading to adulthood. These are times for celebrating their graduation from youth and its frivolity into adulthood and more solemn responsibilities. For backpackers who take on longer nomadic journeys, time is less meaningful as they wander either purposely or casually from place to place, either to avoid the responsibilities of home or to soak up the essence of otherness that helps reform their existential selves.

The constant mobilities and moorings associated with backpacker tourism exist within inimitable spatialities, most notably in transit (e.g. on trains and on trails) and in their enclaved spaces. In the moorings of hostels and enclaves, they find solace and friendship with likeminded others from whom they can learn about the next leg of their journey while sharing their experiences with newcomers. These backpacker spaces perforate the foreignness of the 'other', which most backpackers claim to seek. Yet, they offer refreshment, remedies for homesickness and relief from the stresses of being immersed in a foreign place that for many might be difficult to navigate. For backpackers, the mobility of train travel is much more a part of the experience than it is for many other types of tourists. Here, too, transit spaces and times become true 'places', not just spaces, where they continue to meet others, update their social media and learn to appreciate the corporeal senses associated with riding the train. The mobilities associated with nature paths and heritage trails enable backpackers to socialize, albeit at a greater physical distance than they could in cities, and reflect on their own self-actualization processes.

The culturalities of backpacking come through clearly in the relationships that develop between travellers and with destination residents, with some nationalities preferring to stay within their own enclaved spaces, rarely mingling with local people and interacting only with travellers from their homeland. Most backpackers, however, prefer interacting with as many different travellers and local inhabitants as possible, because this is a large part of what

Backpacker tourist experiences

they desire from their journeys (Enoch & Grossman, 2010). The growth of this type of tourism among non-traditional backpacker markets is illustrative of globalization processes, changing tastes and increasing affluence among younger and older generations. For example, the growing phenomenon of *quiongyou* in China resembles much of the hippie culture of the 1970s in the West, but it differs significantly from the majority of low-budget travel that dominates in the Western world today. These and other culturalities mark dramatic changes in both the supply and demand for backpacker tourism and deserves much more research attention.

Much has been written about backpacker motives and experiences. However, as globalization continues to unfold and its effects become more apparent in new backpacker markets, it is imperative that researchers continue to look outside the normative Global North for answers to questions about backpacker experiences in the temporal, spatial and cultural contexts described in this chapter. It is also important to move beyond these normative times, places and cultural contexts to better understand other manifestations of backpacker tourism and the experiences that follow.

References

Ateljevic, I. and Doorne, S. (2005) Dialectics of authentication: Performing 'exotic otherness' in a backpacker enclave of Dali, China. *Journal of Tourism and Cultural Change*, 3(1), 1–17.

Bae, S. Y. and Chick, G. (2016) A rail pass as a culture code among youth travelers: The case of Rail-ro in Korea', *Journal of Tourism and Cultural Change*, 14(1), 27–44.

Bagnoli, A. (2009) On 'an introspective journey': Identities and travel in young people's lives. *European Societies*, 11(3), 325–345.

Bernstein, J. D. (2019) Begging to travel: Begpacking in Southeast Asia. *Annals of Tourism Research*, 77, 161–163.

Binder, J. (2004) The whole point of backpacking: Anthropological perspectives on the characteristics of backpacking. In G. Richards and J. Wilson (Eds.), *The Global Nomad: Backpacker Travel in Theory and Practice*. Clevedon: Channel View Publications, pp. 92–108.

Bui, H. T., Wilkins, H. and Lee, Y. S. (2014) Liminal experience of East Asian backpackers. *Tourist Studies*, 14(2), 126–143.

Canavan, B. (2018) An existentialist exploration of tourism sustainability: Backpackers fleeing and finding themselves. *Journal of Sustainable Tourism*, 26(4), 551–566.

Cederholm, E. A. (2004) The use of photo-elicitation in tourism research–framing the backpacker experience. *Scandinavian Journal of Hospitality and Tourism*, 4(3), 225–241.

Chen, H. and Weiler, B. (2014) Chinese donkey friends in Tibet: Evidence from the cyberspace community. *Journal of China Tourism Research*, 10(4), 475–492.

Cohen, E. (1973) Nomads from affluence: Notes on the phenomenon of drifter-tourism. *International Journal of Comparative Sociology*, 14(1), 89–103.

Cohen, E. (2003) Backpacking: Diversity and change. *Journal of Tourism and Cultural Change*, 1(2), 95–110.

Cohen, E. (2018) Backpacker enclaves research: Achievements, critique and alternative approaches. *Tourism Recreation Research*, 43(1), 105–116.

Cohen, S. A. (2011) Lifestyle travellers. *Annals of Tourism Research*, 38(4), 1535–1555.

Collins-Kreiner, N. and Kliot, N. (2017) Why do people hike? Hiking the National Israel Trail. *Journal of Economic and Social Geography*, 108(5), 669–687.

Collins-Kreiner, N., Yonay, Y. and Even, M. (2018) Backpacking memories: A retrospective approach to the narratives of young backpackers. *Tourism Recreation Research*, 43(3), 409–412.

Cutler, S., Carmichael, B. and Doherty, S. (2014) The Inca Trail experience: Does the journey matter? *Annals of Tourism Research*, 45, 152–166.

Dayour, F. (2019) Backpackers' experiences with smartphone usage in Ghana. *Anatolia*, 30(3), 390–403.

Dayour, F., Kimbu, A. N. and Park, S. (2017) Backpackers: The need for reconceptualization. *Annals of Tourism Research*, 66, 191–193.

Deville, A., Wearing, S. and McDonald, M. (2016) WWOOFing in Australia: Ideas and lessons for a de-commodified sustainability tourism. *Journal of Sustainable Tourism*, 24(1), 91–113.

Enoch, Y. and Grossman, R. (2010) Blogs of Israeli and Danish backpackers to India. *Annals of Tourism Research*, 37, 520–536.

Franklin, A. and Crang, M. (2001) The trouble with tourism and travel theory? *Tourist Studies*, 1(1), 5–22.

Gemie, S. and Ireland, B. (2017) *The Hippie Trail: A History*. Manchester: Manchester University Press.

Germann Molz, J. and Paris, C. M. (2015) The social affordances of flashpacking: Exploring the mobility nexus of travel and communication. *Mobilities*, 10(2), 173–192.

Giddens, A. (1991) *Modernity and Self-Identity: Self and Society in the Late Modern Age*. Stanford: Stanford University Press.

Hannam, K. and Diekmann, A. (2010) From backpacking to flashpacking: Developments in backpacker tourism research. In K. Hannam, and A. Diekmann (Eds.), *Beyond Backpacker Tourism: Mobilities and Experiences*. Bristol: Channel View Publications, pp. 1–7.

Huxley, L. (2004) Western backpackers and the global experience: An exploration of young people's interaction with local cultures. *Tourism Culture & Communication*, 5(1), 37–44.

Jensen, M. T. Scarles, C. and Cohen, S. (2015) A multisensory phenomenology of Interrail mobilities. *Annals of Tourism Research*, 53, 61–76.

Johnson, J. (2010) Euro-railing: A mobile-ethnography of backpacker train travel. In K. Hannam and A. Diekmann (Eds.), *Beyond Backpacker Tourism: Mobilities and Experiences*. Bristol: Channel View Publications, pp. 102–125.

Kannisto, P. (2016) Extreme mobilities: Challenging the concept of 'travel' *Annals of Tourism Research*, 57, 220–233.

Leinonen, L. (2012) *Suomalaisten Interrail-matkustajien Matkustuskokemuksilleen Antamat Merkitykset*. Unpublished master's thesis, University of Eastern Finland, Joensuu.

Liechty, M. (2005) Building the road to Kathmandu: Notes on the history of tourism in Nepal. *Himalaya*, 25(1), 19–28.

Loker-Murphy, L. and Pearce, P. L. (1995) Young budget travelers: Backpackers in Australia. *Annals of Tourism Research*, 22(4), 819–843.

Luo, X., Huang, S. and Brown, G. (2015) Backpacking in China: A netnographic analysis of donkey friends' travel behavior. *Journal of China Tourism Research*, 11(1), 67–84.

Maoz, D. (2004) The conquerors and the settlers: Two groups of young Israeli backpackers in India. In G. Richards and J. Wilson (Eds.), *The Global Nomad: Backpacker Travel in Theory and Practice*. Clevedon: Channel View Publications, pp. 109–122.

Maoz, D. (2005) Young adult Israeli backpackers in India. In C. Noy and E. Cohen (Eds.), *Israeli Backpackers: From Tourism to Rite of Passage*. Albany: State University of New York Press, pp. 159–188.

Maoz, D. (2007) Backpackers' motivations the role of culture and nationality. *Annals of Tourism Research*, 34, 122–140.

Megerle, A., Hildinger, A. and Ernst, Y. (2015) Linking heritage interpretation with rail and bus line marketing. *Journal of Heritage Tourism*, 10(4), 417–430.

Mertena, I. (2015) *Tourists' Embodied Transport Experiences of Travelling by Train*. Unpublished doctoral thesis, Manchester Metropolitan University.

Mosedale, J. (2009) Woofing in New Zealand as alternative mobility and lifestyle. *Pacific News*, 32, 25–27.

Noy, C. (2004) This trip really changed me: Backpackers' narratives of self-change. *Annals of Tourism Research*, 31, 78–102.

Noy, C. and Cohen, E. (Eds.) (2005) *Israeli Backpackers: From Tourism to Rite of Passage*. Albany: State University of New York Press.

O'Regan, M. (2010) Backpacker hostels: Place and performance. In K. Hannam and A. Diekmann (Eds.), *Beyond Backpacker Tourism: Mobilities and Experiences*. Bristol: Channel View Publications, pp. 85–101.

O'Reilly, C. C. (2006) From drifter to gap year tourist. *Annals of Tourism Research*, 33, 998–1017.

Oliveira-Brochado, A. and Gameiro, C. (2013) Toward a better understanding of backpackers' motivations. *Tékhne*, 11(2), 92–99.

Ooi, N. and Laing, J. H. (2010) Backpacker tourism: Sustainable and purposeful? Investigating the overlap between backpacker tourism and volunteer tourism motivations. *Journal of Sustainable Tourism*, 18(2), 191–206.

Paris, C. M. (2012) Flashpackers: An emerging sub-culture? *Annals of Tourism Research*, 39, 1094–1115.

Paris, C. M. and Teye, V. (2010) Backpacker motivations: A travel career approach. *Journal of Hospitality Marketing & Management*, 19(3), 244–259.

Richards, G. (2015) The new global nomads: Youth travel in a globalizing world. *Tourism Recreation Research*, 40(3), 340–352.

Richards, G. and Wilson, J. (2004) Widening perspectives in backpacker research. In G. Richards and J. Wilson (Eds.), *The Global Nomad: Backpacker Travel in Theory and Practice*. Clevedon: Channel View Publications, pp. 250–279.

Roberson, D. and Babic, V. (2009) Remedy for modernity: Experiences of walkers and hikers on Medvednica Mountain. *Leisure Studies*, 28(1), 105–112.

Ron, A. S. and Timothy, D. J. (2019) *Contemporary Christian Travel: Pilgrimage, Practice and Place*. Bristol: Channel View Publications.

Scheyvens, R. (2002) Backpacker tourism and third world development. *Annals of Tourism Research*, 29, 144–164.

Scherrer, P., Dimmock, K., Lamont, M. and Ripoll González, L. (2021) Rail trails literature: Current status and future research. *Journal of Leisure Research*, 52(1), 97–119

Schlebecker, J. T. (1958) An informal history of hitchhiking. *The Historian*, 20(3), 305–327.

Shulman, S., Blatt, S. J. and Walsh, S. (2006) The extended journey and transition to adulthood: The case of Israeli backpackers. *Journal of Youth Studies*, 9(2), 231–246.

Stoffelen, A. (2018) Tourism trails as tools for cross-border integration: A best practice case study of the Vennbahn cycling route. *Annals of Tourism Research*, 73, 91–102.

Taylor, P., Frost, W. and Laing, J. (2019) Path creation and the role of entrepreneurial actors: The case of the Otago Central Rail Trail. *Annals of Tourism Research*, 77, 79–91.

Timothy, D. J. and Boyd, S. W. (2015) *Tourism and Trails: Cultural, Ecological and Management Issues*. Bristol: Channel View Publications.

Timothy, D. J. and Saarinen, J. (2013) Cross-border co-operation and tourism in Europe. In C. Costa, E. Panyik and D. Buhalis (Eds.), *Trends in European Tourism Planning and Organisation*. Bristol: Channel View Publications, pp. 64–74.

Van Mol, C. and Timmerman, C. (2014) Should I stay or should I go? An analysis of the determinants of intra-European student mobility. *Population, Space and Place*, 20(5), 465–479.

Wearing, S. and McGehee, N. G. (2013) Volunteer tourism: A review. *Tourism Management*, 38, 120–130.

Wilson, J. and Richards, G. (2008) Suspending reality: An exploration of enclaves and the backpacker experience. *Current Issues in Tourism*, 11(2), 187–202.

Xie, J. and Zhu, X. (2019) A sociological analysis of the emergence of 'qiongyou': A comparison between the quiongyouer and the backpacker. *Tourism Tribune*, 34(1), 124–135.

Xie, Y. and Fan, Y. (2017) Tourist experience on a body perspective: Grounded theory analysis on trekking writings and interviews. *Human Geography*, 32(4), 129–137.

Zhang, J., Tucker, H., Morrison, A. M. and Wu, B. (2017) Becoming a backpacker in China: A grounded theory approach to identity construction of backpackers. *Annals of Tourism Research*, 64, 114–125.

Zhu, X. (2009) *A Theoretical and Empirical Study on Backpacker Tourism*. Beijing: China Travel & Tourism Press.

Zhu, X. (2018) The comparative study on authentic experience of Western and Chinese backpacker travelers based on narrative analysis: A case study in Yangshuo, China. *Tourism Tribune*, 33(3), 116–126.

Zhu, X. and Jiang, H. (2019) A study on the hiking experience under the mobility paradigm: A case study on Old Huizhou-Hangzhou Ancient Trail. *Tourism Science*, 33(2), 27–41, 58.

Zhu, X. and Xie, J. (2016) Constructing a typology of backpackers from a cross-cultural perspective. In M. Kozak and N. Kozak (Eds.), *Proceedings of the 8th World Conference for Graduate Research in Tourism, Hospitality and Leisure*. Ankara: Anatolia, pp. 515–519.

19

VOLUNTEER TOURISM

'It's no use going back to yesterday, because I was a different person then'

Alexandra Coghlan

Introduction

A decade ago, volunteer tourism was once considered the 'poster child' of sustainable tourism (Lyons & Wearing, 2008: 6). And yet, as this niche tourism sector grows, defining and shaping the volunteer tourist experience is perhaps more complex than in other tourism sub-sectors. Callanan and Thomas (2005) rightly describe volunteer tourism as eclectic and multi-dimensional. By blending the hedonism of tourism with the altruism of volunteering, these two contrasting concepts create a multitude of competing expectations around volunteer tourism for the tourists themselves, for the hosts, for the third-party providers and, not least, for the academics who study this sometimes controversial phenomenon. The purpose of this chapter, therefore, is to explore how we try to make sense of the volunteer tourist experience, to unpack the expectations around it (and to question whether these are reasonable and/or realistic) and to consider some of the challenges that lead to an implicit tension in this niche sector.

To achieve this, we must first define volunteer tourism. Wearing's (2001: 1) definition is perhaps most commonly used, referring to:

> those tourists who, for various reasons, volunteer in an organised way to undertake holidays that might involve aiding or alleviating the material poverty of some groups in society, the restoration of certain environments or research into aspects of society or environment.

Other definitions are equally useful. For example, McGehee and Santos (2005: 760) define volunteer tourism as 'utilizing discretionary time and income to travel out of the sphere of regular activity to assist others in need' whilst for Keese (2011: 258), it is a 'combination of development work, education and tourism'. Implicit in all definitions, however, are the concepts of travel and the voluntary provision of assistance to others.

It is also useful to understand where volunteer tourism sits in relation to other forms of participatory, immersive, educational travel experiences. Comparable examples include overseas service learning, community-based tourism and conservation tourism, among others. These give some insight into what might (and might not) be expected from the volunteer

262

DOI: 10.4324/9781003219866-23

Volunteer tourism

tourism experience. The chapter will explore some of the most common themes within the volunteer tourism (demand-side) literature, including transformational experiences, authenticity, role ambiguity, the hero's journey, and touch on host-volunteer relations.

Next, we shall consider some of the important challenges facing volunteer tourism and look at the attempts made to address these challenges through codes of conduct, industry guidelines, and certifications. Finally, the chapter will discuss why bringing an ethics-based perspective is useful to understand some of those challenges and conclude by considering whose role it is to fulfil the multitude of expectations that surround volunteer tourism, and how feasible fulfilling those expectations are.

The nature of the sector

In its early days, the prevailing volunteer tourism discourse was the desire for a win-win situation for the responsible, enlightened tourist, the local community and the not-for-profit sector (non-government organizations/NGOs, scientists, community activists, rangers and so forth) who are able to implement their projects and reach out to the public, raising awareness of their work. As such, volunteer tourism has been typically marketed to well-educated, middle class (young) adults as a life-changing experience that combines personal benefits with making 'meaningful contributions'. Such marketing of the experience often includes selling the opportunity to gain personal benefits, such as self-actualization, knowledge /skill acquisition, the development of friendships and the opportunity to make a difference in the world (Lyons, Hanley, Wearing & Neil, 2011; Wearing, 2001). Specifically, the experiences are considered to be highly immersive, authentic and 'backstage', hence offering significant opportunities for self-actualization; Wearing (2002: 239) describes volunteer tourism as offering an 'interactive experience that causes value change, changed consciousness in individuals, which will subsequently influence their lifestyle'.

However, it is arguably this blending of altruism through volunteering, egotism in the form of personal benefits, and enlightenment that creates the tension within volunteer tourism (Sharpley, 2018). And this tension exists in a way that is not present in other, similar forms of niche tourism. International or overseas service learning, for example, is very similar to volunteer tourism, described by Allison, Stott, Felter and Beames (2011: 196) as 'the practice of going overseas to learn through volunteering'. International service learning will often have a social or environmental justice agenda, as well as aiming for critical consciousness raising as an outcome for its participants (Cipolle, 2010). However, service learning also comes with an explicit learning agenda, with in-build pedagogic self-reflection tasks led by a trained teacher. Teaching and learning resources are not only an accepted part of the experience but also an expected part of it, in a manner not present in volunteer tourism. Furthermore, the experience can continue post-trip as teachers remain in touch with their students throughout their educational career, creating opportunities for in-depth debriefing and follow-up activities.

Similarly, many Outward Bound programmes have a similar personal development agenda combined with travel. While variants of the trademarked Outward Bound experience exist as outdoor, adventure education programmes, the original Outward Bound organization explicitly lists experiential learning, reflection, awareness-development and service as core features of their trips (Outward Bound, 2019). As the early studies of this sector indicate, it is also a highly structured experience with explicit goals that are tied to the orchestrating of that experience by trained facilitators (Marsh, Richards & Barnes, 1986; Walsh & Golins, 1976). Their approach is still highly relevant today, targeting many of the same outcomes as volunteer tourism, increasing participants' psychosocial function, employability, intercultural competencies and so forth (Scheinfeld, Rochlen and Russell, 2017; Wang & Zheng, 2015).

While service learning and Outward Bound-style programmes are framed around their pedagogic outcomes and are typically studied by education scholars rather than tourism scholars, there are also a number of tourism sub-sectors that share some similar characteristics to volunteer tourism. One of these is community-based tourism (CBT), which aims to create economic as well as socio-cultural benefits for local communities through tourism development (Okazaki, 2008). CBT is often offered as homestay experiences and appeals more often to international tourists searching for local lifestyles, novelty, personalized service and authentic/genuine social interactions with hosts (Kontogeorgopoulos, Churyen & Duangsaeng, 2015; Mura, 2015; Wang, 2007), particularly in small, and often remote, rural communities. Here, the tourist clearly retains her or his role as visitor, with added benefits of facilitating community development and cultural exchanges through the vehicle of tourism, an outcome often cited as desirable in volunteer tourism.

In a similar vein, conservation tourism and hard ecotourism experiences are expected to offer similar benefits to CBT, but in a natural environment context. On the topic of hard or deep green ecotourists, Wheelan (1991: 16) pointed out over a decade ago that 'ecotourists represent a potential army of recruits with free time and money to spend on sustainable development efforts', perhaps identifying the origins of volunteer tourism. Conservation tourism takes ecotourism a step further, ensuring that tourism delivers direct conservation benefits as tour operators design their products and services to be more conservation-oriented and underpinned by a conservation ethic (Buckley, 2010; Holden, 2009). This may in some circumstances involve elements of citizen science or volunteer activities, but is distinct to volunteer tourism as it does not necessarily include tourists' active participation in conservation. Tourists are aware however, that their visit will contribute to conservation and the tours are sold to them with this conservation focus in mind (Mossaz & Coghlan, 2017).

All of these forms of tourism have explicit pro-social or pro-environmental outcomes that accompany the tourist experience. In that sense, they include the moral dimensions of responsible or sustainable tourism discussed by Holden (2009), Fennell (2006), Sharpley (2012) and others. In addition, community-based tourism, conservation tourism and pro-poor tourism generally include the participatory, immersive and learning components associated with volunteer tourism. Yet, these forms of tourism differ significantly in one important aspect: the role of the participant, and their associated virtues of helper, and the outcomes of enlightenment, intimacy, relationships, self-actualization and transformation.

Volunteer tourists' roles

Selling volunteer tourism becomes a mixed bag of the self-growth benefits of the type associated with service learning and Outward Bound programmes, the 'other'-focused benefits of sustainability outcomes of community-based tourism, pro-poor tourism and conservation tourism, and the global or higher purpose enlightenment of pilgrimages (Smith & Font, 2014). Yet, the commercial nature (discussed below as part of the challenges) of volunteering projects, sold through third-party providers who effectively commodify the benefits listed above, requires a strong business model that ensures financial sustainability of the sector. And in leisure or recreation-based tourism, we know that novelty-seeking, hedonism and R&R (rest and recuperatipon) are the big sellers and major motivators for travel (Malone, McCabe & Smith, 2014). It is not surprising, therefore, that the combined blended nature

Volunteer tourism

of volunteer tourism's benefits and the triadic business model of hosts (project cordinators), volunteer tourists and volunteer tourism brokers creates murky expectations with regard to the experience and the roles of volunteer tourists.

As a direct result, there are a number of studies that explore what Lyons (2003) refers to as 'role ambiguity' in volunteer tourism. This is often framed as a tension between altruism and egotourism (a term coined by Wheeller, 2005). For example, Coghlan and Fennel (2009), Cousins, Evan and Sadler (2009), Mustonen (2007) and Palacios (2010) among others all explore the nature of altruism within volunteer tourism, arguing that while a sense of altruism is present, it is certainly not the primary driver of the sector. Instead, we have witnessed the development of a commodified, hedonic sector replacing the well-intentioned original development agendas of philanthropic host organizations.

One of the earliest researchers to identify the issue was Lyons (2003) in his study of J-1 visitor exchange programmes (work/study exchange programmes with the USA) for young Australians. Lyons identified four simultaneous and ambiguous roles for the participants: (i) a cultural ambassador; (ii) an underpaid employee; (iii) a reluctant volunteer; and (iv) a packaged tourist role. He found that balancing these varied roles 'created frustration and anger that affected the quality of their experience' (Lyons, 2003: 11). His findings are backed up by Blackman and Benson (2010) as well as Zavitz and Butz (2011) who suggest that where volunteer tourists did not feel useful at the project (that is, when they did not have a defined role), disillusionment was likely to follow – a sense neatly captured by Cousins et al.'s (2009) paper entitled: *'I've paid to observe lions, not map roads!'*.

Mustonen (2005), conversely, also acknowledges the shifting roles experienced by volunteer tourists, but accepts that this is part of the experience, as 'the roles of (volunteer) tourists are prone to fluctuate between conventional and altruistic tourists' (Mustonen, 2005: 165). The issue of shifting or ambiguous roles is further explored by Coghlan (2015) using a self-categorization theoretical framework. Drawing on the volunteer tourists' own descriptions of their experiences, Coghlan's study found that respondents' 'I' statements were more commonly related to the hedonic tourist aspects of the experience as well as its personal benefits, while more impersonal 'you' statements described the volunteer work, and its associated pro-social outcomes (co-operation, altruism, empathy), and that respondents continuously shifted between these two self-assigned roles with different foci for the experience depending on their self-categorization.

As part of this shifting identity, some volunteer tourists may struggle to reconcile their identities as tourists with their identities as volunteer tourists, leading to a certain amount of tension and instability around the nature of their travel experience. It is, perhaps, this instability that has led to volunteer tourism's failure to live up to its promise of the delivery of significant and consistent onsite benefits – perhaps one of the most substantial criticisms of volunteer tourism (Guttentag, 2009). Thus, criticisms of the discourse of 'making a difference' and the sometimes over-inflated claims that volunteers are able to assist in significant ways are linked to this sense of role tension between the altruism of volunteering and the hedonism of tourism.

Volunteer tourism and transformation

What is clear from the studies presented above is that the volunteer tourism experience appears to have a strong impact upon a participant's sense of self, or their identity (Bailey & Russel, 2010; Hudson & Inkson, 2006; Lee & Woosnam, 2010; Zahra & McIntosh, 2007). Some authors have argued that the post-trip effects of volunteer tourism, that is, creating informed, engaged world citizens, is as important as the on-site assistance that volunteer tourists may or may not have the capacity to offer. Indeed, the potential for transformative experiences, often associated with concepts of authenticity and even intimacy within the experience (e.g. Conran, 2011), is a prevailing theme in volunteer tourism.

Tomazos and Butler (2010: 373) clearly illustrate the changing self-concept, as their respondents felt that 'their life story was no longer matching who they were'. Another way that this has been conceptualized within the volunteer tourism literature is the hero's journey – this is a theme presented by Zurick (1995: 133) who describes some tourists as seeking a 'mythic quest ... the departure, crossing the threshold into the imagined but still unknown places; the initiation, personal or spiritual anointments that require ritual and supernatural assistance; the return, the conquest of self, the completed quest, and the coming of the hero'. Other researchers, such as Hudson and Inkson (2006) and Tomazos and Butler (2010), have similarly adapted the 'myth of the hero's adventure' to study episodic and long-term overseas volunteering and its impacts on the individual.

Using the well established 'hero's journey' framework (Campbell, 1949), we can identify eight (sometimes 12 or 17) stages that will allow the hero to achieve her or his full potential: (i) the seperation, leaving the ordinary world; (ii) a call to adventure; (iii) crossing the threshold; (iv) confronting new challenges; (v) facing the abyss; (vi) new learning and personal transformation through the experience; (vii) atonement; and finally (viii), returning to the hero's familiar world. Both Hudson and Inkson (2006) and Tomazos and Butler (2010) note these elements in their qualitative studies of overseas volunteers, and provide a clear framework for discussing the transformative potential of travelling and volunteering.

The transformative potential of volunteer tourism reappears as a number of similar constructs in the literature. Mustonen (2005), for example, considers volunteer tourism as a postmodern pilgrimage, whilst Zahra and McIntosh (2007) talk of the cathartic effects of volunteer tourism, and both Coghlan and Gooch (2011) and Coghlan and Weiler (2018) adopt a transformative learning lens to study how the volunteer tourism experience affects its participants. Broadly speaking, all these studies search for the sector's (potential) ability to influence values and attitudes regarding material possession, the value of human beings, relationships and, finally, a sense of justice and individual responsibility towards society and the environment. In a sense, it is tipping the scales not towards altruism, but away from the ego, by breaking the ego's grip on the self.

Of the numerous guiding frameworks of personal transformation (including the hero's journey), it is perhaps Mezirow's (2003: 8) definition that is my preferred. He describes it as 'learning that transforms problematic frames of reference to make them more inclusive, discriminating, reflective, open, and emotionally able to change'. In this sense, it can be applied to any changes in behaviours or attitudes that were not part of your previous self-concept – to sitting quietly by a grieving friend without feeling the need to soothe or cover up their emotions, to calling out a sexist remark by one colleague towards another, to welcoming the banning of plastic bags at supermarkets or a multitude of other seemingly mundane behaviours and attitudes that can actually reflect much deeper processes.

These are all relatively small changes that may be difficult to capture in studies of transformational changes but that reflect the 'dynamic, uniquely individualised process of expanding consciousness' described by Holland-Wade (1998: 713). She reminds us that individuals who undergo transformation will develop a *critical awareness* of the old and new self, leading to a *new self-definition*. As personal transformation is explored in more detail, the notions of an individualized process and a new self-definition emerge as important parameters in the identification and study of transformation in (volunteer) tourists. Panskepp and Northoff (2009)

Volunteer tourism

name this 'metaprocessing', a process of self-reflection that engages the self-related processes of the brain and changes internal working models.

Kottler (2002), meanwhile, describes a process for transformative tourism experience where participants find themselves in an unfamiliar environment, confronting new stimuli, are lost or face adversity, but survive in a way that makes them more resilient. They develop new relationships or magnify levels of intimacy in a current relationship, they gain a new perspective on life and work through the eyes of someone from a different culture and, finally, have their core beliefs shaken to the point that they make major changes upon their return.

Indeed, Leigh (2006) describes issues of re-assimilation into the home environment post-volunteer tourism experience; reverse culture shock may occur amongst volunteer tourists who experienced a sense of connection to their host community and developed new ideas, perceptions and values that align more closely with the host community than their own community. Lee and Woosnam (2010: 1187), conversely, confine their parameters of personal transformation to individuals who 'achieve internal coherence and appropriate relationships with the host community', noting that the participant's identity has been 'modified from one rooted in being a voluntourist from another culture to one that encompasses a greater interculturalness'.

Failings in the experience

A decade on from its responsible tourism 'poster child' status, the more recent research on volunteer tourism often points to its failure to live up to its promises. Notwithstanding the number of studies that are critical of its impacts on host communities, two studies emphatically deny volunteer tourism's transformative potential. Zavitz and Butz (2011: 413) propose five 'transformative failures' at an organic farm in Costa Rica, namely:

i   the hierarchical binary between Northern subject and Southern object on which discourses of international volunteering depend;
ii short-term volunteering's reliance on a tourism infrastructure;
iii the farm's specific characteristics as a volunteering project;
iv the short duration of participants' volunteering stint; and
v   the behavioural outcomes of volunteers' consequent disillusionment with their experience over the course of the trip.

Meanwhile, Blackman and Benson (2010) use the theories of social exchange and psychological contracts to explore the issue of disillusionment that impedes personal positive change in their study of volunteer tourism. Other situations of disillusionment were noted when volunteer tourists felt that the context did not allow them to contribute as much as they would like (e.g. Palacios, 2010; Zavitz & Butz, 2011) or, alternatively, when they felt that their experience did not offer enough fun or opportunities for sight-seeing and other aspects related to the tourism side of volunteer tourism. Again, these issues point to the role ambiguity that arises from the dual nature of volunteer tourism, and has raised a number of concerns that volunteer tourism is actually deepening entrenched 'us' and 'them' stereotypes (Taplin, Dredge & Scherrer, 2014).

Several authors have highlighted that volunteer tourism faces numerous challenges as a sector. Many third-sector organizations are having to make compromises in the area of money *versus* mission, whilst volunteer tourism providers must also face the economic realities of 'doing business', whether they operate within the non-profit or the for-profit business space (Coghlan & Noakes, 2012). Indeed, as far back as 2008, before the rhetoric on volunteer tourism shifted dramatically, Lyons and Wearing (2008) argued that as NGOs began to develop partnerships with corporate entities, they ran the risk of losing sight of their core activity of supporting local communities at all costs instead becoming engaged in the process of commodification of the volunteer tourism experience. Moreover, as volunteer tourism faces increasing competitiveness and complexity through a mixed-market approach and cross-sectoral partnerships, so does the number, scope and diversity of stakeholders to whom they must answer, including donors, clients, staff, funding agencies, volunteers and even mainstream tourists in the voluntourism 'lite' sector.

In addition to increasing the complexity of stakeholder management and accountability, some experts argue that this type of revenue model is the one least directly related to mission performance and is one, therefore, that risks pulling the organization off course and diverting valuable management resources away from activities related to the organization's core mission (Dees, 1998). This is the type of argument that leads back to utterances such as *'I've paid to observe lions, not map roads!'* (Cousins et al., 2009) discussed in the section above on volunteer roles. In addition, the non-profit's multiple roles may also make it more difficult to determine how effectively they are performing their social missions, as the social value outcomes (already less tangible and quantifiable than those of for-profit organizations) of their commercial activity may not be readily apparent to the general public. According to Morris, Webb and Franklin (2011), the ultimate risk may be an inability, or reduced ability, to achieve the social or environmental purpose that the organization set out to achieve.

More recently, a number of authors have considered these issues from a systematic perspective. For example, Burrai and Hannam (2018) focus on five main issues:

i   volunteer tourism's relationship to the neoliberal paradigm, using market-based economics as a solution to global structural issues that promote social inequality.

ii   the focus on the individual as a 'hero' with both the ability and the agency to fix social inequality him or herself and without the need to critically assess and challenge the broader political, economic and social structures that continue to promote inequality and poverty.

iii   the inherent power relations between volunteers and recipients – where care and compassion are no longer social values, but have become commodified and sold as part of one's personal brand.

iv   an extension of the neo-colonial agenda, a notion that is supported by the Eurocentric market-base for volunteer tourism as a sector.

v   the weakened power of regulation when social justice mandates are moved from a macro or societal level to micro-levels of agencies, companies and tourists.

Others, such as Banki and Schonell (2018), argue that volunteer tourism reflects the myriad of development problems found in other, similar sectors. Among such problems they list the fungibility of aid, corruption, representation, worker narratives and temporality. They argue for the implementation of a contract norm between volunteers and their local partners, where 'reciprocity and transparency might practically serve as a corrective to voluntourism's most entrenched problems' (Banki & Schonell, 2018: 1475).

Similar calls for greater accountability for this sector have been made by a range of tourism academics including Barbieri, Santos and Katsube (2012), Fee and Mdee (2011),

Volunteer tourism

Taplin et al. (2014) and Rattan (2015). These authors advocate developing codes of conduct and sectors guidelines, such as those promoted by Comhlámh, the Irish development organization, by The Year Out Group, an association of UK gap year organizations, by Tourism Concern, a former UK-based charity who campaigned on tourism issues, and by Fairtrade Volunteering, an independent group of volunteer tourism organizations, as well as the 'International Voluntourism Guidelines for Commercial Tour Operators' by The International Ecotourism Society (TIES).

These guides and codes of conduct are primarily concerned with how projects are set-up, their social and economic benefits to local communities and the level of support, preparation and debriefing given to volunteers. Their aim is to raise the performance and positive outcomes of volunteer tourism organizations and to increase transparency for stakeholders (local community, funding agencies, tourists and so forth). However, Taplin et al. (2014) do raise concerns that the power differential and dependency relationship between hosts and funders makes the former wary of seeming critical of the latter, thereby skewing evaluation reports.

These guidelines could also allow potential volunteer tourists to carefully consider their choice of sending organization, the impact of their actions and the broader philosophy of combining travel with volunteering. In this regards, McGehee (2014) draws attention to the role that technology now plays in volunteer tourism, particularly with regard to information sharing about the sector, while Smith and Font (2014) warn that current e-marketing contains a lot of greenwashing, is overpositioning and communicating responsibility inconsistently, and requires greater regulation.

One recent development has been the addition of volunteer tourism to the sharing economy platform Airbnb, under their 'experiences' listings. This raises the question of whether the issues associated with volunteer tourism, described above, will intersect with the issues, both positive and negative, associated with Airbnb (Acquier, Daudigeos and Pinkse, 2017; Guttentag, 2015). Certainly, the Airbnb platform will allow for greater market penetration for many small volunteer-based organizations that previously did not have access to volunteer tourism; nevertheless, this development also calls into question the ongoing regulation of this sector.

Many argue, however, that existing guidelines do little to address the broader concerns raised by Burrai and Hannam (2018), Brondo (2015) and others of a commodified 'helper's high' under a neoliberal, neo-colonial agenda. A much more nuanced approach to evaluating the impacts and practices of volunteer tourism has been called for, and Taplin et al. (2014) argue for a 'context first approach' to do just this. They identify five contextual areas that should be considered in this process:

i   The phenomenon and problem, i.e. the issue that the project is trying to address;
ii   The nature of the intervention, i.e. the programme itself;
iii   The broader environment, i.e. the market drivers and stakeholders;
iv   The evaluation context, i.e. the parameters of the actual evaluation; and
v   The decision-making context, i.e. who makes evaluation decisions and how.

In addition, they recommend focusing on the four dimensions of volunteer tourism: the stakeholders, the organizations, the markets and the programmes. Each dimension can vary considerably within the sector, and will influence the context, as identified above. The result is that Taplin et al. (2014) do not offer a suggested evaluation process, but instead refer the readers to a suite of approaches such as empowerment evaluation (Fetterman, 1994,

Fetterman, Kaftarin, Kaftarian & Wandersman, 1996), participatory evaluation (Cousins & Whitmore, 1998), values-engaged evaluation (Greene, 2005, 2012) and evaluation for social justice (Mertens, 2012).

An ethical perspective

While Taplin et al. (2014) remind us that much of our research focus has been on the tourists themselves, with too little attention being given to other stakeholders, the types of evaluation proposed would seem to be useful for a social justice agenda that surely must focus as much on the privileged elite. Thus, Hammersley (2014: 858) asks us to re-cast volunteer tourists as 'facilitators rather than implementors and knowledge conveners rather than knowledge providers'. She reminds us that volunteer tourists are in a position of listener, learner and guest.

The transformative learning agenda advocated by a number of volunteer tourism researchers (and which contributes to the bias towards the volunteer tourist) is arguably a form of social justice in itself (Brondo, 2015). Transformative learning includes themes of shifts or deepening of perspective, feelings and values with regard to what, how and why we perceive, think, feel and act in certain ways, all of which can be difficult to identify and even more difficult to quantify.

These are the types of shifts that are required to solve some of the macro-level, systems-based issue that are highlighted through volunteer tourism. As a result, Coghlan and Gooch (2011) and Hammersley (2014), among others, call for a more structured educational approach to volunteer tourism that includes ongoing critical reflection and debriefing. There is evidence that this approach can lead to longer-term social justice outcomes; for example, Bailey and Russel's (2012) study suggests that volunteer tourists tended to have higher levels of civic engagement, civic attitude, openness, compassion, cognitive drive and reflectivity.

From a tourism perspective (in contrast to a development perspective), an explicit transformative learning agenda would sit within Macbeth's (2005) call for a sixth tourism platform in tourism studies, an ethics platform, which will specifically interrogate the morality of tourism-related actions at all levels. One interesting concept is put forward by Hartman, Paris and Blache-Cohen (2014) through their Fairtrade Learning programme specifically designed for volunteer tourism. Here, they balance community outcomes with volunteer learning, explicitly recognizing the dual purposes of volunteer tourism. Theirs is a useful approach for identifying core principles and accompanying standards across both supply-side stakeholders and student-centred learning.

How widely any of these initiatives will be adopted and by whom – again both within the supply chain of volunteer tourism itself and by volunteer tourists as a market – remains to be seen. Even if these do find an engaging, motivated champion to embed them into the sector's practices, studies of how to teach ethical mindedness (of the type that nurtures pro-social and pro-environmental change) warns of issues so called 'moral muteness'. Moral muteness occurs when people fail to voice moral concerns regarding issues where they hold moral convictions, and is in fact quite common in Western societies (Bird, 2015). Indeed, even when volunteer tourism is successful in addressing issues of social justice, neo-colonialism, power imbalances and so forth, on a person-to-person level there may still be a reluctance to openly discuss and promote value-laden issues, especially once the volunteer tourist has returned to their home environment.

It may be that, in addition to the great tools proposed above – the codes, certifications, guides, evaluation programmes, Fair Trade learning programmes and transformative learning

Volunteer tourism

frameworks, all designed to lift the practice of volunteer tourism and promote its desired social justice outcomes - we need to go one step further and provide volunteer tourists with the tools to voice their new-found values once they return home. Programmes do exist that are designed to do just this; Gentile's (2010) Giving Voice to Values is one example, where she lists seven 'pillars' that will support us in becoming better at voicing our ethical concerns. While Gentile's methods may or may not be suited to the volunteer tourism sector, they do provide a set of tools that can illustrate the scale of work required to overcome an ingrained aversion to speaking up on moral issues in a public or professional sphere.

In conclusion, the volunteer tourism experience is fraught with ambiguity and contradictions – how to reconcile its commercial nature with its original intent is on an ongoing challenge with no solution presenting itself as yet. Indeed, any effort to leverage the benefits of a market-based approach to environmental and social issues within a host community lead back to the very problems of neoliberal and neocolonial critiques of the sector. The dual nature of the sector requires a dual solution, focussing on both maximizing the positive outcomes for host communities, and creating opportunities for participants to engage with some of the macro-level drivers that shape our world. It is a tall order for a niche sector, and one that seems unlikely to be solved by any one solution.

References

Acquier, A., Daudigeos, T. and Pinkse, J. (2017) Promises and paradoxes of the sharing economy: An organizing framework. *Technological Forecasting and Social Change*, 125, 1–10.

Allison, P., Stott, T., Felter, J. and Beames, S. (2011) Overseas youth expeditions. In M. Berry and C. Hodgson (Eds.), *Adventure Education: An Introduction*. Abingdon: Routledge, pp. 187–205.

Bailey, A. and Russel, K. (2010) Predictors of interpersonal growth in volunteer tourism: A latent curve approach. *Leisure Sciences*, 32(4), 352–368.

Bailey, A. and Russel, K. (2012) Volunteer tourism: Powerful programs or predisposed participants? *Journal of Hospitality and Tourism Management*, 19, 123–132.

Banki, S. and Schonell, R. (2018) Voluntourism and the contract corrective. *Third World Quarterly*, 39(8), 1475–1490.

Barbieri, C., Santos, C. A. and Katsube, Y. (2012) Volunteer tourism: On-the-ground observations from Rwanda. *Tourism Management*, 33(3), 509–516.

Bird, F. (2015) Moral muteness. *Wiley Encyclopedia of Management*, 1–4.

Blackman, D. and Benson, A. (2010) The role of the psychological contract in managing research volunteer tourism. *Journal of Travel and Tourism Marketing*, 27, 221–235.

Brondo, K. V. (2015) The spectacle of saving: Conservation voluntourism and the new neoliberal economy on Utila, Honduras. *Journal of Sustainable Tourism*, 23(10), 1405–1425.

Buckley, R. (2010) *Conservation Tourism*. Wallingford: CABI.

Burrai, E. and Hannam, K. (2018) Challenging the responsibility of 'responsible volunteer tourism'. *Journal of Policy Research in Tourism, Leisure and Events*, 10(1), 90–95.

Callanan, M. and Thomas, S. (2005) Volunteer tourism. In M. Noveli (Ed.), *Niche Tourism.: Contemporary Issues, Trends and Cases*. Oxford. Butterworth-Heinemann, pp. 183–200.

Campbell, J. (1949) *The Hero with a Thousand Faces*. Princeton: Princeton University Press.

Cipolle, S. B. (2010) *Service-learning and Social Justice: Engaging Students in Social Change*. Lanham: Rowman & Littlefield Publishers.

Coghlan, A. (2015) Prosocial behaviour in volunteer tourism. *Annals of Tourism Research*, 55, 46–60.

Coghlan, A. and Fennel, D. (2009) Myth or substance: An examination of altruism as the basis of volunteer tourism. *Annals of Leisure Research*, 12(3–4), 377–402.

Coghlan, A. and Gooch, M. (2011) Applying a transformative learning framework to volunteer tourism. *Journal of Sustainable Tourism*, 19(2), 713–728.

Coghlan, A. and Noakes, S. (2012) Towards an understanding of the drivers of commercialization in the volunteer tourism sector. *Tourism Recreation Research*, 37(2), 123–131.

Coghlan, A. and Weiler, B. (2018) Examining transformative processes in volunteer tourism. *Current Issues in Tourism*, 21(5), 567–582.

Conran, M. (2011) They really love me! Intimacy in volunteer tourism. *Annals of Tourism Research*, 38(4), 1454–1473.

Cousins, J. A., Evan, J. and Sadler, J. (2009) Selling conservation? Scientific legitimacy and the commodification of conservation tourism. *Ecology and Society*, 14(1), 32–49.

Cousins, J. B. and Whitmore, E. (1998) Framing participatory evaluation. *New Directions for Evaluation*, Special Issue: Understanding and Practising Participatory Evaluation, 80, 5–23. Available at: https://onlinelibrary.wiley.com/doi/epdf/10.1002/ev.1114

Dees, J. G. (1998) Enterprising nonprofits. *Harvard Business Review*, 76, 55–67.

Fee, L. and Mdee, A. (2011) How does it make a difference? Towards 'accreditation' of the development impact of volunteer tourism. In A. M. Benson (Ed.), *Volunteer Tourism: Theory Framework to Practical Applications*. New York: Routledge, pp. 223–239.

Fennell, D. A. (2006) *Tourism Ethics*. Clevedon: Channel View Publications.

Fetterman, D. M. (1994) Empowerment evaluation. *Evaluation Practice*, 15(1), 1–15.

Fetterman, D. M., Kaftarin, S. J., Kaftarian, S. J. and Wandersman, A. (1996) *Empowerment Evaluation: Knowledge and Tools for Self-assessment and Accountability*. Thousand Oaks: Sage Publications

Gentile, M. C. (2010) *Giving Voice to Values: How to Speak Your Mind When You Know What' Right*. New Haven: Yale University Press.

Greene, J. (2005) A value-engaged approach for evaluating the Bunche-Da Vinci Learning Academy. *New Directions in Evaluation*, 106, 27–45.

Greene, J. (2012) Values-engaged evaluation. My M&E. Retrieved from http://www.mymande. org/index.php?q=content/values-engaged-evaluation.

Guttentag, D. A. (2009) The possible negative impacts of volunteer tourism. *International Journal of Tourism Research*, 11(6), 537–551.

Guttentag, D. A. (2015) Airbnb: Disruptive innovation and the rise of an informal tourism accommodation sector. *Current Issues in Tourism*, 18(12), 1192–1217.

Hammersley, L. A. (2014) Volunteer tourism: Building effective relationships of understanding. *Journal of Sustainable Tourism*, 22(6), 855–873.

Hartman, E., Paris, C. M. and Blache-Cohen, B. (2014) Fair Trade Learning: Ethical standards for community-engaged international volunteer tourism. *Tourism and Hospitality Research*, 14(1–2), 108–116.

Holden, A. (2009) The environment-tourism nexus: Influence of market ethics. *Annals of Tourism Research*, 36(3), 373–389.

Holland-Wade, G. (1998) A concept of analysis of personal transformation. *Journal of Advanced Nursing*, 28(4), 713–719.

Hudson, S. and Inkson, K. (2006) Volunteer overseas development workers: The hero's adventure and personal transformation. *Career Development International*, 11(4), 304–320.

Keese, J. (2011) The geography of volunteer tourism: Place matters. *Tourism Geographies*, 13(2), 257–279.

Kontogeorgopoulos, N., Churyen, A. and Duangsaeng, V. (2015) Homestay tourism and the commercialization of the rural home in Thailand. *Asia Pacific Journal of Tourism Research*, 20(1), 29–50.

Kottler, J. (2002) Transformative travel: International counselling in action. *International Journal for the Advancement of Counselling*, 24, 207–210.

Lee, Y. J. and Woosnam, K. M. (2010) Voluntourist transformation and the theory of integrative cross-cultural adaptation. *Annals of Tourism Research*, 37, 1181–1189.

Leigh, D. (2006) Third cultured volunteer tourists and the process of re-assimilation into home environments. *Australian Journal on Volunteering*, 11(2), 59–67.

Lyons, K. (2003) Ambiguities in volunteer tourism: A case study of Australians participating in a J-1 visitor exchange program. *Tourism Recreation Research*, 28(3), 5–13.

Lyons, K., Hanley, J., Wearing, S. and Neil, J. (2011) Gap year volunteer tourism: Myths of global citizenship? *Annals of Tourism Research*, 39(1), 361–378.

Lyons, K. and Wearing, S. (2008) All for a good cause? The blurred boundaries between volunteering and tourism. In K. Lyons and S. Wearing (Eds.), *Journeys of Discovery in Volunteer Tourism*. Wallingford: CABI, pp. 147–154.

Malone, S., McCabe, S. and Smith, A. P. (2014) The role of hedonism in ethical tourism. *Annals of Tourism Research*, 44, 241–254.

Marsh, H., Richards, G. and Barnes, J. (1986) Multidimensional self-concepts: The effect of participation in an Outward Bound Program. *Journal of Personality and Social Psychology*, 50(1), 195.

MacBeth, J. (2005) Towards an ethics platform for tourism. *Annals of Tourism Research*, 32(4), 962–984.

McGehee, N. (2014) Volunteer tourism: evolution, issues and futures. *Journal of Sustainable Tourism*, 22(6), 847–854.

Volunteer tourism

McGehee, N. and Santos, C. A. (2005) Social change, discourse and volunteer tourism. *Annals of Tourism Research*, 32(3), 760–779.

Mertens, D. M. (2012) Evaluation for social justice. My M&E. Retrieved from http://mymande.org/index.php?q=content/evaluation-social-justice.

Mezirow, J. (2003) Transformative learning as discourse. *Journal of Transformative Education*, 1(1), 58–63.

Morris, M., Webb, J. and Franklin, R. (2011) Understanding the manifestation of entrepreneurial orientation in nonprofit context. *Entrepreneurship Theory and Practice*, 35(5), 1042–2587.

Mossaz, A. and Coghlan, A. (2017) The role of travel agents' ethical concerns when brokering information in the marketing and sale of sustainable tourism. *Journal of Sustainable Tourism*, 25(7), 989–1006.

Mura, P. (2015) Perceptions of authenticity in a Malaysian homestay: A narrative analysis. *Tourism Management*, 51, 225–233.

Mustonen, P. (2005) Volunteer tourism: Postmodern pilgrimage? *Journal of Tourism and Cultural Change*, 3(3), 160–177.

Mustonen, P. (2007) Volunteer tourism – altruism or mere tourism? *Anatolia: An International Journal of Tourism and Hospitality Research*, 18(1), 97–115.

Okazaki, E. (2008) A community-based tourism model: Its conception and use. *Journal of Sustainable Tourism*, 16(5), 511–529.

Outward Bound (2019) Outward Bound: Outcomes. Available at: https://www.outwardbound.org/about-outward-bound/philosophy/outcomes/ (Accessed 13 November 2019).

Palacios, C. M. (2010) Volunteer tourism, development and education in a post-colonial world: Conceiving global connections between aid. *Journal of Sustainable Tourism*, 18(7), 861–878.

Panskepp, J. and Northoff, G. (2009) The trans-species core SELF: The emergence of active cultural and neuro-ecological agents through self-related processing within subcortical-cortical midline networks. *Consciousness & Cognition*, 18(1), 193–215.

Rattan, J. K. (2015) Is certification the answer to creating a more sustainable volunteer tourism sector? *Worldwide Hospitality and Tourism Themes*, 7(2), 107–126.

Scheinfeld, D., Rochlen, A. and Russell, M. (2017) The impact of outward bound programming on psychosocial functioning for male military veterans. *Psychology of Men & Masculinity*, 18(4), 400–408.

Sharpley, R. (2012) Responsible tourism: Whose responsibility? In A. Holden and D. Fennel (Eds.), *Handbook of Tourism & the Environment*. Abingdon: Routledge, pp. 382–391.

Sharpley, R. (2018) Responsible volunteer tourism: tautology or oxymoron? A comment on Burrai and Hannam. *Journal of Policy Research in Tourism, Leisure and Events*, 10(1), 96–100.

Smith, V. and Font, X (2014) Volunteer tourism, greenwashing and understanding responsible marketing using market signalling theory. *Journal of Sustainable Tourism*, 22(6), 942–963.

Taplin, J., Dredge, D. and Scherrer, P. (2014) Monitoring and evaluating volunteer tourism: A review and analytical framework. *Journal Sustainable Tourism*, 22(6), 874–897.

Tomazos, K. and Butler, R. (2010) The volunteer tourist as 'hero'. *Current Issues in Tourism*, 13(4), 363–380.

Walsh, V. and Golins, G. (1976) *The Exploration of the Outward Bound Process*. Research Report, Denver: Colorado Outward Bound School

Wang, Y. (2007) Customized authenticity begins at home. *Annals of Tourism Research* 34(3), 789–804.

Wang, H. and Zheng, T. (2015) A research of outward bound training for college students' general employability competence. *Journal of Teacher Education*, 1, 17.

Wearing, S. (2001) *Volunteer Tourism: Experiences That Make a Difference*. Wallingford: CABI.

Wearing, S. (2002) Re-centering the self in volunteer tourism. In G. Dann (Ed.), *The Tourist as a Metaphor of the Social World*. Wallingford: CABI, pp. 237–262.

Wheelan, T. (1991) *Nature Tourism: Managing for the Environment*. Washington DC: Island Press.

Wheeller, B. (2005) Ecotourism/ egotourism and development. In C. M. Hall and S. Boyd (Eds.). *Nature-based Tourism in Peripheral Areas: Development or Disaster?* Clevedon: Channel View Publications, 263–272.

Zahra, A. and McIntosh, A. (2007) Volunteer tourism: Evidence of cathartic tourist experiences. *Tourism Recreation Research*, 32(1), 115–119.

Zavitz, K. J. and Butz, D. (2011) Not that alternative: Short-term volunteer tourism at an organic farming project in Costa Rica. *ACME: An International E-Journal for Critical Geographies*, 10(3), 412–441.

Zurick, D. (1995) *Errant Journeys: Adventure Travel in a Modern Age*. Austin: University of Texas Press.

20

FEELIN' GROOVY

Exploring slow(ness) in tourism experience

Julia Fallon

Introduction

Slow tourism is described as a form of tourism that connects with the local, respects ecology and is aware of climate change (Dickenson & Lumsdon, 2010). The term, therefore, carries the weight of awareness of the impacts of tourism, a broader empathy with stakeholders in destination communities and an acknowledgement of differences with regard to the tourist experience. It appears, then, that slow tourism is emblematic of a new phase in the development of tourism, one that demonstrates greater care and concern for seeking fairness in tourism demand and supply. Previously, the evolution of tourism has been described as occurring in three phases, those of first, exploration, second, travel and, finally tourism (Fussell, 1980) – see also Chapter 16 in this volume. Rojek (1993) supports this argument regarding the transformation from travel to tourism by highlighting observations made during 1950s of large, over-excited groups of tourists, implying that they were engaging in some form of frenzied experience. He recognizes, too, changes in perceptions of the tourist since the early days of tourism, with a distinction being made between the 'traveller', alone and seeking focused and meaningful experiences and the grouped, passive 'tourist' being rushed about and organized. Although writing almost 30 years ago, Rojek (1993: 179) recognized a world where 'we are so drenched in signs and meanings that we find it difficult to make judgments and commitments about how we should live and what we should do', a kind of cultural or sensory overload that has continued into the twenty-first century. Driven by similar sentiments, Sawday (2008: 10), reacting to being ruled by the gadgetry he possesses, suggests we should simplify our lives by becoming advocates of the Slow movement, which, he explains, 'was born of a regard for the simple pleasures of life'. He translates this thinking into a holiday experience that avoids flying and (in the case of UK residents) encourages visits to Europe rather than, say, Thailand, taking a train along with a bike to become a 'free spirit' (Sawday, 2008: 17).

Such advice may well resonate with some but not all. Hence, the purpose of this chapter is to explore the concept of slow tourism, drawing on the extant related literature to consider aspects of slowness in the tourist experience. Addressing what slowness means for the holiday-maker may reveal some of the limitations of the concept and the need for greater emphasis on the part of both the tourism sector and consumers for slowness to be more widely embraced. Slow thinking in the context of tourism in particular has been a reaction to a faster, globalized world that is coping with dramatic change, and focuses on the significance of time, slowing down and connecting with place (Dickenson & Lumsdon, 2010). More generally, in recognition of the costs of relentless activity and a disconnection with nature and finite resources, there has also been a shift amongst some communities towards embracing slowness as a basis for enhancing community cohesion and well-being therefore creating change. It might also be argued that, at the time of writing, enforced isolation and, to some extent, opting out of society during a global pandemic has crystallized thinking and is resulting in greater awareness that, as Sawday (2008) suggests, slowness means happiness.

Slowness as happiness

The suggestion that slowness is commensurate with happiness is, of course, far from new in thinking about tourism experience: for example, headlines such as 'Lie back and think of the Caribbean' in travel supplements reflect the long-held view of the need to escape to slow down and relax. Many package holiday promotions have favoured popular seaside destinations in the sunny Mediterranean region (Freitag, 2015) where tourists may lie in the sun all day. Activity only commences when the sun sets – a spectacle that is 'ubiquitous in the visual commerce of travel' (Lippard 1999: 50) – heralding the time for eating, drinking and making-merry that encapsulates the perception of the relaxed summer holiday (Roberts, 2004). The emphasis in advertisements and promotions is on being there rather than getting there, the latter being an aspect of the holiday experience that should be seamless and smoothly experienced as quickly as possible. Such an approach is feasible only with fast access to destinations; this first became affordable to the masses with the introduction of jet aircraft and charter flights in the 1960s.

The holiday dream of a quick escape by aeroplane followed by relaxation in the heat of the sun, all conveniently organized by somebody else (traditionally, the tour operator / travel agent) is aligned with the feeling of being carefree and an associated absence of responsibility. Diski (2006) claims that the 'strangeness of getting somewhere else' has never left her; but, from the supply side perspective of a travel agent selling holidays, one packaged destination is easily switch sold for another. The provision of such a circumscribed world (Urry & Larsen 2011: 8), particularly offered by all-inclusive holidays for all age groups, removes any anxiety and uncertainty about budgeting, allowing the holidaymaker to feel calm relaxed and comfortable (Borsay, 2006) – again, sentiments that are generally associated with slowing down. So, whilst the tourism sector was seeing the profitable benefits of packaging accommodation with transport plus extras for selling holidays on the basis of a relaxing (slower) tourist experience, tourism also became seen as a force for international growth and understanding. More specifically, many countries adopted tourism development on the understanding that it was as an easy win for both job creation and increased income from visitor spend (Sharpley, 2015). Furthermore, where countries were endowed with natural resources ripe for exploitation (Crick, 1996), such as guaranteed sunshine, the rapid development of mass tourism inevitably followed (Roberts, 2004).

Mass tourism, underpinned by increasing time and wealth on the part of tourists, innovations within the travel sector and, more recently, rapid advances in information and communication technology allowing tourists to assume greater control in the construction and booking of holidays (Benckendorff, Xiang & Sheldon, 2019) has rendered international travel relatively easy and painless. Low-cost carriers too have opened up an increasing range of places to visit whilst the affordability of holiday experiences such as cruising (even if this is predominantly in the US market), where product differentiation strategies have encouraged a healthier, older generation to now view cruising as a desirable holiday experience (CLIA 2019; Mintel, 2020a; also, Chapter 29 in this volume). The cruising holiday offer is comprehensive and may include travel to the point of boarding the ship, a specific itinerary for the duration of the trip, many inclusive services – such as substantial quantities of food and drink – and amenities, the cabin of a particular category, plus a range of supplementary services (Gibson, 2006). The extent of such organization for pleasure means that the often long-awaited holiday is carefree... and slow.

Aligned with the sense of relaxation and slowness in non-working time, the appeal of escape from the drudge of the everyday, and being distant from it, is also linked to happiness (Peeters et al., 2019). Possibly associated with times past defined in part by manual labour or unrewarding manufacturing jobs, there is compelling contemporary evidence to suggest that people still see their work as something to escape from, that they are unhappy at work (McKinsey, 2019). This dissatisfaction and unhappiness influences behaviour to the extent that people not only seek just non-working time or free time but that such time that is spent meaningfully (Parkin, 2004). 'Meaningfully' is a tricky concept and may be interpreted individually, yet the significance of the expression 'I need a holiday' is loaded with significance, often inferring that taking time away represents both freedom and escape (Mikkelsen & Cohen, 2015), words that are associated with and generally perceived to be necessary for health and well-being. While these words are being articulated more often in the contemporary era, they are not unusual and such sentiments were in evidence in times past. Elizabeth Grosvenor, for example, writing in 1842 (after giving birth to ten children) expressed the need to get away on her yacht where she 'could drift wherever one wished, see the most outlandish sights and still come "home" every evening to civilization on board ship' (Robinson 2001: 106).

While many of today's tourists may well empathize with privileged travellers of the past who were seeking comforts and familiarity, a more recent phenomenon, common to all ages and linking with Pine and Gilmore's (2011: xvi) belief that 'time is the currency of our experiences' is the sharing widely of experiences using social media. Such sharing is a means of tracking how time is spent and the excitement experienced during that time, with the recording of multiple experiences and the creation of sensations generating self-worth and identity. Capturing images of food eaten, places visited and people seen, for example, not only reveals how tourism time is spent, but is also a means of simultaneously seeking validation and approval from peers (Liu, Norman & Pennington-Gray, 2013). Such popularity in evidencing experiences coincidentally connects with the rather old-fashioned concept of time-thrift and the drive to fill waking hours in purposeful pursuits (Foley, 2017). Evidence of a rather disparaging view on what are seen as delinquency in idle pursuits are found in Chamberlain's (1983) description of an English village (as recently as the 1970s), confirming that the only recreation allowed for women was for the improvement of the community, with purely social possibilities only offered to women in their 60s. This is a perspective that clearly demonstrates a throwback to the notion of 'rational recreation' attributed to an aspiring middle class in the newly formed industrial societies. Striving for self-improvement was also a force in thinking and was often shaped by the paternalist and aspirational influences of large employers, such as in the case of the London North West Railway Company dominating the local population and their behaviours in the town of Crewe (Redfern, 1983).

There is no surprise that both transport and access have understandably been powerful influencers and shapers of the tourism experience. As already noted, speed and the mode of transport are evident in our thinking about the relevance of slowness and the slow experience in tourism. Specifically, improvements in transport and communications reinforce an accepted norm that prevarication is a possible weakness whereas directness and speediness are desirable (Parkin, 2004) especially in our wired and connected world. Oftentimes, key to the tourism experience is maximizing opportunities; hence, time-saving and effortlessness in reaching a holiday destination not only demonstrate the conquering of nature but extend the enjoyment of slow time in the destination. Such technological advances continue, increasing the possibility of travelling ever faster. Most recently, this is illustrated by the 2020 Virgin Hyperloop with its speed of 760 miles per hour (see virginhyperloop.com) potentially exaggerating even further the sense of time–space compression that accompanies rapid travel to a destination. Advances in technology and improving infrastructure inform our collective psyche and remove us from evidence in the past that a journey of seven miles by road could take 14 hours and that water transport in Europe was even slower than road travel because it was affected by ice, drought and floods (Black, 2003). It can be seen how the relative comfort and speed of the railways were readily accepted, leading Byron to describe his Blue Train journey to southern Europe as 'Happiness untrammelled' (Fussell, 1980).

Slowing down and connecting with place

Ruskin described early train travel as dehumanizing (Parkin, 2004) and would be surprised to discover that, nowadays, travelling by train is described as a 'relaxing and unhurried opportunity to enjoy the landscapes and rural peace' (Halsall, 2001: 58); ironically, what was initially relatively 'fast' travel has become a form of slower travel. And, following a growing negative reaction to mass tourism from the 1970s onwards, train travel has become part of what Roberts (2004: 68) describes as 'DIY holidays'. To avoid the busyness and the 'one size fits all' offer of time-saving, packaged holiday products, people are increasingly choosing to be independent and make their own travel arrangements. In these instances, tourists seek to manage their own pace and their own journeys rather than being organized into time–space efficiency. Then affords them the opportunity to experience places with greater freedom and a sense of calm (that is, more slowly), which is now seen as being highly beneficial to the tourist experience. And arguably, walking is the ultimate manifestation of slow travel.

Despite the suggestion that discussing walking as integral to the travel experience may be almost banal (Dickinson & Lumsdon 2010: 124), there is no doubt that walking epitomizes the slow tourism experience and connection to place. Wensley and Slade's (2012) study into everyday walking revealed feelings of well-being, social connectedness, the experiencing of nature and the possibility of challenge. Walking, researchers posit, makes participants feel more alive and illustrates an example of meaningful activity that strongly correlates with feelings of happiness (Argyle, 2001). This is elucidated clearly by Lumsdon (2011) who describes walking for ten days covering 110 miles in the Herefordshire in the UK, sharing his view unfolding 'in the vernacular' (Lumsdon 2011: 1) and capturing insights that could only be achieved by going slowly. Walking now encapsulates what is meant by slowness because of the inevitable connection to places, whether strolling in an urban environment like flaneurs, wandering along and observing public spaces (Wearing, Schweinsberg & Johnson, 2019) or undertaking a challenge such as the Exmoor Perambulation (a 30-mile circular walk organized once a year in the Exmoor National Park in the UK, not only to raise money for charity but also to allow walkers to see ordinarily inaccessible parts of the English countryside).

Walking was a mainstay of the back to the land movement in the 1970s that encouraged a resistance to mechanization and mass production and a return to traditional agricultural skills, avoiding the use of chemicals and adopting more natural, organic approaches. At the time, such thinking was believed by many to be old-fashioned or unwise but more recently has gained traction with the impacts of globalization, increased commodification and homogenization (as well as climate change and global warming). Seeing food in packets bearing little or no relation to the original source (and possibly having been transported from the other side of the world) generated resistance with the notion of food miles being of particular concerns. Perhaps epitomized by what Ritzer (2015) refers to as McDonaldization after the emergence of fast food outlets around the world operating on the premise of 'efficiency, calculability, predictability and control' (cited in Roberts, 2004: 154), homogeneity in mass food production inspired the slow food movement (SFM), which was originally established in 1986 in Italy and which offered an emphatic rejection of enforced rationality and its associated thinking of fastness. The SFM highlights the significance of what is seen as is a post-industrialist approach to environmental stewardship that includes an 'educational exploration' of one's own doorstep (Parrinello, 1993: 86). Slow food, therefore, is food that is locally sourced and follows production techniques that are more labour-intensive and, in so doing recreates, what is traditional and sensual. Slow food production and consumption seeks to reconnect consumers with sources and ingredients to stimulate all their senses by production methods that attend to taste, flavour, texture and smell for both uniqueness and authenticity. There is a hint of romanticism and something of the aesthetic in this approach but, while there is an attempt at achieving authenticity, this approach is categorically not about nostalgia and preservation. Rather, adherents to slow food claim that they have an attachment to the uniqueness of place that is valued by all individuals, both hosts and guests, and that by making that attachment transparent they are also encouraging a far more ethical consumption mindset (Cooper & Hall, 2016).

The philosophy and success of the SFM has informed a broader interpretation of slowness (Yurtseven & Kaya 2011). For instance, the so-called Cittaslow emerged in Italy, subsequently evolving into what has become a global movement for towns with populations of less than 50,000 people to adopt slow principles (see cittaslow.com). The slow approach rejects having large numbers of visitors in a concentrated space, thereby seeking to avoid resultant capacity issues and the stress placed on destinations – problems manifested in what is now referred to as overtourism (Milano, Cheer & Novelli, 2019). Cittaslow members are required to follow very specific guidelines based upon seven pillars. These include: energy and environmental guidance including using energy-efficient public transport; specific infrastructural requirements such as cycle pathways; ensuring the of quality of urban life by designating a range of protocols including green spaces; the use of local products and supporting local cultural events; Cittaslow awareness and training for guaranteeing a good welcome to all guests; and, promoting social cohesion by, for example, providing youth group centres and partnerships and supporting projects in developing countries. More detail is provided in Table 20.1.

These examples have much in common with the discourse on sustainable tourism and, in recognition of the fact that there is a finite supply of resources and an ethical responsibility in valuing the local, are designed to ensure that resources endure into the future. The stated agenda for Cittaslow towns has much in common with the United Nations World Tourism Organization's (UNWTO) 2017 One Planet Sustainable Tourism Programme, which is a set of guidelines that aims to drive sustainable change by 2030. The word 'slow' is not included but with the aims of supporting local development, cultures and products and highlighting fragile environments, such as seas and coastal areas, there are clear connections. The programme also recognizes the need for developing, promoting and scaling up sustainable

Slow(ness) in tourism experience

Table 20.1 Cittaslow membership requirements

Energy and environmental

Air quality management, monitoring and reporting
Policies to maintain the quality of water supplies and ensure pollution free water in rivers and waterways
Drinking water use by residents compared with national averages
Purity of sewage wastewater effluent
Percentage of recyclable waste collected in the town (business and residential)
Industrial and domestic composting management
Energy saving in public buildings and other public systems (e.g. transport)
Public energy production from renewable sources
Household electric energy consumption compared with national averages
Reduction of visual pollution (e.g. signage and advertising clutter) and traffic noise
Reduction of public light pollution (e.g. from street lighting)
Conservation of biodiversity

Infrastructure

Cycle paths connecting public buildings
Length of urban cycle paths as a proportion of urban roads
Cycle parking at transport interchanges
Planning for and provision of ecomobility as an alternative to private cars (e.g. buses on demand)
Town planning to promote safe places and spaces and alternative forms of mobility
Infrastructure and buildings that are accessible to all and cater for the diverse needs of people (e.g. families and pregnant women)
Accessibility to medical services
Sustainable distribution of products to and within town centres
Percentage of residents who commute every day to work in another town

Quality of urban life

Planning for urban resilience
Policies to protect and improve civic centres (street furniture, signs, aerials, etc.)
Creation of public green spaces with productive plants/fruit trees
Life/work balance (company hours, nursery provision, etc.)
Reuse of brown sites and waste areas
Use of ICT in the development of interactive services for residents and visitors
Policies and advice to promote eco-friendly architecture
Cable network (fibre/wireless/broadband)
Monitoring and reduction of pollutants (noise, electrical systems, etc.)
Development of home and flexible working
Promotion of private sustainable urban development
Promotion of public sustainable urban development
Promotion of social infrastructure (free recycling projects, time banks)
Creation of productive green spaces within town
Creation of spaces to sell local products
Protection/improvement of workshops and creation of shopping areas for sustainable products
Percentage of built-up areas in relation to green areas in town

Julia Fallon

Local produce and products

Development of sustainable local agriculture

Plans and programmes to protect and support local, traditional, handmade and artisan goods and produce (e.g. through product certification and heritage initiatives)

Increasing the awareness and value of traditional crafts, techniques and methods

Increasing the value of rural areas (greater accessibility to services for residents, promotion and sale of local produce in towns)

Use of local food, if possible organic, in public procurement (school and hospital meals, etc.)

Educational and promotional programmes to encourage and support the purchase of organic and traditionally produced local food by residents and the hospitality industry

Promoting and increasing the value of local cultural events

Additional hotel capacity (beds/people per year)

Prohibiting the use of GMO in agriculture

Innovative plans for land previously used for agriculture

Optional and additional goal

Hospitality, Cittaslow awareness and training

Good welcome – provision of customer service training for all those providing services to visitors, including signs, infrastructure and hours

Increase the awareness of operators and traders on the value of transparent offers, prices and clear tariffs, avoidance of mis-selling and scam offers

Available of 'slow' events and activities in printed material and on web sites

Supporting health education (healthy eating, lifestyles, battle against obesity, diabetes etc)

Ensuring effective community consultations and involvement in the more important administrative decisions

Regular training and awareness on the Cittaslow themes for local government and town partnership, etc. employees

Awareness and promotion of information on Cittaslow to residents

Foster active associations working in partnership with local government and town partnership employees on the Cittaslow themes

Initiatives to involve local business, organizations and opinion formers in promoting Cittaslow and enhancing the town's performance against the membership goals

Use of the Cittaslow logo on printed material and web sites of the local administration and key stakeholders

---

Social cohesion

Policies and programmes to reduce the discrimination of minority groups

Encouragement of social integration in the housing of all ethnic groups

Promote multicultural integration within society e.g. schools

Policies and interventions to integrate disabled people

Encouragement of affordable, accessible, safe and flexible child care, nursery provision, etc.

Encouragement of employment, volunteering, skills development and other training opportunities for young people

Support of initiatives to reduce the percentage of residents living in poverty

Encouragement of thriving community groups and community-based development

Encourage residents and businesses in town to engage with national and local government to help to inform their decisions

Public housing – investment as a percentage of the local budget

Areas for youth activities and youth centres

Partnerships
Support for Cittaslow campaigns and activities
Collaboration with other organizations promoting local and traditional food
Support for twinning projects and cooperation with developing countries for projects that help their development, including through the Cittaslow philosophy

Source: Adapted from Cittaslow (2020) https://www.cittaslow.org.uk/cittaslow-goals/ (Accessed 27 December 2020).

consumption and production practices that boost the efficient use of natural resources, while producing less waste and address the challenges of climate change and biodiversity.

The Cittaslow philosophy and the One Planet Sustainable Tourism Programme would, therefore, appear to be the antithesis of mass tourism. Moreover, their resulting impact on the tourism product might be criticized for being unrealistic because tourists are generally considered to be more concerned with enjoyment than with environmental concerns (McKercher, 1993; Sharpley, 2006). However, there is evidence of their influence and a change in thinking about mass tourism; for instance, Mintel (2020b) report that 62% of people surveyed wanting their travel companies to support local businesses, local economies and local communities. It is also noted that holidaymakers are seeking more special interest activities and here lies the nub of what is happening with regard to some interpretations of slowness in tourism. That is, there typically exists something of a contradictory message in that holiday-makers should reach a place quickly to then experience slowness in the destination, particularly in local forms of transport. This is very much the case, for example, with the Channel Islands of Alderney and Sark, the former being solely dependent upon air access and the latter is entirely car-free.

There are numerous other examples of slow tourism, often highlighted in newspaper supplements. For instance, Moat (2020) writes about cycling across Europe, her slow pace creating an overwhelming connectedness with the places through which she cycles, which, she claims, encourages her joy in nature. Similarly, Ross (2020) proposes paddle boarding along the Cornish coastline, described as both a form of escapism as well as a time for reflection. Other evidence of slow tourism products can be found in YouTube clips that reveal the possibilities of cycling in attractive natural forest or foraging although in such instances it is sometimes difficult to distinguish such experiences from more organized holidays such as stays at 'inland resorts', such as Centerparcs in the UK.

Such developments in the travel offer have led to the re-examination of whether special activity and mass tourism holiday types are polar opposites. Closer investigation of the sustainability of some tourism experiences has revealed questionable behaviours, especially in the supply of ecotourism that claims to be designed to promote the protection of the environment. The reason for this questioning is that ecotourism is often coupled with adventure tourism, raising concerns about the genuine nature-friendliness of the tours (Wheeller, 1994). Moreover, despite small visitor numbers, the motivations of tourism operators have been further questioned because of their avoidance of partnering with local stakeholders (Robinson, Lück & Smith, 2020). Such revelations have led Wearing, Wearing and McDonald (2012: 37) to call for a slow ecotourism, one that adapts to the pace of the destination and which 'has the potential to establish and sustain links between conservation, the tourism industry, communities and nature'.

Prefixing ecotourism with the word slow is suggesting that slow means taking an holistic approach rather than one that simply addresses sustainability, thereby confirming the view that the word slow brings with it a wide interpretation and nuance (Markwell, Fullagar & Wilson, 2012). Slowness (or a slow tourist experience) it is generally agreed, may be achieved by paying attention to the locality, its sounds, the natural surroundings and weather, noticing insects and birds in a locality, making bread, growing vegetables and connecting with animals and so on (Flynn, 2020). In addressing the other slow pillars of fairness, balance and connectedness, the introduction of rewilding spaces (Watson, 2019) is also gaining momentum because it allows nature to be unrestrained, unorganized and unforced. Letting it just be. How this translates into the travel offer is illustrated in a holiday offered by the UK wildlife watching holiday specialist, Nature Trek, who has introduced a new range of low-impact, no-fly group trips that include ferry, boat and train transport for marine wildlife and birdwatching in Spain. The inclusion in this offer of slower lower impact transport throughout allows a more complete slow experience and differs to many other suggestions of aforementioned slow experiences that are concentrated solely in the destination (Guiver & McGrath, 2016).

A tale of slowness

Local women in Vanuatu in the Pacific Islands described visiting Australian backpackers as 'snail women' because they carried their homes on their backs and walked slowly. This description seems apt for a discussion about slow travel and tourism experience; Linda Hill, as one of a handful of visitors, sees herself as one of these snail women who, after arriving by cargo ship from New Zealand (some 2000 miles away), spent over three months in the Pacific islands and on Vanuatu, walking from village to village asking around for accommodation and fitting in with the local community, sharing their food and following local advice on how to cope during her visit (Hill, 1993). In her account as a single woman alone, she describes the warmth and hospitality of the local women who were curious and cared about her. The limited planning, the enjoyment and discovery as one of few visitors being made so welcome meant that Linda Hill was determined to return. This short account fits with a description of slow travel and tourism (Robinson, Lück & Smith, 2020) reinforcing the belief that at the core of tourism is experience (Laing, Wheeler, Reeves & Frost (2014) and that successful long-lasting memories come from the welcome and interaction with locals and their culture (Chandralal & Valenzuela, 2015; Kim, 2014; Mikkelsen & Cohen, 2015).

Such connections with place and local stakeholders distinguish the slow tourism experience (Conway & Timms, 2010). Linda Hill was fortunate in that she had a considerable amount of time to experience the islands and make a deeper connection (especially in a place without an established tourism infrastructure and where there was an informality in her arrangements). Immersing herself in the life of the island and avoiding rushing from place to place typifies what many advocates of slow tourism describe, with their claims of discovering little-known attractions and being away from the main tourist routes. Such an approach, however, may well justify a view of such slow tourists as elitist (Park, 2014) and separating slow tourism from other forms of travel, such as gap-year experiences, remains challenging. Nevertheless, despite these ambiguities, in early 2020, the Association of British Travel Agents (ABTA) identified slow travel as a clearly identifiable trend. Well-being features high in the British psyche and it is accepted that there will be increased interest in the restorative power of connecting with nature helping the ability to wind down. Consumers have too been influenced by ethical concerns about the environment leading to flight-guilt (Mintel, 2020b) and are considering alternatives. Popular holiday destinations are being encouraged to refresh their offer and to include 'slow travel', which sits well with potential holidaymakers seeking alternatives to flying and choosing ferry transport instead – especially with an increase in routes offered (Mintel, 2020b). Such slower forms of travel may indeed lead to a range of benefits that fit with the UNWTO's sustainability goals, including better connectivity between places that are usually flown over (Massey, 1994). There is no doubt that technological developments encourage time-saving and to reject these appears to be rejecting progress, but at what cost is no longer a question raised only by those on the periphery but one that is central to twenty-first-century concerns.

This chapter has addressed the slow experience incorporating aspects of both slow tourism and slow travel and was informed by Dickenson and Lumsdon's (2010) framework that defines slow tourism as equating to quality time, slowing down to enjoy what is on offer including a quality experience that provides meaning and engagement with ecology and diversity. The discussion here has focused on how the supply of the tourism product reflects what many perceive as slowness on holiday and that equates with a carefree and happy experience. Slow tourism and slowness therefore remain open to question, confirming the view that it is a nuanced and contested concept subject to varying interpretation (McGrath & Sharpley, 2017) Being slow and slowness should not simply be equated with niche tourism activity but incorporated into a much wider sustainable agenda where experiences are memorable (Pizam, 2010) and when idle pursuits are valued.

References

ABTA (2020) *Travel Trends Report*. London: Association of British Travel Agents.

Argyle, M. (2001) *The Psychology of Happiness*, 2nd Edn. London: Routledge.

Benckendorff, P., Xiang, Z. and Sheldon, P. (2019) *Tourism Information Technology*, 3rd Edn. Wllingford: CABI.

Black, J. (2003) *The British Abroad: The Grand Tour in the Eighteenth Century*. Stroud: The History Press.

Borsay, P. (2006) *A History of Leisure: The British Experience since 1500*. Basingstoke: Palgrave Macmillan.

Chamberlain, M. (1983) *Fenwomen: A Portrait of Women in an English Village*. London: Routledge and Kegan Paul.

Chandralal, L. and Valenzuela, F. (2015) Memorable tourism experiences: Scale development. *Contemporary Management Research*, 11(3), 291–309.

Cittaslow (2020) Cittaslow Goals. Available at: https://www.cittaslow.org.uk/cittaslow-goals/ (Accessed 27 December 2020).

CLIA (2019) 2019 Cruise Trends and Industry Outlook. Cruise Lines International Association. Available at: https://cruising.org/news-and-research/-/media/CLIA/Research/CLIA-2019-State-of-the-Industry.pdf (Accessed 5 February 2021).

Conway, D. and Timms, B. (2010) Rebranding alternative tourism in the Caribbean: The case for 'slow tourism'. *Tourism and Hospitality Research*, 10(4), 329–344.

Cooper, C. and Hall, C. M. (2016) *Contemporary Tourism: An International Approach*, 3rd Edn. Oxford: Goodfellow Publishers.

Crick, M. (1996) Representations of international tourism in the social sciences: Sun, sex, sights, savings and servility. *Annual Review of Anthropology*, 18, 307–344.

Dickinson, J. and Lumsdon, L. (2010) *Slow Travel and Tourism*. London: Earthscan.

Diski, J. (2006) *On Trying to Keep Still*. London: Little Brown.

Foley, C. (2017) The art of wasting time: Sociability, friendship, community and holidays. *Leisure Studies*, 36(1), 1–20.

Flynn, S. (2020) Taking the slow lane through life. Presenter Kate Humble reveals how a challenge set last year helped her through recent times. *Waitrose and Partners*. Weekend 24 September.

Freitag, R. (2015) *Update on Market Trends in the Mediterranean*. Available at: https://webunwto.s3-eu-west-1.amazonaws.com/imported_images/42775/1_rolf_freitag_autorizado.pdf (Accessed 20 December 2020).

Fussell, P. (1980) *Abroad: British Literary Traveling Between the Wars*. New York: Oxford University Press.

Gibson, P. (2006) *Cruise Operations Management*. Oxford: Butterworth-Heinemann.

Guiver, J. and McGrath, P. (2016) Slow tourism: Exploring the discourses. *Dos Algarves: A Multi-Disciplinary e-Journal*, 27, 11–34.

Halsall, D. A. (2001) Railway heritage and the tourist gaze: Stroomtram Hoorn-Medemblik. *Journal of Transport Geography*, 9(2), 151–160.

Hill, L. (1993) Adventures of a snail woman in the Pacific Islands. In M. Davies and N. Jansz (Eds.), *Women Travel: Adventures, Advice and Experience*. London: Rough Guides Ltd, pp. 360–369.

Kim, J. H. (2014) The antecedents of memorable tourism experiences: The development of a scale to measure the destination attributes associated with memorable experiences. *Tourism Management*, 44, 34–45.

Laing, J., Wheeler, F., Reeves, K. and Frost, W. (2014) Assessing the experiential value of heritage assets: A case study of a Chinese heritage precinct, Bendigo, Australia. *Tourism Management*, 40,180–192.

Lippard, L. R. (1999) *On the Beaten Track: Tourism, Art and Place*. New York: The New Press.

Liu, I., Norman, W. and Pennington-Gray, L. (2013) A flash of culinary tourism: Understanding the influences of online food photography on people's travel planning process on Flickr. *Tourism Culture and Communication*, 3(1), 5–18.

Lumsdon, L. (2011) *A Guide to Slow Travel in the Marches*. Eardisley: Logaston Press.

Markwell, K., Fullagar, S. and Wilson, E. (2012) Reflecting upon slow travel and tourism experiences. In S. Fullagar, K. Markwell and E. Wilson (Eds.), *Slow Tourism, Experiences and Mobilities*. Bristol: Channel View Publications, pp. 227–233.

McKinsey (2019) Happiness and Work: An Interview with Lord Richard Layard. Available at: https://www.mckinsey.com/featured-insights/leadership/happiness-and-work-an-interview-with-lord-richard-layard (Accessed 31 December 2020).

Massey, D. (1994) *Space, Pace and Gender*. Cambridge: Polity Press.

McGrath, P. and Sharpley, R. (2017) Slow travel and tourism: New concept or new label? In M. Clancy (Ed.), *Slow Tourism, Food and Cities: Pace and the Search for the' Good Life'*. Abingdon: Routledge, pp. 49–62.

McKercher, B. (1993) Some fundamental truths about tourism. *Journal of Sustainable Tourism*, 1(1), 6–16.

Mikkelsen, M. V. and Cohen, S. (2015) Freedom in mundane mobilities: Caravanning in Denmark. *Tourism Geographies*, 17(5), 663–681.

Milano, C., Cheer, J. M. and Novelli, M. (Eds.) (2019) *Overtourism: Excesses, Discontents and Measures in Travel and Tourism*. Wallingford: CABI.

Moat, H. (2020) Take me to the rivers a slow cycle from Rotterdam to Istanbul. *The Guardian* 16 May. Available at: https://www.theguardian.com/travel/2020/may/16/cycle-from-netherlands-to-istanbul-turkey-alongside-river-rhine-danube (Accessed 5 February 2021).

Mintel (2020a) *Holidays to Spain: Inc. Impact of COVID 19*. Market Report. London: Mintel. See https://reports.mintel.com/display/990138/

Mintel (2020b) *The Ethical Traveller*. Market Report, London: Mintel. See https://reports.mintel.com/display/987998/

Parrinello, G. (1993) Motivation and anticipation in post-industrial tourism. *Annals of Tourism Research*, 20(2), 233–249.

Park, H Y. (2014) *Heritage Tourism*. Abingdon: Routledge.

Parkin, W. (2004) Out of time: Fast subjects and slow living. *Time and Society*, 13(2/3), 363–382.

Peeters, P., Higham, J., Cohen, S., Eijgelaar, E. and Gossling, S. (2019) Desirable tourism transport futures. *Journal of Sustainable Tourism*, 27(2), 173–189.

Pine, B. J. and Gilmore, J. H. (2011) *The Experience Economy*. Updated Edition. Boston: Harvard Business Review Press.

Pizam, A. (2010) Creating memorable experiences. *International Journal of Hospitality Management*, 29(3), 343.

Redfern, A. (1983) Crewe: Leisure in a railway town. In J. Walton and J. Walvin (Eds.), *Leisure in Britain 1780–1939*.Manchester: Manchester University Press, pp. 117–135.

Ritzer, G. (2015) *The McDonaldisation of Society*, 8th Edn. Thousand Oaks and London: Sage Publications.

Roberts, K. (2004) *The Leisure Industries*. Basingstoke: Palgrave Macmillan.

Robinson J (2001) *Wayward Women: A Guide to Women Travellers*. Oxford: Oxford University Press.

Robinson, P., Lück, M. and Smith, S. (2020) *Tourism*, 2nd Edn. Wallingford: CABI.

Rojek, C. (1993) *Ways of Escape: Modern Transformations in Leisure and Travel.* Basingstoke: Macmillan Press Ltd.

Ross, E. (2020) The perfect post-lockdown activity: Paddleboarding in Cornwall. *The Guardian,* 21 June. Available at: https://www.theguardian.com/travel/2020/jun/21/the-perfect-post-lockdown-activity-paddleboarding-in-cornwall (Accessed 5 February 2021).

Sawday, A. (2008) with *Go Slow England: Special Local Places to Eat, Stay & Savour* (with Gail McKenzie). Bristol: Alistair Sawday Publishing.

Sharpley, R. (2006) Ecotourism: A consumption perspective. *Journal of Ecotourism,* 5(1+2), 7–22.

Sharpley, R. (2015) Tourism: A vehicle for development? In R. Sharpley and T. Telfer (Eds.), *Tourism and Development: Concepts and Issues,* 2nd Edn. Bristol: Channel View Publications, pp. 3–30.

Urry, J. and Larsen, J. (2011) *The Tourist Gaze 3.0.* London: Sage Publications.

Watson, P. (2019) *Slow Travel: Reconnecting With the World at Your Own Pace.* Richmond: Hardie Grant Books.

Wearing, S., Wearing, M. and McDonald, M. (2012) Slow'n down the town to let nature grow: Ecotourism, social justice and sustainability. In S. Fullagar, K. Markwell and E. Wilson (Eds.), *Slow Tourism: Experiences and Mobilities.* Bristol: Channel View Publications, pp. 36–50.

Wearing, S., Schweinsberg, S. and Johnson, P. (2019) Flâneur or choraster: A review of the travel narrator in the formation of the tourist Experience. *Tourism Analysis,* 24(4), 551–562.

Wensley, R. and Slade, A. (2012) Walking as a meaningful leisure occupation: The implications for occupational therapy. *British Journal of Occupational Therapy,* 75(2), 85–92.

Wheeller, B. (1994) Ecotourism: A ruse by any other name. In C. Cooper and L. Lockwood (Eds.), *Progress in Tourism, Recreation and Hospitality Management* (Vol. 6). Chichester: John Wiley & Sons, pp. 3–11.

Yurtseven, H. D. and Kaya, O. (2011) Slow tourists: A comparative research based on Cittaslow principles. *American International Journal of Contemporary Research,* 1(2), 91–98.

21

ECOTOURIST EXPERIENCE

Myth or reality?

Stephen Schweinsberg and Louise O'Flynn

Introduction

Whilst precise figures are hard to come by, the OECD has estimated that ecotourists collectively account for 7% of all international tourist arrivals (101 million ecotourist arrivals in 2018; see The World Counts, 2020). Throughout 2020, as the COVID-19 pandemic has presented an existential threat to the future of global travel (see Gössling, Scott & Hall, 2020; Sharma & Nicolau, 2020; Uğur & Akbıyık, 2020), ecotourism and other supposedly more 'responsible' forms of travel (see Chiu, Lee & Chen, 2014) are perceived to have grown in importance. National associations, such as Ecotourism Australia (see Cardona, 2020), and members of the academic community (e.g. Cherkaoui, Boukherouk, Lakhal, Aghzar & El Youssfi, 2020) have been searching for ways to reset the economic growth trajectory of the tourism industry whilst avoiding the continued perpetuation of the worst impacts of so-called Overtourism. This has been occurring at the same time that ecotourism operators have been heavily impacted by the COVID-19 pandemic. The loss of ecotourist revenue in areas such as the Democratic Republic of the Congo, Australia and Africa has threatened the financial viability of ongoing conservation programmes (see O' Flynn, Schweinsberg and Wearing, 2021, for a discussion of protected area financing), as well as posing a threat to the health of the Great Apes and other parts of the ecotourism product mix (Greenfield & Muiruri, 2020; Holmes, 2020; Luke, 2020). However, with well-managed community-based ecotourism (see Wearing, McDonald, Schweinsberg, Chatterton & Bainbridge, 2020), the opportunity exists for the sector, as in the case of the Mara Naboisho Conservancy (Naboisho, 2020), to empower local communities and provide them with a 'chance to have a stake in their own societies – often for the first time' (Zurab Pololikashvili, UNWTO Secretary-General, in UNWTO, 2020a).

National parks and other ecotourism destinations have long been recognized as having health benefits for visitors and society at large (James, Christiana & Battista, 2019; Runte, 1997). For example, Wen, Kozak, Yang and Liu (2020) have argued that, as the industry responds to the COVID-1 health pandemic, Chinese tourists might look to participate in nature-based travel activities to 'breathe fresh air, connect with something greater than themselves and rejuvenate after the stress of the outbreak'. However, nature-based tourism and ecotourism are distinct in that the former:

286

DOI: 10.4324/9781003219866-25

Ecotourist experience: myth or reality?

Encompasses all forms of tourism – mass tourism, adventure tourism, low impact tourism, ecotourism – which use natural resources in a wild or undeveloped form – including species, habitat, landscape, scenery and salt and fresh water features. Nature tourism is travel for the purpose of enjoying undeveloped natural areas or wildlife.

(Goodwin, 1995 cited in Fennell, 2013: 328)

Ecotourism in contrast is:

Low impact nature tourism, which contributes to the maintenance of species and habitats either directly through a contribution to conservation and/ or indirectly by providing revenue to the local community sufficient for local people to value, and therefore protect, their wildlife heritage area as a source of income.

(Goodwin, 1995, cited in Fennell, 2013: 328)

The question of what an ecotourist is looking for by way of experiences in a COVID-19 world is exacerbated by the notion that, even prior to the pandemic, there was an understanding that we are living in an Anthropocene age and that ecotourism must be willing to address some of the inherent contradictions in its existence. As Fletcher (2019) has argued, ecotourism is an essentially capitalist activity and we must think carefully whether we can continue to advocate for its growth (even as a response to COVID-19) whilst accepting that growth will eventually overwhelm the last vestiges of nature that serve as ecotourism's raison d'être. As Fletcher (2019) also notes, ecotourism's growth trajectory is driven by the demands of consumers. It is ecotourists who are at the heart of the present chapter.

The International Ecotourism Society (hereafter IES) defines ecotourism as 'responsible travel to natural areas that conserves the environment, sustains the well-being of the local people, and involves interpretation and education' (IES, 1995/ 2020). Within these broad parameters, a range of scholarly works have attempted to define what is and is not an ecotourist (e.g. Fennell, 2015b; Page & Dowling, 2001; Wearing & Neil, 2009; Wearing & Schweinsberg, 2018; Weaver, 2011). Attempts to define an ecotourist often involve efforts to account for a virtually limitless set of motivations, socio-demographic and other characteristics and to develop an adaptable ecotourist typology. In this chapter, we will argue that such efforts are of limited value, not simply because the ecotourism market is inherently heterogeneous (see Sharpley, 2006) but because the boundaries of 'ecotourism' and the 'ecotourist' evolve temporally to reflect the evolving standards of the society that practises them. Ecotourism, as indeed all tourism, exists as part of a system that is complex and subject to the effects of evolving stakeholder relations and attitudes to the natural, social and economic world (Baggio, 2008).

The ecotourist experience

Moscardo (2009, cited in Moscardo, 2015: 294) has defined a tourist experience as comprising 'a distinct set of events and/ or activities, occurring in a particular location and within a specific time period, outside of the everyday realm, that provide meaning and significance to the tourist's identity and social interactions'. Whilst Fennell (2020) has argued that modern ecotourism and sustainable development dialogues emerged simultaneously from societal debates around eco-development in 1970s and 1980s, Dowling (2013) has observed that earlier antecedents of ecotourism included the journeys of geographers and writers into 'new' areas in the eighteenth century, including the national parks of the United States and Canada (e.g. Yellowstone and Banff), through to African wildlife safaris and Himalayan treks in the mid-twentieth century. The fact that ecotourism has evolved throughout its history on the basis of a changing understanding of society's relationship to nature (see also Hall, Gössling & Scott, 2015) means that it is not possible to generalize with respect to the ecotourist experience. How one frames an ecotourist experience will be particular to one's background, motivations and goals in travelling. As President Theodore Roosevelt once said in relation to his famed camping trip with the environmentalist John Muir in 1903, which helped precipitate the development of the National Parks Service in 1916:

> I trust I need not tell you (Muir), my dear sir, how happy were the days in the Yosemite I owed to you, and how greatly I appreciated them. I shall never forget our three camps; the first in the solemn temple of the great sequoias; the next in the snow storm among the silver firs near the brink of the cliff; and the third on the floor of the Yosemite, in the open valley fronting the stupendous rocky mass of El Capitan with the falls thundering in the distance on either hand.
>
> *(Roosevelt, 1903)*

Or alternatively, as David Newsome[1] observed in relation to a trip to the Hurulu Ecopark and Biosphere Reserve in Sri Lanka:

> A jeep/tourist/permit is required to enter the reserve, and when cleared for entry as many as 30 vehicles depart and enter the park at approximately the same time and then split off along a network of tracks in search of elephants. When elephants are located, there is close approach at sightings and frequently 10–12 vehicles in attendance … During the sightings elephants were clearly disturbed as evidenced by the aggressive behaviour directed towards closest vehicles. In one case an attack on a vehicle was witnessed and the vehicle was damaged. The occupants of the vehicle said they had found the incident very stressful. Also at sightings there was significant engine noise and the smell of exhaust fumes. Some drivers switched off their engines during a sighting; others in close proximity did not. There seemed to be no rules or protocols regarding the viewing of wildlife and certainly no interpretation …
>
> *(Newsome, 2013: 213)*

As the quote from Roosevelt demonstrates, ecotourism offers opportunities for close and often ephemeral experiences with nature and, when integrated with visitor interpretation and wider destination management approaches, there exists the opportunity to develop truly sustainable ecotourism enterprises (see Bramwell & Lane, 1993; Orams, 1996; Pearce & Moscardo, 1998; Staiff, Bushell & Kennedy, 2002; Wearing & Schweinsberg, 2018). Ham (2016) describes three endgames from interpretation programmes: interpretation as teaching, interpretation as provocation and interpretation as entertainment. What this demonstrates is that whilst the ecotourism industry may generally attract people that have a higher level of environmental awareness and concern in comparison with mass tourists (see Lee & Moscardo, 2005), we cannot at the same time forget that as much as ecotourism is said to be about environmental protection and conservation, it is also about pleasure (Fennell, 2018). Perhaps nowhere is this tension between conservation and pleasure more evident than around elephant treks in localities such as Thailand, Botswana and Sri Lanka. Indeed, Duffy and Moore (2010: 738) have argued that such practices have 'extended and deepened neoliberalism [as it relates to ecotourism] by targeting and opening up new frontiers in nature'. Criticized on an animal welfare front and the perceived need for many in the industry to methodically torture the animals in an effort to make them more docile and able to interact with tourists (see Tourism Concern, n.d.), Schweinsberg and Darcy (2022a) have recently argued that local-scale ecotourist transport options represent an under investigated perspective in ecotourism management. However, for all of their negative impacts, who are we to say in a publication such as this that elephant rides should not occur? Tourists are paying good money for an experience, which even Tourism Concern (n.d.) acknowledges are 'intelligent, social and emotional. In many ways it is the equivalent experience to swimming with dolphins'. Certainly, all sentient creatures need to be treated with the same dignity and respect that we ourselves would expect. However, simply stopping the practice of elephant rides has presented its own challenges; for example, what is to be done with captive elephants when there are no more visitors (see Segarra, 2020 for a discussion of captive elephant management during COVID-19)? There is also the added complication that many of those local workers responsible for cruelty to elephants are often migrant workers who themselves are also subject to abuse and overwork by those in positions of authority (Cadigan, 2016).

The IES (2020) has argued that well-managed ecotourism offers travellers opportunities for immersive experiences of nature that can cultivate greater levels of understanding and potentially cultivate a stewardship and leadership mentality (see Schweinsberg, Heizmann, Darcy, Wearing & Djolic, 2018 for a discussion on sustainability leadership). However, as the elephant trek example illustrates, ecotourist's concern for sustainability principles is often a perspective more honoured in the breach than in the observance. Academics and industry cling to the myth of ecotourism as inherently sustainable and good for the environment (see McKercher & Prideaux, 2014), but is this really the reality? Dolnicar, Yanamandram and Juvan (2013) have noted that there is value in the scientific community being able to rationalize what constitutes an ecotourist, as it is only with consensus on this most fundamental of questions that advancements can occur around sustainable ecotourism management. We do not disagree with this assertion, but would also observe that an ecotourist must also be seen in his or her historical context. In the historical case of Theodore Roosevelt/ John Muir, which is referred to later in this chapter, we can see the early emergence of themes that have come to characterize contemporary discussions of ecotourism's sustainability potential. This includes Muir seeing tourism in national parks as not necessarily something to be lauded but rather as a lesser economic evil when seen in relation to cattle grazing and the commercial clear-cutting of native forest (see Hall, 2010, cited in Wearing & Schweinsberg, 2018). We can also see that whilst the principal protagonist/ consumer, the President of the United States, was perhaps not a committed ecotourist when seen through a contemporary lens, it is nonetheless the case that the actions and behaviours of travellers are never one-dimensional. Roosevelt, it may be said, was an ecotourist of his time as well as a hunter. How travellers manage the multiple independent attributes that collectively characterize their identity will go a long way to determining their sustainability potential.

The sustainable ecotourist

Ecotourism, rightly or wrongly, is a form of tourism that is often treated as being synonymous with notions of sustainability (see Blamey, 2001; Butcher, 2005 for competing perspectives on this issue). However, as Sharpley (2020) has demonstrated, in the past 20 years of scholarly commentary on sustainable tourism, there has been a shift in perspective towards de-growth as a mechanism for understanding the boundaries of sustainable tourism growth (see Fletcher, Murray Mas, Blanco-Romero and Blázquez-Salom, 2019 for a discussion of ecotourism de-growth). If such a change in perspective can occur in a few decades, what can we say about our understanding of what does and does not constitute a sustainable ecotourist over the centuries? Tribe and Liburd (2016) situated history as one of a collection of viewpoints from the arts and humanities that help us comprehend tourism as a complex world making phenomenon and practice through which intercultural understandings and expression unfold. Modern ecotourism is, as we have said, a twentieth-century phenomenon with its origins in the alternative tourism movement that emerged alongside global sustainable development discourse. However, as Wearing and Schweinsberg (2018) demonstrated with respect to the trip that Roosevelt made with Muir into what is now Yosemite National Park in 1903, the antecedents of modern ecotourism potentially go back a lot further in time and must be viewed through the particulars of the time in which they occurred. Fletcher (2014), for example, has argued that modern ecotourists are similar to colonial explorers on account of their interest in the act of exploring and the opportunities that are afforded to them for thrill and adventure, often in the footsteps of earlier colonial explorers (see also Holden & Sparrowhawk, 2002; Wearing, van der Duim & Schweinsberg, 2007). The notion of ecotourism as a traveller fantasy (see Fletcher, 2014) is important for the present discussion on account of the insights that it gives into a traveller's motivation; as Urry and Larsen (2011: 3) argue:

> Places are chosen to be gazed upon because there is anticipation, especially through daydreaming and fantasy, of intense pleasures, either on a different scale or involving different senses from those customarily encountered. Such anticipation is constructed and sustained through a variety of non-tourist technologies, such as film, TV, literature, magazines, CDs, DVDs and videos, constructing and reinforcing the gaze.

Roosevelt was said at the time to be very familiar with the writings of Muir, the instigator of his ecotourist experience. In the course of penning an appreciation piece reminiscing after Muir's death, Roosevelt demonstrated that he was not only well-versed in the power of Muir's writings but that he also had knowledge of the work of Muir's contemporary and intellectual sparring partner, Ralph Waldo Emerson (Roosevelt, 1915). Today, the ecotourist experience is similarly brought to the attention of consumers through mechanisms including travel writing, marketing, travel narration and social media (see Cheng, Wong, Wearing & McDonald, 2017; Maier, 2011; Schweinsberg & Darcy, 2022b; Schweinsberg, Wearing, Kuhn & Grabowski, 2013; Wearing, Schweinsberg & Johnson, 2019). With ecotourists being the ultimate recipients of a marketing message, the choices travellers make will have profound implications for the sustainability of the wider ecotourism system. Schweinsberg and Darcy (2022a: 47) have recently argued with respect to what is now a global ecotourism transportation network that whilst we must never deny the negative environmental impacts of different transport forms, we must also recognize that 'the right to free movement and mobility for all is assured under the International Covenant on Civil and Political Rights'. Resolving these two often competing considerations is not easy; it is, however, essential if ecotourism is to live up to the principles of sustainability that it is often seen as being synonymous with. It is a task made all the more complicated if there is apathy amongst ecotourists. Fennell (2015a: 95) refers to such apathy as 'Akrasia'; where a tourist demonstrates a 'deficient capacity to contain or restrain one's desires, broadly conceived; where the anticipation of pleasure overwhelms good judgement'.

Ecotourist experience: myth or reality?

Understanding the lived experience of ecotourists is, therefore, central to our ability to manage the industry. Much as President Roosevelt entered Yosemite in advance of the provision of what we would categorize as modern visitor infrastructure, so too did early ecotourism demand in the 1990s proceed industry and scholarly understanding. As Diamantis (1998: 515) has observed:

> This growth of demand for ecotourism initially ran ahead of the supply of its products, and created a new challenge for tourism researchers and scholars. In particular, the consumer-driven demand for ecotourism created a dis-equilibrium in academic circles. For example, there are now uncertainties and confusions both in terms of the definition of ecotourism and also in the enumeration of its fundamental principles; confusions which in part are derived from a lack of understanding of the behaviour of ecotourists. Indeed, it can be suggested that until the behaviour of ecotourists is fully explored, it will continue to be difficult to clarify the concept of ecotourism.

Wearing and Schweinsberg (2018) argue that President Roosevelt was an ecotourist because, amongst other things, his time with Muir afforded him the opportunity to be educated on the nature of the Californian environment. Many of the sites he visited are now popular with ecotourist travellers today, including the Coast Redwoods (*sequoia sempervirens*) in California's Redwood National Park, which, along with other species including Australia's Mountain Ash (*eucalyptus regnans*), have been identified as being important for biodiversity preservation and tourism-based economic development (see Hall, James and Baird, 2011). With national parks being home to some of the world's most iconic tourism landscapes, the challenge for ecotourism managers becomes how to 'create a link between people and the environment, working to instil realistic expectations in the minds of visitors and managing expectations in light of conservation realities' (Wearing, Schweinsberg & Tower, 2016: 66). What constitutes a realistic expectation will evolve over time; as Fletcher (2015: 338) has argued, 'the practice of ecotourism is informed by a particular ecotourist gaze'. Therefore, it is on the basis of experience, and a writer's characterization of that experience that reality and myths are framed.

McKercher and Prideaux (2014: 17) observe that a myth can be characterized as 'demonstrably false beliefs that are widely held, long standing and never subjected to deep inspection'. Whilst we would never suggest that academics have been hesitant to subject the ecotourist and more generally the tourist to 'deep inspection', we suggest it is the case that arbitrarily characterizing any belief as 'demonstrably false' runs the risk of subjecting the thinking of people from the past to introspection based on the values and attitudes of the present. Was President Roosevelt on that camping trip to Yosemite with the environmentalist John Muir in the early twentieth century indicative of the values and priorities of an ideal ecotourist, which Weaver and Lawton had in their hard/ soft ecotourist typology (see Weaver & Lawton, 2002) in the early twenty-first century? Probably not. However, does it matter? Whether it is an academic typology or conceptual model (e.g. Wang, Weaver, Li & Zhang, 2016) or a historical event, the power of a myth lies in its ability to shape society's future understanding. There will likely never be a definition of an ecotourist that will universally stand the test of time. Rather, what constitutes an 'ideal' ecotourist will evolve in relation to changing societal expectations regarding the role of tourism more broadly in society. History will then tell us whether an earlier understanding will likely have any salience into the future.

Stephen Schweinsberg and Louise O'Flynn

Evolving ecotourist typologies

When Ceballos-Lascurain composed what is widely held to be the first definition of ecotourism –

> ... travelling to relatively undisturbed or uncontaminated natural areas with the specific objective of studying, admiring, and enjoying the scenery and its wild plants and animals, as well as any existing cultural manifestations (both past and present) found in these areas.
>
> *(Ceballos-Lascurain, 1987: 13)*

he suggested that ecotourists possessed 'an awareness and knowledge about the natural environment and cultural aspects, in such a way that will convert him or her into somebody keenly involved in conservation issues' (Caballos-Lascurian, 1991: 25, cied in Diamantis, 1999: 96). This definition made sense in the context of a period of human history where, as Sharpley (2020) notes, tourism scholars were beginning to recognize the worst excesses of mass tourism and proposing an alternative tourism future for the sector (see also Jafari, 2001). Subsequent to this, however, has been the realization that ecotourism, or indeed any form of tourism, must be subject to critical appraisal regarding the degree to which it actually is sustainable, or simply an opportunity for ego-enhancement masquerading under a veneer of environmental concern (Wheeller, 1993). Scholarship focused on the sustainability potential of whale tourism is emblematic of this trend, with questions being posed regarding the degree to which whale watching is necessarily any more sustainable than whale harvesting (see Cunningham, Huijbens & Wearing, 2012; Kessler, Harcourt & Heller, 2013; Orams, 2000, 2001; Wearing, Cunningham, Schweinsberg & Jobberns, 2014). Ecotourists are recognized as being essential for the development of a sustainable whale watching industry, both on account of the need to self-regulate their own behaviour whilst around the whales but also for the benefits they can bring to host regions and societies (Cunningham et al., 2012).

If we return momentarily to the afore-mentioned IES (1995/2020) definition of ecotourism – 'responsible travel to natural areas that conserves the environment, sustains the well-being of local people, and involves education and interpretation' – we are left with a number of questions related to ecotourist consumers. What does it mean for an ecotourist to act responsibly? What should be the relationship between an ecotourist and the environment (in all of its facets)? And in what way should ecotourists relate to the educational messages provided by ecotourism operators and public sector agencies? In their own way, it is these questions that lie at the heart of previous scholarly attempts to develop typologies to rationalize ecotourist motivations and desired experiences. As Fennell (2015) observed in the fourth edition of his often cited work *Ecotourism*, there has been psychographic scholarship aiming to understand the 'values, lifestyles and [the] various interests of [ecotourists as a] ... specific segment of society' (see also Castellanos-Verdugo, Vega-Vázquez, Oviedo-García & Orgaz-Agüera, 2016). There has also been work to understand the level of experience specialization that ecotourists demand, the rationale being that more committed or 'soft' or 'hard' ecotourists will make varying demands on destination managers and the industry to fulfil (Fennell, 2015). Weaver (2011) similarly talked in terms of ecotourists being an emerging market that developed in response to the environmental movement and a growth in societal perspectives around green paradigms, the effect of which was to draw attention to the presence of a spectrum of ecotourists, the more active of whom have connections to other alternative tourist forms, including volunteer tourism (see also Tomazos & Butler, 2009).

Whilst ecotourist typology scholarship is valuable, work to understand the motivations of ecotourists must always be seen in the context of the distinctiveness of the activities and the congruence that exists to accepted theoretical understanding (Page & Dowling, 2001). For example, if we are to understand the motivations of ecotourists in China, we must acknowledge not only the large number of nature reserves in the country and the provision of infrastructure to encourage ecotourism development, but also the different ways that the Chinese conceive the relationship between human beings and nature. As Wen and Ximing (2008: 567) note, 'Westerners tended to claim man and nature are separate, whereas ancient Chinese traditionally conceived of them within a unity'. In recent years, there has been evidence of scholars publishing ecotourism studies on an increasingly diverse set of geographical locations including Tanzania, Fiji, Mexico, Norway, Rwanda, Sri Lanka, South Korea and Belize (Choi, Oh & Chon, 2021; Gundersen, Vistad, Panzacchi, Strand & van Moorter, 2019; Kwan, Eagles & Gebhardt, 2010; Lemelin & Jaramillo-López, 2019; Mach & Vahradian, 2019; Mafi, Pratt & Trupp, 2019; Newsome, 2013; Olearnik & Barwicka, 2019; Sabuhoro, Wright, Munanura, Nyakabwa & Nibigira, 2017). Such work is welcome in the sense that it acknowledges the sector's inherent heterogeneity, whilst also demonstrating a willingness of the academic community to shake off the blinders of ecotourism's historically western focus. At the same time, however, Wight (2001) argues that it is difficult to definitively state what the ecotourist is (and is not) on account of the tendency for studies to focus on markets in particular destinations and avoid wider questions around the values, predispositions and behaviours of global ecotourism cohorts (for an exception, see Nowaczek & Smale, 2010). The complexity of the tourism experience as it relates to ecotourism was demonstrated by Wheeler (2004: 474) who argued that:

> Definitions of 'new' tourism are equally fallible. Just who actually is an ecotourist? Take, for example, a visit to a waterfall. If I go to Kaieteur or Iguazu, I'm an eco-traveller exploring South America. But what if I go to play the tables at Niagara and glance at the Falls on my way to the surrounding casinos: am I an ecotourist then? Does it actually depend on my purpose of visit, or on the predilections of those 'compiling' the figures? And what, then, if my main purpose of visiting South America is as a sex tourist, and the falls are little more than a diversion? Am I still an eco-tourist?

The importance of considering the relationship between theoretical constructs and place-based circumstance was recently demonstrated by Dodds (2019), who argued that experiences develop across a traveller's lifetime. With reference to Butler's destination life cycle model (see Butler, 1980), Dodds (2019: 218) argued that as tourists mature the

> less touristy they will act and the more they will seek out "other" types of experiences or act less like a traditional tourist and more like a local. They also may feel more responsibility toward the destination as they are more familiar and therefore treat it more like their home.

An evolving ecotourist for an evolving time

As the world continues to be impacted by the COVID-19 pandemic, it is perhaps never more important that those responsible for the management of ecotourism destinations consider what it means to be a responsible eco-traveller. Ecotourism attractions like the Gibbon in Cambodia (Esguerra, 2020) are at threat of infection from COVID-19. Conservation programmes to protect mountain gorillas that were previously supported by revenue from ecotourism operations are now under pressure from declining international tourist revenue (Losh, 2020). A survey of 312 African safari tour operators in September 2020 found that 92% (287) of operators had experienced a decrease of over 75% in actual bookings due to the pandemic (Beekwilder, 2020). This was said to be directly impacting the 16 million people employed directly and indirectly in Africa's tourism industry (Equilibrium Research, 2020). The International Union for the Conservation of Nature (IUCN) has also reported on data drawn from protected area managers in 19 countries, which indicated that protected area agencies had been 'significantly affected their ability to perform basic functions, including payment of salaries and protecting endangered species, monitoring illegal wildlife trade and protecting local communities from damages caused by wildlife' (Waithaka, 2020). At the same time, however, ecotourism is held up as being a major part of global tourism's eventual recovery from COVID-19 (e.g. Cardona, 2020). With its historical focus on environmental protection, local economic development and the provision of more personalized recreational opportunities for travellers, ecotourism is connected to the notion of a 'new normal' post COVID-19 (see also Ateljevic, 2020; Brouder et al., 2020; UNWTO, 2020b).

Romagosa (2020) has argued that ecotourism operators, many of whom are small and medium enterprises, are well placed to be part of a sustainable pandemic recovery in that they combine low visitor numbers with high-quality experiences and a destination value–add. To be successful in this regard, however, will require a critical evaluation of how consumer interests have evolved as a result of the pandemic. Fennell (2020) has explored opportunities for the ecotourism sector to develop capabilities in the provision of personalized, interactive real time tours that can be completed remotely by a traveller away from the real attraction in the destination region (e.g. vEcotourism.org and Wildeverse). Whilst some would question whether virtual reality can ever be anything more than a tool for offering opportunities to augment existing ecotourism experiences, the real question for managers will be whether virtual reality can offset funds that have been lost due to the absence of in-person travellers (Refisch, 2020). This immediately raises the question of how price as an independent variable is factored into the framing of a tourist experience. At the time of writing, studies on the effects of COVID-19 on ecotourist's willingness to pay (WTP) have been absent from mainstream tourism journals; WTP has been considered in the context of broader travel intentions (see Sánchez-Cañizares, Cabeza-Ramírez, Muñoz-Fernández & Fuentes-García, 2020). Rivera and Croes (2010) have previously argued that price is an antecedent of quality in the framing of tourist experiences. Questions for researchers will be whether future ecotourists will adjust their expectations of what they are willing to pay for an experience based on either their experiences with lockdown or other social distancing protocols, or whether the existence of COVID-19 has fundamentally changed travellers' expectations of the appropriateness of travel outside of their immediate community or region?

More broadly, however, we would suggest that the tourism industry needs to consider whether ecotourists have unrealistic expectations over what their experience should encompass. Historically, West and Carrier talked in terms of ecotourists crossing the 'line from "culture" into "nature" in pursuit of a romanticised wilderness space' (West & Carrier, 2004, cited in Fletcher, 2014: 151). Higgins-Desbiolles (2020) has argued that if we are to pursue social and ecological justice goals for tourism post COVID-19, we must think carefully as to whether a reset focused on developing a more environmentally responsible sector is enough? Or instead, do we need to reject established historical myths on what ecotourism is and is not and 'redefine and reorient tourism based on the rights and interests of local communities and local peoples' (Higgins-Desbiolles, 2020: 610). In doing so, we must learn from the past

Ecotourist experience: myth or reality?

but also embrace the reality that a tourism destination is a heterogeneous place based construct subject to often competing histories and contemporary priorities between different stakeholder groups (Buckley, 2020; Schweinsberg, Wearing & Darcy, 2012; Schweinsberg, Wearing & Lai, 2020). The central paradox of ecotourism remains how best to merge consumptive nature and how best to reconcile these to equally important conservation outcomes. Drawing on data collected prior to COVID-19, Beall et al. (2020) recently suggested that travellers will choose ecotourist experiences on the basis of both environmental values and ego-enhancement criteria. But, is this acceptable in the new normal? Or do we have to tighten our framing of sustainable ecotourism and only pursue ecotourist experiences that comport to an understanding that the needs of an ecotourist must be secondary to concerns of local people?

Conclusion

Buckley et al. (2019) recently argued that the 'economic value of protected areas from the improved mental health of visitors ... using quality-adjusted life years, a standard measure in health economics, is US$6 trillion per annum'. This staggering sum indicates the importance of the global ecotourism industry, not only to economies and societies in destination regions (e.g. Hakim, Subanti & Tambunan, 2011) but also to societies in tourism generating regions. Within the United States alone, the US National Parks Service (NPS) manages 417 areas covering around 34 million hectares and, in 2017, over 300 million visitors travelled to NPS managed sites and spending approximately US$18.2 billion in local gateway regions (Cullinane Thomas, 201). This spending sustained 306,000 jobs, and contributed US$11.9 billion in employment income, US$20.3 billion in value-add (contribution to gross domestic product), and US$35.8 billion in economic output (Cullinane Thomas, Koontz& Cornachione, 2018). This chapter has been entitled *Ecotourism: Myth or Reality* to draw attention to the fact that in spite of all its economic value, there is still substantial debate in scholarly communities regarding who an ecotourist actually is. Previous studies typically account for consumer variability by presenting newer tourist typologies. However, with the ever-increasing volume of largely case study-based ecotourism scholarship (see Weaver & Lawton, 2007), it is difficult for any theoretical framing to account for all variability in the data. In this chapter, we have deviated from many previous discussions and instead sought to argue that how a society frames the 'ecotourist' will evolve temporally in a manner that reflects evolving societal understanding of sustainability. There is, we have argued, no definition of 'ecotourist' that will ultimately stand the test of time; there is no permanent reality. There are, however, myths that both inspire travellers at the time to partake in similar activities, whilst also providing future travellers with a reference point to allow them to feel part of group of ecotourists, adventurers, that is bigger than themselves.

Note

1 Associate Professor Murdoch University.

References

Ateljevic, I. (2020) Transforming the (tourism) world for good and (re) generating the potential 'new normal'. *Tourism Geographies*, 22(3), 476–475.

Baggio, R. (2008) Symptoms of complexity in a tourism system. *Tourism Analysis*, 13(1), 1–20.

Beall, J. M., Boley, B. B., Landon, A. C. and Woosnam, K. M. (2020) What drives ecotourism: environmental values or symbolic conspicuous consumption? *Journal of Sustainable Tourism*, 1–20. https://doi.org/10.1080/09669582.2020.1825458

Beekwilder, J. (2020) The Impact of the Coronavirus Pandemic on the Safari Industry (September Update). Available at: https://www.safaribookings.com/blog/coronavirus-outbreak

Blamey, R. (2001) Principles of Ecotourism. *The Encyclopaedia of Ecotourism*. Available at: http://www.cabi-publishing.org/pdf/Books/0851993680/0851993680ch1.pdf

Bramwell, B. and Lane, B. (1993) Interpretation and sustainable tourism: The potential and the pitfalls. *Journal of Sustainable Tourism*, 1(2), 71–80.

Brouder, P., Teoh, S., Salazar, N. B., Mostafanezhad, M., Pung, J. M., Lapointe, D., Higgins-Dsepoilles, F., Haywood, M., Hall, C. M. and Clausen, H. B. (2020). Reflections and discussions: tourism matters in the new normal post COVID-19. *Tourism Geographies*, 22(3), 735–746.

Buckley, R. (2020) Pandemic travel restrictions provide a test of net ecological effects of ecotourism and new research opportunities. *Journal of Travel Research*. https://doi.org/10.1177/0047287520947812

Buckley, R., Brough, P., Hague, L., Chauvenet, A., Fleming, C., Roche, E., Sofija, E. and Harris, N. (2019) Economic value of protected areas via visitor mental health. *Nature Communications*, 10(1), 1–10.

Butcher, J. (2005) The moral authority of ecotourism: A critique. *Current Issues in Tourism*, 8(2–3), 114–124.

Butler, R. (1980) The concept of a tourist area cycle of evolution: implications for management of resources. *The Canadian Geographer/Le Géographe Canadien*, 24(1), 5–12.

Cadigan, H. (2016) The Human Cost of Elephant Tourism: Whilst Western activists focus on the animals, their handlers are often treated as expendable. Available at: https://www.theatlantic.com/science/archive/2016/05/elephants-tourism-thailand/483138/

Cardona, L. (2020) Ecotourism Recovery in Times of COVID-19. Available at: https://www.eco-tourism.org.au/news/ecotourism-recovery-in-times-of-covid-19/ (Accessed 1 November 2020).

Castellanos-Verdugo, M., Vega-Vázquez, M., Oviedo-García, M. Á. and Orgaz-Agüera, F. (2016) The relevance of psychological factors in the ecotourist experience satisfaction through ecotourist site perceived value. *Journal of Cleaner Production*, 124, 226–235.

Ceballos-Lascurain, H. (1987) The future of ecotourism. *Mexico Journal*, 1(17), 13–19.

Cheng, M., Wong, I. A., Wearing, S. and McDonald, M. (2017) Ecotourism social media initiatives in China. *Journal of Sustainable Tourism*, 25(3), 416–432.

Cherkaoui, S., Boukherouk, M., Lakhal, T., Aghzar, A. and El Youssfi, L. (2020) *Conservation Amid COVID-19 Pandemic: Ecotourism Collapse Threatens Communities and Wildlife in Morocco*. Paper presented at the E3S Web of Conferences. https://doi.org/10.1051/e3sconf/202018301003

Chiu, Y.-T. H., Lee, W.-I. and Chen, T.-H. (2014) Environmentally responsible behavior in ecotourism: Antecedents and implications. *Tourism Management*, 40, 321–329.

Choi, Y. E., Oh, C.-O. and Chon, J. (2021) Applying the resilience principles for sustainable ecotourism development: A case study of the Nakdong Estuary, South Korea. *Tourism Management*, 83, 104237. https://doi.org/10.1016/j.tourman.2020.104237

Cullinane Thomas, C., Koontz, L. and Cornachione, E. (2018) *2017 National Park Visitor Spending Effects: Economic Contributions to Local Communities, States, and the Nation*. Natural Resource Report NPS/NRSS/EQD/NRR—2018/1616. Fort Collins: National Park Service.

Cunningham, P. A., Huijbens, E. H. and Wearing, S. L. (2012) From whaling to whale watching: Examining sustainability and cultural rhetoric. *Journal of Sustainable Tourism*, 20(1), 143–161.

Diamantis, D. (1998) Consumer behavior and ecotourism products. *Annals of Tourism Research*, 25(2), 515–528.

Diamantis, D. (1999) The concept of ecotourism: Evolution and trends. *Current Issues in Tourism*, 2(2–3), 93–122.

Dodds, R. (2019) The tourist experience life cycle: A perspective article. *Tourism Review*, 75(1), 216–220.

Dolnicar, S., Yanamandram, Y. and Juvan, E. (2013) The history of ecotourism. In R. Ballantyne and J. Packer (Eds.), *International Handbook on Ecotourism*. Cheltenham: Edward Elgar, pp. 95–107.

Dowling, R. (2013) The history of ecotourism. In R. Ballantyne and J. Packer (Eds.), *International Handbook on Ecotourism*. Cheltenham: Edward Elgar, pp. 15–30.

Duffy, R. and Moore, L. (2010) Neoliberalising nature? Elephant-back tourism in Thailand and Botswana. *Antipode*, 42(3), 742–766.

Equilibrium Research (2020) *Making Money Local: Can Protected Areas Deliver Both Economic Benefits and Conservation Objectives?* Montreal: Secretariat of the Convention on Biological Diversity.

Esguerra, A. (2020) Cambodia's Beautiful Gibbons Could Be Vulnerable to COVID-19, Study Warns. Available at: https://www.vice.com/en/article/akzbn5/cambodias-beautiful-gibbons-could-be-vulnerable-to-covid-19-study-warns

Fennell, D. (2013) Ecotourism. In A. Holden and D. Fennell (Eds.), *The Routledge Handbook of Tourism and the Environment*. Abingdon: Routledge, pp. 321–233.

Fennell, D. (2015a) Akrasia and tourism: Why we sometimes act against our better judgement? *Tourism Recreation Research*, 40(1), 95–106.

Fennell, D. (2015b) *Ecotourism*. Abingdon: Routledge.

Fennell, D. (2018) On tourism, pleasure and the summum bonum. *Journal of Ecotourism*, 17(4), 383–400.

Fennell, D. (2020) Technology and the sustainable tourist in the new age of disruption. *Journal of Sustainable Tourism*, 1–7. https://doi.org/10.1080/09669582.2020.1769639

Fletcher, R. (2014) *Romancing the Wild: Cultural Dimensions of Ecotourism*. Durham: Duke University Press.

Fletcher, R. (2015) Nature is a nice place to save but I wouldn't want to live there: Environmental education and the ecotourist gaze. *Environmental Education Research*, 21(3), 338–350.

Fletcher, R. (2019). Ecotourism after nature: Anthropocene tourism as a new capitalist "fix". *Journal of Sustainable Tourism*, 27(4), 522–535.

Fletcher, R., Murray Mas, I., Blanco-Romero, A. and Blázquez-Salom, M. (2019) Tourism and degrowth: An emerging agenda for research and praxis. *Journal of Sustainable Tourism*, 27(12), 1745–1763.

Gössling, S., Scott, D. and Hall, C. M. (2020) Pandemics, tourism and global change: A rapid assessment of COVID-19. *Journal of Sustainable Tourism*, 29(1), 1–20.

Greenfield, P. and Muiruri, P. (2020) Conservation in crisis: ecotourism collapse threatens communities and wildlife. Available at: https://www.theguardian.com/environment/2020/may/05/conservation-in-crisis-covid-19-coronavirus-ecotourism-collapse-threatens-communities-and-wildlife-aoe (Accessed 20 November 2020).

Gundersen, V., Vistad, O. I., Panzacchi, M., Strand, O. and van Moorter, B. (2019) Large-scale segregation of tourists and wild reindeer in three Norwegian national parks: Management implications. *Tourism Management*, 75, 22–33.

Hakim, A. R., Subanti, S. and Tambunan, M. (2011) Economic valuation of nature-based tourism object in Rawapening, Indonesia: An application of travel cost and contingent valuation method. *Journal of Sustainable Development*, 4(2), 91.

Hall, C. M., Gössling, S. and Scott, D. (2015) The evolution of sustainable development and sustainable tourism. In C. M. Hall, S. Gössling and D. Scott (Eds.), *The Routledge Handbook of Tourism and Sustainability*. Abingdon: Routledge, pp. 15–35.

Hall, C. M., James, M. and Baird, T. (2011) Forests and trees as charismatic mega-flora: implications for heritage tourism and conservation. *Journal of Heritage Tourism*, 6(4), 309–323.

Ham, S. (2016) *Interpretation: Making a Difference on Purpose*. Golden, CO: Fulcrum Publishing.

Higgins-Desbiolles, F. (2020) Socialising tourism for social and ecological justice after COVID-19. *Tourism Geographies*, 22(3), 610–623.

Holden, A. and Sparrowhawk, J. (2002) Understanding the motivations of ecotourists: The case of trekkers in Annapurna, Nepal. *International Journal of Tourism Research*, 4(6), 435–446.

Holmes, B. (2020) Why our close encounters with wildlife are so risky for the animals. Available at: https://www.washingtonpost.com/national/health-science/why-close-human-encounters-with-wildlife-are-so-risky-for-the-animals/2018/11/23/f0bcdf2e-e461-11e8-8f5f-a55347f48762_story.html (Accessed 3 Novemebre 2020).

IES (1995/2020) What is Ecotourism? International Ecotourism Society. Available at: https://ecotourism.org/what-is-ecotourism/

IES (2020) Ecotourism – A Path Towards Better Conservation. International Ecotourism Society. Available at: https://ecotourism.org/news/ecotourism-a-path-towards-better-conservation/

Jafari, J. (2001) The scientification of tourism. In V. Smith and M. Brent (Eds.), *Hosts and Guests Revisited: Tourism Issues of the 21st Century*. New York: Cognizant, pp. 28–41.

James, J. J., Christiana, R. W. and Battista, R. A. (2019) A historical and critical analysis of park prescriptions. *Journal of Leisure Research*, 50(4), 311–329.

Kessler, M., Harcourt, R. and Heller, G. (2013) Swimming with whales in Tonga: Sustainable use or threatening process? *Marine Policy*, 39, 314–316.

Kwan, P., Eagles, P. F. and Gebhardt, A. (2010) Ecolodge patrons' characteristics and motivations: A study of Belize. *Journal of Ecotourism*, 9(1), 1–20.

Lee, W. H. and Moscardo, G. (2005) Understanding the impact of ecotourism resort experiences on tourists' environmental attitudes and behavioural intentions. *Journal of Sustainable Tourism*, 13(6), 546–565.

Lemelin, R. H. and Jaramillo-López, P. F. (2019) Orange, black, and a little bit of white is the new shade of conservation: the role of tourism in Monarch Butterfly Conservation in Mexico. *Journal of Ecotourism*, 1–13. https://doi.org/10.1080/14724049.2019.165672

Losh, J. (2020) Conservation in Crisis: Why Covid-19 Could Push Mountain Gorillas Back to the Brink. Available at: https://www.theguardian.com/environment/2020/may/05/conservation-in-crisis-covid-19-could-push-mountain-gorillas-back-to-the-brink-aoe (Accessed 20 October 2020).

Luke, C. (2020) How COVID-19 Threatens to Collapse the Ecotourism Sector. Available at: https://earth.org/covid-19-threatens-ecotourism/ (Accessed 19 October 2020).

Mach, L. and Vahradian, D. (2019) Tourists want to be spooked, not schooled: sustaining indigenous tourism in the Bastimentos Island National Marine Park, Bocas del Toro, Panama. *Journal of Ecotourism*, 1–15. https://doi.org/10.1080/14724049.2019.1585439

Mafi, M., Pratt, S. and Trupp, A. (2019) Determining ecotourism satisfaction attributes–a case study of an ecolodge in Fiji. *Journal of Ecotourism*, 1–23. https://doi.org/10.1080/14724049.2019.1698585

Maier, K. (2011) Hemingway's Eeotourism: Under Kilimanjaro and the ethics of travel. *Interdisciplinary Studies in Literature and Environment*, 18(4), 717–736.

McKercher, B. and Prideaux, B. (2014) Academic myths of tourism. *Annals of Tourism Research*, 46, 16–28.

Moscardo, G. (2015) Stories of people and places: Interpretation, tourism and sustainability. In C. M. Hall, S. Gossling and D. Scott (Eds.), *The Routledge Handbook of Tourism and Dustainability*. Abingdon: Routledge, pp. 294–304.

Naboisho. (2020) Naboisho Overview. Available at: https://naboisho.com/community-2/

Newsome, D. (2013) An ecotourist's recent experience in Sri Lanka. *Journal of Ecotourism*, 12(3), 210–220.

Nowaczek, A. and Smale, B. (2010) Exploring the predisposition of travellers to qualify as ecotourists: the Ecotourist Predisposition Scale. *Journal of Ecotourism*, 9(1), 45–61.

O'Flynn, L., Schweinsberg, S. and Wearing, S. (2021) Financing protected areas: The social and environmental impact bond's role in terrestrial protected area sustainability. *Journal of Park and Recreation Administration*. https://doi.org/10.18666/JPRA-2021-10870

Olearnik, J. and Barwicka, K. (2019) Chumbe Island Coral Park (Tanzania) as a model of an exemplary ecotourism enterprise. *Journal of Ecotourism*, 1–15. https://doi.org/10.1080/14724049.2019.170051

Orams, M. (1996) Using interpretation to manage nature-based tourism. *Journal of Sustainable Tourism*, 4(2), 81–94.

Orams, M. (2000) Tourists getting close to whales, is it what whale-watching is all about? *Tourism Management*, 21(6), 561–569.

Orams, M. (2001) From whale hunting to whale watching in Tonga: A sustainable future? *Journal of Sustainable Tourism*, 9(2), 128–146.

Page, S. J. and Dowling, R. K. (2001) *Ecotourism*. Harlow: Pearson Education Limited.

Pearce, P. L. and Moscardo, G. (1998) *The Role of Interpretation in Influencing Visitor Satisfaction: A Rainforest Case Study*. Paper presented at the CAUTHE 1998: Progress in tourism and hospitality research: Proceedings of the eighth Australian Tourism and Hospitality Research Conference, 11–14 February 1998, Gold Coast, Queensland, Australia.

Refisch, J. (2020) What COVID-19 Means for Ecotourism. Available at: https://www.unenviron-ment.org/news-and-stories/story/what-covid-19-means-ecotourism

Rivera, M. A. and Croes, R. (2010) Ecotourists' loyalty: Will they tell about the destination or will they return? *Journal of Ecotourism*, 9(2), 85–103.

Romagosa, F. (2020) The COVID-19 crisis: Opportunities for sustainable and proximity tourism. *Tourism Geographies*, 22(3), 690–694.

Roosevelt, T. (1903) Letter from Theodore Roosevelt to John Muir. Available at: https://www.theo-dorerooseveltcenter.org/Research/Digital-Library/Record?libID=o184892

Roosevelt, T. (1915). John Muir: An appreciation. *Outlook*, 109, 27–28.

Runte, A. (1997) *National Parks: The American Experience*: Lincoln: University of Nebraska Press.

Sabuhoro, E., Wright, B., Munanura, I. E., Nyakabwa, I. N. and Nibigira, C. (2017) The potential of ecotourism opportunities to generate support for mountain gorilla conservation among local communities neighboring Volcanoes National Park in Rwanda. *Journal of Ecotourism*, 1–17. https://doi.org/10.1080/14724049.2017.1280043

Sánchez-Cañizares, S. M., Cabeza-Ramírez, L. J., Muñoz-Fernández, G. and Fuentes-García, F. J. (2020) Impact of the perceived risk from Covid-19 on intention to travel. *Current Issues in Tourism*, 1–15. https://doi.org/10.1080/13683500.2020.182957

Schweinsberg, S. and Darcy, S. (2022a) Ecotourism and the trouble with transportation. In D. Fennell (Ed.), *The Routledge Handbook of Ecotourism*. Abingdon: Routledge, pp. 37–52

Schweinsberg, S. & Darcy, S. (2022b). Travel narrator. In D. Buhalis (Ed.), *Encyclopaedia of Tourism Management and Marketing*. Cheltenham: Edward Elgar.

Schweinsberg, S., Heizmann, H., Darcy, S., Wearing, S. and Djolic, M. (2018) Establishing academic leadership praxis in sustainable tourism: Lessons from the past and bridges to the future. *Journal of Sustainable Tourism*, 26(9), 1577–1586.

Schweinsberg, S., Wearing, S. and Darcy, S. (2012) Understanding communities' views of nature in rural industry renewal: the transition from forestry to nature-based tourism in Eden, Australia. *Journal of Sustainable Tourism*, 22(2), 195–213.

Schweinsberg, S., Wearing, S., Kuhn, D. and Grabowski, S. (2013) Marketing national parks for sustainable tourism: Bridging the conservation human usage divide through track/ trail based interpretation. *Australasian Parks and Leisure*, (Winter), 42–48.

Schweinsberg, S., Wearing, S. and Lai, P. (2020) Host communities and last chance tourism *Tourism Geographies*. https://doi.org/10.1080/14616688.2019.1708446

Segarra, C. (2020) Myanmar ponders what to do with its out-of-work elephants. Available at: https://news.mongabay.com/2020/07/myanmar-ponders-what-to-do-with-its-out-of-work-elephants/ (Accessed 19 October 2020).

Sharma, A. and Nicolau, J. L. (2020) An open market valuation of the effects of COVID-19 on the travel and tourism industry. *Annals of Tourism Research*. doi: 10.1016/j.annals.2020.102990

Sharpley, R. (2006) Ecotourism: A consumption perspective. *Journal of Ecotourism*, 5(1–2), 7–22.

Sharpley, R. (2020) Tourism, sustainable development and the theoretical divide: 20 years on. *Journal of Sustainable Tourism*, 28(11), 1932–1946.

Staiff, R., Bushell, R. and Kennedy, P. (2002) Interpretation in national parks: Some critical questions. *Journal of Sustainable Tourism*, 10(2), 97–113.

Tomazos, K. and Butler, R. (2009) Volunteer tourism: The new ecotourism? *Anatolia*, 20(1), 196–211.

Tourism Concern (n.d.) Should You Ride an Elephant? Available at: https://www.tourismconcern.org.uk/campaign/should-you-ride-an-elephant/ (Accessed 20 November 2020).

Tribe, J. and Liburd, J. (2016) The tourism knowledge system. *Annals of Tourism Research*, 57, 44–61.

Uğur, N. G. and Akbıyık, A. (2020) Impacts of COVID-19 on global tourism industry: A cross-regional comparison. *Tourism Management Perspectives*, 36, 100744. https://doi.org/10.1016/j.tmp.2020.100744

UNWTO (2020a) Together We Are Stronger. Available at: https://www.unwto.org/management/zurab-pololikashvili (Accessed 20 November 2020).

UNWTO (2020b) Sustainability as the New Normal. A Vision for the Future of Tourism. UN World Tourism Organization. Available at: https://www.unwto.org/covid-19-oneplanet-responsible-recovery

Urry, J. and Larsen, J. (2011) *The Tourist Gaze 3.0*. London: Sage Publications.

Waithaka, J. (2020) The impact of COVID-19 pandemic on Africa's protected areas operations and programmes. Available at: https://www.iucn.org/news/protected-areas/202007/impact-covid-19-pandemic-africas-protected-areas-operations-and-programmes

Wang, X., Weaver, D. B., Li, X. and Zhang, Y. (2016) In Butler (1980) we trust? Typology of citer motivations. *Annals of Tourism Research*, 61, 216–218.

Wearing, S., Cunningham, P., Schweinsberg, S. and Jobberns, C. (2014) Whale watching as ecotourism: How sustainable is it? *Cosmopolitan Civil Societies: An Interdisciplinary Journal*, 6(1), 38–55.

Wearing, S., McDonald, M., Schweinsberg, S., Chatterton, P. and Bainbridge, T. (2020) Exploring tripartite praxis for the REDD+ forest climate change initiative through community based ecotourism. *Journal of Sustainable Tourism*, 28(3), 377–393.

Wearing, S. and Neil, J. (2009) *Ecotourism*, 2nd Edn. Oxford: Butterworth-Heinemann.

Wearing, S. and Schweinsberg, S. (2018) *Ecotourism: Transitioning to the 22nd Century*. Abingdon: Routledge.

Wearing, S., Schweinsberg, S. and Johnson, P. (2019) Flâneur or choraster: A review of the travel narrator in the formation of the tourist experience. *Tourism Analysis*, 24(4), 551–562.

Wearing, S., Schweinsberg, S. and Tower, J. (2016) *The Marketing of National Parks for Sustainable Tourism*. Clevedon: Channel View Publications.

Wearing, S., van der Duim, R. and Schweinsberg, S. (2007) Equitable representation of local porters: Towards a sustainable Nepalese trekking industry. *Matkailututkimus*, 3(1), 72–93.

Weaver, D. (2011) *Ecotourism*, 2nd Edn. Milton: John Wiley.

Weaver, D. and Lawton, L. (2002) Overnight ecotourist market segmentation in the Gold Coast hinterland of Australia. *Journal of Travel Research*, 40(3), 270–280.

Weaver, D. and Lawton, L. (2007) Twenty years on: The state of contemporary ecotourism research. *Tourism Management*, 28(5), 1168–1179.

Wen, J., Kozak, M., Yang, S. and Liu, F. (2020) COVID-19: Potential effects on Chinese citizens' lifestyle and travel. *Tourism Review*.https://doi.org/10.1108/TR-03-2020-0110

Wen, Y. and Ximing, X. (2008) The differences in ecotourism between China and the West. *Current Issues in Tourism*, 11(6), 567–586.

Wheeller, B. (1993) Sustaining the ego. *Journal of Sustainable Tourism*, 1(2), 121–129.

Wheeller, B. (2004) The truth? The hole truth. Everything but the truth. Tourism and knowledge: A septic sceptic's perspective. *Current Issues in Tourism*, 7(6), 467–477.

Wight, P. (2001) Ecotourists: Not a homogenous market segment. In D. Weaver (Ed.), *The Encyclopaedia of Ecotourism*. Wallingford: CABI Publishing, pp. 387–362.

The World Counts (2020) Number of Eco-tourist Arrivals. Available at: https://www.theworldcounts.com/challenges/consumption/transport-and-tourism/eco-tourism-statistics/story

22

IS IT JUST THE MUSIC?

Understanding the atmosphere in festivalgoers' experience at British rock music festivals

Alyssa Brown

Introduction

Music festivals are a staple feature of the British summertime, attracting roughly 3.7 million tourists a year (UK Music, 2016). However, whilst the music festival industry has grown in popularity and attendance over recent years, it has not been without challenges. For example, in the aftermath of the 2007–2008 global financial crisis, in 2012 more than 50 music festivals were cancelled or postponed for a number of reasons (eFestivals, 2018), including low advance ticket sales, the wettest summer for a century (Met Office, 2012) and the 'Olympics effect' manifested in high demand for venues, suppliers and artists (Shaitly, 2012). Nevertheless, despite these difficulties, the UK festival market has since been identified by entertainment organizations as a 'cash cow' (Stewart, 2016) and has continued to thrive, with events increasing in size, frequency, diversity and attendance (Oliver, 2014; Webster & Exchange, 2014).

However, one of the consequences of this 'festival boom' has been the emergence of a saturated market; festivalgoers (or, as referred to in this chapter, festival tourists) are spoiled for choice, bored with seeing the same thing and, subsequently, increasingly searching for alternative memorable festival experiences. At the same time, the price of tickets to UK festivals are soaring as the costs of and demand for artists increase whilst the price of overseas music festival remains competitive. For example, tickets to the popular Benicassim festival in Spain cost £100 less than those for Glastonbury. It is unsurprising, therefore, that many festival tourists are exploring the music festival scene in warmer countries, combining their music festival and annual holiday with the guarantee of better weather, novel experiences and value for money (Serck, 2013). Hence, it is crucial that festival organizers in the UK, facing the combined challenges of a saturated market, the unreliable British weather and international competition, find a way to survive and sustain the Great British Music Festival.

In the context of this challenging environment facing festival organizers, this chapter seeks to examine the experience of festival tourists at music festivals in the UK. More specifically, drawing on research based upon qualitative semi-structured interviews undertaken amongst attendees at a number of British rock music festivals, it explores what is important to the festival tourist in terms of their experience, thereby potentially informing the future

DOI: 10.4324/9781003219866-26

301

development of such festivals. First, however, the chapter provides a conceptual background to music festivals and tourist experiences before going on to briefly introduce the methods underpinning this research. It then presents and discusses the research findings, revealing the significance of the musixscape, socialscape and overall enjoyment to the creation of the festival atmosphere. Finally, the chapter concludes with a call for further research into the festival atmosphere as a fundamental ingredient of the festival tourist experience.

Understanding the (festival) tourist experience

As such a major social and economic phenomenon, it is surprising that although festivals in general have long been considered in the academic literature (see, for example, Crompton & McKay, 1997; Falassi, 1987; Pieper, 1965; Vaughan, 1979), popular music festivals more specifically have enjoyed only limited academic scrutiny. Moreover, given that music festivals in Britain are not only numerous but also enormously diverse in scope, scale, type and, hence, audience, it is particularly surprising that few if any attempts have been made to explore critically festivalgoers / tourists and the experiences they seek. Therefore, as research in the area of festival and event experiences is still 'scarce and fragmented' (de Geus, Richards & Toepoel, 2016: 276), it is necessary to draw on studies from other disciplines that contribute to the conceptualization of experiences in relation to festivals and events.

Defining the tourist experience

Intangible, continuous, personal and subjective in nature (O'Dell, 2007; Quinlan Cutler & Carmichael, 2010), and as a tacit concept (Jennings, 2010), the term 'experience' is complex to define (Getz & Page, 2016). In fact, 'experience' has often been discussed without the benefit of a clear explanation or definition of the term, leaving individuals to understand the concept through their own perceptions and assumptions (Morgan, 2008; Poulsson & Kale, 2004; Scott, 1991). Typically, dictionary definitions identify experiences as the process or instance of encountering, observing or participating in an occurrence (OED, 2016) yet, although practical in nature, such definitions fail to address the different ways in which experiences may be perceived or understood. In contrast, empirical research across a variety of disciplines such as philosophy (Russon, 2010; Smith, 1970), psychology (Csikszentmihalyi, 2014; Larsen, 2007), social anthropology (Csordas, 1994; Selstad, 2007), marketing (Mossberg, 2008; Tynan & McKechnie, 2009) and economics (Andersson, 2007; Pine & Gilmore, 1999) has attempted to conceptualize the phenomenon and more precise definitions have been proposed within specific real-world contexts.

Examining definitions of experience within the tourism literature typically refers to the interaction between tourists and destinations as the site of the experience (Stamboulis & Skayannis, 2003). However, this focus does not allow for a consideration of the more complex and multifarious factors that contribute to the event tourists experience, especially given the enormous variety of types and scales of events and numerous stakeholder perspectives (Getz & Page, 2016; Jackson, 2014; Jennings, 2010). There is also consensus that the tourist experience is different to everyday experiences (Cohen, 1979; Cohen & Avieli, 2004; Graburn, 2001; Vogt, 1976) – that is, the significance of an event or tourism experience lies in its 'extraordinariness' (see Urry & Larsen, 2011). According to Li's (2000) review of tourist experience literature, definitions often refer to the pursuit of authenticity, the act of consumption, a response to 'ordinary' life and multifaceted leisure activities. However, across the varied and diverse definitions of the tourist experience, the only commonality found was the significance or meaning of the 'occurrence' to the individual.

Understanding atmosphere in festivalgoers' experience

More recently, in an attempt to define more specifically the event experience, de Geus et al. (2016: 276) have proposed a conceptual model that defines the event experience as:

> an interaction between an individual and the event environment (both physical and social), modified by the level of engagement or involvement, involving multiple experiential elements and outputs (such as satisfaction, emotions, behaviours, cognition, memories and learning) that can happen at any point in the event journey.

Whilst de Geus et al.'s (2016) definition and proposed model incorporates a wide range of features that have been highlighted in relevant literature, it does not however clarify the relationship between the experiential elements, no doubt reflecting the overall complexity of experiences. At the same time, nor does it consider the role of value or the importance of particular dimensions of experiences to individuals and stakeholder groups. Therefore, to provide a more comprehensive understanding of the festival and event experience, the following section introduces more specifically how the event / festival experience may be conceptualized.

Conceptualizing the festival tourist experience

The exploration of experience by academics in the field of event tourism has primarily developed from a management perspective. Following the works of Pine and Gilmore (1999), conceptualizing events within the 'experience economy' has encouraged practitioners to explore the concept of experiences within the context of enhancing competitive advantage and organizational success. Generally, research suggests that organizations can add value to their offer by providing memorable and transformational experiences. It has become increasingly clear, however, that not all elements of the consumer experience can be controlled by providers (Verhoef et al., 2009). In fact, the influence from other research disciplines has introduced a wider variety of perspectives and conceptualizations of the phenomenon, which, in turn, has emphasized the interpersonal and emotional nature of experiences. Investigating the festival experience can, therefore, be examined from a variety of perspectives that are divided into six key conceptual approaches:

i Process (the event journey, the duration of the experience, how the experience is consumed)
ii Content (context-specific attributes of the event experience, nature of the activity and intensity, what one experiences)
iii Personal response (cognitive, affective, conative, sensory and emotional responses)
iv Meaning and value (how the experience is interpreted)
v Influencers (motivations and expectations)
vi Outcomes (satisfaction and consumer behaviour).
(Adapted from de Geus et al., 2016; Jackson, 2014; Ritchie & Hudson, 2009)

For the purpose of this chapter, examining what is important in the festival tourist's experience at British rock music festivals focuses primarily on 'content'. The content of an event / festival experience relates to what someone may experience during that event or festival. From an objective and practical perspective, the festival experience consists of a combination of elements that occur within the event's environment, including physical organization, event design and programming of activities, place, entertainment, products, services and comfort amenities (O'Dell, 2007). However, there are also many external and intangible elements that can be consumed, such as online and technological aspects (Hudson & Hudson, 2013; Sundbo & Darmer, 2008); interpersonal interaction, relationships, communitas and other social aspects (O'Dell, 2007; Rihova, Buhalis, Moital & Gouthro, 2013); culture (Andrews & Leopold, 2013; Picard & Robinson, 2006); identity (Connell & Gibson, 2003); the concept of flow (Csikszentmihalyi, 1990); the liminoid and 'out of the ordinary' (de Geus et al., 2016; Turner, 1979); ritual and rites of passage (Turner, 1982); intensity and immersion (Dowd et al., 2004); and learning and transformation (Karlsen, 2007).

Such is the diversity and complexity of the contexts, dimensions and variety of both tangible and intangible content that to consider them all in this chapter would be difficult, if not an impossible task. This is especially so given that the event or festival experience journey involves a number of phases or stages, from first encountering the event through word of mouth or promotional materials, through the booking process and preparing for the event, travelling to and arriving at the event, to the event itself and then post-event interactions through digital media communication, reliving or extending the experience. Furthermore, the multiple and subjective perspectives of what is experienced at an event adds further complications to understanding the concept. Therefore, owing to this complexity, the research discussed in this chapter is limited to and focuses on only what is most important to festival tourists in their experience of a British rock music festival. That is, it does not consider any pre- or post- festival experiences but, rather, on the experience of the festival itself to elicit a deeper analysis of the core event experience.

Investigating the festival atmosphere

As explained above, the aim of the research discussed in this chapter is to explore what is important to festival tourists in their experience at British rock music festivals. Hence, a qualitative approach was adopted to 'tease out some of the more subterranean beliefs and motivations' (Stewart, Smith & Nicholson, 2003: 214). As part of a larger and more comprehensive study (for example, Brown & Sharpley, 2019), a total of 43 semi-structured interviews were conducted on-site with 124 festival attendees at three British rock festivals. These festivals were selected through convenience sampling as access and permission were granted to conduct the research on site. Interview participants were also selected on a convenience basis and were primarily approached away from any main stages so that dialogue could be heard and recorded. Interviews were transcribed verbatim and thematically coded using qualitative data analysis software 'NVIVO'.

The respondents were generally asked to discuss various aspects of their entire music festival experience and, specifically, the most important aspects of the festival experience. Whilst areas from their entire festival experience were discussed, this chapter only incorporates the peri-festival experience; that is, what was most important to the festival tourists whilst they are physically at the festival.

From the interviews, the most popular identified feature of the festival experience was the festival atmosphere. It was most commonly referred to as a motivating attribute for attendance, and the most important aspect of the overall experience. To understand more fully the notion of festival atmosphere, respondents were also asked to define what they considered the atmosphere to be, and why it was most important. Not surprisingly, perhaps, they referred to the atmosphere by identifying a number of features that encompassed a combination of experiential elements. In other words, the festival atmosphere was perceived to be the over-arching term that was used to explain multiple and inter-related festival experience

Understanding atmosphere in festivalgoers' experience

attributes: as one festivalgoer said, 'It's just everything about the festival'. Nevertheless, three primary themes were identified in defining the festival atmosphere; music, social aspects and enjoyment. These core elements were also identified as individually important attributes of the festival experience. Within each area, more specific features were revealed during the interviews, which are now considered in more detail.

Musixscape

Unsurprisingly, music was referred to frequently as one of the most important aspects of the overall festival experience and a key attribute of the festival atmosphere. Music-related features of the festival experience and atmosphere include: the type (artists, genre and line-up) of music; the quality of the performance; physical and sensory responses to music; variety, discovery and exploration of music; and sharing and engaging in music experiences. To capture all of these music-related aspects of the festival atmosphere, this research refers to them collectively as the musixscape.

The respondents often identified strong associations between the 'type' of music and the festival atmosphere:

It's just everyone getting along and having fun and the same interests music wise.

I will buy the ticket on the strength of one band just because I know the atmosphere will be good.

The performance was also identified as a key element in building the festival atmosphere, with references to sound quality, stage presence, 'feeling' the music, and engagement and involvement with the artists:

What you don't get anywhere else is that the music really comes through the ground and up through you, it's so exhilarating.

Some of the bands really get everyone involved and that really makes a difference, its important - the show that they put on.

I was never a big fan of Slipknot, it was always a bit too much for me but after seeing them and their stage presence... when you put the album on it's just you and them, but when they are live you've got the atmosphere, everything and everyone there doing the show and it just makes it so much better!

The findings revealed that the type and quality of music at rock festivals had a strong influence on the perceived atmosphere and enjoyment in the festival tourists' experience. However, this was not limited to the bands and artists that they were familiar with, as the variety and discovery of new music was also identified as an important attribute of the experience:

The variety and having the different stages is obviously important.
I like to discover new music, that makes me excited and happy.

Unsurprisingly, as the core activity at the festival, the importance of music in the festival tourist experience is supported in the literature (for example, Childress & Crompton, 1997; Lee, Lee & Choi, 2011). Music has a positive impact on festival attendees' senses and also their involvement with the festival. However, whilst variety and exploration of new music is important to the festival tourist experience, it was not identified directly as a part of the festival atmosphere. Rather, the enjoyment, excitement and fun that was generated from exploring and discovering new music was attributed to creating the festival atmosphere.

Another important music-related attribute of the festival atmosphere was sharing the music experience with others:

> It's great to see other people enjoying it. That's as much entertainment, seeing other people enjoy the bands.

Co-creation and sharing experiences with others has been found in both tourism and event literature to have a critical impact on engagement and future consumer behaviour (Crompton, 2003; Morgan, 2008; Rihova et al., 2013; Son & Lee, 2011). However, this research also found that this influences the festival atmosphere, and is of critical importance to festival tourists' experiences within the context of British rock music festivals.

Generally, festivalgoers acknowledged that music was an important aspect of the festival experience: 'Obviously the music is key because you wouldn't go if you didn't like the music'. At the same time, however, the respondents all indicated that music was only a part of the experience.

> I go to a lot of gigs …but a festival, it's totally different. You are going for the experience. People go for the music because the music is the main part because that's what makes the festival, but I don't believe it's as important.
>
> Because you say, 'oh look they are playing - let's go and see them; are you coming?' And it starts like that, but once you get here, the bands aren't as important.
>
> It's the whole experience really, the music only plays a small part.

This concurs with research conducted by Anderton (2011), Morgan (2008) and Pegg and Patterson (2010) in that festival tourists have multiple and varied motivations to attend that influence their overall experience. Thus, the following section examines another important and contributing attribute of the festival atmosphere; the social dimension.

Socialscape

In defining the festival atmosphere, the respondents often mentioned a variety of social features of the festival experience, including spending time with friends and family; meeting new people; sharing interests with other festival attendees; friendliness and camaraderie; and feeling a sense of community and belonging. These aspects of the experience were also identified as individually important attributes of the festival experience and are defined in this research as the socialscape of the festival.

Spending quality time with friends or family was identified by all festivalgoers as an important attribute of the festival experience and contributed to building the festival atmosphere.

> I think the actual core of it is definitely your mates.

In fact, many respondents revealed that they believed this to be more important than the music.

> A lot of it is to do with who you go with, the bands are second priority. I think who you are with is the first priority because everyone likes the same kind of music, that's why you're at this particular festival.

Understanding atmosphere in festivalgoers' experience

Many respondents also identified that meeting new people and making friends contributed to the festival atmosphere, and/or occurred as a result of the atmosphere:

You don't normally talk to random people, but you do here.

The festival atmosphere is a unique environment, it's a lot more open socially to talk to completely random strangers. We feel more comfortable to talk to anyone.

It's a positive atmosphere where you make some good friends.

The opportunities to meet new people and make friends was acknowledged to be a result of shared mindsets, interests, values and hobbies that were typical amongst other festival tourists who had preferences for and interests in similar music genres:

Most people come in a group, so if you didn't you would want to feel that you have something in common so that you could make new friends. You always go back to your tent at like 1 a.m. smashed with a bunch of new friends, so it is important.

It's about meeting new people where everyone is so like-minded, they all like the same things so it's good to be surrounded by people like that.

I have seen about 50 Deadpool T-shirts and I like Deadpool, so I'm in good company because they like what I like. See you find people into the same music as you but there are also into the same other things as you.

This reflects and concurs with previous research by Anderton (2011), Brennan and Webster (2010) and Gelder and Robinson (2009), in which reference is made to the importance of 'similar mindsets' and the 'likeminded' nature of the collective festivalgoer community, particularly at rock and metal festivals. Sharing commonalities with other festival tourists was also identified as contributing to the sense of community and belonging at a rock music festival:

Rock festivals are always very friendly, there is always a community atmosphere.

There is quite a big community here, everybody is friendly, and anybody will talk to anybody.

I guess it's like a collective community to come together and enjoy something with other people and share an experience with a large community.

There is a collective mindset.

Thus, the sense of community at rock festivals develops from the shared interests and mindsets of those attending the festivals. In fact, some respondents felt as though they had shared similar previous experiences, such as being bullied or feeling marginalized, and that that they were somehow different to 'the norm' in society. Indeed, many expressed that they felt accepted within the festival community, and that they did not feel like the 'odd one out':

But I like rock festivals because I want to be surrounded by people like me.

There's an underdog type of element that goes on...we are all f★★★ing misfits aren't we...I want to say persecution but not persecution... just like everyone knows where everyone else has come from so everyone has the same understanding, there is no real discrimination like everybody gets on regardless of what happens.

Fantastic people that are like us that don't look at us because we like metal and have tattoos and piercings. Everybody is friendly, and people will help you no matter what.

The atmosphere is when you don't feel like the odd one out.

This reflects the research conducted by Gorman-Murray (2009) and Stone (2009), who report on festivals bringing people together and promoting a sense of communitas (Finkel, 2010). This was aided by the caring and friendly nature of festival tourists. Various stories were told about how they help each other out, such as putting tents up, offering toilet rolls, finding lost wallets and rescuing those in distress:

> We are more tolerant and understanding of the world. We are passionate about lots of things, and people's well-being is one of them. We all want to go out, we want to have fun and enjoy ourselves and we want to help those who can't.
> What you tend to find us festivalgoers are definitely more open-minded as people, we are not really racist or prejudiced in any way shape or form, and we are kind of a bit more civil.

Friendliness and camaraderie amongst festival attendees was also associated with establishing trust and feeling safe at the festival, contributing to the festival atmosphere:

> You get along with everyone, there is no bother, you don't have to worry about anyone trying to pick a fight with you.
> Everybody looks after everybody else.
> Last year I seen some guy drop his wallet and another guy picked it up and went running to give it back. That pretty much sums up the community here.

The friendliness and camaraderie at festivals is confirmed in the literature by Stone (2009) and Turner (1982), whilst Esu and Arrey's (2009) research demonstrate the importance of feeling safe and secure in the festival experience. Sharing things in common with other festival tourists, and the feeling of safety and security that was associated with the festival experience, was important to the overall experience and formed the festival atmosphere.

Another aspect of the socialscape was how important it was for festival tourists to share the experience with others, whether that be their friends, family, strangers or the festival community as a whole:

> It's about being in the same crowd, enjoying the same experience, watching the same bands together.

Consistent with previous studies by Larson (2009), Rihova et al. (2013) and Van Winkle and Bueddefeld (2016), these results demonstrate the importance of shared experiences and co-creation in the festival experience. However, the respondents often suggested that the atmosphere at rock festivals was different than at other music festivals:

> There is no kind of snobbery around, it's not like you don't belong here or whatever everyone is just really welcoming and embracing and I don't know if you necessarily get that in other festivals.
> Late this morning we saw someone going out for a run all kitted up and no one blinked an eye. If that person had gone to V Festival they would be getting looked at and stared down at, it's just here no one cares, everyone is here for the same reason.
> I think you tend to find it is more 'family orientated' as in us rockers are a family.
> I've been to Leeds Festival and I quite like it, it is good, but it didn't feel quite the same because there was a bigger mix of different people that weren't like me. I just didn't

Understanding atmosphere in festivalgoers' experience

have anything in common with them, I guess. It was a bit more isolated, particularly in the arena watching the bands. It wasn't like I was enjoying it with everybody else, I just felt like I was on my own, I just didn't feel like I connected with other people.

From the results, it can be suggested that the atmosphere is experienced differently by rock music festival tourists. However, more research is required to determine whether the festival atmosphere is constructed of the same experiential features at all music festivals, or if this is experienced differently at other festivals. What is clear in this research, however, is the importance of the socialscape to the festival experience and its role in creating the festival atmosphere. That is, the research revealed that it is important for festival tourists to spend time with their friends and family, to meet new people and make friends, to feel part of the festival community through shared interests and to bond with others at the festival. Much of this, however, cannot be managed or controlled by festival organizers; it is co-created between those attending festivals. Thus, festival organizers are able to only support and assist in facilitating these opportunities within the festival environment. Whilst the role of the socialscape and musixscape in the festival atmosphere has been explored, there is also a third dimension: enjoyment.

Enjoyment

Besides the music and social elements of the festival experience, respondents discussed the importance of enjoyment and fun at the festival. They referred to 'good times', the 'buzz', 'being happy', 'relaxed' and 'chilled' when describing the festival atmosphere and, again, these were also identified as critical components of the overall experience. The sense of happiness and enjoyment at the festival was associated by respondents with the sense of freedom that the festival provided:

It's an element of freedom, where you are just enclosed but also surrounded by like-minded people. I think it's the whole thing that the rules are a bit more relaxed at the festival as well isn't it.

You can be yourself and be happy and chilled.

The atmosphere is relaxed, a bit more natural, I think even the people are more laid back. It's not rules, rules, rules, you can have fun and enjoy yourself.

The freedom associated with the festival environment and atmosphere enabled festival tourists to feel as though they could invert their behaviour compared with the everyday. This confirms previous research regarding festive behaviour and the liminality of festival spaces (Anderton, 2011; Pielichaty, 2015). The respondents went on to explain how they behaved differently at festivals.

When you're camping at a festival it is a real let go of all the baggage. There is a real freedom about it that you can only get in that type of environment that is key to relaxing and having a good time.

I think there is a standard mentality when you look at music festivals where you wouldn't act the way you act at a festival if you are just down the pub with your mates. For me for instance, I get completely off the rails and I know I shouldn't act that way in normal society, where a festival seems to give you a bit more leeway than normal but you are aware of it, you are aware that you have a bit more of a social give than when you're at the pub.

Alyssa Brown

Whilst respondents admitted that they behaved differently at the festival, they also associated this with being 'more themselves', as though everyday life limited their authentic self, whilst the festival enabled them to enjoy themselves more. Therefore, it is suggested, in line with Kim and Jamal (2007) and Szmigin et al.'s (2017) research, that music festivals provide a liminal space wherein festival-goers feel free and can express their identity in a safe place that reflects their interests.

> Everyone here is relaxed and promotes a relaxed and comfortable atmosphere – you're comfortable to be yourselves and speak your mind.

The fun and enjoyment felt at the festival was also discussed with reference to stories about previous experiences that were compared with circuses, pantomimes and surreal acts of the unexpected:

> For some reason at the UK festivals, it is about how stupid you are. There is always some idiot a hundred yards away that's done something dumber, and then you go another hundred yards and [it's worse].
> Mankini knees was my favourite last year! There was this guy in massive biker boots with massive great big hair wearing a Mankini.
> We saw someone walking around yesterday with no shoes on, he was f★★★ing w★★★ered in the mud and the rain with all of his stuff off, and it was ten in the morning.

Witnessing unusual behaviour at the festival is, therefore, another form of entertainment that provides feelings of fun and enjoyment. When respondents discussed the importance of enjoyment and freedom at the festival, it was always associated with the music or social elements. In other words, it is the combination of music and people that creates enjoyment and fun at the festival.

> Mine is the atmosphere of, like, you know that everybody is enjoying themselves and having a good time, you can be with your little bubble and you're enjoying it, and you know other people are in a little bubble of their own and enjoying it, then you do get the crossover of people talking to each other like they overheard someone say something and they just join in the conversation without anybody getting angry.
> I like the atmosphere, it's more of a party environment rather than everyone just in a big field getting trashed, it's more of people getting together and enjoying music together, there is more of a community feel.

Therefore, this research suggests that co-creation involves immersing in and engaging with the festival atmosphere through the musixscape, socialscape and enjoyment. What festival tourists value most during the festival experience can therefore be summarized as in Figure 22.1 below. This visual representation demonstrates the overlapping values and the relationship between the experiential attributes that occur or are felt during the festival. At the same time, the three main components that are valued by festival tourists are also what creates the festival atmosphere. Therefore, from this research, it is evident that most important to the festival tourist is the festival atmosphere, which comprises the musixscape (music-related experiential aspects of the festival), socialscape (social-related experiential aspects of the festival) and enjoyment.

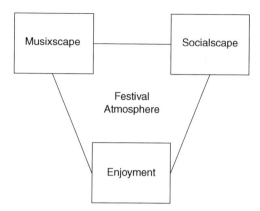

Figure 22.1 The festival atmosphere

Conclusions

This chapter has explored what is most important to festival tourists in their experience of British rock festivals. The results revealed that of most value is the festival atmosphere, which comprises three main components: the musixscape, the socialscape and enjoyment. More specifically, through qualitative interviews with festival tourists, the findings suggest that the relationship between music and social networks at the festival creates enjoyable experiences, which feeds into the festival atmosphere. Whilst the festival atmosphere has been recognized in previous festival literature, it has not been sufficiently explored to understand its value in the festival tourist experience, not least in the context of British rock music festivals. Therefore, this research in this chapter makes an important contribution to the extant literature.

Whilst some of the aspects of the festival atmosphere can be managed by festival organizers, this research demonstrates that there are also many experiential attributes that are not always under the control of festival organizers, such as who festival tourists share their experience with, and how they bond with others. Therefore, opportunities to market or promote such attributes may be limited, or more challenging to advertise. However, managers may consider how the atmosphere can be used to promote and stimulate preferred consumer behaviour.

Owing to the complex nature of the festival experience, the discussion and research in this chapter is limited to conceptualizing the festival atmosphere as the most important experiential dimension at British rock music festivals, and only examines the core or peri-experience phase of the festival tourist journey. In other words, it has not examined the other important attributes of the festival experience, nor the wider experience journey that occurs before or after the festival. Thus, it is suggested that further research is undertaken to explore other aspects of the festival tourist experience, such as pre- and post- experiences, especially acknowledging the growing influence of online digital media on festival tourist experiences.

The findings have also indicated that festival atmospheres may be perceived differently at different types of music festivals and, thus, it is suggested that future research should examine the atmosphere at other festivals of different sizes, locations and music genres. Owing to the importance of the festival atmosphere to the festivalgoer experience at British rock music festivals, further analysis of the influence of this experiential dimension on motivation and consumer behaviour may also provide critical knowledge for festival organizers to strategically improve and manage the festival experience.

Alyssa Brown

References

Andersson, T.D. (2007) The tourist in the experience economy. *Scandinavian Journal of Hospitality and Tourism*, 7(1), 46–58.

Anderton, C. (2011) Music festival sponsorship: between commerce and carnival. *Arts Marketing: An International Journal*, 1(2), 145–158.

Andrews, H. and Leopold, T. (2013) *Events and the Social Sciences*. Abingdon: Routledge.

Brennan, M. and Webster, E. (2010) *The UK Festival Market Report 2010*. The British Music Experience, The O2, London: Official programme of the UK Festival Awards.

Brown, A.E. and Sharpley, R. (2019) Understanding festival-goers and their experience at UK Music Festivals. *Event Management*, 23, 699–720.

Childress, R.D. and Crompton, J.L. (1997) A comparison of alternative direct and discrepancy approaches to measuring quality of performance at a festival. *Journal of Travel Research*, 36(2), 43–57.

Cohen, E. (1979) A phenomenology of tourist experiences. *Sociology*, 13(2), 179–201.

Cohen, E. and Avieli, N. (2004) Food in tourism: Attraction and impediment. *Annals of Tourism Research*, 31(4), 755–778.

Connell, J. and Gibson, C. (2003) *Sound Tracks: Popular Music Identity and Place*. London: Routledge.

Crompton, J.L. (2003) Adapting Herzberg: A conceptualization of the effects of hygiene and motivator attributes on perceptions of event quality. *Journal of Travel Research*, 41(3), 305–310.

Crompton, J.L. and McKay, S.L. (1997) Motives of visitors attending festival events. *Annals of Tourism Research*, 24(2), 425–439.

Csikszentmihalyi, M. (1990) *Flow. The Psychology of Optimal Experience*. New York: Harper Perennial.

Csikszentmihalyi, M. (2014) Toward a psychology of optimal experience. In M. Csikszentmihalyi (Ed.), *Flow and the Foundations of Positive Psychology*. The Netherlands: Springer, pp. 209–226.

Csordas, T.J. (1994) *Embodiment and Experience: The Existential Ground of Culture and Self*. Cambridge: Cambridge University Press.

de Geus, S.D., Richards, G. and Toepoel, V. (.2016) Conceptualisation and operationalisation of event and festival experiences: Creation of an event experience scale. *Scandinavian Journal of Hospitality and Tourism*, 16(3), 274–296.

Dowd, T.J., Liddle, K. and Nelson, J. (2004) Music festivals as scenes: Examples from serious music, womyn's music, and skatepunk. In A. Bennett and R. Peterson (Eds.), *Music Scenes: Local, Translocal and Virtual*. Nashville: Vanderbilt University Press, pp. 149–167.

eFestivals (2018) New Report on Music Concerts and Festivals Reveals Record-Breaking Sales. Available at: http://www.efestivals.co.uk/news/15/151209a.shtml (Accessed 13 May 2018).

Esu, B.B. and Arrey, V.M. (2009) Tourists' satisfaction with cultural tourism festival: A case study of Calabar Carnival Festival, Nigeria. *International Journal of Business and Management*, 4(3), 116–125.

Falassi, A. (1987) *Time Out of Time: Essays on the Festival*. Albuquerque: University of New Mexico Press.

Finkel, R. (2010) 'Dancing Around the Ring of Fire': Social capital, tourism resistance, and gender dichotomies at up Helly Aa in Lerwick, Shetland'. *Event Management*, 14(4), 275–285.

Gelder, G. and Robinson, P. (2009) A critical comparative study of visitor motivations for attending music festivals: A case study of Glastonbury and V Festival. *Event Management*, 13(3), 81–196.

Getz, D. and Page, S.J. (2016) *Event Studies: Theory, Research and Policy for Planned Events*. Abingdon: Routledge.

Gorman-Murray, A. (2009) Intimate mobilities: Emotional embodiment and queer migration. *Social & Cultural Geography*, 10(4), 441–460.

Graburn, N. (2001) Secular ritual: A general theory of tourism. In V. Smith and M. Brent (Eds.), *Hosts and Guests Revisited: Tourism Issues of the 21st Century*. New York: Cognizant Communication Corporation, pp. 42–50.

Hudson, S. and Hudson, R. (2013) Engaging with consumers using social media: A case study of music festivals. *International Journal of Event and Festival Management*, 4(3), 206–223.

Jackson, C. (2014) The festival and event experience. *International Journal of Event and Festival Management*, 15(3), 196–197.

Jennings, G. (2010) *Tourism Research*, 2nd Edn. Chichester: John Wiley & Sons.

Karlsen, S. (2007) The Music Festival as an Arena for Learning: Festspel i Pite Älvdal and Matters of Identity. PhD Thesis, Lulea University of Technology.

Kim, H. and Jamal, T. (2007) Touristic quest for existential authenticity. *Annals of Tourism Research*, 34(1), 181–201.

Larsen, S. (2007) Aspects of a psychology of the tourist experience. *Scandinavian Journal of Hospitality and Tourism*, 7(1), 7–18.

Larson, M., (2009) Festival innovation: Complex and dynamic network interaction. *Scandinavian Journal of Hospitality and Tourism*, 9(2–3), 288–307.

Lee, J., Lee, C. and Choi, Y. (2011) Examining the role of emotional and functional values in festival evaluation. *Journal of Travel Research*, 50(6), 685–696.

Li, Y. (2000) Geographical consciousness and tourism experience. *Annals of Tourism Research*, 27(4), 863–883.

Met Office (2012) 2012: A Wet Year. Available at: https://www.metoffice.gov.uk/weather/learn-about/weather/case-studies/2012-a-wet-year (Accessed 10 July 2019).

Morgan, M. (2008) What makes a good festival? Understanding the event experience. *Event Management*, 12(2), 81–93.

Mossberg, L. (2008) Extraordinary experiences through storytelling. *Scandinavian Journal of Hospitality and Tourism*, 8(3), 195–210.

O'Dell, T. (2007) Tourist experiences and academic junctures. *Scandinavian Journal of Hospitality and Tourism*, 7(1), 34–45.

OED (2016) Experience. Oxford English Dictionary. Available at: https://en.oxforddictionaries.com/definition/experience (Accessed 20 January 2016).

Oliver, R.L. (2014) *Satisfaction: A Behavioural Perspective on the Consumer*. Abingdon: Routledge.

Pegg, S. and Patterson, I. (2010) Rethinking music festivals as a staged event: Gaining insights from understanding visitor motivations and the experiences they seek. *Journal of Convention and Event Tourism*, 11(2), 85–99.

Picard, D. and Robinson, M. (2006) *Festivals, Tourism and Social Change: Remaking Worlds*. Clevedon: Channel View Publications.

Pielichaty, H. (2015) Festival space: gender, liminality and the carnivalesque. *International Journal of Event and Festival Management*, 6(3), 235–250.

Pieper, J. (1965) *In Tune with the World: A Theory of Festivity* (Translated from the German by Ricard and Clara Winston). New York: Harcourt.

Pine, B.J. and Gilmore, J.H. (1999) *The Experience Economy: Work is Theatre & Every Business a Stage*. Boston: Harvard Business Press.

Poulsson, S.H. and Kale, S.H. (2004) The experience economy and commercial experiences. *The Marketing Review*, 4(3), 267–277.

Quinlan Cutler, S. and Carmichael, B. (2010) The dimensions of the tourist experience. In M. Morgan, P. Lugosi, P. and J. Brent Ritchie (Eds.), *The Tourism and Leisure Experience: Consumer and Managerial Perspectives*, Bristol: Channel View Publications, pp. 3–26.

Rihova, I., Buhalis, D., Moital, M. and Gouthro, M. (2013) Social layers of customer-to-customer value co-creation. *Journal of Service Management*, 24(5), 553–566.

Ritchie, J. and Hudson, S. (2009) Understanding and meeting the challenges of consumer/tourist experience research. *International Journal of Tourism Research*, 11(2), 111–126.

Russon, J. (2010) *Human Experience: Philosophy, Neurosis, and the Elements of Everyday Life*. New York: SUNY Press.

Scott, J.W. (1991) The evidence of experience. *Critical Inquiry*, 17(4), 773–797.

Selstad, L. (2007) The social anthropology of the tourist experience. Exploring the 'middle role'. *Scandinavian Journal of Hospitality and Tourism*, 7(1), 19–33.

Serck, L. (2013) Is European festival fever a threat to UK music events? *BBC News*, 7 May. Available at: https://www.bbc.co.uk/news/uk-england-22539977 (Accessed 7 October 2019).

Shaitly, S. (2012) Music festivals try to weather hard times and the Olympics effect. *The Guardian*. Available at: https://www.theguardian.com/music/2012/aug/26/festivals-hard-times-weather-olympics (Accessed 10 July 2019).

Smith, J.E. (1970) *Themes in American Philosophy: Purpose, Experience, and Community*. New York: Harper and Row.

Son, S.M. and Lee, K.M. (2011) Assessing the influences of festival quality and satisfaction on visitor behavioral intentions. *Event Management*, 15(3), 293–303.

Stamboulis, Y. and Skayannis, P. (2003) Innovation strategies and technology for experience-based tourism. *Tourism Management*, 24(1), 35–43.

Stewart, F. (2016) How to Organise a Music Festival #2 The Green Man. Available at: http://drowne-dinsound.com/in_depth/4150355-how-to-organise-a-music-festival-2--green-man (Accessed 10 July 2019).

Stewart, B., Smith, A. and Nicholson, M. (2003) Sport consumer typologies: A critical review. *Sport Marketing Quarterly*, 12(4), 206–216.

Stone, C. (2009) The British pop music festival phenomenon. In J. Ali-Knight, A. Fyall, M. Robertson and A. Ladkin (Eds.), *International Perspectives of Festivals and Events*. London: Elsevier, pp. 205–224.

Sundbo, J. and Darmer, P. (2008) *Creating Experiences in the Experience Economy*. Northampton: Edward Elgar Publishing.

Szmigin, I., Bengry-Howell, A., Morey, Y., Griffin, C. and Riley, S. (2017) Socio-spatial authenticity at co-created music festivals. *Annals of Tourism Research*, 63, 1–11.

Turner, V. (1979) Frame, flow and reflection: Ritual and drama as public liminality. *Japanese Journal of Religious Studies*, 6(4), 465–499.

Turner, V. (1982) *Celebration, Studies in Festivity and Ritual*. Washington: Smithsonian Institution Press.

Tynan, C. and McKechnie, S. (2009) Experience marketing: A review and reassessment. *Journal of Marketing Management*, 25(5–6), 501–517.

UK Music (2016) *Measuring Music 2016 Report*. London: UK Music.

Urry, J. and Larsen, J. (2011) *The Tourist Gaze 3.0*. London: Sage Publications.

Van Winkle, C.M. and Bueddefeld, J.N., (2016) Service-dominant logic and the festival experience. *International Journal of Event and Festival Management*, 7(3), 237–254.

Vaughan, D. (1979) *Does a Festival Pay? A Case Study of the Edinburgh Festival in 1976*. Edinburgh: Tourism and Recreation Research Unit, University of Edinburgh.

Verhoef, P.C., Lemon, K.N., Parasuraman, A., Roggeveen, A., Tsiros, M. and Schlesinger, L.A. (2009) Customer experience creation: Determinants, dynamics and management strategies', *Journal of Retailing*, 85(1), 31–41.

Vogt, J.W. (1976) Wandering: Youth and travel behaviour. *Annals of Tourism Research*, 4(1), 25–41.

Webster, E. and Exchange, L.M. (2014) *Association of Independent Festivals Six-Year Report 2014*. UK: Live Music Exchange. Available at: https://aiforg.com/wp-content/uploads/AIF-Six-Year-Report-2014.pdf

23

THE FILM-INDUCED TOURISM EXPERIENCE

Sue Beeton

Introduction

There was movement at the station, for the word had got around
That the colt from Old Regret had got away ....

(from The Man from Snowy River by Banjo Patterson)

It started with a poem when I was a child, then a movie as a teenager, then as a tourist, tour guide and finally as an educator and researcher, all because of the iconic Australian poem, *The Man from Snowy River*. My personal journey into and with film-induced tourism parallels much of the scholarship in this field. I first consciously engaged as a tourist with film-induced tourism in the 1970s, and even earlier unconsciously. Unknown to me at the time, my love of US Western TV shows and Disney animation as a child set me up for a life of fascination with the emotions of film and the places I got to know via that medium, both real and imaginary (for more on these aspects, see Beeton, 2015). I am led to wonder what will happen next.

I begin the following discussion with the antecedents to the academic study of film-induced tourism - in actual fact, tourists were travelling to famous film sites well before receiving any academic attention. The chapter then moves on to look at selected research into, and discussions of, this phenomenon. As researchers, it is important to acknowledge that the phenomena we study existed well before we studied them, which is also what brought us do so in the first instance. I have had to be selective in this discussion, which is not a definitive 'state of the art' review but one that maps where we have been and presents some indications of where we may be going in our understanding of the film-induced tourist experience. I also trust that the subtleties and layers to tourism that has been induced by film become evident.

Early studies

People travelling to the sites or settings of filming is not new, and has been pre-dated by other forms of tourism induced by popular culture, such as art, poetry, music and literature. While I am not alone in arguing that tourism and film have been linked inextricably

DOI: 10.4324/9781003219866-27

together since the first moving images came into existence over 125 years ago, it is not broadly acknowledged (Beeton, 2015; Strain, 2003).

Gunning (1986) refers to the early era of film (from around 1895 to 1906) as the *cinema of attractions*, where it was the place of filming that was celebrated even more than any storyline, which was limited due to the short length of the film spools lasting only a few minutes. The focus was more on demonstrating this new technology. This is clearly evident in the 'Phantom Rides' of the late nineteenth century, where cameras were attached to moving vehicles (often trains) to showcase the panoramic scenery as the train moved along, with no tourists visible, giving rise to the term. One extant example is Edison's 1903 *Panorama of Gorge Railway*, featuring the landscape near Niagara Falls. As I have noted elsewhere, while '[t]hey were not made to promote tourism per se, [they] contributed to people's desire to visit and experience the sites shown on the screen...' (Beeton, 2011: 53).

While not directly related to tourism, as far back as the middle of the twentieth century there were those who acknowledged the existence of fans' desire to engage with the experiences that their imaginations witnessed. In their classic 1956 paper, Horton and Wohl introduced the concept of *para-social relationships* (Horton & Wohl, 1956) to describe the relationship between the spectator and entertainer during the process of viewing a film or other performance. It is not a stretch to see its relevance to the film-induced tourist experience, particularly in relation to one's imagination (Beeton, 2015; Kim, 2012). When discussing the new mass media of radio, TV and movies, Horton and Wohl (1956: 223) note that, 'the media present opportunities for the playing of roles to which the spectator has – or feels he has – a legitimate claim, but for which he finds no opportunity in his social environment'.

In spite of these commentaries, the intense relationship between film (movies, TV and so on) and tourism, particularly in relation to how tourists experience a place before, during and after their visit, was not seriously contemplated until much later. One early yet brief and primarily unremarked note as to the power of film came from Dean MacCannell in 1976 where he observed that film sites can be significant markers for tourists, giving meaning to places that may on the surface appear extremely 'ordinary'. His example came from the site of the Bonnie and Clyde shoot-out from the movie of the same name:

> As a sight, it amounts to no more than a patch of wild grass, but it was recently provided with an elaborate off-sight marker by the motion picture industry. The fortuitous acquisition of this new marker apparently caught the promoters of the area by surprise as the following information in the brochure is over-stamped in red ink: VISIT THE BONNIE AND CLYDE SHOOTOUT AREA... [The visitors] do not arrive expecting to see anything and are content to be involved with the marker.
>
> *(MacCannell, 1976: 114)*

While MacCannell saw this as something unusual, and even a little odd or quirky, time and time again we see tourists and fans visiting sites that seem, on the surface, to be nondescript but for them are powerfully significant and deeply personal. I have been moved to tears to be at a place that featured in a film that I loved intensely when I was young, never thinking I would actually ever be there (Beeton, 2016). This emotional intensity is due in no small part to the emotions that the films related to these places generate, from fear and longing to joy and excitement, and everything in between. These storytellers have added a layer of emotional content to these places.

Such sites may or may not be marked with a plaque on-site, but with the now common use of GPS devices and mobile phones, film tourists can find these sites with little difficulty.

For example, many of the sites in *The Lord of the Rings* and *The Hobbit* movies in New Zealand are identified in Ian Brodie's publications by their GPS coordinates (Brodie, 2002, 2004, 2011 and 2014).

As a horseback tourist and subsequent tour guide from the mid-1980s to the current day, I have witnessed many people role-playing scenes from *The Man from Snowy River* movies, thundering down mountainsides and quoting lines from the movie and poem around the campfire. Some 30 years after the release of the first of the two movies, I joined a horseback tour with the star of that movie, where people not even born when that first film was made were acting out roles from the film over the entire length of the tour. In fact, they were more familiar with and linked to the story than the actors themselves.

As well as witnessing tourists acting out in the field, tour operators were making many promotional and actual links with movies. Tours in the US of Monument Valley used imagery from films from as long ago as the 1939 Robert Ford movie *Stagecoach* that introduced us to John Wayne, while public access to film studios and sets was also extremely popular. Hollywood Movie Ranches such as Corriganville, where hundreds of Western movies and TV series were filmed, were popular with tourists for many decades from the 1930s (Beeton, 2015; Rothel, 1990; Schneider, 2007). Corriganville even re-created Wild West shoot-outs every day at noon for the masses of tourists and provided opportunities for them to dress in costume, a fore-runner to Cosplay. Singalong bus tours of Vienna to *The Sound of Music* (1965) began shortly after the movie was released and continue today, and daily tours of the sites in the Australian soap, *Neighbours* (1985–) have been running for over 20 years (Beeton, 2016). Yet even so, leading researchers remained somewhat sceptical as to the longevity and power of films to induce tourism. While true in many instances, others demonstrate the powerful resilience of film-induced tourism, particularly for fans.

In one of the early tourism research papers to mention this phenomenon, when writing about media and tourism, Richard Butler speculated on the role of movies and TV programmes as a tourism inducer, but still his musings were not taken further until some years later:

> As people place less importance on reading as a form of getting information about places, and rely more on the visual form of information to gain knowledge, however thin, on almost all items, then what is shown in movies, videos and television will become even more important.
>
> *(Butler, 1990: 51)*

I recall him briefly commenting on this at a conference in the early 1990s where it clearly resonated with me, particularly due to my *Man from Snowy River* experiences. In fact, I would not be in tourism research today if not for that movie and subsequent tourism. When quizzed as to who was doing research in this area, he was not aware of any at that stage. This not only sparked my interest, but led me to my life-long study of this aspect of tourism of which I had direct personal and operational knowledge. In fact, Butler concluded his paper with a prescient observation:

> It can be argued that it is necessary to know much more about how people assimilate knowledge if it is to be understood why people go where they go, and what they expect to get out of going there. Da Vinci, Wordsworth, Scott, and Hemingway may have shaped the tourist destinations into the mid-20th century; George Lucas, Steven Spielberg, Madonna and Michael Jackson may shape destinations into the 21st century.
>
> *(Butler, 1990: 53)*

Apart from starting to take a serious interest in this myself, there was little, if any, academic interest in film-induced tourism following Butler's comments until a group of researchers in the US looked into what they referred to as 'movie-induced tourism'. This included Riley, Tooke, Baker and Van Doren (Riley, 1994; Riley, Baker & Van Doren, 1998; Riley & Van Doren, 1992; Tooke & Baker, 1996). This handful of researchers, while rightly credited with bringing this concept into the academic realm, moved on to other fields of endeavour after a few years, leaving us with some tantalizing data but limited understanding of the film-induced tourist experience. Their work was primarily aimed at demonstrating that this was an area of some importance, focusing on the increased numbers to on-location film sites. They tended to concentrate on management, business and marketing, taking a quantitative approach in which measuring the (primarily economic) 'benefits' of film-induced tourism became a priority.

This attention to the supply-side management of film-induced tourism continues in much of the work in this field, in no small part owing to the fact that many of the academic researchers are based in business faculties where such elements are paramount, as well as the demands of destinations to quantify such economic benefits. This is not 'wrong', but tends to be a little short-sighted as it is difficult to really understand film-induced tourism from such singular attention and misses many significant elements. This is particularly the case when we are looking at the experiences of tourists who are not one homogenous group that can be nailed down to one particular demographic, social cluster or behaviour group.

Owing to these early researchers moving on to other areas of inquiry, there were no deeper nuances, longitudinal studies or researchers concentrating on this fascinating field of tourism in any meaningful way. This presented the opportunity for others to commit to an ongoing interest in this field, of which I was one. I published the first monograph on the topic based on my personal and industry experience as well as some six years of academic research (Beeton, 2005). It was by necessity a wide-ranging work that looked at movies, TV series, theme parks, host communities and the tourists themselves. Such breadth and depth can only be achieved in a book as opposed to a journal article that is shorter and more singular in its premise. So began what has become a lifelong fascination with film-induced tourism scholarship, which has, for me, uncovered layers and layers of this complex field of endeavour.

As my curiosity grew, I became even more convinced that there was far more to this than numbers and marketing, and I grew more and more frustrated with this pervasive focus. I found myself articulating my curiosity about some of the more social equity elements and impacts on host communities, along with a growing fascination with the deep emotions that we experienced as tourists. The tourist experience is so often intertwined with film, especially when the tourist undertakes new experiences because of it, such as my own journey from *The Man from Snowy River* movies to mountain recreation and tour guiding (Beeton, 2008).

Until around 2010, there was virtually no research undertaken on film-induced tourism in Asia, in spite of repeated calls for such research (Beeton, 2005, 2006, 2010; Croy & Heitmann, 2011). Such a lack of interest can be because of many factors, including the pervasiveness of Hollywood in our collective minds, as well as the prevalence of English language academic publishers, which can limit publication success those for whom English is their second language. However, this is changing, not only with an increase in English proficiency and publishing outlets but also through partnerships between western and Asian scholars, along with the western/international education of Asian students, migrants and residents. Nevertheless, there were some Asian studies being undertaken, particularly in Hong Kong and Korea. For example, Yan (2000) and Ng (2008), among others, consider Hong Kong media and film tourism. Examples of Korean studies include work from Kim, S. S., Argusa, Lee and Chon (2007), Kim, S., Long and Robinson (2009) and Kim, S. S., Lee and Chon (2010) (it is important to note here that, as indicated, the authors are two different Kims, namely S. S. Kim and S. Kim).

In their timely publication *Film Tourism in Asia* (Kim & Reijnders, 2018a), the editors continue to bemoan the dearth of Asian studies, noting that 'the great majority of existing studies on film tourism focus exclusively on Western examples, predominantly from the UK, Ireland, Australia and the USA...' (Kim and Reijnders, 2018b: 5), which they strived to address. Their collection includes three chapters in a section entitled 'The Film Tourist Experience' but they fall short in terms of incorporating actual concepts of the tourist experience, which can be the case in some edited publications where the work is not commissioned to cover specific elements. While the publication itself remains a strong contribution to the study of film-induced tourism, it is lacking if we wish to look at the experiences of film-induced tourists; as in all elements of film-induced tourism, there remains great scope for ongoing studies.

Meanwhile, researchers from the social sciences were moving from their studies of film towards tourism, with studies of fan behaviour being included in the tourism mix. While many were undertaking some fascinating and relevant studies, in the early stages they rarely engaged with, or were even aware of, the work from the tourism sector. Spanning such 'siloed' research is a challenge for all researchers, particularly in a field that covers so many disciplines. Bridging this gap became a focus of much of my own work, and remains so (Beeton, 2010). One of the benefits of online databases has meant that when we search now, we are not limited to the publications in our own disciplines, which has helped to broaden the base and scope of our knowledge.

The work done in parallel to these business studies has contributed to expanding and deepening our understanding, while simultaneously confirming the significance of that work.

The film-induced tourist experience

With such hindsight, we can now see the journey towards understanding film-induced tourism outlined above as not quite linear but one that has slowly moved from the supply-side analyses towards considering how the tourist who is induced to visit by film experiences this phenomenon. To look at this in some depth in this chapter, I have chosen not to replicate any of the general reviews of the literature that have been published over the years (see Beeton, 2005, 2010; Cardoso, Estevão, Muniz & Alves 2017; Connell, 2012; Croy & Heitmann, 2011), as there is now such a wide range of literature that such reviews are both almost impossible to undertake and also questionable in their outcomes. Rather, I have taken the liberty of looking at the work of two major research groups in Japan and the Netherlands who are developing theory and knowledge based on this prior work (not only in their own countries), along with my interest of the film-induced tourist experience. Both research groups have produced a range of integrated outputs, from seminars and conferences to journal articles, edited books and monographs, presenting an impressive range of understandings and depth of knowledge.

In the edited publication, *Mediating the Tourist Experience* (edited by Lester and Scarles, 2013), the Japanese notion of *contents tourism* was introduced to a wider international audience. Film and pop-culture based tourism was described in terms of the stories and 'content' of their experience (Beeton, Yamamura & Seaton, 2013). In 2014, a team of researchers based in Japan led by Takayoshi Yamamura and Philip Seaton received an unprecedented five-year funding from the Japan Society for the Promotion of Science for their project, 'International Comparative Research on the Spreading and Reception of Culture through Contents Tourism'. This has seeded ongoing interest and research in this field, particularly in relation to film and anime. Such long-term projects remain crucial to developing knowledge, and the team has continued to gain support for their work.

Kontentsu tzurizumu (contents tourism) had been acknowledged by the Japanese government in 2005, identifying its essence as when tourists add a narrative quality to the places they were visiting, creating a deeper connection and experience. In one of the publications coming out of the Japan Society project noted above, Seaton, Yamamura, Sugawa-Shimada and Jang (2017: 3) define contents tourism as:

> ... travel behaviour motivated fully or partially by narratives, characters, locations, and other creative elements of popular culture forms, including film, television drams, manga, anime, novels and computer games.

In this way, researchers have been able to examine the film tourist experience in some depth and as part of the entire tourism system.

Around the same time (in 2013), in the Netherlands, Stijn Reijnders commenced a four-year project, 'Locating Imagination: An Interdisciplinary Perspective to Literary, Film and Music Tourism'. This project came on the back of his highly regarded 2011 monograph, *Places of the Imagination: Media, Tourism, Culture* (Reijnders, 2011), which sets up the role of the imagination in the media-based film tourist experience by introducing the concept of *lieux d'imagination*. Such places of imagination 'are material reference points like objects or places, which ... serve as material-symbolic references to a common imaginary world' (Reijnders, 2011: 14). This takes MacCannell's (1976) concept of tourism markers referred to early in this chapter and refines it to focus more on the place of the tourist's own imagination and how that connects the stories in film/media with place.

In this monograph, Reijnders presented a circular model of media tourism, which, as with any viable model, has been used as a basis for understanding and incorporated into other models, such as that published in *Travel, Tourism and the Moving Image* (Beeton, 2015). Both models are replicated below with a brief explanation of each.

Reijnders' model presented the creators (of media such as film and literature) as being inspired by physical places (Phase One) and then their stories are transformed into imaginary places (Phase Two) that are subsequently appropriated by fans who then search for a physical place where they can experience their imagined reality (Phases Three and Four). This model is reproduced below (Figure 23.1).

Reijnders' model fed into my concurrent ponderings on how to frame my own work. I did not entirely agree with Reijnders' model in which he separates 'imagination' and 'perception' into two discrete halves of the model. These I consider to be part of each other (or at the very least, having blurred and porous boundaries), so I chose not to delineate between the imagined and physical places in the same way. However, I remain open to a discussion of this approach – often it is through thinking and challenging such models we start to open up to new ways of understanding (Figure 23.2).

Reijnders' team for the Locating Imagination project included three PhD scholars, each focusing on the three distinct areas of media, namely, film, literature and music, while producing interdisciplinary outcomes in the field of media tourism, which is not dissimilar to the Japanese contents tourism project. The aim of the project was to uncover why and how

The film-induced tourism experience

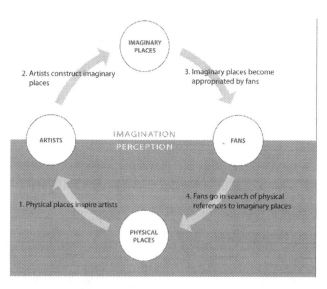

Figure 23.1 Media tourism as part of a circular process
Source: Reijnders (2011: 17) – Reproduced with permission.

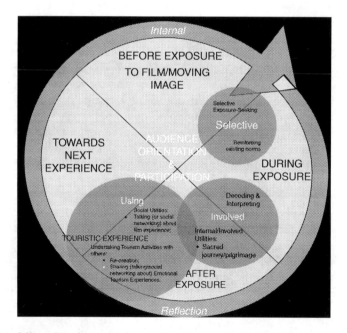

Figure 23.2 Modelling the relationship between audience and tourist activity
Source: Beeton (2015: 29).

popular media gives rise to tourism, focusing on the tourist as well as the location. This focus on the tourist differentiates the work from other studies that were more interested in the media (such as film), location and host destination. They used a combination of qualitative content analysis, ethnographic fieldwork and experimental methods that enabled them to delve deeper than some earlier studies.

Of particular interest here is Waysdorf's (2021) work, in which she studies the experiences of fans at sites of the TV series *The Game of Thrones* (2011–2019), *The Prisoner* (1967–1968) and also at the Universal Studios theme park, *The Wizarding World of Harry Potter*. She found that there were fans of these various series (both TV and film) who had deep experiences at the sites where they were filmed (or other constructed sites such as the theme park). Finding a place where their internal experiences can be re-lived is important to these fan-tourists, even when the places are made-up. She concludes by noting that 'place is important, even, or maybe even more, in a digital and transmedial age, as the physical, "real" experience is still one that can't be duplicated' (Waysdorf, 2021: 294). This supports others' work who have challenged the artifice of 'authenticity' in the film-induced tourist experience, including Beeton, (2005, 2015, 2016), Connell (2012) and Kim and Reijnders (2018b), along with those looking at contents tourism.

This contemplation of the fan as tourist ties in with the work of Yamamura in relation to contents tourism in Japan, particularly when considered in relation to cosplay, where the fan-tourists dress up as their cinematic heroes and heroines, demonstrating a deep connection to what is often seen as fantasy. An excellent example of this is the Toyako Manga Anime Festa in the *onsen* (hot spring) resort of Toyako in Hokkaido, where the entire town is transformed into a venue for fans of all forms of manga (or anime) to experience cosplay. As Yamamura (2015: 44) explains, the town opens up its public spaces that act as a stage 'where both debutantes and proficient cosplayers may enjoy the experience alongside each other'. He argues that this presents us with new forms of tourist experiences where everyone can participate by playing the role of any character they so desire.

While cosplay events can occur anywhere at fan events such as at the numerous Comic-Cons around the world, as well as at Tayako as described above, dressing up when visiting sites depicted in anime (which is often set in a 'real' environment in spite of being animated and as such engaging our imagination) or film is particularly pertinent to tourism and the tourist experience. There is evidence demonstrating that, by taking on the costume of a character, the tourist engages in an even deeper and more powerful emotional experience (Graburn & Yamamura, 2020; Seaton et al., 2017).

In contents tourism research in other parts of the world that is highly relevant to the Japanese studies, demonstrating the global reach of cosplay, is the work of Rastati (2020), which describes the emergence of cosplay in Indonesia. It was initially influenced by Japanese anime gaining popularity in that country in the 1990s, with the concept of cosplay gaining traction towards the end of that decade. While initially focused on Japanese and US characters, it has now developed into a form that also celebrates Indonesian characters and has become an activity reflecting national pride, known as *Indocosu* (a contraction of 'Indonesian cosplay'). This is not only confined to the events, with the cosplayers themselves becoming significant tourist attractions, enhancing not only theirs but others' tourist experiences.

However, even those who do not dress up and participate in cosplay can engage deeply with these sites. As Seaton et al. (2017: 19) explain:

> [o]nce at the destination, fans engage in characteristic behaviours, such as posing for photographs next to important sites related to the contents. On returning home… fans re-engage with the contents in a new light.

These activities of re-enacting and costuming are not isolated to contents tourism per se and have been observed by other researchers around the world, including Buchmann, Moore and Fisher (2010) in relation to *The Lord of the Rings* tourists, and in the work of Knudsen and

Waade (2010) and Larsen (2010) as well as my own early experiences with adventure horse riding (Beeton, 2005). At times these actions suggest deep emotional para-social experiences that verge on the sacred.

Notions of performance and sacredness are examined in work by Jang (2020a), who looks at the ways in which Korean fans bring sacred meaning to a film or pop cultural location via creating their own ritual-like performances. Such performances (and the sharing of them) not only create these sacred places, but also add a level of emotional authentication to them. Such sacredness also connects with notions of secular pilgrimages in tourism, which is not new, but confirms our understanding of the depth of some tourist experiences, particularly in the film-induced tourist experience. Taking the notion of creating sacred sites based on Japanese anime yet further, Jang and Yamamura (2020) have studied a fan-made site in Tasmania, Australia relating to the Japanese anime film, *Kiki's Delivery Service* (1989), which is not set, filmed, or based there. In fact, it was set in Sweden, but it appears that fans have chosen to celebrate a bakery in Tasmania that they consider it to be similar to the one in the anime (Jang & Yamamura, 2020). This raises so many fascinating questions about 'mistaken identities' and the power of fans to construct what they want where they want it, completely challenging all notions of 'authenticity'. In a further twist on the topic of the authenticity of the film-induced tourist experience, Seaton and Beeton (2020) have studied ways in which film can change meanings of two heritage sites in Japan and Australia, where tourists are now more informed by constructed stories through films and other media than any type of reality or authenticity.

The publication, *Contents Tourism and Pop Culture Fandom: Transnational Tourist Experiences* (edited by Yamamura and Seaton, 2020) has sections on both sacredness and pilgrimage from the perspective of contents tourism on an international level. In particular, the chapters from Jang on the religious imagination of Korean contents tourists and Benjamin on her pilgrimage to sites relating to the US series *Breaking Bad* (2008–2013) illustrate how the notion of contents tourism can translate internationally (Jang 2020b; Benjamin, 2020). Coming from a US perspective, Benjamin sees contents tourism as a 'series of touristic experiences motivated by contents' (Benjamin, 2020: 194) and amply illustrates the transnational nature of the concept. To examine her experience of her pilgrimage to sites related to *Breaking Bad*, she applied sensory autoethnography to her contents-related experience, presenting a deep, personal perspective that I find extremely powerful.

With the rapid development of technology over the past two decades, the film-induced fan-tourist experience has changed. As with Jang's work on sacred meaning-making through performance, Ishimori and Yamamura (2009) have noted the emergence of a tourist as also a producer of content, or 'prosumer'. This is due in no small part to the sophistication, democratization and personalization of the media-making process (Ishimori & Yamamura, 2009). Tourists (and fans) can now film themselves re-enacting scenes at the sites of filming and then air them on social media outlets. This is in fact, not new, as I have noted this occurring since the first personal camcorders became available, but they were not as broadly accessible to the producer and consumer ('prosumer') as today, and had limited opportunities to share them outside family home film nights (Beeton, 2015). Today, via the many avenues provided by social media, there is the potential for thousands if not millions of people to be reached.

Yamamura applied his examination of the prosumer to develop a definition of creative fandom in terms of film and contents tourism as 'a community sharing the same contents/ narrative worlds, with unclear borders between the local community, fans, and copyright-holders, and with aspirations of creativity' (Yamamura, 2020: 15). As Graburn and Yamamura (2020: 7) explain, 'fan tourists, as well as contents businesses and local authorities/

communities, are all expressing their creativity in the context of tourism and delivering their contents through a variety of media'. Such blurring of relationships and overlapping experiences is a common element of the tourist experience, which never occurs in a bubble. Yet, we rarely truly acknowledge or grasp such complexity in our studies.

We are also seeing others addressing similar complexities, including those working on the most recent team project from Reijnders, 'Worlds of Imagination: A Comparative Study of Film Tourism in India, Nigeria, Jamaica, South Korea and the United Kingdom'. This study has a focus on the tourist experience and tourists' actions at film sites across a range of countries and cultures. Reijnders brought together an international team to understand film-induced tourism and the experience in more depth as well as across cultures. By examining the visual traditions in the various local media cultures, the effects of local power configurations and the commonalities and differences in motives and experiences, they plan to take a more comprehensive approach to the study of film-induced tourism. At the time of writing, there were some research papers proceeding through the review process as well as PhD dissertations planned to complete in 2021. Of particular interest is the work of Schiavone, who proposes to delve into the interconnected ways in which the various co-producers of film, tourism and heritage professionals are involved in constructing tourist engagements with Scotland (Schiavone & Reijnders, 2020).

Despite the limited publication output from this project at the time of writing, there are some initial outcomes that relate to this discussion, and many more already drafted. Firstly, a deep examination of Bollywood films and tourism is way overdue and now being considered seriously through this project. The focus is on the levels of engagement of the film-induced tourists, particularly in relation to onsite engagement and embodied experiences (Nanjangud & Reijnders, 2020). When studying Indian diaspora in the Netherlands, Nanjangud and Reijnders (2020) found that they did not wish to return to their hometowns or villages, but to the places valorized in the movies, and felt more connected to the India on the screen than the India of their heritage. Even in a study that is so early in their research, they were able to confirm 'the existence of a strong desire for temporary visitation and tourism driven by Bollywood cinema, and seeking difference, yet familiarity' (Nanjangud & Reijnders, 2020: 16). In further exploratory work, Nanjangud (2020) considers the ways that film can affect the ways that film tourists perform their travel, not dissimilar to Horton and Wohl's (1956) concept of para-social behaviour. She argues that 'films not only inspire potential tourism destinations but also promote certain tourism behaviour' (Nanjangud, 2020: 138).

Conclusion

What we can see when we look at selections of the work of these international research teams led by researchers from Japan and the Netherlands is that there is an emerging focus on tourist experiences such as pilgrimage and the ways that fans engage, which is quite different from the 'incidental' film tourist who may visit a film site, but is not driven by his or her specific interest (or fandom) (Beeton, 2005). Fans are highly focused and driven in their desire to experience these destinations and sites or sets of filming.

In spite of the depth of the work outlined above, we are still a long way from truly understanding the film-induced tourist experience. This journey of knowledge that I have outlined in this chapter continues, as does my personal journey, which I have found is moving deeper within myself as I open up emotionally to my own film-induced tourist experiences. It certainly is a never-ending story.

References

Beeton, S. (2005) *Film-Induced Tourism*. Clevedon: Channel View Publications.

Beeton, S. (2006) Understanding film-induced tourism. *Tourism Analysis*, 11(3), 181–188.

Beeton, S. (2008) From the screen to the field: The influence of film on tourism and recreation. *Tourism Recreation Research*, 33(1), 39–47.

Beeton, S. (2010) The advance of film tourism. *Tourism and Hospitality Planning & Development*, 7(1), 1–6.

Beeton, S. (2011) Tourism and the moving image: Incidental tourism promotion. *Tourism Recreation Research*, 36(1), 49–56.

Beeton, S. (2015) *Travel, Tourism and the Moving Image*. Bristol: Channel View Publications.

Beeton, S. (2016) *Film-Induced Tourism*, 2nd Edn. Bristol: Channel View Publications.

Beeton, S., Yamamura, T. and Seaton, P. (2013) The mediatisation of culture: Japans contents tourism and pop culture. In J. Lester and C. Scarles (Eds.), *Mediating the Tourist Experience*. Farnham, Ashgate, pp. 139–154.

Benjamin, S. (2020) Breaking Benjamin: A woman's pilgrimage to New Mexico. In T. Yamamura and P. Seaton (Eds.), *Contents Tourism and Pop Culture Fandom: Transnational Tourist Experiences*. Bristol: Channel View Publications, pp. 189–204.

Brodie, I. (2002) *The Lord of the Rings: A Location Guidebook*. Auckland: Harper Collins Publishers Pty Ltd.

Brodie, I. (2004) *The Lord of the Rings Location Guidebook*, 2nd Edn. Auckland: Harper Collins Publishers.

Brodie, I. (2011) *The Lord of the Rings Location Guidebook: Extended Edition*. Auckland: Harper Collins Publishers.

Brodie, I. (2014) *The Hobbit Motion Picture Trilogy Location Guidebook*. Auckland: Harper Collins Publishers.

Buchmann, A., Moore, K. and Fisher, D. (2010) Experiencing film tourism: Authenticity and fellowship. *Annals of Tourism Research*, 37(1), 229–248.

Butler, R. W. (1990) The influence of the media in shaping international tourist patterns. *Tourism Recreation Research*, 15(2), 46–53.

Cardoso, L., Estevão, C. M., Muniz, A. C. F. and Alves, H. (2017) Film induced tourism: A systematic literature review. *Tourism & Management Studies*, 13(3), 23–30.

Connell, J. (2012) Film tourism: Evolution, progress and prospects. *Tourism Management*, 33(5), 1007–1029.

Croy, G. and Heitmann, S. (2011) Tourism and film. In P. Robinson, S. Heitmann and P. Dieke (Eds.), *Research Themes for Tourism*. Wallingford: CABI, pp. 188–204.

Graburn, N. and Yamamura, T. (2020) Contents tourism: Background, context, and future, *Journal of Tourism and Cultural Change*, 18(1). https://doi.org/10.1080/14766825.2020.1707460

Gunning, T. (1986) The cinema of attraction: Early film, its spectator and the avant-garde, *Wide Angle*, 8(3/4), 63–70.

Horton, D. and Wohl, R. R. (1956) Mass communication and para-social interaction: Observations on intimacy at a distance. *Psychiatry*, 19(3), 215–229.

Ishimori, S. and Yamamura, T. (2009) Jouhou shakai ni okeru kankou kakumei: bunmeishiteki ni mita kankou no gr6baru tornedo [Tourism revolution in information society: Global trend of tourism from the perspective of the world history of civilization]. *JACIC Jouhou*, 94/24(2), 5–17.

Jang, K. (2020a) Creating the sacred places of pop culture in the age of mobility: Fan pilgrimages and authenticity through performance. *Journal of Tourism and Cultural Change*, 18(1), 42–57.

Jang, K. (2020b) Contents tourism and religious imagination. In T. Yamamura and P. Seaton (Eds.), *Contents Tourism and Pop Culture Fandom: Transnational Tourist Experiences*. Bristol: Channel View Publications, pp. 116–127.

Jang, K. and Yamamura, T. (2020) Creative fandoms and the mediatized sacred sites. In C. Cassinger, M. Månsson, A. Buchman and L. Eskilsson (Eds.), *The Routledge Companion to Media and Tourism* Abingdon: Routledge, pp. 307–315.

Kim, S. (2012) Audience involvement and film tourism experiences: Emotional places, emotional experiences. *Tourism Management*, 33(2), 387–396.

Kim, S., Long, P. and Robinson, M. (2009) Small screen, big tourism: The role of popular Korean television dramas in South Korean tourism. *Tourism Geographies*, 11(3), 308–333.

Kim, S. and Reijnders, S. (Eds.) (2018a) *Film Tourism in Asia. Perspectives on Asian Tourism*. Singapore: Springer.

Kim, S. and Reijnders, S. (2018b) Asia on my mind: Understanding film tourism in Asia. In S. Kim and S. Reijnders (Eds.), *Film Tourism in Asia. Perspectives on Asian Tourism*. Singapore: Springer, pp. 1–18.

Kim, S. S., Argusa, J., Lee, H. and Chon, K. (2007) Effects of Korean television dramas on the flow of Japanese tourists. *Tourism Management*, 28(5), 1340–1353.

Kim, S. S., Lee, H. and Chon, K. S. (2010) Segmentation of different types of Hallyu tourists using a multinomial model and its marketing implications. *Journal of Hospitality and Tourism Research*, 34(3), 341–361.

Knudsen, B. T. and Waade, A. M. (2010) Performative authenticity and spatial experience: Rethinking the relation between travel, place and emotion. In B. T. Knudsen and A. M. Waade (Eds.), *Re-Investing Authenticity: Tourism, Place and Emotions*. Bristol: Channel View Publications, pp. 1–19.

Larsen, J. (2010) Goffman and the tourist gaze: A performative perspective on tourism mobilities. In M. H. Jacobsen (Ed.), *The Contemporary Goffman*. New York: Routledge, pp. 313–332

Lester, J and Scarles, C. (Eds.) (2013) *Mediating the Tourist Experience*. Farnham: Ashgate.

MacCannell, D. (1976) *The Tourist: A New Theory of the Leisure Class*. New York: Shocken Books.

Nanjangud, A. (2020) Doing as directed: Analysing representations of travel in contemporary Bollywood cinema. In C. Cassinger, M. Månsson, A. Buchman and L. Eskilsson (Eds.), *The Routledge Companion to Media and Tourism*. Abingdon: Routledge, pp. 132–141.

Nanjangud, A. and Reijnders, S. (2020) Cinematic itineraries and identities: Studying Bollywood tourism among the Hindustanis in the Netherlands. *European Journal of Cultural Studies*. https://doi.org/10.1177/1367549420951577

Ng, B. W. (2008) Hong Kong young people and cultural pilgrimage to Japan: The role of Japanese popular culture in Asian tourism. In J. Cochrane (Ed.), *Asian Tourism: Growth and Change*. Oxford: Elsevier, pp. 183–192.

Rastati, R., (2020) Indonesian cosplay tourism. In T. Yamamura and P. Seaton (Eds.), *Contents Tourism and Pop Culture Fandom: Transnational Tourist Experiences*. Bristol: Channel View Publications, pp. 144–158.

Reijnders, S. (2011) *Places of the Imagination: Media, Tourism, Culture*. Farnham: Ashgate.

Riley, R., Baker, D. and Van Doren, C. S. (1998) Movie induced tourism. *Annals of Tourism Research* 25(4), 919–935.

Riley, R. and Van Doren, C. S. (1992) Movies as tourism promotion: A 'pull' factor in a 'push' location. *Tourism Management*, 13(3), 267–274.

Riley, R. W. (1994) Movie-induced tourism. In A. V. Seaton (Ed.), *Tourism: The State of the Art*. Chichester: John Wiley & Sons.

Rothel, D. (1990) *An Ambush of Ghosts: A Personal Guide to Favourite Western Film Locations*. Madison: Empire Publishing.

Schiavone, R. and Reijnders, S. (2020) Fusing fact and fiction: Placemaking through film tours in Edinburgh. *European Journal of Cultural Studies*, 1–17. https://doi.org/10.1177/1367549420951568

Schneider, J. (2007) *Corriganville: The Definitive True Story of the Ray 'Crash' Corrigan Movie Ranch*. USA: Corriganville Press.

Seaton, P. and Beeton, S. (2020) Rewriting history, revitalizing heritage: Heritage-based contents tourism in the Asia-Pacific region. In C. Cassinger, M. Månsson, A. Buchman and L. Eskilsson (Eds.), *The Routledge Companion to Media and Tourism*. Abingdon: Routledge, pp. 197–204.

Seaton, P., Yamamura, T., Sugawa-Shimada, A. and Jang, K. (2017) *Contents Tourism in Japan: Pilgrimages to the 'Sacred Sites' of Popular Culture*. Cambria: Amherst Publishing.

Strain, E. (2003) *Public Places, Private Journeys. Ethnography, Entertainment and the Tourist Gaze*. New Brunswick: Rutgers University Press.

Tooke, N. and Baker, M. (1996) Seeing is believing: The effect of film on visitor numbers to screened locations. *Tourism Management*, 17(2), 87–94.

Waysdorf, A. S. (2021) Placing Fandom: Reflections on film tourism. In N. van Es, DS. L. Bolderman, A. S. Waysdorf, A. S. and S. L. Reijnders (Eds.), *Locating Imagination: Popular Culture, Tourism, and Belonging*. Abingdon: Routledge, pp. 283–296.

Yamamura, T. (2015) Experience-based consumption in a dramatised space: The history of the Toyako Manga Anime Festa. In K. Nishikawa, P. Seaton and T. Yamamura (Eds.), *The Theory and Practice of Contents Tourism*. Report from Research Faculty of Media and Communication,

Hokkaido University, Japan, pp. 40–45. Available at: https://eprints.lib.hokudai.ac.jp/dspace/bitstream/2115/58300/1/IMC%20Articles%2020150316.pdf (Accessed 17 December 2020).

Yamamura, T. (2020) Contents tourism and creative fandom: The formation process of creative fandom and its transnational expansion in a mixed-media age. *Journal of Tourism and Cultural Change*, 18(1), 12–26. Online: https://doi.org/10.1080/14766825.2020.1707461

Yamamura, T. and Seaton, P. (Eds.). (2020). *Contents Tourism and Pop Culture Fandom: Transnational Tourist Experiences*. Bristol: Channel View Publications.

Yan, C. T. (2000) Star-spangled journey: Hong Kong movie-induced tourism, *The Hong Kong Anthropologist*, 13, 27–33.

24

REMEMBRANCING, REMEMBRANCE GANGS AND CO-OPTED ENCOUNTERS

Loading and reloading dark tourism experiences

Tony Seaton

Introduction

'Harold and Maude' was a low budget film, first released in 1969, which went on to become a cult movie in the 1980s. It was the story of a close relationship between a very old lady and a younger man in his 20s. The film wasn't about romantic love. What brought the asymmetrically aged couple together was a shared taste for attending the funerals of strangers, from the hearse's first arrival until the last handful of earth was scattered over the coffin. After many agreeable, sepulchral trips, the young man, thinking he had found his ideal partner-in-death for life, proposed marriage. But the old lady, though cherishing the graveside moments they had shared together, was not looking for permanent commitment and killed herself, knowing that there would be at least one person at her funeral.

The film offers a cautionary text for approaching the nature of dark tourism experience. Harold and Maude's trips would seem to be an open-and-shut case of dark tourism behaviour to outsiders, but would the couple have seen their sepulchral travel as 'dark' excursions? The question raises a perennial problem in social science inquiry, the insider/outsider dilemma. Should judgements of human behaviour be made by authorized or empowered,[1] external observers, or by the self-defining claims and assertions (and, on occasion, denials) their subjects make about themselves. This is a thorny issue in dark tourism because research respondents have in the past denied that their trips constitute experiences researchers have presumed to be 'dark'. A second issue is whether, even if Harold and Maude had embraced the 'dark tourist' label as self-definition, they would have regarded their activities as representative of all dark tourists or the sectional ones of a minority group *within* it who might be sub-categorized as 'funeral sightseers'.

This chapter addresses these questions in (a) exploring what the common features of dark tourism experiences are; (b) their differences from other kinds of tourism; and (c), the influences that have affected dark tourism experience and may do so in the future.

Dark tourism experience: generic sites and scenarios

The inquiry starts with three preliminary hypotheses. The first is that dark tourism forms part of the aggregate of all recreational tourism that is here understood as the making of

328   DOI: 10.4324/9781003219866-28

periodic visits to destinations, attractions and events to enjoy premeditated activities away from home. The second is that 'all recreational tourism' comprises a number of different, generic tourism forms (one being dark tourism) targeted at, and consumed by, specific audiences. The third is that generic tourism works through a three-way relationship that involves: (a) offering a differentiated product to (b), profiled visitors with specific tastes that (c), delivers visitor experiences that fulfil those visitors' expectations. Examples of generic tourism include sun, sea and sand packaged holidays for families; weekend resort breaks for golfers; skiing holidays for winter sports fans; sea and river cruises for sybaritic sailors, and so on. This segmented model of aggregate and segmented tourism supply and demand is one widely accepted in academic and managerial theory (Seaton & Woodward, 2008). It is also inscribed in the SERVQUAL model applied to tourist behaviour and satisfaction (Ryan, 1997 2012).

But to what extent can it be applied to dark tourism experiences? The starting point in exploring this has to be an appraisal of what dark tourism experiences are, looking to find what they have in common and the ways in which they may differ. What follows are thumbnail samples of dark tourism praxis from around the world that will be used as illustrative mini-cases to anchor the more abstract discussion of remembrance and commemoration that follows. The final section comes back to earth with a second illustrative inventory, this time of some of the forms social remembrancing takes and the ways in which it affects, and is affected by, dark tourism experiences.

Scenario summaries

- *Gothic walks among mummified bodies in the Capuchin Monastery at Palermo in Sicily.* This uniquely creepy experience is commercially offered to tourists in the crypt of the Catacombs where over 200 eighteenth- and nineteenth-century Capuchin monks and others' bodies have been mummified, and are exhibited life size on shelves in their original, tattered and moth-ridden clothes (Catacombe dei Cappuccini, 2020).
- *Volcano watching at the Eimey Museum in Westmanna, Iceland.* Tourists take a boat trip from Reykjavik to the modern, volcano museum on Westmanna Island, which is partly built round the shattered remains of a house destroyed in a volcanic eruption.
- *Homage to John Lennon in Central Park, New York.* This happens at a small memorial space opposite the Dakota Building where Lennon was murdered. New Yorkers pass by it daily; tourists stop and join in informal rituals of commemoration ranging from silent reflection or contemplation to more sociable, guitar-accompanied sing-alongs.
- *Afternoon tea above the sunken village of Llanwddyn in Wales.* In the Edwardian lounge of a sporting hotel at Lake Vyrnwy, visitors take afternoon tea above the great lake that covers the sunken village of Llanwddyn, flooded in 1888 to make the great dam and lake. 40 labourers died in its construction. Most visitors will not know the story unless they walk to a hillside church and burial ground where gravestones from the sunken village church were relocated (Seaton, 2021).
- *Self-catering breaks at the Gothic folly of Lansdown Tower near Bath.* This was once the retreat of William Beckford, a notorious writer, aesthete and collector who built a cemetery and mausoleum in its grounds for himself and his dog. The tower and cemetery are now owned by the Lansdown Trust who let it as one of their heritage properties (Seaton, 2009a).
- *A paid visit to the memorials in Westminster Abbey, London.* This is one of the two great, Anglican, cathedral churches in London, which are the commemorative resting place of dead kings, queens and significant, British cultural figures.

- *Lunch in the Cimetiere des Rois in Geneva or, in Embankment Gardens near Whitehall, London.* In the Swiss cemetery, some city workers and tourists sit and take lunch breaks or wander the graves and memorials, most often looking for that of the writer, Jean-Luis Borges (Dodd, 2015). In Embankment Gardens, tourists in London rest up unaware of its memorial status whilst others take selfies among statues of dead white males, including a Victorian general, Sir James Outram, and William Wycliffe, the first to translate the Bible into English (Byron, 1981).
- *Dining with Dracula, Frankenstein* and *Doctor Jekyll and Mr Hyde.* These celebrated mass killers from gothic fiction are brand name features of restaurants and bars in England, Scotland, America and Japan (*vide*, Google search 2020). In Britain, there are Dracula restaurants in London, Bristol, Coventry and Glasgow.
- *Touring battle sites of World War I fatalities in Gallipoli and the Dardanelles.* These are visited by Australians and New Zealanders as sacred shrines where their national identities were forged, at great human cost, fighting the Turks (Slade, 2003). In Turkish culture, the sites are commemorated as sacred shrines to patriotic martyrs resisting invasion.
- *Witnessing the site of Jewish genocide at the Nazi concentration camp of Auschwitz.* This experience is taken by independent visitors and, in coach excursions as part of package tours of Cracow and its region in Poland lasting up to a day.
- *Walking the city streets of London, passing by memorial statuary and 'blue plaque' signage, marking houses where cultural figures have died.* Blue plaque signage and commemorative statues multiplied in London and Western capitals in the early twentieth century and are features of other metropolitan centres internationally (Byron, 1981; Gleichan, 1928; London County Council, 1901–1930)
- *Riding 'ghost trains' and visiting 'haunted houses'.* Both became fairground and seaside pier attractions in the late nineteenth and twentieth centuries, and still flourish.

To what extent can these mini-cases be collectively subsumed under the generic name of 'dark tourism'? How does a holocaust visit in Poland compare with picnic lunches and selfies among busts of historical figures in a London garden? Are ghost train rides and haunted house visits in the same ball park as walks among tombs and effigies in great national cathedrals? How similar is exposure to mummified corpses in Sicily to viewing the textual and visual narratives in a volcano museum in Iceland? Is an Anzac battlefield tour in Turkey the same order of experience as stopping to read 'blue plaque' names on houses where writers have died? Are family parties in a *Dracula* restaurant in Glasgow having the same eating experience as lunchtime visitors in a Swiss cemetery?

The most obvious experiential features in these scenarios comprise their diversity in timing, duration and activity. Their locations are also diverse, including parks, restaurants, cemeteries, fairgrounds, battle fields, metropolitan streets, atrocity sites, gardens and museums. All contrast with the recognizable homogeneity of most other generic tourism forms that have identifiably, homogeneous settings (e.g. ski slopes, golf courses, sea and sandy beaches, theme parks and so on). The visitor activities pursued in these 'dark' encounters also appear less uniform. They vary from taking photographs in a public garden, encounters with street memorials, riding funfairs, eating in specific restaurants and taking guided tours of battlefields. The experiences also represent contrasts in frequency, timing and duration compared with other tourism forms. Street memorials may be passed in seconds or minutes, a visit to a Holocaust site may be a one-off, afternoon or full-day visit, a battlefield tour may last a week or more.

A second major difference is that dark tourists are more difficult to categorize than the segmented groups that make up demand for other generic forms. They may be tiny minorities like Harold and Maude creating their own, private world of funeral sightseers, or larger numbers of single-focus, mass tourists, such as crowds in Westminster Abbey. They may also be a mixed bunch of foreign tourists walking the city streets, some of whom encounter street memorials by accident, others by design. The question of intentionality is a vexatious factor in dark tourism choice (Jamal & Lelo, 2011). To complicate matters further, research suggests that a single dark tourism site may attract several different kinds of audience; at a historical exhibition of skeletons found under London during building excavations, the audiences included parties of schoolchildren provided with teaching materials to fill in and complete, and adult audiences with no such pedagogic pressures on them (Seaton 2009a).

Since there seems to be no homogenous product and no distinctive consumer grouping in dark tourism behaviour, it fails two criteria typically found in generic tourism forms. Its distinctive appeals must therefore lie in some kind of common mental experiences its visitors share at the sites, which are not readily observable to others.

Death, reification and misrecognition

For more than 20 years, the working assumption, which this writer shared, has been that the unifying experience in all dark tourism was 'actual or symbolic encounters with death' (Seaton, 1996: 240, 2021). There are now reasons for thinking that the first half of this characterization was, and is, false. Dark tourists rarely, if ever, have 'actual contact' with death or the dead unless they witness the dying process. For the most, part, death is reification, an abstraction, rather than a physical object of the tourism gaze. Reification is the process whereby an intangible, hypothetical construct (love, terrorism, greed, hope, death) with no unambiguous physical referent is personified as a living force endowed with its own agency. For centuries, death and the dead have featured as reified presences, personified in literary, religious and artistic texts in which 'the dead speak', though none can recall any specific conversations; and death 'comes to all', though none ever see 'it' arriving in person. The reified presence imputed to death is not physical presence, but the onset of observable absences (of breath, pulse, body heat, etc.), that signify the systemic, internal shutdown of life. Yet, the literary tradition of treating death as real presence has not gone away. A recent book with the provocative title of *The Work of the Dead* (Laqueur 2015) represented death as a collective labour organization whose members were still actively employed in the world. The contents never quite lived up to the hyperbole of the title, but offered what the dust wrapper more reasonably described as an account of, 'how and why the living have cared for the dead'. The evidence for this less fanciful claim was literary texts that spoke *of and for* the dead, rather than work-force evidence of real presence and agency.

Once contact with death is removed from the original conceptualization of dark tourism, what is left is the symbolic level of representation vested in the material signifiers that direct the tourist gaze. In material terms, dark tourist experiences are sensory, travelling encounters with sites, settings and events intended to represent and embody death and the dead. They include memorial gardens, statues, rubrics on buildings and, most of all, funerary architecture and their textual supports (e.g. headstones, epitaphs, photographs on graves). They also include many kinds of artefact in exhibitions and museums (Deetz & Dethlefsen, 1994). These are the only observed and observable physical phenomena in dark tourism. Recognizing this fact brings to light a determination that was previously lost whilst death and the dead were supposed to be the experience. It is that it is the living who control what the tourist is exposed to at dark tourism sites. The dead do not talk, walk or work. They are spoken of, and for, by the remembrance choices of others who mark their memory. This is something that has long been known to the funeral industry that markets its services not to the tastes and desires of the dead but to those of the living, even though the latter may sincerely attempt to articulate 'truths' about the dead in the memorial texts they create for them. Doing the best by the dead is always a matter of doing the best by the living who choose and resource commemorative measures.

Deposing contact with death and substituting encounters with 'remembrance' as the focus of the dark tourism gaze has been ventured in a revised definition of dark tourism as: Travel encounters with engineered and orchestrated remembrance of mortality and fatality (Seaton, 2017, 2018). There follows an account of how this reformulation affects notions of dark tourism experience by opening up to scrutiny factors that were not apparent in death and the dead as the principal encounters, rather than factoring in the nature and origins of commemorative representations that form the business end of 'remembrance'.

Remembrance at the keyboard of imagination

'Remembrance' is a word in wide general currency but one that has attracted no special attention as a 'key word' in cultural and social science analysis. It is not, for example, in Williams' seminal inventory (Williams, 1973). Yet, it is a construct of growing relevance in approaching issues related to the formation of identity and the imagining of society that Williams might well include in 2021. The word has a long pedigree in lexical history that can be traced back to the dictionary of Dr Johnson (Johnson, 1785) and before, to the more modern ones of Webster (1976), the Oxford English Dictionary (OED, 1990) and Collins in the new millennium (Collins, 2000). Despite variations, they share three broad core meanings of 'remembrance' that bear closely on the dark tourism experience.

The first is as a synonym for functioning memory. The relevant entries in the four dictionaries comprise: 'Memory... Retention in memory' (Johnson 1785); 'Faculty or power of remembering or calling to mind' (Webster, 1976); '...memory or recollection in relation to a particular thing' (OED, 1990); '...the act of remembering or state of being remembered' (Collins, 2000). In all these, remembrance is the physical capacity to call things to mind, without adumbrating what they should be and what valuation should be attached to them.

The second order of meaning is remembrance as affective memory of people. The relevant mentions are: 'surviving memory of a person' (Johnson, 1785); 'record of some fact or person' and 'memorial inscription'; (OED, 1990); 'something that serves to keep in or bring to mind' (Webster, 1976); 'the act of honouring some past event, person, etc.' (Collins, 2000). In all these definitions, remembrance is personal recall of private or collective absence and loss and the commemorative measures they produce. This emotional resonance was intensified to an almost sacred degree after the unprecedented carnage of two World Wars. In the years that followed, 'Remembrance' gradually became a concept in upper case, a one-word metonymy that corralled a nexus of ideas: the mass sacrifices of soldiers and civilians killed in wars; the grief of survivors; and the commemorative rituals inaugurated to perpetuate the memory of the dead. Remembrance as this sense of sacralized loss has since been adopted internationally by *post bellum* nations and groups commemorating Jewish holocaust sites in Europe, atom bomb victims in Nagasaki and Hiroshima, as well the dead of two world wars. All have evolved as major dark tourism sites.

The third order of meaning is not about remembrance as sacred memory, but as normative, cautionary reminders of obligations owed by regulated individuals or populations to authorities of some kind: private, commercial or political. The OED (1990) calls this kind of remembrance: 'The act of reminding or putting in mind'. In Webster's (1976) dictionary, it is, 'the state of bearing in mind', a meaning historically exemplified by Roman soldiers instructed to, '... keep the Jews in mind of their provincial status' – that is, of their legal position under Roman law (Webster, 1976). In medieval England there was an appointed, government official whose role it was to remind subjects of the many obligations they owed and must 'bear' in mind to the king. He was called a 'remembrancer'. The name died out, but the functional role lives on in the *praxis* of state and corporate power in *re*-minding people of enforceable obligations that people owe the state in, for example, tax declarations, TV licencing, obeying orders in the armed forces and other domains of public life.

All three orders of meaning operate individually or in some combination, as notes struck on the keyboard of imagination and remembrance, constituting what in Wittgenstein's terms might be termed the 'state of affairs' or 'that which is the case' (Wittgenstein, 1953), in dark tourism experiences as visitors gaze on the material forms of engineered remembrance. Type 1 remembrance is cultural memory among visitors, which, for example, allows them to understand that restaurants and cafes named *Dracula* or *Frankenstein* invite ironic, playful or sceptical gothic performance among family parties and young adults. Type 2 remembrance is person-centred, and comes into play at sites and ritual events where visitors have, or are induced during the experience to feel, an emotional relationship with the dead that calls forth responses of respect and homage, such as those experienced at war memorials and holocaust sites. Type 3 remembrance is a more prescriptive 'bearing in mind', a kind of coercive control directing visitors at certain sites to remember norms of appropriate reaction and conduct that may be signposted as warnings: ('Do not touch the exhibits'; 'Do not leave litter'; 'Private. Stay out!'). The three may at times merge and be difficult to differentiate. Certain national memorial sites and ceremonies might seem to be Type 2 sites where reverence seems voluntary, but not conforming to 'appropriate' norms of visitor behaviour (e.g. in dress, in voice levels, in orderly navigation of the site), might be chastised or sanctioned verbally or non-verbally.

Engineered remembrance of the dead is both creation and consumption. It is a construct manufactured by one group of people to deliver a psychological experience for audiences exposed to the end results. Dark tourism visitation is thus as much a socially produced process as a psychological experience that is dependent on two necessary antecedent conditions: (a) the social selection and evaluation of significant others among the deceased made by living groups motivated to perpetuate their memory; and (b), the choice of material signifiers, judged appropriate by the living groups, for symbolically passing on their preferred memory of the dead to audiences in the present and future (e.g. in epitaphs, memorial tablets, news bulletins and so on).

Mortality and fatality

Centering 'encounters with engineered remembrance' as the core experience in dark tourism makes possible an analytical distinction that is not explicit if it is seen as one with the unilateral abstraction of 'death'. It is that between mortality and fatality.

Mortality comprises deaths of the 'great majority' who live private lives and die from natural causes in regulated conditions at home, or in hospital beds, among family and friends. Their demise attracts few headlines and their funerals are, typically, modest ones with tributes in words and flowers that are followed by more permanent, commemorative textual installations at the grave or on memorial tablets. These are erected by families whose commemorative choices may functionally represent all three of the remembrance variants discussed in that: they are intended to make those who see them cognitively aware of the deceased by name; to feel the affective intensity of loss the departed represent to family and friends; and to discharge the obligatory closure required by society, and one deemed fitting for the deceased by his/her social peers.

Fatality comprises exceptional deaths deemed significant for two different reasons. One is the fact the manner of death has a degree of spectacular pathos and fascination through being premature, sudden, violent or one happening simultaneously to many. Fatality may turn the deaths of unknown, private individuals into overnight celebrities (e.g. murder victims) or into anonymous celebrities in tragic collectives (air crash victims, natural disaster victims). The second kind of fatality comprises that of individuals, the manner of whose death might be unexceptional and thus deemed mortality, but whose acquired fame or celebrity lifts their demise above that of ordinary citizens. This may be signified by the scale of engineered remembrance it attracts after trailered volumes of acclaim and interdiscursive attention they have already attracted during life – through, for example, their work, their wealth, the media and their social connections.

Certain kinds of public commemoration are engineered and orchestrated, less as expressive gestures by family and friends than as attempts by powerful institutions and organizations to influence mass audiences. Commemoration has always been a prime instrument of statecraft organized, financed and conducted by regimes and governments in the development of empires and nations from the Assyrians, Egyptians and Romans of antiquity to latter day ones in Eastern and Western Europe and America. In the days before printing and the mass media following, the prime theatre of commemoration was the outdoor world of public spaces, streets and nodal traffic points (e.g. bridges, harbours, transport terminals) where citizens and visitors went about their daily business, or took their pleasures on foot or as conveyed passengers. The streets have continued to be a major theatre of commemoration as the population size, density and geographical spread of world cities has increased beyond bounds known in antiquity.

Public commemorations and gang shows

Great public memorials are always a collective gang show initiated by a few but consumed by the many. The notion of 'the gang' and 'gangers' is an analogy from the world of building construction, which highlights the fact that memorial installations are a managed combination of human and mechanical resources, a mixture of brain work and brute force. Their beginnings are in resource allocation, then drawing board design, followed by a period of observable construction work. At their conclusion, they are typically signed off by a public launch fronted by an official or celebrity figure. From then on, most traces of their origins disappear; they survive as urban wallpaper that their citizens absorb, by cultural osmosis, as part of their identity. For tourists from abroad, they become navigational landmarks, attractions and icons of the national 'other' they have come to experience. Today London, Washington, Beijing, Delhi and many world capitals commemorate their dead significant others through the silent witnesses of street names, memorial buildings, monuments, memorial gardens and in statuary. Their strategic position makes them hard to avoid, so that to some extent they represent co-opted encounters with commemoration that makes them questionable as authentic, dark tourism choices. What counts as an encounter? Could it be accidental, pass-by exposure or is more prolonged contact required? If so, for how long? Is exposure alone enough, or is some specific perception necessary (e.g. reading and registering the inscription on a monument?). Finally, is some kind of reactive action required t (e.g. taking a selfie at a site? Visiting a house open to the public?). These questions regarding exposure, comprehension, perception and action have parallels with those investigated by researchers trying to measure the effect of outdoor advertising where attempts take place to differentiate audiences functionally into how many walk past a site, notice the advert, register something about its message and act in some way on it. These empirical questions about the more transitory experiences in dark tourism need to be added to those asked about more substantive ones, where intentionality and motivation can be more safely assumed (e.g. Biran, Poria & Oren, 2011; Jamal & Lelo, 2011).

The distinction between the mortality and fatality may be a blurred one, but as a crude rule-of-thumb one it reveals a significant bias in dark tourism visitation and academic research. It is that, though mortality carries off the majority of the dead in all societies, fatality attracts most tourists and dominates academic attention. This pre-occupation with fatality, rather than mortality, supports Stone's premise about the constitutive importance of significant other deaths in dark tourism but raises questions about the sequestration thesis he draws on to explain it. According to this, tourists engage in dark tourism as a way of pursuing *memento mori* reflections on their own mortality through contemplating the death of others in ways sequestered in modern life (Stone, 2011, 2018). If this were so, it might logically be expected that most visitors would do so at sites of mortality, commemorating 'ordinary' people like themselves – in the same way that the medieval, Catholic church constantly reminded its believers that death awaited 'Everyman' – rather than at sites of fatality comprising atrocity, disaster and celebrity deaths more remote from the lives of majority populations. The contemplation of significant other fatalities should logically provoke not self-reflections but sympathy for others or, on occasion, the nastier emotion of *schadenfreude* at their misfortunes. These experiential self/other issues, which may vary at different commemorative sites, have yet to be explored in psychological studies of dark tourism experiences.

When completed, engineered remembrance of fatality and mortality forms the experiential highway that dark tourists travel in their journeys and imaginings. It is not a completed road but one always under construction or, to use a different metaphor, a carousel in which people are constantly allowed on and quietly or violently seen off. This is because the people whose remembered fatality and mortality are the subject of the tourism gaze change as society's knowledge of them changes. Re-evaluation of the dead by the living results in additions and subtractions to the social stocks of the commemorated dead, as well as modifications to narratives told about those already in it. These variations affect dark tourist experiences.

Dark tourism, therefore, raises issues not found in other kinds of generic tourism experiences. It may be a public good provided free by the state, or a commercial product with an admission price. It may be carefully chosen after pre-planning like a trip to Graceland, or a spontaneous picnic lunch in a Swiss cemetery. It may be an organized school trip to view skeletons dug up during road works in London, or a brief street stop just long enough to read a blue plaque recording the house where a famous writer died. It may be crowds queuing to see memorials to dead royalty in Westminster Abbey, or Maude and Harold, an exclusive group of two, edgily situated at a graveside watching the burial of someone they never knew.

The idiosyncrasies of dark tourism experience mean that the notions of planning and appraisal used in other kinds of tourism analysis are difficult to apply. This can be illustrated by looking at a theory first developed in retail in the late 1980s and early 1990s that became influential in hospitality and tourism. This was the SERVQUAL expectation/fulfilment model of customer satisfaction (Parasuraman, Zeithaml & Berry, 1985, 1988, 1991). The model assumes that visitor/guest markets can be segmented into relatively homogenous groups of consumers and that product value can be created for each by first, researching their tastes and expectations, then supplying experiences that fulfil them and, finally, evaluating the results using scaled measures of fulfilment in relation to expectations. The idea was promoted and taken up in hospitality and tourism (see, Ryan, 1997) and still informs much hospitality and tourism marketing. It works well where the choice criteria of experiences and basic benefits sought are clearly known and can be met by discrete products offering customized benefits, located uniformly in one place, at specified times (hotel rooms, leisure facilities, golf courses), and which can be evaluated in before-and-after measurements of satisfaction. Few of these conditions are met in many of the dark tourism encounters discussed here. They do not happen in one kind of place within a fixed time framework, nor do they deliver identically repeatable and predictable outcomes. They may not be constructed packages created organizationally by others, but may be do-it-yourself activities, like those of Maude and Harold, requiring no tourism provider.

Dark tourism also has an additional feature that makes it transactionally unique. Unlike other tourism forms, it is not essentially a two-way relationship between a host/provider who supplies a discrete, ready-made, product package to a tourist/guest. Dark tourism encounters involve a phantom third party, the commemorated dead, an imminent, invisible presence formed, as an epiphenomenon of the tourist gaze on the material signifiers of commemoration that produces the dark tourism experience. The commemorated dead have no physical presence but live on in the minds of visitors as constructs, phantasmagoria with no settled identity. They are always susceptible to remembrance shifts brought about by future re-engineering and re-orchestration efforts of groups or individuals. Remembrance shifts may improve the posthumous standing of the dead or move it into decline or oblivion. They may take place over a long period or happen with dramatic suddenness, and are always beyond the control of either the dead or those who originally commemorated them. This means that some kinds of dark tourism experience are inherently uncontrollable and variable in ways that other kinds of tourism are not. It also makes dark tourism something of a socio-political barometer and lightning conductor, since how visitors react to the commemorated dead when encountering their memorials may provoke basic questions not just about the person commemorated, but about those who authorized, sanctioned and perpetuated it in the present.

Public remembrance and dark tourism experiences

Remembrance and commemoration of events and people have involved debates and controversies that have made them high on news agendas in the early twenty-first century. This chapter concludes with instances that indicate the interface between movements in public remembrance and dark tourism *praxis*. These are typified and inventoried under different headings that suggest how remembrance issues have affected, and been affected by, dark tourism. The typology identifies variations in the momentum and direction of remembrance as a dynamic process, in which it may be characterized as co-created, fast-tracked, excluded, withheld, abandoned, withdrawn, re-narrated in anticipation, radically revised, unconsidered, contested and burlesqued.

Loading and reloading dark tourism experiences

Co-created remembrance

If the SERQUAL model described earlier is of limited use in approaching dark tourism experience, a different one has greater traction. It is that of co-creation. This was a concept promoted in tourism planning and research in the 1990s and still provokes theory and discussion (Prebensen, Chen & Uysal, 2014) – see also Chapter 40 in this volume. Its basis was the belief that a new tourist was emerging who was more demanding than the model of previous ones (Poon, 1993). This 'new tourist' sought greater agency in vacation behaviour and more freedom from one-size-fits-all, tour packaging, allowing more flexible choices and greater participation in making them. Over the next two decades, it appeared to be a prophecy fulfilled. There were seismic increases in internet surfing and shopping around, using websites and social networks in negotiating the timing, costing and booking of travel and touring options. Travel agencies and tour operators, who had once managed these components, went into some decline. However, it gradually transpired that it was the means of recreational travel and tourism – travel costs, the timing and location of flights and accommodation – rather than destination tastes and experiences that were most affected. The latter did not greatly change; sun and sea holidays continued to thrive; and golfing breaks, skiing holidays and theme park trips remained much the same, even if those taking them now shopped around in accessing them and negotiating some of the individual components.

Co-creation, and sometimes self-creation, can play a more substantive role in dark tourism experience than in other forms of tourism. Three points deserve emphasis. One is that although dark tourism experiences may vary from fleeting street contacts to tours lasting days or weeks, they are predominantly brief encounters and short excursions within a repertoire of other experiences on vacation. Secondly, there is no generic provider of dark tourism because there is no single, experiential option that quintessentializes 'engineered remembrance' that can be provided as a standard product. Instead, it constitutes a variety of separable activities, few of which are ones that many tourists would want to spend more than limited time pursuing. Consider… A school holiday lasting a week with the kids in Highgate cemetery? A bank holiday weekend at Auschwitz? A two-day ride on a fair ground ghost train? A honeymoon anniversary among the mummified cadavers in a Palermo crypt? None are tenable options. Dark tourism experiences are mainly less-than-one-day components in the vacation scripting of repertoires, though some may have lasting, emotional impact.

Thirdly, as Harold and Maude demonstrate, there is no need for a 'provider' in all cases. Dark tourism experiences have come into being in which individuals and groups have created their own remembrancing, engineering and orchestrating them in improvised rituals and leave-behind, memorial messages. The mega-example in the late twentieth century was the peoples' shrine to Princess Diana, created outside Buckingham Palace, to which thousands from across Britain travelled as pilgrims to place flowers and mount vigils for weeks after her death (Grünhagen, 2010). Later, a permanent memorial was built and opened to the public by the Spencer family at Althorp, their country home, as a commercial visitor attraction.

However, long before Princess Diana's death, unofficial, do-it-yourself public commemoration had taken hold in Europe and America in the spread of roadside memorials to accident victims, created with flowers, pictures and personal mementos by relatives and friends. From the late 1950s, the deaths of young rock stars elicited outpourings of grief, expressed in vigils and improvised shrines outside their homes, at their death sites and on their graves where fans hung out and left messages. Beneficiaries of this improvised, rock necrophilia included: Eddy Cochran and Marc Bolan, both road accident victims in England; John Lennon, murdered outside his flat opposite Central Park, New York in 1980 where a permanent memorial now exists; and Freddie Mercury and George Michael who died in 1992 and 2016 respectively, at homes where fans gathered, lamented and left trash. After a few years, at the request of families, friends and neighbours, the sites were cleared and further memorial activity ended.

Dark tourism has also included co-created tourism at sites of high profile crimes including terrorism, assassination and serial killing. These typically began as unprompted visits by curious sightseers which grew to require intervention and management by public authorities. Two English examples in the 1970s and 1980s were the homes of serial killers Fred West and Peter Sutcliffe ('The Yorkshire Ripper'). West's home in Gloucester was demolished by local government authorities to end sightseeing. The World Trade Centre site of 9–11 where over 3000 people died in a terrorist attack is a major international instance of tourism that began spontaneously and developed into managed and authorized permanence.

The digital revolution has made possible new commercial kinds of co-created dark tourism; this has included rapid response, *á la carte* guiding for visitors out and about in prime tourist locations. In 2018, for example, customized ghost tours around the City of Oxford were offered and delivered to order by local 'pop-up' flying squads who could travel on foot or by bike and pick up tourists on the streets at points of their choice, from bookings made using choices prompted by smart phones. These 'gig economy' entrepreneurs attracted the hostility of taxi drivers and trained guides who worked from fixed bases at set times during the day.

An edgier kind of sepulchral co-creation has emerged in and around the Catacombs of Paris. These are underground networks of more than 200 miles of galleries, rooms and chambers where, for two centuries, skulls and skeletal remains were stored after clearance from old churchyards and cemeteries to make way for later internments. In the nineteenth century they had featured in tourist guidebooks and had been guided visitor attractions for visiting English. In the mid-twentieth century, small groups of academic visitors began entering them as freelance, subterranean *flaneurs*[2] exploring their history. They called themselves 'cataphiles', and the entrances and exits through which they made illegal entries, '*chatières*' (catflaps). In 2018, a new generation of cataphiles began repurposing them as an avant-garde adventure playground and creative theme park, for art exhibitions and 'happenings'. They opened up closed-off spaces, creating new pathways and decorated them with graffiti murals, carvings and mystic mosaic works involving thousands of tiles, and featuring zombie skulls with popping eyes, tags and fantastic names. They offered guided trips to small parties of intrepid tourists, which included the writer Robert McFarlane. All were supplied with primitive maps to an alterior geography that included underground landmarks named: *The Room of Cubes, The Boutique of Psychosis, Crossroads of the Dead, The Medusa, The Monastery of the Bears* and *Room Z*. Health and safety risks were signposted in remembrance warnings of spots where headroom and spaces were: 'tight', 'very low', 'flooded', 'impracticable', 'impassable', 'humid' or 'unstable' (Macfarlane, 2019). This *bricolage* of co-creation, combining elements of caving, tunnelling, surrealism, fantasy art and the situationist mockeries of Guy Debord (Debord, 1983) links dark tourism with 'experimental tourism' (Antony & Henry, 2005) and psychogeography (Morton, Stone & Jarratt, 2018).

Fast-tracked remembrance

An aspect of engineered remembrance in public agendas in the twenty-first century has been the variety and abundance of celebratory anniversaries, jubilees and memorial tributes with shorter commemorative time-spans. Centenaries were once the gold standard of temporal significance but the celebratory intervals have come down to 75, 50, or even 25 years, particularly in remembering the varying events of the two World Wars. Since commemorative narratives include the deaths of significant others and events with a specific geography (women's issues, gay pride, the start and end of wars), all are dark tourism experiences in the making. In 2016, the 100th anniversary of the Irish uprising was accompanied by a coordinated tourism drive by national and regional tourism organizations to attract international expatriates back to Ireland for the celebrations; this generated 834,000 extra visitors and the highest ever overseas revenue from tourism (Failte Ireland, 2017).

A symptom of this burgeoning era of commemoration is the speed at which new figures, places and issues inspire engineered remembrance. It sometimes took the Catholic Church centuries to authenticate miracles and sanctify new saints; today, public commemoration may sacralize people, causes and agendas in years or even months rather than centuries. This reflects the speed and reach of global and digital communications and the efforts of lobbying groups using them to publicize exemplary others as dead heroes and villains associated with specific causes. Issues once hidden or denied see the light of day. The smart phone has turned every traveller into a photo-journalist manqué, documenting and circulating events caught on camera as enduring remembrance texts. The killing of a black man, George Floyd, in Minneapolis on camera by a white policeman in 2020 became the catalyst for the launch of the 'Black Lives Matter' campaign. Within weeks, it provoked public demonstrations across America and forms of remembrance travel and protest that have been taken up around the world (Floyd, 2020).

A less global but nevertheless remarkable instance of rapid reclamation took place between 1997 and 2019 in Guadeloupe, a former French colony in Africa. It was that of Mulatta Solitude, the daughter of an African slave, who was raped by sailors on a boat whilst being deported into slavery in the early nineteenth century. She later took part in a slavery revolt. For this she was tried and hanged by the French authorities in 1802, one day after giving birth to a baby. No written details of her life survived, her real name is uncertain, and for two centuries she existed only in popular memory. In 1999, however, a memorial statue was placed in her memory on a Guadeloupe street, *Héros aux Abymes Boulevard*, followed in 2007 by a statue, erected in the Île-de-France region in France, celebrating her and the abolition of the slave trade. It was the first memorial to a slavery resistance movement. In 2014, local authorities established a housing estate in the town of Ivry-sur-Seine where one of the roads was named *Allée de la Mulâtresse Solitude*. Six years later, Solitude came to the capital when the Mayor of Paris inaugurated a memorial garden in the *Place of Général-Catroux* with the first statue to a black woman in Paris (Mulatta Solitude, 2020).

Excluded remembrance

Commemoration is clear to all who gaze on its material signifiers. What is not commemorated often passes without notice but may assume great importance later. The sociologist, Macheret, coined the term 'significant silences' to describe literary texts in which what was excluded was as important, or more so, than what remained. Dark tourism has had its share of significant silences that have contributed to the impact of narratives about people and events when finally told and commemorated.

The reasons for exclusion have been many. Politics may make those in positions of official or unofficial power restrict the posthumous voices of people they regard as a threat to their interests, or as witnesses to actions and events they do not want known. In wars, patriotic bias makes almost all countries commemorate their own and their allies' dead but rarely those of their foes. This means that later, when commemorative sites attract visitors from different cultures and countries, they may resent the exclusion or marginalization of their war dead. This was a situation that existed at Waterloo, the first great battlefield to become a mass tourism site where, from 1815 until the 1990s, the French were allowed no memorials, and also at British imperial war sites of the Victorian age in Africa where 'natives' killed in tribal battles with the British had no memorials for their dead (Seaton, 1998; Seaton & Lennon, 2004).

Significant silences may also be imposed for reasons of state security and civilian morale in times of war. In October 1917, during World War I, an explosion in an ammunitions factory at White Lund in Lancaster, England, blew up killing 250 women workers. No news or commemoration of this tragedy was permitted and even relatives of the dead were told to keep silent. In 2017, a century later, the tragedy was first commemorated in a centenary exhibition in a Lancaster museum, and information about it has been available there since. Commemorative absence may also be due to a lack of resources to fund commemoration. In the past, unmarked graves among the poor were common due to the high cost of monumental signage and memorials. Though pauper graves are less common in modern times, financial and cultural capital remains a key influence on the scale, visibility and continuity of commemoration.

Decisions about 'dark' commemoration in public spaces are not just about relations between those who create them and those who visit them. Commemoration inherently is affected by other stakeholders. One group may be residents living near projected sites who may be concerned by the number and type of visitors attracted and also by the nature of the memorial. Not everyone wants the sacred space of home marked down as an atrocity site or workplace catastrophe. Another key stakeholder group is that comprising the descendant communities of the dead, as in the case, for later discussion, of Spaniards seeking details and commemoration of their family members killed by General Franco in the Spanish Civil War. The interaction between different stakeholders at dark tourism sites has been modelled as a heritage 'force field' that may involve conflicting interests (Seaton, 2001: 123–126, 2009b: 75–108).

Remembrance withheld

Remembrance withheld is not suppression of dark commemoration but, rather, the prevention of certain groups from access to it. An international religious and cultural example is that of the historical exclusion of non-Muslim visitors from Mecca, the site of Mohammed's final days on earth. The ban was taken as a challenge by some Victorian literary travellers who regarded access to everywhere as an imperial right and a small number managed to enter Mecca under cover in disguise and duly published their accounts (Ralli 1909). Other reasons for dark exclusions have been: military (concealment of covert operations, weapon testing and 'enhanced interrogation' prisons); risks from environmental hazards and disasters (pollution, radiation levels, famine); and health factors (epidemics, plagues). Secret locations, when they become known, exert considerable dark tourism appeal. It was this that encouraged a publisher in 2012 to commission a guidebook to places people could never visit. It listed 100 international sites and was, unexpectedly, very well illustrated (Smith, 2012).

A different kind of targeted exclusion was that at Lockerbie, one of the blackest of dark tourism sites of the 1980s. Just before Christmas in 1988, a bomb exploded on board a Pan Am flight from London to New York. The aircraft broke up and crashed over the small

Scottish town of Lockerbie, killing 243 passengers, 16 crew and 11 people on the ground. 189 of the passengers were American. The story made headline news across the world and began attracting streams of international journalists as well as voyeuristic sightseers turning off the major motorway nearby to the stricken town. In response, its resident community banded together to deny information, accommodation or cooperative assistance to media teams and inquisitive trippers. The only visitors welcomed were relatives and friends of the victims, a number of whom were Americans who formed close ties with the Lockerbie community in later years. There are memorials at Arlington National Cemetery and Syracuse University in the United States. The main local memorial, a mile west of the town, is now a Garden of Remembrance with the Lockerbie Air Disaster Memorial. A nearby visitors' centre offers information about the area and the disaster, and a Book of Remembrance (Lockerbie, 2020; Sharpley & Wright, 2018: 336–337).

Abandoned remembrance

Abandoned remembrance is commemoration that once was but is no more. It may be a site that still exists but has lost its audience or a memorial that can no longer be read. The reasons may be physical or social. The physical factors include the climatic effects of wind and weather that progressively degrade the materials of commemoration. Flowers fade first and are removed from graves. Wooden crosses rot within a century. The longevity of stone monuments varies with sandstone inscriptions decaying fastest, whilst granite and marble survive longer. Human factors may shorten the life cycle of commemoration more than physical ones, the key one being that the dead in modern towns and cities are soon forgotten. Their graves are rarely visited or tended for more than three generations after their death, which is why burial spaces may be leased for a limited period and discreetly cleared for new occupants when the lease runs out. Abandonment may also be the fate of large communal sites that were once thriving but become derelict as the communities whose dead once filled them change or move away. This kind of sepulchral defection is observable in ex-colonies where Europeans once established their own churches and cemeteries, most of which were closed long ago. There are an estimated 700–1,000 British internment sites across India from the days of the Empire, many of them well-documented (De Rhe-Philipe, 1912; Irving 1910). These already have some dark tourism appeal to military history buffs, family history researchers and other British tourists who form India's main European market.

Archaeology is a mighty agency in the discovery and reclamation of neglected remembrance through its mission to unearth traces of past cultures that have been buried for centuries. Once excavated and exhibited, all sites and artefacts become engineered remembrance of vanished civilizations for the dark tourism gaze. The discovery of Pompeii and Herculaneum in the mid-eighteenth century was the first archaeological exhumation to demonstrate the fascination of what is under the ground for travellers above (Skinner, 2018). Nearly 300 years later, in 1974, the accidental unearthing of the Terracotta Warriors at the funerary site of Qin Shi Huang, the first Emperor of China, became a comparable dark tourism sensation (Anon 2020a, 2020b). In 2012, another royal discovery, the remains of the English King Richard III under a Leicester car park, led to his reburial in Leicester Cathedral and the opening of a Visitor Centre in 2014 on the site of Greyfriars, the medieval friary where he was originally buried. The synergy between archaeology, anthropology and dark tourism is a strong, inter-disciplinary meeting ground for the progress of thanatology.

Tony Seaton

Withdrawn remembrance

Western museums have historically exhibited cross-cultural objects with dark tourism associations (weapons, funerary artefacts, memorial statuary, etc.). These were once put on with curatorial equanimity and accepted uncritically by audiences who were predominantly white, western and Christian. In the 1990s, an interrogative 'new museology' (Vergo, 1989) emerged that recognized the growing diversity of multi-cultural audiences and the issues relating to identity and belief that museum exhibits might provoke (Kaplan, 1994; Rugg & Sedgewick, 2007). In the years following, anticipation of cultural impacts became a high priority for cultural institutions anxious to avoid reactive apologetics. The new orientation did not just affect museum planning before new exhibits went on show; it also led some institutions to review their existing collections as good, cultural housekeeping practice. The Pitt-Rivers Museum in Oxford, a world famous museum of Anthropology and Archaeology, conducted a reviewing of its ethnology collections in 2020, the result of which was the decision to withdraw one of its most popular exhibits from public display. This was a collection of 12 *tsantas*, shrunken heads from Peru and Chile, made by the Shuar and Achuar people in the rainforests of Ecuador and Peru. The problem was not the collection *per se*, but its attribution to 'headhunters' which audience research suggested perpetuated 'racist stereotypes'. The Museum expects to reinstate the heads with a revised textual framing at a later date (Pitt-Rivers, 2020).

Remembrance as anticipatory re-narration

Anticipatory re-narration is a variant of withdrawal. It is the process of changing and/or extending an original commemorative narrative before it provokes comments. A prime example made media headlines in Britain in 2020 when the National Trust, Britain's largest heritage organization, published the results of a survey it had conducted revealing that over 100 of the properties in its custodial portfolio had been established by donors with historical connections to slavery (National Trust, 2020). The connection had been an embarrassing but uncorroborated suspicion for some years, but not one widely disseminated. The admission was a major public revision to the Trust's cultivated emphasis on the 'grace and favour' attributes of its buildings and collections as monuments to the perfected values and taste of lost ages of elegance. It set a precedent in acknowledging the 'dark' contradictions that may co-exist in exhibiting fine art and beautiful objects, and parallels ongoing dilemmas about the marketing of plantation houses in the American south (see Dann & Seaton, 2001). In both the UK and USA, important re-narration may be required as an alternative to withdrawing items in collections.

Remembrance as radical reversal

Radical reversal is a commemorative U turn that removes a positive narrative and replaces it with a negative one, or *vice versa*. A bitter and ongoing example of downgrading is that of the remembrancing of the Civil War in Spain fought in 1937 between international brigades of socialists and communists and fascist nationalists led by General Franco. The Nationalists won and, under Franco's direction, systematically mass murdered their opponents in the years following. Some died as slave labourers in building a granite mausoleum for the dictator outside Madrid. Whilst Franco lived, people feared to challenge his regime. Spain prospered from a tourist boom during which Franco's Mausoleum became

Loading and reloading dark tourism experiences

a tourist attraction. However, since the restoration of democracy in 1974, there have been increasing demands for records on the disappeared victims of Franco's rule to be revealed and for commemoration of them to be made. A first attempt to redress this was with a law of 'historical memory' in 2007, which aimed to remove fascist symbols from public buildings and recognize the mistreatment of Franco's victims. It was only partly implemented. The government has since proposed a law of 'democratic memory' that would go further (Franco, 2019).

Radical reversal upwards has been that of the memory of Alan Turing, a brilliant mathematician who died in ignominy. He had led the Enigma code breaking project during the Second World War at Bletchley in the UK. This was a secret British government team set up to crack coded messages transmitted by the German High Command. Its success ultimately allowed the British and Americans to monitor German communications in real time throughout the later years of the War, gaining advance knowledge of their military intentions and movements. The information was said to have shortened the war and saved thousands of lives. Turing's contribution was unknown to the general public after the war ended but, in 1952, he became notorious through a conviction for homosexual activities, at that time a criminal offence. The disgrace drove him to suicide. It was only after laws against homosexuality were passed in 1967 and the LBGT gay movement lobbied for his recognition that Turing's name and work were honoured. In 2019, a national BBC poll voted him 'Icon of the century', beating Pablo Picasso, Nelson Mandela and Dr Martin Luther King Jr. A statue to his memory was unveiled in Sackville Park near Manchester University where he worked, which is at the heart of the Gay Village (Turing 2019, 2020). Bletchley has become a prime tourist attraction in Central England.

Unconsidered remembrance

Unconsidered remembrance is non-awareness of fatality and mortality as dark tourism resources. This is a geographical issue. As an explicit discourse, dark tourism originated in Western Europe and awareness of it has spread most among English-speaking nations where its novelty value may have led to exaggerated impressions of its consumer dimensions. No data on its national or international scale in visitor numbers or expenditures have ever been presented. However, if its consumer dimensions are uncertain, its mind-boggling potential in supply terms is guaranteed since fatality and mortality, the necessary raw materials of dark tourism, are never going to run out. They are not, however, in themselves a reliable indicator of dark tourism's future. The sufficient condition for this is not the number of the dead but that of the living with the desire and resources to commemorate selectively those events and figures they wish to perpetuate for posterity. It also depends on the recognition of the touristic value of available, historical events and incidents with compelling narratives of fatality and mortality. In Eastern Europe, centuries of tragic conflicts left legacies of drama and melodrama that were better known to the readers of Murray's and Baedeker's guidebooks to Russia in the nineteenth centuries than to most tourists today.

In the West the agendas of dark tourism will be added to form the growing numbers of figures commemorated as significant others in causes once regarded as minority or unimportant ones. In the early twenty-first century, these have included heroes and martyrs reclaimed in movements concerned with: the judicial treatment of ethnic minorities; slavery past and present; women's politics, and LBGT issues. This stretching of commemorative agendas and challenging of old ones has been named 'the politics of commemoration', a linkage to which this chapter will return.

Reclaimed minorities are not the only ones who may be 'remembranced' into the limelight. Little-known narratives relating to larger populations, past and present, may be granted greater bandwidth as part of the intermittent disclosure through the media of things not generally known, a feature of democracies with a liberal commitment to freedom of expression. One example of global fatality is the fate of civilians killed in wars by air strikes. In the past, the commemorated war dead were male soldiers killed in action on the battlefield. Since the late 1930s, however, air power has made home a major killing field of war. Britain was the first to commemorate this when a memorial to those who died in the London Blitz was begun, and ended as the exemplary Civilian War Dead Roll of Honour, a seven volume book containing printed details of 66,375 dead kept in Westminster Abbey and now online (Civilian-war-dead-roll-of-honour, 2020). Japan also remembers its atom bomb dead at Nagasaki and Hiroshima. But there have been no collective memorials mourning the international scale and pathos of aerial annihilation in the past, to which everyone is always vulnerable, and which has happened most to populations with no aerial power of their own to resist. (Fair Play may be another concept whose demise needs remembrancing globally). If the world can unite in solidarity behind the dangers of global warming and pandemic, remembrance of casualties of aerial carnage might be a way of limiting it in the future.

Another posthumous majority of global scale but limited recognition are casualties of industrialization. The Industrial Revolution brought into being the modern world everyone now inhabits, but its history has been selectively narrated, commemorated and exhibited in public terms. Wang's fine study of tourism and modernity includes an insightful and well-documented analysis of industrialization as a driver that produced changing forms of work experience, consciousness and tourism propensity. However, it underplays the differences in physical and social outcomes among the two major players, labour and management, who brought it on (Wang, 2000: 94–116). Until the 1970s, industrial history was only a specialist tributary of economic history, told as a 'gadgets and widgets' account of technology and the elite lives and deaths of inventor and entrepreneurial elites: Mathew Boulton, James Watt, Henry Ford, William Morris and others. There was limited emphasis on the vast work forces involved and, in particular, on the scale of occupational fatality and mortality, which were recorded in exhaustive government reports and inquiries throughout the nineteenth century. This was synthesized in Oliver's classic study (Oliver, 1902) and in a sensational journalistic account, *The White Slaves of England*, by Oscar Wilde's friend, Robert Sherard (Sherard, 1897).

Since the 1970s, an academic boom in social history has greatly expanded scholarship and public awareness of life and labouring conditions, which has been popularized in the tourism creation of open-air, industrial village museums in the UK in the spatial heartlands of the Industrial Revolution in the North at Beamish, in the Midlands near Ironbridge, and at the Black Country Museum between Birmingham and Wolverhampton. In all of them, past working and living environments have been reconstructed by importing buildings and artefacts from defunct collieries, factories and agricultural sites. They recreate a picturesque version of working life but little about working death.

Commemoration of industrial fatality and mortality was, however, inaugurated in 1989 through international, co-operative trade union efforts. The result was the International Commemoration Day for Dead and Injured that takes place on April 28. This is an annual event that represents a movement to workers killed, disabled, injured or made unwell by their work. It is one that has received little mass media coverage, and is therefore largely unknown to the general public. Its dark tourism potential has therefore yet to be judged.

Loading and reloading dark tourism experiences

Contested remembrance

If the 'politics of commemoration' (Hutton, 2016) has added new figures to the honours board of historical memory, a countervailing tendency has been to contest those already on it. Contestation has been described as, 'the social process through which interest groups handle dominance/ subjugation issues in the politics of tourism' (Hollinshead 2000: 108). In tourism terms, contestation has been vandalism at commemorative sites, particularly in military cemeteries and at war memorials. In the first two decades of the twenty-first century, this has proliferated in America, England, Australia, New Zealand, Russia and France. The activists represented different causes: anti-imperialist, fascist, socialist, anti-slavery and nationalist.

Vandalism of commemorations to individuals has targeted Karl Marx's bust in Highgate Cemetery and a Winston Churchill memorial in Australia. Statues and street monuments have also featured. In 2016, students demanded the removal of a statue of the imperialist, Cecil Rhodes, at Corpus Christi College, Oxford and four years later, the decision was taken to do so (Mohdin, Adams & Quinn, 2020). In 2019, another group in Bristol actually tore down a statue to Colston, a philanthropist who had made his fortune through slavery, and threw it into the river Avon (Wall, 2020).

Contestation may be less dramatic and more constructive. In Sparkhill, a Muslim district in Birmingham, a protest against the perceived lack of media comment on Palestinian fatalities in Israeli/Palestine conflicts took the form of chalking graffiti on residents houses that read 'Gaza off our screens but never out of our hearts'. It received no coverage in the news.

For visitors arriving at any of these sites, they would be offered different 'dark' experience from that which might be expected. Herein lies one of the variations to which the dark tourism experience is uniquely susceptible.

Remembrance as dark burlesque

Dark tourism first appeared in academic agendas with a straight face, as a form of solemn inquiry into what was initially treated as a disturbing postmodern phenomenon, an unprecedented taste for visiting sites of atrocity and suffering as tourist attractions (Foley & Lennon, 1996; Lennon & Foley, 2000; Rojek, 1993). This problem-centred orientation has shaped the choice of research subjects and the tone in which they have been addressed. There are reasons to question, however, how fully these represent what dark tourism is or has been. The alleged post-modernism of dark tourism conflicts with evidence that travelling encounters with engineered remembrance go back millennia, and have been frequent and explicit features of tourism since the late eighteenth century. The prevailing focus on 'big time' disaster and atrocity misses the reality that these sites are in a minority and that of the many others, some have carnivalesque and burlesque features. They include excursions to sites and events that would score among the lighter/lightest on dark tourism scales (Sharpley, 2005; Stone, 2006), such as city ghost tours; visiting historic houses said to be haunted; ghost train rides at funfairs; wax work exhibitions of serial killers and their victims; and eating and drinking off 'coffins' in cafes called *Macabre*, *Fantasia* and *Dracula*.

There is also a more basic contradiction about dark tourism experiences. This is that they take place on holiday, a social space stereotypically marked out for having fun with family and friends – and being (self)-photographed in the act. Carnivalesque features prevailed in holidays in the twentieth century when slot-machine amusements on seaside piers and in amusement arcades, showed peep-show murders and hangings, and at Louis Tussauds in

Blackpool exhibits of the horrible include car crashes and diseased lungs as fun fare frighteners. In the present dungeon experiences are global entertainments and serial killers are domesticated in commodified attractions where Jack the Ripper ceases to be a monstrous form of the 'other' and morphs into family entertainment in Madame Tussaud's and East End tours of London.

These serio-comic disjunctions suggest that dark tourism experiences may straddle binary oppositions between: approach and avoidance; fear and love of the 'other'; family values and disruptive transgression. Dark tourism may be exposure to the Biblical *memento mori* message that, in the midst of life we are in death but, far from receiving it as a cautionary lesson, people seem entertained by the fact on holiday. It seems, at times, not to remind them of their own mortality but to celebrate the buoyant feelings of well-being on holiday in the present, contrasted with the dismal fate of others who are literally past it. It remains for research to reveal how the balance between fear and loathing, and laughter and liking are reconciled in dark tourism experience.

Summary

This chapter began with a number of exemplary mini-cases, intended to represent dark tourism in action, as a way of appraising its experiential features as a generic tourism form compared with others. The procedure proved abortive since dark tourism failed two of the defining conditions of generic tourism. The first was that the experiential variety of activities, settings and occasions, observable in the scenarios, lacked the homogeneity found in other niche tourism products and, secondly, it was impossible to identify any specific, delimited group across the scenarios who shared characteristics that marked them off as dark tourists who were different from the rest of the general population.

There was, however, one common feature. All were encounters in different ways with engineered remembrance, embodied in material forms, constructed by intermediaries at commemorative sites representing the dead. These commemorated displays include memorial gardens, gravesites, monuments, blue plaques and symbolic funerary artefacts (see Deetz & Dethlefsen, 1994). Recognition that these representations of death and the dead are engineered and orchestrated through the commemorative choices of others, not the dead themselves, is critical in assessing dark tourism experiences. It makes the claim that dark tourism is direct mediation between the dead and the living untenable. The impression is simply a tribute to the success of commemoration in appearing to offer the audience a transparent window on to the dead, rather than a third party's representation of the deceased at the point of commemoration. The latter, in Wittgenstein's terms, constitutes the constitutive 'state of affairs', which 'is the case' in dark tourism. The dark tourist only becomes a dark tourist by gazing on a representation of death and the dead, allowed and produced by others.

Recognition of this prompts discussion of elements in dark tourism that have received limited attention. The first is the centrality of remembrance, a concept less singular and straightforward than it might appear. The chapter sketches out its importance in shaping individual identity and the exhibited identity of societies, appraising three main ways it has been articulated in lexical discussions as: functioning memory; personal evaluation; and as commanded attention and respect. All have a resonance in dark tourism experiences as the rest of the chapter insists and illustrates.

The second issue is that of power. Power has been evident in tourism analysis for decades (Cheong & Miller, 2000; Church & Coles, 2007; Hall, 1994; MacLeod & Carrier, 2005), but to less of an extent in dark tourism analysis (but see Sharpley 2009 for an explicit governmental perspective). Once engineered and orchestrated remembrance, not death or the dead, are understood as the real focus in dark tourism, the search is on to find 'who dunnit'; that is, who the engineers and the orchestrators are. The account in this chapter, of the institutional origins of public remembrance and commemoration, was an attempt to do so. It suggests that they are often initiated, managed and resourced by the state and governmental agencies that supply the 'gang show' leverage behind major public memorial and rituals around which dark tourism circulates. All are intended to induct those exposed to them into preferred views of the past by their iterated scale and content, and their location in privileged, public spaces with high pedestrian footfall and traffic flows. As such, they are open air exercises in audience-making that may be difficult to avoid, generating co-opted exposures that everyone may have with street names, blue plaque buildings, memorials, statues, and so on. As part of dark tourism, they may be fleeting and accidental encounters, rather than premeditated choices with variable effects, but they never go away.

The longer, premeditated trips to specific commemorative sites and events that form the majority of dark tourism visitations and attract most research are not so different. They are mainly forms of state supported, engineered remembrance (e.g. military cemeteries, cathedrals, holocaust memorials, shrines to cultural figures, etc.). Though longer than street exposures, they are mainly brief encounters that last hours rather than the days or weeks invested in other kinds of tourism, such as packaged holidays. Dark tourism's relations with remembrance and power make it a part of a burgeoning 'politics of commemoration', contemporary debates and controversies in multi-cultural democracies about how the past should be remembered and publicly exhibited. Since dark tourism is by definition about bringing travellers in contact with commemorated fatality and mortality, its contemporary significance is likely to increase. But if it does, both the dark tourism gaze and guidebook accounts may need to change. Viewing commemorative sites may increasingly take on elements of ideological scrutiny never common before. Guidebooks will have to take account of visitor sensitivities that may result in withdrawn narratives, new narratives or the re-narrating of existing ones that reflect more pluralistic content on what is said at memorial sites about the dead and, on occasion, the recognition of what must not be said. The dead will take no part in this; but those who speak for them may one day be called to public account.

Notes

1 Power and authority may coexist in one individual or group; but in democratic societies, it is more common for them to be, or appear to be, separated at the level of public policy determination.
2 *Flaneur* was a term that emerged in the mid-nineteenth century for a species of young Bohemian who cultivated a kind of insider's knowledge of Paris, gained from walking the streets and knowing the places and the people that were "happening", and the secret lives of underclasses. It was a protest ideology adopted in opposition to the bourgeois world of commerce and convention. Its typical representatives were artists and writers among whom the poet, Baudelaire, came to reign supreme. Its ideas have influenced youth cultures ever since.

References

Anon (2020a) Emperor Qin and the Terracotta Army. Available at: https://www.nationalgeographic.com/history/archaeology/emperor-qin/ (Accessed 1 October 2020).
Anon (2020b) The Teracotta Army. Available at: https://en.wikipedia.org/wiki/Terracotta_Army (Accessed 11 October 2020).
Antony, R. and Henry, J. (2005) *The Lonely Planet Guide to Experimental Travel*. Melbourne, Oakland and London: Lonely Planet Publications.

Biran, A., Poria, Y. and Oren, G. (2011) Sought experiences at (dark) heritage sites *Annals of Tourism Research*, 38(3), 820–841.

Byron, A. (1981) *London Statues: A Guide to London Outdoor Statues and Sculpture*. London: Constable.

Catacombe dei Cappuccini (2020) Capuchinj Monks. Available at: https://en.wikipedia.org/wiki/Catacombe_dei_Cappuccini (Accessed 10 November 2020).

Cheong, S. and Miller, M. (2000) Power and tourism: A Foucauldian observation. *Annals of Tourism Research*, 27(2), 371–390.

Church, A. and Coles, T. (2007) *Tourism, Power and Space*. London: Routledge.

Civilian-war-dead-roll-of-honour (2020) Available at: https://www.westminster-abbey.org/abbey-commemorations/commemorations/civilian-war-dead-roll-of-honour-1939-1945 (Accessed 17 November 2020).

Collins (2000) *Dictionary and Thesaurus*. Glasgow: Harper-Collins.

Dann, G. and Seaton, A. V. (2001) *Slavery, Contested Heritage and Thanatourism*. Binghamton and New York: The Haworth Hospitality Press.

De Rhe-Philipe, G. (1912) *A List of Inscriptions on Christian Tombs or Monuments in the Punjab, North-West Frontier Province, Kashmir and Afghanistan Possessing Historical or Archaeological Interest Part 2*. Lahore: Punjab Government Press.

Debord, G. (1983) *Society of Spectacle*. Detroit: Black and Red.

Deetz, l. and Dethlefsen, E. (1994) Death's head, cherub, urn and willow. In S. Pearce (Ed.), *Interpreting Objects and Collections*. London: Routledge, pp. 30–37.

Dodd, S. (2015) Death at lunchtime: An ethnographic study of locals lunching at Cimitiere des Rois. In D. Dumitran and M. Rotar (Eds.), *Places of Memory: Cemeteries and Funerary Practices Throughout Time. Annales Universitatis Apulendsis Series Histororica*, 19(2), pp. 59–68.

Failte Ireland (2017) *Island of Ireland; Overseas Tourism Performance*. Available at: https://www.tourismireland.com/TourismIreland/media/Tourism-Ireland/Press%20Releases/Press%20Releases%202017/Facts-and-Figures-2016.pdf?ext=.pdf. (Accessed 19 November 2020).

Floyd (2020) The Killing of George Floyd. Available at: https://en.wikipedia.org/wiki/Killing_of_George_Floyd. (Accessed 12 November 2020).

Foley, M. and Lennon, J. J. (1996) Editorial: Heart of darkness. *International Journal of Heritage Studies*, 2(4), 195–197.

Franco (2019) The Spanish Government proposes a new law on history. *The Economist*, 19 September. Available at: https://www.economist.com/europe/2020/09/19/the-spanish-government-proposes-a-new-law-on-history (Accessed 11 November 2020).

Gleichan, L. E. (1928) *London's Open-Air Statuary*. London: Longmans, Green and Co.

Grünhagen, C. (2010) 'Our queen of hearts' – The glorification of Lady Diana Spencer: A critical appraisal of the glorification of celebrities and new pilgrimage. *Scripta Instituti Donneriani Aboensis*, 22, 71–86.

Hall, C. M. (1994) *Tourism and Politics: Policy, Power and Place*. Chichester: John Wiley & Sons.

Hollinshead, K. (2000) Contestation. In J. Jafari (Ed.), *Encyclopaedia of Tourism*. London: Routledge, p. 108.

Hutton, P. (2016) The politics of commemoration. In P. Hutton (Ed.), *The Memory Phenomenon in Historical Writing*. New York: Palgrave Macmillan, pp. 49–72.

Irving, M. (1910) *A List of Inscriptions on Christian Tombs or Monuments in the Punjab, North-West Frontier Province*, Kashmir and Afghanistan Possessing Historical and Archaeological Interest, Part 1. Lahore: Punjab Government Press.

Jamal, T. and Lelo, L. (2011) Exploring the conceptual and analytical framework of dark tourism: From darkness to intentionality. In R. Sharpley and P. Stone (Eds.), *Tourist Experience: Contemporary Perspectives*. Abingdon: Routledge, pp. 43–56.

Johnson, S. (1785) *A Dictionary of the English Language*. London: J.F. and C. Rivington.

Kaplan, F. (1994) *Museums and the Making of 'Ourselves: The Role of Objects in National Identity*. Leicester: Leicester University Press,

Laqueur, T. (2015) *The Work of the Dead*. Oxford: Princeton University Press.

Lennon, J. J. and Foley, M. (2000) *Dark Tourism. The Attraction of Death and Disaster*. London: Continuum.

Lockerbie (2020) Garden of Remembrance. Available at: https://www.undiscoveredscotland.co.uk/lockerbie/gardenofremembrance/index.html (Accessed 15 October 2020).

Loading and reloading dark tourism experiences

London County Council (1901–1930) *Indication of Houses of Historical Interest in London.* London: London County Council.

Macfarlane, R. (2019) The invisible city beneath Paris. *New Yorker*, 23 May. Available at: https://www.newyorker.com/news/dispatch/the-invisible-city-beneath-paris (Accessed 26 October 2020).

MacLeod, D. and Carrier, J. (2005) *Tourism, Power and Culture. Anthropological Insights.* Clevedon: Channel View Publications.

Mohdin, A., Adams, R. and Quinn, B. (2020) Oxford college backs removal of Cecil Rhodes statue. *The Guardian,* 17 June https://www.theguardian.com/education/2020/jun/17/end-of-the-rhodes-cecil-oxford-college-ditches-controversial-statue (Accessed 16 November 2020).

Morten, R., Stone, P. and Jarratt, D. (2018) Dark tourism as psychogeography: An initial exploration. In P. Stone, R. Hartmann, A. V. Seaton, R. Sharpley and L. White (Eds.), *Palgrave Handbook of Dark Tourism Studies.* London: Palgrave Macmillan, pp. 227–255.

Mulatta Solitude (2020) La Mulâtresse Solitude. Available at: https://en.wikipedia.org/wiki/La_Mul%C3%A2tresse_Solitude (Accessed 23 October 2020).

National Trust (2020) Addressing the histories of slavery and colonialism at the National Trust. https://www.nationaltrust.org.uk/features/addressing-the-histories-of-slavery-and-colonialism-at-the-national-trust (Accessed 15 November 2020).

OED. (1990) *The Shorter Oxford English Dictionary on Historical Principles.* London: Guild Publishing.

Oliver, T. (1902/1970) *Dangerous Trades. Health and Safety at Work.* London: Thiemmes Contunuum.

Parasuraman, A., Zeithaml, V. A. and Berry, L. L. (1985) A conceptual model of service quality and its implications for future research. *Journal of Marketing*, 49(4), 41–50.

Parasuraman, A., Zeithaml, V. A. and Berry, L. L. (1988) SERVQUAL: A multiple-item scale for measuring consumer perceptions of service quality. *Journal of Retailing*, 64(1), 12–37.

Parasuraman, A., Zeithaml, V. A. and Berry, L. L. (1991) Refinement and reassessment of the SERVQUAL scale. *Journal of Retailing*, 67(4), 420–430.

Pitt-Rivers (2020) Shrunken-heads. Available at: https://www.prm.ox.ac.uk/shrunken-heads, (Accessed 18 September 2020).

Poon, A. (1993) *Tourism, Technology and Competitive Strategies.* Wallingford: CABI.

Prebensen, N., Chen, J. and Uysal, M. (2014) *Creating Experience Value in Tourism.* Wallingford: CABI.

Ralli, A. (1909) *Christians at Mecca.* London: William Heinemann.

Rojek, C. (1993): *Ways of Escape.* Basingstoke: Macmillan.

Rugg, J. and Sedgewick, M. (2007) *Issues in the Curating of Art and Contemporary Performance.* Bristol and Chicago: Intellect.

Ryan, C. (1997) *The Tourist Experience: A New Introduction.* London: Cassell.

Ryan, C. (2012) Ways of conceptualising the tourist experience. In R. Sharpley and P. Stone (Eds.), *Tourist Experience: Contemporary Perspectives.* Abingdon: Routledge, pp. 9–20.

Seaton, A. V. (1996) Guided by the dark: From thanatopsis to thanatourism. *International Journal of Heritage*, 2(4), 234–244.

Seaton, A. V. (1998) War and thanatourism: The Waterloo War 1815–1914. *Annals of Tourism Research,* 26(1), 1–29.

Seaton, A. V. (2001) The silences and disclosures of slavery heritage tourism in the US and UK. In G. Dann and A. V. Seaton (Eds.), *Slavery, Contested Heritage and Thanatourism.* Binghamton. New York: The Haworth Hospitality Press, pp. 107–129.

Seaton, A. V. (2009a) Beckford and the tourists: Gothic performances at Lansdown Tower, Bath. *The Beckford Journal*, 15, 61–82.

Seaton, A. V. (2009b) Purposeful otherness: Approaches to the management of Thanatourism. In Sharpley R. and P. Stone (Eds.), *The Darker Side of Travel. The Theory and Practice of Dark Tourism.* Bristol: Channel View Publications, pp. 101–116.

Seaton, A. V. (2017) Patrimony, engineered remembrance and ancestral vampires: Appraising thanatouristic resources in Ireland and Sicily. In G. Hooper and J. Lennon (Eds.), *Dark Tourism: Practice and Interpretation.* Aldershot: Ashgate, pp. 55–68.

Seaton, A. V. (2018) Encountering engineered and orchestrated remembrance: A situational model of dark tourism and its history. In P. Stone, R. Hartmann, A. V. Seaton, R. Sharpley and L. White (Eds.), *Palgrave Handbook of Dark Tourism Studies.* London: Palgrave Macmillan, pp. 9–32.

Seaton, A. V. (2021, 2022) History of dark tourism. In E. Zuelow and K. James (Eds.), *Oxford Handbook of History of Tourism and Travel.* Oxford: Oxford University Press.

Seaton, A. V. and Lennon, J. (2004) Thanatourism in the early twenty-first century: Moral panics, ulterior motives and alterior desires. In T. V. Singh (Ed.), *New Horizons in Tourism. Strange Experiences and Stranger Practices.* Wallingford: CABI, pp. 63–82.

Seaton, A. V. and Woodward, I. (2008) *Handbook on Tourism Segmentation: Maximising Marketing Effectiveness with Special focus on National Tourism Organisations.* Madrid: UN World Tourism Organization.

Sharpley, R. (2005) Travels to the edge of darkness: Towards a typology of dark tourism. In C. Ryan, S. Page and M. Aiken (Eds.), *Taking Tourism to the Limits: Issues, Concepts and Managerial Perspectives.* Oxford: Elsevier, pp. 217–228.

Sharpley, R. (2009) Dark tourism and political ideology: Towards a governance model. In R. Sharpley and P. Stone (Eds.), *The Darker Side of Travel. The Theory and Practice of Dark Tourism*: Bristol: Channel View Publications, pp. 145–163.

Sharpley, R and Wright, D. (2018) Disasters and disaster tourism: The role of the media. In P. Stone, R. Hartmann, A. V. Seaton, R. Sharpley and L. White (Eds.), *Palgrave Handbook of Dark Tourism Studies.* London: Palgrave Macmillan, pp. 355–354.

Sherard, R. (1897) *The White Slaves of England: Being True Pictures of Certain Social Conditions in the Kingdom of England in the Year 1897.* London: J. Bowden.

Slade, P. (2003) Gallipoli thanatourism. *Annals of Tourism Research,* 33(4), 779–1137.

Skinner, J. (2018) 'The smoke of an eruption and the dust of an earthquake': Dark tourism, the sublime and the re-animation of the disaster location. In P. Stone, R. Hartmann, A. V. Seaton, R. Sharpley and L. White (Eds.), *Palgrave Handbook of Dark Tourism Studies.* London: Palgrave Macmillan, pp. 125–150.

Smith, D. (2012) *100 Places You Will Never Visit. The World's Most Secret Locations.* London: Quercus.

Stone, P. (2006) A dark tourism spectrum: Towards a typology of death and macabre related tourism sites, attractions and exhibitions. *Tourism,* 54(2), pp. b 145–160.

Stone, P. (2011) Dark tourism experiences: Mediating between life and death. In R. Sharpley and P. Stone (Eds.), *Tourist Experience Contemporary Perspectives.* London: Routledge, pp. 21–27.

Stone, P. (2018) Dark tourism in an age of 'spectacular death'. In P. Stone, R. Hartmann, A. V. Seaton, R. Sharpley and L. White, (Eds.), *Palgrave Handbook of Dark Tourism Studies,* London: Palgrave Macmillan, pp. 189–210.

Turing (2019) Alan Turing named most 'iconic' figure of the 20th century. *Manchester Evening News,* 6 February. Available at: https://www.manchestereveningnews.co.uk/news/uk-news/alan-turing-named-most-iconic-15790677. (Accessed 10 November 2020).

Turing (2020) Turing. Available at: https://manchesterhistory.net/manchester/statues/turing.html (Accessed 10 November 2020).

Vergo, P. (1989) *The New Museology.* London: Reaktion Books.

Wall, T. (2020) The day Bristol dumped its hated slave trader in the docks and a nation began to search its soul. *The Guardian,* 14 June. Available at: https://www.theguardian.com/uk-news/2020/jun/14/the-day-bristol-dumped-its-hated-slave-trader-in-the-docks-and-a-nation-began-to-search-its-soul (Accessed 19 November 2020).

Wang, N. (2000) *Tourism and Modernity.* Oxford: Pergamon.

Webster (1976) *Webster's Third New International Dictionary of the English Language.* Chicago and London: Encyclopaedia Britannica, Inc.

Williams, R. (1973) *Keywords: A Vocabulary of Culture and Society.* London: Fontana Press.

Wittgenstein, L. (1953/1968) *Philosophical Investigations* (Trans. G. E. M. Anscombe). Oxford: Basil Blackwell.

25

FRONTIER TOURISM

Transcendence through trial

Jennifer H. Frost

Introduction

According to Belk, Wallendorf and Sherry (1989: 2), consumption in modern society, including travel, can be a vehicle of 'transcendent experience' in people's lives. Transcendence can be understood as a concern with those aspects of life that go beyond petty everyday affairs or a focus on one's immediate needs; it refers to an elevation of thought which is often coupled with spirituality. Piedmont (1999: 988) defines spiritual transcendence as a perspective 'in which a person sees a fundamental unity underlying the diverse strivings of nature and finds a bonding with others that cannot be severed, not even by death'. This suggests a sense of a common humanity, as well as a connection to the natural world and potentially to a deity or higher being. Achieving such transcendence may require certain ingredients to be present. Often there are trials or hardships that prompt it, or the existence of solitude or isolation may be a trigger. In some cases, the act of leaving home and spending time in a new environment seems to be necessary to achieve a transcendent state of being (Moal-Ulvoas, 2017).

The link between travel and transcendence has a long history. This chapter examines this phenomenon through a study of frontier tourists – those travellers who have ventured to the depths of the oceans, the poles, remote deserts, the highest mountain peaks and even outer space – in endeavours and journeys reminiscent of those taken by the characters in Jules Verne's novels or the exploits of the great explorers of the past (Laing & Crouch, 2011; Laing & Frost, 2014). These frontiers, as a cultural construct, have often been conceptualized as spaces in which the immersion in nature or wilderness and the risk inherent in this travel facilitates transcendent or sacred experiences (Laing, 2006; Laing & Frost, 2017; Zurick, 1995). Research is, however, needed to explore this process more fully, including the spiritual meanings of these adventurous and testing pursuits for frontier tourists.

In particular, the 'frontier' nature of their experience may relate as much to emotional/ psychological factors as it does to far-off geographical locations, as the traveller moves from the familiar into the unknown, and faces challenges that are mental and spiritual as well as physical (Laing & Crouch, 2005). The findings of a study of these individuals may, therefore, tell us something about contemporary tourist experiences more broadly, where the individual may push their own boundaries or personal 'frontier' through testing themselves in some way.

DOI: 10.4324/9781003219866-29

351

Jennifer H. Frost

Frontier tourism

Cohen (2004: 332) regards frontier travel experiences as a prime example of 'the quest for extreme authentic otherness ... which in some cases may straddle the boundary between tourism and exploration.' This is, in part, because the concept of a *frontier* naturally changes over time, and what was once a frontier may now be or soon become a much-visited tourist destination (Laing, 2006). Frontier 'trailblazers' will probably be followed in the future by mainstream or mass tourists as development occurs, infrastructure is set up and the frontier areas lose some of their unique qualities. Examples of this phenomenon are already occurring in places such as Antarctica, where tourists are taken to shore from small landing craft carried on luxury cruise ships (Kriwoken & Hardy, 2018), while increasing numbers of tourists are taking guided adventures or expeditions, such as camel treks across deserts (Laing & Crouch, 2005); climbing mountains (Tsaur, Yen & Hsiao, 2013), and travelling underwater on submersibles to see shipwrecks such as the Titanic (Spennemann, 2007). Some of these activities may be, in turn, led by frontier tourists who use the resulting income to help fund their own travel experiences. The path of the frontier tourist is, therefore, a well-trodden one (Laing, 2006; Laing & Crouch, 2011; Zurick, 1995). Even the isolation of the frontier can be questioned, as 'more and more in the future, expeditions to remote places on earth are going to be covered live, in "real time," over the Internet' (Anker & Roberts, 1999: 58). Studying frontier experiences, which might be characterized as being on the fringes or edge of commercial tourism, could therefore provide us with a glimpse of the future of travel. There appears to be a swathe of different motivations for this kind of travel (see Laing, 2006; Laing and Crouch, 2005, 2009a, 2009b, 2009c, 2011; Laing & Frost, 2014, 2017), but some of the dominant reasons include a desire for achievement and/or prestige; a love of nature; the challenge it presents, the aim of personal growth and self-actualization; seeking freedom or escape; and the search for meaning or purpose in life. It is the latter motivation that this chapter is concerned with, in particular the spiritual dimension of frontier tourism.

Laing and Crouch (2006) explored the journeys of frontier tourists using the classic pilgrimage as a lens to study their experiences. This was an exploratory piece of work, with scope to examine this phenomenon more deeply in a follow-up study. This type of journey was characterized as a series of rites, namely: the pre-liminal stage or *rites of separation* as one leaves the home; the liminal stage or *rites of transition*, which occur when undergoing trials; and the post-liminal stage *or rites of incorporation*, which help the traveller connect back to those they left behind and feel a sense of belonging when returning home (Turner & Turner, 1969, 1978). Laing and Crouch found that their study participants underwent intense suffering or a type of penance during their travels, which was seen to have enriched the experience. They were transformed in the process, overcoming fears and personal barriers and becoming more self-aware and sensitive to their surroundings. Those who travelled in groups often referred to the *communitas* that emerged, with the tourists bonding over their common pursuit and the problems that they were forced to overcome together, while the return home was a time for reflection and inspiring others, but also sometimes a period of restlessness, before the call of another 'sacred' journey.

More recently, Laing and Frost (2014) examined the frontier travel experience using the mythological construct of the *hero's journey*, where the individual leaves their homeland to undergo hardship or danger and later returns home renewed and changed by the experience: 'To look death in the face and to return to the living is the ultimate proof of a hero's extraordinary stature' (Van Nortwick, 1992: 28). They found that there are a group of travellers

Frontier tourism

who are 'the hero in their own story' (Laing and Frost, 2014: 241), which incorporates the *call to adventure*, the *journey* and the *return*, following Campbell (1949):

> Part of the myth is that we expect the experience will transform us. We will return as a better, wiser, more interesting person. Our travels will be our travails. They will test us and we will see just how far our boundaries extend.
>
> *(Laing & Frost, 2014: 4)*

Other theoretical lenses might, however, be usefully employed to more fully understand the role of transcendence in the frontier tourist experience.

Transcendence and tourism

There is an extensive literature on transcendence within tourism. However, in the context of this chapter, there is only scope to consider this briefly, focusing on potentially useful theories that might frame this research. In many cases, there is an overlap between the components or elements of transcendence and spirituality, such that they might be regarded as overlapping or similar ideas. The seminal work on transcendence is by Piedmont (1999), who notes some of its components, including *connectedness*; belief in *universality* or an underlying unity and purpose in life; *existentiality*, which refers to living life in the moment but also taking up opportunities for learning or growth; being open to the *paradoxes* in life; *nonjudgementality* or empathy towards others, and *gratitude* for one's life and the world around us. Kujawa (2017) refers to transcendence as one of the three elements of spirituality with respect to tourism, with the other two being *connectedness* and *transformation*. Like the current study, there is an analysis of books, which in this case are characterized as spiritual travel memoir, and Campbell's (1949) hero's journey is utilized as a framework for understanding these travel experiences. Cheer, Belhassen and Kujawa (2017) focus on the *connectivity* of spirituality, whether it be to others, the natural world, life or to oneself. For Willson, McIntosh and Zahra (2013), spiritual tourism involves a search for *meaning, transcendence* and *connectedness*. These researchers also see an element of *self-actualization* in transcendence or 'a focus on growth' (Willson et al., 2013: 153), which links to Piedmont's (1999) notion of existentiality. They similarly refer to the individual achieving their full potential, or going beyond one's usual boundaries. In a spiritual sense, this might involve building one's capabilities, such as the ability to deal with adversity, or overcoming fears and internal barriers. An examination of the potential for spiritual experiences within nature by Sharpley and Jepson (2011) considered connectivity with others and the earth, alongside ideas of being at peace with oneself, a form of existential authenticity. The relationship between the individual and the natural surrounds was discussed, with the observation made that perhaps it was an *emotional response to place* that was described by participants, rather than a spiritual experience per se. The current study may expand upon these findings, given that frontier tourism takes place in some of the most awe-inspiring natural surrounds on and off the planet.

A number of studies have examined transcendence in relation to specific forms of frontier tourism. Tsaur et al. (2013) examined the transcendent experience of mountaineers in Taiwan through a quantitative survey and found that this has a positive effect on happiness, as well as flow, where the skills possessed by the individual and the challenges posed by the activity are finely balanced, and the individual is completely immersed in what they are doing (Csikszentmihalyi, 1975). A qualitative study of polar trekkers in the Arctic by Gyimóthy and Mykletun (2004) considered the role of risk in these pursuits, which was important in providing sufficient or optimal conditions of arousal or excitement, without going too far, and which was linked to the development of competence and the need for deep play. The latter may be seen as akin to transcendence, in that it may involve 'an extraordinary experience that can't be experienced in everyday situations and environments' and may take place within a setting that is remote or unknown, requiring a person to '[cope] with risk, hunger, pain and exhaustion or sometimes even self-torture to inspire vision or insights' (Gyimóthy & Mykletun, 2004: 861). This prior work can be distinguished from the current study, in that spiritual aspects of these experiences were not the central focus.

It is also interesting that much of the research to date has focused on the linkages between spirituality and positive travel experiences, or concentrates on the positive spiritual emotions that can be evoked by tourism. For example, Moal-Ulvoas (2017) interviews a group of older travellers who experience emotions such as awe, wonder, admiration, appreciation and joy on their journeys. According to Willson et al. (2013), there is in contrast a paucity of studies that consider how the search for the spiritual may be achieved through adversity or negative tourist experiences, which they attribute to the fact that some researchers may see these as 'private' moments, or shy away from discussing them due to concerns that this may be taxing, possibly distressing, for both the study participant and the researcher alike. Exceptions include Gyimóthy and Mykletun (2004), who comment about the appeal of hardship to their polar trekkers: 'The rough beauty of the Arctic environment offered a peculiar contrast to physical pain or suffering' (p. 871) and 'many become obsessed and have confronted unimaginable cold, hunger, fear and physical danger to unveil the most inhospitable corners of Earth' (p. 872). Zahra and McIntosh (2007) similarly refer to the exposure of volunteer tourists to suffering, which may result in emotional responses such as tears. These can be cathartic and even life-changing experiences. The current study will extend the work of Gyimóthy and Mykletun (2004) by exploring how the trials of travel can facilitate spiritual outcomes for tourists.

Methodology

A qualitative study was employed, based on an interpretive paradigm. This methodology allows researchers the opportunity to enter the world of the tourist and explore their experiences in depth. The methodological approach was grounded theory, where theory is generated from data, or grounded in the data collected. With grounded theory, the researcher is flexible enough to change the focus of the research and the direction as it happens (Charmaz, 1995). In grounded theory, there is a constant cycling back and forth between development of the theory and analysis of data (Seale, 1999) as more data are collected. This 'constant comparative' method helps to define and refine categories and theory, as data are being collected, with the aim of 'producing thoroughly saturated theoretical accounts' (Seale, 1999: 96). The purpose of the study was to generate a theory of motivations behind frontier tourism. This chapter will focus on the spiritual motivations of the participants, while acknowledging that there may be multifarious reasons that prompt an individual to undergo a frontier tourist experience.

Data were collected in the form of interviews with 37 individuals about their frontier tourism experiences and an analysis of narratives produced by frontier tourists, encompassing 50 autobiographies, two online diaries and two online interviews. Participants in the interviews are identified using a pseudonym, while the authors of biographical texts are identified with their real names and identities, given that this information is in the public domain. Names and contact details for interview participants were found through a variety of sources, such as searches on the Internet (chiefly through search engines like Google, using appropriate keywords), phone books and the researcher's own personal contacts. Some of the texts analysed were possessed by the researcher, while the rest were available in the public domain, such as in libraries and bookshops (including second-hand bookshops), or through suggestions or recommendations of personal contacts. The majority of the interviews were conducted face to face and all were recorded and transcribed. Copies of the transcriptions were sent to participants for their reflections and changes were made where requested; heightening the trustworthiness of the study.

Findings

Seven key themes were elicited from this study, which reveal different facets of the spiritual dimension of frontier tourism.

Self-knowledge/self-awareness

When asked for his overall assessment as to why people would engage in frontier travel, Bryan, a climber, noted: 'Personal growth. I think that's what it's all about'. He went on to unpack that, bringing forward ideas of flow (Tsaur et al., 2013):

> That idea of losing yourself, becoming so absorbed in the action, that you lose any consciousness of self ... You're so focused on what's going on and that's one reason your fear disappears to a large extent. And when you can reach that stage, then you're OK, you know. You can do anything pretty well.

Some climbers referred to personal discovery as an outcome of engaging in high-risk activities. For example, Martin noted:

> Climbing in a way is a search. You are looking for your boundaries. Looking for the boundaries of what you are prepared to put up with. The boundaries of your own ability, the boundaries of your own preparedness to put yourself in danger.

Others linked self-actualization and personal growth to feeling *connected* (Cheer et al., 2017; Piedmont, 1999; Willson et al., 2013). As Liv Arneson, a polar trekker, observed:

> Whether I am skiing through the forest near my cabin in Oslo or paddling through my country's fjords in a kayak, I find a splendor and a deep sense of connectedness that brings peace. I am not a religious person, but the feeling is similar to the one I have heard some religious people describe: It's a reverence that makes everything else make sense. When I am in the wilderness, I know why I am here, what life is about, who I am.
>
> *(Arneson & Bancroft, 2003: 20)*

One participant, Charlie, a desert trekker, described how spending time in nature on long journeys in the Australian Outback gave him greater *insight* into himself and the world around him. There was a self-consciousness expressed with associating this with spirituality or 'enlightenment', but the experience seemed to go beyond an emotional reaction to nature (Sharpley & Jepson, 2011):

> I think for me, there's still some personal, I won't call it enlightenment, or discovery, but there's still something there that I haven't even admitted to or put my finger on or

discovered. Like it's still down the road ... whether it's personal discovery or whatever, maybe something will occur to me in the next day that I've never even thought about. That might affect the way your life goes ... who knows? But certainly I wouldn't get that if I stayed at home.

Jack described a similar effect of a long trek in the desert: 'So when you come out of there it's like you've had a wash, a big wash, because you know then who you are, you know yourself. Big parts of [yourself], I think, which most people don't know'. His use of imagery redolent of being cleansed or *purified*, is explored in more depth later in this chapter.

Harry, an adventurer who often travelled to live in different cultures, felt that it had value in opening him up to different experiences and other people, and thus possibly becoming more empathetic:

> Exploration isn't necessarily about planting flags or conquering nature or mountains, and making your mark. I think we should try and get beyond that and veer to somehow the opposite, in other words opening yourself up and making yourself vulnerable and allowing the place to make its mark on you.

This may be an example of Piedmont's (1999) *nonjudgementality*, but seems to go beyond that. It may be associated with feelings of humility when faced with the sublime, which is discussed later in the chapter.

Self-actualization may also result in greater contentment with oneself and one's life. Kira Salak was attracted to trekking across Papua New Guinea with an expectation of enrichment and found that this began with achieving *one-ness* (Sharpley & Jepson, 2011) or acceptance of oneself, warts and all: 'What I was looking for – what we all look for – can only start from within. All the happiness and love we crave. The self-acceptance. The contentment. Papua New Guinea taught me this' (Salak, 2001: 376).

Gratitude and humility in the face of the sublime

Another part of the spiritual experience of being on the frontier is linking it to the miracle or wonder of life and gaining a new appreciation of what one has. Andrew, a mountain climber, describes being at high altitude in these terms:

> Everything becomes so beautiful and you just become so appreciative of even breathing, of air. Air feels like it's some sort of magical substance, which it is really. You realise at altitude just how we take air for granted, oxygen for granted, you know. You take a breath at altitude and it feels empty, cold and empty. Having something like a cup of tea, tea feels like the best thing in the world! So to me, that's what the sort of spiritual thing is [behind mountaineering], you really do appreciate the wonder of being alive.

Others expressed their feelings as a form of humility, when they exposed themselves to the supremacy of nature and creation and felt insignificant and powerless by comparison with the sublime. Gyimóthy and Mykletun (2004) referred to this phenomenon with respect to their polar trekkers, and connected this back to nineteenth-century romantic views of nature, with 'feelings which may be substitutes for religious experience' (Gyimóthy & Mykletun, (20047: 2). Marinetta Asher explains this sensibility with reference to her Saharan desert experience: 'It makes you feel humble ... All the most advanced machines we've made can't stand against a desert storm. People always talk about conquering nature, but it can't be conquered. We're part of it, aren't we? How can you conquer something that you're a part of?' (Asher, 1988: 168). Her words also suggest perceptions of a strong connection to nature (Sharpley & Jepson, 2011).

For Jon Muir, a trekker, the age of the desert surroundings made him feel small, which he saw in positive terms: 'I just *love* these rounded conical hills. They seem otherwordly, and to me they speak of great age. In this respect I am reduced to a momentary shadow, which feels good' (Muir, 2003: 77). Murray, a mountain climber, made a similar comment: 'It puts a lot of things in perspective. It makes you realize how unimportant you are in the scale of all these other things around you'.

Others, conversely, liked the fact that the power of nature made ultimate 'control' impossible, which they saw as an integral part of the experience. Max, a polar trekker, observed:

> It's the scale of it, the power of the forces at work, and the fact that you've got no control over it is quite shocking for a human being who's used to being able to turn the lights on and off and turn the heating up and down. And to go indoors if it's raining or whatever. Suddenly to be completely exposed, completely at the mercy of the elements of nature is quite a humbling experience!

Heightened consciousness and awareness

Rod, a polar trekker, commented on the spiritual experience in terms of 'consciousness'. There is a crossover with self-actualization and echoes of Piedmont's (1999) existential dimension of spirituality, in terms of living 'in the moment':

> Life is lived so much by the moment, when you're out there, that all of the superfluous stuff of living is shredded away and suddenly you become a different conscious being. And that's a state that I most love being in, out there ... When your body and your mentality and your emotions finally become aligned, and your comfort with the environment too, when they're all aligned, that's when you can start to take things in that you would never otherwise be conscious of.

This was not a long-lasting state however: 'Coming back from that, there was a sense of disappointment that that super-heightened awareness was gone. Back to the mundane!'

Some frontier tourists connect this heightened awareness to the dangers they are exposed to. For example, Ellen MacArthur referred to her focus on 'survival' during her solo ocean voyages: 'I would tune myself into the ocean, and develop once more that awareness of all that was going on around me' (MacArthur, 2003: 364). Chris Bonington described a similar experience while climbing:

> The pattern of lichen on rock, a few blades of grass, the dark, still shape of a lake below, the form of the hills and cloud mountains above might be the same view seen by the passenger on a mountain railway, but transported to his viewpoint among a crowd, he cannot see what I, the climber, can. This is not an elitist ethic, but rather the deeper sensuous involvement that the climber has with the mountains around him, a feeling heightened by the stimulus of risk.

(Bonington, 2000: 7)

Jennifer H. Frost

For Janine, there is a nexus with universality as well as connectedness (Piedmont, 1999): '[Climbing] makes you understand your place in the universe, in the scheme of things, because nothing is in the way. You don't have any distractions. You can really think about what it all means to you. Feel at one with the planet and the universe'. She observed:

> There is something about moving into thin air, which is very different from low altitude. I'm not sure exactly what it is. Maybe it's because you have to breathe very deeply and it seems to me that whatever that is, if it's that or something else, it creates an extraordinary awareness and you feel very much in the now. And that's something that is very hard to replicate in other places.

Sense of meaning and purpose

Seeking meaning in these experiences is often bound up with suffering, which is expanded upon later in this chapter. Eric Weihenmayer, a blind mountaineer, writes of the meaning that climbing gives to his life: 'No one suffers the way one does on a mountain simply for a beautiful view … [It is] indisputable proof that our lives have meaning' (Weihenmayer, 2001: 297). Anatoli Boukreev, another climber, had a similar response to the dangers he faces: 'Something should change in the lives of those who aspire to climb to the summits covered with snow and rock. A human can be transformed by the effort that it takes to breathe the atmosphere above the clouds' (Boukreev, 2001: 167).

Ross links this search for meaning to going beyond his normal boundaries, consistent with the findings of Willson et al. (2013):

> You're taken out of your comfort zone and taken out of that repetitive existence, which you might get or do get anywhere where you're waking up in the same place every day [where] you're less sensitive to finding attachment or finding meaning between what's around you and higher knowledge or higher understandings.

Connectedness

A number of study participants referred to the connections that their travel afforded them. Murray felt that:

> People reconnect with the environment in lots of different ways. Gardening's just a way of reconnecting with the environment. Fishing is, hunting is, all sorts of things are. Most sports are in many ways. [Mountaineering's] just an extreme way of reconnecting with the environment, by putting yourself in an environment that's very hostile.

He contrasts this connectivity with traditional ideas of the conquest of nature:

> I don't think you're against or pitting yourself… you're trying to find a place within nature. When you do it right, you are within [nature]. When you're doing it wrong, you're against or it becomes a struggle against things. If you're doing it right, you're in harmony with those surroundings. When it starts to go wrong, you're not'.

A number referred to connectedness as *communitas*. Andrew, a mountain climber, talked about the camaraderie he experienced with others:

> It's a very profound thing to spend two months risking your lives with other people; you get to know them pretty well. You have to get to know each other *really* well actually, especially at the high altitude because you tend to rely on each other without having to talk too much because even talking's hard work.

Purification

Exposure to nature and, in particular, the risks of nature can lead to a sense that one's life has been purified – stripped down to its essential elements. Catharine Hartley referred to her experience of trekking in Antarctica: 'I had never felt so mentally cleansed. All I had to do was concentrate on putting one foot in front of the other and make mileage ... There was no stress, no rat race and no relationship nightmares' (Hartley, 2002: 164). Robyn Davidson, who trekked across the Australian Outback, is more lyrical in her description of the changes that have been wrought (Davidson, 1980: 154):

> My mind was rinsed clean and sparkling and light. Everything around me was bursting with life and vibrance. The colours danced and glistened in the crisp dawn light. Early morning birds, hundreds of them. My spirits high, I packed up quickly, expertly even, like a precision machine. I felt bigger somehow, expanded.

This process of purification also extended to relationships. As Davidson (1980: 188) observed:

> It was a giant cleansing of all the garbage and muck that had accumulated in my brain, a gentle catharsis. And because of that, I suppose, I could see much more clearly into my present relationships with people and with myself. And I was happy, there is simply no other word for it.

Sailor Jim Shekhdar had a similar experience:

> I was able to sit and ponder how to be a better husband, a better father, a better friend. Rowing across an ocean for nine months could be likened to an extended visit to a health farm: everything was cleansed.
>
> *(Shekhdar, 2001: 5)*

These metaphors of being scoured or rinsed clean suggest a spiritual cleansing or sanctification may occur during these experiences, where the individual is freed from the weight of sin through engaging in a simpler life.

Intense suffering

Intense hardship was described by participants, potentially as a prelude to an ecstatic or rapturous state. They may be likened to the penance stage of the classic pilgrimage

(Turner & Turner, 1969, 1978). For example, Helen, a climber, describes the lure of the unknown in mountaineering based on the stark alternatives it presents: 'It's being on the brink of incredible success or incredible severe consequences of death, a suffering death or suffering and still alive'. Peter Hillary similarly speaks evocatively of the depth of adversity he suffered during his polar treks and its link with a form of 'rapture' or ecstasy: 'The sick madness of living with fear screaming in my ears, and acting against its pleas, is in its finest moments a visionary state unto itself and, in collaboration with external pressures, the conduit to an even greater rapture' (Hillary & Elder, 2003: 116). According to Belk et al. (1989: 8), 'Ecstasy marks the extraordinary character of sacred experience and distinguishes it from the common pleasures of everyday life'. It seems to be a hallmark of a number of frontier tourist experiences and an integral part of its attraction.

Possibly the starkest examples of this phenomenon can be seen in the polar treks of Sir Ranulph Fiennes and Mike Stroud. Their bodies are subjected to terrible privations: 'Within hours our legs became horribly swollen, as with dropsy, we felt sick, giddy and disorientated, and concentrated effort was required even to rise from the lying position. Neither of us could focus our vision' (Fiennes, 1993: 223). They are likened to concentration camp victims:

"'I don't believe it", Mike exclaimed staring at my legs. "You can't pull anything with those. They're Belsen-like'" (p. 163). Fiennes continues:

> On the 75th day I woke from a night of throbbing foot pain with an almost phobic dread of my rigid ski-boots. If some modern-day Gestapo had threatened me with the torture of squeezing my feet into those boots, I would have told all and sold my soul to avoid the experience.
>
> *(Fiennes, 1993: 166)*

Metaphors of Biblical suffering, linked with hell, are used by Fiennes in the language he uses to describe his experiences ('The following day was purgatory' (p. 164)) and his recital of lines from John Bunyan's *Pilgrim's Progress* that ran through his head during the journey: 'And I saw in my dream, that at the end of this valley lay blood, bones, ashes and mangled bodies of men. Death also doth spread his wings over this place' (p. 206). There may be a link to his hero Robert Falcon Scott and almost wanting to suffer to the same degree as a way of 'being' like the explorer (Laing & Crouch, 2011). Fiennes compares his situation to Scott's:

> Our conditions in terms of body deterioration, slow starvation, inadequate clothing, wind chill temperature, altitude and even the day of the year, exactly matched those of Scott and his four companions as they came away from the Pole.
>
> *(Fiennes, 1993: 161)*

Patrick Woodhead alludes to the attraction of suffering in terms of character development and possibly discovery of spiritual truths when he reads Roald Amundsen's book *My Life as an Explorer*, in which Amundsen writes of reading the works of Sir John Franklin as a teenager:

> Slowly starving to death in the High Arctic like Franklin is understandably not something that would attract most people. However, the suffering is really only the byproduct of what people like Amundsen were searching for. It is this strange sort of extremity in life which they were trying to find, the emotions intrinsic to a human at the very edge of their character.
>
> *(Woodhead, 2003: 18)*

The privations of life on the edge appear to be necessary to discover who one really is or to transform into the person that one is meant to be (Piedmont, 1999; Willson et al., 2013).

Discussion and conclusion

The findings suggest that many of these individuals have undergone spiritual journeys, with participants referring to greater self-knowledge or self-awareness, feelings of humility or gratitude experienced in the face of the sublime; heightened consciousness or awareness in risky situations; developing more profound relationships with others, as well as the world around them; the discovery of a deeper sense of meaning or purpose in their lives; purification by spending time in nature; and intense suffering, potentially as a form of penance or prelude to an ecstatic or rapturous state. It appears that exposure to hazards and high levels of physical and emotional challenge, coupled with the grandeur and isolation of the natural surroundings, can create an environment for these spiritual experiences to occur.

These findings equate to many of the components of spiritual transcendence found in the literature, notably connectedness, universality, existentiality and gratefulness (Cheer et al., 2017; Piedmont, 1999; Willson et al., 2013). They suggest that the spiritual dimension of frontier tourism goes beyond merely possessing a similar ritual structure to a pilgrimage or hero's journey (Laing & Crouch, 2006; Laing & Frost, 2017). The frontier tourist experience appears to be inherently transcendent, which may account for its siren-like call for many exponents.

There are moral questions to be faced around the degree of suffering that can occur within these experiences. Apart from the ethical issues that flow from a person deliberately putting themselves in dangerous scenarios and the physical and mental toll that this may take on an individual, there are questions as to whether and when rescue might be required. Apart from the cost of these rescue missions, they may put other lives at jeopardy in the process. There are also risks that could be faced by guides who are travelling with frontier tourists, with high-profile examples of tragedies on Mount Everest (Krakauer, 1998). More recently, we have seen a climbing season cancelled, the result of Sherpas going out on strike to protest against their conditions, with 13 dying in the process of guiding tourists in 2014 (Barnes, 2015). A few of the interview participants alluded to this ethical dilemma, with some expressing the opinion that it was their right to engage in these high-risk activities with the proviso that they do not have the option of rescue available to them. A useful follow-up study might seek to better understand the psychology of these experiences and tease out the ethical issues that potentially flow from them.

The concept of the frontier for these tourists appears to go beyond mere geographic boundaries. These spiritual journeys may bring a tourist up against mental/psychological frontiers, where the individual transcends their own self-imposed limits in terms of what they thought was possible. In the process, they learn more about themselves – and others. This tourist niche might also help us to understand contemporary tourist experiences more generally. Laing and Frost (2017: 237–8) have identified 'a growing trend of travellers who deliberately reject mass tourism and the experience economy and seek to fashion their own experiences, stepping outside their comfort zone and entering the unknown'. They provide an example of the *food explorer*, who enjoys being exposed to new gastronomic experiences while travelling and is drawn to what they perceive as authentic cuisine, as opposed to dining options that have been packaged up for mass tourism. Future research could examine the potential for tourists to be challenged by what they see and do when travelling, beyond the high-risk context of the frontier tourist. The wellness tourist, for example, might share this preference for independence and the seeking out of experiences that change one's perspective on life. The link between suffering and deeper experience has been identified with respect to volunteer tourists (Zahra & McIntosh, 2007) and may be a more widespread phenomenon

Jennifer H. Frost

than is currently identified. There is also scope for research that explores the role of suffering in the broader tourist experience.

It should be acknowledged that there are limitations to the current study. The participants predominantly came from a Western background – Australian, English, Canadian and European – similar to that of the researcher, and this framed the analysis. Future research might examine this phenomenon from a non-Western perspective, to compare the findings cross-culturally. The space tourist also remains under-researched, in part because the population of people who have been able to pursue these experiences is still relatively small. As the opportunities become more concrete for this type of pursuit, this gap will no doubt be addressed by researchers.

References

Anker, C. and Roberts, D. (1999) *The Lost Explorer: Finding Mallory on Mount Everest.* New York: Touchstone.

Arneson, L. and Bancroft, A. with Dahle, C. (2003) *No Horizon Is So Far: Two Women and Their Extraordinary Journey Across Antarctica.* Cambridge: Da Capo Press.

Asher, M. (1988) *Two against the Sahara: On Camelback from Nouakchott to the Nile.* New York: William Morrow.

Barnes, H. (2015) On strike at 8,848 metres: Sherpa and the story of an Everest revolution. *The Guardian*, December 19. https://www.theguardian.com/film/2015/dec/19/on-strike-8848-metres-sherpa-film-everest-revolution (Accessed March 15, 2019).

Belk, R. W., Wallendorf, M. and Sherry, J. (1989) The sacred and the profane in consumer behavior: Theodicy on the Odyssey. *Journal of Consumer Research*, 16(1), 1–38.

Bonington, C. (2000) *Quest for Adventure: Remarkable Feats of Exploration and Adventure 1950–2000.* London: Weidenfeld & Nicolson.

Boukreev, A. (2001) *Above the Clouds: The Diaries of a High-Altitude Mountaineer.* New York: St Martin's Press.

Campbell, J. (1949) *The Hero with a Thousand Faces.* 1993 reprint. London: Fontana Press.

Charmaz, K. (1995) Grounded theory. In J. Smith, R. Harré and L. Van Langenhove (Eds.), *Rethinking Methods of Psychology.* London: Sage Publications, pp. 27–49.

Cheer, J. M., Belhassen, Y. and Kujawa, J. (2017) The search for spirituality in tourism: Toward a conceptual framework for spiritual tourism. *Tourism Management Perspectives*, 24, 252–256.

Cohen, E. (2004) *Contemporary Tourism: Diversity and Change.* Bingley: Emerald.

Csikszentmihalyi, M. (1975) *Beyond Boredom and Anxiety.* San Francisco: Jossey-Bass.

Davidson, R. (1980) *Tracks.* London: Pan Macmillan.

Fiennes, R. (1993) *Mind Over Matter: The Epic Crossing of the Antarctic Continent.* Great Britain: Sinclair-Stevenson.

Gyimóthy, S. and Mykletun, R. J. (2004) Play in adventure tourism: The case of Arctic trekking. *Annals of Tourism Research*, 31(4), 855–878.

Hartley, C. with Chang, Y. (2002) *To the Poles (Without a Beard): The Polar Adventures of a World Record-Breaking Woman.* London: Simon & Schuster.

Hillary, P. and Elder, J. E. (2003) *In the Ghost Country: A Lifetime Spent on the Edge.* Sydney: Random House.

Krakauer, J. (1998) *Into Thin Air: A Personal Account of the Mount Everest Disaster.* London: Pan.

Kriwoken, L. and Hardy, A. (2018) Neo-tribes and Antarctic expedition cruise ship tourists. *Annals of Leisure Research*, 21(2), 161–177.

Kujawa, J. (2017) Spiritual tourism as a quest. *Tourism Management Perspectives*, 24, 193–200.

Laing, J. H. (2006) *Extraordinary Journeys: Motivations behind Frontier Travel Experiences and Implications for Tourism Marketing.* Unpublished PhD thesis. La Trobe University, Melbourne, Australia.

Laing J. H. and Crouch, G. I. (2005) Extraordinary journeys: An exploratory cross-cultural study of tourists on the frontier. *Journal of Vacation Marketing*, 11(3), 209–233.

Laing, J. H. and Crouch, G. I. (2006) From the frontier: Sacred journeys in faraway places. *Tourism: The Spiritual Dimension Conference*, 5–8 April, University of Lincoln, Lincoln.

Frontier tourism

Laing, J. H. and Crouch, G. I. (2009a) Exploring the role of the media in shaping motivations behind frontier travel experiences. *Tourism Analysis*, 14(2), 187–198.

Laing, J. H. and Crouch, G. I. (2009b) Lone wolves? Isolation and solitude within the frontier travel experience. *Geografiska Annaler: Series B, Human Geography*, 91(4), 325–342.

Laing, J. H. and Crouch, G. I. (2009c) Myth, adventure and fantasy at the frontier: Metaphors and imagery behind an extraordinary travel experience. *International Journal of Tourism Research*, 11(2), 127–141.

Laing, J. H. and Crouch, G. I. (2011) Frontier tourism: Retracing mythic journeys. *Annals of Tourism Research*, 38(4), 1516–1534.

Laing, J. and Frost, W. (2014) *Explorer Travellers and Adventure Tourism*. Bristol: Channel View Publications.

Laing, J. and Frost, W. (2017) Nature and well-being: Explorer travel narratives of transformation. In J. Chen and N. Prebensen (Eds.), *Nature Tourism: A Global Perspective*. Abingdon: Routledge, pp. 11–22.

MacArthur, E. (2003) *Taking on the World*. London: Penguin Books.

Moal-Ulvoas, G. (2017) Positive emotions and spirituality in older travelers. *Annals of Tourism Research*, 66, 151–158.

Muir, J. (2003) *Alone across Australia: One Man's Trek across a Continent*. Melbourne: Penguin.

Piedmont, R. L. (1999) Does spirituality represent the sixth factor of personality? Spiritual transcendence and the five-factor model. *Journal of Personality and Social Psychology*, 67(6), 985–1013.

Salak, K. (2001) *Four Corners: A Journey into the Heart of Papua New Guinea*. London: Bantam.

Seale, C. (1999) *The Quality of Qualitative Research*. London: Sage Publications.

Sharpley, R. and Jepson, D. (2011) Rural tourism: A spiritual experience? *Annals of Tourism Research*, 38(1), 52–71.

Shekhdar, J. with Griffiths, E. (2001) *Bold Man of the Sea: My Epic Journey*. London: Hodder & Stoughton.

Spennemann, D. H. (2007) Extreme cultural tourism from Antarctica to the Moon. *Annals of Tourism Research*, 34(4), 98–918.

Tsaur, S. H., Yen, C. H. and Hsiao, S. L. (2013) Transcendent experience, flow and happiness for mountain climbers. *International Journal of Tourism Research*, 15(4), 360–374.

Turner, V. W. and Turner, E. (1969) *The Ritual Process*. London: Routledge.

Turner, V. W. and Turner, E. (1978) *Image and Pilgrimage in Christian Culture*, 2011 Edn. New York: Columbia University Press.

Van Nortwick, T. (1992) *Somewhere I Have Never Travelled: The Second Self and the Hero's Journey in Ancient Epic*. New York: Oxford University Press.

Weihenmayer, E. (2001) *Touch the Top of the World: A Blind Man's Journey to Climb Higher Than the Eye Can See*. Sydney: Hodder Headline Australia.

Willson, G. B., McIntosh, A. J. and Zahra, A. L. (2013) Tourism and spirituality: A phenomenological analysis. *Annals of Tourism Research*, 42, 150–168.

Woodhead, P. (2003) *Misadventures in a White Desert*. London: Hodder & Stoughton.

Zahra, A. and McIntosh, A. J. (2007) Volunteer tourism: Evidence of cathartic tourist experiences. *Tourism Recreation Research*, 32(1), 115–119.

Zurick, D. (1995) *Errant Journeys*. Austin: University of Texas Press.

26
CREATING WELLNESS TOURISM EXPERIENCES

Melanie Kay Smith

Introduction

The aim of this chapter is to analyze the nature of wellness experiences, especially in the context of tourism. Wellness has become one of the most popular contemporary buzzwords and it seems that consumers are increasingly searching for experiences that will improve their wellness or well-being (the difference between these terms will be discussed in due course). The work of Pine and Gilmore (1998) and subsequent experience theorists have argued that experiences can be designed to be personalized, multi-sensory, memorable, engaging and, ideally, co-creative. Many of these principles can be applied to spa design in a wellness context and, indeed, part of this chapter will focus on spa design and experience creation in spa settings. However, it is also important to consider that many wellness experiences are based more generally on rest, relaxation and stress reduction in non-spa settings, such as holistic retreats or natural landscapes. They may be connected to Pine and Gilmore's (2013) notion of the 'transformation' economy or even to spiritual transcendence. One of the important questions to ask is: how should wellness experiences be designed and co-created? And in addition, how far should they be passive rather than active, restful rather than entertaining? The chapter will consider a whole spectrum of wellness experiences, ranging from an escapist 'doing nothing' in a holistic retreat to being entertained in a Japanese spa theme park. Lifestyle trends will be also taken into consideration as well as cultural differences that impact on customers' expectations and preferences.

What is wellness experience?

The term wellness is often confused with well-being, which is a much older and broader concept. In the wider context of research, well-being studies (similarly to quality of life studies) usually include a number of objective and subjective domains such as health, economics, finances, social life, family, work, environment, safety and politics. Subjective well-being is a term that is sometimes used as an alternative to happiness. Dolnicar, Yanamandram and Cliff (2012) include the domains of physical well-being, psychological well-being and social well-being in their study of tourists' subjective well-being. Smith and Diekmann (2017) also discuss the concept of well-being in the context of tourism and build on the work of previous

364

DOI: 10.4324/9781003219866-30

Creating wellness tourism experiences

authors (e.g. McCabe, Joldersma & Li, 2010; Pyke, Hartwell, Blake & Hemingway, 2016), suggesting that well-being refers to both hedonic and eudaimonic elements of experience. The former means experiencing as much pleasure as possible, whereas the latter focuses more on personal growth and transformation, sometimes via processes that are painful or challenging (Knobloch, Robertson & Aitken, 2016). Several authors have discussed how going to wellness or holistic retreats for self-development workshops may be psychologically or emotionally painful at the time but can have long-term cathartic and transformative effects (Fu, Tanyatanaboon & Lehto, 2015; Heintzmann, 2013; Lea, 2008; Reisinger, 2013; Smith, 2013). Voigt, Brown and Howat (2011) suggest that in the context of wellness tourism, more eudaimonic experiences can be gained from spiritual retreats, whereas more hedonic well-being experiences might take place in a beauty spa.

It is important to note that cultural differences may affect factors contributing to well-being the most (Christopher, 1999; Walker & Kavedzija, 2015). For example, people from individualistic cultures may value independence more than those from collective ones who would consider social values first. More specifically, Muslim travellers may feel more comfortable in facilities (e.g. spas, wellness hotels) that have been designed with Halal principles in mind. Uysal, Sirgy, Woo and Kim (2016) also argue that the impact of vacation experience on subjective well-being can depend on gender, age, income level, marital status and so on. For example, some studies have suggested that older people gravitate towards more spiritual experiences (Moal-Ulvoas & Taylor, 2014). Gender also plays a significant role with women traditionally constituting at least 70% of the wellness tourism market (Smith & Puczkó, 2013). Kelly and Smith (2017) examine why middle-aged women tend to be the core market for retreat tourism. It is also important to note that many wellness activities may be connected to lifestage; for example, singles, childless couples and empty nesters are more likely/able to visit a wellness spa for relaxation and quiet time. On the other hand, single young people may have neither the health consciousness nor the disposable income to afford wellness spas and hotels.

Some researchers have attempted to show the short- and long-term impacts or benefits of tourism experiences on well-being. Nawijn and Filep (2016) caution that too much emphasis has been placed on the hedonic aspects of tourism and researchers should not overestimate the benefits of tourism for long-term subjective well-being. On the other hand, some forms of tourism may lead to longer-term well-being than others. Smith and Diekmann (2017) cite Seligman's (2002) distinction between the pleasant life, good life and meaningful life with the latter two contributing more to eudaimonia and greater life satisfaction. In the context of tourism, they argue that these three elements might translate into holidays that provide a combination of pleasure and fun (i.e. hedonism), altruistic activities (e.g. conservation or charity holidays benefitting the local environment and/or community) and meaningful experiences (e.g. education, self-development).

It is important to reiterate that well-being is a much broader concept than wellness, which is more subjective and individual. Nahrstedt (2008) defined wellness as the path to achieving well-being, whereas some might argue that wellness is the 'commercialization' of well-being. The reason for this is that wellness is often defined as being a 'trillion dollar industry' (GWI, 2017) and is the label that tends to be used by commercial spas and luxury wellness hotels. However, in the Finnish context, there is no word for 'wellness' so the term 'wellbeing tourism' has been used for more than ten years now (Konu, Tuohino & Björk, 2013). The Finnish concept of well-being tourism mainly focuses on outdoor recreation and the healing powers of nature, whereas wellness is considered to be a sub-sector of well-being tourism based on pampering or self-indulgence, usually in hotels or spas (Konu, 2014). The most recent globally accepted definition of wellness tourism is the one developed by Smith and Puczkó in the UNWTO/ETC Report (2018), as follows:

> Forms of tourism which aim to improve and balance all of the main domains of human life including physical, mental, emotional, occupational, intellectual and spiritual. The primary motivation for wellness tourists is to engage in preventative, proactive, lifestyle-enhancing activities such as fitness, healthy eating, relaxation, pampering and healing treatments.

The lifestyle-enhancing dimensions of this definition are considered later in the chapter. Voigt et al. (2011) separate wellness tourism into three types: beauty spa visitation; lifestyle resort visitation; and spiritual retreat visitation. This is a useful distinction in terms of experience design and creation. Beauty spas focus more on hedonistic activities that make the customer feel good in the short term (pampering, relaxation, beautification), whereas lifestyle resort visits may contribute to longer-term transformation such as work–life balance, stress reduction or the development of new skills. Spiritual retreats can even be transcendent, meaning that the experiences take the participant beyond the self. The following section provides a deeper analysis of what transformation can mean in the context of wellness tourism.

Towards transformation through wellness tourism

Pine and Gilmore (2013) revisited their concept of the experience economy and argued that people desire experiences because the value lies within them and remains long afterward. They also suggested that buying experiences makes people happier and gives them a greater sense of well-being than purchasing physical goods. They also took their argument a stage further and claimed that the next stage after experience is transformation, whereby the customer is changed by the experience in some appreciable way. They cite examples from the fitness industry, counselling, learning courses and religious excursions, all of which relate quite closely to wellness. The customer is taken beyond merely valuing an experience to being transformed by it, especially when the experience is customized or personalized.

Aho (2001) divides tourism experiences into emotional experiences, informative experiences, practice experiences and transformation experiences. The work of Reisinger (2013, 2015) focuses on transformational tourism, which is viewed as a way of enhancing individual self-development and even changing world views. Reisinger (2015: 5) states that 'Travel can offer physical, psychological, cognitive affective and spiritual experiences that can change one's assumptions, expectations, world views and fundamental structures of the self'. Some authors have suggested that there is a 'true' or 'authentic' self, which is revealed or emerges through travel, especially wellness tourism (Reisinger, 2013; Smith, 2013). Joy (1979) suggested that transformation was connected to spiritual healing and transcendental experiences, whilst Ross (2010) includes visiting sacred sites and participating in rituals, self-exploration through yoga and meditation, as well as being in and connecting with nature in his definition of transformative experiences. Ponder and Holladay (2013) note that yoga tourism is a form of transformational tourism that can lead to self-actualization and spiritual renewal. Reisinger (2013) describes yoga as being a transformational experience that helps people to return to their authentic selves and to enhance their psychological, emotional and spiritual well-being. Garrett (2001) notes that some yoga practitioners might call themselves spiritual, whereas others refer to the idea of 'working on myself'. Bowers and Cheer (2017) analyze the extent to which yoga tourism is connected to spirituality, concluding that individuals may gain wellness benefits or spiritual experiences depending on their own personal and individual perspectives. Sharpley and Jepson (2011) explore the extent to which rural experiences can be considered to be spiritual, finding that that a sense of meaning, harmony and connectedness can emerge, which is linked to respondents' subjective life. The research showed that quiet and remote areas like mountains tend to offer the most transcendental experiences.

If the next stage after experience is transformation, then perhaps the subsequent stage following transformation is transcendence. Williams and Harvey (2001) define transcendence as moments of subjective awareness, intense happiness and freedom, as well as a sense of harmony with the entire world. Wong (2016) argues that self-transcendence is essential for well-being, which includes continual self-improvement and realization of one's potential (connecting again to eudaimonia), whilst Joshanloo (2014) emphasizes the importance of self-transcendence in Eastern philosophy as an important element of well-being. Many Western consumers and travellers are increasingly gravitating towards Eastern philosophies via yoga, Buddhist meditation, spiritual retreats or temple stays. Bandyopadhyaya and Nairb (2019) discuss the growing prominence of spiritual tourism within the rapidly expanding wellness industry. Visiting spiritual destinations like India are experienced by Western tourists as a panacea to hectic modern living and a means of attaining inner harmony. Kujawa (2017) describes spiritual tourism as a transformative experience that often takes place in a collective setting with like-minded people. She develops a definition of spiritual tourism with three elements: transcendence, connectivity and transformation. Cheer, Belhassen and Kujawa (2017) see spiritual travel experiences as a way of reconnecting with ourselves and life in general. There are also increasing overlaps between more hedonic forms of wellness (e.g. spas, beauty) and more eudaimonic ones (e.g. self-development, spirituality). For example, Ashton (2018) describes how the spiritual retreat concept is relatively new in Thailand, but several places offer a combination of mind and body retreats, meditation, inner peace and self-awareness, as well as spa and beauty.

Designing wellness tourism experiences

It can be challenging to design wellness facilities and services that offer transformative and transcendent experiences at a personal and customized level. This section considers two forms of wellness facilities where experiences tend to be carefully designed and staged: spas and retreat centres. Whereas spas tend to include water-based relaxation and recreation in addition to other services, retreats are usually not based on water specifically, but are usually located in peaceful, natural environments. Spas may focus more on beauty and pampering treatments, whereas retreats offer more psychological and creative therapies. However, there is a growing convergence between the two as the spa industry realizes the value of offering transformative self-development experiences as well as rest and stress relief.

Several studies have been undertaken in spa and wellness settings that consider the most important elements for customers' satisfaction. Some of these studies focus more on service quality; for example, Blešić, Čerović and Dragićević (2011) used the ServQual model to analyze five spa hotels' service quality in Serbia. Negative gaps were highlighted between the customer expectations and their perceptions. Similarly, Albayrak, Caber and Öz (2017) also used ServQual and undertook a study of spa and wellness services in a five-star hotel in Antalya. 'Tangibility' was rated highest which related mainly to customers' sanitary and hygiene concerns. The second and third most important elements were 'Credibility & Safety' then 'Competence & Courtesy' of the staff. Lo, Wu and Tsai (2015) examined the impact of spa service quality dimensions on customers' emotions in spas in Southern China. In this research, the responsiveness (behaviour and attitude of employees) and reliability (e.g. times and prices) were the most important elements, followed by empathy (i.e. responding to customer needs) and tangibles (appearance of facilities and environment). Vryoni, Bakirtzoglou and Ioannou's (2017) study in Greek spa centres emphasized the importance of employees' commitment to the comfort of their customers, as well as empathic treatment of customers. Research was also undertaken in Swedish spa hotels by Lagrosen and Lagrosen (2016), who showed that most important elements for customers were related to the physical benefits (e.g. feeling physically better after treatments); mental effects (i.e. feeling more relaxed and less stressed); pleasurable experiences (e.g. pleasant treatments, environment, staff); smoothness and flexibility of the process (e.g. booking, prices). The most important item for customers was the extent to which a calm atmosphere had been created, followed by the relaxation possibilities and treatments, a clean facility with tasty food and friendly staff.

Creating spa experiences

The spa sector is based on creating individual, subjective, intangible and often sensitive services. The financial and emotional investment of consumers is quite considerable and many experienced spa guests will benchmark their experience against past experiences. Ferrari, Puczkó and Smith (2014) discuss the importance of the environment or servicescape within spa experiences, including the aesthetics, design and atmosphere. They emphasize the significance of creating multi-sensory experiences or what Cohen and Bodeker (2008) described as 'sensescapes' that transport the visitor to another realm.

Experience design is clearly a complex field and only a few relevant aspects will be considered here. Tussyadiah (2014) suggests combining different elements when designing experiences for tourism: these include design consciousness, which incorporates value-added factors like aesthetics. In a spa context, aesthetics can be very important, whether the spa experience takes place in a heritage building (e.g. an historic thermal spa) or a newly constructed modern spa. The latter may be designed by a well-known architect, such as the Bad Blumau spa in Austria designed by Hundertwasser or the Marqués de Riscal wine spa in Spain designed by Frank Gehry. The Tschuggen Bergoase spa in Switzerland used the development of a spa with distinctive architectural features to (successfully) attract more guests to its hotel. Spa interiors are also designed with aesthetics in mind such as use of colour and lights to create an atmosphere, as well as opening up the experience to views of nature (e.g. mountains, lakes, beach). According to Georgeson (2011), the key architectural trends that are relevant to the spa and wellness industry include 'jaw-dropping' views, the incorporation of local architectural designs, as well as sustainability and bio-inspired design. This might include the use of natural materials such as locally sourced wood, stone or eco-friendly bamboo as well as designing interior gardens.

Tussyadiah (2014) also mentions 'design thinking' as a way of approaching service delivery and providing solutions to problems in innovative ways. Wellness must be considered to be a holistic experience in terms of the customer journey, which commences from the moment the guest enters a facility. The reception and welcome must be warm and way-finding should be uncomplicated. Information about the existing services must be displayed in a clear and comprehensible way. Many spas have actually reduced the length of their treatment menus to facilitate the process of choice and not to overwhelm the guest with too many options. Therapists need to be professional, calm, but also nurturing. The extent to which co-creation should be included in a spa experience depends very much on the guest and what has already been pre-booked and pre-packaged. It is common for the guest to be offered a male or female therapist and to be asked about their preferences for massage oil, for example. An important element of service design in spas is the way in which the service provider connects to the customer in personal and memorable ways through the creation of moments of engagement or service touchpoints. These can range from the booking system, the welcome from reception, the actual treatment or therapy itself as well as the post-treatment experience. Some spas offer carefully designed signature treatments that connect to their local traditions or rituals and may take 2–3 hours. These can be highly memorable and unique.

The use of technology in experience design and creation is always a subject of debate, especially in this age of over-connection and the trend towards 'digital detox' (hours or days spent without connecting to technology). Spas arguably offer a sanctuary away from technology, although technology can be used to facilitate booking, to provide information, supply post-care and loyalty generation. Smart approaches may be taken to increase energy efficiency or to improve locker room technology. Technology can also help to create interesting effects through lighting or sound.

Pine and Gilmore (1999) suggested that the highest level of consumer engagement is likely to be derived from an escapist experience (rather than an aesthetic, educational or entertaining one). They argue that this should produce a deep and memorable experience. However, such experiences are supposed to entail active participation. Whilst this may be true of retreat centres, spas tend to create more passive experiences where the guest receives treatments from a therapist. Although spa resorts and wellness hotels offer yoga and other active classes, the most popular treatments still tend to be massages and beauty treatments. It could be argued that spas predominantly tend to provide a combination of aesthetic and escapist experiences, but of a passive nature. Entertainment is rarer except in the case of aquaparks or themed spas. The case study of Japanese spas demonstrates this point, but it is debatable as to whether people visit these for wellness reasons or more hedonic ones.

Case study 1: entertaining experiences in Japanese themed spas

Japan has a long history of thermal water and hot spring use in its traditional 'onsen'. The government of Japan has developed a 'Health Japan XXI' programme with guidelines for wellness tourism, which aims to promote preventative healthcare practices within the local population by increasing the use of onsen. In some areas of rural Japan, the traditional onsen is thought to have the potential to constitute an important element of unique and authentic wellness experience development. For example, in the Eastern Hokkaido region of Japan, there are seven onsen areas and the region has over 300 baths and more than 2,000 ryokan or traditional Japanese hotels (Romão, Machino & Nijkamp, 2018).

In addition to these traditional health and wellness facilities, the Japanese have developed themed spas that provide novel experiences for visitors. This includes the Yunessun Spa Resort in Hakone, where there is a relaxing tea bath, as well as a Red Wine Spa, a Japanese Sake Spa, a Coffee Spa and a pepper-water filled Ramen Noodle Spa (Yunessun, 2019). In the so-called 'spa city' of Beppu with its rich thermal waters, a spa theme park was planned for 2017. This included typical amusement park attractions such as ferris wheels, carousels and roller coasters, but instead of seats there were hot tubs. Although questions were asked about whether such rides could be constructed and function safely, the Mayor of Beppu released a YouTube video of the potential attraction and promised internet users that if the video reached one million views, then the 'spa-musement park' would become a reality. It opened in 2017 partly thanks to 75,000,000 yen (£500,000/$650,000) worth of voluntary contributions (Yoshida, 2017).

Melanie Kay Smith

Cultural differences, expectations and preferences ideally need to be considered in spa experience management where possible. This can range from the type of décor that is used (for example, a minimalist Zen or Scandinavian design or a more opulent Middle Eastern or Indian style full of colour and scents). Hindley and Smith (2017) provide an analysis of the different expectations of consumers in hospitality and tourism according to their cultural backgrounds. They quote research by Tooman, Tomasberg and Smith (2013) which showed that Russian, Finnish, Latvian and Swedish guests in Estonian spas had quite different expectations and preferences. Some nationalities or cultural groups are unused to being naked in spas (which is common in Germany, Austria, Netherlands, Scandinavia), especially in a mixed gender environment. In particular, Islamic spas most certainly need to provide separate spaces for women as well as female therapists (Yaman, Alias & Ishak, 2012). Spas may be considered to be quiet spaces where talking and socializing is not tolerated (e.g. Germany, Austria), whereas in others, they are an integral part of everyday life and may encourage socializing with family or friends, even drinking alcohol (e.g. Finland, Russia). The word spa may conjure up different images in the minds of different nationalities. For most Western tourists, a spa would be considered to be a place for pampering and luxury whereas for Eastern Europeans, the associations are more to do with medical thermal waters and rehabilitation. Korean spas or Jjimjilbangs function more like multi-entertainment centres with televisions, restaurants, gyms, karaoke rooms and use of mobile phones is acceptable and widespread.

One further consideration for both spas and retreat centres is the extent to which they are adopting principles of sustainability. It has been more challenging for spas to adapt, as they are often luxury facilities within four or five star hotels. Retreats, on the other hand, tend to be small-scale venues in the countryside. However, progress has been made and The Little Green Book for Spas was designed by Six Senses and provides recommendations on how spas should operate in a more sustainable way. The International Spa Association (ISPA) embraces the three pillars of sustainability, namely, planet, people and prosperity, and they have introduced guidelines for sustainable spas. The Green Spa Network was officially incorporated as a not-for-profit trade association in 2007. As stated earlier, bio-inspired design and architecture are desirable and there is now a growing trend to connect both sustainability and wellness.

Compared with spas, retreat centres often offer more educational and escapist experiences of a more interactive and participatory nature. The next section shows how retreats design experiences that can lead to transformation and even transcendence.

Creating holistic and spiritual retreat experiences

Retreat-based tourism has grown exponentially in the past decade, offering holidays for those people who want to escape from everyday stress but also to engage in processes of self-development. The Retreat Company (2019), which represents more than 500 retreat centres in the UK and Europe, report that their most popular requests are for yoga holidays, followed by getting away into nature, and doing nothing at all as well as detoxification programmes. Retreats tend to offer themed packages of several days that combine activities depending on the needs of the guest. So the focus can be on stress management, life coaching, relationship counselling, creative development and much more. Retreat Finder (2019) lists over 2,500 retreats with at least 20 categories of retreat, including some of the following: yoga, meditation, art, movement, nature/wildlife, outdoor/adventure, spiritual/pilgrimage. Retreat centres tend to be located in peaceful natural environments and there is a growing

Creating wellness tourism experiences

trend for eco-retreats. Kelly and Smith (2017) categorized retreats and the experiences they offer into the following categories:

- **Religious and Spiritual retreats:** e.g. meditation centres, temple stays, monasteries
- **Yoga retreats:** retreats focusing mainly on yoga or combining it with other activities such as meditation, pilates, dance or sports
- **Health retreats:** focused on lifestyle and general health improvements, such as diet, exercise, stress management
- **Fitness retreats:** these concentrate more on physical activities and sports, often combined with controlled nutrition
- **Mind-based retreats:** these may offer meditation, mindfulness, but also counselling or coaching
- **Body–Mind–Spirit:** these retreats may offer carefully selected programmes and workshops to balance physical, mental, psychological and spiritual well-being.
- **Miscellaneous:** these retreats are often located in landscapes that have specific connections to nature, for example, silent retreats in deserts or eco-retreats in jungles

Kelly's (2012) research shows that the main motivations for going to retreats are to de-stress and unwind, as well as enhancing health more generally. Participants may want to improve a specific practice, such as yoga, or seek spiritual and social benefits. Lea (2008) emphasizes the benefits of removing oneself from everyday life to rest and recuperate; however, escapism is only one part of the experience in retreat tourism. Self-development and longer-term transformation is also a major focus of this type of tourism (Smith, 2013). Processes of transformation may sometime only be possible via experiences that are negative and uncomfortable (Lea, 2008), involving elements of risk or insecurity, even trauma (Reisinger (2013). Heintzmann (2013) notes that some tourists visit retreat centres to work through negative life events, such as serious illness, bereavement or relationship breakdowns. Retreats may also encourage participants to rediscover the joy in their lives, an approach advocated by Dina Glouberman who co-founded the still successful Skyros holistic holidays in 1979. She also emphasizes the importance of being with like-minded communities (Glouberman & Cloutier, 2017).

Experience design in retreats is often carefully constructed around themes like stress management or work–life balance. Expert therapists and teachers will be invited to give workshops and courses to participants. There will be a certain degree of co-creation in some retreats (e.g. Skyros offers participants a choice of several courses from which they may choose two per week) in addition to yoga classes and group social activities. The following case study of Cortijo Romero in Spain shows how experience creation can work in a holistic retreat context.

Case study 2: experience design in an holistic retreat: Cortijo Romero

Cortijo Romero was established in 1986 to offer personal development holidays. One of the aims is that the holidays should be 'taken home' by the participant, meaning that the effects should last way beyond the holiday. It is very much orientated towards individuals and their needs at a particular time in their life. Individuals can choose a course that is relevant to them, which may be relaxing and rejuvenating, creative or well-being-enhancing or focused on personal transformation and change. The course facilitators tend to be leaders in their field ranging from bodywork to psychotherapy to the creative arts. Current categories for course include:

Well-being for Body & Mind: benefits to take home include feeling more relaxed, deepening an existing practice or discovering a new one and achieving greater clarity of mind.

Transformation & Change: this course can help to create deeper, happier relationships, increase confidence or give a clearer direction in life to help make meaningful changes.

Relax & Rejuvenate: these weeks allow participants the chance to just 'be' and feel renewed, nurtured and gain a fresh perspective on life.

Arts, Creativity & Expression: a week learning singing, art, dancing, music, photography or writing can help participants to feel more free and live a fuller life.

An example of a Well-being course is titled 'Six Keys to Well-being' and includes the cultivation of gratitude, mindfulness, connection, forgiveness, kindness and awe or wonder. In the Transformation category, 'Coming Home to Yourself' encourages digital detox.

Each course offers 18–20 hours of group time, spread over morning and afternoon sessions, and sometimes one or more evening sessions instead of in the afternoon. Optional yoga or Tai Chi classes are offered before breakfast. Individual sessions of massage and coaching can be booked for an additional fee. The food is vegetarian (but special diets can be arranged for an extra fee) and it is local, fresh and organic.

Most participants visit alone, although some come with a partner or a friend. Although space and solitude are offered, the group dynamic and social environment are important aspects of the experience. It attracts small groups of around 20–30 guests at one time who are usually split between two courses.

(Source: Cortijo Romero, 2019)

Spiritual retreats are becoming more popular with non-religious Western tourists and, therefore, deserve a special mention. The Retreat Company (2019) makes very little reference to religion or faith of any kind, preferring to use the term 'Spiritual Awareness'. Within this category, around 50 options are available in a range of countries around the world. For example, Jiang, Ryan and Zhang (2018) estimate that there are over 100 Chinese temples that offer meditation stays. They suggest that non-religious tourists tend to derive a 'sacred-spiritual' experience, which they divide into 'Search for Meaning' and 'Search for Escape'.

The last section of this chapter considers some of the lifestyle trends that are currently influencing the wellness sector and shaping the creation of experiences.

Lifestyle trends and new wellness experiences

As mentioned earlier, sustainability and the greening of spas is one of the most prevalent trends of the past decade or more. This has also extended to the food and catering sector in which debates are currently raging about whether veganism is healthier and more sustainable than eating meat. Less radical approaches to catering include trying to minimize

Creating wellness tourism experiences

food waste, but also to encourage portion control. Hotel buffets are notorious for not only creating massive food waste but also contributing to over-eating. The slow food movement has extended to numerous countries around the world influencing the consumption of more local and organic foods.

One particularly interesting development that has emerged in recent years is the healthy hotel concept, as considered in Case Study 3.

Case study 3: the healthy hotel concept

Although all four- or five-star hotels nowadays tend to have a spa (whether guests use them or not and regardless of the lack of profit), infusing rooms and catering with wellness is a relatively new approach. Although it is debatable as to how far the healthy hotel concept is working as a business model, several hotels have taken measures that aim to improve the healthiness of their rooms. Hoisington (2013) explains the emergence of the healthy hotel concept as a result of business traveller surveys that had revealed that a significant number of guests wanted to maintain a healthy diet and exercise regime whilst travelling. Delos Living (a wellness design company) was employed in several hotels to design so-called 'Stay Well' rooms that include healthy mini-bars and room service menus, air purification systems, water filtration systems, light therapy, blackout shades and vitamin C shower infusions. These have been endorsed in online promotional videos by the well-known 'guru' of wellness Deepak Chopra. Around a 25% premium tends to be charged for such rooms. In 2014, IHG (InterContinental Hotels Group) opened Even-branded hotels, which placed wellness at the core of the brand rather than being a mere after-thought. The rooms are designed using natural eucalyptus fibre and high thread count linens and the bath products are natural. Colour LED lighting is used to change the mood. These hotels also offer in-room fitness experiences with videos, equipment and yoga mats, flexible spaces for working, menus with fresh, organic ingredients and clearly labelled food, as well as free filtered water. Other examples include Marriott Westin properties that offer a running concierge gear-lending, a SuperFoodSRx menu and bedside aromatherapy balms. Fairmont lends its Loyalty guests Reebok apparel, running shoes and route maps for their stay. Swissôtel offers in-room equipment: aero steps, Swiss balls, TheraBands, Pilates ring and exercise cards.

Kantar Consulting (2018) provide a detailed analysis of consumer lifestyle trends. They emphasize the importance of health and well-being and the fact that consumers want to eat, drink and live to better optimize their bodies' systems. According to their survey, 75% of consumers globally say that they are likely to buy products and services that enhance their sense of emotional well-being in the next 12 months. On the other hand, lifestyle diseases and obesity are growing fast and 86 percent of people say that lack of sleep is causing them stress. This may be connected to overwork or to overuse of technology. For example, research in Korea shows that long working hours are common (over 48 hours a week) and have an adverse effect on emotional well-being, such as depression, disturbed sleep, negative impact on relationship and occurrence of illness (Lee, Kim, Kim, Kang, Yun, Park, Song & Lee, 2013). Responsible and sustainable living is important to at least a third of consumers but it is growing all the time, including both environmental consciousness and social responsibility.

Melanie Kay Smith

Some 90% of global consumers say that they prioritize experiences over material possessions (especially Millennials). It seems that growing numbers of people, especially the young, are looking for experiences and sensations that liven up their everyday activities. Consumers want to have their uniqueness and creativity respected and celebrated and to receive engaging experiences. This would re-confirm the need for personal, customized and co-created services. Self-development might also be a priority, as consumers want to lead fuller and more productive lives helped rather than hindered by technology. 67% of people want to simplify their lives, so although they want to lead fuller lives, this may involve less complexity. People are getting married later or not at all, which means that the singles market is an important one.

The importance of re-connecting with nature may also become even more important as 80% of urban dwellers are living in air quality that has exceeded safe levels, according to the Kantar (2018) report. For many decades, environmental psychology and eco-therapy have been used to enhance health and well-being. Brymer, Cuddhiy and Sharma-Brymer (2010) provide a very comprehensive overview of this literature insofar as it relates to wellness. They conclude that the nature-based experiences that are the most likely to provide optimal wellness are those where a person can truly make contact with and connect with non-human nature. This may take place in the increasingly more sustainable and green spas or eco-retreats, as well as the growing number of green festivals, as well as holidaying in slow cities or eco-villages. The term 're-wilding' is being used increasingly to describe experiences of foraging, herbal healing, outdoor fitness and survival skills, as well as forest therapy. Forest therapy is becoming more and more popular in many countries and the well-being effects of forest-related nature-based tourism have been studied by researchers in Japan, Korea and Finland, amongst others. For example, Ohe, Ikei, Song and Miyazaki (2017) claim that forest therapy could decrease blood pressure, reduce the pulse rate and increase the parasympathetic nervous activity that is enhanced in relaxing situations, and also show that physiological and psychological relaxation effects last three to five days. Komppula and Konu (2017) show how forest therapy experiences can be designed using an example of Japanese tourists in Finnish forests. Different packages were designed for different persona-inspired groups and tested both virtually and face-to-face.

Conclusion

This chapter has demonstrated that the wellness sector can offer a broad spectrum of educational, aesthetic, escapist or even entertaining experiences. Education can be offered in the form of personal development courses; aesthetics is present in the design and atmosphere of spa facilities; escapism is offered via interactive programmes in retreat centres; and entertainment may be experienced in themed spas. The benefits for the customer are also varied, with more hedonic spa treatments offering relaxation and temporary stress relief; retreat programmes can help transform one's life and to develop new skills, whereas spiritual practices can be transcendent leading to a new sense of self and purpose.

Different wellness experiences may be desired according to age and gender, cultural and religious background, as well as life-stage. For this reason, co-creation of wellness experiences tends to take place in the choice of relevant spa treatments and the nature of their delivery or in the choice and combination of retreat programmes and courses. Wellness experiences can also be personalized or customized according to individual characteristics and personality traits or even the guest's mood at that moment. In terms of experience creation, previous research on spa and wellness facilities highlighted the importance of an attractive, clean environment and calm atmosphere, friendly empathetic staff and a smooth, reliable

Creating wellness tourism experiences

process. Retreat centre research suggests that many guests are looking for a recuperative experience that helps them to recalibrate their life. It is important to observe and monitor recent lifestyle trends when planning wellness experiences, especially the growing connections between sustainability and human well-being, the need to address lifestyle diseases, stress and overwork, as well as using technology to enhance rather than diminish feelings of wellness. Regardless of their age, gender or cultural background, humans naturally graviate towards wanting to be well and are prepared to invest in the future of their wellness. This makes the need for innovative wellness experience creation an important social and business proposition for many years to come.

References

Aho, S. K. (2001) Towards a general theory of touristic experiences: Modelling experience process in tourism. *Tourism Review*, 56 (3/4), 33–37.

Albayrak, T., Caber, M. and Öz, E. K. (2017) Assessing recreational activities' service quality in hotels: An examination of animation and spa & wellness services. *Journal of Quality Assurance in Hospitality & Tourism*, 18(2), 218–234.

Ashton, A. S. (2018) Spiritual retreat tourism development in the Asia Pacific region: Investigating the impact of tourist satisfaction and intention to revisit. A Chiang Mai, Thailand case study. *Asia Pacific Journal of Tourism Research*, 23(11), 1098–1114.

Bandyopadhyaya, R. and Nairb, B. B. (2019) Marketing Kerala in India as *God's Own Country!* for tourists' spiritual transformation, rejuvenation and well-being. *Journal of Destination Marketing & Management*, 14, 100369. https://doi.org/10.1016/j.jdmm.2019.100369

Blešić, I., Čerović, S. and Dragićević, V. (2011) Improving the service quality as a socially responsible activity of hotel companies. *Economic Interferences*, 13(29), 273–286.

Bowers, H. and Cheer, J. M. (2017) Yoga tourism: Commodification and western embracement of eastern spiritual practice. *Tourism Management Perspectives*, 24, 208–216.

Brymer, E. G., Cuddihy, T. and Sharma-Brymer, V. (2010) The role of nature-based experiences in the development and maintenance of wellness. *Asia-Pacific Journal of Health, Sport and Physical Education*, 1(2), 21–27.

Cheer, J. M., Belhassen, Y. and Kujawa, J. (2017) The search for spirituality in tourism: Toward a conceptual framework for spiritual tourism. *Tourism Management Perspectives* 24, 252–256.

Christopher, J. (1999) Situating psychological well-being: Exploring the cultural roots of its theory and research. *Journal of Counseling & Development*, 77, 141–152.

Cohen, M. and Bodeker, G. (2008) *Understanding the Global Spa Industry.* Oxford: Butterworth Heinemann.

Cortijo Romero (2019) A Different Kind of Holiday. Available at www.cortijo-romero.co.uk (Accessed 10 January 2020).

Dolnicar, S., Yanamandram, V. and Cliff, K. (2012) The contribution of vacations to quality of life. *Annals of Tourism Research*, 39(1), 59–83.

Ferrari, S., Puczkó, L. and Smith, M. (2014) Co-creating spa customer experience. In J. Kandampully (Ed.), *Customer Experience Management: Enhancing Experience and Value through Service Management.* Dubuque, Iowa: Kendall Hunt, pp. 187–203.

Fu, X., Tanyatanaboon, M. and Lehto, X. Y. (2015) Conceptualizing transformative guest experience at retreat centres. *International Journal of Hospitality Management*, 49, 83–92.

Garrett, C. (2001) Transcendental meditation, reiki and yoga: Suffering, ritual and self-transformation. *Journal of Contemporary Religion*, 16(3), 329–342.

Georgeson, A. (2011) Innovations in architecture and design for spa. *1st Brazilian Spa Conference*, Sao Paolo, 28 August.

Glouberman, D. and Cloutier, J. (2017) Community as holistic healer on health holiday retreats: The case of Skyros. In M. K. Smith and L. Puczkó (Eds.), *The Routledge Handbook of Health Tourism.* Abingdon: Routledge, pp. 152–167.

GWI (2017) *Global Wellness Economy Monitor.* Miami: Global Wellness Institute.

Heintzmann, P. (2013) Retreat tourism. In Y. Reisinger (Ed.), *Transformational Tourism Tourist Perspectives*, Wallingford: CABI, pp. 68–81.

Hindley, C. and Smith, M. K. (2017) Cross-cultural issues of consumer behaviour in hospitality and tourism. In S. K. Dixit (Ed.), *Routledge Handbook of Consumer Behaviour in Hospitality and Tourism,* Abingdon: Routledge, pp. 86–95.

Hoisington, A. (2013) Brands focus on health and wellness in design. *Hotel News Now,* 15 October. Available at: http://www.hotelnewsnow.com/Articles/20616/Brands-focus-on-health-and-wellness-in-design (Accessed 10 January 2010).

Jiang, T., Ryan, C. and Zhang, C. (2018) The spiritual or secular tourist? The experience of Zen meditation in Chinese temples. *Tourism Management,* 65, 187–199.

Joshanloo, M. (2014) Eastern conceptualizations of happiness: Fundamental differences with Western views. *Journal of Happiness Studies,* 15, 475–493.

Joy, W. B. (1979) *Joy's Way: A Map for the Transformational Journey: An Introduction to the Potentials for Healing with Body Energies.* Los Angeles: J. P. Tarcher, Inc.

Kantar Consulting. (2018) Consumer Lifestyle Trends. Available at https://www.ifsa.eu.com/uploads/1/2/0/2/120245019/global_consumer_lifestyle_trends_-_grace_binchy_bord_bia.pdf (Accessed 10 January 2020).

Kelly, C. (2012) Wellness tourism: Retreat visitor motivations and experiences. *Tourism Recreation Research,* 37(3), 205–213.

Kelly, C. and Smith, M. K. (2017) Journeys of the self: The need to retreat. In M. K. Smith and L. Puczkó (Eds.), *The Routledge Handbook of Health Tourism.* Abingdon: Routledge, pp. 138–151.

Knobloch, U., Robertson, K. and Aitken, R. (2016) Experience, emotion and eudaimonia: A consideration of tourist experiences and well-being, *Journal of Travel Research,* 56(5), 651–662.

Komppula, R. and Konu, H. (2017) Designing forest-based wellbeing tourism services for Japanese customers – a case study from Finland. In N. K. Prebensen, J. S. Chen and M. S. Uysal (Eds.), *Co-Creation in Tourist Experiences.* Abingdon: Routledge, pp. 50–63.

Konu, H. (2014) *Defining and Developing Wellbeing Tourism.* Licentiate thesis Joensuu, University of Eastern Finland.

Konu, H., Tuohino, A. and Björk, P. (2013) Wellbeing tourism in Finland. In M. K. Smith and L. Puczkó (Eds.), *Health, Tourism and Hospitality: Spas, Wellness and Medical Travel.* Abingdon: Routledge, pp. 345–350.

Kujawa, J. (2017) Spiritual tourism as quest, *Tourism Management Perspectives,* 24, 193–200.

Lagrosen, Y. and Lagrosen, S. (2016) Customer perceptions of quality – a study in the SPA industry. *European Business Review,* 28(6), 657–675.

Lea, J. (2008) Retreating to nature: Rethinking 'therapeutic landscapes'. *Area,* 40(1), 90–98.

Lee, K. H., Kim, J. E., Kim, Y. K., Kang, D. M., Yun, M. J., Park, S. G., Song, J. S. and Lee, S. G. (2013) Long working hours and emotional well-being in Korean manufacturing industry employees. *Annals of Occupational and Environmental Medicine,* 25(38). doi:10.1186/2052-4374-25-3. Available at: https://aoemj.biomedcentral.com/track/pdf/10.1186/2052-4374-25-38

Lo, A., Wu, C. and Tsai, H. (2015) The impact of service quality on positive consumption emotions in resort and hotel spa experiences. *Journal of Hospitality Marketing & Management,* 24(2), 155–179.

McCabe, S., Joldersma, T. and Li, C. (2010) Understanding the benefits of social tourism: Linking participation to subjective well-being and quality of life. *International Journal of Tourism Research,* 12(6), 761–773.

Moal-Ulvoas, G. and Taylor, V. A. (2014) The spiritual benefits of travel for senior tourists. *Journal of Consumer Behaviour,* 13, 453–462.

Nahrstedt, W. (2008) *Wellnessbildung: Gesundheitssteigerung in der Wohlfühlgesellschaft,* Berlin: Erich Schmidt Verlag.

Nawijn, J. and Filep, S. (2016) Two directions for future tourism well-being research. *Annals of Tourism Research,* 61, 221–223.

Ohe, Y., Ikei, H., Song, C. and Miyazaki, Y. (2017) Evaluating the relaxation effects of emerging forest-therapy tourism: A multidisciplinary approach, *Tourism Management,* 62, 322–334.

Pine, B. J. and Gilmore, J. H. (1998) Welcome to the experience economy. *Harvard Business Review,* 76(4), 97–105.

Pine, J. B. and Gilmore, J. H. (1999) *The Experience Economy: Work is a Theatre and Every Business a Stage.* Boston: Harvard Business School Press.

Pine, J. B. and Gilmore, J. H. (2013) The experience economy: Past, present and future. In J. Sundbo and F. Sorensen, F. (Eds.), *Handbook on the Experience Economy.* Cheltenham: Edward Elgar Publishing, pp. 21–44.

Pyke, S., Hartwell, H., Blake, A. and Hemingway, A. (2016) Exploring well-being as a tourism product resource. *Tourism Management*, 55, 94–105.

Ponder, L. M. and Holladay, P. J. (2013) The transformative power of yoga tourism. In Y. Reisinger (Ed.), *Transformational Tourism: Tourist Perspectives*. Wallingford: CABI, pp. 98–108.

Reisinger, Y. (2013) *Transformational Tourism: Tourist Perspectives*. Wallingford: CABI.

Reisinger, Y. (2015) *Transformational Tourism: Host Perspectives*. Wallingford: CABI.

Retreat Company (2019) Retreat Hideaways. Available at: theretreatcompany.com (Accessed 27 June 2019).

Retreat Finder (2019) Find a Retreat. Available at: www.retreatfinder.com (Accessed 26 June 2019).

Romão, J., Machino, K. and Nijkamp, P. (2018) Integrative diversification of wellness tourism services in rural areas – an operational framework model applied to east Hokkaido (Japan). *Asia Pacific Journal of Tourism Research*, 23(7), 734–746.

Ross, S. (2010) Transformative travel: An enjoyable way to foster radical change, *Re(vision)*, 32(1), 54–61.

Seligman, M. E. P. (2002) *Authentic Happiness*. New York: Free Press.

Sharpley, R. and Jepson, D. (2011) Rural tourism: A spiritual experience? *Annals of Tourism Research*, 38(1), 52–71.

Smith, M. K. (2013) Wellness tourism and its transformational practices. In Y. Reisinger (Ed.), *Transformational Tourism Tourist Perspectives*. Wallingford: CABI, pp. 55–67.

Smith, M. K. and Diekmann, A. (2017) Tourism and wellbeing. *Annals of Tourism Research*, 66, 1–13.

Smith, M. K. and Puczkó, L. (2013) *Health, Tourism and Hospitality: Spas, Wellness and Medical Travel*. Abingdon: Routledge.

Tooman, H., Tomasberg, K. and Smith, M. K. (2013) Cross-cultural Iisues in health and wellness services in Estonia. In J. Kampandully (Ed.), *Health and Wellness Services*. Dubuque: Kendall Hunt Publishers, pp. 347–361.

Tussyadiah, L. P. (2014) Toward a theoretical foundation for experience design in tourism. *Journal of Travel Research*, 53(5), 543–564.

UNWTO/ETC (2018) *Exploring Health Tourism*. Madrid: UN World Tourism Organization.

Uysal, M., Sirgy, M. J., Woo, E. and Kim, H. L. (2016) Quality of life (QOL) and well-being research in tourism. *Tourism Management*, 53, 244–261.

Voigt, C., Brown, G. and Howat, G. (2011) Wellness tourists: In search of transformation. *Tourism Review*, 66(1/2), 16–30.

Vryoni, S., Bakirtzoglou, P. and Ioannou, P. (2017) Customers' satisfaction and service quality of spa centers in Greece. *Acta Kinesiologica*, 11(1), 12–18.

Walker, H. and Kavedzija, I. (2015) Values of happiness, *HAU: Journal of Ethnographic Theory*, 5(3), 1–23.

Williams, K. J. H. and Harvey, D. (2001) Transcendent experience in forest environments. *Journal of Environmental Psychology*, 21(3), 249–260.

Wong, P. T. P. (2016) Meaning-seeking, self-transcendence and well-being. In A. Batthyany (Ed.), *Logotherapy and Existential Analysis: Proceedings of the Viktor Frankl Institute*. Cham: Springer, pp. 311–322.

Yaman, Alias and Ishak (2012) Beauty treatment and spa design from Islamic perspective. *Procedia – Social and Behavioural Sciences*, 50, 492–501.

Yoshida, R. (2017) Beppu makes splash with bathtub theme park. *Japan Times*, July 29. Available at: https://www.japantimes.co.jp/news/2017/07/29/national/beppu-makes-splash-bathtub-theme-park/#.XhwsUMhKjIU

Yunessun. (2019) Welcome to Hot Spring Paradise. Available at: https://www.yunessun.com/global/en/ (Accessed 10 January 2020).

27

SEEKING THE UNUSUAL BUT SUSTAINABLE

Scuba diving experience

Caglar Bideci and Mujde Bideci

Introduction

The tourist experience is recognized as being a complex phenomenon (Bideci & Albayrak, 2018). Typically, the outcome of individual encounters with products, services and places, it is determined by a variety tangible and intangible factors, both personal and external to the individual. However, whilst complex, the tourist experience is often linked to some degree of the unusual, such as a peak experience (Maslow, 1964), an extraordinary experience (Arnould & Price, 1993) or a memorable consumer experience (Pine & Gilmore, 1999). Also, a common feature of the tourist experience is that, more often than not, it occurs in planned (business) physical environments, because service providers have the ability to control the process of formation and delivery of experience/s. Moreover, from the perspective of the 'aesthetic' realm of experiences, tourists seek a positive or satisfying experience usually without trying to change the nature of the environment presented to them (Oh, Fiore & Jeoung, 2007).

However, one notable exception is when the tourist experience occurs underwater; that is, in an unplanned, unknown and dynamic environment that differs from the usual environment in which people live. The structure of an underwater tourism experience, particularly diving, is affected by not only the tourist's personal knowledge, experience, interests and engagement with the services provided, but also the environment and its active components; the underwater environment is in a state of constant flux. Even if there are planned underwater structures, such as artificial reefs and wrecks, their surroundings may be shaped in various ways, and this can add variety to the perceived experience. As a consequence, underwater experiences, such as scuba diving, should be considered, evaluated and reinterpreted on the basis of their unpredictable merits and on the specified dimensions of scuba divers' experiences, including the great variety of potential scuba diving motivations.

This chapter aims to contribute to knowledge and understanding of the scuba diving experience. Indeed, a comprehensive understanding of scuba diving experiences is essential both to underpinning further research and to inform its effective planning and management, both currently and in the future. But what is a scuba diving experience? Scuba diving, as a recreational activity that by definition takes place beneath the water, is a relatively new and increasingly popular 'experience' in the form of gravity control and aesthetic pleasure

378   DOI: 10.4324/9781003219866-31

(Musa & Dimmock, 2013), which results from the relationship between people and the underwater environment that lies waiting to be discovered. In addition, however, it is a type of tourism 'product', and, for this reason, touristic services also contribute to this experience. In other words, a consideration of demand alone is insufficient to understand scuba diving as an emerging tourism product as it involves a variety of other touristic services, such as the need for accommodation facilities, transportation, food and beverage, health care (for example, decompression chambers and hyperbaric medical care for scuba divers more generally). The following sections now discuss the evolution of scuba diving tourism and its experiential characteristics before going on to consider how that experience might be developed within the principles of sustainability.

Scuba diving tourism: an overview

Now I flew without wings.

(Cousteau, 1953: 16)

This quotation by Jacques-Yves Cousteau (1910–1997), the well-known French naval officer who was also an ocean explorer, conservationist and filmmaker, perhaps inspired a new era of underwater exploration and adventure. Moreover, Cousteau made a significant contribution to the growth and popularity of underwater activities through his co-invention (with French engineer Émile Gagnan) in 1943 of the Aqua-Lung, better known as SCUBA, or 'self-contained underwater breathing apparatus'.

The word scuba usually relates to diving tourism or recreative diving activities. Scuba diving tourism can be characterized as a tourism product that occurs in marine environments and that attracts people seeking to discover the underwater environment facilitated by the use of specialist breathing apparatus. In a general sense, then, the concept of scuba diving tourism comprises, first, scuba diving tourists or scuba divers who are keen on exploring the sub-aquatic environment, second, the scuba diving experience and third, scuba diving destinations.

Scuba diving tourists are defined by Tabata (1989) as those who dive less than 30 m deep – 30 m/100ft. is the maximum depth that recreational divers with advanced open water certification should descend to – and seek coral reefs, planned scenery, shipwrecks, different vehicles, man-made structures / artificial reefs and diverse marine biology (Rouphael & Hanafy, 2007). Scuba divers expect to enjoy a subaqueous experience in pristine natural surroundings or well-planned underwater marine environments, in a sense encountering the unseen, the unknown in a place beyond limits.

The popularity of scuba diving has increased significantly in recent decades (Dimmock & Musa, 2015). According to the OECD (2016), marine and coastal tourism will account for about 26% of the total value of the ocean economy by 2030; more specifically, after cruise and coastal tourism development, scuba diving will be the third greatest driver of the tourism-related ocean economy. Indeed, although some researchers have referred to scuba diving tourism as a 'niche market' segment (Arin & Kramer, 2002; Davis & Tisdell, 1995; Dimmock, 2009; Karacsonyi, 2004) amongst many forms of tourism and touristic products, both natural coral reefs and artificial reef areas have been transformed from niche attractions into a billion-dollar tourism industry (Cope, 2003; de Groot and Bush, 2010; Hawkins, Roberts, Kooistra, Buchan & White, 2005; Lucrezi, Milanese, Markantonatou, Cerrano, Sarà, Palma & Saayman, 2017; Wongthong & Harvey, 2014). Nowadays, as Garrod and Gössling (2008) observe, scuba diving tourism has become a form of mass tourism. For example, in the Similan Islands in Thailand, the annual revenue generated through the use of the coral reefs as a touristic attraction increased more than 20-fold between 1999 and 2003, from US$22,000 to US$460,000 (Tapsuwan & Asafu-Adjaye, 2008). In addition, according to the National Oceanic and Atmospheric Administration (NOAA, 2012), coral reefs more generally attract very lucrative tourism markets globally, generating about US$10 billion in 2012 (see also Huang & Coelho, 2017). In the state of Florida alone, scuba diving creates over 13,000 jobs, in excess of $1 billion output, about $417 million income and approximately $80 million in state revenue, collectively constituting for over 33% of income in this coastal tourism economy (Huth, Morgan & Burkart, 2015). In short, the revenue accruing from contemporary touristic activities in coral reef areas amounts to about $30 billion annually; more than 350 million people travel to visit these pristine environments (Oceanwealth, 2020), in so doing also providing numerous benefits for various stakeholders (Anderson & Loomis, 2011). Hence, there is clear evidence to support the argument that the scuba diving tourism sector is an important source of recurring revenue for coastal destinations.

From a destinational perspective, the most popular sites for scuba diving tourists are, perhaps unsurprisingly, coral reefs and their surroundings where the fish population is abundant and various marine species can be seen. These include the Great Barrier Reef in Australia, the Coral Triangle in southeast Asia and the reefs in the Red Sea, Egypt. However, in addition, the natural the physical and ecological environment of coral reefs, 'manufactured' scuba diving areas, such as those offering artificial reefs, are also popular amongst scuba diving tourists (Barker & Roberts, 2004; Medio, Ormond & Pearson, 1997; Rouphael & Hanafy, 2007; Rouphael & Inglis, 1997, 2001), offering a culturally authentic subaqueous experience (Bideci & Cater, 2019a). Currently, there are at least 91 regions promoting their (natural and/or artificial) coral reefs assets (Dimmock & Musa, 2015). In addition to oceanic or coastal sites, there also exist thousands of areas around the world in lakes and rivers (Musa & Dimmock, 2013), which attract the attention of considerable numbers of people who seek unusual experiences for different scuba diving purposes. Overall, then, there are innumerable planned underwater visiting places, including natural wildlife marine areas, historical or artificial wrecks, marine protected areas and caves that attract millions of tourists to the underwater world and offer them the opportunity to engage in scuba diving (Bideci & Cater, 2019b).

Scuba diving attracts both inexperienced (beginners, novice) and more experienced (certified or advanced) scuba diving tourists, from those who simply want to try it out to those who dive regularly, and who travel specifically to participate in scuba diving or engage in it whilst travelling. According to PADI (Professional Association of Diving Instructors), as stated in its Worldwide Corporate Statistics Report, there are more than 27 million certified scuba divers who have qualified since 1967, and every year about one million people train for the certificate for scuba diving (PADI, 2019). To be more precise, it is estimated that there are about six million active scuba divers worldwide (DEMA, 2020), with over 2.84 million scuba divers in the USA alone in 2019 (SFIA, 2020). A variety of factors have driven this demand; developments in technology (specifically, more advanced scuba diving equipment), an increasing interest and curiosity in exploring underwater environments, and greater social interaction (through both social and visual media), awareness, education and accessibility have incentivized tourists and novelty seekers to go scuba diving in specific environments beneath the water (Bideci & Cater, 2019b). This trend has also both stimulated and been supported by the development of a diverse range of scuba diving activities and courses, from open water, night, or technical to adventure diving (for example, wreck) courses, as well as those offering training in deep scuba diving and different master classes for both tourists and professionals. Consequently, such diversity with the underwater environment offers

Scuba-diving experience

the opportunity for a variety of different experiences for both novelty and thrill-seekers (Bideci & Cater, 2019a). It is to this that the next section turns to evaluate the characteristics of this experience.

Characteristics of the scuba diving experience

The characteristics of the scuba diving tourist experience have been considered from a variety of perspectives. On the one hand, it is often described as 'unique and as a touristic activity exciting' (Cater & Cater, 2007; Dimmock, 2009; O'Sullivan, 2008). Because of varying underwater natural settings, each dive offers a different, special and unique experience (Dimmock, 2010; Kler & Moskwa, 2013; Kruger & Jakes, 2003), and provides scuba divers with new knowledge different from that gained from preceding dives. On the other hand, scuba diving experiences can be seen as 'dynamic and emergent, not static and discrete' (Kler & Moskwa, 2013: 140) by reason of taking place in a changing and erratic underwater environment. Therefore, the nature of each scuba diving experience may be determined by not only an individual diver's characteristics, including the number of dives performed, their level of certification, their motivations, and their personal interpretation and risk perceptions of underwater places, but also external environmental conditions, such as location, local culture and people, wildlife, geographic identifiers (e.g. climate, temperature, water quality) and the engagement of different stakeholders.

Significantly, scuba diving is a potentially dangerous activity (Ewert, 1989; Musa, Kadir & Lee, 2006; Musa, Seng, Thinaranjeney & Masoud, 2010); it can be regarded as a type of adventure sport and, for this reason, the perceived experience is considered adventurous, thrilling and unusual. By way of illustration, according to DAN (Divers Alert Network), the total number of scuba diving fatalities in 2016 was 169 whilst 10.320 scuba divers suffered diving-related injuries the same year (Buzzacott & Denoble, 2018). Alternatively, Kler and Moskwa (2013: 135) define the scuba diving experience as 'positive feelings of excitement, adventure, freedom and relaxation'. To be more precise,

> people get a lot of satisfaction from participating in dangerous sport... Danger and fear are exiting; excitement within limits is pleasant; therefore, danger is pleasant as long as limited, controllable or under control, vicarious, or make-believe-and is known to be such.
>
> *(Scitovsky, 1992: 41)*

Seeking circumscribed danger in the activity is an attractive point of departure for excitement within the context of individual experience: 'Threat or danger clearly play an important role in both focusing our attention and determining the pleasantness of stimulation' (Scitovsky, 1992; 45). From this perspective, scuba diving must be seen as distinctive from other adventure sports activities in terms of feeling danger because not only does it take place in an unfamiliar environment but also participants rely on essential life support – a reliable air supply– whilst engaging in the activity. Yet, in terms of experience, it may be argued that the adventure motive is not the sole trigger for participating in scuba diving tourism; that is, other factors should be taken into account. For example, in comparison with other types of adventure sports, such as mountain or rock climbing, scuba divers are unable to see what is happening underwater until they actively dive in and become part of the marine environment and, even then, the range of vision might be limited and indefinite. But at the same time, scuba diving offers participants a kind of free movement against gravity. Unlike other sports, when diving, people can move in three dimensions (forwards and backwards, up and down, or left and right) like a fish or bird (Musa & Dimmock, 2013), though within the limitation of their movement ability. Hence, although it can be considered a relatively dangerous activity, the underwater environment encourages people to engage in scuba diving to discover the new.

More specifically, what makes scuba diving special and distinctive in terms of stimulation and excitement is its ability is to satisfy curiosity, provide novelty and to engender a sense of wonder in the underwater environment. What is more, whilst the scuba diving, tourists not only try to identify their surroundings, but also they tend to interpret everything they see according to their individual values and emotions by attributing meaningful symbolic characters in the performance of a 'discover-it-yourself experience'. In other words, 'sense of place' (Kler & Moskwa, 2013) is also a significant constituent to the scuba diving experience. Eventually, each scuba diving experience may have a meaning, which is shaped by a 'personal connection to place' (Kler & Moskwa, 2013) for tourists.

To summarize, then, scuba diving tourism provides scuba divers with a contemporary tourist experience in an unpredictable environment. Scuba divers are motivated by search for difference in what is, in essence, an alien environment for the human race (Cater, 2008). In a sense, they can be described as people who are 'curious borderline' (Scitovsky, 1992) or 'hardy adventurists' (Musa & Dimmock, 2012). Scuba diving combines attraction and surprise by offering a unique experience at every turn.

Since the 1970s, researchers have focused on scuba diving as a tourism experience, attempting to identify and define its particular characteristics. As can be seen in Table 27.1, different themes and issues related to the scuba diving experience have emerged over the years as the research has evolved and matured. The first study, published in 1989, was concerned with the topic of perceived risk but, in the following years motivation became, and has remained, a dominant theme in scuba diving studies. For example, the main motivations for tourists to go scuba diving have been identified as: observing, seeing and exploring marine life (Ditton, Osburn, Baker & Thailing, 2002; Edney, 2012); adventure, excitement, social interaction, fun, relaxation (Dearden, Bennett & Rollins, 2006; Kler & Tribe, 2012; Meisel-Lusby & Cottrell, 2008); stature, personal challenge (Todd, Graefe & Mann, 2002); and enjoyment (Lucrezi, Saayman & van der Merwe, 2013; Shafer & Inglis, 2000). These motivations can be found to be related to various demographic factors, such as socio-economic status (Duffus & Dearden, 1990). More recently, a majority of researchers have become more interested in scuba divers' behaviours and attitudes. It has been found that, perhaps unsurprisingly, scuba divers have a tendency to develop their diving skills (gain certification) and learn more about the underwater environments (Hammerton Dimmock, Hahn, Dalton & Smith, 2012; Todd, Graefe & Mann, 2002; Worachananant, Carter, Hockings & Reopanichkul, 2008), which, in turn, contributes to an enhanced experience. It is also suggested that these improved scuba diving skills can reduce detrimental effects on the marine environment that are caused by scuba divers' direct interaction, which reflects intensity of use and a lack of diving experience (Kirkbride-Smith, Wheeler & Johnson, 2013). Historically speaking, the development of the research can be seen as following the early stages of scuba diving tourism, then its increasing popularity and the emergence and use of alternative dive sites and consequently focusing on the increase in damage to coral reefs and marine surroundings caused by scuba divers. However, it can be argued that the sustainability of the scuba diving experience has yet to be sufficiently considered. Table 27.1 summarizes the extant research into the scuba diving experience phenomenon.

The quality of the scuba diving experience is the most significant element of marine-based tourism destinations (Garrod, 2008). For this reason, a better understanding of that experience may help to enhance the quality of tourism services in this activity. With an improved

Scuba-diving experience

Table 27.1 Studies focusing on scuba diving tourism experience

Author/s	Year	Subject/s of experience
Roos	1989	Perceived risk
Wilks	1991	Risk
Todd, Graefe and Mann	2002	Motivation and skill
Meyer, Thapa and Pennington-Gray	2003	Motivation
Miller and Taubman-Ben-Ari	2004	Risk-taking
Stolk, Markwell and Jenkins	2005	Perceptions of artificial reefs
Musa, Kadir and Lee	2006	Satisfaction
Tschapka	2006	Motivation
Thapa, Graefe and Meyer	2006	Specialization and marine based Environmental behaviours
Meisel-Lusby and Cottrell	2008	Motivations and expectations
Cater	2008	Embodiment
Dimmock	2009	Comfort (adventure)
Musa, Seng, Thinaranjeney and Masoud	2010	Underwater behaviour
Anderson and Loomis	2011	Specialization and behaviour norms
Szuster, Needham and McClure	2011	Perceptions and evaluations of crowding underwater
Ong and Musa	2011	Underwater behaviour
Ong and Musa	2012	Underwater responsible behaviour
Kler and Tribe	2012	Pursuit
Paterson, Young, Loomis and Obenour	2012	Satisfaction
Edney	2012	Characteristics, motivations and attitudes
Salim, Bahauddin and Mohamed	2013	Underwater behaviour
Kirkbride-Smith, Wheeler and Johnson	2013	Experience levels and perceptions
Toyoshima and Nadaoka	2015	Environmental briefing and buoyancy control
Schoeman, Van der Merwe and Slabbert	2016	Perceived value
Bentz, Lopes, Calado and Dearden	2016	Motivation and specialization
Naidoo, Ramseook-Munhurrun and Li	2018	Sustainability based on online reviews
Mylonopoulos and Moira	2019	Motivation
Gregory and Edney	2019	The mature aged female diver
Verkoeyen and Nepal	2019	Response to coral bleaching
Albayrak, Caber and Cater	2019	Motivation

knowledge of scuba diving activities, authorities and businesses can develop appropriate marketing initiatives, gain competitive advantage (Schoeman, Van der Merwe & Slabbert, 2016) and have better risk management (Cater, 2008). In turn, this facilitates an increase in customer satisfaction whilst, moreover, addressing scuba divers' needs and expectations and understanding the dimensions of their attitudes and experiences are important for setting up management norms (Bentz, Lopes, Calado & Dearden 2016) that also help to create a sustainable industry with an attractive choice of investment opportunities (Dikou & Troumbis, 2006). For instance, there are three indicators to be aware with regard to scuba divers' attitudes: (i) personal motivations; (ii) seeking memorable scuba diving experiences; and (iii) reflections on the social aspects of scuba diving (Cater, 2008). However, giving priority only to scuba divers' needs and their satisfaction is insufficient to create a unique experience; an unusual and satisfying scuba diving experience is dependent on reliable conditions in protected marine environments that offer diversifying natural areas with abundant wildlife, and sustainable usage through ensuring economic stability and improving life quality for locals. By addressing all these constituents, the scuba diving industry may develop more sustainable and contemporary experiences according to the needs of scuba divers balanced with local requirements for the marine environment in the long term.

Improving the scuba diving experience based on sustainable principles

Scuba diving has a strong nature-based orientation (Stolk, Markwell & Jenkins, 2005) in marine surroundings. Unplanned and unsustainable scuba diving tourism developments or a focus on maximizing scuba divers' experiences may impact negatively on the marine environment, leading to economic disparity, decreased standards for living for local communities and dissatisfaction for tourists. In addition, the lack of an integrated strategy and management plan for developing scuba diving tourism may ultimately result in lost future benefits (Bentz et al, 2016). However, a well-planned management concept with an equal degree of involvement on the part of tourists, communities and industry stakeholders that takes into account the capacity of local resources may help to ensure the sustainable development on scuba diving tourism (Canavan, 2016; Chaperon & Bramwell, 2013), encouraging its maintenance and promotion and improving the quality of the scuba diving experience (Haddock-Fraser & Hampton, 2012; Hillmer-Pegram, 2014; Mota & Frausto, 2014; Su & Swanson, 2017; Townsend, 2008).

To provide the basis for a sustainable scuba diving experience, a number of contemporary strategies are in evidence in both the literature and in practice. One of the more common policies is the substitution of coral reefs with artificial reef (wreck) areas. It is believed that this may be an effective solution to reduce the destructive effect of scuba diving and to maintain the health of both coral reefs (and artificial reefs) and to increase the satisfaction of scuba divers (Anderson & Loomis, 2011). The main objective of this policy is to redirect intensive scuba diving activities from fragile natural environments to artificially created areas, such as wrecks and structured submerged recreative attractions. Amongst the wide variety of marine-based attractions, artificial wrecks in particular may offer scuba divers more interesting, challenging and diverse experiences (Edney, 2017) with picturesque opportunities. Compared with shallow scuba diving on coral reefs, artificial wrecks can be found in different sizes and at different depths. Moreover, the diving experience may be more challenging owing to the wreck itself, including deep diving and entering the wreck. In addition, such a challenging scuba diving experience also provides continuity in skill development; scuba divers can obtain an advanced certificate, permitting them to dive into deeper and more challenging wrecks. Moreover, to extend the time spent underwater, they can have training in more technical forms of scuba diving using, for example, enriched air nitrox, trimix or rebreather equipment. Consequently, the scuba diving experience may become continuously challenging.

In other respects, scuba diving tourists' knowledge of sustainable behaviour can be thought of as inadequate (Garrod, 2007; Higham & Lück, 2007). Recent studies have identified detrimental effects that are caused by different types of unsustainable levels of scuba diving activities at popular sites (Au, Zhang, Chung & Qiu, 2014; Hasler & Ott, 2008; Toyoshima & Nadaoka, 2015; Zakai & Chadwick-Furman, 2002). Surprisingly, most damage has been caused by taking photographs with the use of heavy equipment (Barker & Roberts, 2004; Krieger & Chadwick, 2013; Rouphael & Inglis, 2001). However, to ensure reliable and authentic scuba diving experiences, a set of methods has been suggested to control the behaviour of scuba divers (Ong & Musa, 2011, 2012), such as comprehensive pre-dive briefings and specialized education before interacting with fragile marine environments (Barker & Roberts, 2004; Davis & Tisdell, 1995; Medio, Ormond & Pearson, 1997; Worachananant et al., 2008). Alongside education, managing or restricting the number of scuba divers at certain times to regulate the locations in which scuba diving activities occur is another contemporary approach (Roche et al., 2016). Controlling the types of equipment used and implementing conservation programmes, such as Project Aware by PADI or Green Fins, promoting codes of conduct for both operators and tourists with guidelines from avoiding stepping on coral to joining conservation projects, are other suggested responses to manage the behaviour of scuba divers. In so doing, scuba divers may be encouraged to engage in a conscious and sophisticated experience.

Improving the sustainability of scuba diving experiences focuses on the significance of natural resources and artificial attractions and creates conditions for the preservation of these areas (Girard & Nijkamp, 2009). Moreover, the objectives are not only about maintaining an optimum experience for scuba diving tourists but also ensuring commercial profits, meeting local people's requirements and maintaining the balance of value and recreational uses of the fragile marine environment (Dimmock & Musa, 2015). One means of ensuring a sustainable experience is to pursue a balance between the economic benefit accruing from scuba diving tourism and its potential ecological threats. In addition, providing education and training on environmental issues and raising their environmental awareness amongst scuba diving tourists to may be the most effective means of managing the adverse impacts of diving on the marine environment. In other words, applying sustainability principles in the scuba diving experience may not be difficult and, at the same time, it can add more value to the experience in a positive and specialized way.

Conclusion

Creating scuba diving tourist experiences depends on multi-directional, individual, in-situ, administrative and monitoring strategies with regard to scuba divers and sustainability. To achieve this, a number of contemporary approaches exist to improve the quality of the scuba diving experience, such as maintaining the balance between economic benefits and social equity whilst protecting the marine environment. More specifically, better understanding of the characteristics of scuba diving and the divers' experiences and, in particular, greater knowledge of the preferences and attitudes of scuba diving tourists, is a significant step in reaching the desired outcomes, not least because this can inform the design and management of destinations based on scuba divers' needs. Moreover, establishing guidelines or codes of conduct to manage scuba divers' behaviours, particularly underwater, may also contribute to ensuring unique in-situ experiences. However, the connection between the personal involvement of scuba divers and the protection of the natural area is a complicated process. As Fath (2015) and Rodríguez (2017) suggest, understanding the relationship between tourist behaviour and the protection of natural resources may point to ways of managing scuba diving in natural areas within sustainable principles. Another solution is to offer alternative scuba diving areas, such as artificial reefs and wrecks, where designed and managed recreational activities may generate unusual but sustainable scuba diving experiences. Together, such strategies may help to create an integrated scuba diving experience for both tourists and all stakeholders involved in this industry.

Nevertheless, as suggested in this chapter, scuba diving itself is continually an exploratory experience process. That is, unlike other forms of tourism types, the scuba diving tourist experience is erratic and unpredictable in the sense that the marine environment is dynamic;

it cannot be guaranteed that the experience of a particular dive will be either unpleasant or pleasurable owing to a number of variables, from the overall trip experience to, for example, a lack of marine life or local underwater conditions that might diminish quality of the experience. In addition, the nature of physical interaction with the underwater environment and an individual's expectations, attitudes and previous diving experience may be influential. Therefore, having a good or unpleasant scuba diving experience is dependent on a variety of personal and external factors.

In summary, then, scuba diving tourism both in natural reef-based and alternative / artificial areas has the potential to contribute substantially to the conservation of marine ecosystems (Lucrezi, Saayman & van der Merwe, 2013) and bring benefits to local communities in coastal destinations. Through the appropriate planning and management of scuba diving, it is possible to reduce detrimental effects on natural habitats or artificially created resources, to provide economic benefits for stakeholders and to provide unique experiences to scuba diving tourists whilst, through raising awareness of environmental issues amongst scuba divers, scuba diving can be transformed from an environmental threat into a potential tool for conservation (Bentz et al, 2016; Dearden, Bennett & Rollins, 2006; Tapsuwan & Asafu-Adjaye, 2008; Zeppel & Muloin, 2008). In other words, if undertaken within the principles of sustainability, the scuba diving experience has the potential to make a positive contribution to environmental protection, social equality and an increase public awareness without sacrificing its economic benefits or the novel subaqueous scuba diving tourist experience.

References

Albayrak, T., Caber, M. and Cater, C. (2019) Mass tourism underwater: A segmentation approach to motivations of scuba diving holiday tourists. *Tourism Geographies*, Online: https://doi.org/10.1080/14616688.2019.169688

Anderson, L. E. and Loomis, D. K. (2011) Scuba diver specialization and behaviour norms at coral reefs. *Coastal Management*, 39(5), 478–491.

Arin, T. and Kramer, R. A. (2002) Divers' willingness to pay to visit marine sanctuaries: An exploratory study. *Ocean and Coastal Management*, 45(2–3), 171–183.

Arnould, E. J. and Price, L. L. (1993) River magic: Extraordinary experience and the extended service encounter. *Journal of Consumer Research*, 20(1), 24–45.

Au, A. C. S., Zhang, L., Chung, S. S. and Qiu, J. W. (2014) Diving associated coral breakage in Hong Kong: Differential susceptibility to damage. *Marine Pollution Bulletin*, 85(2), 789–796.

Barker, N. H. and Roberts, C. M. (2004) Scuba diver behaviour and the management of diving impacts on coral reefs. *Biological Conservation*, 120(4), 481–489.

Bentz, J., Lopes, F., Calado, H. and Dearden, P. (2016) Understanding diver motivation and specialization for improved scuba management. *Tourism in Marine Environments*, 12(1), 35–49.

Bideci, C. and Cater, C. (2019a). In search of underwater atmosphere: A new diving world on artificial reefs. In M. Volgger and D. Pfister (Eds.), *Atmospheric Turn in Culture and Tourism: Place, Design and Process Impacts on Customer Behaviour, Marketing and Branding*. Bingley: Emerald Publishing Limited, pp. 245–257.

Bideci, C. and Cater, C. (2019b) Dive and novelty seeking in experimental artificial reefs. *Journal on Tourism & Sustainability*, 3(1), 22–31.

Bideci, M. and Albayrak, T. (2018) An investigation of the domestic and foreign tourists' museum visit experiences. *International Journal of Culture, Tourism and Hospitality Research*, 12(3), 366–377.

Buzzacott, P. and Denoble, P. J. (2018) *DAN Annual Diving Report 2018 Edition: A Report on 2016 Diving Fatalities, Injuries, and Incidents*. Durham: Divers Alert Network.

Canavan, B. (2016) Tourism culture; Nexus, characteristics context and sustainability. *Tourism Management*, 53, 229–243.

Cater, C. and Cater, E. (2007) *Marine Ecotourism: Between the Devil and the Deep Blue Sea*. Wallingford: CABI.

Scuba-diving experience

Cater, C. I. (2008) The life aquatic: Scuba diving and the experiential imperative. *Tourism in Marine Environments*, 5(4), 233–244.

Chaperon, S. and Bramwell, B. (2013) Dependency and agency in peripheral tourism development. *Annals of Tourism Research*, 40,132–154.

Cope, R. (2003) The international diving market. *Travel and Tourism Analyst*, 6, 1–39.

Cousteau, J. Y. (1953) *The Silent World*. London: Hamish Hamilton.

Davis, D. and Tisdell, C. (1995) Recreational scuba-diving and carrying capacity in marine protected areas. *Ocean and Coastal Management*, 26(1), 19–40.

de Groot, J. and Bush, S. R. (2010) The potential for dive tourism led entrepreneurial marine protected areas in Curacao. *Marine Policy*, 34(5), 1051–1059.

Dearden, P., Bennett, M. and Rollins, R. (2006) Implications for coral reef conservation of diver specialization. *Environmental Conservation*, 33(4), 353–363.

DEMA (2020) *Fast Facts: Recreational Scuba Diving and Snorkelling*. Diving Equipment and Marketing Association. Available at: https://www.dema.org/store/download.aspx?id=7811B097-8882-4707-A160-F999B49614B6 (Accessed 27 March 2020).

Dikou, A. and Troumbis, A. (2006) Dive tourism in north Aegean, Greece: Potential and prospects. *Tourism in Marine Environments*, 3(2), 131–143.

Dimmock, K. (2009) Finding comfort in adventure: Experiences of recreational SCUBA divers. *Leisure Studies*, 28(3), 279–295.

Dimmock, K. (2010) CCN: Towards a model of comfort, constraints, and negotiation in recreational scuba diving. *Tourism in Marine Environments*, 6(4), 145–160.

Dimmock, K. and Musa, G. (2015) Scuba diving tourism system: A framework for collaborative management and sustainability. *Marine Policy*, 54, 52–58.

Ditton, R. B., Osburn, H. R., Baker, T. L. and Thailing, C. E. (2002) Demographics, attitudes, and reef management preferences of sport divers in offshore Texas waters. *ICES Journal of Marine Science*, 59 (suppl.), 186–191.

Duffus, D. A. and Dearden, P. (1990) Non-consumptive wildlife-oriented recreation: A conceptual framework. *Biological Conservation*, 53(3), 213–231.

Edney, J. (2012) Diver characteristics, motivations, and attitudes: Chuuk Lagoon. *Tourism in Marine Environments*, 8(1–2), 7–18.

Edney, J. (2017) Human dimensions of wreck diving and management: Case studies from Australia and Micronesia. *Tourism in Marine Environments*, 12(3–4), 169–182.

Ewert, A. W. (1989) *Outdoor Adventure Pursuits: Foundations, Models, and Theories*. Scottsdale: Publishing Horizons.

Fath, B. D. (2015) Quantifying economic and ecological sustainability. *Ocean and Coastal Management*, 108, 13–19.

Garrod, B. (2007) Marine wildlife tourism and ethics. In J. Higham and M. Lück (Eds.), *Marine Wildlife and Tourism Management: Insights from the Natural and Social S*. Wallingford: CABI, pp. 257–271.

Garrod, B. (2008) Market segments and tourist typologies for diving tourism. In B. Garrod, B andS. Gössling (Eds.), *New Frontiers in Marine Tourism: Diving Experiences, Sustainability, Management*. Amsterdam: Elsevier, pp. 31–48.

Garrod, B. and Gössling, S. (2008) Introduction. In B. Garrod and S. Gössling (Eds.), *New Frontiers in Marine Tourism: Diving Experiences, Sustainability, Management*. Amsterdam: Elsevier, pp. 8–29.

Girard, L. F. and Nijkamp, P. (Eds.) (2009) *Cultural Tourism and Sustainable Local Development*. Farnham: Ashgate Publishing.

Gregory, S. F. and Edney, J. (2019) Divers or divas? A market analysis of the mature aged female diver: An Australian perspective. *Tourism in Marine Environments*, 14(3), 143–162.

Haddock-Fraser, J. and Hampton, M. P. (2012) Multistakeholder values on the sustainability of dive tourism: case studies of Sipadan and Perhentian Islands, Malaysia. *Tourism Analysis*, 17(1), 27–41.

Hammerton, Z., Dimmock, K., Hahn, C., Dalton, S. J. and Smith, S. D. (2012) Scuba diving and marine conservation: Collaboration at two Australian subtropical destinations. *Tourism in Marine Environments*, 8(1–2), 77–90.

Hasler, H. and Ott, J. A. (2008) Diving down the reefs? Intensive diving tourism threatens the reefs of the northern Red Sea. *Marine Pollution Bulletin*, 56(10), 1788–1794.

Hawkins, J. P., Roberts, C. M., Kooistra, D., Buchan, K. and White, S. (2005) Sustainability of scuba diving tourism on coral reefs of Saba. *Coastal Management*, 33(4), 373–387.

Higham, J. E. S. and Lück, M. (2007) Marine wildlife and tourism management: In search of scientific approaches to sustainability. In J. Higham and M. Lück (Eds.), *Marine Wildlife and Tourism Management: Insights from the Natural and Social S.* Wallingford: CABI, pp.1–18.

Hillmer-Pegram, K. C. (2014) Understanding the resilience of dive tourism to complex change. *Tourism Geographies*, 16(4), 598–614.

Huang, Y. and Coelho, V. R. (2017) Sustainability performance assessment focusing on coral reef protection by the tourism industry in the Coral Triangle region. *Tourism Management*, 59, 510–527.

Huth, B., Morgan, A. and Burkart, C. (2015) Measuring Florida artificial reef economic benefits: A synthesis. *Florida Artificial Reef Summit*. Clearwater: University of Florida/Florida Sea Grant.

Karacsonyi, T. (2004) Malapascua diving: Flamboyants, threshers and ghost pipefish. *Divelog*, October, pp. 44–45.

Kirkbride-Smith, A. E., Wheeler, P. M. and Johnson, M. L. (2013) The relationship between diver experience levels and perceptions of attractiveness of artificial reefs-examination of a potential management tool. *PloS One*, 8(7). https://doi.org/10.1371/journal.pone.0068899

Kler, B. and Moskwa, E. (2013) Experience, interpretation and meanings. In G. Musa and K. Dimmock (Eds.), *Scuba Diving Tourism*. Abingdon: Routledge, pp.134–151.

Kler, B. K. and Tribe, J. (2012) Flourishing through SCUBA: Understanding the pursuit of dive experiences. *Tourism in Marine Environments*, 8(1–2), 19–32.

Krieger, J. R. and Chadwick, N. E. (2013) Recreational diving impacts and the use of pre-dive briefings as a management strategy on Florida coral reefs. *Journal of Coastal Conservation*, 17(1), 179–189.

Kruger, L. E. and Jakes, P. J. (2003) The importance of place: Advances in science and application. *Forest Science*, 49(6), 819–821.

Lucrezi, S., Milanese, M., Markantonatou, V., Cerrano, C., Sarà, A., Palma, M. and Saayman, M. (2017) Scuba diving tourism systems and sustainability: Perceptions by the scuba diving industry in two Marine Protected Areas. *Tourism Management*, 59, 385–403.

Lucrezi, S., Saayman, M. and van der Merwe, P. (2013) Managing diving impacts on reef ecosystems: Analysis of putative influences of motivations, marine life preferences and experience on divers' environmental perceptions. *Ocean and Coastal Management*, 76, 52–63.

Maslow, A. H. (1964) *Religions, Values, and Peak Experiences*. Columbus: Ohio State University Press.

Medio, D., Ormond, R. F. G. and Pearson, M. (1997) Effect of briefings on rates of damage to corals by scuba divers. *Biological Conservation*, 79(1), 91–95.

Meisel-Lusby, C. and Cottrell, S. (2008) Understanding motivations and expectations of scuba divers. *Tourism in Marine Environments*, 5(1), 1–14.

Meyer, L. A., Thapa, B. and Pennington-Gray, L. (2003) An exploration of motivations among scuba divers in North Central Florida. In R. Schuster (Ed.), *Proceedings of the 2002 Northeastern Recreation Research Symposium*. Syracuse: State University of New York, pp. 292–295.

Miller, G. and Taubman–Ben-Ari, O. (2004) Scuba diving risk taking: A terror management theory perspective. *Journal of Sport and Exercise Psychology*, 26(2), 269–282.

Mota, L. and Frausto, O. (2014) The use of scuba diving tourism for marine protected area management. *International Journal of Social, Management, Economics and Business Engineering*, 8, 3159–3164.

Musa, G. and Dimmock, K. (2012) Scuba diving tourism: Introduction to special issue. *Tourism in Marine Environments*, 8(1–2), 1–5.

Musa, G. and Dimmock, K. (2013) Introduction: Scuba diving tourism. In G. Musa and K. Dimmock (Eds.), *Scuba Diving Tourism*. Abingdon: Routledge, pp. 21–31.

Musa, G., Kadir, S. and Lee, L. (2006) Layang Layang: An empirical study on SCUBA divers' satisfaction. *Tourism in Marine Environments*, 2(2), 89–102.

Musa, G., Seng, W., Thinaranjeney, T. and Masoud, A. (2010) The influence of scuba divers' personality, experience, and demographic profile on their underwater behaviour. *Tourism in Marine Environments*, 7(1), 1–14.

Mylonopoulos, D. and Moira, P. (2019) Exploring the profiles and motives of recreational divers: Case study from Greece. *TIMS. Acta*, 13(1), 5–14.

Naidoo, P., Ramseook-Munhurrun, P. and Li, J. (2018) Scuba diving experience and sustainability: An assessment of online travel reviews. *The Gaze: Journal of Tourism and Hospitality*, 9, 43–52.

NOAA (2012) *Tourism and Recreation*. National Oceanic and Atmospheric Administration. Available at: https://coralreef.noaa.gov/aboutcorals/values/tourismrecreation/ (Accessed 10 August 2016).

Oceanwealth (2020) *Benefits of Nature Based Tourism*. The Nature Conservancy. Available at: https://oceanwealth.org/ecosystem-services/recreation-tourism/ (Accessed 16 April 2020).

OECD (2016) *The Future of the Ocean Economy 2030*. Paris: OECD Publishing. Available at: https://read.oecd-ilibrary.org/economics/the-ocean-economy-in-2030_9789264251724-en#page1 (Accessed: 15 May 2020).

Oh, H., Fiore, A. M. and Jeoung, M. (2007) Measuring experience economy concepts: Tourism applications. *Journal of Travel Research*, 46(2), 119–132.

Ong, T. F. and Musa, G. (2011) An examination of recreational divers' underwater behaviour by attitude–behaviour theories. *Current issues in Tourism*, 14(8), 779–795.

Ong, T. F. and Musa, G. (2012) Examining the influences of experience, personality and attitude on SCUBA divers' underwater behaviour: A structural equation model. *Tourism Management*, 33(6), 1521–1534.

O'Sullivan, K. (2008) The comfort of strangeness. *Sydney Morning Herald*, March 22: 33.

PADI (2019) *Worldwide Corporate Statistics*. Professional Association of Diving Instructors Available at: https://www.padi.com/sites/default/files/documents/2019-02/2019%20PADI%20Worldwide%20Statistics.pdf (Accessed 27 March 2020).

Paterson, S., Young, S., Loomis, D. K. and Obenour, W. (2012) Resource attributes that contribute to non-resident diver satisfaction in the Florida Keys, USA. *Tourism in Marine Environments*, 8(1–2), 47–60.

Pine, B. J. and Gilmore, J. H. (1999) *The Experience Economy: Work is Theatre and Every Business a Stage*. Boston: Harvard Business Press.

Roche, R. C., Harvey, C. V., Harvey, J. J., Kavanagh, A. P., McDonald, M., Stein-Rostaing, V. R. and Turner, J. R. (2016) Recreational diving impacts on coral reefs and the adoption of environmentally responsible practices within the SCUBA diving industry. *Environmental Management*, 58(1), 107–116.

Rodríguez, A. M. (2017) *The Secret of the Scuba Diving Spider … and More!* New York: Enslow Publishing, LLC.

Roos, R. (1989) Are the risks of sport scuba diving being underestimated? *The Physician and Sportsmedicine*, 17(7), 132–142.

Rouphael, A. B. and Hanafy, M. (2007) An alternative management framework to limit the impact of SCUBA divers on coral assemblages. *Journal of Sustainable Tourism*, 15(1), 91–103.

Rouphael, A. B. and Inglis, G. J. (1997) Impacts of recreational scuba diving at sites with different reef topographies. *Biological conservation*, 82(3), 329–336.

Rouphael, A. B. and Inglis, G. J. (2001) 'Take only photographs and leave only footprints'? An Experimental study of the impacts of underwater photography on coral reef dive sites. *Biological Conservation*, 100(3), 281–287.

Salim, N., Bahauddin, A. and Mohamed, B. (2013) Influence of scuba divers' specialization on their underwater behavior. *Worldwide Hospitality and Tourism Themes*, 5(4), 388–397.

Schoeman, K., Van der Merwe, P. and Slabbert, E. (2016) The perceived value of a scuba diving experience. *Journal of Coastal Research*, 32(5), 1071–1080.

Scitovsky, T. (1992) *The Joyless Economy: The Psychology of Human Satisfaction*, Revised Edition. New York: Oxford University Press USA.

SFIA (2020) *Scuba Diving Participation Report 2019*. Sports and Fitness Industry Association. Available at: https://www.sfia.org/reports/796_Scuba-Diving-Participation-Report-2019 (Accessed 27 March 2020).

Shafer, C. S. and Inglis, G. J. (2000) Influence of social, biophysical, and managerial conditions on tourism experiences within the Great Barrier Reef World Heritage Area. *Environmental Management*, 26(1), 73–87.

Stolk, P., Markwell, K. and Jenkins, J. (2005) Perceptions of artificial reefs as scuba diving resources: a study of Australian recreational scuba divers. *Annals of Leisure Research*, 8(2–3), 153–166.

Su, L. and Swanson, S. R. (2017) The effect of destination social responsibility on tourist environmentally responsible behavior: Compared analysis of first-time and repeat tourists. *Tourism Management*, 60, 308–321.

Szuster, B. W., Needham, M. D. and McClure, B. P. (2011) Scuba diver perceptions and evaluations of crowding underwater. *Tourism in Marine Environments*, 7(3–4), 153–165.

Tabata, R. S. (1989) The use of nearshore dive sites by recreational dive operations in Hawaii. In O. Magoon, H. Converse, D. Miner, L. T. Tobin and D. Clark (Eds.), *Coastal Zone '89: Proceedings of the Sixth Annual Conference on Coastal Zone Management*. Reston: American Society of Civil Engineers, pp. 2865–2876.

Tapsuwan, S. and Asafu-Adjaye, J. (2008) Estimating the economic benefit of SCUBA diving in the Similan Islands, Thailand. *Coastal Management*, 36(5), 431–442.

Thapa, B., Graefe, A. R. and Meyer, L. A. (2006) Specialization and marine based environmental behaviors among SCUBA divers. *Journal of Leisure Research*, 38(4), 601–615.

Todd, S., Graefe, A. and Mann, W. (2002) Differences in SCUBA diver motivations based on level of development. In S. Todd (Ed.), *Proceedings of the 2001 Northeastern Recreation Research Symposium*. Cortland: State University of New York.

Townsend, C. (2008) Dive tourism, sustainable tourism, and social responsibility: A growing agenda. In B. Garrod and S. Gössling (Eds.), *New Frontiers in Marine Tourism: Diving Experiences, Sustainability, Management*. Amsterdam: Elsevier, pp. 140–152.

Toyoshima, J. and Nadaoka, K. (2015) Importance of environmental briefing and buoyancy control on reducing negative impacts of SCUBA diving on coral reefs. *Ocean and Coastal Management*, 116, 20–26.

Tschapka, M. K. (2006) *Involvement, Motivations and Setting Preference of Participants in the Adventure Tourism Activity of Scuba Diving*. Canberra: University of Canberra.

Verkoeyen, S. and Nepal, S. K. (2019) Understanding scuba divers' response to coral bleaching: An application of Protection Motivation Theory. *Journal of Environmental Management*, 231, 869–877.

Wilks, J. (1991) Diving dropouts: The Australian experience. *Australian Journal of Science and Medicine in Sport*, 23, 17–20.

Wongthong, P. and Harvey, N. (2014) Integrated coastal management and sustainable tourism: A case study of the reef-based SCUBA dive industry from Thailand. *Ocean and Coastal Management*, 95, 138–146.

Worachananant, S., Carter, R. W., Hockings, M. and Reopanichkul, P. (2008) Managing the impacts of SCUBA divers on Thailand's coral reefs. *Journal of Sustainable Tourism*, 16(6), 645–663.

Zakai, D. and Chadwick-Furman, N. E. (2002) Impacts of intensive recreational diving on reef corals at Eilat, northern Red Sea. *Biological Conservation*, 105(2), 179–187.

Zeppel, H. and Muloin, S. (2008) Conservation and education benefits of interpretation on marine wildlife tours. *Tourism in Marine Environments*, 5(2–3), 215–227.

28

RELIGIOUS TOURISM

A spiritual or touristic experience?

Daniel H. Olsen

Introduction: the problem of understanding experience

Writing a chapter on the experiences of people who engage in religious tourism, as well as categorizing and evaluating research on such experiences, is fraught with difficulty. For example, any such discussion should include a broader elucidation on subjects such as motivation, embodiment, emotion, affect, personal and group identity formation and activity types, as well as the temporal, socio-cultural and geographical contexts within which these experiences occur. In addition, an examination of what constitutes religious pilgrimage, religious tourism and spiritual tourism in the context of (post)modernity must also be discussed, particularly considering the hybridization of pilgrimage/tourism and the sacred/secular in both theory and practice (e.g., Collins-Kreiner, 2010; della Dora, 2012; Kaelber, 2006; Olsen, 2010; Thomas, White & Samuel, 2018).

Another difficulty arises when trying to group, categorize or typologize religious tourism experiences. Typologizing or segmenting tourist types is standard practice by scholars who (sometimes unconsciously) follow the business model of tourism by grouping people within a widely heterogeneous tourism marketplace into homogenous niche categories to better understand the phenomenon under consideration (e.g., Dolnicar, 2008). This has been the case with religious tourism. However, a fundamental problem with typologies is that they are not always based on the 'conscious, immediate experience' (Mannell & Iso-Aloha, 1987: 316) of religious tourists and, as such, may be unreliable because they are grounded in some cases by time- and distance-decayed and biased recollections of on-site experiences. Also, categorizations of visitors based on participant observation do not necessarily reveal why people visit sacred sites, which often are a syncretic blend of spiritual, habitual and recreational reasons (Nelson, 1996). In addition, attempting to create experiential and motivational typologies of religious tourists based on a single case study while ignoring the broader socio-cultural milieus within which religious tourism takes place and without attempting some sort of broader validation and refinement effort makes universalistic typological efforts regional, contextual and reductionist in nature. In addition, as Olsen (2010: 849) notes, 'From a postmodern and poststructuralist perspective it is difficult to accept anachronistic and abstract universal travel typologies that place binary opposites as an "everything/nothing" concept where types of travel and travelers fit into tidy categories.' As

DOI: 10.4324/9781003219866-32

such, these typologies are 'useful only for classifying various sub-markets of contemporary pilgrimage as the continuum does not reflect the multi-layered meanings of pilgrimage and tourism in the modern era' (Olsen, 2010: 849).

The rise of the 'experience economy' also complicates an understanding of the religious tourism experience. According to Pine and Gilmore (2011), as economies mature and evolve over time, they diversify their commodity offerings from low-order and valued goods, such as extractive resources and manufactured commodities, to higher-order, intangible and more expensive products or goods, such as services and staged experiences. These higher-order goods are in many instances customizable for individualistic consumption, and the more customizable the consumed experience, the more people are willing to pay for such experiences. As such, top-down, company-centric tourism development has been slowly replaced by 'co-creative' business models, where tourist demand determines the types of tourist experiences that are created in 'experience space' (Prahalad & Ramaswamy, 2003; see Binkhorst & Den Dekker, 2009; Campos, Mendes, Valle & Scott, 2018). This means that tourist activities and experiences – including religious tourism activities and experiences – are negotiated between tourists and experience providers, with these experiences becoming increasingly modified and commodified to meet the various taste preferences of an increasingly individualized and fragmented tourism market.

This, then, raises questions regarding the role of authenticity and authentication within travel experiences, religious or otherwise. While discussions regarding authenticity within tourism studies revolve around three types of authenticity – objective, constructive or symbolic and existential (Wang, 1999) – and which types are instrumental in the construction of tourism experiences (Chhabra, 2019), authentication refers to the socio-political process of how something is defined as being authentic (Cohen & Cohen, 2012). Indeed, deliberations revolving around the creation and construction of authentic experiences have long occupied tourism scholars. Some argue that many tourists actively seek contrived, inauthentic 'pseudo-events' (e.g., Boorstin, 1987; Urry & Larsen, 2011), while others contend that tourists seek or 'quest' for unmediated, authentic, embodied, real and 'ordinary' encounters with the cultures and places within which they visit. However, those arguing the second position admit that these encounters and their matching experiences rarely occur, even within a postmodern and relativistic society, because of the mediatized, strategic and staged nature of tourism promotion and consumption (e.g., Jansson, 2002; MacCannell, 1973, 1976; Pine & Gilmore, 2008; Roodenburg, 2004). These arguments regarding authenticity are problematized further by the rise of virtual and media-mediated realities that parrot real-world experiences through simulated mobilities (Campbell, 2013; Jansson, 2002).

According to Bremer (2004: 3–7), while many tourists are generally concerned with aesthetic (primarily authentic) experiences as they journey, which frame their experiences of and with religion, religious travellers seek authentic religious experiences that can be enhanced through aesthetics. While religiously motivated tourists may search for 'religious authenticity' through authentic religious experiences (Bremer 2001, 2004), is it truly possible today to find 'real' and meaningful experiences with the 'numinous' or the 'holy' (Eliade, 1959; Otto, 1950), particularly when considering the mediated nature of travel to and interpretation at sacred destinations which create a particular 'sense of place' (Shackley, 2001) designed to lead visitors toward certain expected behaviors and experiences? As such, a distinction needs to be made between what experiences religious tourists want to have, the experiences tour agencies promise these tourists will have, the experiences sacred site managers want them to have, and the experiences religious tourists actually have. In addition, what happens to the overall travel experience when the expected experiences do not materialize (e.g., Kaell, 2016)? All of this is a part of understanding what is meant by authentic expected experiences in a religious tourism context (Olsen, 2013).

The purpose of this chapter is to work through some of these difficulties and concerns, albeit in a cursory manner, by focusing on how academics have attempted to describe and typologize the experiences of religious tourists. After deconstructing the intersection of religion and tourism through the term 'religious tourism', a brief review of the literature on religious tourist motivations and experiences is presented with an accompanying model of religious tourism experience. The differences between religious and tourist experiences are then discussed before concluding with a less than definitive answer to the question posed in the title of this chapter.

Deconstructing religious tourism

The label and practice of 'religious tourism,' serving as an intersectional marker between religion and tourism, has become an increasingly naturalized focus of study among many tourism and religious studies scholars (e.g., Badone & Roseman, 2004; Butler & Suntikul, 2018; de Oliveira, 2017; El-Gohary, Edwards & Eid, 2017; Raj & Griffin, 2015; Stausberg, 2011; Timothy & Olsen, 2006a). However, while some scholars have debated whether these two terms are synergistic or a syntomic and dichotomous contradiction of terms (e.g., Giumbelli, 2018; Stausberg, 2014), a brief deconstruction of the two words in this syntagma is necessary when considering the experiences of religious tourists to determine the answer to the question this chapter seeks to address: is religious tourism a spiritual or a touristic experience?

The term 'religion' revolves around 'a set of beliefs or discourses, which give rise to a set of practices around which a community is defined, which is regulated by an institution that regulates these beliefs, discourses and practices the community follows' (Olsen, 2008: 22). The term 'tourism', as defined by the author, refers to

> an activity that involves taking a temporary trip that takes place within the principles of a capitalistic production system comprised of industries, intermediaries and private and government institutions that regulate tourist motivations based on supply and demand issues and mediate the complex interactions and variety of experiences between tourists and the host communities and their environments.
>
> *(Olsen, 2008: 20)*

One of the commonalities that these seemingly disparate terms have to each other is that they both involve some sort of *practice*, and the practice that bridges the gap between these two concepts is mobility – or more specifically, the act of pilgrimage.

Pilgrimage has been defined by Barber (1991: 1) as a 'journey to a distant sacred goal.' This definition implies that the motivation for a journey and the experiences that are desired by a person participating in a pilgrimage are religious and sacred in nature. The word pilgrimage itself came about in the early seventeenth century to describe different types of (European) religious travel under one umbrella term (Eade & Albera, 2016: 6–9) and then, like the term 'religion', used as a conceptual and comparative term to study similar modes and types of travel in non-Western cultures (Braun, 2000; Smith, 1988, 1998). However, while pilgrimage has historically referred to religiously motivated travel to sites owned and managed by religious organizations and institutions, in the present (post)modern era, what constitutes a pilgrimage has been metaphorically and playfully expanded to include 'any journey undertaken by a person in quest of a place or a state that he or she believes to embody a *valued ideal*' (Morinis, 1992: 4, emphasis added; see Knox & Hannam, 2014; Olsen, 2014). Therefore, what constitutes a pilgrimage in the present era has been expanded to include travel to non-religious sites, such as travelling to sporting events; the gravesites of famous people; sites of civil religion; places related to film, anime and other aspects popular culture; and really any hedonistic recreational activity where meaningful experiences occur (e.g., Alderman, 2002; Gammon, 2004; Knox & Hannam, 2014; Sugawa-Shimada, 2015; West, 2008).

Like 'pilgrimage', 'tourism' is a more modern term to describe types of past and present mobilities. It was not until the late 1800s that the word 'tourism' was utilized to describe circular trips performed by people during their leisure time. Prior to this time, terms such as 'journeying', 'travel' and 'travail' were used to describe such trips (Leiper, 1983). While tourism in this context refers to the act of travel regardless of motivation, some tourism theorists have compared modern tourism with religious pilgrimage, in that both forms of mobility seem to exhibit similar structural and experiential similarities. For example, Brown (2013; see also Wang, 1999) argues that the act of tourism can serve as a catalyst for existential authenticity, leading a person to engage in 'authentic living' as they travel in search of their authentic 'self'. In doing so, tourists enter a realm of 'non-ordinary flotation' (Jafari, 1987) or a state of hyperreality (Eco, 1983; Holmberg, 1993), experience a non-ordinary sacred 'high' (Graburn 1989) and then return to their profane lives. As such, tourism is seen as 'symbolically sacred and morally on a higher plane than the regards of the ordinary workday world' (Graburn 1989: 28), with the tourist experience being analogous to the pilgrim experience (Osterrieth, 1997).

Granted, as noted earlier, some scholars rightfully note that tourism contains elements of inauthenticity and hedonistic motivations and activities, with many people assuming the title 'traveller' to distinguish their altruistic and morally superior motives from the 'tourist', who is both symbolic of the economic, socio-cultural and environmental problems and the superficial and inauthentic experiences associated with modern mass tourism (e.g., Boorstin, 1987; Redfoot, 1984; Week, 2012). However, while pilgrimage and tourism are often contrasted by using the image of the pious pilgrim and the superficial tourist or 'nitwit' (Cohen, 1979), historically, religious pilgrims combined sacred and recreational motivations and pursuits while travelling for religious purposes (Olsen, 2010; Turner & Turner, 1978). As such, the mixing of religious and touristic motivations and experiences historically have not been incongruent or incompatible with each other. As Olsen (2010) notes, the main characters in Chaucer's *The Canterbury Tales* engaged in a mix of religious and hedonistic activities and therefore had religious and non-religious experiences as they travelled. Because of this blending of sacred/morally superior and recreational/inauthentic motivations and activities, Turner and Turner (1978: 20) argue that 'a tourist is half a pilgrim, if a pilgrim is half a tourist.' This tension between pilgrimage and tourism can be seen in how different people describe themselves when visiting religious sites. As Di Giovine (2016; see Hughes, Bond & Ballantyne, 2013) notes, religiously motivated tourists tend to think of pilgrimage and tourism as diametrically opposed; that they are conducting a 'pilgrimage' and are not tourists per se. At the same time, Collins-Kreiner and Kliot (2000) found that there was a range of self-labeling between visitors to Israel who considered themselves either a pilgrim, a blend of pilgrim–tourist, or a tourist, while Bond, Packer and Ballantyne (2015) argue that many people who visit religious sites and events do not consider themselves pilgrims or even at times religious tourists – just visitors. As such, 'visitors' perceptions of themselves at a sacred site vary according to their religion and level of belief' (Kim & Kim, 2019a: 532).

Religious tourism

'Religious tourism', then, refers in part to a blending of sacred and secular motivations when travelling to sacred destinations and attractions. The inclusion of motivations and attractions in trying to understand the dynamics of the religious tourism market, however, has led to questions regarding whether this tourism niche market should be defined from a supply side or demand side perspective. For example, from a supply side view, tourism niche markets are defined by the types of activities people engage in while travelling. As Timothy and Olsen (2006b: 77) note, 'a person traveling to participate in a cultural festival would be considered a cultural tourist, while a person wanting to experience the thrill of skydiving may be considered an adventure tourist'. As such, religious tourism is defined from an industry perspective as 'people who visit sacred sites during their journeys to other attractions and destinations', with pilgrims being considered 'a type of tourist who travels for religious or spiritual reasons'. However, from a demand side perspective, religious tourism 'is separate from other forms of tourism because it is characterized by its aims, motivations, and destinations', which is a much more difficult way to determine tourism market niches.

While seemingly a trivial and purely academic issue, the acknowledgement of this supply/demand issue has led more practically to a fragmentation of the religious tourism market, which can be divided into four distinct but overlapping tourism niche markets: religious tourism; pilgrimage or faith tourism; spiritual tourism market; and New Age tourism (Olsen, in press). As noted above, religious tourism focuses on combining religious and secular motivations and activities as a part of a broader cultural and/or heritage itinerary regardless of the motivations of those who are participating in said itineraries. Pilgrimage or faith tourism, however, is more focused on people who are motivated to travel because of religion and focuses specifically on 'believer[s] as tourist[s]' (Terzidou, Scarles & Saunders, 2018). While this is not to say that pilgrimage or faith tourists do not engage in leisure or recreational pursuits while travelling, this tourism niche market focuses on 'developing faith-friendly offerings to address consumers' religious sentiments' (Izberk-Bilgin & Nakata, 2016: 286) – travelling to sites related to the religious persuasion of tourists for educational and ritual purposes and to experience communitas with other individuals of their faith. The spiritual tourism market is tied strongly to both the religious and pilgrimage/faith tourism markets in that many spiritual tourists travel to sites owned and maintained by institutionalized faiths. However, spiritual tourists view religion as an uneasy model of interpretation and a barrier to unmediated self-realization and identity formation, and as such also look outside of religion and religious institutions in their search for meaning and the 'self'. The New Age marketplace is just that – a marketplace of sometimes seemingly disparate spiritual, religious and 'beyond the planet' traditions and conspiracies (see Asprem & Dyrendal, 2015) that allows people to experiment with different religious and spiritual traditions in an 'eclectic meaning-making' process (Cusack, 2022).

Typologies of and research on religious tourism experiences

A quick search of the academic literature on the religious tourism market reveals some research emphasizing the motivations of religious and non-religious tourists who visit religious sites (e.g., Battour, Ismail, Battor & Awais, 2017; Blackwell, 2007; Buzinde, Kalavar, Kohli & Manuel-Navarrete, 2014; Dowson, Yaqub & Raj, 2019; Drule, Chiş, Băcilă & Ciornea, 2012; Haque & Momen, 2017; Kamenidou & Vourou, 2015; Robina Ramírez & Fernández Portillo, 2020; Terzidou 2010; Terzidou, Scarles & Saunders, 2018; Wang, Chen & Huang, 2016). This research finds that visitors have highly diversified motivations to visit these sites, ranging from purely religious motives to cultural and heritage appreciation, learning or education and curious sightseeing. This focus on understanding motivations for travel is typical for academics as well as tourism practitioners when trying to understand and develop a particular tourism niche market (e.g., Cohen, 1979; McKercher & Du Cros, 2003; Mo, Howard & Havitz, 1993; Plog, 1974). This is also the case with academic research on religious tourism, which is a relatively newer research entry in tourism studies (Rashid, 2018). While the religious tourism market is a multi-billion dollar niche market with between 300 and 600 million religious tourists travelling the world each year (Timothy, 2021; UNWTO, 2011, 2014), there is still much work that needs to be done to better understand the structure, motivations and experiences related to those who create and participate in this market. Unfortunately, as Bond (2015), and Kim, Kim and King (2016) lament, there is not much literature on the experiences of people who visit religious sites and several questions remain. For example, what types of experiences do people want or expect to have when visiting these sites? How are these experiences tied to their motivations for travel? What are the actual outcomes for people who visit and interact with religious sites in various ways? However, there is a small but growing literature on the experiences of visitors at religious sites, which, along with the literature on motivations, is briefly examined here.

One of the first typologies that focused on the differing motivations of religious tourists was an oft-cited continuum created by Smith (1992) which, in placing the tourist and the pilgrim on opposite sides of a spectrum, suggested that people who travel fall somewhere along a sliding range between being a true secular tourist seeking hedonistic pleasure to a pure pilgrim seeking sacred places and experiences. Between these two poles lie an infinite number of sacred-secular combinations, with the middle of these two poles representing a person being half a pilgrim and half a tourist – in essence a religious tourist. This continuum implies that where a person is located between being a 'pure pilgrim' and a 'pure tourist' will determine their motivations for travelling, their choice of destination and the types of experiences they expect to have.

Since Smith's pilgrim–tourist continuum, there have been several attempts to further understand and segment the religious tourist into more specific sacred–secular combinations. For example, based on the geographic, demographic and psychographic characteristics of Jewish pilgrims, Collins-Kreiner (2010) typologizes these pilgrims into 'pure pilgrims', 'pilgrim-tourists', 'traditional believers' and 'secular visitors', noting that religious affiliation and intensity contributes to the categorization of these pilgrims – the more religious a person in practice, the closer toward 'pure pilgrim' they were. Albayrak et al. (2018) also noted that religious tourism experiences differed among visitors to Jerusalem depending on their religious preferences. Ron (2009) created a typology of Christian travel based on travel activities or products: 'pilgrimage' based on travel related to scriptural geographies (e.g., Old and New Testaments, The Book of Mormon) and 'other forms of pilgrimage travel' related to dramatic plays and pageants, volunteer tourism, contrived attractions such as religious theme parks, conferences and conventions, and visiting local Christian and non-Christian communities. While little was written about motivation, Ron's typology also suggests that religiosity may play a role in the choice of the types of activities or products religious tourists chose to consume. Ebadi (2014) categorized visitors to the Khaled Nabi shrine in Iran into six discrete types based on motivations and experiences sought: religious pilgrims; spiritual pilgrims/tourists; ecotourists; ethnic tourists; Turkmen cultural/historical tourists; and non-Turkmen cultural/historical tourists. Ebadi (2014) notes that the number of people 'exclusively' motivated by religion were in the minority. In their study of visitors to Mount Kailash, a mountain held sacred by adherents to Tibetan Buddhism, Hinduism, Bön and Jainism in the Tibet Autonomous Region, Wang, Luo, Huang and Yang (2020) classified

Religious tourism

visitors as 'pilgrims', 'spiritual inquirers', 'hobbyists' and 'accidental tourists', noting that classifications differ based on their experiences sought (i.e., personal to social/group) and perceived educational benefits (i.e., spiritual to secular).

While not about the religious tourist experience per se, from a supply and geographical perspective, Nolan and Nolan (1992) developed a three-tiered typology of tourist usages of religious sites – pilgrimage shrines, centers of interest for religious tourism and sites related to religious folklore and festivals – and suggest that these different site attributes may influence travel motivations and offer different types of experiences. Bond, Packer and Ballantyne (2015) note this in their study of three different Christian religious heritage sites, including the Shrine of Our Lady of Walsingham (pilgrimage shrine), Canterbury Cathedral (centers of interest for religious tourism) and the Glastonbury Abbey Christian pilgrimage festival (religious folklore and festivals). From their research, they discovered five types of experiences that people are seeking through their engagement with religious heritage sites and activities. These experiences include:

i   *Connecting spiritually and emotionally*: with something outside of themselves;
ii   *Discovering new things*: wanting to experience something out of the ordinary;
iii   *Engaging mentally*: or seeking educational experiences;
iv   *Interacting and belonging*: experiences that led to social interaction and bonding; and
v   *Relaxing and finding peace*: experiences related to rejuvenation and relaxation.

Their findings also indicated that while connecting spiritually and emotionally was tied to all five experiential types, experiences relating to relaxing and finding peace was the most important experience as noted by participants, overshadowing even spiritual or cognitive experiences. Moreover, they found differences in the types of visitors, the activities they participated in, and the experiences visitors had at these different sites/events. Olsen (2013), in his discussion of 'expectations of experience', or what religious tourists are expecting to experience when they travel, takes a more geographic approach, dividing religious tourism experiences based on whether religious tourists are travelling to a specific point (e.g., religious site), along a line (e.g., a religiously themed route) or through an area (e.g., a broader religious region such as the Holy Land). Olsen (2013) notes that temporally there are differences regarding the motivations and the types of experiences people have who travel to religious points versus along religious lines and religious areas.

Similar to Bond, Packer and Ballantyne (2015), other work regarding religious tourism typologies has focused on visitors to cathedrals and monasteries. For example, Davis (1992) developed a typology of four types of visitors to cathedrals: 'gawpers', who come as visitors but have unexpected religious or spiritual experiences (see Jackson & Hudman, 1995); 'cultured despisers', who enjoy visiting cathedrals but bristle when presented with religious messaging; 'prayer-makers', who are interested in praying or having others pray for them; and 'true believers', who are interested in receiving religious messaging during their visit. Francis, Williams, Annis and Robbins (2008; see also Francis, Mansfield, Williams & Village, 2010) examined St. David's Cathedral in Wales and Chester Cathedral in England using a Jungian approach to create several Jungian psychological visitor profiles or types. They found that cathedrals tend to attract more introverts than extroverts, sensing types (i.e., focus on details than the overall picture) than intuitive types (i.e., focus on the overall picture), more judging types (i.e., structure their outer world through actively judging external stimuli) than perceiving types (i.e., structure their outer world through passively judging external stimuli), and an equal mix of thinking types (i.e., make decisions based on objective, impersonal logic) and feeling types (i.e., make decisions based on subjecting, personal values). Griffiths (2011), researching the motivations of visitors to the St Patrick's and Sacred Heart Cathedrals in Australia, found that visitors came for a mix of religious and educational reasons, including public worship, architectural appreciation, to learn more about the history of these cathedrals, spiritual reasons and private prayer. Rodrigues and McIntosh (2014) found that visitors to a Catholic monastery in New Zealand were searching for three main experiential themes: 'religious experience', 'personal experience' and 'social experience'. Focusing on non-religious visitors to a Romania monastery, Drule et al. (2012: 433) found that these visitors were motivated mainly by self-actualization – the 'desire to become a better person'. Andriotis (2009), examining the experiences of male tourists to Mount Athos, Greece, divided visitor experience into five 'elements':

i   *Spiritual element*: visitors who are motivated by faith;
ii *Cultural element*: visitors who seek cultural experiences within a religious architectural frame untouched by modernity;
iii *Secular element*: visitors who seek relaxing, socially cohesive experiences;
iv *Environmental element*: visitors who seek solitude or quiet in an aesthetically pleasing natural setting; and
v   *Educational element*: visitors who seek experiences that invite learning and education.

More recently, there has been a shift to expand understanding of religious tourism experiences through 'means-end chain theory'. According to Costa, Dekker and Jongen (2004: 403), means–end chain theory involves examining 'how concrete product attributes are linked to self-relevant consequences of consumption and personal life values (or goals)'. In other words, this theory 'views consumers as goal-oriented decision-makers, who choose to perform behaviors that seem most likely to lead to desired outcomes' (Costa et al., 2004: 404). The means–end chain theory generally uses 'laddering' as a qualitative technique to identify relationships between product attributes (A), benefits or consequences derived from the consumption of a chosen product (C), or in this case, the benefits or consequences that are 'generated through religious tourism experiences' (Kim & Kim, 2019a: 533), and how this these benefits affect personal, higher-order values (V) – values that are defined as 'a crucial belief that directly affects the behavior of individuals' (Kim & Kim, 2019a: 535) – such as happiness, sense of belonging, achievement and security. The relationship between these three aspects of means–end chain theory are generally summarized as A–C–V.

In the context of religious tourism, in using means–end theory and laddering, Kim, Kim and King (2016) found that for both Christian and non-Christian pilgrims walking along Camino de Santiago de Compostela, the most important value was happiness (V), which was tied directly to their interactions with the natural environment and the opportunity for long contemplation (A), and which led to both a growing appreciation for nature and being recharged through reflection and contemplation (C). They also found, among other findings, that the opportunity for physical exercise (A) led to people feeling healthier (C) while fulfilling the value 'pursuit of a healthy life' (V). Kim and Kim (2019a) also used means–end chain theory and laddering to investigate the hierarchal value map of religious tourists visiting Vatican City. They also identified several A–C–V links or chains, the most important being 'the opportunity to explore the traditions and history of sites' (A); 'had a genuinely religious experience' (C); 'learned about the history of my religion' (C); and 'enhancement of faith and spirituality' (V). Progano, Kato and Cheer (2020) also use the same methodology to compare the similarities and differences in the A–C–V chains of Japanese and Australian visitors walking the Nakahechi section of the Kumano Kodo pilgrimage trail in Japan. Pezeshki et al. (2019: 14) similarly found that visiting a pilgrimage site associated with their faith tradition (A) led to 'relaxation' (C), which led to 'inner peace' (C), 'a contemplation with God's creations' (C) and a relief from the 'burden of their sin' (C), which in turn led to 'a sense of salvation in their lives' (V).

In related research, other scholars have focused more specifically on the 'benefits' or 'consequences' and 'values' related to religious tourism. For example, Bond, Packer and Ballantyne (2015) found that some of the benefits derived from visiting cathedrals included personal fulfillment, spiritual growth, cognitive insight (i.e., learning/education), social bonding and restoration (i.e., sense of peace, rejuvenation and relaxation). While not using the means–end chain theory per se, Lee, Jan and Lin (2020) suggest that the desire for authentic experiences (A) among first-time and repeat visitors to the Dajia Mazu pilgrimage in Taiwan leads them to attend and participate in the pilgrimage. While there are 'costs' to participating in the pilgrimage – monetarily, temporally and environmentally – because the benefits derived from the pilgrimage (C) outweigh the costs, pilgrimage participants tend to support further tourism development to ensure the Dajia Mazu pilgrimage continues into the future. In the same vein, Kim and Kim (2019b) suggest that religious tourism experiences positively enhance the values of 'happiness' and 'self-satisfaction/fulfillment'. Huang, Pearce, Guo and Shen (2019), interviewed visitors to the four great Buddhist mountains in China and categorized visitor values into seven themes: 'a new window for life', 'the need for religious belief', 'importance of closer relationships', 'inspiration from others', enlightenment from natural features', 'the symbolism of wild animals and insects' and 'sacredness of symbolic properties'.

With this discussion in mind, Figure 28.1 provides a simple diagram to outline a tentative understanding of the religious tourism experience. In Stage 1, following Collins-Kreiner (2010), a person's level of religiosity may lead them to choose a destination or attraction based on its religious attributes. Those who are more religiously motivated may visit a pilgrimage shrine that specifically caters to the performance of religious rituals, while those who are more inclined toward learning about religious culture (even their own) might gravitate toward religious tourism centres or sites related to religious folklore and festivals (Bond, Packer & Ballantyne, 2015; Nolan & Nolan, 1992). In Stage 2, in a twist to the A–C–V chain, Collins-Kreiner (2010) puts values next, as, in many cases, religiosity informs people's values (V) and decision-making. Stage 3 focuses on the attributes of potential destinations (A), followed by the 'perceived benefits' or 'perceived consequences' that people might accrue based on those destination attributes, benefits or consequences (C_1), which are influenced in part by tourism marketing that shapes consumer behavior and choices. Stage 5 involves travel to religious sites, the liminal stage of the religious tourism experience in which people enter a state 'betwixt and between' everyday life and the unknown that allows people potentially have life-altering experiences (Beech, 2011; Turner & Turner, 1978). Stage 6 involves the activities in which people engage at religious sites. Stage 7 involves the benefits and experiences that occur through engagement with these activities and the material and immaterial aspects of these sites (C_2). These experiences then realign people's values, and either strengthen religiosity if the experiences they were expecting to have were positive or weaken religiosity if their experiences were negative in nature (see Kaell, 2016).

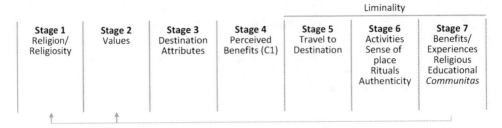

Figure 28.1 A model of religious tourism experience

Religious and touristic experiences

The typologies and A–C–V chains noted above are generally useful in trying to understand the diverse motivations and experiences of religious tourists, and highlight that while many people travel to religious sites to have religious or spiritual experiences, they also have other educational, cultural, wellness or leisure-oriented motivations and sought-after experiences. However, one could rightfully ask how fundamentally different the experiences of spiritual tourists and religious tourists are, particularly considering that as spirituality is generally viewed as being located 'both within and beyond' religion (Stausberg, 2011: 355). This is one reason, as noted above, why the religious tourism and spiritual tourism markets are viewed as interrelated and yet separate tourism niche markets (see Norman, 2011; Sharpley, 2009; Willson, 2016).

While this question is one that deserves future academic attention, the more pertinent question is how the experiences of religious tourists differ from people that engage in leisure and recreationally based travel and tourism. While tourism is often seen as comprising superficial experiences, the earlier discussion on the similarities between pilgrimage and tourism point to more than just a structural relationship. Indeed, many tourists seek authentic, life-altering experiences when they travel–transformative, even epiphanic, experiences whereby they receive 'moments of sudden and significant insight' (Wearing, McDonald & Ankor, 2016: 159). Such moments lead to

> life-altering experiences that go beyond mere education or the development of a new skill to affect a person so fully that previous worldviews, ideas, and values are no longer relevant, and where new values and ways of life are integrated into the tourist's daily life.
> *(Olsen 2017: 120)*

Tourism, like pilgrimage and religious tourism, is an identity-building exercise (Bauman, 1996) in which people travel to find a deeper meaning than what they experience in their daily lives (Cohen, 1979). This search for meaning, embodied in the questions 'why do I live', 'what do I live for' (Kirillova, Lehto & Cai, 2017: 499) and 'what is the meaning of my life?' (Olsen & Guelke, 2004: 595), leads millions of people a year to visit religious sites and monasteries and engage in temple stays in faith communities outside of their own (e.g., Chun, Roh & Spralls, 2017; Song et al. 2015). This search also leads people to walk traditional religious pilgrimage trails in search of spiritual and personal meaning (e.g., Digance, 2006; Hitchner, Schelhas, Brosius & Nibbelink, 2019; Kato & Progano, 2017; Olsen & Trono, 2018; Slavin, 2003).

In many ways, comparing religious experiences to tourism experiences is valid. For example, in the same way that religious tourists develop strong attachments and place special

Religious tourism

meanings on religious sites, tourists do the same for destinations in which they have transformative experiences (Bremer, 2004; Kirillova, Lehto & Cai, 2017). Indeed, as Bremer (2004) notes, in many cases, both religious followers and tourists hold the same places to be special, such as religious sites. Also, both religious adherents and tourists participate in travel to have different and distinct experiences from their everyday lives, experiences that have the potential to be life-altering and transformative and lead to 'profound inter-personal changes' (Kirillova, Lehto & Cai, 2017: 498) that last well beyond the return home (Wearing, McDonald & Ankor, 2016). These experiences and changes are often described as being spiritual and transcendent in nature and, as such, some tourist journeys 'cannot be classified as conventional tourism' (Jirásek, 2014: 50; see Cheer, Belhassen & Kujawa, 2017; Robledo, 2015; Sharpley & Jepson 2011; Sharpley & Sundaram 2005; Willson, McIntosh & Zahra, 2013). As a case in point, many people who participate in volunteer tourism claim that many of their experiences are spiritual in nature (McGehee, 2014; Mustonen, 2006; Zahra, 2006). These spiritual or transcendent experiences, according to Kirillova, Lehto and Cai (2017), are triggered by several interrelated factors, including unity with nature and others, introspection, spontaneity and novelty, self-development and aesthetic experiences. While these spiritual or transcendent experiences can occur at any point in a journey, these triggering factors or episodes, as Kirillova, Lehto and Cai (2017) point out, generally occur at the end of a journey, such as during the return home or at the end of travelling along a pilgrimage trail (Lopez, 2013).

Wearing, McDonald and Ankor (2016: 157) suggest that 'epiphanic experience[s]' are most effective when a person engages in 'unpredictable travel that contains such an openness to the unknown and the Other that [it] result[s] in epiphanic experiences'. They also suggest that these experiences best occur in an atmosphere where people have unmediated experiences – where it is 'individual practices and performances, not representations' (Olsen, 2017: 121), through which these experiences are manifest. However, it is nearly impossible to have an unmediated experience, considering the ways in which religious leaders and tourism marketers influence the perceived attributes and benefits of visiting religious tourism destinations. In addition, in many cases, the aesthetics and interpretation at religious tourism sites are specifically designed to elicit certain emotions and experiences within visitors (Olsen, 2012; Shackley, 2001; Thouki, 2019). Instead, religious tourists and sacred site managers engage in a dialectical co-creation of religious tourism experiences. As Bremer (2006: 27) argues, 'the meaningfulness of a particular place derive from practices that establish them and maintain them, and from the discursive force of those practices in the communities that regard them as special or peculiar'. As such, religious tourists, other visitors and site managers imbue sacred sites with religious authenticity (Bremer, 2001).

So, are there differences in the experiences that people who are motivated by religion to religious sites and have spiritual or transformative experiences and those who are not motivated by religion but visit the same sites and have similar experiences? The interpretation of whether an experience – both individual and collective – is spiritual or transformative or not is based on the lenses through which a person interprets their experience. A person who is motivated by non-religious reasons to visit religious sites will interpret their experiences through the lens of what Falque (2016: 90) refers to as *perceptive faith*, which points to a 'conviction that there is something' within the known world that will reveal to a person an idea of truth or authentic life. This can be differentiated from the religious tourist, who, 'through' religious faith, believes that their travel is related to the idea of transcendence, seeking experiences that occur above and beyond the normal or physical world. In this case, while both religiously and non-religiously motivated persons may be searching for 'the authentic self', for a non-religious person, this searching and finding does not lead to any change in status in the afterlife. This is opposed to religious persons who are focused on afterlife concerns, seek a relationship with a godly 'other' (Falque, 2016) and look for immanence or the divine as manifested in the material world.

Religious tourism: a spiritual or touristic experience?

Religion has long been a critical part of the human experience (Nelson, 2009). For centuries, people have travelled both to religious and non-religious sites in search for meaning. As such, travel is about identity construction. For the leisure-oriented tourist, lying on a beach may be a part of their lifestyle and therefore a part of maintaining their personal identity, but for cultural-heritage, educational and religious tourists, their personal identity is formed and informed by the search for spiritual and transcendental experiences that provide meaning and, in the case of religiously motivated persons, a better afterlife. As such, returning to the question posed at the outset of this chapter, the answer, while simplistic in nature, is *contextual*. Not everyone who travels to a religious site is motivated by religion or seeking a spiritual experience. While visitors to religious sites may have what they consider to be unexpected religious or spiritual experiences, this is not the main reason why they came. Conversely, others travel to these same sites expecting transcendent experiences. As such, each person. In the same way that one person's sacred site is another person's leisure playground, what may be a spiritual experience for a person may not translate in the same way to the person who is having a similar, even shared, experience.

In the context of religious tourism which, as noted above, was defined in this chapter as travel to religious sites regardless of motivation, to be a religious tourist means that religion and religious motivation and its associated sought-after experiences do not need to be the only travel style or identity. Even those that label themselves as strictly pilgrims can find it difficult to be a pilgrim all the time. As such, there is room for 'play' regarding engagement with religious, spiritual and touristy types of activities and experiences. Religious tourism is therefore both a spiritual and a touristic experience depending on how an individual understands and interprets their experiences. If a person views their motivations and experiences through the lens of religion, then they will relate their experiences to some sort of religious worldview, whereas those travelling for leisure or recreational experiences relate to their experiences within a secular humanist perspective. In this sense, a religious tourist is open to both the recreational/leisure aspects of travel as well as the potential for transformational experiences (Olsen, 2017).

References

Albayrak, T., Herstein, R., Caber, M., Drori, N., Bideci, M. and Berger, R. (2018) Exploring religious tourist experiences in Jerusalem: The intersection of Abrahamic religions. *Tourism Management*, 69, 285–296.

Alderman, D. H. (2002) Writing on the Graceland Wall: On the importance of authorship in pilgrimage landscapes. *Tourism Recreation Research*, 27(2), 27–33.

Andriotis, K. (2009) Sacred site experience: A phenomenological study. *Annals of Tourism Research*, 36(1), 64–84.

Asprem, E. and Dyrendal, A. (2015) Conspirituality reconsidered: How surprising and how new is the confluence of spirituality and conspiracy theory? *Journal of Contemporary Religion*, 30(3), 367–382.

Badone, E. and Roseman, S. R. (2004) *Intersecting Journeys: The Anthropology of Pilgrimage and Tourism*. Chicago: University of Illinois Press.

Barber, R. (1991) *Pilgrimage*. Woodbridge: Boydell & Brewer Ltd.

Religious tourism

Battour, M., Ismail, M. N., Battor, M. and Awais, M. (2017) Islamic tourism: An empirical examination of travel motivation and satisfaction in Malaysia. *Current Issues in Tourism*, 20(1), 50–67.

Bauman, Z. (1996) From pilgrim to tourist: or a short history of identity. In S. Hall and P. du Gay (Eds.), *Questions of Cultural Identity*. London: Sage Publications, pp. 18–36.

Beech, N. (2011) Liminality and the practices of identity reconstruction. *Human Relations*, 64(2), 285–302.

Binkhorst, E. and Den Dekker, T. (2009) Agenda for co-creation tourism experience research. *Journal of Hospitality Marketing & Management*, 18, 311–327.

Blackwell, R. (2007) Motivations for religious tourism, pilgrimage, festivals and events. In R. Raj and K. Griffin (Eds.), *Religious Tourism and Pilgrimage Festivals Management: An International Perspective*. Wallingford: CABI, pp. 35–47.

Bond, N. (2015) Exploring pilgrimage and religious heritage tourism experiences. In R. Raj and K. Griffin (Eds.), *Religious Tourism and Pilgrimage Management: An International Perspective*, 2nd Edn. Wallingford: CABI, pp. 118–129.

Bond, N., Packer, J. and Ballantyne, R. (2015) Exploring visitor experiences, activities and benefits at three religious tourism sites. *International Journal of Tourism Research*, 17(5), 471–481.

Boorstin, D. J. (1987) *The Image: A Guide to Pseudo-Events in America*. New York: Atheneum.

Braun, W. (2000) Religion. In W. Braun and R. T. McChutcheon (Eds.), *Guide to the Study of Religion*. New York: Cassell, pp. 3–18.

Bremer, T. S. (2001) Religion on Display: Tourists, Sacred Places, and Identity at the San Antonio Missions. PhD Dissertation, Princeton University.

Bremer, T. S. (2004) *Blessed with Tourists: The Borderlands of Religion and Tourism in San Antonio*. Chapel Hill: The University of North Carolina Press.

Bremer, T. S. (2006) Sacred space and tourist places. In D. J. Timothy and D. H. Olsen (Eds.), *Tourism, Religion and Spiritual Journeys*. London: Routledge, pp. 5–35.

Brown, L. (2013) Tourism: A catalyst for existential authenticity. *Annals of Tourism Research*, 40, 176–190.

Butler, R. and Suntikul, W. (Eds.) (2018) *Tourism and Religion: Issues and Implications*. Bristol: Channel View Publications.

Buzinde, C. N., Kalavar, J. M., Kohli, N. and Manuel-Navarrete, D. (2014) Emic understandings of Kumbh Mela pilgrimage experiences. *Annals of Tourism Research*, 49, 1–18.

Campbell, H. (Ed.) (2013) *Digital Religion. Understanding Religious Practice in New Media Worlds*. Abingdon: Routledge.

Campos, A. C., Mendes, J., Valle, P. O. D. and Scott, N. (2018) Co-creation of tourist experiences: A literature review. *Current Issues in Tourism*, 21(4), 369–400.

Cheer, J. M., Belhassen, Y. and Kujawa, J. (2017) The search for spirituality in tourism: Toward a conceptual framework for spiritual tourism. *Tourism Management Perspectives*, 24, 252–256.

Chhabra, D. (2019) Authenticity and the authentication of heritage: Dialogical perceptiveness. *Journal of Heritage Tourism*, 14(5/6), 389–395.

Chun, B., Roh, E. Y. and Spralls III, S. A. (2017) Living like a monk: Motivations and experiences of international participants in templestay. *International Journal of Religious Tourism and Pilgrimage*, 5(1), 39–55.

Cohen, E. (1979) A phenomenology of tourist experiences. *Sociology*, 13(2), 179–201.

Cohen, E. and Cohen, S. A. (2012) Authentication: Hot and cool. *Annals of Tourism Research*, 39(3), 1295–1314.

Collins-Kreiner, N. (2010) Current Jewish pilgrimage tourism: Modes and models of development. *Tourism*, 58(3), 259–270.

Collins-Kreiner, N. and Kliot, N. (2000) Pilgrimage tourism in the Holy Land: The behavioural characteristics of Christian pilgrims. *Geojournal*, 50, 55–67.

Costa, A. D. A., Dekker, M. and Jongen, W. M. F. (2004) An overview of means-end theory: Potential application in consumer-oriented food product design. *Trends in Food Science & Technology*, 15(7–8), 403–415.

Cusack, C. M. (2022) The new spiritual marketplace: Comparing New Age and new religious movements in an age of spiritual and religious tourism. In D. H. Olsen and D. J. Timothy (Eds.), *Routledge Handbook of Religious and Spiritual Tourism*. Abingdon: Routledge, pp. 79–89.

Davis, B. R. (1992) Not strangers but pilgrims: A case study of the phenomenon of the God-quest among visitors in cathedrals. *Dialogue and Alliance*, 6, 21–31.

de Oliveira, C. (2017) *Religious Tourism and Heritage in Brazil*. Cham: Springer International Publishing.

della Dora, V. (2012) Setting and blurring boundaries: Pilgrims, tourists, and landscape in Mount Athos and Meteora. *Annals of Tourism Research*, 39(2), 951–974.

Di Giovine, M. A. (2016) A higher purpose: Sacred journeys as spaces for peace in Christianity. In A. M. Pazos (Ed.), *Pilgrims and Pilgrimages as Peacemakers in Christianity, Judaism and Islam*. Abingdon: Routledge, pp. 9–38.

Digance, J. (2006) Religious and secular pilgrimage: Journeys redolent with meaning. In D. J. Timothy and D. H. Olsen (Eds.), *Tourism, Religion and Spiritual Journeys*. London Routledge, pp. 52–64.

Dolnicar, S. (2008) Market segmentation in tourism. In A. Woodside and D. Martin (Eds.), *Tourism Management: Analysis, Behaviour and Strategy*. Wallingford: CABI, pp. 129–150.

Dowson, R., Yaqub, J. and Raj, R. (Eds.) (2019) *Spiritual and Religious Tourism: Motivations and Management*. Wallingford: CABI.

Drule, A. M., Chiş, A., Băcilă, M. F. and Ciornea, R. (2012) A new perspective of non-religious motivations of visitors to sacred sites: evidence from Romania. *Procedia-Social and Behavioral Sciences*, 62, 431–435.

Eade, J. and Albera, D. (2016) Pilgrimage studies in global perspective. In D. Albera and J. Eade (Eds.), *New Pathways in Pilgrimage Studies: Global Perspectives*. Abingdon: Routledge, pp.1–17.

Ebadi, M. (2014) Typologies of the visitors at Khaled Nabi shrine, Iran: Tourists or pilgrims? *International Journal of Culture, Tourism and Hospitality Research*, 8(3), 310–321.

Eco, U. (1983) *Travels in Hyperreality*. San Diego: Harcourt Brace Jovanovich Publishers.

El-Gohary, H., Edwards, D. J. and Eid, R. (Eds.) (2017) *Global Perspectives on Religious Tourism and Pilgrimage*. Hershey, PA: IGI Global.

Eliade, M. (1959) *The Sacred and the Profane: The Nature of Religion*. Orlando, FL: Harcourt, Inc.

Falque, E. (2016) *Crossing the Rubicon: The Borderlands of Philosophy and Theology*. New York: Fordham University Press.

Francis L. J., Williams, E., Annis, J. and Robbins M. (2008) Understanding cathedral visitors: Psychological type and individual differences in experience and appreciation. *Tourism Analysis*, 13(1), 71–80.

Francis, L. J., Mansfield, S., Williams, E. and Village, A. (2010) Applying psychological type theory to cathedral visitors: A case study of two cathedrals in England and Wales. *Visitor Studies*, 13(2), 175–186.

Gammon, S. (2004) Secular pilgrimage and sport tourism. In B. W. Ritchie and D. Adair (Eds.), *Sport Tourism: Interrelationships, Impacts and Issues*. Clevedon: Channel View Publications, pp. 30–45.

Giumbelli, E. (2018) Religious tourism: Analytical routes through multiple meanings. *Religion and Society: Advances in Research*, 9, 24–38.

Graburn, N. (1989) Tourism: The sacred journey. In V. L. Smith (Ed.), *Hosts and Guests: The Anthropology of Tourism*, 2nd Edn. Philadelphia: University of Pennsylvania Press, pp. 21–36.

Griffiths, M. (2011) Those who come to pray and those who come to look: Interactions between visitors and congregations. *Journal of Heritage Tourism*, 6(1), 63–72.

Haque, A. and Momen, A. (2017) A model of Islamic tourism towards religious motivation and tourist satisfaction in Malaysia. In F. L. Gaol and F. D. Hutagalung (Eds.), *Social Interactions and Networking in Cyber Society*. Singapore: Springer, pp. 153–167.

Hitchner, S., Schelhas, J., Brosius, J. P. and Nibbelink, N. (2019) Thru-hiking the John Muir Trail as a modern pilgrimage: Implications for natural resource management. *Journal of Ecotourism*, 18(1), 82–99.

Holmberg, C. B. (1993) Spiritual pilgrimages: Traditional and hyperreal motivations for travel and tourism. *Visions of Leisure and Business*, 12(2), 18–27.

Huang, K., Pearce, P., Guo, Q. and Shen, S. (2019) Visitors' spiritual values and relevant influencing factors in religious tourism destinations. *International Journal of Tourism Research*, 22(3), 314–324.

Hughes, K., Bond, N. and Ballantyne, R. (2013) Designing and managing interpretive experiences at religious sites: Visitors' perceptions of Canterbury Cathedral. *Tourism Management*, 36, 210–220.

Izberk-Bilgin, E. and Nakata, C. C. (2016) A new look at faith-based marketing: The global halal market. *Business Horizons*, 59(3), 285–292.

Jackson, R. H. and Hudman, L. (1995) Pilgrimage tourism and English cathedrals: The role of religion in travel. *The Tourist Review*, 50(4), 40–48.

Jafari, J. (1987) Tourism models: The sociocultural aspects. *Tourism Management*, 8(2), 151–159.

Jansson, A. (2002) Spatial phantasmagoria: The mediatization of tourism experience. *European Journal of Communication*, 17(4), 429–443.

Jirásek, I. (2014) Pilgrimage-tourism continuum once again: Matrix of sacred, spiritual and profane connectedness to authenticity. *Journal of Martial Arts Anthropology*, 14(4), 46–53.

Religious tourism

Kaelber, L. (2006) Paradigms of travel: From medieval pilgrimage to the postmodern virtual tour. In D. J. Timothy and D. H. Olsen (Eds.), *Tourism, Religion and Spiritual Journeys*. London and New York: Routledge, pp. 65–79.

Kaell, H. (2016) Can pilgrimage fail? Intent, efficacy, and evangelical trips to the Holy Land. *Journal of Contemporary Religion*, 31(3), 393–408.

Kamenidou, I. and Vourou, R. (2015) Motivation factors for visiting religious sites: The case of Lesvos Island. *European Journal of Tourism Research*, 9, 78–91.

Kato, K. and Progano, R. N. (2017) Spiritual (walking) tourism as a foundation for sustainable destination development: Kumano-kodo pilgrimage, Wakayama, Japan. *Tourism Management Perspectives*, 24, 243–251.

Kim, B. and Kim, S. S. (2019a) Hierarchal value map of religious tourists visiting the Vatican City/Rome. *Tourism Geographies*, 21(3), 529–550.

Kim, B. and Kim, S. S. (2019b) The effect of religious tourism experiences on personal values. *International Journal of Religious and Pilgrimage Tourism*, 7(2), 85–93.

Kim, B., Kim, S. S. and King, B. (2016) The sacred and the profane: Identifying pilgrim traveler value orientations using means-end theory. *Tourism Management*, 56, 142–155.

Kirillova, K., Lehto, X. and Cai, L. (2017) What triggers transformative tourism experiences? *Tourism Recreation Research*, 42(4), 498–511.

Knox, D. and Hannam, K. (2014) Is a tourist a secular pilgrim or a hedonist in search of pleasure? *Tourism Recreation Research*, 39(2), 236–242.

Lee, Y. H. Jan, F-H. and Lin, Y. H. (2020) How authentic experience affects traditional religious tourism development: Evidence from the Dajia Mazu pilgrimage, Taiwan. *Journal of Travel Research*. https://doi.org/10.1177/0047287520921240

Leiper, N. (1983) An etymology of 'tourism. *Annals of Tourism Research*, 10(2), 277–280.

Lopez, L. (2013) How long does the pilgrimage tourism experience to Santiago de Compostela last? *International Journal of Religious Tourism and Pilgrimage*, 1(1), 1–14.

MacCannell, D. (1973) Staged authenticity: Arrangements of social space in tourist settings. *American Journal of Sociology*, 79(3), 589–603.

MacCannell, D. (1976) *The Tourist: A New Theory of the Leisure Class*. New York: Schocken.

Mannell, R. C. and Iso-Aloha, S. E. (1987) Psychological nature of leisure and tourism experience. *Annals of Tourism Research*, 14(2), 314–331.

McGehee, N. G. (2014) Volunteer tourism: Evolution, issues and futures. *Journal of Sustainable Tourism*, 22(6), 847–854.

McKercher, B. and Du Cros, H. (2003) Testing a cultural tourism typology. *International Journal of Tourism Research*, 5(1), 45–58.

Mo, C. M., Howard, D. R. and Havitz, M. E. (1993) Testing an international tourist role typology. *Annals of Tourism Research*, 20(2), 319–335.

Morinis, A. (1992) Introduction: The territory of the anthropology of pilgrimage. In A. Morinis (Ed.), *Sacred Journeys: The Anthropology of Pilgrimage*. Westport: Greenwood Press, pp. 1–28.

Mustonen, P. (2006) Volunteer tourism: Postmodern pilgrimage? *Journal of Tourism and Cultural Change*, 3(3), 160–177.

Nelson, J. K. (1996) Freedom of expression: The very modern practice of visiting a Shinto shrine. *Japanese Journal of Religious Studies*, 23(1/2), 117–153.

Nelson, J. M. (2009) *Psychology, Religion, and Spirituality*. New York: Springer.

Nolan, M. L. and Nolan, L. (1992) Religious sites as tourism attractions in Europe. *Annals of Tourism Research*, 19(1), 68–78.

Norman, A. (2011) *Spiritual Tourism: Travel and Religious Practice in Western Society*. New York: Bloomsbury Publishing.

Olsen, D. H. (2008) Contesting Identity, Space and Sacred Site Management at Temple Square in Salt Lake City, Utah. PhD Thesis. Waterloo: University of Waterloo.

Olsen, D. H. (2010) Pilgrims, tourists, and Weber's 'ideal types'. *Annals of Tourism Research*, 37(3), 848–851.

Olsen, D. H. (2012) Teaching truth in 'third space': The use of religious history as a pedagogical instrument at Temple Square in Salt Lake City, Utah. *Tourism Recreation Research*, 37, 227–237.

Olsen, D. H. (2013) A scalar comparison of motivations and expectations of experience within the religious tourism market. *International Journal of Religious Tourism and Pilgrimage*, 1(1), 41–61.

Olsen, D. H. (2014) Metaphors, typologies, secularization, and pilgrim as hedonist: A response. *Tourism Recreation Research*, 39(2), 248–258.

Olsen, D. H. (2017) Other journeys of creation: Non-representational theory, co-creation, failure, and the soul. *Tourism Recreation Research*, 42(1), 120–124.

Olsen, D. H. (in press) Faith, New Age spirituality, and religion: Negotiating the religious tourism niche market. In M. Novelli, M., J. Cheer, J., C. Dolezal, A. Jones and Milano, C. (Eds.), *Handbook of Niche Tourism*. Cheltenham: Edward Elgar.

Olsen, D. H. and Guelke, J. K. (2004) 'Nourishing the soul': Geography and matters of meaning. In D. Janelle, B. Warf and K. Hansen (Eds.), *WorldMinds: Geographical Perspectives on 100 Problems*. Dordrecht: Kluwer Academic Associates, pp. 595–599.

Olsen, D. H. and Trono, A. (Eds.) (2018) *Religious Pilgrimage Routes and Trails: Sustainable Development and Management*. Wallingford: CABI.

Osterrieth, A. (1997) Pilgrimage, travel and existential quest. In R. H. Stoddard and A. Morinis. (Eds.), *Sacred Places, Sacred Spaces: The Geography of Pilgrimages*. Baton Rouge, LA: Department of Geography and Anthropology, Louisiana State University, pp. 25–39.

Otto, R. (1950) *The Idea of the Holy*. Oxford: Oxford University Press.

Pezeshki, F., Ardekani, S. S., Khodadadi, M., Almodarresi, S. M. A. and Hosseini, F. S. (2019) Cognitive structures of Iranian senior tourists towards domestic tourism destinations: A means-end chain approach. *Journal of Hospitality and Tourism Management*, 39, 9–19.

Pine, B. J. and Gilmore, J. H. (2008) The eight principles of strategic authenticity. *Strategy & Leadership*, 36(3), 35–40.

Pine, B. J. and Gilmore, J. H. (2011) *The Experience Economy: Work is a Theatre & Every Business a Stage*. Boston: Harvard Business Review Press.

Plog, S. C. (1974) Why destination areas rise and fall in popularity. *Cornell Hotel and Restaurant Administration Quarterly*, 14(4), 55–58.

Prahalad, C. K. and Ramaswamy, V. (2003) The new frontier of experience innovation. *MIT Sloan Management Review*, 44(4), 12–18.

Progano, R. N., Kato, K. and Cheer, J. M. (2020) Visitor diversification in pilgrimage destinations: Comparing national and international visitors through means-end. *Tourism Geographies*. https://doi.org/10.1080/14616688.2020.1765013

Raj, R. and Griffin, K. (Eds.) (2015) *Religious Tourism and Pilgrimage Management: An International Perspective*, 2nd Edn. Wallingford: CABI.

Rashid, A. G. (2018) Religious tourism: A review of the literature. *Journal of Hospitality and Tourism Insights*, 1(2), 150–167.

Redfoot, D. L. (1984) Touristic authenticity, touristic angst, and modern reality. *Qualitative Sociology*, 7(4), 291–309.

Robina Ramírez, R. and Fernández Portillo, A. (2020) What role does tourists' educational motivation play in promoting religious tourism among travellers? *Annals of Leisure Research*, 23(3), 407–428.

Robledo, M. A. (2015) Tourism of spiritual growth as a voyage of discovery. In D. Chambers and T. Rakic (Eds.), *Tourism Research Frontiers: Beyond the Boundaries of Knowledge*. Bingley: Emerald Group Publishing Limited, pp. 71–86.

Rodrigues, S. and McIntosh, A. (2014) Motivations, experiences and perceived impacts of visitation at a Catholic monastery in New Zealand. *Journal of Heritage Tourism*, 9(4), 271–284.

Ron, A. S. (2009) Towards a typological model of contemporary Christian travel. *Journal of Heritage Tourism*, 4(4), 287–297.

Roodenburg, H. (2004) Pierre Bourdieu: Issues of embodiment and authenticity. *Etnofoor*, 17(1/2), 215–226.

Shackley, M. (2001) *Managing Sacred Sites: Service Provision and Visitor Experience*. London and New York: Continuum.

Sharpley, R. (2009) Tourism, religion and spirituality. In T. Jamal and M. Robinison (Eds.), *The Sage Handbook of Tourism Studies*. London: Sage Publications, pp. 237–253.

Sharpley, R. and Jepson, D. (2011) Rural tourism: A spiritual experience? *Annals of Tourism Research*, 38(1), 52–71.

Sharpley, R. and Sundaram, P. (2005) Tourism: A sacred journey? The case of ashram tourism, India. *International Journal of Tourism Research*, 7(3), 161–171.

Slavin, S. (2003) Walking as spiritual practice: The pilgrimage to Santiago de Compostela. *Body & Society*, 9(3), 1–18.

Smith, J. Z. (1988) 'Religion' and 'religious studies': No difference at all. *Soundings*, 71, 231–244.

Religious tourism

Smith, J. Z. (1998) Religion, religions, religious. In M. C. Taylor (Ed.), *Critical Terms for Religious Studies*. Chicago: University of Chicago Press, pp. 269–284.

Smith, V. L. (1992) The quest in guest. *Annals of Tourism Research*, 19(1), 1–17.

Song, H. J., Lee, C. K., Park, J. A., Hwang, Y. H. and Reisinger, Y. (2015) The influence of tourist experience on perceived value and satisfaction with temple stays: The experience economy theory. *Journal of Travel & Tourism Marketing*, 32(4), 401–415.

Stausberg, M. (2011) *Religion and Tourism: Crossroads, Destinations and Encounters*. Abingdon: Routledge.

Stausberg, M. (2014) Religion and spirituality in tourism. In A. Lew, C. M. Hall and A. Williams (Eds.), *The Wiley Blackwell Companion to Tourism*. Hoboken: John Wiley & Sons, pp. 349–360.

Sugawa-Shimada, A. (2015) Rekijo, pilgrimage and 'pop-spiritualism': Pop-culture-induced heritage tourism of/for young women. *Japan Forum* 27(1), 37–58.

Terzidou, M. (2010) Religion as a motivation to travel: The case of Tinos island in Greece. *Tourism and Hospitality Planning & Development*, 5(2), 113–129.

Terzidou, M., Scarles, C. and Saunders, M. N. (2018) The complexities of religious tourism motivations: Sacred places, vows and visions. *Annals of Tourism Research*, 70, 54–65.

Thomas, S., White, G. R. and Samuel, A. (2018) To pray and to play: Post-postmodern pilgrimage at Lourdes. *Tourism Management*, 68, 412–422.

Thouki, A. (2019) The role of ontology in religious tourism education: Exploring the application of the postmodern cultural paradigm in European religious sites. *Religions*, 10. https://doi.org/10.3390/rel10120649

Timothy, D. J. (2021) *Cultural Heritage and Tourism: An Introduction*, 2nd Edn. Bristol: Channel View Publications.

Timothy, D. J. and Olsen, D. H. (2006b) Conclusion: Whither religion and tourism? In D. J. Timothy and D. H. Olsen (Eds.), *Tourism, Religion and Spiritual Journeys*. London: Routledge, pp. 271–278.

Timothy, D. J. and Olsen, D. H. (Eds.) (2006a) *Tourism, Religion and Spiritual Journeys*. London: Routledge.

Turner, V. and Turner, E. (1978) *Image and Pilgrimage in Christian Culture*. New York: Columbia University Press.

UNWTO. (2011) *Religious Tourism in Asia and the Pacific*. Madrid: World Tourism Organization.

UNWTO. (2014) Tourism can protect and promote religious heritage. Available at: https://www.unwto.org/archive/europe/press-release/2014-12-10/tourism-can-protect-and-promote-religious-heritage (Accessed 30 November 2020).

Urry, J. and Larsen, J. (2011) *The Tourist Gaze 3.0*. London: Sage Publications.

Wang, J., Luo, Q., Huang, S. S. and Yang, R. (2020) Restoration in the exhausted body? Tourists on the rugged path of pilgrimage: Motives, experiences, and benefits. *Journal of Destination Marketing & Management*, 15. https://doi.org/10.1016/j.jdmm.2019.100407

Wang, N. (1999) Rethinking authenticity in tourism experience. *Annals of Tourism Research*, 26(2), 349–370.

Wang, W., Chen, J. S. and Huang, K. (2016) Religious tourist motivation in Buddhist Mountain: The case from China. *Asia Pacific Journal of Tourism Research*, 21(1), 57–72.

Wearing, S., McDonald, M. and Ankor, J. (2016) Journeys of creation: Experiencing the unknown, the other and authenticity as an epiphany of the self. *Tourism Recreation Research*, 41(2), 157–167.

Week, L. (2012) I am not a tourist: Aims and implications of 'traveling'. *Tourist Studies*, 12(2), 186–203.

West, B. (2008) Enchanting pasts: The role of international civil religious pilgrimage in reimagining national collective memory. *Sociological Theory*, 26(3), 258–270.

Willson, G. B. (2016) Conceptualizing spiritual tourism: Cultural considerations and a comparison with religious tourism. *Tourism Culture & Communication*, 16(3), 161–168.

Willson, G. B., McIntosh, A. J. and Zahra, A. L. (2013) Tourism and spirituality: A phenomenological analysis. *Annals of Tourism Research*, 42, 150–168.

Zahra, A. (2006) The unexpected road to spirituality via volunteer tourism. *Tourism*, 54(2), 173–185.

29

THE CONTEMPORARY CRUISE TOURIST EXPERIENCE

Jo-Anne Lester, Jennifer Holland and Catherine Palmer

Introduction

Taking a socio-cultural perspective, this chapter deconstructs the nature of experience for cruise tourists in relation to the spatial context and unique characteristics of vacationing at sea. Attempting to define a contemporary cruise tourist experience is challenging, particularly in the context of an industry characterized by product proliferation, design innovation and an increasingly diverse customer base. Hence, there is no single tourist experience but, rather, a myriad of experiences depending upon the individual, the type of cruise selected and the approach adopted. Moreover, the word experience itself can be conceptualized and understood in different ways depending upon the disciplinary focus. For example, anthropology, philosophy and management all have extensive bodies of literature exploring the meaning of or the management of experience across a range of situations and cultural contexts, including the context of tourism (see Andrews, 2009; Davey, 2016; Richards, 2001; Sharpley & Stone, 2012; Turner & Bruner, 1986). Terzidou, Scarles and Saunders' (2017: 117) analysis of experience; in relation to pilgrimage tourism, offers a useful illustration of the approach to experience adopted here when they argue that the pilgrimage experience is a complex '… series of performances where movements intertwine with religious prescriptions, embodied spaces of production and consumption, inter-subjective interactions and material encounters in tourist spaces…'.

Given the above, this chapter adopts a holistic approach to the nature of experience by focusing on selected overarching themes, as follows: architecture and the materiality of cruise ship space (including the architecture of technology); the body; and the cruise community. This focus moves the discussion away from a socio-economic understanding of experience exemplified by the 'experience economy' approach (Klingman, 2007; Pine & Gilmore, 1999; Richards, 2001) and beyond the cruise experience in terms of business, management and operational aspects such as service delivery, customer satisfaction and initiatives to maximize on board revenue (see Huang & Hsu, 2010; Petrick, 2004; Weaver, 2005a). In doing so, the discussion provides an alternative and a more nuanced understanding of experience as it relates to cruise tourists.

While acknowledging that the cruise experience reaches beyond the physical boundaries of the ship, this chapter focuses on the onboard experience in relation to the spatial

408

DOI: 10.4324/9781003219866-33

characteristics of cruise ships. Clearly, onshore activities are a significant part of the cruise experience, as is the relationship between the ship and the sea; however, a detailed consideration of these aspects falls beyond the scope of this chapter (see Andriotis & Agiomirgianakis 2010; Bennett, 2016; Jaakson, 2004a; Lester, 2011; Weaver, 2014). Lefebvre's (1991) spatial triad comprising spatial practice (perceived space), representations of space (conceived space) and representational space (lived space) is a useful starting point for a focus on architecture, cruise ship space and experience. For Lefebvre, the experience of space emerges out of the dynamic relationship between these three elements. In particular, representational space is space as conceived and created by professionals and technical experts such as architects, urban planners, engineers and designers. Contemporary cruise ships are examples of such spaces being the product of technological advancements that have enabled architects and engineers to design and build huge spatial structures capable of accommodating thousands of passengers. The representational cruise ship space created by architects and designers is inhabited or, more precisely, embodied, by people – by thinking, feeling bodies. Once embodied by a cruise ship community, the built environment, what Tuan (1977) refers to as architectural space, plays a fundamental role in creating the social roles and structures that influence how individuals and communities behave. Architectural space reveals, instructs and articulates the social order (Tuan, 1977) and, as such, the architectural space of a cruise ship plays a significant role in creating, mediating and controlling the cruise tourist experience. It is a constituting partner in the architecture of experience.

Appreciating the relationship between spatial developments and innovations in ship building and experience(s), the focus here acknowledges the segment of the market serviced by modern mega vessels. These exceed 100,000 gross registered tonnage and offer a significant increase in spatial capacities than other cruise vessels preceding the contemporary era of passenger ship building (Lunn, 2009). Such ships illustrate technological innovations in shipbuilding and exemplify the concept of a ship as 'floating cities' (Lunn 2009), a 'floating resort' or 'marine resort' (UNWTO, 2010). Given this focus, the following section provides a brief overview of the spatial characteristics and developments in passenger ship building in the context of such mega ships. Thereafter, the chapter addresses the relationship between embodiment and experience in the context of cruise ship architecture with the third and final section focusing on experience as it relates to the concept of an onboard community.

Cruise ship space and the architecture of experience

Architecture, like experience, is conceived and understood in a variety of different ways, ranging from design and construction to biology, culture, technology and physics (Buchli, 2013; Mallgrave, 2010; Pallasmaa, 2005; Rovelli, 2015). There is also significant literature exploring the relationship between architecture and tourism (Graburn, Gravari-Barbas & Staszak, 2019; McLaren, 2006; Morosan & Fesenmaier, 2007; Palmer, 2018; Scerri, Edwards & Foley, 2019). For the purpose of this section, the discussion focuses on architecture both in relation to the built environment and the architecture of technology as these two illustrate Lefebvre's representations of space; space that is conceived and created by professionals and technical experts.

Cruise ships as architectures of the sea are feats of engineering and innovation in terms of their mechanical workings and spatial design (Quartermaine, 1996; Quartermaine & Peter, 2006). As bounded vacation spaces 'out at sea', cruise ships have been noted for their enclavic characteristics (Jaakson, 2004a; Lester & Weeden, 2004; Weaver, 2005a; Wood, 2000).

Indeed, Bennett's (2016: 51) analysis of cruise ship space utilizes the concept of omnitopia to explore the all-encompassing nature of these holiday environments packaging everything...

> ...designed to be experienced as a simulated all-encompassing vast interior. As passengers move from place to place, engaging with various sites on the ship, they encounter the spaces as if cocooned in a bubble that causes the exterior natural world of the ocean to appear unthreatening and distant.

According to Lester (2011, 2017) and Noy (2014), the purposefully designed 'closed' or cocooned environment of a cruise ship has much in common with the architectural model of the panopticon (Bentham, 1995; Foucault, 1995) that exemplifies how spatial design influences and shapes behaviour. Most often associated with the self-regulating function of prison architecture, when applied to a cruise ship, the concept of the panopticon reveals the ways in which behaviour and, hence, experience is shaped by the notion of 'looking' and being 'looked at' (Lester, 2017). In this sense, cruise ship architecture creates spaces of containment that insulate the passengers from the land-based world of the everyday. This aligns with Foucault's (1986) concept of heterotopic space, space that is different or 'other' (Wealleans, 2006), although the notion of cruise ships as heterotopic spaces is not without its critics (Rankin & Collins, 2017; Weaver, 2005b). Indeed, Rankin and Collins (2017: 226) prefer the phrase 'heterotopic assemblages' to refer to the complex, fluid and multifaceted spatial dynamics of cruise ships. Nevertheless, as argued in the chapter, heterotopia is a useful framing concept for considering experience as it relates to cruise tourists.

It is clear from the above that unpicking the contemporary cruise experience is far more complex than it perhaps once was, not least because technological innovations have enabled ship designers and architects to radically influence the nature of the cruise experience through the construction of ships that can accommodate in excess of 6,000 passengers. Royal Caribbean International's (RCI) Oasis-class ships exemplify the scale, scope and new directions in passenger shipbuilding and the concept of a holiday resort at sea.[1] Designed around a 'neighbourhood' concept, *Symphony of the Seas* (228,081 GRT), with 18 decks and a passenger occupancy totalling 6,680 at full capacity, is currently the world's largest cruise ship.[2] The sheer physical scale of such vessels creates a visual spectacle when viewed from the dock side or when encountered out at sea. The sensory opulence of the ships is mediated through the aesthetics of luxury interior design (Wealleans, 2006) that extends to the use of culture as a constituent element of experience. For example, Celebrity Cruises promote their ships as art galleries complete with auctions at sea created by bringing '... together teams of world-class architects, interior designers, stylists, and landscape artists to create a showcase of the most inspiring spaces at sea'.[3]

Architecture in relation to technology such as artificial intelligence, virtual reality (VR), augmented reality, robotics and so on create a more personalized onboard experience. Technical innovations, such as RCI's WOWBand wristband[4] and Princess Cruise's OceanMedallion pendant,[5] replace the room key card, moreover, are not only used to access cabins or for onboard purchases; they also hold personalized information, such as food allergies. Furthermore, as the app is downloaded onto a passenger's phone, the device can track and locate other members of their travel group. Through the app, staff know the name of a passenger as s/he approaches and drinks can be pre-ordered for the theatre with staff able to track the location of individuals so that they can deliver what has been ordered.

The availability and affordability of digital technologies have transformed the onboard experience. Celebrity Cruises offer onboard virtual tours of their ships facilitated by digital

The contemporary cruise tourist experience

media, allowing passengers to explore previously difficult to access areas of the ship such as the bridge. Moreover, digital platforms mediate the passenger gaze beyond the physical boundaries of the ship, enabling destinations to be vicariously experienced ahead of arrival to facilitate planning of the onshore experience (see RCI and Venice[6]). The architecture of technology driving the development in virtual shore excursions means that if a cruise passenger chooses to do so, s/he can experience other places and other cultures without leaving the structural confines of the ship. The extent to which cruise passengers of the future may decide to remain onboard is as yet unknown, but doing so will dramatically affect how the cruise tourist experience is conceptualized, experienced and understood. In terms of onboard VR, RCI provide headsets that deliver a virtual trampolining experience while those of TUI's *Marella Discovery 2* provide an immersive VR gaming experience.[7]

Although it is not possible to draw attention to all the ways in which the architecture of technology influences experience, these examples illustrate the ways in which technologies are woven into the physical fabric of the onboard cruise experience. On the one hand, technological innovation offers enhanced and novel onboard experiences, customized and personalized services that highlight the agency of passengers when it comes to deciding the type and nature of the onboard experience. On the other hand, the use of technology can be seen as a means of contriving, managing and controlling experiences, pointing to the organized nature of these seemingly individualized experiences. That is, passengers are enchanted by technology into believing they are individuals, free to move in and around the cruise ship, when in fact they are inhabiting highly controlled environments designed to encourage passengers to consume and to spend.

While innovations in the spatial design of mega cruise ships have a significant influence on the cruise tourist experience, it is important to acknowledge the mediated nature of this experience, specifically through the pre-cruise and pre-excursion promotional strategies adopted by cruise companies (Lallani, 2017; Lester, 2017) and the construction and organization of onboard spaces of engagement. These spaces fulfil a mediating function that encourages cruise passengers to engage with the activities and entertainment strategies on offer. Participating in onboard activities is not, however, just about taking part or joining in on a practical level; it is also about engaging the physical, emotional and sensory body of the tourist. As such, it is important to understand the role and influence of the body and bodies in shaping the cruise tourist experience.

The embodied cruise ship experience

The cruise experience is one that is co-constructed through the coming together of people, space and materiality to create meaningful encounters that shape what it means to be a cruise tourist and to have a cruise tourist experience. As people move about the ship, they encounter other people (both passengers and crew), and they engage in activities and with technology, with the schedules and routines associated with being at sea and with the numerous available spaces from cabins to restaurants, theatres, fitness studios, decks and swimming pools. These encounters are not merely social in terms of conversations between people; they are physical and emotional performances that co-create the experience of taking a cruise holiday. This experience comes into being through the thinking, feeling body of the tourist — it is an embodied experience. As such, the body is a key constituent of what we referred to earlier as the architecture of experience.

The term 'embodied' and, by association, 'embodiment' refers to the ways in which understanding, social values, behaviour and experience are shaped by and through the human body (Csordas, 1994; Mauss, 1979). Hence, the body and bodies are moulded by culture, by the values and belief systems of a particular society. So it is through culture and the social context that a body acquires knowledge about how to move in any given situation. For Mauss (1979), the repertoire of culturally conditioned bodily uses and techniques specific to a particular group or society, what he refers to as a *habitus*, produce particular ways of running, swimming, dancing and digging that enable group members to recognize each other. Such bodily techniques serve to distinguish one group from another, such that squatting societies are distinguishable from sitting societies (Mauss, 1979). Squatting or sitting bodies produce different experiences of the material environments in which they move. So, in terms of cruise tourism, how a body moves around and 'uses' the onboard places and spaces of the ship influences the experience created, an experience structured by the architecture of the ship.

As a social context inhabited by people, a cruise ship can be understood as a specific, albeit temporary, form of society whose members have all acquired the necessary knowledge to enable them to function as members of that society. Bourdieu (1977) is instructive here as he extends the concept of *habitus* to encompass the structures, processes and practices that construct and internalize body behaviours. Embodied knowledge of how to behave emerges through engagement with the everyday practices of a particular habitus, which, in this instance, is the habitus of a cruise ship. The body of a cruise tourist learns how to dress and how to behave on board the ship and seeks confirmation of what is the correct way to behave by noticing, even if unconsciously, the behaviour and dress of other cruise tourists (Lester, 2017). These codes of behaviour coalesce to form a common sense understanding of what is and what is not acceptable within any given group. Even though not every individual will 'obey' the behavioural codes established, these codes still have a powerful, normative conditioning influence (Schrock & Boyd, 2006). As Palmer (2018: 37) argues, a tourist habitus is associated with and defined in relation to specific activities, practices and behaviours, which coalesce to form '... an embodied history of how to behave as a tourist reinforced by the reactions of other tourists that this is the correct way of being a tourist'.

In terms of the social context of cruise tourism, individuals learn how to behave as a cruise tourist both before and after arriving on the ship. While onboard the ship, bodies learn how to be a cruise tourist through safety announcements, signage, schedules and routines and, before joining the ship, through reading the information and instructions on embarkation and about the expectations of life onboard. In relation to backpacking, O'Regan (2016: 333) notes that, '[e]ven before the journey, the backpacker body is made fit-for-purpose, with vaccinations, travel insurance and first-aid kits incorporated, performed and rendered through the body as embodied expressions of backpacker consciousness'. All forms of tourism teach potential tourists what to expect and how to behave and, in doing so, start to build a picture of the sort of experience that can be expected. A body learns behaviour associated with being a particular type of tourist, how to walk and to sightsee as a tourist (Palmer, 2018), and cruise tourists are no exception. Before setting foot on the ship, bodies are prepared and pre-conditioned on how to be a cruise tourist, not solely through the information provided by the cruise company but also by, for example, past experiences of cruising or visiting online forums such as *Cruise Critic*. Interestingly, *Cruise Critic* includes a link to a discussion thread entitled *Lose Before You Cruise* which provides '[a] place for cruisers to share their stories of how to lose weight before a cruise. Virtual snacks allowed, but only in small quantities' (Cruise Critic, 2020). Such discussion threads can be found on other cruise sites and blogs, such as *Life Well Cruised*, and illustrate the extent to which the cruise tourist experience is constructed in relation to a specific, idealized body image, an idealized image of what a cruise body should look like.

Turning the body of home into the body of away involves imagining the body in different onboard places and spaces engaging in a range of activities and experiences, such as eating, drinking, sunbathing, lounging, exercising, dancing and promenading. The cruise body of away will encounter other bodies, including those of the cruise staff and those of fellow passengers, so *Lose Before You Cruise* is about creating the right type of cruise body; a body that will be gazed upon by other people, by other bodies. Bodily preparation is also a feature of other types of tourism, as is the existence of a holiday wardrobe distinct from that associated with work and the routines of life at home (Andrews, 2011; Hyde & Olesen, 2011; Jack & Phipps, 2005). However, what to pack, what to wear in relation to each cruising activity and how to interpret the codes associated with descriptions such as casual, formal and informal dress have a heightened significance when applied to a cruise holiday because of the long-standing traditions associated with ocean cruising (Lester, 2017). Such traditions produce a socially controlled bodily experience where dressing for a cruise was and still is about the display of cultural capital and understandings of social class.

How a cruise body is dressed directly affects experience. Cruise company advice about what to wear is about removing any anxieties new or returning passengers may have, but this advice also serves to control how people should look in particular spaces and, thereby, the sort of experience delivered. In this way, the architecture of the ship constructs experience in relation to a body that is conditioned and controlled. For example, the website for P&O Cruises includes pages on what to wear that states:

We have a few policies in place to ensure your time on board feels special. Here's a useful guide to what to expect on board in terms of dress codes so you can step out in style... Black Tie nights, offer a chance to get dressed to the nines in glamorous evening wear..... For Evening Casual nights, dress as you would for dinner in a nice restaurant... but no tracksuits, football shirts or trainers.... The dress code during the day is just your typical holiday wardrobe.... Away from the pool, we ask for shoes to be worn and no pool wear in the ship's lounges, inside bars, restaurants or reception.

(P&O Cruises, 2020)

The above advice illustrates the social context created by going on a cruise holiday and the type of behaviour expected, reproduced and internalized as *experience*, behaviour that over time represents the embodied knowledge of the cruise habitus. This embodied history is further influenced by technological innovations that alter the cruise tourist's relationship with and experience of nature, specifically the sea. This relationship takes place in spaces that are specifically designed to trigger an embodied, sensory experience. Indeed, the architecture of technology creates immersive spaces where experience is heightened through the stimulation of the senses. For example, in inside cabins, webcams create virtual balconies or portholes that live stream external footage of sea views in real time. RCI also installed digital walls into its cabins, and '[t]he effect is completed by piping in the rhythmic sounds of calming waves or gentle rain showers, and having a faux sunrise serve as an alarm clock and the night sky revealed on the concept cabin's ceiling' (Locker, 2017). Other innovations include, for example, Disney's magic portholes that combine a sea view with fantasy and movie characters that can be themed as appropriate.[8]

The architecture of technology enables cruise companies to provide a diverse range of sensory experiences, with the result that the creation of a multisensory experience occurs in different ways. RCI have, for example, built a garden of living trees and plants called Central Park on some ships, enabling passengers to enjoy walking through a park accompanied by the smell and feel of a land-based garden.[9] Likewise, Celebrity's Solstice Class ships boast The Lawn Club, a lawn of real grass where passengers walk, play games or listen to live music; usually co-located with restaurants or outside cafés, '[t]here's nothing quite like the feeling of relaxing on the lawn while, in reality, you're miles away from land'.[10] These examples highlight the embodied multisensory nature of experience both generally and specifically in relation to tourism (see Buzova, Cervera-Taule & Sanz-Blas, 2020; Merchant, 2011; Palmer & Andrews, 2020). While engagement with the sea has always been inextricably tied to all forms of maritime transport, the simulated nature of this sensory experience has developed exponentially, driven by the possibilities arising from innovations in technology.

Such innovations neatly illustrate what Gell (1992) has referred to as the technology of enchantment and the enchantment of technology. The tourism sector as a whole relies upon the aesthetics of enchantment, the techniques of construction and interior design to attract tourists and to create meaningful experiences (Palmer, 2018). The opulence and aesthetic appeal of cruise ships as spaces to inhabit, even if temporarily, creates a discourse of enchantment (see Bennett, 2001). In this sense, the cruise tourist experience is an enchanted embodied experience, imagined and co-constructed in relation to the structural and technological architecture of the cruise ship. However, ever larger ships and the expansion of the range and scale of onboard activities can lead to diminishing connections with the sea, which, when coupled with operational challenges such as crowding, queues at check-in, embarkation/debarkation and catering services, entertainment schedules and shore excursions, can result in experiences quickly becoming disenchanted experiences (Chin, 2008; Kwortnik, 2008). The behaviour of other passengers can also cause disenchantment when an out-of-place aesthetic disturbs a cruiser's expectation of a safe and relaxing space, as Rankin and Collins' analysis of cruise blogs illustrates,

> ...I bought a coffee at the Explorers Cafe and then sat down .... The Crows Nest was very crowded and I noticed a number of people making faces about the ... very loud RAP MUSIC. I went to the bartender and asked ... him to notice that the room was full of primarily old people, doing puzzles and reading books. Did he really think that they were interested in hearing RAP!
>
> *(cited in Rankin & Collins, 2017: 235–6, emphasis in original)*

Cruise tourists encounter the social spaces of the cruise ship and draw upon a shared repertoire of learned behaviours to co-construct an individual and collective experience of being on a cruise holiday. A traditional part of this social world is promenading, or walking around the deck and experiencing the movement, sounds, smells and feel of the sea in relation to the structural solidness of the ships architecture. However, innovations in ship design and technology have significantly altered the cruise tourist experience as imagined and understood in relation to promenading and moving around the ship. Promenading has much in common with what Symonds, Brown and Lo Iacono (2017) and others have referred to as wayfinding, a way of moving and locating the self that engages the whole physical and sensate body (see Ingold, 2000; Vannini, 2016). Technology has remodelled passenger relationships with the sea by changing the nature of promenading, changing how the inside and the outside of the ship is experienced.

Most large ships no longer have accessible decks that allow passengers to circumnavigate the ship uninterrupted. Technology has also changed the way cruisers move around and find their way onboard. For example, companies such as MSC Cruises use geo-location apps that operate in a similar way to the Google maps navigation feature. Passengers can be directed around the ship and even locate their companions via their smart devices, thereby creating an onboard experience almost totally devoid of risk in relation to anxieties about losing one's way. This illustrates how the architecture of technology creates an experience by training, regulating and insulating the body of the passenger from the very environment that makes a cruise holiday distinctive, namely, the sea outside and the material characteristics of maritime transport. Furthermore, the spatial layout of a ship influences how time is organized and experienced through the demarcation of spaces as cabins, recreation or dining areas, entertainment spaces, viewing platforms and so on. Itineraries and schedules move bodies from one activity to another and this movement is also controlled and directed largely, although not exclusively, by technology, the previously mentioned RCI's WOW wristband being one example.

In common with other forms of tourism, the cruise ship experience is based upon a different understanding of and relationship with time. This experience is assisted by the lack of clocks onboard, although a clock can be found at the purser's desk. The following cruiser blog entry illustrates the disorientating effect of 'invisible' time:

> NO CLOCK – we used to be able to get the time from the web cam channel on the TV but that does not happen now. You have no idea of the time especially (for the 1st time) being in an inside cabin, ALONG WITH REGULARLY CROSSING DIFFERENT TIME ZONES. No we don't wear watches.
> *(Cited in Rankin & Collins, 2017: 234, emphasis in original)*

Clearly, passengers can access 'the time' via their mobile devices and through the television in their cabin. However, such access is purposeful, meaning that it is possible for awareness of 'the time' to be avoided, overlooked or even forgotten. Cruise ship time can be disorientating as ships frequently pass through different time zones and many passengers may only become aware of the change once they arrive in port. Changes in time zones affect onboard schedules, such as meal times, and although such changes are communicated through onboard announcements, these can go unnoticed unless a passenger is actively seeking out 'the time'. Consequently, meals may be taken later than expected or missed all together. Conversely food can be an essential activity for ordering the sense of time: '…time on the cruise ships is no longer ordered by hours and minutes, but by the practice of smelling, feeling and tasting food, which works to knit together an "other" kind of time and place' (Rankin & Collins, 2017: 235). In this sense, the sensory aesthetic of food serves to locate the body of the cruise tourist in both time and space.

The above illustrates that the daily rhythms of away are different to the rhythms of home; the body-clock routines of home are rearranged in relation to the schedules and structures of the ship and of being at sea. Many cruise lines continue the tradition of ringing the ships' bell both at noon as a marker of time and, in particular, at the time when daily announcements are made by the Captain. The noon bell not only marks time but also reminds passengers that they are experiencing cruise time, time organized in relation to being at sea rather than being on land. Cruise time has different rhythms that are dictated by the ocean and by the commercial imperatives of cruise lines. As Stein (2012: 342) demonstrates through research into vacation time as a form of social control, '[t]he experience onboard a cruise ship illustrates how much of the vacation is oriented towards meeting an idealized experience that eliminates or alters the schedules and temporal constraints of everyday life'. She concludes that '[t]he ways in which individuals experience the passage of time can be manipulated by social ecologies' (Stein, 2012: 351). Architecture is the controlling social ecology of a cruise ship, whether in terms of structural design aesthetics or through the architecture of technology. This controlling hand of architecture constructs a cruise tourist experience based on being part of a floating onboard community.

Experience of and through the onboard community

As already argued, a cruise ship can be understood as a specific, albeit temporary, form of society, and this society is experienced as a community often perceived as a collective of likeminded individuals. This community comprises both passengers and crew who collectively co-construct the onboard experience. The spaces, schedules and activities provide opportunities for solo passengers and passengers travelling in different-sized groups to come together and create a shared social experience. However, the sense of belonging traditionally associated with being a member of a community has been transformed by advancements in cruise ship design and engineering; the sense of being part of an onboard community is still created, but it is a different experience to that associated with the smaller-sized vessels of 10–20 years ago.

The emergence of mega vessels and the resulting growth in passenger numbers has transformed the social experience of being at sea. Although there remain many opportunities for people to come together, the ability to remain anonymous in the sense of being able to avoid other passengers is facilitated by the size and complexity of contemporary cruise ship design. For example, the number of restaurants was once limited by the size of the ship so that passengers had to share tables and engage in a shared social experience, often with the same people every night. Nowadays, however, it is possible on many ships for two people to dine alone every time, including sitting at tables when watching shows in the entertainment spaces. This results in an experience based upon the ability to create relative anonymity within the wider cruise ship community. Clearly, not every passenger seeks out such an experience and in fact most passengers fully engage with other people, while there are some activities that all passengers are required to engage with, such as safety drills and (dis)embarkation processes. However, contemporary cruise ships do enable a more individualized experience and, thereby, provide greater opportunities for some passengers to opt in or out of the wider onboard community created by the way in which the ship is designed and built. The contemporary cruise tourist experience is, thus, one where being part of a community of like-minded people is more fluid and open than perhaps it once was. This is the cruise community as heterotopia.

As previously mentioned, the concept of heterotopia, or 'other place', was conceived by Foucault (1986) as being real sites or spaces that actually exist. This is in contrast to utopias, which are idealized spaces or societies formed in the imagination and, hence, do not exist and are unreal. Heterotopic spaces exist alongside but outside the ordinary spaces of daily life. They are outside in the sense that they are isolated or set apart from the everyday, with controls put in place to regulate who is allowed to enter and leave. These controls may be economic, affecting an individual's ability to pay for access, or based upon meeting specified legal requirements and, as such, heterotopias influence social behaviour and relationships. Foucault's examples of such spaces include the cemetery, prisons, brothels, festivals and transportation such as boats. These spaces illustrate an important feature of heterotopias; that is, their association with different experiences of time. Everyday time is disrupted or altered when, for example, watching a film in a cinema, travelling on a ship or visiting a theme park (Bruchansky, 2010; Ivakhiv, 2011; Lester 2011; Weaver, 2005b).

Boats and ships are located outside daily life because they are transient, mobile and physically isolated from the onshore spaces where life is actually lived while reflecting back on or

The contemporary cruise tourist experience

representing aspects of the 'real world'. Characteristics such as these explain why Foucault (1986: 27, emphasis in original) described the ship as '...the heterotopia *par excellence*. In civilizations without boats, dreams dry up...'. This association of boats with dreaming highlights an important identifying feature of heterotopias. For Foucault, heterotopias are sites of the imagination, sites of illusion that are experientially detached from the spaces of daily life and, as such, they are experienced differently. They may reflect or, as Foucault refers to it, mirror sites of everyday life, but they create different, idealized experiences. So it is no surprise that cruise ships have been described as 'floating utopias' (Berger, 2004), 'hedonistic floating pleasure palaces' (Jaakson, 2004b) and 'imagined worlds of excess, indulgence and escape' (Lester, 2011).

Within a heterotopia, such as a ship, an idealized view of society can be found, one where the routines, obligations and constraints of life at home are represented, contested and reversed. Low's (2008) discussion of the American gated community as heterotopia is instructive here, arguing that gated communities are marked by a blurring of public and private boundaries because they permit collective private ownership of what is in effect public space. According to Low, gated communities illustrate the social construction of a new type of space specifically designed to create safe havens as a sanctuary from the challenges of society. However, these safe havens are only available for those who can afford them. In gated communities,

> residents experience a sense of community, through the imposition of the external barrier and economic restrictions on who can enter. This heterotopian characteristic is magnified in the gated community because of the walls and gates, but also by the internal processes of control that residents are willing to 'put up with' in order to maintain the sense of oneness and safety at home.
>
> *(Low, 2008: 159)*

Cruise tourism operates in much the same way by providing a home away from home where the challenges and constraints of daily life are suspended and exchanged for experiences marked by freedom, freedom from responsibility and from the realities of everyday life, such as fear of crime and hardship. While much the same can be argued for other types of tourism, for example all-inclusive holidays, the difference with cruise tourism is that the sense of freedom it creates is markedly different and, arguably, more significant. This is because a ship at sea isolates and cocoons passengers from the challenges of daily life to a greater extent than the land-based bubble of an all-inclusive resort. Nevertheless, the sense of freedom associated with being on a cruise is to an extent a mirage since negative events do occur; people fall overboard and instances of crime, including sexual assault, are more frequent than the images of escape and freedom associated with cruise tourism might suggest (Klein & Poulston, 2011; Panko & Henthorne, 2019). A mirage of freedom exists because a cruise ship is actually a highly secure environment where passengers are protected by strategies they may not necessarily be aware of, such as the installation of discrete security devices such as CCTV. The mirage of freedom emphasizes the discourse of enchantment associated with cruise ship space, a discourse reinforced by the distance that exists between the ship, the land and the organized routines and obligations associated with home.

Being onboard a cruise ship involves being physically separated from the land with both the ship and the sea acting as protective barriers that limit who can belong by keeping out individuals who do not, such as non-cruisers or people unable to afford the cost of a cruise. At the same time, they protect passengers from social harms. Moreover, onboard safety drills are examples of the type of internal control processes that passengers are prepared to put up with to stay physically safe in an environment that is isolated, unfamiliar and mobile. Attendance at such drills is compulsory with cruise lines such as Disney relying on state-of-the-art automated systems to ensure guests have checked-in at assembly stations or drill locations. In this manner, a cruise community of interdependent members is created in which each member is aware that their behaviour affects the safety of other passengers. In other words, the safety drill encourages a heterotopian cruise experience based upon being part of a community characterized by an understanding that 'we are all in this together' magnified by the protective barriers of the ship and the sea. That said, technology is starting to change the face of such mandatory protocols with RCI's introduction of e-Muster drills[11] whereby passengers can choose to undertake this activity in their own time, thereby avoiding collective activity at sea.

In addition to the passengers and crew, the interdependent cruise ship community also includes the family and friends of the passengers back home. Over the years, innovations in technology have enabled passengers to stay in contact with friends and family far more effectively and cheaply than was previously possible. Although this has been the case with land-based tourism for many years (see Molz, 2012), onboard communication technologies have advanced significantly utilizing satellite technology and the internet. The sense of isolation of being at sea, away from land and in a closed environment diminishes with the use of social media, the internet, Skype, mobile phones, smart technology and so on, enabling connections to be maintained with home. As the following post from the *Cruzely* marketing website illustrates:

> Part of the fun of going on vacation? These days, it's letting everyone know that you went on vacation. And there is no better way to let people know you had a blast on your cruise than with Facebook, Instagram, Twitter, Snapchat and other apps that help you keep in touch back home while you are away.
>
> *(Callais, 2018)*

With technological advances, ship-to-shore communication has become characterized by the taken-for-granted assumption that contact is instantaneous, even though this may not be the case when factors such as time differences or technological interruptions are taken into account. As a result, for those passengers who choose to stay connected, the onboard cruise tourist experience is one characterized by what Gergen (2004) refers to as 'absent presence':

> One is physically present but is absorbed by a technologically mediated world of elsewhere. …. a world of relationships, both active and vicarious, within which domains of meaning are being created or sustained. Increasingly, these domains of alterior meaning insinuate themselves into the world of full presence – the world in which one is otherwise absorbed….
>
> *(Gergen, 2004: 227)*

For example, through the use of Apple hubs on Celebrity Cruises, friends and family can 'join' in with an individual or group cruise experience, helping to co-construct it and being temporarily invited into the onboard community. As Kathy writes in her blog *The Quiet Cruiser*, although Carnival Cruises offer The Hub app, 'I've found that the easiest way for my family and I to communicate is to start a secret Facebook group with only us in it, then buy internet service for a day or two mid-cruise... That way we can all keep in touch with each other...'.[12] On the *Caribbean Princess*, the interdependent cruise ship community comprises a virtual 3D avatar called *Tagalong* connected to Princess's Ocean Medallion worn around the neck or on the wrist. The primary purpose of the medallion is similar to RCI's WOWBand referred to earlier, namely, the provision of a digitally enhanced passenger experience. However, the avatars linked to the *Tagalong* Medallions remain within the reach of the passenger as they move around the ship, appearing on deck screens and on passenger mobile devices (Gaudiosi, 2019). As such, membership of a cruise community is not limited to being human, to the extent that the cruise tourist experience of and through community is both corporeal and simulated.

As previously noted, there is no one, single cruise tourist experience. Moreover, in terms of community, some cruisers may extend their experience beyond the end of the holiday as is often the case with repeat cruisers. A post-cruise community is reinforced and perpetuated through the virtual world of social media, enabling both first-time and experienced cruisers to share experiences and to ask for and receive advice. Passengers can engage with websites and networks both during and after a cruise, further maintaining the sense and the experience of being part of a community of like-minded individuals. As Vogel and Oschmann (2012: 12) state '[w]ebsites like cruise-addicts.com, cruisemates. com or cruisecritic.com would not exist without thousands of cruise passengers willing to invest time and effort into communicating their experiences and keeping each other up to date'. It should also be noted that the experience of community varies dependent on complex factors such as the type of cruise, the cruise line, cruise duration, the itinerary of destinations and so forth.

Interestingly, some passengers come with an already well-established sense of community and belonging that contributes to a more intense, immersive experience *through* community. Such is the case on themed cruises designed to attract individuals who are part of an existing sub-culture of shared interest, or fandom. Here the cruise appeals to and reinforces existing bonds that continue long after the cruise is over. As Mittermeier (2019) argues in relation to *Star Trek: The Cruise*, a floating extension of the land based *Star Trek* conventions attracting fans of the television series and film franchise:

> ...the immersivity of the cruise stems less from the actual physical theming of space than from the shared community of fans. Although this is also true for the regular convention experience, the 'bubble' of the ship acts as an added catalyst for it and makes the experience uniquely immersive.
>
> *(Mittermeier, 2019: 1380–1381)*

Conclusion

This chapter has highlighted some of the ways in which the cruise tourist experience is co-constructed through embodied, relational encounters between the architecture and materiality of cruise ship space (including the architecture of technology). In so doing, the growth and development of cruise ships as floating holiday/pleasure spaces has been foregrounded, acknowledging the extent to which advancements and innovations in the spatial design of passenger ships have transformed what it means to have an experience at sea, separated from the land. However, and as noted in the introduction, adopting an holistic approach to the term 'experience' should not be taken to mean that the cruise tourist experience is collective or homogenous; myriad experiences exist depending upon factors such as cruise type and culture. Furthermore, the ever-evolving complexities of cruise ships as architectural spaces at sea, together with the spatial dynamics resulting from innovations in engineering and technology, will continue to radically transform what and how passengers co-construct, engage with and consume 'the cruise experience'. Hence, the notion of the cruise experience is context specific with the cruise tourist having greater agency in what defines individual experience(s). To conclude, while it is not possible to provide an all-encompassing exploration of 'the cruise experience', this chapter has set out some key themes, thereby offering an alternative and more nuanced understanding of experience as it relates to cruise tourists. Moreover, these themes are intended to stimulate discussion about the fluid and relational nature of experience rather than provide a point of closure that defines what experience is, or how it should be conceived and understood.

Notes

1 https://www.royalcaribbean.com/gbr/en/cruise-ships/largest-ships-oasis-class [accessed 14/01/21]
2 Fact sheet, RCI https://www.royalcaribbeanpresscenter.com/fact-sheet/31/symphony-of-the-seas/ [accessed 30/11/20]
3 https://www.celebritycruises.com/gb/about-us/our-distinction/stunning-design [accessed 31/12/20].
4 https://www.royalcaribbeanblog.com/category/category/wowband [accessed 30/11/20].
5 https://www.princess.com/cruise-tips-vacation-ideas/video/onboard-experience/the-oceanmedallion.html [accessed 30/11/20].
6 https://www.youtube.com/watch?v=Fkha8nysDUc [accessed 30/11/20].
7 https://www.tui.co.uk/cruise/ships/marella-discovery-2/facilities/ [accessed 6 January 2021].
8 https://disneyparks.disney.go.com/blog/2012/01/magical-portholes-on-the-disney-fantasy [accessed 14/01/21].
9 https://www.royalcaribbeanpresscenter.com/video/824/landscaping-at-sea-maintaining-harmony-of-the-seas-central-park/ [accessed 15/01/2021].
10 https://www.celebritycruises.co.uk/onboard/venues-and-activities/the-lawn-club/ [accessed 15/01/2021].
11 https://www.royalcaribbean.com/blog/royal-caribbean-changes-the-game-with-muster-2-0/ [accessed 14/1/21].
12 https://quietcruiser.com/2019/02/19/how-do-i-keep-in-touch/ [accessed 6 January 2021].

References

Andrews, H. (2009) Tourism as a 'moment of being'. *Suomen Antropologi: Journal of the Finnish Anthropological Society*, 34(2), 5–21.
Andrews, H. (2011) *The British on Holiday: Charter Tourism, Identity and Consumption*. Bristol: Channel View publications.
Andriotis, K. and Agiomirgianakis, G. (2010) Cruise visitors' experience in a Mediterranean port of call. *International Journal of Tourism Research*, 12(4), 390–404.
Bennett, J. (2001) *The Enchantment of Modern Life: Attachments, Crossings, and Ethics*. Princeton: Princeton University Press.
Bennett, M. (2016) Competing with the sea: Contemporary cruise ships as omnitopias. *Performance Research: A Journal of the Performing Arts*, 21(2), 50–57.
Bentham, J. (1995) *The Panopticon Writings*. London: Verso.
Berger, A. A. (2004) *Ocean Travel and Cruising: A Cultural Analysis*. New York: Haworth Hospitality Press.
Bourdieu, P. (1977) *Outline of a Theory of Practice*. Cambridge: Cambridge University Press.
Bruchansky, C. (2010) The heterotopia of Disney World. *Philosophy Now*, 77 (Feb/Mar), 15–17.
Buchli, V. (2013) *An Anthropology of Architecture*. London: Bloomsbury.
Buzova, D., Cervera-Taule, A. and Sanz-Blas, S. (2020) Exploring multisensory place experiences through cruise blog analysis. *Psychology & Marketing*, 37(1), 131–140.

The contemporary cruise tourist experience

Callais, T. (2018) How to access Facebook, Instagram, Twitter (& Mmre) on a cruise. Available from: https://cruzely.com/how-to-access-facebook-instagram-twitter-more-on-a-cruise/ (Accessed 11 December 2020).

Chin, C. B. N. (2008) *Cruising in the Global Economy: Profits, Pleasure and Work at Sea*. Aldershot: Ashgate.

Cruise Critic. (2020) Lose Before You Cruise. Available at: https://boards.cruisecritic.com/forum/90-lose-before-you-cruise/ (Accessed 24 November 2020).

Csordas, T. J. (1994) *Embodiment and Experience. The Existential Ground of Culture and Self*. Cambridge: Cambridge University Press.

Davey, N. (2016) Lived experience: Erlebnis *and* Erfahrung. In N. Keane and C. Lawn (Eds.), *The Blackwell Companion to Hermeneutics*. Chichester: Wiley, pp. 326–332.

Foucault, M. (1986) Of Other Spaces. *Diacritics*, 16(1), 22–27.

Foucault, M. (1995) *Discipline and Punish. The Birth of the Prison*. New York: Vintage Books.

Gaudiosi, J. (2019) Your personal avatar can now board a cruise ship with you. Available at: https://www.wired.com/story/carnival-medallion-cruise-tagalong-avatar/ (Accessed 17 December 2020).

Gell, A. (1992) The technology of enchantment and the enchantment of technology. In J. Coote and A. Sheldon (Eds.), *Anthropology, Art and Aesthetics*. Oxford: Oxford University Press, pp. 40–63.

Gergen, K. (2004) The challenge of absent presence. In J. Katz and M. Aakhus (Eds.), *In Perpetual Contact: Mobile Communications, Private Talk, Public Performance*. Cambridge: Cambridge University Press, pp. 227–241.

Graburn, N., Gravari-Barbas, M. and Staszak, J-F. (2019) Simulacra, architecture, tourism and the uncanny. *Journal of Tourism and Cultural Change*, 17(1), 1–12.

Huang, J. and Hsu, C. H. C. (2010) The impact of customer-to-customer interaction on cruise experience and vacation satisfaction. *Journal of Travel Research*, 49(1), 79–92.

Hyde, K. and Olesen, K. (2011) Packing for touristic performances. *Annals of Tourism Research*, 38(3), 900–919.

Ingold, T. (2000) *The Perception of the Environment: Essays on Livelihood, Dwelling and Skill*. London: Routledge.

Ivakhiv, A. (2011) Cinema of the not-yet: The utopian promise of film as heterotopia. *Journal for the Study of Religion, Nature & Culture*, 5(2), 186–209.

Jaakson, R. (2004a) Beyond the tourist bubble? Cruiseship passengers in port. *Annals of Tourism Research*, 31(1), 44–60.

Jaakson, R. (2004b) Globalisation and neocolonialist tourism. In C. M. Hall and H. Tucker (Eds.), *Tourism and Postcolonialism: Contested Discourses, Identities and Representations*. London: Routledge, pp. 169–183.

Jack, G. and Phipps, A. (2005) *Tourism and Intercultural Exchange. Why Tourism Matters*. Clevedon: Channel View.

Klein, R. and Poulston, J. (2011) Sex at sea: Sexual crimes aboard cruise ships. *Tourism in Marine Environments*, 7(2), 67–80.

Klingman, A. (2007) *Brandscapes. Architecture in the Experience Economy*. Cambridge: Massachusetts Institute of Technology.

Kwortnik, R. J. (2008) Shipscape influence on the leisure cruise experience. *International Journal of Culture, Tourism and Hospitality Research*, 2(4), 289–311.

Lallani, S. S. (2017) Mediating cultural encounters at sea: Dining in the modern cruise industry. *Journal of Tourism History*, 9(2–3), 160–177.

Lefebvre, H. (1991[1974]) *The Production of Space* (Trans D. Nicholson-Smith). Oxford: Blackwell Publishing

Lester, J. (2011) Tourism and Film: Real, 'Reel' and Imagined Spaces of Cruise Ships. (unpublished Ph.D.), Cardiff: Cardiff Metropolitan University

Lester, J. (2017) Mediating the cruise experience. In R. Dowling and C. Weeden (Eds.), *Cruise Ship Tourism*, 2nd Edn. Wallingford: CABI, pp. 188–204.

Lester, J. A. and Weeden, C. (2004) Stakeholders, the natural environment and the future of Caribbean cruise tourism. *International Journal of Tourism Research*, 6(1), 39–50.

Locker, M. (2017) Inside Royal Caribbean's Wild, Tech-Filled Cruise of the Future. Fast Company [online]. Available at: https://www.fastcompany.com/40495733/inside-royal-caribbeans-wild-tech-filled-cruise-of-the-future (Accessed 24 November 2020).

Low, S. (2008) The gated community as heterotopia. In M. Dehaene and L. De Cauter (Eds.), *Heterotopia and the City: Public Space in a Postcivil Society*. Abingdon: Routledge, pp.153–164.

Lunn, G. (2009) *Building the Biggest: From Ironships to Cruise Liners*. Stroud: The History Press.

Mallgrave, F. (2010) *The Architect's Brain: Neuroscience, Creativity and Architecture*. Chichester: Wiley-Blackwell.

Mauss, M. (1979) *Sociology and Psychology: Essays by Marcel Mauss*. London: Routledge.

McLaren, B. (2006) *Architecture and Tourism in Italian Colonial Libya*. Seattle: University of Washington Press.

Merchant, S. (2011) Negotiating underwater space: The sensorium, the body and the practice of scuba-diving. *Tourist Studies*, 11(3), 215–234.

Mittermeier, S. (2019) (Un)conventional voyages? Star Trek: The cruise and the themed cruise experience. *The Journal of Popular Culture*, 52(6): 1372–1386.

Molz, J. G. (2012) *Travel Connections. Tourism, Technology and Togetherness in a Mobile World*. Abingdon: Routledge.

Morosan, C. and Fesenmaier, D. R. (2007) A conceptual framework of persuasive architecture of tourism websites: Propositions and implications. In M. Sigala, L. Mich and J. Murphy (Eds.), *Information and Communication Technologies in Tourism 2007*. Proceedings of the International Conference, Ljubljana, Slovenia. New York: Springer, pp. 243–254.

Noy, C. (2014) Staging portraits: Tourism's panoptic photo-industry. *Annals of Tourism Research*, 47, 48–62.

O'Regan, M. (2016) A backpacker habitus: The body and dress, embodiment and the self. *Annals of Leisure Research*, 19(3), 329–346.

P&O Cruises (2020) What to Wear. Available at: https://www.pocruises.com/what-to-wear (Accessed 24 November 2020).

Pallasmaa, J. (2005) *The Eyes of the Skin: Architecture and the Senses*. Chichester: Wiley-Blackwell.

Palmer, C. (2018) *Being and Dwelling through Tourism: An Anthropological Perspective*. Abingdon: Routledge.

Palmer, C. and Andrews, A. (Eds.) (2020) *Embodiment and Tourism*. Abingdon: Routledge.

Panko, T. and Henthorne, T. (2019) Crimes at sea: A review of crime onboard cruise ships. *International Journal of Safety and Security in Tourism/Hospitality*, 20, 1–23.

Petrick, J. F. (2004) First timers' and repeaters' perceived value. *Journal of Travel Research*, 43(1), 29–38.

Pine, J. and Gilmore, J. (1999) *The Experience Economy: Work is Theatre & Every Business a Stage*. Boston: Harvard Business School.

Quartermaine, P. (1996) *Building on the Sea: Form and Meaning in Modern Ship Architecture*. London: Academy Group Ltd and national Maritime Museum.

Quartermaine, P. and Peter, B. (2006) *Cruise, Identity, Design and Culture*. London: Laurence King Publishing Ltd.

Rankin, J. R. and Collins, F. L. (2017) Enclosing difference and disruption: Assemblage, heterotopia and the cruise ship. *Social & Cultural Geography*, 18(2), 224–244.

Richards, G. (2001) The experience industry and the creation of attractions. In G. Richards (Ed.), *Cultural Attractions and European Tourism*. Wallingford: CABI, pp. 55–69.

Rovelli, C. (2015) *Seven Brief Lessons on Physics* (Trans S. Carnell and E. Segre). London: Penguin.

Scerri, M., Edwards, D. and Foley, C. (2019) Design, architecture and the value to tourism. *Tourism Economics*, 25(5), 695–710.

Schrock, D. and Boyd, E. (2006) Reflexive transembodiment. In D. Waskul and P. Vannini (Eds.), *Body/Embodiment: Symbolic Interaction and the Sociology of the Body*. Aldershot: Ashgate, pp. 51–66.

Sharpley, R. and Stone, P. R. Eds. (2012) *Contemporary Tourist Experience. Concepts and Consequences*. Abingdon: Routledge.

Stein, R. (2012) Time off: The social experience of time on vacation. *Qualitative Sociology*, 35(3), 335–353.

Symonds, P., Brown, D. and Lo Iacono, V. (2017) Exploring absent presence: Wayfinding as an embodied sociocultural experience. *Sociological Research Online*, 22(1), 5. Available at: http://www.socresonline.org.uk/22/1/5.html DOI: 10.5153/sro.4185 (Accessed 18 January 2021)

Terzidou, M., Scarles, C. and Saunders, M. K. N. (2017) Religiousness as tourist performances: A case study of Greek Orthodox pilgrimage. *Annals of Tourism Research*, 66, 116–129.

Tuan, Y-F., (1977) *Space and Place: The Perspective of Experience*. London, Edward Arnold.

The contemporary cruise tourist experience

Turner, V. W. and Bruner, E. (Eds.) (1986) *The Anthropology of Experience*. Urbana and Chicago: University of Illinois Press.

UNWTO (2010) *Cruise Tourism – Current Situation and Trends*. Madrid: UN World Tourism Organization.

Vannini, P. (2016) How to Climb Mount Fuji (at your earliest convenience). A non-representational approach. In B. H. Brewster and A. J Puddephatt (Eds.), *Microsociological Perspectives for Environmental Sociology*. Abingdon: Routledge, pp. 48–60.

Vogel, M. and Oschmann, C. (2012) The demand for ocean cruisers: Three perspectives. In M. Vogel., A. Papathanassis and B. Wolber (Eds.), *The Business and Management of Ocean Cruises*. Wallingford: CABI, pp. 3–18.

Wealleans, A. (2006) *Designing Liners: A History of Interior Design Afloat*. London: Routledge.

Weaver, A. (2005a) Spaces of containment and revenue capture: 'Super-sized' cruise ships as mobile tourism enclaves. *Tourism Geographies*, 7(2), 165–184.

Weaver, A. (2005b) Representation and obfuscation: Cruise travel and the mystification of production. *Tourism Culture & Communication*, 5(3), 165–176.

Weaver, A. (2014) Representation, commerce, and consumption: The cruise industry and the ocean. In T. Cusack (Ed.), *Framing the Ocean, 1700 to the Present*. Abingdon: Routledge, pp. 117–129.

Wood, R. E. (2000) Caribbean cruise tourism: Globalisation at sea. *Annals of Tourism Research*, 27(2), 345–370

30

KEY COMPONENTS OF SPORT TOURIST EXPERIENCES

Sean Gammon

Introduction

Similar to the study of tourism in general, the experiences of the sport tourist in particular lie at the centre of what sport tourism is and what it encompasses. Also, much like in tourism, there has been a notable oversimplification as to what constitutes a sport tourist experience. On a very basic level it involves the experience of sport as a tourist. This chimes with Kurtzman's (1995: 6) broad definition of the field, who views sport tourism encompassing '...the use of sports as a vehicle for tourism endeavours.' However, this suggests that sport is always the driver of tourism – and not *vice versa* – and does not account for the different types of sport–tourism interaction and touristic contexts involved. For example, whether a tourist has travelled to play, spectate or visit a specific sport attraction will profoundly affect their experience(s) (Gammon, 2015; Gibson, 2005a). Likewise, the distance travelled, along with the chosen level of hospitality, will heavily influence any ensuing sport tourist experience (Higham & Hinch, 2018). When such contexts are combined with other variables, such as individual motives, identity factors, personality traits, emotional investment, expectations and previous sport and/or tourist experiences, we are left with an almost incalculable number of experiential outcomes.

Therefore, it will come as little surprise that this chapter does not aim to identify a list of such experiences but, rather, to first illustrate the diversity of the sport tourism landscape and second, to highlight those experiences that are unusual and/or unique to sport tourism. Such distinctions are important, not only to make a case for stronger acquiescence of the field's identity and existence (see Gammon, Ramshaw & Wright, 2017) but also to help bring to light those critical components that help form and frame its very nature.

The sport tourism landscape

Before exploring the key components that influence sport tourist experiences, it is first necessary to make clearer what sport tourism is and what it contains. Whilst the field (or sub-field) of sport tourism is a relative newcomer to the academic arena, its practice can be traced back over millennia (Huggins, 2013; Standeven & De Knop, 1998; Weed & Bull, 2009). It is likely that the first organized sports event that generated tourism was the Olympic Games

424   DOI: 10.4324/9781003219866-34

Key components of sport tourist experiences

that dates from 776 BC. It was common for both athletes and spectators to travel considerable distances to compete in and watch events that could attract as many as 40,000 people from all over Greece. Interest and research into the early development of sport events and their impacts have occupied the attention of predominantly historians (see Berryman, 1973; Guttmann, 1981), though studies specifically focusing on the tourism connections to sports participation is a relatively recent academic evolvement. In fact, the term sport tourism (at least in English) was first documented as late as 1966 in a paper for the Council of Physical Recreation UK (Anthony, 1966). It was not until the 1980s that serious academic attention was paid to the significance of sport-related tourism, stemming from a paper that explored the policy and provision for active sport tourists in Western Europe (Glyptis, 1982). However, it was in the 1990s that a noteworthy and sustained interest started to gain momentum.

In conjunction with numerous sport event impact analyses, it was during this period that researchers turned their attention to both defining and delineating sport tourism. Much of the discussion concerning definitions can be found in Van Rheenen, Cernaianu and Sobry's (2017) analyses of contributions made in the *Journal of Sport and Tourism* – and its predecessor, the *Journal of Sport Tourism*. Their study found that since 1992, 30 distinct definitions had been suggested that highlight five paradigmatic dimensions: sport as motivation for travel, space, time, participant experience and economic motivations. Very few definitions proffer a single dimension that suggests the multi-influential nature of sport tourism experiences and situations. Therefore, current definitions offer variations on a theme that has arguably led to a sense of apathy and indifference within the academy of accepting a single interpretation. Whilst it is beyond the scope of this chapter to explore the strengths and weaknesses of all the key contributors to sport tourism definitions (see Higham & Hinch, 2018), it is important (given the emphasis of this collection) to focus on those definitions and conceptualizations that have an experiential component to them.

Standeven and De Knop (1998) were amongst the first authors to suggest that the nature of sport tourism consists of an *experience* of physical activity tied to an *experience* of place (emphasis added). This perspective was augmented further by Weed and Bull (2009: 63) who conceptualize sport tourism as '…arising from the unique interaction of activity, people and place'. Both contributions draw attention to the important synergetic qualities of sport tourism experiences, though without pinning down the essence of what the culminating experience might be. The manner in which the experience of sport and tourism interact has also been suggested by other authors who focus on the motivational dimensions of sport tourism manifestations (Gammon & Robinson, 1997, 2003; Ritchie, Mosedale & King, 2001; Sofield, 2003). These studies argue that the experience of sport tourism is largely determined by the primary and secondary purposes of the trip. For example, Gammon and Robinson (1997) argue that sport tourist experiences are partially dependent upon the motivational drives of the constituent parts. In other words, the extent in which sport or tourism act as the primary or secondary purpose of a trip will lead to very different experiential outcomes. By applying the theory of secondary reinforcement (Calder & Staw, 1976), it was suggested that secondary motives can act as a reinforcing or enriching drive to the primary motives. This culminated in the design of a consumer framework that divided the relationship between sport and tourism to either *sport tourism* that refers to those who travel primarily to experience sport in some way, and *tourism sport* that refers to those where sport is a secondary or incidental consideration (Robinson & Gammon, 2004).

However, adopting a binary approach towards sport tourism has had its distractors. For example, Weed and Bull (2009: 61) claim that emphasizing the dominance of its constituent parts '…establishes a subordinate role for either tourism or for sport' and in doing so neglects both the synergistic and holistic qualities of the term. Furthermore, they argue that binary-based approaches distract from the unique qualities of sport tourism that are founded on the interaction of people, place and activity. In reality, however, there is little difference between the arguments outlined above, as they both adhere to the conflation of sport and tourism creating an outcome that is both existentially and, therefore, experientially distinct. Weed and Bull (2009), therefore, place much emphasis on the unique and holistic qualities of the term that escalate sport tourism to a standing that is more than the sum of its parts – a position that is shared by others (see Downward, 2005; Pigeassou, Bui-Xuan & Gleyse, 2003). Whilst Robinson and Gammon (2004) concur with this conclusion, they differ in that they believe that the fusion of sport and tourism results in *many* distinct yet differing states that are determined by the dominance of either sport or tourism:

> Put simply, sport tourism is unquestionably a blend of two phenomena that will in turn create many differing yet related manifestations. In the same way that the colour green is made up from yellow and blue and will vary in hue depending on the dominance of its constituent colours - so will sport tourism.
>
> *(Gammon, 2015: 112)*

This position has also been supported, applied and adapted within the literature (see Hudson & Hudson, 2010; Smith, 2010) with Higham and Hinch (2018: 41) concluding that this perspective helps to gain '...a better understanding of sport tourism markets, which provides insights into the distinct sport and tourism-related services and experiences required by each'.

The above discussion should not be viewed as an aimless exercise in semantics but, rather, as an opportunity to identify potential salient components that make up sport tourist experiences. Furthermore, a decision has to be made so as to identify the specific experiential circumstances that qualify it as sport-related tourism. In other words, we must ask whether a sport tourist experience only occurs when there is perfect union between its binary constituents, or whether to consider all sport–tourist interactions – irrespective of their importance or dominance to the individual. As it is likely that experiences will differ depending on how significant or dominant each binary part is to the other (Gammon, 2015), the following discussion will consider all combinations where the experience of sport and tourism takes place – including where each is as important as the other.

A further factor to consider is the many contexts where sport tourism takes place. For example, Kurtzman and Zauhar (1997), taking a core-product perspective, identified five sport tourism categories: *tours*; *resorts*; *attractions*; *cruises*; and *events* (*adventure* being a category added later). However, the most commonly utilized is Gibson's (1998) tripartite typology that delineates sport tourism into *active sport tourism, event sport tourism* and *nostalgia sport tourism*. There have been some misgivings using the term nostalgia, as it describes a specific emotional response that could potentially occur at any of the other two types (Weed & Bull, 2009). Therefore, the term *sport tourism attraction* (Gibson, 2005b) may be a more appropriate term as it refers to those sport places that are visited for reasons different from watching events or active participation. Ramshaw and Gammon (2007) suggest that the term *heritage sport tourism* may better frame this category as it widens its breadth whilst also acknowledging the significance of nostalgia in many sport tourism episodes. Also, the term *event sport tourism* has been thought of as too broad as it encompasses two major event types that delineate events that are predominantly participant or spectator driven. This has led to more recent typologies, expanding on the types outlined above: *spectator events*; *participation events*; *active sport*; and *sport heritage* (Higham & Hinch, 2018).

Key components of sport tourist experiences

Lastly, there has been much debate concerning the importance of authenticity in sport tourism episodes (Gammon, 2011; Hinch & Higham, 2005; Hurych, 2017) – yet surprisingly this is a consideration rarely incorporated in the definitions outlined earlier. The significance of authenticity within the tourism domain has produced much debate, initially generated by the polarized positions outlined by MacCannell (1989) and Boorstin (1964) (see also Chapter 6 in this volume). And whilst there remains a theoretical fluidity concerning the extent in which authenticity is a key determinant in tourist experiences (Heitmann, 2011), the same cannot be said for sport. A key attribute for any competitive sport event is that the result must be unknown – however likely the outcome may be (Gammon, 2020). Consequently, experiences relating to watching sport are intimately tied with the presumption that the competition and, therefore, the result, are authentic. Similarly, authenticity runs through much of the experiences relating to the many forms of sport tourism outlined above. For the sport tourist, sport offers existential, cultural and social encounters that offer insights into the self, the destination and its people.

As outlined in the introduction, the aim of this chapter is not to list the innumerable experiences that emanate from sport tourism episodes but, rather, to identify those salient components that are mostly likely to influence them. By doing so, it will draw attention to the unique experiential properties that distinguish sport tourism from other tourist types. Drawing on those definitional and conceptual debates on sport tourism summarized above, the key components that are more likely to influence sport tourist experiences are *activity, motivation, authenticity* and *place* (conveniently producing the acronym: A MAP). It is important to point out that each of these components are interrelated and play an equal part in sport tourism experience – whilst also acting as umbrella terms for a host of other influencing factors.

Place

The significance of place in all forms of tourism has occupied a good deal of discussion; after all tourism, in very simple terms, involves leaving one place to visit another. Sport-related tourism is no different yet, whilst more traditional conceptualizations of tourist experience accentuate the quest for strangeness or difference (Cohen, 1979; Smith, 1978), the experience of the sport tourist is more nuanced, embracing the familiar within and around the unfamiliar. For example, the travelling fan will often encounter fields of play that appear similar to those experienced back home – yet when juxtaposed with sites and sights that they are less accustomed to will generate simultaneous experiences of familiarity and strangeness. Whilst such experiences are not unique to sport tourism, having been discussed in more general tourism terms (Cohen, 1972, 1979; Lee & Crompton, 1992), they remain a significant signature of the sport tourist encounter. This blend of familiarity and strangeness is not just limited to the travelling fan or spectator but also to the active sport tourist whose experience of playing a sport will be affected by the surroundings in which the sport takes place. Factors relating to home and away advantage for professional sports people is a topic that has been explored in some depth (for example, Carron, Loughhead & Bray, 2005; Courneya & Carron, 1992) but has not been significantly investigated in terms of how the experience of being a tourist affects the experience of sport – and of course *vice versa*.

Cohen's (1979) widely referred to tourist experience categories identify five modes of experience that are based upon differing levels of superficiality, ranging from recreational (most superficial), diversionary, experiential, experimental and existential (least superficial). Given the often playful nature of sport participation, it would be tempting to place such experiences within the most superficial recreational mode, yet this would ignore the significance

427

that sport-related places hold for many who travel to them. Gammon (2004) refers to these places as special sites/sights of sporting significance, which are capable of initiating secular pilgrimages and feelings of awe and respect. With regard to the active sport tourist, the term apprenticeship pilgrimage can be used (Griffith, 2013) to describe those journeys taken by enthusiasts to places where a deeper connection to an interest and passion is sought.

Such places can be far from the 'pilgrim's' home but are considered worthy of the journey as they offer transformative experiences under the tutelage of masters or recognized experts. The travelling fan or spectator will also seek out sport event experiences at venues that hold significant personal or collective meaning. In the same way that Wagnerian fans view the *Bayreuth Festspielhaus* as the ultimate venue in which to experience the composer's music, so too will sports fans desire to experience specific sports at specific places. Of course, the perceived significance of sport venues is largely subjective, yet there remains a collective acquiescence that some are more important than others (e.g., Fenway Park: Baseball; Wimbledon: Tennis; Augusta National: Golf; Lord's Cricket Ground). In many cases, it is the history of a venue that increases its notoriety and esteem. This led to the design of retro stadia (predominantly baseball parks in the 1990s) that were built incorporating features from the parks of the 1920s and 1930s. The primary aim of these ball parks was to offer the spectator and fan a taste of what it was like to watch baseball in its heyday – an experience that was deemed lost and inaccessible in most modern venues. Whilst it is easy to dismiss such places as nothing more than romantic facsimiles of the original(s), offering, at best, experiences founded on unashamed staged authenticity (see following section), it must be taken on board that some have become attractions in their own right. Ramshaw and Gammon's (forthcoming) analysis of the Oriole Park at Camden Yards (OPCY) in Baltimore (the first of the retro ball parks) conclude that the park is slowly becoming what it first set out to imitate: a famous sporting venue that has its own identity and signature – perhaps illustrating McCannell's (1989) observations on emergent authenticity.

So important are such places they have become visitor attractions in their own right, generating significant interest from those who wish to just experience the place rather than the events they usually host. Tours of iconic sports venues are commonplace across the globe and have become integral features of many destinations' tourism portfolios (Gammon & Fear, 2005; Higham & Hinch, 2018; Ramshaw, 2020; Ramshaw & Gammon, 2010). Place may also be a central consideration when visiting sports museums and halls of fame, especially when the place in some way validates the curatorial decisions and objects that are housed within them. For example, the National Baseball Hall of Fame and Museum in Cooperstown (NY) is inextricably linked with the symbolic home of the sport, as is the cricket museum at Lord's cricket ground. In these cases, there is a relationship between sports places and the places that surround and legitimize them – a process that Malpas (1998) describes as the *folding and unfolding* of place (see Gammon, 2015 for sport tourism examples). This form of place corroboration illustrates effectively the interrelatedness of the key components, especially the significance of authenticity in numerous sport tourism episodes.

Authenticity

As indicated earlier, a fundamental element of all competitive sport is that the result must never be known in advance. For those who either actively participate or watch sport, any suspicion that the result is in any way predetermined will compromise both the sport and the meaningfulness of the experience. Yet, for all this piety, there is evidence that some tourist events that have a sporting theme are solely performed for the paying customer. Whether it be heritage-based enactments or perhaps exhibition matches, the competitiveness is often secondary to the performance (Wood, 2005), illustrating perhaps McCannell's (1989) views on staged authenticity. But this should not detract from the importance of authenticity to the overwhelming majority of sport tourism episodes. As Higham and Hinch (2018: 73) note, 'to a larger extent, authenticity is what makes sport so compelling'.

There is no doubt that the significance of authenticity in the study of tourism has exercised the minds of tourism scholars for many decades (Sharpley, 2018). Initial discussions revolved around the importance of authenticity in the decision-making process of the tourist, with later debates focusing on those specific aspects of authenticity that are more relevant to the study of tourism (Lau, 2010; Wang, 1999). Put simply, authenticity can be viewed first in objective terms that are mostly associated with objects and cultural practices that have been verified and authenticated by 'experts' as real – or second, in subjective terms that focus more on the experiences and interpretations of the tourist. Moreover, Wang (1999) suggests that such experiences enable the tourist to connect to and/or to find their true selves. He refers to this as existential authenticity, which differs from object-based category as it

> ...can often have nothing to do with the issue of whether toured objects are real. In search of tourist experience which is existentially authentic, tourists are preoccupied with an existential state of Being activated by certain tourist activities.
>
> *(Wang, 1999: 359)*

For the active sport tourist, it is likely that a reciprocity takes place between objective and subjective authenticity, whereby the environment will validate and support the chosen activity and, in so doing, help nurture feelings of personal expressiveness (Waterman, 1993). Furthermore, the tourism context will allow individuals to focus more on the activity rather than being distracted by any concerns that the home environment may activate. As a result, an increase in awareness of the physicality-based dimensions of a sport will often be accentuated, which will in turn (re)affirm a sense of personal and social identity (Lamont, 2014; Rickly-Boyd, 2012; Shipway & Jones, 2008). Wang (1999) refers to this dimension of existential authenticity as intra-personal authenticity, which is connected to *bodily feelings* and *self-making*.

Of course, the extent in which such sport tourist activities nurture and accentuate a more authentic sense of self is very much dependent upon the degree of seriousness that an individual has for a sport. For those tourists who engage in sport in a more casual manner – as no more than an entertaining diversion – the likelihood of experiencing the identity-affirming outcomes detailed above will be less common. However, there will be others who take a more playful approach to the sport activities on offer, who are prepared to experiment with both the activity and the potential identity it offers. This form of experimentation has been discussed extensively within the leisure literature and brings to light the self-contained nature found in many leisure situations that sport and tourism are often attached (Kelly, 1983). This means that individuals can safely experiment with sport-related identities away from the home environment, making it less likely to be judged or ridiculed by those that know them.

There are also opportunities to engage in sport fantasy-based experiences through participating in one of the many fantasy camps offered predominantly in North America (Gammon & Ramshaw, 2013). The camps are designed so that fans of a team and/or a sport can directly interact with players and coaches from the past. The primary aim of the camps is essentially to provide wish fulfilment to those adults (usually over the age of 35) who want to realize their childhood dreams of playing alongside their heroes in the higher echelons of their chosen sport. In this case the experience of authenticity is more socially constructed (see Wang, 1999) though undoubtedly self-aware, as participants are fully cognisant that their levels of expertise and ability fall well below that of a professional athlete. Therefore, the authenticity is more object-based as the ex-professional players are manifestly the genuine articles, as are the venues in which the matches and coaching takes place. From an emotional perspective, nostalgia has also been linked to the fantasy camp experience (Gammon, 2002), though how this combines with feelings of wish fulfilment and fantasy is unclear.

The sport event tourist's experiences are as equally complex as the active participant, though displaying very different connections to notions of authenticity. For example, there has been much discussion concerning the ability of sports events to exude authentic representations of both a people and their culture (Higham & Hinch, 2009; Jarvie, 2012; Nauright, 1996). It can offer a backstage glimpse into the values, passions and traditions of a nation or region, where the action and the fervour of the event acts as camouflage to the hidden spectating tourist. Giulianotti (2005: 132) refers to this type of sport spectator as an example of the contemporary *flaneur* who can '...guide in semi-detached fashion, through a cornucopia of experiences.' Any team or player allegiances are rarely serious, though supportive performances will still take place, if only to build on the necessary subterfuge.

However, the influence of authenticity upon the more serious travelling fan will be primarily dependent on the sport, the context of the event, the level of fan identity and the ensuing motives that drive attendance (see next section). As a result, the significance of authenticity on the fan experience will be largely dependent upon individuals' specific biographies. But where fans spend time together whilst travelling to and from away events, it is likely that an increased sense of *communitas* will take place. Wang (1999: 365), derived from the work of Turner (1973), refers to this as inter-personal authenticity, where the democratized make-up of the travelling groups leads to a sense of social equality:

> ...tourists can ease themselves of the pressures stemming from inauthentic social hierarchy and status distinctions. Rather they approach one another in a natural, friendly, and authentic way.

This is not to suggest, as Hinch and Higham (2005) observe, that such sub-cultural groups have little hierarchical structures themselves, only that membership can boost feelings relating to personal identity creation and affirmation.

The search for authenticity may be more obvious in those that seek out sport-related attractions such as museums, halls of fame and other sites of special sporting significance. Most of these examples are housed within the heritage sport tourism domain and so are predominantly associated with visitors seeking out important, genuine artefacts from the past. Consequently, experiences will include (amongst others) feelings of wonder and awe, personal and collective nostalgia or just general fascination. The degree of impact that such objects will engender will unsurprisingly be dependent on the motives of the visitors and the degree of seriousness connected to the sport and/or sports on display. On some occasions, the historical significance of where the objects are housed will add further reverence and status, especially when the attraction is treated with similar veneration (Ramshaw, Gammon & Tobar, 2019). Whilst it could be argued that tours of famous sports stadia and other significant sporting places will generate similar responses, the degree of authenticity will be staged, as backstage areas are carefully prepared for the curious visitor (Gammon, 2011). Nevertheless, the experience is often valued as it represents a symbolic reversal, where visitors are temporarily given access to areas that are usually reserved for the great and privileged (Couldry, 1998).

Motivation

The study of motivation within tourism and sport has spawned much debate, incorporating a wide range of theories and approaches. In tourism alone, there exists a bewildering diversity of studies that explore the motivational intricacies of what drives tourists to travel (see Sharpley, 2018). Similarly, sport has occupied researchers' time in identifying not only what initiates competitive and recreational participation, but also what does not (Clancy, Herring, MacIntyre & Campbell, 2016; Konstantinos, Charalambos & Grouios, 2002). To add to the complexity, both academic fields have applied motivational studies from an array of academic disciplines, each of which is situated round specific theoretical frameworks. As could be expected, motivational research in sport tourism has been inspired by its parent fields (see Weed & Bull, 2009), culminating in various theories and approaches that also display great variety and heterogeneity.

It would be easy to dismiss any attempts to identify an all-encompassing motivational theory for sport tourism as foolhardy, yet this would overlook the influence that motivation has upon the sport tourist experience (Higham & Hinch, 2018). Therefore, it may be more helpful to conclude that each of the approaches outlined in the literature contribute to gaining a better understanding of why sport tourists do what they do (Gibson, 2005a) whilst also drawing attention to the extent to which motives affect experience. In simple terms, there appear to be three levels of motivational approaches outlined in the sport tourism literature: *macro* approaches, *meso* approaches and *micro* approaches, each of which offers equally important contributions to the field. Macro approaches refer to those theories and propositions that aim to highlight the foundational drives that are common across all sport tourism episodes. For example, Weed and Bull (2009) bring attention to the 'pleasure principle' (emanating from the work of Freud) that posits that a salient determinant of sport tourism involvement is the opportunity to engage in enjoyable sport-related activities whilst taking advantage of the agreeable experiences of being on vacation. This is linked with Robinson and Gammon's (2004) contention that consumers either consider sport as the primary motive (*sport tourism*) or tourism (*tourism sport*). As previously noted, this approach adapts secondary reinforcement theory (Calder & Staw, 1976) and postulates that secondary considerations can reinforce and enrich primary ones.

In contrast, meso approaches include those studies that aim in identifying what motivates individuals in engaging in specific sport tourism episodes. Therefore, these approaches acknowledge that different types of sport tourism generate different motives. For instance, in the context of active sport tourism, whilst some highlight factors relating to opportunities for personal and social identity affirmation (Shipway & Jones, 2008), others focus on kinaesthetic-related experiences and place (Geffroy, 2017), serious leisure (Gibson, Willming & Holdnak, 2002) or self-determination theory (Aicher & Brenner, 2015). The work of Gibson and Pennington-Gray (2005), centred on the influence of role theory to golf tourist behaviour, may also be grouped in this approach as the role model may well influence the nature of the motives to participate. Studies that explore the motives of the sport event tourist display equally diverse approaches, such as those that focus on cultural opportunities (Nauright, 1996), nostalgia (Fairley, 2003; Kulczycki & Hyatt, 2007), social belonging (Smith and Stewart, 2007), fantasy (Gammon, 2002) or theories relating to hooliganism (Weed, 2002). The motives for those who visit sporting attractions have also engaged research framed round secular pilgrimage (Gammon, 2004), education (Moore, 2012) and nostalgia (Vamplew, 1998).

Micro approaches are the least implemented within sport tourism motives as they aim to identify those deeper psychological needs that often lie behind many of the motives indicated in the other approaches listed above. For example, hidden motives (see Simler & Hanson, 2018) go some way in explaining why individuals desire to seek identity affirmation, self-expression, nostalgia or serious leisure and so on. Therefore, the impulse to achieve stronger feelings of personal and social identity may stem from an absence of opportunity to express the self in other life contexts, such as local community, family or work. These hidden drives are further complicated by the fact that they are often unknown to the individual, a problem featured in both the study of tourism (Dann, 1981; Sharpley, 2018) and sport (Roberts, 1992). Equally the same applies for sport tourist motives, with Kurtzman and Zauhar (2005: 21) noting that sport tourists often make decisions '…without truly being aware of the subtle or hidden forces shaping or attracting their sport destination selection'. This, of course, creates some interesting methodological decisions for those researching in motivation, especially concerning what data to obtain and why, as well as what method(s) to choose.

Sport tourism-related studies that have considered underlying motives are relatively few – though some have considered the deeper antecedent roots to nostalgia, such as feelings of alienation in the present and uncertainty of the future (Gammon & Ramshaw, 2013), whilst others have commented on the desire for adventure-based tourism stemming from existential anxieties and the quest for meaningful life experiences (Beedie, 2013). Whilst hidden motives are undoubtedly problematic to identify, they can reveal potentially important reasons for what draws individuals to specific experiences, all of which have implications for both providers and participants of sport tourism episodes. However, there remains hesitation as to how much emphasis should be placed upon motives in predicting sport tourist behaviours as motives can be multi-dimensional, transitory and change during a trip (Weed & Bull, 2009). Nevertheless, this should not detract from the fact that individuals' motives undeniably influence expectations, which in turn shapes the final experience (Gnoth, 1997).

Activity

On a very basic level, sport tourism is about directly and/or indirectly engaging in sport as a tourist. Some have suggested (Hall, 1992; Standeven & De Knop, 1998) that the nature of such engagement is either passive or active, distinguishing between those who physically take part in sport and those who watch sport or visit sport-related attractions. However, Weed (2005) suggests that, especially in the case of supporters, the term *passive* may overlook the active engagement that many fans display when watching their teams. In this case, Weed (2005) proposes that the sport is experienced *vicariously* rather than passively and that the same could be applied to those who visit sport attractions, where objects, sites or sights trigger imagined activities, real or otherwise (see Gammon, 2002).

Active sport tourist experiences are deeply rooted in the physical elements of whatever sport is being played and, therefore, have been explained in kinaesthetic and embodied terms connected to play and space (Geffroy, 2017). Yet there is still a lack of clarity and agreement that explains how the experience of sport alters when in the role of a tourist. Whilst it was suggested above that the experience of tourism potentially helps individuals to be less distracted by the concerns and distractions of home, it does not account for the possibility that unfamiliar places offer their own distractions. Nevertheless, for the recreational active sport tourist, the combination of tourism and sport-related experiences can generate a sense of permissiveness that accentuates feelings of freedom and enjoyment. This draws attention to the enabling qualities that tourism environments can provide for many activities – not just sport (Gammon, 2015).

Key components of sport tourist experiences

In contrast to this perspective, Cherrington, Black and Tiller (2020) found that the environment is not always considered in such positive terms. Their ethnographic study of ultramarathons revealed that the powerful natural environment was considered as something to endure and overcome, which, in turn, brought about feelings of fragility and mortality.

Experiences of activity as a sport event tourist differs in that the interaction with the sport is vicarious and is very much dependent upon the importance of the result and the level of fandom (Wann, Melnick, Russell & Pease, 2001). Similarly, the extent that the experience of the activity varies as a tourist is yet unknown, as is the impact of the result on the image of the destination and resulting intention to revisit. However, it is likely that fans and spectators will, at the very least, experience a similar range of emotions that home fans encounter. But sports events do not just attract fans and spectators. An additional group that is often not considered in event tourism are the officials working at the events and those working for the media. In these cases, it is likely that the experiences will comprise feelings related to both work and leisure. The term *bleisure* has been proffered (Lichy & McLeay, 2018) to describe situations where travel incorporates both business and leisure, though studies in this area tend to separate the culminating experiences rather than conflating them. Volunteers too will often qualify as sport tourists, though it appears that their experiences are predominantly focused upon their sport-related responsibilities with tourism being only a minor secondary consideration (Jarvis & Blank, 2011).

The experiences of activities encountered at sport attractions, such has museums and halls of fame, tend to occur mnemonically through the sites, objects and images encountered within and around them (Gammon & Fear, 2005). They will often generate reflections and remembrances of when visitors played a particular sport or when they watched a specific game or particular player. Furthermore, historic attractions will often stimulate imagined activities and events that pre-date the memories of the visitors, spawning nostalgic reflections, which are more learned than lived (Fairley & Gammon, 2005).

Conclusion

As indicated throughout this chapter, sport tourist experiences are many and varied, and are influenced by numerous personal, social, cultural and environmental factors. To assume that it is simply a culmination of sport and tourism experiences is as misleading as it is inaccurate. The influence of the combined internal and external variables alluded to throughout this discussion produce innumerable experiences that will differ from one person to another. It is, therefore conceivable that two individuals engaging in identical sport tourism activities will encounter quite different experiences. Furthermore, it is equally possible for an individual to face inconsistent experiences when repeating the same activity.

As is the case for all sport and tourism episodes, to identify the myriad influences that in some way impact upon the resulting experience will almost certainly obfuscate an already complex and contentious area of investigation and debate. Consequently, in an attempt to simplify future research, four key experiential components have been proposed: place, authenticity, motivation and activity. Each of these components are offered as broad umbrella terms that contain further influencing factors (that can be placed in more than one of the components) that have been eluded to within this brief summary. For example, personality may have a bearing on individual sport tourist choices (motivation), which, in turn, could provide situations that enable more authentic (authenticity) behaviours and experiences. The key components themselves unquestionably interact too, which leads to very specific experiences, though determining exactly how and in what ways requires further investigation and research.

Over the past 30 years, much emphasis has rightly been placed on the economic impacts of sport tourism to both specific destinations and national economies. And whilst such research is vital in determining the potential global worth of sport tourism, it has drawn attention away from the deeply personal value(s) that sport tourism has upon those that experience it. As a result, acknowledging the significance of the experiential components by those providing sport tourism experiences can lead to more sensitively considered product designs and delivery.

References

Aicher, T. and Brenner, J. (2015) Individuals' motivation to participate in sport tourism: A self-determination theory perspective. *International Journal of Sport Management, Recreation and Tourism*, 18, 56–81.

Anthony, D. (1966) *Sport and Tourism*. CCPR/ICSPE, Bureau for Public Relations.

Beedie, P. (2013) Playing the great outdoors: Risk and adventure activities in the twenty-first century. In S. Elkington and S. Gammon (Eds.), *Contemporary Perspectives in Leisure: Meanings, Motives and Life-Long Learning*. Abingdon: Routledge, pp. 79–92.

Berryman, J. W. (1973) Sport history as social history? *Quest*, 20(1), 65–73.

Boorstin, D. (1964) *The Image: A Guide to Pseudo-Events in America*. New York: Harper and Row.

Calder, B. J. and Staw, B. (1976) Self-perception of intrinsic and extrinsic motivation. *Journal of Personality and Social Psychology*, 31(4), 599–605.

Carron, A. V., Loughhead, T. M. and Bray, S. R. (2005) The home advantage in sport competitions: Courneya and Carron's (1992) conceptual framework a decade later. *Journal of Sports Sciences*, 3(4), 395–417.

Cherrington, J., Black, J. and Tiller, N. (2020) Running away from the taskscape: Ultramarathon as 'dark ecology' *Annals of Leisure Research*, 23(2), 243–263.

Clancy, R. B., Herring, M. P., MacIntyre, T. E. and Campbell, M. J. (2016) A review of competitive sport motivation research. *Psychology of Sport and Exercise*, 27, 232–242.

Cohen, E. (1972) Toward a sociology of international tourism. *Social Research*, 39, 164–182.

Cohen, E. (1979) A phenomenology of tourist experiences. *Sociology*, 13(2), 178–201.

Couldry, N. (1998) The view from inside the 'simulacrum': Visitors' tales from the set of Coronation Street. *Leisure Studies*, 17(2), 94–107.

Courneya, K. S. and Carron, A. V. (1992) The home advantage in sport competition: A literature review. *Journal of Sport and Exercise Psychology*, 14, 13–27.

Dann, G. (1981) Tourist motivation: An appraisal. *Annals of Tourism Research*, 8(2), 187–219.

Downward, P. (2005) Critical (realist) reflection on policy and management research in sport, tourism and sports tourism. *European Sport Management Quarterly*, 5(3), 302–322.

Fairley, S. and Gammon, S. (2005) Something lived, something learned: Nostalgia's expanding role in sport tourism. *The Journal of Sport in Society: Cultures, Commerce, Media, Politics*, 8(2), 182–197.

Fairley, S. (2003) In search of relived social experience: Group-based nostalgia sport tourism. *Journal of Sport Management*, 17(3), 284–304.

Gammon, S and Fear, V. (2005) Stadia tours and the power of backstage. *The Journal of Sport Tourism*, 10(4), 243–252.

Gammon, S. (2002) Fantasy, nostalgia and the pursuit of what never was. In S. Gammon and J. Kurtzman (Eds.), *Sport Tourism: Principles and Practice*. Eastbourne: LSA Publication, 76, pp. 61–71.

Gammon, S. (2004) Secular pilgrimage and sport tourism. In B. Ritchie and D. Adair (Eds.), *Sport Tourism: Interrelationships, Impacts and Issues*. Clevedon: Channel View Publications, pp. 40–45.

Gammon, S. (2011) 'Sporting' new attractions? The commodification of the sleeping stadium. In R. Sharpley and P. Stone (Eds.), *Tourism Experiences: Contemporary Perspectives*. London: Routledge, pp. 115–126.

Gammon, S. (2015) Sport tourism finding its place? In S. Elkington and S. Gammon (Eds.), *Landscapes of Leisure: Space, Place and Identities*. London: Palgrave Macmillan, pp. 110–123.

Gammon, S. (2020) Sports events: Typologies, people and place. In S. Page and J. Connell (Eds.), *The Routledge Handbook of Events*, 2nd Edn. Abingdon: Routledge, pp. 104–119.

Gammon, S. and Ramshaw, G. (2013) Nostalgia and sport. In A. Fyall, A. and B. Garrod (Eds.), *Contemporary Cases in Sport*. London: Goodfellow Publishers, pp. 201–219.

Gammon, S. and Robinson, T. (1997) Sport and tourism: A conceptual framework. *Journal of Sport Tourism*, 4(3), 11–18.

Gammon, S. and Robinson, T. (2003) Sport and tourism: A conceptual framework. *Journal of Sport and Tourism*, 8(1), 21–26.

Gammon, S., Ramshaw, G. and Wright R. (2017) Theory in sport tourism: Some critical reflections. *Journal of Sport and Tourism*, 21(2), 69–74.

Geffroy, V. (2017) 'Playing with space': A conceptual basis for investigating active sport tourism practices. *Journal of Sport and Tourism*, 21(2), 95–113.

Gibson, H. (1998) Sport tourism: A critical analysis of research. *Sport Management Review*, 1, 45–76.

Gibson, H. (2005a) Towards an understanding of 'why sport tourists do what they do'. *Sport in Society*, 8(2), 198–217.

Gibson, H. (2005b) Sport tourism: Concepts and theories. An introduction. *Sport in Society. Cultures, Commerce, Media, Politics*, 1(2), 133–141.

Gibson, H. and Pennington-Gray, L. (2005) Insights from role theory: Understanding golf tourism. *European Sport Management Quarterly*, 5(4), 443–468.

Gibson, H., Willming, C. and Holdnak, A. (2002) 'We're Gators … Not just Gator fans': Serious leisure and University of Florida football. *Journal of Leisure Research*, 34(4), 397–425.

Giulianotti, R. (2005) *Sport: A Critical Sociology*. Cambridge: Polity Press

Glyptis, S. (1982) *Sport and Tourism in Western Europe*. London: British Travel Education Trust.

Gnoth, J. (1997) Tourism motivation and expectation formation. *Annals of Tourism Research*, 24(2), 283–304.

Griffith, L. M. (2013) Apprenticeship pilgrims and the acquisition of legitimacy. *Journal of Sport and Tourism*, 18(1), 1–15.

Guttmann, A. (1981) Sports spectators from antiquity to the Renaissance. *Journal of Sport History*, (8)2, 5–27.

Hall, C. M. (1992) Adventure, sport and health. In C. M. Hall and B. Weiler (Eds.), *Special Interest Tourism*. London: Belhaven Press, pp. 141–158.

Heitmann, S. (2011) Authenticity in tourism. In P. Robinson, S. Heitmann and P. Dieke (Eds.), *Research Themes for Tourism*. Wallingford: CABI, pp. 45–58.

Higham, J. and Hinch, T. (2009) *Sport and Tourism: Globalization, Mobility and Identity*. London: Butterworth-Heinemann.

Higham, J. and Hinch, T. (2018) *Sport Tourism Development*. Bristol: Channel View Publications.

Hinch, T. and Higham, J. (2005) Sport tourism and authenticity. *European Sport Management Quarterly*, 5(3), 243–256.

Hudson, S. and Hudson, L. (2010) *Golf Tourism*. Oxford: Goodfellow Publishers Limited.

Huggins, M. (2013) Sport, tourism and history: Current historiography and future prospects. *Journal of Tourism History*, 5(2), 107–130.

Hurych, E. (2017) Authenticity in the perspective of sport tourism: Some selected examples. *Physical Culture and Sport. Studies and Research*, 73(1), 44–53

Jarvie, G. (2012) *Sport, Culture and Society: An Introduction*. Abingdon: Routledge.

Jarvis, N. and Blank, C. (2011) The importance of tourism motivations among sport event volunteers at the 2007 World Artistic Gymnastics Championships, Stuttgart, Germany. *Journal of Sport and Tourism*, 16(2), 129–147.

Kelly, J. (1983) *Leisure Identities and Interactions*. London: George Allen and Unwin.

Konstantinos, A., Charalambos, T. and Grouios, G. (2002) Perceived constraints on recreational sport participation: Investigating their relationship with intrinsic motivation, extrinsic motivation and amotivation. *Journal of Leisure Research*, 34(3), 233–252.

Kulczycki, C. and Hyatt, C (2007) Expanding the conceptualization of nostalgia sport tourism: Lessons learned from fans left behind after sport franchise relocation. In S. Gammon and G. Ramshaw (Eds.), *Heritage, Sport and Tourism: Sporting Pasts – Tourist Futures*. London: Routledge, pp. 53–73.

Kurtzman, J. (1995) Sports tourism categories revisited. *Journal of Sport Tourism*, 2(3), 6–11.

Kurtzman, J. and Zauhar, J. (1997) A wave in time – the sports tourism phenomena. *Journal of Sport Tourism*, 4(2), 7–24.

Kurtzman, J. and Zauhar, J. (2005) Sports tourism consumer motivation. *Journal of Sport Tourism*, 10(1), 21–31.

Lamont, M. (2014) Authentication in sport tourism. *Annals of Tourism Research*, 45, 1–17.

Lau, R. (2010) Revisiting authenticity: A social realist approach. *Annals of Tourism Research*, 37(2), 478–498.

Lee, T. and Crompton, J. (1992) Measuring novelty seeking in tourism. *Annals of Tourism Research*, 19(4), 732–751.

Lichy, J and McLeay, F. (2018) Bleisure: Motivations and typologies. *Journal of Travel & Tourism Marketing*, 35(4), 517–530.

MacCannell, D. (1989) *The Tourist: A New Theory of the Leisure Class*, 2nd Edn New York: Shocken Books.

Malpas, J. (1998) Finding place: spatiality, locality, and subjectivity. In A. Light and J. Smith (Eds.), *Philosophy and Geography III: Philosophies of Place*. Lanham: Rowman & Littlefield Publishers, Inc. pp. 21–34.

Moore, K. (2012) Sport in museums and museums of sport: An overview. In J. Hill, K. Moore and J. Wood J. (Eds.), *Sport, History and Heritage: Studies in Public Representation*. Woolbridge: The Boydell Press, pp. 93–106.

Nauright, J. (1996) 'A Besieged Tribe'?: Nostalgia, white cultural identity and the role of rugby in a changing South Africa. *International Review for the Sociology of Sport*, 31(1), 69–85.

Pigeassou, C, Bui-Xuan, G. and Gleyse, J. (2003) Epistemological issues on sport tourism: Challenges for a new scientific field. *Journal of Sport Tourism*, 8(1), 27–34.

Ramshaw, G. (2020) *Heritage and Sport: An Introduction*. Bristol: Channel View Publications.

Ramshaw, G. and Gammon, S. (2007) More than nostalgia? Exploring the heritage/sport tourism nexus. In S. Gammon and G. Ramshaw (Eds.), *Heritage, Sport and Tourism: Sporting Pasts – Tourist Futures*. London: Routledge, 9–23.

Ramshaw, G. and Gammon, S. (2010) On home ground? Twickenham stadium tours and the construction of sport heritage. *Journal of Heritage Tourism*, 5(2), 87–102.

Ramshaw, G. and Gammon, S. (forthcoming) The historicization of a heritage icon: The three ages of Oriole Park at Camden Yards. In G. Ramshaw and S. Gammon (Eds.), *Baseball and Heritage: People, Place and Promotion*. Gainesville: Florida Press.

Ramshaw, G., Gammon, S. and Tobar, F. (2019) Negotiating the cultural and economic outcomes of sport heritage attractions: The case of the National Baseball Hall of Fame. *Journal of Sport & Tourism*, 23(2–3), 79–95.

Rickly-Boyd, J. M. (2012) Lifestyle climbing: Toward existential authenticity. *Journal of Sport and Tourism*, 17(2), 85–104.

Ritchie, B., Mosedale, L. and King, J. (2001) Profiling sport tourism: The case of super12 rugby union in Canberra. *Journal of Sport and Tourism*, 6(2), 15–16.

Roberts, G. C. (Ed.) (1992) *Motivation in Sport Exercise*. Leeds: Human Kinetics.

Robinson, T. and Gammon, S. (2004) Revisiting and applying the sport tourism framework: A question of primary and secondary motives. *The Journal of Sport Tourism*, 9(3), 221–233.

Sharpley, R. (2018) *Tourism, Tourists and Society*, 5th Edn. Abingdon: Routledge.

Shipway, R. and Jones, I. (2008) The great suburban Everest: An 'insiders' perspective on experiences at the 2007 Flora London Marathon. *Journal of Sport and Tourism*, 13(1), 61–77.

Simler, K. and Hanson, R. (2018) *Hidden Motives in Everyday Life: The Elephant in the Brain*. New York: Oxford University Press.

Smith, A. (2010) The development of 'sports-city' zones and their potential value as tourism resources for urban areas. *European Planning Studies*, 18(3), 385–410.

Smith, A. and Stewart, B. (2007) The travelling fan: Understanding the mechanisms of sport fan consumption in a sport tourism setting, *Journal of Sport and Tourism*, 12(3–4), 155–181.

Smith, V. (1978) *Hosts and Guest: The Anthropology of Tourism*. Philadelphia: University of Pennsylvania Press.

Sofield, T. H. (2003) Sports tourism: From binary division to quadripartite construct. *Journal of Sport Tourism*, 8(3), 144–165.

Standeven, J. and De Knop, P. (1998) *Sport Tourism*. Leeds: Human Kinetics.

Turner, V. (1973) The centre out there: The pilgrim's goal. *History of Religions*, 10, 191–230.

Vamplew, W. (1998) Facts and artifacts: Sports historians and sports museums. *Journal of Sport History*, 25(2), 268–282.

Van Rheenen, D., Cernaianu, S. and Sobry, C. (2017) Defining sport tourism: A content analysis of an evolving epistemology. *Journal of Sport and Tourism*, 21(3), 75–95.

Wang, N. (1999) Rethinking authenticity in tourism experience. *Annals of Tourism Research*, 26(2), 349–370.

Key components of sport tourist experiences

Wann, D., Melnick, M., Russell, G and Pease, D. (2001) *Sport Fans: The Psychology and Social Impact of Spectators*. London: Routledge.

Waterman, A. S. (1993) Two conceptions of happiness: Contrasts of personal expressiveness (eudaimonia) and hedonic enjoyment. *Journal of Personality and Social Psychology*, 64(4), 678–691.

Weed, M. (2002) Football hooligans as undesirable sports tourists: Some meta analytical speculations. In S. Gammon and J. Kurtzman (Eds.), *Sport Tourism: Principles and Practice*, Eastbourne: LSA publications, pp. 35–52.

Weed, M. (2005) Sports tourism theory and method: Concepts, issues and epistemologies. *European Sport Management Quarterly*, 5(3), 229–242.

Weed, M. and Bull, C. (2009) *Sports Tourism: Participants, Policy and Providers*. Oxford: Butterworth-Heinemann.

Wood, J. (2005) Olympic opportunities: Realizing the value of sports heritage for tourism in the UK. *The Journal of Sport and Tourism*, 10(4), 307–321.

31

PHOTOGRAPHY AND THE TOURIST EXPERIENCE

From cameras to smartphones

Richard Sharpley

Introduction

Tourism, according to Urry (2002), is motivated by the opportunity to 'gaze' on people, places and attractions that are 'out of the ordinary' (Urry, 2002: 1). What tourists choose to gaze upon may be determined by images they have seen in newspapers, promotional materials, guidebooks or, in this digital age, on the Internet but, for Urry, the 'tourist gaze' essentially defines the tourist experience. And of course, the visual consumption of tourist places is not limited to simply gazing on (and remembering) sites and attractions; since sightseeing first emerged as a social practice (Adler, 1989), tourists have not only gazed on places but also sought to record them materially. Initially, this was in the form of paintings or drawings (Taylor, 1994) but, following its invention in the early nineteenth century, photography has become virtually synonymous with tourism. 'Although people have for centuries engaged in various forms of tourism... Louis Daguerre's invention of photography in 1839 virtually co-incided with Thomas Cook's first organized tour in 1841, an event that for many represented the beginning of modern mass tourism' (Li, Sharpley & Gammon, 2017: 1). Since then, the histories of tourism and photography have been intertwined (Teymur, 1993: 6) or, as Belk and Yeh (2011: 345) observe, 'the emergence of mass tourism and popular photography owe a great deal to one another'. Consequently, tourism and photography go hand in hand – 'to be a tourist... is to be, almost by necessity, a photographer' (Markwell, 1997: 131).

Putting it more succinctly, photography has always been fundamental to the tourist experience; 'tourism and photography are modern twins' (Larsen, 2006: 241). And unsurprisingly, the relationship between these 'twins' has long attracted academic attention, although it was the cultural commentator Susan Sontag who first explored this relationship in her seminal work *On Photography* (Sontag, 1977). Arguing that photography more generally subsumes reality into a world of images, she suggested that tourists in particular are complicit in this process; not only do they take photographs compulsively as necessary evidence of their holiday experience but also, implicitly, the purpose of tourism becomes the collection of photographic images. In other words, for Sontag, the distinction between an experience (touristic or otherwise) and material images of that experience dissolves in the social practice of photography; 'Ultimately, having an experience becomes identical with taking a photograph of it... Today everything exists to end in a photograph' (Sontag, 1977: 24).

438

DOI: 10.4324/9781003219866-35

Photography and the tourist experience

As discussed shortly, Sontag's work provided the foundation for much of the subsequent academic study of the tourism–photography relationship (and, as this chapter will go on to suggest, remains relevant today), not least contributing much to the development of Urry's (2002) concept of the tourist gaze. The important point here, however, is that the relationship between tourism and photography is now understood as more complex and dynamic than initially proposed by Sontag. Certainly, at the time she was writing, the nature of tourism, the more general significance of photography as a social practice (Bourdieu, 1996) – that is, the recording of non-ordinary or special social events – and, indeed, the technological parameters of photography were such that the tourist experience was defined deterministically by prevailing tourist photographic practices. Typically, for example, a relatively small number of photographs of places visited, and of tourists themselves in those places as a record or proof of being there, would be captured; these would then be sent for processing and printing, with the anticipation and subsequent ritual viewing of the photographs (and the compilation of the photo album) being an intrinsic element of the tourist experience.

Since then, not only has it been argued that tourists have come to play a more proactive, performative role in their photographic practices (Haldrup & Larsen, 2010; Larsen, 2005; Scarles, 2009; Stylianou-Lambert, 2012) but also, of specific relevance to this chapter, advances in information and communication technology and, in particular, the advent and affordances of the smartphone have fundamentally transformed the practice of tourist photography and its significance to the tourist experience. Indeed, as this chapter will propose, the almost universal use of the smartphone by tourists for capturing and sharing photographs (which is not to deny the continuing popularity of digital cameras, whether compact or single lens reflex (SLR) with interchangeable lenses, among many tourists) arguably challenges traditional understandings of the spatial and temporal meaning of tourism – that is, the experience of out-of-the-ordinary time and place. Before doing so, however, it first briefly reviews the more general debates surrounding the contribution of photography to the tourist experience, in particular the extent to which tourists adopt either a passive, reproductive role in selecting what to gaze on and photograph or a more active, participatory or productive role.

Tourist photography: competing perspectives

As observed in the introduction to this chapter – and by most commentators on the topic of tourist photography – photography has, for as long as it has existed, been integral to the tourist experience; 'taking photographs is an emblematic tourist practice; it is almost unthinkable to travel for pleasure without bringing the light-weight camera along and returning home without snapshot memories' (Haldrup & Larsen, 2003: 24). However, tourist photography cannot be thought of in simple, practical terms as a tourist just 'capturing a moment' or, in a sense, creating personal souvenirs for later consumption. Certainly, a photograph is, on the one hand, 'an automatic record through the mediation of light of a given event' (Berger, 2013: 19); the camera records what it 'sees' at a particular moment, the determining factor being not what is being photographed but the moment at which the photograph is taken. On the other hand, however, a camera is an unthinking 'instrument of recording' (Price, 1994: 4) and, therefore, the camera records but the photographer chooses what to record – or what not to record (Wright & Sharpley, 2018). Hence, the significance of a photograph lies in the fact that it records something that, for the photographer, is worth recording (Berger, 2013: 18). The questions then are: what is it that renders something, from the tourist's perspective, worth recording? And, what factors determine how that something is recorded?

Putting it another way, the relationship between photography and tourism is and always has been complex, reflecting Chalfen's (1979: 436) suggestion that both tourism and photography are 'kinds of social interaction'. The practice of tourist photography is socially (and culturally) influenced, and also represents a form of social interaction between the tourist and the places and people they are photographing; the camera mediates between the social worlds of the photographer and the photographed. And it is this complex relationship that has been the focus of academic attention, with research addressing a variety of issues, from how and why tourists take photographs and the significance of the images they produce to the potential impacts on local people as the willing (or unwilling) subjects of tourist photography (Scarles, 2013).

Principal among these issues explored in the literature is the question of why particular sites/sights or moments are selected for recording photographically and the degree of agency on the part of the tourist in making such choices. Undoubtedly, it was Sontag's (1977) ground-breaking work that stimulated wider research into this question, while Urry (2002) continued the debate by highlighting what he sees as a causal relationship between images of a place, their influence on motivating travel to that place and tourists' subsequent desire to create their own photographic records of it. As he explains:

> The objects and technologies of cameras and films have constituted the very nature of travel, as sites turn into sights, they have constructed what is worth going to 'sightsee' and what images and memories should be brought back.
>
> *(Urry, 2002: 129)*

In so doing, he alludes to an argument widely proposed in the literature that 'tourists are… passive consumers of foreign destinations who reproduce with their own photographs images they have encountered in promotional material such as guidebooks, postcards, websites, etc.' (Stylianou-Lambert, 2012: 1817). In other words, as has long been recognized, images/photographs of places are, or can be, a powerful influence on where people travel and how they view places. Not only are they fundamental to the creation of destination image (Beerli & Martín, 2004; Gallarza, Saura & García, 2002), but also they frequently define the places that tourists should visit (Markwell, 1997). In short, photographs act as 'markers' of a destination or attraction (MacCannell, 1989); they mark them out as worthy of visiting. Consequently, tourists travel to particular sites or attractions to consume not the site/sight itself, but previously seen images (or markers) of it. Additionally, they consume the site/sight by taking their own photographs, reproducing as far as possible the pictures they have already seen (Jenkins, 2003). Thus, through photography, tourists do not consume actual places or experiences but images of those places or experiences and, in that process, they verify their own anticipated experience. In so doing, they complete, as Albers and James (1988: 136) put it, 'a hermeneutic circle, which begins with the photographic appearances that advertise and anticipate a trip… and ends up with travelers certifying and sealing the very same images in their own photographic productions'. Implicitly, then, the successful completion of the hermeneutic circle provides tourists with a satisfying experience. Others, conversely, are more ambivalent about the hermeneutic circle as means of conceptualizing tourist photography (Garrod, 2008) while, from a more practical perspective, it may not always be possible, for technical or other reasons, to compete that hermeneutic circle. Certain places may be unphotographable (Garlick, 2002) in the sense that the image created by another photograph cannot be recreated. This, in turn, may result in a disappointment for the tourist.

Photography and the tourist experience

Inevitably, the 'verification' photographs that individual tourists take of a particular place may differ for, as Chalfen (1979) argues, the photographic practices of tourists vary according to their motives, expectations and touristic behaviours. Just as places are subject to interpretations that vary according to the socio-cultural background of those encountering them, so too will tourists' photographs of places be similarly determined. Hence, it is erroneous to generalize about tourists' photographic practices (Chalfen, 1979), although research has shown that even tourists who engage proactively with a destination take photographs that reveal 'ideologies of Western power and dominance' (Caton & Santos, 2008: 7). Nevertheless, it has been popularly considered that tourists seek to reproduce, through their own photographic practices, previously seen images of places and attractions. Whether or not they place themselves in their photographs by requesting others to take over the role of photographer in the production of the indisputable evidence that 'I was here' (Bell & Lyall, 2005), they are passive participants in 'the game of directed viewing' (Scarles, 2009: 478) and, in playing that game, they arguably achieve a satisfying experience.

In contrast, it has been suggested more recently that tourist photography has become a more proactive, embodied activity, reflecting the arguments that not only is tourism more generally now being performed by tourists (Bærenholdt et al., 2004) but also they are participants in the co-creation of their experiences (Prebensen & Foss, 2011; see also Chapter 40 in this volume). In other words, rather than being a passive form of consumption whereby tourists capture predetermined images of places and people, some argue that photography is becoming a performance that 'lights up the tourist experience' (Scarles, 2009: 465). Tourist photography is now 'less concerned with spectatorship and "consuming places" than with *producing* place myths, social roles, and social relationships' (Larsen, 2005: 417, emphasis in original). As Scarles (2009: 471) explains, tourist photography has not only become a 'reflexive performance [in which] only desirable or aesthetically pleasing experiences that reinforce desired experience and place narratives' are captured, but also one based on imposing imagination on reality, overlaying 'physical space with imagine space' (Scarles, 2009: 472–3) to create images that represent the lived and experienced moment, combining reality and imagination and the self and the other, when the photograph is taken.

Arguably, this more proactive, embodied engagement of tourists in their photographic practices has not only been encouraged and facilitated by the evolution of digital photography and, specifically, the smartphone. It has also, perhaps, become inevitable as the cultural significance and practice of photography more generally has been transformed by and, indeed, merged into wider contemporary social practices related to the pervasive use of information and communication technologies, central to which has been the increasingly widespread use of the smartphone. And as this chapter goes on to consider, this 'digital shift' in tourist photography has not only influenced how tourists engage in photography and the type of images they seek to capture but also the use and significance of these images – the 'selfie' is perhaps the most evident manifestation of this (Dinhopl & Gretzel, 2016; Kohn, 2018). In short, the smartphone has irrevocably changed the role of photography in tourism with commensurate implications for the nature of the tourist experience more generally. By way of introduction, the following section reviews briefly the shift in photographic technology from traditional cameras to the smartphone.

From cameras to smartphones

For more than 150 years, although it became progressively simpler, cheaper and more convenient, photography – as a social practice – remained film-based. As a result, people tended to take relatively few photographs, limited by the number of frames on a film and the costs of purchasing films and of processing and printing. Moreover, with the exception of Polaroid 'instant film' cameras that were particularly popular in the 1970s (Buse, 2010) – and which recently have enjoyed something of a nostalgic renaissance (Mullally, 2019) – a time-lag existed between taking the photograph and seeing the resultant print. As suggested earlier in this chapter, an essential element of holiday experience for many tourists was receiving, with some anticipation, the pack of prints from the processors after returning home. Hence, taking photographs was typically reserved for special occasions such as birthdays, weddings, family gatherings and, of course, holidays; the social function of photography was essentially to record special or non-ordinary events (Bourdieu, 1996).

Following the introduction of digital photography from the late 1980s onwards and latterly the smartphone-camera (the first smartphone, IBM's Simon Personal Communicator, became commercially available in the mid-1990s, but it was only in 2007 that the ubiquitous Apple iPhone was first launched), this function of photography did not disappear. Rather, it dissolved into the increasingly voluminous production of images of the everyday. That is, as digital cameras served to 'elevate otherwise ordinary objects and events to photo-worthy occurrences' (Okabe & Ito, 2003: 26), the traditional purpose of taking pictures was transformed. Originally (and ironically) developed by Kodak – the evolution of digital photography led to the company filing for bankruptcy in 2012, although it still exists today – digital cameras have over the past two decades become increasingly widely used. In particular, following the introduction of the smartphone, the taking and sharing of photographs on a variety of Web 2.0-supported social media platforms has become not only widespread but, for many people, an integral element of contemporary social life.

The popularity of smartphones with their picture-taking affordances lies in both their convenience, removing the need to carry a separate and perhaps bulky camera, and their technological functionality. Tourist-photographers are now able to take innumerable images, inspecting them instantaneously on screen and discarding/deleting (and if necessary re-taking) 'unsuccessful' pictures; the risk of disappointment no longer exists. Hence, not only has the significance of the practice of photography been transformed, with the often immediate consumption or viewing of images becoming an essential element of producing photographs, but also the tourist has much more control over the manner in which people and places are represented (Haldrup & Larsen, 2010). At the same time, the practice of photography has become playful; the shared viewing of images (usually of the self and others) on-screen contributes to group social experiences (Li, Sharpley & Gammon, 2017) while images produced by/in smartphones are now mobile. In other words, also increasingly integral to tourist smartphone photography is the practice of uploading of images onto social media sites. And it is this, along with other functions and capabilities of smartphones, that has fundamental implications for the tourist experience.

Smartphones and the tourist experience

The principal focus of this chapter is on the role and influence of photography on the tourist experience and, specifically, transformations in that experience brought about by the almost universal use of the smartphone as a means of taking photographs. It is, for example, estimated that around 1.2 trillion digital photographs were taken in 2017, with 85 percent being taken on mobile phones (eksposure, 2020). This remarkable volume of images reflects the fact that not only do people always carry their smartphones with them but also use them to take photographs of anything and everything, however trivial. In short, the opportunity to capture an image is never missed.

In addition to becoming the contemporary camera of choice, however, the smartphone offers other more functional affordances that impact more widely on the tourist experience and, therefore, deserve some consideration here.

Smartphones: functional affordances and the tourist experience

Inevitably, much academic attention has been paid over the past two decades to the consequences of advances in information and communication technology (ITC), or what might be referred to as the digital revolution, for tourism and the tourist experience (Benckendorff, Xiang & Sheldon, 2019; Buhalis, 2003; Egger & Buhalis, 2008; Navío-Marco, Ruiz-Gómez & Sevilla-Sevilla, 2018; Xiang, 2018). Much of the literature focuses on the application of ITC to the travel and tourism sector; that is, on how ITC can contribute to more effective operations in the hospitality, transport and other related sectors as well as to facilitating destination marketing and management and the development of the 'smart' destination (Jovicic, 2019; see also Chapter 45).

However, research has also increasingly focused on the functional benefits that the smartphone in particular has brought to tourists themselves and their experiences. Notably, Wang and Fesenmaier (2013) identify a number of purposes for which smartphones are used and, significantly, how they have transformed tourists' behaviour and experience, or how their feelings and sensations during the trip might be influenced by the use of their smartphones. They (2013) propose four categories of smartphone use, all mostly related to the connectivity provided through access to the Internet (hence the potential negative impact on the tourist experience if such connectivity is sporadic or unobtainable). Two of these ('facilitation' and 'information search') are functional uses that influence tourist behaviour in different ways, including:

- More time spent searching for information and planning. Travel decisions are consequently based on 'richer' knowledge and, therefore, tourists are more confident in their purchase and, hence, may have a more satisfying experience.
- Alternatively, the flexibility and ease afforded by smartphones render the tourist experience equally flexible, enhanced by the sense of freedom to 'make it up as we go along'. This flexibility, along with the enormous variety of information available, also enables people to participate in tourism more frequently, although this of course remains constrained by personal financial and temporal resources.

The two other uses of smartphones identified by Wang and Fesenmaier (2013) relate more directly to the tourist experience. First, given the multiple functions of smartphones, they are commonly and frequently used as self-entertainment devices, which, as discussed in more detail shortly, includes the taking and sharing of photographs. Hence, smartphones contribute to the hedonic aspect of the tourist experience; they are a source of entertainment and fun, contributing to a more relaxing, less stressful experience. And second, smartphones are, by definition, communication devices and it is this that, arguably has had most influence on the tourist experience, in a number of ways.

Principally, irrespective of the extent to which they use their smartphones, tourists feel more connected to the 'outside' world beyond the liminal zone that is the destination (see Chapter 7 in this volume). And this sense of connectedness adds a positive dimension to the tourist experience through, for example, being able to share novel experiences with family and friends or, indeed, hearing about what others 'back home' are doing. Tourists may also be more comfortable and relaxed knowing that they can easily be contacted if necessary. In other words, the connectivity afforded by smartphones diminishes the emotional, if not physical distance between home and the destination, an outcome that may on the one hand be beneficial but, on the other hand, may mean the tourist is never fully 'on holiday'.

Second, tourists feel more informed, more knowledgeable and, hence more empowered. Being able to familiarize themselves with the destination, to seek out the amenities and facilities that suit them best (and to avoid those that, according to the online reviews of other tourists, should be avoided), tourists feel more in control of their holiday experience. In other words, they feel less dependent on the (profit-motivated) travel organizer, though perhaps more dependent on, but also more trusting of, the on-line 'word-of-mouth' recommendations of other tourists. Indeed, research has shown generally 'that CGC [consumer-generated content] is perceived as more trustworthy when compared to content from official destination websites, travel agents, and mass media' (Filieri, Alguezaui & McLeay, 2015: 175). In addition, the availability of mobile 'augmented reality' applications contributes to their knowledge and enjoyment of sites and attractions where such application are available (Yung & Khoo-Lattimore, 2019).

Finally, and importantly, the tourist experience is enhanced by the sense of security implicit in the communication opportunities provided by smartphones. Such security may emanate simply from remaining in touch with those home while, from a more practical perspective, being able to quickly find a hotel room or a taxi (for example, using the Uber app) reduces the challenges or the sense of uncertainty when, for instance, a tourist arrives late at night in an unfamiliar city. However, the sense of security provided by smartphone ownership and use is not unique to tourism. Some years ago, the increasing incidence of the so-called 'nomophobia' (no-mo(bile) phone phobia) was identified within contemporary society (Archer, 2013). Now a recognized problematic consequence of smartphone use (Bhattacharya, Bashar, Srivastava & Singh, 2019), it refers to the increasing dependence on and addiction to smartphones to the extent that, according to Archer (2013), 40 percent of people live in fear of being without their phones.

In all likelihood, most people would recognize their own dependence on smartphones and admit to their unease if they misplace it; moreover, the extent to which smartphones intrude into everyday social life is more than evident to the casual observer. Such use of and dependence on smartphones is pervasive in most spheres of contemporary life, including tourism, and in addition to the benefits outlined above, may well impact negatively on the tourist experience. Generally, for example, Tribe and Mkono (2017) argue that the digital revolution is resulting in what they refer to as a condition of 'e-lienation' among tourists; whereas tourism was once motivated by the need to escape from the alienated, anomic condition of contemporary society and to seek meaning and reality elsewhere (MacCannell, 1989), the use of smartphones to facilitate participation in tourism may, ironically, enhance a sense of alienation.

More specifically, as Sharpley (2018) discusses, smartphone use may serve to diminish the tourist experience in a number of ways. Most importantly, the constant connectivity afforded by smartphones means that the tourist is never truly away, never truly immersed in the 'Other'; although they may be physically in the destination, they remain socially and psychologically rooted 'at home'. In addition, the traditional lure of tourism (for many) – the opportunity for adventure, discovery or serendipitous experiences – has been lost to the now fully-informed tourist who travels fully prepared. Every part of the trip can be pre-planned

Photography and the tourist experience

and pre-booked online with decisions being made on the basis of a thorough informa-tion search including tourist review sites. As such, the tourist has, in a sense, experienced their holiday before even leaving home. Moreover, the use of smartphones, and the ever-increasing number of 'apps' on offer, precludes immersed, authentic experiences. Rather, the destination is not experienced through visual or emotional engagement with it, but through technology. For example, augmented reality apps may enhance a tourist's knowledge or un-derstanding of a place, but may limit their sense of being 'in' that place.

Collectively, these outcomes support the argument that the pervasive use of smartphones by tourists has increasingly challenged a fundamental element of the tourist experience, namely, to be in an experiencing place. According to Minca (2000: 389) 'tourism is, above all, a spatial phenomenon'; it involves the movement of people from one meaningful place or to another, typically in pursuit of new, meaningful experiences. In other words, the 'very idea of a "holiday" is ... based on the opportunity to shift or change spatial context' (Minca, 2000: 390). In turn, this suggests that tourists purposefully seek out specific places in the ex-pectation of satisfying and distinctive experiences that such places promise (Suvantola, 2002) and, hence, that tourism can only be understood in terms of 'the social, cultural and psycho-logical interactions that visitors have with the place' (Jepson & Sharpley, 2015: 1159). For much of the history of the modern phenomenon of tourism, this has undoubtedly remained the case although, more recently, two transformations have served to weaken the between place and the tourist experience. First, tourist places have, in a postmodern sense, become de-differentiated from 'ordinary' places; although people still travel to places as tourists, everywhere (as opposed to 'somewhere else') has become a destination (Urry, 1994). And to return to the main emphasis of this chapter, the second transformation has been the advent of the smartphone and, in particular, its contemporary dominant role in tourist photogra-phy. As the next section now considers, the almost ubiquitous use of smartphones for both the taking and (reflecting the connectivity smartphones afford) sharing of photographs has led to a fundamental reshaping of the relationship between tourism and photography and a commensurate deconstruction of the tourist experience.

Smartphone photography and the tourist experience

The consequences of the increasing touristic use of smartphones on the nature of the nature of the experience discussed above can be summarized as a process of disconnection between the tourist and the destination or place. Specifically, the connectivity of smartphones means that although tourists are corporeally in place, psychologically or emotionally they are not. Notably, this disconnection process is amplified in particular by the use of smartphones for the taking and online sharing of photographs, not least through the increasing ubiquity of the 'selfie' (Holiday et al., 2016), a practice which is coming to define people's experiences both as tourists and more generally. As Korin (2016: 50–1) laments:

> ...the preoccupation with recording rather than the experiencing is a staple in vid-eos and photographs that plague social media sites and streams in the contemporary world... [tourists] ...are increasingly invested in producing user-centred self-executed visual narratives, frequently sacrificing an engaged participation in the situation that they work so hard to preserve.

Providing examples of tourists capturing adventurous experiences on their smartphones for instantaneous upload or attendees at music events turning their backs to the stage both to record the performance and to confirm their being there, Korin (2016) describes the perhaps more frivolous versions of a practice that can be increasingly witnessed at tourism and leisure destinations and events around the world. And it is a practice that also has a darker side as commentators increasingly consider, for example, the ethical dimensions of tourist selfies at disaster sites (Ibrahim, 2015), what Hodalska (2017: 405) refers to as 'ghoulish souvenirs providing emotional detachment', as well as the increasing incidence of serious injury or death among tourists seeking the ultimate selfie (Maddox, 2017; Weiler, Gstaettner & Scherrer, 2021). A discussion of these particular issues is beyond the scope of this chapter but, more generally, given that often significant financial and other resources are invested in the consumption of tourist experiences, Korin (2016: 51) logically goes on to ask, 'how such a seemingly contradictory practice has gained preponderance and become a dominant cultural practice'. The answer, he proposes, lies in 'nowstalgia', a contemporary culturally defined condition which encourages people, through their photographic practices, to detach themselves from present action and situations; in short, to detach themselves from being in place.

To understand the concept of 'nowstalgia', it is first necessary to briefly review that of nostalgia from which it derives. Although 'nostalgia has probably always been part of the human condition' (Gammon & Ramshaw, 2013: 201), the actual term first emerged in the late seventeenth century. Derived from the Greek words 'nostos' (meaning homecoming) and 'algos' (pain), it was coined to describe a form of homesickness so extreme that it was considered to be neurological disease (Sekikides, Wildschut & Basen, 2004: 200–1). Over the next two centuries, it became more widely seen as a condition of depression or melancholy, though often still associated with homesickness, loss or grief but, by the twentieth century it had acquired its contemporary and more positive interpretation as a form of wistful longing for happy (or happier) past times or places. In other words, nostalgia can be thought of as an arguably rose-tinted 'yearning to return to or relive a past period' (Fairley & Gammon, 2005: 183) that is, implicitly, better or more desirable than the present.

Nostalgia, then, is inextricably linked to memory; something cannot be yearned for if it is not remembered. However, this immediately raises the distinction between individual and collective memory and its association with nostalgia, with some arguing that it is only possible for people to be nostalgic about a period that they have actually lived through (Davis, 1979). Others, conversely, consider it possible to be nostalgic toward periods experienced by previous generations but maintained as a collective, if not entirely accurate – memory (Goulding, 2002). For example, it has long been suggested that contemporary rural tourism, at least in developed, industrialized nations, is in part motivated by a desire to experience 'rurality', a socially constructed, nostalgic vision of an arcadian, pre-modern countryside (Sharpley & Sharpley, 1997). Either way, the important point here is that although nostalgia is concerned with the past, the nostalgic past is becoming ever closer to the present in a world defined by rapid technological advance and socio-cultural change and a pervasive postmodern anomie that encourages people to seek identity and meaning in what might be described as a 'present-past'. As a consequence, in circumstances facilitated by contemporary technology – specifically smartphones – nostalgia is becoming replaced by 'nowstalgia'.

According to Korin (2016: 52–3), 'nowstalgia' can be defined as:

> ...the production and distribution of visual documents with potential future nostalgic value by an individual who become increasingly engaged in its documentation and sacrifices her participation in the activity or situation deemed likely memorable in a time to come.

Photography and the tourist experience

In other words, by focusing entirely on the photographing of places or events on a smart-phone and, in the particular case of 'selfies', locating the self in that recording, thereby directing the viewer (the self or another) toward the photographer, the significance of the experience lies not in the place or event but in the expectation of nostalgic feelings in the future when viewing the photograph. Putting it another way, rather than experiencing the place or event itself, the tourist–photographer experiences in the present the anticipation of nostalgic yearnings in the future to relive the place or event; they experience the process of 'nowstalgia'. And in so doing, the tourist is no longer 'in place' and their experience is no longer defined by place; rather, they become, in a sense a conduit for the experience of the place by others viewing uploaded images and for their own future nostalgic satisfaction.

Conclusion

It would be erroneous to suggest that all (smartphone-based) tourist photography is inspired by 'nowstalgic' desires. Undoubtedly, many tourists take photographs on their smartphones in the process of completing the hermeneutic circle – that is, capturing and recreating im-ages previously viewed elsewhere images and, which, in some cases, might be collated and reproduced in a physical album. Indeed, the only difference between this and traditional tourist photography is that, rather than sending the film away for printing and processing, pre-selected and collated digital images are uploaded to the website of one of the many com-panies offering printing services. Equally, not all tourists share their photographs on social media sites while on holiday. Nevertheless, the position of photography within the tourist experience has been irrevocably altered with the advent of the smartphone; de-materialized, digital images can be instantly viewed, enhanced, shared or deleted and, hence, tourist pho-tography in the digital revolution has become less about creating future memories and more about creating and sharing images as an element of the actual tourist experience.

Yet, the placing of the self in photographs, a common practice throughout the history of tourist photography but now manifested in the ubiquitous 'selfie', combined with the often instantaneous sharing of such images on social media sites – something that will inevitably become ever more widespread given the extent to which it is practiced by the younger 'digital native' generations – has had an arguably more significant influence on the tourist experience. Little has perhaps changed with regard to the link between photography and the tourist experience; to repeat Sontag's observation cited earlier in this chapter: 'Ultimately, having an experience becomes identical with taking a photograph of it... Today everything exists to end in a photograph' (Sontag, 1977: 24). However, the experience, as well as the taking of photographs of it, has changed. The recording in images of the place and the self in anticipation of nostalgic yearning not only represents a curious fusion of past and future that occurs in the present, but also denies tourists the experience of the present time and present place. In effect, the 'real' tourist experience is being lost within both the functional uses of smartphones and in particular, contemporary smartphone-based photographic practices.

References

Adler, J. (1989) Origins of sightseeing. *Annals of Tourism Research*, 16(1), 7–29.
Albers, P. and James, W. (1988) Travel photography: A methodological approach. *Annals of Tourism Research*, 15(2), 134–158.
Archer, D. (2013) Smartphone addiction. *Psychology Today*. Available at: https://www.psychology-today.com/blog/reading-between-the-headlines/201307/smartphone-addiction (Accessed 13 October 2017).

Bærenholdt, J., Haldrup, M. and Urry, J. (2004) *Performing Tourist Places.* London: Routledge.

Beerli, A. and Martín, J. (2004) Factors influencing destination image. *Annals of Tourism Research,* 31(3), 657–681.

Belk, R. and Yeh, J. (2011) Tourist photographs: Signs of self. *International Journal of Culture, Tourism and Hospitality Research,* 5(4), 345–353.

Bell, C. and Lyall, J. (2005) 'I was here': Pixilated evidence. In D. Crouch, R. Jackson and F. Thompson (Eds.), *The Media and the Tourist Imagination: Converging Cultures.* Abingdon: Routledge, pp. 135–142.

Benckendorff, P., Xiang, Z. and Sheldon, P. (2019) *Tourism Information Technology,* 3rd Edn. Wllingford: CABI.

Berger, J. (2013) *Understanding a Photograph* (edited/introduced by G. Dyer). London: Penguin Books.

Bhattacharya, S., Bashar, M. A., Srivastava, A. and Singh, A. (2019) NOMOPHOBIA: No mobile phone phobia. *Journal of Family Medicine and Primary Care,* 8(4), 1297–1300.

Bourdieu, P. (1996) *Photography: A Middle-Brow Art.* Cambridge: Polity Press.

Buhalis, D. (2003) *eTourism: Information Technology for Strategic Management.* Harlow: Pearson Education.

Buse, P. (2010) Polaroid into digital: Technology, cultural form, and the social practices of snapshot photography. *Continuum,* 24(2), 215–230.

Caton, K. and Santos, C. (2008) Closing the hermeneutic circle? Photographic encounters with the other. *Annals of Tourism Research,* 35(1), 7–26.

Chalfen, R. M. (1979) Photograph's role in tourism: Some unexplored relationships. *Annals of Tourism Research,* 6(4), 435–447.

Davis, F. (1979) *A Yearning for Yesterday: A Sociology of Nostalgia.* New York: Free Press.

Dinhopl, A. and Gretzel, U. (2016) Selfie-taking as touristic looking. *Annals of Tourism Research,* 57, 126–139.

Egger, R. an Buhalis, D. (2008) *eTourism: Case Studies.* Oxford: Butterworth Heinemann.

eksposure (2020) 11 Mobile Photography Statistics and How It's Changing Our World. *eksposure.* Available at: https://www.eksposure.com/mobile-photography-statistics/ (Accessed 4 December 2020).

Fairley, S. and Gammon, S. (2005) Something lived, something learned: Nostaglia's expanding role in sport tourism. *Sport in Society,* 8(2), 182–197.

Filieri, R., Alguezaui, S. and McLeay, F. (2015) Why do travelers trust TripAdvisor? Antecedents of trust towards consumer-generated media and its influence on recommendation adoption and word of mouth. *Tourism Management,* 51, 174–185.

Gallarza, M., Saura, I. G. and Garcia, H. C. (2002) Destination image: Towards a conceptual framework. *Annals of Tourism Research,* 29(1), 56–78.

Gammon, S. and Ramshaw, G. (2013) Nostalgia and sport. In B. Garrod and A. Fyall (Eds.), *Contemporary Cases in Sport.* Oxford: Goodfellow Publishers, pp. 201–219.

Garlick, S. (2002) Revealing the unseen: Tourism, art and photography. *Cultural Studies,* 16(2), 289–305.

Garrod, B, (2008) Understanding the relationship between tourism destination imagery and tourist photography. *Journal of Travel Research,* 47(3), 346–358.

Goulding, C. (2002) An exploratory study of age related vicarious nostalgia and aesthetic consumption. *Advances in Consumer Research,* 29(1), 542–546.

Haldrup, M. and J. Larsen (2003) The family gaze. *Tourist Studies,* 3(1), 23–45.

Haldrup, M. and Larsen, J. (2010) *Tourism, Performance and the Everyday: Consuming the Orient.* Abingdon: Routledge.

Hodalska, M. (2017) Selfies at horror sites: Dark tourism, ghoulish souvenirs and digital narcissism. *Zeszyty Prasoznawcze,* 60(2), 405–423.

Holiday, S., Lewis, M. J., Nielsen, R., Anderson, H. D. and Elinzano, M. (2016) The selfie study: Archetypes and motivations in modern self-photography. *Visual Communication Quarterly,* 23(3), 175–187.

Ibrahim, Y. (2015) Self-representation and the disaster event: Self-imaging, morality and immortality. *Journal of Media Practice,* 16(3), 211–227.

Jenkins, O. (2003) Photography and travel brochures: The circle of representation. *Tourism Geographies,* 5(3), 305–328.

Jepson, D. and Sharpley, R. (2015) More than sense of place? Exploring the emotional dimension of rural tourism experiences. *Journal of Sustainable Tourism,* 23(8–9), 1157–1178.

Jovicic, D. (2019) From the traditional understanding of tourism destination to the smart tourism destination. *Current Issues in Tourism*, 22(3), 276–282.

Kohn, T. (2018) 'Backs' to nature: Musing on tourist selfies. In S. Gmelch and A. Kaul (Eds.), *Tourists and Tourism: A Reader*, 3rd Edn. Long Grove, IL: Waveland Press Inc., pp. 69–77.

Korin, E. (2016) Nowstalgia: Articulating future pasts through selfies and GoPro-ing, *Meiden & Zeit*, 31(4), 50–60. Available at: https://medienundzeit.at/wp-content/uploads/2017/02/MZ-2016-4-online-ed.pdf#page=52 (Accessed 14 December 2020).

Larsen, J. (2005) Families seen sightseeing: Performativity of tourist photography. *Space and Culture*, 8(4), 416–434.

Larsen, J. (2006) Geographies of tourist photography. In J. Falkheimer and A. Jansson (Eds.), *Geographies of Communication: The Spatial Turn in Media Studies*. Gothenburg: Nordicom, pp. 241–257.

Li, M., Sharpley, R. and Gammon, S. (2017) Towards an understanding of Chinese tourist photography: Evidence from the UK. *Current Issues in Tourism*, 22(5), 505–521.

MacCannell, D. (1989) *The Tourist: A New Theory of the Leisure Class*, 2nd Edn. New York: Shocken Books.

Maddox, J. (2017) 'Guns don't kill people… selfies do': Rethinking narcissism as exhibitionism in selfie-related deaths. *Critical Studies in Media Communication*, 34(3), 193–205.

Markwell, K. (1997) Dimensions of photography in a nature-based tour. *Annals of Tourism Research*, 24(1), 131–155.

Minca, C. (2000) 'The Bali Syndrome': The explosion an implosion of 'exotic' tourist spaces, *Tourism Geographies*, 2(4), 389–403.

Mullally, U. (2019) Shake it like a Polaroid picture: the return of instant photography. *Irish Times*, 5 January. Available at: https://www.irishtimes.com/culture/art-and-design/visual-art/shake-it-like-a-polaroid-picture-the-return-of-instant-photography-1.3729075 (Accessed 4 December 2020).

Navío-Marco, J., Ruiz-Gómez, L. M. and Sevilla-Sevilla, C. (2018) Progress in information technology and tourism management: 30 years on and 20 years after the internet-Revisiting Buhalis & Law's landmark study about eTourism. *Tourism Management*, 69, 460–470.

Okabe, D. and Ito, M. (2003) *Personal, Portable, Pedestrian: Mobile Phones in Japanese Life*. Cambridge: MIT Press.

Prebensen, N. K. and Foss, L. (2011) Coping and co-creating in tourist experiences. *International Journal of Tourism Research*, 13(1), 54–67.

Price, M. (1994) *The Photograph: A Strange, Confined Space*. Stanford: Stanford University Press.

Scarles, C. (2009) Becoming tourist: Renegotiating the visual in the tourist experience. *Environment and Planning D: Society and Space*, 27(3), 465–488.

Scarles, C. (2013) The ethics of tourist photography: Tourists' experiences of photographing locals in Peru. *Environment and Planning D: Society and Space*, 31(5), 897–917.

Sekikides, C, Wildschut, T. and Basen, D. (2004) Nostalgia: Conceptual issues and existential functions. In L. Greenberg, J. Koole and T. Pyszczynski, T. (Eds.), *Handbook of Experimental Existential Psychology*. New York: The Guildford Press, pp. 200–214.

Sharpley, R. (2018) *Tourism, Tourists and Society*, 5th Edn. Abingdon: Routledge.

Sharpley, R. and Sharpley, J. (1997) *Rural Tourism: An Introduction*. London: International Thomson Business Press

Sontag, S. (1977) Sontag, S. (1977) *On Photography*. London: Penguin Books.

Stylianou-Lambert, T. (2012) Tourists with cameras: Reproducing or producing? *Annals of Tourism Research*, 39(4), 1817–1838.

Suvantola, J. (2002) *Tourist Experience of Place*. Aldershot: Ashgate.

Taylor, J. (1994) *A Dream of England: Landscape, Photography and the Tourist's Imagination*. Manchester: Manchester University Press.

Teymur, N. (1993) Phototourism – or the epistemology of photography in tourism. *Tourism in Focus*, 6, pp. 6 and 16.

Tribe, J. and Mkono, M. (2017) Not such smart tourism? The concept of e-lienation. *Annals of Tourism Research*, 66, 105–115.

Urry, J. (2002) *The Tourist Gaze*, 2nd Edn. London: Sage Publications.

Urry, J. (1994) Cultural change and contemporary tourism. *Leisure Studies*, 13(4), 233–238.

Wang, D. and Fesenmaier, D. (2013) Transforming the travel experience: The use of smartphones for travel. In L. Cantoni an X. Xiang (Eds.), *Information and Communication Technologies in Tourism 2013*. Berlin/Heidelberg: Springer, pp. 58–69.

Weiler, B., Gstaettner, A. M. and Scherrer, P. (2021) Selfies to die for: A review of research on self-photography associated with injury/death in tourism and recreation. *Tourism Management Perspectives*, 37. https://doi.org/10.1016/j.tmp.2020.100778

Wright, D. and Sharpley, R. (2018) The photograph: Tourist responses to a visual interpretation of a disaster. *Tourism Recreation Research*, 43(2), 161–174.

Xiang, Z. (2018) From digitization to the age of acceleration: On information technology and tourism. *Tourism Management Perspectives*, 25, 147–150.

Yung, R. and Khoo-Lattimore, C. (2019) New realities: A systematic literature review on virtual reality and augmented reality in tourism research. *Current Issues in Tourism*, 22(17), 2056–2081.

32

ACCESSIBLE TOURIST EXPERIENCES

Marcus Hansen and Alan Fyall

Introduction

The disabled population is a critical consumer segment that is currently largely ignored or misunderstood by the tourism industry (Loi & Kong, 2017; Tchetchik, Eichhorn & Biran 2018). The World Bank (2019) estimates that 15 percent of the global population have a disability with around 190 million experiencing considerable challenges in functioning. Further, it is anticipated that by 2030, 100 million people will be living with a disability in the US alone (Tchetchik et al., 2018). Indeed, it is expected that the number of people living with a disability (PLwD) will increase to 1.2 billion by 2050 globally (World Bank, 2019). Other societal factors make such figures concerning. According to the United Nations (2015a), the number of people aged 60 or over will more than double to 2.1 billion by 2050. As a society, we are experiencing longer life expectancy, yet fertility rates are also falling, meaning that the global population is increasingly ageing (Lee & King, 2019). As an example, the percentage of the global population over 65 years old has increased from 4.1 percent in 1900 to 16 percent in 2016 (Turner & Morken, 2016). This development has, in turn, meant that ageing is today one of the greatest economic and social challenges (Duedahl, Blichfeldt & Liburd, 2020). These challenges are further exacerbated as a result of the often times accompanying age-related disabilities (Vila, Darcy & González, 2015). Indeed, PLwD and seniors make up in excess of 20 percent of the global population (Vila et al. 2015).

As a result, societies across the world are faced with significant challenges, especially with an increasing focus on accessibility and inclusion in all areas of life (Michopoulou, Darcy, Ambrose & Buhalis, 2015). Yet, a study by the European Commission (2013) found that 70 percent of those requiring accessibility had both the financial and physical capabilities to travel and that PLwD tend to take longer vacations and spend more. The links between tourism and quality of life are well documented, with it improving physical, psychological and mental health (Hartwell et al., 2018; Lee, Agarwal & Kim, 2012; Moura, Kastenholz & Pereira, 2018). Indeed, tourism has the ability of contributing positive emotions, life satisfaction and personal development (Agovino, Casaccia, Garofalo & Marchesano, 2017; Evcil, 2018; Yau, McKercher & Packer, 2004). Furthermore, tourism may also contribute to society

DOI: 10.4324/9781003219866-36

451

through a realization of social equality, social integration and the reduction of social adaptation expenses (Eichhorn, Miller & Tribe, 2013; Lee et al., 2012).

In 1948, the United Nations General Assembly recognized the right to leisure and international travel as human rights under the Universal Declaration of Human Rights (United Nations, 2015b; also McCabe & Diekmann, 2015). Although there have been debates surrounding the extent these rights encompass tourism (Breakley & Breakley, 2013), many Western nations have interpreted them as such (McCabe & Diekmann, 2015). Nevertheless, within the developed world, the rights of people with disabilities are much more clearly defined. In 2006, the United Nations' Convention on the Rights of People with Disabilities (CRPWD) recognized the rights of PLwD to access services from all areas of citizenship, including transport and the built environment (Article 9), as well as all areas of cultural life (Article 30) (Michopoulou et al., 2015). Indeed, accessibility and inclusion are critical parts of the CRPWD, with the emphasis on living independently and enabling participation within society, including leisure, sport and tourism, as well as community inclusion (Darcy & Burke, 2018).

More recently, the UN has included 'Reduced Inequalities' as one of the 17 Sustainable Development Goals (SDGs), expanding the importance of accessibility (UNWTO, 2015). Likewise, the European Disability strategy 2010–2020 recognized accessibility as one of eight areas for joint action between the EU countries under the European Disability Strategy 2010–2020 (Agovino et al., 2017). Importantly, many of these principles are captured in disability legislation, such as the Equality Act 2010 in the UK (UK, 2010) and the Americans with Disabilities Act (1990) in the US (Department of Justice, 2010; Nyanjom, Boxall & Slaven, 2018; Shaw & Veitch, 2011), which further extend the UN's CRPWD as they focus particularly on the access needs of various areas of disability, including mobility, vision, hearing, intellectual/cognitive, mental health and sensitivities. Tourism is specifically included under such legislation, with legislation prohibiting service providers, such as accommodation, visitor attractions and restaurants, from denying full and equal access to services based on an individual's disability (Card et al., 2006). Nevertheless, access issues for PLwD are well-documented within the tourism industry (Buhalis & Darcy, 2011; Mesquita & Carneira, 2016; Nyanjom et al., 2018).

Experiences are at the heart of tourism (Tussyadiah, 2014). Indeed, to remain competitive, destinations seek to create and deliver memorable experiences to their visitors (Kim & Ritchie, 2014). Yet, tourist experiences are predominantly framed as hedonic with the focus overwhelmingly on stimulating positive emotions (Sedgley et al., 2017), and barriers to full participation in tourism experiences for PLwD remain (McKercher & Darcy, 2018). Some argue that tourist activities remain a distant dream for PLwD, with social exclusion a common reality (Pagán, 2015; Sedgley, Pritchard, Morgan & Hanna, 2017). Previous studies have, for example, highlighted various barriers to full participation in tourism experiences and these are believed to be one of many reasons why PLwD tend to have lower quality tourism experiences than those of the general population (McKercher & Darcy, 2018). In fact, the benefits of tourism experiences are largely inaccessible to PLwD, despite the obvious relevance to a demographic often deprived of opportunities to develop their physical, intellectual and social capacities (Kastenholz, Eusébio & Figueiredo, 2015).

The numerous barriers to PLwD participation in tourism include physical, environmental, economic and social barriers (Agovino et al., 2017). Perhaps not surprisingly, therefore, the concept of accessible tourism has become increasingly popular and viewed with growing importance within both academia and practice (Buhalis & Darcy, 2011; Cohen, Prayag &

Accessible tourist experiences

Moital, 2014; Vila et al., 2015). Yet, in reality, access issues remain common whilst scholars and practitioners alike continue to struggle to comprehend the needs of the wider disability spectrum (Bauer, 2018). In fact, the tourism industry has arguably neglected and, indeed, excluded PLwD and their carer(s), focusing instead on the ideal tourist (Small, Darcy & Packer, 2012). As such, the need exists to design experiences with the end-user in mind and in which the service provider emphasizes with the tourist (Lam, Chan & Peters, 2020). Tussyadiah (2014) refers to this as human-centred design, whereby experiences are designed with a focus on stimuli such as senses, cognition, emotions and affect.

Accessible tourism

Accessible tourism promotes accessible services to PLwD and is an increasingly important focus-area within both academia and industry (Buhalis & Darcy, 2011; Rickly, 2018). The focus of accessible tourism is on inclusion as well as on the removal of barriers to travel for PLwD (Lam et al., 2020; McKercher & Darcy, 2018). In contrast to much medical research, accessible tourism adheres to the social model of disability, whereby it is the way in which the environment and society is organized that is considered to be disabling as opposed to it being the 'fault' of the individual (Gillovic, McIntosh, Darcy & Cockburn-Wootten, 2018; Randle & Dolnicar, 2019). The theoretical underpinnings of the social model revolve around the way in which organizations, structures, processes and practices exclude, omit, overlook or deliberately discriminate against PLwD (McKercher & Darcy, 2018; Shakespeare, Watson & Alghaib, 2017). As such, the social model of disability recognizes that impairments are an inherent part of society and, therefore, the role of society is to enable full participation as opposed to disable people (Randle & Dolnicar, 2019). Hence, the model focuses on identifying barriers to participation and on either eliminating them or at least minimizing their impact (Randle & Dolnicar, 2019). By removing barriers to access to participation that effectively limit the functioning of PLwD, quality of life and well-being is improved (McIntosh, 2020). In fact, it is widely believed that tourist experiences may benefit socially marginalized groups of people by improving self-worth and thereby quality of life and well-being (McCabe, 2009; Sedgley et al., 2017).

Nevertheless, barriers to travel and participation remain and discourage people with disabilities from engaging in tourism (Bauer, 2018; Connell & Page, 2019a; McKercher & Darcy, 2018). Moreover, hostile attitudes towards people with disability are not uncommon and are often founded in a lack of awareness, education and training towards disability (McKercher & Darcy, 2018; Rickly, Halpern, McCabe & Hansen, 2020). However, somewhat worryingly, it has also been argued that owing to the growing importance of superior customer experience, managers in hospitality are wary of adopting positive attitudes towards PLwD over concerns of customer incompatibility (Tchetchik et al., 2018).

Accessible tourism is, at times, referred to as 'disabled tourism', 'disability tourism', 'easy-access tourism', 'barrier-free tourism', 'inclusive tourism' and 'universal tourism' (Lam et al., 2020). Critical to these concepts is the desire for accessible and inclusive experiences, meaning the removal of barriers for PLwD is key (Agovino et al., 2017; Lam et al., 2020). In their seminal work, Buhalis and Darcy (2011:10) defined accessible tourism as:

> a form of tourism [...] that enables people with access requirements, including mobility, vision, hearing and cognitive dimensions of access, to function independently and with equity and dignity through the delivery of universally designed tourism products, services and environments.

Accessibility is considered to be contingent on the nexus between legislation and the built environment (Bohdanowicz-Godfrey, Zientara & Bąk, 2019). In fact, in many Western countries, service providers have a legal responsibility to comply with disability legislation, such as that in the UK and the US referred to above. Nevertheless, it is widely believed that the legislation is outdated as it typically only covers major disabilities, meaning the wider and growing disability spectrum, such as hidden and visual disabilities, are often disregarded (Devile & Kastenholz, 2018; Mesquita & Carneiro, 2016; Rickly, 2018). Or, as Randle and Dolnicar (2019) discovered, the Americans with Disabilities Act (1990) in the US effectively contained inadvertent loopholes owing to the growth of the sharing economy and organizations such as Airbnb. In that case, it was found that hosts with five rooms or less and where the owner resides at the property were able to disregard the legislation. In addition, previous research indicates that tourism service providers fail to provide accessible services to people with disabilities through an apparent lack of education and awareness (Connell & Page, 2019a; Rickly et al., 2020). As an example, service providers within destinations often assume that by being wheelchair accessible, they are naturally accessible to all disabilities (Kong & Loi, 2017). Yet, this is a particularly complex demographic, including many types and levels of disabilities, meaning a one-size-fits-all approach is highly ineffective (Mckercher & Darcy, 2018). However, this is not just an issue for immediate tourism stakeholders as it seemingly reflects systemic issues across society, with architects, designers and planners also tending to reduce disability to medical and stereotypical notions, thereby disregarding the diversity and complexity of disability (Rebernik, Favero & Bahillo, 2020).

However, PLwD have a desire to travel. Indeed, their desire to participate in tourism experiences is considered the same as that of the non-disabled (Tutuncu, 2017). Yet, the literature on accessible tourism experiences, particularly with regard to participation, is still in its early stages (Devile & Kastenholz, 2018). Nevertheless, this demographic is considered an underdeveloped market for the tourism industry, meaning destinations have an opportunity to seize a potential competitive advantage as well as an avenue to combat seasonality (Lee & King, 2019; Visit Scotland, 2019). As an example, the Purple Pound, the spending power of PLwD in the UK, is estimated to be worth over £249 billion and contributes £12bn to tourism in England (Visit England, 2016; We Are Purple, 2019). Furthermore, research also indicates that three out of four customers living with a disability have moved their business elsewhere due to disability awareness of businesses (Visit Scotland, 2019). Thus, it is incredibly important and relevant to understand the travel behaviours of PLwD and the factors that influence their experience, such as the barriers to full participation (Devile & Kastenholz, 2018). This is particularly so with regard to the development of accessible destinations and tourist products, especially with the goal of creating a civil society where PLwD are treated equally compared with others (Connell & Page, 2019a; Devile & Kastenholz, 2018). The need has been recognized for a change in attitude to facilitate, encourage and support accessible tourism experiences, with the understanding that these can be beneficial to PLwD's personal development, well-being, improving the ability to cope with stress, improve health conditions, self-esteem, satisfaction and social inclusion (Devile & Kastenholz, 2018; Tutuncu, 2017).

Nevertheless, research has revealed that the tourism industry itself has struggled to consider, and indeed understand, the significance of this emerging demographic as a tourist market and its implications, with a disregard towards the wider disability spectrum beyond the wheelchair with regard to the needs of PLwD (Tchetchik et al., 2018). This is seemingly down to a question of education and awareness (Nyanjom et al., 2018). Indeed, delivering a satisfactory experience for PLwD at a destination level becomes even more complex

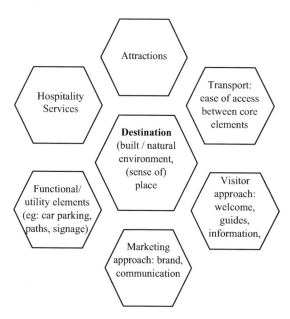

Figure 32.1 Destination accessibility touchpoints
Source: Adapted from Connell and Page (2019a).

owing to the fragmented nature of the destination, given that such an experience involves various different entities that all need to be accessible to PLwD and their carer(s) (Nyanjom et al., 2018). These include, amongst others, accessible transportation, hospitality facilities and visitor attractions (Vila et al., 2015). Connell and Page (2019a) further outline the many touchpoints within the destination influencing accessibility and inclusivity. These are summarized below (see Figure 32.1). Evidently, delivering accessible tourist experiences is a major challenge.

Barriers and constraints to tourism

Key to accessible tourism is the design and delivery of experiences that adhere to its core values: independence, equality and dignity (Buhalis & Darcy, 2011). However, many barriers remain still today, such as attitudinal, physical and informational barriers, preventing this from becoming the reality (Lam et al., 2020; Randle & Dolnicar, 2019). The removal of barriers is a complex and challenging issue owing to heterogeneous access requirements of PLwD. Furthermore, McKercher and Darcy (2018) found that the literature tends to focus on physical and mobility disabilities, thereby neglecting other equally important fields, such as vision and hearing, families with children and intellectual disabilities. In this regard, design thinking, which is a process to solve challenges for the creation of tourism experience and successful tourism development (Sheldon, Fesenmaier & Xiang, 2017), would be able to drive innovative technological solutions to fulfil the access requirement of PLwD.

PLwD are confronted with various barriers and constraints to participation when engaging in tourism experiences (Lee et al., 2012). The literature on constraints draws on leisure constraints theory and focuses on why individuals are unable to participate in travel or why travel preferences are changed as a result of the constraints (Crawford & Godbey, 1987; Jackson, Crawford & Godbey, 1993; Karl, Bauer, Ritchie & Passauer, 2020). Smith's (1987) seminal work categorizes barriers that PLwD experienced whilst travelling. He developed three categories: intrinsic (relating to a person's physical, cognitive or psychological state), environment (relating to infrastructure in place, such as buildings and transportation) and interactive (relating to the barriers disrupting the interaction of people and society). However, constraints do not necessarily prevent travel, but may force the tourist to adapt their travel behaviour from what it would be in the absence of constraints (Karl et al., 2020). This is referred to as the constraints negotiation model (Ying et al., 2020).

Crawford and Godbey (1987) categorized barriers to travel as intrapersonal, interpersonal and structural. Intrapersonal barriers revolve around the individual's psychological and physical characteristics, such as sensory impairment, motivation to participate and lack of sufficient knowledge (Huber, Milne & Hyde, 2018; Karl et al., 2020; Lam et al., 2020). Interpersonal barriers include barriers to interacting with service providers, travel companions and strangers during travelling (Lam et al., 2020). Finally, structural barriers revolve around the infrastructure of the destination, getting to and from the destination, but also financial resources (Lam et al., 2020). McKercher and Chen (2015) later added a fourth category, namely lack of interest; no amount of barrier removal would stimulate the desire to travel, if the PLwD simply has no interest in travel. The categories are organized into a hierarchy with intrapersonal barriers at the bottom, meaning PLwD have to negotiate their way sequentially through the constraints successfully to participate in tourist experiences (Crawford, Jackson & Godbey, 1991).

Key to this argument is the understanding that whilst constraints may discourage participation, the motivation to travel may also break down such barriers (Karl et al., 2020). This may be achieved through coping strategies. Jackson and Rucks (1995), for example, identified two types of coping strategies: cognitive and behavioural. On the one hand, cognitive strategies relate to changes in cognition to cope with cognitive dissonance to accommodate leisure needs (Ying et al., 2021). On the other hand, behavioural strategies revolve around changes made to travel behaviour, such as rescheduling of activities and changes to the time or frequency of participation (Ying et al., 2020). Previous studies indicate that the likelihood of PLwD attempting to negotiate through barriers depends on variables such as motivation, attitudes and perceived benefits (Lyu, 2012; Ying et al., 2020). McKercher and Darcy's (2018) hierarchical and interactive framework, adapted and simplified in Figure 32.2 below, provides further structure to our understanding of the barriers that are experienced by PLwD. As in the previously discussed frameworks, this too is sequential although barriers at one level may influence barriers at another. In addition, it highlights the increasing specificity of needs by categorizing barriers that impact on influencing those barriers that are unique to PLwD, taking into account the dynamicity of disability (Mckercher & Darcy, 2018).

However, barriers to participation can also lead to a state of learned helplessness. This is not, perhaps, surprising; the barriers they face, societal overprotection and even levels of enforced dependency may result in PLwD eventually succumbing to a lack of confidence and demonstrating 'expected' behaviours as proposed in the theory of learned helplessness (Bauer, 2018). Although only limited research has been undertaken into the incidence of learned helplessness in the context of tourist experiences (Lee et al., 2012; Wen, Huang & Goh, 2020), it does provide a deeper understanding of why PLwD may opt out of travel and tourism, particularly once we have understood the constraints to participation experienced by PLwD. Seligman (1975: 33), who developed the theory, defined it as 'an effect resulting from the uncontrollability of aversive events'. Essentially, as PLwD continue to experience barriers and challenges to participation in tourist experiences, they will inevitably expect negative outcomes, meaning non-participation, and therefore stop attempting further

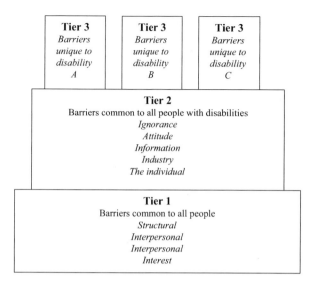

Figure 32.2 Hierarchy of barriers to travel by people with disabilities
Source: Adapted from McKercher and Darcy (2018).

participation in the future (Lee et al., 2012). Likewise, Smith (1987) argued that as a consequence of the impact of the barriers that PLwD experience, their decision-making process is influenced by a variety of personal characteristics, including self-helplessness. Barriers to participation are, nevertheless, experienced differently amongst PLwD, because they do not comprise a homogenous group (Vila et al., 2015). To further explore how these barriers are experienced by PLwD, impairments can be categorized into three groups: physical/mobility impairments, sensory impairments and cognitive impairments (Domínguez, Fraiz & Alén, 2013). The following sections will provide some examples of barriers that PLwD might encounter within the tourist experience.

Travelling with a physical impairment

Physical and mobility impairments include those that lead to physical mobility restrictions affecting limbs, back and/or neck. Such impairments can cause difficulty with physical and motor tasks, independent movement and performing tasks in daily life (Buhalis & Darcy, 2011; Domínguez, Fraiz & Alén, 2013). People who use mobility devices, such as wheelchairs, experience many access issues including getting in and out of transportation vehicles and disembarking at ports as well as when using hospitality services (Tutuncu, 2017). Issues surrounding travelling in a wheelchair at airports and on aeroplanes in particular are well documented (Bauer, 2018; Poria, Reichel & Brandt, 2011). The sheer size of some airports makes them particularly inaccessible to people with mobility impairments, with challenges including long waits in uncomfortable temporary wheelchairs as well as long distances to gates and toilets (Bauer, 2018). However, once on the plane, there is also the issue of the transfer from the wheelchair to the seat which, in some cases, has caused pain to the tourist and led to undignified experiences whilst front-line staff appear ill-aware and lack appropriate training and education in the handling of passengers with disabilities (Poria et al., 2011). In addition, toilets on board the planes are largely inaccessible to people using mobility devices; Bauer (2018) describes them as painful, embarrassing and humiliating to use. Indeed, it would appear that passengers using mobility devices are prepared to go to lengths to avoid using these facilities by using nappies, catheters or bottles (Poria et al., 2011). However, others split their flight journeys to allow for toilet trips at the airport (Bauer, 2018). A further problem is that wheelchairs have to be stowed in the hold during the flight, and it is not uncommon for them to be returned damaged or even sometimes to go missing, meaning that the trip may be over before it has even started (Bauer, 2018). Thus, despite much of the focus related to tourist accessibility being on wheelchair access, barriers facing wheelchair users whilst travelling are not uncommon.

Travelling with a sensory impairment

Participating in tourism goes beyond mere physical access (Yau et al., 2004). Sensory impairment refers to those who have limited or no vision, live with an audiological impairment or have limited, impaired or delayed capacities to use expressive or receptive language (Buhalis & Darcy, 2011; Domínguez et al., 2013). PLwD may struggle with tasks requiring clear vision, clear hearing, written or oral communication, understanding information presented visually or auditorily or general speech capabilities, and have issues with conveying, understanding or using written and spoken language (Buhalis & Darcy, 2011; Domínguez et al., 2013; Vila et al., 2015). A number of impairments would therefore fall under this category, including the perhaps more obvious ones such as audiological and visual impairment, but conditions such as dementia, epilepsy and autism also involve sensory impairments (Connell & Page, 2019b; McIntosh, 2020; Sedgley et al., 2017; Vila et al., 2015). Indeed, these latter conditions are considered to be hidden disabilities in the sense that there is no immediately obvious signifier of disability, such as a wheelchair or a guide dog, which presents further challenges (Connell & Page, 2019a; McIntosh, 2020). Yet, the conditions play a critical role in travel experiences.

Given the increasing interest in the phenomenon that is accessible tourism, it is surprising that travelling with a visual impairment has to date been largely neglected (Bauer, 2018; Devile & Kastenholz, 2018; Richards et al., 2010). People with vision impairment (PwVI) experience similar barriers to other PLwD through a hostile society and inaccessible environments. However, unlike many impairments, PwVI often rely on a guide dog as a mobility aid that in itself may be problematic within tourism, for example, with transport and in accommodation facilities (Rickly et al., 2020). Indeed, Rickly et al. (2020) encountered hostile environments towards guide dogs, despite their importance both as a mobility aid and also to the emotional well-being of the PwVI. Specifically, Rickly et al.'s study identified barriers similar to those discussed earlier in this chapter at airports, train stations, hotels and restaurants, including poorly trained front-line staff, a lack of awareness amongst the general public and front-line staff, as well as poorly designed environments.

At the same time, it is important to note that travel and tourism is also largely geared towards sighted people, promoting experiences dominated by words such as 'sightseeing' (Lam, Chan & Peters, 2020). The World Health Organization (2020) estimates that, globally, up to one billion people live with a visual impairment that could have been prevented or has yet to be addressed (WHO, 2020), whilst in the UK it is estimated that over two million people are visually impaired, a figure that is expected to increase owing to an ageing population and other underlying health issues (Small, 2015). It is further believed that PwVI are less likely to travel compared with those with other impairments, particularly in the context of international travel (Loi & Kong, 2017; Small & Darcy, 2010). Issues such as the fear of missing information, including information such as changes to flight details or train platforms, particularly in noisy environments, have been identified as a source of travel anxiety for PwVI (Poria et al., 2011). Another barrier to travel for PwVI revolves around the challenge of memorizing journeys, often a prerequisite owing to inaccessible environments. Basic aspects, such as signage and lighting, for example, are typically unsuitable for PwVI and indeed people living with sensory impairments, such as dementia (Connell & Page, 2019a; Darcy & Dickson, 2009). This becomes a particular problem when travelling (Bauer, 2018) and, as such, independence and confidence have a considerable bearing on travel behaviour (Loi & Kong, 2017).

Travelling with a cognitive impairment

Most research on accessible tourism has, to date, focused on visible disabilities such as physical impairments (McIntosh, 2020). Consequently, it is perhaps not surprising that industry and scholars alike struggle to comprehend the wider disability spectrum and, specifically, those surrounding cognitive impairment, also known as hidden or invisible disabilities. Matthews and Harrington (2000: 405) define hidden disability as 'one that is hidden: not to be immediately noticed by an observer except under unusual circumstances or by disclosure from the disabled person or other outside source'. Hidden disabilities revolve around intellectual and mental health and are life-long illnesses that effectively lead to behavioural disorders (Vila et al., 2015). As a result, people living with a cognitive impairment may struggle to learn, have disorganized patterns of learning, struggle with adaptive behaviour, struggle to comprehend abstract concepts, have limited control of cognitive functioning, struggle with sensory, motor and speech skills and have restrictive life functions (Buhalis & Darcy, 2011; Domínguez et al., 2013). Impairments that fall into this category include autism, dementia and epilepsy (Connell & Page, 2019b; McIntosh, 2020; Sedgley et al., 2017), and quality of life is considered to be reduced for those living with such impairments owing to the limiting factors with regard to positive life experiences and personal control (McIntosh, 2020). Nevertheless, research in these fields is extremely limited and only recently has any significant attention been paid to these areas.

According to Kong and Loi (2017), some simply assume that people living with a cognitive impairment have no interest in participating in tourism experiences (Kong & Loi, 2017). This, however, is not necessarily the case; people living with cognitive impairments still have a desire to engage in tourism experiences but, unfortunately, tend not to feel supported and that places are inaccessible (Connell & Page, 2019b). As an example, research indicates that access issues for people living with dementia can be numerous and revolve around mobility, memory-loss, visual perception and spatial awareness, information provision (including websites), interaction with the environment, accommodation and paying for goods and services, but also with regard to the design and colour of the infrastructure, including transport and signage (Connell & Page, 2019b; Klug et al., 2017). Yet, many of these issues are also relevant for someone living with autism, and indeed other cognitive impairments.

Social exclusion is a common factor amongst people living with cognitive impairments (McIntosh, 2020). This can have severe consequences; people living with autism, for example, have increased chances of experiencing depression, and anxiety as a result of social exclusion (Sedgley et al., 2017). In such instances, once again, barriers remain person-centred as well as societal, arguably presenting levels of intrapersonal, interpersonal and structural barriers (Crawford & Godbey, 1987). Barriers within society are largely a result of a lack of training and education amongst front-line staff and a lack of awareness within wider society (Connell & Page, 2019a; McIntosh, 2020; Sedgley et al., 2017). This has led to a poor understanding of cognitive impairments and, in turn, has created a stigma that has caused misconceptions and negative stereotypes, thereby leading to social exclusion (McIntosh, 2020). As a result, cognitive impairments do not just affect the person psychologically, but also socially (McIntosh, 2020). Indeed, people living with autism or dementia, for example, often struggle with social interaction and imagination, find communication problematic and many may find it difficult to understand social norms and struggle to comprehend others' emotions.

The challenge for destinations, and the tourism industry more broadly, is that society has yet to fully comprehend what these impairments mean to the people living with them (Connell & Page, 2019a). However, this is slowly changing. The UK, for example, is at the forefront of dementia care, where the focus is not on only on finding a cure for the disease but also on how to live well with it (Klug et al., 2017). For example, Visit Scotland (2019) published a dementia-friendly toolkit for the Scottish tourism industry, providing guidelines on how to deliver dementia-friendly experiences. It is hoped that such initiatives will also help educate society and remove the current prevalent stigma surrounding people with dementia, and indeed that they may be useful for addressing other cognitive impairments, such as autism and epilepsy.

The following section provides a small case study of an award-winning family vacation resort in Denmark, called Feriecenter Slettestrand, which prides itself on its disability-friendly facilities. The analysis of the resort and its facilities was carried out using information from their website as well as the resort's Instagram page and Access Denmark, an organization founded in 2003 in collaboration with Visit Denmark, HORESTA (Hotel, Restaurant and Tourism industry) and Disabled Peoples' Organizations Denmark (Access Denmark, 2020). The websites accessed are listed separately at the end of the chapter.

Feriecenter Slettestrand, Denmark

Feriecenter Slettestrand, which will be referred to simply as Slettestrand in what follows, is a vacation resort on the north-western coast of Denmark close to one hour's drive from the city of Aalborg. It has been family owned since 1999, when John and Inger-Marie Kronborg purchased the resort. John and Inger-Marie both had backgrounds in special education, working with children living with various impairments. As such, their aim was, and remains, to deliver an experience where people, irrespective of their circumstances, are able to participate equally and experience nature. They refer to this as vacations with freedom.

Today, Slettestrand is well-known across Denmark as a prime resort for people with or without impairments. It was awarded the North-Jutland Disability prize in 2005, the Danish Prize of Initiative, owing to its unique and accessible facilities; it has also received a five-star rating by Handi-Travel-Info and is recognized as meeting all seven accessibility criteria by Access Denmark. These accessibility criteria revolve around: (i) wheelchair users; (ii) people living with motor impairments; (iii) people living with visual impairment; (iv) people living with audiological impairment; (v) people living with asthma and other allergies; (vi) people living with cognitive impairment; and (vii) people living with reading difficulties. Slettestrand promotes an experience with a focus on the self rather than the disability, with the understanding that it is the environment that disables as opposed to it being the fault of the visitor. This approach is very much along the lines of the social model of disability (Randle & Dolnicar, 2019).

Accessible tourist experiences

The resort boasts various facilities, including swimming pools that are accessible to wheelchairs and that are also used for rehabilitation exercises, and apartments with lifts, whilst activities include customized horse carriages and specialized bikes and vehicles. As such, the resort has removed many barriers to participation for people with a physical impairment, avoiding the aforementioned challenges of uncomfortable transport in temporary wheelchairs (Bauer, 2018). However, rather unfortunately, there is no indication that Slettestrand is accessible to disabilities beyond those requiring wheelchair access, apart from a statement declaring they meet all seven accessibility requirements of Access Denmark (a statement that is nevertheless supported by Access Denmark on their website). As an example, the resort's disability-friendly page on the website highlights only the needs of those in wheelchairs. In contrast, no mention is made of how Slettestrand is accessible to people living with a sensory or cognitive impairment and, hence, it is not possible to ascertain the extent to which the resort remains accessible to PLwD beyond those of the physical nature, despite this being advertised rather prominently.

Thus, one can refer back to the accessible tourism literature in which Kong and Loi (2017) argue that many tourism stakeholders believe that by being wheelchair accessible, they are accessible to all disabilities. Certainly, that is the immediate impression a potential visitor to Slettestrand would have. Indeed, much like the literature on accessible tourism (McKercher & Darcy, 2018), the resort appears to focus predominantly on physical and mobility disabilities. This would further indicate that attitudinal, informational and physical barriers remain for those with sensory and/or cognitive impairments, as argued by Lam, Chan and Peters (2020). Whether this links back to the issue of customer compatibility remains unclear (Tchetchik et al., 2018), yet it is easy to see how a resort promoting activities that are particularly physical in nature may discourage PLwD from participation.

However, Slettestrand is not just for PLwD but also people without disabilities who, in general, are in pursuit of an active vacation. Certainly, on the resort's Instagram page, it is outdoor walks and mountain bike-related activities that are mainly promoted as opposed to anything more closely related to an accessible vacation (See Figure 32.3). In fact, beyond family values and environmentally friendly behaviour, the resort's Instagram page primarily appears to promote adrenaline-fuelled activities more akin to those offered by an adventure tourism visitor attraction (Hansen, Fyall & Spyriadis, 2020), with little regard to highlighting their disability-friendly features. Yet, online features such as websites and social-media pages are also considered part of the accessibility equation in the context of the ease of access of destination infrastructure (Connell & Page, 2019a). As such, owing to the lack of information provided on Slettestrand's website and Instagram page, people living with sensory and/ or cognitive impairments may be confused and look elsewhere for a vacation resort, despite the promise of the resort being accessible to various disabilities.

Conclusion

Accessible tourism is a concept attracting increasing attention within both academic and tourism sector circles. With people with disabilities becoming increasingly common, in part reflecting changing demographics around the world, contemporary society is facing one of the greatest economic and social challenges. Most developed countries have some form of disability legislation to enable equal access across society for PLwD. Indeed, the creation of a civil society has become a priority for many countries, whilst 'reducing inequalities' is 1 of the 17 Sustainable Development Goals established by the United Nations. Yet, as

Figure 32.3 Feriecenter Slettestrand
Source: Instagram (2020).

considered in this chapter, various barriers to accessible tourism experiences for PLwD continue to exist. The desire to participate in tourism is evident amongst PLwD, yet the industry is clearly struggling to facilitate such experiences. This arguably reflects a lack of awareness, understanding and training within the industry and, indeed, across society more generally.

This chapter has highlighted how some of the more obvious disabilities, such as physical and mobile impairments, tend to attract more attention both within the literature and in practice, undoubtedly adding to this lack of awareness. Not only is this discussed widely in the literature explored for the chapter but also exemplified in the mini case study of Feriecenter Slettestrand in Denmark, a resort in which experiences are marketed as being widely accessible but are primarily focused on physical and mobile impairments. This lack of awareness is most likely also adding to the current stigma surrounding many disabilities, such as autism, epilepsy and dementia, which in turn has added to levels of social exclusion. Certainly, it contributes to the barriers experienced by PLwD when travelling.

This chapter has also highlighted how infrastructure may contribute to barriers to participation. This is perhaps the more obvious type of barrier, yet the mini case study demonstrated how a resort promoting itself as disability-friendly one may quickly discourage PLwD from participating owing to an ambiguous website in which it claims to be accessible to seven different types of impairments but only describes its facilities in relation to physical and motor-related impairments. Connell and Page (2019) specifically referred to information provision, including that of websites, as one of a number of infrastructural barriers causing access issues for PLwD. In addition, this chapter has explored the many different types of barriers to participation in tourism experiences for PLwD and it is clear that industry is some way off of being able to deliver such experiences.

Accessible tourist experiences

Nevertheless, as suggested here, tourism experiences can alleviate social exclusion and contribute to well-being and quality of life. Equally, from the service provider's perspective, providing accessible experiences is not only a legal and, perhaps even moral obligation, but may also very well contribute to a competitive advantage. Further research is, however, required, particularly in the fields of tourist experiences, in relation to cognitive impairments. It is also likely that many in the tourism industry, as well as many tourism scholars, do not possess expertise in accessibility issues and hence, are unable to deliver such experiences. Thus, future research would benefit from an interdisciplinary focus on accessible tourism.

Websites accessed for the case study

https://nordjyske.dk/nyheder/pris-til-feriecenter-slettestrand/5d77cf7f-86ae-4b03-a722-947bd01f3924

https://handi-travel-info.dk/Rejsemaal.aspx?id=36

https://slettestrand.dk/handicapvenlig/

https://slettestrand.dk/

https://slettestrand.dk/om-os/

https://www.instagram.com/feriecenter_slettestrand/

http://accessdenmark.com/

http://accessdenmark.com/purpose-of-the-labelsystem/purpose-of-the-label-system-105

http://accessdenmark.com/factsheet/feriecenter-slettestrand-2371-1

https://www.instagram.com/feriecenter_slettestrand/

References

Agovino, M., Casaccia, M., Garofalo, A. and Marchesano, K. (2017) Tourism and disability in Italy. Limits and opportunities. *Tourism Management Perspectives*, 23, 58–67.

Bauer, I. (2018) When travel is a challenge: Travel medicine and the 'dis-abled' traveller. *Travel Medicine and Infectious Disease*, 22, 66–72.

Bohdanowicz-Godfrey, P., Zientara, P. and Bąk, M. (2019) Towards an accessible hotel: A case study of Scandic. *Current Issues in Tourism*, 22(10), 1133–1137.

Breakley, N. and Breakley, H. (2013) Is there a right to tourism? *Tourism Analysis*, 18, 139–148.

Buhalis, D. and Darcy, S. (Eds.) (2011). *Accessible tourism: Concepts and Issues*. Bristol: Channel View Publications.

Card, J. A., Cole, S. T. and Humphrey, A. H. (2006) A comparison of the accessibility and attitudinal barriers model: Travel providers and travelers with physical disabilities. *Asia Pacific Journal of Tourism Research*, 11(2), 161–175.

Cohen, S. A., Prayag, G. and Moital, M., (2014) Consumer behaviour in tourism: Concepts, influences and opportunities. *Current Issues in Tourism*, 17(10), 872–909.

Connell, J. and Page, S. J. (2019a) Case study: Destination readiness for dementia-friendly visitor experiences: A scoping study. *Tourism Management*, 70, 29–41.

Connell, J. and Page, S. (2019b) Tourism, ageing and the demographic time bomb – The implications of dementia for the visitor economy: A perspective paper. *Tourism Review*, 75(1), 81–85.

Crawford, D. W. and Godbey, G. (1987) Reconceptualizing barriers to family leisure. *Leisure Sciences*, 9(2), 119–127.

Crawford, D.W., Jackson, E.L. and Godbey, G. (1991) A hierarchical model of leisure constraints. *Leisure Sciences*, 13(4), 309–320.

Darcy, S. and Burke, P. F. (2018) On the road again: The barriers and benefits of automobility for people with disability. *Transportation Research Part A: Policy and Practice*, 107, 229–245.

Darcy, S. and Dickson, T. J. (2009) A whole-of-life approach to tourism: The case for accessible tourism experiences. *Journal of Hospitality and Tourism Management*, 16(1), 32–44.

Department of Justice. (2010) *US Department of Justice Americans with Disabilities Act Title III Regulations*. Available at: https://www.ada.gov/regs2010/titleIII_2010/titleIII_2010_regulations.htm (Accessed 18 November 2020).

Devile, E. and Kastenholz, E. (2018) Accessible tourism experiences: The voice of people with visual disabilities. *Journal of Policy Research in Tourism, Leisure and Events*, 10(3), 265–285.

Domínguez, T., Fraiz, J. A. and Alén, E. (2013) Economic profitability of accessible tourism for the tourism sector in Spain. *Tourism Economics*, 19(6), 1385–1399.

Duedahl, E., Blichfeldt, B. and Liburd, J. (2020) How engaging with nature can facilitate active healthy ageing. *Tourism Geographies*. https://doi.org/10.1080/14616688.2020.1819398

Eichhorn, V., Miller, G. and Tribe, J. (2013) Tourism: A site of resistance strategies of individuals with a disability. *Annals of Tourism Research*, 43, 578–600.

European Commission. (2013) *Economic Impact and Travel Patterns of Accessible Tourism in Europe*. Final Report, Service Contract SI2. ACPROCE052481700. European Commission, DG.

Evcil, A. N. (2018) Barriers and preferences to leisure activities for wheelchair users in historic places. *Tourism Geographies*, 20(4), 698–715.

Gillovic, B., McIntosh, A., Darcy, S. and Cockburn-Wootten, C. (2018) Enabling the language of accessible tourism. *Journal of Sustainable Tourism*, 26(4), 615–630.

Hansen, M., Fyall, A. and Spyriadis, T. (2020) Adventure or amusement? Image and identity challenges for the aerial adventure industry and implications for positioning and policy. *Anatolia*, 31(3), 423–435.

Hartwell, H., Fyall, A., Willis, C., Page, S., Ladkin, A. and Hemingway, A. (2018) Progress in tourism and destination wellbeing research. *Current Issues in Tourism*, 21(16), 1830–1892.

Huber, D., Milne, S. and Hyde, K. F. (2018) Constraints and facilitators for senior tourism. *Tourism Management Perspectives*, 27, 55–67.

Instgram (2020) Feriecenter_slettestrand [Instragram] Available at: https://www.instagram.com/feriecenter_slettestrand/ (Accessed 1 December 2020).

Jackson, E. L., Crawford, D. W. and Godbey, G. (1993) Negotiation of leisure constraints. *Leisure Sciences*, 15(1), 1–11.

Jackson, E. L. and Rucks, V. C. (1995) Negotiation of leisure constraints by junior-high and high-school students: An exploratory study. *Journal of leisure Research*, 27(1), 85–105.

Karl, M., Bauer, A., Ritchie, W. B. and Passauer, M. (2020) The impact of travel constraints on travel decision-making: A comparative approach of travel frequencies and intended travel participation. *Journal of Destination Marketing & Management*, 18. https://doi.org/10.1016/j.jdmm.2020.100471

Kastenholz, E., Eusébio, C. and Figueiredo, E. (2015) Contributions of tourism to social inclusion of persons with disability. *Disability & Society*, 30(8), 1259–1281.

Kim, J. and Ritchie, J. R. B. (2014) Cross-cultural validation of a Memorable Tourism Experience Scale (MTES). *Journal of Travel Research*, 53(3), 323–335.

Klug, K., Page, S. J., Connell, J., Robson, D. and Bould, E. (2017) Rethinking heritage: A guide to help make your site more dementia-friendly. Available at: https://uhra.herts.ac.uk/handle/2299/23348 (Accessed 10 September 2019).

Kong, W. H. and Loi, K. I. (2017) The barriers to holiday-taking for visually impaired tourists and their families. *Journal of Hospitality and Tourism Management*, 32, 99–107.

Lam, K. L., Chan, C. S. and Peters, M. (2020) Understanding technological contributions to accessible tourism from the perspective of destination design for visually impaired visitors in Hong Kong. *Journal of Destination Marketing & Management*, 17. https://doi.org/10.1016/j.jdmm.2020.100434.

Lee, B. K., Agarwal, S. and Kim, H. J. (2012) Influences of travel constraints on the people with disabilities' intention to travel: An application of Seligman's helplessness theory. *Tourism Management*, 33(3), 569–579.

Lee, C. F. and King, B. (2019) Determinants of attractiveness for a seniors-friendly destination: A hierarchical approach. *Current Issues in Tourism*, 22(1), 71–90.

Loi, K. I. and Kong, W. H. (2017) Tourism for all: Challenges and issues faced by people with vision impairment. *Tourism Planning & Development*, 14(2), 181–197.

Lyu, S. O. (2012) Using the Leisure Constraints Negotiation Process to Understand Participants' Leisure Involvement and Benefit Realization. PhD Thesis, Michigan State University. Community, Agriculture, Recreation and Resource Studies.

Matthews, C. K. and Harrington, N. G. (2000) Invisible disability. In D. O. Braithwaite and T. L. Thompson (Eds.), *Handbook of Communication and People with Disabilities*. Mahwah, NJ: Lawrence Erlbaum, pp. 405–421.

McCabe, S. (2009) Who needs a holiday? Evaluating social tourism. *Annals of Tourism Research*, 36(4), 667–688.

McCabe, S. and Diekmann, A. (2015) The rights to tourism: Reflections on social tourism and human rights. *Tourism Recreation Research*, 40(2), 194–204.

McIntosh, A. J. (2020) The hidden side of travel: Epilepsy and tourism. *Annals of Tourism Research*, 81. https://doi.org/10.1016/j.annals.2019.102856

McKercher, B. and Chen, F. (2015) Travel as a life priority? *Asia Pacific Journal of Tourism Research*, 20(7), 715–729.

McKercher, B. and Darcy, S. (2018) Re-conceptualizing barriers to travel by people with disabilities. *Tourism Management Perspectives*, 26, 59–66.

Mesquita, S. and Carneiro, M. J. (2016) Accessibility of European museums to visitors with visual impairments. *Disability & Society*, 31(3), 373–388.

Michopoulou, E., Darcy, S., Ambrose, I. and Buhalis, D. (2015) Accessible tourism futures: The world we dream to live in and the opportunities we hope to have. *Journal of Tourism Futures*, 1(3), 179–188.

Moura, A. F. A., Kastenholz, E. and Pereira, A. M. S. (2018) Accessible tourism and its benefits for coping with stress. *Journal of Policy Research in Tourism, Leisure and Events*, 10(3), 241–264.

Nyanjom, J., Boxall, K. and Slaven, J. (2018) Towards inclusive tourism? Stakeholder collaboration in the development of accessible tourism. *Tourism Geographies*, 20(4), 675–697.

Pagán, R. (2015) The contribution of holiday trips to life satisfaction: The case of people with disabilities. *Current Issues in Tourism*, 18(6), 524–538.

Poria, Y., Reichel, A. and Brandt, Y. (2011) Dimensions of hotel experience of people with disabilities: An exploratory study. *International Journal of Contemporary Hospitality Management*, 23(5), 571–591.

Randle, M. and Dolnicar, S. (2019) Enabling people with impairments to use Airbnb. *Annals of Tourism Research*, 76, 278–289.

Rebernik, N., Favero, P. and Bahillo, A. (2020) Using digital tools and ethnography for rethinking disability inclusive city design: Exploring material and immaterial dialogues, *Disability & Society*. https://doi.org/10.1080/09687599.2020.1779035

Richards, V., Pritchard, A. and Morgan, N. (2010) (Re)envisioning tourism and visual impairment. *Annals of Tourism Research*, 37(4), 1097–1116.

Rickly, J. M. (2018) Considering service animals in tourism. *Annals of Tourism Research*, 71, 57–58.

Rickly, J., Halpern, N., McCabe, S. and Hansen, M. (2020) *Guide Dogs on Holiday: Guide Dog Owner Experiences in the Travel and Tourism Sector*. http://doi.org/10.17639/nott.7038

Sedgley, D., Pritchard, A., Morgan, N. and Hanna, P. (2017) Tourism and autism: Journeys of mixed emotions. *Annals of Tourism Research*, 66, 14–25.

Seligman, M. E. (1975) *Helplessness: On Depression, Development and Death*. San Francisco: W.H. Freeman.

Shakespeare, T., Watson, N. and Alghaib, O. A. (2017) Blaming the victim, all over again: Waddell and Aylward's biopsychosocial (BPS) model of disability. *Critical Social Policy*, 37(1), 22–41.

Shaw, G. and Veitch, C. (2011) Demographic drivers of change in tourism and the challenge of inclusive products. In D. Buhalis and S. Darcy (Eds.), *Accessible tourism: Concepts and Issues*. Bristol: Channel View Publication, pp. 46–61.

Sheldon, P. J., Fesenmaier, D. R. and Xiang, Z. (2017) *Design Science in Tourism: Foundations of Destination Management (Tourism on the Verge)*. Cham: Springer International Publishing.

Small, J. (2015) Interconnecting mobilities on tour: Tourists with vision impairment partnered with sighted tourists. *Tourism Geographies*, 17(1), 76–90.

Small, J. and Darcy, S. (2010) Tourism, disability and mobility. In S. Cole and N. Morgan (Eds.), *Tourism and Inequality: Problems and Prospects*. Wallingford: CABI, pp. 1–21.

Small, J., Darcy, S. and Packer, T. (2012) The embodied tourist experiences of people with vision impairment: Management implications beyond the visual gaze. *Tourism Management*, 33(4), 941–950.

Smith, R. W. (1987) Leisure of disabled tourists: Barriers to participation. *Annals of Tourism Research*, 14(3), 376–389.

Tchetchik, A., Eichhorn, V. and Biran, A. (2018) 'Not on my vacation': Service encounters between able-bodied and disabled consumers – The case of high-contact service. *Journal of Policy Research in Tourism, Leisure and Events*, 10(3), 204–220.

Turner, N. and Morken, L. (2016) *Better Together: A Comparative Analysis of Age-friendly and Dementia Friendly Communities*. Washington, DC: AARP. Available at: https://www.aarp.org/content/dam/aarp/livable-communities/livable-documents/documents-2016/Better-Together-Research-Report.pdf (Accessed 22 October 2018).

Tussyadiah, I. P. (2014) Toward a theoretical foundation for experience design in tourism. *Journal of Travel Research*, 53(5), 543–564.

Tutuncu, O. (2017) Investigating the accessibility factors affecting hotel satisfaction of people with physical disabilities. *International Journal of Hospitality Management*, 65, 29–36.

UK. (2010) *Equality Act*. London: UK Government. Available at: http://www.legislation.gov.uk/ukpga/2010/15/pdfs/ukpga_20100015_en.pdf (Accessed 29 September 2018).

United Nations. (2015a) *World Population Ageing 2015*. United Nations, Department of Economic and Social Affairs. Population Division. Available at: http://www.un.org/en/development/desa/population/publications/pdf/ageing/WPA2015_Report.pdf (Accessed 20 March 2020).

United Nations. (2015b) Universal Declaration of Human Rights. Available at: http://un.org/en/udhrhandbook/pdf/udhr_booklet_en_web.pdf (Accessed 15 December 2020).

UNWTO. (2015) Annual Report 2015. UN World Tourism Organization. Available at: https://sdgs.un.org/sites/default/files/publications/2619annual_report_2015_lr.pdf (Accessed 05/11/20).

Vila, T. D., Darcy, S. and González, E. A. (2015) Competing for the disability tourism market: A comparative exploration of the factors of accessible tourism competitiveness in Spain and Australia. *Tourism Management*, 47, 261–272.

Visit England. (2016) *The Purple Pound: Volume and Value of Accessible Tourism in England. Visit England.* Available at: https://www.visitbritain.org/sites/default/files/vb-corporate/business-hub/resources/purple_pound_infographic.pdf (Accessed 20 March 2020).

Visit Scotland. (2019) Become More Dementia Friendly. Available at: https://www.visitscotland.org/news/2019/dementiaguide (Accessed 3 October 2019).

We Are Purple. (2019) The Purple Pound: Infographic. Available at: https://wearepurple.org.uk/the-purple-pound-infographic/ (Accessed 30 September 2019).

Wen, J., Huang, S. S. and Goh, E. (2020) Effects of perceived constraints and negotiation on learned helplessness: A study of Chinese senior outbound tourists. *Tourism Management*, 78.https://doi.org/10.1016/j.tourman.2019.104059

WHO. (2020) *Blindness and Vision Impairment*. World Health Organization. Available at: https://www.who.int/news-room/fact-sheets/detail/blindness-and-visual-impairment (Accessed 16 December 2020).

World Bank. (2019) Disability Inclusion. The Word Bank. Available at: https://www.worldbank.org/en/topic/disability (Accessed 20 March 2020).

Yau, M. K. S., McKercher, B. and Packer, T. L. (2004) Traveling with a disability: More than an access issue. *Annals of Tourism Research*, 31(4), 946–960.

Ying, T., Tang, J., Wen, J., Ye, S., Zhou, Y. and Li, F. S. (2021) Traveling with pets: Constraints, negotiation, and learned helplessness. *Tourism Management*, 82. https://doi.org/10.1016/j.tourman.2020.104183

SECTION 4

The tourist experience and place

33

MARKETING A SENSE OF PLACE TO TOURISTS

A critical perspective

Maria Lichrou and Aggelos Panayiotopoulos

Introduction

An enduring image of the island of Santorini, one of Greece's popular tourism destinations, is that of 'large clusters of whitewashed buildings nesting at dizzying heights, spilling down cliff sides and offering gasp-inducing views from land or sea' (Bain, 2019). It is precisely this perpetual image of the island that a photographic exhibition entitled *SantoREni: work in progress* (Anonymous, 2012) disrupted. Photos in the exhibition depicted traffic, chaotic buildings, unfinished construction sites, supermarket outlets and parked motorbikes lined up in a street. One might wonder what best captures Santorini's sense of place. Is it the former, the eternal awe-inspiring view from the Caldera? Or the hustle and bustle of the main square in Fira, the capital town? Is it the vernacular architecture or the concrete imitations sprawling on the surface of the island? The contrast between the postcard imagery, emanating a sense of timelessness and Santorini's daily life prompted us to reflect on the experience of place, the interconnections between material aspects and symbolic meanings, and marketing's role in (co)creating a sense of place for tourists.

Places are not simply geographic locations with objective physical attributes, but are generally understood in terms of three core elements: location, locale and sense of place (Cresswell, 2009). Location refers to the geographical position of a place, its coordinates on a map, while locale refers to its physical characteristics, such as the visible and tangible aspects of its landscape (Cresswell, 2009). Sense of place is a more elusive and ambiguous concept that broadly refers to how people relate to places through lived experience (Agnew, 2011). Sense of place has been examined by researchers from diverse disciplines, including anthropologists, geographers, environmental psychologists, architects and sociologists. Exploring various definitions of sense of place, including Yi-Fu Tuan's *topophilia* (the affective bond between people and place) and Setha Low's *place attachment* (attachment of culturally shared emotional meanings to a particular space), Cross (2001) draws attention to how people relate to places in emotional, experiential and symbolic ways. Sense of place, then, refers to subjective perceptions of place and the affective bonds that people develop with a place or setting, which are culturally significant.

Sense of place is sometimes discussed in tandem with the concept of 'genius loci', or spirit of place, which, while originally associated with deities and spirits thought to reside

DOI: 10.4324/9781003219866-38

469

in places, has come to refer to a place's special 'feel' (Steele, 1981) or distinctive character (Relph, 1997). According to Malpas (2008: 199–200),

> '[s]ense of place' refers us, on the face of it, both to a sense of the character or identity that belongs to certain places or locales, as well as to a sense of our own identity as shaped in relation to those places - to a sense of 'belonging to' those places.

Thus, sense of place is our ability to connect with and be aware of places (Relph, 1997), and genius loci is the distinctive identity we associate with a particular place (Relph, 2007). Sense of place offers marketing thought and practice an important yet challenging concept to understand how people emotionally connect with and interpret places. Importantly, while sense of place involves emotional reactions to a place and interpretations of that place, a sense of place is also bounded by physical form and location (Stedman, 2003). Sense of place can therefore also involve the interaction between physical elements and socially constructed meanings (Campelo, Aitken, Thyne & Gnoth, 2014; Young, 1999).

In this chapter we explore the growing interest in sense of place among place marketing and branding scholars. We trace a trajectory of place marketing thought from a functional approach that treats places as products, towards representational perspectives that focus on perceptions, identity and image and, more recently, participatory perspectives that seek to engage with people's sense of place. In doing so, we explore the significance of symbolic meanings and narratives of place. Finally, we offer a critical discussion of sense of place with an emphasis on the interconnections between material and symbolic, and existential and political dimensions of place.

Place product

The extension of conventional marketing thinking and practice on geographical entities (e.g. Kotler & Gertner, 2004) necessitated the conception of places as products. Drawing on notions of place as object and location (Ashworth & Voogd, 1990a; 1990b), the place–product is conceived both as a set of products and experiences provided locally and as a product in its own right. For example, the urban product is separated into *contributory* elements, such as the specific services or even a particular isolated characteristic of the city, and the *nuclear product*, which is the city as a whole (Sleipen, 1988; cited in Ashworth & Voogd, 1990b). Similarly, a tourist destination is both 'the point of consumption of the complex of activities that comprises the tourism experience and [...] ultimately what is sold by place promotion agencies on the tourism market' (Ashworth & Voogd, 1990a: 7). Accordingly, place marketing has the task of designing a desirable 'place mix' (Kotler, Haider & Rein 1993), referring to the selection, development and promotion of place attributes and positioning the place product in the market through segmentation (Boisen, Terlouw & van Gorp, 2011), and the promotion of attractive images of place (Ashworth & Voogd 1994). Attributes such as physiography, culture and history have long been considered sources of a place's competitive advantage (Crouch & Ritchie, 1999). Places are essentially conceived as packages of attributes, including natural and cultural attractions, services and available infrastructure (see, for example, Buhalis, 2000; Murphy, Pritchard & Smith, 2000). Arguably, this perspective focuses on physical and functional aspects of place in an effort to sell and promote places.

Marketers may have found some comfort in the place product construct in the form of an integrated and standardized framework amenable to the application of marketing tools. Yet, the complexity and fluidity of places is challenging conventional marketing practice and the very notion of a unified place product (see, for example, Warnaby & Medway, 2013). Places are living entities, constantly evolving through time. They are multifaceted and multipurpose, involving multiple individuals and communities with diverse interests and claims to place (Goodwin, 1993). Residents, visitors, investors and commuters all have different stakes. This calls for a collaborative marketing effort that acknowledges and brings together the wishes of different actors.

Marketers, tourists and local communities 'co-create' place products. Importantly, local communities and their different ways of attachment to a place are an important factor of the place product (Warnaby & Medway, 2013) and should not be excluded from the marketer's frame of reference (Hall, 2000). This questions the appropriateness of marketing orientation for places, because adapting a place's resources solely for the satisfaction of the tourists' needs may neglect the needs of the locals (Haywood, 1990). Places may indeed become objectified, evident historically in the experience of negative tourism impacts internationally (Crick, 1996), such as in the case of Mediterranean tourism destinations (e.g. Lichrou, O'Malley & Patterson, 2017; Panayiotopoulos & Pisano, 2019). More recently, negative impacts and local resistance to tourism phenomenon are examined under the term overtourism (Milano, Cheer & Novelli, 2019; Milano, Novelli & Cheer, 2019).

The complexity of places and, consequently, the complexity of management processes involved (e.g. Boisen, Terlouw, Groote & Couwenberg, 2018; Skinner, 2008), have prompted a rethinking of the role of marketing in the context of place (Warnaby & Medway, 2013; Warnaby, Medway & Bennison, 2010), recognizing that place values form a living and constantly evolving relational system (Gnoth, 2007). Specifically, terminology evolved from 'place marketing' to 'place branding', marking a shift of attention from functional to representational understandings of place (see Giovanardi, Lucarelli & Pasquinelli, 2013), and from places as physical entities to subjective perceptions or images and interpretations. To paraphrase Kavaratzis (2004), encounters with places happen through perceptions and images; thus, the object of place marketing is not the place itself, but its image. What is more, images are not created solely by marketers, nor are marketers in control of the images perceived by tourists. Accordingly, place meanings are co-constructed, and while marketers are not in control, they capitalize on particular images and meanings.

Place meanings

The production of tourist space is 'as much a symbolic order of meaning as a form of material production' (Meethan, 2001: 168). Socio-cultural accounts of tourism and place (Framke, 2002; Morgan & Pritchard, 1998) emphasize the role of symbolic meanings as constitutive of places (Voase, 1999). Rather than static, objective or a priori phenomena (McCabe & Stokoe, 2004), places represent specific historical and cultural phases in society (Saarinen, 1998). Thus, places are not simply physical spaces, but fluid, dynamic contexts of social interaction and collective memory (Stokowski, 2002). From this perspective, culture is not simply a resource or attribute of the 'place-product', but a dynamic process implicated in the construction and interpretation of places. Furthermore, the experience of place entails interpretation of material aspects, such as the landscape, which represents something, and in that sense the experience of place can be conceived as a story (Suvantola, 2002).

We develop a sense of place for different places in the world without even having been there (Relph, 1997). Meanings about places are formed through exposure and interactions with media, popular culture, fiction and the stories of others (Iwashita, 2006; Santos, 2004). For instance, an advertisement for Greek-style yogurt in the UK can also be implicated in the construction of particular perceptions of Greece through the reproduction of particular (stereotypical) images of Greek people and culture. It is within the tourist's own cultural framework that knowledge, expectations and fantasies, as well as perceptions of the identities of tourism destinations, are created (Iwashita, 2006). Thus, tourist places are culturally significant; they engender representational cultures, which increase the accessibility of sites in everyday life (Rojek, 1997). What is more, signs, images and symbols make the site familiar to tourists in their ordinary culture through the process of indexing (Rojek, 1997), which involves the creation of visual, textual and symbolic representations of places through the media and the semiotic conventions associated with signifying a site (Hughes, 1998). Examples of such media include travellers' tales, printed texts such as travel brochures, as well as novels and poems, dramatic and cinematic traditions and television. Through our screens, books, music and social interactions (physical or online through various social media), we become part of the circuit of cultural representations of places.

People seek to experience 'in reality' the pleasurable dramas they have already experienced in their imagination (Campbell, 1987, cited in Urry, 1990: 13). The tourist imagination constructs ideas, images, myths and fantasies about different places (Selwyn, 1996). The consumption of places involves symbolic interaction processes involved through which tourists create their personal dramas (Voase, 1999). Metaphorical, allegorical and false information is a resource for tourists as an object of reverie, dreaming and speculation (Rojek, 1997). It seems, then, that the 'mythical' is unavoidable in discussions of travel and tourism and, to some degree, the social construction of places always involves the mobilization of myth (Rojek, 1997). Traditional as well as contemporary mythologies are sources of the imagery that surrounds places. For example, the imagery of Ireland as a tourism destination still relies to a great extent on 'pre-modern' associations with friendly inhabitants and empty spaces. This imagery continues in spite of the dramatic changes to both the people and the landscape evinced by the 'Celtic Tiger' (Foley & Fahy, 2004) and, more recently, the financial crisis. There are numerous examples of the role of mythical discourses in the construction of popular tourism places. Urry (1995) discusses the influence of Romantic poetry on perceptions of the English countryside and its aesthetic appreciation. Costa (1998) examines the paradisal discourses involved in the marketing and consumption of Hawaii.

Appreciating the role of language in the way people construct places, Stokowski (2002) argues that sense of place is rooted in narration. Through stories, we experience and remember places (Trapp-Fallon, 2003). Individuals make sense of their experiences in the world mainly in the form of narrative and consequently their experiences are also structured in narrative form (Bruner, 1991; 2004). For example, places receive visitors 'through the narrative morsels' they plant themselves 'that are put in circulation by others' (Bendix, 2002: 476). Through her analysis of travel articles, Santos (2004) shows how such stories frame the way readers make sense of various places. Seen as texts and sets of spatial narratives (Meethan, 1996; Voase, 1999), places involve 'not only written media such as documents, books and brochures, but also spoken, visual and non-verbal media' (Stokowski, 2002: 372). Tourist narratives are, thus, place-making tools (Rickly-Boyd, 2009), including stories that people share online (Munar, 2011). In this sense, marketing and branding communication efforts can be thought of as part of the cultural media for the creation and circulation of place narratives.

It is important to note that narratives are not only structures of meaning, but also structures of power (Santos, 2004). The 'ability to assign meaning to a place is an act of power which has real effects on the people living in it' (Human, 1999: 83). Symbolic values and meanings are not given, but contested and actively involving processes and the construction of place entails the interests or positions of dominant groups (Meethan, 1996). This has political and ethical implications, because representations of people and places have the potential not only to construct the way societies see different places but also to powerfully shape the way the people living in these places see themselves (Borgerson & Schroeder, 2002). For example, a semiotic analysis of six postcards from the colonial era, portraying Arab men and women in an 'orientalist' fashion, reveals how the postcards encompass multiple meanings implicated in the construction of notions of 'us' and 'them' and how they 'capture the essence of the culture of colonial travels, power and discourse' (Burns, 2004: 273). Tourism places are often promoted through mystification, fantasy, associations with Disney world and indulgence in unreality (Britton, 1979). This is reflected in western tourists' perceptions of destinations in the third world often being shaped by myths that construct particular places as unchanged, unrestrained and uncivilized (Echtner & Prasad, 2003). Therefore, an understanding of place requires the exploration of the social relations that underlie the production of text (Gotham, 2002), as image and symbolic meaning are not neutral but political.

Place brand

The shift of discourse from function/object towards representation/meaning has resulted in discussions of the place brand as representation of a place's identity. The place brand, as a complex construct, incorporates both internal and external audiences. In the context of cities, Graham (2002) makes a distinction between the 'external city', that which is marketed to tourists and investors, and the 'internal city', which is that in which people ground their everyday lives. Place brand is thus 'a representation of identity, building a favourable internal (those who deliver the experience) and external (with visitors) image (leading to brand satisfaction and loyalty; name awareness; perceived quality; and other favourable brand associations)' (Govers & Go, 2016: 17).

Capitalizing upon imagery that distinguishes a place from ordinary/everyday places, place branding strives to evoke a distinct sense of place. For example, tourism destinations are demarcated from everyday/ordinary places by signifiers in the landscape and the marketing industry (Shaw & Williams, 2004) by virtue of their natural, historical or cultural extraordinariness (Rojek, 1997). Yet, in their struggle for differentiation, those responsible for the branding of places are often driven to similar policy formulas (Turok, 2009). Preoccupied with engendering development and growth, such practices often consist of quick yield but highly speculative and ephemeral projects (Harvey, 1989), such as serial reproduction of cultural attractions (Richards & Wilson, 2006), themed environments (Amin & Thrift, 2002), flagship projects and catchy slogans (Colomb & Kalandides, 2010).

In essence, places are reimagined from spaces of production to spaces of consumption (Lash & Urry, 1994) and this reimagining rests largely on image and aestheticization (Miles, 2010) as places try to become attractive to tourists and visitors for shopping, entertainment and tourism activities. Critics point out to the fact that, paradoxically, in pursuing difference, place marketing produces sameness (Griffiths, 1998) and homogeneity across places. Places may become commodified, due to the decontextualization of culture to mobilize sensations, dreams and play for profit (Amin & Thrift, 2002). This process of commodification can be detrimental for those living in places as it promotes an uncritical relationship with a place's culture and the past (Kearns & Philo, 1993). Besides, '[i]t would be a caricature to imagine place and space being occupied only by passive consumers in the role of tourists and a congenial, compliant local population' (Burns, 2006: 391). In this regard, place marketing practices may contribute to an apparent loss of a sense of place (Malpas, 2008).

In taking these issues into consideration, Kavaratzis and Hatch (2013) argue that effective place branding should simultaneously involve the following processes: *expressing*, which concerns the place's cultural understandings with increased attention to the meanings that local populations attach to a place; *reflecting*, which brings new meanings into culture thus altering place identity; *impressing*, which seeks to leave impressions on others and inform their perceptions, and; *mirroring*, which concerns the mirroring of changes in external images in the brand (Kavaratzis & Hatch, 2013: 80–1). A participatory turn in place branding is reflected in the growing body of work advocating bottom-up, participative approaches as a path to enhanced brand authenticity, stakeholder identification and commitment and brand sustainability (Aitken & Campelo, 2011; Insch & Stuart, 2015; Jernsand & Kraff 2015; Karavatzis, Giovanardi & Lichrou, 2017; Kavaratzis, 2012; Lindstedt, 2011; Zenker & Erfgen, 2014).

These challenges, together with heightened concerns regarding those living in a place and how they are affected by or implicated in the place branding process, have resulted in discussions about the role of sense of place in place branding (Campelo *et al.*, 2014). In this sense, the process of branding as a reflexive, dynamic and collaborative process is far more important than its output as it is a process that can facilitate community engagement with a place (e.g. Lichrou, Patterson, O'Malley & O'Leary, 2017). Furthermore, branding efforts increasingly attempt to incorporate and convey a sense of place as this is experienced by the diverse people living, working and visiting a place. This can be seen in the cases of Belfast and Berlin, discussed by Northover (2010) and Colomb and Kalandides (2010) respectively, where residents' personal stories and experiences (in)formed the two cities' branding campaigns.

A critical marketing perspective on sense of place

The production and consumption of places involves the entanglement of material, discursive and embodied performances (Rabbiosi, 2016). Exploring place brand essence, Skinner (2011) discusses the role of the physical elements of place as well as symbolic meanings and sensory experiences. Marketing, then, seeks to appreciate the aforementioned elements, to capitalize on and promote particular senses of place. Returning to Santorini, it is not surprising that the most widely circulated sense of place centres on the experience of the Caldera, which has fascinated artists, scientists and visitors alike and is often the pride of local residents (Lichrou, O'Malley & Patterson, 2014). In the words of a Greek photographer:

> It is not easy to describe Santorini with words, as is the case with everything unique. Once you stand on the Caldera you feel awe before the almightiness of nature. Nowhere else one encounters so closely life and death, white and black, tame and wild, light and darkness. [...] Which artist isn't inspired by this theme? Which photographer will remain unmoved by Santorini?
>
> *(Talianes, 1998: front inside cover, author's translation)*

Undeniably, the experience described above is the most distinct aspect of Santorini for visitors. To borrow Casey's (2001) concept, the *impressionism* of Santorini is rooted in the experience of the Caldera, an experience characterized by a certain intensity. By 'impressionism of place', Casey refers to the mark a place can leave on us, because 'the presence of a place remains lodged in our body long after we have left it, ready to be revived when the appropriate impression or sensation arises' (Casey, 2001: 688). Sense of place is an embodied experience involving corporeal, cognitive and affective processes involved (Rakić &

Marketing a sense of place

Chambers, 2012). For Tuan (1977: 6–7), it is important to give attention to the ways 'people feel about space and place, to take into account the different modes of experience (sensorimotor, tactile, visual, conceptual), and to interpret space and place as images of complex—often ambivalent—feelings'.

However, a sense of Santorini is not confined to the awe-inspiring view of the Caldera but involves a multiplicity of experiences, from extraordinary to mundane, from pleasant to unpleasant. These include the traffic of the main road of the island, the music and other noises coming out of nightclubs, the bustle of shops, the smells of the traditional produce at the local food market, walking on the cobbled alleys, drinking cocktails at the bars in the evening, sunbathing on a black sand beach and so on. It is precisely this multiplicity of experiences that the exhibition (*SantoREni: work in progress*), cited in the introduction of this chapter, addressed, challenging the fixation to the postcard imagery of the Caldera. This shifts attention to other less celebrated senses of place. Opening the exhibition, visual artist Assimis (2012) talked about how 'Santorini is ten different Santorinies', and described how the different senses of place change as one experiences different geographical locations of the island at different times of the year. The artist, explained the purpose of the work as follows:

> The photographs, as well as the video, attempt to depict and explore this new landscape, which is always in motion. The aim is to first understand it, and then to move away from this postcard-like perpetual image of Santorini -not because it doesn't exist- but because it doesn't exist outside the social reality of today.
>
> *(cited in Anonymous, 2012: online)*

The aforementioned event thus prompts a rethinking of the sense of place of Santorini in this case, but also a sense of place in general. It sheds light on the diversity of experiences as well as the temporality and social embeddedness of sense of place. In this regard, sense of place is existential and political. Relph (1997) describes how a sense of place is in part an 'innate facility' that we all possess to some extent. It is our awareness of and ability to connect with one's surroundings. However, he also understands sense of place as a learned skill, offering the example of geography as a discipline that engenders a 'critical environmental awareness' (Relph, 1997). Recognizing sense of place as both an innate ability and a learned skill, we can argue that sense of place is influenced by the social reality in which one is embedded. To give one example, talking about his experiences growing up in Santorini, a young entrepreneur (in his 30s) recalls:

> I have experienced tourism since I was 6 years old. I remember that I opened my eyes and I was selling coca colas and orangeades. This is how I remember it, this is how it started. [...] I grew up within this, talking to the American, interacting with the tourists, with customers who were passing by, with [...] people from the first cruise ships that had started arriving [...].
>
> *(cited in Lichrou et al., 2017: 112)*

As such, a sense of place as a form of relation to and belonging to place (Cross, 2001) develops within particular social, political and economic circumstances. For instance, Lichrou et al. (2014), focusing on local narratives of Santorini, discussed three distinct and competing senses of place and associated forms of belongingness. The first two were clearly associated with tourism; 'harsh beauty' expressed primarily a tourist sense of place focusing on the intense aesthetic experience of the island's landscape, and 'service business' expressed an entrepreneurial sense, focusing on commercial success and facilitation of customer satisfaction for tourists (Lichrou et al., 2014). Third, a sense of Santorini as 'home' was demarcated both spatially and temporally from tourism (Lichrou et al., 2014).

The different senses exposed not only a diversity of experiences and perspectives among different participants, some of whom identified more as entrepreneurs and others as residents, but also different moments in a single participant's narrative as the same participant often embodied different roles. Thus, we see how their relationship with and experience of place did not take place in a vacuum, but was embedded, shaped by and, in turn, shaped the social, political and economic life of the island. Elsewhere, Lichrou *et al.* (2017) discuss the discontent expressed by participants due to the rapid changes caused by touristification and local efforts (reflected in the exhibition discussed earlier) to move beyond a single image to confront and make sense of the changes taking place and to imagine alternatives for the island's future. Researching sense of place should therefore be open to the multiplicity of place experiences and to 'challenge notions of past authenticities' and the 'possibility of change in the future (Massey, 1999: 288, cited in Agnew, 2011: 325).

Conclusion

Following the recognition that places are open, dynamic and contested, and appreciating the role of sense of place in the place branding process, a critical marketing approach considers the dialectical process through which the physical space is imbued with symbolic meaning (Meethan, 1996; 2001), the entanglement of material, discursive and embodied performances in the production and consumption of places (Rabbiosi, 2016) as well as the corporeal, cognitive and affective processes involved (Rakić & Chambers, 2012). Reflecting on these issues, this chapter has explored sense of place from a critical marketing perspective. In doing so, we have presented different understandings of place, combining tourism and marketing literatures. We have traced a trajectory from functional to representational and participatory understandings of place. Finally, we have discussed sense of place drawing attention to the dialectical relationship between material and symbolic, as well as existential and political dimensions.

From a critical marketing perspective, sense of place should not be seen in isolation from other elements of place such as a place's materiality, the practices and structures of social interactions, the institutions that regulate them, and the systems of representations involved in the production of place meanings (Kavaratzis & Kalandides, 2015). Such an approach offers possibilities both for scholars of place marketing/branding as well as practitioners. An open, dynamic and relational understanding of sense of place helps towards moving away from romanticized, static understandings of place. In this regard, marketing a sense of place is not a one-dimensional process focusing merely on tourist imagery and needs. The experiences and meanings of those living and working in a place are a critical dimension. Through a critical participatory approach, we can challenge notions of the past and open up possibilities for progressive change in the future.

References

Agnew, J. (2011) Space and place. In J. Agnew and D. Livingstone (Eds.), *The Sage Handbook of Geographical Knowledge*. London: Sage, pp. 316–330.

Aitken, R. and Campelo, A. (2011) The four Rs of place branding. *Journal of Marketing Management*, 27(9–10), 913–933.

Amin, A. and Thrift, N. (2002) *Cities: Reimagining the Urban*. Cambridge: Polity Press.

Marketing a sense of place

Anonymous (2012) On Friday is the grand opening of the exhibition 'santoR.Eni': Work in progress [translation from Greek]. *Atlantea*. Available at: https://atlantea.news/tin_paraskevi_ta_egkainia_tis_ekthesis_santoreni_ergo_se_exelixi/ (Accessed 5 December 2019).

Ashworth, G. J. and Voodg, H. (1990a) Can places be sold for tourism? In G. Ashworth and B. Goodall (Eds.), *Marketing Tourism Places*. London and New York: Routledge, pp. 1–16.

Ashworth, G. J. and Voogd, H. (1990b) *Selling the City: Marketing Approaches in Public Sector Urban Planning*. London: Belhaven Press.

Ashworth, G. J. and Voogd, H. (1994) Marketing and place promotion. In J. R. Gold and S. Ward (Eds.), *Place Promotion: The Use of Publicity and Marketing to Sell Towns and Regions*. Chichester: John Wiley & Sons, pp. 39–52.

Assimis, K. (2012) Santorini is ten different Santorinies [translation from Greek]. Talk at the opening of Zoe Hatziyannaki's photographic exhibition *SantoR.Eni: Work in progress*, featured in *Atlantea*. Available at: https://atlantea.news/i_santorini_einai_deka_diaforetikes_santorines/ (Accessed 4 December 2019).

Bain, C. (2019) Santorini for first-timers. *Lonely Planet*, online featured article Available at: https://www.lonelyplanet.com/articles/santorini-for-first-timers (Accessed 30 December 2019).

Bendix, R. (2002) Capitalizing on memories past, present, and future: Observations on the intertwining of tourism and narration. *Anthropological Theory*, 2(4), 469–487.

Boisen, M., Terlouw, K. and van Gorp, B. (2011) The selective nature of place branding and the layering of spatial identities. *Journal of Place Management and Development*, 4(2), 135–147.

Boisen, M., Terlouw, K., Groote, P. and Couwenberg, O. (2018) Reframing place promotion, place marketing, and place branding-moving beyond conceptual confusion. *Cities*, 80, 4–11.

Borgerson, J. L. and Schroeder, J. E. (2002) Ethical issues of global marketing: Avoiding bad faith in visual representation. *European Journal of Marketing*, 36(5/6), 570–594.

Britton, R. A. (1979) The image of the Third World in tourism marketing. *Annals of Tourism Research*, 6(3), 318–329.

Bruner, J. (1991) The narrative construction of reality. *Critical Inquiry*, 18(1), 1–21.

Bruner, J. (2004) Life as narrative. *Social Research: An International Quarterly*, 71(3), 691–710.

Buhalis, D. (2000) Marketing the competitive destination of the future. *Tourism Management*, 21(1), 97–116.

Burns, P. M. (2004) Six postcards from Arabia: A visual discourse of colonial travels in the Orient. *Tourist Studies*, 4(3), 255–275.

Burns, P. M. (2006) Social identities and the cultural politics of tourism. In P. M. Burns and M. Novelli (Eds.), *Tourism and Social Identities*. Oxford: Elsevier, pp. 29–40.

Campelo, A., Aitken, R., Thyne, M. and Gnoth, J. (2014) Sense of place: The importance for destination branding. *Journal of Travel Research*, 53(2), 154–166.

Casey, E. S. (2001) Between geography and philosophy: What does it mean to be in the place-world? *Annals of the Association of American Geographers*, 91(4), 683–693.

Colomb, C. and Kalandides, A. (2010) The 'be Berlin' campaign: Old wine in new bottles or innovative form of participatory place branding. In G. Ashworth and M. Kavaratzis (Eds.), *Towards Effective Place Brand Management: Branding European Cities and Regions*. Cheltenham: Edward Elgar, pp. 173–190.

Costa, J. A. (1998) Paradisal discourse: A critical analysis of marketing and consuming Hawaii. *Consumption, Markets and Culture*, 1(4), 303–346.

Cresswell, T. (2009) Place. In R. Kitchin and N. Thrift (Eds.), *International Encyclopedia of Human Geography*, 8, 169–177.

Crick, M. (1996) Representations of international tourism in the social sciences: Sun, sex, sights, savings, and servility, In G. Apostolopoulos, S. Leivadi and A. Yiannakis (Eds.), *The Sociology of Tourism: Theoretical and Empirical Investigations*. London: Routledge, pp. 15–50.

Cross, J. E. (2001). What is sense of place? Paper prepared for the 12th Headwaters Conference, Western State College, November 2–4, 2001. Colorado State University Libraries.

Crouch, G. I. and Ritchie, J. B. (1999) Tourism, competitiveness, and societal prosperity. *Journal of Business Research*, 44(3), 137–152.

Echtner, C. M. and Prasad, P. (2003) The context of third world tourism marketing. *Annals of Tourism Research*, 30(3), 660–682.

Foley, A. and Fahy, J. (2004) Incongruity between expression and experience: The role of imagery in supporting the positioning of a tourism destination brand. *Journal of Brand Management*, 11(3), 209–217.

Framke, W. (2002) The destination as a concept: A discussion of the business-related perspective versus the socio-cultural approach in tourism theory. *Scandinavian Journal of Hospitality and Tourism*, 2(2), 92–108.

Giovanardi, M., Lucarelli, A. and Pasquinelli, C. (2013) Towards brand ecology: An analytical semiotic framework for interpreting the emergence of place brands. *Marketing Theory*, 13(3), 365–383.

Gnoth, J. (2007) The structure of destination brands: Leveraging values. *Tourism Analysis*, 12(5–6), 345–358.

Goodwin, M. (1993) The city as commodity: The contested spaces of urban development. In G. Kearns and C. Philo, C. (Eds.), *Selling Places: The City as Cultural Capital, Past and Present*, Oxford: Pergamon Press, pp. 145–162.

Gotham, K. F. (2002) Marketing Mardi Gras: Commodification, spectacle and the political economy of tourism in New Orleans. *Urban Studies*, 39(10), 1735–1756.

Govers, R. and Go, F. (2016) *Place Branding: Glocal, Virtual and Physical Identities, Constructed, Imagined and Experienced*. Basingstoke: Palgrave Macmillan.

Graham, B. (2002) Heritage as knowledge: Capital or culture? *Urban Studies*, 39(5–6), 1003–1017.

Griffiths, R. (1998) Making sameness: Place marketing and the new urban entrepreneurialism. In N. Oatley (Ed.), *Cities, Economic Competition and Urban Policy*. London: Sage Publications, pp. 41–57.

Hall, C. M. (2000) *Tourism Planning: Policies, Processes and Relationships*. Harlow: Prentice Hall.

Harvey, D. (1989) From managerialism to entrepreneurialism: The transformation in urban governance in late capitalism. *Geografiska Annaler, Series B, Human Geography*, 71(1), 3–17.

Haywood, K. M. (1990) Revising and implementing the marketing concept as it applies to tourism. *Tourism Management*, 11(3), 195–205.

Hughes, G. (1998) Tourism and the semiological realization of space. In G. Ringer (Ed.), *Destinations: Cultural Landscapes of Tourism*. London: Routledge, pp. 17–32.

Human, B. (1999) Kodachrome icons: Photography, place and the theft of identity. *International Journal of Contemporary Hospitality Management*, 11(2/3), 80–84.

Insch, A. and Stuart, M. (2015) Understanding resident city brand disengagement. *Journal of Place Management and Development*, 8(3), 172–186.

Iwashita, C. (2006) Media representation of the UK as a destination for Japanese tourists: Popular culture and tourism. *Tourist Studies*, 6(1), 59–77.

Jernsand, E. M. and Kraff, H. (2015) Participatory place branding through design: The case of Dunga beach in Kisumu, Kenya. *Place Branding and Public Diplomacy*, 11(3), 226–242.

Karavatzis, M., Giovanardi, M. and Lichrou, M. (Eds.) (2017) *Inclusive Place Branding: Critical Perspectives on Theory and Practice*. Abingdon, Routledge.

Kavaratzis, M. (2004) From city marketing to city branding: Towards a theoretical framework for developing city brands. *Place Branding and Public Diplomacy*, 1(1), 58–73.

Kavaratzis, M. (2012) From 'necessary evil' to necessity: Stakeholders' involvement in place branding. *Journal of Place Management and Development*, 5(1), 7–19.

Kavaratzis, M. and Hatch, M. J. (2013) The dynamics of place brands: An identity-based approach to place branding theory. *Marketing Theory*, 13(1), 69–86.

Kavaratzis, M. and Kalandides, A. (2015) Rethinking the place brand: The interactive formation of place brands and the role of participatory place branding. *Environment and Planning A*, 47(6), 1368–1382.

Kearns, G. and Philo, C. (1993) *Selling Places: The City as Cultural Capital, Past and Present*. Oxford: Pergamon.

Kotler, P. and Gertner, D. (2004) Country ad brand, product and beyond: A place marketing and brand management perspective. In N. Morgan, A. Pritchard and R. Pride (Eds.), *Destination Branding: Creating the Unique Destination Proposition*. Oxford: Elsevier Butterworth-Heinemann, pp. 40–56.

Kotler, P., Haider, D. H. and Rein, I. J. (1993) *Marketing Places: Attracting Investment, Industry, and Tourism to Cities, States, and Nations*. New York: Free Press.

Lash, S. and Urry, J. (1994) *Economies of Signs and Space*. London: Sage Publications.

Lichrou, M., O'Malley, L. and Patterson, M. (2014) On the marketing implications of place narratives. *Journal of Marketing Management*, 30(9–10), 832–856.

Lichrou, M., O'Malley, L. and Patterson, M. (2017) Making Santorini: Reflecting on the past, imagining the future. *Journal of Place Management and Development*, 10(2), 106–120.

Lichrou, M., Patterson, M., O'Malley, L. and O'Leary, K. (2017) Place branding and place narratives. In A. Campelo (Ed.), *Handbook on Place Branding and Marketing*. Chichester: Edward Elgar, pp. 160–177.

Marketing a sense of place

Lindstedt, J. (2011) Place, identity and the socially responsible construction of place brands. *Place Branding and Public Diplomacy*, 7(1), 42–49.

Malpas, J. (2008) New media, cultural heritage and the sense of place: Mapping the conceptual ground. *International Journal of Heritage Studies*, 14(3), 197–209.

McCabe, S. and Stokoe, E. H. (2004) Place and identity in tourists' accounts. *Annals of Tourism Research*, 31(3), 601–622.

Meethan, K. (1996) Consuming (in) the civilized city. *Annals of Tourism Research*, 23(2), 322–340.

Meethan, K. (2001) *Tourism in Global Society: Place, Culture, Consumption*. Basingstoke: Palgrave.

Milano, C., Cheer, J. M. and Novelli, M. (Eds.) (2019) *Overtourism: Excesses, Discontents and Measures in Travel and Tourism*. Wallingford: CABI.

Milano, C., Novelli, M. and Cheer, J. M. (2019) Overtourism and degrowth: A social movements perspective. *Journal of Sustainable Tourism*, 27(12), 1857–1875.

Miles, S. (2010) *Spaces for Consumption*. London: Sage Publications.

Morgan, N. and Pritchard, A. (1998) *Tourism Promotion and Power: Creating Images, Creating Identities*. Chichester: John Wiley & Sons Ltd.

Munar, M. A. (2011) Tourist-created content: Rethinking destination branding. *International Journal of Culture, Tourism and Hospitality Research*, 5(3), 291–305.

Murphy, P., Pritchard, M. P. and Smith, B. (2000) The destination product and its impact on traveller perceptions. *Tourism Management*, 21(1), 43–52.

Northover, J. (2010) A brand for Belfast: How can branding a city influence change? *Place Branding and Public Diplomacy*, 6(2), 104–111.

Panayiotopoulos, A. and Pisano, C. (2019) Overtourism dystopias and socialist utopias: Towards an urban armature for Dubrovnik. *Tourism Planning & Development* 16(4), 393–410.

Rabbiosi, C. (2016) Place branding performances in tourist local food shops. *Annals of Tourism Research*, 60, 154–168.

Rakić, T. and Chambers, D. (2012) Rethinking the consumption of places. *Annals of Tourism Research*, 39(3), 1612–1633.

Relph, E. (1997) Sense of place. In S. Hanson (Ed.), *Ten Geographic Ideas that Changed the World*. New Brunswick: Rutgers University Press, 205–226.

Relph, E. (2007) Spirit of place and sense of place in virtual realities. *Techné: Research in Philosophy and Technology*, 10(3), 17–25.

Richards, G. and Wilson, J. (2006) Developing creativity in tourist experiences: A solution to the serial reproduction of culture? *Tourism Management*, 27(6), 1209–1223.

Rickly-Boyd, J. M. (2009) The tourist narrative. *Tourist Studies*, 9(3), 259–280.

Rojek, C. (1997) Indexing, dragging and the social construction of tourist sights. In J. Urry and C. Rojek (Eds.), *Touring Cultures: Transformations of Travel and Theory*. London: Routledge, pp. 62–84.

Saarinen, J. (1998) The social construction of tourist destinations: The process of transformation of the Saariselkä tourism region in Finnish Lapland. In G. Ringer (Ed.), *Destinations: Cultural Landscapes of Tourism*. London: Routledge, pp. 54–73.

Santos, C. A. (2004) Framing Portugal: Representational dynamics. *Annals of Tourism Research*, 31(1), 122–138.

Selwyn, T. (1996) *The Tourist Image: Myths and Myth Making in Tourism*. Chichester: John Wiley & Sons.

Shaw, G. and Williams, A. M. (2004) *Tourism and Tourism Spaces*. London: Sage Publications.

Skinner, H. (2008) The emergence and development of place marketing's confused identity. *Journal of Marketing Management*, 24(9–10), 915–928.

Skinner, H. (2011) In search of the genius loci: The essence of a place brand. *The Marketing Review*, 11(3), 281–292.

Stedman, R. C. (2003) Is it really just a social construction? The contribution of the physical environment to sense of place. *Society & Natural Resources*, 16(8), 671–685.

Steele, F. (1981) *The Sense of Place*. Boston: CBI Publishing Company, Inc.

Stokowski, P. A. (2002) Languages of place and discourses of power: Constructing new senses of place. *Journal of Leisure Research*, 34(4), 368–382.

Suvantola, J. (2002) *Tourist's Experience of Place: New Directions in Tourism Analysis*. Farnham: Ashgate.

Talianes, D. (1998) *Santorini: And the Sea 'Gave Birth to the Land'*. Athens: Topio Publications.

Trapp-Fallon, J. M. (2003) Searching for rich narratives of tourism and leisure experience: How oral history could provide an answer. *Tourism and Hospitality Research*, 4(4), 297–305.

Tuan, Y. F. (1977) *Space and Place: The Perspective of Experience*. Minneapolis: University of Minnesota Press.

Turok, I. (2009) The distinctive city: Pitfalls in the pursuit of differential advantage. *Environment and Planning A*, 41(1), 13–30.

Urry, J. (1990) *The Tourist Gaze: Leisure and Travel in Contemporary Societies*. London: Sage Publications.

Urry, J. (1995) *Consuming Places*. London: Routledge.

Voase, R. (1999) 'Consuming' tourist sites/sights: A note on York. *Leisure Studies*, 18(4), 289–296.

Warnaby, G. and Medway, D. (2013) What about the 'place' in place marketing? *Marketing Theory*, 13(3), 345–363.

Warnaby, G., Medway, D. and Bennison, D. (2010) Notions of materiality and linearity: The challenges of marketing the Hadrian's Wall place 'product'. *Environment and Planning A*, 42(6), 1365–1382.

Young, M. (1999) The social construction of tourist places. *Australian Geographer*, 30(3), 373–389.

Zenker, S. and Erfgen, C. (2014) Let them do the work: A participatory place branding approach. *Journal of Place Management and Development*, 7(3), 225–234.

34

THE IMPORTANCE OF BUILT HERITAGE IN THE ENGLISH SEASIDE EXPERIENCE

David Jarratt

Introduction

The United Nations estimates that approximately half of tourists visit a coastal area whilst, within the European Union, 51% of all hotel bed capacity is concentrated in coastal areas and in the UK, seaside locations account for 39% of holiday nights (European Commission, n.d.; UNWTO, 2013; Visit Britain, 2016). So, a high proportion of all leisure tourism is coastal tourism – which can be defined as 'the full range of tourism, leisure, and recreationally oriented activities that take place in the coastal zone and the offshore coastal waters' (Hall, 2001: 602). At this point, one may question if coastal tourism in general and seaside tourism in particular differ? In other words, what do we mean by 'seaside'? A quick survey of dictionary definitions suggests that the most common definition of seaside is, first and foremost, a place by the sea, but *especially* a holiday area – most commonly a resort. So, in common usage the 'seaside' embraces an element of leisure or tourism; this, in turn, reflects how most inland dwellers access this coast – as visitors. Hence, the concepts of coastal tourism and seaside tourism are in some respects very similar, although the latter implies an increased emphasis on popular forms of tourism and, therefore, resorts. As such, it is the correct term for this chapter, the focus of which is on the most popular form of coastal leisure tourism in England – visiting a traditional seaside resort.

There are no earlier examples of mass tourism than these seaside resorts which, in the nineteenth century, grew rapidly to accommodate demand from the residents of the new towns and cities of the Industrial Revolution. By the early twentieth century, their scale and complexity was unmatched. Despite economic restructuring, increased competition and other challenges, they remain popular today; indeed, when one considers that these places are products of the Industrial Revolution, they have proven remarkably adaptive and resilient (Walton, 2000). There now exists, of course, a significant variety of seaside resorts across the globe and they offer a range of experiences but, arguably, the combined historical and contemporary cultural significance of the English resorts offers a unique opportunity to consider the touristic experience of the seaside.

The purpose of this chapter, then, is to consider the visitor experience of the English seaside resorts of today. Inevitably, such experiences will vary a great deal, for seaside visitors comprise a large, heterogeneous group and the way in which they experience the coast

DOI: 10.4324/9781003219866-39

481

will inevitably differ, just as seaside places across England also differ. Nonetheless, if the seaside experience is explored from the perspective of broader cultural themes and meanings associated with English resorts, then a number of patterns emerge. The seaside is on the limen of the built environment and the ocean, which represents nature or even wilderness to modern man (see Gillis, 2012), and can therefore be considered as a culture–nature interface. The natural element of this interface holds a popular appeal that transcends any one country or culture. Specifically, natural spaces are more likely to facilitate topophilia, or place-attachment, for those living in urban-based cultures (Beery, Jönsson & Elmberg, 2015; Tuan, 1974). So, in contemporary Western culture, a positive genius loci and emotionally charged experiences are more likely to be associated with these spaces (Tuan, 1974). The seaside is one example of natural spaces but, whilst the appeal of nature may seem universal, the cultural element of the coastal nature–culture interface is more specific and one with which, arguably, visitors are likely to identify. Elborough (2010: 8) describes the English seaside as 'deeply cultural', a place which is often part of personal history, as well as of national history. In particular, therefore, this chapter explores the experiential elements of this seaside sense of place. Specifically, it considers the English seaside resort as an enduring socio-cultural construction that is framed by the physically constructed, or *built*, environment. The buildings and built heritage of the seaside are absolutely essential to its character and to the seaside experience.

The seaside as a cultural space

There appears to be a disconnect between the seaside in our head (or *heart*) and the physical reality of these resorts. For one thing, there is quite a variety of English seaside resorts. For instance, Brighton is a successful and cosmopolitan city by the sea, whilst Blackpool has managed to retain its popular/working-class appeal as the Las Vegas of the North. The small coastal town of Grange-over-Sands now functions as a retirement town for the middle classes and a place for day-trippers, and regenerated Margate is seen by some as 'Shoreditch by the Sea' (Shoreditch is a fashionable residential are in east London). Conversely, New Brighton, on the Mersey Estuary, embodies the most pessimistic potential outcomes of the Tourism Area Life Cycle Model (Butler, 1980) – the end of tourism. Interestingly, Grange-over-Sands, in complete contrast to New Brighton, never witnessed decline (Walton, 2000). This variety of seaside histories demonstrates that there is neither an inevitable seaside narrative nor a single experience of English seaside resorts. Instead, there is a complex interaction of macro and micro factors, from the global to the local, which determine why some resorts fair better than others. It is clear that many seaside resorts fell from grace during the second half of the twentieth century as mobility, wealth, visitor aspirations and competition were in a state of flux. The medium-sized working class resorts, such as Clacton or Morecambe, seemed to be especially hard hit – they were too small to keep attracting tourists but too big to become exclusive (Jarratt, 2019). Yet, despite the variety in scale, economic fortune, class connotations and other differences, all of these places are a part of the seaside – not just because of their coastal locations but because of a particular set of cultural features and visitor beliefs/behaviour that distinguish them. So, apart from proximity to the ocean, what makes the seaside the seaside – what is its genius loci or sense of place?

Before addressing this last question, we briefly consider place and 'sense of place' more generally. Place is a concept that can be interpreted in a number of different ways but, in simple terms, it can be defined as space that has been ascribed meaning: 'place = space + meaning' (Turner & Turner, 2006: 205). Furthermore, it is fluid, subjective and socially constructed. Tuan, one of the foremost scholars of place, focuses upon experience that is a 'cover-all term for the various modes through which a person knows and constructs a reality' (Tuan, 2011: 8). He stresses that experience and place cannot be fully separated (Tuan, 1974). Indeed, place is the crucible in which experience is forged.

Sense of place is referred to when place identity is significant enough to be experienced; it is the emotional attachment people have to place(s). Jorgenson and Stedman (2001) refer to sense of place as the relationship or bond with a place that is experienced through the individual's conscious and unconscious feelings, ideas and perceptions regarding that environment/place. These different elements interact with each other. For example, Ettenger (2015) identifies how the sense of place of cultural tourists is much influenced not only by their direct experience but also by what they have heard beforehand. In line with these scholars, this chapter adopts the definition offered by Jarratt, Phelan, Wain and Dale (2019: 410): sense of place is

> The fluid and multi-faceted way in which we know notable or memorable places through sensing, experiencing, and remembering a geographical location and its features. It is, therefore, a combination of our interaction with a physical environment and the meanings that we (as individuals and a society) bestow upon it, at the time or subsequently.

Some have considered the genius loci of the seaside. A number explain, in part, this 'indefinable seaside spirit' (Lindley, 1973: 11) through liminality and marginality (Bennett, 1986; Shields, 1991; Webb, 2005). Since industrialization, this zone has hosted the healthy seaside, the carnivalesque seaside and other versions of the seaside in which social actors play their part (Baerenholdt, Haldrup, Larsen & Urry, 2004; Shields, 1991). The culture–nature interface that is the seaside (Preston-Whyte, 2004) grew to be socio-culturally distinct to fulfil its role as a place for tourists to reconnect with nature and with themselves; that is, their authentic selves as opposed to public roles (Wang, 1999). In particular, Wang (1999) suggests that nostalgia or romanticism represent the ideal of the tourist's search for authenticity and it is not, perhaps, coincidental that the traditional British seaside resort is often associated with family holidays, childhood, a romantic view of the past and nostalgia (Walton, 2000, 2010).

These theories point towards the seaside as a distinctive place that hosts a variety of potential meanings, but it is more ambiguous than it is truly transgressive (Chase, 1999). These meanings and the distinctive experience offered by the seaside are now explored in more detail.

Seasideness: sense of place at the seaside

There has been little research that maps the visitors' sense of place at the seaside, although in an attempt to do so, Jarratt (2015) conceptualizes such a sense of place as 'seasideness' – see Figure 34.1.

Seasideness is a distinct sense of place associated with seaside resorts as experienced by visitors to these coastal destinations. It comprises a combination of factors, including the distinctive natural environment, leisure activities undertaken and the built environment of coastal resorts. It is 'a distinctive experience which is centred around the inter-related themes of nostalgia, wellness and spirituality' (Jarratt, 2015: 351). So, this seaside experience is associated with various feelings, especially feelings of restoration and subjective well-being – which embraces a semi-spiritual element. Visitors consider the seaside to be a place of relaxation where the mind is free to wander and where they can experience a sense

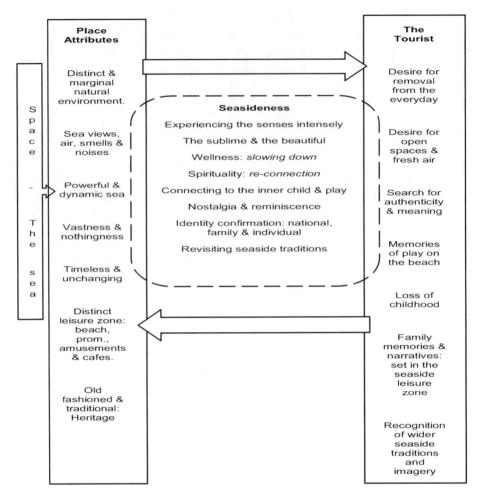

Figure 34.1 Seasideness
Source: Jarratt (2015).

of connection to something bigger and more significant than themselves. This 'something' most often takes the form of 'nature' but can also be something more akin to religious thought (Jarratt & Sharpley, 2017). Wellness also is central to seasideness, perhaps second only to feelings of nostalgia, which is now discussed in more detail.

It is well recognized that nostalgia is a fundamental component of visitor motivation for a variety of tourism experiences (Davis, 1979; Vesey & Dimanche, 2003). Yet, whilst seaside heritage is increasingly recognized; contemporary nostalgia for the seaside rarely affords anything more than a passing comment, although notable exceptions include historian John Walton and the sociologist John Urry. Thirty years ago, the latter commented that seaside resorts should not try to resist the trend to nostalgia but should instead embrace it before further deterioration to tourism occurs (Urry, 1990). More recently, Jarratt and Gammon (2016) discussed seaside nostalgia, primarily based around a definition of nostalgia as an idealized, selective and, therefore, adapted reflection of the past but one which also incorporates a dissatisfaction or frustration with the present – we cannot return to 'the good old days'.

However, nostalgia is not that simple. For example, the extent of the aforementioned dissatisfaction will vary a great deal and it operates on a number of levels, from the individual to the national or another collective. Furthermore, nostalgia does not necessarily rely on personal memories, for stimulated nostalgia is vicarious in nature and can be evoked from images, objects and collective narratives (Goulding, 1999). In essence, nostalgic experiences are intertwined with identity because it facilitates a meaningful narrative from the past. Nostalgic images associated with the seaside are instantly recognizable as 'part of England's collective consciousnesses, our folk memory' (Elborough, 2010: 7). Such nostalgia feeds into national identity; the English shoreline and seaside resort has become a symbol of Englishness (some might say Britishness but the focus here is on England) with one foot in the past (Jarratt, 2015). The decline of resort infrastructure can, of course, lead to physical demolition but, in the stages preceding this, resorts can adopt a faded grandeur that some people find attractive, affirming and deeply nostalgic. In considering the seaside, Bracewell (2004) attempts to explain this:

> For a little while though, within those fading grand hotels, silent boarding houses, dormant ornamental gardens and windswept piers is both an ultimate expression of Englishness and its plangent requiem – the 'sense of something lost', perhaps, prompting nostalgia for a former innocence.

As we saw earlier, the seasideness model reflects the meeting of place and the visitor. Just as the visitor is influenced by their feelings, memories and experiences, the place in question is shaped by distinctive buildings and the sea itself which dominate the somatic environment and, therefore, the visitor experience. Yet, in the study of tourism more generally, the emphasis is more often on the tourist experience rather than on sense of place with which it is bound; indeed, tourism has been associated the very opposite of sense of place – placelessness, and an erosion of 'authentic' landscapes (Relph, 1976). Robinson and Picard (2009) argue that an individual's social experience is more important than the scene in which the tourism experience occurs. Indeed, familiarity with places is an important element of touristic motivation, whether they be 'authentic' or not (Leisen, 2001). Furthermore, the experience of authenticity can be more social and existential than reliant on an objective authenticity (Wang, 1999). Also, any clearly stated sense of place can never be entirely representative of place owing to the dynamic, relational and subjective nature of place in general (Massey, 1997). So, offering a perhaps simplified notion of sense of place, as proposed in the seasideness model (Figure 34.1), does have its limitations. Nevertheless, it is useful as a key component and determining factor in the tourist experience; place is rather more than just the stage upon which tourism is played out. For instance, the seaside's liminal/liminoid nature, which is sometimes described as a part of its appeal, flavours the experience (see also Chapter 7 in this volume).

So, seasideness, as discussed by Jarratt (2015), reflects an experience that spans the boundary of two zones and can be described as limonoid. In other words, the marginal seaside setting is a place where nature physically meets culture in the form of the man-made and

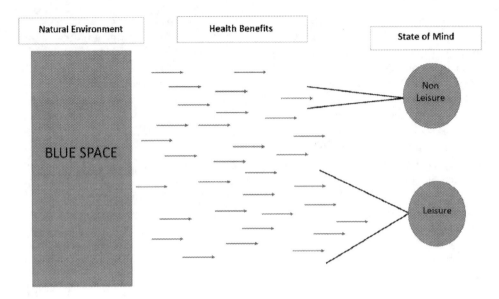

Figure 34.2 Leisure health receptor model
Source: Gammon and Jarratt (2019).

built environment. The multi-sensory sea, which represents wilderness to urban man, can have a Proustian effect. Environmental psychologists tell us that blue spaces offer just the right level of somatic stimulation and exposure to them can have more powerful wellness impacts than green spaces (White et al., 2010). This connection between the coast and wellness is a longstanding one of course; indeed, the word 'resort' comes from the Old French 'restortir' – something you turn to for help or assistance. In addition to the health benefits of blue spaces, the leisure state of mind could also be an intervening factor in this coastal wellness (see Figure 34.2).

What seems to have attracted less attention, however, is the impact of exposure to built elements of the seaside, the most obvious manifestation of the cultural side of this boundary. The marginal setting seems to be an appropriate one for the traditional limonoid or carnivalesque seaside behaviours. These tended to take place on the beach, promenade or in the buildings that line the coast. In other words, these places served a purpose. Many couples were to meet in The Winter Gardens and dance halls and piers around the English coast, The Grand (hotel) in Brighton is synonymous with the 'dirty weekend' and all piers have an element of romance. The quote from Gray, in the next section, sums this up well.

Seaside architecture – framing seasideness

At some point in their lives, most people in Western societies have, in search of leisure and pleasure, holidayed in resorts by the sea. These experiences, together with a multitude of seaside images from postcards to films, and from novels to advertisements, leave people with complex memories and feelings about the seaside. Cut through and sequenced by time and place, these might include sunburnt childhood holidays on a beach littered, depending on the place, with deckchairs and windbreaks or sun loungers and parasols; teenagers having fun in the sea or open air lido; fumbled first sexual encounters under a pier; a family stroll along a promenade or boardwalk or a cliff-top park; visits to seaside entertainment complexes, from funfairs to casinos; or old people sitting in a seafront shelter watching the world go by. These examples, of course, are deliberately chosen to make the point that the resort experience is frequently framed and conditioned by seaside architecture: the buildings and built form, the open spaces and design detail, that go to make up resorts.

(Gray, 2006: 7)

The promenade and the buildings along *the front* are vital to the identity of the seaside resort and a wealth of distinctive seaside architectural survives along the British coast. This built heritage spans many different times and places and cannot be easily summarized here (see, for example, Brodie, 2018; Brodie & Winter, 2007; Gray, 2006). One distinguishing feature of seaside architectural heritage, however, is a tendency towards the out-of-the-ordinary and fantastic, especially from the nineteenth century onwards. Orientalism and other 'exotic' architectural designs have come to represent seaside architecture and are important to the 'otherness' of the seaside (Ferry, 2009; Gray, 2006). Examples include the Morecambe's Central Pier, which was once known as the 'The Taj Mahal of the North' because of its intricate domes although this structure has now sadly disappeared (Ferry, 2009: 102), Marine Parade in Bexhill, the impressive Royal Pavilion in Brighton as well as a variety of shelters and bandstands (see Figure 34.3). This exoticism feeds into a distinctive sense of place that Elborough (2010: 227) captures well:

The seaside, though, was always about being somewhere else, in English life. Historically, literally points of departure for travelers, its stock in trade was offering a departure from normality. The architecture, from ornamental iron balustrades and Raj bandstands to the glitterball-lit ball rooms and neon-signed amusement arcades, seduced by transporting visitors into realms of fantasy.

The tendency towards the out of the ordinary continued and in the inter-war and post-war period, seaside architecture took an art-deco and modernist direction(s) which was equally distinct (see Steele, 2015 and Figures 34.4, 34.5 and 34.6).

The seaside experience of resorts is one that has remained surprisingly unscathed in the minds of many English visitors, and there can be little doubt that a hazy nostalgia has played a role in this. Yet, the physical reality is somewhat different. Tourism has continued through the years but there have been causalities in terms of seaside heritage. With the ravages of time and changing leisure and tourism patterns, the built heritage at the seaside has suffered; structures and buildings have disappeared or changed usage (Jarratt, 2019). The removal of seaside heritage is still taking place today. Most seaside heritage has remained outside the authorized heritage discourse (the traditional/mainstream view of heritage as sanctioned by experts) but in this century, a growing number of voices have begun to consider it significant (Smith, 2006).

In 2001, the English Tourism Council observed that 'Seaside resorts have made an enormous contribution to the cultural identity of England and contain some of the finest examples of our built heritage. This is overlooked rather than promoted' (ETC, 2001: 23). However, since then it seems that surviving seaside heritage is overlooked less frequently. For example, the grade two listed Blackpool Winter Gardens now boasts heritage tours and

Figure 34.3 Brighton's Western Bandstand – Orientalism from the Victorian period
Source: Kathryn Ferry (reproduced with permission).

Blackpool museum will soon be under construction. Dreamland in Margate, which is now grade two listed, has reopened. Weston-Super-Mare's Grand Pier was reopened in 2010 after investment of over £51 million following a fire. Britain has a National Pier Society (see https://piers.org.uk/) and these vulnerable structures are the objects of 'affectionate nostalgia' (Walton, 2010: 1). English Heritage has shown an interest in seaside heritage and surveyed resorts in 2002 (Brodie & Winter, 2007) and more recently the sea front itself has been carefully examined (Brodie, 2018). The overdue recognition of seaside architecture is underway, yet working-class resorts are still subject to stigma (see Walton & Wood, 2009). One reason for this delay in recognition is the focus on the heritage of production rather than consumption – seaside resorts are still in use, quite unlike most industrial heritage sites in the UK which are representative of something more clearly consigned to the past. With time, we may see an even wider recognition and nostalgic appreciation of English seaside heritage through the experiences of coastal visitors.

Case-study: Morecambe

Morecambe, in Lancashire in north-west England, is a medium-sized seaside resort that developed in the nineteenth century. During the twentieth century, it boomed as a working-class

The importance of built heritage

Figure 34.4 Blackpool pleasure beach and casino, designed in the international modern style by Joseph Emberton and built during 1937–1940
Source: Jenny Steele (reproduced with permission).

resort before falling into a very sharp decline during the 1970s and 1980s. Much of the original resort infrastructure, including the two piers, a large lido, a variety of popular entertainment venues and the majority of accommodation providers were lost (see Jarratt, 2019 for more detail). By the turn of the new millennium, regeneration was underway, but progress was slow. Today, the resort offers a popular promenade, a well-known hotel, some early to mid-twentieth century built heritage and, as always, impressive views across Morecambe Bay towards the Lake District, but little else in terms of tourism infrastructure.

The research discussed here formed part of a wider study that looked at the seaside experience in Morecambe (see Jarratt, 2013). It revolved around semi-structured interviews and aimed to reflect a perspective in some depth, rather than a population, as is common in studies of this type (Smith, Flowers & Larkin, 2009). Interviewees were aged 55–74 years, resided in the North of England and were repeat visitors, thereby reflecting the typical profile of a visitor to Morecambe.

For the interviewees, the place identity of the British seaside, specifically Morecambe, operated on different, interconnected, levels. These meanings were both individual and collective. In broad terms, place-related meanings operated on the basis of the individual, family and nationality. Typically, childhood holidays with loved ones were remembered on the one hand and a sense of tradition and national identity was expressed on the other. Morecambe reminded visitors of Englishness (the term Britishness was also used), chiefly because it is considered an old-fashioned place rich in English leisure traditions and history. In a similar fashion, cultural signifiers, such as sticks of rock, Bed and Breakfasts, sandcastles and the windswept front were all identified as symbols of the English seaside. Cultural signifiers constitute the building blocks of place identity and sense of place. For the interviewees, cultural signifiers mark the past and are intertwined with memory:

> I think a lot of people sort of my age in a way, remember about the seaside, would be the typical visit to the seaside, spending time on the beach, the ice cream, the building sand castles, they…the paddling, all those sort of things that would be a typical seaside visit for kids my age back in, in the you know, the sort of 50s, early 60s.

The beach and the built environment held more cultural signifiers than any other aspect of the seaside environment. When asked what, if any, changes they would like to see to the resort, the interviewees referred to new or improved swimming pools, theatres and more cafes. The suggestions were always attractions that Morecambe already had or had lost over the years. The interviewees wanted Morecambe to be a traditional seaside resort, just a *better one* or one more like the way it used to be, with built heritage being a key part of this. They viewed the Tern Project (the regenerated promenade with various artworks) favourably but considered the regeneration of the resort as piecemeal and incomplete. Tangible heritage was considered a positive defining characteristic of Morecambe by interviewees. The Victorian and inter-war periods were often referred to and the related tangible heritage appeared to be valued:

> Them old buildings are, are the… they were built a lot in Victorian times but they're still fine buildings, and that is what when you go to a seaside and you look at all bed and breakfasts' along the front and, and they are the essence of, of the seaside anyway…

For the respondents, built heritage offered an appealing tradition and tangible link to the past, but also cemented a distinct place identity. One interviewee thought that many contemporary towns and cities lacked the distinctiveness still offered by seaside resorts that have retained something of what they were:

> When we were youngsters if you went to a… Well like it you just went to Preston or Wigan you would get a variety of shops that were owned by different people and I mean now you just go and they're all the same…

However, this distinctiveness is not entirely positive, as the image of seaside towns as old-fashioned and even run-down was recognized:

> I think that's the image you get and sort of almost all of them have seen their heyday and they're not as they were.

Such negative assertions do not entirely go against visitor appeal; rather, they feed into a bitter-sweet nostalgia for the past. Such decay marks a stage further back; it allows a connection to a golden age. One interviewee acknowledged some changes to the resort since his youth but overlooked decay to enjoy a place rich in narrative and meaning. He distinguished between the physical characteristics of place and the meaning he continues to ascribe to such resorts:

> Physically obviously everything changes. But I think in our minds, culturally, it's a great place to go and enjoy yourself.

Nostalgia not only allowed such enjoyment but appeared to very much underpin visitor appeal. Nostalgia was savoured; interviewees considered it to be one of the primary reasons to visit, as the following quote suggests:

> ...it's a trip down memory lane really when we go to Morecambe. And I, I certainly enjoy it myself. It's not too far, and essentially that's why we go.

One interviewee described the seaside as a type of nostalgia that is 'bred into the English people' as part of our national identity, a birth-right, and clarified the importance of personal childhood memories: 'your childhood memories always bring you back...'. Another interviewee pointed out that reminiscing about the past was very often a shared, social and pleasurable experience:

> ...I mean your whole life when you get older is your memories and, you know, you become boring because you're repeating them, you know, 'Oh do you remember when...' you do and often with affection.

These nostalgic interviewees considered a visit to the old-fashioned seaside to be reassuring and enjoyable. Furthermore, it provided a contrast to and perhaps a temporary escape from everyday life. Built heritage and specific seaside sites were a key component of this appeal as they were linked to memories and family narratives. Notably, interviewees placed a high value upon the built heritage of the seaside, and all of them wanted these buildings to be restored and used:

> I just think that the... the buildings that they... the old buildings that they have should be utilised and should be, you know, made more accessible to people, or... they should do some... they shouldn't knock them... certainly shouldn't pull them down. You know, the Winter Gardens, for example...

Half the respondents brought up the significance of the Midland Hotel to Morecambe as a destination during their interviews. The restored and reopened Modernist hotel (see Figures 33.5 and 33.6) attracted a good deal of attention nationally as a unique piece of architecture and potential barometer of change – a symbol of successful regeneration and therefore a symbol of a potentially brighter future (Sharman, 2007). This was reflected in the comments of the interviewees for whom it represents the best of Morecambe: '...the Midland Hotel just looks... it's just an icon, isn't it, really?' Most often the interviewees considered the re-invented Midland as a symbol of the resort's past when it attracted a wealthy and glamorous clientele as a destination hotel: 'It was sort of the place to be.'

Furthermore, a modern-day visit to this hotel acted as a tangible link to an idealized and selective version of the past. Interviewees even described this experience as reliving a

Figure 34.5 The Midland Hotel, which was designed by Oliver Hill and dates to 1933, during the 2015 Vintage by the Sea Festival

Source: Jenny Steele (reproduced with permission).

Figure 34.6 The main stairway of the Midland Hotel with a medallion relief by Eric Gill

Source: Jenny Steele (reproduced with permission).

The importance of built heritage

decadent past – an imagined past influenced by postcards, a television episode of 'Poirot', which was filmed there and other images. This distinctive building appears to allow or encourage an experience of escape or fantasy:

> You're thinking... 'cos it did have a, a part in history when it was the venue of all the rich. Big cars were parked outside, I've seen photographs. Very rich people using it in the 20s and 30s. And so you're now able to go there and it, it's like reliving that, you know.

The Midland Hotel is the resort's most obvious and best-known built heritage site. Indeed, it was the most consistently discussed site across the interviews. It usually appeared to be the objective of a collective nostalgia for times gone by as opposed to more personal memories. However, other less obvious, less grand and more varied sites of heritage were revealed by the interviews. These places were linked to specific personal memories of family holiday experiences that they hosted. Therefore, these places within the resort were linked to family narratives and memories of loved ones. In most cases, these were childhood memories and often involved parents who have now passed away or children who have now grown up. For example, traditional cafes were sites that had meaning attached to them. Indeed, for some it appears that nostalgia and retelling a family narrative is a key reason to visit particular eating places where family members once gathered. One interviewee claimed to visit Morecambe chiefly for the sea-views and nostalgia associated with a particular café. He observes that visiting Brucciani's café (which was built in 1939 and appears to have changed remarkably little over the past 50 years or more – (see Figure 34.7) is a 'trip down memory lane' for him and especially his wife:

> We have to go into Brucciani's because this is a kind of period piece, and I get the same tale – I get the same tale every time we go in: this is where she and her sister came with her mum and dad and they had an ice cream and so on. So, that's the kind of thing I mean by memory lane. But, but it's not just Brucciani's; of course these other places are significant in her memory.

Nostalgia for the loss of childhood was usually, but not always, that of the interviewee themselves. Another interviewee suggests that a different café is linked to very specific memories of his daughter who has long since grown-up and moved out. He recalled how she always ordered the same prawn sandwiches.

The specific seaside scenes of reminiscence or nostalgia varied and included cafes, old railway stations, penny arcades as well as the beach or promenade. In each case, the setting was traditional and can still be visited today. Without the physical presence of these sites, perhaps, the appropriate neuronic triggers could not facilitate a connection with selected elements of the past. These scenes were all positive re-telling of a seaside narrative and very often a family narrative too, thereby underpinning individual and collective identity through nostalgia. Lowenthal (2011) points out that, for many people, this type of identification with the past is achieved through attachment to certain places that hold memories or meaning. Such places are often shaped over time, preserved to some degree but need not be magnificent.

This case study echoes the observation of Gray (2006), Brodie (2018) and others that built heritage is a vitally important aspect of the seaside visitor experience. Diverse places were

Figure 34.7 Brucciani's café window
Source: Jenny Steele (reproduced with permission).

the sites of meaningful experiences and memories to the interviewees. These traditional places hold a nostalgic appeal, underpin sense of place and feed into personal and collective identities, both of people and place. It is interesting that the Midland Hotel appeared to inform collective elements of identity, whilst the other sites (such as cafes) tended to inform personal elements. The Midland symbolized elements of the past in general of collective nostalgia rather than family narratives, particular memories of childhood and personal nostalgia. Interviewees often referred to the traditional built seaside environment in generic terms which could describe any such resort; however, these references were often punctuated by specific reference to landmarks and sites in Morecambe. These informed Morecambe's sense of place, which, in turn, fed into a more transferable seaside sense of place, or seasideness. Whether one's focus is Morecambe or seaside resorts more generally, distinctiveness was vitally important to their appeal.

Conclusion

This chapter has observed that seaside nostalgia has endured and seaside heritage has been rediscovered of late, inferring that seaside resorts are no longer places of recovery, but places in recovery as they move back into the cultural mainstream (Steele & Jarratt, 2019). Elborough (2010) observes that our 'rapprochement' with the seaside has been underway since the start of the twentieth-first century when the artist Tracy Emin sold her Whitstable beach hut to Charles Satchi for £75,000 – which would soon reflect the real-world inflation of beach hut prices in Southern England. He also points to the popular BBCTV series Coast, which was first aired in 2005. Gentrification is now well established in many coastal resorts, especially those within commuting distance from major economic centres. This does not necessarily diminish the serious socio-economic challenges facing residents in many coastal communities though (BBC News, 2019). Nevertheless, those migrating to and visiting these seaside towns want distinctive towns that afford access to blue spaces. Built heritage is at the centre of this distinctiveness which, as discussed in this chapter, is an important part of the seaside experience (Jarratt, 2015). This distinct resort experience, or seasideness, is framed and conditioned by the sea but also by the built environment. Seasideness relies on the culture of the coast just as much as it does nature. So, it is vital that the struggle to preserve remaining seaside heritage continues; it appears the tide is now moving in this direction. Equally, any new developments in resorts that wish to be popular destinations should wherever possible be distinctive from today's 'blandscapes' and foster their appeal as *somewhere else*. In short, this distinctive seaside heritage and design remain crucial to the visitor experience of English resorts and, therefore, to the future of the seaside.

References

Baerenholdt, J., Haldrup, M., Larsen, J. and Urry, J. (2004) *Performing Tourist Places*. Aldershot: Ashgate Publishing.

BBC News (2019) England's most deprived areas named as Jaywick and Blackpool. BBC News, 26 September. Available at: https://www.bbc.co.uk/news/uk-england-49812519, (Accessed 27 September 2019).

Beery, T., Jönsson, K. and Elmberg, J. (2015) From environmental connectedness to sustainable futures: Topophilia and human affiliation with nature. *Sustainability*, 7(7), 8837–8854. Available at: http://dx.doi.org/10.3390/su7078837.

Bennett, T. (1986) Hegemony, ideology, pleasure: Blackpool. In: T. Bennett, C. Mercer and J. Woollacott (Eds), *Popular Culture and Social Relations*. Milton Keynes: Open University Press, pp. 135–154

Bracewell, M. (2004) The Last Resort. Available at: The Independent On Line: https://www.independent.co.uk/news/uk/this-britain/the-last-resort-5539247.html (Accessed 22 October 2020).

Brodie, A. (2018) *The Sea Front*. Swindon: English Heritage Books.

Brodie, A and Winter, G. (2007) *England's Seaside Resorts*. Swindon: English Heritage Books.

Butler, R. (1980) The concept of a tourist area cycle of evolution: Implications of management resources. *Canadian Geographer*, 24(1), 5–12.

Chase, L. (1999) *Creation of Place Image in Inter-War Clacton and Frinton*. Unpublished Ph.D. thesis, University of Essex.

Davis, F. (1979) *Yearning for Yesterday*. New York: The Free Press.

Elborough, T. (2010) *Wish You Were Here: England on Sea*. London: Hodder & Stoughton.

ETC. (2001). *Sea Changes – Creating World Class Resorts in England*. London: English Tourism Council.

Ettenger, K. (2015) The other Maine guides: How the humanities create sense of place and enrich tourism. *Maine Policy Review*, 24(1), 73–79.

European Commission. (n.d.) *Integrated Marine Policy: Coastal and Marine Tourism*. EU Commission: Available at: https://ec.europa.eu/maritimeaffairs/policy/coastal_tourism_en (Accessed 5 November 2020).

Ferry, K. (2009) *The British Seaside Holiday*. Oxford: Shire Publications.

Gammon, S. and Jarratt, D. (2019) Keeping leisure in mind: The intervening role of leisure in the blue space – health nexus. In R. Foley, R. Kearns, T. Kistemann and B. Wheeler (Eds.), *Blue Space, Health and Wellbeing: Hydrophilia Unbounded*. Routledge: Abingdon, pp.38–52.

Gillis, J. (2012) *The Human Shore: Seacoasts in History*. Chicago: Chicago University Press.

Goulding, C. (1999) Heritage, nostalgia and the grey consumer. *Journal of Marketing Practice: Applied Marketing Science*, 5(6), 177–199.

Gray, F. (2006) *Designing The Seaside*. London: Reaktion Books.

Hall, M. C. (2001) Trends in ocean and coastal tourism: The end of the last frontier. *Ocean & Coastal Management*, 44, (9–10), 601–618

Jarratt, D. (2013) A Socio-cultural Analysis of the Traditional Seaside Resort and Its Contemporary Meaning to Tourists with Specific Reference to Morecambe, UK. Ph.D. thesis, University of

Central Lancashire. Available at: https://clok.uclan.ac.uk/9621/1/Jarratt%20David%20Final%20 eThesis%20%28Master%20Copy%29.pdf (Accessed 1 October 2020).

Jarratt, D. (2015) Sense of place at a British coastal resort: Exploring 'seasideness' in Morecambe. *Tourism: An International Interdisciplinary Journal*, 63(3), 351–363.

Jarratt, D. (2019) The development and decline of Morecambe in the nineteenth and twentieth centuries: A resort caught in the tide. *Journal of Tourism History*, 11(3), 263–283.

Jarratt, D. and Gammon, S. (2016). 'We had the most wonderful times': Seaside nostalgia at a British resort. *Tourism, Recreation Research*, 41(2), 123–133.

Jarratt, D., Phelan, C., Wain, J. and Dale, S. (2019) Developing a sense of place toolkit: Identifying destination uniqueness. *Tourism and Hospitality Research*, 19(4), 408–421

Jarratt, D. and Sharpley, R. (2017) Tourists at the seaside: Exploring the spiritual dimension. *Tourist Studies*, 17(4), 349–368.

Jorgenson, B. and Stedman, R. (2001) Sense of place as an attitude: Lakeshore owner's attitudes toward their properties. *Journal of Environmental Psychology*, 21(3), 233–248.

Leisen, B (2001) Image segmentation: The case of a tourism destination. *Journal of Services Marketing*, 15(1), 49–66.

Lindley, K. (1973) *Seaside Architecture*. London: Hugh Evelyn.

Lowenthal, D. (2011) *The Past is a Foreign Country*. Cambridge: Cambridge University Press.

Massey, D. (1997) A global sense of place. In T. Barnes and G. Gregory (Eds.), *Reading Human Geography*. London: Arnold, pp. 315–323.

Preston-Whyte, R. (2004) The beach as a liminal space. In A. Lew, M. Hall and A. Williams (Eds.), *A Companion for Tourism*. Oxford: Blackwell, pp. 349–359.

Relph, E. (1976) *Place and Placelessness*. London: Pion Limited.

Robinson, M. and Picard, D. (2009) *The Framed World: Tourists, Tourism and Photography*. Aldershot: Ashgate.

Sharman, R. (Producer & Director). (2007). Southport to Whitehaven [Television series episode]. In S. Evanson (Series Producer), *Coast – Series 3*. London: BBC2.

Shields, R. (1991) *Places on the Margin: Alternative Geographies of Modernity*. London: Routledge.

Smith, J. A., Flowers and Larkin, M. (2009) *Interpretative Phenomenological Analysis: Theory Method and Research*. London: Sage.

Smith, L. J. (2006) *Uses of Heritage*. London: Routledge.

Steele, J. (2015). Looking Back Moving Forward [Blog]. Available at: https://lookingbackmovingforward2014.wordpress.com/ (Accessed 1 November 2020).

Steele, J. and Jarratt, D. (2019) The seaside resort: Nostlagia and restoration. In E. Speight (Ed.), *Practising Place: Creative and Critical Reflections on Place*. Sunderland: Art Editions North, The University of Sunderland, pp. 132–150.

Tuan, Y-F. (1974) *Topophilia: A Study of Environmental Perception, Attitudes, and Values*. London: Prentice-Hall.

Tuan, Y-F. (2011) *Space and Place: The perspective of Experience*. Minneapolis: University of Minnesota Press.

Turner, P. and Turner, S. (2006). Place, sense of place, and presence. *Presence*, 15(2), 204–217.

UNWTO. (2013) *Sustainable Marine Tourism: Expert Group Meeting on Oceans, Seas and Sustainable Development: Implementation and Follow-up to Rio+20*, 18–19 April 2013. New York: UN.

Urry, J. (1990) *The Tourist Gaze: Leisure and Travel in Contemporary Societies*. London: Sage Publications.

Vesey, C. and Dimanche, F. (2003) From Storyville to Bourbon Street: Vice, nostalgia and tourism. *Journal of Tourism and Cultural Change*, 1(1), 54–70.

Visit Britain. (2016) The GB Tourist: Statistics 2015. Available at: Visit Britain: https://www.visitbritain.org/sites/default/files/vb-corporate/Documents-Library/documents/England-documents/gb_tourist_report_2015.pdf (Accessed 5 November 2020).

Walton, J. K. (2000) *The British Seaside: Holidays and Resorts in the Twentieth Century*. Manchester: Manchester University Press.

Walton, J. K. (2010) The Victorian Seaside. Available at: http://www.bbc.co.uk/history/british/victorians/seaside_01.shtml. (Accessed 17 November 2020).

Walton, J. K. and Wood, J. (2009) Reputation and regeneration: History and the heritage of the recent past in the re-making of Blackpool. In L. Gibson and J. Pendlebury (Eds.), *Valuing Historic Environments*. Aldershot: Ashgate, pp. 15–137.

The importance of built heritage

Wang, W. (1999) Rethinking authenticity in tourism experience. *Annals of Tourism Research*, 26(2), 349–370.

Webb, D. (2005) Bakhtin at the seaside: Utopia, modernity and the carnivalesque. *Theory Culture and Society*, 22(3), 121–138.

White, M., Smith, A., Humphryes, K., Pahl, S. Snelling, D. and Depledge, M. (2010). Blue space: The importance of water for preference, affect, and restorativeness ratings of natural and built scenes. *Journal of Environmental Psychology*, 30(4), 482–493.

35

ISLAND TOURIST EXPERIENCES

Godfrey Baldacchino

Introduction

That there is such a chapter title in this collection begs the question: to what extent can one talk about *island* tourism, and especially from an experiential perspective? Is it at all possible to sustain an island tourism experience that is different from a mainland tourism one? And should this answer persist in spite of the obvious differences that characterize the many islands around the world? Putting it another way, there are frequent claims made about the uniqueness of islands as destinations and the consequentially just-as-unique island tourist experiences. However, are such claims valid and scientifically tenable, or are they simply evidence or part of that aggressive marketing pitch meant to entice travellers to island destinations?

This chapter proposes to unpack this argument by first hypothesizing the reasons why such a question should be raised in the first place, and at this time. I then go on to suggest five geo-political qualities that apply to islands (and which, I would argue, do not apply, or apply differently, to mainlands). It is important to note that here I am using the term mainlands to represent non-islands, even though I realize that this is not always a clear-cut distinction based on mutual exclusion. There are islands that 'become' parts of mainlands and/or peninsulae at low tide; for example, Holy Island (also known as Lindisfarne), lying off the coast of north-east England, benefits from vehicular access via a causeway at low tide. And what about islands that are linked to mainlands via bridges or tunnels? Do such permanent links negate their island status or perceptions thereof? Irrespective of these debates, I argue that these five qualities provide the materialist basis for any plausible psychological or experiential consequences that illuminate what it means to be a tourist in such island locales. Once explained conceptually, illustrative case material is then provided to flesh out each of these qualities in concrete contexts, and with reference to both 'warm water' and 'cold water' islands. A final section concludes.

The material strikes back

Like it was for Robinson Crusoe, interest in islands has tended to be accidental. However, recent decades have seen a renewed interest in the study of islands, and this goes beyond the disciplines of biogeography and anthropology that have looked naturally at islands as fieldwork sites for at least a century (Mead, 1924; Wallace, 1880). Island Studies now has its research and teaching programmes in such universities as that of Malta (in Malta), of Tasmania (in Australia), of Prince

498

DOI: 10.4324/9781003219866-40

Edward Island (in Canada), Kagoshima and Okinawa (Japan) and of the Highlands and Islands of Scotland (in the UK). Island Studies has its own flagship, peer-reviewed and open access *Island Studies Journal* (since 2006) and an *International Handbook of Island Studies* (since 2018) (Baldacchino, 2018). This renaissance is a welcome respite to a strong wave of both structuralist-Marxist and post-modernist scholarship which, from widely different epistemological positions have, on one hand, affirmed the exclusive centrality of social class or, on the other hand, sought to dismiss the role of the material in human behaviour and social science generally. Mainstream theories of space and place have displaced the primacy and legitimacy of rational scientific doctrines (e.g. space as container; the world as a given and a 'stand alone' reality), and replaced them with relational and subjectivist renditions (e.g. space as socially constructed; existing only through the eyes of the beholder/actor). Thus, places are not only features in inhabitants' narratives; they are narratives in their own right (Rodman, 1992).

These developments in social geography were necessary to foreground the vital role of subjects in shaping their world via its interpretation; moreover, they were also debunking crass and uncorroborated interpretations of how, deterministically, environmental features 'caused' certain behavioural traits (e.g. Brunhes, 1926; Semple, 1911). However, the switch may have gone too far, dismissing and denigrating the potential of material places – including islands – to somehow influence human behaviour, or their perception, or both.

The business of lived spatiality has become a significant *problematique* at a time when 'area studies' is finally emerging from this deep epistemological slumber (Goss & Wesley-Smith, 2010: ix). The status of place in a globalizing world where there is no rest needs to be carefully critiqued; glib and simplistic classificatory premises that have rested at the heart of many arguments in the social sciences are to be rejected (Barth, 1969). And yet, we must acknowledge that there is a keen 'awhereness' in play everywhere (Thrift, 2011: 9). Context matters; there is a stubborn, visceral materiality in what we do. I argued this in a journal article that looked at replacing the materiality of sand, albeit in a Western cultural driven sense (Baldacchino, 2010; Baldacchino & Clark, 2013).

Five attributes

This is why I propose five material qualifiers unapologetically. I propose each and support my choice with statements that match the scientific conditions of rigour, repeatability and systematicity. The five attributes – identity, scale, distance, peripherality and archipelagicity – are graphically represented in Figure 35.1 below. They are intimately interrelated but will each be reviewed in turn for the sake of analytical clarity.

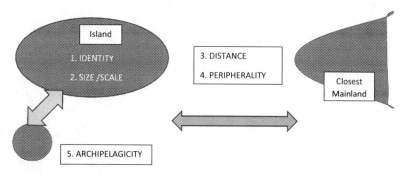

Figure 35.1 Five attributes of islands
Source: The author.

One caveat here. There are bound to be a few exceptions – some of which I may high-light myself – which may suggest that the argument being made below is untenable and invalid. I would counter by saying that these are precisely the exceptions that justify the general rule.

Identity

The first and pivotal condition that distinguishes islands from any other land mass is that they are self-evident as pieces of land surrounded by water. Island identity is easily surmised from the natural boundaries offered by the aquatic medium. While mainland borders can be drawn and redrawn, change and shift over time, mainly because of human military and diplomatic action, conquest and defeat, the fully coastal boundaries of islands change largely because of natural forces, namely, accretion and erosion. Any such changes also occur in the long term, unless we factor in daily tidal highs and lows, and the occasional huge storm or a volcano's lateral collapse, which can change coastlines in very short timespans.

The power of this observation can easily escape us. However, a look at the political map of the world suggests that all mainlands are shared between multiple numbers of jurisdic-tions. For example, the European continent – itself geographically part of EurAsia – has no less than 51 different independent states. In contrast, all inhabited islands in the world *except ten* are controlled by, or are configured as, one single country. Moreover, it appears that a border on an island comes across as some kind of nuisance or aberration (Baldacchino, 2013). Indeed, the polities sharing these ten islands have had a history of uneasy relations, some more so than others. Some elude an enduring settlement yet manage to establish and main-tain strained relations, such as between the Greek and Turkish communities on the island of Cyprus (Scott, 2012). Somewhat bizarrely, the enduring Cyprus Problem adds a twist to tourist experiences there; the opportunity exists for tourists to cross the Green Line, visit the 'other side' and hear different interpretations of who is to blame and what needs to be done –if they are so interested in knowing more.

The singular exception here is probably Australia, the world's only continent and, hence, a mainland, which is, however, configured as a single (albeit federal) sovereign state. (Here, I am tempted to accept the claims to sovereignty of the Principality of Hutt River, an un-recognized micronation, which would support my thesis of multiple states per mainland [de Castro & Kober, 2018]; but, I will resist.) This situation to me suggests that Australia (and not smaller Greenland) qualifies as the world's largest island, irrespective of its status as a continent (on its own terms, or as part of Oceania) (Perera, 2009).

This is not to dismiss or denigrate the internal divisions that would exist *within* island societies or communities. From Jamaica to Fiji, and from Trinidad to New Caledonia, there are powerful schisms at work, discernible along political party and/or ethnic lines. And yet, rarely do these schisms threaten or jeopardize the territorial integrity of the state *qua* island. (One exception here could be Mindanao, in the Philippines, with sepa-ratist groups effectively running part of the island). There is only one island that I know of with two names for two different constituent parts: Lewis and Harris, in the Western Isles of Scotland.

The identity label permits a type of tourism marketing that suggests an appropriation of the full island experience: 'doing', say, Bermuda or Ibiza or Tahiti is easier and conceptually tenable because the target is framed. Islands are naturally places that you can, imaginatively, get your arms around.

Island tourist experiences

Small size / scale

This task is rendered easier by small(er) size. Of course, there are small states, particularly in Europe, that are not islands. Without getting side-tracked onto the hopeless task of defining smallness, it is clear that the combination of small size or small scale and being surrounded by water makes for an enticing tourism experience. Hence 'doing' Bermuda can happen not just because Bermuda fits nicely onto a clear conceptual mental map, but also because Bermuda is small and so 'taking it all in' is a fantasy that can yet be psychologically fulfilled.

Additionally, the smaller the island, the more its island characteristics come to the fore. The dependence on the (typically single) ferry service, on its (typically single) airport and the nagging presence of the sea crashing incessantly on its shores, never far away, are suggestive of island life, and can be quickly stamped on tourist experiences, especially if transport logistics need to be carefully juggled. Take Pitcairn, one of the world's most remote island jurisdictions, which is trying to build a tourism industry (Amoamo, 2011). Would-be visitors, however, need to be careful; if they decide to stay longer than a couple of hours, they lose the opportunity to leave the island with the same vessel that transported them there and the very next ship to visit may be two months' away.

Distance from the mainland

Indeed, the distance from the mainland introduces another variable, namely, the obligation to cross a stretch of water. In the case of oceanic islands in the high seas, travel to and from the island is often dependent on expensive air travel whilst for continental or near islands, the options would include ferry services and even bridges or tunnels.

This situation creates the psychological experience of a crossing, an inevitable transition over an aquatic medium to and from an island. This journey can serve as part of the almost spiritual catharsis implicit in some island tourism advertising: the release from the tensions and stresses of urban living; the taking on of a different mode of living (so-called 'island time'); the mental preparation to 'take it all in' while one succumbs to the island's own pace and rhythm. And then there is the return journey, equally inevitable: time to take stock, build psychological reserves to last you until your next holiday as you once again prepare to take on the real world and its rat race and unforgiving stresses.

Distance from the mainland obliges entry and access to islands via very specific chokepoints in the form of airports and seaports. The arrivals lounges of these infrastructures become the first 'sites' that tourists experience although, in the case of international travel, these often sadly involve exasperatingly long queues to go through customs and immigration. Departures are similarly organized through these conduits. Most small island capital cities are port cities and island airports, where they exist, are typically not far away. (I can think of two islands whose capital is not a port, namely Cyprus with Nicosia and Anguilla with The Valley.) Hence, the transport infrastructures consolidate the urban and more mass-oriented aspects of island life. Indeed:

> on small islands, the [capital] city can tower over the rest of the [island] community, commanding a considerable proportion of the population; the island's settlement pattern could be totally dominated by the urban sprawl emerging away from and out of its capital (and typically main port) city.
>
> *(Baldacchino, 2014: 138)*

In contrast to the tourist brochures, where congestion is non-existent and population density is light (if not zero), island life is different; most tourists will need to navigate across roads clogged with traffic and along a road network that often radiates out of the capital-cum-port city. Taken as a global average (and excluding the largely empty island of Greenland and the largely empty continents of Australia and Antarctica), the world's islands have a population density *three times larger* than mainlands (Baldacchino, 2007). Of the 13 jurisdictions with the highest population density in the world, nine are islands or mainly islands. Macao tops the list, followed by Singapore, Hong Kong, Malta, Bermuda, Bahrain, Maldives, Guernsey and Jersey (Baldacchino, 2012a: xxvii).

Distance from the mainland, and the separation from main species pools that it implies, sets the stage for distinct evolutionary processes, especially on high-altitude oceanic islands (Steinbauer et al., 2016). From the Komodo dragon (on Komodo Island, Indonesia) to the giant tortoise (on the Galapagos Islands, Ecuador; as well as Aldabra Atoll, Seychelles), the lemur of Madagascar and the Tasmanian devil (on Tasmania, Australia), endemic species have become iconic attractions for specific tourist experiences. The geo-physical forces that have shaped these islands have also created some spectacular landscapes that have become tourist allures in their own right. These include Bora Bora (French Polynesia), Hạ Long Bay (Vietnam), Big Island, Hawai'i (USA), Santorini (Greece), Soqotra (Yemen), Prince Edward Island (Canada), Yakushima (Japan) and the part-time island of Mont St Michel (France). And the manner in which humans have sought to master or engineer island landscapes has ushered in other unique, cultural-cum-natural formations, which draw the curious from all over the world – think of the islands of Gorée (Senegal), Hashima (Japan), Lindisfarne (UK), Skellig Michael (Ireland), Zanzibar stone town (Tanzania) and the megalithic temples in Gozo (Malta). Not surprisingly, all these sites are inscribed on the UNESCO World Heritage List. In fact, almost one-sixth of these World Heritage Sites are either on islands, or are islands *in toto*.

UNESCO's initiative to develop its World Heritage Site List has triggered a hedonistic streak of tourism that is playfully gathering trophies and ticking off check lists (Harrison & Hitchcock, 2005). Islands may be more difficult and expensive to get to, but the smaller exponents facilitate the sense of a psychologically comprehensive assessment that I have already alluded to in this chapter. Hence, the aficionados' rush to 'bag' even more islands and proudly claim to have seen and absorbed their UNESCO heritage allure, adding to one's growing *curriculum vitae*. For example, island geographer Stephen Royle counts the different islands he visits; he has shared his 700-plus island experience in print (Royle, 2015).

With endemism comes the risk of extinction. Tourists also flock to locations to find out about the facts and myth of extinct species, to witness first-hand members of species faced with extinction, or to help in conservation efforts to prevent such from happening. Thus, Mauritius was home to the dodo (*Raphus cucullatus*), a species of flightless, oversized pigeon that was rendered extinct within 100 years of being discovered by Europeans. At the same time, the Mauritius Kestrel, the Mauritius Parakeet and the Pink Pigeon have all tethered on the brink of extinction but are now recovering, thanks to keen conservation efforts that have involved various international volunteers.

People and lived-in habitats – and not just birds, mammals and reptiles – become the objects of such a systematic and reductionist 'tourist gaze' (Urry, 2002). The threats posed by global warming and sea-level rise have ushered in a streak of dark, morbid, voyeuristic tourism; 'the global warming clock is ticking, so see these places while you can' (Farbotko, 2010). Tourists have rushed to take in and experience the 'disappearing' Maldives and 'sinking'

Venice, adding to the environmental strains that jeopardise these sites' survivability. Ironically, these tourist adventures are often abetted by the marketing strategies of these very same threatened countries and regions.

Peripherality

The separation between island and mainland, necessitated by the existence of the water medium, also has political implications. In most (but not all) cases – Singapore is a dramatic exception (Barter, 2006) – the mainland is the stronger player in the dyad. There is an asymmetric power relationship, rendered even more unequal when the political clout of the island is insignificant compared with that of the mainland. Smaller island populations, and their limited economic or strategic value, lock islands into dependency relationships that can be hard to avoid or resist (Baldacchino, 2012b). These tensions come to the fore every time this relationship threatens to become locked in by means of a fixed link through the building of a permanent connection, such as a bridge, tunnel or causeway (Baldacchino, 2008). Near continental islands run the major risk of such an incorporation; islands further away from mainlands can nurture some level of autonomy (Baldacchino, 2019). Distance matters.

The implications for tourism are varied. First, the trajectory of tourism development becomes more likely to be impacted, or even determined, by mainland interests and capital. Second, the nature and frequency of transport connectivities become controlled by politico-economic elites who are motivated by interests and priorities that do not necessary align with island benefits and needs. Third, domestic mass tourism from the mainland may take over the island economy – especially in the case of the smaller islands – causing serious environmental pressures (Starc, 2020). The sway of the mainland over the island is best mitigated when islands are their own jurisdictions, and possibly their own sovereign states.

Archipelagicity

We often say island, but we really mean archipelago. This is because most island units are made up of more than one single stretch of coral, limestone or basalt. And therefore, the issues of identity, scale, distance and peripherality already discussed above can all take on a new life and meaning *within* the island unit.

Again, there are exceptions: Barbados, Cyprus and Nauru are effectively single island jurisdictions: but these cases are clearly rare. Malta, the smallest member state of the European Union since 2004, has three inhabited islands – the main island, also called Malta, plus Gozo and Comino – but includes some 20 other named 'satellite' islets and rocks (Sciberras & Sciberras, 2010). Visiting all of these makes for an interesting day-long boat trip.

Tasmania, for example, is the smallest and single island state of Australia. Its main island is also called Tasmania. But there are, officially, another 333 named islands that take up 6% of the land area of this (archipelagic) state. Some are uninhabited (including nature reserves), some are off limits (16 are privately owned), while others are inhabited and want their own piece of the tourist action. These will have their own concerns about access and connectivity, the type and seasonality of visitations experienced and preferred, whether they should have their own ferries and airports, and so on. The debates I have already highlighted between mainland and island are reproduced, at a smaller scale, within the island *qua* archipelago, introducing situations of multiple insularity. A complementarity of the tourism product and experience across different islands in the group may be deemed to be a logical pursuit and a rationally shared objective. In the Seychelles, for example, the islands that are farther out from Mahé, the main island – effectively, the mainland for and to the smaller islands – are configured as more exclusive destinations, offering higher levels of quality of service and more exclusive experiences at a suitably higher price (Seetaram & Joubert, 2018). But the tourism industry in the Seychelles has been crafted during a long period of one-party rule (Wilson, 1994). Even the number of hotel beds is capped, to the envy of governments elsewhere where such a measure, while scientifically sound and speaks to issues of 'carrying capacity' that are so quickly reached in small islands, is bound to be unpopular with the local business lobby. Alas, in democratic contexts, jealousy, rivalry and political pressure from entrepreneurs and citizens in small island constituencies may lead to a replication of both tourism infrastructure and tourism product. Consider, for example, the Canaries or the Azores, with multiple international airports on most of the constituent islands (and, in the case of Tenerife, *two* international airports) (Baldacchino, 2015; Baldacchino & Ferreira, 2013).

Discussion

I would expect that, for tourist experiences on islands to be packaged or consumed smartly in ways that foreground the (small) *island* experience, then they would invoke and exploit the combined effects of identity, scale, distance from mainland, power asymmetry and archipelagicity. Arrival is essentially by boat/ferry or plane; the point of access is typically at or close to the port-cum-capital city; and the sojourn is made memorable by the intensity of the experience, by how much can be taken in – including unique landscapes, flora or fauna – over what is typically a small land area. The prospect of island-hopping entices and permits visits to the smaller (and more pristine?) islands within the archipelago. But the experience is bedevilled by the risks and vulnerabilities that a guided tour, boat, ferry or a flight might be late or cancelled (and with hardly any alternative options available for travel) and so jeopardize one's schedule, a harrowing prospect to those who plan their vacations meticulously. There is also a lot of waiting, for the boat, for the plane, for a special package tour. In such situations, one can better appreciate what it means to be isolated; in July 2018, for example, some 700 tourists from 26 countries were trapped on the Indonesian island of Lombok after a devastating earthquake killed more than a dozen people (CNN, 2018).

These observations are removed from the glossy exotic (and at times erotic) stereotypes of island spaces, and their island peoples (Apostolopoulos & Gayle, 2002; Baum, 1997; Connell, 2003; Lockhart, 1997). Islands and islanders are in a perennial struggle to shape suitable representations of themselves, representations that are sufficiently authentic to reflect reality but also sufficiently scripted to entice and seduce, especially so if they happen to be warm water destinations that depend on tourism revenues (Edmond & Smith, 2003). Servile and accommodating island folk – including, in some locales, the provision of sexual services – can be assumed as part of the tourist experience package. Regretfully, the smaller the island, the less its island populace tends to control how it appears on internet browser searches and travel agency websites and brochures. Islands find themselves presented as locales of desire, platforms of paradise, habitual sites of fascination, emotional offloading or religious pilgrimage. Indeed, Hay (2006: 26) argues that the metaphoric deployment of 'island', with the associated attributes of small physical size and warm water, is possibly *the* central gripping metaphor in Western discourse (emphasis in original). Similarly, Tuan (1990: 247) claims that four natural environments have figured prominently in humanity's (including non-Western) enduring and endearing dreams of the ideal world. These are the forest, the shore, the valley ... and the island.

The ultimate island experience is perhaps one that, again, distinguishes islands from mainlands: the private island. Private property must typically contend with neighbours, but not when it comprises a whole island surrounded by water. The market for private islands is hot; on the one hand, there are those with deep pockets – for example, Sir Richard Branson, Johnny Depp or Celine Dion – who are searching for privacy, exclusivity and escape from pestering paparazzi while fulfilling the dream of absolute control. Visitors, desired or otherwise, cannot so easily drop by unannounced. On the other hand, cruise ship companies are developing their own private islands to maximize revenue when their passengers are off ship, while guaranteeing quality of service and security (Showalter, 1995). And if a naturally occurring private island does not quite cut it, failing to match one's exact expectations, then why not build one's own? Artificial islands are now available in various locations, from Hulhumale in the Maldives to the Palm and Jumeirah Islands in Dubai (Jackson and della Dora, 2009). These geo-engineered spaces may qualify as the ultimate, spectacular enclosures of hope (Jackson and della Dora, 2011).

Conclusion

'Islands are special places' (Matvejević, 1999: 16). Historically, they have served to host those societal segments that were deemed best not to mix with the mainstream, such as lepers, criminals, political refugees, hermits and monks. What is left of these sites – from the leper colony on Molokai, Hawaii to Alcatraz Prison in San Francisco Bay – has become an attraction in its own right, a museum drawing in crowds of curious tourists. In the twenty-first century, islands have become sites of privilege and exclusivity, driven by the same, enduring desire to avoid mixing with the mainstream; one example is the hyper-luxurious Burj Al Arab, a '7-star' hotel in Dubai, which, of course, had to be built on an artificial island so as to better 'protect' and insulate/isolate its clients (Hazbun, 2006). In 300 years, Robinson Crusoe has come a long way (Defoe, 1719).

References

Amoamo, M. (2011) Remoteness and myth making: Tourism development on Pitcairn Island. *Tourism Planning & Development*, 8(1), 1–19.

Apostolopoulos, Y. and Gayle, D. J. (2002) *Island Tourism and Sustainable Development: Caribbean, Pacific, and Mediterranean Experiences*. New York: Praeger.

Baldacchino, G. (Ed.) (2007) *A World of Islands: An Island Studies Reader*. Charlottetown: University of Prince Edward Island, Institute of Island Studies Press.

Baldacchino, G. (2008) *Bridging Islands: The Impact of Fixed Links*. Charlottetown: Acorn Press.

Baldacchino, G. (2010) Re-placing materiality: A Western anthropology of sand. *Annals of Tourism Research*, 37(4), 763–778.

Baldacchino, G. (2012a) Geography, land use conflict and heritage management: The instructive role of densely populated islands. In G. Baldacchino (Ed.), *Extreme Heritage Management: The Practices and Policies of Densely Populated Islands*. New York: Berghahn Books, pp. xxv–xli.

Baldacchino G. (2012b) The lure of the island: A spatial analysis of power relations. *Journal of Marine and Island Cultures*, 1(1), 55–62.

Baldacchino, G. (Ed.) (2013) *The Political Economy of Divided Islands: Unified Geographies, Multiple Polities*. New York: Palgrave Macmillan.

Baldacchino, G. (2014) Capital and port cities on small islands sallying forth beyond their walls: A Mediterranean exercise. *Journal of Mediterranean Studies*, 23(2), 137–151.

Baldacchino, G. (2015) *Archipelago Tourism: Policies and practices*. Farnham: Ashgate.

Baldacchino, G. (Ed.) (2018) *The Routledge International Handbook of Island Studies*. Abingdon: Routledge.

Baldacchino, G. (2019) How far can one go? How distance matters in island development. *Island Studies Journal*, 15(1), 25–42.

Baldacchino, G. and Clark, E. (2013) Guest editorial introduction: Islanding cultural geographies. *Cultural Geographies*, 20(2), 129–134.

Baldacchino, G. and Ferreira, E. D. C. (2013) Competing notions of diversity in archipelago tourism: Transport logistics, official rhetoric and inter-island rivalry in the Azores. *Island Studies Journal*, 8(1), 84–104.

Barter, P. A. (2006) 'Central' Singapore island, 'peripheral' mainland Johor: Making the link. In G. Baldacchino (Ed.), *Bridging Islands: The Impact of Fixed Links*. Charlottetown: Acorn Press, pp. 251–261.

Barth, F. (1969) Introduction. In F. Barth (Ed.), *Ethnic Groups and Boundaries: The Social Organization of Culture Difference*. Boston: Little, Brown & Co, pp. 9–38.

Baum, T. G. (1997) The fascination of islands: A tourist perspective. In D. G. Lockhart and D. Drakakis-Smith (Eds.), *Island Tourism: Problems and Perspectives*. London: Mansell, pp. 21–35.

Brunhes, J. (1926/ 1954) *Géographie humaine: Essai de classification positive*. Paris: Alcan. Published as: *Human Geography: An Attempt at a Positive Classification* (Trans I. C. LeCompte). London: George C. Harrap (1971).

CNN (2018) July 30. Hundreds of Tourists Trapped by Indonesia Quake Descending Volcano, 30 July. Available at: https://www.cbsnews.com/news/tourists-stranded-on-indonesia-volcano-mount-rinjani-by-earthquake-landslides/

Connell, J. (2003) Island dreaming: The contemplation of Polynesian paradise. *Journal of Historical Geography*, 29(4), 554–581.

de Castro, V. B. and Kober, R. (2018) The principality of Hutt River: A territory marooned in the Western Australian Outback. *Shima*, 12(1), 143–159.

Defoe, D. (1719) *The Life and Strange Surprising Adventures of Robinson Crusoe, of York, Mariner*. London: William Taylor.

Edmond, R. S. and Smith, V. (2003) *Islands in History and Representation*. London: Routledge.

Farbotko, C. (2010) 'The global warming clock is ticking so see these places while you can': Voyeuristic tourism and model environmental citizens on Tuvalu's disappearing islands. *Singapore Journal of Tropical Geography*, 31(2), 224–238.

Goss, J. and Wesley-Smith, T. (2010) *Remaking Area Studies: Teaching and Learning across Asia and the Pacific*. Honolulu: University of Hawai`i Press.

Harrison, D. and Hitchcock, M. (Eds.) (2005) *The Politics of World Heritage: Negotiating Tourism and Conservation*. Clevedon: Channel View Publications.

Hay, P. (2006) A phenomenology of islands. *Island Studies Journal*, 1(1), 19–42.

Hazbun, W. (2006) Explaining the Arab Middle East tourism paradox. *The Arab World Geographer*, 9(3), 201–214.

Jackson, M. S. and della Dora, V. (2009) 'Dreams so big only the sea can hold them': Man-made islands as anxious spaces, cultural icons, and travelling visions. *Environment & Planning A: Economy and Space*, 41(9), 2086–2104.

Jackson, M. S. and della Dora, V. (2011) Spectacular enclosures of hope. In R. Shields, O. Park and T. Davidson (Eds.), *Ecologies of Affect: Placing Nostalgia, Desire and Hope*. Waterloo, Canada: Wilfred Laurier University Press, pp. 293–316.

Lockhart, D. G. (1997) Islands and tourism: An overview. In D. G. Lockhart and D. Drakakis-Smith (Eds.), *Island Tourism: Problems and Perspectives*. London: Mansell, pp. 3–20.

Matvejević, P. (1999) *Mediterranean: A Cultural Landscape*. (Trans M. H. Heim). Berkeley: University of California Press.

Mead, M. (1924/1943) *Coming of Age in Samoa: A Study of Adolescence and Sex in Primitive Societies*. Harmondsworth: Penguin.

Perera, S. (2009) *Australia and the Insular Imagination: Beaches, Borders, Boats, and Bodies*. New York: Springer.

Rodman, M. C. (1992) Empowering place: Multilocality and multivocality. *American Anthropologist*, 94(3), 640–656.

Royle, S. A. (2015) Navigating a world of islands: A 767 island odyssey. In G. Baldacchino (Ed.), *Archipelago Tourism: Policies and Practices*. Farnham: Ashgate, pp. 43–56.

Sciberras, J. and Sciberras, A. (2010) Topography and flora of the satellite islets surrounding the Maltese archipelago. *The Central Mediterranean Naturalist*, 5(2), 31–42.

Island tourist experiences

Scott, J. (2012) Tourism, civil society and peace in Cyprus. *Annals of Tourism Research*, 39(4), 2114–2132.

Seetaram, N. and Joubert, B. (2018) Tourism in the Seychelles: Trends and experiences. In M. McLeod and R. Croes (Eds.), *Tourism Management in Warm-water Island Destinations*. Wallingford: CABI, pp. 131–146.

Semple, E. C. (1911) *Influences of the Geographic Environment*. London: Constable.

Showalter, G. R. (1995) Cruise ships and private islands in the Caribbean. *Journal of Travel & Tourism Marketing*, 3(4), 107–118.

Starc, N. (Ed.) (2020) *The Notion of Near Islands: The Croatian Archipelago*. Lanham: Rowman & Littlefield International.

Steinbauer, M. J., Field, R., Grytnes, J. A., Trigas, P., Ah-Peng, C., Attorre, F., Birks, H. J. B., Borges, P. A., Cardoso, P., Chou, C. H. and De Sanctis, M. (2016) Topography-driven isolation, speciation and a global increase of endemism with elevation. *Global Ecology and Biogeography*, 25(9), 1097–1107.

Thrift, N. J. (2011) Lifeworld Inc.: And what to do about it. *Environment & Planning D: Society and Space*, 29(1), 5–26.

Tuan, Y-F. (1990) *Topophilia: A Study of Environmental Perception, Attitudes and Values*, 2nd Edn. New York: Columbia University Press.

Urry, J. (2002) *The Tourist Gaze*, 2nd Edn. Thousand Oaks: Sage Publications.

Wallace, A. R. (1880) *Island Life: Or, The Phenomena and Causes of Insular Faunas and Floras, Including a Revision and Attempted Solution of the Problem of Geological Climates*. London: Macmillan & Co.

Wilson, D. (1994) Unique by a thousand miles: Seychelles tourism revisited. *Annals of Tourism Research*, 21(1), 20–45.

36

DELIVERING APPEALING AND COMPETITIVE RURAL WINE TOURISM EXPERIENCES

Elisabeth Kastenholz and Bernard Lane

Introduction

For over 40 years, rural tourism has been considered as an effective low-cost tool for the sustainable development of many economically relatively less dynamic rural regions with few resources, populations with lower than average incomes and with poor supporting social and economic services. Usually, these problems have resulted from agricultural change and modernization, falling agricultural prices and the impacts of globalization (Lane, 1994a, b; Lane & Kastenholz, 2015; OECD, 1994; Sharpley & Roberts, 2004). However, many rural areas also often hold a wide variety of underused, but potentially valuable, natural and cultural heritage attractions and unique traditions. Many tourists are now increasingly seeking such authentic, engaging, meaningful and sensory-rich tourist experiences (Agapito, Valle& Mendes, 2014; Garrod, Wornell & Youel, 2006; Kastenholz, Carneiro & Marques, 2012; Pan & Ryan, 2009; Sidali, Kastenholz & Bianchi, 2015). These attributes and experiences can be nostalgically embellished to attract tourist expenditures, and can also help communities in search of lost or jeopardized local/regional identities (Christou, Farmaki & Evangelou, 2018; Figueiredo, Kastenholz & Lima, 2013; Rodrigues, Kastenholz & Morais, 2012).

One particularly interesting cultural resource that is very much dependent on the natural conditions of the place where it is produced is that of local food and its associated traditions (Pereiro & Conde, 2005; Sidali, Kastenholz & Bianchi, 2015; Sims, 2009). Local food is increasingly recognized as a manifestation and symbol of the particular place, its agriculture, soils and climate conditions and the ways that local people have produced food items that are traditionally easiest to obtain and most highly valued by their communities. Particular traditions in food production and consumption have, in recent years, become one of the most valued elements of many rural tourist experiences; traditional, small-scale agriculture and its associated landscapes are both found to be highly appealing (Carneiro, Lima & Silva, 2015; Sidali, et al., 2015). This is relatively new. Twenty-five years ago, Hjalager (1996: 110) pointed out that, 'the eating culture is a distinctive feature which is utterly underestimated in the tourism sector in general, and paradoxically so in rural tourism', but that has changed rapidly. Sims (2009) and Everett and Slocum (2013) sum up in two now heavily read and cited papers the recent dramatic rise in the interest from rural visitors in food and drink tourism. This chapter looks at issues surrounding the delivery of one niche market in the rural

508   DOI: 10.4324/9781003219866-41

Rural wine tourist experiences

food tourism experience, that of local wine tourism. It pays special attention to the issues and opportunities of product development to create those experiences.

Wine tourism can be seen as a particular type of rural tourism, located in and inspired by rural wine-producing territories, linked to local wine producers and their neighbouring communities and engaging with those territories' rural resources and traditions (Alonso, 2009; Popp & McCole, 2016). Wine tourism can sometimes also be enjoyed in an urban context (for example, in Portugal in the Oporto wine cellars located on the southern banks of the Douro river in the city of Vila Nova de Gaia), with tensions and bridges between urban and rural realities and imaginaries being a prolific field of debate increasingly affecting the rural tourism research agenda (Garau, 2015; Paniagua, 2002). But wine tourism is predominantly based in rural areas, and growing in many parts of the world. It is also often considered as a form of 'special interest tourism' (Bruwer, 2003) or integrated into food tourism, with wine being typically consumed as part of and in combination with meals, associated with particular dishes and enhancing the value of local gastronomy (Etcheverria, 2016).

As a speciality type of tourism, wine tourism is very place-bound with the concept of 'terroir' being central to wine production and corresponding wine brands, with a specific combination of soil, climate and long-lasting local and regional agricultural traditions being responsible for particular types of grapes and resulting wines, as visible in officially demarcated wine-producing regions and labels. This 'terroir' is of particular interest to wine lovers, but also to any visitor enjoying the beautifully shaped wine-growing landscapes, created by local farmers, sometimes arranged in terraces along rivers and reflecting cultural identities, making them particularly attractive and meaningful (Holland, Smit & Jones, 2017; Lavrador, Kastenholz & Lima, 2012; Mitchell, Charters & Albrecht, 2012).

Although wine tourism has become increasingly attractive, there are still many wine tourism businesses and destinations that focus largely on wine and wine production, apparently neglecting the overall rural destination experience such areas may provide (Holland et al, 2017; Riscinto-Kozub & Childs, 2012). This may be due to the difficulty of many agricultural businesses to diversify into tourism, which is a demanding and distinct sector (Hjalager, 1996; Sharpley, 2002). But it may also be due to the enthusiasm of specialist wine producers, who sometimes only target sophisticated wine lovers, neither understanding nor seeking opportunities for addressing non-specialist wine terroir visitors, or even novices in wine consumption, especially if still working in an earlier stage of development of the suggested wine tourism life cycle (Tomljenović & Getz, 2009).

It is particularly the countries of the so-called 'New World' that have only relatively recently started producing wine that show more innovative, experience-orientated wine tourism approaches, while those from the 'Old World' tend to present relatively fewer experience options (Alonso & Yi Liu, 2012; Charters, 2009). It seems that in the former, wine tourism has been strategically integrated into a kind of modern lifestyle-orientated wine business from the beginning, while in the 'old world', wine tourism was added as a perhaps non-essential complement to a traditional, nearly 'sacred' way of doing things in wine production. Other tourism motivations, different from expert tasting and information delivery about grapes, soil and wine production, often relate to stories or community experiences outside the vineyard or cellar door, and might not have been considered as relevant to visitor experiences by traditional winemakers.

It is in this context that a destination and experience approach seems to be crucial, trying to integrate into tourist experiences as many relevant, appealing and unique materials, local resources, stories and curiosities as possible. This approach can be delivered in two distinct ways: (i) as a packaged experience product, prepared by incoming tour operators or (ii) as a destination opportunity package, made available by destination marketing organizations (DMOs), local agents' networks or wine routes for both tour operators and for numerous independent travellers experiencing co-creation. Despite the role of incoming tour operators, we next focus on the second approach, typically chosen by independent travellers, exploring regions spontaneously but aided by local businesses, networks and good heritage and tourism information. This latter group appears to have greatest potential for growth and income but requires a skilled and competitive approach.

We first debate the role of terroir in rural wine tourism and then examine the wine tourist and his/her experience expectations. Next, we consider the importance of routes, networks and holistic governance structures to address and fulfil such expectations, lessons and innovations from heritage interpretation, while not neglecting the role of the internet in experience provision and facilitation nor that of co-creation in developing involving and successful rural wine destination experiences.

From wine production to tourism experiences

Wine tourism is often defined as a type of tourism based on travel and visitation to wineries and wine-producing destinations, centred on specific attractions such as wine cellars, museums and events associated with wine, to enjoy experiences related to aspects of wine as the main visitor motivation (Hall, Johnson, Longo & Mitchell, 2000). It is sometimes viewed as a part of special interest tourism (Bruwer, 2003; Charters & Ali-Knight, 2002). Getz and Brown (2006) identify three core dimensions of wine tourism: the 'core wine product', the 'core destination appeal' and the 'cultural product', revealing an interest that goes beyond wine and its tasting.

Research increasingly shows that many wine tourists engaging in winery and wine destination visitation are also driven by a general interest in exploring rural territories in which wine is produced and where wine represents one motivation and experience amongst many others (Guedes & Joukes, 2016; Kastenholz, Cunha, Eletxigerra, Carvalho & Silva, 2021; Popp & McCole, 2016). Accordingly, one may distinguish tourists as either 'specialist winery tourists' or 'generalist visitors' (Johnson, 1998, in Galloway et al., 2008), depending on the role of wine and wineries as their main or rather complementary travel purpose. These findings apply to many forms of special interest tourism and, in terms of income generation and eventually ongoing wine sales, are extremely important. Moreover, such a distinction is crucial for tourism product development that needs to target each group with a particular experience offering to yield the best possible outcome in terms of satisfaction, on-site wine sales but also loyalty towards both wines and wine destinations.

In Palacio and McCool's (1997) now old but far-seeing paper on segmenting ecotourists in Belize, it was surprisingly found that ecotourists, as measured by the combination of benefits that they perceived on the trip, comprised only 18% of the visitors, even though they visited many of the same attractions and destinations in Belize as other segments. Ecotourists rated being with others as an important benefit of their visit. One of the largest groups travelling to ecotourism sites, but with no real interest in ecotourism, comprised 26.9% of the sample. They were labelled as 'Passive Players'. Later work has found that passive players are common to many forms of special interest tourism. They feature strongly in consultants' surveys undertaken for many destinations, where they are often simply known as 'family and friends'. Those surveys usually note that destinations that offer additional experiences to 'passive players' tend to gain longer stays, greater expenditure and repeat visits.

Rural wine tourist experiences

Wine tourism has frequently, especially in 'old world' European wine-producing countries with long wine traditions, started as a cellar-centric activity, helping wineries increase profitable sales (from the wine producers' perspective); wine tourism was seen as a secondary activity to wine sales (Charters, 2009). But this perspective has changed in recent decades. This not only mirrors the previously identified market changes, with an increasing popularity of wine tourism as a complementary experience while exploring rural areas; it is also based on the understanding of new opportunities of enhancing a wine's and a region's brand name and creating additional appeal for rural destinations with multiple, scattered heritage elements (Quattrone, Tomaselli, Riguccio & Russo, 2007).

In this context, Holland, Smit and Jones (2017) suggest the term '*Terroir Tourism*' for more holistic rural wine tourism experiences anchored in particular areas with a unique identity associated with a specific type of wine and its source region. This broader framing of wine tourism as a niche market within rural tourism (Popp & McCole, 2016) also reveals its potential for enhancing the broader sustainable development of rural areas (Pellin & Vieira, 2015). Here, tourism not only helps maintain an important agro-sector – wine production – but additionally stimulates other economic, social and cultural activities within the region (e.g. local food production, accommodation and hospitality provision), increasing locally retained value and encouraging the conservation of natural and cultural heritage, sometimes within newly designed tourism experience products, as well as enhancing a territories' cultural identity and creating a regional 'brand for wine sales as well as tourism. (Darnay, 2016; Guedes & Joukes, 2016; Pellin & Vieira, 2015).

Wine tourism is nowadays recognized as a regional and tourism destination diversification tool, a valuable complementary activity to wine production and sales (Correia, Vaughan, Edwards & Silva, 2014), as a sector creating multiple impacts on other economic activities and adding value to other destination attractions (Pellin & Vieira, 2015). However, the move towards tourism means a huge challenge for many farmers (Sharpley, 2002), which is also true for wine production. In many places, producers still consider the wine business as their primary activity with wine tourism producing some kind of promotional or branding effect. It is, therefore, considered as a marketing investment (Bruwer, Coode, Saliba & Herbst, 2013) or as a means of increasing cellar door sales (Carlsen, 2011).

Understanding the rural wine tourism market

But what do we know about the wine tourist, the visitor to wineries and wine destinations? Despite diverse empirical evidence reported in the literature, several authors (e.g., Beverland et al., 1998; Byrd et al., 2016; Macionis & Cambourne, 1998; Mitchell, Hall & Mclntosh, 2000) have described the typical wine tourist as middle aged, highly educated, with professional and administrative occupations, above average income and mainly being a domestic traveller. A literature review comparing 'old' and 'new world' wine tourism destinations (Cunha, Carneiro & Kastenholz, 2020) only found an observable difference between the two destination types regarding gender, with 'old world wine tourism destinations' being apparently dominated by men and 'new world' destinations dominated by female wine tourists. The authors suggest this intriguing result may be due to distinct gender stereotypes associated with wine consumption, as well as with the fact that in the 'old world' wine-producing countries, wine tourism is mostly focused on wine, while in the 'new world' a much wider tourism experience is offered, frequently integrating diverse heritage elements and service experiences.

Moreover, several authors have explored the diversity within the wine tourism market, conducting segmentation studies and identifying differences, mainly based on travel motivation (more or less focused on wine) and/or involvement with wine. Apart from Johnson's previously mentioned distinction between 'specialist winery tourists' or 'generalist visitors' (Johnson 1998, in Galloway et al., 2008), one of the most cited typologies of wine tourist is that proposed by Hall (1996, cited in Hall & Macionis, 1998). He proposes three categories of wine tourists based on motivation, intention to purchase wine and wine involvement: (i) the 'wine lover', an experienced and very interested winery visitor, mature and with high income and education; (ii) the 'wine interested', likely to have visited other wine regions, but wine not being the only purpose of the visit, with moderate to high income and university educated; and (iii) the 'curious tourist', with only moderate interest in wine and wineries, moderate income and education. Pratt (2014) later added a fourth category – the 'disinterested wine tourist', visiting wineries as part of a group, and considering them an alternative to a bar, with no interest in learning about wine.

Charters and Ali-Knight (2002) proposed a similar five group model of wine tourists: (i) The wine lover; (ii) the connoisseur (a highly knowledgeable sub-group of the wine lover); (iii) the wine interested; (iv) the wine novice (corresponding to the curious tourist); and (v) the hangers-on, not interested in wine; for them the wine-related attraction is just another tourist attraction. Pratt's (2014) empirical study of the Australian wine tourist market found that most tourists fall into the category of 'wine interested' (55%), followed by the 'wine curious' tourist (17%), the 'wine lover' (15%), with 12% classified as 'disinterested wine tourists'.

There is no consensus in empirical studies as to which group dominates, which probably depends on the features of the region studied, with those integrating a larger variety of attractions and located close to flagship attractions or cities attracting many visitors, probably attracting more 'generalist' visitors, wine novices, 'hanger-ons' or disinterested wine tourists. However, as in other tourism contexts (see Palacio & McCool, 1997), it is expected that the 'specialist wine tourist', 'connoisseur' or pure 'wine lover' should comprise a minority group of winery and wine destination visitors, as also found by Pratt (2014). This reality should be considered by wine business and destination managers to successfully cater to a diverse wine tourism market, typically motivated by more than wine tasting and purchase, while these may be an interesting and valuable ingredient in a broader 'wine terroir experience product'.

Designing and marketing experiences: the role of routes, governance and networks

Not all rural areas host flagship attractions (Sharpley, 2007) or have highly attractive natural scenery and, therefore, those areas need to work hard to attract tourists. That rule applies to all forms of rural tourism, including wine tourism. And, now that rural tourism has become both well established and widespread, rural regions compete strongly between themselves for market share. There is also increasing competition from other growing and innovative forms of tourism experience, including city-based cultural tourism, electric cycling and Nordic walking, ocean and river cruising. Wine tourism in rural areas must, therefore, work hard to both attract visitors and increase their lengths of stay and spend. Businesses need to become better organized and more professional (Lane & Kastenholz, 2015). And they need to overcome the great weakness of almost all most forms of rural tourism: businesses are small, often untrained, and they rarely work together. To achieve success, they have to work together

Rural wine tourist experiences

with other wine tourism businesses, local tourism businesses and offer a wider range of informed and attractive experiences. The 'passive players' or 'generalist visitors' must become more interested and excited.

There are three central techniques to achieve these aims. They all require skills, time and financial investments.

1   Routes, corridors and greenways can be devised and used to create both marketing opportunities and new, spatially and thematically organized experiences, provided by businesses and places strung along a narrow route. Corridors are wider, encompassing valleys or wider routes perhaps containing roads, railways and rivers. Greenways are similar to routes and corridors, but emphasize non-motorized links and the beauty of the landscape through which they deliberately pass – as walking, cycle or driving routes. All add new aspects to the wine tourism experience, encouraging a sense of travel, achievement, even physical effort and completion to the wine tourism experience, while immersing visitors in meaningful scenically beautiful cultural landscapes (Quattrone, Tomaselli, Riguccio & Russo, 2017).

2   Routes can also take the wine tourism experience into a more sophisticated situation by creating a linear destination. That can help create incentives to form local partnerships. Partnerships – because of their size and their ability to get public sector support – can hire experts to survey visitors to find more about their interests, and to develop new experiences ranging from wine heritage centres, to interpreted wine walks.

3   Partnerships can also create branded experience marketing strategies, ranging from print material to web sites. Cai (2002) shows the advantages of cooperative branding to create a consistent and strong destination image and brand identity, especially for a rural region. Brunori and Rossi (2000) describe the high values released by the partnership-making process in rural Italy, a key step along the way to effective tourism governance, and towards second-generation rural tourism (Lane & Kastenholz, 2015). Koutsouris (2009) provides information about the role of social learning in rural tourism regions in Greece.

Networks of wine tourism destinations can also be created, typically regionally and/ or nationally (see Hall, 2005; Hall, Cambourne, Macionis & Johnson, 1997). Networks are rarely directly involved in experience creation, but they do encourage the spread of good practice in experience creation and marketing practice. They can also assist, trial and disseminate the use of training sessions in tourism management for businesses, communities and the public sector.

Regional heritage elements may be more professionally integrated into the experience and marketing mix through the use of greenways, routes or itineraries to enhance the region's overall tourism appeal (Popp & McCole, 2016; Quattrone et al., 2007), while the tourists themselves often already informally integrate them while exploring destinations, their resources, services and attractions (Gnoth, 2003; Kastenholz et al., 2021).

There are, therefore, perhaps unintended but valuable results from encouraging the creation of new, appealing, distinctive and eventually more articulated visitor experiences. The process can be useful in providing marketing themes. Importantly, to create and market such experiences and themes, wine tourism businesses need to work together and research their markets. Those businesses should then realize that partnerships can be useful, a potential precursor to the creation of linear wine tourism destinations and resorts, perhaps decentralized, but nevertheless a valuable marketing, innovation and governance concept.

Coping with an effective internet presence

The internet has transformed many rural tourism destinations. For relatively low investments, web sites enable remote rural destinations to market themselves worldwide and 24/7. But the internet has done much more than open 24/7 information possibilities. Hughes and Moscardo (2019: 237) sum up the still evolving situation: 'The existing discussion of Information and Communication Technologies (ICT) and tourism has mostly focused on ways in which new technologies can automate or make existing tasks more efficient (doing old things better) or ways that expand and alter existing tasks (doing old things in new ways)'. For a very up-to-date review of the fast-growing role of the internet in tourism, see Gössling (2021).

Three examples illustrate that there is far to go in using the internet in wine tourism. First, the marketing of destinations is often now carried out remotely – and by visitors themselves – using social media. Social media users can become very excited about telling others of great / fascinating / new experiences (see Alalwan, Rana, Dwivedi & Algharabat, 2017) and, hence, monitoring social media may be useful for better understanding markets, their destination and service evaluations, preferences and desires. This knowledge contributes to experience development and market communication decisions (Kastenholz et al., 2021).

Second, researchers now find it relatively quick and economical to use contractors to use e-mail and internet to interrogate focus groups, or Facebook members, to find out about how tourists rate created experiences, and what future experiences they crave (and what they do not). This process allows the researcher to select the geographic areas to concentrate on by postcode or distance from the wine tourism location.

Third, it is well known that heritage interpretation can bring new experiences to life for tourists (Bramwell & Lane, 1993). In the past, that was done via fixed information boards or live human guides. The boards gave few details, were sometimes vandalized and could be quite dull for users. Human guides are expensive and have to be booked in advance. The use of experiences in heritage interpretation to convey messages dates back to Freeman Tilden's pioneering and remarkably effective work for the National Park Service of the USA in the 1970s (Tilden, 1975). But the internet has brought, via smart phones and easily accessible web sites, a whole new approach to telling experiences, including poetry and music. Try https://soundcloud.com/tom_lane/tom-lane-stream-of-consciousness/s-2NthNpv1gCe to experience a guided walk along the famous River Liffey in Ireland's capital, Dublin. This concept has also made it possible to transform – for example – long train journeys into enlightening experiences. Web sites and smart phones can react accurately to the users' position to make geographically accurate statements, which may be particularly interesting when exploring rural, heritage-rich territories along wine routes.

There are however, downsides as well as upsides to most new developments. Gössling and Lane (2015) found that web-based accommodation booking systems were very effective (e.g.: booking.com), especially in rural areas. But they have been so effective and low cost that many local rural tourism associations that once provided training and discussion by charging for making accommodation reservations have collapsed. Equally, low-cost and effective marketing options for wine tourism destinations in well-read daily papers have been lost by the closure of many newspapers that suffered the loss of advertising to web sites (Herndon, 2012).

Co-creating innovative and diversified terror experiences

The so-called 'new experience paradigm' (Pine & Gilmore, 1998; Schmitt, 1999) places consumer experience as central to adding value at a time when experiences are valued more

Rural wine tourist experiences

than material possessions, with complex sensory-rich, emotional and symbolic features being preferred to the functionality of products and services within a social framework sometimes coined the 'experience society' (Schulze, 1996). This paradigm describes what has always been the core of tourism, sometimes referred to as an industry for 'selling dreams' (Holloway, 1995), yielding the fulfilment of needs tourists hardly can fulfil in their ordinary lives at home and sometimes even allowing the transformation of self (Wolf, Ainsworth & Crowley, 2017). These high experience expectations are projected into special localities, permitting the enjoyment of a particular place, interaction with its features and people, immersion into diverse intriguing 'realities' and even 'escape' from ordinary life (Pine & Gilmore, 1998). Tourist experience is currently recognized as crucial to the appeal and competitiveness of a tourist destination or service (Aho, 2001; Binkhorst & Dekker, 2009; Campos, Mendes, do Valle & Scott, 2015; Minkiewicz, Evans & Bridson, 2014; Prebensen & Dahl, 2013). This is also particularly true for rural wine tourist experiences, typically complex place and people experiences, marked by specific features of the geographical, social and cultural context that visitors to rural territories seek to explore (Kastenholz, Carneiro, Marques & Lima, 2012) and actively engage with (Carvalho, Lima, Kastenholz & Sousa, 2016). This active engagement and involvement with local resources and others in the experiencescape has been coined 'co-creation' (Binkhorst & Dekker, 2009; Campos, Mendes, do Valle & Scott, 2015; Minkiewicz, Evans & Bridson, 2014; Prebensen & Dahl, 2013).

Tourists are showing growing interest in being an active part of their holidays. Many want to learn, discover and explore new places, to get to know new people, particularly the local community, and are also seeking interactive, authentic and memorable experiences (Binkhorst & Dekker, 2009). Binkhorst and Dekker (2009: 315) suggest that co-creation in tourism may be defined as 'the interaction of an individual at a specific place and time and within the context of a specific act'. Many authors suggest 'tourist participation' and 'social interaction' as the central dimensions of co-creation in tourism (Binkhorst & Dekker, 2009; Campos et al., 2015; Prebensen & Dahl, 2013). Campos et al. (2015) propose a model of co-creation focusing on the experience at the destination, where the tourist plays a central part interacting with others and the environment, engaging both mentally and physically and going through a set of psychological events, leading to experience memorability.

Social interaction between visitors and local residents was found as essential to the wine tourist experience (Carmichael, 2005), while 'hands-on' activities are known to be popular agro-tourism experiences. Japanese tourists were introduced by one of the authors of this chapter to the experience of harvesting – under supervision – their own rice. British and Austrian tourists pay much higher fares to be able to drive heritage steam trains (again – under supervision), that may significantly add intensity to the experience of rural territories.

Considering experience co-creation in wine tourism, both a rural and cultural tourism pursuit, all these elements should be part of an involving, memorable wine tourism experience, permitting active, individually distinct forms of participation. This can include walking through vineyards, talking to wine producers, tasting and pairing wines with food, participating in a guided tour, asking questions, touching leaves, grapes, barrels and bottles, cold and humid cellar walls, talking with other visitors, with the local sales employee in the wine shop, with people from the nearby village or town, who eventually also produce their own wines and may share curious stories, talking to the waiter in a local restaurant, enjoying the landscape, driving, cycling or walking through it, appreciating it from the window of a rural tourism accommodation unit, experimenting with the destination experiencescape with and in all senses, emotions, moving through it and, importantly, staying within it for more than a brief cellar visit, so as to absorb as much of it as possible to construct meaning and attachment.

Conclusions

Wine tourism businesses and destinations need to revise their strategy and practice to better attend to their visitors' needs and expectations in light of current trends, but also to make the best of the opportunities embedded in wine-producing territories associated with their natural, cultural and social identities and the manifestations of those identities. These processes will not be easy. But they could be assisted by on-the-spot integrated academic research into the training necessary and the results of various methodologies. This would be a new development for all three parties involved (see Higuchi & Yamanaka, 2017).

It is most important to understand the motivations, behaviour patterns and experience expectations of a particular wine-producing destination to attract and satisfy visitors and help them enjoy as much as possible complementary resources and attractions. That way, a complete, appealing, special and authentic rural wine tourism experience may be provided that should be much more than visiting cellar doors and wine tasting, giving an involving, interesting and enjoyable experience of exploring wine terroirs and stories, landscapes, cultural peculiarities, foods and local people. The dimensions of the rural tourist experience are highlighted by Kastenholz, Carneiro, Marques and Lima (2012), with sensory, emotional and social interaction elements standing out in a rather unique, peaceful, 'slow tourism' context associated with perceived 'authenticity', ideally leading to place attachment (Kastenholz, Marques & Carneiro, 2020). These elements, as well as co-creative experience opportunities, should be similarly relevant in rural wine tourism, where wine is a part, albeit an important one, of an overall, involved and memorable destination experience.

A further development of synergies between tourism experiences and wine sales growth would be to market wine tourism destinations on the labels of wine bottles. The existence of local and regional web sites renders that process much easier than it was when tried 30 years ago.

And the future?

This chapter has explored the issues around wine tourism's product development to regenerate rural economies, by creating and marketing strong and appealing visitor experiences. In writing the chapter, it became clear that growing visitor demand for in-depth experiences is now perhaps replacing the strong interest in briefly visiting more and more places, an activity that adds to emissions and to climate change pressures. Is ticking off more and more destinations on personal 'bucket lists' about to change in favour of in-depth experiences? Could a better understanding of experience creation and their delivery become an important agent of behavioural change? Could it help speed up slow tourism's journey to greater popularity? There is much in-depth research to be done and much to learn for destination and marketing managers.

Note (funding)

This chapter was developed in the scope of the research project TWINE – Co-creating sustainable Tourism & WINe Experiences in rural areas – PTDC/GES-GCE/32259/2017 – POCI-01–0145-FEDER-032259, funded by the ERDF through the COMPETE 2020 – Operational Programme Competitiveness and Internationalization (POCI), and Portugal's national funds (OPTDC/GES-GCE/32259/2017-E), through the FCT/MCTES.

References

Agapito, D., Valle, P. and Mendes, J. (2014) The sensory dimension of tourist experiences: Capturing meaningful sensory-based themes in Southwest Portugal. *Tourism Management*, 42, 224–237.

Aho, S. K. (2001) Towards a general theory of touristic experiences: Modelling experience process in tourism. *Tourism Review*, 56(3/4), 33–37.

Alalwan, A. A., Rana, N. P., Dwivedi, Y. K. and Algharabat, R. (2017) Social media in marketing: A review and analysis of the existing literature. *Telematics and Informatics*, 34(7), 1177–1190.

Alonso, A. D. (2009) Wine, tourism and experience in the Canary Islands' context *Tourism*, 57(1), 7–22.

Alonso, A. D. and Yi, L. (2012) Old wine region, new concept and sustainable development: Winery entrepreneurs' perceived benefits from wine tourism on Spain's Canary Islands. *Journal of Sustainable Tourism*, 20(7) 991–1009.

Beverland, M., James, K., James, M., Porter, C. and Stace, G. (1998) Wine tourism: Missed opportunities in West Auckland. *Australian & New Zealand Wine Industry Journal*, 13(4), 403–407.

Binkhorst, E. and Dekker, T. (2009) Agenda for co-creation tourism experience research. *Journal of Hospitality Marketing & Management*, 18(2–3), 311–327.

Bramwell, B. and Lane, B. (1993) Interpretation and sustainable tourism: The potential and the pitfalls, *Journal of Sustainable Tourism*, 1(2), 71–80.

Brunori, G. and Rossi, A. (2000) Synergy and coherence through collective action: Some insights from wine routes in Tuscany. *Sociologia Ruralis*, 40(4), 409–423.

Bruwer, J. (2003) South African wine routes: Some perspectives on the wine tourism industry's structural dimensions and wine tourism product. *Tourism Management*, 24(4), 423–435.

Bruwer, J., Coode, M., Saliba, A. and Herbst, F. (2013) Wine tourism experience effects of the tasting room on consumer brand loyalty. *Tourism Analysis*, 18(4), 399–414.

Byrd, E. T., Canziani, B., Hsieh, Y. C. J., Debbage, K. and Sonmez, S. (2016) Wine tourism: Motivating visitors through core and supplementary services. *Tourism Management*, 52, 19–29.

Cai, L. A. (2002) Cooperative branding for rural destinations. *Annals of Tourism Research*, 29(3), 720–742.

Campos, A., Mendes, J., do Valle, P. and Scott, N. (2015) Co-creation of tourist experiences: A literature review. *Current Issues in Tourism*, 21(4), 369–400.

Carlsen, J. (2011) Assessing service quality at wineries and cellar doors through service mapping. *International Journal of Wine Business Research*, 23(3), 271–290.

Carmichael, B. (2005) Understanding the wine tourism experience for winery visitors in the Niagara Region, Ontario, Canada. *Tourism Geographies*, 7(2), 185–204.

Carneiro, M. J., Lima, J. and Silva, A. L. (2015) Landscape and the rural tourism experience: Identifying key elements, addressing potential, and implications for the future. *Journal of Sustainable Tourism*, 23(8–9), 1217–1235.

Carvalho, M., Lima, J., Kastenholz, E. and Sousa. A. J. (2016) Co-Creative rural tourism experiences: Connecting tourists, community and local resources. In E. Kastenholz, M. J. Carneiro, C. Eusébio and E. Figueiredo (Eds.), *Meeting Challenges for Rural Tourism Through Co-creation of Sustainable Tourist Experiences*. Newcastle upon Tyne: Cambridge Scholars Publishing, pp. 83–106.

Charters, S. (2009) New World and Mediterranean wine tourism: A comparative analysis. *Tourism*, 57(4), 369–379.

Charters, S. and Ali-Knight, J. (2002) Who is the wine tourist? *Tourism Management*, 23(3), 311–319.

Christou, P., Farmaki, A. and Evangelou, G. (2018) Nurturing nostalgia? A response from rural tourism stakeholders. *Tourism Management*, 69, 42–51.

Correia, A., Vaughan, R., Edwards, J. and Silva, G. (2014) The potential for cooperation between wine and tourism businesses in the provision of tourism experiences: The case of the Douro valley of Portugal. *Revista Portuguesa de Estudos Regionais*, (36), 43–55.

Cunha, D., Carneiro, M. J. and Kastenholz, E. (2020) 'Velho Mundo' versus 'Novo Mundo': Diferentes perfis e comportamento de viagem do enoturista?. ['Old World' versus 'New World': Distinct profiles and travel behavior amongst wine tourists?] *Journal of Tourism and Development*, 34, 113–128.

Darnay, S. (2016) Quality of landscape and sustainability benefit to wine tourism: Contexts and commitments. In M. Peris-Ortiz, M. de la Cruz Del Río Rama and C. Rueda-Armengot, (Eds.), *Wine and Tourism: A Strategic Segment for Sustainable Economic Development*. Cham: Springer, pp. 15–25.

Etcheverria, O. (2016) Wine tourism and gastronomy. In M. Peris-Ortiz, M. de la Cruz Del Río Rama and C. Rueda-Armengot (Eds.), *Wine and Tourism: A Strategic Segment for Sustainable Economic Development*. Cham: Springer International Publishing, pp. 161–177.

Everett, S. and Slocum, S. L. (2013) Food and tourism: An effective partnership? A UK-based review. *Journal of Sustainable Tourism*, 21(6), 789–809.

Figueiredo, E., Kastenholz, E. and Lima, J. (2013) Recreating rurality – Visions of hosts and guests in two Portuguese villages. In E. Figueiredo and A. Raschi (Eds.), *Fertile Links? Connections between Tourism Activities, Socioeconomic Contexts and Local Development in European Rural Areas*. Florence: Florence University Press, pp. 43–70.

Galloway, G., Mitchell, R., Getz, D., Crouch, G. and Ong, B. (2008) Sensation seeking and the prediction of attitudes and behaviours of wine tourists. *Tourism Management*, 29(5), 950–966.

Garau, C. (2015) Perspectives on cultural and sustainable rural tourism in a smart region: The case study of Marmilla in Sardinia (Italy). *Sustainability*, 7(6), 6412–6434.

Garrod, B., Wornell, R. and Youel, R. (2006) Re-conceptualising rural resources as countryside capital: The case of rural tourism. *Journal of Rural Studies*, 22(1), 117–128.

Getz, D. and Brown, G. (2006) Critical success factors for wine tourism regions: A demand analysis. *Tourism Management*, 27(1), 146–158.

Gnoth, J. (2003) Consumer activated services networks: Towards a dynamic model for tourism destinations. Proceedings of the 32nd EMAC Conference (University of Strathclyde, Glasgow).

Gössling, S. (2021) Tourism, technology and ICT: A critical review of affordances and concessions. *Journal of Sustainable Tourism*. doi.org/10.1080/09669582.2021.1873353

Gössling, S. and Lane, B. (2015) Rural tourism and the development of Internet-based accommodation booking platforms: A study in the advantages, dangers and implications of innovation. *Journal of Sustainable Tourism,* 23(8–9), 1386–1403.

Guedes, A. and Joukes, V. (2016) Hotel ships on the Douro River and their relationship with the terroir. In M. Peris-Ortiz, M. Del Río Rama and C. Rueda-Armengot (Eds.), *Wine and Tourism: A Strategic Segment for Sustainable Economic Development*. Cham: Springer, pp. 87–105.

Hall, C. M. (2005) Rural wine and food tourism cluster and network development. In D. Hall, I. Kirkpatrick and M. Mitchell (Eds.), *Rural Tourism and Sustainable Business*. Clevedon: Channel View Publications, pp. 149–164.

Hall, C. M., Cambourne, B., Macionis, N. and Johnson, G. (1997) Wine tourism and network development in Australia and New Zealand: Review, establishment and prospects. *International Journal of Wine Marketing*, 9(2), 5–31.

Hall, C. M., Johnson, G., Longo, A. M. and Mitchell, R. (2000) Paying for tastings: The New Zealand experience. In *Proceedings of the First New Zealand Wine Tourism Conference*, Marlborough, November 21–23, pp. 21–23.

Hall, C. M. and Macionis, N. (1998) Wine tourism in Australia and New Zealand. In R. Butler, C. M. Hall and J. Jenkins (Eds.), *Tourism and Recreation in Rural Areas*. Chichester: John Wiley & Sons, pp. 197–221.

Herndon, K. (2012) *The Decline of the Daily Newspaper: How an American Institution Lost the Online Revolution*. New York: Peter Lang.

Higuchi, Y. and Yamanaka, Y. (2017) Knowledge sharing between academic researchers and tourism practitioners: A Japanese study of the practical value of embeddedness, trust and co-creation. *Journal of Sustainable Tourism*, 25(10), 1456–1473.

Hjalager, A. M. (1996) Agricultural diversification into tourism: Evidence of a European Community development programme. *Tourism Management*, 17(2), 103–111.

Holland, T., Smit, B. and Jones, G. (2017) Toward a conceptual framework of terroir tourism: A case study of the Prince Edward County, Ontario wine region. *Tourism Planning & Development*, 11(3), 275–291.

Holloway, J. C. (1995) *The Business of Tourism*, 4th Edn. London: Longman.

Hughes, K. and Moscardo, G. (2019) ICT and the future of tourist management. *Journal of Tourism Futures*, 5(3), 228–240.

Kastenholz, E., Carneiro, M. J. and Marques, C. (2012) Marketing the rural tourism experience. In R. Tsiotsou and R. Goldsmith (Eds.), *Strategic Marketing in Tourism Services*. Bingley: Emerald, pp. 247–264.

Kastenholz, E., Carneiro, M. J., Marques, C. P. and Lima, J. (2012) Understanding and managing the rural tourism experience – the case of a historical village in Portugal. *Tourism Management Perspectives*, 4, 207–214.

Rural wine tourist experiences

Kastenholz, E., Cunha, D., Eletxigerra, A., Carvalho, M. and Silva, I. (2021) Exploring wine terroir experiences: A social media analysis. In A. Abreu, D. Liberato, E. A. González and J. C. Garcia Ojeda (Eds.), *Advances in Tourism, Technology and Systems. ICOTTS 2020. Vol. 2.* Singapore: Springer, pp. 402–420.

Kastenholz, E., Marques, C. P. and Carneiro, M. J. (2020) Place attachment through sensory-rich, emotion-generating place experiences in rural tourism. *Journal of Destination Marketing & Management*, 17. doi.org/10.1016/j.jdmm.2020.100455.

Koutsouris, A. (2009) Social learning and sustainable tourism development; local quality conventions in tourism: A Greek case study. *Journal of Sustainable Tourism*, 17(5), 567–581.

Lane, B. (1994a) What is rural tourism? *Journal of Sustainable Tourism*, 2(1–2), 7–21.

Lane, B. (1994b) Sustainable rural tourism strategies: A tool for development and conservation. *Journal of Sustainable Tourism*, 2(1–2), 102–111.

Lane, B. and Kastenholz, E. (2015) Rural tourism: The evolution of practice and research approaches – towards a new generation concept? *Journal of Sustainable Tourism*, 23(8–9), 1133–1156.

Lavrador Silva, A., Kastenholz, E. and Lima, J. (2012) O papel da Paisagem na experiência de Enoturismo – o caso de Favaios [The role of landscape in the wine tourism experience- the case of Favaios] *RTD/Journal of Tourism and Development*, 17/18, 1257–1270.

Macionis, N. and Cambourne, B. (1998) Wine tourism: Just what is it all about? *Wine Industry Journal*, 13(1), 41–47.

Minkiewicz, J., Evans, J. and Bridson, K. (2014) How do consumers co-create their experiences? An exploration in the heritage sector. *Journal of Marketing Management*, 30(1–2), 30–59.

Mitchell, R., Charters, S. and Albrecht, J. N. (2012) Cultural systems and the wine tourism product. *Annals of Tourism Research*, 39(1), 311–335.

Mitchell, R., Hall, C. M. and McIntosh, A. (2000) Wine tourism and consumer behavior. In C. M. Hall, L. Sharples, B. Cambourne and N. Macionis (Eds.), *Wine Tourism Around the World: Development, Management and Markets.* Oxford: Butterworth-Heinemann, pp. 115–135.

OECD. (1994) *Tourism Strategies and Rural Development.* Organisation for Economic Co-operation and Development. Available at: https://www.oecd.org/cfe/tourism/2755218.pdf https://www.oecd.org/cfe/tourism/2755218.pdf (Accessed 16 January 2021).

Palacio, V. and McCool, S. F. (1997) Identifying ecotourists in Belize through benefit segmentation: A preliminary analysis. *Journal of Sustainable Tourism*, 5(3), 234–243.

Pan, S. and Ryan, C. (2009) Tourism sense-making: The role of the senses and travel journalism. *Journal of Travel & Tourism Marketing*, 26(7), 625–639.

Paniagua, A. (2002) Urban-rural migration, tourism entrepreneurs and rural restructuring in Spain. *Tourism Geographies*, 4(4), 349–371.

Pellin, V. and Vieira, A. C. P. (2015) Contributions of geographical indications for territorial strengthening in rural space: A case study in southern Brazil *Espacios*, 36(8), 7–7.

Pereiro, X. and Conde, S. P. (2005) Turismo e oferta gastronómica na comarca de Ulloa (Galiza): Análise de uma experiência de desenvolvimento local [Tourism and gastronomic offer in the region of Ulloa (Galicia): Analysis of a local development experience]. *Pasos – Revista de Turismo y Patrimonio Cultural*, 3(1), 109–123.

Pine, J. and Gilmore, J. (1998) Welcome to the experience economy. *Harvard Business Review.* Available at: https://hbr.org/1998/07/welcome-to-the-experience-economy (Accessed 27 January 2021).

Popp, L. and McCole, D. (2016) Understanding tourists' itineraries in emerging rural tourism regions: The application of paper-based itinerary mapping methodology to a wine tourism region in Michigan. *Current Issues in Tourism*, 19(10), 988–1004.

Pratt, M. (2014) Four Wine Tourist Profiles. Paper presented at AWBR 8th International Conference, Germany. Available at: http://academyofwinebusiness.com/wp-content/uploads/2014/07/TE06_Pratt_Marlene.pdf (Accessed 28 January 2021).

Prebensen, N. and Dahl, J. (2013) Value co-creation significance of tourist resources. *Annals of Tourism Research*, 42, 240–261.

Quattrone, M., Tomaselli, G., Riguccio, L. and Russo, P. (2017) Assessment of the territorial suitability for the creation of the greenways networks: Methodological application in the Sicilian landscape context. *Journal of Agricultural Engineering*, 48(4), 209–222.

Riscinto-Kozub, K. and Childs, N. (2012) Conversion of local winery awareness: An exploratory study in visitor vs non-visitor attitude and perception. *International Journal of Wine Business Research*, 24(4), 287–301.

Rodrigues, Á., Kastenholz, E. and Morais, D. (2012) Travel constraints and nostalgia as determinants of cross-Atlantic legacy tourism. In H. Pechlaner, T. J. Lee and G. G. Bò (Eds.), *New Minorities and Tourism*. Bozen: Europaeische Akademie Bozen, pp. 75–92.

Schmitt, B. (1999) Experiential marketing. *Journal of Marketing Management*, 15(1–3), 53–67.

Schulze, G. (1996) *The Experience Society*. London: Sage Publications.

Sharpley, R. (2002) Rural tourism and the challenge of tourism diversification: The case of Cyprus. *Tourism Management*, 23(3), 233–244.

Sharpley, R. (2007) Flagship attractions and sustainable rural tourism development: The case of the Alnwick Garden, England. *Journal of Sustainable Tourism*, 15(2), 125–143.

Sharpley, R. and Roberts, L. (2004) Rural tourism: 10 years on. *International Journal of Tourism Research*, 6(3), 119–124.

Sidali, K., Kastenholz, E. and Bianchi, R. (2015) Food tourism, niche markets and products in rural tourism: Combining the intimacy model and the experience economy as a rural development strategy. *Journal of Sustainable Tourism*, 23(8–9), 1179–1197.

Sims, R. (2009) Food, place and authenticity: Local food and the sustainable tourism experience. *Journal of Sustainable Tourism*, 17(3), 321–336.

Tilden, F. (1975) *Interpreting Our Heritage*. Chapel Hill: University of North Carolina Press.

Tomljenović, R. and Getz, D. (2009) Life-cycle stages in wine tourism development: A comparison of wine regions in Croatia. *Tourism Review International*, 13(1), 31–49.

Wolf, I. D., Ainsworth, G. and Crowley, J. (2017) Transformative travel as a sustainable market niche for protected areas: A new development, marketing and conservation model. *Journal of Sustainable Tourism*, 25(11), 1650–1673.

37

WILDERNESS TOURISM

Nature-based tourist experiences in wild places

Jarkko Saarinen

Introduction

The connection between tourism and the wilderness may seem paradoxical. On the one hand, wilderness is often considered a place where wildlife and natural processes rule and humans and human activities should not really exist. The United States Wilderness Act of 1964, for example, states that 'a wilderness, in contrast with those areas where man and his own works dominate the landscape, is hereby recognized as an area where the earth and its community of life are untrammelled by man' (Wilderness Act, 1964). The Act is not just another policy document. In a similar way to establishing the world's first national park at Yellowstone (USA) in 1872, the world's first wilderness act created a model for global conservation and defining wilderness areas as places that offer 'outstanding opportunities for solitude' (Wilderness Act, 1964), for example.

On the other hand, tourism is obviously a human activity, whose presence per se may conflict with the above kinds of notions of a wilderness as a non-human environment (see Saarinen, 2019). In addition, the very nature of tourism is that it creates changes to places where it exists and which it utilizes (Holden, 2006; Mathieson & Wall, 1982). Tourism is also seen as a process that evolves from small-scale activities to larger ones with an increasing number of visitors and impacts following the crowd (see Butler, 1980; 2010). Thus, touristic use can make wilderness areas and natural environments so popular that it may become very challenging to find solitude and experience untrammelled nature by those visitors seeking these kinds of nature-based tourism experiences.

However, despite the Western ideal of wildernesses as the last vestiges and places beyond civilization and human influence, untouched by the modern world, they are deeply integrated to human systems (Saarinen, 2016). Nowadays, they are increasingly promoted as sites for tourism consumption and tourist experiences (Buckley, 1999, 2006; Sæþórsdóttir, Hall & Saarinen, 2011; Wall-Reinius, 2012). In tourism advertising, positive images, such as the experience of solitude, freedom and naturalness are connected to the wilderness as tourism products related to a variety of activities that a wild, harsh and rugged nature could offer for visitors (see Saarinen, 2005; Sæþórsdóttir 2010a, b; Thorhallsdottir, 2007). Although these kinds of active and visible uses of wilderness characteristics in tourism promotion may be a relatively new issue, wilderness areas have long been associated with tourism

DOI: 10.4324/9781003219866-42

521

(Frost & Hall, 2010). For example, creating the first national park at Yellowstone was aimed at limiting human settlements, occupancy, sale, indigenous uses and the expansion of extractive resource industries in the area (Nash 1967: 108). By doing so, the national park was 'dedicated and set apart as a public park or pleasuring-ground for the benefit and enjoyment of the people' (Yellowstone National Park Protection Act, 1872). Similarly, the Wilderness Act (1964) explicitly indicates that wilderness areas should also provide opportunities to practise 'a primitive and unconfined type of recreation' in a place 'where man himself is a visitor who does not remain.' These kinds of temporal recreational mobilities by visitors and references to the 'enjoyment of people' are nowadays widely conceptualized and practiced as tourism.

Thus, wilderness areas and national parks are profoundly related to tourism and the recreational use of those areas by non-local people. From the very beginning of the conservation movement and the evolution of the modern tourism industry, wilderness environments were considered targets and co-products of the global tourism phenomenon that was constantly calling for new and different kinds of attractions. However, to provide nature experiences and outstanding opportunities for solitude, for example, there needs to be some regulation of the touristic use of these areas. Indeed, due to the very nature of tourism as a growth-oriented catalyst of change, wilderness and nature experiences (as we now conceptualize them) are not infinite in the hands of the tourism industry.

Originally, the attempts to limit the growth of tourism in wild areas was based on a carrying capacity thinking (Butler, 2010; Lucas, 1964; Wagar, 1964, 1974). It meant that researchers and managers tried to define the maximum number of tourists in a given space and time, without causing unacceptable changes in the physical, economic and socio-cultural environment and to visitors' satisfaction (Butler, 1996, 1999; Getz, 1983; Mathieson & Wall, 1982). Nowadays, governance approaches to managing the relationship between tourism and wilderness conservation are based on area-specific models (see Hendee, Stankey & Lucas, 1990) or broader sustainability and responsibility thinking in tourism (see Blackstock, White, McCrum, Scott & Hunter, 2008; Saarinen, 2014a; Sharpley, 2000, 2009, 2013). This chapter discusses the nature and role of wilderness environments and wild places in tourism. First, the idea of the wilderness and its relationship with land ethics are introduced, followed by a discussion on the wilderness as a tourist attraction and a place for nature-based tourist experiences. Finally, management and governance needs for wilderness tourism are briefly debated, followed by conclusions.

Wilderness use and land ethics

Wilderness environments are considered to represent the last existing fragments of untrammelled nature, untouched by civilization and human activities. The International Union for Conserving Nature (IUCN), for example, has labelled the 'highest' protection area category as Strict Nature Reserves (1a) and 'wilderness' (1b) (Saarinen, 2019). According to the IUCN, wildernesses are considered to be large, unmodified or slightly modified areas, retaining their natural character without permanent or significant human habitation. In this respect, the wilderness represents a space external and in opposition to people, culture and civilization (see Cronon, 1998; Nash, 1967). At the same time, however, wilderness areas are defined and redefined, managed and used by people.

The wilderness may conjure up distinct meanings and images based on the natural characteristics of those environments. Still, different kinds of objectives and values, often contradictory ones, are connected with the idea and use of the wilderness (Saarinen, 1998a, 2005). The wilderness is a value-bounded and ethically loaded idea and place, and our notion of a

Wilderness tourism

wilderness as a place reflects our specific relationships to it and the types and levels of activities we consider acceptable in a place called a wilderness. As stated by Tuan (1974: 112), the wilderness is 'a state of mind'. Due to this personally, socially and culturally coded nature of the wilderness, it is difficult to find any single and universally accepted definition for the wilderness concept (see Short, 1991; Nash, 1967). For land management and conservation uses, various 'objective' or technical definitions have been outlined. In the United States, for example, the minimum size for a wilderness area is 2020 hectares, and their basic characteristics are that they should be in a natural state, have no roads and contain natural fauna (Wilderness Act, 1964). The corresponding minimum size in Finland is 15,000, in Australia 25,000 and in Sweden 50,000 hectares (Saarinen, 1998a). Thus, even these objective (numerical) measurements vary depending on the societal context.

The early conservation movement of wilderness areas and wild places in general was not purely ecological or biocentric aiming to conserve the natural environment for the sake of nature itself (Butler, 1998; Hall, 1992; Nash, 1967). There was an implicit emphasis on what we would now call a sustainable use of natural resources (see Enders & Remig, 2015a). Indeed, Crober (2015) and many other scholars connect early the conservation movement with sustainability thinking by arguing that the basic principles of sustainable development, in general, has its origins in the eighteenth century idea of 'sustained yield' in forestry (i.e. natural resource use and management) and especially in nineteenth century nature conservation (Enders & Remig, 2015b; Hall, 1998). Influenced by the sustained yield approach. Gifford Pinchot, the first Chief of the United States Forest Service in the 1910s, introduced a so-called wise use, or utilitarian conservation approach, in natural resource management, which is often seen as a historical antecedent of sustainable development thinking (Butler, 1998).

It is challenging to evaluate how these historical centuries-old processes actually influenced the politics and institutionalization of sustainable development in the 1980s (Saarinen & Gill, 2019), but they all have common ground with anthropocentric attitudes towards the environment. The classic Brundtland Commission definition, stating that sustainable development is development that 'meets the needs of the present without compromising the ability of future generations to meet their own needs' (WCED, 1987) primarily focuses on human needs with an argument that caring for the environment and natural systems is not only good but indispensable for us and for our future.

In addition to the broad idea of anthropocentrism, there are numerous different approaches, categorizations and attitudes towards nature and the wilderness and their uses, such as biocentrism and ecocentrism (see Bauer, Vasile & Mondini, 2018; Fennell, 2006; Glacken, 1992; Jamal, 2019). Pietarinen (1987), for example, has outlined four basic attitudes towards forest and wilderness environment: utilism, humanism, mysticism and primitivism. With the exception of the last one, these attitudes are anthropocentric to different degrees. Utilism underlines the unrestricted right of people to use the natural environment and the wilderness as a source of raw materials. Even highly excessive exploitation can be accepted and later compensated for through ever-advancing technological solutions. From a humanism perspective, the use of a wilderness environment should promote human development attaining ethical, aesthetic and mental equilibrium, that is, not only as a source of raw materials for economic growth that is still considered necessary for societal development. Mysticism connects humans to a larger spiritual entity formed by nature, emphasizing an experiential unity between us, the natural and the 'divine'. Primitivism (i.e. biocentrism or deep ecology) underlines the need to recognize the intrinsic value of the wilderness environment that is an equal entity with human systems. From this perspective, humans have no special rights to exploit nature and human well-being should not rest on a foundation that causes negative impacts and damage to the wilderness (see Fennell, 2006; Saarinen, 1998a).

Obviously, biocentric or deep ecology approaches do not support a touristic use of the wilderness, as they evidently cause negative impacts on the environment. From the anthropocentric perspective and for the touristic use of wilderness areas, Aldo Leopold's (1949) idea of land ethics is interesting as it connects the use of the wilderness with the current notion of and need for sustainability. In his seminal work *A Sand County Almanac*, Leopold suggests a new kind of ethics to deal with people's relationship with the land and the animals and plants that live and grow upon it. In his land ethics, 'a thing is right when it tends to preserve the integrity, stability, and beauty of the biotic community. It is wrong when it tends otherwise' (Leopold, 1949: 224–225). Therefore, we can utilize the wilderness in different ways, including for aesthetic, recreation and tourism reasons, but with a great responsibility: while using the wilderness, humans need to limit their effect on it, otherwise we may destroy the natural capital our own existence depends on. As pointed out earlier, this is also the message of the need for sustainable development by the Brundtland's Commission (WCED, 1987).

Although Leopold was critical of recreational development, as he considered it fragmenting wilderness, in principle his land ethics acknowledges that a change is inevitable in human–nature relations, and to cope with the change in a 'sustained' way, there needs to be 'flexibility in the structure' but also adjustments; that is, regulations (Leopold, 1949: 216). The land ethics approach connects humans with the wilderness in a way that partly challenges traditional Western understanding of human–nature relations, being based on an opposition between organized society and wilderness or culture and nature (see Castree, 2014, 2015; Saarinen, 2019). In this respect, land ethics can help us see that there have never been humans without nature and vice versa, empowering us to think that tourism and the wilderness can coexist but with certain conditions and ethical guidelines.

The wilderness as a tourism environment

Compared with many extractive industries, such as forestry and mining, tourism represents a different kind of economy in terms of the use of wilderness environments (see Sæþórsdóttir & Saarinen, 2016a; 2016b). Despite being a large, global-scale activity, the tourism industry is often seen as being 'softer' towards (destination) environments in its operations (Holden, 2003, 2006). Nowadays, wilderness environments attract a substantial amount of tourists, and some wilderness areas may have millions of visitors per year (see Saarinen, 2013, 2014b; Sæþórsdóttir, 2011). Countries where wild natural areas still exist can treat them as a capital asset and earn money by exporting the 'wilderness experience' (Sæþórsdóttir, 2010a; 2010b), which is also seen as providing a rationale for protecting wilderness areas in many places (see Butler & Boyd, 2000; Hall & Boyd, 2005).

The link between conserving wild places and tourism is probably as old as the history of protected areas (Frost & Hall, 2010). Still, the wilderness and its key characteristics have not always been positively perceived attraction elements for people and their recreational and touristic consumption needs. According to Short (1991: 6) 'fear of the wilderness was one of the strongest elements in European attitudes to wilderness up to the nineteenth century', and Europeans transferred that fear or even hate towards wild places to their colonies in North America, Africa and Australia, for example (see Connor, 2014; Hall, 1992, 1998; Tuan, 1979). The wilderness was considered a place that is inhabited by 'wild beasts' and that is beyond civilization and the sphere of human control (Nash, 1967: 1–2).

Wilderness tourism

In general, the growing demand for tourists to experience wilderness areas has been based on the altered positive attitudes towards the environment (see Frost & Hall, 2010; Sæþórsdóttir, Hall & Saarinen, 2011), and the development of transportation systems and accessibility has integrated even the most remote wild places closely to the global tourism market and its economic circuits (Saarinen, 2005; Sæþórsdóttir, 2011). As a result, wild natural environments are 'universally regarded as a source of pleasure' (Wang, 2000: 80) and the tourism industry has become a significant user, stakeholder and element of change in wilderness environments (Buckley, 1999, 2006; Saarinen, 2013).

Wilderness tourism is usually considered an independent or individualistic form of tourism. Traditionally, activities such as backpacking and hiking have been linked to wilderness recreation (Brown, 1980; Pigram & Jenkins, 1999; Wolfe, 1964). However, in the past two or three decades, the growth of wilderness tourism has been largely based on a rise in organized forms of nature-based and adventure tourism (Buckley, 2006; Cloke & Perkins, 2002; Sæþórsdóttir, 2010a). These new tourism forms in the wilderness involve activities such as mountain biking, snowmobile trekking, rafting, horse riding, hiking, sport fishing, husky safaris, motorized boat tours and even four-wheel drives. All these activities can play with the images of naturalness, freedom, solitude and wildness but, in practice, they may also be in conflict with traditional wilderness characteristics and cause conflicts among wilderness users and negative changes to wilderness experiences (see Buckley, 1999; Manning, 1985; Vail & Heldt, 2004; Vaske, Shelby, Graefe & Heberlein 1986).

Based on a wide variety of current tourism activities in wilderness areas, there is obviously a diverse scale of tourist experiences and motivations that can be linked to touristic visits to the wilderness. As indicated earlier, solitude is often listed as the key quality and a desirable state of mind for wilderness visitors (see Hendee, Stankey & Lucas, 1990; Roggenbuck, Williams & Watson, 1993). Solitude and especially the conditions for experiencing solitude is also one of the most studied issues in wilderness tourism (see Hammitt, 1982; Manning, 1985; 2003; Williams, Roggenbuck & Bange, 1991). The basic question is how many visitors can a wilderness, or a certain trail, river route or camping area, host in a given time without jeopardizing the opportunity to experience solitude by the visitors. These kinds of practical wilderness management questions have led to conceptually interesting research on crowding, encounter norms and social carrying capacity, for example (see Lucas, 1964; McCool & Lime, 2001; Saarinen, 1998b, 2013, 2014b; Williams et al., 1991).

However, these issues turned out to be both theoretically and practically complex questions that are contextual and highly dependent on a large number of 'variables'. The encounter norms, for example, have been noted to vary depending on the numbers of people that one comes into contact with at a certain time and space in a wilderness visit, but also group size (both one's own and the one contacted), behaviour, activities, ethnicity, pets and so on may have an effect. In addition, different kinds of values and nature attitudes, as well as environmental and many other situational factors can play a major role in terms of how individuals and/or groups evaluate contacts as acceptable or unacceptable in wilderness settings (see Patterson & Hammitt, 1990; Vaske et al., 1986).

Many of the studies focusing on visitor perceptions on encounters and crowding rely on the measurement of (overall) visitor satisfaction (Connelly, 1987), which has also turned out to be a problematic concept for wilderness management (Hendee, Stankey & Lucas, 1990) as overall satisfaction may depend on many elements other than encounters or perceived crowding alone. In addition, human satisfaction is obviously a subjective matter and, as noted by Manning (2003: 109), 'the same type of recreation opportunity might be judged as

Jarkko Saarinen

very satisfying to one visitor and substantially less satisfying to another visitor.' In a situation where the touristic use of a wilderness area is increasing, this leads to a serious management problem based on what is termed the displacement process. Visitors who are sensitive to crowding, for example, will search for other areas for their wilderness visits and, thus, the user segments of a particular site may turn to 'visitors less sensitive to crowding' (Manning, 2003: 109). Therefore, wilderness tourism management and governing the tourism industry cannot be based on perceived impacts and satisfaction of the visiting tourists alone. There needs to be factors other than the visitor satisfaction or the industry's ethics alone involved.

Thinking about the limits to growth in wilderness tourism management

In some places the scale of wilderness tourism may have reached a level that questions the softer side of the industry compared with some other economic uses of the wild. Indeed, the increasing popularity of tourism in wilderness areas poses a threat to the biodiversity values of these areas (Buckley, 1999, 2006). Increasing tourism can also conflict with wilderness experiences focusing on an unconfined type of recreation (Higham, 1998). This resembles Hardin's (1968) tragedy of commons situation. Although the tragedy of commons is a complex and problematic framework in practice (see Ostrom, 1990), it can be applied to the wilderness experience context at a general level. In the tragedy of commons situation, increased and unrestricted public access to a common resource (wilderness area) would ultimately deplete the shared limited resource, that is, wilderness experiences based on a primitive and unconfined type of recreation. In this respect, it is quite evident that the increased touristic attractiveness of wilderness areas has this kind of challenges for the carrying capacity and management in many wilderness areas (Hendee, Stankey & Lucas, 1990: 401). This has created a need to set a limit to growth in wilderness tourism, but the exercise of determining maximum use levels has turned out to be a complex task (see Butler, 1996; Lindberg, McCool & Stankey, 1997; Saarinen, 2013).

Traditionally, wilderness management has focused on two related but often conflicting elements: environmental conditions and use levels (Lindberg, McCool & Stankey, 1997). The former refers to wilderness characteristics and how they are protected, while the latter focuses on how many visitors and/or different kinds of visitors and visitor groups can be allowed to enter an area in a given time period. This focus on visitor numbers is based on carrying capacity thinking in resource and tourism management (see Butler, 1996, 2010; Hendee, Stankey & Lucas, 1990; Lucas, 1964; Wagar, 1974). However, these two aims focusing on resource conditions and use levels are connected in complex ways owing to, for example, the noted contextual nature of wilderness experience, encounter norms, visitor satisfaction and (social) carrying capacity. In general, this complexity creates what Lindberg, McCool and Stankey (1997: 462) call 'a confusion of inputs and outputs' in wilderness management. For example, a general objective for wilderness management can be to provide a high-quality visitor experience while sustaining the wilderness and its functions in a material way. For these two kinds of goals to be achieved in wilderness tourism management, Lindberg, McCool and Stankey (1997) have listed several conditions for it. These include objectives such as a need for a widely accepted agreement on the type of desired social and resource conditions, an agreement on the desired level of these conditions and a need to understand the relationship between use levels and impacts for a selected set of (objective) indicators. According to Lindberg, McCool and Stankey (1997: 463), these kinds of 'requirements are rarely, if ever, met', which makes the focus on tourist numbers and the use of carrying capacity thinking alone challenging in wilderness tourism management.

Wilderness tourism

Alternative wilderness tourism management approaches are based on the recreational opportunity spectrum (ROS) and the limits of acceptable change (LAC) approaches. ROS is a practical tool used for managing a diverse set of wilderness recreation and tourism opportunities based on different physical, social and managerial settings (see Manning, 2003; Brown, Driver & McConnell, 1978). By describing a range of these settings, selected types of touristic offerings and opportunities can be defined for wilderness visitors. According to Kliskey (1998: 79), the ROS 'is based on the assumption that the more variation in the environment, the more the variation in the types of experiences a typical user could enjoy'. Based on this call for variation, the ROS involves a zoning approach that aims to provide a diversity of touristic opportunities on a continuum from 'developed' to 'undeveloped' environments (Brown, Driver & McConnell, 1978; Clark & Stankey, 1979) from which wilderness visitors can decide where to go based on the settings they prefer to seek (Sæþórsdóttir, 2011). Past research has demonstrated that some wilderness tourist groups do value developed facilities, structures, services and security backup by the wilderness area management, while other groups prefer freedom and unregulated settings (see Saarinen, 2013). The ROS thinking helps managers to plan diversity in touristic opportunities and to decide how much development, that is, facilities and infrastructure, should be provided in different kind of areas (zones). Thus, the same wilderness area could provide a variety of wilderness experiences without fully displacing any visitor segment out of the area.

The LAC model was developed for managing wilderness areas by defining what tourism impacts on the environment can be considered acceptable (Clark & Stankey, 1979; Stankey, Cole, Lucas, Petersen & Frissell, 1985), and what management actions and guidelines are needed to ensure that the tourism activities and their impacts remain constrained within the defined LAC (Hendee, Stankey & Lucas, 1990). Therefore, LAC thinking acknowledges that tourism activities do mean impacts on the wilderness and, thus, to have tourism there needs to be a framework that defines the accepted limits of impacts. LAC thinking originates partly from carrying capacity thinking, as it focuses on how much and what kind of tourism use would be too much in a certain wilderness area or sub-area (Stankey et al., 1985; see also Lucas, 1964; Wagar, 1964). These kinds of questions are increasingly relevant in the current situation, where use levels and forms of tourism can rapidly grow and change (Butler 1996, 2010). This has even led the Responsible Tourism Partnership (2019) network to suggest that the LAC approach would be the most useful methodology 'for avoiding or managing overtourism', in general. Due to the complexity and scale of the overtourism phenomenon and its management, however, that may be an unrealistic expectation. Overtourism includes not only having too many tourists in the same space in a given time period (crowding), but also wider structural socio-economic changes in host–guest and other stakeholder relations (see Milano, Cheer & Novelli, 2019; Nofre, Giordano, Eldridge, Martins & Sequera 2018). These may be rather difficult to manage by a framework that has been designed for public lands and activities that take place mainly in natural settings.

Unlike the ROS, the LAC approach emphasizes the use of various integrated planning processes to determine indicators for identifying appropriate management strategies and plans (Hendee, Stankey & Lucas, 1990; Manning, 2003). The LAC process involves four key elements: the identification of acceptable and achievable social and resource conditions; a creation of understanding of the relationship between existing conditions and those judged acceptable; defining management actions that will assist in achieving these conditions; and a monitoring and constant evaluation of the management and use processes (Stankey et. al., 1985). The use of the LAC model has also revitalized carrying capacity thinking in tourism (see Butler, 2010; Cocossis & Mexa, 2004). Interestingly, carrying capacity has been occasionally interpreted as an application of sustainable tourism (Butler, 1999). The carrying capacity approach aims to offer time- and space-specific answers to sustainable tourism development at the local level (Hunter, 1995; Saarinen, 2013). There are some similarities between the concepts (see Butler 1996; Cocossis & Mexa 2004), including the shared challenges of the past, such as providing unrealistic expectations of simple solutions based on an ideological rhetoric (see Lindberg, McCool & Stankey, 1997; McCool & Lime, 2001; Saarinen, 2014a; Sharpley, 2000, 2009).

However, sustainability thinking in wilderness management may have the capacity to evolve towards practical structures and frameworks aiming to guide wilderness tourism development towards more responsible and ethical ways of utilizing wild places in tourism (see Sæþórsdóttir, 2011). This is urgently needed, as many of the traditional planning and management models treat wilderness environments as 'islands', or territorial units with strong boundaries. In reality, however, wilderness environments are relational spaces with porous boundaries connecting these areas and their changes to wider regional, economic and global processes. Indeed, sustainable wilderness tourism should include a systemic approach that goes beyond a single area management focus alone, involving adjacent lands and communities. In addition, in the Anthropocene age and with climate change policies, the sustainability management of wilderness tourism should involve compensation measures (e.g. carbon offsetting) considering tourists' journeys from and back to home. This has turned out to be a major challenge for the tourism industry in general and the aviation sector in particular, but it may be a reality in a relatively near future (see IATA, 2019).

Conclusions

Remaining wilderness areas have become integral parts of modern tourism and its constantly evolving operations. It is evident that tourism and different forms of nature-based tourism will increase in wilderness areas in the future. Already today, there is a diverse scale of tourist motivations and experiences that are linked to visits in wilderness environments, and many of these motivations go beyond the traditional ideas of experiencing solitude and primitive and unconfined types of recreation in wilderness environments.

Growing tourism and the increasing presence of the tourism industry is often regarded as a major threat to wilderness values and characteristics. Based on this, there is an increasing need for context- or zone-specific wilderness management guiding and also setting limits to growth for wilderness tourism. This is nothing new. However, the present scale of the tourism industry and its growth needs represent a new level of challenge for wilderness tourism management. Due to the estimated growth of global tourism and the rapidly evolving nature-based tourism activities, the traditional wilderness values and characteristics of a given area may be lost in the future. Buckley (1999; 2006) has stated that the current trend of growing commercial tourism is important to recognize, as it is likely to create major challenges for wilderness management and managers. The reason is that compared with 'unconfined types of recreation', commercial tourism is an economically and politically highly influential and powerful activity, especially in peripheral regions with limited livelihood options other than evolving tourism that demands more access to the remaining wilderness environments (Saarinen, 2013). For Buckley (1999) this causes concerns about the political capacity of wilderness managers to steer these areas towards conservation and limit the growth of tourism if management for tourism and tourism development is to be 'given a higher priority' in the future (Buckley, 1999: 191).

Wilderness tourism

Indeed, wilderness areas are vulnerable resources for tourism and its impacts. As noted by Higham (1998: 27) 'wilderness areas are arguably the most sensitive physical resources for tourism'. While this is correct, and probably increasingly so, there is also a long symbiotic relationship between tourism and wilderness conservation (see Frost & Hall, 2010; Hall, 1992). Based on this, tourism has not necessarily been a negative issue for wilderness conservation and adjacent local communities (see Fennell, 1999). However, due to the current pace of growth of the tourism industry, this potentially symbiotic but also potentially conflicting relationship between wilderness conservation and tourism calls for wilderness management thinking that does not only acknowledge the co-existence between humans and nature, but also realizes the related threats in the growth of wilderness tourism. In this way, tourism could be 'viewed as a renewable resource that, if cared for properly, can be utilized indefinitely' (Hollenhorst, Houge-MacKenzie & Ostergren, 2014: 306). Indeed, this 'proper caring' refers to the need to set the limits to the growth in tourism by creating structures and collaborative processes and practices that lead the industry on a sustainable development path within an overall sustainability framework (Bramwell, 2011; Saarinen & Gill, 2019). Approaches such as land ethics could help us to set such limits, but only if there are wider structures, regulations and actions that govern the industry and its impacts not only inside but also beyond the (porous) boundaries of wilderness areas.

References

Bauer, N., Vasile, M. and Mondini, M. (2018) Attitudes towards nature, wilderness and protected areas: A way to sustainable stewardship in the South-Western Carpathians. *Journal of Environmental Planning and Management*, 61(5–6), 857–877.

Blackstock, K. L., White, V., McCrum, G., Scott, A. and Hunter, C. (2008) Measuring responsibility: An appraisal of a Scottish national park's sustainable tourism indicators. *Journal of Sustainable Tourism*, 16(3), 276–297.

Bramwell, B. (2011) Governance, the state and sustainable tourism: A political economy approach. *Journal of Sustainable Tourism*, 19(4–5), 459–477.

Brown, P. J. (1980) Defining the recreation experience. In R. W. Rowe and L. G. Chesnut (Eds.), *Managing Air Quality and Scenic Resources at National Parks ands Wilderness Areas*. Colorado: Westview Press, pp. 3–12.

Brown, P. J., Driver, B. L., and McConnell, C. (1978) *The Opportunity Spectrum Concept and Behavioral Information in Outdoor Recreation Resource Supply Inventories: Background and Application*. Fort Collins, CO: Department of Agriculture, Forest Service, Rocky Mountain Forest and Range Experiment Station.

Buckley, R. (1999) Wilderness in Australia. In S. McCool, D. Cole, B. Borrie and J. O'Loughlin, (Comps), *Wilderness Science in a Time of Change Conference, Volume 2*. Ogden: U.S. Department of Agriculture, Forest Service, Rocky Mountain Research Station, pp.190–193.

Buckley, R. (2006) *Adventure Tourism*. Wallingford: CABI.

Butler, R. (1980) The concept of a tourism area cycle of evolution. *Canadian Geographer*, 24, 5–12.

Butler R. (1996) The concept of carrying capacity for tourism destinations: Dead or merely buried? *Progress in Tourism and Hospitality Research*, 2, 283–293.

Butler, R. (1998) Sustainable tourism: Looking backwards in order to progress? In C. M. Hall and A. A. Lew (Eds.), *Sustainable Tourism: A Geographical Perspective*. New York: Longman, pp. 25–34.

Butler, R. (1999) Sustainable tourism: A state-of-the-art review. *Tourism Geographies*, 1(1), 7–25.

Butler, R. (2010) Carrying capacity in tourism. In D. G. Pearce and R. Butler (Eds.), *Tourism Research: A 20–20 vision*. Oxford: Goodfellow Publishers, pp. 53–64.

Butler, R. and S. Boyd (Eds.) (2000) *Tourism and National Parks: Issues and implications*. Chichester: Wiley & Sons.

Castree, N. (2014) The Anthropocene and geography I: The back story. *Geography Compass*, 8(7), 436–49.

Castree, N. (2015) Geography and global change science: Relationships necessary, absent, and possible. *Geographical Research*, 53(1), 1–5.

Clark, R. N. and Stankey, G. H. (1979) *The Recreation Opportunity Spectrum: A Framework for Planning, Management, and Research*. Portland: U.S. Department of Agriculture-Forest Service.

Cloke, P. and Perkins, H. (2002) Commodification and adventure in New Zealand. *Current Issues in Tourism*, 5(6), 521–549.

Cocossis, H. and Mexa, A. (2004) *The Challenge of Tourism Carrying Capacity Assessment: Theory and Practice*. Aldershot: Ashgate.

Connelly, N. (1987) Critical factors and their threshold for camper satisfaction at two campgrounds. *Journal of Leisure Research*, 19(3), 159–173.

Connor, T. (2014) *Conserved Spaces, Ancestral Places*. Pietermaritzburg: University of KwaZulu-Natal Press.

Crober, U. (2015) The discovery of sustainability: A genealogy of a term. In J. C. Enders and M. Remig (Eds.), *Theories of Sustainable Development*. Abingdon: Routledge, pp. 6–15.

Cronon, W. (1998) The trouble with wilderness, or getting back to the wrong nature. In J. Callicott and M. Nelson (Eds.), *The Great New Wilderness Debate*. Athens: University of Georgia Press, pp. 471–499.

Enders. J. C. and Remig, M. (2015a) Theories of sustainable development: An introduction. In J. C. Enders and M. Remig (Eds.), *Theories of Sustainable Development*. Abingdon: Routledge, pp.1–5.

Enders. J. C. and Remig, M. (Eds.) (2015b) *Theories of Sustainable Development*. London: Routledge.

Fennell, D. (1999) *Ecotourism: An Introduction*. New York: Routledge.

Fennell, D. (2006) *Tourism Ethics*. Clevedon: Channel View Publications.

Frost, W. and C.M Hall (Eds.) (2010) *Tourism and National Parks*. London: Routledge.

Getz, D. (1983) Capacity to absorb tourism: Concepts and implications for strategic planning. *Annals of Tourism Research*, 10(2), 239–263.

Glacken, C. (1992) Reflections on the history of Western attitudes to nature. *Geojournal*, 26(2), 103–111.

Hall, C. M. (1992) *Wasteland to World Heritage: Preserving Australia's Wilderness*. Melbourne: Melbourne University Press.

Hall, C. M. (1998) Historical antecedents of sustainable development and ecotourism: New labels on old bottles? In C. M. Hall and A. A. Lew (Eds.), *Sustainable Tourism: A Geographical Perspective*. New York: Longman, pp. 13–14.

Hall, C. M and Boyd, S. (Eds.) (2005) *Nature-based Tourism in Peripheral Areas: Development or Disaster?* Clevedon: Channel View Publications.

Hammitt, W. E. (1982) Cognitive dimensions of wilderness solitude. *Environment and Behaviour*, 14(4), 478–493.

Hendee, J., G. Stankey and Lucas, R. (1990) *Wilderness Management*. Golden: Fulcrum.

Hardin, G. (1968). Tragedy of the Commons. *Science*, 162, 1243–1248.

Higham, J. (1998) Sustaining the physical and social dimensions of wilderness tourism: The perceptual approach to wilderness management in New Zealand. *Journal of Sustainable Tourism*, 6(1), 26–51.

Holden, A. (2003) In need of new environmental ethics for tourism. *Annals of Tourism Research*, 30(1), 94–108.

Holden, A. (2006) *Environment and Tourism*. London: Routledge.

Hollenhorst, S. J., Houge-MacKenzie, S. and Ostergren, D. M. (2014) The trouble with tourism. *Tourism Recreation Research*, 39(3), 305–319.

Hunter, C. J. (1995) On the need to re-conceptualise sustainable tourism development. *Journal of Sustainable Tourism*, 3(3), 155–165.

IATA. (2019) Carbon Offsetting Scheme for International Aviation (CORSIA). The International Air Transport Association. Available at: https://www.iata.org/en/policy/environment/corsia/ (Accessed 10 December 2019).

Jamal, T. (2019) *Justice and Ethics in Tourism*. Abingdon: Routledge.

Kliskey, A. D. (1998) Linking the wilderness perception mapping concept to the recreation opportunity spectrum. *Environmental Management*, 22(1), 1, 79–88.

Leopold, A. (1949) *From a Sand County Almanac*. Oxford: Oxford University Press.

Lindberg, K., McCool, S. and Stankey, G. (1997) Rethinking carrying capacity. *Annals of Tourism Research*, 24(2), 461–465.

Wilderness tourism

Lucas, R. (1964) Wilderness perception and use: The example of the Boundary Waters Canoe area. *Natural Resource Journal*, 3(3), 394–411.

Manning, R. (1985) Crowding norms in backcountry settings: A review and synthesis. *Journal of Leisure Research*, 17(2), 75–89.

Manning, R. (2003) What to do about crowding and solitude in parks and wilderness? A reply to Stewart and Cole. *Journal of Leisure Research*, 35(1), 107–118.

Mathieson, A. and Wall, G. (1982) *Tourism: Economic, Physical and Social Impacts*. New York: Longman.

McCool, S. and Lime, D. W. (2001) Tourism carrying capacity: Tempting fantast or useful reality. *Journal of Sustainable Tourism*, 9(5), 372–388.

Milano, C., Cheer, J.M. and Novelli, M. (Eds.) (2019) *Overtourism: Excesses, Discontents and Measures in Travel and Tourism*. Wallingford: CABI.

Nash, R. (1967) *Wilderness and the American Mind*. London: Yale University Press.

Nofre, J., Giordano, G., Eldridge, A., Martins, J. and Sequera, J. (2018) Tourism, nightlife and planning: Challenges and opportunities for community liveability in La Barceloneta. *Tourism Geographies*, 20(3), 377–396.

Ostrom, E. (1990) *Governing the Commons*. Cambridge: Cambridge University Press.

Patterson, M. and Hammitt, W. (1990) Backcountry encounter norms, actual reported encounters, and their relationship to wilderness solitude. *Journal of Leisure Research*, 22(3), 259–275.

Pietarinen, J. (1987) Human and forest: Four basic attitudes (in Finnish). *Silva Fennica*, 21(4), 323–331.

Pigram, J. J. and Jenkins, J. M. (1999) *Outdoor Recreation Management*. London: Routledge.

Responsible Tourism Partnership. (2019) Limits of Acceptable Change. Available at: https://responsibletourismpartnership.org/limits-of-acceptable-change/ (Accessed 12 December 2019).

Roggenbuck, J., Williams, D. and Watson, A. (1993) Defining acceptable conditions in wilderness. *Environmental Management*, 17(2), 187–197.

Saarinen, J. (1998a) Wilderness, tourism development and sustainability: Wilderness attitudes and place ethics. In A. E. Watson and G. Aplet (Comps), *Personal, Societal, and Ecological Values of Wilderness: Sixth World Wilderness Congress Proceedings on Research, Management, and Allocation, Vol. I. General Technical Report*. Ogden: USDA Forest Service, Rocky Mountain Research Station, pp. 29–34.

Saarinen, J. (1998b) Cultural influence on response to wilderness encounters: A case study from Finland. *International Journal of Wilderness*, 4(1), 28–32.

Saarinen, J. (2005) Tourism in northern wildernesses: Nature-based tourism development in northern Finland. In C.M. Hall and S. Boyd (Eds.), *Nature-based Tourism in Peripheral Areas: Development or Disaster?* Clevedon: Channelview Publications, pp. 36–49.

Saarinen, J. (2013) Tourism into the wild: The limits of tourism in wilderness. In A. Holden and D. Fennell (Eds.), *The Routledge Handbook of Tourism and the Environment*. Abingdon: Routledge, pp. 145–154.

Saarinen, J. (2014a) Critical sustainability: Setting the limits to growth and responsibility in tourism. *Sustainability*, 6(11), 1–17.

Saarinen, J. (2014b) Tourism and tourists in nature, national parks and wilderness. In C. M. Hall, A. Lew and A. Williams (Eds.), *The Wiley Blackwell Companion to Tourism*. Chichester: Blackwell, pp. 500–512.

Saarinen, J. (2016) Wilderness conservation and tourism: What do we protect for and from whom? *Tourism Geographies*, 18(1), 1–8.

Saarinen, J (2019) What are wilderness areas for? Tourism and political ecologies of wilderness uses and management in the Anthropocene. *Journal of Sustainable Tourism*, 27(4), 472–487.

Saarinen, J. and Gill, A. M. (2019) Tourism, resilience and governance strategies in the transition towards sustainability. In J. Saarinen and A. M. Gill (Eds.), *Resilient Destinations: Governance Strategies in the Transition towards Sustainability in Tourism*. Abingdon: Routledge, pp. 15–33.

Sæþórsdóttir, A. D. (2010a) Planning nature tourism in Iceland based on tourist attitudes. *Tourism Geographies*, 12(1), 25–52.

Sæþórsdóttir, A. D. (2010b) Tourism struggling as the wilderness is developed. *Scandinavian Journal of Hospitality and Tourism*, 10(3), 334–357.

Sæþórsdóttir, A. D. (2011) Wilderness tourism in Iceland – land use and conflicts with power production. *Nordia Geographical Publications*, 40(2), pp. 1–133.

Sæþórsdóttir, A. D. and Saarinen, J. (2016a) Challenges due to changing ideas of natural resources: Tourism and power plant development in the Icelandic wilderness. *Polar Record*, 52(1), 82–91.

Sæþórsdóttir, A. D. and Saarinen, J. (2016b). Changing ideas about natural resources: Tourists' perspectives on the wilderness and power production in Iceland. *Scandinavian Journal of Hospitality and Tourism*, 16(4), 404–421.

Sæþórsdóttir, A. D., Hall, C. M. and Saarinen, J. (2011) Making wilderness: Tourism and the history of the wilderness idea in Iceland. *Polar Geography*, 34(4), 249–273.

Sharpley, R. (2000) Tourism and sustainable development: Exploring the theoretical divide. *Journal of Sustainable Tourism*, 8(1), 1–19.

Sharpley, R. (2009) *Tourism Development and the Environment: Beyond Sustainability?* London: Earthscan.

Sharpley, R. (2013) Responsible tourism: Whose responsibility? In A. Holden and D. Fennell (Eds.), *The Routledge Handbook of Tourism and Environment*. London: Routledge, pp. 382–391.

Short, J.R. (1991) *Imagined Country: Society, Culture and Environment*. London: Routledge.

Stankey, G., Cole, D., Lucas, R., Petersen, M. and Frissell, S. (1985) *The Limits of Acceptable Change (LAC) System for Wilderness Planning*. USDA Forest Service General Technical Report, INT-176. Ogden: Intermountain Forest and Experiment Station.

Thorhallsdottir, T. E. (2007) Environment and energy in Iceland: A comparative analysis of values and impacts. *Environmental Impact Assessment Review*, 27, 522–544.

Tuan, Y-F. (1974) *Topophilia: A Study on Environmental Perception, Attitudes and Values*. New York: Prentice-Hall.

Tuan, Y-F. (1979) *Landscapes of Fear*. Oxford: Blackwell.

Vail, D. and Heldt, T. (2004) Governing snowmobilers in multiple-use landscapes: Swedish and Maine (USA) cases. *Ecological Economics*, 48(4), 469–483.

Vaske, J.J., Shelby, B. Graefe, A. and Heberlein, T. (1986) Backcountry encounter norms: Theory, method and empirical evidence. *Journal of Leisure Research*, 18(3), 137–153.

Wang, N. (2000) *Tourism and Modernity*. Amsterdam: Pergamon.

Wagar, A. (1964) The carrying capacity of the wild lands for recreation. *Forest Science Monograph*, 7, 1–24.

Wagar, A. (1974) Recreational carrying capacity reconsidered. *Journal of Forestry*, 72(5), 274–278.

Wall-Reinius, S. (2012) Wilderness and culture: Tourist views and experiences in the Laponian World Heritage Area. *Society and Natural Resources*, 25(7), 621–632.

WCED. (1987) *Our Common Future*. World Commission on Environment and Development. New York: United Nations. Available at: http://www.un-documents.net/our-common-future.pdf (Accessed 17 December 2019).

Wilderness Act. (1964) Public Law 88–577. 88th Congress, September 3, 1964. Available at: https://www.nps.gov/orgs/1981/upload/WAct_508.pdf (Accessed 7 December 2019).

Williams, D., Roggenbuck, J. and Bange, S. (1991) The effect of norm-encounter compatibility on crowding perceptions, experience and behavior in river recreation settings. *Journal of Leisure Research*, 23(2), 154–172.

Wolfe, R. (1964) Perspective on outdoor recreation: A bibliographical survey. *The Geographical Review*, 54(2), 203–238.

Yellowstone National Park Protection Act. (1872) Available at: https://memory.loc.gov/cgi-bin/ampage?collId=llsl&fileName=017/llsl017.db&recNum=73 (Accessed 11 December 2019).

SECTION 5

Creating and mediating the tourist experience

38

DESIGNING THE TOURIST EXPERIENCE

A marketing perspective

Dora Agapito

Introduction

Along with changes in contemporary societies, transformations in tourism both in scope and scale have made contemporary tourist experiences more complex, dynamic and diverse in their forms (Sharpley & Stone, 2011). In this context, the process of designing quality tourist experiences has been deemed pivotal within the marketing and management of travel destinations (Agapito, 2020; Morgan, Lugosi & Ritchie, 2010; Ritchie & Hudson, 2009; Tung & Ritchie, 2011; Tussyadiah, 2014; Walls, Okumus, Wang & Kwun, 2011a). Whilst within marketing a tourist experience is regarded as a consumer experience (Moutinho, 1987), destination marketing and management organizations (DMOs), accommodation units, visitor attraction providers, event organizers and tourist firms seek to enhance visitor experiences by providing the optimal conditions for positive experiences to emerge. Decision-makers anticipate that the destination environment in the broader sense carries potential to be perceived as meaningful and valued personally by tourists and, as such, may lead to favourable outcomes, such as satisfaction and positive post-consumption behaviours in the long run (Scott, Gao & Ma, 2017; Sotiriadis & Gursoy, 2016).

From a marketing perspective, the experience economy paradigm has set the tone by regarding consumer experiences as holistic products with a distinct economic value and a premium position when compared with commodities, goods and services (Pine & Gilmore, 1998). This approach emphasizes that, although personal, experiences can be partially *designed or staged* (Agapito, Mendes & Valle 2013; Carù & Cova, 2003; Duerden et al., 2018) to facilitate individuals to be 'engaged on an emotional, physical, intellectual or even spiritual level' (Pine & Gilmore, 1998: 99). Inasmuch as 'everything tourists go through at a destination can be experience' (Oh, Fiore & Jeoung, 2007: 120), such as lodging, gastronomy, transportation, souvenirs, resources and leisure activities, the use of the construct *experiencescape* has been preferred in the experience design approach within the visitor economy sector (Chen, Suntikul & King, 2020; O'Dell & Billing, 2005) as an extension of the *servicescape* concept that stems from services marketing (Bitner, 1992; Pizam & Tasci, 2019). The notion of *experiencescape* involves the composition of diverse external stimuli surrounding tourism consumption encounters, which can be partially designed to actively and emotionally engage individuals within travel destinations (Mossberg, 2007). This external environment

DOI: 10.4324/9781003219866-44

mediates visitors' attention by offering cues that aid tourists in consistently framing and adding meaning to their experiences (Ooi, 2005).

Indeed, despite the several uses of the expression *design*, the process of designing the consumer experience from a managerial perspective is related to the planning of the consumption environment in a consistent and holistic manner to accrue perceived value and meaning for the experiences (Tussyadiah, 2014). The relevance of this approach is supported by research demonstrating that stimuli are mediated by internal processes, such as perception, resulting in approach or avoidance behaviours (Mehrabian & Russel, 1974). This idea is aligned with the classical stimuli–organism–response (S-O-R) theory in environmental psychology (Belk, 1975), which has been widely used in hospitality and tourism contexts to explain consumer behaviour (for example, Dedeoğlu, Bilgihan, Ye, Buonincontri & Okumus, 2018; Liu & Jang, 2009; Mody, Suess & Lehto, 2017). The tourist experience design approach is also aligned with congruity theory, which advocates that individuals are more likely to develop positive attitudes towards products (in the broader sense) when the elements composing the consumption environment are perceived as consistent (Osgood & Tannenbaum, 1955).

Accordingly, the experiential marketing approach to tourism proposes a number of external stimuli that can be addressed in the process of designing the tourist experience, such as sensory and physical stimuli (corporeal and virtual) and human-related stimuli, and products and themes (Agapito, Mendes & Valle, 2013; Agapito, Pinto, Ascensão & Tuominen, 2020; Mossberg, 2007). Despite some concerns that this approach will impact on the authenticity of the tourist experience and local communities (Hall, 2008), current studies suggest that while focusing on local resources, social interactions and the involvement of different stakeholders in the design of experiencescapes, this process has the potential to contribute to conceptualizing and facilitating distinct, creative and responsible experiences that fit destination positioning, segmentation/targeting, branding and communication goals in a more consistent and sustainable way (Agapito et al., 2020; Agapito, Valle & Mendes, 2014; Duxbury & Richards, 2019; Fesenmaier & Xiang, 2017a; Gnoth, 2017; Kastenholz, Carneiro & Marques, 2012). Moreover, whilst experience design is not prescriptive, as experiences are formed individually, this process can offer the proper stage encouraging particular emotional responses and mindsets through a coherent bundle of design elements that can be perceived as authentic (Rickly & McCabe, 2017).

Against this background, this chapter aims to outline and discuss the role of external stimuli to the tourist that are proposed in the literature as key to the process of designing tourist experiences through the theoretical lens of experiential marketing. To this end, following a review of the concept of tourist experience informed by an experiential marketing perspective, the chapter goes on to portray particular external factors (sensory and physical stimuli, human-related stimuli, products and themes) that have been advocated as key to shaping compelling tourist experiences, regardless of their type. A reflection is then offered in light of contemporary debates and current trends in research that aids the discussion of the contribution of this marketing approach to the design of tourist experiences and, subsequently, to the dynamic creation and communication of competitive experiential offerings while catering to more responsible tourism for destinations and tourism firms.

The tourist experience concept: A marketing perspective

Although tourism has been identified in foundational research in the 1970s as encompassing experiences (Cohen, 1979; MacCannell, 1976), a stream of contemporary tourism studies

Designing the tourist experience

focusing on a marketing perspective has adopted the experiential approach and experience design principles to address tourist experiences in their diverse forms (Agapito, 2020; Fesenmaier & Xiang 2017a; Gilmore & Pine, 2002; Godovykh & Tasci 2020; Morgan, Elbe & Curiel, 2009; Mossberg, 2007; Scott et al., 2017; Sotiriadis & Gursoy, 2016; Volo, 2009). The experiential paradigm highlights the importance of the process involved in consumption over products, services and corresponding functional elements *per se* (Holbrook, 1999; Holbrook & Hirschman, 1982). Indeed, Hirschman and Holbrook (1986: 166) state that 'long-sought-after consumption experience must be viewed as an emergent property that results from the inter-relationships and overlaps among person, environment, thought, emotion, activity and value'.

Accordingly, Pine and Gilmore use the expression *staging experiences* in the sense that a consumer experience occurs when a company 'intentionally uses services as the stage and goods as props to engage customers in a way that creates a memorable event' (Pine & Gilmore, 1998: 98). Provider intentionality is, therefore, the key aspect that differentiates a 'designed experience' from a 'spontaneous experience' (Duerden et al., 2018: 198). Moreover, the multidimensional aspect of the consumer experience within an experiential marketing approach is also documented in literature. For example, Schmitt (1999: 57) proposes that consumer experiences are composed by strategic experiential modules and should 'provide sensory, emotional, cognitive, behavioural, and relational values that replace functional values'. These ideas were further developed by researchers following experience theory such as Svabo, Larsen, Haldrup and Berenholdt (2013: 316) who discuss the role of spatial design in the experience economy and, in doing so, approach the experience as a 'process where people undergo the influence of things, environments, situations and events, and a wide range of materials play active roles as mediator of experience'. In the same vein, Verhoef and colleagues outline the customer experience construct as 'holistic in nature' and involving the 'customer's cognitive, affective, emotional, social and physical responses' (Verhoef, Lemon, Parasuraman, Roggeveen, Tsiros & Schlesinger, 2009: 32).

Against this background, Volo (2009), in her work on conceptualizing the experience in specific tourism contexts following a marketing approach, concludes that the tourist experience is holistic and comprises the events that occur to an individual outside the 'usual environment', involving cognitive processes of sensation, perception and memory. The focus on psychological processes is also stressed by Gnoth and Matteucci (2014: 4), who define the experience in a tourism context as the 'conflux of what is sensually perceived, how it is processed, and how it is retained in the resulting experience'.

Accordingly, models and frameworks focusing on the multidimensional aspect of the consumer experience in tourism (Godovykh & Tasci 2020; Quinlan Cutler & Carmichael, 2010; Walls et al., 2011a) highlight the phasic nature of the tourist experience (anticipation phase, on-site visitation and reflection phase), as well as the influence of factors internal to the individual (for example, psychographic and sociodemographic characteristics) and situational factors (for example, travel companions) in the perception of experience, expectations, attitudinal and behavioural outcomes (Agapito et al., 2013; Gnoth, 1997; Walls, Okumus, Wang & Kwun, 2011b). Ultimately, the experiential approach to tourism views tourists as peak consumers looking for extraordinary and added valued experiences (Duerden et al., 2018; Mossberg, 2007; Wang, 2002). This is witnessed in a context where tourists are increasingly more educated, informed and experienced in travel, with more and easier access to competitive tourism offerings (Tussyadiah, 2014; Williams, 2006). In this sense, the experience is co-created by providers and consumers in drawing desirable value (Gnoth, 2017).

In short, an experiential marketing approach to consumer experiences in tourism contexts should take into consideration that:

a   Tourist experiences are multidimensional and perceived holistically;
b   Positive and memorable tourist experiences are perceived as 'extraordinary' and are of a hedonic nature;
c   Factors situational and internal to the individual determine the formation of tourist experiences that are co-created for desired value;
d   Tourist experiences are of a phasic nature;
e   The consumption environments are composed of external stimuli, which can be designed consistently to actively and emotionally engage visitors; a process that can contribute to impact on attitudinal and behavioural outcomes.

Designing the tourist experience and external stimuli

The design of innovative and creative experiences is key for firms in the visitor economy sectors (Jernsand, Kraff & Mossberg, 2015; Scott, Laws & Boksberger, 2009; Williams, 2006). The concept of experience design has been transferred to the experiential marketing approach and applied to tourism based on the idea that values and meanings can be planned and evoked through contextual elements by orchestrating external stimuli (which will be captured by the human senses) in a compelling, engaging and purposeful manner (Agapito, 2020; Agapito et al., 2013, 2020; Fesenmaier & Xiang, 2017b; Tussyadiah, 2014). This approach is supported by environmental psychology, which is concerned with the relationship between human behaviour and the surrounding environment (Crouch, Perdue, Timmermans & Uysal, 2004).

In her work on a theoretical foundation for experience design in tourism, Tussyadiah (2014) posits that aspects such as the holistic nature of the experience, the iterative and dynamic approach and the human-centric perspective of design are the core of tourism experience design. In particular, the human-centric perspective is informed by a consumer-focus approach to designing tourism experiences, often referred to in the literature as *empathic design*, which is focused on human connections and engagement (Leonard & Rayport, 1997). Technology-assisted interactions are also actively incorporated in this approach, with an emphasis on designing improved tourist experiences (Tussyadiah, 2014). Indeed, if well managed, this component can aid marketing management efforts in the process of designing more accessible and quality experiences (e.g., using principles of universal design) by addressing the experience in its different phases and optimizing the use of a variety of stimuli other than visual elements in the environment, both corporeal and virtual (Agapito, 2020; Agapito et al., 2013; Cantero, 2018; Tussyadiah & Fesenmaier, 2009). In summary, Fesenmaier and Xiang, following works from pioneer scholars in tourism such as Clare Gunn (see *Vacationscape*, 1972) argue that the paradigm of *Design Science in Tourism* provides a contemporary 'basic logic for conducting research and designing tourism places' in an innovative way, contributing to 'improve people's lives as well as their travel experiences' (Fesenmaier & Xiang 2017b: 4) and, subsequently, their well-being.

In this context, frameworks following an experiential marketing and holistic approach to tourist experiences (for example, Agapito et al., 2013, 2020; Mossberg, 2007) recommend that the design of compelling tourist experiences should address several external stimuli, such as sensory and physical stimuli, human stimuli, products-related stimuli and themes. These stimuli are discussed in the following sub-sections.

Designing the tourist experience

Sensory and physical stimuli

Psychology indicates that human perception is a 'conscious sensory experience' and encompasses a 'sequence of processes that work together to determine our experience of a reaction to stimuli in the environment' (Goldstein, 2010: 5). Accordingly, sensory stimuli have been deemed central to the process of designing consumer experiences (Pine & Gilmore, 1999). Along these lines, sensory marketing aims to engage the consumer's senses, a process that affects individuals' perception, judgement and behaviour (Krishna, 2012). 'Sensory stimuli' refers thus to visual, olfactory, hearing, gastronomic and haptic stimulations in consumption encounters, which can trigger approach or avoidance behaviours (Krishna, 2012; Mattila & Gao, 2017). Whilst Kotler (1973) refers to sensory stimuli as atmospherics and presents it as a marketing tool, Bitner (1992) popularized the construct servicescape by dividing the physical surroundings of a service encounter into: (a) ambient conditions, which include the sensory stimuli; (b) spatial layout and functionality and (c) signs, symbols and artefacts, which are displayed in service environments. The physical environment, which also includes aspects such as cleanliness and comfort, is offered as encompassing the potential to impact the experience and, thus, organizations' image and individuals' emotions, attitudes and behaviour (Agapito et al., 2020; Bitner, 1992; Krishna, 2012; Mattila & Gao, 2017; Walls, Okumus, Wang & Kwun, 2011b).

In addition to psychology, consumer behaviour, marketing and management studies, and contemporary tourism studies with a managerial approach to tourism experiences have also borrowed the term *sensescapes* from human geography (Agapito et al., 2013) and followed the idea that, apart from sight, other senses can be spatially ordered (smellscapes, soundscapes, tastescapes or geographies of touch) and, subsequently, contribute to the sense of place (Porteous, 1985; Rodaway, 1994; Tuan, 1977; Urry, 2002). Moreover, a multisensory approach to experience design has been used to aid the marketing management of more inclusive experiences for tourists with sensory disabilities (Cantero, 2018; Dann & Dann, 2012; Richards, Pritchard & Morgan, 2010; Small, Darcy & Packer, 2012).

Practical applications in hospitality and tourism contexts are numerous. From menus displaying different options for pillow textures to the use of specific sounds, scents, lighting and gastronomic delights, sensory and physical stimuli have become part of the factors considered in the marketing and management of visitor experiences in events, accommodation businesses, museums, restaurants and other tourism-related contexts. In 2014, to encouraging visitors to engage with unique resources and attractions, York DMO launched their scent-based visitor guide 'Smell York', which was infused by 12 scents related to local attractions. For example, while the railway heritage was olfactorily depicted by an infusion combining coal, steam, engine oil and iron scents, chocolate heritage was presented by the scent of cocoa, butter, sugar and nuts, whilst rural Yorkshire more generally was embodied by the scent of fresh wild heather (Smith, 2014). The same year, multisensory stimuli inspired by the Loch Lomond and the Trossachs National Park were displayed at the international arrivals walkway at Glasgow Airport to creatively provide international visitors with an informed sensory experience based on the Scottish woodland trail and to encourage tourists to visit this distinct nature-based attraction. At their arrival, visitors are thus able to hear specific birdsong sounds, visualize wildlife existing in the park, experience forest-related scents, and sit on wooden benches (Deighton, 2014).

Product-related factors

Whilst depicted as 'tangible symbol in the tourists' consumption' (Mossberg, 2007: 68), products and souvenirs in tourism contexts are part of the experiencescape, affect the experience by triggering approach or avoidance behaviours, and act as cues for memory recollection (Agapito et al., 2013, 2020; Ooi, 2005; Swanson, 2004). In particular, the acquisition of souvenirs is part of the experience, acting as symbolic evidence of visitation and engaging tourists emotionally, as many of these memorabilia will be offered to friends and family. As such, souvenirs are part of the process of sharing stories and word of mouth (Brown, 1992; Mossberg, 2007; Wilkins, 2011). Hence, while making available what can be perceived as unique and meaningful products and souvenirs, such as local gastronomy and beverage, visual arts, music and handicraft, destinations and tourist firms are in a better condition to fulfil tourists' desire for authenticity while also contributing to the local economy (Kastenholz, Eusébio & Carneiro, 2016; Swanson, 2004).

In this context, a number of hotel businesses are acknowledging the importance of *localness* in relation to the products and souvenirs they present to tourists, as well as its impact on the memorability of the experience. For example, Anantara Vilamoura resort, in Portugal, has teamed up with the TASA Project (TASA, 2015) that unites young designers and local craft artisans in making unique products to be available in their lodging units, with guests being able to engage, for example, with woven pool bags, locally sourced cork coasters, and signature Algarvian ceramic fruit bowls.

Human-related stimuli

Human interactions are part of the experiencescape and can be facilitated by the experience design (Walls et al., 2011a, 2011b). These interactions relate to employees' performance (host–guest), social encounters between the tourist and other customers, and interactions between tourists and locals (Agapito et al., 2020; Mossberg, 2007; Nickerson, 2006). The literature on services marketing stresses that personnel skills should be of both a procedural (technical-based) and convivial (communicative-related) nature (Dong & Siu, 2013; Martin, 1991). For example, by following the SERVQUAL model rationale, Albacete-Sáez, Fuentes-Fuentes and Lloréns-Montes (2007) consider that the technical component is related to the promptness of front-desk employees to address guest demands in a fast, reliable and knowledgeable way, whilst tourist relations refer to endeavours to discuss with the customer information about the culture, traditions and activities within the surrounding destination setting. The experiential approach follows the recommendation of the services marketing literature that the process of designing the consumption environment should also include stimuli that facilitate interactions between guests and other customers (Baker, 1987; Tombs & McColl-Kennedy, 2003). Moreover, the inclusion of the development of *communitas* in the planning of guest experiences, by encouraging interactions between tourists and locals, can boost the feeling of *communion* with others (Arnould & Price, 1993). These short-lived emotional bonds are referred to as *communitesque moments*, which can contribute to enhancing tourist experiences by making them more active, immersive and memorable (Lugosi, 2008).

DMOs and tourism and hospitality firms have long recognized the role of employee performances and are now increasingly acknowledging the importance of facilitating social interactions in enhancing tourist experiences. Especially in rural areas, Kastenholz et al. (2012) stress that residents can be directly involved in the global tourist experience and in personalized interactions between locals and tourists, facilitated by including residents in roles such as tour guides, managers of recreational activities and coordinators of thematic workshops related to local elements. In addition, tourism-related projects such as *With Locals* (https://www.withlocals.com/), *Backstreet* (https://www.backstreetacademy.com/) and *Human Connections* (https://humanconnections.org/) focus particularly on the relationships between

Designing the tourist experience

guests and local hosts. In a different context, historical and film recreations and tours are also a relevant example of the processes of facilitating social interactions (companions, personnel and other customers) through design elements. Rickly and McCabe (2017) use the study of *Lord of the Rings* tourism in New Zealand (Buchmann, Moore & Fisher, 2010) as an example to illustrate how an experience of 'fellowship' can be encouraged by a designed environment centred around a particular theme.

Theme

According to the experiential approach to tourism, the existence of a theme is essential to the process around experience design (Agapito et al., 2020; Jernsand et al., 2015; Mossberg, 2007; Pine & Gilmore, 1999). Accordingly, themes have been posed as a powerful marketing tool to differentiate and enhance tourism offerings (Åstrøm, 2018; Güzel, 2016; Schmitt & Simonson, 1997). A theme is the main idea or concept enveloping and overarching the customer experience in a symbolic way (Åstrøm, 2017; Carù & Cova, 2007; Strömberg, 2015). This helps individuals to organize and frame impressions in a consistent manner, as well as to accrue value to the holistic experience (Agapito et al., 2014; Åstrøm, 2017; Ellis & Rossman, 2008; Morgan, 2006; Mossberg, 2007; Oh, Fiore & Jeoung, 2007). Hence, the existence of a theme supports narratives that offer structure and meaning to otherwise incongruent experience elements (Åstrøm, 2017; Pine & Gilmore, 1999). Subsequently, these external stimuli have the potential to aid the process of facilitating tourists' engagement and recollection of the tourist experience. Indeed, the design of purposeful themed environments can be related to unique cultural and natural endogenous resources that are part of the local identity (Agapito et al., 2014; Agapito, Pinto & Mendes, 2017; Moscardo, 2010; Pikkemaat, Peters, Boksberger & Secco, 2009). Moreover, designed themes should be perceived as authentic (Åstrøm, 2019) and support branding and targeting strategies that are inclusive and serve community goals (Hall, 2008; Pikkemaat et al., 2009).

Examples of the use of creative and focused themes can be found in numerous hospitality and tourism contexts. Brighton's rock 'n' roll boutique hotel Pelirocco themed its rooms and activities using music-related multisensory stimuli for branding and targeting purposes, while engaging their customers with activities focused on this music genre. In S. Brás de Alportel in Algarve, Portugal, cork oak trees and their uses (for example, wine bottle stoppers, clothing, shoes, fashion accessories, furniture, surfboards and skates) is the theme of a visitor route aiming to engage visitors with this particular local product (https://www.visitportugal.com/en/content/the-cork). Vintage heritage has also become an important theme in rural areas where unique types of wine are produced. The design of this theme can be found, for example, in the wine museum Enoteca in Douro, Portugal, where visitors can engage with multiple stimuli orchestrated around a narrative based on local endogenous resources as a global experience (Kastenholz et al., 2012).

Contemporary reflections on designing the tourist experience from a marketing perspective

While there still remains some criticism with regard to the process of tourism design as opposed to authentic tourist experiences, following the works of Cohen (1979) and MacCannell (1976), the approach to the concept as being synonymous with originality and genuineness has evolved into a more flexible and contemporary perspective, supporting the utmost importance of experience design in tourism (Åstrøm, 2019; Rickly & McCabe, 2017). The discussion has moved from objectivist focus to one on a constructivist approach, which is more concerned with the symbolic and narrative aspects of the tourist experience.

Wang (1999) furthers the discussions by proposing existential authenticity as a form of authenticity related to the activities performed by tourists, thus embedded with notions of identity and embodiment. In a critical reflection on the evolution of the construct, Rickly and McCabe (2017: 61) clarify that 'existential authenticity points to the power of subtle stating, atmosphere, companionship amongst travellers and intersubjectivity', inasmuch as 'tourism is a performative act'. In this context, the *staging* acts only as a reference that directs attention, encourages particular emotions and points towards particular behaviours (Ooi, 2005). Hence, it is 'up to the individual tourists to work with this raw material in relation to the motivations that inspired their visit to actually perform the space' (Rickly & McCabe, 2017: 23). Accordingly, although the focus of this chapter is on the external stimuli of experience design, it is important to acknowledge that those factors internal and situational to the individual that determine the formation of the tourist experience are aspects that should be also taken into consideration in the tourism design process (Agapito et al., 2013; Gnoth, 2017; Walls et al., 2011a).

Whilst memorable and positive tourist experiences rely on tourists' acknowledgement of meaning, value and authenticity, the process of providing desirable experiences is crucial to sustainable competitiveness for destinations and firms (Gnoth, 2017; Scott et al., 2017; Sotiriadis & Gursoy, 2016). The current literature, although still predominantly theoretical, emphasizes the process of designing holistic tourist experiences as a potential responsible approach to tourism. This follows the rationale that an experiential marketing approach to tourism can be focused on external stimuli that are sensory-informed, product-related, human-based and thematic-informed, which can be inspired by endogenous resources and local identities while offering platforms of collaboration between a variety of stakeholders (Agapito et al., 2013, 2020; Kastenholz et al., 2012).

Specifically, rural tourism, community-based tourism and creative tourism are strongly linked areas where the approach to experience design involving collaborative approaches within the community has recently been particularly productive, both in practical and research applications with a focus on culture, people and environment (Duxbury & Richards, 2019). The CREATOUR research-and-application project (see http://creatour.pt/en/), developed in Portugal, is an insightful example that illustrates a tourism design process by focusing on endogenous resources in rural areas, encouraging interactions and co-creation between visitors and local residents in a process that is conceptualized and implemented by residents for community benefit.

Whilst Richards (2011) highlights the significance of creativity in the planning and development of cultural tourism, creative tourism has been defined as 'travel directed toward an engaged and authentic experience, with participative learning in the arts, heritage, or special character of a place, and it provides a connection with those who reside in this place and create this living cultural' (UNESCO, 2006: 3). Hence, creativity has become an important element in the making of places by incorporating symbolic aspects linked to intangible heritage and local identity within the physical and sensory design. Practical examples of this approach are illustrated in the creative tourism toolkit developed by the Designated Areas for Sustainable Tourism Administration (DASTA) in Thailand (Richards, Wisansing & Paschinger, 2019).

In addition, while consciously addressing a diversity of external stimuli, the experience becomes more inclusive for all walks of life, a process that can be optimized by technology (Cantero, 2018). In fact, ICT can be an enabler of personalized experiences at different stages

Designing the tourist experience

of the experience and play an important role in the process of staging desired environments, both corporeal and virtual. This can be realized by using ICT to find solutions for issues such as overcrowding peaks by aiding crowd management, for example (Fesenmaier & Xiang, 2017b). In situations of vulnerable environments, a simulacrum of external stimuli can also be utilized in online environments and interpretation centres aiming to preserving resources while ensuring vivid and engaged interactions between people, resources, places and environments (Agapito et al., 2013).

Final remarks

This chapter outlines a contemporary trend in research on a marketing approach to tourist experiences, which is focused on a managerial mindset that privileges the process of designing quality experiences based on a combination of external stimuli – such as sensory and physical stimuli, human-related stimuli, products and themes – in a systematic way. Experiential marketing studies in tourism contexts, supported by disciplines such as environmental psychology, demonstrate that this approach has the potential to facilitate memorable and compelling experiences by actively engaging individuals, a process that has the potential to favourably impact tourists' attitudes and behaviours towards tourism destinations. Nevertheless, it is important to acknowledge that the environment in which the experience takes place can only be partially designed, as factors situational and internal to the individual play an important part in the experience and other stimuli are not under the control of decision makers (Agapito et al., 2013; Gnoth, 2017; Rickly & McCabe, 2017).

Whilst diverse external stimuli can be addressed in a marketing perspective (i.e. the relationship between external stimuli resulting from tourism experience design, individual tourist experiences and tourist outcomes), this should be done in a consistent way with a view to enhancing the overall tourist experience, considering that the experience is perceived holistically. If well-managed, experiential marketing of the experience design in tourism can help destinations and tourism firms to align desired experiences to positioning, branding and targeting goals, as well as contribute to communities' well-being and place-making. External stimuli can direct visitors' attention, signal key messages and set boundaries mitigating inappropriate tourist behaviours that can negatively affect the experiences of others. In fact, if stimuli in the environment are not managed, disparate elements of the external environment will still be part of the customer experience. A conscious, systematic and holistic approach to external stimuli can thus help to frame and accrue value and meaning for the experience while contributing to the development of innovative processes that benefit different stakeholders. This can be developed at different scales, since this approach can be applied to contexts such as events, attractions, hotels, cities or regions. Accordingly, the focus on external stimuli in the experience design can encourage the development of networks and local partnerships to creatively address unique selling prepositions based on local resources and identities that can value destinations, firms and communities.

This chapter has also offered some insights on how the process of experience design focused on external stimuli can encourage the development of responsible and effective marketing practices. In contemporary contexts, responsible marketing management is critical to maintaining positive relationships between involved stakeholders, balancing customers' needs and wants with the organization's specific goals, while ensuring supportive public attitudes. Indeed, in tourism destinations, the support of local communities is critical to the successful development of tourism. In a context where current debates are focused on the economic, social, cultural and environmental costs generated by tourism and negatively impacting residents' lives (Milano, Cheer & Novelli, 2019; Nunkoo & Gursoy, 2019), a marketing approach to responsibly designing tourist experiences may offer some contributions to the process of enhancing tourists' experiences aimed at people's well-being and sustainable competitiveness of destinations and tourism and firms.

Acknowledgement

This work is financed by National Funds provided by FCT – Foundation for Science and Technology (Portugal) through project UIDB/04020/2020.

References

Agapito, D. (2020) The senses in tourism design: A bibliometric review. *Annals of Tourism Research,* 83. https://doi.org/10.1016/j.annals.2020.102934

Agapito, D., Mendes, J. and Valle, P. (2013) Exploring the conceptualization of the sensory dimension of tourist experiences. *Journal of Destination Marketing & Management,* 2(2), 62–73.

Agapito, D., Pinto, P., Ascenção, M. P. and Tuominen, P. (2020) Designing compelling accommodationscape: Testing a framework in a rural context. *Tourism and Hospitality and Hospitality Research,* 1–16. https://doi.org/10.1177/1467358420972753

Agapito, D., Pinto, P. and Mendes, J. (2017) Tourists' memories, sensory impressions and loyalty: In loco and post-visit study in Southwest Portugal. *Tourism Management,* 58, 108–118.

Agapito, D., Valle, P. and Mendes, J. (2014) The sensory dimension of tourist experiences: Capturing meaningful sensory-based themes in Southwest Portugal. *Tourism Management,* 42, 224–237.

Albacete-Sáez, C. A., Fuentes-Fuentes, M. M. and Lloréns-Montes, F. J. (2007) Service quality measurement in rural accommodation. *Annals of Tourism Research,* 34(1), 45–65.

Arnould, E. J. and Price, L. L. (1993) River magic: Extraordinary experience and extended service encounter. *Journal of Consumer Research,* 20(1), 24–45.

Åstrøm, J. K. (2017) Theme factors that drive the tourist customer experience. *International Journal of Culture, Tourism and Hospitality Research,* 11(2), 125–141.

Åstrøm, J. K. (2018) Exploring theming dimensions in a tourism context. *European Journal of Tourism Research,* 20, 5–27.

Åstrøm, J. K. (2019) Why theming? Identifying the purposes of theming in tourism. *Journal of Quality Assurance in Hospitality & Tourism,* 21(3), 245–266.

Baker, J. (1987) The role of the environment in marketing services: The consumer perspective. In J. A. Czepiel, C. A. Congram and J. Shanahan (Eds.), *The Services Challenge: Integrating for Competitive Advantage.* Chicago: American Marketing Association, pp. 79–84.

Belk, R. W. (1975) Situational variables and consumer behavior. *Journal of Consumer Research,* 2(3), 157–164.

Bitner, M. J. (1992) Servicescapes: The impact of physical surroundings on customers and employees. *Journal of Marketing,* 56(2), 57–71.

Brown, G. (1992) Tourism and symbolic consumption. In P. Johnson and B. Thomas (Eds.), *Choice and Demand in Tourism.* London: Mansell Publishing, pp. 57–71.

Buchmann, A., Moore, K. and Fisher, D. (2010) Experiencing film tourism: Authenticity and fellowship. *Annals of Tourism Research,* 37, 229–248.

Cantero, K. N. G. (2018) Theoretical analysis on the foundations of sensory-based tourism for the blind. *Journal of American Academic Research,* 6(4), 120–126.

Carù, A. and Cova, B. (2003) Revisiting consumption experience: A more humble but complete view of the concept. *Marketing Theory,* 3(2), 267–286.

Chen, Z., Suntikul, W. & King, B. (2020) Research on tourism experiencescapes: The journey from art to science. *Current Issues in Tourism,* 23(11), 1407–1425.

Cohen. E. (1979) A phenomenology of tourist experiences. *Sociology,* 13(2), 179–201.

Crouch, G., Perdue, R., Timmermans, H. and Uysal, U. (2004) Building foundations for understanding the consumer psychology of tourism, hospitality and leisure. In G. Crouch, R. Perdue, H. Timmermans and M. Uysal (Eds.), *Consumer Psychology of Tourism, Hospitality and Leisure,* Vol. 3. Wallingford: CABI, pp. 1–9.

Designing the tourist experience

Dann, E. and Dann, G. M. S. (2012) Sightseeing for the sightless and soundless: Tourism experiences of the deafblind. *Tourism, Culture and Communication*, 12(2), 125–140.

Dedeoğlu, B. B., Bilgihan, A., Ye, B. H., Buonincontri, P. and Okumus, F. (2018) The impact of servicescape on hedonic value and behavioral intentions: The importance of previous experience. *International Journal of Hospitality Management*, 72, 10–20.

Deighton, K. (2014) Event TV: Glasgow Airport arrivals transformed into loch-side woodland. Campaign, 13 August. Available at: https://www.campaignlive.co.uk/article/event-tv-glasgow-airport-arrivals-transformed-loch-side-woodland/1307682 (Accessed 17 October 2019).

Dong, P. and Siu, N. Y. M. (2013) Servicescape elements, customer predispositions and service experience: The case of theme park visitors. *Tourism Management*, 36, 541–551.

Duerden M. D., Lundberg, N. R., Ward, P., Taniguchi, S. T., Hill, B., Widmer, M. A. and Zabriskie, R. (2018) From ordinary to extraordinary: A framework of experience types. *Journal of Leisure Research*, 49(3–5), 196–216.

Duxbury, N. and Richards, G. (2019) *A Research Agenda for Creative Tourism*. Cheltenham: Edward Elgar.

Ellis, G. D. and Rossman, J. R. (2008) Creating value for participants through experience staging: Parks, recreation, and tourism in the experience industry. *Journal of Park and Recreation Administration*, 26(4), 1–20.

Fesenmaier, D. F. and Xiang, Z. (2017a) *Design Science in Tourism: Foundations of Destinations Management*. Cham, Switzerland: Springer.

Fesenmaier, D. F. and Xiang, Z. (2017b) *Introduction to Tourism Design and Design Science in Tourism*. In D. F. Fesenmaier and Z. Xiang (Eds.), *Design Science in Tourism: Foundations of Destinations Management*. Cham, Switzerland: Springer, pp. 3–16.

Gilmore, J. H. and Pine, B. J. (2002) Differentiating hospitality operations via experiences: Why selling services is not enough. *Cornell Hotel and Restaurant Quarterly*, 43(3), 87–96.

Gnoth, J. (1997) Tourism motivation and expectation formation. *Annals of Tourism Research*, 24(2), 283–304.

Gnoth, J. (2017) Destinations and value co-creation: Designing experiences as processes. In D. F. Fesenmaier and Z. Xiang, Z. (Eds.), *Design Science in Tourism: Foundations of Destinations Management*. Switzerland: Springer, pp. 125–138.

Gnoth, J. and Matteucci, X. (2014) Response to Pearce and McCabe's critiques. *International Journal of Culture, Tourism & Hospitality Research*, 8(2). https://doi.org/10.1108/IJCTHR-04-2014-0029

Godovykh, M. and Tasci, A. D. A. (2020) Customer experience in tourism: A review of definitions, components, and measurements. *Tourism Management Perspectives*, 35. https://doi.org/10.1016/j.tmp.2020.100694

Goldstein, E. B. (2010) *Sensation and Perception*, 8th Edn. Belmonte: Wadsworth.

Gunn, C. (1972) *Vacationscape: Designing Tourist Areas*. Austin: The University of Texas Press.

Güzel, O. (2016) Experience-based service design. In M. Sotiriadis and D. Gursoy (Eds.). *The Handbook of Managing and Marketing Tourism Experiences*. Bingley: Emerald, pp. 3–20.

Hall, C. M. (2008) Servicescapes, designs capes, branding, and the creation of place-identity: South of Litchfield, Christchurch. *Journal of Travel and Tourism Marketing*, 25(3), 233–250.

Hirschman, E. and Holbrook, M. (1986) Expanding the ontology and methodology of research on the consumption experience. In D. Brinberg, and R. J. Lutz (Eds.), *Perspectives on Methodology in Consumer Research*. New York: Springer-Verlag, pp. 213–251.

Holbrook, M. (1999) *Consumer Value: A Framework for Analysis and Research*. London: Routledge.

Holbrook, M. and Hirschman, E. (1982) The experiential aspects of consumption: Consumer fantasies, feelings, and fun. *Journal of Consumer Research*, 9, 132–140.

Jernsand, E. M., Kraff, H. and Mossberg, L. (2015) Tourism experience innovation through design. *Scandinavian Journal of Hospitality and Tourism*, 15(1), 98–119.

Kastenholz, E., Carneiro, M. J. A. and Marques, C. P. (2012) Marketing the rural tourism experience. In R. H. Tsiotsou and R. E. Goldsmith (Ed.), *Strategic Marketing in Tourism Services*. Bingley: Emerald, pp. 247–264.

Kastenholz, E., Eusébio, C. and Carneiro, M. J. (2016) Purchase of local products within the rural tourist experience context. *Tourism Economics*, 22(4), 729–748.

Kotler, P. (1973). Atmospherics as a marketing tool. *Journal of Retailing*, 49(4), 48–64.

Krishna, A. (2012) An integrative review of sensory marketing: Engaging the senses to affect perception, judgment and behavior. *Journal of Consumer Psychology*, 22(3), 332–351.

Leonard, D. and J. F. Rayport. (1997) Spark innovation through empathic design. *Harvard Business Review*, 75(6), 102–113.

Liu, Y. and Jang, S. (2009) The effects of dining atmospherics: An extended Mehrabian–Russell model. *International Journal of Hospitality Management*, 28(4), 494–503.

Lugosi, P. (2008) Hospitality spaces, hospitable moments: consumer encounters and affective experiences in commercial settings. *Journal of Foodservice*, 19(2), 139–149.

MacCannell, D. (1976) *The Tourist: A New Theory of the Leisure Class*. New York: Schocken Books.

Martin, W. B. (1991) *Quality Service: The Restaurant Manager's Bible*. Ithaca, NY: Cornell University, School of Hotel Administration.

Mattila, A. S. and Gao, L. Y. (2017) Atmospherics and the tourist experience. In D. F. Fesenmaier and Z. Xiang, Z. (Eds.), *Design Science in Tourism: Foundations of Destinations Management*. Cham, Switzerland: Springer, pp. 151–160.

Mehrabian, A. and Russel, J. A. (1974) *An Approach to Environmental Psychology*. Cambridge, MA: Massachusetts Institute of Technology.

Milano, C., Cheer, J. and Novelli, M. (2019) *Overtourism: Excesses, Discontents and Measures in Travel and Tourism*. Wallingford: CABI.

Mody, M., Suess, C. and Lehto, X. (2017) The accommodation experiencescape: A comparative assessment of hotels and Airbnb. *International Journal Contemporary Hospitality Management*, 29(9), 2377–2404.

Morgan, M. (2006) Making space for experiences. *Journal of Retail & Leisure Property*, 5(4), 305–313.

Morgan, M., Elbe, J. and de Esteban Curiel, J. (2009) Has the experience economy arrived? The views of destination managers in three visitor-dependent areas. *International Journal of Tourism Research*, 11(2), 201–216.

Morgan, M., Lugosi, L. and Ritchie J. R. B. (2010) *The Tourism and Leisure Experience: Consumer and Managerial Perspectives*. Bristol: Channel View Publications.

Moscardo, G. (2010) The shaping of tourist experience: The importance of stories and themes. In M. Morgan, P. Lugosi and J. R. B. Ritchie (Eds.), *The Tourism and Leisure Experience: Consumer and Managerial Perspectives*. Bristol: Channel View Publications, pp. 43–58.

Mossberg, L. (2007) A marketing approach to the tourist experience. *Scandinavian Journal of Hospitality and Tourism,* 7(1), 59–74.

Moutinho, L. (1987) Consumer behaviour in tourism. *European Journal of Marketing*, 21, 5–44.

Nickerson, N. (2006) Some reflections on quality tourism experiences. In G. Jennings and N. Nickerson (Eds.), *Quality Tourism Experiences*. Burlington: Elsevier, pp. 227–235.

Nunkoo, R. and Gursoy, D. (2019) *The Routledge Handbook of Tourism Impacts: Theoretical and Applied Perspectives*. Abingdon: Routledge.

O'Dell, T. and Billing, P. (2005) *Experiencescapes: Tourism, Culture and Economy*. Copenhagen: Copenhagen Business School Press.

Oh, H., Fiore, A. M. and Jeoung, M. (2007) Measuring experience economy concepts: Tourism applications. *Journal of Travel Research*, 46(2), 119–132.

Ooi, C. (2005) A theory of tourism experiences: The management of attention. In T. O'Dell and P. Billing (Eds.), *Experiencescapes:Tourism, Culture, and Economy*. Denmark: Copenhagen Business School Press, pp. 51–68.

Osgood, C. E. and Tannenbaum, P. H. (1955) The principle of congruity in the prediction of attitude change. *Psychological Review*, 62(1), 42–55.

Pikkemaat, B., Peters, M., Boksberger, P. and Secco, M. (2009) The staging of experiences in wine tourism. *Journal of Hospitality Marketing & Management*, 18(2/3), 237–253.

Pine, J. and Gilmore, J. H. (1998) Welcome to the experience economy. *Harvard Business Review*, 76(4), 97–105.

Pine, B. J. and Gilmore, J. H. (1999) *The Experience Economy: Work is Theatre & Every Business a Stage*. Boston, MA: Harvard Business School Press.

Pizam, A. and Tasci, A. D. A. (2019) Experienscape: Expanding the concept of servicescape with a multi-stakeholder and multi-disciplinary approach (invited paper for 'luminaries' special issue of international journal of hospitality management). *International Journal of Hospitality Management*, 76, 25–37.

Porteous, J. D. (1985) Smellscape. *Progress in Physical Geography*, 9, 356–378.

Quinlan Cutler, S. and Carmichael, B. (2010) The dimensions of the tourist experience. In L. Morgan, P. Lugosi and J. R. B. Ritchie (Eds.), *The Tourism and Leisure Experience: Consumer and Managerial Perspectives*. Bristol: Channel View Publications, pp. 3–36.

Richards, G. (2011) Creativity and tourism: The state of the art. *Annals of tourism research*, 38(4), 1225–1253.

Richards, G., Wisansing, J. J. and Paschinger, E. (2019) Creating Creative Tourism Toolkit. DASTA, Thailand. Available at: https://perfectlink.co.th/wp-content/uploads/2019/01/Creating-Creative-Tourism-Toolkit_Version-Eng.pdf (Accessed 20 April 2019).

Richards, V., Pritchard, A. and Morgan, N. (2010) (Re)envisioning) tourism and visual impairment. *Annals of Tourism Research*, 37(4), 1097–1116.

Rickly, J. M. and McCabe, S. (2017) Authenticity for tourism design and experience. In D. F. Fesenmaier and Z. Xiang, Z. (Eds.), *Design Science in Tourism: Foundations of Destinations Management*. Cham, Switzerland: Springer, pp. 55–68.

Ritchie, J. R. B. and Hudson, S. (2009) Understanding and meeting the challenges of consumer/tourist experience research. *International Journal of Tourism Research*, 11(2), 111–126.

Rodaway, P. (1994) *Sensuous Geographies: Body, Sense and Place*. London: Routledge.

Schmitt, B. (1999) Experiential marketing. *Journal of Marketing Management*, 15(1–3), 53–67.

Schmitt, B. and Simonson, A. (1997) *Marketing Aesthetics: The Strategic Management of Brands, Identity and Image*. New York: The Free Press.

Scott, N., Gao, J. and Ma, J. (2017) *Visitor Experience Design*. Wallingford: CABI.

Scott, N., Laws, E. and Boksberger, P. (2009) The marketing of hospitality and leisure experiences. *Journal of Hospitality Marketing & Management*, 18(2–3), 99–110.

Sharpley, R. and Stone, P. R. (2011) *Tourist Experience: Contemporary Perspectives*. Abingdon: Routledge.

Small, J., Darcy, S. and Packer, T. (2012) The embodied tourist experiences of people with vision impairment: management implications beyond the visual gaze. *Tourism Management*, 33(4), 941–950.

Smith, O. (2014) Smell York: Tourist board launches tourist guide. The Telegraph, 7 March. Available at: https://www.telegraph.co.uk/travel/destinations/europe/united-kingdom/england/yorkshire/york/articles/Smell-York-tourist-board-launches-scented-guide/ (Accessed 17 October 2019).

Sotiriadis, M. and Gursoy, D. (2016) *The Handbook of Managing and Marketing Tourism Experiences*. Bingley: Emerald.

Strömberg, P. (2015) Theming. In D. T. Cook and J. M. Ryan (Eds.), *The Wiley Blackwell Encyclopedia of Consumption and Consumer Studies*. Chichester: John Wiley & Sons, pp. 545–549.

Svabo, C., Larsen, J., Haldrup, O. and Berenholdt, J. O. (2013) Experiencing spatial design. In J. Sunbo and F. Sørensen (Eds.), *Handbook on the Experience Economy*. Cheltenham: Edward Elgar, pp. 310–324.

Swanson, K. K. (2004) Tourists' and retailers' perceptions of souvenirs. *Journal of Vacation Marketing*, 10(4), 363–377.

TASA (2015) TASA Project – Ancestral Techniques Current Solutions. Available at: https://projecto-tasa.com/?lang=en (Accessed 17 October 2019).

Tombs, A. and McColl-Kennedy, J. R. (2003) Social-servicescape conceptual model. *Marketing Theory*, 3(4), 447–475.

Tuan, Yi-Fu (1977) *Space and Place: The Perspective of Experience*. Minneapolis: University of Minnesota Press.

Tung, V. W. S. and Ritchie, J. R. B. (2011) Exploring the essence of memorable tourism experiences. *Annals of Tourism Research*, 38(4), 1367–1386.

Tussyadiah, I. P. (2014) Toward theoretical foundation for experience design in tourism. *Journal of Travel Research*, 53(5), 543–564.

Tussyadiah, I. P. and Fesenmaier, D. R. (2009) Mediating tourist experiences: Access to places via shared videos. *Annals of Tourism Research*, 36(1), 24–40.

UNESCO Creative Cities Network (2006) Towards Sustainable Strategies for Creative Tourism: Discussion Report of the Planning Meeting for 2008 International Conference on Creative Tourism. Paris: UNESCO. Available at: https://unesdoc.unesco.org/ark:/48223/pf0000159811 (Accessed 20 April 2019).

Urry, J. (2002) *The Tourist Gaze*, 2nd Edn. London: Sage Publications.

Verhoef, P. C., Lemon, K. N., Parasuraman, A., Roggeveen, A., Tsiros, M. and Schlesinger, L. A. (2009) Customer experience creation: Determinants, dynamics and management strategies. *Journal of Retailing*, 85(1), 31–41.

Volo, S. (2009) Conceptualizing experience: A tourist based approach. *Journal of Hospitality Marketing & Management*, 18(2–3), 111–126.

Walls, A., Okumus, F., Wang, Y. and Kwun, D. (2011a) An epistemological view of consumer experiences. *International Journal of Hospitality Management*, 30(1), 10–12.

Walls, A., Okumus, F., Wang, Y. and Kwun, D. (2011b) Understanding the consumer experience: An exploratory study of luxury hotels. *Journal of Hospitality Marketing & Management*, 20(2), 166–197.

Wang, N. (1999) Rethinking authenticity in tourism experience. *Annals of Tourism Research*, 26, 349–370.

Wang, N. (2002) The tourist as peak consumer. In G. M. S. Dann (Ed.), *The Tourist as a Metaphor of the Social World*. Wallingford: CABI, pp. 181–295.

Wilkins, H. (2011) Souvenirs: What and why we buy. *Journal of Travel Research*, 50(3), 239–247.

Williams, A. (2006) Tourism and hospitality marketing: Fantasy, feeling and fun. *International Journal of Contemporary Hospitality Management*, 18(6), 482–495.

39

TOURIST EXPERIENCE

A marketing perspective

Serena Volo

Introduction

Scholars, practitioners and destinations have paid increasing attention to the tourist experience, its definition, its constituents and measurements and its evaluation. Since the 1970s, the topic has been extensively investigated (Gunn, 1972; Cohen, 1979) and since then, given the experiential nature of tourism, it has received constant and increasing attention in the literature (Scott & Le, 2017; Uriely, 2005; Volo, 2009). Over the decades, several disciplines have inspired scholars in their investigation of tourist experiences. From sociologists to computer scientists, researchers have explored this multi-faceted concept and presented different approaches to its definition, measurement and assessment. Despite the abundance of studies, however, many issues continue to be debated in the tourism literature and, to do justice to such a complex construct, authors argue on the need for alternative approaches. Indeed, theoretical and empirical studies still discuss the concept and meaning of the tourist experience, the multiple ways in which tourists themselves conceive their experiences, the influencing determinants on them, their different phases and tourists' final evaluations of lived experiences.

Arguably one of the richest topics in tourism literature, then, the tourist experience remains an evolving concept and, thus, an interesting and popular area of research. Studies on definitions, conceptualizations and the operationalization of the tourist experience have flourished, offering some common ground on the construct but also nourishing fierce debates surrounding the foundations of the experience concept (e.g.: Mannell & Iso-Ahola, 1987; Sharpley & Stone, 2012a; Uriely, 2005; Volo, 2009). For example, tourist experience typologies and different tourist segments have been extensively investigated in the context of multiple environments and contexts (e.g.: Beeho & Prentice, 1997; Bouchet, Lebrun & Auvergne, 2004; Chan, 2009; Larsen, 2007; Moon & Han, 2019; Prentice, 2001; Sharpley & Stone, 2012b), providing numerous setting-based typologies of experiences and segment-based type of tourists and, thus, opening many opportunities for research (Scott & Le, 2017). The investigations of the tourist experience have also explored, albeit in a limited way, the different phases of the experience, with some authors distinguishing between sequential stages of an experience and others focusing exclusively on one stage. Addressing the entire holiday experience, however, most scholars distinguish between the typical pre-,

DOI: 10.4324/9781003219866-45

549

during and post-travel stages (e.g.: Aho, 2001; Hull, Stewart & Yi, 1992; Park & Santos, 2017). In addition, several have pointed to the relevance of the active role of tourists in experiencing their vacations and in engaging in the co-creation process (e.g.: Binkhorst & Den Dekker, 2009; Li & Petrick, 2008; Volo, 2009) whilst, over the past decade, the attention of scholars has leaned towards the co-creation of experiences with an increasing effort to recognize, codify and empirically explore the relevance of tourists' engagement in the production of the experience (Andrades & Dimanche, 2014; Campos, Mendes, Valle & Scott, N, 2018; Minkiewicz, Evans, & Bridson, 2013; Prebensen, Chen & Uysal, 2017).

The purpose of this chapter is to review the most relevant contributions, themes and models related to the tourism experience from a tourism marketing perspective. The core of the chapter focuses on three aspects of tourist experience that have substantial relevance in marketing, namely: (i) conceptual developments; (ii) the type of tourist experience; and (iii), the role of co-creation in the tourist experience. Thus, the following section reviews the extent literature with a focus on definitions and frameworks characterized by a variety of disciplinary approaches. Subsequently, different types of tourism experiences are described and the related literature is presented to highlight the variety of marketing touchpoints available to reach out for tourists. The chapter then goes on to discuss selected research on the co-creation of tourist experiences offering an overview of the theoretical perspectives adopted, the different stakeholders involved and the dimensions of experience co-creation investigated in the literature. Finally, the chapter concludes with an overall discussion on tourist experience research, offering tourism marketing scholars and practitioners the tools to understand the conditions necessary to keep up with increasingly sophisticated experience seekers. The conclusion also identifies advances and shortcomings in the research and areas for further research.

Conceptual developments in the tourist experience

The complexity of the tourist experience is widely acknowledged in the literature. In early work, Cohen considered tourist experiences from a sociological perspective as opportunities for differentiation from everyday life (Cohen, 1972, 1979) whereas, from a psychological point of view, Mannell and Iso-Ahola (1987) emphasized the uniquely individual nature of tourism and leisure experiences. Since then, researchers from different disciplines have addressed the definition and conceptualization of the tourist experience, offering alternative but also complementary visions; Lash and Urry (1994), for example, question the work–everyday life dichotomy by extending the tourist experience to virtual reality settings. Generally, however, the lack of a 'single theory that defines the meaning and extent of tourist experiences' was soon acknowledged (Chhetri et al., 2004: 34), although Quan and Wang (2004) conceptualize tourist experience as an organic whole but, nevertheless, propose a distinction between peak and supporting experiences that complement each other. Volo (2009: 119) entrenches in the 'tourist experience essence' the sensation–perception–interpretation sequence that each individual experiences while on vacation, that is, outside the individual's daily environment and routines. The relative nature of such experiences is also asserted, as individuals have different emotional experiences even when engaging in the same activities at the same place and at the same time (Volo, 2009). Indeed, experiences are subjective and personal (Knobloch, Robertson & Aitken, 2017; Ryan 2002a). Furthermore, the variability of experiences sought by different types of tourists ought to be considered as tourists of different target markets participate in different experiences (Sharpley & Stone, 2011; Uriely, 2005).

Overall, then, many studies have acknowledged the difficulties in defining the tourist experience and in identifying and measuring its components when taking into account the characteristics of the individual tourist. Often, however, the conceptualization of the tourist experience integrates the dimensions of space and time (Cohen, 1972; Li, 2000; Sharpley & Stone, 2011; Volo, 2009); indeed, the tourist experience has been defined as 'the culmination of a given experience' formed by tourists 'when they are visiting and spending time in a given tourist location' (Graefe & Vaske, 1987, cited in Page, Brunt, Busby & Connell, 2001: 412). Furthermore, Ryan (2002b) emphasizes the perceptions, role and use made of time during a holiday, which he defines as 'a process of displacement [...] into another place and a special time' (Ryan, 2002b: 206). An example of hedonic consumption, the tourist experience is 'what the tourist is seeking' (Volo, 2005: 205), and it remains a 'complicated psychological process' (Quinlan Cutler & Carmichael, 2010: 3). Indeed, complex and multifaceted, tourist experiences can be seen on the one hand as the bundle of services consumed by tourists during their vacations or, on the other hand, simply as the experience of being a tourist (Sharpley & Stone, 2011). While the latter consolidates the sociological and psychological perspective, the former opens up the experience realm to marketing scholars. Indeed, marketers have for many years discussed experiences as equivalent of offerings and being particularly experiential in nature, tourism products have certainly contributed to such approach with experiential marketing seen as essential for hospitality and tourism (Li, 2000; Oh, Fiore & Jeoung, 2007; Williams, 2006). Considered a desirable commodity (O'Dell, 2007), tourism has been referred to as the 'marketplace of experiences' in which the challenge for business lies in transforming staged offerings into personal experiences (Volo, 2009).

The marketing approach to experience is based on the centrality of the tourist (Moutinho, 1987; Swarbrooke & Horner, 1999) and places emphasis on the consumer-centric experience. With the tourist at the core of the experience, marketing-based studies explore, for example, different typologies of activities, the satisfaction or quality experienced by tourists, the importance of human interactions, the role of external stimuli, prior knowledge and past experience, and creativity (e.g.: Baum, 2002; Go, 2005; Gursoy & McCleary, 2004; Volo, 2009). Uriely (2005) recognizes the shift to a post-modernist approach to tourist experience identifying the determinants that have accompanied the process: a re-conjunction between leisure and work/everyday life activities (Lash & Urry, 1994; Munt, 1994; Pizam, Uriely & Reichel, 2000; Ryan, 2002a), the search for 'micro-types' of tourism activities (Wickens, 2002) and a focus on the 'subject' in shaping the experience (e.g.: Uriely, Yonay & Simchai 2002; Wickens, 2002). According to experience embodiment theorists, a holistic experience has two elements: a phenomenological level, of which consumers are fully aware, and a cognitive level where transformation and learning occur (Tsai, 2005). Sundbo and Hagedorn-Rasmussen (2008), define an experience as a 'mental journey' in which the consumer has accomplished alternative purposes (having fun, learning or participating in something special) of which s/he has memories. In conceptualizing the tourist experience, Volo (2009) similarly asserts that tourism is 'essentially a marketplace of experience and tourists are the "mental places" where the tourist experience happens' (Volo, 2009: 119). Thus, experiences are very personal. In this vein, researchers can attempt observation but necessarily require interaction with the tourist to collect data that not only refer to the tourism offerings available in the marketplace but also tell the story of the individual experience.

Some authors point out the dual usage of the word experience both as a noun and a verb and as its evoking role: subjectivity, involvement, emotion and learning (Gao, Scott & Ding, 2010; Scott, Gao & Ma, 2017). The relevance of both business and consumer perspectives of experience is also pointed out by scholars attempting to conceptualize experiences in tourism and hospitality (Walls, Okumus, Wang & Kwun 2011). Owing to the subjectivity of an individual's response to similar tourism activities and offerings, scholars call for attention to be paid to conceptualizing and theorizing experiences and several reviews of literature give justice to such a complex topic (Adhikari & Bhattacharya, 2015; Jensen, Lindberg & Østergaard, 2015; Komppula & Gartner, 2013; Ritchie, Tung & Ritchie, 2011; Scott & Le, 2017; Sharpley & Stone, 2012b; Volo, 2009).

Typologies of tourist experience

Individualism, multiplicity and diversity characterize tourist experiences. Over the decades, tourism marketers' efforts have moved in the direction of amplifying the once monotonic offering and, thus, proposing to tourists a plethora of alternative experiences. Indeed, with the aim of improving the aggregate of tourists' outcomes (value, quality, satisfaction, memorability), marketing efforts have moved in the directions of creating alternative types of experiences. In most cases, marketers simply propose 'alternative offerings', although some authors point out that, focusing on a collective perspective, marketing has focused attention on experiences that can please the average tourism consumer (Scott & Le, 2017). Nevertheless, both approaches to the experience – the individual experience distinctive of psychological studies and the experience as offering typical of marketing studies – can have validity and be usefully applied. Indeed, while the first one is highly subjective and may demystify the role of tourism entrepreneurs in creating the experience, the second one heavily relies on the sought experiences and the targeted offerings in the marketplace. Therefore, there is a variety of 'objects' or typologies of experience offerings necessary for the tourist experience to occur. In reconciling these aspects, it is useful to consider the typologies of the tourist experience as discussed in the literature.

Regarding typologies, three aspects can possibly be used to reframe the existing research in this area: the spatial dimension, tourist traits and emotional outcomes. Table 39.1 provides a summary of experience typologies according to their discriminating factors and their focus; examples are also provided that are then further discussed in this section.

Typologies according to spatial–geographical dimensions

The spatial dimension of the experience has often been used to conceptualize and categorize different tourist experience typologies and, consequently, different tourist segments. Indeed, multiple physical environments and contexts have been used to differentiate among experiences and to cluster similar ones together. This approach to typologies is very common in

Table 39.1 Synopsis of typologies of tourist experience

Focus	Discriminating factors	Examples of experiences
Where	Spatial–Geographical Dimensions	Urban, theme park, restaurant, hotel, festival, cultural, wildlife, museum, restaurant; cruise, virtual, Artic, Chinese, South-African...
Who	Tourist Traits	Female, obese, family, children, gay, lesbian, backpacker, pilgrim, air traveller, solo traveller, generation Z, millennials...
How	Experience Outcomes	Quality, satisfying, valuable, memorable, emotion related...

Tourist experience: marketing perspective

marketing and it is certainly beneficial to practitioners in the field. It simply permits grouping according to relevant characteristics, such as, for example: the cultural versus the natural tourism experience; the urban versus the rural; the museum experience; the theme park experience; the restaurant or food experience; the cruising experience the festival experience; the peer-to-peer accommodation experience; and so on (e.g.: Axelsen & Swan, 2010; Ballantyne, Packer & Sutherland, 2011; Bigne, Andreu & Gnoth, 2005; Curtin, 2010; Hosany & Witham, 2010; Jepson & Sharpley, 2015; Kastenholz, Carneiro, Marques & Loureiro, 2018; Page, 2002; Quan & Wang, 2004; Ryu & Han, 2011; Selby, 2004; Sthapit, Coudounaris & Björk, 2019; Therkelsen, 2015; Torres, Fu & Lehto, 2014; Trischler & Zehrer, 2012; Tussyadiah & Zach, 2017). In this category can also be included various geographical perspectives – for example, island experiences, destination experiences, Chinese, Artic, South-African – which are often used to frame the experience (e.g.: Huang, Tang & Weaver, 2017; Hudson & Ritchie, 2009) and even digital, virtual and augmented reality experiences (e.g.: Bec et al, 2019; Martins et al., 2017). Yet, when (forced by external unforeseeable reasons) individuals are limited in their travelling mobility and cannot find the same pleasure in virtual tourist experiences, one could make much of Cohen's (1995) reference to the space dimension of tourist experiences and debating his question would be more than appropriate 'if any experience could be virtually had in any location, no experience will be place-bound anymore; then why should people travel?' (Cohen 1995: 20). Reflecting on this quest brings meaning to our scholarly field and to public and private tourism industry activities. Notwithstanding the importance of technology-enhanced experiences (Neuhofer, Buhalis & Ladkin, 2012), however, on site experiential fulfillment is what has made tourism one of the world's largest social global phenomena. The subjective interactions of tourists with destinations and places, with people, attractions and artefacts are deemed essential in the experience, and these happen in a tourist destination contextualized by some spatial and geographical characteristics (Tussyadiah & Zach, 2012). In addition, combining geo-spatial and chronological dimensions, tourists can have on-site experiences – that is, tourism experiences at the destinations – and *en-route* experience derived from travelling to and returning from the destination (Tussyadiah & Zach, 2012).

Typologies according to tourist traits

Tourists' characteristics have been also extensively used to identify and frame different types of experiences. Tourists' demographics, sexual preferences, physical traits and travelling preferences are seen as dominant influencers on the experience. The individualistic nature of human experience is uncovered in many studies, with qualitative research methods and interpretivist paradigms being used widely. This approach is more consumer behaviour-oriented and recognizes the individual's role at the centre of the tourism experience. Undoubtedly, recognizing the variety of traits, features and characteristics of tourists offers nuances that traditional marketing clusters cannot capture, allowing scholars to better tailor theoretical and practical suggestions. Some examples worth mentioning include studies on the experience of the female tourists, family or children, gay men and lesbian women, millennials, Gen Z, backpackers, air travellers and pilgrims (Belhassen, Caton & Stewart, 2008; Brown & Osman, 2017; Haddouche & Salomone, 2018; Jordan & Aitchison, 2008; Mohd, Ismail, Isa & Jaafar, 2019; Poria, 2006; Wattanacharoensil, Schuckert, Graham & Dean, 2017; Wilson & Little, 2008; Wilson & Richards, 2008; Wu, Wall, Zu & Ying, 2019). These studies offer the benefit of accommodating some daily traits of the analyzed vacationers in their contextual travel experience, thus overcoming the criticism pointed out by McCabe (2002), namely, that the tourism literature overlooks the blurred borders between daily life and tourism. Close attention should, however, be paid to avoiding the excessive fragmentation of the analysis of the tourist experience as individuals' multiple identities and role may shape the experience differently (a solo female traveller can be a business traveller one day or a pilgrim another). Indeed, blurring the borders between daily life and tourism means acknowledging the multiplicities and the inconsistencies of individuals' preferences, choices and behaviours in their tourism activities, which render a holiday like a small-scale version of life that, in return, might lead to bringing back, expanding and merging the tourist experience in – to use McCabe's (2002: 70) words – the 'microcosm of everyday life'. This points to a somewhat circular process in which the characteristics, profiles and traits of tourists ought to be carefully used by marketers and in which the experience outcomes, below discussed, move beyond possible direct cause–effect relationships.

Typologies according to experience outcomes

Tourists seek experiences as a means of achieving valuable outcomes that are mostly related to their emotional status, learning opportunities or transformational occasions. Certainly, outcomes such as satisfaction, quality and value permeated the early studies on the tourist experience and some remain relevant, with authors focusing, for example, on tourist experience value, on the impact of the type and dimensions of experiences on satisfaction, or on investigating quality experiences, typically to capture the behavioural consequences that are relevant for marketing purposes (e.g.: Björk, 2014; Cole & Scott, 2004; Haven-Tang & Jones, 2010; Jennings, 2010; Kastenholz et al., 2018; Lin & Kuo, 2016; Volo, 2009). The last decade has witnessed a sharp increase in studies focusing on the memorability of the experience. The significance of tourist experiences – intended as evaluated experiences according to Cutler and Carmichael (2010) – is related not only to short-term outcomes but to their ability to remain imprinted in the individual or collective memory of tourists. Thus, several scholars have investigated the so-called memorable tourism experience (e.g.: Coudounaris & Sthapit, 2017; Kim & Ritchie, 2014; Kim, Ritchie & McCormick, 2012; Servidio & Ruffolo, 2016; Sthapit & Coudounaris, 2018; Tung & Ritchie, 2011). Indeed, the relevance of recollection and memory is acknowledged by those who consider the psychological aspects of experience (these constructs are naturally embedded in their theoretical frameworks) but also by marketing scholars for whom the focus is on the activation of other outcome processes (repeat purchasing behaviour, loyalty, positive recommendations), which is possible when individuals can recognize, recollect or remember certain lived experiences associated with destinations or businesses and their brands or products.

Growing interest in the emotional outcomes of tourist experiences is also recently documented. Indeed, the diverse elements of a tourist experience are believed to generate emotive outcomes (i.e., feelings, moods, arousal), which may create affective transformation (Volo, 2009) and allow for further related outcomes relevant for marketing. Initial attempts document an effort to link emotions and tourist experiences (e.g.: Hosany & Gilbert, 2010; Hosany et al., 2015; Prayag, Hosany, & Odeh, 2013), with some pointing out that emotions deriving from tourist experiences remain a somewhat neglected area of research and hence the need exists to further explore their relationship (Scott & Le, 2017; Volo, 2017). The importance of emotion as an outcome in the tourist experience is seen as relevant from a scholarly perspective (Cohen, Prayag & Moital, 2014), and also from the tourism providers' perspective. Loyalty, intention to revisit or post-positive online reviews and recommendations to visit a destination or an attraction are typical by-products of those experiences that stimulate emotional outcomes. Undeniably, the emotional language is easily used in tourism

Tourist experience: marketing perspective

experience assessments for its ability to simply and universally convey tourists' evaluations. Thus, scholars have recently attempted to measure emotional outcomes of tourist experiences offering useful evidence to policy makers and marketing managers (e.g.: Bastiaansen et al., 2019; Kim & Fesenmaier, 2015; Knobloch, Robertson & Aitken, 2017; Li, Scott & Walters, 2015). Recent studies combined traditional surveying techniques with psychophysiological measures of emotion in an attempt to provide fine-grained emotional outcomes that can then be used to better design tourism experiences (Jordan, Spencer, & Prayag, 2019; Kim & Fesenmaier, 2015; Li, Walters, Packer & Scott, 2018; Shoval, Schvimer & Tamir, 2018; Tussyadiah, 2014). The findings of these novel research approaches are however still exploratory. Emotions are certainly connected with tourist experiences, but they are also shaped by personal mental associations and individuals' biological makeup (Volo, 2017). Thus, the association between emotions and tourist experience evaluation is still controversial and needs closer investigation (Mitas et al., 2021; Volo, 2020).

Co-creation in tourist experience

Since the start of the new millennium, tourism scholarship has witnessed a shift from the traditional dichotomic view of tourist experiences – namely, the producer and user standpoints – into a merged experiential process in which tourists co-create their experiences together with the supply side in such ways that are more inspirational, meaningful and transformational (see also Chapter 40). Thus, the attention of industry and academia has moved into the so-called co-creation of tourist experiences that sees tourists having an active role in creating their own experiences (e.g.: Andrades & Dimanche, 2014; Binkhorst & Den Dekker, 2009; Cabiddu, Lui & Piccoli, 2013; Go, 2005; Prebensen & Foss, 2011). The value of these co-creative behaviours has been reported by many authors who point out the relevance of engagement, personalization, interaction and empowerment that this approach offers to tourists in creating their experiences; they also highlight the benefits that tourism businesses could harvest (Chathoth et al., 2012; Minkiewicz et al., 2013; Pera, 2017). This mirrors the work of others who consider co-creative tourism experiences to those relating to high levels of active participation and interaction during consumption (Campos, Mendes, Valle & Scott, 2017, 2018). The relevance of the networked nature of tourism and the multiplicity of actors and stakeholders actively engaging in taking part in the co-creation process has also been noted (Binkhorst & Den Dekker, 2009; Lugosi, 2014; Sfandla & Björk, 2012). Indeed, tourism destinations and businesses have increasingly provided tourists with the opportunity to collaborate not only through to the final stage of consumption but also in tourism innovation and idea generations processes (Campos et al., 2017; Volo, 2006).

In a recent review of co-creation in tourism (Campos et al., 2018), two perspectives were identified, namely, the supply perspective and the tourist perspective. On the organization/destination side, Campos et al. (2018) propose that integrative networks, systems and processes can stimulate tourists' participation not only in consumption but also the design and production of experiences. Therefore, co-creation can happen at all phases of the overall tourism experience: pre-trip, during the experience consumption interacting with tourists, providers and other tourism actors, and also after the holiday when engaging in sharing experiences through traditional or social media channels (Neuhofer et al. 2012; Kim & Fesenmaier, 2017). From the supply side, there remains the interest in understanding, managing and systematizing the processes that can favour such co-creation, even when these processes require organizational or structural changes (Bharwani & Jauhari, 2013; Campos et al., 2018; Lugosi & Walls, 2013). Providers of tourism experiences are thus required to grow their awareness of the relevant role they play in facilitating not just the consumption of final experiences but the overall experiential tourism process. From the perspective of tourists, Campos et al. (2018) suggest a behavioural and psychological approach that see experiences still related to the different phases pre, during and post consumption. In their review, the authors frame past literature around some relevant aspects of participation, namely: (i) the partial tourist participation in which tourists contribute only to one or more stages or aspects of the experience co-creation; (ii) the co-creation contribution to the overall experience; (iii) the on-site co-creation activities participation *per se*; (iv) the on-site co-creation activities with others; and (v), the on-site subjective co-creation of experiences. Focusing on on-site co-creation, Campos et al. (2018) conclude their work presenting a conceptual framework that enables a psychological interpretation of the *experiencescape* onsite and emphasizing the role of marketing managers in offering their customers intensive and close interaction and participation during the onsite experience that, in return, boosts effectiveness and competitiveness.

Finally, recent studies stress the importance of investigating the peak moments of the tourist co-creation experience (Campos et al., 2018), reinvigorating the need to discriminate between low and high co-creation contexts, to investigate the influence of co-creation on the tourism experience and revisit intentions (Sugathan & Ranjan, 2019) and to deepen the understanding of the tourist-to-tourist interaction impact on experiences (Lin, Zhang, Gursoy & Fu, 2019). Overall, the extant literature concurs on the need to consider the complexity of the tourism experience, its actors, phases and environments and on the necessity to strengthen the methodologies adopted to measure co-creation effects on tourists' experiences.

Conclusion

This chapter has sought to provide insights into the most relevant contributions, themes and models relevant to the tourist experience from a tourism marketing perspective. In this sense, the literature reviewed reflects only partially the existing contributions on tourists' experiences. Yet, the theoretical and empirical studies discussed here assist in framing some of the current and most relevant issues that scholars and practitioners are facing. There is indeed a growing need to understand the conditions necessary to keep up with the increasingly sophisticated experience seekers.

Some decades have passed since scholars started to devote attention to the tourist experience and certainly, several advancements are noticeable. First, the reviewed literature concurs on the complexity of the tourism experience, on the multiplicity of its actors and on some overall phases in which tourists experience their vacations (Campos et al., 2018; Scott & Le, 2017; Sharpley & Stone, 2012b). These are relevant points that contribute to shape a framework in which marketing scholars and practitioners can elaborate their theoretical and practical contributions. It is evident that different disciplinary approaches can, and must, be used to explore both the experience as the 'essence' and the experience as 'offering'. Although some authors advocate for the supremacy of discipline over the others, the extant literature reveals that a variety of approaches can enrich theory and model development, and this it is certainly beneficial to the scientific community.

Second, the investigation of a multiplicity of tourists' types reveals a variety of perspectives to the study of tourist experiences. Whether geographically distinguished or based on the characteristics of tourists, these experiences define segmentation and targeting opportunities for marketers who are seeking to differentiate. In contrast, the outcome-based

Tourist experience: marketing perspective

experience literature has remained mostly focused on satisfaction and quality, though more recently it has slowly embraced the concept of value. The bulk of outcome-related literature seems, however, to address the issue of memorable tourists' experiences as those seem to trigger most of the behavioural output relevant for tourism marketing. Less attention is devoted to the emotional experiences, with some authors pointing to the utmost relevance of the emotive components (Knobloch, Robertson & Aitken 2017; Mitas et al., 2021; Scott & Le, 2017; Volo, 2017, 2020).

Third, from a marketing perspective, the shift from a passive tourist to an active one and from tourist interaction to tourist co-creation are among the most relevant advances that have enabled the industry to develop, and even to lead, some experiential features in the context of the overall service marketing discipline. Moreover, through the co-creation of experiences, industry stakeholders are able to gather information on the processes underpinning anticipated experiences and gain valuable clues on how to create valuable offerings. Furthermore, social media platforms have created novel opportunities for sharing and co-creating experiences at different stages of the vacation. From the early blogs and their content analysis to big data and their algorithms, the tourist experience has been at the core of scholars' attempts to capture and investigate tourists' spontaneous annotations about their experiences (Volo, 2018). Together with the online narratives, tourists nowadays have a plethora of tools to simultaneously share their experiences with family and friends around the world. The value of textual and visual data to explore the tourist experience is widely documented and the effect on experiences can be further investigated (e.g.: Bornarel et al., 2020; Volo & Irimiás, 2020). Marketers and tourists have preferential communication channels for evaluations of experiences, and both seem to benefit from this constant, fast and dynamic opportunity to document the lived experience.

However, a number of shortcomings also emerge from the literature that can offer fertile soil for future investigations. For example, some authors criticize the descriptive approach adopted in much of the tourism literature that focuses on the experience of individuals but undervalues the psychological mechanisms behind experiential processes (Scott & Le, 2017). Scholars in the field of psychology and cognitive science warn against a simplification of the experience construct. The centrality of 'the tourist' in the experience and the focus on the 'experience essence' gives emphasis to the individual's ability to create experiences independently from the 'tourist experience' sold in the marketplace (Volo, 2009). In short, one can say that: as beauty is in the eye of the beholder, experiences are in the minds of individuals. In other words, the 'tourist experience, or what people experience as tourists, is unique to the individual; thus, there are as many forms of tourist experience as there are tourists' (Sharpley & Stone, 2014: 2). Interesting and thought-provoking, this can be one of the challenges for the new generation of tourism consumer behaviour theorists and practitioners.

Other scholars point to the lack of dialogue between certain types of tourism firms and their customers; maintaining an open exchange with customers would enable micro-tourism firms to acquire more information about their experiences and, therefore, better design their value propositions (Yachin, 2018). Equally, despite the variety of tourism environment studies, the literature lacks comprehensive models that combine spatially or geographically identified experiences with a direct investigation of the marketing efforts of such areas or destinations. That is, more can still be done by discussing with the providers of tourist experiences onsite and over time. In this respect, the marketing literature seems to be bound to the tourist experience perspective in neglecting insights and developments from the supply side.

Furthermore, recent studies implicitly or explicitly address the issue of non-linearity in the influence of emotion on overall tourism experience evaluations (Mitas et al., 2021; Volo, 2020) and call for an understanding of emotional baselines (Volo, 2017), for studying emotional intelligence in relation to tourism (Prentice, 2019) and for encouraging the identification of moment-by-moment experience triggers (Kim & Fesenmaier, 2015; Mitas et al., 2021). The discussion on emotional outcomes in tourism experiences is often dominated by a marketing-driven approach and that is unable to cope with the changes in the mainstream emotion research (Volo, 2020). More collaborations across disciplines and attention to research issues, from data collection to methodological choices, are suggested to strengthen the methodologies adopted to measure experiences and the related emotional outcomes. Finally, given the human capacity to anticipate, sort and reinterpret experiences, and the constant opportunity for tourists and marketers to interact in the real or virtual marketspace, there is plenty of room left for marketers' actions and scholarly investigations in exploring the role of marketing stimuli or the mental sequence of tourist experiences.

References

Adhikari, A. and Bhattacharya, S. (2015) Appraisal of literature on customer experience in tourism sector: Review and framework. *Current Issues in Tourism* 19(4), 296–321.

Aho, S. K. (2001) Towards a general theory of touristic experiences: Modelling experience process in tourism. *Tourism Review*, 56(3–4), 33–37.

Andrades, L. and Dimanche, F. (2014) Co-creation of experience value: A tourist behaviour approach. In M. Chen and J. Uysal (Eds.), *Creating Experience Value in Tourism*. Wallingford: CABI, pp. 95–112.

Axelsen, M. and Swan, T. (2010) Designing festival experiences to influence visitor perceptions: The case of a wine and food festival. *Journal of Travel Research*, 49(4), 436–450.

Ballantyne, R., Packer, J. and Sutherland, L. A. (2011) Visitors' memories of wildlife tourism: Implications for the design of powerful interpretive experiences. *Tourism Management*, 32(4), 770–779.

Bastiaansen, M., Lub, X., Mitas, O., Jung, T. H., Passos Acenção, M., Han, D., Moilanen, T., Smit, B. and Strijbosch, W. (2019) Emotions as core building blocks of an experience. *International Journal of Contemporary Hospitality Management*, 31(2), 651–668.

Baum, T. (2002) Making or breaking the tourist experience: The role of human resource management. In C. Ryan (Ed.), *The Tourist Experience: A New Introduction*, 2nd Edn. London: Continuum, pp. 94–111.

Bec, A., Moyle, B., Timms, K., Schaffer, V., Skavronskaya, L. and Little, C. (2019) Management of immersive heritage tourism experiences: A conceptual model. *Tourism Management*, 72, 117–120.

Beeho A. and Prentice R. (1997) Conceptualizing the experiences of heritage tourists: A case study of New Lanark World Heritage Village. *Tourism Management*, 18(2), 75–87.

Belhassen, Y., Caton, K. and Stewart, W. P. (2008) The search for authenticity in the pilgrim experience. *Annals of Tourism Research*, 35(3), 668–689.

Bharwani, S. and Jauhari, V. (2013) An exploratory study of competencies required to co-create memorable customer experiences in the hospitality industry. *International Journal of Contemporary Hospitality Management*, 25(6), 823–843.

Bigne, J. E., Andreu, L. and Gnoth, J. (2005) The theme park experience: An analysis of pleasure, arousal and satisfaction. *Tourism Management* 26(6), 833–844.

Binkhorst, E. and Den Dekker, T. (2009) Agenda for co-creation tourism experience research. *Journal of Hospitality Marketing and Management*, 18(2), 311–327.

Björk, P. (2014) Tourist experience value: Tourist experience and life satisfaction. In N. Prebensen, J. Cheer and M. Uysal (Eds.), *Creating Experience Value in Tourism*. Wallingford: CABI, pp. 22–32.

Bornarel, F., Delacour, H., Liarte, S. and Virgili, S. (2020) Exploring travellers' experiences when visiting Verdun battlefield: A TripAdvisor case study. *Current Issues in Tourism*, 1–18.Online: https://doi.org/10.1080/13683500.2020.1751593

Bouchet, P. Lebrun A.-M. and Auvergne, S. (2004) Sport tourism consumer experiences: A comprehensive model. *Journal of Sport Tourism*, 9(2), 127–140.

Brown, L. and Osman, H. (2017) The female tourist experience in Egypt as an Islamic destination. *Annals of Tourism Research*, 63, 12–22.

Tourist experience: marketing perspective

Cabiddu, F., Lui, T.-W. and Piccoli, G. (2013) Managing value co-creation in the tourism industry. *Annals of Tourism Research*, 42, 86–107.

Campos, A. C., Mendes, J., Valle, P. and Scott, N. (2017) Attentive tourists: The importance of co-creative experiences. In N. Scott, J. Gao and J. Ma (Eds.), *Visitor Experience Design*. Wallingford: CABI, pp. 93–109.

Campos, A. C., Mendes, J., Valle, P. and Scott, N. (2018) Co-creation of tourist experiences: A literature review. *Current Issues in Tourism*, 21(4), 369–400.

Chan, J. (2009) The consumption of museum service experiences: Benefits and value of museum experiences. *Journal of Hospitality Marketing & Management*, 18(2–3), 173–196.

Chathoth, P., Altinay, L., Harrington, R. J., Okumus, F. and Chan, E. S. W. (2012) Co-production versus co-creation: A process based continuum in the hotel service context. *International Journal of Hospitality Management*, 32, 11–20.

Chhetri, P., Arrowsmith, C. and Jackson, M. (2004) Determining hiking experiences in nature-based tourist destinations *Tourism Management*, 25(1), 31–43.

Cohen, E. (1972) Towards a sociology of international tourism. *Social Research*, 39, 164–189.

Cohen, E. (1979) A phenomenology of tourist experiences. *Sociology*, 13(2), 179–201.

Cohen, E. (1995) Contemporary tourism-trends and challenges: Sustainable authenticity or contrived post-modernity? In R. Butler and D. Pearce (Eds.), *Change in Tourism: People, Places, Processes*. London: Routledge, pp.12–29.

Cohen, S. A., Prayag, G. and Moital, M. (2014) Consumer behaviour in tourism: Concepts, influences and opportunities. *Current issues in Tourism*, 17(10), 872–909.

Cole S. T. and Scott, D. (2004) Examining the mediating role of experience quality in a model of tourists experiences. *Journal of Travel and Tourism Marketing*, 16(1), 77–88.

Coudounaris, D. N. and Sthapit, E. (2017) Antecedents of memorable tourism experience related to behavioral intentions. *Psychology & Marketing*, 34(12), 1084–1093.

Curtin, S. (2010) Managing the wildlife tourism experience: The importance of tour leaders. *International Journal of Tourism Research*, 12(3), 219–236.

Gao, L., Scott, N. and Ding, P. (2010) Design of memorable cultural heritage attraction experiences for tourists. In V. C. Nguyen (Ed.), Proceedings of the International Scientific Conference: *Culture in the Integrated World*. Hanoi: Hanoi University of Culture, pp. 330–348.

Go, F. M. (2005) Co-creative tourists: An idea whose time has come. In P. Keller, and T. Bieger (Eds.), AIEST 55th Congress: *Innovation in Tourism – Creating Customer Value*, AIEST 55th Congress. St. Gallen, Switzerland: AIEST, pp. 77–89.

Graefe, A. and Vaske J. (1987) A framework for managing quality in the tourist experience. *Annals of Tourism Research*, 14(3), 390–404.

Gunn, C. (1972) *Vacationscape: Designing Tourist Regions*. Austin, Texas: University of Texas at Austin.

Gursoy, D. and McCleary, K. W. (2004) Travelers' prior knowledge and its impact on their information search behavior. *Journal of Hospitality & Tourism Research*, 28(1), 66–94.

Haddouche, H. and Salomone, C. (2018) Generation Z and the tourist experience: Tourist stories and use of social networks. *Journal of Tourism Futures*, 4(1), 69–79.

Haven-Tang, C. and Jones, E. (2010) Delivering quality experiences for sustainable tourism development: Harnessing a sense of place in Monmouthshire. In M. Morgan, P. Lugose and J. R. B. Ritchie (Eds.), *The Tourism and Leisure Experience: Consumer and Managerial Perspectives*. Bristol: Channel View Publications, pp. 163–181.

Hosany, S. and Gilbert, D. (2010) Measuring tourists' emotional experiences toward hedonic holiday destinations. *Journal of Travel Research*, 49(4), 513–526.

Hosany, S., Prayag, G., Deesilatham, S., Causevic, S. and Odeh, K. (2015) Measuring tourists' emotional experiences: Further validation of the destination emotion scale. *Journal of Travel Research*, 54(4), 482–495.

Hosany, S. and Witham, M. (2010) Dimensions of cruisers' experiences, satisfaction, and intention to recommend. *Journal of Travel Research* 49(3), 351–364.

Huang, M. F., Tang, C. and Weaver, D. (2017) The Arctic tourism experience from an evolving Chinese perspective. In Y-S. Lee, D. Weaver and N. Prebensen (Eds.), *Arctic Tourism Experiences: Production, Consumption and Sustainability*. Wallingford: CABI, pp. 89–99.

Hudson, S. and Ritchie, J. B. (2009) Branding a memorable destination experience. The case of 'Brand Canada'. *International Journal of Tourism Research*, 11(2), 217–228.

Hull, R., Stewart, W. and Yi, Y. (1992) Experience patterns: Capturing the dynamic nature of a recreation experience. *Journal of Leisure Research*, 24(3), 240–252.

Jennings, G. R. (2010) Research processes for evaluating quality experiences: Reflections from the 'experiences'. In M. Morgan, P. Lugose and J. R. B. Ritchie (Eds.), *The Tourism and Leisure Experience: Consumer and Managerial Perspectives*. Bristol: Channel View Publications, pp. 81–98.

Jensen, Ø., Lindberg, F. and Østergaard, P. (2015) How can consumer research contribute to increased understanding of tourist experiences? A conceptual review. *Scandinavian Journal of Hospitality and Tourism*, 15(suppl. 1), 9–27.

Jepson, D. and Sharpley, R. (2015) More than sense of place? Exploring the emotional dimension of rural tourism experiences. *Journal of Sustainable Tourism*, 23(8–9), 1157–1178.

Jordan, E. J., Spencer, D. M. and Prayag, G. (2019) Tourism impacts, emotions and stress. *Annals of Tourism Research*, 75, 213–226.

Jordan, F. and Aitchison, C. (2008) Tourism and the sexualisation of the gaze: Solo female tourists' experiences of gendered power, surveillance and embodiment. *Leisure Studies*, 27(3), 329–349.

Kastenholz, E., Carneiro, M. J., Marques, C. P. and Loureiro, S. M. C. (2018) The dimensions of rural tourism experience: Impacts on arousal, memory, and satisfaction. *Journal of Travel & Tourism Marketing*, 35(2), 189–201.

Kim, J. and Fesenmaier, D. (2015) Measuring emotions in real time: Implications for tourism experience design. *Journal of Travel Research*, 54(4), 419–429.

Kim, J. and Fesenmaier, D. (2017) Sharing tourism experiences: The post-trip experience. *Journal of Travel Research*, 56(1), 28–40.

Kim, J. and Ritchie, J. B. (2014) Cross-cultural validation of a memorable tourism experience scale (MTES). *Journal of Travel Research*, 53(3), 323–335.

Kim, J., Ritchie, J. R. B. and McCormick, B. (2012) Development of a scale to measure memorable tourism experiences. *Journal of Travel Research*, 51(1), 12–25.

Knobloch, U., Robertson, K. and Aitken, R. (2017) Experience, emotion, and eudaimonia: A consideration of tourist experiences and well-being. *Journal of Travel Research*, 56(5), 651–662.

Komppula, R. and Gartner, W. C. (2013) Hunting as a travel experience: An auto-ethnographic study of hunting tourism in Finland and the USA. *Tourism Management*, 35, 168–180.

Larsen, S. (2007) Aspects of a psychology of the tourist experience. *Scandinavian Journal of Hospitality and Tourism*, 7(1), 7–18.

Lash, S. and Urry, J. (1994) *Economies of Signs and Space*. London: Sage Publications.

Li, S., Scott, N. and Walters, G. (2015) Current and potential methods for measuring emotion in tourism experiences: A review. *Current Issues in Tourism*, 18(9), 805–827.

Li, S., Walters, G., Packer, J., and Scott, N. (2018) Using skin conductance and facial electromyography to measure emotional responses to tourism advertising. *Current Issues in Tourism*, 21(15), 1761–1783.

Li, X. and Petrick, J. F. (2008) Tourism marketing in an era of paradigm shift. *Journal of Travel Research*, 46(3), 235–244.

Li, Y. (2000) Geographical consciousness and tourism experience. *Annals of Tourism Research*, 27(4), 863–883.

Lin, C. H. and Kuo, B. Z. L. (2016) The behavioral consequences of tourist experience. *Tourism Management Perspectives*, 18, 84–91.

Lin, H., Zhang, M., Gursoy, D. and Fu, X. (2019) Impact of tourist-to-tourist interaction on tourism experience: The mediating role of cohesion and intimacy. *Annals of Tourism Research*, 76, 153–167.

Lugosi, P. (2014) Mobilising identity and culture in experience co-creation and venue operation. *Tourism Management*, 40, 165–179.

Lugosi, P. and Walls, A. R. (2013) Researching destination experiences: Themes, perspectives and challenges. *Journal of Destination Marketing & Management*, 2(2), 51–58.

Mannell, R. and Iso-Ahola, S. (1987) Psychological nature of leisure and tourism experience. *Annals of Tourism Research*, 14(3), 314–331.

Martins, J., Gonçalves, R., Branco, F., Barbosa, L., Melo, M. and Bessa, M. (2017) A multisensory virtual experience model for thematic tourism: A Port wine tourism application proposal. *Journal of Destination Marketing & Management*, 6(2), 103–109.

McCabe, S. (2002) The tourist experience and everyday life. In G. Gann (Ed.), *The Tourist as a Metaphor of the Social World*. Wallingford: CABI, pp. 61–75.

Minkiewicz, J., Evans, J. and Bridson, K. (2013) How do consumers co-create their experiences? An exploration in the heritage sector. *Journal of Marketing Management*, 30(1–2), 30–59.

Tourist experience: marketing perspective

Mitas, O., Mitasova, H., Millar, G., Boode, W., Neveu, V., Hover, M., van den Eijnden, F. and Bastiaansen, M. (2021) More is not better: The emotional dynamics of an excellent experience. *Journal of Hospitality & Tourism Research*. https://doi.org/10.1177/109634802095707

Mohd, N. S., Ismail, H. N., Isa, N., and Jaafar, S. (2019) Millennial tourist emotional experience in technological engagement at destination. *International Journal of Built Environment and Sustainability*, 6(1–2), 129–135.

Moon, H. and Han, H. (2019) Tourist experience quality and loyalty to an island destination: The moderating impact of destination image. *Journal of Travel & Tourism Marketing*, 36(1), 43–59.

Moutinho, L. (1987) Consumer behaviour in tourism. *European Journal of Marketing*, 21(10), 3–44.

Munt, I. (1994) The 'other' postmodern tourism: Culture, travel and the new middle class. *Theory, Culture and Society*, 11(3), 101–123.

Neuhofer, B., Buhalis, D. and Ladkin, A. (2012) Conceptualising technology enhanced destination experiences. Journal of Destination Marketing & Management, 1(1–2), 36–46

Oh, H., Fiore, A. M. and Jeoung, M. (2007) Measuring experience economy concepts: Tourism applications. *Journal of Travel Research*, 46(2), 119–132.

O'Dell, T. (2007) Tourist experiences and academic junctures. *Scandinavian Journal of Hospitality and Tourism*, 7(1), 34–45.

Page S. J., Brunt, P., Busby, G. and Connell, J. (2001) *Tourism: A Modern Synthesis*. London: Thomson Learning.

Page, S. J. (2002) Urban tourism: Evaluating tourists' experience of urban places. In C. Ryan (Ed.), *The Tourist Experience: A New Introduction*, 2nd Edn. London: Continuum, pp 112–136.

Park, S. and Santos, C. A. (2017) Exploring the tourist experience: A sequential approach. *Journal of Travel Research*, 56(1), 16–27.

Pera, R. (2017) Empowering the new traveller: Storytelling as a co-creative behaviour in tourism. *Current Issues in Tourism*, 20(4), 331–338.

Pizam, A. Uriely, N. and Reichel, A. (2000) The intensity of tourist-host social relationship and its effect on satisfaction and change of attitudes: The case of working tourists in Israel. *Tourism Management*, 21(4), 395–406.

Poria, Y. (2006) Assessing gay men and lesbian women's hotel experiences: An exploratory study of sexual orientation in the travel industry. *Journal of Travel Research*, 44(3), 327–334.

Prayag, G., Hosany, S. and Odeh, K. (2013) The role of tourists' emotional experiences and satisfaction in understanding behavioral intentions. *Journal of Destination Marketing & Management*, 2(2), 118–127.

Prebensen, N, Chen, J. and Uysal, M. (Eds.) (2017) *Co-creation in Tourist Experiences*. Abingdon: Routledge

Prebensen, N. K. and Foss, L. (2011) Coping and co-creating in tourist experiences. *International Journal of Tourism Research*, 13(1), 54–67.

Prentice, C. (2019) Emotional intelligence and tourist experience: A perspective article. *Tourism Review*, 75(1), 52–55.

Prentice, R. (2001) Experiential cultural tourism: Museums and the marketing of the new romanticism of evoked authenticity. *Museum Management and Curatorship*, 19(1), 5–26.

Quan, S. and Wang, N. (2004) Towards a structural model of the tourist experience: an illustration from food experiences in tourism. *Tourism Management*, 25(3), 297–305.

Quinlan Cutler, S. and Carmichael, B. (2010) The dimensions of the tourist experience. In M. Morgan, P. Lugosi and J. Ritchie (Eds.), *The Leisure and Tourism Experience: Consumer and Managerial Perspectives*. Bristol: Channel View Publications, pp. 3–26.

Ritchie, J. R. B., Tung, V. W. S. and Ritchie, R. J. B. (2011) Tourism experience management research: Emergence, evolution and future directions. *International Journal of Contemporary Hospitality Management*, 23(4), 419–438.

Ryan, C. (2002a) Stages, gazes and constructions of tourism. In C. Ryan (Ed.), *The Tourist Experience: A New Introduction*, 2nd Edn. London: Continuum, pp. 1–26.

Ryan, C. (2002b) 'The time of our lives' or time for our lives? An examination of time in holidaying. In C. Ryan (Ed.), *The Tourist Experience: A New Introduction*, 2nd Edn. London: Continuum, pp. 210–212.

Ryu, K. and Han, H. (2011) New or repeat customers: How does physical environment influence their restaurant experience? *International Journal of Hospitality Management*, 30(3), 599–611.

Scott, N. and Le, D. (2017) Tourism experience: A review. In N. Scott, J. Gao and J. Ma (Eds.), *Visitor Experience Design*. Wallingford: CABI, pp. 30–49.

Scott, N., Gao, J. and Ma, J. (Eds.) (2017) *Visitor Experience Design*. Wallingford: CABI.

Selby, M. (2004) *Understanding Urban Tourism, Image, Culture and Experience: Tourism, Retailing and Consumption*. London: I.B. Tauris.

Servidio, R. and Ruffolo, I. (2016) Exploring the relationship between emotions and memorable tourism experiences through narratives. *Tourism Management Perspectives*, 20, 151–160.

Sfandla, C. and Björk, P. (2012) Tourism experience network: Co-creation of experiences in interactive processes. *International Journal of Tourism Research*, 15(5), 495–506.

Sharpley, R. and Stone, P. (2011) Introduction: Thinking about the tourist experience. In R. Sharpley and P. Stone (Eds.), *Tourist Experience: Contemporary Perspectives*. Abingdon: Routledge, pp. 1–8.

Sharpley, R. and Stone, P. (2012a) Introduction: Experiencing tourism, experiencing happiness? In R. Sharpley and P. R. Stone (Eds.), *Contemporary Tourist Experience*. Abingdon: Routledge, pp. 1–8.

Sharpley, R. and Stone, P. (Eds.) (2012b) *Contemporary Tourist Experience: Concepts and Consequences*. Abingdon: Routledge.

Shoval, N., Schvimer, Y. and Tamir, M. (2018) Real-time measurement of tourists' objective and subjective emotions in time and space. *Journal of Travel Research*, 57(1), 3–16.

Sthapit, E. and Coudounaris, D. N. (2018) Memorable tourism experiences: Antecedents and outcomes. *Scandinavian Journal of Hospitality and Tourism*, 18(1), 72–94.

Sthapit, E., Coudounaris, D. N. and Björk, P. (2019) Extending the memorable tourism experience construct: An investigation of memories of local food experiences. *Scandinavian Journal of Hospitality and Tourism*, 19(4–5), 333–353.

Sugathan, P. and Ranjan, K. R. (2019) Co-creating the tourism experience. *Journal of Business Research*, 100, 207–217.

Sundbo, J. and Hagedorn-Rasmussen, P. (2008) The backstaging of experience production. In J. Sundbo and P. Darmer (Eds.), *Creating Experiences in the Experience Economy*. Cheltenham: Edward Elgar Publishing, pp. 83–110.

Swarbrooke, J. and Horner S. (1999) *Consumer Behaviour in Tourism*. Oxford: Butterworth-Heinemann.

Therkelsen, A. (2015) Catering for yourself: Food experiences of self-catering tourists. *Tourist Studies*, 15(3), 316–333.

Torres, E. N., Fu, X. and Lehto, X. (2014) Examining key drivers of customer delight in a hotel experience: A cross-cultural perspective. *International Journal of Hospitality Management*, 36, 255–262.

Trischler, J. and Zehrer, A. (2012) Service design: Suggesting a qualitative multistep approach for analyzing and examining theme park experiences. *Journal of Vacation Marketing*, 18(1), 57–71.

Tsai, S. (2005) Integrated marketing as management of holistic consumer experience. *Business Horizons*, 48(5), 431–441.

Tung, V. W. S. and Ritchie, J. R. B. (2011) Exploring the essence of memorable tourism experiences. *Annals of Tourism Research*, 38(4), 1367–1386.

Tussyadiah, I. P. (2014) Toward a theoretical foundation for experience design in tourism. *Journal of Travel Research*, 53(5), 543–564.

Tussyadiah, I. P. and Zach, F. J. (2012) The role of geo-based technology in place experiences. *Annals of Tourism Research*, 39(2), 780–800.

Tussyadiah, I. P. and Zach, F. J. (2017) Identifying salient attributes of peer-to-peer accommodation experience. *Journal of Travel & Tourism Marketing*, 34(5), 636–652.

Uriely, N. (2005) The tourist experience: Conceptual developments. *Annals of Tourism Research*, 32(1), 199–216.

Uriely, N., Yonay, Y. and Simchai, D. (2002) Backpacking experiences: A type and form analysis. *Annals of Tourism Research*, 29(2), 520–538.

Volo, S. (2005) Tourism destination innovativeness. In P. Kellet and T. Bieger (Eds.), *Innovation in Tourism: Creating Customer Value*. AIEST 55th Congress. St. Gallen, Switzerland: AIEST, pp. 199–211.

Volo, S. (2006) A consumer-based measurement of tourism innovation. *Journal of Quality Assurance in Hospitality & Tourism*, 6(3–4), 73–87.

Volo, S. (2009) Conceptualizing experience: A tourist-based approach. *Journal of Hospitality Marketing & Management*, 18(2/3), 111–126

Volo, S. (2017) Emotions in tourism: From exploration to design. In D. Fesenmaier and Z. Xiang (Eds.), *Design Science in Tourism: Foundations of Destination Management*. Dordrecht: Springer, pp. 31–40.

Volo, S. (2018) Tourism data sources: From official statistics to big data. In C. Cooper, S. Volo and W. Gartner (Eds.), *The Sage Handbook of Tourism Management*. London, Sage Publications, pp. 193–201.

Volo, S. (2020) The experience of emotion: Directions for tourism design. *Annals of Tourism Research*, 86, https://doi.org/10.1016/j.annals.2020.103097

Volo, S. and Irimiás, A. (2020) Instagram: Visual methods in tourism research. *Annals of Tourism Research*, p.103098.

Walls, A., Okumus, F., Wang, Y. and Kwun, D. J-W. (2011) An epistemological view of consumer experiences. *International Journal of Hospitality Management*, 30(1), 10–21.

Wattanacharoensil, W., Schuckert, M., Graham, A. and Dean, A. (2017) An analysis of the airport experience from an air traveler perspective. *Journal of Hospitality and Tourism Management*, 32, 124–135.

Wickens, E. (2002) The sacred and the profane: A tourist Typology. *Annals of Tourism Research*, 29(3), 834–51.

Williams, A. (2006) Tourism and hospitality marketing: Fantasy, feeling and fun. *International Journal of Contemporary Hospitality Management*, 18(6), 482–495.

Wilson, E. and Little, D. E. (2008) The solo female travel experience: Exploring the 'geography of women's fear'. *Current Issues in Tourism*, 11(2), 167–186.

Wilson, J. and Richards, G. (2008) Suspending reality: An exploration of enclaves and the backpacker experience. *Current Issues in Tourism*, 11(2), 187–202.

Wu, M. Y., Wall, G., Zu, Y and Ying, T. (2019) Chinese children's family tourism experiences. *Tourism Management Perspectives*, 29, 166–175.

Yachin, J. M. (2018) The 'customer journey': Learning from customers in tourism experience encounters. *Tourism Management Perspectives*, 28, 201–210.

40

VALUE CO-CREATION IN TOURISM ECO-SYSTEMS

Operant and operand resources

Nina K. Prebensen and Muzaffer S. Uysal

Introduction

The concept of value co-creation is used to describe a shift from the organization as a definer of value to a more participative process in which people and organizations together develop meaning (e.g., Ind & Coates, 2013). The purpose of this chapter is to explore the role of the actors in this process and the way they participate in creating value for both themselves and others (that is, who and how). In particular, the resources used in value co-creation will be outlined.

Consider, for instance, a tourist visiting Northern Norway, travelling with her partner. Before the journey, they look for information on the Internet, buy an airline ticket and rent a car in Tromsø. They search for information on the area in terms of climate (what to wear), transportation, tourist activities and attractions (what to do), restaurants (what and where to eat) and hotels (where to stay). They find various travel suggestions and offers.

The tourists buy some of these services in advance, but they prefer to deal with many activities, such as dining and overnight stays, during the journey. While they perform all the preparatory activities, they utilize their previous knowledge and experiences and gain new knowledge based on the search behaviour. However, an additional aim of these tourists is to enjoy the autonomy to experience something novel and different; hence, quite a few decisions will have to be made during the journey. They might also be busy in the time prior to their journey and, accordingly, leave some decisions and actions to be made during their travels. Arriving back home, they may reflect on and memorize their experiences in various ways. These reflections will influence them telling others about their experiences (word of mouth) as well as their intention to return to the destination in the future (co-creation activities after the journey).

Despite the advances in research on the importance of the actors' role in adding value to the final consumer experience (e.g. Payne, Storbacka & Frow, 2008), few have explored the type of resources that the actors utilize and the ways in which the consumers actually add value to their final experience of the services. Overall, then, the process of a vacation is, as the foregoing example shows, about co-creating experiences while visiting another place over a period of time, a process that can be viewed as the

564

DOI: 10.4324/9781003219866-46

Value co-creation in tourism eco-systems

reconfiguration of value-creating systems before, during and after the journey (Chen et al., 2018). In this vein, value co-creation refers to the processes whereby providers collaboratively engage with customers to create value (Prahalad & Ramaswamy, 2004). Research has demonstrated the imperative of active participation to create satisfying experiences (Prebensen, Woo, Chen & Uysal, 2014; Prebensen, Woo & Uysal, 2014; Prebensen & Xie, 2017). Active participation may reflect physical as well as psychological dimensions of the value creation process.

One of the premises within the perspective of service-dominant logic (SD logic) (Vargo & Lusch, 2004, 2008) is that 'all social and economic actors are resource integrators'. This proposition designates the need to understand better 'the commonalities of activities of the actors that constitute the market(s)' (Vargo & Lusch, 2010: 6) and the nature of networks that are linked together by 'the trinity of competences, relationships and information' (Lusch, Vargo & Tanniru, 2010, p. 21). SD logic assumes a co-dependent relationship between providers and customers, both of whom will benefit from the interactions. Following this line of thinking, the service provider proposes value for the customer to actualize by utilizing skills and knowledge from the network (e.g., Aarikka-Stenroos & Jaakkola, 2012; Jaakkola, Helkkula & Aarikka-Stenroos, 2015). Consequently, tourists play an essential role in the value co-creation process by integrating resources beyond the firm–customer exchange, including customers' self-generated activities. However, value co-creation implies mutual interaction through service exchange (Grönroos, 2011) based on the goal, target and product type. The positive (or negative) output from the resources used offers benefits (or detriments) for all the actors (Lusch & Vargo, 2014), which should lead to a positive (or negative) appraisal of co-created value. In the S-D logic approach, actors are viewed as 'operant resources'; that is, they integrate skills and knowledge into co-creation processes. Often, the actors also use natural resources and infrastructure, that is, operand resources, to co-create value for the customer and other actors.

Operant resources are the typical factors related to people, organization, communication and relationships, while operand resources are described in terms of material properties, such as financial resources, infrastructure and legal ownership (Constantin & Lusch, 1994). Hunt (2004) designated operant resources as typically human (e.g., the skills and knowledge of individual employees), organizational (e.g., controls, routines, cultures, competences), informational (e.g., knowledge about market segments, competitors and technology), and relational (e.g., relationships with competitors, suppliers and customers), and operand resources as typically physical (e.g. raw materials, products and facilities).

As consumers are perceived as 'value driven', tourism firms, to sustain their competitiveness, should recognize what their customers value. Perceived value is depicted as a vital strategic instrument for firms to be successful in the marketplace (Woodruff, 1997). As value perception is depicted as a critical element of consumption and decision-making behaviour and is considered to influence tourists' satisfaction and future intentions (Gallarza & Gil-Saura, 2006), the tourism industry will benefit from this knowledge to meet customers' needs in a valuable way. Value is delineated as 'always uniquely and phenomenologically determined by the beneficiary' (Vargo & Lusch, 2008: 7). However, the processes of the service encounter between the actors influences its creation. Effective co-creation in the encounter may lead to value building, whereas ineffective integration of actor resources could lead to value destruction (Echeverri & Skålén, 2011; Plé & Cáceres, 2010). Operant resources, such as knowledge and skills, are therefore core to define and develop value for all collaborating participants, including the tourist.

Nina K. Prebensen and Muzaffer S. Uysal

Theoretical perspectives

Co-creation, interaction and integration of resources

Co-creation of value is considered to be derived from the opportunity for interaction and integration of resources (Gummesson & Mele, 2010). All the actors participating in value co-creation are integrated into social networks in which they exchange experiences that will influence their own experiences. Thus, every social and economic actor effectively becomes an integrator of resources. In these networks of resources, actors integrate with other actors and apply their knowledge and skills to determine how and when to respond. Subsequently, each actor provides something of value to these networks. Gummesson and Mele (2010) held that these network-based interactions stimulate the integration of resources and empower value creation. Value networks remain amalgamated as each respective actor holds competences, relationships and shared information.

Observing a tourist destination, the actors participate in various ways to create value for themselves or for others utilizing both operant and operand resources in the service system (Buhalis, 2000). Service systems are defined as 'value-co-creation configurations of people, technology, value propositions connecting internal and external service systems, and shared information' (Maglio & Spohrer, 2008: 18), and may reflect individuals interacting as well as larger systems comprising the global economy. Normann (2001) outlines a value creating system as a provider and a customer connected by value propositions in value chains and value networks.

Vargo and Lusch (2016: 6) argued for a more 'holistic, dynamic, and realistic perspective of value creation, through exchange, among a wider, more comprehensive (than firm and customer) configuration of actors'. As such, they discussed the importance of the institutional and macro-level view of value creation. From this perspective, the structure of the institution – that is, its rules, norms, meanings, symbols and practices – influence collaboration. Institutions such as destination companies are extraordinary examples of resource-integrating networks (see Figure 40.1).

Value integrators

Co-creating experiences as a theoretical construct reflects the consumer, in addition to the service provider, as taking an active part in consuming and producing value (Arnould, Price & Malshe, 2006; Baron, Patterson, Warnaby & Harris, 2010; Price, Arnould & Malshe, 2006). Consequently, value integrators are all actors participating in defining, designing and performing various aspects of the experience. Knowledge, learning and communication – that is, operant resources – are subsequently imperative constructs in value co-creation. Given the significance of recognizing all the participating actors as value creators in tourist destination experiences, it is imperative that tourism planners and experience providers know how to plan and provide a platform for value to be co-created.

Interactions in systems can result in multiple outcomes (Edvardsson, Tronvoll & Gruber, 2011), and the use and integration of the operand and operant resources may be motivated by a variety of reasons dependent on what the actors value. The resources utilized and integrated can be based on personal value and/or business reasons. The actors' role and position in the value-creating process is therefore an important aspect. Within the tourism system, the key

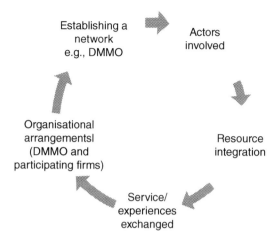

Figure 40.1 A destination eco-system
Source: Adapted from Vargo and Lusch (2016: 7).

actors are the tourists, transportation companies, accommodation companies, food and beverage companies, companies providing nature and/or culture-based activities/experiences, museums and governmental organizations. In addition to the tourists, a key factor in integrating resources is the destination marketing and management organization (DMMO). However, it is through acknowledgment and support (customer integration) in meeting the needs of the customers that the DMMOs will succeed.

Perceived value for the customer

As tourists have different motivations and needs for travelling during their vacation, pleasure is derived from diverse activities providing various types of experience value. Customer value as a construct has received increased attention over the past decade (e.g., Gallarza, Saura & Holbrook, 2011), and the use of a multidimensional framework has been recognized (Holbrook, 1994; Sheth, Newman & Gross, 1990; Sweeney & Soutar, 2001). In particular, customer value research has been acknowledged as a more complete measure of customers' overall evaluation of services and products than just quality and service perception.

Product quality and service perception measures reflect customers' evaluation of the service provider, such measures including tangibility, reliability, responsiveness, assurance, empathy and convenience (Zeithaml, Berry & Parasuraman, 1988). Value perception measures also reflect customers' evaluation of the feelings and emotions co-created in the situation, such as value for money, functional value, emotional value, social value and epistemic value (Sheth et al., 1990; Williams & Soutar, 2009). Value perception thus reflects not only the service providers but also the tourists partaking in creating value. For tourists, value could emerge through various consumer experiences within the consumption system of services.

Recent research has shown how tourist value is influenced by the level of skills, perceived mastery and competency and psychological and physiological participation in an activity (Prebensen & Xie, 2017), the same study revealing that satisfaction is influenced indirectly through value perception. This supports Cronin, Brady and Hult's (2000) assertion that the consumer decision-making process for service products is best modelled as a complex system in which consumers' value perceptions affect behavioural intentions directly and indirectly through satisfaction.

Perceived value by actors (service providers)

In tourism ecosystems, institutions lead interactions in value co-creation and therefore signify the 'rules' of resource integration and coordinate actors' efforts to make joint value co-creation likely. Tourism providers, including DMMOs, aim to attract the right number of customers and the right type of customers so that all the collaborating partners can meet their business goals.

The tourism industry, similar to many other industries, is struggling to become more sustainable. A baseline in sustainable tourism is a conscious and consistent effort on all matters concerning the environment, social matters and local prosperity. The social, physical and cultural well-being of communities are also dependent on healthy ecosystems. Value co-creation and sustainability share an outlook in which the key role of the firm in its operating context focuses on 'wealth, welfare and wellbeing, over time' (Kuhlman & Farrington, 2010: 3441).

Firm/organizational resources

Resource-based theory (RBT), also known as the resource-based view, emphasizes resources as being essential for building an organizational competitive advantage (Barney, 1991; Peteraf, 1993). RBT further suggests that firms are required to focus on intangible, dynamic operant resources to enhance their competitive advantage and performance.

To identify marketing resources that help to co-create customer value, Ceric, d'Alessandro, Soutar and Johnson (2016) used resource-based theory (RBT) as a theoretical underpinning. RBT helps practitioners to focus on key aspects of their businesses and networks, which can provide a long-term competitive advantage. The critical aspect is to find the resources and capabilities that are the most important for a specific organization. Ceric et al. (2016) built on the foundation of RBT that a resource is valuable when it can improve organizational effectiveness and efficiency through dimensions such as rarity and non-imitativeness. Rarity indicates that only a few current and potential actors have access to that resource, whilst a resource is non-imitable when actors cannot obtain, imitate, purchase or duplicate that resource. Capabilities are important in facilitating the use of resources in the marketplace (Hooley, Broderick & Möller, 1998). Day (1994: 38) defined capabilities as a 'complex bundle of skills and accumulated knowledge that enable firms to coordinate activities and make use of their assets'.

In s similar vein, resource advantage theory (Madhavaram & Hunt, 2008) holds that firms should focus on intangible, dynamic operant resources to enhance their competitive advantage and performance. A firm's operant resources, such as reputation, employees' skills/knowledge, relationships and organization culture, play a vital role in the value-creating process. Operant resources are described as dynamic and infinite and can create additional operant resources (Vargo & Lusch, 2004). The way in which firms and organizations (service systems) facilitate the co-creation of their resources with collaborating actors, including customers, are therefore essential. The providers of services offer their resources, competencies and processes to customers (Grönroos, 2004). Baron and Warnaby (2011)

Value co-creation in tourism eco-systems

categorized the operant resources of firms into three elements: representational resources (reputation, credibility and comfort), cultural resources (knowledge, management skills, capacity, quality of service and technical expertise) and social resources (the friendliness of staff, relationships and networking). During service interactions, customers may evaluate firms' operant resources, which are demonstrated through the frontline staff's capability and skills or cultural resources.

Facilitating for value co-creation

Environmental psychology (Clayton et al., 2016) underpins ideas and perspectives that individuals may react differently to physical surroundings such as nature, physical products and infrastructure (operand resources). Based on this thinking and claiming that individuals may react to places with two contradictory types of behaviour, namely, approach or avoidance, Bitner (1992) developed a model of consumption encounters including both place and people referred to as the Servicescape model. Approach behaviour is delineated to include all positive behaviours that might be directed at a particular place, while avoidance behaviours embrace the opposite. These two types of behaviour can be viewed as opposing reactions to certain places and situations. To explore individuals' reactions in various servicescapes, also named experiencescape by Mossberg (2007), it is imperative to know the degree to which consumers co-create strategies and coping mechanisms to various situations (Prebensen & Foss, 2011). The Prebensen and Foss (2011) study reveals various types of coping and co-creation strategies based on different servicescapes, such as at a destination when the tourist is either alone or together with family or friends, and towards whom the interaction is directed (other tourists or the host).

As coping and co-creation reflect the type and level of activities taken, knowledge and skills (operant resources) are affecting the action taken in encountering operand as well as operant resources. Tourism providers should therefore concentrate on developing knowledge and skills in facilitating and proposing successful experiences to be co-created together with its customers. Arnould et al. (2006) show that consumers have a substantial but also unpredictable impact on value-creation processes. The Arnould et al. (2006) study allocates consumer operant resources into cultural (i.e. specialized knowledge/skills, history, imagination), social (i.e. family relationships, consumer communities, commercial relations) and physical (i.e. physical and mental endowment, energy, emotion, strength). The service provider should employ these resources when developing value propositions for their customers and in facilitating for value co-creation.

The tourists' resources

Tourism researchers, such as Brondoni (2016) and Salvioni (2016), argue that tourists nowadays focus on their self-identification, perceptions and sensations rather than on destination hardware such as accommodation, transport and airports. However, as tourists have various degrees of resources and travel experiences, providing different degrees of knowledge, involvement, motivation and self-efficacy, they hold various types and degrees of operant resources.

Building on the social-cognitive theory of Bandura (1977) reveals the importance of self-efficacy or self-perceived mastering in co-creating experience value when visiting a destination. Another study of tourist resource reveals that time and effort make a positive contribution to the perceived value of a tourist vacation (Prebensen, Vittersø & Dahl, 2013). The explanation for this is that since experience-based consumption to a large extent focuses on hedonic value for the customer (Holbrook, 2005), the time and effort spent on such travels (before, during and after) are operant resources in such co-creation situations. Carù & Cova (2007: 7) observe that it is 'widely accepted within an experiential perspective that consumers are not passive agents reacting to a stimulus, but instead, the actors and producers of their own experiences...' Tourists resources are exposed by the tourists being at the destination and taking part in producing and enjoying various experiences while there (Sandström, Edvardsson, Kristensson & Magnusson, 2008).

Co-creation is further understood to include physical and psychological participation, implying that participants as consumers bring both their physical presence and resources but also their emotional engagement and immersion into the process of consumption. Energy, emotion and strength are forms of operant resources. Resources are consequently related to the individual willingness to partake as well as to the knowledge and skills (ability) to participate and master the situation and activity in value creation processes. To some extent, these resources are the software of value creation and are deemed essential for value to be

Table 40.1 Examples of operant and operand resources in the tourism network ecosystem

	Operant resources used (typical)	*Operand resources used (typical)*
The tourists	Previous experiences, Information searching skills, previous behaviours, motivation, involvement, social skills	Internet, social media, nature – scenery, woods, mountains, cultural sites
The DMMO	Communication and information skills, analytical skills (segmentation etc.), system skills, collaborative skills and knowledge, producing appealing materials for the various actors, collaboration, creating collaborative platforms (physical and online), nudging, the rules, norms, meanings, symbols, practices developed and shared in the network★	Infrastructure, WEB, social media, nature, culture and history of the destination
Transportation companies	Logistic, collaboration, segmentation, value chain, relationships, organization culture★	Infrastructure (roads, maps signs), transportation vehicles
Accommodation companies	Yield management, communication, motivation, brand relationships, organization culture★	Infrastructure, physical units and appearance
Museums and historical sites (often public)	Staging, communicating, informing, relationships, organization culture★	Infrastructure, authentic sites, history
Culture-based activity providers	Staging, communicating, informing, storytelling, engaging, relationships, organization culture★	Infrastructure, local culture and history
Nature-based activity providers	Staging, communicating, informing, storytelling, engaging, relationships, organization culture★	Infrastructure, nature, animals, paths
Food and beverage companies	Producing food and beverages, staging, tasting, segmenting, yield management, relationships, organization culture★	Infrastructure, raw materials produced in nature

★ Representational resources (reputation, credibility and comfort), cultural resources (knowledge, management skills, capacity, quality of service and technical expertise) and social resources (the friendliness of staff, relations, networking) (Baron & Warnaby, 2011).

Value co-creation in tourism eco-systems

co-created. It is also important to recognize that operant resources (or resources in general) could have a hierarchy of importance in their use and reconfiguration depending on the setting and context, implying that competitive advantage could be built upon resource–advantage theory's notion of basic resources and higher-order resources, and interconnected operant resources (Madhavaram & Hunt, 2008). Table 40.1 above outlines examples of operand and operant resources in a tourism ecosystem.

A resource integration framework in tourism

Resource integration in tourism denotes that value is co-created in a service system or, alternatively, is a constellation of networked actors accessing or acquiring scarce resources. Middleton and Hawkins (1998) describes a destination as a unique and complex product of the tourism industry, comprising, among other factors, an area's climate, infrastructure and suprastructure, services, and natural and cultural attributes. Gretzel et al. (2015) apply the term 'ecosystem' suggested by Investopedia (2015) to describe the relationships between economic entities (producers, distributors, consumers, government agencies, etc.). Through competition and/or cooperation, the economic entities of producers, distributors, consumers, government agencies facilitate, independently, or in some combination, the creation and distribution of a product or service.

Designating a destination as a complex ecosystem includes both operand and operant resources where the actors' knowledge, skills and the integration of these resources are vital. Destinations thus include numerous firms and individuals providing and enjoying various types and numbers of activities, services and benefits, embracing the overall experience (Gunn & Var, 2002; Uysal, Berbekova & Kim, 2020) providing value for the guests and the hosts. The culture and structure of interactions and information between and among the actors are core within this ecosystem. Integration of operant resources is of particular importance, given their role as the fundamental source of strategic benefit.

As indicated by Gunn and Var (2002), in its simplest form, a tourism system/network consists of an origin, representing demand, and a destination, representing supply. Supply and demand interaction are an essential reality in shaping up the production and consumption of tourism goods and services. Thus, the nature of this interaction should be the most fundamental concept in creating tourism experiences. What do we mean by this interaction and why is it important in integrating resources? Putting it simply, demand refers to desires or needs of buyers and consumers, whilst supply refers to available resources and constraints, and how the market reacts to demand. Employing a similar approach, the tourism system consists of an origin and a destination in its simplest form (Gunn & Var, 2002). An origin represents the demand side of tourism from which visitors generate. A destination, on the other hand, refers to the supply side of tourism that may have certain attractiveness power. In other words, the interaction is the one that forms the sphere of experience settings based on goals, targets and market types. In this vein, the configuration of resources is essential not only for creation of tourism experience but also for quality of experience. The functioning tourism network system in the modern world presents a bundle of different tangible and intangible resources provided by both the supply and the demand side that the integration of resources forms the tourist experience (Prebensen, Uysal & Chen, 2018). This experience then spans through phases of the trip as the tourist plans, travels and returns to the destination of origin (Uysal, Harrill & Woo, 2011). Thus, to facilitate and create tourism experience, the nature and types of resources are integrated to create value and this needs to be acknowledged. The operand resources of tourism destinations may typically include

Nina K. Prebensen and Muzaffer S. Uysal

the destination setting (nature, infrastructure, amenities, attractions, nature of attractions, accessibility), people in the destination (tourism industry employees, locals, other tourists), information and communication technologies. The operant resources consist of knowledge, skills and information (Table 40.1). Some of these resources may be ranked higher in their significance (Prebensen Uysal & Chen, 2018). However, which of these resources are active in the tourism experience depends very much on the tourist. The operant resources are viewed as dominant in value co-creation. Similarly, while the available tangible resources at the destination are of importance, creating a quality or co-created experience is only possible when operant resources from both the supply and demand sides are applied as well. The formation and thus the nature of operant resources in the tourism system network is influenced by a host of factors, including sociocultural context, tourists' needs/expectations and tourism development level of the destination (Uysal, Berbekova & Kim, 2020). These contextual factors shape the knowledge, information and skill levels of actors involved in the tourism experience co-creation. Moreover, the integration of tangible and intangible resources from the perspective of the firm in the processes of creating a quality experience further enhances the operant resources of the actors involved (Bruce et al., 2019). It is clear that the setting as a function of demand and supply interaction affects the process of creating value – experiences and desired outcomes. The participant interacts with the setting – without which there is less opportunity to create. Therefore, the elements of the setting or experience dimensions should involve the tourist emotionally, physically, spiritually and intellectually (Gountas, 2017; Grönroos, 2006; Mossberg, 2007). Furthermore, the elements of the setting are augmented with technological agents.

Bajarin (2011) describes the concept of the digital ecosystem to include interactions among technological agents (devices, databases, programs, etc.) where information flows and forms the infrastructure for digital business ecosystems. The knowledge of this digital business ecosystem allows connection between the demand and supply side and the interaction between the two for value creation at a destination. Consequently, a successful development of a destination as a functioning tourism ecosystem is about merging, coordinating and integrating new knowledge with traditional infrastructure.

Destination management and marketing organizations operate numerous operand resources related to nature, culture and infrastructure. Some of these resources may overlap and, in some cases, could have a hierarchy of operant resources from basic to composite and interconnected resources (Madhavaram & Hunt, 2008), implying that they may not be necessarily mutually exclusive but complimentary in nature based on context and the setting. These resources present value for destinations, firms and customers. However, firms may create value for their customers through the operant resources. Then these actors may also help enhance value for the customers and themselves by involving, teaching and motivating the customer to participate in and master various types of activities before, during and after the trip (Chen, Prebensen & Uysal, 2018).

A framework of the destination integration system is suggested below (Figure 40.2). Located in the centre of the ecosystem is the destination, often organized as a destination management and marketing organization (DMMO), where different stakeholders of the production and consumption system of tourism, including the tourist interact depending on the role goal, and target. The interactions may happen before (online or through another medium), during the journey or after the journey (memorizing). Tourists and service providers utilize operant and operand resources, integrated by the various actors to fulfill their goals, needs and wants. These goals, needs and wants are reflected through the actors' value perceptions. Value perceptions differ according to the actors' roles—as a tourist, as an employee

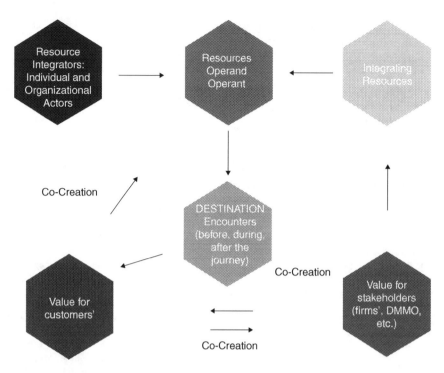

Figure 40.2 Destination resource integration framework

or as a manager, or as representing an organization, a host or a network, such as a DMMO company. Co-creation processes between the actors occur throughout the whole process of a tourist journey, between the actors.

Conclusion

The co-creation of tourism experience is formed and realized by integrating both operand and operant resources in tourism. The degree to which this happens is influenced by how actors of the functioning tourism network system utilize and allocate their resources in the sphere of experience setting. The setting as physical or digital space in which tourism experiences take place plays a crucial role in configuring use of resources stemming from both providers and tourists as a function of tourism interaction. The development and modifications of resource configurations have to take into account changes in consumer preferences and expectations so that destinations and the tourism enterprise can ensure facilitating for quality experience while sustaining business success. People and their knowledge and skills serve as a facilitator of added value to the process of co-creation of experiences in the consumption of both tangible and intangible tourism goods, services and experiences.

It is important to remember that the value co-creation between the service providers and the customers is only possible through interaction that could take place throughout the duration of different phases of a tourism/travel consumption experience. When there is no interaction, the value is created separately by customers and by firms. The value co-creation implies a mutual interaction through services exchange (Grönroos, 2012) based on goal, target and product type.

Nina K. Prebensen and Muzaffer S. Uysal

The key challenge for the tourism industry is to match competency and capabilities with the ever-changing expectations of tourists as key actors in the process of co-creation of experience value. However, to better understand the tourism eco-system, expectations and value by the various hosts, i.e., strategic benefits, should be matched with the value perception of the tourist. To be successful in the marketplace, the authors of the current chapter argue for the service providers to facilitate the customer to partake in creating valuable experiences for themselves and others.

References

Aarikka-Stenroos, L. and Jaakkola, E. (2012) Value co-creation in knowledge intensive business services: A dyadic perspective on the joint problem-solving process. *Industrial Marketing Management*, 41(1), 15–26.

Arnould, E. J., Price, L. L. and Malshe, A. (2006) Toward a cultural resource-based theory of the customer. In R. F. Lusch and S. L. Vargo (Eds.), *The Service-dominant Logic of Marketing: Dialog, Debate, and Directions*. Abingdon: Routledge, pp. 91–104.

Bajarin, B. (2011) Why it's all about the digital ecosystem. Techpinions.com.

Bandura, A. (1977) Self-efficacy: Toward a unifying theory of behavioral change. *Psychological Review*, 84(2), 191–215.

Barney, J. (1991) Firm resources and sustained competitive advantage. *Journal of Management*, 17(1), 99–120.

Baron, S. and Warnaby, G. (2011). Individual customers' use and integration of resources: Empirical findings and organizational implications in the context of value co-creation. *Industrial Marketing Management*, 40(2), 211–218.

Baron, S., Patterson, A., Warnaby, G. and Harris, K. (2010) Service-dominant logic: Marketing research implications and opportunities. *Journal of Customer Behaviour*, 9(3), 253–264.

Bitner, M. J. (1992) Servicescapes: The impact of physical surroundings on customers and employees. *Journal of Marketing*, 56(2), 57–71.

Brondoni, S. M. (2016) Global tourism management. Mass, experience and sensations tourism. *Symphonya. Emerging Issues in Management*, 1, 7–24.

Bruce, H. L., Wilson, H. N., MacDonald, E. K. and Clarke, B. (2019) Resource integration, value creation and value destruction in collective consumption contexts. *Journal of Business Research*, 103, 173–185.

Buhalis, D. (2000) Marketing the competitive destination of the future. *Tourism Management*, 21(1), 97–116.

Carù, A. and Cova, B. (Eds.) (2007) *Consuming Experience*. London: Routledge.

Ceric, A., D'Alessandro, S., Soutar, G. and Johnson, L. (2016) Using blueprinting and benchmarking to identify marketing resources that help co-create customer value. *Journal of Business Research*, 69(12), 5653–5661.

Chen, J. S., Prebensen, N. K. and Uysal, M. (2018) Dynamic drivers of tourist experiences. In N. K. Prebensen, J. S. Chen and M. Uysal (Eds.), *Creating Experience Value in Tourism*. Wallingford: CABI, pp. 11–21.

Clayton, S., Devine-Wright, P., Swim, J., Bonnes, M., Steg, L., Whitmarsh, L. and Carrico, A. (2016) Expanding the role for psychology in addressing environmental challenges. *American Psychologist*, 71(3), 199–215.

Constantin, J. A. and Lusch, R. F. (1994) *Understanding Resource Management*. Oxford: The Planning Forum.

Cronin Jr, J. J., Brady, M. K. and Hult, G. T. M. (2000) Assessing the effects of quality, value, and customer satisfaction on consumer behavioral intentions in service environments. *Journal of Retailing*, 76(2), 193–218.

Day, G. S. (1994) The capabilities of market-driven organizations. *Journal of Marketing*, 58(4), 37–52.

Echeverri, P. and Skålén, P. (2011) Co-creation and co-destruction: A practice-theory based study of interactive value formation. *Marketing Theory*, 11(3), 351–373.

Edvardsson, B., Tronvoll, B. and Gruber, T. (2011) Expanding understanding of service exchange and value co-creation: A social construction approach. *Journal of the Academy of Marketing Science*, 39(2), 327–339.

Value co-creation in tourism eco-systems

Gallarza, M. G. and Saura, I. G. (2006) Value dimensions, perceived value, satisfaction and loyalty: An investigation of university students' travel behaviour. *Tourism Management*, 27(3), 437–452.

Gallarza, M. G., Gil-Saura, I. and Holbrook, M. B. (2011) The value of value: Further excursions on the meaning and role of customer value. *Journal of Consumer Behaviour*, 10(4), 179–191.

Gountas, S. (2017) Creating emotional platforms. In N.K. Prebensen, J. Chen and M.S Uysal (Eds.), *Co-creation in Tourist Experiences*. Abingdon: Routledge, pp. 10–21.

Gretzel, U., Koo, C., Sigala, M. and Xiang, Z. (2015). Special issue on smart tourism: Convergence of information technologies, experiences, and theories. *Electronic Markets*, 25(3), 175–177.

Grönroos, C. (2004) The relationship marketing process: Communication, interaction, dialogue, value. *Journal of Business & Industrial Marketing*, 19(2), 99–113.

Grönroos, C. (2006) Adopting a service logic for marketing. *Marketing Theory*, 6(3), 317–333.

Grönroos, C. (2011) Value co-creation in service logic: A critical analysis. *Marketing Theory*, 11(3), 279–301.

Grönroos, C. (2012) Conceptualising value co-creation: A journey to the 1970s and back to the future. *Journal of Marketing Management*, 28(13/14), 1520–1534.

Gummesson, E. and Mele, C. (2010) Marketing as value co-creation through network interaction and resource integration. *Journal of Business Market Management*, 4(4), 181–198.

Gunn, C. A. and Var, T. (2002) *Tourism Planning: Basics, Concepts, Cases*. New York: Routledge.

Holbrook, M. B. (1994) The nature of customer value: An axiology of services in the consumption experience. *Service Quality: New Directions in Theory and Practice*, 21(1), 21–71.

Holbrook, M. B. (2005) Customer value and autoethnography: Subjective personal introspection and the meanings of a photograph collection. *Journal of Business Research*, 58(1), 45–61.

Hooley, G., Broderick, A. and Möller, K. (1998) Competitive positioning and the resource based view of the firm. *Journal of Strategic Marketing*, 6(2), 97–116.

Hunt, S. D. (2004) On the service-centered dominant logic of marketing. *Journal of Marketing*, 68(1), 21–22.

Ind, N. and Coates, N. (2013) The meanings of co-creation. *European Business Review*, 25(1), 86–95.

Jaakkola, E., Helkkula, A. and Aarikka-Stenroos, L. (2015). Service experience co-creation: Conceptualization, implications, and future research directions. *Journal of Service Management*, 26(2), 182–205.

Kuhlman, T. and Farrington, J. (2010) What is sustainability? *Sustainability*, 2(11), 3436–3448.

Lusch, R. F. and Vargo, S. L. (2014) *The Service-Dominant Logic of Marketing: Dialog, Debate, and Directions*. Abingdon: Routledge.

Lusch, R. F., Vargo, S. L. and Tanniru, M. (2010) Service, value networks, and learning. *Journal of the Academy of Marketing Science*, 38, 19–31.

Madhavaram, S. and Hunt, S. D. (2008) The service-dominant logic and a hierarchy of operant resources: Developing masterful operant resources and implications for marketing strategy. *Journal of the Academy of Marketing Science*, 36(1), 67–82.

Maglio, P. P. and Spohrer, J. (2008) Fundamentals of service science. *Journal of the Academy of Marketing Science*, 36(1), 18–20.

Middleton, V. T. and Hawkins, R. (1998) *Sustainable Tourism: A Marketing Perspective*. London: Routledge.

Mossberg, L. (2007) A marketing approach to the tourist experience. *Scandinavian Journal of Hospitality and Tourism*, 7(1), 59–74.

Normann, R. (2001) *Reframing Business: When the Map Changes the Landscape*. Hoboken: John Wiley & Sons.

Payne, A. F., Storbacka, K. and Frow, P. (2008) Managing the co-creation of value. *Journal of the Academy of Marketing Science*, 36(1), 83–96.

Peteraf, M. A. (1993). The cornerstones of competitive advantage: A resource-based view. *Strategic Management Journal*, 14(3), 179–191.

Plé, L. and Cáceres, R. C. (2010) Not always co-creation: Introducing interactional co-destruction of value in service-dominant logic. *Journal of Services Marketing*, 24(6), 430–437.

Prahalad, C. K. and Ramaswamy, V. (2004) Co-creation experiences: The next practice in value creation. *Journal of Interactive Marketing*, 18(3), 5–14.

Prebensen, N. K. and Foss, L. (2011) Coping and co-creating in tourist experiences. *International Journal of Tourism Research*, 13(1), 54–67.

575

Prebensen, N. K., Uysal, M. S. and Chen, J. S. (2018) Perspectives on value creation: Resource configuration. In N. K. Prebensen, J. S. Chen and M. S. Uysal (Eds.), *Experience Value in Tourism*. Wallingford: CABI, pp. 228–237.

Prebensen, N. K., Vittersø, J. and Dahl, T. I. (2013) Value co-creation significance of tourist resources. *Annals of Tourism Research*, 42, 240–261.

Prebensen, N. K., Woo, E. and Uysal, M. (2014) Experience value: Antecedents and consequences. *Current Issues in Tourism*, 17(10), 910–928.

Prebensen, N. K., Woo, E., Chen, J. S. and Uysal, M. (2014) Motivation and involvement as antecedents of the perceived value of the destination experience. *Journal of Travel Research*, 52(2), 253–264.

Prebensen, N. K. and Xie, J. (2017) Efficacy of co-creation and mastering on perceived value and satisfaction in tourists' consumption. *Tourism Management*, 60, 166–176.

Price, L. L., Arnould, E. J. and Malshe, A. (2006) Toward a cultural resource-based theory of the customer. In R. F. Lusch and S. L. Vargo (Eds.), *The New Service-Dominant Logic in Marketing*. Armonk: ME Sharpe, pp. 91–104.

Salvioni, D. (2016) Hotel chains and the sharing economy in global tourism. *Symphonya: Emerging Issues in Management*, 1, 31–44.

Sandström, S., Edvardsson, B., Kristensson, P. and Magnusson, P. (2008) Value in use through service experience. *Managing Service Quality: An International Journal*, 18(2), 112–126.

Sheth, J. N., Newman, B. I. and Gross, B. (1990) *Why We Buy What We Buy: A Theory of Consumption Values*. Cincinnati: South-Western Publishing Co.

Sweeney, J. C. and Soutar, G. N. (2001) Consumer perceived value: The development of a multiple item scale. *Journal of Retailing*, 77(2), 203–220.

Uysal, M., Berbekova, A. and Kim, H. (2020) Designing for quality of life. *Annals of Tourism Research*, 83, 102944.

Uysal, M., Harrill, R. and Woo, E. (2011) Destination marketing research: Issues and challenges. In Y. Wang and A.Pizam (Eds.), *Destination Marketing and Management: Theories and Applications*. Wallingford: CABI, pp. 99–112.

Vargo, S. L. and Lusch, R. F. (2004) Evolving to a new dominant logic for marketing. *Journal of Marketing*, 68(1), 1–17.

Vargo, S. L. and Lusch, R. F. (2008) Service-dominant logic: Continuing the evolution. *Journal of the Academy of Marketing Science*, 36(1), 1–10.

Vargo, S. L. and Lusch, R. F. (2010) From repeat patronage to value co-creation in service ecosystems: A transcending conceptualization of relationship. *Journal of Business Market Management*, 4(4), 169–179.

Vargo, S.L. and Lusch, R. F. (2016) Institutions and axioms: An extension and update of service-dominant logic. *Journal of the Academy of marketing Science*, 44(1), 5–23.

Williams, P. and Soutar, G. N. (2009) Value, satisfaction and behavioral intentions in an adventure tourism context. *Annals of Tourism Research*, 36(3), 413–438.

Woodruff, R. (1997) Customer value: The next source for competitive advantage. *Journal of the Academy of Marketing Science*, 25, 139–153.

Zeithaml, V. A., Berry, L. L. and Parasuraman, A. (1988) SERVQUAL: A multiple-item scale for measuring consumer perceptions of service quality. *Journal of Retailing*, 64(1), 12–40.

41

PLACE-BASED EDUCATION, CEMETERY VISITATION AND THE TOURIST EXPERIENCE

Siow-Kian Tan and Siow-Hooi Tan

Introduction

Any place, though especially a World Heritage Site (WHS), may mean different things to different stakeholders. For the local community, it is a place in which to live and work; for tourists, it is a place to visit and revisit. And to sustain itself, a WHS should retain its heritage status while attracting visitors, fundamental to which is the concept of place attachment. Place attachment is vital not only for the local community for whom the place is home; it is also important for tourists to feel attached to a place.

Place attachment or, alternatively, sense of place, can be understood or considered from several perspectives. It can, for example, be seen as place dependency and place identity (Williams & Vaske, 2003) or it might be considered to consist of affective, cognitive and behavioural dimensions that will motivate people to do something to sustain the heritage (Tan, Tan, Kok & Choon, 2018). In general, it is a bond or link between people and place (Hidalgo et al., 2001; Scannell & Gifford, 2010).

Place-based education (PBE) has been seen as 'education in a community' (Newmann & Oliver, 1967). Its purpose is to enhance a sense of place amongst both learners and instructors, to emphasize enculturation and human development with the welfare of community life and to promote local ecological and cultural sustainability over competitiveness and resource exploitation (Gruenewald & Smith, 2014; Rodriguez, 2008; Semken & Freeman, 2008; Smith & Sobel, 2010; Sobel, 2004). As place-based education is vital for sustaining cultural heritage, Tan and Tan (2020) propose a place-based approach for nurturing a sense of place amongst local people at a WHS. The ontological construct of place, which consists of place as visual attributes, place as a product, place as a process and place as meanings (Arefi & Triantafillou, 2005; Sun, Chan & Chen, 2016) has been used as an underpinning theory to develop the above-mentioned framework.

The facilitation of tourists developing a sense of attachment can be achieved through either educational tours or tour-guiding learning. Nevertheless, Nairn (2005: 301) argues that 'direct experiences' in an educational tour may help the participants to 'reproduce, rather than contest, existing ideological systems' and, therefore, create psychological distance from the local events and populations that they encounter during the tour. In other words, educational tours could end up maintaining, rather than narrowing, the epistemological

DOI: 10.4324/9781003219866-47

distance between the learner-tourists and the people and events at their destination (Suzuki, 2016). That is to say, contemporary educational tours or tour-guiding learning may not be able to contribute to the tourist experience by enhancing their sense of place towards the destination.

Using the ontological construct of place (Arefi & Triantafillou, 2005; Sun et al., 2016) and the five dimensions of place-based education framework (Tan & Tan, 2020), this chapter aims to discuss ways of enhancing the tourist experience through tour-guiding learning that emphasizes the place-based content for a better engagement with a place. It is based on research undertaken at Bukit China, the oldest traditional Chinese cemetery (Cartier, 1993; MCAH, 2011) in the world located in Melaka, a UNESCO WHS in Malaysia. Cemeteries may reveal the history of a place. Certainly, in Western countries, the presence of graves, monuments and consecrated buildings contributes to the perception of cemeteries as historically and culturally valuable places (Nordh, Evensen & Skår, 2017). Moreover, this combination of history, culture and nature enhances the attraction of cemeteries as places for tourists to visit and explore. Consequently, cemetery tourism is a well-established activity, particularly in Europe and the United States (Del Lama, 2018). It has been categorized as a light-type of 'dark tourism' (Fonseca, Seabra & Silva, 2016). The motives of visiting cemeteries are varied, and include the desire to be in a peaceful environment or an interest in seeing the graves of famous people. For example, the Père Lachaise cemetery in Paris is one of the most famous cemeteries in the world, where renowned personalities of the music scene, such as Jim Morison, Edith Piaf and Frédéric Chopin, poets, including Honoré de Balzac, Oscar Wilde and Marcel Proust, and artists and sculptors, such as Eugène Delacroix and Maz Ernst, are buried (Fonseca et al., 2016).

When visiting such cemeteries where well-known people are interred, the visitor experience may be enhanced by opportunities to learn more about the people whose graves tourists gaze upon. Indeed, this is undoubtedly one of the reasons that an increasing number of guided tours are nowadays being organized to visit cemeteries. However, most of these 'popular' cemeteries are those where notable, famous or, perhaps, infamous people are buried, and where tourists purposely visit to pay respect to these personalities. In contrast, there is relatively little understanding of cemeteries as a whole as tourist attractions and, in particular, how the visitor experience may be enhanced through promoting or encouraging sense of place. In addition, in Eastern countries, and especially in Chinese society, cemeteries have always been associated with death and the inauspicious, with people typically visiting a cemetery once or twice a year for certain occasions, such as burial ceremonies, or during Qing Ming ('Tomb Sweeping Day') when they visit to pray to their ancestors and make ritual offerings. Nevertheless, old cemeteries contain numerous histories related to place, yet people seldom perceive a cemetery as a resource that can be utilized to nurture a sense of place and enhance the tourist experience. Hence, the study discussed in the sections below seek to address this gap in knowledge, in particular exploring the following questions: (i) What are the elements of a cemetery that can be used in tour-guiding learning? And (ii), how might these elements be utilized to enhance the tourist experience?

The context of the study – Bukit China, Melaka, Malaysia

Located in the heart of Melaka City, the Chinese cemetery on Bukit China is probably the world's oldest remaining traditional Chinese burial ground in the world (Cartier, 1993). Sprawling over 42 hectares of undulating terrain along the southeastern fringe of the central city, it contains more than 12,500 traditional graves, including some 60 graves of Muslims,

Place-based education

probably Acehnese leaders, the majority with unknown identities (Cartier, 1993; MCAH, 2011; T. K. Wong, 2016).

'Bukit China', which translates from Malay as 'China Hill, actually consists of three hills, namely: China Hill, Tempurung Hill and Gedong Hill. 'Bukit China' was originally known as 'Bukit Tinggi' dating back to the time of the ancient Melaka dynasty. It was later named Bukit China owing to a legendary marriage between the sixth Malaccan Sultan, Mansur Shah and a princess of Ming Dynasty named Hang Li-Po. Although the authenticity of this legendary marriage remains unascertained, it was mentioned in the 'Sejarah Melayu', or 'The Malay Annals'[1] (T. K. Wong, 2016). In 1685, the second Chinese Kapitan (Captain) Li Wei Jing bought the hill(s) from the Dutch government and dedicated them to the Chinese community for the burial purposes. He then handed over the management of the land to the Cheng Hoon Teng Temple (MCAH, 2011, 2014). However, when Bukit China was first used as a burial site remains unknown. The earliest tombs that have been identified were dated 1614 and 1622 (W.-B. Wong, 2013).

Chinese cemeteries in Malaysia, especially Bukit China, have faced several challenges over the years owing to development. During the middle of British colonial era in the nineteenth century, Bukit China was approximately twice its current size. However, colonial road building halted the expansion of the burial area and effectively marked the current boundaries of the cemetery (Cartier, 1993). Later, in 1984, the Melaka state government announced an urban development plan that would transform Bukit China into residential condominiums, retail and office space (TheStar, 1984). Perhaps inevitably, this development proposal led to a politically inflamed debate in Melaka city and the wider state and, finally, combined pressure from political and community groups successfully led to the area retaining its status as a cemetery. It was later transformed into an historic open space (Cartier, 1993).

Nevertheless, as time has passed by, the importance of this history had not been told. Not only was Bukit China abandoned by local people, as few are happy to use it as a public space for walking or jogging, but also even the Chinese community itself ignored it, with some leaders perceiving it to be an 'inauspicious' place (MCAH, 2014). To challenge this negative image, some individuals, especially Lye Phat Chin, along with the Melaka Chinese Assembly Hall (MCAH) Youth Section took the initiative to collect data, create a cultural map, organize an annual cultural event and, since 2007, organize guided tours to visit the cemetery (MCAH, 2011, 2014).

The number of visitors who register on these tours has remained quite stable since then, although the overall audience for the tours is limited. Two reasons can be suggested for this. First, the guided tours around Bukit China are led by committee members of MCAH, a non-government organization (NGO), and they do so on a voluntary basis. Hence, they can only guide tours when there is request from a group, and during certain periods, such as school holidays, public holidays or weekends. Second, the majority of the participants are Chinese as it is a Chinese cemetery; although it 'witnessed' the history and development of Melaka, the state government seldom links Bukit China to the history of the area.

Method

In-depth interviews were conducted with a guide who initiated the fieldwork and data collection of Bukit China, and with members of the NGO committee that organizes and leads the guided tours of the site. In addition, the authors participated in a guided tour to Bukit China and relevant documentation, such as books, maps and literature, was accessed.

Given that the aim of the study was to explore how the tourist experience could be enhanced though tour-guided learning that emphasizes place-based content, the dimensions of place (Arefi & Triantafillou, 2005; Sun et al., 2016; Tan & Tan, 2020) were used as a guideline for the interview and data analysis. Eight documents, which included three interview transcripts (labelled as I1–I3), a guided tour observation (labelled as T1), a book, a cultural map and four articles (labelled as D1–D4) were used for content analysis. The documents were read and re-read several times to have a clearer idea about the overall picture of Bukit China and other related issues, and for an understanding of place-based themes.

Findings

Firstly, place-related concepts were extracted from the documents using open coding. From this, a total of 26 concepts emerged. Subsequently, these 26 concepts were grouped under 12 subthemes using axial coding and, lastly, these subthemes were categorized under five main themes using selective coding, as shown in Table 41.1.

Table 41.1 Concepts, subthemes and themes of a cemetery tour

Concepts (open coding)	Subthemes (axial coding)	Themes (selective coding)
• Individual/Family	Forms	Visual attributes
• Kongsi/clan association		
• Material used	Design-related	
• Structure – Tombstone; Tomb shoulder; Tomb hand; Altar table; Grave courtyard; Tomb mound; Tomb rear shore; 'Hou-tu' (God-of-earth); Stone sculpture; Tomb pavilion		
• Shapes – gable end: Earth; Fire; Wood; Water; Metal		
• Epitaph		
• A resting place	Burial site	Functions
• Common grave and Spiritual		
• Leisure activity	Public space	
• Cultural event		
• Flora	Ecosystem habitat	
• Fauna		
• Pre-Kapitan period	History	Process (restructuring through time)
• Kapitan period		
• Urban development	Obliterations	
• Death and inauspicious		
• Cultural heritage	Revive	
• Community development		
• Socio-cultural	People	Meanings
• Heritage/Feng-Shui		
• Development	Government/ local authority	
• Preservation		
• Other places	Spatial	Critical reflexivity
• Different background		
• Past	Temporal	
• Future		

Place-based education

Theme 1: visual attributes – form, designs

Visual attributes are something that can be seen and observed, and can be used to trigger the curiosity of visitors. Six concepts (individual/family tomb, kongsi/clan association, material used, structure, shapes and epitaph) have been categorized into two subthemes (forms and design-related) under this theme. There are two 'forms' of tombs: (i) 'individual/family tombs; and, (ii) kongsi/clan association'.

'Individual/family tombs' are the most common type of graves, either individual or husband and wife, or husband and wives, or family tombs. In a feudal society, it was common for men, especially those who were rich, to marry several wives, sometimes because of succession issues. These Chinese immigrants stayed and died in Melaka without going back to their homeland, either because of wars or conflicts occurring at that time or because they had already settled in Melaka and perceived this place as their home. In contrast, 'kongsi/clan association' tell another part of Malaccan history. Generally, Chinese cemeteries had common graves belonging to different kongsi/clan associations. These clan associations were established to assist their clan people who migrated and worked in this new land. The common graves are for remembrance of the clan's spirit and clan people without family/identity.

There are four 'design-related' characteristics of the tombs, of which (i) 'materials used; (ii) structure; (iii) shapes; and, (iv) epitaph' may tell some interesting stories. With regard to materials used, one interviewee explained:

> When you walk up to the hill from the entrance behind the primary school, you will see some dark red brownish color tombs. The material is the same as what you can see at the ancient fortress such as the A'Famosa, that's laterite rock. They get the laterite rock from an island nearby called Pulau Upeh. This rock is rich in iron, it is soft when immersed in sea water and therefore it's easy to cut and transport from the island to the inland. When it's exposed to the air, it becomes hard and solid.
>
> *(I2)*

The 'structure' of the tomb includes the tombstone, tomb shoulder, grave courtyard, tomb mound, tomb rear shore, stone sculpture and tomb pavilion. Additionally, a typical Chinese tomb will have a 'Hou-Tu' or God-of-earth beside the tomb. This is to protect the owners and their successions. '"Hou-tu" is at the left side of the Cantonese's tomb, while it is located at the right side of the tomb of a Hokkien' (MCAH, 2011).

> The tomb mound always looks like a turtle's shell as the Chinese believe that the turtle is the guardian of the tomb.
>
> *(T1)*

The 'shapes' of the tomb represent the five elements of 'Yin-Yang'; these shapes can also be found in the upper part of some heritage buildings at the old town. 'The square-ish end represents Earth, the spiky end represents Fire, the wavy end represents Water, the upright end represents Wood, and the rounded end represents Metal.' (MCAH, 2011). Visual attributes are important, as the visitors will first be attracted to what they see, and this will enhance the cognitive components of their sense of place.

Theme 2: functions – burial site, public space, ecosystem habitat

Six concepts (a place to rest, common grave, leisure activity, event, flora and fauna) were categorized into three subthemes (burial site, public space and ecosystem habitat) under the second theme – functions. In other words, a cemetery is not just for burial purposes but also serves as a public space/park and a habitat within the ecosystem.

There are two concepts under 'burial site': (i) it is 'a place to rest' permanently for those who had settled down here and (ii) a 'common grave' for those without identity or family, or as a symbolic sign to represent the spirit of the clan.

> No one knows when Bukit China was first used as a burial ground. A stone inscription set up in 1795 by the monk Kunshan, mentions that at the time the Baoshan ting, or funerary temple was established at the foot of the Bukit China Cemetery, there were already many graves on the hill.
>
> *(D1)*

> The common grave of Eng Chun (a clan of Hokkien) Kongsi is located at the top of this hill. It is not for burial purposes, but for placing the things that represent the clan's spirit, such as the five grains."
>
> *(D2)*

Under the second subtheme – 'public space' – there are two concepts: (i) 'leisure activities and (ii) event gathering point':

> It's a place where you can walk and jog, but it's better for you to come with friends as this place is really quiet.
>
> *(I2)*

It is also the venue and gathering point for annual cultural events, such as the Chinese cultural event known as the 'Climbing three hills on the Ninth day of the Ninth month'.

> In ancient China, on the Ninth day of the Ninth month of Chinese Lunar Calendar, people climb the hill to enjoy the scenery and good weather. According to this tradition, the purpose of this day is to celebrate the harvest and to ward off evil. 'In Malaysia, we seldom celebrate this festival. However, starting 2007, we organized this event here. We chose this event as according to tradition, people go for climbing and hiking on this day.'
>
> *(I2).*

In addition, the cemetery area is an 'ecosystem habitat' for flora and fauna.

> This is the pong pong tree. Although the fruit looks delicious, you cannot eat it. Some people squeeze its juice for poisoning rats. There, another plant, it's what we call neem. You can boil its leaf in water, and the water can be used to relieve itching.
>
> *(I1)*

> You can see dusky leaf monkey here; it is a very cute-looking monkey. In addition, you will be able to see several types of frog and a variety of birds.
>
> *(I2)*

Place-based education

In conclusion, the second theme – the functions of the cemetery – might also be able to enhance the tourist experience by accumulating the cognitive components of sense of place.

Theme 3: process and development – history, obliterations, revive

As the cemetery existed centuries ago, it witnessed the development of Melaka. Six concepts (pre-Kapitan period, Kapitan period, urban development, death and inauspicious, cultural heritage and community development) emerged from the analysis and were then categorized into three subthemes (history, obliterations and revival) under the third theme.

Two concepts emerged under 'history': (i) 'pre-Kapitan period and (ii) Kapitan period'.

> The earliest tomb that has been identified dates back to 1614, another was dated in 1622. That time was Ming Dynasty in China. These ancient tombs show that four hundred years ago, the Chinese were already here in Malaya.
>
> *(I2)*

> There were some Muslims' tombs there at Bukit Gedong. These tombs dated back to 16th 17th centuries. That was during the Portuguese occupation.
>
> *(T1)*

There are two concepts – (i) 'urban development and (ii) death and inauspicious' emerged under the second subtheme – 'obliterations':

> Before the 1980s, Bukit China was a very desolate place. The thatch and weedy morass was overgrown, and could be up to an adult's waist level. Normally people wouldn't visit there other than for the 'Qing-Ming' festival.
>
> *(I3)*

> In 1984, the state government wanted to level down the hills for commercial purposes. Some Chinese leaders were against the proposal, however, and led the community to protect, preserve and beautify the cemetery.
>
> *(I2)*

This incident in 1980s led to a politically inflamed debate in Melaka city and state. Subsequently, however, the area was transformed into an open space for people to jog and for leisure activities.

> In 1989, Melaka Chinese community organized the 6th Chinese Cultural Festival, the 'cultural torch/flame' which lit up the hilltop. Since then, the festival commences from the top of Bukit China no matter which state organizing the event.
>
> *(T1)*

However, two decades later, conflicts began within the Chinese association itself.

> Later in the 2000s, within our own association, some committee members had some arguments amongst themselves. Some said that the cemetery represents death and the inauspicious, hence, cultural events should not be organized there. Others even argued, this was the reason that cultural event was not able to attract youngsters.
>
> *(I2).*

Two concepts that include (i) 'cultural heritage and (ii) community development' were emerged under the third subtheme – 'revival'. The next 'preservation movement' started in 2007, when the youths of the Melaka Chinese Assembly Hall became conscious about the importance of reviving their cultural heritage:

> The Chinese have the perception that when we go to a cemetery, we should not wear bright colours, as the cemetery is inauspicious. We wanted to change this perception. Therefore, we used red as the colour of our T-shirts (for cultural activities), we wished to change the old mindset. This cemetery is the resting place of our ancestors; we should appreciate their contributions to our place here, we should be thankful and respectful. Only through this are we able to tell our youngster the stories of our ancestors.
>
> *(I2)*

The third theme – process and development of Bukit China, refers to not only enhancing the cognitive component, for instance, knowledge about the place, but also awakening a sense of loss, sense of justice and sense of mission among the participants.

Theme 4: meanings – people, government/local authority

Four concepts (socio-cultural, heritage, development and preservation) were categorized into two subthemes (people and government/local authority) under the fourth theme. Two concepts, (i) 'socio-cultural and (ii) heritage' emerged under 'people'.

From the Chinese perspective, the cemetery carries many meanings in addition to just being a burial site. It is a memorable place, especially from a historical perspective:

> Bukit China is not only meant for Melaka's Chinese, but also for the Chinese community of Malaysia, as it showed the historical trails of our ancestors.
>
> *(I2)*

It also shows the differences between an Eastern and Western perspective. It challenges the Westerner's perception of a cemetery, as thousands of tombs were not orderly arranged but positioned according to a belief in 'feng-shui' (Cartier, 1993). Moreover, as there are also some Muslim Acehnese tombs on the hill, it was seen as a harmonious place where people of different ethnic origins rest together forever and peacefully.

> Although it's called Bukit China, it's not just a resting place for Chinese. There were also quite a number of Muslim tombs there. It's meant for everyone in this land.
>
> *(I1)*

Two concepts, which include (i) 'development and (ii) preservation' emerged under 'government/local authority' sub-theme. After the development controversy in 1984 had been resolved, the state government recognized the significance of Bukit China (Cartier, 1993).

> The government later recognized its status and began promoting this as one of the tourist spots of Melaka. Therefore, sometimes you will see some foreign tourists visit this place.
>
> *(I1)*

Place-based education

The tomb of Panglima Pidi, an Acehnese Warrior, can bring you back to the Portuguese occupation period, as this warrior and his comrades helped to free Melaka from foreign occupation. Later, in the 17th century, many Chinese migrated here to earn their living, and the ancient Chinese tombs tell the story of Chinese immigrants.

(I3)

In 2008, Melaka city and George Town Penang were declared UNESCO World Heritage Site (WHS). Bukit China was classified as the buffer zone of Melaka WHS. This inscription seems to be 'protecting' Bukit China from being developed; however, if no one is keen to know its story, this effort will become meaningless.

The fourth theme – meanings – should include different perspectives, as people do not live in isolation. That is, over time, people migrated from their homelands to seek better living. In that process, they interacted with each other and these interactions generated different socio-cultural practices and heritages. These 'outcomes' should be told and understood. Not only that, the authorities' perspective should be conveyed as well as these stakeholders often have contradictory opinions reflecting conflicts of interest.

This theme not only enhances the cognitive component but, more importantly, emphasizes a sense of loss and a sense of justice of visitors, especially when conflicts such as the issue of development emerge, encouraging them to consider what can be done.

Theme 5: critical reflexivity – spatial, temporal

Four concepts (other places, different background, past and future) were categorized into two subthemes (spatial and temporal) under the fifth theme. Two concepts: (i) 'other places, and, (ii) different background' emerged under 'spatial':

Bukit China can be transformed into an open learning center, to educate the community about the history of their place, especially the relationship with China, the homeland of Chinese ancestors.

(D4)

It is not just a burial ground, it's a cultural and creativity incubator center. The challenge here is, how are we going to transform the cultural activities into something that might attract people from different backgrounds to join and know about us?

(D4)

Wars or social conflicts caused many people to migrate to other places. Slowly, this migration shaped and reshaped to form the current social demographic. Although people originate from different places, many came to perceive this place as their hometown. No one 'owns' or is 'owned by' a place.

Two concepts, namely (i) 'past' and (ii) future' emerged under the 'temporal' sub-theme. There are more than 12,500 graves at Bukit China, the size/scale of which varies significantly. However, what is evident is that, irrespective of the size of a grave, everyone ended up with a small resting place, as shown in an epitaph beneath the altar of a grave:

We have a meaningful epitaph here: 'Passers-by, stop and see! What I was, you are now. What I am, you shall be.' The deceased is telling us that everyone will die, why should we pursue so many unnecessary things in our live'.

(T1)

We seldom think about our past, where are we from, why are we here. It's time for us to find out the answer. When you get to know about your own self, you will be more appreciative of what you have now.

(I3)

Our mindset should not stop at 30 years ago. We have to move forward. What can be done to enhance the sense of community, self-esteem and self-pride?

(D4)

The fifth theme – critical reflexivity – emphasizes the behavioural component, which is the sense of mission of the participants. Actions have to be taken to make changes to ourselves, place, community or society. Visitors are therefore encouraged to engage in self-reflection throughout the visiting process. This is important as without interaction with the 'inner-self', the information will not remain long in their memories. In addition, without 'touching' the senses, visitors will not feel 'attached' to the place, and will not be motivated to 'do something'.

Conclusion

The study discussed in the chapter aimed to identify how to enhance the visitor experience by tour-guiding learning that emphasizes the place-based content for a better engagement with a place. Hence, the elements of a place that could be used as guidelines for a guided tour, for engaging and enhancing visitors experience in a WHS, were identified. A total of 26 concepts and 12 subthemes that were categorized under five themes were emerged from the data. These themes can be used as guidelines for a cemetery to generate a better understanding a place and to enhance the visitor experience.

Nevertheless, although a cemetery such as Bukit China might be used to nurture tourists' sense of place and enhance their experience, not all cemeteries are rich in history and culture. At the same time, tour-guiding learning may be more about enhancing local tourists' sense of place rather than that of international tourists, as local people will feel more engaged and attached to a place such as Bukit China than foreigners. Furthermore, not all tourists are willing to learn about a place through visiting a cemetery, especially in Eastern countries. In addition, not only do local tour guides have to be trained to provide proper explanations about a place; other stakeholders, such as local authority, should also play a role. Nevertheless, the brief study discussed here has indicated how particular elements of a WHS (in this case, a cemetery) can be harnessed in the design and delivery of a guided-learning tourism to promote a sense of place amongst tourists and thereby enhance their experiences.

Note

1 Sejarah Melayu or Malay Annals, also known as Sulalatus Salatin (Genealogy of Kings), is the literary and historical work on the history of the Malaccan sultanate.

References

Arefi, M. and Triantafillou, M. (2005) Reflections on the pedagogy of place in planning and urban design. *Journal of Planning Education and Research*, 25(1), 75–88.

Cartier, C. L. (1993) Creating historic open space in Melaka. *Geographical Review*, 83(4), 359–373.

Place-based education

Del Lama, E. A. (2018) Potential for urban geotourism: Churches and cemeteries. *Geoheritage*, 11(3), 717–728.

Fonseca, A. P., Seabra, C. and Silva, C. (2016) Dark tourism: Concepts, typologies and sites. *Journal of Tourism Research and Hospitality*, S2(002), 1–6.

Gruenewald, D. A. and Smith, G. A. (2014) Introduction: Making room for the local. In D. A. Gruenewald and G. A. Smith (Eds.), *Place-Based Education in the Global Age: Local Diversity* New York/London: Psychology Press, pp. xiii–xxiii.

Hidalgo, M. C., Hernandez, B. and Hidalgo MC, H. B. (2001) Place attachment: Conceptual and empirical questions. *Journal of Environmental Psychology*, 21, 271–281.

MCAH (2011) *Community of Bukit China and Bukit China – Cultural Map*. Melaka Chinese Assembly Hall Youth Section.

MCAH. (2014) *Cultural Map of Historical Malacca*. Melaka Chinese Assembly Hall Youth Section.

Nairn, K. (2005) The problems of utilizing "direct experience" in geography education. *Journal of Geography in Higher Education*, 29(2), 293–309.

Newmann, F. M. and Oliver, D. W. (1967) Education and community. *Harvard Educational Review*, 37(1), 61–106.

Nordh, H., Evensen, K. H. and Skår, M. (2017) A peaceful place in the city—A qualitative study of restorative components of the cemetery. *Landscape and Urban Planning*, 167(May), 108–117.

Rodriguez, A. (2008) *The Multiple Faces of Agency: Innovative Strategies for Effecting Change in Urban School Contexts*. Rotterdam: Sense Publishers.

Scannell, L. and Gifford, R. (2010) Defining place attachment: A tripartite organizing framework. *Journal of Environmental Psychology*, 30(1), 1–10.

Semken, S. and Freeman, C. B. (2008) Sense of place in the practice and assessment of place-based science teaching. *Science Education*, 92(6), 1042–1057.

Smith, G. and Sobel, D. (2010) *Place and Community-Based Education in Schools*. London: Routledge.

Sobel, D. (2004) *Place-Based Education: Connecting Classrooms & Communities*. Great Barrington: Orion Society.

The Star (1984) Why did the govt choose this land? *The Star*, 18 July.

Sun, Y., Chan, R. C. K., and Chen, H. (2016). Learning with geographical sensitivity: Place-based education and its praxis. *Professional Geographer*, 68(4), 574–583.

Suzuki, T. (2016) Bridging between 'here/now' and 'there/then': Guiding Japanese mainland school 'peace education' tours in Okinawa. *Journal of Cultural Geography*, 33(1), 100–125.

Tan, S.-K. and Tan, S.-H. (2020) Clan/geographical association heritage as a place-based approach for nurturing the sense of place for locals at a World Heritage Site. *Journal of Hospitality and Tourism Management*, 45, 592–603.

Tan, S. K., Tan, S. H., Kok, Y. S., and Choon, S. W. (2018) Sense of place and sustainability of intangible cultural heritage - the case of George Town and Melaka. *Tourism Management*, 67, 376–387.

Williams, D. R., and Vaske, J. J. (2003) The measurement of place attachment: Validity and generalizability of a psychometric approach. *Forest Science*, 49(6), 830–840.

Wong, T. K. (2016) Early Chinese presence in Malaysia as reflected by three cemeteries (17th–19th c.). *Archipel*, 92, 9–21.

Wong, W.-B. (2013) *A Collection of Tombstone Inscriptions of Bukit China, Malacca (1614–1820)* 馬六甲三寶山墓碑輯錄. Malaysian Chinese Research Centre.

42

SERVICE EXPERIENCES AND INNOVATION IN THE HOSPITALITY INDUSTRY

Thais González-Torres, Eva Pelechano-Barahona and Fernando E. García-Muiña

Introduction

The increasing demand for unique and memorable experiences is requiring tourism firms to develop distinct value-added provisions for products and services (Chang, 2018). The marketing literature provides a rich body of knowledge on the key attributes fundamental to the design service experiences capable of satisfying customers in the tourism industry. This helps us answer the question: what factors are needed to provide service experiences? (e.g. Hosany & Witham, 2010; Le Bel, 2005). However, the analysis of the relationship between service attributes and their impact on customer satisfaction is insufficient to enhance our understanding of how firms can design and manage service experiences.

Traditional and current research considers the tourism industry as a mere technology adopter as well as a 'non-knowledge-intensive service', which has led to an underestimation of its innovative potential. However, from a management perspective, innovating on the attributes of the service experience can make tourism experiences memorable, as well as improve business performance. Innovation is a crucial mechanism to gain competitive advantage and create value by transforming services into more compelling and unique experiences to exceed guests' expectations (Chandralal &Valenzuela, 2015; Ottenbacher & Gnoth, 2005). Thus, the need to adapt to the changing tourist environment points to innovation as an essential condition not only to succeed, but also to survive (Gomezelj, 2016).

With a few exceptions (e.g. Martín-Rios & Ciobanu, 2019), research on innovation in the hospitality industry is still scarce, especially in terms of empirical results (Gomezelj, 2016). Innovation is a differentiating factor capable of generating competitive advantage and economic returns by improving quality and reputation, reducing service costs and increasing productivity and efficacy (Hernández-Perlines, Ariza-Montes, Han & Law, 2019; Tang, Wang & Tang, 2015). Focusing collectively on these issues can help us answer the question: how can firms design service experiences and improve their performance?

The literature on the experience economy suggest that, in service experiences, innovation takes place in four distinct design areas: (i) the physical environment (product innovation); (ii) the service delivery process (process innovation); (iii) back office support (organizational innovation); and (iv), marketing activities (marketing innovations) (Stamboulis & Skayannis, 2003; Voss & Zomerdijk, 2007). Given the lack of research addressing these issues in

588

DOI: 10.4324/9781003219866-48

Service experiences and innovation

tourism, the main objective of this chapter is to better understand the multidimensional nature of innovation in the experiences of services provided by hospitality companies. To do so, and following a review of the relevant literature, a statistical analysis of the EU's Community Innovation Survey is presented. Based on an Exploratory Factor Analysis (EFA) of 1913 enterprises in NACE-2009 classification Sector I (Accommodation and food service activities), two major contributions are made:

i   the identification of and relationship between innovation areas and service experience attributes.
ii the identification of the dimensions of innovative service experiences in the hospitality industry: marketing, organizational and the combined component service-process innovation.

The chapter is structured as follows. The following section deals with the theoretical framework proposed to approach the service experience and innovation in the hospitality industry. The third and fourth sections then describe the research methodology and results and, finally, the fifth section presents the discussion, conclusions, limitations and areas for future research.

Theoretical framework: the service experience in the tourism and hospitality industries

Recent literature reveals that the tourism and hospitality industry is currently facing various economic trends that are particularly challenging. An important trend is that clients no longer buy products; rather, they buy benefits and experiences that goods and services provide for them (Io, 2017; Pikkemaat & Zehrer, 2016). This implies that customer satisfaction not only comes from the basic functional qualities of the product, but also from its emotional dimensions such as security, happiness or social acceptance (Berry, Carbone & Haeckel, 2002). More specifically, the marketing literature describes the experience as a key motivator of consumption. Numerous authors associate it with customer satisfaction, image, loyalty and word-of-mouth communication (e.g. Jain, Aagja & Bagdare, 2017; Vasconcelos, Barichello, Lezana, Forcellini, Ferreira & Cauchick Miguel, 2015). In addition, the experience can also be presented as a strategic success factor for business given that it comprises both functional characteristics and customer emotions, representing an effective tool for differentiation, the generation of sustainable competitive advantage and the creation of value (Chang, 2018; Eide, Fuglsang & Sundbo, 2017; Kandampully, Zhang & Jaakkola, 2018; Zehrer, 2009).

Research in tourism has mainly addressed the notion of experience based on detailed descriptions of a great heterogeneity of attributes that can be related both to the characteristics of the service and to the emotions or feelings of the customer. These factors can also be of a physical or non-physical nature (e.g. Hosany & Witham, 2010; Le Bel, 2005) (see Table 42.1). Firms must focus on these areas to connect with the customer and generate the experience, thus leading to outcomes such as satisfaction, loyalty, word of mouth and revisiting intention (Helkkula, 2011; Klaus & Maklan, 2012).

Regarding the characteristics of the service, diverse authors suggest that service providers can enhance memorable and authentic tourist experiences by focusing on the physical evidence – location, rooms, bathrooms, parking space, architectural design, furniture, signage and variety of tourism offerings, among others. Websites and social media are also

Table *42.1* Service experience attributes in tourism research

Attribute nature	Associated with service characteristics	Associated with customer emotions or sensations
Physical	Location (appealing, convenient); Physical evidence (furniture, signage, attractive architectural design, ambience, cleanliness and décor); Stay and ambience (attractive architectural design, ambience, cleanliness and décor); Means of communication (to communicate the experiential brand promise); Quality and variety of tourism offerings (entertainment, socialization, leisure activities and gaming); Website and social media experience (accurate information, online reviews, social media)	
Non-physical	Sensory experiences (smell, visual, aesthetic, etc.); Communication (information about attendance times) Procedural service (tasks and steps) Themes (dominant idea or organizing principle); Core service (meeting needs, reliability, superiority, good, quality) Servicescape (Up-to-date, attractive and suiting service type facilities, neat employees); Employee service (prompt service, willingness to help, availability, trust, transactions safety, politeness, personal attention; skills and expertise, social skills, supportiveness); Service validity (matching between customers' needs and agreed upon service specifications); Service reliability (service performance quality) Peace-of-mind (service provider's expertise); Product experience (having choices, compare offerings); Outcome focus (customers' transaction cost reduction) Price (to assess perceptions and expectations)	*Hedonic component* Hedonism (pleasure, excitement and enjoyment); Entertainment (amusement, fun); Escapism (escape from reality, forgetting daily routine, being someone else, being in a different world); Convivial service (customer´s emotions and appreciation of the service) Novelty (unique experiences) Authentic local experiences (local culture, real day-to-day life of locals); *Involvement component* Social experience-involvement (other customers, group, guide; with travel companies, service staff and other tourists); Authentic local experiences (local culture, real day-to-day life of locals); *Learning component* Education (knowledge, learning, curiosity stimulus, educational nature, skills enhancement); Self-beneficial experiences (self-confidence improvement, personal identity development, learning about him or herself, new skills acquisition) Knowledge (exploration and acquisition)

Service experiences and innovation

acknowledged as crucial elements in improving the service experience. It could be said that these attributes can help to eliminate confusion, ensure a pleasant stay and invoke feelings that stimulate positive responses to the brand (Gilmore & Pine, 2002; Io, 2017; Le Bel, 2005; So & King, 2010).

There are also nonphysical attributes associated with the characteristics of the service that can be managed to design and stage pleasurable experiences. For example, So & King (2010) consider that it is essential to develop the functional aspects of the service to meet the primary needs of customers. More specifically, Le Bel (2005) stresses the importance of focusing on procedural services or tasks and steps such as checking in customers, moving equipment, tracking and delivering baggage, and so on. Other studies highlight the significance of staff competence, especially with regard to skills and expertise, efficiency, commitment and professionalism (Chandralal & Valenzuela, 2015; Flanagan, Johnston & Talbot, 2005). In addition, price is another non-physical attribute characterizing the service that helps assess customers' quality perceptions and expectations, rather than attract them (Johnson, Lervik Olsen & Wallin Andreassen, 2009; Sathish & Venkatesakumar, 2011). In the same line of thought, Gilmore and Pine (2002) refer to themes as dominant ideas or organizing principles to create a coherent experience for guests' worthy of commanding added fees.

In addition to the service characteristics, several studies explore the relationships between customer emotions and non-physical attributes. A majority of them identifies a hedonic attribute associated with sensations such as pleasure, excitement, inspiration, enjoyment and spiritual fulfillment, among others (e.g. Pine & Gilmore; 1999; Zatori, Smith & Puczko, 2018). Customer involvement is another attribute since clients can be emotionally and mentally involved with service providers, local residents and even other guests (Flanagan et al., 2005; Khan & Rahman, 2017). Finally, there is a set of non-physical attributes associated with the customer desire to learn. This implies that the experience may include a learning experience for the guest, or that it is designed to help the guest learn something new either about the environment or about himself or herself (Hwang & Lyu, 2015; Oh, Fiore & Jeoung, 2007) (see Table 42.1).

To adapt to changing customer needs, tourism firms must shift their managerial focus from the delivery of tourism services to the provision of tourism experiences. In other words, businesses need to change their paradigm from the mere service delivery to the 'staged' experience economy focused on the creation of memorable consumption experiences (Brent Ritchie, Wing Sun Tung & Ritchie, 2011; Pikkemaat & Zehrer, 2016; Pine & Gilmore, 1999; Zehrer, 2009). When customers enjoy memorable experiences, they show more willingness to pay for the portfolio of experiences encountered during their time spent in the place. Moreover, memories lead to future transactions and repetition of purchase (Pine & Gilmore, 1999). Hence, it is particularly interesting to understand what customers perceive as memorable.

Experiences are valuable only when they are stored and remembered by customers (Pine & Gilmore, 1999; Kim, Ritchie & McCormick, 2012). Customers perceive that a service is distinctive if they can enjoy novel and unique experiences that have little in common with other events. Novelty will lead to enhanced memories about the experience (Chandralal & Valenzuela, 2015). Therefore, it could be said that innovation represents an important tool to transform services into more compelling and unique experiences, making tourists feel satisfied and engaged with the firm (Gilmore & Pine, 2002; Tang et al., 2015).

An innovative capacity to continuously renew experiences is crucial for tourism and hospitality firms to respond to or exceed customer expectations (Tang et al., 2015; Voss &

Zomerdijk, 2007). Aimed at designing and managing service experiences, firms need to be committed to the continuous identification of factors to differentiate from the typical mainstream tourism products (Chandralal & Valenzuela, 2015).

Relation between the service experience and business innovation in the tourism and hospitality industries

The latest edition of the *Oslo Manual* (OECD, 2018: 20) defines a business innovation as the introduction of 'a new or improved product or business process (or combination thereof) that differs significantly from the firm's previous products or business processes and that has been introduced on the market or brought into use by the firm'. In services, a business product innovation may include significant improvements in how they are provided (efficiency or speed), the addition of new functions or characteristics, or the introduction of entirely new services (OECD, 2005). On the other hand, business process innovations may affect a firm's core activity of producing and delivering products for sale as well as all the ancillary or supporting activities, thus including those of an organizational and marketing nature (see Table 42.2).

Consistent with these notions of innovation, the literature on the experience economy suggests that, as noted above, innovation takes place in four distinct design areas that directly or indirectly influence the customer engagement. On this basis, it is proposed that innovation in service experiences has a multidimensional nature according to the different areas of innovation: product, process, marketing and organization (see Table 42.3). The following paragraphs seek to describe the main characteristics and examples to provide a better understanding of the mechanisms to innovate in service experiences.

Product innovation is defined as 'the introduction of a good or service that is new or significantly improved with respect to its characteristics or intended uses' (OECD, 2005: 48). In services, this may include significant improvements in how they are provided (efficiency or speed), the addition of new functions or characteristics, or the introduction of entirely new services (OECD, 2005). A good example of product innovation in the hospitality industry is

Table 42.2 Business innovation dimensions and areas

Business innovation		Areas of innovation
Product		Goods or services
		New services (new functions or characteristics; provision improvements)
PROCESS	. Production	Operation processes
		Logistics, delivery or distribution methods
		Ancillary activities
	Marketing	Design or packaging
		Media or techniques for product promotion
		Methods for product placement or sales channels
		Methods of pricing
	Organization	Business practices for organizing procedures
		Methods of organizing work responsibilities and decision-making
		Methods of organizing external relations

Source: Adapted from OECD (2005, 2018).

Table 42.3 Innovation areas and service experience attributes

Type of innovation		Concept	Service experience attributes	
			Associated with service characteristics	*Associated with customer emotions or sensations*
Product		– New services – New functions or characteristics – Provision improvements	**Physical:** Facilities, equipment, room, breakfast, housekeeping, restaurant, location, variety of tourism offerings, up-to-date, attractive service facilities. **Non-physical:** Service level in reception, reliability, superiority, neat employees, cleanliness, smell, quietness, temperature, atmospherics, maintenance, external and internal visual appealing, colour combination, attractive architectural design and décor.	**Hedonism:** Customer's emotions perception, sense of harmony, pleasure, attractiveness. **Involvement:** Gentle guests, contact with local culture **Learning:** Knowledge, learning, curiosity stimulus, educational nature, skills enhancement, learning about him or herself, new skills acquisition.
Process	Production	– Changes in equipment and software – Changes in procedures or techniques – Operation processes – Logistics, delivery or distribution methods – Ancillary activities	**Tasks and steps:** Checking in customers, moving equipment and items for onboard service, tracking and delivering baggage. **Employee service and competences:** Prompt service, willingness to help, availability, trust, transactions safety, politeness, personal attention, communication, responsiveness, information provision, welcoming, helpful and friendly appearance, attentiveness, social skills, supportiveness.	–
	Marketing	– Changes product design – New sales channels – Changes in promotion – Changes in pricing strategy	Means of communication: Website and social media experience. Price: Price vs quality, price vs other hotels; price vs expectations.	Hedonism: Pleasure, excitement and enjoyment. Entertainment: Amusement, fun. Escapism: Escape from reality, forgetting daily routine, being someone else, being in a different world. Convivial service: Customer´s emotions and appreciation of the service. Novelty: Unique experience.
	Organization	– New methods in business practices – New methods in workplace organization – New methods in external relations	**Service design:** Staff empowerment to design and deliver the experience. **Systems:** Self-organizing	–

the incorporation of additional services related to wellness and health, such as workout gear in rooms and personal yoga spaces. This type of innovation is closely related to physical and non-physical attributes associated with service characteristics identified by the service experience literature. Regarding physical evidence, facilities, equipment, room, service level in reception, housekeeping and so on are the most widely recognized elements in the literature (e.g. Johnson et al., 2009; Khan & Rahman, 2017). Besides these factors, non-physical aspects, such as cleanliness and reliability, among others, are also crucial to achieve memorable experiences (Le Bel, 2005). Moreover, the objective of the introduction of new services is clearly related to the development of customer attributes associated with hedonic pleasure as well as learning desires of the experience.

Within process innovations, a production innovation refers to 'the implementation of a new or significantly improved production or delivery method' (OECD, 2005: 49), usually intended to decrease production costs, increase quality or deliver new or significantly improved products. Thus, it can involve significant changes in equipment and software or in the procedures or techniques that are employed to deliver services, including ancillary support activities, such as purchasing and accounting. As an example, the introduction of a new reservation system is a process innovation.

The literature on services experiences refers to production innovation in non-physical attributes associated with service characteristics such as tasks and steps, employee service and competences (Chandralal & Valenzuela, 2015; Zatori et al., 2018). Moreover, the process has to do with the emotional attributes of experience involvement, especially regarding interactions with service providers. On the other hand, changes in the equipment and software can also affect the service experience, especially websites and devices to connect with customers (Khan & Rahman, 2017).

In a similar vein, a marketing innovation is 'the implementation of a new marketing method involving significant changes in product design or packaging, product placement, product promotion or pricing' (OECD, 2005: 49). This type of innovation is aimed at better addressing customer needs, opening up new markets or newly positioning a firm's product on the market with the objective of increasing the firm's sales. In services industries, new marketing concepts imply significant changes in the service design while maintaining basic functionalities. In addition, marketing innovation also includes new sales channels, new promotion concepts and new pricing strategies. The introduction of revenue management systems or the introduction of a new method enabling customers to choose desired product specifications and price on the firm's website are examples of marketing innovations in tourism firms.

As already noted, the literature on services experiences has a marketing-oriented nature. We can relate to marketing innovations attributes associated with the service characteristics: means of communication, website, attractive architectural design, ambience, etc. (Khan & Rahman, 2017; Le Bel, 2005). Furthermore, marketing theory is particularly focused on customer satisfaction and, by extension, on attributes related to hedonic sensations such as pleasure, excitement and enjoyment (Hosany & Witham, 2010; Kim et al., 2012).

Finally, organizational innovation refers to 'the implementation of a new organizational method in the firm's business practices, workplace organization or external relations' (OECD, 2005: 51). This type of innovation is aimed at increasing the firm's performance by reducing administrative costs or transaction costs, improving workplace satisfaction, gaining access to non-tradable assets or reducing costs of supplies. To do so, it may involve the implementation of new methods for organizing routines and procedures, the introduction of new methods for distributing responsibilities and decision-making as well as new

Service experiences and innovation

concepts for the structuring of activities and finally, new ways of organizing relations with the stakeholders. Examples of organizational innovations are the implementation of practices for codifying knowledge like databases or practices for employee development and retention.

It seems that this organizational innovation is not directly related to the service experience given the difficulty for customers to directly perceive this kind of internal changes. Consequently, there is a lack of attributes related to organizational aspects in service experience literature. Only Nixon and Rieple (2010) refer to attributes like staff empowerment and self-organization to design and deliver memorable experience in the particular case of Ritz Carlton Hotels. Thus, from the research discussed in the following sections, it is proposed that organizational innovations may be perceived by customers since methods for organizing routines and procedures will derive in improving experience characteristics such as speed, efficiency and connection with customers (Voss & Zomerdijk, 2007).

In light of the foregoing, it is proposed that the service experience notion comprises four dimensions – product, production, marketing, organization – on which action can be taken to achieve better firm performance.

The research: method

The initial study sample is made up of 1913 companies that responded to the Community Innovation Survey (CIS) during 2008–2014. The sample comprises European companies in NACE-2009 classification (statistical classification of economic activities in the European Community) Sector I – Accommodation and Food Service Activities.

The Community Innovation Survey (CIS) is an initiative of the EU's Innovation Program and the Statistical Office of the European Communities (EUROSTAT), undertaken within the framework of the European Innovation Monitoring System (EIMS). The CIS survey uses the principles of the *Oslo Manual*, which is an international and official reference source of guidelines for the collection and use of data on innovation activities in industry (OECD, 2005). A number of studies related to innovative performance have used this survey (e.g. Cricelli, Greco & Grimaldi, 2016; Moreira, Silva, Simoes & Sousa, 2012; Teixeira & Santos, 2016). However, there are very few studies that employ CIS to analyze hospitality industries (e.g. Bečić, Črnjar and Licul, 2014; Nordli, 2017); rather, researchers usually design ad hoc questionnaires leading to cross-sectional data.

According to the *Oslo Manual* (OECD, 2005), which is the main reference guide to develop the Community Innovation Survey (CIS), innovation occurs when the firm introduces into the market new or improved products, processes, marketing methods and/or organizational methods. The Community Innovation Survey addresses the four dimensions of innovation. Thus, it provides information about the introduction in the market of new or significantly improved goods and services. Regarding production innovation, it shows if firms have introduced new or significantly improved methods of production, distribution systems or supporting activities such as maintenance systems or operations for purchasing, accounting or computing. With respect to marketing innovation, CIS addresses the introduction of significant changes to the aesthetic design, new media or techniques for product promotion, new sales channels and new methods of pricing. Finally, organizational innovation provides information about the introduction of new business practices for organizing procedures, new methods of organizing work responsibilities and decision-making and new methods of organizing external relations (see Table 42.4 for a summary)

Thais González-Torres et al.

Table 42.4 Summary of variables

Type of innovation		Variable	Description	Measure
Product		Good-	Introduction in the market of new or significantly improved goods	Quantitative
		Service	Introduction in the market of new or significantly improved services	Quantitative
Process	Production	Operations	Introduction in the market of methods of production	Quantitative
		Distribution logistics	Introduction in the market of logistic, delivery or distribution system	Quantitative
		Supporting activities	Introduction in the market of supporting activities for the processes (maintenance systems or operations for purchasing, accounting or computing)	Quantitative
	Marketing	Promotion	Introduction in the market of new media or techniques for product promotion	Quantitative
		Sales channels	Introduction in the market of new methods for product placement or sales channels	Quantitative
		Pricing	Introduction in the market of methods of pricing goods or services	Quantitative
	Organizational	Business practices	Introduction in the market of new business practices for organizing procedures	Quantitative
		Organizing work	Introduction in the market of new methods of organizing work responsibilities and decision-making	Quantitative
		External relations	Introduction in the market of new methods of organizing external relations	Quantitative

Source: Adapted from OECD (2005).

To identify the dimensions of innovative experiences in the hospitality industry, once the variables have been typified, we carried out an Exploratory Factor Analysis (EFA) (main components, varimax rotation). The main purpose of factor analysis is to reduce dimensionality of measurable and observable variables to fewer latent variables that share a common variance (Bartholomew, Knotts, & Moustaki, 2011). Accordingly, EFA has been used to regroup the variables related to the different types of innovation into a limited set of clusters.

Research: results

The results of this analysis made it possible to identify three factors: service, marketing and organization (see Table 42.5). The results also lead us to eliminate measures such as the introduction of new or significantly improved goods (within the product innovation) and the introduction of supporting activities (within the production innovation).

Service experiences and innovation

Table 42.5 Factorial exploratory analysis: results for the innovative experience

Innovative experience			
KMO	0,923		
Bartlett test	Sig: 0,000		
Components of innovative service experience	**Service**	**Marketing**	**Organization**
Service innovation	**0,722**	0,325	0,064
Production: operations	**0,789**	0,073	0,094
Production: distribution logistics	**0,772**	0,020	0,207
Marketing: promotion	0,114	**0,835**	0,260
Marketing: sales channels	0,142	**0,807**	0,178
Marketing: pricing	0,118	**0,720**	0,273
Organization: business practices	0,193	0,226	**0,791**
Organization: organizing work	0,175	0,285	**0,797**
Organization: external relations	0,053	0,179	**0,720**
Reliability: Cronbach alpha	0,718	0,787	0,752

Thus, an innovative experience in hospitality industries comprises the combination of service-production, marketing and the organizational the combination of service-production innovation. Given the characteristics of services, product (service) and production are joined in a unique variable. In other words, an innovative experience results from the service functionalities and delivery (service innovation); emotional engagement and how it is sold (marketing innovation) and how it is provided at an organizational level (organizational innovation). Even though customers do not directly perceive organizational innovation, internal improvements in business practices, work responsibilities or external relations may influence the experience perceived by them.

Discussion and conclusions

Innovation in the tourism and hospitality industry is a key factor for firms to adapt to the changing environment (Gomezelj, 2016). In addition, these companies must design unique and memorable experiences capable of engaging customers while remaining competitive (Chang, 2018). While novelty can lead to enhanced memories about the experience, innovation is capable of transforming services into unique experiences, making tourists feel satisfied and engaged with the firm (Chandralal & Valenzuela, 2015; Gilmore & Pine, 2002; Tang et al., 2015). Thus, from a management perspective, innovating on the attributes of the experience – which can be related both to the characteristics of the service and to the emotions of the customer – can make tourism experiences memorable, as well as improve business performance.

Following the *Oslo Manual* (OECD, 2018: 20), a business innovation represents the introduction of a new or improved product or business process – delivery, ancillary or supporting activities, including those of organizational and marketing nature. According to our results, innovation in hospitality service experiences results from the service functionalities and delivery (service innovation); the emotional engagement and how it is sold (marketing innovation) and how it is provided at an organizational level (organizational innovation) (see Table 42.6).

Thais González-Torres et al.

Table 42.6 Business innovation dimensions and areas in hospitality firms

Business innovations: Oslo Manual (2005, 2018)			*Areas of innovation*		*Business innovations in hospitality*	
Product		✓	Goods	✗	*Service*	
		✓	Services	✓		
Process	*Production*	✓	Operation processes	✓		
		✓	Logistics, delivery or distribution methods	✓		
		✓	Ancillary activities	✗		
	Marketing	✓	Design or packaging	✗	*Marketing*	*Process*
		✓	Media or techniques for product promotion	✓		
		✓	Methods for product placement or sales channels	✓		
		✓	Methods of pricing	✓		
	Organization	✓	Business practices for organizing procedures	✓	*Organization*	
		✓	Methods of organizing work responsibilities and decision-making	✓		
		✓	Methods of organizing external relations	✓		

Hospitality firms aiming at engaging customers through experiences can introduce new or improved services focusing particularly on physical attributes such as facilities, room characteristics, breakfasts and so on. In addition, non-physical factors also related to the delivery process are also crucial – reliability, cleanliness, maintenance and employee service, and competences, among others. Special attention should be paid to achieving customer emotions like hedonism, involvement and learning.

From the marketing perspective, innovating in new or improved means of communication, promotion and pricing strategy can lead to memorable experiences by affecting customer emotions like entertainment and escapism sensation. And finally, even though customers do not directly perceive the organizational innovation, internal improvements in business practices, work responsibilities or external relations may influence the experience perceived by them. Thus, innovating in business practices to better design and providing the experience as well as in workplace organization can also be relevant.

The results summarized above must be interpreted with caution owing to the limitations inherent in its methodological design. To begin with, this research is focused on the analysis of a sample of hospitality firms. Therefore, the results may not be generalizable for application in other contexts. Future research may also examine the relation between innovation and experience in other sectors within the tourism industry. Using a database as a secondary source of information represents another difficulty in generalizing results. In this vein, conclusions have to be limited to the established spatial and temporal context. Shortcomings of CIS-based studies may lead to some limitations. Firstly, a limited number of countries

Service experiences and innovation

were present within the industry of hospitality. Taking into account that innovation results are moderated by country, an increased number of participating countries would make the results more robust.

References

Bartholomew, D., Knotts, M. and Moustaki, I. (2011) *Latent Variable Models and Factor Analysis: A Unified Approach*, 3rd Edn. Chichester: John Wiley & Sons.

Bečić, E., Črnjar, K. and Licul, M. (2014) Measures of innovation activities in tourism according to CIS survey. In Faculty of Tourism and Hospitality Management in Opatija (Ed.), *Biennial International Congress. Tourism & Hospitality Industry.* University of Rijeka, Faculty of Tourism & Hospitality Management, p. 90.

Berry, L. L., Carbone, L. P. and Haeckel, S. H. (2002) Managing the total customer experience. *MIT Sloan Management Review*, 43(3), 85–89.

Brent Ritchie, J. R., Wing Sun Tung, V. and Ritchie, R. (2011) Tourism experience management research: Emergence, evolution and future directions. *International Journal of Contemporary Hospitality Management*, 23(4), 419–438.

Chandralal, L. and Valenzuela, F. R. (2015) Memorable tourism experiences: Scale development. *Contemporary Management Research*, 11(3), 291–310.

Chang, S. (2018) Experience economy in hospitality and tourism: Gain and loss values for service and experience. *Tourism Management*, 64, 55–63.

Cricelli, L., Greco, M. and Grimaldi, M. (2016) Assessing the open innovation trends by means of the Eurostat Community Innovation Survey. *International Journal of Innovation Management*, 20(3), 1650039.

Eide, D., Fuglsang, L. and Sundbo, J. (2017) Management challenges with the maintenance of tourism experience concept innovations: Toward a new research agenda. *Tourism Management*, 63, 452–463.

Flanagan, P., Johnston, R. and Talbot, D. (2005) Customer confidence: The development of a 'pre-experience' concept. *International Journal of Service Industry Management*, 16(4), 373–384.

Gilmore, J. H. and Pine, B. J. (2002) Differentiating hospitality operations via experiences: Why selling services is not enough. *Cornell Hotel and Restaurant Administration Quarterly*, 43(3), 87–96.

Gomezelj, D. O. (2016) A systematic review of research on innovation in hospitality and tourism. *International Journal of Contemporary Hospitality Management*, 28(3), 516–558.

Helkkula, A. (2011) Characterising the concept of service experience. *Journal of Service Management*, 22(3), 367–389.

Hernández-Perlines, F., Ariza-Montes, A., Han, H. and Law, R. (2019) Innovative capacity, quality certification and performance in the hotel sector. *International Journal of Hospitality Management*, 82, 220–230.

Hosany, S. and Witham, M. (2010) Dimensions of cruisers' experiences, satisfaction, and intention to recommend. *Journal of Travel Research*, 49(3), 351–364.

Hwang, J. and Lyu, S. O. (2015) The antecedents and consequences of well-being perception: An application of the experience economy to golf tournament tourists. *Journal of Destination Marketing & Management*, 4(4), 248–257.

Io, M. U. (2017) Understanding the effects of multi-dimensional tourism experiences on tourists' positive emotions and satisfaction in the context of casino hotels. *International Journal of Culture, Tourism and Hospitality Research*, 11(2), 142–156.

Jain, R., Aagja, J. and Bagdare, S. (2017) Customer experience: A review and research agenda. *Journal of Service Theory and Practice*, 27(3), 642–662.

Johnson, M. D., Lervik Olsen, L. and Wallin Andreassen, T. (2009) Joy and disappointment in the hotel experience: managing relationship segments. *Managing Service Quality: An International Journal*, 19(1), 4–30.

Kandampully, J., Zhang, T. and Jaakkola, E. (2018) Customer experience management in hospitality: A literature synthesis, new understanding and research agenda. *International Journal of Contemporary Hospitality Management*, 30(1), 21–56.

Khan, I. and Rahman, Z. (2017) Development of a scale to measure hotel brand experiences. *International Journal of Contemporary Hospitality Management*, 29(1), 268–287.

Kim, J. H., Ritchie, J. B. and McCormick, B. (2012) Development of a scale to measure memorable tourism experiences. *Journal of Travel Research*, 51(1), 12–25.

Klaus, P. and Maklan, S. (2012) EXQ: A multiple-item scale for assessing service experience. *Journal of Service Management*, 23(1), 5–33.

Le Bel, J. L. (2005) Beyond the friendly skies: An integrative framework for managing the air travel experience. *Managing Service Quality: An International Journal*, 15(5), 437–451.

Martín-Ríos, C. and Ciobanu, T. (2019) Hospitality innovation strategies: An analysis of success factors and challenges. *Tourism Management*, 70, 218–229.

Moreira, J., Silva, M. J., Simoes, J. and Sousa, G. (2012) Marketing innovation: Study of determinants of innovation in the design and packaging of goods and services – Application to Portuguese firms. *Contemporary Management Research*, 8(2). https://doi.org/10.7903/cmr.11047

Nixon, N. W. and Rieple, A. (2010) Luxury redesigned: How the Ritz-Carlton uses experiential service design to position abundance in times of scarcity. *Design Management Journal*, 5(1), 40–49.

Nordli, A. J. (2017) Measuring innovation in tourism with Community Innovation Survey: A first step towards a more valid innovation instruments. *Scandinavian Journal of Hospitality and Tourism*, 17(4), 423–440.

Oh, H., Fiore, A. M. and Jeoung, M. (2007) Measuring experience economy concepts: Tourism applications. *Journal of Travel Research*, 46(2), 119–132.

OECD. (2005) *Oslo Manual: Guidelines for Collecting and Interpreting Innovation Data*. Paris: OECD Publishing.

OECD. (2018) *Oslo Manual: Guidelines for Collecting and Interpreting Innovation Data*. Paris: OECD Publishing.

Ottenbacher, M. and Gnoth, J. (2005) How to develop successful hospitality innovation. *Cornell Hotel and Restaurant Administration Quarterly*, 46(2), 205–222.

Pikkemaat, B. and Zehrer, A. (2016) Innovation and service experiences in small tourism family firms. *International Journal of Culture, Tourism and Hospitality Research*, 10(4), 343–360.

Pine, B. J. and Gilmore, J. H. (1999) *The Experience Economy: Work Is Theatre and Every Business a Stage*. Boston: Harvard Business Press.

Sathish, A. S. and Venkatesakumar, R. (2011) Coffee experience and drivers of satisfaction, loyalty in a coffee outlet – With special reference to 'café coffee day'. *Journal of Contemporary Management Research*, 5(2), 1–13.

So, K. and King, C. (2010) 'When experience matters': Building and measuring hotel brand equity: The customers' perspective. *International Journal of Contemporary Hospitality Management*, 22(5), 589–608.

Stamboulis, Y. and Skayannis, P. (2003) Innovation strategies and technology for experience-based tourism. *Tourism Management*, 24(1), 35–43.

Tang, T. W., Wang, M. C. H. and Tang, Y. Y. (2015) Developing service innovation capability in the hotel industry. *Service Business*, 9(1), 97–113.

Teixeira, A. A. and Santos, L. C. B. D. (2016) Innovation performance in service companies and KIBS vis-à-vis manufacturing: the relevance of absorptive capacity and openness. *Revista Brasileira de Gestão de Negócios*, 18(59), 43–66.

Vasconcelos, A. M., Barichello, R., Lezana, Á., Forcellini, F. A., Ferreira, M. G. G. and Miguel, P. A. C. (2015) Conceptualisation of the service experience by means of a literature review. *Benchmarking: An International Journal*, 22(7), 1301–1314.

Voss, C. and Zomerdijk, L. (2007) *Innovation in Experiential Services: An Empirical View*. London Business School: AIM Research.

Zatori, A., Smith, M. K. and Puczko, L. (2018) Experience-involvement, memorability and authenticity: The service provider's effect on tourist experience. *Tourism Management*, 67, 111–126.

Zehrer, A. (2009) Service experience and service design: concepts and application in tourism SMEs. *Managing Service Quality: An International Journal*, 19(3), 332–349.

43

TOUR GUIDES AS MEDIATORS OF COMMEMORATION, EDUCATION AND HOLIDAY MAKING

The anthropology of the dark tourism experience in Berlin

Asaf Leshem

Introduction

The purpose of this chapter is to consider the role of the tour guide within the frame of the tourist experience. More specifically, it sets out to explore the mediating position of guides – who are commonly tasked with ensuring that tourists are having fun, the main goal of their tour experience – in the context of dark tourism. That is, it focuses on how tour guides fulfil their role at tourism sites of death and tragedy that typically present emotional, intellectual and even politically charged difficult heritages.

More generally, of course, an important role of the tour guide is to enhance the tourist experience (Pond, 1993). For example, when on a tour of an old cathedral, the interpretation by a guide may not only inform tourists about the building but also give meaning to its wider historical and cultural significance. Alternatively, during a walk in a nature reserve, the guide might, in addition to identifying and discussing particular flora and fauna, contextualize them within contemporary debates surrounding nature conservation and sustainability. Either way, the contribution of the tour guide has a great impact on what the tourist takes back home with them, on their holiday memories and on their satisfaction. And importantly, these are usually positive experiences that are, in a sense, relatively benign. Arguably, however, this is not the case with tour guiding related to the dark tourism experience. As this chapter will propose through the case of dark tourism in Berlin, although customer satisfaction remains the prime goal of tour guiding, the emotional impact of tour guide interpretation on the tourist experience is not benign. In other words, the contemplation of death, human tragedy or genocide undoubtedly has potentially powerful and long-lasting impacts on tourists, and tour guides may play a fundamental role in how tourists confront and understand dark sites.

DOI: 10.4324/9781003219866-49

601

Asaf Leshem

Tour guides in context: from the past to the present

Berlin's tour guides comprise street/urban guides, museum docents and tour leaders, the latter commonly travelling to the city with their tour groups either from foreign countries or from other German states. In most cases, tour guides in Berlin are not residents of the city. Some are very experienced and knowledgeable; others, however, are very often 'shallow experts' on many destinations and, moreover, their work as guides is one of several duties they have to perform.

As a first step to understanding the role tour guides in Berlin play in the construction of the dark tourism experience, it is useful to offer a brief review of the historical roots and evolution of the contemporary tour guiding profession. According to Cohen (1985), the earliest evidence of tour guiding can be traced back as far 3,000 B.C. Cohen describes the two main functions guides performed at this time involved being pathfinders and mentors. Others, such as Pond (1993), similarly refer to early manifestations of tour guides as pathfinders, cicerones (those who provide information about places of interest to sightseers) and geographical guides. Thus, these forerunners of the modern guide both helped visitors to find their way to and around an unfamiliar place and also, in some cases, assisted them in familiarizing themselves with the local culture. In Greco-Roman times, this basic role expanded to include not only finding the way but also the arrangement of accommodation and other travel services (Cohen, 1985; Holloway, 1981). As such, these early guides performed roles that may be compared with those undertaken by today's tour leaders – part guiding, part representing their tour companies and, in general, being responsible for all the tourism services provided to the tourist (Pond, 1993; Weiler & Black, 2015).

It was not until the age of the Grand Tour from the late seventeenth century onwards, and in parallel to the evolution of modern tourism, that we can see a major step in the development of tour guiding into the profession that we see nowadays. During the late Renaissance and, in particular, on the Grand Tour, guides became companions, personal tutors, pathfinders, language teachers and translators of local cultures (Mead, 1914; Pond, 1993). And with the subsequent evolution and growth of the tourism industry into its modern form and magnitude, the various roles of tour guides, tour leaders and museum docents have, to some extent, speciated to contribute to different elements of the tourist experience (Hu & Wall, 2012; Weiler & Black, 2015).

In the contemporary era, tour guides, as Rabotic (2009, 2010) argues, function as a form of cultural mediator, performing instrumental, social, communicative and interactive roles. Yu, Weiler and Ham (2004) observe that this cultural mediation is vital in delivering memorable and positive tourist experiences, whilst Hu and Wall (2012) argue further that guide mediation and its potential contribution to the tourist experience is one necessary element of sustainable practices at the destination. Hence, rather than just acting as information providers, tour guides today provide part of the tourist experience. As Andersson (2007) explains, through their practices in a particular space and time, including the consumption of accommodation and transport services or participation in particular activities, tourists seek experiences that will provide the highest utility. Putting it more simply, tourism services, including the tour guide, are collectively provided for the tourist to have a good time (Andersson, 2007; Stasiak, 2013).

However, the manner in which tour guides contribute to the tourist experience varies by context; that is, their mediating role may be more or less influential depending on the nature of the site or attraction. In particular, the role or performance of tour guides as well as the interpretation they provide may arguably be distinctive in tourism destinations that present historical heritage that is difficult, sensitive and often controversial – in short, at dark tourism sites. As noted above, to explore this issue, thereby enhancing understanding of the anthropology of tour guiding, this chapter draws on a study of Berlin where tour guiding is positioned between the city's darker heritage and its more contemporary attractions. More specifically, this chapter was born from a larger-scale ethnographic study of tour guide interpretation of dark tourism in Berlin. It aims to look at the tourist experience of dark tourism sites in Berlin with a particular focus on the tour guide's mediating role as part of that experience. Through this analysis, I seek to position the tour guide within the tourist experience of dark tourism sites and to describe the changing nature of the tourist experience within the frame of guided tours at such sites. Such exploration requires us first to consider briefly not only dark tourism in general, but also the specific forms of dark tourism that occur in Berlin. Hence, by way of introduction, we must first briefly touch upon the multi-layered complexity of the city's dark attractiveness.

Berlin, difficult heritage and dark tourism

Berlin's history of the last two centuries can be divided into relatively easily defined chapters, each providing a developmental background to the next and each riddled with political and social events, most of which left a mark on heritage extending far beyond the city itself. If, for the sake of an historical exercise, we looked at the life of a person who was born in 1900 and died in 2000, we would see that this person lived in Otto von Bismark's imperial Germany, in the democratic Weimar Republic, in fascist Nazi Germany, in either the socialist East Germany or the neo-liberal democratic West Germany and, finally, in today's reunited Federal Republic of Germany.

The historical chapters that our imaginary person experienced are now a source of fascination for millions of tourists, both domestic and international. Nevertheless, tourists visit Berlin for a variety of reasons; for some, the main purpose is business whilst others might be on an urban holiday or 'city break'. Yet others regularly travel to the city to visit their friends or family members. Whatever the purpose, however, Berlin in the second decade of the twenty-first century is a destination that offers a diverse array of attractions, from a seemingly endless choice of shopping opportunities and musical concerts to more than 500 galleries and some 180 museums. And the average tourist is likely to divide their time between wandering around leisurely, engaging in shopping, eating or visiting a light-themed museum and the arguably more challenging experience of visiting one of the many sites presenting the painful heritage of the Holocaust, the Second World War and the Cold War.

Several scholars have argued that Berlin's memorial sites and museums were initially designed to commemorate the victims and allow both mourning by survivors and, for the German people, a platform for confronting their troubled past (see, for example, Bookheimer, 2015; Frank, 2015; Ladd, 1997). Today, however, these sites are visited by millions of people, most of whom have no direct relation to the historical events they represent. Tourists in Berlin walk in the Memorial for the Murdered Jews of Europe, listen to audio guides in the Topography of Terror museum, take a guided tour in the Sachsenhausen Museum and Memorial and walk along the Berlin Wall Memorial. In doing so, they are participating in a phenomenon most commonly referred to as dark tourism (Light, 2017).

As in any discussion of particular cases within the phenomenon of dark tourism, it is first important to establish the most relevant definition of the concept in which to frame the case and, second, to narrow down the type of dark tourism and its position on Stone's spectrum of dark to light (Stone, 2006) – see also Chapter 25 for a more extensive discussion of dark tourism. For example, Foley and Lennon's (1996: 198) early definition – 'the presentation and consumption (by visitors) of real and commodified death and disaster sites' – is too broad for this study; they also go on to use the word tragedy, which may again be too inclusive. In contrast, Tarlow (2005: 48) defines dark tourism as 'visitations to places where tragedies or historically noteworthy death has occurred and that continue to impact our lives'. Certainly, as this chapter discusses, in the context of tourist sites related to the Second World War and the Cold War, the ongoing impact of these events is undeniably present. Nevertheless, for the purposes of this chapter, Preece and Price (2005: 192) offer the most suitable definition, embracing as it does the memorial sites, museums, monuments and other buildings visited by tourists in Berlin. With a minor adaptation (the removal of the word 'disaster'), dark tourism in Berlin can then be best defined as 'travel to sites associated with death, acts of violence, tragedy, scenes of death and crimes against humanity'.

The geographical space in which dark tourism occurs also demands particular attention in much the same way that the type of dark tourism in the city needs to be accurately defined. Through developing the concept of dark–darker sites, Miles (2000, 2002) distinguishes between museums, memorials and monuments, each with varying degrees of presentation of the macabre, the level of severity of the atrocity that occurred on the site and, in particular, whether it is the actual site of an event or is more broadly associated with the event. Also notable in Miles's argument is the timescale; in Germany, sites of dark tourism have undergone a shift from being purposefully designed for commemoration to commemoration and education and, from the early 2000s, further evolving as tourist attractions (Bookheimer, 2015; Frank, 2015; Gross, 2006; Ladd, 1998). Building on Miles' dark to darker categorization, Stone (2006) suggests a spectrum of lightest to darkest supply of dark tourism.

In Berlin, sites with histories and stories related to the Berlin Wall and Second World War and the Holocaust (by definition dark tourism sites) may be categorized into four types, as follows:

i   Memorial sites – notably, the memorial site for the Berlin Wall at Bernauer Strasse, the Sachsenhausen Memorial and Museum (Figures 43.1 and 43.2), the Memorial for the murdered Jews of Europe (Figure 43.3), the Memorial for Victims of War and Tyranny (Neue Wache), the Memorial at Platform 17 and several others.
ii   Museums – Topography of Terror, the Stasi Museum, Otto Weidt Workshop for the Blind, the German History Museum (DHM), House of the Wannsee Conference, the Jewish Museum, the Berlin Story Museum and others.
iii   Historical buildings
iv   Monuments/statues/information signs.

Inevitably, there are several limitations to this categorization. Firstly, some memorial sites now function both as a memorial and as a museum, usually with ongoing development of new exhibitions. Secondly, some museums as a whole focus on a part of the story, whereas others have sections that cover the topic as a historical chapter, such as the Holocaust in the German History Museum. Thirdly, some historical buildings are also museums, such as the House of the Wannsee Conference. And lastly, the distinction between memorials and monuments may not always prove to be straightforward. For example, the 'Presence of Absence' by Micha Ulman is an underground monument shaped like an empty library functioning as a memorial site to the Nazi book burning of the 10th of May, 1933.

Figure 43.1 Sachsenhausen Memorial and Museum

Figure 43.2 Sachsenhausen Memorial and Museum

Nevertheless, the characterization of these sites as darkest sites on Stone's (2006) spectrum is especially useful. Roughly generalized for the purpose of this chapter, the sites are of high political significance (Frank, 2015; Ladd, 1997), they commemorate death and suffering, they are education and commemoration oriented (though this I will contest later in this chapter), they are authentic in location and largely authentic in interpretation (with the problematic exception of Checkpoint Charlie), and they are still relatively close in their time scale to the event. Positioning Berlin's dark tourism sites on the light to dark spectrum also helps us to create an accurate picture that differentiates them from other forms of dark

Figure 43.3 Memorial to the Murdered Jews of Europe

tourism, such as visitation to Chernobyl (Stone, 2013), to Jim Morrison's grave in Paris (Sharpley, 2005) or to the London Dungeon attraction (Stone, 2009). This distinction is more meaningful as these sites potentially differ in terms of the motivations of people to visit them, in how death is perceived and perhaps commodified, in the site interpretation and in their political significance (Light, 2017; Sharpley, 2005; Stone, 2006).

Although it may be challenging to confirm through research, it can be safe to argue that some visitors to dark sites in Berlin are consciously motivated by *schadenfreude* (NB: public denial of the Holocaust is illegal in Germany, and guides in Sachsenhausen are instructed to call the police if displays of *schadenfreude* are witnessed on the premises. Similarly, inappropriate displays of happiness at the Wall Memorial are frowned upon). Indeed, some commentators (see, for example Foley & Lennon, 1997; Gross, 2006; Sharpley, 2009) suggest that *schadenfreude*, along with entertainment, voyeurism and morbid curiosity, may draw visitors to dark sites. More relevant to Berlin's sites, however, confronting death, commemoration and seeking knowledge and understanding, as well as simply being the thing to do (Hughes, 2008; Tarlow, 2005), are considered to be amongst the most common motivations for people to visit such sites (Ashworth & Hartmann, 2005; Seaton, 1996; Sharpley & Stone, 2009). The motivation to visit dark tourism sites is arguably the first step in the experience itself, akin perhaps to the anticipation or excitement of planning a holiday being part of the overall tourist experience (Parrinello, 1993; Urry, 1990).

Interpretation, however, is crucial to the dark tourism experience itself, providing meaning to the visit as well as being a determinant of both the perceived character of the site and the intellectual substance the tourist will take away with them. It may be used to rewrite people's lives and deaths (Sharpley, 2009) and even as a potential means of demonstrating peaceful collaboration between past enemies (Gelbman & Maoz, 2012). Sharpley's (2009) point with regard to the power of dark tourism interpretation is made clear by Macdonald (2009, 2013) who argues that dark tourism sites were first developed by people who wanted primarily to remember victims of the atrocities the sites commemorate, and later by others who were more concerned with education and as a means of supporting whole societies to deal with the troubled past. And in some cases, according to Macdonald (2009, 2013), dealing with the past means forgetting it.

Interpretation may be understood as language translation and it is important to understand that, in the context of this chapter, it has two overlapping meanings: (i) interpretation of dark tourism through, for example, exhibitions, information signs, audio guides and so on (see for example, White & Frew, 2013) and (ii) interpretation specifically undertaken by tour guides. As one of the roles of the tour guides, interpretation may at various tourism sites be controversial, touching on moral and political issues (Pond, 1993; Weiler & Black, 2015; Wynn, 2011). The term 'cultural brokers', first introduced by Holloway (1981: 387), points to the powerful and, perhaps, problematic position of tour guides in their work. Simply put, tour guides have, on the one hand, the power to present history and cultures in a false way (Pearce, 1984) or, on the other hand, to be an ambassador of social and political sustainability (Hu & Wall, 2012).

As previously established, this chapter draws on a wider study of tour guiding at dark tourism sites in Berlin. That study, as the following section explains, combined both ethnographic and auto-ethnographic research.

Ethnography and autoethnography

There are many tourists who visit memorial sites in and around Berlin, such as Sachsenhausen, on their own. In so doing, they may be guided by reading the exhibition's information boards or listening to audio guides. However, as a researcher, I chose to focus on tour guides' interpretation rather than its more static counterpart, not least because of the scale of guided tours to sites of dark tourism in Berlin. An average full-time guide in one of the major five public companies (running tours open to the public, also known as 'walk ins') may guide between 15 and 30 or more tourists a day during the high season. Tours based on the theme of dark tourism comprise more than half of all tours offered in Berlin; these include tours based on the themes of the Third Reich, Jewish Heritage, the former concentration camp of Sachsenhausen and the Cold War.

I am one of the several hundred tour guides working in Berlin. For me, guiding and observing other guides as an ethnographer is more than Macdonald's concept of 'hanging around' (Macdonald, 2013); working as guide enabled me to observe and interact with my peers, hence the choice of ethnography and indeed auto-ethnography as a research strategy. In doing so, I avoided disguising my own voice as neutral, whilst still applying scientific methods (Cole, 2005).

Over time, I observed with permission more than 40 guides and interviewed many others. The analysis in this chapter is based on these observations, including interpretations I made on my tours.

Analysis of the guided dark tourism experience in Berlin

Correlating interpretation with its target audience

The way in which tour guides decide how to interpret starts from the type of tour they are undertaking. If they are guiding a public tour, in advance they will only know the overall theme of the tour and the language to be spoken. They will then assess how best to progress with the tour and what form of interpretation to undertake when meeting the tourists. In contrast, when guiding private tours, different approaches will be adopted when receiving the booking from another guide or agency or if the customer contacted the guide directly. In the first case, the guide usually receives some details from the agency, perhaps including some or all of: names (an indication of the tourists' origin); language; the numbers of people and sometimes the relations between them; the theme of the tour and what sites are to be shown; the level of knowledge and interest the tourists may have; the tourists' age and gender. However, when there has been direct contact between the customer and the guide, perhaps by email, the guide may know a lot more, including the profession of the guests, whether they have previously visited Berlin, the extent of their interest in dark or even general history and other background details.

Nevertheless, in all cases and in a more or less systematic way, guides try to assemble a collection of parameters that will eventually determine how they will interpret the dark chapters of Berlin's history to particular groups of tourists. These may include: names, language/s, country of origin, country of residence, previous visit to Berlin, age/s, gender, profession/s, group size, the dynamic among the people in the group, level of knowledge (this is a particularly important one), who paid for the tour, the reason for visiting Berlin, the reason for visiting dark tourism sites – in particular Sachsenhausen – their duration of stay in Berlin, when the tourists arrived (are they tired from their flight?), the political views of the tourist, their levels of patience, their mood and even if they seem nice. Quinn and Ryan (2015) point out that guides also take into account external influences, such as governmental agencies and destination management.

Importantly, guides do not have all these details all the time and will often gather only the most important details, such as language, level of knowledge, nationality and group dynamics and connection (family, friends, colleagues or complete strangers). Moreover, for smaller private tours, they will typically make a much greater effort to provide a more suitable, tailored interpretation with a greater degree of detail and explanation than when guiding a larger, heterogeneous group of tourists.

The interpretation

Tour guides use a variety of methods, techniques and dramaturgical skills to interpret the sites during their tours. Although with experience these techniques develop to the extent that some guides are very aware of their 'game' (Wynn, 2011), others take more time and just do what comes naturally. Owing to the sensitive nature of interpretation of dark tourism, even a single word or phrase can have an important effect on the meaning of the story, and how it is understood by the tourists. In this research, guides were observed using three levels of interpretation (as shown in Table 43.1 below); they make interpretation choices using these three levels – words, anecdotes and narrative (of the whole tour). These choices may reveal the guide's level of knowledge, their knowledge of the group they are guiding and even their political opinion or value system.

The psychological, social and cultural process of how tourists make sense of their experience in dark tourism sites is yet to be fully researched. However, this research demonstrates the considerable control guides have over the way tourists obtain information and how it may affect them in a variety of ways. This controlled interpretation of dark events may be used, for example, as a deliberation tool to discuss contemporary social and political issues. It

Tour guides as mediators of commemoration

Table 43.1 The three levels of interpretation

	Content	*Performance*
Word	Selecting words to fit narratives, e.g. murdered or killed or died, Hitler or Adolf, saying Soviets or socialists or communists to mean the same thing, damaged or ruined, etc.	Emphasis on a particular word, words that have stronger or softer meanings, words that are generic or specific, slow vowel prolongation, etc.
Anecdote	Using statistics to prove a point, a short story strategically placed to interpret a particular location, playing the 'what if' game – e.g. "do you think that if Hitler wouldn't have invaded Russia they would have won the war?"	Raising voice, changing pace, changing tone, acting a character, putting on accents, monotonous up to five minutes, transition from happy to sad voice or vice versa, etc.
Narrative	• 'feed' the tourist • Correcting perspective • Political ideology personal • Political ideology aimed for a specific target market, • no narrative/completely adaptive to the tourist type and characteristics.	• Telling the tourists what they want to hear – often racists or stereotypical – usually hot interpretation • Incorporating messages • A combination of the first two • Gathering more parameters, and giving little bias, and at times more analytical interpretation, usually cold interpretation

can also be used to enhance positive or negative feelings of the destination, build on existing stereotypes or make tourists question their perspective or moral views on certain topics.

The tourists

As explained above, these interpretation techniques in part reflect the characteristics of individual guides (their knowledge, skills and experience) and in part are a response to the needs of tourists. During the research, when casually asked, most tourists between the ages of 40 and 60 indicated that they wanted to split their time in Berlin between what they considered to be fun activities (shopping, going out, visiting light topic museums, etc.) and 'dark' activities, such as taking a Third Reich or Sachsenhausen tour, or visiting the Topography of Terror museum and others like it. For most, the ratio of fun to dark activities was about 50–50, but with fluctuations of up to 40–60 either way. Visitors with personal connections to the story – that is, second generation holocaust survivors or those who visited Berlin during the time of the Berlin Wall – typically displayed a different ratio of up to 70–30 dark to light/fun.

Those visitors who were on return visits usually talked about the desire to learn several new angles to the story and to develop new ideas that they previously were not aware of. Indeed, a tour can be thought of as the process of planting ideas. In some cases, this occurs only to a limited extent; in others, the impact is very significant. In both cases, however, tourists – especially younger ones – will take a long time to 'digest' the new information.

As a general rule, guides always aspire to make tourists, their customers, feel satisfied with their tour experience. That rule will only be broken for the following reasons: guides will 'allow' the tourist to express a different opinion to their own, but not something that is factually false. Guides will generally not continue the tour as normal if they receive a personal insult (of racist, homophobic or other natures). Finally, Holocaust denial is considered by all the guides I spoke to as a 'red line' not to be crossed by the tourist. In public tours, holocaust deniers are ejected from the tour and their money refunded. In private premium tours, although a very rare occurrence, one or two guides related how the tour was ruined once a tourist expressed such views. In these cases, guides know they may receive negative reviews or even complaints, but overlook these because the radical views of some tourists are 'unacceptable' and, in Germany, even illegal.

Group dynamics

In tour guiding, the tourist is almost never a single entity; an interesting part of every tour is its group dynamics (Cohen, 1985; Pond, 1993; Wynn, 2011). Visitation to sites presenting atrocity and genocide are by their nature significantly more sensitive than any other tourist site. Tourists are faced with what they expected to get from the visitation but de facto their expectations are laced with the social interaction that is essentially tourism (Urry, 1990). These social circles of expectation may be conceptualized as in Figure 43.4.

From the perspective of the individual, they are at the centre of the circle but there are several circles around them with different expectations as to what they are supposed to get from the visitation. To a lesser or greater extent, tour guides are forced to be alert, reacting constantly to these dynamics. Their interpretation is ideally aimed to produce a satisfied customer and, with it, for the guide to be happy with their own performance as they perceive it. From the perspective of the tourist, however, there are many more layers of how the interpretation is received and later digested (Figure 43.4).

Tourist experience and the dark tourism sites

As it is almost unavoidable to go on a tour in Berlin without seeing a monument or a memorial, tourists become judges of commemoration art. In interpreting these memorials, I often suggested to my guests to think about the purpose of the memorials and who were they created for. In so doing, they will be able to consider whether the memorials are good or not, or whether they serve their purpose. Tourists are often encouraged by myself and my peers to

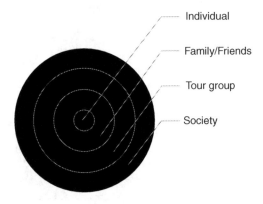

Figure 43.4 The social circles of the tour group

Tour guides as mediators of commemoration

be judges and tell them if the memorial works. Famously, for example, Peter Eisenman, the designer of the Memorial for the Murdered Jews of Europe, declared that he wants people to be the judges and to decide the meaning of the memorial.

The temporality of the experience

In undertaking this analysis, the temporal aspect must be taken into account. Sites and even small memorials evolve over time. They are presented in a different way according to the current government and political atmosphere (Lowenthal, 1985; Sharpley, 2009). Large memorial sites develop more exhibitions, the environments around statues change and even the political atmosphere evolves, leading to different ways in which the visitors view the memorials. And of course, new generations are born more temporally distant from the events that sites wish to commemorate; they will have different social knowledge and will face different social challenges (Lowenthal, 1985).

Old and new generations are also becoming more aware. The guide's mediating role in dark heritage is therefore required to undergo a new phase in its evolution. Quinn and Ryan (2015) support this point, arguing that tour guiding, along with the interpretation of sites, must be subjected to a reworking of memory. Partly, this means that guides must interpret historical events in a cultural language that fits current socio-political atmospheres. With this in mind, the guide's work is always responsive to their guests, and at the same time to the site itself.

It may be argued that dealing with a destination's past whilst it also functions as a tourist destination may be counterproductive. Hohenhaus (2013), for example, discusses sites commemorating the genocide in Rwanda, where there exists a potential clash of motivations between Rwandan mourners and tourist outsiders (Hohenhaus, 2013). In Berlin, as Ladd (1997) and Frank (2015) argue, many memorials were first built for the reunited German people to deal with their traumatic past. Moreover, many were designed and constructed when annual visitor numbers were less than one million. By the time this research was conducted, annual visitor numbers had risen to 14 million with an additional 33 million overnight stays of friends and relatives (VFRs). Berlin's memorials, then, are no longer experienced only by its own long-term residents, but are now shared by German and international visitors from around the world. This unplanned sharing of memorials may result in a conflict, whereby Berliners could feel that walking around memorial sites and sharing them with thousands of outsiders who did not experience the same things they did might feel like going to a nudist beach flooded with voyeuristic intruders.

Undoubtedly, dark heritage functions in opposition to those more common heritage sites presenting the cultures of 'our past'. Here, there is not an illusion of history (Hewison, 1987); rather, the dark chapters of history are not (usually) something local people are proud of. Memorial sites present those events (of the Cold War and the Holocaust) inevitably with different levels of drama and unpleasant sensations. Although correlation and causation may not always be presented to the tourists with such direct clarity, it is nevertheless implied in the underlying messages of interpretation. In other words, events are related by tour guides in certain ways that allow their guests to experience dark tourism sites in a way that may be argued to have an added value. For example, tour guides may interpret the psychological propaganda tools used by the National Socialist Ministry of Propaganda, pointing implicitly to the outcomes of state policies of enticing hatred and persecution. And often, it is unavoidable for tourists to create an immediate correlation between past events and contemporary social and political situations familiar to them from their own countries (the Israeli–Palestinian conflict, the Catalan demand for independence, Trump's presidency, Brexit and many others).

At all times, guides struggle to manage the conflict between their own ego and personal agenda to the ultimate need of keeping the tourist experience satisfactory. These may collide if, for example, the guide adds messages of a certain political bias in a transparent way and, as a result, the guests may feel that 'guide shoved his opinions down our throats'. Distinguishable from most other forms of heritage tourism, it can be argued that dark tourism is more emotional and is taken more personally by many visitors.

Discussion and conclusion

The business of tourism is often perceived as important but not life threatening. Although tour operators and guides take their jobs seriously, they are also aware that if they make a mistake, it is unlikely to have serious ramifications. Nevertheless, this chapter has sought to demonstrate the role tour guides have in the dark tourism experience. Tour guides are faced with challenging professional elasticity and skill, as their interpretive role means that they educate people about difficult and sensitive themes, whilst keeping their role as service givers.

Furthermore, most tourists are emotionally involved when visiting dark sites, such as a former concentration camp, a memorial to victims of a genocide or a museum depicting other forms of atrocity or human tragedy. In light of both that and the fact that the subject matter of dark tourism sites is considered more serious, the mediating role of the guides becomes one where the tourists are less passive, more opinionated and ultimately more conversational.

The sensitivity of the job

Tourists are becoming more and more aware of the tourism industry and its workings and operations. One guide attested to the fact that to give their guest the best possible experience, he acts – without pretending – as the guest's friend, and walks around and shows them sites in the same way they would show it to their real friends or family. Nevertheless, the guide said that it is obvious to both parties that the tour is a business transaction but that, so as not to ruin the positive experience, both guides and tourists prefer not to deal with payment during the tour itself. In other words, even though neither the guide nor the tourist would not wish to over-romanticise the authenticity of the experience, they would still rather keep some of the magic of being friends for the duration of the tour. In the case of dark tourism, this guide–tourist dynamic is further amplified as the sensitivity of the topic requires a level of trust in the process of a natural conversation; a conversation that hypothetically could take place between real friends.

As explained earlier in the chapter, tourists are not one homogeneous group. More precisely, they are increasingly diverse in their backgrounds, and smarter about their travel choices and aims. And as also explained above, guides are in a unique position that is more dynamic and intimate. The mediating nature of this relationship differs from that of the more static nature of dark tourism sites and museums in that it allows them the potential to be a more successful link between the dark event and the tourist. In other words, guides are better positioned (as illustrated in Figure 43.5 below) in the balancing act of dark tourism being both a social activity of education and commemoration whilst remaining a commercial tourism activity.

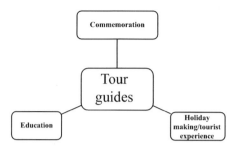

Figure 43.5 Tour guide position in the dark tourism experience

Tourist experience as a dialogue

Guides perceive guiding dark tourism – particularly in Sachsenhausen – as more important than 'just a job'. Though not referring to a dark tourism tour as potentially fun, guides nevertheless endeavour to guide the tour so as to leave the tourists with a feeling of satisfaction. And yet in the dark tourism experience, it was observed in this research that guides will not interpret events in such a way that they would feel competes with the historical truth or with the messages conveyed by the story (e.g. regarding the victims of the Berlin Wall, or stories related to the prisoners of Sachsenhausen concentration camp). In other words, unique to the dark tourism experience, guides will seek to guide the tour for the tourists *as well as* for the topic.

Another relevant point here pertains to the dynamic nature of a guided tour. Perhaps in contrast to other more conventional guided tours, in a dark tourism tour there is continuous discussion and feedback between guides and their guests, constantly bringing changes to the experience on the tour. Guides are aware of how dark tourism events as related by them to the tourists have a strong emotional impact, in part owing to contemporary connections tourists make. In addition, in the dark tourism experience, guides consider tourist engagement and good questions to be a very important part of the tour so as to ensure better understanding on the part of tourists of the interpretation of social and political historical processes.

Crucially, this research has also shed light on the uniquely challenging nature of mediating – or translating – dark tourism events in a dissimilar way to how other forms of local culture or heritage are interpreted. Here, the potential for difficult heritage to serve as what Morsch and Ley (2010) refer to as educational and humanitarian purposes is acknowledged by the guides. Unsurprisingly perhaps, tourists too are often aware of this unique interaction. When asked, almost every tourist I spoke to casually on my tours told me that beyond personal commemoration, to them the importance of these sites is so that 'we (as global society) don't forget and learn not to repeat the mistakes of the past'. Effectively, guides' interpretation of dark tourism for several hours of a tour integrates commemoration and education into their guests' holiday time.

Putting it another way, the observed tours in this research typically provided evidence of guides functioning in their traditional guide role of a mentor (Cohen, 1985), using their interpretation to contribute to social sustainability (as suggested by Hu and Wall, 2012 earlier in this chapter). However, the integration of education into holiday making is not without its risks and pitfalls. This research, then, confirms the findings of Poria and Ashworth's (2009) study that suggests that the interpretation in these sites often reflects nationalistic, heroic messages, and is there to encourage an ideological national narrative and the visitor's sense of belonging to society. Similarly, guides' selection of interpretation method employing the

Asaf Leshem

three levels of interpretation discussed in this chapter may also be used to reinforce negative stereotypes or world views.

Finally, in reference to our particular position in time, I would contest the current management paradigm whereby commemoration and education as the principal aims of dark tourism sites are perceived as separate from and, indeed, considered morally superior to the more traditional escapism aims of tourism (i.e. as part of the visitation of holiday makers). Rather, the outcomes of the research discussed in this chapter perhaps reflect the contemporary evolution from collective to social memory (Lowenthal, 1985, 1988) inasmuch as the potentially valuable contribution of tour guides' interpretation of dark tourism sites and events to tourists knowledge and understanding should be acknowledged as being in tandem with a more positive perspective of dark tourism being part of the contemporary holiday making.

References

Andersson, T. B. (2007) The tourist in the experience economy. *Scandinavian Journal of Hospitality and Tourism*, 7(1), 46–58.

Ashworth, G. and Hartmann, R. (2005) *Horror and Human Tragedy Revisited. The Management of Sites of Atrocities for Tourism.* New York: Congnizant Communication Corporation.

Bookheimer, B. J. (2015) The Layers of Memory at Sachsenhausen. From the GDR to Contemporary Germany. Honours thesis, University of Tennessee Chattanooga.

Cohen, E. (1985) The tourist guide: The origins, structure and dynamics of a role. *Annals of Tourism Research*, 12(1), 5–29.

Cole, S. (2005) Action ethnograpy: Using participant observation. In B. W. Richie, P. Burns and C. Palmer (Eds.), *Tourism Research Methods: Integrating Theory with Practice*. Wallingford: CABI, pp. 63–72.

Frank, S. (2015) *Wall Memorials and Heritage. The Heritage Industry of Berlin's Checkpoint Charlie.* Abingdon: Routledge.

Foley, M. and Lennon, J. (1996) JFK and dark tourism: A fascination with assassination. *International Journal of Heritage Studies*, 2(4), 198–211.

Foley, M. and Lennon, J. (1997) Dark tourism: An ethical dilemma. In M. Foley, J. Lennon and G. Maxwell (Eds.), *Hospitality, Tourism and Leisure Management: Issues in Strategy and Culture.* London: Cassell, pp. 153–164.

Gelbman, A. and Maoz, D. (2012) Island of peace or island of war: Tourist guiding. *Annals of Tourism Research*, 39(1), 108–133.

Gross, A. S. (2006) Holocaust tourism in Berlin: Global memory, trauma, and the 'negative sublime'. *Journeys*, 7(2), 73–100.

Hewison, R. (1987) *The Heritage Industry: Britain in a Climate of Decline.* London: Methuen.

Hohenhaus, P. (2013) Commemorating and commodifying the Rwandan genocide: Memorial sites in a political difficult context. In L. White and E. Frew (Eds.), *Dark Tourism and Place Identity. Managing and Interpreting Dark Places.* Abingdon: Routledge, pp. 142–155.

Holloway, J. C. (1981) The guided tour: A sociological approach. *Annals of Tourism Research*, 8(3), 377–402.

Hu, W. and Wall, G. (2012) Interpretive guiding and sustainable development: A framework. *Tourism Management Perspectives*, 4, 80–85.

Hughes, R. (2008) Dutiful tourism: Encountering the Cambodian genocide. *Asia Pacific Viewpoint*, 49(3), 318–330.

Ladd, B. (1997) *The Ghosts of Berlin. Confronting German History in the German Landscape.* Chicago and London: The University Chicago Press.

Light, D. (2017) Progress in dark tourism and thanatourism research: An uneasy relationship with heritage tourism. *Tourism Management*, 61, 275–301.

Lowenthal, D. (1985) *The Past is a Foreign Country.* Cambridge: Cambridge University Press.

Lowenthal, D. (1998) Fabricating heritage. *History & Memory*, 10(1), 5–24.

Macdonald, S. J. (2009) *Difficult Heritage.* University of Michigan. Available at: https://www.youtube.com/watch?v=IjTOw5NcRwg (Accessed 20 January 2019).

Macdonald, S. J. (2013) *Memorylands: Heritage and Identity in Europe Today.* Abingdon: Routledge.

Mead, W. E. (1914) The Grand Tour in the Eighteenth Century. Available at: http://aughty.org/pdf/grand_tour_18th_century.pdf (Accessed 13 October 2016).

Miles, W. (2000) Post-communist Holocaust commemoration in Poland and Germany. *The Journal of Holocaust Education*, 9(1), 33–50.

Miles, W. (2002) Auschwitz: Museum interpretation and darker tourism. *Annals of Tourism Research*, 29(4), 1175–1178.

Morsch, G. and Ley, A. (2010) *Sachsenhausen Concentration Camp, 1936–1945. Events and Development.* Berlin: Metropol.

Parrinello, G. L. (1993) Motivation and anticipation in post-industrial tourism. *Annals of Tourism Research*, 20(2), 233–249.

Pearce, P. L. (1984) Tourist-guide interaction. *Annals of Tourism Research*, 11(1), 129–146.

Pond, K. L. (1993) *The Professional Guide: Dynamics of Tour Guiding*. London: Chapman and Hall.

Poria, Y. and Ashworth, G. (2009) Heritage tourism: Current resource for conflict. *Annals of Tourism Research*, 36 (3), 522–525.

Preece, T. and Price, G.G. (2005) Motivations of participants in dark tourism: A case study of Port Arthur, Tasmania. In C. Ryan, S, Page and M. Aicken M. (Eds.), *Taking Tourism to the Limits: Issues, Concepts and Managerial Perspectives*. Oxford: Elsevier, pp. 191–197.

Quinn, B. and Ryan, T. (2015) Tour guide and the mediation of difficult memories: The of Dublin Castle, Ireland. *Current Issues in Tourism*, 19(4), 322–337.

Rabotic, B. (2009) The creative role of tour guiding. Paper presented at the *Cities as Creative Spaces for Cultural Tourism Conference*, Boğazici University, Istanbul. Available at: https://tuygar.boun.edu.tr/sites/tuygar.boun.edu.tr/files/RABOT%C4%B0C%2C%20THE%20CREATIVE%20ROLE%20OF%20TOURIST%20GUIDING.pdf (Accessed 6 January 2021).

Rabotic, B. (2010) Professional tourist guided: The importance of interpretation for tourist experiences. *20th Biennial International Congress: New Trends in Tourism and Hotel Management*, Opatija, Croatia, Book of Abstracts, pp. 6–8.

Seaton, A. V. (1996) Guided by the dark: From thanatopsis to thanatourism. *International Journal of Heritage Studies*, 2(4), 234–244.

Sharpley, R. (2005) Travels to the edge of darkness: Towards a typology of dark tourism. In C. Ryan, S. Page and M. Aicken (Eds.), *Taking Tourism to the Limit: Issues, Concepts and Managerial Perspectives*. Oxford: Elsevier, pp. 215–226.

Sharpley, R. (2009) Dark tourism and political ideology: Towards a governance model. In R. Sharpley R. and P. Stone (Eds.), *The Darker Side of Travel: The Theory and Practice of Dark Tourism*. Bristol: Channel View Publications, pp. 145–163.

Sharpley, R. and Stone, P. (Eds.) (2009) *The Darker Side of Travel: The Theory and Practice of Dark Tourism*. Bristol: Channel View Publications.

Stasiak, A. (2013) Tourist product in experience economy. *Tourism*, 23(1), 27–35.

Stone, P. (2006) A dark tourism spectrum: Towards a typology of death and macabre related tourist sites, attractions and exhibitions, *Tourism: An Interdisciplinary International Journal*, 54(2), 145–160.

Stone, P. (2009) 'It's a Bloody Guide': Fun, fear and a lighter side of dark tourism at the The Dungeon Visitor Attractions, UK. In R. Sharpley and P. Stone (Eds.), *The Darker Side of Travel: The Theory and Practice of Dark Tourism*. Bristol: Channel View Publications, pp. 167–185.

Stone, P. (2013) Dark tourism, heterotopias and post-apocalyptic places: The case of Chernobyl. In L. White and E. Frew (Eds.), *Dark Tourism and Place Identity. Managing and Interpreting Dark Places*. Abingdon: Routledge, pp. 79–94.

Tarlow, P. (2005) Dark tourism: The appealing 'dark' side of tourism and more. In M. Novelli (Ed.), *Niche Tourism: Contemporary Issues, Trends and Cases*. Oxford: Elsevier, pp. 47–57.

Urry, J. (1990) *The Tourist Gaze*. London: Sage Publications.

Weiler, B. and Black, R. (2015) The changing face of the tour guide: One-way communicator to choreographer to co-creator of the tourist experience. *Tourism Recreation Research*, 40(3), 364–378.

White, L. and Frew, E. (2013) *Dark Tourism and Place Identity: Managing and Interpreting Dark Places*. Abingdon: Routledge.

Wynn, J. R. (2011) *The tour Guide: Walking and Talking New York*. Chicago: University of Chicago Press.

Yu, X., Wailer, B. and Ham, S. (2004) Cultural mediation in guided tour experiences: A case study of Australian guides of Chinese tour groups. In G. R. Jennings (Ed.), *New Frontiers in Tourism Research: Proceedings of the Annual Conference of Research and Academic Papers* (Vol. XVI). International Society of Travel and Tourism Educators, pp. 83–95.

44

EXPERIENCE DESIGN IN THE SMART TOURISM DESTINATION

Barbara Neuhofer and Dimitrios Buhalis

Introduction

The topic of tourist experiences has received widespread attention since the early 1960s (Boorstin, 1964). The theoretical foundations of the tourist experience have been expanded upon ever since, with a wide spectrum of concepts focusing on motivations, attitudes, behaviours, types and complexities around the tourist experience (Cohen, 1979; Ryan, 2010). With the advent of the digital age and its rapid proliferation of information and communication technologies (ICTs) in tourism, the literature of the 2000s has called for a discussion of the tourist experience in the digital domain (Neuhofer, Buhalis & Ladkin, 2012; Tussyadiah & Fesenmaier, 2009). While traditionally the tourist experience has been portrayed as distinct to everyday life (White & White, 2004), digital technologies have transformed the nature of the tourist experience by offering new possibilities for connection, interaction and co-creation before, during and after travel (Neuhofer et al., 2012, 2014). In this context, ICTs have not been merely an add on to a tourist experience but have fundamentally changed its nature though enhancing, substituting, extending, recording and reliving experiences through digital means (Neuhofer et al., 2012). These developments have opened a distinct research field – one at the intersection of the tourist experience and digital technology – with Neuhofer et al. (2012) coining the notion of technology-enhanced tourist experiences.

The digital transformation continues to transform all life domains, including work, leisure and tourism. The most recent eTourism literature reflects this development as we witness more holistic conversations that focus on the integration of ICTs in wider tourism and life ecosystems (Buhalis, 2019). For contemporary tourism management, one of the core areas of interest is the question of how tourism can harvest the immense potential of the interconnectivity of ICTs and become truly 'smart'. All around the globe, cities and destinations collaborate to bring smart tourism initiatives to the market. Likewise, tourists increasingly seek experiences that are co-created, smart and highly personalized (Buhalis, 2019; Femenia-Serra, Neuhofer & Ivars-Baidal, 2019). With major opportunities and challenges evolving around the synchronization of technology hardware, software, networks, data, people and systems (Buhalis, 2019), the smart tourism agenda has evolved fast. From the early beginnings of defining what smartness means (Boes, Buhalis & Inversini, 2016), research is now concerned with how it can be

616

DOI: 10.4324/9781003219866-50

Experience design

operationalized in practice, and how tourists themselves and their lived experiences can become smart and smarter (Femenia-Serra et al., 2019).

In parallel with the academic interest in smart tourism, we can see a wide range of smart tourism developments in the global business landscape. For instance, in China, the government has introduced a wide range of end-user devices to connect tourists, organizations and destinations (Wang, Li & Li, 2013). Destination marketing organizations (DMOs) in Korea have recognized the value of ICTs in future smart tourism developments by integrating webpages, social media and mobile applications in various travel stages. In Spain, smart innovation is promoted to link both the public and private sectors in tourism (Ivars-Baidal, Celdrán-Bernabeu, Mazón & Perles-Ivar, 2019).

As we move into an era of technology integration in which technology-enhanced tourist experiences take centrestage (Neuhofer et al., 2012), the smart tourism discourse is evolving too (Benckendorff, Xiang & Sheldon, 2019). In particular, there is evidence that smart tourism shifts from a rather technology-centred conversation to more experiential questions (Femenia-Serra et al., 2019). In fact, the interconnection of systems, social media, Internet of Things (IoT), travel apps and multiple forms of ICTs are transforming not only the way destinations operate, but also how tourists co-create experience value in the experience ecosystem (Buhalis, 2003; Femenia-Serra et al., 2019). With a growing demand for individualization in all consumption and life contexts, tourists seek higher-level experiences that are not only technology-enhanced but truly personalized, memorable and offer value creation and transformation in the long term (Neuhofer, 2022; Neuhofer, Celuch & To, 2020; Sheldon, 2020).

The synergy between the digital age and the experience economy (Neuhofer et al., 2014; Pine & Gilmore, 2011) creates a fertile ground for smart ecosystems to evolve towards integrated living systems that allow for the co-creation of individualized experiences and mutual value for all stakeholders involved. With this vision of what may come next, this chapter seeks to open a conversation that places the human experience and value co-creation at the centre of smart tourism development. It asks the question: How can we intentionally design and facilitate individual smart tourism experiences? This question requires a shift towards the field of human-centred experience design to understand how to create human-driven smart tourist experiences with the possibilities of emerging technologies in mind.

The chapter is divided into four main sections. The first section provides a theoretical overview of smart tourism research and a deep dive into the concept of smartness, smart tourism and smart tourism destinations. The second part focuses on tourist experiences in relation to resource integration and value co-creation. The third ventures into the design field and brings new perspectives for human-centred and tourism experience design. Following the review of the literature, the fourth part integrates the knowledge into a practical experience design roadmap that shows how to intentionally design for tourist experiences in the smart tourism destination ecosystem.

Smartness, smart tourism and the smart tourism destination

The concept of smartness emerged in the late twentieth century and focuses on digital and intelligent connections of urban infrastructure to foster economic and social development (Boes et al., 2016). Generally, the notion of smartness can be described by its capabilities in monitoring, controlling, optimizing and creating a high level of autonomy (Porter & Heppelmann, 2014). On a technological level, smart components can range from the integration of sensors, data storage, hardware, software, operating systems and enhanced user interfaces, among many others (Porter & Heppelmann, 2014). However, these devices and systems alone do not create smartness. Aristotle famously said 'The whole is greater than the sum of the parts'; transferring this statement to the contemporary smart tourism context, this is also true for smartness. The key to smartness is interconnectivity and interoperability of ICTs that lead to a radical redesign of the whole system (Buhalis, 2019). Driven by the philosophy of open innovation (Boes et al., 2016), smartness promotes a dynamic collaboration of networks and empowers all stakeholders within a given ecosystem to co-create value and elevate collective competitiveness.

One industry often integrated into the wider smart urban development agenda is tourism (Xiang, Tussyadiah & Buhalis, 2015). Similar to the concept of 'smart city', which aims to improve sustainability and the quality of life of its citizens through technologies (Gretzel, Sigala, Xiang & Koo, 2015), smart tourism can be defined as:

> a tourism system that takes advantage of smart technology in creating, managing and delivering intelligent touristic services/experiences and is characterized by intensive information sharing and value co-creation.
>
> *(Gretzel, Werthner, Koo & Lamsfus, 2015: 3)*

In a similar vein, smartness:

> takes advantage of interconnectivity and interoperability of integrated technologies to reengineer processes and data in order to produce innovative services, products and procedures towards maximising value for all stakeholders.
>
> *(Buhalis, 2022)*

What these definitions have in common is the necessity to connect technologies, create integrated and communicative systems that yield innovation, enhanced experiences and co-create shared value for all actors in a determined ecosystem. What is particularly noteworthy in the smart tourism discourse is that there is an ongoing debate that technological infrastructures alone do not guarantee a destination to be smart. Technological infrastructures, such as cloud computing, smartphones, location-based services, radio-frequency-identification, sensors, wearable devices and Wi-Fi, are pivotal to the development of smart tourism systems. However, besides hard smartness (e.g. technology), it is indeed the integration of soft smartness (e.g. innovation, social and human capital and leadership and value creation) that is indispensable to the development of successful smart tourism destinations (Boes et al., 2016; Buhalis, 2019).

Technology discussions in tourism have come a long way, from techno-centric debates and a focus on the practical implementation of ICTs to the establishment of the field of eTourism. The development of smart tourism systems goes further, namely, towards integrated ambient intelligence tourism systems (Buhalis, 2019). While the eTourism literature mainly concentrates on the Web 2.0 and efforts in the digital realm (Buhalis, 2003), smart tourism takes the conversation one level higher. It bridges both digital and physical environments, combines public–private-consumer collaboration (Gretzel et al., 2015) and takes advantage of technology as interconnected Internet of Things (IoT) and ambient intelligence (Femenia-Serra et al., 2019).

What is of particular relevance is that smart tourism is far from static, as it is constantly evolving and developing as technological innovation progresses. As a result, the opportunities

Experience design

for smart tourism destinations are closely linked to the breakthrough of more disruptive technologies on the horizon. For instance, we can see sensors, gamification, wearable devices, blockchain and artificial intelligence (AI) (Buhalis, 2019; Neuhofer, Magnus & Celuch, 2020) that drastically change market structures at the micro-individual and macro-societal level (Buhalis & Sinarta, 2019; Buhalis et al., 2019). In the smart tourism ecosystem, all stakeholders (e.g. tourists, locals, governments, cities, tour operators and general institutions) are connected through ICTs infrastructure and involved in the process of value creation and exchange of resources (Koo, Mendes, Filho & Buhalis, 2019). The role of technology is central in that it serves as the connector – a medium that allows for all interactions and collaborations among actors to occur (Femenia-Serra et al., 2019). Smartness thus is 'the glue' of interconnected systems that seeks to co-create value for everyone involved (Buhalis, 2015).

When it comes to considering tourist experiences in the smart tourism context, we thus need to recognise three important aspects, namely that:

i   ICTs are the glue for interconnected and interoperable smart tourism destinations (Buhalis, 2015);
ii   smart tourism is a multifaceted and complex phenomenon (Gretzel, Sigala, Xiang & Koo, 2015);
iii the tourist experience and value co-creation for all tourists and stakeholders is at the core of the smart tourism destination (Femenia-Serra et al., 2019)

Tourists increasingly step into smart technology-enhanced environments developed, orchestrated and designed by the DMOs. At the same time, tourists integrate their own resources, smart devices and applications. This creates an interconnected playing field with the potential for smart, context-aware, ambience-intelligent and highly individual experiences to emerge. The next part of the chapter thus shifts the focus on to the concept of tourist experiences and discusses their potential and embeddedness in smart tourism destinations.

Tourist experiences, resource integration and value co-creation in smart tourism destinations

As technology resource integration intensifies (Gretzel, Werthner, Koo & Lamsfus, 2015) and value co-creation occurs in the physical and digital realm at the same time (Neuhofer et al., 2012), tourist experiences take on new dimensions. A wide spectrum of technology-enhanced tourist experiences can unfold. However, the specific kind of technology-enhanced tourist experience that occurs is dependent upon two main factors, namely: (i) the intensity of technology integration and (ii), the intensity of co-creation (Neuhofer et al., 2014). Depending on the low or high manifestation of these characteristics in a matrix, Neuhofer et al. (2014) conceptualize a typology of four types of technology-enhanced tourist experiences, including:

i   conventional offline experiences (low technology, low co-creation)
ii   technology-assisted experiences (high technology, limited co-creation)
iii technology-enhanced experiences (high technology, some co-creation)
iv   technology-empowered experiences (high technology, high co-creation)

Considering the experience hierarchy model by Neuhofer et al. (2014), it is evident that a smart tourist experience does not only rely on technology as a key factor, but needs the exchange and integration of resources and value co-creation (Koo et al., 2019). Value co-creation has become a widely used term in the services marketing and tourism literature. It originates from the service-dominant (S-D) logic and suggests that value occurs in a mutually beneficial process and value is always created *with* and determined *by* the consumer in the consumption process (Vargo & Lusch, 2017).

For value to be realized, the process of resource integration needs to occur, which can be understood as a collaborative process between organizations and consumers and wider stakeholders in a service ecosystem (Neuhofer et al., 2012). In any consumption and smart tourism contexts alike, resources consist of knowledge, skills, competencies and technologies that need to be integrated for value to be formed (Boes et al., 2016). Depending on the actors involved and the resources integrated, value formation can occur in various forms. It is important to note that value co-creation may not always be merely positive; in fact, value can be co-created (positive) as well as co-destroyed (negative) or co-recovered (negative turned into positive) (Camilleri & Neuhofer, 2017; Fan, Hsu & Lin, 2020).

Why does value formation matter in the smart tourism context? One main reason is that with ICTs as a key resource involved, technological issues, insufficiencies and interruptions may be a realistic scenario. For an integrated view of smart tourism, it is thus critical to consider the positive and negative impact of technology on tourist experiences and value co-creation. With a focus on its value-adding nature, recent literature has discussed a wide array of use cases on how tourists co-create value in technology-enhanced tourist contexts. Value co-creation as a mindset, activity and outcome has become paramount in tourism. A focus on tourist co-creation boosts consumer participation and empowers tourists to control their desired outcomes (Sugathan & Ranjan, 2019). This is particularly relevant for smart tourism; experiences are not just passively consumed by tourists, but actively co-created with ICTs throughout the entire customer journey from the anticipatory, experiential, to the reflective phase (Neuhofer et al., 2012; Tussyadiah & Fesenmaier, 2009).

In the pre-experience phase, tourists start dreaming, seeking inspiration and exploring the desired destination online (Neuhofer et al., 2012). For instance, recent ICTs, such as virtual reality (VR), offer a glimpse into a destination before the physical travel and advance the tourist experience to a more intensive level (Beck, Rainoldi & Egger, 2019). Once at the destination, a wide range of technological systems are interconnected to empower tourists to make decisions on the go (Neuhofer et al., 2012) and to co-create experiential value through social interactions and encounters (Fan et al., 2020). Regarding the post-experience stage, tourist experiences and memories can be re-collected and re-shared in interconnected systems of stakeholders, ranging from online users to tourism organizations within the visited destination (Neuhofer et al., 2012). These consumer-integrated ICTs applications are just but a few technological resources at play.

Smart tourist experiences and individual tourist activities do not happen in a vacuum. Instead, they occur in a system of connected networks, devices, sensors and big data across the IoT infrastructure (Buhalis, 2022). Resources thus take on a central role in the successful co-creation of value. This is particularly true for smart tourism destinations, which depend upon complex IoT systems (Buhalis, 2022; Porter & Heppelmann, 2014), in which it is important that each technology in itself and all technologies connected form a harmonious resource environment for smart tourist experiences to unleash their full potential. Resource integration and, thus, value co-creation of smart tourist experiences occurs on two main levels:

i   resource integration on the individual tourist level;
ii resource integration on the systematic DMO and ecosystem level.

Experience design

Particularly as we move towards artificial-intelligence and ambient-intelligence systems, tourist experiences will not be so much pre-designed, but co-created dynamically in the *now*. For instance, tourists integrate their own smart applications to co-create experiences and value (Neuhofer & Buhalis, 2017) and support various touchpoints of travel in real-time (Buhalis, 2019; Buhalis & Sinarta, 2019; Xiang et al., 2015). In a smart destination scenario, tourists look for information that is easily accessible, personalized, context-relevant and often updated and available in real time (Buhalis, 2022; Buhalis & Sinarta, 2019). Thus, one of the key elements that sets smart tourist experiences apart from non-technology-mediated experiences is that they allow for personalization based on context and data in real time (Femenia-Serra & Neuhofer, 2018).

For instance, the weather in a destination suddenly changes, the overcrowding of an attraction calls for a change of plan or delays in public transport require the search for alternatives. These are scenarios that are realistic, occur frequently and invite the full potential of smartness. Context-aware ICTs and AI can use live data, make suggestions and present refined itineraries. The biggest role of technology is in the effective interconnection of systems, and synchronization of data offers real-time updates. While this is already happening globally in some areas, the full potential of smartness is still to come. What this means for tourist experiences is that this new generation of ICTs can elevate the state of a smart tourism destination to an unprecedented level of 'nowness' (Buhalis & Sinarta, 2019). For businesses and governments, resource integration thus means to envision, develop and make use of an interconnected technological infrastructure to best take advantage of information and big data (Femenia-Serra & Neuhofer, 2018) in a non-intrusive manner (Gretzel, Werthner, Koo & Lamsfus, 2015) to facilitate better experiences for tourists. Increased processing power and ubiquitous connectivity have enabled a re-engineering of tourism services and experiences on a micro and macro level (Buhalis & Sinarta, 2019).

Beyond the idea of nowness, tourist experiences will become more intelligent, situational and contextual. Particularly as AI technology enters the field (e.g. chatbots and robots), real-time contextualization and personalization is expected to be a key feature in the value proposition of smart tourism destinations (Grundner & Neuhofer, 2021). For instance, latest studies show that in transportation hubs, such as airports, service robots and autonomous trolleys can help manage visitor flows and the well-being of employees. When the tourist is on the go, on-demand information and proactive suggestions delivered through AI can support effective decision-making as tourists are navigating through smart destinations (Grundner & Neuhofer, 2021; Wang et al., 2020). Futures studies indicate that AI is expected to become even more of a game changer for smart destinations, as AI progresses from narrow AI (e.g. performing a specific activity) to general artificial intelligence (i.e. equals human intelligence) and super intelligence (outperforms human intelligence) levels (Grundner & Neuhofer, 2021). Not only will AI serve tourists as a valuable resource in the realization of experiences, but we can expect AI to take on the role as an actor in human-AI co-creation relations. Tourist experiences are co-created in a symbiotic interaction, fuelled by big data and consumer preferences and precisely calculated and adapted to the current context and situation.

In painting a present and future picture of technology in smart tourism destinations, it is important to keep a human-centred approach in mind. Smart destinations should not think of experience design in terms of the creation of 'pre-packaged smart experiences'. Instead, the goal is to offer value propositions for tourists that support smart contextualized co-creation – when, where and however needed – that can then potentially lead to more personalized experiences, value and memories in the long term. One of the most intriguing open areas in recent smart tourism research is how to learn more from the design field. How can we maximize technological capacities while creating an experience that is not a high-tech but indeed high-touch one with the human at the centre stage? The next section turns to the field of experience design to borrow insights from human-centred design to discuss how we may orchestrate future smart tourism environments that give rise to consumer-centric, personalized and contextually smart tourist experiences.

Human-centred experience design: how can we design smart tourist experiences?

In the marketing and design literature, there is a longstanding tradition emphasizing the importance of the 'consumer' in service encounters and customer journeys. Human-centred design and experience design are emerging fields that call for a deeper understanding of and connection with individuals (Tussyadiah, 2017). It is partly thanks to the digital revolution that a focus on user-centred experiences and user-experience design (UX) has emerged, laying the groundwork for a focus on human-centeredness (Gulati & Oldroyd, 2005). One of the core arguments of human-centred design is that technological artefacts are not designed for the sake of technology and abstract end-users, but for real people with real needs.

This is where experience design comes into play. As a highly interdisciplinary field, it draws on psychology, ethnography, cultural studies, linguistics and information sciences to explain human behaviours and interactions within an ecosystem (Tussyadiah, 2014). The notion of 'design thinking' is thereby particularly relevant (Arenas, Goh & Urueña, 2019). Design thinking represents a unique philosophy, a mindset, a toolset and a process (Brenner, Uebernickel & Abrell, 2016). Generally, scholars differentiate between design (as the noun form) and designing (as the verb form) (Love, 2002). Designing refers to intentional human activities, whereas design suggests the plan or the process as the basis for human actions to occur (Love, 2002). The ultimate goal of experience design is to deliberately design, shape, influence and transform human behaviours. When we talk about experience design, the experience is not a by-product but the centre of the effort. Most importantly, experience design stands for 'intentionality'. This means that experiences do not happen by chance, but are intentionally and strategically designed along a customer journey to allow for a desired outcome, e.g. positive emotions, value, memories or transformation to emerge (Neuhofer, Celuch & To, 2020).

Experiences generally involve complex interactions between design attributes, the psychological states of the consumer and the surrounding sociocultural and contextual environment (Neuhofer, 2022; Neuhofer, Celuch & To, 2020). Tourist experiences are pursued for their uniqueness, sensations, emotions, spirituality and memorable recollections (Park & Stangl, 2020; Sterchele, 2020). Different from mass products or service encounters, the intangible and subjective nature illustrate tourism as a design context to evoke emotions and escalate experiences through human interactions (Tussyadiah, 2014). It is precisely in this interesting interplay of personal states, social interactions and interactions with the physical environment that experience design is most adept to serve. In fact, tourism is a predestined context in which experience design can show its potential and application.

Several scholars, including Fesenmaier and Xiang (2017) and Tussyadiah (2014) conceptualize fundamental approaches to the process of tourism experience design. First, drawing from human factors and ergonomics, experience design evolves around *human-centeredness* by focusing on the inner states and desires of the end-user (Tussyadiah, 2014). Second,

Experience design

experience design is an *iterative process* of design thinking that involves prototyping, testing, analyzing and refining to better understand humans and enhance their experiences (Arenas et al., 2019). Third, experience design focuses on offering a *holistic design concept* that emerges from a design process and considers the interactions between design features and contextual details in a comprehensive way to elevate meanings and values (Arenas et al., 2019).

One area that is gaining increasing attention in experience design is humanistic and positive psychology (Seligman & Csikszentmihalyi, 2014). Experience design is not only about the process of design thinking, but inherently about the design of specific psychological and behavioural outcomes. In a recent study, Neuhofer, Celuch and To (2020) examined the context of events and festivals as a vehicle for memorable and transformative experiences. By building on Seligman's original PERMA (Positive Emotion, Engagement, Relationships, Meaning, Achievement) model, Neuhofer, Celuch and To (2020) explored a series of psychological and contextual dimensions that are necessary to create a 'transformative vehicle that can be transferred to any human encounter and consumption context, including tourism destinations. The developed transformative vehicle encompasses six main design dimensions that are proposed for designing any 'time and space' in tourism, events and wider services contexts, creating the extended abbreviation PERMAL:

i   design for positive emotions (e.g. emotions, surprises, excitement, appreciation)
ii   design for engagement (e.g. interactions, chance encounters, communitas)
iii   design for relations (new encounters, reconnecting with others and the self)
iv   design for meaning (anticipation, self-expression, sense of unity)
v   design for accomplishment (self-actualization, self-discovery, fulfilment, memory)
vi   design for liminality (escapism, ambience, senses, aesthetics, storytelling)

With an inherent focus on humans, experience design means designing in a human way on multiple levels, from micro to macro, from the individual to objects and the surrounding environment (Neuhofer, Celuch & To, 2020). In this frame, the smart tourism destination can be considered as an environment that is rich in internal and external stimuli, rendering it an ideal 'playground' for intentional design towards desired human behaviours, experiences and value outcomes. This chapter now turns to linking the concepts of the tourist experience, smart tourism destination and experience design to propose an integrated theoretical view and practical roadmap on how to use intentional experience design in smart tourist experience settings.

Experience design in the smart tourism destination

Several key areas are identified that, together, form a 'roadmap' in which experience design can be used to facilitate tourist experience and value co-creation in the smart tourism destination. Three main steps are identified, including: (i) the intentional experience design process; (ii) the smart tourist or more simply, smart human; and (iii) the smart tourism destination environment. These dimensions are supported with guiding questions relevant for each step of the design process. One of the core philosophies of experience design is the need to identify the right question and problem before trying to find a solution. Accordingly, the exemplary questions should be inspirational and useful for design teams designing smart tourist experiences.

Designing the intentional experience design process

From the field of experience design, we can learn that experiences are first and foremost a product arising from a contemplative and co-creative idea-generation process, a design thinking approach and intentional design – from idea to idea and prototype – being put into place. Design requires a process. Design requires a method. Design requires intentionality. Design thinking is a field rich with hands-on tools, canvas templates and methods that can be borrowed to guide all phases of the experience design process of tourist experiences. Design thinking represents a problem-solving approach by building empathy and understanding towards the consequences and the impacts of each action to optimize tourist experiences (Arenas et al., 2019). When it comes to designing experiences within the smart tourism destination scenario, it is critical to note that design does not refer to the design of technology. Technological hardware, software and data infrastructure is often proclaimed as a proud centre of many smart tourism innovations. And while technological developments are valuable and, in fact, essential for the progress of smartness, experience design invites us to shift the focus as we move:

- From technology design to human experience design
- From a chance aggregation of experiences to an intentional design of experiences and touchpoints along a personalized customer journey
- From static and long processes to dynamic and co-creative iterations and prototypes

What we can learn from the field of design is not only how to design for an outcome, but also to design the design process itself. Guiding questions in this process can be:

- *What methods shall be used in the idea generation, user research, ideation and prototyping process?*
- *What user research methods will be used to gather real human insights into the tourists' needs, wants, aspirations and desired experiences and values?*
- *What insights can we learn from inductively examining existing big data to gather insights that complement the early phases of the design process?*
- *Which stakeholders in the smart tourism system do we need to involve in the design process?*

Designing for the smart human

Following the process of intentional design and implementation of the design in a real-life setting, the smart tourism experience is ready to unfold. It is through the lived experience of the tourist that the full complexity of the integration of interconnected technological systems and the designed contextual environment takes shape and form. The human is the starting point of this process. Some important questions to ask are:

- *What is the entry state when the tourist arrives at the destination?*
- *What are their expectations and goals?*
- *What are their aspirations?*
- *What is the value they seek?*
- What is the goal they seek to fulfil?
- What is the exit psychological state and exit behaviour when the tourist has lived an experience and leaves the smart tourism destination?

Experience design

These exemplary questions help in the early phases of the design process to develop empathy and put oneself into the shoes of the tourist. It is a first starting point, which will be followed by more in-depth contemplation of the current and desired psychological states of the tourists that subsequently inform the design of the experience and value proposition. Only once these states have been reflected upon, it is recommended to ask: *What technological infrastructure, applications or data are needed to accomplish these goals and achieve these psychological and experiential states?* As should be noted, the sequence of contemplation is (i) human first and (ii) technology and environment second. Human factors, people's desires, interests and deeper psychological needs must be considered before machines (Stankov & Gretzel, 2020).

Rooted in the literature of positive psychology, experiences must be crafted so that they address tourists' inner needs that match their personal traits and, hence, can potentially foster personal human flourishing. By considering the six PERMAL dimensions introduced above (Neuhofer, Celuch & To, 2020), experience design for smart tourism destinations requires designers to take an intentional look at finer psychological layers. While these layers are prone to emerge in immersive, high-touch and socially dense contexts, such as festivals (Neuhofer, Celuch & To, 2020), it is indeed possible to translate the core learnings to technology-mediated and more high-tech environments. What this means for the particular context of smart tourism destinations can be guided by the following question: *What technological infrastructure, applications or data are needed to trigger, create and foster each dimension of positive emotions, engagement, relations, meaning, accomplishment and liminality?*

Designing the smart tourism destination experience

In synthesizing the insights from the foregone design process and the developed empathic understanding of the tourist, the smart tourism destination experience can be designed. While the second step largely focuses on the psychological state of the tourist, the third step seeks to design and manifest the ambient reality of the smart tourism destination. In this way, this step moves from the individual micro to the macro environmental level and opens up to include the consideration of the destination with its entire tangible, intangible and technological infrastructure and stakeholders. While questions may be numerous in this stage, a few starting points include:

- *How can value be co-created for the smart tourist and all stakeholders in the smart tourism ecosystem?*
- *How can smart technology help enhance the tourist's -insert-* of the lived experience? (*e.g. flow, personalization, co-creation, information, social interaction, transformation).*
- *What technological resources can be used, interconnected and interconnected from both the destination and tourists to facilitate one seamless experience?*
- *What data is the tourist willing to share for the most individual experience to be created?*
- *How can the smart tourism destination serve as a vehicle for the highest individualized, relevant and meaningful experience in the right place and time?*

From an environmental design perspective, designing a smart tourism destination is a complex yet interesting task. Intentional design processes help break down the process in sizeable parts and, thus, reduce the complexity of designing the whole system. What sets the smart tourist experience design apart from offline experiences is the consideration of vast technological resources and how to use them most effectively. The fact that smart tourist experiences are recognized as a shared goal in the ecosystem (Gretzel, Reino, Kopera & Koo, 2015) urges tourism businesses to come up with effective solutions through co-creation (Sugathan & Ranjan, 2019). Although it appears that tourist experiences are often placed at the centre of smart tourism destinations, it is important to note that the design should be holistic, encompassing compassionately all stakeholders and residents' well-being and quality of life (Garcia, Aciar, Mendoza & Puello, 2018). By having a clear picture regarding who is involved, and where and how experiences occur in smart tourism destinations (Neuhofer et al., 2012), much attention can be given at every stage to intentionally design experiences and induce long-lasting memories through a human-centred approach (Tussyadiah, 2014).

Discussion and conclusions

The proliferation of ICTs and the emerging concept on human experience design have paved a paradigm shift from consumer-focused thinking to human-centred perspectives in the smart tourism ecosystem. By bridging tourist experiences with smart tourism and experience design, this chapter highlights the importance of the humanistic aspect of the design in future tourist experiences. While digital transformation has opened interoperability, virtualization, automation, decentralization, capability analysis and real-time data collection (Pencarelli, 2019), the ultimate quest is to fulfil a human need through the capacities that these technological resources invite us to explore.

The ultimate sophistication of the tourist experience lies in its individuality (Wei, Zhao, Zhang & Huang, 2019). This widely acknowledged statement is of particular relevance when considering tourist experience in the smart tourism destination context. The fact that no two experiences are alike implies the quest for personalization through digital connectivity (Neuhofer, Buhalis & Ladkin, 2015). What, however, changes is that with unprecedented smart, ambient and artificial-intelligence technologies on the horizon, tourist experiences will move from the known level of personalization to a yet unknown level of individualization. As the technological interoperability of systems becomes more established, more human experience approaches will be needed (Buhalis & Leung, 2018).

Amidst a global acceleration and redefinition of human values in the COVID-19 global pandemic, the nature of smart tourist experiences is expected to further evolve and gain in relevance. Smart technology offers affordances that will play a key role in shaping experiences in post-pandemic realities by helping tourists deal with prevailing ambivalences around information, safety, health, transportation and social distancing. On a wider humanistic level, values are being reformed giving rise to tourism scenarios that transcend hedonistic consumption patterns in quest for deeper, more human, social and spiritual dimensions. Personal growth, spiritual awakening and consciousness development (Sheldon, 2020) are only a few of the wider topics that will require the symbiosis of all stakeholders and resources in a system for mutual value creation and true transformation. Coupled with the need to design clean and safe technology-mediated and transformative experiences, the emergence of refined tourist experiences is on the horizon. While we have witnessed early traces of technology-mediating experiences for human transformation, this demand can be expected to grow. Designing tourist experiences for smart tourism destinations means not only focusing on experiential aspects, but focusing on collective happiness and well-being of the ecosystem in the long term (Sheldon, 2020).

Experience design

References

Arenas, A. E., Goh, J. M. and Urueña, A. (2019) How does IT affect design centricity approaches? Evidence from Spain's smart tourism ecosystem. *International Journal of Information Management*, 45, 149–162.

Beck, J., Rainoldi, M. and Egger, R. (2019) Virtual reality in tourism: A state-of-the-art review. *Tourism Review*, 74(3), 586–612.

Benckendorff, P. J., Xiang, Z. and Sheldon, P. J. (2019) *Tourism Information Technology*. Wallingford: CABI.

Boes, K., Buhalis, D. and Inversini, A. (2016) Smart tourism destinations: Ecosystems for tourism destination competitiveness. *International Journal of Tourism Cities*, 2(2), 108–124.

Boorstin, D. J. (1964) *The Image: A Guide to Pseudo-Events in America*. New York: Harper.

Brenner, W., Uebernickel, F. and Abrell, T. (2016) Design thinking as mindset, process, and toolbox. In W. Brenner and F. Uebernickel (Eds.), *Design Science in Tourism*. Cham: Springer, pp. 3–21.

Buhalis, D. (2003) *eTourism: Information Technology for Strategic Tourism Management*. Harlow: Pearson Education.

Buhalis, D. (2015) Working definitions of smartness and smart tourism destination. *Dimitrios Journeys*. Available at: http://buhalis.blogspot.co.uk/2014/12/working-definitions-of-smartness-and.html

Buhalis, D. (2019) Technology in tourism. From information communication technologies to eTourism and smart tourism towards ambient intelligence tourism: A perspective article. *Tourism Review*, 75(1), 267–272.

Buhalis, D. (2022) Smart tourism. In D. Buhalis (Ed.), *Encyclopedia of Tourism Management and Marketing*. Cheltenham: Edward Elgar Publishing. https://doi.org/10.4337/9781800377486.smart.tourism

Buhalis, D., Harwood, T., Bogicevic, V., Viglia, G., Beldona, S. and Hofacker, C. (2019) Technological disruptions in services: Lessons from tourism and hospitality. *Journal of Service Management*, 30(4), 484–506.

Buhalis, D. and Leung, R. (2018) Smart hospitality: Interconnectivity and interoperability towards an ecosystem. *International Journal of Hospitality Management*, 71, 41–50.

Buhalis, D. and Sinarta, Y. (2019) Real-time co-creation and nowness service: Lessons from tourism and hospitality. *Journal of Travel & Tourism Marketing*, 36(5), 563–582.

Camilleri, J. and Neuhofer, B. (2017) Value co-creation and co-destruction in the Airbnb sharing economy. *International Journal of Contemporary Hospitality Management*, 29(9), 2322–2340.

Cohen, E. (1979) A phenomenology of tourist experiences. *Sociology*, 13(2), 179–201.

Fan, D. X. F., Hsu, C. H. C. and Lin, B. (2020) Tourists' experiential value co-creation through online social contacts: Customer-dominant logic perspective. *Journal of Business Research*, 108, 163–173.

Femenia-Serra, F. and Neuhofer, B. (2018) Smart tourism experiences: conceptualisation, key dimensions and research agenda. *Investigaciones Regionales-Journal of Regional Research*, 42, 129–150.

Femenia-Serra, F., Neuhofer, B. and Ivars-Baidal, J. A. (2019) Towards a conceptualisation of smart tourists and their role within the smart destination scenario. *The Service Industries Journal*, 39(2), 109–133.

Fesenmaier, D. R. and Xiang, Z. (2017) Introduction to tourism design and design science in tourism. In D. Fesenmaier and Z. Xiang (Eds.), *Design Science in Tourism*. Cham: Springer, pp. 3–16.

Garcia, L. M., Aciar, S., Mendoza, R. and Puello, J. J. (2018) Smart tourism platform based on micro-service architecture and recommender services. In M. Younas, I. Awan, G. Ghinea and M. Catalan Cid (Eds.), *Mobile Web and Intelligent Information Systems*. Cham: Springer, pp. 167–180.

Gretzel, U., Reino, S., Kopera, S. and Koo, C. (2015) Smart tourism challenges. *Journal of Tourism*, 16(1), 41–47.

Gretzel, U., Sigala, M., Xiang, Z. and Koo, C. (2015) Smart tourism: Foundations and developments. *Electron Markets*, 25(3), 179–188.

Gretzel, U., Werthner, H., Koo, C. and Lamsfus, C. (2015) Conceptual foundations for understanding smart tourism ecosystems. *Computers in Human Behavior*, 50, 558–563.

Grundner, L. and Neuhofer, B. (2021) The bright and dark sides of Artificial Intelligence: A futures perspective on tourist experiences. *Journal of Destination Marketing and Management*. 19. https://doi.org/10.1016/j.jdmm.2020.100511

Gulati, R. and Oldroyd, J. B. (2005) The quest for customer focus. *Harvard Business Review*, 83(4), 92–101.

Ivars-Baidal, J. A., Celdrán-Bernabeu, M. A., Mazón, J. N. and Perles-Ivars, Á. F., (2019) Smart destinations and the evolution of ICTs: A new scenario for destination management? *Current Issues in Tourism*, 22(13), 1581–1600.

Koo, C., Mendes Filho, L. and Buhalis, D. (2019) Smart tourism and competitive advantage for stakeholders. *Tourism Review*, 74(1), 1–128.

Love, T. (2002) Constructing a coherent cross-disciplinary body of theory about designing and designs: Some philosophical issues. *Design Studies*, 25(3), 345–361.

Neuhofer, B. (2022) Experience design. In D. Buhalis (Ed.), *Encyclopedia of Tourism Management and Marketing*. Cheltenham: Edward Elgar Publishing. https://doi.org/10.4337/9781800377486.experience.design

Neuhofer, B. and Buhalis, D. (2017) Service-dominant logic in the social media landscape: New perspectives on experience and value co-creation. In M. Sigala and U. Gretzel (Eds.), *Advances in Social Media for Travel, Tourism and Hospitality*. Abingdon: Routledge, pp. 13–25

Neuhofer, B., Buhalis, D. and Ladkin, A. (2012) Conceptualising technology enhanced destination experiences. *Journal of Destination Marketing & Management*, 1(1–2), 36–46.

Neuhofer, B., Buhalis, D. and Ladkin, A. (2014) A typology of technology-enhanced tourism experiences. *International Journal of Tourism Research*, 16(4), 340–350.

Neuhofer, B., Buhalis, D. and Ladkin, A. (2015) Smart technologies for personalized experiences: A case study in the hospitality domain. *Electronic Markets*, 25(3), 243–254.

Neuhofer, B., Celuch, K. and To, L. (2020) Experience design and the dimensions of transformative festival experiences. *International Journal of Contemporary Hospitality Management*, 32(9), 2881–2901.

Neuhofer, B., Magnus, B. and Celuch, K. (2020) The impact of artificial intelligence on event experiences: A scenario technique approach. *Electronic Markets*. pp.1–17. https://doi.org/10.1007/s12525-020-00433-4

Park, S. and Stangl, B. (2020) Augmented reality experiences and sensation seeking. *Tourism Management*, 77, 1–11.

Pencarelli, T. (2019) The digital revolution in the travel and tourism industry. *Information Technology & Tourism*, 1–22. https://doi.org/10.1007/s40558-019-00160-3

Pine, B. J. and Gilmore, J. H. (2011) *The Experience Economy: Work is Theatre & Every Business a Stage*. Boston: Harvard Business School Press.

Porter, M. and Heppelmann, J. (2014) How smart, connected products are transforming competition. *Harvard Business Review*, 92(11), 64–88.

Ryan, C. (2010) Ways of conceptualizing the tourist experience: A review of literature. *Tourism Recreation Research*, 35(1), 37–46.

Seligman, M. E. and Csikszentmihalyi, M. (2014) Positive psychology: An introduction. In M. Csikszentmihalyi (Ed.), *Flow and the Foundations of Positive Psychology: The Collected Works of Mihaly Csikszentmihalyi*. Dordrecht: Springer, pp. 279–298.

Sheldon, P. J. (2020) Designing tourism experiences for inner transformation. *Annals of Tourism Research*, 83, 1–12.

Stankov, U. and Gretzel, U. (2020) Tourism 4.0 technologies and tourist experiences: A human-centered design perspective. *Information Technology & Tourism*, 1–12. https://doi.org/10.1007/s40558-020-00186-y

Sterchele, D. (2020) Memorable tourism experiences and their consequences: An interaction ritual (IR) theory approach. *Annals of Tourism Research*, 81, 1–13.

Sugathan, P. and Ranjan, K. R. (2019) Co-creating the tourism experience. *Journal of Business Research*, 100, 207–217.

Tussyadiah, I. P. (2014) Toward a theoretical foundation for experience design in tourism. *Journal of Travel Research*, 53(5), 543–564.

Tussyadiah, I. P. (2017) Technology and behavioral design in tourism. In D. Fesenmaier and Z. Xiang (Eds.), *Design Science in Tourism*. Cham: Springer, pp 173–191.

Tussyadiah, I. P. and Fesenmaier, D. R. (2009) Mediating tourist experiences. *Annals of Tourism Research*, 36(1), 24–40.

Vargo, S. L. and Lusch, R. F. (2017) Service-dominant logic 2025. *International Journal of Research in Marketing*, 34(1), 46–67.

Wang, D., Li, X. and Li, Y. (2013) China's 'smart tourism destination' initiative: A taste of the service-dominant logic. *Journal of Destination Marketing & Management*, 2(2), 59–61.

Experience design

Wang, J., Xie, C., Huang, Q. and Morrison, A. M. (2020) Smart tourism destination experiences: The mediating impact of arousal levels. *Tourism Management Perspectives*, 35. https://doi.org/10.1016/j.tmp.2020.100707

Wei, C., Zhao, W., Zhang, C. and Huang, K. (2019) Psychological factors affecting memorable tourism experiences. *Asia Pacific Journal of Tourism Research*, 24(7), 619–632.

White, N. R. and White, P. B. (2004) Travel as transition. *Annals of Tourism Research*, 31(1), 200–218.

Xiang, Z., Tussyadiah, I. and Buhalis, D. (2015) Smart destinations: Foundations, analytics, and applications. *Journal of Destination Marketing & Management*, 4(3), 143–144.

INDEX

accessible tourism 453–455
Acts of Wanton Wonder 84
adventure tourism 96, 103, 117, 147, 154, 160, 162, 187, 250, 259, 281, 287, 352, 381, 426, 432, 525
affective realism 40, 41, 44, 46
Africa 50, 56, 249, 286, 288, 294, 339, 340, 524, 552, 553
Airbnb 17, 226, 250, 269, 454
alienation 38, 39, 78, 97, 147, 170, 177, 432, 444
allocentric 108, 171, 189, 190, 219
altruism 262, 263, 265, 266
analogy 51, 52, 334
anime 320, 322, 323, 394
anomie 170, 201, 202, 446
anti-structure 92, 93, 94, 95, 96
approach-avoidance model 202, 203
architecture: of experience 409; of technology 413, 415
artificial intelligence (AI) 410, 619, 621, 626
attention: economy 116; merchants 116–117, 122; structure framework 113–116
attraction-distraction arenas 118
attributes: interactional 69, 70, 71, 72, 73; physical/tangible 68, 70, 71, 72, 73; service-based 72, 73
augmented reality 18, 22, 243, 410, 445, 553
aura 77, 78, 85, 86; auratic object 77
Auschwitz 28, 38, 330, 337
Australia 50, 56, 116, 117, 172, 250, 251, 252, 253, 265, 282, 286, 291, 315, 37, 319, 323, 356, 245, 355, 359, 380, 398, 399, 499, 500, 502, 503, 512, 523, 524
Austria 58, 368, 370, 515
authentication 77, 78, 79, 80, 81, 82, 83, 85, 86, 323, 392

authenticity: constructive 78, 79, 147, 392; existential 39, 78, 79, 147, 229, 236, 353, 392, 394, 427, 429, 485, 542; objective 78, 79, 147, 392, 429, 485; paradox of 217; religious 392; simulated 80, 83, 85, 86; staged 3, 39, 78, 79, 82, 83, 119, 145, 236, 244, 245, 392, 428, 429
autoethnography 323, 607

backpacker 204, 217, 218, 226, 235, 244, 245, 249–259, 282, 412, 557, 553
backstage 78, 170, 187, 289, 430
barriers (to tourism) 452, 453, 454, 455–457, 462
Berlin: Memorial for the Murdered Jews of Europe 604, 606, 611; Wall Memorial 603–604
blog, travel 31, 223, 225, 258, 412, 414, 415, 418, 557; blogger 223, 226
blue space 160, 486, 495
Bodleian Library 84, 85
Botanic Gardens, Oxford 84
brand illusion 136–137
Brighton 90, 96, 482, 486, 487, 488, 541
bucket list 114, 230, 516
Bukit China Cemetery 578, 579, 580, 582, 583, 584, 586
bungee jumping 97
Burning Man Festival 238, 241, 242

camel ride 57
camera 16, 141, 223, 230, 316, 339, 439, 440, 411–412, 442
Camino de Santiago 161, 257, 398
Canada 50, 83, 253, 288, 499, 502
Cape Town 146
capitalism 13, 15; disorganized 15
carnivalesque 122, 345, 483, 486
Catacombs of Paris 338

Index

Cathedral 56, 81, 82, 329, 330, 341, 347, 397, 398, 399, 601
cemeteries, Chinese 578, 584
cemetery tourism 329, 330, 335, 337, 345, 578, 586
chaos theory 51
Children's University Tasmania 115
China 30, 83, 210, 207, 251, 252, 253, 254, 259, 293, 341, 367, 399, 583, 617
Church of England 155
Cittaslow 278, 279–281
Claude glass 141
coastal tourism 379, 380, 481, 487
co-creation, value 564–574
codes of conduct 145, 263, 269, 385
cognition 26, 54, 67, 73, 113, 122, 143
cognitive: evaluation 66, 67; impairment 457, 459–460, 461; psychology 50, 65
commoditization 78
communitas 92–93, 96, 97, 98, 161, 241, 242, 245, 304, 308, 352, 359, 395, 400, 430, 540, 623
community-based tourism 264, 542
Community Innovation Survey 595
connectedness 157, 160, 162, 277, 281, 287, 353, 355, 358–359, 361, 444
consumer society 13
contents tourism 319, 320, 322, 323
continuum, familiarity-strangerhood 188
coral reef 227, 379, 380, 382, 384, 385
Coronavirus 12, 22, 228
Corriganville 317
Covid-19 1, 2, 228, 286, 287, 289, 293, 294, 295, 626
cruise: community 408, 409, 416–419; embodied experience 411–416; ship space 409–411; tourist 408–419
Cyprus 241, 500, 501, 503

Dajia Mazu pilgrimage 399
dark heritage 611
dark tourism 55, 57, 117, 227, 328–342, 578, 601–614
data mining 68
death 26, 28, 45, 321, 331–332, 333, 334, 335, 337, 338, 341, 344, 346, 347, 351, 352, 360, 446, 578, 601, 605, 606
deconstruction 18, 20, 21, 22, 79, 393
democratization 14, 184, 224
desert tourism 30, 96, 357
digital: ecosystem 572, 617, 619, 626; media 19, 304, 311, 322, 410, 411; nomadism 37; photography 134, 439, 442; revolution 338, 443, 444, 447, 622; technology 154, 410, 411, 413, 616, 617, 618, 626; transformation 616, 626
disability 451, 452, 453, 454, 456, 458, 459, 460, 461, 462

disabled population 451
discourse analysis 19, 20, 21
Disneyland 116, 123
dwelling 144

ecotourism 22, 160, 224, 264, 281, 286, 287, 288, 289, 290, 291, 292, 293, 294, 295, 519; slow 281
ecotourist 190, 240, 264, 286–295, 396, 510; sustainable 289–291
edgework 45
educational tours 577, 578
ego-enhancement 201, 202, 292, 295
egotourism 265
Eiffel Tower 122, 129
elephant treks 288
embodiment 44, 80, 81, 140–149, 387, 391, 409, 411, 542, 551
emotions: basic 40, 55, 64; constructed 40; definitions 39–40
empathy 265, 274, 353, 368, 567, 624
empowerment 251, 265, 555, 593, 595
enclave 238; backpacker 244, 250, 252, 256–257, 258
English Heritage 83, 488
Enlightenment, The 9, 11, 215
environmental bubble 188, 190, 238, 240, 245, 257
epiphanic experience 400
epistemology 17
erfahrung 52, 56, 60, 192
erlebnis 4, 52, 56, 60, 192
escaping-seeking framework 200, 202–203, 204, 208
ethics 19, 21, 38, 59, 149, 263, 270, 522, 524, 526, 529
eTourism 616, 618
eudaimonia 26, 31, 157, 365, 367
Everest, Mount 41, 42, 43, 44, 46, 227, 361
existential anxiety 37, 39
existential-authentic experience 30
experience: economy 303, 361, 392, 588, 591, 592, 617; epiphanic 400, 401; felt 117, 118, 113, 157; festival 301–311; frontier 95, 161, 352–353, 354, 361–362; hospitality 64–74; liminal 91–94, 97; liminoid 93–94, 304, 485; lived 81, 191, 251, 291, 469, 549, 617; memorable 71, 73, 301, 369, 383, 446, 452, 515, 538, 547, 543, 557, 588, 589, 591, 594, 595, 597, 598, 617, 623; negative 59, 117, 118, 187, 202, 203, 230, 269, 354, 371, 399, 443, 444, 525, 543, 565, 620; peak 26, 106, 107, 172, 236, 244; remembered 25, 52, 56, 58, 59, 60, 591; service 589–592; spiritual 96, 153–163, 351, 352, 353, 354, 355, 356, 357, 359, 361, 365, 366, 367, 370–372, 391–401; transformative 39, 45, 46, 54, 93, 94, 95, 96, 97, 158, 161, 186, 196, 238, 266, 267, 365, 366, 367, 400, 401, 428, 623, 626

632

Index

Experience Africa 50
experience design: external stimuli 538, 541, 542, 543; human-related stimuli 540–541; sensory stimuli 539; theme 541
Experience Fluctuation Model 108
Experience Sampling Method 108
experiencescape 240, 515, 535, 536, 539, 540, 556, 569
experiential: dissonance 119; episodes 25, 60
experiment, spiritual 160–161

fatality 332, 333–334, 335, 343, 344, 347
Feriecenter Slettestrand, Denmark 460–461
festival 2, 81, 93, 175, 29, 238, 241, 242, 245, 374, 395, 397, 416, 553, 582, 583, 623, 625; experience 302–304; music 96, 301–311
flaneur 347
flashpacker 250
flow: and experience 104–107; micro 104, 105, 107, 110; and play 103–104; and work 107–108
Flow State Scale 109
food tourism 508, 509
Fordist/Fordism 15, 21
Foucault 12, 135, 410, 416, 417
Four Channel Model 108
frontstage 84, 187

Game of Thrones 322
gap year 37, 175, 249, 250, 252, 253, 269, 282
gendered bodies 37, 39, 43, 44, 46
generic perspectives 170, 171, 180, 181
genius loci 469, 470, 482, 483
Gettysburg National Park 146
ghost tours 84, 116, 330, 337, 338, 345
globalization 12, 13, 14, 22, 224, 259, 278, 508
Grand Tour 141, 223, 224, 249, 252
Great Barrier Reef 380
green space 159, 160, 278, 279, 486
guest-host interactions 114, 119

habitus 412, 413
happiness, conceptualization of 24–27
Harold and Maude 328, 331, 335, 336, 337
Harry Potter 80, 82, 83, 84, 85, 86, 322
Healing 159–160, 365, 366, 374
healthy hotel 373
hedonia 26, 31, 186
hedonism 256, 262, 264, 265, 365, 590, 593, 598
hermeneutic circle 440, 447
heroism 41
hero's journey 263, 266, 352, 353, 361
heterotopia 410, 416, 417, 418
heterotopic 238; assemblages 410; spaces 410, 416
Hierarchical Value Map 205
hierarchy of needs 172, 192, 203, 204, 221
hiking 143, 148, 249, 252, 253, 257–258, 525, 582

hippie 221, 249, 250, 254, 259; trail 249
hitchhiking 231, 249
Hollywood 317, 318
Holocaust 38, 330, 332, 333, 347, 603, 604, 606, 609, 610, 611
Hong Kong 206, 318, 319, 502
hospitality experience 64–74
human-centred design 453, 617, 621, 622–623, 626
humanism 11, 523
humility 356, 361
humour 50, 56, 57
hyperreality 17, 45, 80, 81, 82, 83, 85, 147, 394

identity 28, 29, 92, 96, 97, 98, 107, 114, 148, 157, 171, 175, 193, 195, 218, 222, 225, 230, 238, 239, 254, 255, 256, 258, 265, 267, 287, 289, 304, 310, 332, 334, 336, 356, 391, 395, 400, 502, 429, 430, 431, 437, 446, 483, 487, 491, 493, 494, 500, 547
immersion 26, 55, 81, 103, 106, 107, 187, 190, 249, 254, 304, 351, 515, 570
inauthenticity 79, 81, 216, 394
in-betweenness 92
India 45, 143, 223, 225, 256, 324, 341, 367, 370
individualism 11, 15, 207, 251, 552
Indonesia 50, 57, 179, 180, 322, 502, 504
information and communication technology (ICT) 243, 275, 439, 443, 616
innovation, technological 409, 410, 413, 414, 418, 618, 624
intelligence: ambient 618; artificial 410, 619, 621, 626
International Ecotourism Society (IES) 287
Internet of Things (IoT) 243
interoceptive 40, 43, 45
interpretation, three levels 608–609
Interrail 250, 255–256
intersubjectivity 42, 82, 144, 542
Ireland 249, 319, 339, 472, 502, 514
irreality 80
islands: archipelagicity 503–504; distance from mainland 501–503; identity 500; peripherality 503; size 500
Israel/Israeli 38, 208, 250, 253, 256, 258, 345, 394, 612

Japan 114, 161, 207, 319, 320, 322, 323, 324, 330, 344, 364, 365, 374, 399, 502

Kailash, Mount 396
Kaiser Wilhelm Memorial Church, Berlin 119
Khaled Nabi shrine 396
Korea 175, 179, 204, 293, 319, 323, 324, 370, 373, 374, 617
Kumano Kodo 161, 399

Index

language 10, 18, 19, 41–42, 51, 131, 141, 223, 224, 251, 252, 256, 318, 360, 458, 477, 554, 607, 608, 611
lifestyle: advertising 131; traveller 250
liminality 90, 91–94, 309, 400, 483, 623, 625; of tourist experiences 97
liminal zone 90, 93, 95–96, 97, 443, 485
limits of acceptable change 527
limits to growth 526–529
local food 250, 256, 280, 281, 475, 508, 511, 515
Lord of the Rings 81, 147, 317, 322, 541
low cost airline 95, 226
loyalty 250, 256, 280, 281, 475, 508, 511, 515

Malaysia 118, 179, 180, 578, 579, 582, 584
Marriott 373
Marxism 11
mass tourism 14, 17, 21, 78, 187, 188, 189, 190, 217, 220, 224, 235–245, 275, 277, 287, 288, 297, 340, 361
Mauritius 502
meaning of life 28, 29, 31
means-end chain theory 398, 399
Melaka City 578, 579, 583, 585
mementos 128, 133–134, 137, 337
memorability 25, 64, 68, 70, 71, 72, 73, 74, 231, 515, 540, 554
memory 25, 29, 42, 53, 55, 69, 133, 332, 333, 339, 342, 345, 346, 446, 459, 471, 465, 490, 491, 493, 537, 540, 554, 611, 623
metaphor 50, 51, 52, 54, 60, 115, 137, 145, 147, 174, 226, 335, 366, 472, 504
metatourism 229
Midland Hotel, Morecambe 491, 492, 493, 494
mindful tourist 190, 204, 371, 372
mobile phone 16, 116, 316, 370, 418, 442, 444
mobilities 148, 149, 237, 250, 252, 256, 258, 392, 394, 522
mobility impairments 457, 458, 459
modernity 12, 239, 344, 391, 398; inauthentic 39
moral muteness 270
moralism 11
morals 38, 155
Morecambe 482, 487, 488–494
mortality 31, 332, 333–334, 335, 343, 344, 346, 347, 433
motivation: pull 67, 72, 117, 171, 200, 201–202, 205, 208; push 67. 72, 117, 143, 171, 172, 181, 200, 201–202, 205, 208
mountaineering 29, 44, 45, 104, 356, 358, 360
Muir, John 288, 289, 290, 291
musixscape 302, 305–306, 309, 310, 311
Muslim 179, 180, 340, 345, 365, 578, 583, 584

narrative, fantasy 77–86
national park 160, 286, 288, 289, 290, 291, 521, 522

National Park Service (NPS) 288, 295, 514
nature-authentic experience 30
nature based tourism 286, 374, 521–529
Netherlands 58, 319, 320, 321, 370
neuroscience 40, 50, 52, 177, 178
new moral tourist 224–225
New Salem 78, 80, 81, 83
new tourist 337
New Zealand 81, 97, 147, 193, 194, 195, 196, 251, 252, 282, 317, 330, 345, 398, 541
nomophobia 444
non-institutionalized tourist 188, 189, 238, 239
non-representational theory 140, 142, 144, 149
nostalgia 85, 175, 176, 179, 180, 204, 278, 426, 430, 431, 432, 446, 483, 484, 485, 482, 490, 491, 493, 494
nowstalgia 446, 447

onboard community 409, 416–419
onsen 322, 369
operand/operant resources 565, 566, 567, 569, 570, 571, 572, 573
orchestra model 50–61; affective component 54–55; behavioural component 55; cognitive component 55; relationships component 55; sensory component 54
outward bound 263, 264
overtourism 226–227, 278, 286, 471, 527

package tour/tourism 14, 15, 16, 21, 56, 94, 123, 185, 186, 218, 224, 225, 237, 240, 241, 244, 275, 329, 330, 336, 347, 370, 374
paranormal tourism 50, 56, 57, 227
peak experience 26, 106, 107, 172, 236, 244
performativeturn 142, 145
peri-festival experience 304
PERMA model 177, 623
photo album 141, 439, 447
photographic practices 439, 440, 441, 446, 447
photography 56, 133, 134, 137, 141, 230, 438–447
pilgrim 158, 161, 220, 221, 241, 257, 337, 395, 396, 397, 398, 402, 552, 553
pilgrimage 28, 31, 41, 91, 92, 94, 154, 158, 161, 162, 170, 257, 264, 266, 323, 324, 359, 361, 370, 391, 392, 393, 394, 395, 391, 397, 399, 400, 401, 408, 428, 431, 504; secular 91, 94, 154, 158, 161, 162, 323, 391, 395, 396, 428, 431
pilgrim-tourist 396
place: attachment 258, 278, 358, 400, 469, 471, 481, 483, 493, 515, 511, 577; brand 83, 113, 118, 137, 226, 227, 471, 472, 473, 474, 476, 511, 543; marketing 113, 469–476, 500, 513, 514, 543
place-based education 577, 578
planned behaviour, theory of 206

Index

Platform Nine and Three Quarters 85, 86
Port Arthur Historic Park 117
positive psychology 108, 176, 177, 623, 625
post-Fordist/Fordism 15
postmodern consumption 14–17
postmodernity 4–29
post-tourist 16, 17, 22, 228, 229
powerscape 221
pre-experience phase 620
Princess Diana 134, 337
prosumer 323
pseudo-event 78, 79, 186, 216, 220, 392
psychocentric 108, 171, 189, 219
pull (motives) 67, 72, 117, 171, 200, 201–202, 205, 208
Purple Pound 454
push (motives) 67. 72, 117, 143, 171, 172, 181, 200, 201–202, 205, 208
push-pull model 200, 201–202, 205, 208

quest 41, 137, 153, 154, 157, 158, 159, 161, 162, 170, 171, 220, 227, 231, 266, 357, 427, 432
quiongyou 252, 259

rail travel 222, 250, 255–256, 277
rationalism 11
recreational opportunity spectrum 527
reefs, coral 227, 379, 380, 382, 384, 385
referent 52, 130, 131, 132, 144, 331
relativism 10, 18
religion: commodification of 158
religiosity 154, 155–156, 157, 158, 396, 399, 400
religious: experience 42, 155–156, 158–159, 391–393, 395–397, 400–402; tourism 153, 155, 156, 157, 158–159, 391–402
remembered experiences 25, 52, 56, 58, 59, 60, 591
remembrance: abandoned 341; contested 345; engineered 332, 333, 334, 335, 337, 338, 339, 341, 345, 346, 347; excluded 339–340; fast-tracked 338–339; unconsidered 343–345; withdrawn 342
resource-based theory 568–569
retreat tourism 364, 365, 366, 367, 369, 370–372, 374
rite: liminal 89–98; of passage 91, 92, 93, 94, 95, 242, 245, 253, 303; preliminal 91; postliminal 91
rural tourism 446, 508, 509, 511, 512, 513, 514, 515, 516
Rwanda 293, 611

Sachsenhausen 28, 603, 604, 605, 606, 607, 608, 609, 613
sacred site 21, 119, 158, 257, 323, 330, 366, 391, 392, 394, 395, 396, 399, 401, 402
Sagrada Familia Cathedral 82

Santorini 469, 474, 475, 476
satisfaction: attribute-level 65, 67, 68; definitions of 65–67; emotional 67, 71, 72, 73; transactions approach 65
schadenfreude 335, 606
scuba diving 378–386
seaside: architecture 486–488; heritage 481–495; nostaglia 483, 484, 485, 487, 488, 490, 491, 493, 494; resorts 90, 94, 95, 96, 242, 481–495
seasideness 483–486, 494, 495
self actualization 157, 173, 174, 176, 180, 201, 203, 204, 221, 231, 251, 252, 256, 257, 258, 263, 264, 352, 353, 355, 356, 357, 366, 398, 623
selfie 441, 445, 456
semiology 128, 129, 130
semiotic: analysis 20, 128, 131, 137, 473; toolbox 129–130, 137
sense of place 118, 400, 455, 469–476, 483, 494, 586
sensory impairment 456, 457, 458–459, 461
serious leisure 103, 109, 180, 431, 432
service: class 132; learning 263–264
servicescape 368, 535, 539, 569, 590
service-dominant logic 565, 620
Seychelles 502, 503, 504
sightseeing 18, 140, 141, 143, 145, 208, 216, 238, 251, 338, 396, 438, 458
signifier 129, 130
signs: iconic 129, 132, 135, 222; indexical 129, 132, 134, 135; symbolic 129, 130, 472
simile 51, 52
Singapore 59, 117, 120, 502, 503
slow: ecotourism 281; food 278, 373; tourism 274–283, 516
slowness 274, 275–277, 278, 281, 282, 283
smart: destination 243, 244, 245, 443, 616–626; tourism / tourist 243, 244, 245, 616–626
smartness 243, 617, 618, 619, 621, 624
smartphone 16, 30, 95, 250, 439, 441, 442, 443–447, 618
smellscape 141, 255, 539
socialscape 302, 306–309, 310–311
social networks 13, 145, 234, 311, 337, 561
South West Coast Path 144
souvenirs 20, 56, 120, 18, 133, 137, 439, 446, 535, 539, 540
spa: experiences 368–370; resort 322, 366, 369
Spain 58, 123, 161, 282, 301, 342, 361, 371, 617
spatialization 147
special interest tourism 10, 15, 17, 21, 509, 510
spiritual: centre 97, 189, 220; search 400, 401, 402; tourism 154, 157, 159–161, 162, 353, 400–401; transcendence 102, 103, 104, 105, 106, 107, 114, 351, 353–354, 361, 364, 367, 370, 401
spirituality 156–157
sport: fantasy camps 429; heritage 426, 430

Index

sport tourism: activity 432–433; authenticity 428–430; landscape 424–427; motivation 431–432; place 427–428
Spring Hill Pioneer Village 80, 81
Sri Lanka 288, 293
storyscape 83
sunlust 188
swastika 114
syntagmatic relationships 129, 133, 134, 135

Tasmania 117, 119, 323, 498, 502, 503
technology of enchantment 414
temple stay 162, 367, 371, 372, 400
terroir 509, 510, 511, 512, 516
Thailand 50, 57, 274, 288, 367, 380, 547
thanatourism 277
topophilia 469, 482
tour group dynamics 610
tour guides: cultural mediator 602, 607; pathfinders 602
tourism: accessible 453–455; adventure 96, 103, 117, 147, 154, 160, 162, 187, 250, 259, 281, 287, 352, 381, 426, 432, 525; coastal 379, 380, 481, 487; contents 319, 320, 322, 323; cruise 30, 206, 216, 226, 238; mass 14, 17, 21, 78, 187, 188, 189, 190, 217, 220, 224, 235–245, 275, 277, 287, 288, 297, 340, 361; rural 446, 508, 509, 511, 512, 513, 514, 515, 516; serious 103; slow 274–283, 516; smart 243, 244, 245, 616–626; spiritual 154, 157, 159–161, 162, 353, 400–401; sport 424–427; zone 95, 97, 98, 190–191, 256
tourist: body 142–145; existential 97, 153, 170, 189, 200; gaze 16, 54, 89, 90, 114, 140, 141, 145, 149, 255, 331, 336, 438, 439, 502; institutionalized 188, 218, 238, 239, 253; mindful 190, 204, 371, 372; new 337; new moral 224–225; non-institutionalized 188, 189, 238, 239; recreational 97, 170, 189, 202, 220, 236, 329; religious 158, 159, 161, 163, 221, 391–401; responsible 119, 190, 191, 263, 267, 286, 292, 293, 547; smart 243, 244, 245, 616–626
Tourist Area Life Cycle 219, 482
transcendence 102, 103, 104, 105, 106, 107, 114, 351, 353–354, 361, 364, 367, 370, 401
transition 91, 92, 134, 254, 352
travel career: ladder 51, 172, 173, 192, 200, 203–204; pattern 169, 174–176, 177, 178, 179, 180, 181, 192, 200, 203–204
traveller-tourist dichotomy 186–187
trekking 257, 258, 356, 359, 525
TripAdvisor 15, 57
Turkey 69, 74, 207, 223, 330

typology, tourist 3, 59, 153, 186, 188, 189, 195, 202, 203, 220, 221, 231, 236, 238, 287, 291, 293, 396, 397, 426, 619

Uber 17, 444
Ulysses factor 169–170
underwater: environment 379, 380, 381, 382, 386; tourism 378
United States / USA 50, 85, 146, 171, 219, 249, 253, 288, 289, 295, 341, 521, 523, 578
utilitarian values 68

value: integrators 573; perception 265, 567, 568, 573
Vanuatu 282
Vatican Museum 118, 398
venturesomeness 196
Viking museums 119, 120
Viking Ship Museum 146
virtual reality 16, 18, 22, 29, 81, 294, 410, 550, 553
vision impairment 458
visionscape 141
volunteer tourism 29, 103, 105, 250, 252, 262–271, 292, 354, 361, 396, 401, 433, 502

Wakes Weeks 94
walking 107, 110, 143, 144, 146, 147, 160, 161, 257, 277, 282, 330, 331, 398, 399, 413, 414, 475, 512, 513, 515, 579, 611
Walt Disney World 79
wanderlust 2, 188, 190
wellbeing, subjective 39, 365
wellnessexperience 364–366
whale watching 292
wheelchair 454, 457, 458, 460, 461
white knuckle ride 97
white water rafting 97, 103, 109
wilderness: biocentrism 523; conservation 522; environment 524–526; humanism 523; land ethics 522, 524, 529; limits to growth 526–528; primitivism 523; tourism 521–529; utilism 523
wine: New World 509, 511; Old World 509, 511; Tourism 508–511; tourism market 511–512
World Heritage Site 79, 502, 577, 585
World Wide Web 14, 15

Yellowstone 288, 521, 522
yoga 143, 160, 366, 367, 369, 370, 371, 372, 373, 594
Yosemite 288, 290, 291

Zen 30, 370

Printed in the United States
by Baker & Taylor Publisher Services